Alan Greenwood and his wife, Cleo, are the publishers of *Vintage Guitar* magazine, which they launched in 1986. *Vintage Guitar* is the largest monthly publication for guitar collectors, enthusiasts, and dealers. They also publish *Vintage Guitar®* Online at www.vintageguitar. com, and the fine line of Vintage Guitar Books. His collection includes several vintage instruments from the '50s, '60s and '70s, as well as newer production and custom-made guitars and amps. He lives in Bismarck, North Dakota.

Gil Hembree began collecting guitars in 1966 as a college student working at Kitt's Music on G Street in Washington, DC. He graduated from American University in 1969 with a BSBA and two days after graduation he was hired by the General Motors Corporation. He held several assignments with GM including Financial Administrator of the Wichita Falls, Texas plant (where he obtained his MBA from Midwestern State University), and Supervisor of Corporate Audit in Detroit. In January of 2000, after a 30-year career, he retired from GM and he was immediately contracted by Vintage Guitar to co-author the Vintage Guitar Price Guide. Hembree maintains a small collection of '50s and '60s Fender and Gibson guitars and amps. He lives with his wife, Jane, in Austin, Texas.

The Official Vintage Guitar® Magazine Price Guide
By Alan Greenwood and Gil Hembree

Vintage Guitar Books
An imprint of Vintage Guitar Inc., PO Box 7301, Bismarck, ND 58507, (701) 255-1197, Fax (701) 255-0250, publishers of *Vintage Guitar®* magazine and Vintage Guitar® Online at www.vintageguitar.com. Vintage Guitar is a registered trademark of Vintage Guitar, Inc.

ISBN 1-884883-16-8

Cover and Back photos: Ward Meeker/Doug Yellow Bird. Instruments courtesy of Dave Rogers/Dave's Guitars.

Cover Design: Doug Yellow Bird/Vintage Guitar, Inc.

Printed in the United States of America

VI

Acme Guitar Works
Just The Good Stuff!

- Complete Fender® guitar kits with genuine Fender® body, neck, case, hardware
- Customize with your choice of our prewired Strat® assemblies, on your choice of genuine Fender® pickguards
- Nitrocellulose lacquer finish
- Full factory parts warranty
- Choose from several fretwire and radius options
- Full assembly available, with warranty
- Configure yours today using our custom online configurator, or call for details

- We build prewired assemblies using the finest pickups available
- Built to order, you select the options, we build it
- Genuine Fender® pickguards and knobs, or choose our cardboard template option and use your existing pickguard
- CTS pots and Orange Drop caps made exclusively for Acme to the tightest tolerances in the industry
- Ultra clean, rock-solid wiring
- Configure yours today using our custom online configurator, or call for details
- 3 solder joints to make (solderless option available) for a complete rewire in minutes
- Aged pickguards and knobs available by Bill Nash (Nashguitars)

Cardboard Template

Tele® Assembly

Solderless Option

Fender® Cases

Prewired Strat® Assemblies

Prewired Tele® Assemblies

Lindy Fralin Pickups

Jason Lollar Pickups

John Suhr Pickups

Fender® Pickups

Lace Pickups

Guitar Electronic Parts

CTS Pots

CRL Switches

Orange Drop Capacitors

Wiring Kits

Genuine Fender® Guitar Kits

Genuine Fender® Bodies and Necks

Genuine Fender® Hardware

Genuine Fender® Knobs

Genuine Fender® Pickguards

Genuine Fender® Cases

George L's Cable

Cool Hendrix T-Shirts

Pedalboards

The finest pickups, always in stock. Listen to MP3 clips on our website! Choose from the following manufacturers:

www.acmeguitarworks.com **302-836-5301**

Fender®, Strat®, and Tele® are registered trademarks of Fender Musical Instruments Corp. Acme Guitar Works is an Authorized Fender Dealer and an Authorized Fender Service Center (Gold Level).

www.texasguitarshows.com

The 4 Amigos Present **arlington 2005** World's Largest

OCTOBER 15-16

ARLINGTON CONVENTION CENTER
1200 Ballpark Way • Arlington, Texas 76011
800-453-SHOW (7469)
888-473-6059

California world guitar shows
TEXAS AMIGOS PRODUCTIONS

2005 SHOWS

Bay Area World Guitar Show
Marin Civic • San Rafael • January 8-9

Orange County World Guitar Show
OC Fairgrounds • Costa Mesa • January 15-16

Phoenix World Guitar Show
TBA

Bay Area World Guitar Show
Marin Civic • San Rafael • July 30-31

Santa Monica World Guitar Show
Santa Monica Civic Auditorium • August 6-7

San Diego World Guitar Show
Del Mar Fairgrounds • September 24-25

Tex★US Guitar Shows, Inc.
800-525-7273
larryb@stringswest.com
918-288-2222

Texas Guitar Shows, LLC

presents . . .

Austin Guitar Show 2005
Crockett Center • March 12-13

Chicago Guitar Show 2005
Odeum Expo Center • Villa Park • May 21-22

Chicago Guitar Show 2005
Odeum Expo Center • Villa Park • Sept. 10-11

888-473-6059
Fax 817-473-1089

417-869-3325
Fax 417-863-7767

X

What's it really worth?

Right now.

Gruhn Guitars offers an easy-to-use online appraisal service.

When you need more than a range of values, get a *fast, accurate appraisal* from the best in the business.

400 Broadway, Nashville, TN 37203
615 256-2033 * FAX 615 255-2021 * gruhn@gruhn.com

Appraisals by mail or email.
Visit our website for up-to-date inventory and photos.

w w w . g r u h n . c o m

BuffaloBrosGuitars.Com
Thousands of Guitars ~ New, Used & Vintage!
4901 El Camino Real, Carslbad, CA 92009 ~ E-Mail: BuffaloBros@aol.com ~ Phone (760) 434-4567
Great Selection ~ Friendly Folks ~ Great Prices

Home of the 100% Upgrade Policy!

Buy a new, used or vintage guitar from us and trade it in for what you paid toward an upgrade guitar! See website for details! Mastercard / Visa Accepted!

Why buy elsewhere?

Table of Contents

Fine Fretted Instruments

1238 Boston Post Road
Guilford, CT 06437
(203) 458-2525

brian@acousticmusic.org

Acoustic Music.Org®

Using The Vintage Guitar Price Guide

Understanding the Values

The Official Vintage Guitar Price Guide conveys specific values for excellent-condition, all-original instruments. *The Guide*'s definition of excellent condition allows for some wear, but the instrument should be well-maintained, with no significant blemishes, wear, repairs, or damage. An all-original instrument has the parts and finish it had when it left the factory. Replacement parts and refinishes can greatly affect value, as can the appropriate case (or cover) in excellent condition. In many instances, a "wrong" case will not greatly affect value, but with the top-dollar collectibles, it can.

Repairs affect value differently. Some repair is necessary to keep an instrument in playable condition, and the primary concern is the level of expertise displayed in the work. An amateurish repair will lower the value more than one that is obviously professional. A refinished guitar, regardless of the quality of the work, is generally worth 50% or less of the values shown in *The Guide*. A poorly executed neck repair or significant body repair can mean a 50% reduction in a guitar's value. A professional re-fret or minor, nearly invisible body repair will reduce a guitar's value by only 5%.

The values in the *The Guide* are for unfaded finishes. Slight color fade reduces the value by only 5%, but heavily faded examples can reduce the value by 25% to 50%.

We use a range of excellent-condition values, as there is seldom agreement on a single price point for vintage and used instruments. A tighter range suggests there is a general consensus, while a wide range means the market isn't in strict agreement. A mint-condition instrument can be worth more than the values listed here, and anything in less-than-excellent condition will have a reduced value.

Finding the Information

The table of contents shows the major sections. Each is organized in alphabetical order by brand, then by model. In a few instances, there are separate sections for a company's most popular models, especially when there is a large variety of similar instruments. Examples include Fender's Stratocasters, Telecasters, Precision and Jazz basses, and Gibson's Les Pauls. The outer top corner of each page uses a dictionary-type header that tells the models or brands on that page. This provides a quick way to navigate each section. The index at the back shows the page numbers for each type of instrument, by brand, and is a great place to start when looking for a specific model or brand.

The Guide has excellent brand histories and in most cases the guitar section has the most detailed information for each brand. When possible, *The Guide* lists each model's years of availability and any design changes that affect values.

More information on many of the brands covered in *The Guide* is available in the pages of *Vintage Guitar* magazine and on the "Brand Pages" section of our website, www.vintage-guitar.com.

The authors of *The Guide* always appreciate your help, so if you find any errors, or have additional information on certain brands or models, we'd like to hear from you. We are especially looking for info on any brand not yet listed. Whatever you may have to contribute, feel free to drop us a line at al@vguitar.com.

New Retail Pricing Information

The Guide continues to add information on individual luthiers and smaller shops. It's difficult to develop values on used instruments produced by these builders because much of their output is custom work, production is low, and/or they haven't been producing for a period of time sufficient to see their instruments enter the used/resale market. To give you an idea about their instruments, we've developed five grades of retail values for new instruments. These convey only the prices charged by the builder, and are not indicative of the quality of construction. *The Guide* applies this scale to all builders and manufacturers of new instruments.

The five retail-price grades are:
Budget - up to $250,
Intermediate - $251 to $1,000,
Professional - $1,001 to $3,000,
Premium - $3,001 to $10,000,
Presentation - more than $10,000.

The Guide uses the terms "production" and "custom" to differentiate between builders who do true custom work versus those who offer a widely available line of instruments. "Production" means the company offers specific models, with no variations. "Custom" means they do only custom orders, and "production/custom" indicates they do both. Here's an example:

Hembree Guitars
1967-present. Luthier Gil Hembree builds his professional-grade, custom, archtop guitars in Austin, Texas. He also builds basses.

This tells who the builder is, the type of instruments they build, where they build them, how long they've been operating under that brand, that they do only custom work, and that they ask between $1,000 and $3,000 for their guitars (professional-grade).

Again, we've applied the retail price grades and production and/or custom labels to most new-instrument manufacturers.

Introduction

The Vintage Market

The market for classic vintage guitars continues to defy the laws of gravity; what goes up does not always come down. The average vintage guitar and bass in our Guitar Collectors Index is worth 38% more now than it was just a year ago.

The Guitar Collectors Index was developed to track the values of classic American instruments. It now consists of 42 guitars and basses, and its numbers represent the overall average value of those instruments. We selected excellent-condition examples of instruments made in the 1960s or earlier - 14 each from Fender, Gibson, and Martin, generally accepted as being among the top guitar companies of that era. We intentionally omitted the top collectibles of each brand, like the '58 Les Paul Standard, the pre-war Martin D-45 and the '50s custom-color Fender Stratocasters, but the Index still represents a good cross-section of the instruments available from those companies during that time. Plus, it would be one very cool collection to own!

Chart 1 shows the overall average dollar value of the 42 instruments (excellent-condition examples) that make up the Index. In 1991, the average instrument in the group was valued

THE 42 INDEX

FROM FENDER	
1952 blond Precision Bass	
1952 blond Esquire	
1953 blond Telecaster	
1956 sunburst Stratocaster	
1958 sunburst Jazzmaster	
1958 blond Telecaster	
1960 sunburst Stratocaster	
1961 sunburst, stack knob, Jazz Bass	
1962 sunburst, 3-knob, Jazz Bass	
1963 sunburst Telecaster Custom	
1963 sunburst Esquire Custom	

1964 Lake Placid Blue Jaguar
1964 sunburst Precision Bass
1966 Candy Apple Red Stratocaster

FROM GIBSON
1952 sunburst ES-5
1952 Les Paul Model
1954 Les Paul Jr.
1958 sunburst EB-2 Bass
1958 Les Paul Custom
1958 natural ES-335
1958 Super 400CES
1959 Les Paul Jr.
1959 J-160E
1961 sunburst ES-355
1961 Les Paul SG

1964 sunburst Thunderbird II Bass
1965 EB-3 Bass
1969 sunburst Citation

FROM MARTIN
1931 OM-28
1932 00-28 special order
1935 D-18
1944 scalloped-brace 000-28
1944 D-28
1950 D-28
1958 000-18
1959 D-18
1959 D-28E
1962 D-28
1967 GT-75
1968 000-18
1969 N-20
1969 D-45

Guitar Dealer Participants

The information refined on these pages comes from several sources, including the input of many knowledgeable guitar dealers. Without the help of these individuals, it would be very hard for us to provide the information here and in each issue of *Vintage Guitar* magazine. We deeply appreciate the time and effort they provide.

Andy Eder
Andy's Guitars

Tim Page & Bob Page
Buffalo Brothers

Norm Moren
Cold Springs Electrical Works

Stan Werbin
Elderly Instruments

Dave Hussong
Fretware Guitars

Gary Dick
Gary's Classic Guitars

Dave Belzer & Drew Berlin
Guitar Center

Jimmy Brown
Guitar Emporium (KY)

Dave Hinson
Killer Vintage

Timm Kummer
Kummer's Vintage Instruments

Buzzy Levine
Lark Street Music

Larry Wexer
Laurence Wexer, Ltd.

Stan Jay
Mandolin Brothers

Bob November
McKenzie River Music

Mike Reeder
Mike's Music

Jay Jacus
New Jersey Guitar & Bass Center

Eliot Michael
Rumble Seat Music

Chris Clayton
Pick of the Ricks

Richard Friedman
Sam Ash & Manny's Music

David Davidson
Sam Ash Music - Carle Place

Eric Schoenberg
Schoenberg Guitars

Bruce Barnes & Kenny Rardin
Solidbodyguitar.com

Gil Southworth
Southworth Guitars

Scott Freilich
Top Shelf Music

John DeSilva
Straight Shooter Guitars

Nate Westgor
Willie's American Guitars

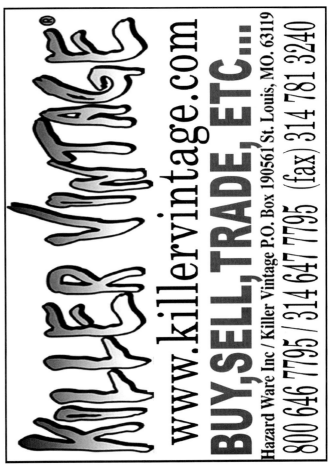

at $3,660. Fourteen years later, that average is $11,094.

Chart 2 shows the annual accumulative appreciation of the average instrument in the Index. Since 1991 the average guitar or bass has increased by 213%. It has been an impressive ride, with the average annual increase approximating 24%.

But, have the values of the three brands in our sample group – Martin, Fender, and Gibson – changed at the same rate? Have people preferred Fenders to Martins? No! Gibsons, Fenders, and Martins have appreciated at amazingly similar rates. Chart 3 represents the appreciation of each brand and shows that as Fenders have risen in value, Martins and Gibsons have matched those increases. A rising tide apparently raises all boats.

Charts 1, 2, and 3 are based on averages. But be careful – each guitar's trend line is different. For example, three of the 42, or 7% of our collection, actually dropped in value. The first three charts look at groups of instruments, so Chart 4 demonstrates variances in two individual guitars. This chart compares the Index's best performer (the one that appreciated the most) with the worst performer, a guitar that actually declined in value from '02. The two had similar changes in value up to '01.

So, what's hot and what's not? We've shown that most classic vintage guitars are increasing in value. But certain models have rockets, while others have anchors. The instrument listed in Chart 4 as the Index's worst performer is a member of the full-body acoustic archtop group. This type of guitar, as well-made and beautiful as it is, is not appreciating. Rather, it is often declining in value – a trend that has been noticed for

Authors Alan Greenwood and Gil Hembree.

several years. Thus, the market for that instrument is considered "soft" or "flat."

Quite the opposite is the vintage solidbody market. 1950s solidbodies are a perfect example – more people want them and more people play them. Les Pauls and Stratocasters from the '50s are certainly hot items. Any classic vintage guitar with a custom finish is also hot. Any "excellent" to "near-mint" vintage guitar is hot. People want condition and originality. Vintage flat-top guitars are consistent performers and pre-war Martins continue to perform well.

A market sector that is definitely not hot is vintage pedals. Pedals caught fire in the mid 1990s and maxed out in '99. While the market is soft, the overall use of pedals has never been higher. At the end of the last decade, some dealers were doing

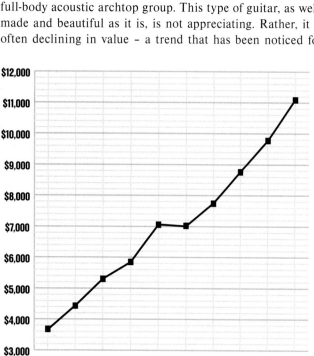

**#1   Average Price of a Vintage Guitar in
The 42 Index (an index of 42 vintage guitars)**

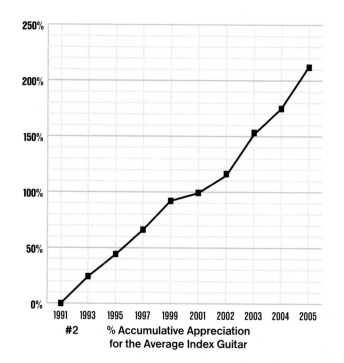

**#2   % Accumulative Appreciation
for the Average Index Guitar**

nothing but pedals. Those days are gone, but certain pedals, like an original Tube Screamer, are still sought after. Chart 5 demonstrates how the pedal market has fallen in relation to guitar values. One reason is eBay, where small, inexpensive, easy-to-ship items flourish to the point of driving prices down. Chart 5 shows that while the guitars in our Index appreciated over 140%, vintage pedals from the 1970s appreciated only 7%. The average effects pedal is worth less now than in 1999.

The percent of appreciation for the average vintage lap steel from 1940 to 1960 is shown in Chart 6, with trends for laps in general, then Gibson and Fender models, and all other brands. Other brands have been flat, and again, vintage Gibsons and

Fenders lead the way.

In the current market, amplifiers are in demand, with Fenders from the 1950s and '60s, and '70s Marshalls being the standard. The amp market is smaller than that for guitars and basses, and fewer dealers stock them because they're not as easy to ship.

Expectations are very high for 2005. The vintage stringed instrument market has been one of increasing values, increasing passion, and increasing numbers of hobbyists/collectors/musicians. In the '60s, the market grew because players were seeking better instruments. As the market matured, condition and originality became more important. This is certainly the decade

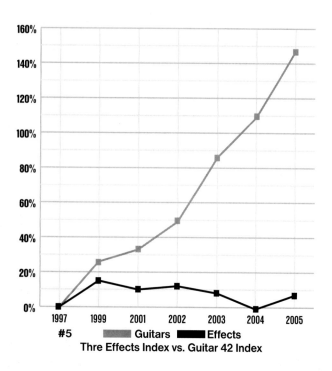

#3   ■ Martin   Gibson   Fender

% Appreciation By Brand

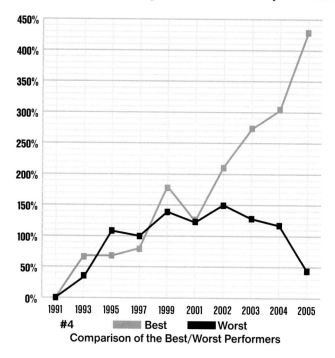

#4   Best   ■ Worst

Comparison of the Best/Worst Performers

#5   Guitars   ■ Effects

Thre Effects Index vs. Guitar 42 Index

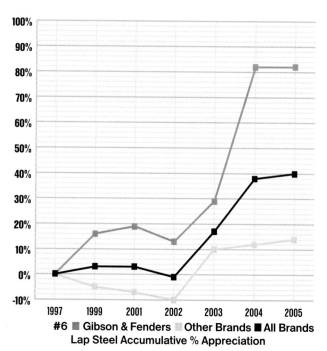

#6   ■ Gibson & Fenders   Other Brands   ■ All Brands

Lap Steel Accumulative % Appreciation

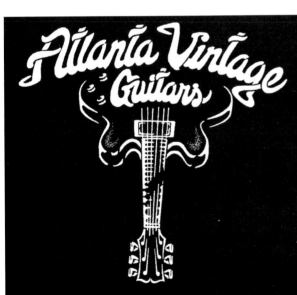

of the investor, where condition and originality reign supreme. Excellent, original, classic vintage guitars are more difficult to find, but dealers and collectors are up to the challenge. The dedicated, passionate collectors and vintage dealers will find a way to maintain a supply of fine vintage instruments. 2005 promises to be another great year, and guitars continue to be a great way to invest your time and money.

Les Pauls and Stratocasters from the 1950s and Martins from the '30s and '40s may eventually attain Stradivarius-level fame and fortune. Models from many modern builders will someday enter the realm of the elite, alongside classic models by Martin, Fender, and Gibson. What will they be? You're on your own there, but it sure is a good reason to try as many guitars as you can.

You can keep up with the latest news by reading *Vintage Guitar* magazine's "Dealer News" column, where dealers discuss past, present, and future trends. There's a lot of knowledge out there, and *Vintage Guitar* keeps you connected.

The New Market

The musical instrument (MI) market covers the spectrum of new products, from pianos to drums, guitars, violins, etc. MI does not include used and vintage guitars. So why discuss it here? Because today's new guitar buyer will likely be tomorrow's vintage guitar buyer. Is the guitar popular with today's new-instrument buyer? Are young people playing them? The MI and vintage markets are directly and indirectly related. Buyers who opt for a vintage piece may be foregoing a new-guitar purchase. Buyers who opt for an "aged" guitar may be foregoing a vintage piece.

The future of the vintage guitar business is dependent upon a successful new-guitar market. History has shown that adults retain the passion for the instruments of their youth. In 40 years, will the teenager of today pursue his or her youthful passion, and sustain the culture of the guitar?

Chart A, with data compiled from *The Music Trades* magazine, shows that fretted instruments (guitars, banjos, steels, mandolins, basses, etc.) and amplifiers make up the most popular new-musical-instrument group. This has been constant for many years.

Chart B, with data from a 2003 Gallup poll for the musical instrument industry group NAMM, shows that today's youth market is more active, musically, than other age groups, including members of the Baby Boom generation (born 1946 to 1964). This chart also demonstrates that the new and used market is broad-based – people of all ages are playing. Since the guitar is the number-one-selling instrument, it could be argued that Chart B refutes "The Baby Boom Dropout Theory" which says that as babyboomers age and lose interest in vintage guitars, the vintage

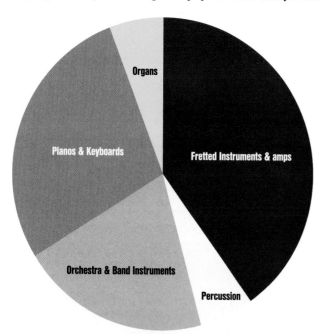

Chart A - Musical Industry Breakdown

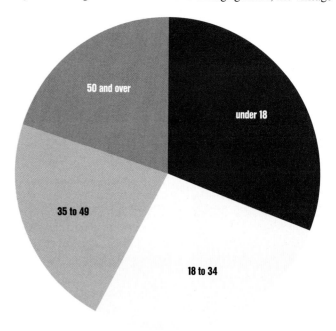

Chart B - Musical Instrument Players by Age

Builder Updates and Corrections

If you produce instruments for sale and would like to be included in the next *VG Price Guide*, send your infomation to al@vguitar.com. Include info on the types of instruments you build, model names and prices, yearly production, the year you started, where you are located and a short bio about yourself.

If you spot errors in the information about brands and models in this guide, or have information on a brand you'd like to see included, please contact us at the above email address. Your help is appreciated.

market bubble will burst. But Chart B shows that well over half of today's guitar enthusiasts are not babyboomers. Combine this with this decade's love affair with the guitar, and you'll find a strong statement that new and vintage guitars are important to popular culture.

Chart C shows the percentage of improving sales in the 1990s and 2000s. Guitar sales show no sign of weakness; in fact they are better than ever. This bodes well for the guitar culture and influences the future of the vintage guitar business.

More Information

Vintage Guitar's website, vintageguitar.com, is updated five times a week from the magazine's inventory of articles. This expanding resource includes interviews with many of your favorite guitarists, reviews of new gear and recordings, and historic information on many of the brands and models covered in this book.

If a model is missing from *the Guide* or if you'd like something clarified, please write us at gil@vguitar.com. If you're a builder and would like to be included, want to correct your info, or have information on your favorite brand, please drop a line to al@vguitar.com.

Acknowledgments

Compiling The *Official Vintage Guitar Price Guide* is a massive undertaking that requires the talents of many people. We use many sources to determine the values, but the vintage instrument dealers who give their time and expertise to provide market information play an important role. Many of them provide info on brands and models, and they are acknowledged throughout the Guide.

Randy Klimpert provided the information and photos in the ukulele section. Many of the brand histories used in this edition are based on the work of Michael Wright, the longtime "Different Strummer" columnist for *VG*.

Several people at *VG* played an important role, as well. Sandi

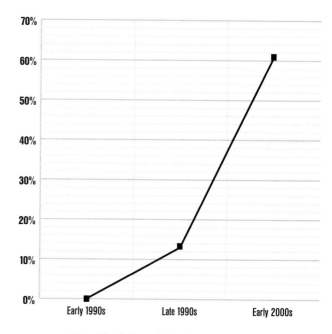

Chart C - Guitars Sales % of Improvement

Stayton did the big job of compiling and cataloging information. Doug Yellow Bird designs the cover and the inside pages and does most of the layout. Jeanine Shea assists with editing and, with James Jiskra, compiles the ads and dealer directory. Ward Meeker selects all the photos. We thank all of them for their usual fine work.

As always, we welcome suggestions, criticisms, and ideas to make future guides better. Contact us at *Vintage Guitar*, Inc., PO Box 7301, Bismarck, ND 58507, or by email at gil@vguitar. com or al@vguitar.com.

Thank you,

Alan Greenwood and Gil Hembree

Guitars

Abyss Custom single-cut

*1963 Airline Super III
Res-O-Glas*

MODEL YEAR	FEATURES	EXC. COND. LOW	HIGH

A Fuller Sound

1998-present. Professional and premium grade, custom nylon and steel-string flat-tops built by Luthier Warren Fuller in Oakland, California.

Abel

1994-present. Custom aircraft-grade aluminum body, wood neck, guitars built by twins Jim and Jeff Abel in Evanston, Wyoming. They offered the Abel Axe from 1994-'96 and 2000-2001, and still do custom orders. They also made the Rogue Aluminator in the late '90s.

Axe

1994-1996. Offset double-cut aluminum body with dozens of holes in the body, wood neck, various colors by annodizing the aluminum body. Abel Axe logo on the headstock.

1994-1996	Non-trem model	$700	$900
1994-1996	Trem model	$700	$900

Abilene

Budget and intermediate grade, production, acoustic and electric guitars imported by Samick.

Acoustic Guitars

Recent import copies.

2000-2002		$75	$125

Electric Guitars

Solidbody and hollowbody electrics, designs often based on classic American models.

2000-2002		$65	$115

Abyss

1997-present. Luthier Kevin Pederson builds his premium grade, production/custom, hollowbody and solidbody guitars in Forest City, Iowa.

5th Anniversary Super Cut

2002. Limited edition model in honor of the firm's 5th anniversary. Single-cut solidbody, high end appointments.

2002	Flamed maple top	$2,300	$2,500

Acoustic

Ca. 1965-ca. 1987, present. Mainly known for solidstate amps, the Acoustic Control Corp. of Los Angeles, California, did offer guitars and basses from around '69 to late '74. The brand was revived by Samick a few years ago on a line of amps.

Black Widow Guitar

1969-1970, 1972-1974. Both versions featured an unique Black equal double cutaway body with German carve, two pickups, a zero fret, and a protective "spider design" pad on back. The early version (called the AC500 Black Widow) had 22 frets, an "Ebonite" fingerboard, and pickups with one row of adjustable polepieces (described as "steel guitar dual pickups" in sales text). The later version was 24 frets, a rosewood 'board, and humbuckers with two rows of adjustable pole pieces (some '72s have the older style pickup). The jack and four control knobs were configured differently on the two versions. Acoustic outsourced the production of the guitars, possibly to Japan, but final

MODEL YEAR	FEATURES	EXC. COND. LOW	HIGH

200 or so guitars produced by Semie Moseley. The AC700 Black Widow 12-string was also available for '69-'70.

1969-1970		$850	$950
1972-1974		$850	$950

Agile

1985-present. Budget grade, production, acoustic and electric guitars imported by Rondo Music of Union, New Jersey. They also offer mandolins.

Solidbody Electrics

Import from Epiphone supplier factory, similar to Epiphone Les Paul or SG-style.

2000s		$150	$200

Aims

Ca. 1974-ca. 1976. Aims instruments, distributed by Randall Instruments in the mid-'70s, were copies of classic American guitar and bass models. Randall also offered a line of Aims amps during the same time.

Airline

Ca. 1958-1968. Airline was a brand used by Montgomery Ward on acoustic, electric archtop and solidbody guitars and basses, amplifiers, steels, and possibly banjos and mandolins. Instruments manufactured by Kay, Harmony and Valco.

Acoustic Archtops (higher end)

1950s		$300	$500
1960s		$300	$500

Acoustic Archtops (lower end)

1950s		$125	$300
1960s		$125	$300

Acoustic Res-O-Glas Resonator

Res-o-glas, coverplate with M-shaped holes, asymmetrical peghead.

1964		$550	$850

Amp-In-Case Model

1960s. Double cut, single pickup, short-scale guitar with amplifier built into the case, Airline on grille.

1960s		$275	$350

Electric Hollowbodies

1950s	Barney Kessel copy	$550	$750
1960s	ES-175 copy	$450	$650
1960s	Harmony H-54 Rocket II copy	$200	$450
1960s	Harmony H-75 (335-style) copy	$400	$600

Electric Res-O-Glas

Res-o-glas is a form of fiberglass. The bodies and sometimes the necks were made of this material.

1960s		$600	$1,000

Electric Res-O-Glas Resonator

Res-o-glas is a form of fiberglass. These models have resonator cones in the body.

1960s		$550	$850

Electric Solidbodies (deluxe-higher end)

Appointments may include multiple pickups, block inlays, additional logos, more binding.

1950s		$500	$900

MODEL YEAR	FEATURES	EXC. COND. LOW	HIGH
Electric Solidbodies (standard-lower end)			
1960s		$300	$500
Flat-Top (lower end, 13" body)			
1960s		$50	$100

Alamo
1947-1982. Founded by Charles Eilenberg, Milton Fink, and Southern Music, San Antonio, TX, and distributed by Bruno & Sons. Alamo started out making radios, phonographs, and instrument cases. In 1949 they added amplifiers and lap steels. From '60 to '70, the company produced beginner-grade solidbody and hollow-core body electric Spanish guitars. The amps were all-tube until the '70s. Except for a few Valco-made examples, all instruments were built in San Antonio. See *Guitar Stories Volume II*, by Michael Wright, for a complete history of Alamo with detailed model listings.

Electric Hollowbodies
| 1960s | | $175 | $350 |

Electric Solidbodies
| 1960s | | $175 | $350 |

Alamo Guitars
2000-present. The Alamo name has been revived for a line of handcrafted, professional grade, production/custom, guitars by Alamo Music Products, which also offers Robin and Metropolitan brand guitars and Rio Grande pickups.

Alan Carruth
1970-present. Professional and premium grade, production/custom, classical and archtop guitars built by luthier Alan Carruth in Newport, New Hampshire. He also builds violins, harps and dulcimers. He started out building dulcimers and added guitars in '74.

Alberico, Fabrizio
1998-present. Luthier Fabrizio Alberico builds his premium grade, custom, flat-top and classical guitars in Cheltenham, Ontario.

Alembic
1969-present. Premium and presentation grade, production/custom, guitars, baritones, and 12-strings built in Santa Rosa, California. They also build basses. Established in San Francisco by Ron and Susan Wickersham, Alembic started out as a studio working with the Grateful Dead and other bands on a variety of sound gear. By '70 they were building custom basses, later adding guitars and cabinets. By '73, standardized models were being offered.

California Special
1988-present. Double cut neck-thru solidbody, six-on-a-side tuners, various colors.
| 1990s | | $1,600 | $1,800 |

Orion
1990-present. Offset double cut glued neck solidbody, various colors.
| 1990s | | $1,400 | $1,600 |

Pan-Alembic
1980s. Single cut body, maple fretboard, logo on pickguard, blade bridge pickup.
| 1980s | | $250 | $350 |

Series I
Early-1970s-present. Neck-through, double cut solidbody with bookmatched koa and black walnut core, three pickups in a single-coil and hum cancelling configuration, optional body styles available, natural.
| 1970s | | $2,500 | $2,800 |

Allen Guitars
1982-present. Premium grade, production resonators, steel-string flat-tops, and mandolins built by Luthier Randy Allen, Colfax, California.

Aloha
1935-1960s. Private branded by Aloha Publishing and Musical Instruments Company, Chicago, Illinois. Made by others. There was also the Aloha Manufacturing Company of Honolulu which made musical instruments from around 1911 to the late '20s.

Alray
1967. Electrics and acoustics built by the Holman-Woodell guitar factory in Neodesha, Kansas, who also marketed similar models under the Holman brand.

Alvarez
1965-present. Intermediate and professional grade, production, acoustic guitars imported by St. Louis Music. They also offer banjos and mandolins. Initially high-quality handmade Yairi guitars were exclusively distributed, followed by lower-priced Alvarez line. In 1990 the Westone brand used on electric guitars and basses was replaced with the Alvarez name; these Alvarez electrics were offered until 2002. Many Alvarez electric models designed by luthier Dana Sutcliffe; several models designed by Dan Armstrong.

Classic I, II, III
1994-1999. Designs based on classic solidbody American models.
| 1994-1999 | | $150 | $200 |

Flat-Top (lower end)
1966-present. Beginner-grade instruments, solid or laminate tops, laminate back and sides, little or no extra appointments. Some are acoustic/electric.
1970s		$50	$100
1980s		$75	$125
1990s		$100	$150

1964 Alamo Fiesta I

Alembic Skylark

GUITARS

Alvarez-Yairi DY-58 9-string

1969 Dan Armstrong lucite

MODEL YEAR	FEATURES	EXC. COND. LOW	HIGH

Flat-Top (mid-level)
1966-present. Solid tops, laminated back and sides, lower appointments such as bound fingerboards and headstocks, nickel hardware and pearl inlay.

1970s		$125	$225
1980s		$125	$225
1990s		$125	$225

Flat-Top (mid-to-high-end)
1966-present. Solid spruce tops, solid mahogany or rosewood backs, laminated mahogany or rosewood sides, may have scalloped bracing, mid-level appointments like abalone headstock inlay, soundhole rosettes and herringbone body binding.

1970s		$250	$350
1980s		$250	$350
1990s		$250	$350

Flat-Top (high end)
1966-present. Solid rosewood and/or mahogany backs and sides, solid spruce tops, may have dovetail neck joint, highest appointments like abalone inlay and real maple binding.

1980s		$500	$600

Fusion Series (with piezo and EQ)
1981-present. Single cutaway, acoustic/electrics with EQ and transducer/piezo pickups. Earlier models had spruce tops with spruce or mahogany back and sides. More recent models have maple tops, backs and sides.

1980s		$300	$400
1990s		$300	$400

Alvarez Yairi
1966-present. Alvarez Yairi guitars are hand-crafted and imported by St. Louis Music.

Flat-Top (mid-level)
Solid top of cedar or spruce, depending on model, mid-level appointments.

1970s		$400	$500
1980s		$400	$500
1990s		$400	$500

Flat-Top (higher-end)
Solid top of cedar or spruce, depending on model, higher-end appointments.

1970s		$700	$900
1980s		$700	$900
1990s		$700	$900

Flat-Top 9-String (DY-58)
Flat-top acoustic with 9 strings (doubles on the 3 high strings).

1989	Natural	$700	$800

Fusion Series (with piezo and EQ)
1998-2002. Piezo bridge with volume and tone controls, higher-end appointments.

1990s		$700	$800

Alvarez, Juan
1960s. Made in Spain by Juan Alvarez, imported to the U.S.A. by Juan. J. Fernandez.

MODEL YEAR	FEATURES	EXC. COND. LOW	HIGH

American Acoustech
1993-2001. Production steel string flat-tops made by Tom Lockwood (former plant manager for Guild) and Dave Stutzman (of Stutzman's Guitar Center) as ESVL Inc. in Rochester, New York.

American Archtop Guitars
1995-present. Premium and presentation grade, custom six- and seven-string archtops by luthier Dale Unger, in Stroudsburg, Pennsylvania.

American Conservatory (Lyon & Healy)
Late-1800s-early-1900s. Mainly catalog sales guitars and mandolins from the Chicago maker. Mid-level Lyon & Healy offering, above Lyon & Healy Lakeside brand, and generally under Lyon & Healy Washburn brand.

Harp Guitar Style G2210
Early-1900s. Two six-string necks with standard tuners, one neck fretless, rosewood back and sides, spruce top, fancy rope colored wood inlay around soundhole, sides and down the back center seam.

1917	Natural	$2,000	$3,500

American Showster
1986-present. Established by Bill Meeker and David Haines, Bayville, New Jersey. The Custom Series is made in the U.S.A., while the Standard Series (introduced in '97) is made in Czechoslovakia.

AS-57 Classic (original '57)
1987-present. Body styled like a 1957 Chevy tail fin, basswood body, bolt-on neck, one humbucker or three single-coil pickups, various colors.

1987-1997		$2,000	$2,500

Ampeg
1949-present. Founded in '49 by Everett Hull as the Ampeg Bassamp Company in New York and has built amplifiers throughout its history. In '62 the company added instruments with the introduction of their Baby Bass and from '63 to '65, they carried a line of guitars and basses built by Burns of London and imported from England. In '66 the company introduced its own line of basses. In '67, Ampeg was acquired by Unimusic, Inc. From '69-'71 contracted with Dan Armstrong to produce lucite "see-through" guitars and basses with replaceable slide-in pickup design. In '71 the company merged with Magnavox. Beginning around '72 until '75, Ampeg imported the Stud Series copy guitars from Japan. Ampeg shut down production in the spring of '80. MTI bought the company and started importing amps. In '86 St. Louis Music purchased the company. In '97 Ampeg introduced new and reissue American-made guitar and bass models. They discontinued the guitar line in 2001.

MODEL YEAR	FEATURES	EXC. COND. LOW	HIGH

AMG1

1999-2001. Dan Amstrong guitar features, but with mahogany body with quilted maple top, two P-90-style or humbucker-style pickups.

1999	Humbuckers, gold hardware	$900	$1,000
1999	Kent Armstrong pickups	$400	$600
1999	P-90s, standard hardware	$400	$600

Dan Armstrong Lucite Guitar

1969-1971. Clear plexiglas solidbody, with interchangable pickups. Dan Armstrong reports that around 9,000 guitars were produced. Introduced in '69, but primary production was in '70-'71. Reissued in '98.

1969		$2,000	$3,000
1970		$2,000	$3,000
1971		$2,000	$3,000

Dan Armstrong Lucite Guitar Reissue

1998-2001. Produced by pickup designer Kent Armstrong (son of Dan Armstrong). Offered in "smoked" (ADAG2) or "clear" (ADAG1).

1998-2001		$700	$850

Heavy Stud (GE-150/GEH-150)

1973-1975. Import from Japan. Single cut body, inexpensive materials, weight added for sustain.

1970s		$275	$375

Sonic Six (By Burns)

1964-1965. Solidbody, 2 pickups, tremolo, cherry finish. Same as the Burns Nu-Sonic guitar.

1960s		$400	$500

Stud (GE-100/GET-100)

1973-1975. Import from Japan. SG body style, inexpensive materials, weight added for sustain. GET-100 included '70s-style SG tremolo assembly.

1970s		$250	$350

Super Stud (GE-500)

1973-1975. Import from Japan. SG body style, inexpensive materials, weight added for sustain. Top-of-the-line in the Stud Series.

1970s		$300	$400

Thinline (By Burns)

1963-1964. Semi-hollowbody, 2 F-holes, 2 pickups, double cut, tremolo. Import by Burns of London. Same as the Burns TR2 guitar.

1963-1964		$350	$450

Wild Dog (By Burns)

1963-1964. Solidbody, 3 pickups, shorter scale, tremolo, sunburst. Import by Burns of London. Same as the Burns Split Sound.

1963-1964		$600	$850

Wild Dog De Luxe (By Burns)

1963-1964. Solidbody, 3 pickups, bound neck, tremolo, sunburst. Import by Burns of London. Same as the Burns Split Sonic guitar.

1963-1964		$500	$650

Andersen Stringed Instruments

1978-present. Luthier Steve Andersen builds premium and presentation grade, production/custom flat-tops and archtops in Seattle, Washington. He also builds mandolins.

Metropolitan

1990s. Large body, soft cutaway, electric archtop, single gold-plated neck humbucker pickup, top quality wood figured back and rims.

1990s		$7,500	$8,500

Andreas

1995-present. Luthier Andreas Pichler builds his aluminium-necked, solidbody guitars and basses in Dollach, Austria.

Angelica

Ca. 1967-1972. Entry-level guitars imported from Japan.

Electric Solidbodies

Japanese import.

1970s		$100	$150

Angus

1976-present. Professional and premium grade, custom-made steel and nylon string flat-tops built by Mark Angus in Laguna Beach, California.

Antares

1990s. Korean-made budget acoustic guitars imported by Vega Music International of Brea, California.

Antique Acoustics

1970s-present. Luthier Rudolph Blazer builds production/custom flat-tops, 12-strings, and archtops in Tubingen, Germany.

Apollo

Ca. 1967-1972. Entry-level guitars imported by St. Louis Music. They also had effects.

Electric Guitars

Japanese imports.

1970s		$100	$125

Applause

1976-present. Budget and intermediate grade, production, acoustic and acoustic/electric guitars. They also offer basses, mandolins and ukes. Kaman Music's entry-level Ovation-styled brand. The instruments were made in the U.S. until around '82, when production was moved to Korea. On the U.S.-made guitars, the back of the neck was molded Urelite, with a cast aluminum neck combining an I-beam neck reinforcement, fingerboard, and frets in one unit. The Korean models have traditional wood necks.

AA Models (acoustic)

Imported. Laminate top, plastic or composition body. Specs and features can vary on AA Models.

1976-1981	U.S.-made	$100	$150
1980s	Import	$75	$100

1963 Ampeg Wild Dog Deluxe

*Antique Acoustics
Blazer Memphis Custom*

Aria Pro II Urchin Deluxe

1855 Ashborn Model 2

MODEL YEAR / FEATURES	EXC. COND. LOW	HIGH
AE Models (acoustic/electric)		
Imported. Laminate top, plastic or composition body. Specs and features can vary on AE Models.		
1976-1981 U.S.-made	$225	$275
1980s	$200	$250
1990s	$200	$250

Arbor

Late-1980s imports by Midco International. Student level to mid-level near copies of classic and popular American models.

MODEL YEAR / FEATURES	EXC. COND. LOW	HIGH
Electric Guitars		
1980s.		
1980s	$175	$275

Arch Kraft

1933-1934. Full-size acoustic archtop and flat-top guitars. Budget brand produced by the Kay Musical Instrument Company and sold through various distributors.

MODEL YEAR / FEATURES	EXC. COND. LOW	HIGH
Acoustic Guitars (archtops or flat-tops)		
1930s	$200	$350

Aria Diamond

Aria established in Japan in 1953, Aria Diamonds were marketed in the 1960s.

MODEL YEAR / FEATURES	EXC. COND. LOW	HIGH
Electric Guitars		
Various models and appointments in the '60s.		
1960s	$300	$400

Aria Pro II/Aria

1960-present. Budget and intermediate grade, production, electric, acoustic, acoustic/electric, and classical guitars. They also make basses, mandolins, and banjos. Aria was established in Japan in '53 and started production of instruments in '60 using the Arai, Aria, Aria Diamond, and Diamond brandnames. The brand was renamed Aria Pro II in '75. The name Aria Pro II was used mainly on electric guitars, with Aria used on others. Over the years, they have produced a variety of acoustic guitars, banjos, mandolins, electric solidbody guitars and basses, amplifiers, and effects. Around '87 Aria moved production of cheaper models to Korea, reserving Japanese manufacturing for more expensive models. In around '95 some models were made in United States, though most contemporary guitars sold in U.S. are Korean. Models have been consolidated by sector unless specifically noted. Model series tend to run for several years and then discontinued.

MODEL YEAR / FEATURES	EXC. COND. LOW	HIGH
Acoustic Solid Wood Top Guitars		
1960s-present. Steel string models, various appointments, generally mid-level imports.		
1980s	$100	$150
Acoustic Veneer Wood Top Guitars		
1960s-present. Steel string models, various appointments, generally entry-level imports.		
1980s	$75	$100

MODEL YEAR / FEATURES	EXC. COND. LOW	HIGH
Classical Solid Wood Top Guitars		
1960s-present. Various models, various appointments, generally mid-level imports.		
1980s	$100	$200
Classical Veneer Wood Top Guitars		
1960s-present. Various models, various appointments, generally entry-level imports.		
1980s	$50	$100
Fullerton Series		
1995-2000. Various models with different appointments and configurations based on the classic offset double cut solidbody.		
1995-2000	$175	$250
Herb Ellis (PE-175/FA-DLX)		
1978-1987 (Model PE-175) and 1988-1993 (Model FA-DLX). Archtop hollowbody, ebony fingerboard, two humbuckers.		
1977-1987	$400	$600
Semi-Solid Electrics		
1980s-present. Various models, various appointments, generally mid-level imports.		
1980s	$250	$350
Solidbody Guitars		
1960s-present. Various models, various appointments, generally mid-level imports.		
1960-1990	$250	$350

Armstrong, Rob

1971-present. Custom steel- and nylon-string flat-tops, 12-strings, and parlor guitars made in Coventry, England by luthier Rob Armstrong. He also builds mandolins and basses.

Arpeggio Korina

1995-present. Professional, premium and presentation grade, production/custom, korina wood solidbody guitars built by luthier Ron Kayfield in Pennsylvania.

Artesano

Professional grade, production, classical guitars built in Valencia, Spain, and distributed by Juan Orozco. Orozco also made higher-end classical Orozco Models 8, 10 and 15.

MODEL YEAR / FEATURES	EXC. COND. LOW	HIGH
Models 20 to 50		
Classical solid tops.		
1985	$175	$275

Artinger Custom Guitars

1997-present. Luthier Matt Artinger builds his professional and premium grade, production/custom, hollow, semi-hollow, and chambered solidbody guitars in Emmaus, Pennsylvania. He also builds basses.

Ashborn

1848-1864. James Ashborn, of Wolcottville, Connecticut, operated one of the largest guitar making factories of the mid-1800s. Models were small parlor-sized instruments with ladder bracing and gut strings. Most of these guitars will need repair.

MODEL		EXC. COND.	
YEAR	FEATURES	LOW	HIGH

Often of more interest as historical artifacts or museum pieces versus guitar collections.

Model 2
1848-1864. Flat-top, plain appointments, no position markers on the neck, identified by Model number.

| 1850s | Fully repaired | $400 | $600 |

Model 5
1848-1864. Flat-top, higher appointments.

| 1850s | Fully repaired | $1,200 | $1,500 |

Atkin Guitars
1993-present. Luthier Alister Atkin builds his production/custom steel and nylon string flat-tops in Canterbury, England. He also builds mandolins.

Audiovox
Ca. 1935-ca. 1950. Paul Tutmarc's Audiovox Manufacturing, of Seattle, Washington, was a pioneer in electric lap steels, basses, guitars and amps.

Austin
1999-present. Budget and intermediate grade, production, acoustic, acoustic/electric, resonator, and electric guitars imported by St. Louis Music. They also offer basses, mandolins and banjos.

Era '62 Standard
2001-present. Tele-style body and configuration, solid hardware body, maple neck and rosewood fretboard.

| 2001 | | $125 | $150 |

Austin Hatchet
Mid-1970s-mid-1980s. Trademark of distributor Targ and Dinner, Chicago, Illinois.

Hatchet
Travel guitar.

| 1980s | | $175 | $200 |

Avanti
1960s. Import from Europe.

Electric Solidbody
1960s. Solidbody with triple single-coil pickups, dot markers, six-on-a-side tuners.

| 1960s | | $100 | $150 |

Bacon & Day
Established in 1921 by David Day and Paul Bacon, primarily known for fine quality tenor and plectrum banjos in the '20s and '30s. Purchased by Gretsch circa '40.

Belmont
Gretsch era, two DeArmond pickups. Natural

| 1950s | | $1,000 | $1,100 |

Ramona Archtop
| 1930s | Sunburst | $500 | $800 |
| 1940s | Sunburst | $500 | $800 |

Senorita Guitar
Sunburst, mahogany back and sides.

| 1940s | | $700 | $1,000 |

Sultana I
1930s. Large 18 1/4" acoustic archtop, Sultana engraved on tailpiece, block markers, bound top and back.

| 1930s | | $3,500 | $3,900 |

Baker U.S.A.
1997-present. Professional and premium grade, production/custom, solidbody electric guitars. Established by master builder Gene Baker after working at the Custom Shops of Gibson and Fender. Baker produced a line of professional and premium grade, production/custom, solid- and hollowbody guitars in Santa Maria, California. They also built basses. Baker produced the Mean Gene brand of guitars from '88-'90. In September '03, the company was liquidated and the Baker U.S.A. name was sold to Robert English and Ed Roman. Gene Baker currently works for Ernie Ball and is no longer involved with Baker U.S.A.

B1/B1 Chambered/B1 Hollow
1997-present. Double cut mahogany body, maple top, with a wide variety of options including chambered and hollowbody construction, set-neck.

| 1997-2003 | | $1,800 | $2,200 |

BJ/BJ Hollow
1997-2003. Double cut mahogany body, P-90-type pickups, several options available, set-neck.

| 1997-2003 | | $1,500 | $1,800 |

BNT
1997-2000. Mahogany solidbody, maple top, with a wide variety of options, neck-through body.

| 1997-2000 | | $1,800 | $2,000 |

Baldwin
1965-1970. The Baldwin company was founded in 1862, in Cincinnati, Ohio when reed organ and violin teacher named Dwight Hamilton Baldwin opened a music store that eventually became one of the largest piano retailers in the Midwest. In 1890, Baldwin began manufacturing upright pianos. In 1935, Baldwin pioneered electronic organs and developed the electronic church organ. By '65, the Baldwin Piano and Organ company was ready to buy into the guitar market but was outbid by CBS for the Fender company. Baldwin did procure Burns of London in September '65, and sold the guitars in the U.S. under the Baldwin name. Baldwin purchased the Gretsch guitar company in '67. English production of Baldwin guitars ends in '70, after which Baldwin concentrates on the Gretsch brand.

Baby Bison (Model 560 by mid-1966)
1966-1970. Double cut solidbody, V headstock, 2 pickups, shorter scale, tremolo, black, red or white finishes.

| 1966-1970 | | $800 | $950 |

Bison (Model 511 by mid-1966)
1965-1970. Double cut solidbody, scroll headstock, 3 pickups, tremolo, black or white finishes.

| 1965-1970 | | $1,100 | $1,300 |

Baker BJ Elite

1967 Baldwin Baby Bison

GUITARS

Baldwin Marvin

1900 Bay State parlour guitar

MODEL YEAR	FEATURES	EXC. COND. LOW	HIGH

Double Six (Model 525 by mid-1966)
1965-1970. Offset double cut solidbody, 12 strings, 3 pickups, green or red sunburst.

| 1965-1970 | | $1,100 | $1,300 |

G.B. 66 De Luxe
1965-1966. Same as Standard with added "density control" on treble horn, golden sunburst.

| 1965-1966 | | $650 | $750 |

G.B. 66 Standard
1965-1970. Thinline Electric archtop, dual Ultra-Sonic pickups, offset cutaways, red sunburst.

| 1965-1970 | | $600 | $700 |

Jazz Split Sound/Split Sound (Model 503 mid-1966)
1965-1970. Offset double cut solidbody, scroll headstock, 3 pickups, tremolo, red sunburst or solid colors.

| 1965-1970 | | $700 | $950 |

Marvin (Model 524 by mid-1966)
1965-1970. Offset double cut solidbody, scroll headstock, 3 pickups, tremolo, white or brown finish.

| 1965-1970 | | $750 | $850 |

Model 706
1967-1970. Double cut semi-hollowbody, scroll headstock, 2 pickups, 2 F-holes, no vibrato, red or golden sunburst.

| 1967-1970 | | $550 | $600 |

Model 706 V
1967-1970. Model 706 with vibrato.

| 1967-1970 | | $550 | $600 |

Model 712 R Electric XII
1967-1970. Model 712 with "regular" neck, 335-style body, red or gold sunburst.

| 1967-1970 | | $550 | $600 |

Model 712 T Electric XII
1967-1970. Model 712 with "thin" neck, 335-style body, red or gold sunburst.

| 1960s | | $550 | $600 |

Nu-Sonic
1965-1970. Solidbody electric student model, six-on-a-side tuners, black or cherry finish.

| 1960s | | $400 | $500 |

Vibraslim (Model 548 by late-1966)
1965-1970. Double cut semi-hollowbody, 2 pickups, tremolo, 2 F-holes, red or golden sunburst.

| 1960s | | $550 | $700 |

Virginian (Model 550 by mid-1966)
1965-1970. Single cut flat-top with 2 pickups, one on each side of soundhole, scroll headstock, tremolo, natural.

| 1960s | | $900 | $1,000 |

Baranik Guitars
1995-present. Premium grade, production/custom steel-string flat-tops made in Tempe, Arizona by luthier Mike Baranik.

Barclay
1960s. Thinline acoustic/electric archtops, solidbody electric guitars and basses imported from Japan. Generally shorter scale beginner guitars.

MODEL YEAR	FEATURES	EXC. COND. LOW	HIGH

Electric Solidbody Guitars
Various models.

| 1960s | Various models | $125 | $225 |

Barcus-Berry
1964-present. Founded by John Berry and Les Barcus introducing the first piezocrystal transducer. Martin guitar/Barcus-Berry products were offered in the mid-1980s. They also offered a line of amps from around '76 to ca. '80.

Model 2510
Steel strings, acoustic bridge pickups, active volume and tone controls, various colors.

| 1980s | | $250 | $350 |

Model 2520 Two-Way
Semi-hollowbody cutaway, acoustic/electric, acoustic bridge pickup, neck magnetic pickup, active mixer, various colors.

| 1980s | | $250 | $350 |

Model 2530 Three-Way
Semi-hollowbody acoustic/electric, acoustic bridge pickup, bridge and neck magnetic pickups, active mixer, various colors.

| 1980s | | $250 | $350 |

Barrington
1988-1991. Imports offered by Barrington Guitar Werks, of Barrington, Illinois. Models included solidbody guitars and basses, archtop electrics, and acoustic flat-tops. Barrington Music Products is still in the music biz, offering LA saxophones and other products.

BGW-800 (acoustic/electric)
1988-1991. Acoustic/electric, flat-top single cutaway with typical round soundhole, opaque White.

| 1988-1991 | | $400 | $500 |

BRG-883 T (solidbody)
1988-ca 1991. Barrington's line of pointy headstock, double cut solidbodies.

| 1988-1991 | | $175 | $225 |

Bartell of California
1964-1969. Founded by Paul Barth (Magnatone) and Ted Peckles. Mosrite-inspired designs.

Electric 12
Mosrite-style body.

| 1964-1969 | | $1,100 | $1,300 |

Bay State
1865-ca.1910. Bay State was a trademark for Boston's John C. Haynes Co.

BC Rich
Ca. 1966/67-present. Budget, intermediate, and premium grade, production/custom, import and U.S.-made, electric and acoustic guitars. They also offer basses. Founded by Bernardo Chavez Rico in Los Angeles, California. As a boy he worked for his guitar-maker father Bernardo Mason Rico (Valencian Guitar Shop, Casa Rico, Bernardo's Guitar Shop), building first koa ukes and later, guitars, steel

MODEL		EXC. COND.	
YEAR	FEATURES	LOW	HIGH

guitars and Martin 12-string conversions. He started using the BC Rich name ca. '66-'67 and made about 300 acoustics until '68, when first solidbody electric made using a Fender neck.

Rich's early models were based on Gibson and Fender designs. First production instruments were in '69 with ten fancy Gibson EB-3 bass and ten matching Les Paul copies, all carved out of single block of mahogany. Early guitars with Gibson humbuckers, then Guild humbuckers, and, from '74-'86, DiMarzio humbuckers. Around 150 BC Rich Eagles were imported from Japan in '76. Ca. '76 or '77 some bolt-neck guitars with parts made by Wayne Charvel were offered. Acoustic production ended in '82 (acoustics were again offered in '95).

For '83-'86 the BC Rich N.J. Series ("N.J." Nagoya, Japan) was built by Masan Tarada. U.S. Production Series (U.S.-assembled Korean kits) in '84. From '86 on, the N.J. Series was made by Cort in Korea. Korean Rave and Platinum series begin around '86. In '87, Rich agrees to let Class Axe of New Jersey market the Korean Rave, Platinum and N.J. Series. Class Axe (with Neil Moser) introduces Virgin in '87 and in '88 Rave and Platinum names are licensed to Class Axe. In '89, Rico licensed the BC Rich name to Class Axe. Both imported and American-made BC Riches are offered during Class Axe management. In 2000, BC Rich became a division of Hanser Holdings. During '90-'91, Rico begins making his upscale Mason Bernard guitars (approx. 225 made). In '94, Rico resumes making BC Rich guitars in California.

First 340-360 U.S.-built guitars were numbered sequentially beginning in '72. Beginning in '74, serial numbers change to YYZZZ pattern (year plus consecutive production). As production increased in the late-'70s, the year number began getting ahead of itself. By '80 it was two years ahead; by '81 as much as four years ahead. No serial number codes on imports.

Assassin

1986-1998. Double cut body, 2 humbuckers, maple through-neck dot markers, various colors.

1986-1989		$700	$800
1990-1998		$700	$800

Assassin (N.J. Series)

1986-2001. Import model

1986-2001		$300	$350

B-28 Acoustic

Ca.1967-1982. Acoustic flat-top, hand-built, solid spruce top, rosewood back and sides, herringbone trim, large pearl R logo on headstock. Known to have its own voice, not exactly similar to a Martin or Gibson flat-top.

1970-1982		$600	$900

B-30 Acoustic

Ca.1967-1982. Acoustic flat-top.

1967-1982		$600	$900

B-38 Acoustic

Ca.1967-1982. Acoustic flat-top, cocobolo back and sides, herringbone trim.

1967-1982		$600	$900

B-45 Acoustic

Hand built, D-style rosewood body.

1970s		$2,400	$2,700

Bich (N.J. Series)

1983-present. Imported bolt-neck version.

1980s		$250	$350
1990s		$250	$350

Bich (U.S.A. assembly)

1976-1998. Four-point sleek body style. Assembly in U.S.A. Came in Standard top or Supreme with highly figured maple body.

1970s	Supreme top	$1,500	$1,900
1980s	Standard top	$1,000	$1,200
1980s	Supreme top	$1,300	$1,500
1990s	Standard top	$900	$1,100

Bich 10-String

1976-1990s. Doubles on four low strings.

1979-1982		$2,300	$2,700

Bich Doubleneck

Six/twelve doubleneck.

1980s		$2,100	$2,600

Black Hole

1988. Bolt-on neck, rosewood 'board, integrated pickup design, Floyd Rose.

1988		$175	$275

Eagle Doubleneck

Rosewood, cloud inlay.

1975		$3,300	$3,900

Eagle Special

1977-ca.1982. Koa.

1981	Natural	$900	$1,200

Eagle Supreme

1977-present.

1977		$1,300	$1,700

Exclusive EM2

1996-1998. Double cut solidbody, three-on-a-side tuners, dual humbuckers, various colors.

1996-1998		$175	$250

G-String

Kahler tremolo.

1980s		$250	$400

Gunslinger

1987-1999. Inverted headstock, one (Gunslinger I) or two (Gunslinger II) humbuckers. Recessed cutout behind Floyd Rose allows player to pull notes up two full steps.

1980s	Black, maple neck	$450	$600
1980s	Various artist designs (e.g. Nagal)	$700	$800
1990s	Red Sparkle	$400	$550

Ironbird

1981-present. Pointy body and headstock.

1981-1989		$600	$800

Ironbird Doubleneck

Six/twelve doubleneck.

1980s		$1,800	$2,300

Mockingbird

1976-present. Maple or koa.

1970s	Earlier short horn style	$1,800	$2,000

1982 BC Rich Bich

BC Rich Ironbird

BC Rich Mockingbird

Benedetto Fratello

MODEL YEAR	FEATURES	EXC. COND. LOW	HIGH
1970s	Later long horn style	$1,900	$2,100
1980s		$1,400	$1,600
Mockingbird (N.J. Series)			
1983-present. Import model.			
1980s		$300	$375
Mockingbird Supreme			
1976-present. Offset rosewood body with sharp treble horn, cloud inlays, U.S.A.-made.			
1976-1979		$1,900	$2,200
1990s		$1,300	$1,600
Nighthawk			
1978-ca.1982. Bolt-on neck.			
1978-1982		$500	$700
Outlaw			
1987-ca. 1993. N.J. Series, like Gunslinger with reverse headstock.			
1987-1993		$1,000	$1,100
Phoenix			
1977-ca.1982. Bolt-on neck.			
1977-1982		$300	$550
Seagull			
1972-1976. Single cutaway solidbody, neck-through, two humbuckers.			
1972-1976		$1,300	$1,700
Seagull Doubleneck			
Koa.			
1979		$3,200	$3,800
Seagull II			
1976. Double cut solidbody, neck-through, two humbuckers.			
1976		$1,000	$1,300
Seagull Supreme			
1970s		$1,600	$2,000
ST Platinum Series (import)			
1986-1998. Solidbody, import from Korea.			
1986-1989		$250	$400
ST-III (U.S.A.-made)			
Solidbody electric, bolt-on maple neck, two single-coils and one humbucker, Kahler tremolo, Black hardware. Variety of bold colors.			
1980s		$400	$700
1990s		$400	$700
Stealth I Series II			
1983-1989. Mahogany body and neck, dot inlays, 24-fret neck, 2 pickups.			
1983-1989		$800	$900
Stealth I Standard			
1983-1989. Maple body, two pickups, 24-fret neck, diamond-shaped inlays.			
1983-1989		$800	$900
The Mag			
U.S. Handcrafted Series Mockingbird Acoustic Supreme, with solid spruce top, quilted maple back and sides, pickup with preamp and EQ optional.			
2000	Dark Sunburst	$950	$1,000
Virgin (N.J. Series)			
1987-1993, 2000-present. Import from Japan and Korea.			
1987-1993		$325	$375

MODEL YEAR	FEATURES	EXC. COND. LOW	HIGH
Warlock			
1981-present. Four-point sleek body style with widow headstock.			
1980s		$900	$1,200
1990s		$900	$1,200
Warlock (N.J. Series)			
Imported bolt-neck.			
1990s		$350	$500
Warlock (Platinum Series import)			
1988-present. Lower-end import.			
1988-2000		$300	$375
Warlock Supreme			
1980s. Solid peghead vs. widow headstock.			
1980s		$1,100	$1,700

Bear Creek Guitars

1995-present. Luthier Bill Hardin worked for OMI Dobro and Santa Cruz Guitar before introducing his own line of professional and premium grade, custom-made Wessenborn-style guitars, made in Kula, Hawaii. He also builds ukuleles.

Beardsell Guitars

1996-present. Production/custom flat-tops, classical and electric solidbody guitars built by luthier Allan Beardsell in Toronto, Ontario.

Beltona

1991-present. Production/custom metal body resonator guitars made in New Zealand by Steve Evans and Bill Johnson. Beltona was originally located in England.

Beltone

1930s-1940s. Lower-end models.

Resonator Copy

1930s-1940s. Resonator copy but without a real resonator, rather just an aluminum plate on a wooden top, body mahogany plywood.

1938		$250	$300

Benedetto

1968-present. Archtop guitars, violins and a few solidbodies hand-crafted by Robert Benedetto in East Stroudsburg, PA. He is especially known for refining the seven-string guitar. As of '99, Benedetto only makes special order instruments. He licensed the names of his standard models to Guild, which now makes them in their Custom Shop in Nashville, TN. (Refer to Benedetto FMIC for post-'99 instruments.)

Benny

Electric semi-hollow, 14 1/2" body, cutaway, chambered Sitka spruce top.

1990s	Natural	$4,000	$5,000

Benny Deluxe

Electric semi-hollow, chambered spruce top, abalone inlays, deluxe version of the Benny.

1990s	Sunburst	$5,000	$6,000

MODEL YEAR	FEATURES	EXC. COND. LOW	HIGH

Cremona
Acoustic/electric archtop, single cutaway, 17" body, Natural.

1988-1991		$19,000	$22,000

Fratello
1988-1999. Acoustic archtop, single cutaway, 17" body, blond or sunburst.

1980s	Blond or sunburst	$13,000	$15,000
1990s	Honey blond	$13,000	$15,000

La Venezia
Acoustic archtop, single cutaway, 17" body.

1990s	Sunburst	$16,000	$17,000

Limelite Custom
1993. Single-cutaway, neck pickup, select aged wood, Blond.

1993		$20,000	$25,000

Manhattan
1989-1999. Archtop with 16" body, neck pickup, Blond.

1989-1999		$12,000	$14,000

Manhattan Custom
Carved 17" body, Blond.

1990s		$14,000	$16,000

Benedetto (FMIC)
1999-present. Premium and presentation, production/custom, acoustic and electric archtops. In '99, Bob Benedetto entered into an agreement with Fender (FMIC) to have the FMIC Guild Custom Shop, Nashville, TN, build Benedetto guitars under his guidance and supervision.

Artist
2000- .

2001		$5,000	$5,500

Manhattan
2000-present. 17" single cut archtop (3" deep), suspended mini-humbucking pickup.

2000		$10,000	$11,000

Bently
ca.1985-1998. Student and intermediate grade copy style acoustic and electric guitars imported by St. Louis Music Supply. Includes the Series 10 electrics and the Songwriter acoustics (which have a double reversed B crown logo on the headstock). St. Louis Music replaced the Bently line with the Austin brand.

2230/2231/2232
Double cut solidbody, 3 pickups, dot markers, sunburst, red or black.

1980s		$75	$125

Songwriter Dreadnought 5111
Spruce top, mahogany, Natural.

1980s		$50	$100

Bertoncini Stringed Instruments
1995-present. Luthier Dave Bertoncini builds his premium grade, custom, flat-top guitars in Olympia, Washington. He has also built solidbody electrics, archtops, mandolins and banjos.

Beyond The Trees
1976-present. Luthier Fred Carlson offers a variety of innovative designs for his professional and presentation grade, production/custom six- and 12-string flat-tops in Santa Cruz, California. He also produces the Sympitar (a six-string with added sympathetic strings) and the Dreadnautilus (a unique shaped headless acoustic).

Bigsby
1946-present. Pedal steel guitars, hollow-chambered electric Spanish guitars, electric mandolins, doublenecks, replacement necks on acoustic guitars, hand vibratos, all handmade by Paul Arthur Bigsby, machinist and motorcycle enthusiast (designer of '30s Crocker motorcycles), in Downey, California. Initially built for special orders.

Bigsby was a pioneer in developing pedal steels. He designed a hand vibrato for Merle Travis. In '48, his neck-through hollow electrics (with Merle Travis) influenced Leo Fender, and Bigsby employed young Semie Moseley. In '56, he designed the Magnatone Mark series guitars and one Hawaiian lap steel.

He built less than 50 Spanish guitars, six mandolins, 125 to 150 pedal steels and 12 or so neck replacements. SN was stamped on the end of fingerboard: MMDDYY. In '65, the company was sold to Gibson president Ted McCarty who moved the tremolo/vibrato work to Kalamazoo. Bigsby died in '68.

Fred Gretsch purchased the Bigsby company from Ted McCarty in '99. A solidbody guitar and a pedal steel based upon the original Paul Bigsby designs were introduced January, 2002. Early Bigsby guitars command high value on the collectible market.

Solidbody Guitars
Late-1940s-early-1950s.

1948-1952	Natural	$18,000	$25,000

Bil Mitchell Guitars
1979-present. Luthier Bil Mitchell builds his professional and premium grade, production/custom, flat-top and archtop guitars in Wall, New Jersey.

Bischoff Guitars
1975-present. Professional and premium-grade, custom-made flat-tops built by luthier Gordy Bischoff in Eau Claire, Wisconsin.

Bishline Guitars
1985-present. Luthier Robert Bishline builds custom-made flat-tops and resonators in Tulsa, Oklahoma. He also builds mandolins and banjos.

Black Jack
1960s. Violin-body hollowbody electric guitars and basses, possibly others. Imported from Japan by unidentified distributor. Manufacturers unknown, but some may be Arai.

1985 Bently Series 10 graphite

1952 Bigsby Grady Martin Doubleneck

GUITARS

Blade RH4

Bolin Cobra

MODEL YEAR	FEATURES	EXC. COND. LOW	HIGH

Blackshear, Tom

1958-present. Premium and presentation grade, production, classical and flamenco guitars made by luthier Tom Blackshear in San Antonio, Texas.

Blade

1987-present. Intermediate and professional grade, production, solidbody guitars from luthier Gary Levinson, who started repairing guitars in '64 and started Levinson Music Products Ltd. in Switzerland in '87 to produce Blade guitars. He also builds basses.

California Custom
1994-present. California Standard with maple top and high-end appointments.

1994-1999		$700	$1,000

California Deluxe
1994-1995. Standard with mahogany body and maple top.

1994-1995		$600	$700

California Hybrid
1998-1999. Standard with piezo bridge pickup.

1998-1999		$550	$650

California Standard
1994-present. Offset double cut, swamp ash body, bolt neck, five-way switch.

1994-1999		$350	$450

R 3
1988-1993. Offset double cut maple solidbody, opaque finishes, bolt maple neck, 3 single-coils or single/single/humbucker.

1988-1993		$400	$500

R 4
1988-1993. R 3 with ash body and see-thru color finishes.

1988-1993		$500	$600

Blanchard Guitars

1994-present. Luthier Mark Blanchard builds premium grade, custom steel-string and classical guitars originally in Mammoth Lakes, California, and since May '03, in northwest Montana.

Blue Star

1984-present. Luthier Bruce Herron builds his production/custom guitars in Fennville, Michigan. He also builds mandolins, lap steels, dulcimers and ukes.

Travelmaster

1990s		$200	$250

Bluebird

1930s. Private brand with Bluebird painted on headstock, probably made by Harmony or another Chicago mass-producer.

13" Flat-Top
1930s. Private brand with Bluebird painted on headstock.

1938		$75	$150

Blueridge

Early 1980s-present. Intermediate and professional grade, production, solid-top acoustic guitars distributed by Saga. In '00, the product line was redesigned with the input of luthier Greg Rich (Rich and Taylor guitars).

Boaz Elkayam Guitars

1985-present. Presentation grade, custom steel, nylon, and flamenco guitars made by luthier Boaz Elkayam in Chatsworth, California.

Bohmann

1878-ca. 1926. Acoustic flat top guitars, harp guitars, mandolins, banjos, violins made in Chicago, by Joseph Bohmann (born 1848, Neumarkt, Bohemia, Czechoslovakia). Bohmann's American Musical Industry founded 1878. Guitar body widths are 12", 13", 14", 15". He had 13 grades of guitars by 1900 (Standard, Concert, Grand Concert sizes). Early American use of plywood. Some painted wood finishes. Special amber-oil varnishes. Tuner bushings. Early ovalled fingerboards. Patented tuner plates and bridge design. Steel engraved label inside. Probably succeeded by son Joseph Frederick Bohmann.

Ca. 1896 12" body faux rosewood, 13", 14" and 15" body faux rosewood birch, 12", 13", 14" and 15" body Sunburst maple, 12", 13", 14" and 15" body rosewood.

By 1900 Styles 0, 1, 2 and 3 Standard, Concert and Grand Concert maple, Styles 1, 2, 3, 4, 5, 6, 7, 8, 9, 10, 11 and 12 in Standard, Concert, and Grand Concert rosewood.

14 3/4" Flat-Top
Solid spruce top, veneered Brazilian rosewood back and sides, wood marquetry around top and soundhole, Natural. Each Bohmann should be valued on a case-by-case basis.

1900		$1,100	$1,400

Bolin

1978-present. Professional and premium grade, production/custom, solidbody guitars built by luthier John Bolin in Boise, Idaho. Bolin is well-known for his custom work. His Cobra guitars are promoted and distributed by Sanderson Sales and Marketing as part of the "Icons of America" Series.

NS
1996-present. Slot-headstock, bolt-on neck, single cutaway solidbody, Seymour Duncan passive pickups or EMG active. From 1996 to the fall of 2001 custom-built serial numbers to 0050 then from the fall of 2001 to the present production model build starting with SN 0051.

2001-2003	Standard production	$2,000	$2,100

Bond

1984-1985. Andrew Bond made around 1,400 Electraglide guitars in Scotland. Logo says 'Bond Guitars, London.'

MODEL YEAR	FEATURES	EXC. COND. LOW	HIGH

Digital Guitar
1983-1986. Double cut solid carbon-composite body and neck, digital LED display, special power supply required and used with special cable, black.
1983-1986 $1,100 $1,200

ElectraGlide
1984-1985. Black carbon graphite one-piece body and neck, double cut, 3 single-coils (2 humbuckers were also supposedly available), digital LED controls that required a separate transformer.
1984-1985 $900 $1,000

Graphite Guitar
1983-1986. Double cut (more Gisbon-style than Fender) black graphite body, 3 pickups, special power supply required, special cable required.
1983-1986 $1,000 $1,300

Bourgeois
1993-1999, 2000-present. Luthier Dana Bourgeois builds his professional and premium grade, production/custom, acoustic and archtop guitars in Lewiston, Maine. Bourgeois co-founded Schoenberg guitars and built Schoenberg models from '86-'90. Bourgeois' 20th Anniversary model was issued in '97. Bourgeois Guitars, per se, went of business at the end of '99. Patrick Theimer created Pantheon Guitars, which included seven luthiers (including Bourgeois) working in an old 1840s textile mill in Lewiston, Maine and Bourgeois models continue to be made as part of the Pantheon organization.

Serial Number List
1993	1-70
1994	71-205
1995	206-350
1996	351-665
1997	666-1040
1998	1041-1450
1999	1451-1975

Country Boy
1990s-present. Pre-war D-style model designed for Ricky Skaggs with Sitka spruce top, select mahogany back and sides, Bourgeois script logo headstock inlay, individually labeled with a Ricky Skaggs label, Natural.
1990s $1,800 $2,200

Custom OMS
1990s. Triple 0-size, 12-fret, Indian rosewood back and sides, Englemann spruce top.
1990s $3,000 $3,300

D - 20th Anniversary
1997. Special production of 20 instruments, 'bearclaw' spruce top, select rosewood back and sides, luminescent mother-of-pearl fingerboard inlaid with ornate abalone floral pattern, fancy abalone rosette and border, Natural.
1997 $3,300 $3,500

JOM (Brazilian rosewood)
Jumbo Orchestra Model flat-top, 15 5/8", spruce top, Brazilian rosewood back and sides.
1990s $3,100 $3,900

JOM (mahogany)
Jumbo Orchestra Model flat-top, 15 5/8", cedar top, mahogany back and sides.
1990s $1,300 $1,600

JR-A
Artisan Series, 15 5/8", spruce top, rosewood back and sides.
1990s $900 $1,100

Martin Simpson
1997-2003. Grand auditorium with unusual cutaway that removes one-half of the upper treble bout, Englemann spruce top, Indian rosewood back and sides, Natural.
1997-2003 $2,600 $2,700

OMC (Brazilian rosewood)
1990s-present. Full-sized, soft cutaway flat-top, Adirondack spruce top, figured Brick Red Brazilian rosewood back and sides, Natural.
1990s $5,000 $5,200

OMS (Indian rosewood)
1990s. Full body, non-cutaway, Indian rosewood back and sides, size is 000 with 12-fret neck.
1990s $2,700 $3,000

Slope D
D-size, 16", spruce top, mahogany back and sides.
1990s $1,700 $2,000

Bourgeois D-150

Bown Guitars
1981-present. Luthier Ralph Bown builds custom steel-string, nylon-string, baritone, and harp guitars in Walmgate, England.

Bozo
1964-present. Bozo (pronounced Bo-zho) Padunovac learned instrument building in his Yugoslavian homeland and arrived in the United States in 1959. He '64 he opened his own shop and has built a variety of high-end, handmade, acoustic instruments, many being one-of-a-kind. He has built around 570 guitars over the years. There were several thousand Japanese-made (K. Yairi shop) Bell Western models bearing his name made from '79-'80; most of these were sold in Europe. He currently builds premium and presentation grade, production/custom guitars in Lindenhurst, Illinois.

Cutaway 12-String
Often old world Balkan ornamentation, generally Sitka spruce top, Indian rosewood back and sides, Widow-style headstock, ornamentation can vary.

1977	Standard ornamentation	$2,000	$2,500
1993	Elaborate ornamentation	$5,000	$6,000
1998	Elaborate custom ornamentation	$6,500	$7,500

Bradford
Mid-1960s. Brand name used by the W.T. Grant Company, one of the old "5 & 10" style retail stores similar to F.W. Woolworth and Kresge.

Bozo 40th Anniversary

GUITARS

Breedlove Balance

1990s Brian Moore MC/1

MODEL YEAR	FEATURES	EXC. COND. LOW	HIGH

Many of these instruments were made in Japan by Guyatone.

Acoustic Flat-Tops
Various colors.

1960s		$100	$200

Electric Solidbody Guitars
Various colors.

1960s		$100	$200

Breedlove

1990-present. Founded by Larry Breedlove and Steve Henderson. Professional, premium, and presentation grade, production/custom, steel and nylon string flat-tops built in Tumalo, Oregon. They also build mandolins. Several available custom options may add to the values listed here.

C1 (C10)
1990-present. Shallow concert-sized flat-top, non-cutaway, solid spruce top, mahogany back and sides, natural.

1994-1995		$1,400	$1,600

C15/R
1990-present. Concert-size C1 with soft rounded cutaway, and optional cedar top and rosewood back and sides, gold tuners.

1997		$1,800	$2,000

N25E
Classical electric, 15 1/4" with Fishman pickup, solid red cedar top, solid rosewood back and sides, abalone soundhole rosette, offset dot markers.

2002		$1,800	$2,000

RD20 X/R
Indian rosewood back and sides, sitka spruce top, winged bridge, abalone soundhole rosette.

1999		$1,800	$1,900

SC20-Z Custom
Mid-size with deep body, flat-top, Zircote back and sides, sitka spruce top.

1999		$1,800	$2,000

SJ20-12 W
12-string, walnut (W) back and sides.

2000		$1,800	$2,000

Brian Moore

1992-present. Founded by Patrick Cummings, Brian Moore and Kevin Kalagher in Brewster, New York; they introduced their first guitars in '94. Initially expensive custom shop guitars with carbon-resin bodies with highly figured wood tops; later went to all wood bodies cut on CNC machines. The intermediate and professional grade, production, iGuitar/i2000series was introduced in 2000 and made in Korea, but set up in the U.S. Currently the premium grade, production/custom, Custom Shop Series guitars are handcrafted in La Grange, NY. They also build basses and electric mandolins.

C-45
1999-2001. Solidbody, mahogany body, bolt-on neck, two P-90-type pickups.

1990s		$900	$1,000

C-55
1997-present. Solidbody, burl maple body, bolt-on neck. Currently produced as a limited edition.

1997-1999		$900	$1,000

C-90
1996-present. Solidbody, figured maple top on mahogany body, bolt-on neck, hum-single-hum pickups.

1996-2000	Red Sunburst	$1,100	$1,300

DC1
1997-present. High quality quilted maple top, double humbucker, single cutaway option, gold hardware.

1997-2000		$1,600	$1,900

iGuitar 2.13
2000-present. Solidbody Midi controller, dual humbuckers and piezo bridge pickup, figured maple top, gold hardware, made in Korea, sold in conjunction with a Roland processor.

2000-2003		$600	$800

MC1
1994-present. High-end model, quilted maple top, various pickup options including piezo and midi, gold hardware. Should be evaluated on a case-by-case basis.

1994-2000	Various options	$2,500	$4,000

Brian Stone Classical Guitars

Luthier Brian Stone builds his classical guitars in Corvallis, Oregon.

Brook Guitars

1993-present. Simon Smidmore and Andy Petherick build their production/custom Brook steel-string, nylon-strings, and archtops in Dartmoor, England.

Bruné, R. E.

1966-present. Luthier Richard Bruné builds his premium and presentation grade, custom, classical and flamenco guitars in Evanston, Illinois. He also offers his professional and premium grade Model 20 and Model 30, which are handmade in a leading guitar workshop in Japan. Bruné's "Guitars with Guts" column appears quarterly in *Vintage Guitar* magazine.

Bruno and Sons

1834-present. Established in 1834 by Charles Bruno, primarily as a distributor, Bruno and Sons marketed a variety of brandnames, including their own; currently part of Kaman.

Harp Guitar

1924		$1,500	$2,500

Hollowbody Electrics
1960s-1970s. Various imported models.

1960s		$200	$250

Parlor Guitar
Brazilian rosewood back and sides.

1880-1920		$750	$1,000

MODEL		EXC. COND.	
YEAR	FEATURES	LOW	HIGH

Bunker

1961-present. Founded by guitarist Dave Bunker, who started building custom guitars and basses while performing in Las Vegas in the '60s. Bunker began building guitars with his father and developed a number of innovations. Around '92 Bunker began PBC Guitar Technology in Allentown, PA, building American-made instruments for Ibanez. PBC closed in '97 and Bunker moved back to Washington State to start Bunker Guitar Technology and resumed production of several Bunker models. In early 2002, Bunker Guitars became part of Maple Valley Tone Woods of Port Angeles, Washington. Currently Bunker offers intermediate, professional, and premium grade, production/custom, guitars and basses built in Port Angeles.

Most early Bunker guitars were pretty much custom-made in low quantities.

Electric Solidbody or Archtop Guitars
Various colors.

1960s		$750	$850
1970s		$750	$850
1980s		$750	$850
1990s		$750	$850

Burns

Late 1950s-1970, 1992-present. Intermediate and professional grade, production, electric guitars built in England. Reissue-style models include the Bison, Elite Custom, Marquee, Marquee Special. They also build basses.

Jim Burns began building guitars in the late-1950s. Baldwin Organ (see Baldwin listing) purchased the company in '65 and offered the instruments until '70. The Burns name was revived in '91 by Barry Gibson as Burns London, with Jim Burns' involvement, offering reproductions of some of the classic Burns models of the '60s (distributed in the U.S. by Burns USA). Jim Burns passed away in August '98.

Bison
1964-1965. Double cut solidbody, 3 pickups, tremolo, black or white.

1964-1965		$1,150	$1,350

Flyte
1974-1977. Fighter jet-shaped solidbody, pointed headstock, 2 humbucking pickups, silver.

1974-1977		$700	$900

Jazz Split Sound
1962-1965. Offset double cut solidbody, 3 pickups, tremolo, red sunburst.

1962-1965		$700	$950

Marvin
1964-1965. Offset double cut solidbody, scroll headstock, 3 pickups, tremolo, white.

1964-1965		$800	$900

Nu-Sonic
1964-1965. Solidbody, 2 pickups, tremolo, white.

1965		$400	$500

Split Sonic
1962-1964. Solidbody, 3 pickups, bound neck, tremolo, sunburst.

1962-1964		$550	$700

TR-2
1963-1964. Semi-acoustic model.

1963-1964		$350	$450

Virginian
1964-1965. Burns of London model, later offered as Baldwin Virginian in 1965.

1964-1965		$950	$1,050

Burnside

1987-1988. Budget solidbody guitars imported by Guild.

Solidbody Electric/Blade
1987-1988. Kramer-style solidbody, fat pointy headstock.

1987-1988	Red-Orange Sunburst	$325	$375

Burton Guitars

1980-present. Custom classical guitars built by luthier Cynthia Burton in Portland, Oregon.

Buscarino Guitars

1981-present. Luthier John Buscarino builds his premium and presentation grade, custom archtops and steel-string and nylon-string flat-tops in Franklin, North Carolina.

Byers, Gregory

1984-present. Premium grade, custom classical and Flamenco guitars built by luthier Gregory Byers in Willits, California.

C. Fox

1997-2002. Luthier Charles Fox built his premium grade, production/custom flat-tops in Healdsburg, California. In 2002 he closed C. Fox Guitars and move to Portland, Oregon to build Charles Fox Guitars.

CA (Composite Acoustics)

1999-present. Professional grade, production, carbon fiber composite guitars built in Lafayette, Louisiana.

Callaham

1989-present. Professional, production/custom, solidbody electric guitars built by luthier Bill Callaham in Winchester, Virginia. They also make tube amp heads.

Campellone

1978-present. Luthier Mark Campellone builds his premium grade, custom archtops in Smithfield, Rhode Island. He also made electrics and basses in the '70s and '80s, switching to archtops around 1990.

Brian Moore i2p

Burns Vitasonic

Campellone Cameo

Carvin DC-135

MODEL YEAR FEATURES	EXC. COND. LOW	HIGH

Deluxe
1990-present. 17", middle of the company product line, archtop, Blond or Sunburst.
1990-1995 — $5,500 — $6,000

Special
1994-present. 16" to 18" archtop, carved spruce top, carved flamed maple back, flamed maple sides, Blond or Sunburst.
199-1999 — $6,500 — $7,000

Carbonaro
1974-present. Luthier Robert Carbonaro builds his premium grade, production/custom, archtop and flat-top guitars in Santa Fe, New Mexico.

Carlos
ca.1976-late 1980s. Imported copies of classic American acoustics distributed by Coast Wholesale Music.

Model 240
1970s. D-18 copy with mahogany (laminate?) back and sides, spruce top, Natural.
1978 — $150 — $300

Model 275
1970s. D-35 copy with rosewood (laminate?) sides and three-piece back, spruce top, Natural.
1978 — $175 — $350

Carvin
1946-present. Intermediate and professional grade, production/custom, acoustic and electric guitars. They also offer basses and amps. Founded in Los Angeles by Hawaiian guitarist and recording artist Lowell C. Kiesel as the L.C. Kiesel Co. making pickups for guitars. Bakelite Kiesel-brand electric Hawaiian lap steels are introduced in early-'47. Small tube amps introduced ca. '47. By late-'49, the Carvin brandname is introduced, combining parts of names of sons Carson and Gavin. Carvin acoustic and electric Spanish archtops are introduced in '54. Instruments are sold by mail-order only. The company relocated to Covina, California in '49 and to Escondido, California in '68. Two retail stores opened in Hollywood and Santa Ana, California in '91.
   Approx. 2,000-4,000 guitars made prior to '70 with no serial number. First serial number appeared in '70, stamped on end of fingerboard, beginning with #5000. All are consecutive. Later SN on neck plates. Approximate SN ranges include:
1970:   First serial number #5000.
1980-83: Serial numbers in 11000 range (approx. 1000/year) [koa DC200K #11815, 1981].
1983-84: #13000-15000.
1985-86: #17000-20000.
1988-89: #22000-25000.
1989-91: #26000-33000.
1992:   #35000-ff.

AE185
1994-present. Single cut acoustic/electric, F-hole.
1994-2000 — $600 — $900

MODEL YEAR FEATURES	EXC. COND. LOW	HIGH

BC130
1989-1990. Neck-through-body, double cut, three pickups, trem.
1989-1990 — $350 — $450

CM130
1976-early-1980s. Single cutaway solidbody, two humbucking pickups, phase and coil split switches.
1976-1982 — $500 — $600

DB-630 Doubleneck
1970s. Six/four (bass) doubleneck.
1977 — $700 — $1,000

DBS-98 B Doubleneck
1970s. Three pickups, four/six strings. Natural.
1970s — $700 — $1,000

DC-100
1980s. Double cutaway solidbody.
1980s — $350 — $450

DC-125
1991-1996. Double cutaway solidbody, one humbucking pickup.
1991-1996 — $500 — $600

DC-127
1991-present.
1991-2000 — $500 — $600

DC-135
1991-present. Double cut, neck-through construction, single-single-hum pickups.
1991-1999 — $500 — $700

DC-150
1977-1991, 2002-present. Double cut solidbody, 2 humbuckers, stereo wiring.
1977-1991 — $500 — $700

DC-200
1980-present. Double cut solidbody, block inlays, 2 humbuckers.
1980s — $500 — $700

DC-400
1993-present. Double cut, koa body, flamed maple top, neck-through, and higher appointments.
1993-2000 — $600 — $800

DN-612 Doubleneck
1981-1996. Twelve-string and six-string doubleneck, double cutaway.
1981-1990 — $800 — $1,000

DT-650 Doubleneck
Late-1970s. Doubleneck with 12/6 strings, maple body and necks, block inlays, two split-coil humbuckers for each neck.
1970s — $800 — $1,000

SGB
1955-1962. Single-cutaway slab body, two single-coil pickups (later humbuckers), dot markers.
1955-1958 — P-90-style pickups — $500 — $600
1959-1962 — Humbucker-style pickups — $500 — $600

SH-225
Semi-hollowbody.
1981 — $500 — $600

MODEL YEAR	FEATURES	EXC. COND. LOW	HIGH

TL-60 (T)
1993-present. Single cut, neck-thru solidbody, 2 single coils. The earlier T version had 1 humbucker, 1 single coil.

1993-1999		$500	$600

Ultra V
1988-1993. V-shaped solidbody with bass wing shorter than treble side, block inlays, two humbucking pickups.

1988-1993		$500	$600

Casa Montalvo
1987-present. Intermediate and professional grade, production/custom flamenco and classical guitars made in Mexico for George Katechis of Berkeley Musical Instrument Exchange.

Casio
1987-1988. Digital guitars imported from Japan, plastic body, synthesizer features.

DG10
1987. Self-contained digital guitar.

1987		$75	$150

DG20
Midi-capable digital guitar.

1987		$175	$250

Chandler
1984-present. Intermediate and professional grade, production/custom, solidbody electric guitars built by luthiers Paul and Adrian Chandler in Chico, California. He also builds basses, laptops and pickups. Chandler started making pickguards and accessories in the '70s, adding electric guitars, basses, and effects in '84.

555 Model
1992-present. John Lennon Rickenbacker-style body, Firebird-style pickups, retro slotted headstock.

1992	TV Yellow	$500	$600

Austin Special
1991-1999. Resembles futuristic Danelectro, lipstick pickups, available in five-string version.

1991-1999		$500	$600

Austin Special Baritone
1994-1999. Nicknamed "Elvis," Gold Metal-Flake finish, mother-of-toilet-seat binding, tremolo, baritone.

1994-1999		$500	$600

Metro
1994-present. Double cut slab body, P-90 in neck position and humbucker in the bridge position.

1994-2000		$500	$700

Telepathic
1994-2000. Classic single cut style, three models; Basic, Standard, Deluxe.

1990s	Basic	$400	$450
1990s	Deluxe 1122 Model	$600	$700
1990s	Standard	$500	$600

Chapin
Professional and premium grade, production/custom, semi-hollow, solidbody, and acoustic electric guitars built by luthiers Bill Chapin and Fred Campbell in San Jose, California.

Chapman
1970-present. Made by Emmett Chapman, the Stick features 10 strings and is played by tapping both hands. The Grand Stick features 12 strings.

Stick
Ten or 12 strings, touch-tap hybrid electric instrument.

1970-1999	10 strings	$900	$1,000
1970-1999	12 strings	$1,100	$1,200
2000-2003	10 strings	$1,100	$1,300

Charles Fox Guitars
1968-present. Luthier Charles Fox builds his premium and presentation grade, custom, steel and nylon string guitars in Portland, Oregon. He also produced GRD acoustic and electric guitars for 1978-'82 and C. Fox acoustic guitars for '97-'02. He also operates The American School of Lutherie in Portland.

Charles Shifflett Acoustic Guitars
1990-present. Premium grade, custom, classical, flamenco, resonator, and harp guitars built by luthier Charles Shifflett in High River, Alberta. He also builds basses and banjos.

Charvel
1978-present. Intermediate and professional grade, production, solidbody electric guitars. Founded by Wayne Charvel in California. U.S.-made '78-'85, a combination of imports and U.S.-made post-'85. Charvel also manufactured the Jackson brand. The earliest San Dimas Charvels were custom-built with wild graphics, locking trems, high-output pickups, and pointy headstocks.

Charvel licensed its trademark to IMC in '85 and IMC moved the factory to Ontario, CA in '86. On October 25, 2002, Fender Musical Instruments Corp. (FMIC) took ownership of Jackson/Charvel Manufacturing Inc.

Electric guitar manufacturing info

1986-1989	Japanese-made Models 1 through 8
1989-1991	Japanese-made 550 XL, 650 XL/Custom, 750 XL (XL=neck-through)
1989-1992	Japanese-made Models 275, 375, 475, 575
1990-1991	Korean-made Charvette models
1992-1994	Korean-made Models 325, 425

275 Deluxe Dinky
1989-1991. Made in Japan, offset double-cut solidbody, one single-coil and one humbucker ('89), three stacked humbuckers ('90-'91), trem.

1989	1 single, 1 humbucker	$300	$400
1990-1991	Stacked humbuckers	$300	$400

Chandler Lectra-Slide

Charles Fox steel-string

GUITARS

1986 Charvel Model 2

Charvel Model 5

MODEL YEAR	FEATURES	EXC. COND. LOW	HIGH
325SL			
	1992-1994. Dot inlays.		
1992-1994		$300	$400
325SLX			
	1992-1994. Surfcaster-like thinline acoustic/electric, dual cutaways, F-hole, on-board chorus, shark inlays, made in Korea.		
1992-1994		$300	$400
375 Deluxe			
	1989-1992. Maple or rosewood fingerboard, dot inlays, single-single-humbucker.		
1989-1992		$300	$400
475			
	1989-1992. Humbucker-single-single configuration, bolt-on neck, dot markers.		
1989-1992		$300	$400
475 Deluxe/Special			
	1989-1992. Introduced as Special, discontinued as Deluxe, bound rosewood fingerboard, shark fin markers, two oval stacked humbuckers and single bridge humbucker.		
1989-1992		$300	$400
625F/625ACEL			
	1992-2000. Acoustic-electric cutaway.		
1992-2000		$275	$400
Avenger			
	1990-1991. Randy Rhoads-style batwing-shaped solidbody, 3 stacked humbuckers, trem, made in Japan.		
1990-1991		$300	$400
Charvette			
	1990-1991. Charvette Series made in Korea, super-Strat-style, model number series 100 through 300.		
1990-1991		$175	$250
Fusion Deluxe			
	1989-1991. Double cut solidbody, trem, one humbucker and one single-coil pickup, made in Japan.		
1989-1991		$250	$325
Fusion Standard/AS FX 1			
	1993-1996. Double cut solidbody, trem, one regular and two mini humbuckers, made in Japan, also named AS FX1.		
1993-1996		$225	$325
Model 1			
	1986-1989. Offset double cut solidbody, maple neck, dot inlays, 1 humbucker, tremolo, made in Japan.		
1986-1989		$250	$300
Model 1A			
	1986-1989. As Model 1, but with 3 single-coils.		
1980s		$250	$300
Model 1C			
	1986-1989. As Model 1, but with 1 humbucker, 2 single coils.		
1986-1989		$275	$325
Model 2			
	1986-1989. As Model 1, but with rosewood 'board.		
1980s		$275	$325
Model 3			
	1986-1989. As Model 2, but with 1 humbucker, 2 single coils.		
1986-1989		$275	$325

MODEL YEAR	FEATURES	EXC. COND. LOW	HIGH
Model 3A			
	1986-1988. As Model 3, but with 2 humbuckers.		
1986-1988		$275	$325
Model 3DR			
	1988-1989. As Model 3, but with 1 humbucker and 1 single-coil.		
1988-1989		$275	$325
Model 4			
	1986-1989. As Model 2, but with 1 regular humbucker and 2 stacked humbuckers mounted in the body (no pickguard), and with active electronics.		
1986-1989		$300	$400
Model 4A			
	1986-1989. As Model 4, but with two regular humbuckers.		
1986-1989		$300	$400
Model 5			
	1986-1989. As Model 4A, but is neck-thru construction, with JE1000TG active elctronics.		
1987		$300	$400
Model 5A			
	1988. Single humbucker and single knob version of Model 5, limited production, made in Japan.		
1988		$300	$325
Model 6			
	1986-1989. As Model 4, but with shark's tooth fingerboard inlays.		
1986-1989		$400	$600
Model 7			
	1988-1989. Single cut solidbody, bound top, reversed headstock, two single-coils, made in Japan.		
1988-1989		$400	$600
Model 88 LTD			
	1988. Double cut solidbody, one slanted humbucker, shark fin inlay, 1000 built, made in Japan.		
1988		$500	$700
San Dimas Bolt-On (U.S.-made)			
	1981-1986. U.S.-made with San Dimas neck plate, bolt-on neck, Strat-style headstock early production, pointy headstock late production, reissued in mid-1990s. Serialization starts with 1001 (not1), serial numbers end with 5491 in early-1986.		
	Serialization as follows, *1981 1001-1095, 1982 1096-1724, 1983 1725-2938, 1984 2939-4261, 1985 4262-5303, 1986 5304-5491*		
1981-1982	Strat-style soft headstock shape	$1,300	$2,500
1982-1986	Jackson-style pointy headstock shape	$1,300	$1,500
ST Custom			
	1990-1992. Offset double cut ash solidbody, 2 single-coils and 1 humbucker, rosewood 'board, trem, made in Japan.		
1990s		$300	$350
ST Deluxe			
	1990-1992. Same as ST Custom but with maple 'board.		
1990s		$275	$325

MODEL YEAR	FEATURES	EXC. COND. LOW	HIGH

Surfcaster
1991-1994. Offset double cut, F-hole, 2 single-coils, bound body, trem, made in Japan.

| 1991-1994 | | $600 | $750 |

Surfcaster 12
1991-1994. 12-string version of Surfcaster, no trem, made in Japan.

| 1991-1994 | | $600 | $750 |

Surfcaster HT (Model SC 1)
1992-1996. Hardtail (no trem) version of the Surfcaster, made in Japan.

| 1992-1996 | | $450 | $550 |

Chiquita

1979-present. Intermediate grade, production guitars made by Erlewine Guitars in Austin, Texas (see that listing). There was also a mini amp available.

Travel Guitar
1979-present. Developed by Mark Erlewine and ZZ Top's Billy Gibbons. 27" overall length solidbody.

| 1980s | Blond, Natural or Yellow | $200 | $225 |
| 1980s | Red option | $250 | $275 |

Chrysalis Guitars

1998-present. Luthier Tim White builds his premium grade, production/custom Chrysalis Guitar System, which includes interchangeable components that can be quickly assembled into a full-size electric/acoustic guitar, in New Boston, New Hampshire. A variety of instruments may be created, including 6- and 12- string electrics and acoustics, electric and acoustic mandocello and acoustic basses.

Cipher

1960s. Solidbody electric guitars and basses imported from Japan by Inter-Mark. Generally strange-shaped bodies.

Electric Solidbody Guitars
Student-level import.

| 1960s | | $75 | $150 |

Citron

1995-present. Luthier Harvey Citron builds his professional and premium grade, production/custom solidbody guitars in Woodstock, New York. He also builds basses. In 1975, Citron and Joe Veillette founded Veillette-Citron, which was known for handcrafted, neck-thru guitars and basses. That company closed in 1983.

Custom-Made Electrics
2000s. A variety of solidbody and thin hollowbody mid- to high-end electrics.

| 2000s | | $1,600 | $2,600 |

Collings

1986-present. Professional, premium, and presentation grade, production/custom, flat-top and archtop guitars built in Austin, Texas. They also build mandolins. Bill Collings started with guitar repair and began custom building guitars around '73. In '80, his relocated his shop from Houston to Austin and started Collings Guitars in '86.

00-41 (Brazilian rosewood)
2001. Premium Brazilian rosewood back and sides, Adirondack spruce top, abalone top purfling.

| 2001 | | $7,000 | $7,500 |

000-2H (Indian rosewood)
1994-present. 15" 000-size, Indian rosewood back and sides, spruce top, slotted headstock, 12-fret neck, dot markers.

| 1994-2000 | | $2,500 | $3,500 |

C-10 (mahogany)
1994-present. 000-style, spruce top, mahogany back and sides, natural.

| 1995-2000 | | $2,000 | $2,500 |

C-10 Deluxe (Indian rosewood)
1994-present. Indian rosewood back and sides C-10, natural.

| 1994-2002 | | $2,300 | $3,000 |

C-100 (mahogany)
1994-1995. Quadruple 0-style, spruce top, mahogany back and sides, natural. Replaced by CJ Jumbo.

| 1994-1995 | | $2,000 | $2,500 |

CJ Jumbo (Indian rosewood)
1995-present. Quadruple 0-style, spruce top, Indian rosewood back and sides, Natural.

| 1995-2000 | | $2,500 | $3,000 |

D-1
1994-present. D-style, 15 5/8", spruce top, mahogany back and sides, natural.

| 1995 | | $2,000 | $2,500 |

D-1A Custom
Upgrade D-1 with Adirondack spruce top and higher appointments, natural.

| 1999-2002 | | $2,300 | $3,200 |

D-1SB
Sunburst finish option for D-1 model.

| 2001 | | $2,300 | $2,800 |

D-2 (Indian rosewood)
1986-1995. D-1 with Indian rosewood back and sides, natural.

| 1986-1995 | | $2,400 | $2,900 |

D-2H (Indian rosewood)
1986-present. Dreadnought. Same as D-2 with herringbone purfling around top edge.

| 1986-2001 | | $2,500 | $3,000 |

D-2H/D-2HBZ (Brazilian rosewood)
Grade AA Brazilian rosewood, spruce top.

| 1994-2001 | | $5,500 | $6,000 |

D-3 (Brazilian rosewood)
Similar to D-2H but with abalone purfling/rosette.

| 1991 | | $6,000 | $6,500 |

OM-1 (mahogany)
1994-present. Grand concert, Sitka spruce top, mahogany back and sides, natural.

| 1994-2000 | | $2,000 | $2,500 |

OM-2H (Indian rosewood)
2000s.

| 2000s | | $2,500 | $3,000 |

Charvel Surfcaster

Collings D-2H

Collings CJ Jumbo

Comins Chester Avenue

MODEL YEAR	FEATURES	EXC. COND. LOW	HIGH

OM-2HAV (Brazilian rosewood)
Adirondack spruce top, Brazilian rosewood back and sides, ivoroid-bound body.
1998 — $5,500 — $6,500

OM-3 (Brazilian rosewood)
Brazilian rosewood back and sides, Adirondack spruce top, fancy rosette.
1998 — $6,000 — $6,500

OM-3 (Indian rosewood)
2002 — $2,500 — $3,000

OM-3HC (Indian rosewood)
Single rounded cutaway, 15", spruce top, Indian rosewood back and sides, herringbone purfling.
1986 — $2,800 — $3,200

OM-42B (Brazilian rosewood)
Brazilian rosewood back and sides, Adirondack spruce top, fancy rosette and binding.
2000 — $7,000 — $7,500

SJ (Indian rosewood)
Sitka spruce top, Indian rosewood or quilted maple back and sides.
1992 — $3,000 — $3,800

SJ-41 (Brazilian rosewood)
Cedar top, Brazilian rosewood back and sides.
1996 — $7,000 — $7,500

Comins
1992-present. Premium grade, custom archtops built by luthier Bill Comins in Willow Grove, Pennsylvania. He also offers a combo amp built in collaboration with George Alessandro.
Chester Avenue
1994-present. Electric archtop, solid spruce top and back, 17" or 18" cutaway, options can vary.
1994-1999 17" — $5,500 — $6,500
1994-1999 18" — $6,000 — $7,000
Classic
1995-present. Classic archtop jazz model, 17" cutaway, pickguard mounted neck pickup, block markers.
1995-1999 — $5,000 — $5,500
Parlor
1995-present. 14" archtop with viola styling.
1995-1999 — $3,000 — $3,500
Renaissance
1996-present. 17" archtop cutaway, carved European spruce top, solid curly maple back and sides, unique removable sound baffles, blond.
1996-1999 — $5,500 — $6,000

Concertone
Ca.1914-1930s. Concertone was a brandname made by Chicago's Slingerland and distributed by Montgomery Ward. The brand was also used on other instruments such as ukuleles.

Conklin
1984-present. Intermediate, professional and premium grade, production/custom, 6, 7, 8, and 12 string solid and hollowbody electrics, by luthier Bill Conklin. He also builds basses. Originally located

in Lebanon, Missouri, in '88 the company moved to Springfield, Missouri. Conklin instruments are made in the U.S. and overseas.

Conn
Ca. 1968-ca.1978. Student to mid-quality classical and acoustic guitars, some with bolt-on necks. Imported from Japan by band instrument manufacturer and distributor Conn/Continental Music Company, Elkhart, Indiana.
Acoustic Guitars
Japanese imports.
1970s — $150 — $200
1980s — $150 — $200
Classical Guitars
Student-level Japanese imports.
1970s — $150 — $200

Connor, Stephan
1995-present. Luthier Stephan Connor builds his premium grade, custom nylon-string guitars in Waltham, Massachusetts.

Conrad
Ca. 1968-1978. Mid- to better-quality copies of glued-neck Martin and Gibson acoustics and bolt-neck Gibson and Fender solidbodies. Also mandolins and banjos. Imported from Japan by David Wexler and Company, Chicago, Illinois.
Acoustical Slimline 12-String 40100
1970s. ES-335-style, two DeArmond-style pickups, rosewood fingerboard, 12 strings, dot markers.
1970s — $100 — $300
Acoustical Slimline 40080/40085
1970s. ES-335-style, two or three DeArmond-style pickups, rosewood fingerboard, block markers.
1970s — $100 — $300
Bison (40035/40030/40065/40005)
1970s. Bison copy, one through four pickups available, rosewood fingerboard with dot markers, six-on-side headstock.
1970s — $100 — $200
Bumper (40223)
1970s. Armstrong Lucite copy, import.
1974 — $225 — $275
De Luxe Folk Guitar
1970s. Resonator acoustic, mahogany back, sides and neck, Japanese import.
1974 — $175 — $250
Master Size 40178
1972-1977. Byrdland copy.
1970s — $350 — $400
Violin-Shaped 12-String Electric 40176
1970s. Scroll headstock, two pickups, 500/1 control panel, bass side dot markers.
1970s — $100 — $300
Violin-Shaped Electric 40175
1970s. Scroll headstock, two pickups, 500/1 control panel, bass side dot markers, vibrato.
1970s — $100 — $300

MODEL YEAR	FEATURES	EXC. COND. LOW	HIGH

White Styrene 1280 (solidbody)
1970s. Solid maple body covered with white styrene, two pickups, trem, bass side dot markers, White.

1970s		$100	$300

Contreras (Manuel Contreras)
See listing for Manuel Contreras.

Coral
Refer to Danelectro section.

Córdoba
Line of classical guitars handmade in Portugal and imported by Guitar Salon International.

Cordova
1960s. Classical nylon string guitars imported by David Wexler of Chicago.
Grand Concert Model WC-026
1960s. Highest model offered by Cordova, one-piece rosewood back, laminated rosewood sides, spruce top, Natural.

1963		$175	$300

Coriani, Paolo
1984-present. Production/custom nylon-string guitars and hurdy-gurdys built by luthier Paolo Coriani in Modeila, Italy.

Cort
1973-present. North Brook, Illinois-based Cort offers budget, intermediate and professional grade, production/custom, acoustic and solidbody, semi-hollow, hollow body electric guitars built in Korea. They also offer basses.
Doubleneck
Cherry, six/twelve necks, SG-style, Asian import.

1970s		$250	$450

Electric Guitars
1973-present. A variety of models were offered, often copy guitars. These guitars were heavily distributed in the 1980s.

1973-1989		$175	$400
1990-1999		$50	$300

Crafter
2000-present. Line of intermediate and professional grade, production, acoustic and acoustic/electric guitars from Hohner. They also offer mandolins and a bass.

Crafters of Tennessee
See listing under Tennessee.

Cranium
1996-present. Professional grade, production/custom, hollow, semi-hollow, and solidbody electrics built by luthier Wayne O'Connor in Peterborough, Ontario.

Crescent Moon
1999-present. Professional grade, production/custom, solidbody guitars and basses built by luthier Craig Muller in Baltimore, Maryland.

Crestwood
1970s. Copies of the popular classical guitars, flat-tops, electric solidbodies and basses of the era, imported by La Playa Distributing Company of Detroit.
Electric Guitars
1970s. Includes near copies of the 335 (Crestwood model 2043, 2045 and 2047), Les Paul Custom (2020), Strat (2073), Jazzmaster (2078), Tele (2082), and the SG Custom (2084).

1970s		$100	$300

Cromwell
1935-1939. Budget model brand built by Gibson and distributed by mail-order businesses like Grossman, Continental, and Richter & Phillips.
Acoustic Archtops
1935-1936. Archtop acoustic, F-holes, pressed mahogany back and sides, carved and bound top, bound back, pickguard and 'board, no truss rod.

1935-1939		$500	$800

Crown
1960s. Violin-shaped hollowbody electrics, solidbody electric guitars and basses, possibly others. Imported from Japan.
Barney Kessel Copy
Double pointed cutaways, two humbucking pickups, laminated top, full-depth body.

1969		$400	$500

Electric Solidbody Guitars
Student-level Japanese import.

1960s		$100	$200

Crucianelli
Early 1960s. Italian guitars imported into the U.S. by Bennett Brothers of New York and Chicago around 1963 to '64. Crucianelli also made the Imperial brand guitars for the Imperial Accordion Company of Chicago.

Cumpiano
1974-present. Professional and premium grade, custom steel-string and nylon-string guitars, and acoustic basses built by luthier William Cumpiano in Northampton, Massachusetts.

Custom
1980s. Line of solidbody guitars and basses introduced in the early 1980s by Charles Lawing and Chris Lovell, owners of Strings & Things in Memphis.

D'Agostino
1976-early 1990s. Acoustic and electric solidbody guitars and basses imported by PMS Music,

1974 Conrad doubleneck

Cort Larry Coryell

1981 D'Agostino LP-500

D'Angelico plectrum guitar

MODEL YEAR	FEATURES	EXC. COND. LOW	HIGH

founded in New York City by former Maestro executive Pat D'Agostino, his brother Steven D'Agostino, and Mike Confortti.

First dreadnought acoustic guitars imported from Japan in '76. First solidbodies manufactured by the EKO custom shop beginning in '77. In '82 solidbody production moved to Japan. Beginning in '84, D'Agostinos were made in Korea. Overall, about 60% of guitars were Japanese, 40% Korean.

Acoustic Flat-Tops
1976-1990. Early production in Japan, by mid-'80s, most production in Korea.

1970s		$150	$300

Electric Semi-Hollowbody Guitars
1981-early 1990s. Early production in Japan, later versions from Korea.

1980s		$250	$350

Electric Solidbody Guitars
1977-early 1990s. Early models made in Italy, later versions from Japan and Korea.

1970s		$250	$350

D'Ambrosio
2001-present. Luthier Otto D'Ambrosio builds his premium grade, custom/production, acoustic and electric archtop guitars in Providence, Rhode Island.

D'Angelico
John D'Angelico built his own line of archtop guitars, mandolins and violins from 1932 until his death in 1964. His instruments are some of the most sought-after by collectors.

D'Angelico (L-5 Snakehead)
1932-1935. D'Angelico's L-5-style copy with snakehead headstock, his first model.

1932-1935	Sunburst	$12,000	$17,000

Excel/Exel (non-cutaway)
1936-1949. Non-cutaway, 17" width, one-three-ply bound F-hole. Natural finishes were typically not offered in the 1930s. Non-cut Excels were generally not offered after 1949 in deference to the Excel cutaway.

1936-1939	Sunburst, straight F-hole	$18,000	$25,000
1938-1939	Sunburst, standard F-hole	$18,000	$20,000
1940-1949	Natural	$18,000	$21,000
1940-1949	Sunburst, standard F-hole	$16,000	$20,000

Excel/Exel Cutaway
1947-1964. Cutaway, 17" width, one-three-ply bound F-hole. Larry Wexer noted from 1950-1957, D'Angelico guitars suffer from severe binding problems and many have replaced bindings. Replaced bindings make the guitar non-original and these repaired guitars have lower values.

1947-1949	Natural, original binding	$35,000	$45,000
1947-1949	Natural, non-original binding	$20,000	$25,000

MODEL YEAR	FEATURES	EXC. COND. LOW	HIGH
1947-1949	Sunburst, original binding	$35,000	$38,000
1947-1949	Sunburst, non-original binding	$15,000	$20,000
1950-1959	Natural, original binding	$35,000	$45,000
1950-1959	Natural, non-original binding	$20,000	$25,000
1950-1959	Sunburst, original binding	$35,000	$40,000
1950-1959	Sunburst, non-original binding	$15,000	$20,000
1960-1964	Natural	$35,000	$45,000
1960-1964	Sunburst	$35,000	$40,000

New Yorker (non-cutaway)
1936-1949. Non-cutaway, 18" width, five-ply-bound F-hole. New Yorker non-cutaway orders were overshadowed by the cutaway model orders starting in '47. All prices noted are for original bindings. Non-original (replaced) bindings will reduce the value by 33%-50%.

1936-1939	Sunburst	$20,000	$27,000
1940-1949	Natural	$25,000	$32,000
1940-1949	Sunburst	$20,000	$30,000

New Yorker Cutaway
1947-1964. Cutaway, 18" width, 5-ply-bound F-hole. New Yorker non-cutaway orders were overshadowed by the cutaway model orders starting in 1947. All prices noted are for original bindings. Non-original (replaced) bindings will reduce the value by 33%-50%.

1947-1949	Natural, 4 made	$60,000	$75,000
1947-1949	Sunburst	$45,000	$60,000
1950-1959	Natural	$70,000	$75,000
1950-1959	Sunburst	$45,000	$60,000
1960-1964	Natural	$60,000	$75,000
1960-1964	Sunburst	$50,000	$60,000

New Yorker Special
1947-1964. Cutaway, 17" width, also called Excel New Yorker or Excel Cutaway New Yorker, has New Yorker styling. All prices noted are for original bindings. Non-original (replaced) bindings will reduce the value by 33%-50%. Not to be confused with D'Angelico Special (A and B style).

1947-1949	Natural	$35,000	$45,000
1947-1949	Sunburst	$35,000	$38,000
1950-1959	Natural	$35,000	$45,000
1950-1959	Sunburst	$35,000	$40,000
1960-1964	Natural	$35,000	$45,000
1960-1964	Sunburst	$35,000	$40,000

Special
1947-1964. Generally Style A and B-type instruments made for musicians on a budget, plain specs with little ornamentation, not to be confused with New Yorker Special.

1947-1964	Natural	$15,000	$18,000
1947-1964	Sunburst	$12,000	$15,000

Style A
1936-1945. Archtop, 17" width, unbound F-holes, block fingerboard inlays, multi-pointed headstock, nickel-plated metal parts.

1936-1939	Sunburst	$12,000	$13,000
1940-1945	Sunburst	$11,000	$12,000

MODEL YEAR	FEATURES	EXC. COND. LOW	HIGH

Style A-1
1936-1945. Unbound F-holes, 17" width, arched headstock, nickel-plated metal parts.

1936-1939	Sunburst	$12,000	$13,000
1940-1945	Sunburst	$11,000	$12,000

Style B
1933-1948. Archtop 17" wide, unbound F-holes, block fingerboard inlays, gold-plated parts.

1936-1939	Sunburst	$13,000	$15,000
1940-1948	Sunburst	$12,000	$14,000

Style B Special
1933-1948. D'Angelico described variations from standard features with a 'Special' designation. Vintage dealers may also describe these instruments as 'Special'.

1936-1939	Sunburst	$14,000	$17,000
1940-1948	Sunburst	$14,000	$17,000

D'Angelico (Vestax)
1988-present. Premium and presentation grade, production/custom, archtop, flat-top, and solidbody guitars built by luthier Hidesato Shino and Vestax near Tokyo, Japan. Distributed in the U.S. by D'Angelico Guitars of America, in Westfield, New Jersey.

D'Angelico II
Mid-1990s. Archtops built in the U.S. and distributed by Archtop Enterprises of Merrick, New York.

Jazz Classic
1990s. Electric archtop, cutaway, carved spruce top, figured maple back and sides, single neck pickup.

1990s		$3,800	$4,000

D'Aquisto
1965-1995. James D'Aquisto apprenticed under D'Angelico until the latter's death, at age 59, in 1964. He started making his own brand instruments in '65 and built archtop and flat top acoustic guitars, solidbody and hollowbody electric guitars. He also designed guitars for Hagstrom and Fender. He died in '95, at age 59.

Avant Garde
1987-1994. 18" wide, non-traditional futuristic model, approximately five or six instruments were reportedly made. Because of low production this pricing is for guidance only.

1990	Blond	$75,000	$125,000

Centura/Centura Deluxe
1994 only. 17" wide, non-traditional art deco futuristic archtop, approximately 10 made, the last guitars made by this luthier. Due to the low production this pricing is for guidance only.

1994	Blond	$75,000	$100,000

Excel (cutaway)
1965-1992. Archtop, 17" width, with modern thin-logo started in 1981.

1965-1967	Blond	$53,000	$57,000
1965-1969	Sunburst	$45,000	$55,000
1968-1979	Blond	$43,000	$47,000
1968-1979	Sunburst	$35,000	$40,000
1980-1989	Blond	$53,000	$57,000
1980-1989	Sunburst	$40,000	$42,000
1990-1992	Blond	$53,000	$57,000
1990-1992	Sunburst	$40,000	$42,000

Excel (flat-top)
1980s. Flat-top, 16", flamed maple back and sides, Sitka spruce top, about 15 made, narrow Excel-style headstock, oval soundhole, D'Aquisto script logo on headstock.

1980s		$15,000	$20,000

HollowElectric
Early model with bar pickup, D'Aquisto headstock, 1970s model with humbuckers.

1965	Sunburst	$10,000	$12,000
1972	Sunburst	$10,000	$12,000

Jim Hall Model (hollow electric)

1965	Laminate top	$10,000	$12,000
1978	Solid top	$10,000	$12,000

New Yorker Classic (solidbody)
1980s. Only two were reported to be made, therefore this pricing is for guidance only.

1980s		$17,000	$19,000

New Yorker Deluxe (cutaway)
1965-1992. Most are 18" wide.

1965-1967	Blond	$55,000	$65,000
1965-1967	Sunburst	$55,000	$65,000
1968-1979	Blond	$45,000	$50,000
1968-1979	Sunburst	$45,000	$50,000
1980-1989	Blond	$47,000	$50,000
1980-1989	Sunburst	$47,000	$50,000
1990-1992	Blond	$53,000	$57,000
1990-1992	Sunburst	$53,000	$57,000

New Yorker Special (cutaway)
1966-1992. Most are 17" wide.

1966-1967	Blond	$55,000	$65,000
1966-1967	Sunburst	$55,000	$65,000
1970-1979	Blond	$45,000	$50,000
1970-1979	Sunburst	$45,000	$50,000
1980-1989	Blond	$47,000	$50,000
1980-1989	Sunburst	$47,000	$50,000
1990-1992	Blond	$53,000	$57,000
1990-1992	Sunburst	$53,000	$57,000

New Yorker Special 7-String
1980s. Limited production 7-string, single cutaway, sunburst.

1980s		$47,000	$50,000

Solo/Solo Deluxe
1992-1993. 18" wide, non-traditional non-cutaway art deco model, only two reported made. Because of low production this pricing is for guidance only.

1992-1993	Blond	$85,000	$97,000

D'Aquisto (Aria)
May 2002-present. Premium grade, production, D'Aquisto designs licensed to Aria of Japan by D'Aquisto Strings, Inc., Deer Park, New York.

Centura Electric
2002-present. Chambered solidbody.

2002	Blond option	$2,400	$2,600

1960 D'Angelico New Yorker

D'Aquisto custom oval-hole

Daisy Rock Heartbreaker

Danelectro Convertible

MODEL YEAR	FEATURES	EXC. COND. LOW	HIGH

D'Leco Guitars

1991-present. Luthier James W. Dale builds his premium grade, production/custom archtops in Oklahoma City, Oklahoma.

D'Pergo Custom Guitars

2002-present. Professional, premium, and presentation grade, production/custom, solidbody guitars built in Windham, New Hampshire. Every component of the guitars are built by D'Pergo.

Daily Guitars

1976-present. Luthier David Daily builds his premium grade, production/custom classical guitars in Sparks, Nevada.

Daion

1978-1985. Mid- to higher-quality copies imported from Japan. Original designs introduced in the '80s.

555 Headhunter

1980s. ES-335-style body.

1980-1985		$700	$900

Caribou

1980s. Acoustic/electric, cutaway body.

1980-1985		$500	$700

Mark I, II, III, IV

1978-1985. D-style, cedar or spruce top, various hardwood back and sides.

1978-1985	Natural	$300	$400

Mark X

1980s.

1980-1985		$600	$800

Power X

1978-1985. Slightly offset double cutaway slab through-body construction, no body binding, two humbuckers, four control knobs, two toggles including coil tap, see-through finish.

1978-1985		$400	$600

Savage

1978-1985. Offset double cutaway solidbody with pronounced lower bass bout, two humbucker standard set-up, opaque solid colors.

1978-1985		$400	$450

Daisy Rock

2001-present. Budget and intermediate grade, production, full-scale and 3/4 scale, solidbody, semi-hollow, acoustic, and acoustic/electric guitars. Founded by Tish Ciravolo as a Division of Schecter Guitars, the Daisy line is focused on female customers. Initial offerings included daisy and heart-shaped electric guitars and basses.

Dan Armstrong

Dan Armstrong started playing jazz in Cleveland in the late-'50s. He moved to New York and also started doing repairs, eventually opening his own store on 48th Street in '65. By the late-'60s he was designing his Lucite guitars for Ampeg (see Ampeg for those listings). He moved to England in '71, where he developed his line of colored stomp boxes. He returned to the States in '75. Armstrong died in '04.

Wood Body Guitar

1973-1975. Sliding pickup, wood body.

1973-1975	Brown	$1,200	$1,500

Danelectro

1946-1969, 1996-present. Founded in Red Bank, New Jersey, by Nathan I. "Nate" or "Nat" Daniel, an electronics enthusiast with amplifier experience. In 1933, Daniel built amps for Thor's Bargain Basement in New York. In '34 he was recruited by Epiphone's Herb Sunshine to build earliest Electar amps and pickup-making equipment. From '35 to '42, he operated Daniel Electric Laboratories in Manhattan, supplying Epiphone. He started Danelectro in '46 and made his first amps for Montgomery Ward in '47. Over the years, Danelectro made amplifiers, solidbody, semi-hollow and hollowbody electric guitars and basses, electric sitar, and the Bellzouki under the Danelectro, Silvertone, Coral, and Dane, brand names. In '48, began supplying Silvertone amps for Sears (various coverings), with his own brand (brown leatherette) distributed by Targ and Dinner as Danelectro and S.S. Maxwell. He developed an electronic vibrato in '48 on his Vibravox series amps. In '50 he developed a microphone with volume and tone controls and outboard "Echo Box" reverb unit. In the fall of '54, Danelectro replaced Harmony as provider of Silvertone solidbody guitars for Sears. Also in '54, the first danelectro brand guitars appeared with tweed covering, bell headstock, and pickups under the pickguard. The Coke bottle headstock debuts as Silvertone "Lightning Bolt" in '54, and is used on Danelectros for '56 to '66.

The company moved to Red Bank, New Jersey in '57, and in '58 relocated to Neptune, New Jersey. In '59, Harmony and Kay guitars replace all but three Danelectros in Sears catalog. In '66, MCA buys the company (Daniel remains with company), but by mid-'69, MCA halts production and closes the doors. Some leftover stock is sold to Dan Armstrong, who had a shop in New York at the time. Armstrong assembled several hundred Danelectro guitars as "Dan Armstrong Modified" with his own pickup design.

Rights to name acquired by Anthony Mark in late-'80s, who assembled a number of thinline hollowbody guitars, many with "Longhorn" shape, using Japanese-made bodies and original Danelectro necks and hardware. In '96, the Evets Corporation, of San Clemente, California, introduced a line of effects bearing the Danelectro name. Amps and guitars, many of which were reissues of the earlier instruments, soon followed. In early 2003, Evets discontinued the guitar and amp lines, but still offers Danelectro effects.

MCA-Danelectro made guitars were called the "Dane Series". Dane A model numbers start with Alpha A (e.g. A2V), Dame B models start

MODEL YEAR	FEATURES	EXC. COND. LOW	HIGH

with alpha B (e.g. B3V), Dane C (e.g. C2N), and Dane D (e.g. D2N). The least expensive series was the Dane A, going up to the most expensive Dane D series. All Dane Series instruments had Jazzmaster/Jaguar-style bodies and came with single, double or triple pickups and with hand vibrato options. The Dane Series were made from 1967 to 1969. MCA did carry over the Convertible, Guitarlin 4123, Long Horn Bass-4 and Bass-6 and Doubleneck 3923. MCA also offered the Bellzouki Double Pickup 7021. Each Dane Series includes an electric 12-string.

Bellzouki Double Pickup
1961-1969. Twelve-string electric, modified teardrop shape with two body points on both treble and bass bouts. Sunburst finish.

1961-1969		$850	$1,050

Bellzouki Single Pickup
1961-1969. Twelve-string electric, teardrop-shaped body. Sunburst finish.

1961-1969		$750	$850

Convertible
1959-1969. Acoustic/electric, double cutaway. Guitar was sold with or without the removable single pickup.

1950s	Pickup installed	$450	$550
1960s	Acoustic, no pickup	$250	$350
1960s	Pickup installed	$350	$450

Coral Firefly
1967-1969. ES-335-shaped body, F-holes, two pickups. Sold with or without vibrato.

1967-1969		$350	$450

Coral Hornet 2
1967-1969. Jaguar-type body, two pickups. Sold with or without vibrato.

1967-1969		$400	$550

Coral Sitar
1967-1969. Six-string guitar with 13 drone strings and three pickups (two under the six strings, one under the drones). Kind of a USA-shaped body.

1967-1969		$1,800	$2,800

Deluxe Double Pickup (6028)
Double cutaway, two pointer knobs, two pickups, standard-size pickguard, master control knob. White (6026), Dark Walnut (6027), Honey Walnut (6028).

1960s		$600	$700

Deluxe Triple Pickup (6037)
Double cutaway, 3 pointer knobs, 3 pickups, standard-size pickguard, master control knob. White (6036), dark walnut (6037), honey walnut (6038).

1960s		$900	$1,050

Doubleneck (3923)
1959-1969. A "Shorthorn" double cutaway, bass and six-string necks, one pickup on each neck, Coke bottle headstocks.

1959-1969	White Sunburst	$1,250	$1,550

Electric Sitar
1967-1969. Traditional looking, oval-bodied sitar. No drone strings as on the Coral Sitar of the same period.

1967-1969		$750	$950

Guitaralin (4123)
1963-1969. The "longhorn" guitar, with two huge cutaways, 32-fret neck, and two pickups.

1963-1969		$1,350	$1,450

Hand Vibrato Double Pickup (4021)
1960s. Two pickups, double cutaway, batwing headstock, simple design vibrato.

1960s	Black	$500	$600

Hand Vibrato Single Pickup (4011)
1960s. One pickup, double cutaway, batwing headstock, simple design vibrato.

1960s	Black	$300	$500

Model C
1955-ca.1958. Single cutaway, one pickup.

1955-1958		$300	$400

Pro 1
1963-ca.1964. Odd-shaped double cutaway electric with squared off corners, one pickup.

1963-1964		$300	$500

Standard Double Pickup
1959-1967. A "Shorthorn" double cutaway, two pickups, two stacked, concentric volume/tone controls, seal-shaped pickguard, Coke bottle headstock. The Black version of this guitar is often referred to as the Jimmy Page model because he occasionally used one.

1950s	Black	$950	$1,150
1960s		$600	$800

Standard Single Pickup
1958-1967. A "Shorthorn" double cutaway, one pickup, two regular control knobs, seal-shaped pickguard, Coke bottle headstock.

1958-1967		$400	$550

U-1
1956-ca.1960. Single cutaway, one pickup, Coke bottle headstock.

1956-1960	Custom color	$750	$850
1956-1960	Standard color	$350	$450

U-1 '56 Reissue
1998-1999. Single cut semi-hollow, masonite top and bottom, bolt-on neck, reissue of 1956 U-1, with single 'lipstick tube' pickup, various colors.

1998-1999		$75	$125

U-2
1956-1959. Single cutaway, two pickups, stacked concentric volume/tone controls, Coke bottle headstock.

1956-1959	Standard color	$450	$850

U-2 '56 Reissue
1998-2003.

1998-2003		$100	$175

U-3 '56 Reissue
1999-2003. Single cut reissue of 1956 U-3 with 3 'lipstick tube' pickups, various colors.

1999-2003		$150	$225

Dave Maize Acoustic Guitars
1991-present. Luthier Dave Maize builds his professional and premium grade, production/custom, flat-tops in Cave Junction, Oregon. He also builds basses.

Danelectro Doubleneck 6/4

Danelectro Guitarlin

David Thomas McNaught
Vintage Double-Cut

1983 Dean Bel Air

David Thomas McNaught

1989-present. Professional, premium, and presentation grade, custom, solidbody guitars built by luthier David Thomas McNaught and finished by Dave Mansel in Locust, North Carolina. In '97, they added the production/custom DTM line of guitars.

Vintage Double Cut
Classic/modern offset double cutaway, figured maple top, twin exposed humbuckers.

2002		$3,000	$3,500

Vintage Standard
Classic solidbody single cutaway design, through-neck construction, two-piece figured maple top, exposed humbucking-style pickups with standard control layout.

2003		$3,000	$3,500

Davis, J. Thomas

1975-present. Premium and presentation grade, custom, steel-string flattops, 12-strings, classicals, archtops, Irish citterns and flattop Irish bouzoukis made by luthier J. Thomas Davis in Columbus, Ohio.

Davoli

See Wandre listing.

de Jonge, Sergei

1972-present. Premium grade, production/custom classical and steel-string guitars built by luthier Sergei de Jonge in Oshawa, Ontario.

De Paule Stringed Instruments

1969-1980, 1993-present. Custom steel-string, nylon-string, archtop, resonator, and Hawaiian guitars built by luthier C. Andrew De Paule in Eugene, Oregon.

Dean

1976-present. Intermediate, professional and premium grade, production/custom, solidbody, hollowbody, acoustic, acoustic/electric, and resonator guitars made in the U.S., Korea, the Czech Republic and China. They also offer basses, banjos, mandolins, and amps. Founded in Evanston, Illinois, by Dean Zelinsky. Original models were upscale versions of Gibson designs with glued necks, fancy tops, DiMarzio pickups and distinctive winged headstocks (V, Z and ML), with production beginning in '77. In '80 the factory was relocated to Chicago. Dean's American manufacturing ends in '86 when all production shifts to Korea. In '91 Zelinsky sold the company to Tropical Music in Miami, Florida. For '93-'94 there was again limited U.S. (California) production of the E'Lite, Cadillac and ML models under the supervision of Zelinsky and Cory Wadley. Korean versions were also produced. In '95, Elliott Rubinson's Armadillo Enterprises, of Clearwater, Florida, bought the Dean brand. In

'97 and '98, Dean offered higher-end USA Custom Shop models. In '98, they reintroduced acoustics. In 2000, Zelinsky once again became involved in the company.
Dating American models: first two digits are year of manufacture. Imports have no date codes.

Baby ML
1982-1986. Downsized version of ML model.

1980s	Import	$350	$400
1980s	U.S.-made	$400	$500

Baby V
1982-1986. Downsized version of the Flying V-shaped V model.

1980s	Import	$300	$350
1980s	U.S.-made	$350	$450

Baby Z
1982-1986. Downsized version of the Explorer-shaped Z model.

1980s	Import	$300	$350
1980s	U.S.-made	$350	$450

Bel Aire
1983-1984. Solidbody, possibly the first production guitar with humbucker/single/single pickup layout, U.S.A.-made. An import model from Asia was introduced in '87

1980s	Import	$300	$350
1980s	U.S.-made	$500	$550

Budweiser Guitar
Ca.1987. Shaped like Bud logo.

1987		$450	$500

Cadillac (USA)
1979-1985. Single long treble horn on slab body.

1979-1982		$800	$1,000

Cadillac Deluxe (USA)
1993-1994, 1996-1997. Single long-horn shape, American-made, various colors..

1993-1994		$1,000	$1,200
1996-1997		$1,000	$1,200

Cadillac Reissue (import)
1992-1994. Single long-horn shape, two humbuckers, various colors.

1992-1994		$350	$400

Cadillac Standard
1996-1997. Slab body version.

1996-1997		$800	$1,000

Cadillac Time Capsule 25th Anniversary
2003. 100 made, U.S.-made, flamed maple top.

2003		$1,000	$1,500

E'Lite
1978-1985, 1994-1996. Single-horn shape.

1979-1985		$800	$900

E'Lite Deluxe
Single-horn shape.

1980s		$1,000	$1,200

Eighty-Eight
1987-1990. Offset double cut solidbody, import.

1987-1990		$150	$275

Golden E'Lite
Single pointy treble cutaway, fork headstock, gold hardware, ebony fingerboard, Sunburst.

1980s		$1,000	$1,200

MODEL YEAR	FEATURES	EXC. COND. LOW	HIGH

Hollywood Z (import)
1985-1986. Bolt-neck Japanese copy of Baby Z, Explorer shape.

| 1985-1986 | | $150 | $175 |

Jammer (import)
1987-1989. Offset double cutaway body, bolt-on neck, dot markers, six-on-a-side tuners, various colors offered.

| 1987-1989 | | $150 | $175 |

Mach I (import)
1985-1986. Limited run from Korea. Mach V with six-on-a-side tunes, various colors.

| 1985-1986 | | $150 | $175 |

Mach V (import)
1985-1986. Pointed solidbody, two humbucking pickups, maple neck, ebony 'board, locking trem, various colors. Limited run from Korea.

| 1985-1986 | | $150 | $175 |

Mach VII (USA)
1985-1986. Mach I styling, made in America, offered in unusual finishes.

| 1985-1986 | | $800 | $1,000 |

ML (import)
1983-1990. Korean-made.

| 1983-1990 | | $250 | $300 |

ML (ML Standard/US-made)
1977-1986. There is a 'flame' model and a 'standard' model.

| 1977-1982 | | $1,100 | $1,300 |

V (V flamed)
Flamed maple version of V Standard.

| 1977-1981 | Unbound | $800 | $1,000 |

V (V Standard)
1977-1986. V copy, there is a 'standard' and a 'flame' model offered.

| 1977-1986 | Bound | $1,100 | $1,300 |

Z (Z Standard)
1977-1986. Explorer copy.

| 1977-1983 | U.S.-made, bound | $1,200 | $1,400 |
| 1983-1986 | Japanese import | $250 | $350 |

Z Autograph (import)
1985-1987. The first Dean import from Korea offset double cutaway, bolt-on neck, dot markers, offered in several standard colors.

| 1985-1987 | | $150 | $200 |

Z Coupe/Z Deluxe (USA Custom Shop)
1997-1998. Explore-style mahogany body offered in several standard colors, Z Deluxe with Floyd Rose tremolo.

| 1997-1998 | | $800 | $1,100 |

Z Korina (USA Custom Shop)
1997-1998. Explorer Z Coupe with korina body, various standard colors.

| 1997-1998 | | $800 | $1,100 |

Z LTD (USA Custom Shop)
1997-1998. Z Coupe with bound neck and headstock, offered in several standard colors.

| 1997-1998 | | $800 | $1,100 |

Dean Markley

The string and pickup manufacturer offered a limited line of guitars and basses for a time in the '80s. They were introduced in '84.

Concert
1987. Solidbody, either 3 single-coils,1 humbucker and 2 single-coils, or 1 humbucker.

| 1987 | | $225 | $325 |

Custom Vintage
1987. Solidbody, dot or shark-tooth inlays, either 1 humbucker, 2 single-coils and 1 humbucker, 2 humbuckers, or 3 single-coils.

| 1987 | | $225 | $325 |

Vintage
1987. Solidbody, vintage-style with either 3 single-coils or 1 humbucker and 2 single-coils.

| 1987 | | $225 | $275 |

Dearstone

1993-present. Luthier Ray Dearstone builds his professional and premium grade, custom, archtop and acoustic/electric guitars in Blountville, Tennessee. He also builds mandolin family instruments and violins.

DeCava Guitars

1983-present. Professional and premium grade, production/custom, archtop and classical guitars built by luthier Jim DeCava in Stratford, Connecticut. He also builds ukes, banjos, and mandolins.

DeGennaro

2003-present. Premium grade, custom/production, acoustic, archtop, semi-hollow and solidbody guitars built by luthier Degennaro in Grand Rapids, Michigan. He also builds basses and mandolins.

Dynasty
2004-present. Handcrafted, semi-hollowbody, through-neck, solid spruce top, figured maple back, two pickups with option Baggs piezo pickup.

| 2004 | | $1,000 | $1,500 |

Dell'Arte

1997-present. Production/custom Maccaferri-style guitars from John Kinnard and Alain Cola. In '96, luthier John Kinnard opened a small shop called Finegold Guitars and Mandolins. In '98 he met Alain Cola, a long time jazz guitarist who was selling Mexican-made copies of Selmer/Maccaferri guitars under the Dell'Arte brandname. Cola wanted better workmanship for his guitars, and in October '98, Finegold and Dell'Arte merged. As of May '99 all production is in California.

Anouman Custom

| 1990s | | $2,000 | $2,200 |

Dennis Hill Guitars

1991-present. Premium and presentation grade, production/custom, classical and flamenco guitars built by luthier Dennis Hill in Panama City, Florida. He has also built dulcimers, mandolins, and violins.

Dean Baby ML

Early-'80s Dean Z

DeVoe archtop

Ditson model 1-45

MODEL YEAR	FEATURES	EXC. COND. LOW	HIGH

Desmond Guitars

1991-present. Luthier Robert B. Desmond builds his premium grade, production/custom classical guitars in Orlando, Florida.

DeTemple

1995-present. Premium grade, production/custom, solidbody electric guitars built by luthier Michael DeTemple in Sherman Oaks, California. He also builds basses.

DeVoe Guitars

1975-present. Luthier Lester DeVoe builds his premium grade, production/custom flamenco and classical guitars in Nipomo, California.

Dick, Edward Victor

1975-present. Luthier Edward Dick currently builds his premium grade, custom, classical guitars in Denver, Colorado (he lived in Peterborough and Ottawa, Ontario until '95). He also operates the Colorado School of Luthrie.

Dickerson

1937-1947. Founded by the Dickerson brothers in 1937, primarily for electric lap steels and small amps. Instruments were also private branded for Cleveland's Oahu company, and for the Gourley brand. By '47, the company changed ownership and was renamed Magna Electronics (Magnatone).

Dillion

2000-present. Dillion, of Cary, North Carolina, offers intermediate grade, production, acoustic, acoustic/electric, hollow-body and solidbody guitars made in Korea and Vietnam. They also have basses and mandolins.

DFV58K

V, Korina, gold hardware, 2 humbuckers.

2003		$325	$350

DMG75

Mosrite Ventures copy, Bigsby, 2 humbuckers.

2003		$350	$400

DR500

Double cut solidbody, 2 humbuckers.

2003		$350	$400

Dillon

1975-present. Professional and premium grade, custom, flat-tops built by luthier John Dillon originally in Taos, New Mexico ('75-'81), then in Bloomsburg, Pennsylvania ('81-'01), and since 2001 back in Taos. He also builds basses.

DiPinto

1995-present. Intermediate and professional grade, production retro-vibe guitars from luthier Chris DiPinto of Philadelphia, Pennsylvania. He also builds basses. Until late '99, all instruments built in the U.S., since then all built in Korea.

Ditson

1916-1930. Ditson guitars were made by Martin and sold by the Oliver Ditson Company of Boston. The majority of production was from 1916 to '22 with over 500 units sold in '21.

Concert Model Style 2

1916-1922. Similar in size to Martin Size 0.

1916-1922		$2,300	$2,500

Standard Model Style 1

1916-1922. Small body similar to Martin size 3, plain styling.

1916-1922		$1,200	$1,500

Standard Model Style 2

1916-1922. Small body similar to Martin size 3, plain styling.

1916-1922		$1,500	$1,800

Standard Model Style 3

1916-1922. Small body similar to Martin size 3, styling similar to D-28.

1916-1922		$2,300	$2,500

Dobro

1929-1942, ca. 1954-present. Currently, professional and premium grade, production, wood and metal body resophonic guitars offered by Gibson.

Founded 1929 in Los Angeles by John Dopyera, Rudy Dopyera, Ed Dopyera and Vic Smith (Dobro stands for "Dopyera Brothers"). Made instruments sold under the Dobro, Regal, Norwood Chimes, Angelus, Rex, Broman, Montgomery Ward, Penetro, Bruno, Alhambra, More Harmony, Orpheum, and Magn-o-tone brands.

Dobro instruments have a single cone facing outward with a "spider bridge" structure and competed with National products. Generally, model names are numbers referring to list price and therefore materials and workmanship (e.g., a No. 65 cost $65). Because of this, the same model number may apply to various different instruments. However, model numbers are never identified on instruments!

In '30, the company name was changed to Dobro Corporation, Ltd. In '32, Louis Dopyera buys Ted Kleinmeyer's share of National. Louis, Rudy and Ed now hold controlling interest in National, but in '32 John Dopyera left Dobro to pursue idea of metal resophonic violin. In December of '34 Ed Dopyera joins National's board of directors (he's also still on Dobro board), and by March of '35 Dobro and National have merged to become the National Dobro Corporation. Dobro moves into National's larger factory but continues to maintain separate production, sales and distribution until relocation to Chicago is complete. Beginning in early-'36 National Dobro starts relocating its offices to Chicago. L.A. production of Dobros continues until '37, after which some guitars continue to be assembled from parts until '39, when the L.A. operations were closed down.

All resonator production ended in '42. Victor Smith, Al Frost and Louis Dopyera buy the company and change the name to the Valco Manufacturing Company. The Dobro name does not appear when production resumes after World War II.

In mid-'50s – some sources say as early as '54 – Rudy and Ed Dopyera began assembling wood-bodied "Dobros" from old parts using the name DB Original. In about '59, some 12-fret DB Originals were made for Standel, carrying both DB Original and Standel logos. In around '61, production was moved to Gardena, California, and Louis Dopyera and Valco transferred the Dobro name to Rudy and Ed, who produce the so-called Gardena Dobros. At this time, the "modern Dobro" logo appeared with a lyre that looks like two back-to-back "6s." Dobro Original debuts ca. '62. In late-'64 the Dobro name was licensed to Ed's son Emil (Ed, Jr.) Dopyera. Ed, Jr. designs a more rounded Dobro (very similar to later Mosrites) and has falling out with Rudy over it.

In '66 Semi Moseley acquires the rights to the Dobro brand, building some in Gardena, and later moving to Bakersfield, California. Moseley introduced Ed, Jr's design plus a thinline double-cutaway Dobro. Moseley Dobros use either Dobro or National cones. In '67 Ed, Sr., Rudy and Gabriella Lazar start the Original Music Instrument Company (OMI) and produce Hound Dog brand Dobros. In '68 Moseley goes bankrupt and in '70 OMI obtains the rights to the Dobro brand and begin production of OMI Dobros. In '75 Gabriella's son and daughter, Ron Lazar and Dee Garland, take over OMI.

Rudy Dupyera makes and sells Safari brand resonator mandolins. Ed, Sr. dies in '77 and Rudy in '78. In '84 OMI was sold to Chester and Betty Lizak. Both wood and metal-bodied Dobros produced in Huntington Beach, California. Chester Lizak died in '92. Gibson purchased Dobro in '93 and now makes Dobros in Nashville, Tennessee.

Dobros generally feature a serial number which, combined with historical information, provides a clue to dating. For prewar L.A. guitars, see approximation chart below adapted from Gruhn and Carter's *Gruhn's Guide to Vintage Guitars* (Miller Freeman, 1991). No information exists on DB Originals.

Gardena Dobros had D prefix plus three digits beginning with 100 and going into the 500s (reportedly under 500 made). No information is available on Moseley Dobros.

OMI Dobros from '70-'79 have either D prefix for wood bodies or B prefix for metal bodies, plus three or four numbers for ranking, space, then a single digit for year (D XXXX Y or B XXX Y; e.g., "D 172 8" would be wood body #172 from '78). For '80-'87 OMI Dobros, start with first number of year (decade) plus three or four ranking numbers, space, then year and either D for wood or B for metal bodies (8 XXXX YD or 8 XXX YB; e.g., "8 2006 5B" would be metal body #2008 from '85). From '88-'92, at least, a letter and number indicate guitar style, plus three or four digits for ranking, letter for neck style, two digits for year, and letter for body style (AX XXXX NYYD or AX XXX NYYB).

MODEL YEAR	FEATURES	EXC. COND. LOW	HIGH

L.A. Guitars (approx. number ranges, not actual production totals)

1928-30	900-2999	
1930-31	3000-3999	
1931-32	BXXX (Cyclops models only)	
1932-33	5000-5599	
1934-36	5700-7699	
1937-42	8000-9999	

Angelus
1933-1937. Wood body, round neck, two-tone Walnut finish. Continues as Model 19 in Regal-made guitars.

1933-1937		$900	$1,000

Cyclops 45
Square neck.

1931		$1,700	$1,800

DS33/Steel 33
1995-2000. Steel body with light Amber Sunburst finish, resonator with coverplate, biscuit bridge.

1995-2000		$1,100	$1,300

Hula Blues
Brown, painted Hawaiian scenes, round neck.

1991		$700	$800

Model 1
Nickel.

1930s		$2,500	$3,000

Model 125 De Luxe
1929-1934. Black walnut body, round or square neck, Dobro De Luxe engraved, triple-bound top, back and fingerboard, nickel-plated hardware. Natural.

192-1934	Round neck	$3,000	$3,500

Model 27
1933-1937. Regal-made, wooden body.

1933-1937	Round neck	$1,500	$2,000

Model 27 (OMI)

1980s		$1,000	$1,200

Model 33

1980s		$1,000	$1,500

Model 33 D
1971-1987 (OMI), 1995-1997 (Gibson). Chrome-plated brass body, etched diamond, floral, and then lattice design on front. Available with round neck or square neck.

1970s		$1,000	$1,500

Model 33 H
1973-1997 (OMI & Gibson). Same as 33 D, but with etched Hawaiian scenes. Available as round or square neck.

1980s	Round neck	$1,200	$1,500

Model 36
1932-1934. Wood body with resonator.

1932-1934		$1,200	$2,000

Model 36 S
1980s. Chrome-plated brass body, square neck, slotted headstock, dot markers, engraved rose floral art.

1980s		$1,200	$1,400

Model 37
1933-1937. Regal-made wood body, bound body and fingerboard, 12-fret neck.

1933-1937	Sunburst, square neck	$1,600	$2,100

1937 Dobro Model 27 (squareneck)

1930s Dobro Model 45

1931 Dobro Model 66

1967 Domino Baron

MODEL YEAR	FEATURES	EXC. COND. LOW	HIGH
Model 37 G			
1933-1937. California-made wood body, 12-fret round neck.			
1933-1937		$1,500	$1,800
Model 37 Tenor			
1933-1937 (Regal). Tenor version of No. 37.			
1933-1937		$600	$800
Model 42			
1930s		$1,500	$1,600
Model 45			
1929-1933. California-made, wood body, round or square neck, dark stain.			
1929-1933	Natural, square neck	$1,700	$1,800
Model 55			
1920-1930s. Unbound wood body, metal resonator, bound neck, Sunburst.			
1920s		$1,900	$2,000
1930s		$1,900	$2,000
Model 60 Cyclops			
1932-1933.			
1932-1933		$2,500	$3,000
Model 60/Model 60 D (OMI)			
1970-1993. Wood body (laminated maple) with Dobro resonator cone. Model 60 until '73 when renamed 60 D, and various 60 model features offered. Post-1993 was Gibson-owned production.			
1970s		$950	$1,050
1980s		$850	$950
1990s		$800	$900
Model 65			
1920s-1930s. Wood body with sandblasted ornamental design top and back, metal resonator.			
1928	Sunburst	$3,100	$3,500
Model 66 (Cyclops)			
1972-1995 (OMI & Gibson). Round neck and slotted peghead. Sunburst.			
1970s	Round neck	$800	$1,000
Model 90 (Duolian) (OMI)			
1972-1993. Chrome-plated, F-holes, etched Hawaiian scene.			
1980s		$1,300	$1,400
Regal Tenor 27-1/2			
1933-1937. Tenor version of Model 27.			
1930s		$800	$900
Regal/Dobro 37			
1933-1937. Regal-made wood body, bound body and fingerboard, 12-fret neck.			
1930s	Mahogany, round neck	$1,500	$2,000
1930s	Mahogany, square neck	$2,000	$2,500
Regal/Dobro 46			
1935-1942. Aluminum body, 14 frets, slotted peghead. Silver finish. Listed as No. 47 in 1939-1942.			
1940s	Round neck	$1,100	$1,300
Regal/Dobro 47			
1939-1942. Continuation of 46.			
1940s	Degraded finish (common problem)	$900	$1,000

MODEL YEAR	FEATURES	EXC. COND. LOW	HIGH
1940s	Round neck, original finish	$1,500	$2,000
Regal/Dobro 62			
1935-1942. Nickel-plated brass body, Spanish dancer etching. Continued as No. 65 for 1939-'42.			
1940s	Round neck	$3,000	$3,500
1940s	Square neck	$1,500	$2,000
Regal/Dobro Leader 14 M/14 H			
1934-1935. Nickel-plated brass body, round or square neck, solid peghead.			
1934-1935	Round neck	$2,000	$2,500
1934-1935	Square neck	$1,500	$1,800
Regal/Dobro Professional 15 M/15 H			
1934-1935. Engraved nickel body, round or square neck, solid peghead.			
1934-1935	Round neck	$3,000	$3,500
1934-1935	Square neck	$2,000	$2,500

Dodge

1996-present. Luthier Rick Dodge builds his intermediate and professional grade, production, solidbody guitars with changeable electronic modules in Tallahassee, Florida. He also builds basses.

DC Classic/Convertible DC Classic

1996-present. Offset-style body, bolt-on neck, rear-mounted convertible electronic modules, various colors.

1996-1999		$600	$750

Domino

Ca. 1967-1968. Solidbody and hollowbody electric guitars and basses imported from Japan by Maurice Lipsky Music Co. of New York, New York, previously responsible for marketing the Orpheum brand. Models are primarily near-copies of EKO, Vox, and Fender designs, plus some originals. Models were made by Arai or Kawai. Earlier models may have been imported, but this is not yet documented.

Baron

1967-1968. Double cut body, three pickups, tremolo.

1967-1968		$250	$500

Californian

1967-1968. Odd, squared body, copy of a Vox Phantom, two pickups, tremolo.

1967-1968		$250	$500

Californian Rebel

1967-1968. Odd, squared-off, triangle-shaped body, one F-hole, two or three pickups, tremolo.

1967-1968		$250	$500

Dawson

1967-1968. ES-335-style, two F-holes, two or three pickups.

1967-1968		$250	$500

Don Musser Guitars

1976-present. Custom, classical and flat-top guitars built by luthier Don Musser in Cotopaxi, Colorado.

MODEL YEAR	FEATURES	EXC. COND. LOW	HIGH

Doolin Guitars

1997-present. Luthier Mike Doolin builds his premium grade, production/custom acoutics featuring his unique double cutaway in Portland, Oregon.

Dorado

Ca. 1972-1973. Six- and twelve-string acoustic guitars, solidbody electrics and basses. Brand name used briefly by Baldwin/Gretsch on line of Japanese imports.

Acoustic Flat-Top/Acoustic Dobro
Introduced in 1972. Imported, includes folk D-style, Jumbo Western-style, Grand Concert-style (with laminated (?) rosewood back and sides), and Dobro-style.

1970s		$175	$250

Solidbody Electric
Introduced in 1972. Imported, includes Model 5985 Solidbody, which is a Strat-style with two P-90-style pickups, two knobs and a single toggle, Dorado on the headstock.

1970s		$150	$250

Dragge Guitars

1982-present. Luthier Peter Dragge builds his custom, steel-string and nylon-string guitars in Ojai, California.

Dragonfly Guitars

1994-present. Professional grade, production/custom, sloped cutaway flat-tops, semi-hollow body electrics, and dulcitars built by luthier Dan Richter in Roberts Creek, British Columbia.

DTM

1997-present. See David Thomas McNaught listing.

Dunwell Guitars

1996-present. Professional and premium grade, custom, flat-tops built by luthier Alan Dunwell in Nederland, Colorado.

Dupont

Luthier Maurice Dupont builds his classical, archtop, Weissenborn-style and Selmer-style guitars in Cognac, France.

MD-50-E
Selmer-style cutaway flat-top, large bridge.

2001		$2,500	$2,700

Earthwood

1972-1985. Acoustic designs by Ernie Ball with input from George Fullerton. One of the first to offer acoustic basses.

Eastman

1992-present. Professional and premium grade, production, archtop and flat-top guitars mainly built in China, with some from Germany and Romania. Beijing, China-based Eastman Strings started out building violins and cellos. They added guitars in '02 and mandolins in '04.

Eaton, William

1976-present. Luthier William Eaton builds custom specialty instruments such as vihuelas, harp guitars, and lyres in Phoenix, Arizona. He is also the Director of the Robetto-Venn School of Luthiery.

Ed Claxton Guitars

1972-present. Premium grade, custom flat-tops made by luthier Ed Claxton, first in Austin, Texas, and currently in Santa Cruz, California.

Egmond

1960-1972. Entry-level import from Holland. Prices include original guitar case, and an example without the case is worth considerably less.

Electric Guitar
Solidbody or semi-hollow entry-level.

1960-1972		$300	$450

Ehlers

1985-present. Luthier Rob Ehlers builds his premium grade, production/custom, flat-top acoustic guitars in Oregon.

15 CRC
Cutaway, western red cedar top, Indian rosewood back and sides.

1996		$2,700	$2,900

15 SRC
Cutaway, European spruce top, Indian rosewood back and sides.

1998		$2,800	$3,000

16 BTM
European spruce top, mahogany back and sides, Troubadour peghead, Black lacquer finish.

1998		$2,800	$3,000

16 SK Concert
Sixteen inch lower bout, relatively small upper bout, small waist, European spruce top, flamed Koa back and sides, diamond markers, Natural.

1993		$2,300	$2,500

16 SM
European spruce top, mahogany back and sides.

1999		$2,300	$2,400

16 SSC
Cutaway, European spruce top, English sycamore back and sides.

1996		$2,900	$3,100

25 C
Limited Edition Anniversary Model, European spruce top, Indian rosewood back and sides, abalone top border.

2001		$3,800	$4,000

Eichelbaum Guitars

1994-present. Luthier David Eichelbaum builds his premium grade, custom, flat-tops in Santa Barbara, California.

Don Musser dreadnought

Dunwell parlor guitar

1982 EKO CO-2 Cobra

EKO 500/4V

EKO

1959-1985, present. Acoustic, acoustic/electric, electric thinline and full-size archtop hollowbody, solidbody electric guitars and basses built by Oliviero Pigini and Company in Recanati, Italy, and imported by LoDuca Brothers, Milwaukee, Radio and Television Equipment Company in Santa Ana, California and others. First acoustic guitars followed by sparkle plastic-covered electrics by '62. Sparkle finishes are gone ca. '66. Pigini dies ca. '67. LoDuca Bros. phases out in early-'70s. By '75 EKO offers some copy guitars and they purchased a custom shop to make other brands by '78. Solidbody EKO guitars and basses are again being made in Recanati, Italy.

Barracuda
1966-ca.1978. ES-335 copy, two pickups.
1966-1978 $400 $450

Barracuda 12-String
1966-ca.1970. 12-string ES-335 copy, two pickups.
1966-1970 $350 $400

Cobra I
1966-1978. Double cut solidbody, single pickup, two knobs.
1966-1978 $275 $325

Cobra II
1966-1978. Double cut solidbody, dual pickups, two knobs.
1966-1978 $300 $350

Cobra III
1966-1978. Double cut solidbody, three pickups, two knobs.
1966-1978 $325 $375

Cobra XII
1967-ca.1969. Double cut solidbody 12-string, two pickups.
1967-1969 $350 $475

Condor
1966-ca.1969. Double cut solidbody with three or four pickups.
1966-1969 $400 $500

Dragon
1967-ca.1969. Single cutaway archtop, two F-holes, three pickups, tremolo.
1967-1969 $400 $500

Flat-Top Acoustic
1960s. Various student-level flat-top acoustic models.
1960s $125 $225

Florentine
1964-ca.1969. Double cut archtop, two pickups.
1964-1969 $475 $550

Kadett
1967-ca.1978. Double cut solidbody with point on lower bass side of body, three pickups, tremolo.
1967-1978 $400 $500

Kadett XII
1968-ca.1969. Double cut solidbody 12-string, with point on lower bass side of body.
1968-1969 $450 $500

Lancer

1967-ca.1969. Double cut solidbody, two pickups.
1967-1969 $250 $325

Lark I
Sunburst, thin hollow cutaway, one pickup.
1970 $375 $425

Lark II
Sunburst, thin hollow cutaway, two pickups.
1970 $375 $425

Model 500/1
1961-1964. Single pickup, plastic covered body.
1961-1964 $300 $400

Model 500/3V
1961-1964. Three pickups, vibrato, plastic covered body.
1961-1964 Plastic sparkle $525 $625

Model 500/4
1961-1964. Four pickups, non-vibrato, plastic covered body.
1961-1964 $625 $725

Model 500/4V
1961-1964. Four pickups, vibrato, plastic covered body.
1961-1964 Blue Sparkle $675 $775

Model 540 (Classical)
1960s. Nylon-string classical guitar.
1960s $150 $200

Model 700/3V (Map-shape)
1961-1964. Three pickups, vibrato, map-shaped plastic body.
1961-1964 Woodgrain plastic $950 $1,025

Model 700/4V (Map-shape)
1961-1967. Sort of map-shaped body, electric, with regular or sparkle top.
1960s Standard finish $950 $1,025
1961-1967 Red, Blue, Silver Sparkle $1,150 $1,225

Ranger 12
1967-ca.1982. Flat-top 12-string, acoustic or with pickup with tone and volume control.
1967-1982 $350 $400

Rocket VI/Rokes
1967-ca.1969. Rocket-shape design, solidbody, six-string, says "Rokes" on the headstock. The Rokes were a popular English band that endorsed EKO guitars. Marketed as the Rocket VI in the U.S.; and as the Rokes in Europe. Often called the Rok.
1967-1969 $600 $800

Rocket XII
1967-ca.1969. Rocket-shape design, 12-string solidbody. Often called the Rok.
1967-1969 $600 $750

El Degas
Early-1970s. Japanese-made copies of classic American electrics and acoustics, imported by Buegeleisen & Jacobson of New York, New York.

Let's Play
Early-1970s. Les Paul single cut copy, black, block markers, 2 pickups.
1970s $125 $175

| MODEL | | EXC. COND. | |
| YEAR | FEATURES | LOW | HIGH |

Electar

See Epiphone listing.

Electra

1971-1984. Imported from Japan by St. Louis Music. Most instruments made by Matsumoku in Matsumoto, Japan. The Electra line replaced SLM's Japanese-made Apollo and U.S.-made Custom Kraft lines. First guitar, simply called The Electra, was a copy of the Ampeg Dan Armstrong lucite guitar and issued in '71, followed quickly by a variety of bolt-neck copies of other brands. In '75 the Tree of Life guitars debut with a leaf pattern carved into the top, and the Electra line expanded to 25 models. Gibson-style headstocks changed to wave or fan shape by '78. By around '81 ties with Matsumoku further solidified and decision eventually made to merge SLM's Electra brand with Matsumoku's Westone brand. Some Korean production begins in early-'80s. In the fall of '83, the Electra Brand becomes Electra Phoenix. By beginning of '84, the brand name becomes Electra-Westone and by the end of '84 just Westone. Matsumoku-made guitars have serial number in which first one or two digits represent the year of manufacture. Thus a guitar with a serial number beginning in 0 or 80 would be from 1980.

Elvin Bishop
1976-ca.1980. ES-335 copy with tree-of-life inlay.

1977-1980		$550	$650

MPC Outlaw
1976-1983. Has separate modules that plug in for different effects.

1976-1983		$350	$550

Phoenix
1980-1984. Double cut solidbody.

1980-1984		$200	$325

Rock
1971-1973. Les Paul copy. Becomes the Super Rock in 1973.

1971-1973		$200	$300

Super Rock
1973-ca.1978. Les Paul copy. Renamed from Rock (1971-1973).

1973-1978		$225	$325

Electro

The Electro line was manufactured by Electro String Instruments and distributed by Radio-Tel. The Electro logo appeared on the headstock rather than Rickenbacker. Refer to the Rickenbacker section.

Elliott Guitars

1966-present. Premium and presentation grade, custom, nylon-string classical and steel-string guitars built by luthier Jeffrey Elliott in Portland, Oregon.

Emperador

1966-1992. Imported from Japan by Westheimer Musical Instruments. Early models appear to be made by either Teisco or Kawai; later models were made by Cort.

Acoustic Archtop Guitars
Japanese import.

1960s		$200	$300

Electric Solidbody Guitars
Japanese import.

1960s		$200	$300

Epiphone

Ca. 1873-present. Budget, intermediate and professional grade, production, solidbody, archtop, acoustic, acoustic/electric, resonator, and classical guitars made in the U.S. and overseas. They also offer basses, amps, mandolins and banjos. Founded in Smyrna, Turkey, by Anastasios Stathopoulos and early instruments had his label. He emigrated to the U.S. in 1903 and changed the name to Stathoupoulo. Anastasios died in 1915 and his son, Epaminondas ("Epi") took over. The name changed to House of Stathopoulo in '17 and the company incorporated in '23. In '24 the line of Epiphone Recording banjos debut and in '28 the company name was changed to the Epiphone Banjo Company. In '43 Epi Stathopoulo died and sons Orphie and Frixo took over. Labor trouble shut down the NYC factory in '51 and the company cut a deal with Conn/Continental and relocated to Philadelphia in '52. Frixo died in '57 and Gibson bought the company. Kalamazoo-made Gibson Epiphones debut in '58. In '69 American production ceased and Japanese imports began. Some Taiwanese guitars imported from '79-'81. Limited U.S. production resumed in '82 but sourcing shifted to Korea in '83. In '85 Norlin sold Gibson to Henry Juszkiewicz, Dave Barryman and Gary Zebrowski. In '92 Jim Rosenberg became president of the new Epiphone division.

1958 Korina Explorer
1997-present. Explorer with typical appointments, korina body.

1997-2000		$450	$500

1958 Korina Flying V
1997-present. Typical Flying V configuration, korina body.

1997-2000		$450	$550

1963 Firebird VII
2000-present. 3 mini-humbuckers, gold hardware, Maestro-style vibrato, block markers, Firebird Red, reverse body.

2000		$425	$500

Barcelone (classical)
1963-1968. Highest model of Epiphone 1960s classical guitars.

1963-1965		$700	$900
1966-1968		$700	$800

1981 Electra Outlaw

Jeffrey Elliot classical

1966 Epiphone Casino

1962 Epiphone Coronet

MODEL YEAR	FEATURES	EXC. COND. LOW	HIGH
Bard 12-String			
1962-1969. Flat-top, mahogany back and sides, Natural or Sunburst.			
1962-1964		$1,800	$2,300
1965-1969		$1,400	$1,900
Blackstone			
1931-1950. Acoustic archtop, Sunburst, F-holes.			
1933-1934	Masterbuilt	$1,400	$1,600
1935-1937		$1,200	$1,400
1938-1939		$1,100	$1,300
1940-1941		$1,000	$1,200
1948-1949		$900	$1,200
Broadway (Acoustic)			
1931-1958. Non-cutaway acoustic archtop.			
1931-1938	Sunburst, walnut body	$2,400	$3,600
1939-1942	Sunburst, maple body	$2,400	$3,600
1946-1949	Natural	$2,400	$3,300
1946-1949	Sunburst	$2,300	$3,000
1950-1958	Sunburst	$2,400	$2,900
Broadway (Electric)			
1958-1969. Gibson-made electric archtop, single cutaway, two New York pickups (mini-humbucking pickups by '61), Frequensator tailpiece, block inlays. Sunburst or Natural finish with Cherry optional in '67 only.			
1958-1964	Natural	$4,000	$5,000
1958-1964	Sunburst	$3,900	$4,900
1965-1969	Sunburst	$3,000	$4,700
1966-1968	Natural	$3,300	$4,800
1967	Cherry option	$3,300	$4,800
Broadway Regent (Acoustic Cutaway)			
1950-1958. Single cutaway acoustic archtop, Sunburst.			
1950-1958		$2,900	$3,200
Broadway Tenor			
1937-1953. Acoustic archtop, Sunburst.			
1939		$1,000	$1,200
1950		$800	$1,000
Byron			
1949-ca.1955. Acoustic archtop, mahogany back and sides, Sunburst.			
1949-1955		$400	$700
Caiola Custom			
1963-1970. Introduced as Caiola, renamed Caiola Custom in '66. Electric thinbody archtop, two mini-humbuckers, multi-bound top and back, block inlays. Walnut or Sunburst finish (Walnut only by '68).			
1963-1964	Sunburst or Walnut	$3,300	$4,200
1965-1966	Sunburst or Walnut	$3,100	$4,000
1967-1968	Sunburst or Walnut	$2,900	$4,000
1969-1970	Walnut	$2,900	$3,800
Caiola Standard			
1966-1970. Electric thinbody archtop, two P-90s, single-bound top and back, dot inlays. Sunburst or Cherry.			
1966		$2,700	$3,600
1967-1968		$2,600	$3,500
1969-1970		$2,500	$3,400

MODEL YEAR	FEATURES	EXC. COND. LOW	HIGH
Casino (one pickup)			
1961-1970. Thinline hollowbody, double cutaway, one P-90 pickup, trapeze tailpiece, tune-o-matic bridge, vibrato optional by '62. Sunburst or Royal Tan finish (Cherry optional in '67).			
1961-1964	Sunburst	$2,300	$2,700
1965-1966	Sunburst	$2,100	$2,500
1967-1968	Sunburst or optional cherry	$2,000	$2,300
1969-1970	Sunburst or optional cherry	$1,900	$2,200
Casino (two pickups)			
1961-1970. Two pickup (P-90) version.			
1961-1963	Royal Tan or Sunburst, Black covers	$3,000	$3,500
1963-1964	Sunburst, chrome covers	$3,500	$4,000
1965-1966	Sunburst	$3,500	$4,000
1967-1968	Cherry option	$2,500	$3,000
1967-1968	Sunburst	$3,000	$3,500
1969-1970	Sunburst or optional cherry	$2,900	$3,200
Casino Reissue			
1995-present. Sunburst.			
1995		$650	$700
Century			
1939-1970. Thinline archtop, non-cutaway, one pickup, trapeze tailpiece, Walnut finish. Sunburst finish available in '58, Royal Burgundy available '61 and only Sunburst finish available by '68.			
1949	Large rectangular pickup	$1,000	$1,600
1950	New York pickup	$1,000	$1,600
1951-1957	Sunburst	$1,000	$1,600
1958-1964	P-90 pickup	$1,000	$1,600
1965-1970		$900	$1,500
Classic (Classical)			
1963-1970. Includes the Madrid, Entrada, Seville, Classic, Espana, and Barcelone models.			
1963-1965		$500	$600
1966-1970		$450	$550
Coronet (Electric Archtop)			
1939-1949. Electric archtop, laminated mahogany body, one pickup, trapeze tailpiece, Sunburst. Name continued as an electric solidbody in '58.			
1939-1949		$900	$1,400
Coronet (Solidbody)			
1958-1969. Solidbody electric, one New York pickup ('58-'59), one P-90 ('59-'69). Cherry or Black finish, Silver Fox finish available by '63. Reintroduced as Coronet USA '91-'94, Korean-made '95-'98.			
1958	Sunburst	$1,500	$2,100
1959	Sunburst	$1,500	$2,000
1960	Cherry	$1,500	$2,000
1961	Cherry	$1,400	$1,900
1962	Cherry	$1,300	$1,800
1963	Cherry or Silver Fox	$1,200	$1,700
1963	Green Stain (faded Pacific Blue)	$1,200	$1,700

MODEL YEAR	FEATURES	EXC. COND. LOW	HIGH
1964	Cherry or Silver Fox	$1,100	$1,600
1964	Green Stain (faded Pacific Blue)	$1,100	$1,600
1965	Cherry or Silver Fox	$1,000	$1,500
1965	Green Stain (faded Pacific Blue)	$1,000	$1,500
1966-1969	Cherry	$900	$1,400

Coronet (Import)

1970s. Import electric, Sunburst.

1970s		$250	$350

Crestwood Custom

1958-1970. Solidbody, two New York pickups ('58-'60), two mini-humbuckers ('61-'70), symmetrical body ('58-'62), asymmetrical ('63-'70), slab body with no Gibson equivalent model.

1958-1960	Cherry, New York pickups	$2,700	$3,200
1961-1964	Cherry, mini-humbuckers	$2,400	$2,900
1961-1964	White, mini-humbuckers	$2,600	$3,100
1964-1966	Pacific Blue	$2,600	$3,100
1965-1966	Cherry	$2,000	$2,500
1965-1966	White	$2,200	$2,700
1967-1968	Cherry	$1,900	$2,400
1967-1968	White	$2,000	$2,500
1969-1970	Cherry or White	$1,900	$2,400

Crestwood Deluxe

1963-1969. Solidbody with three mini-humbuckers, block inlay. Cherry or White finish.

1963-1964	Cherry	$3,000	$3,500
1963-1964	White	$3,100	$3,600
1965-1966	Cherry	$2,800	$3,300
1965-1966	White	$3,000	$3,500
1967-1968	Cherry	$2,600	$3,100
1967-1968	White	$2,700	$3,200
1969	Cherry or White	$2,400	$2,900

De Luxe

1931-1957. Non-cutaway acoustic archtop, maple back and sides, trapeze tailpiece ('31-'37), frequensator tailpiece ('37-'57), gold-plated hardware. Sunburst or Natural finish.

1931-1934	Sunburst	$4,600	$5,600
1935-1939	Sunburst	$4,500	$5,500
1939	Natural, 1st year option	$5,500	$6,000
1940-1944	Natural	$5,300	$5,800
1940-1944	Sunburst	$4,300	$5,300
1945-1949	Natural	$4,600	$5,100
1945-1949	Sunburst	$3,600	$4,600
1950-1957	Natural	$3,200	$4,700
1950-1957	Sunburst	$2,700	$4,200

De Luxe Cutaway/Deluxe Cutaway

1953-1970. Renamed from De Luxe Regent, cataloged Deluxe Cutaway by Gibson in 1958. Special order by 1964 with limited production because acoustic archtops were pretty much replaced by electric archtops.

1953-1957	Epiphone NY-made	$3,800	$5,700

MODEL YEAR	FEATURES	EXC. COND. LOW	HIGH
1958-1965	Gibson Kalamazoo, rounded cutaway	$3,800	$5,700
1965-1970	Special order only	$3,800	$7,000

De Luxe Electric (Archtop)

1954-1957. Single cutaway electric archtop, two pickups. Called the Zephyr De Luxe Regent from '48-'54.

1954-1957	Natural or Sunburst	$3,500	$4,500

De Luxe Regent (acoustic archtop)

1948-1952. Acoustic cutaway archtop, high-end appointments, rounded cutaway, renamed De Luxe Cutaway in 1953.

1948-1952		$3,900	$6,000

Del Ray

1995-2000. Offset double cut, 2 blade humbuckers, dot markers, tune-o-matic, flamed maple top.

1995-2000		$325	$350

Devon

1949-1957. Acoustic archtop, non-cutaway, mahogany back and sides. Sunburst finish, optional Natural finish by '54.

1950-1953	Sunburst	$1,500	$1,700
1954-1957	Natural option	$1,700	$2,000
1954-1957	Sunburst	$1,400	$1,600

Dot (ES-335 Dot)

1997-present. Ephiphone's dot-neck 335 guitar.

1997-2000		$375	$450

Dwight

1963, 1967. Coronet labeled as "Dwight" for dealer. 75 made in '63 and 36 in '67.

1963	Cherry	$1,200	$1,700
1964	Cherry	$1,100	$1,600
1965	Cherry	$1,000	$1,500
1966-1967	Cherry	$900	$1,400

El Diablo

1990s. Offset double cut acoustic/electric, on-board piezo and 3-band EQ, composite back and sides, spruce top, cherry sunburst.

1990s		$300	$325

El Dorado FT 90

1963-1970. Dreadnought flat-top acoustic, mahogany back and sides, multi-bound front and back, Natural.

1963-1964		$2,200	$2,700
1965-1970		$1,500	$2,500

Electar Model M

1935-1939. Epiphone's initial entry into the new electric guitar market of the mid-1930s. 14-3/4" laminate maple archtop, horseshoe pickup, trap door on back for installing electronics, Electar (not Epiphone) logo on headstock, oblong pickup replaces horseshoe pickup in late-1937.

1935-1936	Two control knobs	$1,200	$1,400
1937-1939	Three control knobs	$1,200	$1,400

Emperor (Acoustic Archtop)

1935-1957. Acoustic archtop, non-cutaway, maple back and sides, multi-bound body, gold-plated hardware. Sunburst, optional Natural finish by 1939.

1936-1938	Sunburst	$5,900	$6,900

Epiphone Crestwood

1946 Epiphone Emperor

1961 Epiphone Emperor

Epiphone FT-110

MODEL YEAR	FEATURES	EXC. COND. LOW	HIGH
1939-1949	Natural	$6,000	$7,000
1939-1949	Sunburst	$5,800	$6,800
1950-1954	Natural	$3,800	$6,500
1950-1954	Sunburst	$3,700	$6,300

Emperor (Thinline Electric)
1958-1969. Single cutaway, thinline archtop, three New York pickups in '58-'60, three mini-humbuckers '61 on, multi-bound, gold-plated hardware. Sunburst or Natural finish until '65 when only Sunburst was made.

1958-1960	Natural	$9,500	$11,500
1958-1960	Sunburst	$9,000	$11,000
1961-1962	Natural	$9,000	$11,000
1961-1962	Sunburst	$8,500	$10,500
1963-1968	Special order only	$8,500	$10,500

Emperor Cutaway (formerly Emperor Regent)
1953-1970 (Gibson-made 1958 on). Renamed from Emperor Regent. Acoustic archtop, single cutaway, maple back and sides, multi-bound body, gold-plated hardware. Sunburst or Natural finish.

1953-1958	Natural	$7,700	$9,200
1953-1958	Sunburst	$6,300	$7,800

Emperor Electric
1953-1957. Archtop, single cutaway, three pickups, multi-bound body, Sunburst. Called the Zephyr Emperor Regent in '50-'53.

1953-1957		$4,500	$6,500

Emperor Regent
1948-1953. Acoustic archtop with rounded cutaway. Renamed Emperor Cutaway in 1953.

1948-1953	Natural	$7,700	$9,200
1948-1953	Sunburst	$6,500	$8,000

Entrada (Classical)
1963-1968. Flat-top classical, Natural.

1963-1965		$400	$600
1966-1968		$350	$550

Espana (Classical)
1962-1968. Classical, maple back and sides, U.S.-made, natural. Imported in 1969 from Japan.

1962-1965		$600	$800
1966-1968		$550	$750

Firebird 300
1986-1988. Korean import, Firebird Red.

1987		$250	$350

Firebird 500
1986-1988. Korean import, Firebird Red.

1987		$275	$375

Firebird II/III
1995-2000. 2 mini-humbuckers, Firebird Red, dot markers.

1995-2000		$375	$400

Folkster FT 95
1966-1969. Fourteen inch small body, mahogany back and sides, double White pickguards.

1966-1969	Natural	$900	$1,000

FT 30
1941-1949. Acoustic flat-top, Brown stain, mahogany back and sides. Reintroduced as Gibson-made FT 30 Caballero in 1958.

1941-1949		$950	$1,100

FT 30 Caballero
1958-1970. Reintroduced from Epiphone-made FT 30. Gibson-made acoustic flat-top, Natural, all mahogany body, dot inlay. Tenor available 1963-1968.

1959-1960		$900	$1,050
1961-1964		$700	$900
1965-1970		$600	$750

FT 45
1941-1948. Acoustic flat-top, walnut back and sides, cherry neck, rosewood fingerboard. Natural top. Reintroduced as Gibson-made FT 45 Cortez in 1958.

1941-1948		$1,400	$1,800

FT 45 Cortez
1958-1969. Reintroduced from Epiphone-made FT 45. Gibson-made acoustic flat-top, mahogany back and sides. Sunburst or Natural top (Sunburst only in '59-'62).

1958-1961	Sunburst	$1,000	$1,500
1962-1964	Sunburst	$1,000	$1,400
1965-1969	Sunburst	$900	$1,200

FT 79
1941-1958. Acoustic 16" flat-top, square shoulder D-style, walnut back and sides until '49 and laminated maple back and sides '49 on, Natural. Renamed FT 79 Texan by Gibson in '58.

1941-1949	Walnut back & sides	$3,000	$3,300
1949-1958	Laminated pressed maple body	$2,500	$2,800

FT 79 Texan
1958-1970, 1993-1995. Renamed from Epiphone FT 79. Gibson-made acoustic flat-top, mahogany back and sides. Sunburst or Natural top. Gibson Montana made 170 in '93-'95.

1958-1961		$2,500	$2,800
1962-1964		$2,200	$2,700
1965-1966		$1,900	$2,500
1967-1968		$1,600	$2,300
1969-1970		$1,300	$2,000

FT 110
1941-1958. Acoustic flat-top, Natural. Renamed the FT 110 Frontier by Gibson in 1958.

1941-1949	Square shoulder	$2,500	$3,000
1949-1954	Round shoulder	$1,800	$2,800
1954-1958	Mahogany neck	$1,800	$2,800

FT 110 Frontier
1958-1970, 1994. Renamed from FT 110. Acoustic flat-top, Natural or Sunburst. Gibson Montana made 30 in 1994.

1958-1966		$1,800	$2,800
1967-1969		$1,500	$2,500

G-310
1989-present. SG-style model with large pickguard.

1989-1999	With gig bag, not case	$225	$275

G-400 Deluxe
1999-present. SG-style model with flamed maple top, 2 exposed humbuckers.

1999-2002		$425	$450

MODEL YEAR	FEATURES	EXC. COND. LOW	HIGH

Genesis
1979-1980 Double cut solidbody, 2 humbuckers with coil-taps, carved top, Red or Black. Available as Custom, Deluxe, and Standard models. Tawainese import.

| 1979-1980 | | $300 | $400 |

Goth 1958 Explorer
2002-present. Flat black finish.

| 2002-2003 | | $400 | $500 |

Granada (Non-cutaway Thinbody)
1962-1969. Non-cutaway thinline archtop, one F-hole, one pickup, trapeze tailpiece. Sunburst finish.

| 1962-1966 | | $850 | $950 |
| 1967-1969 | | $550 | $750 |

Granada Cutaway
1965-1970. Single cutaway thinline archtop, one F-hole, one pickup, Sunburst.

| 1965-1966 | | $800 | $1,000 |
| 1967-1970 | | $750 | $950 |

Howard Roberts Custom
1965-1970. Single cutaway archtop, bound front and back, one pickup. Walnut finish (Natural offered 1966 only).

| 1965-1967 | | $2,800 | $3,700 |
| 1968-1970 | | $2,200 | $3,400 |

Howard Roberts III
1987-1991. Two pickups, various colors.

| 1987-1991 | | $600 | $650 |

Howard Roberts Standard
1964-1970. Single cutaway acoustic archtop, bound front and back. Cherry or Sunburst finish. Listed in catalog as acoustic but built as electric.

1964-1965		$2,600	$3,500
1966-1967		$2,500	$3,400
1968-1970		$2,000	$3,200

Joe Pass Emperor II
1994-present. ES-175-style with rounded cutaway, block markers, 2 humbuckers.

| 1994-2000 | | $600 | $650 |

Les Paul Custom
1988-present. Various colors.

| 1988-2000 | | $400 | $500 |

Les Paul Deluxe
1998-2000. Typical mini-humbucker pickups.

| 1998-2000 | | $400 | $500 |

Les Paul Special Double Cut
1995-2000. Bolt-on neck.

| 1995-2000 | | $200 | $250 |

Les Paul Standard
1989-present. Solid mahogany body, carved maple top, two humbuckers.

| 1989-2000 | Sunburst, foto-flame top | $350 | $450 |

Les Paul XII
1998-2000. 12-string solidbody, trapeze tailpiece, flamed maple sunburst, standard configuration.

| 1998-2000 | | $550 | $650 |

Madrid (Classical)
1962-1969. Classical, Natural.

| 1962-1969 | | $300 | $400 |

Navarre
1931-1940. Flat-top, mahogany back and sides, bound top and back, dot inlay. Brown finish.

| 1936 | Hawaiian, Masterbilt label | $1,400 | $1,600 |

Nighthawk Standard
1995-2000. Epiphone's version of the Gibson Nighthawk, single cut, bolt neck, figured top.

| 1995-2000 | | $325 | $375 |

Olympic (3/4 Scale Solidbody)
1960-1963. Twenty-two inch scale.

| 1960-1963 | Sunburst | $650 | $750 |

Olympic (Acoustic Archtop)
1931-1949. Mahogany back and sides.

| 1931-1949 | | $600 | $800 |

Olympic Double (Solidbody)
1960-1969. Slab body, the same as the mid-1960s Coronet, Wilshire and Crestwood Series, single cut '60-'62, asymmetrical cut '63-'70, 2 Melody Maker single-coils, vibrato optional in '64 and standard by '65.

1960-1962	Sunburst, single cutaway	$850	$1,050
1963-1965	Sunburst, double cutaway	$850	$1,050
1966-1969	Cherry or Sunburst	$800	$950

Olympic Single (Solidbody)
1960-1970. Slab body, the same as the mid-1960s Coronet, Wilshire and Crestwood Series, single cutaway 1960-1962, asymmetrical double cutaway 1963-1970, two Melody maker single-coil pickups, vibrato optional in 1964 and standard by 1965.

1960-1962	Sunburst, single cutaway	$750	$950
1963-1965	Sunburst, double cutaway	$700	$950
1966-1967	Cherry or Sunburst	$675	$850
1968-1970	Cherry or Sunburst	$675	$850

Olympic Special (Solidbody)
1962-1970. Short neck with neck body joint at the 16th fret (instead of the 22nd), single Melody Maker-style single-coil bridge pickup, small headstock, double cutaway slab body, dot markers, Maestro or Epiphone vibrato optional 1964-1965, slab body contour changes in 1965 from symmetrical to asymmetrical with slightly longer bass horn, Sunburst.

1964-1965		$650	$850
1966-1967		$600	$800
1968-1970		$550	$750

PR-200 (EA-20)
1992-present. Imported D-style, spruce top with satin finish, mahogany back and sides, Natural.

| 1992-1999 | | $150 | $250 |

PR-350
1984-1999. Acoustic flat-top, mahogany D-style body. Also available with a pickup.

| 1984-1999 | | $175 | $275 |

PR-350-CE
1989-1999. Acoustic flat-top, cutaway, mahogany D-style body. Also available with a pickup.

| 1989-1999 | | $250 | $350 |

1965 Epiphone Howard Roberts

1965 Epiphone Olympic

GUITARS

1966 Epiphone Riviera

Epiphone Sheraton

MODEL YEAR	FEATURES	EXC. COND. LOW	HIGH
PR-600 ACS/ASB/N			
1980s. Import 000-size flat-top, glued bridge, dot markers, Sunburst, from Japan.			
1985-1988		$250	$400
Pro 1			
1989-1996. Solidbody, double cutaway, one single-coil and one humbucking pickup, bolt-on neck, various colors.			
1989-1996		$300	$400
Pro 2			
1995-1998. Higher-end Pro I with Steinberger DB bridge, various colors.			
1995-1998		$325	$400
Professional			
1962-1967. Double cutaway, thinline archtop, one pickup. Mahogany finish.			
1962-1967	With matching Professional Amp	$1,800	$2,000
Recording A			
1928-1931.			
1928-1931		$1,300	$1,500
Recording B			
1928-1931. Asymmetrical body, cutaway bouts, flat-top, arched back, laminated maple back.			
1928-1931		$2,000	$2,200
Recording C			
1928-1931.			
1928-1931		$2,400	$2,800
Recording D			
1928-1931.			
1928-1931		$3,000	$3,400
Recording E			
1928-1931.			
1928-1931		$4,000	$4,500
Riviera			
1962-1970, 1993-1994. Double cut thinline archtop, 2 mini-humbuckers. Royal Tan standard finish changing to sunburst in '65, cherry optional by '66-'70. An additional 250 were made in Nashville in '93-'94. A Riviera import was available in '82 and for '94-present.			
1962-1964	Tan or custom cherry	$2,500	$3,500
1965-1966	Sunburst or cherry	$2,500	$3,500
1966-1967	Burgundy Mist	$2,500	$3,500
1967-1968	Sunburst or cherry	$2,200	$3,500
1967-1968	Walnut	$2,100	$3,400
1969	Sunburst or cherry	$2,000	$3,200
Riviera (import)			
1970s.			
1978		$500	$600
Riviera 12-String			
1965-1970. Double cutaway, 12 strings, thinline archtop, two mini-humbuckers.			
1965	Sunburst or cherry	$2,000	$2,300
1966	Sunburst or cherry	$1,900	$2,200
1967	Sunburst or cherry	$1,700	$2,000
1968-1970	Cherry	$1,600	$1,900
Riviera 12-String Reissue			
1997-present. Korean-made reissue.			
1997-2002	Natural	$450	$650

MODEL YEAR	FEATURES	EXC. COND. LOW	HIGH
Riviera Reissue			
1994-present. Korean-made reissue.			
1994-2002	Natural	$400	$450
S-900			
1986-1989. Neck-through-body, locking Bender tremolo system, two pickups with individual switching and a coil-tap control.			
1986-1989		$350	$400
Serenader 12-String FT 85			
1963-1969. Twelve strings, mahogany back and sides, dot inlay, Natural.			
1963-1964		$900	$1,100
1965-1966		$700	$900
1967-1969		$600	$800
Seville (Classical)			
1938-1941, 1961-1969 (Gibson-made). Classical guitar, mahogany back and sides, Natural. The '61-'63 version also available with a pickup.			
1961-1965		$400	$600
1966-1969		$350	$550
Sheraton			
1958-1970, 1993-1994. Double cut thinline archtop, 2 New York pickups '58-'60, 2 mini-humbuckers '61 on, frequensator tailpiece, multi-bound, gold-plated hardware. Sunburst or natural finish with cherry optional by '65. An additional 250 American-made Sheratons were built from '93-'94.			
1958-1959	Natural, New York pickups	$9,000	$11,000
1960	Natural, New York pickups	$8,000	$10,000
1961-1963	Natural, mini-humbuckers	$7,500	$9,000
1961-1963	Sunburst, mini-humbuckers	$6,800	$8,000
1964-1965	Natural	$6,500	$7,500
1964-1965	Sunburst	$6,000	$7,000
1965	Cherry	$6,200	$7,200
1966	Sunburst or cherry	$5,500	$6,500
1967	Sunburst or cherry	$5,000	$6,300
1968	Sunburst or cherry	$4,800	$6,000
1969	Sunburst	$4,500	$5,500
1993-1994	Model reintroduced	$550	$650
Sheraton (Japan)			
1978-1983. Early reissue, not to be confused with Sheraton II issued in late-1990s, Natural or Sunburst.			
1978-1983		$550	$650
Sheraton II (reissue)			
1997-present. Contemporary reissue, Natural or Sunburst.			
1997-1999		$425	$475
Sorrento (one pickup)			
1960-1970. Single cut thinline archtop, 1 pickup in neck position, tune-o-matic bridge, nickel-plated hardware, sunburst, natural or Royal Olive finish (cherry or sunburst by '68).			
1960-1965		$1,600	$2,000
1966-1968		$1,400	$1,900
1969-1970		$1,200	$1,900

GUITARS

MODEL YEAR	FEATURES	EXC. COND. LOW	HIGH

Sorrento (two pickups)

1960-1970. Single cutaway thinline archtop, two pickups, tune-o-matic bridge, nickel-plated hardware. Sunburst, Natural or Royal Olive finish (Cherry or Sunburst by 1968).

1960-1965		$1,800	$2,400
1966-1968		$1,600	$2,300
1969-1970		$1,400	$2,300

Sorrento (Reissue)

1997-2000.

1997-2000		$400	$450

Spartan

1934-1949. Acoustic archtop, multi-bound, trapeze tailpiece, Sunburst.

1930s		$800	$1,100
1940s		$700	$900

Spirit

1979-1983. American-made electric solidbody, double cutaway, carved top with two humbuckers, various colors.

1979-1983		$650	$750

Triumph

1931-1957. 15-1/4" '31-'33, 16-3/8" '33-'36, 17-3/8" '36-'57. Walnut back and sides until '33, laminated maple back and sides '33, solid maple back and sides '34, natural or sunburst.

1931-1932	Sunburst, laminated walnut body	$1,000	$1,700
1933	Sunburst, laminated maple body	$1,000	$1,700
1934-1935	Sunburst, solid maple body	$1,400	$1,800
1936-1940	Sunburst 17 3/8" body	$1,700	$2,400
1941-1949	Natural	$1,700	$2,400
1941-1949	Sunburst	$1,600	$2,200
1950-1957	Natural	$1,600	$2,200
1950-1957	Sunburst	$1,400	$1,800

Triumph Regent (Cutaway)

1948-1969. Acoustic archtop, single cutaway, F-holes. Renamed Triumph Cutaway in '53, then Gibson listed this model as just the Triumph from '58-'69.

1948-1958	Natural	$2,300	$3,000
1948-1958	Sunburst	$2,200	$2,800
1959-1965	Sunburst	$2,100	$2,700
1966-1968	Sunburst	$2,100	$2,600

Troubadour FT 98

1963-1969. 16" square shoulders, D-style, maple back and sides, gold-plated hardware, classical width fingerboard.

1963-1969		$1,500	$2,000

USA Map Guitar

1982-1983. Solidbody electric, mahogany body shaped like U.S. map, two pickups, American-made promotional model, natural.

1982-1983		$1,800	$2,000

Vee-Wee (Mini Flying V)

2003. Mini Flying V student guitar, Flying V shape with single bridge pickup, gig bag, solid opaque finish.

2003		$115	$125

Wilshire

1959-1970. Double cutaway solidbody, two pickups, tune-o-matic bridge, Cherry.

1959	Symmetrical body	$2,600	$3,100
1960-1962	Thinner-style body, P-90s	$2,500	$3,000
1962	Mini-humbuckers	$2,300	$2,800
1963-1964	Asymmetrical body	$2,200	$2,700
1965-1966		$1,800	$2,300
1967-1968		$1,700	$2,200
1969-1970		$1,600	$2,100

Wilshire 12-String

1966-1968. Solidbody, two pickups, Cherry.

1966		$2,200	$2,700
1967-1968		$2,000	$2,500

Wilshire II

1984-1985. Solidbody, maple body, neck and fingerboard, two humbuckers, three-way switch, coil-tap, one tone and one volume control, various colors.

1984		$250	$300

Windsor

1959-1962. Archtop, one or two pickups, single cutaway thinline. Sunburst or Natural finish.

1959-1960	New York pickup	$1,600	$2,000
1961-1962	Mini-humbucker	$1,600	$2,000

X-1000

1986-1989. Electric solidbody, Korean-made, various colors.

1987		$250	$300

Zenith

1931-1969. Acoustic archtop, bound front and back, F-holes, Sunburst.

1931-1933		$900	$1,100
1934-1935	Larger 14 3/4" body	$900	$1,100
1936-1949	Still larger 16 3/8" body	$900	$1,100
1950-1958		$800	$1,000
1959-1961		$550	$950
1963-1964		$500	$900

Zephyr

1939-1957. Non-cutaway electric archtop, one pickup, bound front and back, Blond or Sunburst. Name continued '58-'64 on thinline cutaway, two pickup model.

1939	Oblong pickup	$1,400	$2,000
1940-1943		$1,400	$2,000
1944-1946	Top mounted pickup	$1,300	$1,900
1947-1948	Metal covered pickup	$1,200	$1,800
1949-1957	New York pickup	$1,100	$1,700

Zephyr (Thinline Cutaway)

1958-1964. Gibson-made version, thinline archtop, single cutaway, two pickups. Natural or Sunburst finish.

1958-1959		$2,000	$2,600
1960-1964		$1,800	$2,400

Epiphone Wilshire

1944 Epiphone Zenith

The *Vintage Guitar Price Guide* shows low to high values for items in all-original excellent condition, and, where applicable, with original case or cover.

Epiphone Zephyr De Luxe Regent

ESP XTone PS-2V

MODEL YEAR	FEATURES	EXC. COND. LOW	HIGH

Zephyr De Luxe (Non-cutaway)
1941-1954. Non-cutaway electric archtop, one or two pickups, multi-bound front and back, gold-plated hardware, Blond or Sunburst.

1941-1942		$2,500	$3,300
1945-1949		$2,500	$3,400
1951-1954		$2,000	$2,700

Zephyr De Luxe Regent (Cutaway)
1948-1954. Single cutaway electric archtop, one or two pickups until '50, then only two, gold-plated hardware. Sunburst or Natural finish. Renamed Deluxe Electric in '54.

1948-1954	Natural or Sunburst	$3,500	$4,500

Zephyr Emperor Regent
1950-1954. Archtop, single rounded cutaway, multi-bound body, three pickups. Sunburst or Natural finish. Renamed Emperor Electric in 1954.

1950-1951	Natural	$4,500	$5,200
1950-1951	Sunburst	$4,300	$5,000
1952-1953	Natural	$4,300	$5,000
1952-1953	Sunburst	$4,100	$4,800
1954	Natural	$4,100	$4,800
1954	Sunburst	$3,800	$4,500

Zephyr Regent
1950-1958. Single cutaway electric archtop, one pickup, Natural or Sunburst. Called Zephyr Electric for '54-'58.

1950		$1,400	$2,700
1951		$1,300	$2,600
1953		$1,200	$2,500
1954		$1,100	$2,300
1955		$1,000	$2,200
1957		$900	$2,100

Erlewine
1979-present. Professional and premium grade, production/custom guitars built by luthier Mark Erlewine in Austin, Texas. Erlewine also produces the Chiquita brand travel guitar.

ESP
1983-present. Hisatake Shibuya's Electronic Sound Prodicts (ESP), a chain of retail stores, began to produce replacement parts for electric guitars in 1983. In 1985, ESP started to make custom-made guitars for special customers. ESP was originally known as a custom low-volume high-quality builder, and ESP continues with those roots today. In 1987 volume was so great that a factory was opened in Tokyo with a continued Emphasis on a high quality product. In 1986, ESP opened a sales office in New York, selling custom guitars ($2,000-$9,000 in today's dollars) and production models ($1,500-#3,500). In 1996, ESP introduced the entry-level competitively priced (starting at $300) LTD Series. The entry-level product line was so successful that ESP began to be considered an economy brand, even though it had its origins as a high-end custom builder. Owner Hisatake Shibuya is known as a major vintage guitar collector. He operated a vintage guitar show 48th Street Custom Guitars during the

1990s but he closed that shop in 2003. By 2004, the ESP product line includes over 100 models.

20th Anniversary
1995. Solidbody, double cut, ESP95 inlaid at 12th fret.

1995	Gold	$1,000	$1,200

Eclipse Custom (USA)
1998-2000. U.S. Custom Shop-built single cut mahogany body and maple top, various colors offered.

1998-2000		$800	$1,100

Eclipse Custom/Custom T (import)
1986-1988. Single cut mahogany solidbody, earliest model with bolt-on dot marker neck, 2nd version with neck-through design and block markers. The Custom T adds double locking tremolo.

1986	Bolt-on neck, dot markers	$450	$550
1987	Bolt-on neck, dot markers	$450	$550
1987	Neck-through, block markers	$550	$650
1987	Neck-through, Custom T	$550	$650
1988	Neck-through, block markers	$550	$650
1988	Neck-through, Custom T	$550	$650

Eclipse Deluxe
1986-1988. Single cut solidbody, one single-coil and one humbucker pickup, vibrato.

1986-1988	Black	$400	$550

Horizon
1986, 1996-2001. Double cut neck-thru body, bound ebony 'board, one single-coil and one humbucker, buffer preamp circuit, various colors. Reintroduced 1996-2001 with bolt-on neck, curved rounded point headstock.

1986		$350	$450
1996-2001		$250	$300

Horizon Classic (USA)
1993-1995. U.S.-made, carved mahogany body, set-neck, dot markers, various colors. Optional mahogany body with figured maple top also offered.

1993-1995	Figured maple top option	$1,200	$1,500
1993-1995	Standard mahogany body	$1,100	$1,300

Horizon Custom (USA)
1998-present. U.S. Custom Shop-made, mahogany body, figured maple top, bolt-on neck, mostly translucent finish in various colors.

1998		$1,100	$1,300

Horizon Deluxe (import)
1989-1992. Horizon Custom with bolt-on neck, various colors.

1989		$550	$650

Hybrid I (import)
1986 only. Offset double cutaway body, bolt-on maple neck, dot markers, six-on-a-side tuners, standard vibrato, various colors.

1986		$250	$350

MODEL YEAR FEATURES	EXC. COND. LOW	HIGH

Hybrid II (import)
Offset double cutaway, rosewood board on maple bolt-on neck, lipstick neck pickup, humbucker bridge pickup, Hybrid II logo on headstock.

1980s	$300	$400

LTD EC-300
2002-present. Single cut solidbody, 2 humbuckers, Korean-made.

2000s	$350	$400

LTD EC-1000
2002-present. Deluxe appointments including abalone inlays and figured-top, 2 humbuckers, Korean-made.

2000s	$650	$750

LTD H-100
1998-present. Offset double-cut solidbody, 2 humbuckers, made in Korea.

2000s	$150	$175

LTD Viper
2000-present. Double cut SG style solidbody, 2 humbuckers.

2000s	$325	$425

M-I Custom
1987-1994. Offset double cutaway through-neck body, offset block markers, various colors.

1987-1994	$650	$750

M-I Deluxe
1987-1989. Double cut solidbody, rosewood 'board, two single-coils and one humbucker, various colors.

1987-1989	$550	$650

M-II
1989-1994, 1996-2000. Double cut solidbody, reverse headstock, bolt-on maple or rosewood cap neck, dot markers, various colors.

1989-1994	$700	$800

M-II Custom
1990-1994. Double cut solidbody, reverse headstock, neck-through maple neck, rosewood cap, dot markers, various colors.

1990-1994	$900	$1,000

M-II Deluxe
1990-1994. Double cut solidbody, reverse headstock, Custom with bolt-on neck, various colors.

1990-1994	$800	$900

Maverick/Maverick Deluxe
1989-1992. Offset double cutaway, bolt-on maple or rosewood cap neck, dot markers, double locking vibrola, six-on-a-side tuners, various colors.

1989	$250	$350

Metal I
1986 only. Offset double cutaway, bolt-on maple neck with rosewood cap, dot markers, various colors.

1986	$250	$350

Metal II
1986 only. Single horn V-style body, bolt on maple neck with rosewood cap, dot markers, various colors.

1986	$250	$350

Metal III
1986 only. Reverse offset body, bolt-on maple neck with maple cap, dot markers, Gold hardware, various colors.

1986	$300	$400

Mirage Custom
1986-1990. Double cut neck-thru solidbody, two-octave ebony fingerboard, block markers, one humbuck and two single-coil pickups, locking trem, various colors.

1986-1990	$500	$600

Mirage Standard
1986 only. Single pickup version of Mirage Custom, various colors.

1986	$275	$350

Phoenix
1987 only. Offset, narrow waist-style, through-neck mahogany body, Black hardware, dot markers, various colors.

1987	$450	$550

Phoenix Contemporary
Late-1990s. Firebird copy, three pickups vs. two on the earlier offering.

1998	$800	$850

S-454/S-456
1986-1987. Offset double cutaway, bolt-on maple or rosewood cap neck, dot markers, various colors.

1986-1987	$250	$500

S-500
1991-1993. Double cut figured ash body, bolt-on neck, six-on-a-side tuners, various colors.

1991-1993	$500	$700

Traditional
1989-1990. Double cutaway, three pickups, tremolo, various colors.

1989-1990	$500	$600

Vintage/Vintage Plus S
1995-1998. Offset double cutaway, bolt-on maple or rosewood cap neck, dot markers, Floyd Rose locking vibrato or standard Strat-type vibrato, various colors.

1995-1998	$600	$900

Espana
Early-1960s-early-1970s. Distributed by catalog wholesalers. Built in Sweden.

Classical
Early-1960s-early-1970s. Guitars with white spruce fan-braced tops with either walnut, mahogany, or rosewood back and sides.

1970s	$125	$175

EL-36
1969-early-1970s. Thin hollow doublecut, two pickups, Natural.

1970s	$150	$200

Jumbo Folk
1969-early-1970s. Natural.

1970s	$125	$200

S-1 Classical
1969-early-1970s. Natural.

1970s	$125	$175

ESP H100 ASB

1986 ESP Traditional

Evergreen Mountain tenor guitar

1957 Fender Stratocaster

MODEL		EXC. COND.	
YEAR	FEATURES	LOW	HIGH

Essex (SX)

1985-present. Budget grade, production, electric and acoustic guitars imported by Rondo Music of Union, New Jersey. They also offer basses.

Euphonon

1934-1944. This Larson-made brand was intended to compete with the competition's new larger body, 14-fret, solid peghead (unslotted) models. Standard and D-style models were offered. Three models were offered ranging from the small 13 3/4" student model, to the top end 15" and 16" models.

Ornamentation and features are as important as rosewood vs. mahogany. Euphonons with truss rods were marketed as Prairie State models.

D-Style/Standard 16" D-46 Appointments

1934-1944		$25,000	$30,000

D-Style/Standard 16" Fancy Binding

1934-1944		$15,000	$17,000

D-Style/Standard 16" Pearl Trim

1934-1944		$20,000	$25,000

Standard 13"-15" Fancy Binding

1934-1944		$8,000	$10,000

Everett Guitars

1977-present. Luthier Kent Everett builds his premium grade, production/custom, steel-string and classical guitars in Atlanta, Georgia. He has also built archtops, semi-hollow and solidbody electrics, Dobro-styles, and mandolins.

Evergreen Mountain

1971-present. Professional grade, custom, flat-top and tenor guitars built by luthier Jerry Nolte in Cove, Oregon. He also builds basses and mandolins and built over 100 dulcimers in the '70s.

Everly Guitars

1982-2001. Luthier Robert Steinegger built these premium grade, production/custom flat-tops in Portland, Oregon (also see Steinegger Guitars).

Falk

Custom archtop guitars built by luthier Dave Falk in Independence, Missouri.

Farnell

1989-present. Luthier Al Farnell builds his professional grade, production, solidbody guitars in Ontario, California. He also offers his intermediate grade, production, "C" Series which is imported from China. He also builds basses.

Favilla

1890-1973. Founded by the Favilla family in New York, the company began to import guitars in 1970, but folded in '73. American-made models have the Favilla family crest on the headstock. Import models used a script logo on the headstock.

Fender

1946 (1945)-present. Budget, intermediate, professional and premium grade, production/custom, electric, acoustic, acoustic/electric, classical, and resonator guitars built in the U.S. and overseas. They also build amps, basses, mandolins, banjos, bouzoukis and violins. Ca. 1939 Leo Fender opened a radio and record store called Fender Radio Service, where he met Clayton Orr "Doc" Kauffman, and in '45 they started KF Company to build lap steels and amps. In '46 Kauffman left and Fender started the Fender Electric Instrument Company. By '50 Fender's products were distributed by F.C. Hall's Radio & Television Electronics Company (Radio-Tel, later owners of Rickenbacker). In '53 Radio-Tel is replaced by the Fender Sales Company which was ran by Don Randall. In January '65 CBS purchased the company for $13 million and re-named it Fender Musical Instruments Corporation. The CBS takeover is synonymous with a decline in quality - whether true or not is still debated, but the perception persists among musicians and collectors, and "Pre-CBS" Fenders are more valuable. Fender experienced some quality problems in the late-'60s. Small headstock is enlarged in '65 and the four-bolt neck is replaced by the three-bolt in '71. With high value and relative scarcity of Pre-CBS Fenders, even CBS-era instruments are now sought by collectors. Leo Fender kept on as consultant until '70. Fender went on to design guitars for Music Man and G&L.

Bill Schultz and Dan Smith were hired from Yamaha in '81. In '82 Fender Japan is established to produce licensed Fender "copies" for sale in Japan. Also in '82, the Fender Squire brand debuts on Japanese-made instruments for the European market and by '83 they were imported into U.S.

In '84 CBS put Fender up for sale and the company was purchased by an investor group headed by Bill Schultz but the purchase does not include the Fullerton factory. While a new factory was being established at Corona, CA, all Fender Contemporary Stratocasters and Telecasters were made either by Fender Japan or in Seoul, Korea. U.S. production resumes in '86 with American Standard Stratocaster. The Fender Custom Shop, run by Michael Stevens and John Page, opens in '87. The Mexican Fender factory is established in '90. In '95, Fender purchased the Guild guitar company. On January 3, 2002, Fender Musical Instruments Corporation (FMIC) announced the sale of holdings in the company. FMIC recapitalized a minority portion of the common stock. The recapitalization partners included Roland Corporation U.S. (Los Angeles) and Weston Presidio, a private equity firm (San Francisco). As of January 1, 2003, Fred Gretsch Enterprises, Ltd granted Fender the exclusive rights to develop, produce, market and distribute Gretsch guitars worldwide where FMIC is responsible for all aspects of the Gretsch product lines and brand-names, including development of new products. Fred Gretsch consulted during the changeover and will also consult on product development and

MODEL YEAR	FEATURES	EXC. COND. LOW	HIGH

quality control. Around the same time, Fender also acquired the Jackson/Charvel Guitar Company. As of 2004 FMIC brands also include Guild, Squire, DeArmond, Benedetto, Rodriguez, Sunn, SWR amps, Brand X amps and Floyd Rose.

Dating older Fender guitars is an imprecise art form at best. While serial numbers were used, they were frequently not in sequence, although a lower number will frequently be older than a substantially higher number. Often necks were dated, but only with the date the neck was finished, not when the guitar was assembled. Generally, dating requires triangulating between serial numbers, neck dates, pot dates, construction details and model histories.

From '50 through roughly '65, guitars had more-or-less sequential numbers in either four or five digits, though some higher numbers may have an initial 0 or - prefix. These can range from 0001 to 99XXX.

From '63 into '65, some instruments had serial numbers beginning with an L prefix plus 5 digits (LXXXXX). Beginning in '65 with the CBS takeover into '76, 6-digit serial numbers were stamped on F neckplates roughly sequentially from 10XXXX to 71XXXX. In '76 the serial number was shifted to the headstock decal. From '76-'77, the serial number began with a bold-face 76 or S6 plus 5 digits (76XXXXX).

From '77 on, serial numbers consisted of a two-place prefix plus 5 digits (sometimes 6 beginning in '91): '77 (S7, S8), '78 (S7, S8, S9), '79 (S9, E0), '80-'81 (S9, E0, E1), '82 (E1, E2, E3), '84-'85 (E4), '85-'86 (no U.S. production), '87 (E4), '88 (E4, E8), '89 (E8, E9), '90 (E9, N9, N0), '91 (N0), '92 (N2).

Serial numbers on guitars made by Fender Japan consist of either a two-place prefix plus 5 digits or a single prefix letter plus 6 digits: '82-'84 (JV), '83-'84 (SQ), '84-'87 (E), '85-'86+ (A, B, C), '86-'87 (F), '87-'88+ (G), '88-'89 (H), '89-'90 (I, J), '90-'91 (K), '91-'92 (L), '92-'93 (M).

Factors affecting Fender values: The sale to CBS in '65 is a major point in Fender instrument values as CBS made many changes that collectors feel affected quality. The '70s introduced the three-bolt neck and other design changes that aren't that popular with guitarists. Custom color instruments, especially Strats from the '50s and early-'60s, can be valued much more than the standard Sunburst finishes. In '75 Fender dropped the optional custom colors and started issuing the guitars in a variety of standard colors.

The various Telecaster and Stratocaster models are grouped under those general headings.

Avalon
1984-1995. Acoustic, mahogany neck, back and sides (nato after 1993), spruce top.

1984	Wine Red	$350	$450

Broadcaster
Mid-1950-early-1951. For a short time in early-1951, before being renamed the Telecaster, models had no Broadcaster decal; these are called "No-casters" by collectors.

1950	Blond	$25,000	$35,000
1951	Clipped decal, "No Caster"	$25,000	$30,000

Broadcaster Leo Fender Custom Shop
1999 only. Leo Fender script logo signature replaces Fender logo on headstock. Custom Shop Certificate signed by Phyllis Fender, Fred Gretsch, and William Schultz. Includes glass display case and poodle guitar case.

1999		$7,000	$8,000

Custom Shop '50s Relic/'51 No Caster
1996-present. Called the '50s Relic Nocaster for '96-'99, and '51 Nocaster in "NOS," "Relic," or "Closet Classic" versions at present, with the Relic Series being the highest offering.

1990s	Relic No Caster	$1,700	$1,900
2000s	Closet Classic	$1,200	$1,400

Bronco
1967-1980. Slab solidbody, 1 pickup, tremolo, red.

1967-1969		$650	$750
1970-1975		$550	$650
1976-1980		$500	$600

Bullet
1981-1983. Solidbody, came in 2- and 3-pickup versions (single-coil and humbucker), and single and double cut models. A later Squire version was also offered.

1981-1983	3 pickups	$350	$400
1981-1983	2 pickups	$300	$350

Squire Bullet
1985-1988. Fender Japan was established in 1982. Squire production began in 1983. Production was shifted to Korea in 1987.

1985-1988	Sunburst, humbuckers	$250	$350
1985-1988	White	$175	$300

Concert
1963-1970. Acoustic flat-top slightly shorter than King/Kingman, spruce body, mahogany back and sides (optional Brazilian or Indian rosewood, zebrawood or vermillion), natural, sunburst optional by 1968.

1963-1965	Natural	$650	$950
1966-1968	Natural or Sunburst	$550	$850
1979-1970	Natural or Sunburst	$550	$750

Coronado I
1966-1970. Thinline semi-hollowbody, double cut, tremolo, 1 pickup, single-bound, dot inlay.

1966-1967	Blue custom color	$1,100	$1,400
1966-1967	Cherry Red	$750	$850
1966-1967	Orange custom color	$950	$1,350
1966-1967	Sunburst	$750	$850
1966-1967	White (unfaded)	$1,000	$1,200
1968-1970	Sunburst	$600	$750

Fender Avalon

Fender Broadcaster

Fender Coronado II (Antigua)

1970s Fender Custom

MODEL YEAR	FEATURES	EXC. COND. LOW	HIGH

Coronado II
1966-1969 (Antigua finish offered until 1970). Thinline semi-hollowbody, double cut, tremolo optional, two pickups, single-bound, block inlay. Available in standard finishes but special issues offered in Antigua and six different Wildwood finishes. Wildwood finishes were achieved by injecting dye into growing trees.

MODEL YEAR	FEATURES	LOW	HIGH
1966-1967	Blue custom color	$1,200	$1,400
1966-1967	Cherry Red	$800	$1,000
1966-1967	Olympic White custom color	$1,100	$1,300
1966-1967	Orange custom color	$1,200	$1,400
1966-1967	Silver custom color	$1,200	$1,400
1966-1967	Sunburst	$800	$1,000
1966-1967	Wildwood (unfaded)	$1,200	$1,400
1967	Blue custom color	$1,200	$1,400
1967-1968	Antigua	$1,200	$1,400
1968	Cherry Red	$700	$900
1968	Orange custom color	$1,100	$1,300
1968	Sunburst	$700	$900
1968	Wildwood	$1,100	$1,300
1969	Antigua	$1,000	$1,300
1969	Cherry Red	$600	$800
1969	Orange custom color	$1,000	$1,200
1969	Sunburst	$600	$800
1969	Wildwood	$1,000	$1,200
1970	Antigua	$900	$1,200

Coronado XII
1966-1969 (Antigua finish offered until 1970). Thinline semi-hollowbody, double cutaway, 12 strings, two pickups, block inlay. Standard, Antigua and Wildwood finishes available.

MODEL YEAR	FEATURES	LOW	HIGH
1966-1967	Cherry Red	$800	$1,000
1966-1967	Orange custom color	$1,200	$1,400
1966-1967	Sunburst	$800	$1,000
1966-1967	Wildwood Green	$1,200	$1,400
1968	Cherry Red	$700	$900
1968	Orange custom color	$1,100	$1,300
1968	Sunburst	$700	$900
1968	Wildwood Rainbow Gold	$1,100	$1,300
1969	Antigua	$1,000	$1,300
1969	Cherry Red	$600	$800
1969	Orange custom color	$1,000	$1,200
1969	Sunburst	$600	$800
1969	Wildwood	$1,000	$1,200

Custom
1969-1971. Six-string solidbody that used up parts from discontinued Electric XII. Asymmetrical cutaway, long headstock, two split pickups. Also marketed as the Maverick.

MODEL YEAR	FEATURES	LOW	HIGH
1969-1970	Sunburst	$1,200	$1,500

Cyclone
1998-present. Mexican import, solidbody, contoured offset waist, poplar body. Various colors.

MODEL YEAR	FEATURES	LOW	HIGH
1998-2000		$325	$375

D'Aquisto Elite
1984, 1989-1995. Part of Fender's Master Series. Archtop, single cut, glued neck, one pickup, gold-plated hardware, made in Japan until '94. In '94 the Fender Custom Shop issued a version that retailed at $6,000. Various colors.

MODEL YEAR	FEATURES	LOW	HIGH
1984	Japan made	$1,900	$2,100
1989-1994	Japan made	$1,900	$2,100

D'Aquisto Standard
1984 (Serial numbers could range from 1983-1985). Part of Fender's Master Series. Archtop, single cutaway, glued neck, two pickups, made in Japan. Various colors.

MODEL YEAR	FEATURES	LOW	HIGH
1984		$1,700	$1,900

D'Aquisto Ultra
1994-2000, Custom Shop, made under the supervision of James D'Aquisto. Flamed maple back and sides, spruce top, ebony tailpiece, bridge and pickguard, all hand carved.

MODEL YEAR	FEATURES	LOW	HIGH
1990s		$7,500	$8,500

Duo-Sonic
1957-1969. Solidbody, 3/4-size, 2 pickups, short- and long-scale necks. Short-scale necks listed here (see Duo-Sonic II for long-scale). Reissued Mexican-made in 1994.

MODEL YEAR	FEATURES	LOW	HIGH
1957-1959	Sand/Natural, maple neck	$1,100	$1,300
1957-1963	Sand/Natural, rosewood board	$1,000	$1,200
1964-1965	Blue, Red or White	$900	$1,100
1966-1969	Blue, Red or White	$800	$1,000

Duo-Sonic II
1965-1969. Solidbody, 2 pickups, long-scale neck. Though the long-scale neck Duo-Sonic was not known as the Duo-Sonic II until 1965, we have lumped all long-scales under the II for the purposes of this Guide.

MODEL YEAR	FEATURES	LOW	HIGH
1965-1969	Blue, Red, or White	$1,000	$1,300

Duo-Sonic Reissue
1994-1997. Made in Mexico.

MODEL YEAR	FEATURES	LOW	HIGH
1994-1997	Black, Red, White	$175	$225

Electric Violin
1958-1976. Sunburst is the standard finish.

MODEL YEAR	FEATURES	LOW	HIGH
1958-1960	Natural, with bow	$1,400	$1,500
1960-1969	Natural, with bow	$1,300	$1,400
1970-1976	Natural, with bow	$1,200	$1,300

Electric XII
1965-1969. Solidbody, 12 strings, long headstock, 2 split pickups. Custom colors can fade or become darker; for example Lake Placid Blue changes to green. The price ranges below are for instruments that are relatively unfaded. Many older guitars have some color fade and minor fade is factored into these values. Each custom color should be evaluated on a case-by-case basis.

Custom color Fenders can be forged and bogus finishes have been a problem. As the value of custom color Fenders has increased, so has the problem of bogus non-original finishes. The prices in the Guide

MODEL YEAR	FEATURES	EXC. COND. LOW	HIGH

are for factory original finishes in excellent condition. The prices noted do not take into account market factors such as fake instruments, which can have the effect of lowering a guitar's market value unless the guitar's provenance can be validated.

1965	Black	$2,300	$2,800
1965	Blue Ice	$2,600	$3,200
1965	Candy Apple Red	$2,300	$2,800
1965	Firemist Gold	$2,600	$3,000
1965	Lake Placid Blue	$2,300	$2,800
1965	Ocean Turquoise	$2,700	$3,700
1965	Olympic White	$2,300	$2,800
1965	Sherwood Green	$2,800	$3,300
1965	Shoreline Gold	$2,700	$3,200
1965	Sonic Blue	$2,700	$3,200
1965	Sunburst	$1,900	$2,300
1965	Surf Green	$2,800	$3,300
1966	Black	$2,100	$2,700
1966	Blue Ice	$2,400	$3,100
1966	Burgundy Mist	$2,400	$3,200
1966	Candy Apple Red	$2,100	$2,700
1966	Charcoal Frost	$2,400	$3,100
1966	Dakota Red	$2,200	$3,000
1966	Daphne Blue	$2,200	$3,000
1966	Fiesta Red	$2,200	$3,000
1966	Firemist Gold	$2,400	$3,100
1966	Firemist Silver	$2,400	$3,100
1966	Foam Green	$2,400	$3,100
1966	Inca Silver	$2,400	$3,100
1966	Lake Placid Blue	$2,100	$2,700
1966	Ocean Turquoise	$2,400	$3,100
1966	Olympic White	$2,100	$2,700
1966	Sherwood Green	$2,600	$3,200
1966	Shoreline Gold	$2,500	$3,100
1966	Sonic Blue	$2,500	$3,100
1966	Sunburst (late '66), block	$1,600	$1,900
1966	Sunburst, dot inlay, unbound	$1,700	$2,100
1966	Surf Green	$2,600	$3,200
1966	Teal Green	$2,600	$3,200
1967	Lake Placid Blue	$2,000	$2,300
1967	Sunburst, block	$1,600	$1,800
1968	Sunburst	$1,500	$1,800
1969	Candy Apple Red	$1,900	$2,200
1969	Sunburst	$1,500	$1,700

Elite Telecaster
1983-1985. Two active humbuckers, 3-way switch, 2 volume knobs, 1 presence and filter controls, chrome hardware, various colors.

1983-1985		$800	$900

Esprit Elite
1984. Part of the Master Series, made in Japan, double cut, semi-hollow, carved maple top, 2 humbuckers, bound rosewood 'board, snowflake inlays.

1984		$750	$1,050

Esprit Standard
1984. Part of the Master Series, made in Japan, double cut, semi-hollow, carved maple top, two humbuckers, bound rosewood 'board, dot inlays.

1984	.	$700	$1,000

Esprit Ultra
1984. Double cut, semi-hollow, carved spruce top, two humbuckers, bound rosewood 'board, split-block inlays, sunburst, gold hardware. Part of the Master Series, made in Japan.

1984		$800	$1,100

Esquire
1950-1970. Ash body, single cut, 1 pickup, maple neck, black pickguard 1950-1954, white pickguard 1954 on.

1951	Blond, Black pickguard	$12,000	$15,000
1952-1954	Blond, Black pickguard	$11,000	$14,000
1954-1955	Blond, White pickguard	$8,500	$10,000
1956-1957	Blond	$7,500	$8,000
1958	Blond	$7,000	$9,700
1959	Blond, maple board	$6,000	$7,000
1959	Blond, slab board	$5,900	$6,500
1960	Blond	$5,800	$6,400
1960	Sunburst	$6,500	$8,500
1961	Blond	$5,700	$6,200
1961	Sunburst	$6,400	$8,400
1962	Blond	$5,500	$6,000
1963	Blond	$5,100	$5,400
1963	Candy Apple Red	$7,000	$8,000
1963	Lake Placid Blue	$7,000	$8,000
1963	Olympic White	$7,000	$8,000
1963	Sunburst	$5,300	$5,600
1964	Blond	$5,000	$5,300
1964	Burgundy Mist	$7,500	$13,000
1965	Blond	$4,800	$5,100
1965	Lake Placid Blue	$5,800	$7,000
1966	Blond	$5,000	$5,300
1966	Olympic White	$5,500	$6,300
1967	Blond	$3,800	$4,600
1967	Ice Blue Metallic	$6,000	$7,300
1967	Lake Placid Blue	$5,300	$6,900
1967	Olympic White	$5,100	$6,300
1968	Blond	$3,500	$4,400
1968	Sunburst	$3,600	$4,500
1969	Blond	$3,100	$4,100
1969	Sunburst	$3,100	$4,100
1970	Blond	$2,900	$3,900

Esquire Custom
1959-1970. Same as Esquire, but with bound alder sunburst body and rosewood fingerboard.

1959		$13,000	$16,000
1960		$12,000	$15,000
1961-1962	Slab board	$10,000	$12,000
1962-1964	Curve board	$9,000	$11,000
1965-1967		$5,500	$7,000
1968-1970		$5,000	$6,300

Esquire Custom GT/Celtic/Scorpion
2003-present. Single cut solidbody, 1 humbucker, 1 knob (volume), solid colors.

2003		$350	$425

Esquire Custom Shop
Various colors.

1990s		$1,800	$2,200

1970s Fender Electric XII

1956 Fender Esquire

Fender Flame Ultra

1961 Fender Jaguar

F-Series Dreadnought Flat-Top
1969-1979. The F-Series were Japanese-made acoustics. Included were Concert- and Dreadnought-size instruments with features running from plain to bound necks and headstocks and fancy inlays. There was also a line of F-Series classical, nylon string guitars.

Model Year	Features	Low	High
1969-1979		$175	$200

Flame Elite
1984. Part of the Master Series, made in Japan, neck-thru, double cut, solidbody, 2 humbuckers, rosewood 'board, snowflake inlays.

| 1984 | | $800 | $1,000 |

Flame Standard
1984. Master Series, made in Japan, neck-thru, double cut, solidbody, 2 humbuckers, rosewood 'board, dot inlays.

| 1984 | | $700 | $850 |

Flame Ultra
1984. Master Series, made in Japan, neck-thru, double cut, solidbody, 2 humbuckers, rosewood 'board, split block inlays (some with snowflakes), gold hardware.

| 1984 | | $900 | $1,100 |

Gemini I
1984-ca.1989. Imported inexpensive classical nylon string acoustic.

| 1984-1989 | Sunburst | $125 | $175 |

Gemini II
1984-ca.1989. Imported Inexpensive dreadnought steel string acoustic.

| 1984-1989 | Sunburst | $175 | $225 |

Gemini III
1984-ca.1989. Imported acoustic.

| 1984-1989 | Black | $200 | $250 |

Harmony-Made Series
Early-1970s-mid-1970s. Harmony-made with White stencil Fender logo, mahogany. Natural or Sunburst.

| 1970s | | $75 | $175 |

Jag-Stang
1996-1999. Japanese-made, designed by Curt Cobain, body similar to Jaguar, tremolo, one pickup, oversize Strat peghead. Fiesta Red or Sonic Blue.

| 1996 | 1st issue, 50th Anniv. Label | $450 | $550 |
| 1997-1999 | | $400 | $500 |

Jaguar
1962-1975. Reintroduced as Jaguar '62 in '95-'99. Custom colors can fade and often the faded color has very little similarity to the original color. The values below are for an instrument that is relatively unfaded. Each custom color should be evaluated on a case-by-case basis. Custom color Fenders can be forged and bogus finishes have been a problem. As the value of custom color Fenders has increased, so has the problem of bogus non-original finishes. The prices in the Guide are for factory original finishes in excellent condition. The prices noted do not take into account market factors such as fake instruments, which can have the effect of lowering a guitar's market value unless the guitar's provenance can be validated.

Model Year	Features	Low	High
1962	Black	$3,100	$3,400
1962	Blond	$3,100	$3,400
1962	Burgundy Mist	$4,200	$5,000
1962	Dakota Red	$3,700	$4,000
1962	Daphne Blue	$3,700	$4,000
1962	Fiesta Red	$3,700	$4,000
1962	Foam Green	$4,200	$5,000
1962	Inca Silver	$4,200	$4,500
1962	Lake Pacid Blue	$3,200	$3,500
1962	Olympic White (unfaded)	$3,200	$3,400
1962	Shell Pink	$4,700	$5,000
1962	Sherwood Green	$3,700	$4,000
1962	Shoreline Gold	$3,700	$4,000
1962	Sonic Blue	$3,700	$4,000
1962	Sunburst	$2,200	$2,700
1962	Surf Green	$4,200	$5,000
1963	Black	$3,000	$3,300
1963	Candy Apple Red	$3,000	$3,300
1963	Fiesta Red	$3,500	$3,800
1963	Lake Placid Blue	$3,100	$3,400
1963	Lake Placid Blue, Gold hardware	$3,700	$3,900
1963	Olympic White	$3,000	$3,300
1963	Shoreline Gold	$3,600	$3,900
1963	Sonic Blue	$3,600	$3,900
1963	Sunburst	$2,100	$2,300
1964	Black	$2,900	$3,300
1964	Burgundy Mist	$3,700	$4,000
1964	Candy Apple Red	$2,900	$3,300
1964	Fiesta Red	$3,200	$3,800
1964	Lake Placid Blue	$2,900	$3,300
1964	Olympic White	$2,900	$3,300
1964	Sonic Blue	$3,500	$3,900
1964	Sunburst	$2,000	$2,200
1965	Black	$2,500	$3,200
1965	Blue Ice	$3,200	$3,700
1965	Burgundy Mist	$3,400	$4,000
1965	Candy Apple Red	$2,600	$3,300
1965	Fiesta Red	$3,100	$3,800
1965	Firemist Gold	$3,100	$3,800
1965	Lake Placid Blue	$2,600	$3,300
1965	Ocean Turquoise	$3,100	$3,800
1965	Olympic White	$2,600	$3,300
1965	Shoreline Gold	$3,100	$3,800
1965	Sonic Blue	$3,100	$3,800
1965	Sunburst	$1,900	$2,100
1965	Teal Green	$3,100	$3,800
1966	Black	$2,400	$3,100
1966	Blond	$3,100	$4,000
1966	Blue Ice	$3,200	$3,700
1966	Candy Apple Red	$2,500	$3,200
1966	Fiesta Red	$2,900	$3,600
1966	Firemist Gold	$3,000	$3,800
1966	Lake Placid Blue	$2,500	$3,200
1966	Olympic White	$2,500	$3,200
1966	Sonic Blue	$2,900	$3,600
1966	Sunburst, block markers	$1,500	$1,900
1966	Sunburst, dot markers (early '66)	$1,700	$2,100

MODEL YEAR	FEATURES	EXC. COND. LOW	EXC. COND. HIGH
1967	Black	$2,300	$3,000
1967	Candy Apple Red	$2,500	$3,200
1967	Lake Placid Blue	$2,500	$3,200
1967	Sunburst	$1,500	$1,900
1968	Black	$2,200	$2,900
1968	Blue Ice	$2,600	$3,300
1968	Candy Apple Red	$2,300	$3,000
1968	Lake Placid Blue	$2,300	$3,000
1968	Olympic White	$2,300	$3,000
1968	Sunburst	$1,400	$1,850
1969	Black	$2,200	$2,800
1969	Blond	$2,200	$2,800
1969	Candy Apple Red	$2,200	$2,800
1969	Firemist Gold	$3,000	$3,300
1969	Firemist Silver	$3,000	$3,300
1969	Lake Placid Blue	$2,200	$2,800
1969	Ocean Turquoise	$3,200	$3,700
1969	Olympic White	$2,200	$2,800
1969	Sonic Blue	$3,000	$3,300
1969	Sunburst	$1,400	$1,800
1970	Sunburst	$1,400	$1,750
1971	Black	$1,800	$2,300
1971-1972	Candy Apple Red	$1,900	$2,400
1971-1975	Sunburst	$1,200	$1,600

'62 Jaguar

1995-present. Reintroduction of Jaguar, Japanese-made until 1999, then U.S.-made, basswood body, rosewood fingerboard. Various colors.

1995-1999	Import	$450	$550
1999-2003	U.S.A.-made	$950	$1,000

Jazzmaster

1958-1980. Contoured body, 2 pickups, rosewood fingerboard, clay dot inlay. Reintroduced as Japanese-made Jazzmaster '62 in '96. Custom color Fenders can be forged and bogus finishes have been a problem. As the value of custom color Fenders has increased, so has the problem of bogus non-original finishes. The prices in the Guide are for factory original finishes in excellent condition. The prices noted do not take into account market factors such as fake instruments, which can have the effect of lowering a guitar's market value unless the guitar's provenance can be validated.

1958	Sunburst	$3,700	$4,700
1958	Sunburst, rare maple fingerboard	$5,700	$6,500
1959	Olympic White	$4,700	$5,500
1959	Sonic Blue	$5,200	$6,300
1959	Sunburst	$3,700	$4,700
1960	Blond	$5,000	$5,800
1960	Olympic White	$4,600	$5,500
1960	Sunburst	$3,200	$4,200
1961	Blond	$5,200	$6,300
1961	Olympic White	$4,500	$5,500
1961	Shell Pink	$5,900	$7,200
1961	Sunburst	$3,100	$3,300
1962	Black, matching headstock	$4,700	$5,700
1962	Blond see-through over ash	$4,900	$6,200
1962	Burgundy Mist, slab board	$5,700	$7,000

MODEL YEAR	FEATURES	EXC. COND. LOW	EXC. COND. HIGH
1962	Fiesta Red, curve board	$4,700	$5,300
1962	Fiesta Red, slab board	$5,200	$6,300
1962	Lake Placid Blue, matching headstock, slab	$4,700	$5,800
1962	Lake Placid Blue, slab board	$4,600	$5,700
1962	Olympic White, slab board	$4,400	$5,500
1962	Shell Pink, slab board	$5,800	$7,100
1962	Shoreline Gold Metallic	$5,700	$7,000
1962	Sunburst, curve board	$2,800	$3,100
1962	Sunburst, slab board	$3,500	$3,600
1963	Blond	$4,700	$5,100
1963	Candy Apple Red	$4,700	$5,100
1963	Dakota Red	$4,700	$6,000
1963	Lake Placid Blue	$4,500	$5,100
1963	Olympic White	$4,300	$4,900
1963	Shoreline Gold	$5,400	$6,200
1963	Sunburst	$2,700	$3,000
1964	Blond	$4,200	$5,000
1964	Burgundy Mist	$4,600	$6,000
1964	Candy Apple Red	$4,400	$4,500
1964	Fiesta Red	$4,500	$6,000
1964	Ice Blue Metallic	$4,500	$6,000
1964	Lake Placid Blue	$4,400	$4,500
1964	Olympic White	$4,100	$4,300
1964	Sunburst	$2,600	$3,000
1965	Blond	$4,100	$5,000
1965	Candy Apple Red	$3,900	$4,200
1965	Dakota Red	$4,400	$6,000
1965	Fiesta Red	$4,400	$6,000
1965	Firemist Gold	$4,400	$6,000
1965	Ice Blue Metallic	$4,400	$6,000
1965	Lake Placid Blue	$4,000	$4,200
1965	Natural	$3,700	$4,000
1965	Olympic White	$3,700	$4,000
1965	Sonic Blue	$4,400	$6,000
1965	Sunburst	$2,000	$2,500
1966	Candy Apple Red	$3,600	$4,000
1966	Dakota Red	$4,200	$5,500
1966	Ice Blue Metallic	$4,200	$5,500
1966	Lake Placid Blue	$3,700	$4,000
1966	Olympic White	$3,600	$3,900
1966	Sunburst, blocks, bound	$1,900	$2,300
1966	Sunburst, dot markers (early '66)	$2,100	$2,400
1967	Candy Apple Red	$2,900	$3,600
1967	Lake Placid Blue	$2,900	$3,600
1967	Sunburst	$1,800	$2,300
1968	Black	$2,600	$3,300
1968	Blue Ice	$3,000	$3,700
1968	Candy Apple Red	$2,700	$3,400
1968	Lake Placid Blue	$2,700	$3,400

1966 Fender Jaguar

1960 Fender Jazzmaster

The *Vintage Guitar Price Guide* shows low to high values for items in all-original excellent condition, and, where applicable, with original case or cover.

1966 Fender Jazzmaster

1964 Fender Musicmaster

MODEL YEAR	FEATURES	EXC. COND. LOW	HIGH
1968	Olympic White	$2,700	$3,400
1968	Sunburst	$1,800	$2,200
1969	Black	$2,600	$3,200
1969	Blond	$2,600	$3,200
1969	Candy Apple Red	$2,600	$3,200
1969	Firemist Gold	$3,400	$3,700
1969	Firemist Silver	$3,400	$3,700
1969	Lake Placid Blue	$2,600	$3,200
1969	Ocean Turquoise	$3,600	$4,100
1969	Olympic White	$2,600	$3,200
1969	Sonic Blue	$3,400	$3,700
1969	Sunburst	$1,700	$2,200
1970	Sunburst	$1,500	$1,900
1970-1972	Candy Apple Red	$2,100	$2,600
1971-1975	Sunburst	$1,400	$1,700
1973-1974	Natural	$1,400	$1,800
1976-1982	Sunburst	$1,100	$1,600

Jazzmaster '62
1996-present. Japanese-made reintroduction of Jazzmaster. Basswood body, rosewood fingerboard, U.S.-made from 1999. Various colors.

1996-1999	Import	$450	$550
1999-2003	U.S.A.-made	$950	$1,000

Jazzmaster The Ventures Limited Edition
1996. Japanese-made, ash body, 2 pickups, block inlay.

1996	Transparent Purple/Black	$950	$1,150

Katana
1985-1986. Import, wedge-shaped body, bridge pickup.

1985-1986	Black	$250	$350

King
1963-1965. Full-size 15 5/8" wide acoustic. Renamed Kingman in 1966.

1963-1965	Natural	$800	$1,000

Kingman
1966-1971. Full-size 15 5/8" wide acoustic. Slightly smaller by 1970. Offered in three Wildwood colors, referred to as the Wildwood acoustic which is a Kingman with dyed wood.

1966-1968		$800	$1,000
1969-1971		$800	$950

Lead I
1979-1982. Double cut solidbody with 1 humbucker, black or brown.

1979-1982		$300	$400

Lead II
1979-1982. Double cut solidbody, 2 pickups, black or brown.

1979-1982		$350	$425

Lead III
1982. Double cut solidbody with 2 split-coil humbuckers, 2 3-way switches, black or brown.

1982		$400	$450

LTD
1969-1975. Archtop electric, single cut, gold-plated hardware, carved top and back, 1 pickup, multi-bound, bolt-on neck.

1969-1975	Sunburst	$3,500	$5,000

Malibu
1965-1970. Acoustic flat top, spruce top, mahogany back and sides, black, mahogany and sunburst.

1965-1970		$550	$650

Marauder
1965 only. The Marauder has 3 pickups, and some have slanted frets. Only 8 were made, thus it is very rare.

1965	First generation, hidden pickups	$6,500	$11,500
1965	2nd generation, exposed pickups	$5,000	$10,000

Montego I
1968-1975. Electric archtop, single cut, bolt neck, 1 pickup, chrome-plated hardware.

1968-1975		$1,700	$2,500

Montego II
1968-1975. Electric archtop, single cut, bolt neck, 2 pickups, chrome-plated hardware.

1968-1975	Sunburst	$2,000	$2,700

Musiclander
1969-1972. Also called Swinger and Arrow. Solidbody, 1 pickup, arrow-shaped headstock, no model name on peghead. Red, White, and Blue.

1969-1972		$1,200	$1,600

Musicmaster
1956-1980. Solidbody, 1 pickup, short-scale (3/4) neck, blond. Restyled in '64 like Mustang with Red, White and Blue available that year. Regular-scale necks were optional and are called Musicmaster II from '64 to '69. After '69, II is dropped and Musicmaster continues with regular-scale neck.

1956-1959	Blond	$800	$950
1960-1964	Blond	$700	$900
1964-1969	Blue, red, or white	$600	$700
1970-1974	Blue, red, or white	$500	$600
1975-1980	Black or white	$400	$500

Musicmaster II
1964-1969. Solidbody, 1 pickup, long regular-scale neck version of Musicmaster, red, white, and blue.

1964-1969		$650	$750

Mustang
1964-1982, 1997-1998. Solidbody, 2 pickups. Reissued as '69 Mustang in 1996 and name changed back to Mustang 1997-1998. Dakota Red, Daphne Blue and Olympic White with Competition Red, Blue and Orange finishes added ca. 1969-1972. Competition finishes featured a racing stripe on the front of the body.

1964-1965	Various colors	$1,300	$1,400
1966-1969	Various colors	$1,200	$1,300
1970-1979	Various colors	$1,100	$1,200
1980-1982	Various colors	$800	$1,100

Mustang '69 Reissue
1996-1999. Japanese-made reissue of Mustang. Name changed back to Mustang in 1997-1998.

1996-1999	Blue or White	$475	$550

Newporter
1965-1971. Acoustic flat-top, mahogany back and sides.

1965-1968	Spruce top	$450	$550

MODEL		EXC. COND.	
YEAR	FEATURES	LOW	HIGH
1968-1971	Mahogany top	$350	$450

Palomino

1965-1970. Acoustic flat-top, spruce top, mahogany back and sides, triple-bound, black or mahogany.

1965-1970		$550	$650

Performer

1985-1986. Imported Swinger-like body design, 2 slanted humbuckers.

1985-1986		$875	$925

Prodigy

1991-1995. Electric solidbody, double cut, chrome-plated hardware, 2 single-coil and 1 humbucker, blue or black.

1991		$300	$375

Redondo

1969-1971. Mid-size flat-top, 14 3/8" wide. Replaces Newport spruce top model.

1969-1971		$450	$550

Robben Ford

1989-1994. Symmetrical double cut, 2 pickups, glued-in neck, solidbody with tone chambers, multi-bound, gold-plated hardware. After 1994 made in Fender Custom Shop.

1989-1994	Sunburst	$800	$1,000

Shenandoah 12-String

1965-1971. Acoustic flat-top, spruce top, mahogany back and sides.

1965-1968	Antigua	$950	$1,250
1965-1968	Blond	$700	$850
1969-1971	Antigua	$850	$1,150
1969-1971	Blond	$600	$800

Showmaster FMT (Custom Shop)

2000-present. Strat-style with bound figured maple top (FMT), 2 single-coils and a bridge position humbucker, maple neck, Custom Shop certificate.

2000-2002		$1,000	$1,400

Starcaster

1974-1980. Double cut, thinline semi-hollowbody, 2 humbuckers. Fender currently uses the Starcaster name on a line of budget guitars sold through Costco stores.

1974-1980	Most colors	$1,700	$2,000
1974-1980	Natural, mildly figured top	$2,000	$2,300

Stratocaster

The following are all variations of the Stratocaster. The first four listings are for the main U.S.-made models. All other Stratocaster models are listed alphabetically after that in the following order.

Stratocaster
Standard Stratocaster (includes 'Smith Strat')
American Standard Stratocaster
American Series Stratocaster
'50s Stratocaster
'54 Stratocaster FMT
'57 Stratocaster
'60s Stratocaster
'62 Stratocaster
'68 Stratocaster

'72 Stratocaster
25th Anniversary Stratocaster
40th Anniversary Stratocaster
American Classic Stratocaster
American Deluxe Fat Stratocaster
American Deluxe Stratocaster
Big Apple Stratocaster
Bill Carson Stratocaster
Blue Flower Stratocaster
Bowling Ball/Marble Stratocaster
Buddy Guy Stratocaster
California Stratocaster
Collector's Edition Stratocaster
Contemporary Stratocaster
Custom Shop '54 Stratocaster
Custom Shop '56 Stratocaster
Custom Shop '57 Special Stratocaster
Custom Shop '57 Stratocaster
Custom Shop '58 Stratocaster
Custom Shop '60 FMT Stratocaster
Custom Shop '60 Stratocaster
Custom Shop '65 Stratocaster
Custom Shop '68 Stratocaster
Custom Shop '69 Stratocaster
Custom Shop 21st Century Limited Ed. Stratocaster
Custom Shop 35th Anniversary Stratocaster
Custom Shop 40th Ann. Diamond Ed. Stratocaster
Custom Shop 50th Anniversary Stratocaster
Custom Shop 50th Anniversary Stratocaster Relic
Custom Shop Aluminum Stratocaster
Custom Shop Contemporary Stratocaster (U.S.A.)
Custom Shop Dick Dale Stratocaster
Custom Shop Floyd Rose Relic Stratocaster
Custom Shop Freddy Tavares Aloha Stratocaster
Custom Shop Hellecaster Stratocaster
Custom Shop HLE Stratocaster
Custom Shop Holoflake Stratocaster
Custom Shop Homer Haynes Ltd Ed Stratocaster
Custom Shop Hot Wheels Stratocaster
Custom Shop Jimi Hendrix Monterey Pop Stratocaster
Custom Shop Moto Limited Edition Stratocaster
Custom Shop Moto Set Stratocaster
Custom Shop Playboy 40th Anniversary Stratocaster
Custom Shop Relic '50s Stratocaster
Custom Shop Relic '60s Stratocaster
Custom Shop Set-Neck Stratocaster
Custom Shop Texas Special Stratocaster
Deluxe Strat Plus
Elite Stratocaster
Eric Clapton Stratocaster
Floyd Rose Classic Stratocaster
Foto Flame Stratocaster
Gold Stratocaster
Gold Elite Stratocaster

Fender Performer

1995 Fender Moto Stratocaster

1954 Fender Stratocaster

1956 Fender Stratocaster

Hank Marvin Stratocaster
Harley-Davidson 90th Anniversary Stratocaster
Hellecaster John Jorgenson Stratocaster
HM Stratocaster
HRR Stratocaster
Jeff Beck Stratocaster
Jimi Hendrix Tribute Stratocaster
Jimi Hendrix Voodoo Stratocaster
Jimmy Vaughan Tex-Mex Stratocaster
Lone Star Stratocaster
Paisley Stratocaster
Powerhouse/Powerhouse Deluxe Stratocaster
Richie Sambora Stratocaster
Roadhouse Stratocaster
Robert Cray Stratocaster
Roland Stratocaster (Mexico)
Short-Scale (7/8) Stratocaster
Squier Stratocaster II
Squier Stratocaster Standard
Standard Stratocaster
Stevie Ray Vaughan Stratocaster
Strat Plus
Stratocaster Special
Stratocaster XII
Sub Sonic Stratocaster
Super/Deluxe Super Stratocaster
Tanqurey Tonic Stratocaster
The Strat
U.S. Strat Ultra
Ventures Limited Edition Stratocaster
Walnut Elite Stratocaster
Walnut Stratocaster
Yngwie Malmsteen Stratocaster

Stratocaster

1954-1981. Two-tone Sunburst until '58, three-tone after. Custom color finishes were quite rare in the '50s and early-'60s and are much more valuable than the standard Sunburst finish. By the '70s, color finishes were much more common and do not affect the value near as much. In '75 Fender dropped the optional custom colors and started issuing the guitars in a variety of standard colors (sunburst, blond, white, natural, walnut and black). Three-bolt neck '72-'81, otherwise four-bolt.

Custom color Fenders can be forged and bogus finishes have been a problem. As the value of custom color Fenders has increased, so has the problem of bogus non-original finishes. The prices in the Guide are for factory original finishes in excellent condition. The prices noted do not take into account market factors such as fake instruments, which can have the effect of lowering a guitar's market value unless the guitar's provenance can be validated.

See Standard Stratocaster for 1982-1984 (following listing), and American Standard Stratocaster for 1986-2000. Currently called the American Series Stratocaster.

Unless noted, all Stratocasters listed have the Fender tremolo system. Non-tremolo models (aka hardtails) typically sell for less than a tremolo model. Many vintage authorities suggest that the tremolo block helps produce a fuller range of sound. The

non-tremolo models are often noted to have a more shrill tone. On average, many-many more tremolo models were made. One year, 1958, seems to be a year where a greater percentage of non-tremolo models were made. Tremolo vs. non-tremolo valuation should be taken on a brand by brand basis; for example, a pre-1965 Gibson ES-335 non-tremolo model is worth more than a tremolo equipped model.

MODEL YEAR	FEATURES	EXC. COND. LOW	EXC. COND. HIGH
1954	Sunburst 2-tone, ash body	$30,000	$33,000
1955	Sunburst 2-tone, ash body	$26,000	$29,000
1956	Blond, ash body, nickel hardware	$29,000	$34,000
1956	Mary Kaye Blond, ash body, gold hardware	$33,000	$42,000
1956	Sunburst, ash body	$25,000	$28,000
1957	Blond, nickel hardware	$29,000	$34,000
1957	Custom color, special order	$35,000	$41,000
1957	Mary Kaye Blond, Gold hardware, alder	$33,000	$42,000
1957	Sunburst, alder body	$21,000	$25,000
1958	Black	$23,000	$28,000
1958	Blond, nickel hardware	$29,000	$34,000
1958	Fiesta Red	$29,000	$34,000
1958	Mary Kaye Blond, gold hardware	$31,000	$40,000
1958	Sunburst	$16,000	$20,000
1958	Sunburst, non-trem	$12,000	$16,000
1959	Blond, nickel hardware	$26,000	$35,000
1959	Mary Kaye Blond, gold hardware	$29,000	$41,000
1959	Sunburst 3-tone, maple board	$14,000	$18,000
1959	Sunburst, slab board	$13,000	$17,000
1959	Sunburst, slab, non-trem.	$10,000	$13,000
1960	Black	$23,200	$25,520
1960	Blond	$17,000	$20,000
1960	Burgundy Mist	$29,000	$32,000
1960	Dakota Red	$27,000	$31,000
1960	Daphne Blue	$21,000	$26,000
1960	Fiesta Red	$27,000	$31,000
1960	Foam Green	$30,000	$35,000
1960	Inca Silver	$23,000	$26,000
1960	Lake Placid Blue	$19,000	$20,000
1960	Olympic White	$17,000	$19,000
1960	Shell Pink	$34,000	$38,000
1960	Sherwood Green	$27,000	$31,000
1960	Shoreline Gold	$23,000	$26,000
1960	Sonic Blue	$21,000	$26,000

MODEL YEAR	FEATURES	EXC. COND. LOW	HIGH
1960	Sunburst	$13,000	$16,000
1960	Surf Green	$30,000	$35,000
1961	Black	$21,000	$23,000
1961	Burgundy Mist	$27,000	$30,000
1961	Dakota Red	$24,000	$29,000
1961	Daphne Blue	$18,000	$23,000
1961	Lake Placid Blue	$16,000	$18,000
1961	Olympic White	$15,000	$17,000
1961	Sea Foam Green	$28,000	$32,000
1961	Sherwood Green Metallic	$24,000	$29,000
1961	Shoreline Gold	$21,000	$23,000
1961	Sonic Blue	$18,000	$23,000
1961	Sunburst	$12,000	$15,000
1962	Black, curved board	$15,000	$17,000
1962	Black, slab board	$18,000	$21,000
1962	Candy Apple Red, curved board	$14,000	$16,000
1962	Candy Apple Red, slab board	$16,000	$20,000
1962	Fiesta Red, curved board	$16,000	$18,000
1962	Fiesta Red, slab board	$18,000	$23,000
1962	Olympic White, curved board	$13,000	$15,000
1962	Olympic White, slab board	$15,000	$17,000
1962	Sonic Blue, curved board	$16,000	$21,000
1962	Sonic Blue, slab board	$18,000	$23,000
1962	Sunburst, curved board	$10,000	$12,000
1962	Sunburst, slab board	$12,000	$15,000
1963	Black	$14,000	$16,000
1963	Blond	$16,000	$18,000
1963	Candy Apple Red	$14,000	$16,000
1963	Dakota Red	$16,000	$18,000
1963	Fiesta Red	$16,000	$18,000
1963	Lake Placid Blue	$15,000	$17,000
1963	Olympic White	$13,000	$15,000
1963	Sea Foam Green	$20,000	$23,000
1963	Shoreline Gold	$18,000	$22,000
1963	Sonic Blue	$14,000	$19,000
1963	Sunburst	$9,500	$11,000
1964	Black	$13,000	$15,000
1964	Blond	$14,000	$16,000
1964	Burgundy Mist, faded	$21,000	$23,000
1964	Burgundy Mist, unfaded	$22,000	$25,000
1964	Candy Apple Red	$13,000	$15,000
1964	Daphne Blue	$17,000	$21,000
1964	Fiesta Red	$15,000	$17,000
1964	Inca Silver, faded	$18,000	$21,000
1964	Inca Silver, unfaded	$20,000	$23,000
1964	Lake Placid Blue	$15,000	$17,000

MODEL YEAR	FEATURES	EXC. COND. LOW	HIGH
1964	Olympic White	$12,000	$14,000
1964	Shoreline Gold	$17,000	$21,000
1964	Sonic Blue	$14,000	$17,000
1964	Sunburst	$8,500	$10,000
1965	Black, L-Series	$11,000	$13,000
1965	Blond, "F" plate	$11,000	$13,000
1965	Burgundy Mist, mild fade	$21,000	$23,000
1965	Candy Apple Red	$11,000	$13,000
1965	Candy Apple Red, gold hardware	$12,000	$14,000
1965	Charcoal Frost	$13,000	$15,000
1965	Dakota Red, L-series	$12,000	$14,000
1965	Firemist Silver, faded	$14,000	$16,000
1965	Firemist Silver, unfaded	$16,000	$18,000
1965	Ice Blue Metallic	$14,000	$16,000
1965	Inca Silver	$15,000	$17,000
1965	Inca Silver, L-Series	$16,000	$18,000
1965	Lake Placid Blue	$12,000	$14,000
1965	Ocean Turquoise	$16,000	$18,000
1965	Olympic White	$10,000	$12,000
1965	Sea Foam Green	$16,000	$18,000
1965	Sonic Blue, "F" plate	$14,000	$16,000
1965	Sunburst, early '65 Green guard	$8,000	$9,500
1965	Sunburst, later '65 White guard	$7,000	$7,500
1966	Black	$10,000	$12,000
1966	Blond	$10,000	$12,000
1966	Candy Apple Red	$10,000	$12,000
1966	Ice Blue Metallic	$11,000	$13,000
1966	Inca Silver	$12,000	$14,000
1966	Lake Placid Blue	$11,000	$13,000
1966	Lake Placid Blue, gold hardware	$12,000	$14,000
1966	Sonic Blue	$12,000	$14,000
1966	Sunburst	$6,500	$7,500
1967	Fiesta Red	$11,000	$13,000
1967	Lake Placid Blue	$10,500	$12,000
1967	Sonic Blue	$11,000	$13,000
1967	Sunburst, maple cap	$7,000	$8,000
1967	Sunburst, rosewood neck	$6,000	$7,000
1968	Blond	$9,000	$10,000
1968	Candy Apple Red, maple cap	$10,000	$12,000
1968	Candy Apple Red, rosewood cap	$9,000	$10,000
1968	Dakota Red, maple cap	$12,000	$14,000
1968	Dakota Red, rosewood cap	$10,000	$12,000
1968	Fiesta Red, maple cap	$12,000	$14,000

1958 Fender Stratocaster Mary Kaye

1964 Fender Stratocaster

The *Vintage Guitar Price Guide* shows low to high values for items in all-original excellent condition, and, where applicable, with original case or cover.

GUITARS

1963 Fender Stratocaster

*1973 Fender Stratocaster
(hardtail)*

MODEL YEAR	FEATURES	EXC. COND. LOW	EXC. COND. HIGH
1968	Fiesta Red, rosewood cap	$10,000	$12,000
1968	Lake Placid Blue, maple cap	$10,000	$12,000
1968	Lake Placid Blue, rosewood cap	$9,500	$11,000
1968	Olympic White, maple cap	$9,000	$10,000
1968	Olympic White, rosewood cap	$8,500	$10,000
1968	Sonic Blue, maple cap	$12,000	$14,000
1968	Sonic Blue, rosewood cap	$10,000	$12,000
1968	Sunburst, maple cap	$7,000	$8,000
1968	Sunburst, rosewood cap	$6,000	$7,000
1969	Candy Apple Red	$9,500	$11,000
1969	Firemist Gold	$10,000	$12,000
1969	Lake Placid Blue	$9,500	$11,000
1969	Natural	$7,500	$9,000
1969	Olympic White	$8,500	$10,000
1969	Sonic Blue, maple cap	$11,000	$13,000
1969	Sonic Blue, rosewood cap	$10,000	$12,000
1969	Sunburst	$5,500	$6,000
1970	Black, maple cap	$8,000	$9,000
1970	Black, rosewood cap	$6,000	$7,500
1970	Blond, maple cap	$7,000	$9,000
1970	Blond, rosewood cap	$6,000	$7,500
1970	Candy Apple Red, maple cap	$8,000	$9,000
1970	Candy Apple Red, rosewood cap	$6,000	$7,500
1970	Firemist Gold, maple cap	$9,000	$10,000
1970	Firemist Gold, rosewood cap	$7,500	$9,000
1970	Firemist Silver, maple cap	$9,000	$10,000
1970	Firemist Silver, rosewood cap	$7,500	$9,000
1970	Lake Placid Blue, maple cap	$8,000	$9,000
1970	Lake Placid Blue, rosewood cap	$6,000	$7,500
1970	Ocean Turquoise, maple cap	$9,000	$10,000
1970	Ocean Turquoise, rosewood cap	$7,500	$9,000
1970	Olympic White, maple cap	$8,000	$9,000
1970	Olympic White, rosewood cap	$6,000	$7,500
1970	Sonic Blue, maple cap	$8,000	$9,000

MODEL YEAR	FEATURES	EXC. COND. LOW	EXC. COND. HIGH
1970	Sonic Blue, rosewood cap	$7,000	$8,000
1970	Sunburst, maple cap	$6,000	$7,000
1970	Sunburst, roswood cap	$5,000	$6,000
1971	Black, 4-bolt neck	$6,000	$7,000
1971	Candy Apple Red, 4-bolt neck	$6,000	$7,000
1971	Natural, 4-bolt neck	$5,000	$6,000
1971	Olympic White, 4-bolt neck, maple cap	$7,500	$9,000
1971	Olympic White, rosewood cap	$6,000	$7,000
1971	Sunburst, 4-bolt neck, rosewood cap	$4,500	$6,000
1972	Black, 3-bolt neck	$2,100	$2,900
1972	Blond, 3-bolt neck	$2,100	$2,900
1972	Candy Apple Red, 3-bolt neck	$2,100	$2,900
1972	Lake Placid Blue, 3-bolt neck	$2,100	$2,900
1972	Natural	$2,100	$2,900
1972	Olympic White, 3-bolt neck	$2,100	$2,900
1972	Sunburst, 3-bolt neck	$2,100	$2,700
1972	Transparent Blond	$2,100	$2,900
1973	Black	$2,000	$2,700
1973	Blond	$2,100	$2,900
1973	Blond, non-trem.	$1,800	$2,500
1973	Candy Apple Red	$2,100	$2,800
1973	Lake Placid Blue	$2,100	$2,800
1973	Natural	$2,000	$2,700
1973	Natural, non-trem.	$1,700	$2,300
1973	Olympic White	$2,000	$2,700
1973	Olympic White, non-trem.	$1,700	$2,300
1973	Sunburst	$2,000	$2,600
1973	Sunburst, non-trem.	$1,700	$2,300
1973	Walnut	$2,000	$2,700
1973	Walnut, non-trem.	$1,700	$2,300
1974	Black	$1,600	$2,500
1974	Black, non-trem.	$1,300	$2,000
1974	Blond	$1,700	$2,700
1974	Lake Placid Blue	$1,700	$2,700
1974	Natural	$1,500	$2,400
1974	Olympic White	$1,600	$2,500
1974	Sunburst, staggered poles	$1,700	$2,500
1974	Walnut	$1,700	$2,500
1974	Walnut, non-trem.	$1,400	$2,000
1974	Wine Red	$1,700	$2,500
1975	Black	$1,500	$1,900
1975	Blond (transparent)	$1,500	$1,900
1975	Cream	$1,500	$1,900
1975	Natural	$1,500	$1,900
1975	Olympic White	$1,500	$1,900
1975	Sunburst	$1,500	$1,900
1975	Walnut	$1,500	$1,900

The *Vintage Guitar Price Guide* shows low to high values for items in all-original excellent condition, and, where applicable, with original case or cover.

MODEL YEAR	FEATURES	EXC. COND. LOW	HIGH
1976	Black	$1,400	$1,800
1976	Natural	$1,400	$1,800
1976	Sunburst	$1,400	$1,800
1976	Sunburst, non-trem.	$1,100	$1,500
1976	Walnut	$1,400	$1,800
1976	White	$1,400	$1,800
1977	Black	$1,200	$1,700
1977	Blond	$1,200	$1,700
1977	Cream	$1,200	$1,700
1977	Natural	$1,200	$1,700
1977	Sunburst	$1,200	$1,700
1977	Sunburst, non-trem.	$900	$1,300
1977	Walnut	$1,200	$1,700
1977	White, faded	$900	$1,300
1977	White, unfaded	$1,200	$1,700
1978	Antigua	$1,400	$1,600
1978	Black	$1,200	$1,600
1978	Blond	$1,200	$1,600
1978	Burgundy/Trans. Red	$1,200	$1,600
1978	Cream (opaque), Black guard	$1,200	$1,600
1978	Natural	$1,200	$1,600
1978	Sunburst	$1,000	$1,500
1978	Sunburst, non-trem.	$700	$1,100
1978	Walnut	$1,000	$1,500
1979	Antigua	$1,400	$1,600
1979	Antigua, non-trem.	$1,300	$1,500
1979	Black	$1,000	$1,500
1979	Black, non-trem.	$900	$1,200
1979	Blond	$1,000	$1,500
1979	Burgundy/Trans. Red	$1,000	$1,500
1979	Natural	$1,000	$1,500
1979	Sunburst	$1,000	$1,600
1979	Walnut	$1,000	$1,500
1979	White	$1,000	$1,500
1979	White, non-trem.	$900	$1,100
1980	Black	$1,000	$1,500
1980	Ivory	$1,000	$1,500
1980	Natural	$1,000	$1,500
1980	Sunburst	$1,000	$1,600
1980	White	$1,000	$1,500
1981	Black	$900	$1,300
1981	Capri Orange	$1,000	$1,600
1981	Cathay Ebony	$1,000	$1,600
1981	Maui Blue	$1,000	$1,600
1981	Monaco Yellow	$1,000	$1,600
1981	Morocco Red	$1,000	$1,600
1981	Natural	$900	$1,300
1981	Ruby Red	$900	$1,300
1981	Sahara Taupe	$900	$1,300
1981	Sunburst	$900	$1,300

Standard Stratocaster (includes 'Smith Strat')

1981-1984. Replaces the Stratocaster. Renamed the American Standard Stratocaster for '86-'00 (see next listing). Renamed American Series Stratocaster in '00. From '81/'82 to mid-'83, four knobs same as regular Strat but with four-bolt neck. In August '81, Dan Smith was hired by Bill Schultz and Fender

produced an alder body, four-bolt neck, 21-fret, small headstock Standard Stratocaster that has been nick-named the 'Smith Strat' (made from Dec. '81-'83). Mid-'83 to the end of '84 two knobs and pickguard mounted input jack. Not to be confused with current Standard Stratocaster, which is made in Mexico.

1981-1983	"Smith Strat", 4-bolt, 3 knobs	$1,100	$1,300
1983-1984	Various colors, 2 knobs	$700	$900

American Standard Stratocaster

1986-2000. See Stratocaster and Standard Stratocaster for earlier models. Renamed American Series Stratocaster in 2000.

1986-1989	Various colors	$700	$900
1989	Mary Kaye Limited Edition	$850	$950
1990-1999	Various colors	$600	$725
1995	Limited edition matching headstock	$850	$900

American Series Stratocaster

2000-present. Fender's updated standard produc-tion model, ash or alder body, rosewood fingerboard, dot markers, 3 staggered single-coil pickups, five-way switch, hand polished fret edges.

2000-2002	Blond finish on ash body	$600	$700
2000-2002	Various colors	$500	$600

'50s Stratocaster (import)

1992-present. Part of Collectables Series, made in Japan, V-neck with skunk stripe, 8 screw single ply pickguard, various colors.

1992-1999		$450	$600

'54 Stratocaster FMT

1993-1998. Custom Classic reissue. FMT means Flame Maple Top. Also comes in gold hardware edi-tion.

1993-1998	Flame maple top	$1,600	$1,800
1993-1998	Gold hardware option	$1,700	$1,900

'57 Stratocaster (U.S.-made)

1982-present. U.S.A.-made at the Fullerton, CA plant (1982-1985) and at the Corona, CA plant (1985-present).

1982-1984	Various colors	$1,000	$1,200
1986-1989	Blond, ash body	$1,100	$1,400
1986-1989	Various colors	$1,000	$1,200
1990-1999	Blond finish on ash body	$1,100	$1,400
1990-1999	Various colors	$1,000	$1,200

'57 Vintage Stratocaster (Japan)

1984-1985. Japanese-made. Various colors.

1984-1985		$450	$600

'60s Stratocaster (Japan)

1992-present. Part of Collectables Series, made in Japan, U-neck slab board, various colors, some with foto flame.

1992-1999	Foto-flame option	$450	$600
1992-1999	Various colors	$450	$600

1981 Fender Stratocaster

1982 Fender '57 Stratocaster

1979 Fender Silver Anniversary Stratocaster

1983 Bowling Ball Stratocaster

MODEL YEAR	FEATURES	EXC. COND. LOW	HIGH
'62 Stratocaster			
1982-present. U.S.A.-made at Fullerton, CA plant (1982-1985) then at Corona, CA plant (1985-present).			
1982-1984	Various colors	$1,100	$1,400
1986-1989	Transparent blond	$1,300	$1,600
1986-1989	Various colors	$1,100	$1,400
1990-1999	Various colors	$1,100	$1,400
'62 Stratocaster (Japan)			
1984-1985.			
1984-1985	White	$500	$600
'68 Stratocaster (Japan)			
1997-1999. Import from Japan, ash body, 1968 specs including large headstock, part of Collectables Series, sunburst, natural, Olympic White.			
1997-1999		$500	$600
'72 Stratocaster			
1988-1993. Made in Japan.			
1988-1993	White	$500	$600
25th Anniversary Stratocaster			
1979-1980. Has "ANNIVERSARY" on upper body horn. Silver Metallic or white pearlescent finish.			
1979	White, 1st issue	$1,300	$1,400
1979-1980	Silver (faded to Gold)	$1,050	$1,150
1979-1980	Silver (unfaded)	$1,250	$1,350
40th Anniversary Stratocaster			
1994 only. American Standard model (not Custom Shop model). Plain top, appearance similar to a 1954 maple-neck Stratocaster. Not to be confused with the Custom Shop 40th Anniversary Diamond Edition.			
1994	Sunburst	$1,400	$1,700
American Classic Stratocaster			
1993-present. Custom Shop version of American Standard, 3 pickups, tremolo, rosewood fingerboard, nickel or gold-plated hardware.			
1993-1999	Transparent Blond finish on ash body	$1,500	$1,700
1993-1999	Various colors and options	$1,400	$1,600
American Deluxe Fat Stratocaster			
1998-2003. Fender DH-1 bridge humbucker for 'fat sound', made in the U.S.A., premium alder or ash body.			
1998-2003	Transparent finish on ash body	$950	$1,050
1998-2003	Various colors	$850	$950
American Deluxe Stratocaster (U.S.-made)			
1998-present. Premium alder or ash body, made in the U.S.A.			
1998-1999	Transparent finish on ash body	$950	$1,050
1998-1999	Various colors	$850	$950
Big Apple Stratocaster			
1997-2000. Two humbucking pickups, five-way switch, rosewood fingerboard or maple neck, non-trem optional.			
1997-2000	Various colors	$725	$775

MODEL YEAR	FEATURES	EXC. COND. LOW	HIGH
Bill Carson Stratocaster			
Ca. 1992. Based on the 1957 Strat, with bird's-eye maple neck and Cimarron Red finish. One left-handed and 100 right-handed guitars produced, serial numbers MT000-MT100. Made in Fender Custom Shop, the project was initiated by The Music Trader (MT) in Florida. Bill Carson was presented with MT007.			
1992		$1,700	$2,200
Blue Flower Stratocaster			
1988-1993. 1972 Strat reissue with a reissue 1968 Tele Blue Floral finish. Japanese-made.			
1988-1993		$600	$800
Bonnie Raitt Stratocaster			
1995-2000. Alder body, often in Blueburst, Bonnie Raitt's signature on headstock.			
1995-2000		$900	$1,100
Bowling Ball/Marble Stratocaster			
Ca.1983-1984. Standard Strat with 1 tone and 1 volume control, jack on pickguard. Called 'Bowling Ball Strat' due to the swirling, colored finish.			
1984		$1,800	$2,300
Buddy Guy Stratocaster			
1995-present. Maple neck, 3 Gold Lace Sensor pickups, ash body, signature model.			
1995	Blond or Sunburst	$900	$1,100
Buddy Guy Stratocaster (Mexico)			
Maple neck, polka dot finish.			
1990s		$425	$450
California Stratocaster			
1997-1999. Made in the U.S., painted in Mexico, 2 pickups.			
1997-1999	Various colors	$450	$550
Collector's Edition Stratocaster ('62 reissue)			
1997. Pearl inlaid 1997 on 12th fret, rosewood fingerboard, alder body, gold hardware, tortoise guard, nitro finish, 1997 made.			
1997	Sunburst	$1,100	$1,300
Contemporary Stratocaster (import)			
1985-1987. Import model used while the new Fender re-organized, black headstock with silver-white logo, black or white 'guard, 2 humbucker pickups or single-coil and humbucker, 2 knobs and slider switch.			
1985-1987		$250	$300
Custom Shop '54 Stratocaster			
1993-1998 (Custom Shop Classic reissue), 1997-present. Ash body, Custom '50s pickups, gold-plated hardware.			
1993-1998	Various options	$1,400	$1,700
Custom Shop '54 Stratocaster FMT			
1993-1998. Flame maple top version.			
1993-1998		$1,600	$1,800
1993-1998	Gold hardware option	$1,700	$1,900
Custom Shop '56 Stratocaster			
1999-present. Most detailed replica (and most expensive to date) of 1956 Strat, including electronics and pickups.			
1999-2004	Closet Classic	$1,700	$1,800
1999-2004	NOS Mary Kaye Blond, ash body	$1,500	$1,600

MODEL YEAR	FEATURES	EXC. COND. LOW	HIGH
1999-2004	NOS Sunburst, alder body	$1,400	$1,500
1999-2004	Relic custom color	$2,000	$2,100
1999-2004	Relic Mary Kaye	$1,900	$2,000

Custom Shop '57 Special Stratocaster

1992-1993. Flamed maple top, bird's-eye maple neck, run of 60 made, sunburst.

1992-1993		$1,800	$1,900

Custom Shop '57 Stratocaster

Mid-1990s. Custom Shop, replaced by the more authentic, higher-detailed '56 Custom Shop Stratocaster by 1999. Custom Shop models can be distinguished by the original certificate that comes with the guitar.

1994-1996	Sunburst	$1,300	$1,400
1994-1997	Transparent Blond, ash body	$1,500	$1,600

Custom Shop '58 Stratocaster

1996-present. Ash body, Fat '50s pickups, chrome or gold hardware. Custom Shop models can be distinguished by the original certificate that comes with the guitar.

1996-1999	Custom color, gold hardware	$1,600	$1,800
1996-1999	Sunburst, chrome hardware	$1,400	$1,500
1996-1999	Sunburst, gold hardware	$1,500	$1,600

Custom Shop '58 Stratocaster (Dakota Red)

1996. Run of 30 made in Dakota Red with matching headstock, maple neck, Texas special pickups, gold hardware.

1996		$1,600	$1,800

Custom Shop '60 FMT Stratocaster

1997-1999. Flame maple top.

1997-1999		$1,600	$1,800

Custom Shop '60 Stratocaster

1999-present. Most detailed replica (and most expensive to date) of 1960 Strat, including electronics and pickups.

1999-2004	Closet Classic option	$1,700	$1,800
1999-2004	NOS Mary Kaye Blond, ash body	$1,500	$1,600
1999-2004	NOS various colors	$1,400	$1,500
1999-2004	Relic Mary Kaye	$1,900	$2,000

Custom Shop '60 Stratocaster (short-run)

Short-run production during the 1990s, permanent product line 1999-present. Various colors.

1994		$1,500	$1,700

Custom Shop '65 Stratocaster

1998-1999. Built to 1965 small-headstock specs with rosewood or maple cap fingerboard, transition logo.

1998-1999	Maple cap board	$1,700	$1,800
1998-1999	Rosewood board	$1,700	$1,800

Custom Shop '68 Stratocaster

1990s. Jimi Hendrix-style, maple cap neck.

1990s		$1,700	$1,800

Custom Shop '69 Stratocaster

2000s. Large headstock, U-shaped maple neck with rosewood or maple cap options, '69-style finish.

2000s	Closet Classic option	$1,700	$1,800

MODEL YEAR	FEATURES	EXC. COND. LOW	HIGH

Custom Shop 21st Century Limited Ed. Stratocaster

2000. One of first 100 to leave Fender in 2000, certificate with CEO William C. Schultz, 21st logo on headstock.

2000		$1,100	$1,200

Custom Shop 35th Anniversary Stratocaster

1989-1991. Custom Shop model, figured maple top, Lace Sensor pickups, Eric Clapton preamp circuit.

1989-1991	Sunburst	$1,800	$2,400

Custom Shop 40th Ann. Diamond Ed. Stratocaster

1994. 40th anniversary headstock inlay, flamed maple top on ash body, 1954-1994 inlay at 12th fret, gold etched pickguard, gold hardware.

1994	Sunburst	$4,500	$6,000

Custom Shop 50th Anniversary Stratocaster

1995-1996. Flame maple top, three vintage-style pickups, gold hardware, gold 50th Anniversary coin on back of the headstock, 2500 made.

1995-1996	Sunburst	$1,400	$1,500

Custom Shop 50th Anniversary Stratocaster Relic

1995-1996. Relic aged 'played-in' feel, diamond headstock inlay, 200 units planned.

1995-1996	Shoreline Gold	$2,600	$2,800

Custom Shop Aluminum Stratocaster

1994-1995. Aluminum with anodized marble-variant finish.

1994-1995		$1,500	$1,800

Custom Shop Contemporary Stratocaster (U.S.A.)

1989-1998. U.S.A.-made, 7/8 scale body, hum/single/single pickups.

1989-1998	Various colors	$1,100	$1,400

Custom Shop Dick Dale Stratocaster

1994-present. Alder body, reverse headstock, chartreuse sparkle finish.

1994-2000		$1,600	$1,800

Custom Shop Floyd Rose Relic Stratocaster

1998-1999. Late '60s large headstock, 1 humbucker and 2 Strat pickups.

1998-1999		$1,400	$1,600

Custom Shop Freddy Tavares Aloha Stratocaster

1993-1994. Hollow aluminum body with hand engraved Hawaiian scenes, custom inlay on neck, 153 made.

1993-1994		$4,000	$4,500

Custom Shop Hellecaster Stratocaster

1997. Gold sparkle 'guard, gold hardware, split single-coils, rosewood 'board.

1997		$1,300	$1,700

Custom Shop HLE Stratocaster

1988-1990.

1988-1990	Gold	$1,400	$1,600

1994 Fender Custom Shop Aluminum Stratocaster

Fender '60s Closet Classic Stratocaster

1983 Fender Elite Stratocaster

Fender Eric Clapton Stratocaster

MODEL YEAR	FEATURES	EXC. COND. LOW	HIGH

Custom Shop Holoflake Stratocaster

1992-1993. Sparkle finish, maple neck, alder body.

1992-1993		$1,300	$1,500

Custom Shop Homer Haynes Ltd Ed Stratocaster

1988. 1959 Strat basics with gold finish, gold anodized guard, and gold hardware.

1988		$1,500	$1,900

Custom Shop Hot Wheels Stratocaster

2003. Commissioned by Hot Wheels, 16 made, orange flames over blue background, large Hot Wheels logo.

2003		$3,100	$3,500

Custom Shop Jimi Hendrix Monterey Pop Stratocaster

1997-1998. Near replica of Monterey Pop Festival "sacrifice" guitar.

1997-1998	Red psychedelic-style finish	$6,500	$7,500

Custom Shop Moto Limited Edition Stratocaster

1990s. Pearloid cover in various colors, includes Certificate of Authenticity, not to be confused with White pearloid Moto Strat which is part of a guitar and amp set (as listed below).

1990s		$1,500	$1,700

Custom Shop Moto Set Stratocaster

1995-1996. Custom Shop set including guitar, case, amp and amp stand.

1995-1996	White Pearloid	$3,800	$4,200

Custom Shop Playboy 40th Anniversary Stratocaster

1994. Nude Marilyn Monroe graphic on body.

1994		$5,500	$6,000

Custom Shop Relic '50s Stratocaster

1996-1999. Relatively faithful reproduction of 1950s (ca. 1957) era Strat with 'played-in' feel, replaced by 1956 Strat.

1996-1999	Gold hardware	$1,600	$2,000
1996-1999	Mary Kaye Blond over ash	$1,600	$2,000
1996-1999	Various colors	$1,400	$1,800

Custom Shop Relic '60s Stratocaster

1996-1999. Relatively faithful reproduction of 1960s era Strat with 'played-in' feel, replaced by 1960 Relic.

1996-1999	Gold hardware	$1,600	$2,000
1996-1999	Various colors	$1,400	$1,800

Custom Shop Set-Neck Stratocaster

1992-1999. Mahogany body and figured maple top, four pickups, glued-in neck, active electronics. By 1996 ash body.

1992-1996		$1,200	$1,400

Custom Shop Texas Special Stratocaster

1991-1992. State of Texas map stamped on neck plate, Texas Special pickups, maple fretboard, 50 made.

1991-1992	Sunburst	$1,700	$2,000

MODEL YEAR	FEATURES	EXC. COND. LOW	HIGH

Deluxe Strat Plus

1987-1998. Three Lace Sensor pickups, Floyd Rose, alder (poplar available earlier) body with ash veneer on front and back, various colors. Also see Strat Plus.

1987-1998		$650	$800

Elite Stratocaster

1983-1984. The Elite Series feature active electronics and noise-cancelling pickups, push buttons instead of three-way switch, various colors. Also see Gold Elite Stratocaster and Walnut Elite Stratocaster.

1983-1984		$800	$900

Eric Clapton Stratocaster

1988-present. U.S.A.-made, 1957 reissue features, active electronics, three Lace Sensors, maple neck, various colors.

1988-1999		$850	$950

Floyd Rose Classic Stratocaster

1992-1997. 2 single-coils, bridge humbucker, Floyd Rose trem, various colors.

1992-1997		$700	$800

Foto Flame Stratocaster

1994-1996, 2000. Japanese-made Collectables model, alder and basswood body with Foto Flame (simulated woodgrain) finish on top cap and back of neck.

1994-1996		$450	$500
2000		$450	$525

Gold Stratocaster

1981-1983. Gold metallic finish and gold-plated brass hardware.

1981-1983		$1,100	$1,300

Gold Elite Stratocaster

1983-1984. The Elite series feature active electronics and noise-cancelling pickups. The Gold Elite has gold hardware and pearloid tuner buttons. Also see Elite Stratocaster and Walnut Elite Stratocaster.

1983		$1,000	$1,200

Hank Marvin Stratocaster

1995-1996. Feista Red.

1995		$1,400	$1,700

Harley-Davidson 90th Anniversary Stratocaster

1993. Custom Shop, 109 total made, Harley-Davidson and Custom Shop V logo on headstock (Diamond Edition, 40 units), nine units produced for the Harley-Davidson company without diamond logo, 60 units were not Diamond Edition, chrome-plated engraved metal body, engraved guard, Custom Shop Certificate important attribute.

1993		$11,000	$12,000

Hellecaster John Jorgenson Stratocaster

1997-1998. Gold sparkle 'guard, gold hardware, split single-coils, rosewood 'board, made in Japan.

1997		$900	$1,100

MODEL		EXC. COND.	
YEAR	FEATURES	LOW	HIGH

HM Stratocaster (U.S.-made)

1988-1992 ('88 Japanese-made, '89-'90 U.S.- and Japanese-made, '91-'92 U.S.-made). Heavy Metal Strat. Floyd Rose, regular or pointy headstock, black hardware, 1 or 2 humbuckers, 1 single-coil and 1 humbucker, or 2 single-coils and 1 humbucker. Later models have choice of 2 humbuckers and 1 single-coil or 2 single-coils and 1 humbucker.

| 1989-1992 | U.S. production | $275 | $375 |

HM Stratocaster (import)

1988-1992 (Imported 1988, U.S. and import production 1989-1990, U.S. only 1991-1992).

| 1988-1990 | Bud Dry logo finish | $350 | $450 |
| 1988-1990 | Import | $200 | $250 |

HRR Stratocaster

1990-1995. Japanese-made, "hot-rodded" vintage-style Strat, Floyd Rose Tremolo system, three pickups, maple neck. Foto Flame, black, Olympic White or sunburst.

| 1990-1995 | | $300 | $400 |

Jeff Beck Stratocaster

1994-present. Alder body, Lace Sensor pickups, special designed trem, various colors but mostly Surf Green.

| 1990s | | $800 | $1,000 |

Jimi Hendrix Tribute Stratocaster

1997-2000. Left-handed guitar strung right-handed, maple cap neck, Olympic White finish.

| 1997-1999 | | $1,000 | $1,100 |

Jimi Hendrix Voodoo Stratocaster

1998-2002. Right-handed body with reverse peghead, maple neck, sunburst, Olympic White, or black.

| 1998-1999 | | $1,100 | $1,300 |

Jimmy Vaughan Tex-Mex Stratocaster

1997-present. Poplar body, maple 'board, Jimmy Vaughan signature on headstock, three Tex-Mex pickups. Various colors.

| 1997-1999 | | $350 | $450 |

Lone Star Stratocaster

1996-2000. Alder body, 1 humbucker and 2 single-coils, rosewood fingerboard or maple neck. Various colors.

| 1996-1999 | | $700 | $750 |

Paisley Stratocaster

1988-1995. Japanese-made 1972 Strat reissue with a reissue 1968 Tele Pink Paisley finish.

| 1988-1995 | | $800 | $1,100 |

Powerhouse/Powerhouse Deluxe Stratocaster

1997-present. Import Standard Strat configuration with pearloid pickguard, various colors, some colors discontinued.

| 1997-1999 | | $400 | $450 |

Richie Sambora Stratocaster

1993-2002. Alder body, Floyd Rose trem, maple neck.

| 1993-2002 | Sunburst | $1,000 | $1,200 |

Roadhouse Stratocaster

1997-2000. U.S.-made, poplar body, tortoise shell pickguard, maple fingerboard, three Texas Special pickups. Various colors.

| 1997-2000 | | $650 | $700 |

Robert Cray Stratocaster

1991-present. Custom Shop signature model, rosewood fingerboard, chunky neck, lighter weight, hard-tail non-tremolo, alder body, gold-plated hardware. Various colors.

| 1991-1999 | | $1,150 | $1,250 |

Roland Stratocaster (Mexico)

1990s. Single synth pickup and 3 standard single-coils, made in Mexico.

| 1990s | | $450 | $550 |

Short-Scale (7/8) Stratocaster

1989-1994. Similar to Standard Strat, but with 2 control knobs and switch, 24-inch scale vs. 25-inch scale, sometimes called a 'mini-Strat', Japanese import. Various colors.

| 1989-1994 | | $550 | $600 |

Squier Stratocaster II

1989-1990. Import from India.

| 1989-1990 | | $80 | $125 |

Squier Stratocaster Standard

1982-1998. Fender Japan was established in '82 with Squier production beginning in '83. Production was shifted to Korea in '87 and later allocated to China, India (Squier II '89-'90) and Mexico. This model is the low-cost Stratocaster Standard version of the Squier line. Various colors.

| 1982-1989 | | $200 | $350 |
| 1990-1998 | | $150 | $275 |

Squier Stratocaster Standard (Affinity Series)

Three single-coil pickups, made in China.

| 1999 | | $75 | $100 |

Squier Stratocaster Standard (Double Fat Strat)

Large headstock, two humbucker pickups, made in China.

| 1999 | | $100 | $150 |

Standard Stratocaster (Japan)

1985. Interim production in Japan while the new Fender reorganized, standard pickup configuration and tremolo system, three knobs with switch, traditional style input jack, traditional shaped headstock (Natural Maple color).

| 1985 | Black or Red, White guard | $500 | $700 |

Standard Stratocaster (Mexico)

Fender Mexico started production in 1991. Not to be confused with the American-made Standard Stratocaster of '81-'84. High end of range includes a hard guitar case, while the low end of the range includes only a gig bag. Various colors.

| 1991-1999 | Black | $225 | $300 |
| 1991-1999 | Other colors | $275 | $325 |

Fender Jeff Beck Stratocaster

Fender Jimmie Vaughan Tex Mex Stratocaster

Fender Stevie Ray Vaughan Stratocaster

Fender Walnut Elite Stratocaster

MODEL YEAR	FEATURES	EXC. COND. LOW	HIGH

Stevie Ray Vaughan Stratocaster
1992-present. U.S.A.-made, alder body, sunburst, gold hardware, SRV pickguard, lefty trem unit, Brazilian rosewood fingerboard (pau ferro by 1993).

1992-1999		$1,050	$1,150

Strat Plus
1987-1998. Three Lace Sensor pickups, alder (poplar available earlier) body, trem, rosewood fingerboard or maple neck, various colors. See Deluxe Strat Plus for ash veneer version.

1987-1989		$700	$800
1990-1998		$650	$750

Stratocaster Special (Mexico)
1993-1995. A humbucker and a single-coil pickup, 1 volume, 1 tone.

1993-1995		$300	$350

Stratocaster XII
1988-1995. Alder body, maple neck, 21-fret rosewood fingerboard, 3 vintage Strat pickups, Japanese-made. Various colors.

1988-1995		$550	$650

Sub Sonic Stratocaster
2000-2001. Baritone model tuned B-E-A-D-G-B, single-single-hum pickup configuration, Strat-styling.

2000-2001		$900	$1,100

Super/Deluxe Super Stratocaster
1997-2003. Import made in Mexico, part of Deluxe Series, Standard Strat features with maple neck.

1997-2003		$275	$300

Tanqurey Tonic Stratocaster
1988. Made for a Tanqurey Tonic liquor ad campaign giveaway in 1988, many were given to winners around the country. Ads said that they could also be purchased through Tanqurey, but that apparently didn't happen.

1988	Tanqurey Tonic Green	$950	$1,100

The Strat
1980-1983. Alder body, four-bolt neck, large "Strat" on painted peghead, gold-plated brass hardware. Various colors.

1980-1983	Rare colors	$1,200	$1,500
1980-1983	Various common colors	$1,000	$1,200

U.S. Strat Ultra
1990-1997. Alder body with figured maple veneer on front and back, single Lace Sensor pickups in neck and middle, double Sensor at bridge, Ebony fingerboard.

1990-1997	Sunburst	$800	$1,000

Ventures Limited Edition Stratocaster
1996. Japanese-made tribute model, matches Jazzmaster equivalent.

1996	Black	$900	$1,000

Walnut Elite Stratocaster
1983-1984. The Elite Series feature active electronics and noise-cancelling pickups. Walnut Elite has a walnut body and neck, gold-plated hardware and pearloid tuner buttons. Also see Elite Stratocaster and Gold Elite Stratocaster.

1983-1984	Natural Walnut	$2,000	$2,300

Walnut Stratocaster
1981-1983. American Black Walnut body and one-piece neck/fingerboard.

1981-1983	Natural Walnut	$1,700	$2,100

Yngwie Malmsteen Stratocaster
1988-present. U.S.-made, maple neck, scalloped fingerboard, three single-coil pickups. Blue, Red, White.

1988-1999		$950	$1,150

Telecaster
The following are all variations of the Stratocaster. The first four listings are for the main U.S.-made models. All other Stratocaster models are listed alphabetically after that in the following order.

Telecaster
Standard Telecaster
American Standard Telecaster
American Series Telecaster
'50s Telecaster
'52 Telecaster
'60 Telecaster Custom (Custom Shop)
'62 Custom Telecaster
'69 Blue Flower Telecaster
'69 Pink Paisley Telecaster
'69 Rosewood Telecaster
'69 Telecaster Thinline
'72 Custom Telecaster
'72 Telecaster Thinline
'90s Telecaster Thinline
Albert Collins Telecaster
Aluminum Telecaster
American Deluxe Telecaster
Black and Gold Telecaster
California Fat Telecaster
California Telecaster
Contemporary Telecaster
Custom Shop '63 Closet Classic Telecaster
Custom Shop 40th Anniversary Telecaster
Custom Shop 50th Anniversary Telecaster
Custom Shop American Classic Holoflake Telecaster
Custom Shop American Classic Telecaster
Custom Shop Buck Owens Telecaster
Custom Shop Custom Classic Telecaster
Custom Shop Jerry Donahue Telecaster
Custom Shop John Jorgenson Telecaster
Custom Shop Sparkle Telecaster
Custom Shop Thinline Telecaster
Danny Gatton Telecaster
Deluxe Telecaster
Foto Flame Telecaster
HMT Telecaster
James Burton Telecaster
Rosewood Telecaster
Set-Neck Telecaster
Squier Telecaster
Squier Telecaster Affinity
Standard Telecaster (Mexico)
Tele Jr./Set Neck Tele Jr.

Telecaster Custom
Telecaster Deluxe
Telecaster Deluxe Nashville
Telecaster Plus Standard
Telecaster Thinline/Thinline II

Telecaster

1951-1982. See Standard Telecaster (following listing) for 1982-1985, and American Standard Telecaster for 1988-2000. Currently called American Series Telecaster.

MODEL YEAR	FEATURES	EXC. COND. LOW	HIGH
1951	Blond, black pickguard	$19,000	$23,000
1952	Blond, black pickguard	$18,000	$22,000
1953	Blond, black pickguard	$16,000	$21,000
1954	Blond, black pickguard	$15,000	$20,000
1954	Blond, white pickguard	$13,000	$16,000
1955	Blond, white pickguard	$12,000	$16,000
1956	Blond	$11,000	$15,000
1957	Blond	$10,000	$14,000
1957	Custom color (various)	$25,000	$30,000
1958	Blond	$9,000	$11,000
1958	Sunburst	$11,000	$13,000
1959	Blond, early slab board	$8,000	$10,000
1959	Blond, maple neck	$9,000	$11,000
1960	Blond	$8,000	$10,000
1960	Sunburst	$10,500	$12,500
1961	Black	$10,000	$12,000
1961	Blond	$7,500	$10,000
1961	Dakota Red	$16,000	$18,000
1961	Fiesta Red	$16,000	$18,000
1961	Lake Placid Blue	$10,000	$12,000
1962	Blond, curved board	$7,000	$9,000
1962	Blond, slab board	$7,500	$9,500
1962	Fiesta Red, slab board	$15,000	$17,000
1962	Inca Silver, slab board	$14,000	$16,000
1962	Lake Placid Blue, curved board	$9,200	$11,200
1962	Lake Placid Blue, slab board	$10,000	$12,000
1962	Sea Foam Green, slab board	$15,000	$17,000
1962	Sherwood Green, slab board	$13,000	$16,000
1962	Shoreline Gold, slab board	$13,000	$16,000
1962	Sonic Blue, slab board	$12,000	$14,000
1962	Surf Green, slab board	$15,000	$17,000
1963	Black	$9,000	$11,000
1963	Blond	$7,000	$8,500

MODEL YEAR	FEATURES	EXC. COND. LOW	HIGH
1963	Burgundy Mist	$13,000	$15,000
1963	Dakota Red	$12,000	$15,000
1963	Daphne Blue	$11,000	$13,000
1963	Fiesta Red	$14,000	$16,000
1963	Inca Silver	$13,000	$15,000
1963	Lake Placid Blue	$9,000	$11,000
1963	Olympic White	$9,000	$11,000
1963	Sea Foam Green	$14,000	$16,000
1963	Shell Pink	$16,000	$21,000
1963	Sherwood Green	$12,000	$14,000
1963	Shoreline Gold	$11,000	$13,000
1963	Sonic Blue	$11,000	$13,000
1963	Sunburst	$7,500	$9,000
1963	Surf Green	$14,000	$16,000
1964	Blond	$6,500	$8,200
1964	Sonic Blue	$11,000	$13,000
1965	Blond	$6,000	$7,500
1965	Candy Apple Red	$7,200	$8,200
1965	Lake Placid Blue	$7,000	$8,200
1966	Blond	$5,500	$6,500
1966	Candy Apple Red	$6,500	$8,000
1966	Firemist Gold	$7,000	$8,700
1966	Lake Placid Blue	$6,200	$7,700
1966	Olympic White	$6,000	$7,500
1966	Sunburst	$4,700	$6,200
1967	Black	$5,500	$7,000
1967	Blond	$4,200	$5,500
1967	Blond, Bigsby	$3,500	$5,000
1967	Blond, maple cap	$4,500	$6,000
1967	Candy Apple Red	$6,300	$7,800
1967	Ice Blue Metallic	$7,000	$8,200
1967	Lake Placid Blue	$6,300	$7,800
1967	Olympic White	$6,000	$7,500
1967	Sunburst	$4,500	$6,000
1968	Black	$5,000	$6,500
1968	Blond	$3,700	$5,000
1968	Blond, factory Bigsby	$3,000	$4,000
1968	Blue floral	$6,800	$8,300
1968	Candy Apple Red	$6,300	$7,800
1968	Dakota Red	$6,700	$8,200
1968	Lake Placid Blue	$6,300	$7,800
1968	Pink Paisley	$7,100	$8,600
1968	Sunburst	$4,000	$5,500
1969	Blond	$3,300	$4,200
1969	Blue Floral	$6,800	$8,300
1969	Candy Apple Red	$5,300	$6,800
1969	Pink Paisley	$7,100	$8,600
1969	Sunburst	$3,500	$4,500
1969	White	$4,000	$5,500
1970	Blond	$3,000	$4,000
1970	Blond, Fender Bigsby	$2,300	$3,200
1970	Candy Apple Red	$4,100	$5,800
1970	Firemist Gold	$4,700	$6,400
1970	Sunburst	$2,900	$4,100
1971	Black	$2,300	$3,400
1971	Blond	$2,300	$3,400
1971	Candy Apple Red	$3,200	$4,500
1971	Sunburst	$2,300	$3,400
1971	Transparent Brown	$2,300	$3,400

1958 Fender Telecaster

1965 Fender Telecaster

The *Vintage Guitar Price Guide* shows low to high values for items in all-original excellent condition, and, where applicable, with original case or cover.

GUITARS

Fender Albert Collins Telecaster

Fender '69 Telecaster Thinline

MODEL YEAR	FEATURES	EXC. COND. LOW	HIGH
1971	White	$2,600	$3,900
1972	Black	$2,600	$3,100
1972	Blond	$2,200	$2,500
1972	Candy Apple Red	$2,900	$3,400
1972	Natural	$2,000	$2,400
1972	Olympic White	$2,300	$2,900
1972	Sunburst	$2,000	$2,400
1973	Various colors	$1,900	$2,500
1974	Various colors	$1,800	$2,400
1975	Various colors	$1,600	$1,900
1976	Various colors	$1,500	$1,800
1977	Various colors	$1,300	$1,700
1978	Various colors	$1,100	$1,700
1979	Various colors	$1,100	$1,600
1980	Various colors	$1,100	$1,500
1981	Various colors	$1,000	$1,400
1982	Various colors	$900	$1,400

Standard Telecaster
1982-1985. See Telecaster for 1951-1982, and American Standard Telecaster (following listing) for 1988-2000. Not to be confused with the current Standard Telecaster, which is made in Mexico.

1982-1985	Blond	$700	$1,100

American Standard Telecaster
1988-2000. See Telecaster for 1951-1983, and Telecaster Standard for 1983-1985. All 1994 models have a metal 40th Anniversary pin on the headstock, but should not be confused with the actual 40th Anniversary Telecaster model (see separate listing). All standard colors. Renamed the American Series Telecaster in 2000.

1988-1989		$675	$850
1990-1999		$625	$725

American Series Telecaster
2000-present.

2000-2002		$500	$600

'50s Telecaster (import)
1992-1999. Import from Japan, basswood body, blond finish, Black guard.

1992-1999		$450	$550

'52 Telecaster
1982-present. 1952 Telecaster reissue, ash body, with maple neck or rosewood fingerboard.

1982-1999	Blond	$800	$1,000
1990-1999	Copper (limited number)	$800	$1,000

'60 Telecaster Custom (Custom Shop)
1997-present. U.S.A. custom shop, alder body, black or custom colors.

1997-2002		$1,300	$1,500

'62 Custom Telecaster (import)
1985-1999. Made in Japan, bound top and back, rosewood fretboard.

1985-1999	Sunburst or Red	$450	$550

'69 Blue Flower Telecaster
Ca.1986-1994. Import, Blue Flower finish.

1986-1989		$800	$950
1990-1994		$500	$800

'69 Pink Paisley Telecaster
Ca.1986-1998. Import, Pink Paisley finish.

1986-1989		$800	$950
1990-1998		$500	$800

MODEL YEAR	FEATURES	EXC. COND. LOW	HIGH

'69 Rosewood Telecaster
1986-1996. Japanese-made reissue, rosewood.

1986-1996		$1,300	$1,700

'69 Telecaster Thinline
1988-1998. Import, 2 Tele pickups.

1988-1998	Natural	$450	$550

'72 Custom Telecaster
1986-1999. Import.

1986-1999	Black or red	$600	$650

'72 Telecaster Thinline
1988-1998. Import, humbuckers.

1988-1998	Natural	$450	$550

'90s Telecaster Thinline
1998-2000. Ash body, single F-hole, natural Foto-Flame or transparent crimson.

1998-2000		$900	$1,100

Albert Collins Telecaster
1990-present. U.S.-made Custom Shop signature model, bound swamp ash body, humbucker pickup in neck position.

1990-1999	Natural	$1,100	$1,300
1995	Silver Sparkle	$1,200	$1,400

Aluminum Telecaster
1994-1995. Aluminum with anodized marble-variant finish.

1994-1995		$1,500	$1,800

American Deluxe Telecaster
1998-present. Premium ash or alder body with see-through finishes.

1998-1999		$850	$950

Black and Gold Telecaster
1981-1982. Black finish, gold-plated brass hardware.

1981-1982		$1,100	$1,300

California Fat Telecaster
1997-1998. Alder body, maple fretboard, Tex-Mex humbucker and Tele pickup configuration.

1997-1998		$450	$550

California Telecaster
1997-1998. Alder body, maple fretboard, Tex-Mex Strat and Tele pickup configuration.

1997-1998	Sunburst	$450	$550

Contemporary Telecaster (import)
1985-1987. Japanese-made while the new Fender reorganized, 2 or 3 pickups, vibrato, Black chrome hardware, rosewood fingerboard.

1985-1987		$250	$300

Custom Shop '63 Closet Classic Telecaster
1999-present. Alder body (or blond on ash), original spec pickups, C-shaped neck, rosewood fingerboard.

1999	Blond on ash	$1,800	$1,900
1999	Candy Apple Red on alder	$1,600	$1,700

Custom Shop 40th Anniversary Telecaster
1988, 1999. Custom shop limited edition run of 300, two-piece flamed maple top, gold hardware (1988), flamed maple top over ash body, gold hardware (1999).

1988	1st run, high-end	$3,200	$3,700
1999	2nd run, plain top	$1,200	$1,500

MODEL YEAR	FEATURES	EXC. COND. LOW	HIGH

Custom Shop 50th Anniversary Telecaster

1995-1996. Flame maple top, 2 vintage-style pickups, gold hardware, gold 50th Anniversary coin on back of the headstock, 1250 made.

1995-1996	Sunburst	$1,300	$1,400

Custom Shop American Classic Holoflake Telecaster

1996-present.

1996-2000		$1,300	$1,500

Custom Shop American Classic Telecaster

1993-2000. Handcrafted version of American Standard, thin lacquer-finished ash body, maple or rosewood 'board. Earlier versions had gold hardware and custom-color options.

1993-2000	Various colors and options	$1,300	$1,500

Custom Shop Buck Owens Ltd Edition Telecaster

1998-2002. Red, white and blue sparkle finish, gold hardware, gold 'guard, rosewood 'board, by Fender Japan.

1998-2002		$850	$950

Custom Shop Custom Classic Telecaster

2000-present. U.S.A. Custom Shop version of American Series, alder body, maple or rosewood 'board.

2000-2002		$1,200	$1,400

Custom Shop Jerry Donahue Telecaster

1992-2001. Designed by Donahue, Tele bridge pickup and Strat neck pickup, bird's-eye maple neck and top, basswood body, special passive circuitry. There was also a Japanese J.D. Telecaster.

1992-1999	Custom color, Gold hardware	$1,500	$1,700
1992-1999	Sunburst	$1,200	$1,300

Custom Shop John Jorgenson Telecaster

1998-2001. Custom Shop, double-coil stacked pickups, sparkle or black finish. Early models had korina body.

1998-2001	Gold Sparkle	$1,300	$1,700

Custom Shop Sparkle Telecaster

1993-1995. Poplar body, white pickguard, sparkle finish: champagne, gold, silver

1993-1995		$1,300	$1,500

Custom Shop Thinline Telecaster

1990s	Gold sparkle	$1,500	$1,700

Danny Gatton Telecaster

1990-present. Custom Shop signature model like 1953 Telecaster, maple neck, 2 humbucking pickups.

1990-2000	Frost Gold	$1,800	$2,000

Deluxe Telecaster (U.S.A.-made)

1972-1981. Two humbuckers.

1972-1978	Various colors	$1,800	$2,100
1972-1981	Blond	$1,900	$2,200
1978	Antigua	$1,900	$2,200

Foto Flame Telecaster

1994-1996. Import, sunburst or transparent.

1994-1996		$450	$500

HMT Telecaster

1990-1993. Japanese-made "Metal-rock" Tele, available with or without Floyd Rose tremolo, one Fender Lace Sensor pickup and one DiMarzio bridge humbucker pickup.

1990-1993	Black	$200	$250

James Burton Telecaster

1990-present. Ash body, 3 Fender Lace pickups. Available in black with gold paisley, black with Candy Red paisley, pearl white, and Frost Red.

1990-1999	Black and gold paisley, gold hardware	$800	$1,100
1990-1999	Frost Red, black hardware	$500	$800
1990-1999	Pearl White, gold hardware	$500	$800
1990-2000	Black and red paisley, black hardware	$800	$1,100

Rosewood Telecaster

1969-1972. Rosewood body and neck.

1969-1972		$4,000	$6,000

Set-Neck Telecaster

1990-1996. Glued-in neck, Custom Shop, 2 humbuckers. Set Neck CA "Country Artist" has one humbucker and one Tele pickup. Various colors.

1990-1996		$1,100	$1,300

Squier Telecaster

1983-1998. Fender Japan was established in '82 with Squier production beginning in '83. Production was shifted to Korea in '87 and later allocated to China, India (Squier II '89-'90) and Mexico. This model is the low-cost version of the Telecaster for Squier.

1983-1984	Blond, 1st year '70s-style logo	$250	$350
1985-1989	Black or blond	$200	$300

Squier Telecaster Affinity (China)

Made in China, standard Telecaster styling. Various colors.

1999		$75	$100

Standard Telecaster (Mexico)

Production at the Mexico facility started in 1991. High end of range includes a hard guitar case, while the low end of the range includes only a gig bag. Various colors.

1991-1999		$300	$350

Tele Jr./Set Neck Tele Jr. (Custom Shop)

1994, 1997-2000. Transparent blond ash body, two P-90-style pickups, set neck, 11 tone chambers. 100 made in '94, reintroduced in '97.

1994		$1,600	$1,800

Telecaster Custom

1959-1972. Body bound top and back, rosewood fingerboard, 2 Tele pickups. See Telecaster Custom (2nd Edition) for the one Tele/one humbucker version.

1959	Sunburst, maple	$14,000	$20,000
1960	Sunburst	$13,000	$17,000
1961	Black	$16,000	$18,500

Fender James Burton Telecaster

1965 Fender Telecaster Custom

1971 Telecaster Thinline

1974 Telecaster Thinline

MODEL YEAR	FEATURES	EXC. COND. LOW	HIGH
1961	Dakota Red	$19,000	$23,000
1961	Fiesta Red	$19,000	$23,000
1961	Lake Placid Blue	$16,000	$18,500
1961	Sunburst	$12,000	$16,000
1962	Fiesta Red, slab board	$18,000	$21,000
1962	Inca Silver, slab board	$18,000	$21,000
1962	Lake Placid Blue, slab board	$16,000	$18,500
1962	Sea Foam Green, slab board	$20,000	$23,300
1962	Sherwood Green, slab board	$17,000	$19,800
1962	Shoreline Gold, slab board	$17,000	$19,800
1962	Sonic Blue, slab board	$18,000	$21,000
1962	Sunburst	$11,000	$12,900
1962	Surf Green, slab board	$20,000	$23,300
1963	Sunburst	$10,000	$11,600
1964	Sunburst	$9,000	$10,500
1965	Candy Apple Red	$11,000	$12,800
1965	Sunburst	$7,500	$8,700
1966	Sunburst	$6,500	$7,600
1967	Lake Placid Blue	$9,000	$10,500
1967	Sunburst	$6,000	$7,000
1968	Candy Apple Red, maple cap	$8,500	$9,900
1968	Firemist Gold, rosewood cap	$9,000	$11,000
1968	Sunburst, maple cap	$6,500	$7,500
1968	Sunburst, rosewood cap	$6,000	$7,000
1968	White	$8,000	$9,300
1969	Sunburst	$5,500	$6,500
1970	Sunburst	$5,400	$6,300
1971	Sunburst, 3-bolt neck	$3,300	$3,900
1971	Sunburst, 4-bolt neck	$4,000	$4,700
1972	Sunburst, 3-bolt neck	$3,100	$3,600

Telecaster Custom (II)
1972-1981. One humbucking and 1 Tele pickup, standard colors. See above for two Tele pickup version. Also called Custom Telecaster.

1972-1975		$1,600	$2,100
1976-1981		$1,500	$1,900

Telecaster Deluxe (import)
1995-1998. Import, 1 Tele-style bridge pickup and 2 Strat-style pickups, rosewood fingerboard, Foto Flame '95-'97 and non-Foto Flame '97-'98.

1995-1998	Sunburst	$450	$500

Telecaster Deluxe Nashville (Mexico)
1998-present. Tex-Mex Strat and Tele pickup configuration, various colors.

1998-1999		$450	$500

Telecaster Plus Standard
1990-1997. Two Lace Sensor pickups, 1 single-coil, 1 double. Different model, called Telecaster Plus (no standard) offered 1994-1997. Various colors.

MODEL YEAR	FEATURES	EXC. COND. LOW	HIGH
1990-1997		$650	$800

Telecaster Thinline/Thinline II
1968-1980. Semi-hollowbody, 1 F-hole, 2 Tele pickups, ash or mahogany body. In late-1971, the "tilt neck" was added and the two Tele pickups were switched to 2 humbuckers.

MODEL YEAR	FEATURES	EXC. COND. LOW	HIGH
1968	Custom color (more common)	$3,800	$4,400
1968	Custom color (rare)	$6,500	$7,500
1968	Natural Ash	$3,500	$4,200
1968	Natural mahogany	$4,500	$5,000
1968	Sunburst	$3,500	$4,200
1969	Custom color (more common)	$3,800	$4,200
1969	Custom color (rare)	$6,500	$7,500
1969	Natural ash	$3,300	$3,800
1969	Natural mahogany	$4,300	$4,800
1969	Sunburst	$3,300	$3,800
1970	Custom color (more common)	$3,800	$4,100
1970	Custom color (rare)	$6,500	$7,400
1970	Natural ash	$3,300	$3,700
1970	Natural mahogany	$4,300	$4,700
1970	Sunburst	$3,300	$3,700
1971	Custom color (more common)	$3,500	$4,000
1971	Custom color (rare)	$6,400	$7,300
1971	Natural ash, 3-bolt neck	$2,700	$3,000
1971	Natural mahogany, 3-bolt neck	$3,200	$3,500
1971	Sunburst, 3-bolt neck	$2,700	$3,000
1972-1974	Black, humbuckers	$3,000	$3,500
1972-1974	Blond, custom option	$3,000	$3,500
1972-1974	Mahogany, humbuckers	$2,800	$3,200
1972-1974	Natural ash, humbuckers	$2,500	$3,000
1972-1974	Sunburst, humbuckers	$2,500	$3,000
1972-1974	Walnut	$2,400	$2,900
1972-1974	White	$2,500	$3,000
1975-1978	Black, humbuckers	$2,400	$3,100
1975-1978	Blond, custom option	$2,400	$3,100
1975-1978	Natural ash, humbuckers	$1,800	$2,500
1975-1978	Sunburst, humbuckers	$1,800	$2,500
1975-1978	Walnut	$1,700	$2,400
1975-1978	White	$1,700	$2,400

MODEL		EXC. COND.	
YEAR	FEATURES	LOW	HIGH

Toronado/Toronado Deluxe

1999-present. Contoured offset-waist body with 2 Atomic Humbucker pickups. Offered in Black, Arctic White, Candy Apple Red, and Brown Sunburst.

1999-2001	Atomic humbuckers	$400	$500
1999-2001	DE-9000 P-90s	$400	$500

Villager 12-String

1965-1971. Acoustic flat top, spruce top, mahogany back and sides, 12 strings. Natural.

1965-1968		$600	$750
1969-1971		$550	$700

Wildwood

1967-1969. Acoustic flat top with wildwood dyed top.

1967-1969	Various (faded)	$850	$1,000
1967-1969	Various (unfaded)	$1,200	$1,500

Fernandes

1969-present. Established in Tokyo. Early efforts were classical guitars, but they now offer a variety of guitars and basses.

AFR-120

1988-1998. Bolt-on neck, locking tremolo, graphic finishes, Natural.

1988		$300	$450

APG-100

1989-1996. Carved and bound maple top, mahogany back, maple neck, rosewood fingerboard, various pickup configurations, Sunburst.

1991-1996		$500	$600

FR-552

Introduced in 1987. One-piece maple neck, 24-fret fingerboard, deep cutaway, Fernandes Floyd Rose locking tremolo.

1988	Black	$200	$275

LE-1

Introduced in 1987. Double cut alder body, maple or rosewood fingerboard, various colors.

1987		$200	$275

LE-2 G

1991-1998. LE-2 with gold hardware.

1991-1998	Sunburst	$300	$400

LE-2/LE-2X

1991-1998. Double cut, hum-single-single non-pole pickups, Floyd-style vibrato (LE-2X double-locking), various colors.

1990s		$250	$350

TE-3

1993-1998. Natural.

1997		$450	$550

TE-59/60

Introduced in 1987. Single cut alder body, Natural.

1987		$200	$300

Fina

Production classical and steel-string guitars built at the Kwo Hsiao Music Wooden Factory in Huiyang City, Guang Dong, mainland China. They also build acoustic basses.

Fine Resophonic

1988-present. Professional and premium grade, production/custom, wood and metal-bodied resophonic guitars (including reso-electrics) built by luthiers Mike Lewis and Pierre Avocat in Vitry Sur Seine, France. They also build ukes and mandolins.

Fleishman Instruments

1974-present. Premium and presentation grade, custom flat-tops made by luthier Harry Fleishman in Sebastopol, California. He also offers basses and electric uprights. Fleishman is the director of Luthiers School International.

Fletcher Brock Stringed Instruments

1992-present. Custom flat-tops and archtops made by luthier Fletcher Brock in Ketchum, Idaho. He also builds mandolin family instruments.

Flowers Guitars

Premium grade, custom, archtop guitars built by luthier Gary Flowers in Baltimore, Maryland.

Floyd Rose

2004-present. Floyd Rose, inventor of the revolutionary Floyd Rose Locking Tremolo, introduced a guitar line at Winter NAMM, January 2004. Innovations accompany the new models, including the SpeedLoader headstock nut and automatic electronic tuner that eliminates the need for tuning keys. The Redmond Series includes six models simply named Model 1 through Model 5, plus the Model K (made of 'Karina" limba).

Fontanilla Guitars

1987-present. Luthier Allan Fontanilla builds his premium grade, production/custom, classical guitars in San Francisco, California.

Fouilleul

1978-present. Production/custom, classical guitars made by luthier Jean-Marie Fouilleul in Cuguen, France.

Frame Works

1995-present. Professional grade, production/custom, steel- and nylon-string guitars built by luthier Frank Krocker in Burghausen, Germany. The instruments feature a neck mounted on a guitar-shaped frame. Krocker has also built traditional archtops, flat-tops, and classicals.

Framus

1946-1975, 1996-present. Professional and premium grade, production/custom, guitars made in Markneukirchen, Germany. They also build basses and amps.

"Frankische Musikindustrie" (Framus) founded in Erlangen, Germany by Fred Wilfer, relocated to

Fender Toronado

Floyd Rose Redmond

Framus Strato-Melodie 9-string

Froggy Bottom Model K

Bubenreuth in '54, and to Pretzfeld in '67. Begun as an acoustic instrument manufacturer, Framus added electrics in the mid-'50s. Earliest electrics were mostly acoustics with pickups attached. Electric designs begin in early-'60s. Unique feature was a laminated maple neck with many thin plies. By around '64-'65 upscale models featured the "organtone," often called a "spigot," a spring-loaded volume control that allowed you to simulate a Leslie speaker effect. Better models often had mutes and lots of switches. In the '60s, Framus instruments were imported into the U.S. by Philadelphia Music Company. Resurgence of interest in ca. '74 with the Jan Akkermann hollowbody followed by original mid-'70s design called the Nashville, the product of an alliance with some American financing. The brand was revived in '96 by Hans Peter Wilfer, the president of Warwick, with production in Warwick's factory in Germany. Distributed in the U.S. by Dana B. Goods.

Atilla Zoller AZ 10
Early-1960s-late-1970s. Single cut archtop, 2 pickups, neck glued-in until the 1970s, bolt-on after. Model 5/65 30% lower in value than Model 5/67.

1960s	Sunburst	$750	$900

Big 18 Solid Doubleneck 5/200
196s	Sunburst	$550	$700

Billy Lorento
Ca.1958-1977. Semi-hollowbody, single cut thinline, 2 pickups.

1958-1977	$500	$800

Caravelle 5/117
Ca.1965-1977. Double cut archtop, tremolo, 2 pickups, cherry or sunburst.

1965-1977	$400	$500

Golden Television 5/118
Ca. 1967-ca. 1970. Semi-hollowbody, natural light-colored solid spruce top, double cut, 3 pickups, gold hardware, cherry or sunburst.

1967-1970	$500	$700

Jan Akkerman
1974-1977. Single cut semi-hollowbody, 2 pickups, gold hardware.

1974-1977	$600	$800

King 5/98
Single cutaway flat-top.

1960s	$400	$600

Missouri 5/60 (E Framus Missouri)
Ca.1960-1977. Non-cutaway acoustic archtop until 1965, single cut with 2 pickups after, Natural or Sunburst.

1960-1977	$450	$650

Nashville
1974-1977.

1974-1977	$425	$575

Sorella 5/59
Ca.1955-1977. Single cut acoustic archtop.

1955-1977	$475	$675

Strato de Luxe 5/168
Ca.1964-1972. Fender Jaguar-shaped solidbody, 1, 2, or 3 pickups, some models have gold hardware.

1964-1972	Sunburst	$450	$550

Strato de Luxe 12-String 5/068
Ca.1964-1972. 12 strings, 2 pickups, tremolo.

1964-1972	Sunburst	$400	$500

Strato Melodie 9-String
Ca.1963-1970. Solidbody, offset double cut, doubles on 3 high strings, 2 single-coil pickups, tremolo.

1963-1970	Sunburst	$500	$700

Tennessee Custom
1996-present. Double cut hollowbody, f-hole, flame maple top, 2 humbuckers, tremolo.

1990s	$1,700	$1,750

Texan 12-String Flat-Top 5/296
1960s	Natural or Sunburst	$250	$300

Fresher
1973-1985. The Japanese-made Fresher brand was introduced in '73. The guitars were mainly copies of popular brands and were not imported into the U.S., but they do show up at guitar shows.

Solidbody Electrics
Japanese import.

1970s	$200	$350

Froggy Bottom Guitars
1970-present. Luthier Michael Millard builds his premium and presentation grade, production/custom flat-tops in Newfane, Vermont (until 1984 production was in Richmond, New Hampshire).

Fukuoka Musical Instruments
1993-present. Custom steel and nylon-string flat-tops and archtops built in Japan.

Futurama
Late 1950s-mid to late 1960s. Futurama was a brand name used by Selmer in the U.K. Early instruments made in Czechoslovakia, models for 1963-'64 made by Sweden's Hagstrom company. Some later '60s instruments may have been made in Japan. Hobbyists will recognize the brand name as Beatle George Harrison's first electric.

Futurama III
1963-1964. Vague Strat meets Jazzmaster solidbody, 3 pickups, 3 push button levels, 2 knobs, Futurama logo on pickguard.

1963	Harrison exact specifications	$4,000	$6,000

Fylde Guitars
1973-present. Luthier Roger Bucknall builds his professional and premium grade, production/custom acoustic guitars in Penrith, Cumbria, United Kingdom. He also builds basses, mandolins, mandolas, bouzoukis, and citterns.

MODEL YEAR	FEATURES	EXC. COND. LOW	HIGH

G & L

1980-present. Intermediate and professional grade, production/custom, solidbody and semi-hollowbody electric guitars made in the U.S. and overseas. They also make basses. Founded by Leo Fender and George Fullerton following the severance of ties between Fender's CLF Research and Music Man. Company sold to John MacLaren and BBE Sound, when Leo Fender died in '91. In '98 they added their Custom Creations Department. In '03 G & L introduced the Korean-made G & L Tribute Series. Several of the following price ranges were developed with help from Tim Page.

ASAT
1986-1998. Called the Broadcaster in 1985. 2 or 3 single-coil or 2 single-coil/one humbucker pickup configurations until early-'90s, 2 single-coils after.

1986		$700	$800
1987	Leo Fender sig. on headstock	$750	$850
1988-1991	Leo Fender sig. on body	$850	$950
1992-1998		$600	$700

ASAT '50
1999. Limited run of 10 instruments.

1999		$1,000	$1,250

ASAT 20th Anniversary
2000. Limited Edition of 50, ash body, tinted bird's-eye maple neck, two-tone Sunburst.

2000		$1,300	$1,500

ASAT Blues Boy Limited Edition
1999. Limited edition of 20.

1999		$1,000	$1,200

ASAT Blues Boy Semi-Hollow Limited Edition
1999. Limited edition, thin semi-hollow, limited edition of 12 units.

1999		$1,000	$1,400

ASAT Classic
1990-present. Two single-coil pickups, individually adjustable bridge saddles, neck-tilt adjustment and tapered string posts.

1990-1991	Signature on neck	$850	$1,050
1992-1997	3-bolt neck	$750	$950
1997-2003	4-bolt neck	$700	$900

ASAT Classic B-Bender
1997. 12 made with factory-original B-Bender.

1997		$1,100	$1,200

ASAT Classic Blues Boy
2001-present. Humbucker neck pickup, single-coil at bridge.

2001-2003		$750	$900

ASAT Classic Blues Boy Semi-Hollow
1997-present. Chambered Classic with F-holes.

1997-1999		$800	$950

ASAT Classic Commemorative
1991-1992. Leo Fender signature and birth/death dating.

1991	Australian lacewood, 6 made	$4,000	$6,000

1991-1992	Cherryburst, 350 made	$2,400	$2,600

ASAT Classic Custom
1996-1997, 2002-present.

1996-1997	1st version	$850	$950
2002-2003	2nd version, 4-bolt neck	$700	$750

ASAT Classic Custom Semi-Hollow
2002-present.

2002-2003		$750	$850

ASAT Classic Semi-Hollow
1997-present.

1997-2003		$700	$800

ASAT Classic Three
1998. Limited Edition of 100 units.

1998		$1,000	$1,400

ASAT Deluxe
1997-present. Two humbuckers, flamed maple top, bound body.

1997	3-bolt neck, less than 100 made	$1,000	$1,400
1997-2003	4-bolt neck	$1,000	$1,100

ASAT Deluxe Semi-Hollow
1997-present. Two humbuckers.

1997-2003		$1,100	$1,300

ASAT III
1988-1991, 1996-1998. Single cutaway body, three single-coil pickups.

1988-1991	1st version, Leo era, 150 made	$950	$1,050
1996-1998	Post Leo era	$700	$800

ASAT Junior Limited Edition
1998-2002. Single cut semi-hollowbody, 2 single-coil pickups, short run of 250 units.

1998-2002		$900	$1,100

ASAT S-3
1998-2000. Three soap-bar single-coil pickups, limited production.

1998-2000		$700	$900

ASAT Semi-Hollow
1997-present. Semi-hollow version of ASAT Special.

1997-2003		$700	$800

ASAT Special
1992-present. Like ASAT, but with two larger P-90-type pickups, chrome hardware, various colors.

1992-1997	3-bolt neck	$600	$800
1997-1998	4-bolt neck	$600	$750

ASAT Special Deluxe
2001-present. No pickguard version of the Special with figured maple top.

2001-2003		$800	$850

ASAT Z-2 Limited Edition
1999. Limited edition of ten instruments, semi-hollow construction, Natural ash, tortoise bound, engraved neckplate.

1999		$950	$1,050

ASAT Z-3
1998-present. Three offset-style Z-3 high output pickups.

1998-2003		$700	$800

G&L ASAT Classic Blues Boy

G&L ASAT III

The *Vintage Guitar Price Guide* shows low to high values for items in all-original excellent condition, and, where applicable, with original case or cover.

G&L ASAT Z-3 Semi-Hollow

G&L Legacy

MODEL YEAR	FEATURES	EXC. COND. LOW	HIGH

ASAT Z-3 Semi-Hollow
1998-present. Semi-hollowbody-style, three offset-style Z-3 high output pickups.

1998-2003		$800	$900

Broadcaster
1985-1986. Solidbody, two single-coil pickups with adjustable polepieces act in humbucking mode with selector switch in the center position. Black parts and finish. Name changed to ASAT in early-1986.

1985-1986	Signed by Leo, ebony board	$1,800	$2,100
1985-1986	Signed by Leo, maple board	$1,800	$2,200

Cavalier
1983-1986. Offset double cutaway, two humbuckers, 700 made.

1983-1986		$700	$1,000

Climax
1992-1996. Offset double cut, bolt maple neck, six-on-a-side tuners, double locking vibrato.

1992-1996	Blue	$750	$850

Climax Plus
1992-1996. Two humbuckers replace single-coils of the Climax, plus one single-coil.

1992-1996		$750	$850

Climax XL
1992-1996. Two humbuckers only.

1992-1996		$750	$850

Comanche V
1988-1991. Solidbody, three Z-shaped single-coil humbucking pickups, five-position selector switch, hard rock maple neck in choice of three radii, 22-fret rosewood fingerboard, vibrato, fine tuners, Leo Fender's signature on the body.

1988-1991	Sunburst	$850	$950

Comanche VI
1990-1991. Leo Fender's signature on the body, six mini-toggles.

1990-1991		$1,000	$1,300

Comanche (reintroduced)
1998-present. Reissue with either swamp ash or alder body, bolt-on maple neck, 3 Z-coil pickups, standard or premium finish options.

1998-2003	Premium finish, flame top	$900	$1,000
1998-2003	Standard finish	$750	$850

Commemorative
1992-1997. About 350 made, Leo Fender signature on upper bass bout.

1992-1997	Sunburst	$2,000	$2,400

F-100 (Model I and II)
1980-1986. Offset double cut solidbody, 2 humbuckers. Came in a I and II model - only difference is the radius of the fingerboard.

1980-1986	Natural	$700	$900

F-100 E (Model I and II)
1980-1982. Offset double cut solidbody, 2 humbuckers, active electronics, pre-amp. Came in a I and II model - only difference is the radius of the fingerboard.

1980-1982	Natural	$700	$900

MODEL YEAR	FEATURES	EXC. COND. LOW	HIGH

G-200
1981-1982. Mahogany solidbody, maple neck, ebony fingerboard, two humbucking pickups, coil-split switches, Natural or Sunburst, 209 made.

1981-1982		$1,000	$1,300

GBL-LE (Guitars by Leo Limited Edition)
1999. Limited edition of 25, semi-hollowbody, three pickups.

1999		$1,000	$1,300

George Fullerton Signature
1995-present. Double cut solidbody, sunburst.

1995-1997	3-bolt neck	$800	$1,000
1997-2003	4-bolt neck	$700	$800

HG-1
1982-1983 Offset double cut, 1 humbucker, dot inlays.

1982-1983		$1,900	$2,100

HG-2
1982-1984. 2 humbucker HG.

1982-1984		$1,000	$1,500

Interceptor
1983-1991. Until 1986 it was sort of an X-shaped solidbody (1987-1989 was an offset double cut solidbody), either 3 single-coils, 2 humbuckers, or 1 humbucker and 2 single-coils.

1983-1985	1st X-body, about 70 made	$1,200	$1,400
1985-1986	2nd X-body, about 12 made	$1,500	$1,700
1988-1991	Double cut body	$700	$900

Invader
1984-1991, 1998-present. Double cut solidbody, two single-coil and one humbucker pickups.

1984-1991	1st version	$500	$700
1998-2003	2nd version	$800	$900

Invader Plus
1998-present. Two humbuckers and single blade pickup in the middle position.

1998-2003		$800	$900

Invader XL
1998-present. Two humbuckers.

1998-2003		$750	$850

John Jorgenson Signature Model ASAT
1995. About 190 made, Silver Metalflake finish.

1995		$1,000	$1,500

Legacy
1992-present. Classic double cut configuration, various colors.

1992-1994	3-bolt neck, Duncan SSLs	$650	$800
1995-1997	3-bolt neck, Alnicos	$600	$750
1997-2003	4-bolt neck, Alnicos	$550	$700

Legacy 2HB
2001-present. Two humbucker pickups.

2001-2003		$550	$700

Legacy Deluxe
2001-present. No pickguard, figured maple top.

2001-2003		$700	$850

MODEL YEAR	FEATURES	EXC. COND. LOW	HIGH

Legacy HB
2001-present. One humbucker pickup at bridge position plus 2 single-coil pickups.

2001-2003		$600	$750

Legacy Special
1993-present. Legacy with 3 humbuckers, various colors.

1993-1997	3-bolt neck	$600	$700
1998-2003	4-bolt neck	$550	$600

Nighthawk
1983. Offset double cut solidbody, 3 single-coil pickups, 269 made. Name changed to Skyhawk in 1984.

1983	Sunburst	$650	$950

Rampage
1984-1991. Offset double cut solidbody, hard rock maple neck, ebony fingerboard, one bridge-position humbucker pickup.

1984-1991	Sunburst	$600	$800

Rampage (reissue)
2000. Limited Edition of 70 units, supplied with gig bag and not hard case, Ivory finish.

2000	.	$500	$700

S-500
1982-present. Double cut mahogany or ash solidbody, maple neck, ebony or maple fingerboard, three single-coil pickups, vibrato.

1982-1987	No mini-toggle	$600	$800
1988-1991	Mini-toggle, Leo's signature on body	$800	$1,000
1992-1997	3-bolt neck	$650	$800
1997-2003	4-bolt neck	$600	$700

S-500 Deluxe
2001-present. Deluxe Series features, including no pickguard and flamed maple top.

2001-2003	Natural	$800	$900

SC-1
1982-1983. Offset double cut solidbody, one single-coil pickup, tremolo, 250 made.

1982-1983	Sunburst	$600	$800

SC-2
1982-1983. Offset double cut solidbody, 2 MFD "soapbar" pickups, about 600 made.

1982-1983	Mustang-style body	$500	$700
1983	Strat-style body	$500	$600

SC-3
1982-1991. Offset double cut solidbody, 3 single-coil pickups, tremolo.

1982-1983	Mustang-style body	$550	$750
1984-1987	Strat-style body, no pickguard	$500	$700
1988-1991	Strat-style body with pickguard	$500	$600

Skyhawk
1984-1987. Renamed from Nighthawk. Offset double cut solidbody, 3 single-coil pickups with five-position switch, signature on headstock '84-'87, then on body '88-'91.

1984-1987	Signature on headstock	$650	$750
1988-1991	Signature on body	$750	$850

Superhawk
1984-1987. Offset double cut solidbody, hard rock maple neck, ebony fingerboard, G&L or Kahler tremolos, 2 humbucker pickups, signature on the headstock.

1984-1987		$550	$750

Will Ray Signature Model
2002-present. Will Ray signature on headstock, three Z-coil pickups, Hipshot B-Bender.

2002-2003		$900	$1,000

G.L. Stiles

1960-1994. Built by Gilbert Lee Stiles (b. October 2, 1914, Independence, WV; d. 1994) primarily in the Miami, Florida area. First solidbody, including pickups and all hardware, built by hand in his garage. Stiles favored scrolls, fancy carving and walnut fingerboards. His later instruments were considerably more fancy and refined. He moved to Hialeah, Florida by '63 and began making acoustic guitars and other instruments. His acoustics featured double stressed (bent) backs for increased tension. He later taught for the Augusta Heritage Program and Davis and Elkins College in Elkins, West Virginia. Only his solidbodies had consecutive serial numbers. Stiles made approximately 1000 solidbodies and 500 acoustics.

Gabriel's Guitar Workshop

1979-present. Production/custom steel- and nylon-stringed guitars built by luthier Gabriel Ochoteco in Germany until '84 and in Brisbane Australia since.

Gagnon

1998-present. Luthier Bill Gagnon builds his premium and presentation grade, production/custom, archtop guitars in Beaverton, Oregon.

Galanti

Ca.1962-ca.1967. Electric guitars offered by the longtime Italian accordion maker. They may have also offered acoustics.

Galiano

New Yorkers Antonio Cerrito and Raphael Ciani offered guitars under the Galiano brand during the early part of the last century. They used the brand both on guitars built by them and others, including The Oscar Schmidt Company.

Gallagher

1965-present. Professional and premium grade, production/custom, flat-top guitars built in Wartrace, Tennessee. J. W. Gallagher started building Shelby brand guitars in the Slingerland Drum factory in Shelbyville, Tennessee in 1963. In '65 he and his son Don made the first Gallagher guitar, the G-50. Doc Watson began using Gallagher guitars in 1968. In '76, Don assumed operation of the business when J. W. semi-retired. J. W. died in '79.

G&L Legacy Special

*Gallagher
Doc Watson*

GUITARS

Ganz Babe

Garrison G-25

MODEL YEAR	FEATURES	EXC. COND. LOW	HIGH
71 Special			
1970-present. Indian rosewood, herringbone trim, Natural.			
1970-1979		$1,700	$1,900
A-70 Ragtime Special			
1978-present. Smaller (auditorium/00) body size, spruce top, mahogany back and sides, G logo, Natural.			
1990-1999		$1,700	$1,800
Custom 12-String			
Introduced in 1965. Mahogany, 12-fret neck, Natural.			
1965		$1,000	$1,300
Doc Watson 12-String			
1995-2000		$1,500	$1,700
Doc Watson Model			
1974-present. Spruce top, mahogany back and sides, scalloped bracing, ebony fingerboard, herringbone trim, Natural.			
1974-1999		$1,500	$1,700
Doc Watson Model (cutaway)			
1975-present. Spruce top, mahogany back and sides, scalloped bracing, ebony fingerboard, herringbone trim, Natural.			
1985		$1,600	$1,800
G-45			
1970-present. Acoustic flat-top, mahogany back and sides, spruce top, rosewood fingerboard, Natural.			
1980		$900	$1,100
G-70			
1978-present. Flat-top, rosewood back and sides, herringbone trim on top and soundhole, mother-of-pearl diamond fingerboard inlays, bound headstock, natural.			
1978-1998		$1,300	$1,600

Gallagher, Kevin

1996. Kevin Gallagher, luthier, changed name brand to Omega to avoid confusion with J.W. Gallagher. See Omega listing.

Galloup Guitars

1994-present. Luthier Bryan Galloup builds his professional and premium grade, production/custom flat-tops in Big Rapids, Michigan. He also operates the Galloup School of Lutherie and The Guitar Hospital repair and restoration business.

Gamble & O'Toole

1978-present. Premium grade, custom classical and steel string guitars built by luthier Arnie Gamble in Sacramento, California, with design input and inlay work from his wife Erin O'Toole.

Ganz Guitars

1995-present. Luthier Steve Ganz builds his professional grade, production/custom classical guitars in Bellingham, Washington.

Garcia

Made by luthier Federico Garcia in Spain until late-1960s or very early-'70s when production moved to Japan.

MODEL YEAR	FEATURES	EXC. COND. LOW	HIGH
Classical (mahogany)			
1960s. Made in Spain, mid-level, solid mahogany back and sides, solid spruce top.			
1960s		$225	$275
Classical (rosewood)			
1960s. Made in Spain, mid-level, solid rosewood back and sides, solid spruce top.			
1960s		$450	$500
Classical (walnut/pine)			
1970s. Made in Japan, mid-level, walnut back and sides, Spanish pine top.			
1970s		$125	$150
Classical (walnut/spruce)			
1960s. Made in Spain, mid-level, walnut back and sides, solid spruce top.			
1960s		$400	$450

Garrison

2000-present. Intermediate and professional grade, production, acoustic and acoustic/electric guitars designed by luthier Chris Griffiths using the "Griffiths Active Bracing System" (a single integrated glass-fiber bracing system inside a solid wood body). He started Griffiths Guitar Works in 1993 in St. John's, Newfoundland, and introduced Garrison guitars in 2000.

MODEL YEAR	FEATURES	EXC. COND. LOW	HIGH
G-20			
2000-present. D-style, solid western red cedar top, solid birch back and sides.			
2000-2002		$300	$325
G-30			
2000-present. D-style, solid spruce top, solid birch back and sides, dot markers.			
2000-2002		$350	$375
G-40 CE			
2000-present. Single cut, D-size.			
2000-2002		$575	$650

Giannini

1900-present. Founded by guitar-builder Tranquill Giannini, an Italian who traveled to Brazil in 1980 and discovered the exotic woods of Brazil. This large Brazilian manufacturer located in Salto, SP, Brazil near Sao Paolo, was producing 30,000 instruments a year by 1930. Their acoustic instruments were being heavily imported into the U.S. by 1963. They added electric guitars in '60, but these weren't imported as much, if at all. Gianninis from this era used much Brazilian Rosewood. Currently Giannini offers a variety of stringed instruments.

MODEL YEAR	FEATURES	EXC. COND. LOW	HIGH
Classical			
Early-1970s. Nylon string import, small body.			
1970s		$150	$300

MODEL YEAR	FEATURES	EXC. COND. LOW	HIGH

CraViola
1970s. Kidney bean-shaped rosewood body, acoustic. Line included a classical, a steel string, and a 12-string.

1972-1974	Natural	$200	$325

CraViola 12-String
Early-1970s. Kidney'bean shaped body, 12 strings.

1972-1974		$275	$325

Gibson
1880s (1902)-present. Intermediate, professional, and premium grade, production/custom, acoustic and electric guitars made in the U.S. They also build basses, mandolins, amps, and banjos under the Gibson name. Gibson also offers instruments under the Epiphone, Kramer, Steinberger, Dobro, Tobias, Valley Arts, Slingerland (drums), Baldwin (pianos), Trace Elliot, Electar (amps), Maestro, Gibson Labs, Oberheim, and Echoplex brands.

Founded in Kalamazoo, Michigan by Orville Gibson, a musician and luthier who developed instruments with tops, sides and backs carved out of solid pieces of wood. Early instruments included mandolins, archtop guitars and harp guitars. By 1896 Gibson had opened a shop. In 1902 Gibson was bought out by a group of investors who incorporated the business as Gibson Mandolin-Guitar Manufacturing Company, Limited. The company was purchased by Chicago Musical Instrument Company (CMI) in '44. In '57 CMI also purchased the Epiphone guitar company, transferring production from Philadelphia to the Gibson plant in Kalamazoo. Gibson was purchased by Norlin in late-'69 and a new factory was opened in Nashville, Tennessee in '74. The Kalamazoo factory ceased production in '84. In '85, Gibson was sold to a group headed by Henry Juskewiscz. Gibson purchased the Flatiron Company in '87 and built a new factory in '89, moving acoustic instrument production to Bozeman, Montana.

The various models of Firebirds, Flying Vs, Les Pauls, SGs, and Super 400s are grouped together under those general headings. Custom Shop and Historic instruments are listed with their respective main model (for example, the '39 Super 400 Historical Collection model is listed with the Super 400s).

335 S Custom
1980-1981. Solidbody, 335-shaped, mahogany body, unbound rosewood 'board, 2 exposed Dirty Finger humbuckers, coil-tap, TP-6 tailpiece.

1980-1981	Sunburst	$700	$900

335 S Deluxe
1980-1982. Same as 335 S Custom but with bound ebony 'board, brass nut.

1980-1982	Cherry	$700	$900
1980-1982	Silverburst	$800	$1,100
1980-1982	Sunburst	$700	$900

335 S Standard
1980-1981. Solidbody, 335-shaped, maple body and neck, 2 exposed split-coil humbuckers, stop tailpiece, no coil-tap, unbound 'board.

1980-1981	Sunburst	$650	$750

Advanced Jumbo
1936-1940. Dreadnought, 16" wide, round shoulders, Brazilian rosewood back and sides, Sunburst. Reintroduced 1990-1997.

1936-1937		$35,000	$40,000
1938-1940		$32,000	$40,000

Advance Jumbo (reissue)
1990-1999, 2001-present. Issued as a standard production model, but soon available only as a special order for most of the '90s; currently offered as standard production. Renamed 1936 Advanced Jumbo for 1997-1998. There were also some limited-edition AJs offered during the '90s.

1990-1999		$1,600	$2,000
2001-2002	Reintroduced	$1,700	$1,900

B-15
1967-1971. Mahogany, spruce top, student model. Natural finish.

1967-1971		$450	$700

B-25
1962-1977. Flat-top, mahogany, bound body. Cherry Sunburst (Natural finish is the B-25 N).

1962-1964		$1,200	$1,500
1965-1966		$1,000	$1,300
1967-1968		$800	$1,100
1969-1977		$700	$900

B-25 3/4
1962-1968. Short-scale version, flat-top, mahogany body. Cherry Sunburst (Natural finish is the B-25 3/4 N).

1962-1964		$800	$1,100
1965-1966		$700	$900
1967-1968		$600	$800

B-25 N
1962-1977. Flat-top, mahogany, bound body. Natural (Cherry Sunburst finish is the B-25).

1962-1964		$1,200	$1,500
1965-1966		$900	$1,100
1967-1968		$700	$1,000
1969-1977		$600	$900

B-25 N 3/4
1966-1968. Short-scale version, flat-top, mahogany body. Natural (Cherry Sunburst finish is the B-25 3/4).

1966-1968		$600	$900

B-25-12
1962-1970. Flat-top 12-string version, mahogany, bound body. Cherry Sunburst (Natural finish is the B-25-12 N).

1962-1964		$900	$1,100
1965-1966		$700	$900
1967-1968		$600	$800
1969-1970		$500	$700

Giannini CraViola

Gibson Advanced Jumbo reissue

GUITARS

1965 Gibson B-25-12 N

1957 Gibson Byrdland

MODEL YEAR	FEATURES	EXC. COND. LOW	HIGH
B-25-12 N			

1962-1977. Flat-top 12-string version, mahogany, bound body. Natural (Cherry Sunburst is the B-25-12).

MODEL YEAR	FEATURES	LOW	HIGH
1962-1964		$1,000	$1,200
1965-1966		$800	$1,000
1967-1968		$700	$900
1969-1977		$600	$800
B-45-12			

1961-1979. Flat-top 12-string, mahogany, round shoulders for 1961, square after. Sunburst (Natural finish is the B-45-12 N).

1961-1962	Round shoulders	$2,000	$2,500
1962-1964	Square shoulders	$1,800	$2,300
1965-1969	Non-pin bridge introduced	$1,400	$1,900
1970-1979	Pin bridge reintroduced	$1,000	$1,400
B-45-12 N			

1962-1979. Flat-top 12-string, mahogany. Natural (Cherry Sunburst finish is the B-45-12).

1962-1964	Square shoulders	$1,800	$2,300
1965-1969	Non-pin bridge introduced	$1,400	$1,900
1970-1979	Pin bridge reintroduced	$1,000	$1,400
B-45-12 Limited Edition			

1991-1992. Limited edition reissue with rosewood back and sides, natural.

1991-1992		$1,250	$1,350
B.B. King Custom			

1980-1988. Lucille on peghead, two pickups, multi-bound, gold-plated parts, Vari-tone, Cherry or Ebony. Renamed B.B. King Lucille in 1988.

1980-1988		$1,500	$1,600
B.B. King Lucille			

1988-present. Introduced as B.B. King Custom, renamed B.B. King Lucille. Lucille on peghead, two pickups, multi-bound, gold-plated parts, Vari-tone, Cherry or Ebony.

1988-2001		$1,500	$1,600
B.B. King Standard			

1980-1985. Like B.B. King Custom, but with stereo electronics and chrome-plated parts, Cherry or Ebony.

1980-1985		$1,400	$1,500
Barney Kessel Custom			

1961-1973. Double cut archtop, 2 humbuckers, gold hardware, cherry sunburst.

1961-1964		$3,200	$3,900
1965-1966		$3,100	$3,700
1967-1969		$2,900	$3,200
1970-1973		$2,500	$3,000
Barney Kessel Regular			

1961-1974. Double cut archtop, 2 humbuckers, nickel hardware, cherry sunburst.

1961-1964		$2,900	$3,200
1965-1966		$2,700	$3,000
1967-1969		$2,500	$2,900
1970-1973		$2,200	$2,700

MODEL YEAR	FEATURES	EXC. COND. LOW	HIGH
Blue Ridge			

1968-1979, 1989-1990. Flat-top, dreadnought, laminated rosewood back and sides. Natural finish. Reintroduced for 1989-1990.

1968-1969		$1,100	$1,300
1970-1971		$1,000	$1,200
1972-1979		$950	$1,100
1989-1990		$800	$1,000
Blue Ridge 12			

1970-1978. Flat-top, 12 strings, laminated rosewood back and sides. Natural finish.

1972-1978		$700	$900
Blueshawk			

1996-present. Small Les Paul single cutaway-type body with F-holes, two single-coil hum cancelling Blues 90 pickups, six-way Varitone rotary dial.

1996-2002		$450	$650
Byrdland			

1955-1992. Thinline archtop, single cutaway (rounded until late-1960, pointed 1960-late-1969, rounded after 1969, rounded or pointed 1998-present), two pickups. Now part of the Historic Collection.

1956-1957	Natural, P-90s	$9,500	$10,000
1956-1957	Sunburst, P-90s	$7,500	$8,000
1958-1959	Natural, PAFs	$8,800	$11,000
1958-1959	Sunburst, PAFs	$7,800	$9,000
1960-1962	Natural, PAFs	$8,300	$10,000
1960-1962	Sunburst, PAFs	$7,300	$8,000
1963-1964	Natural, Pat #	$7,300	$8,000
1963-1964	Sunburst, Pat #	$6,800	$7,500
1965-1969	Natural	$5,300	$6,300
1965-1969	Sunburst	$4,300	$5,500
1970-1979	Natural	$3,000	$4,800
1970-1979	Various other colors	$3,000	$4,300
1980-1992	Various colors	$3,800	$4,500
Byrdland Historic Collection			

Various colors.

1993-2002	Natural	$4,100	$4,500
1993-2002	Sunburst	$3,600	$3,900
1993-2002	Wine Red	$3,000	$3,200
C-0 Classical			

1962-1971. Spruce top, mahogany back and sides, bound top. Natural.

1962-1971		$250	$375
C-1 Classical			

1957-1971. Spruce top, mahogany back and sides, bound body. Natural.

1957-1971		$325	$425
C-1 E Classical Electric			

1960-1967. C-1 with ceramic bridge pickup, catalog notes special matched amplifier that filters out fingering noises.

1960-1967		$425	$550
C-1 S Petite Classical			

1961-1966. Petite 13 1/4" body, natural spruce top, mahogany back and sides.

1961-1966		$300	$400
C-2 Classical			

1960-1971. Maple back and sides, bound body. Natural.

1960-1971		$500	$700

MODEL YEAR	FEATURES	EXC. COND. LOW	HIGH

C-4 Classical
1962-1968. Maple back and sides. Natural.
| 1962-1968 | | $725 | $900 |

C-6 Classical
1958-1971. Rosewood back and sides, Gold hardware, Natural.
| 1958-1971 | | $800 | $1,000 |

C-8 Classical
1962-1969. Rosewood back and sides. Natural.
| 1962-1969 | | $1,000 | $1,300 |

CF-100
1950-1958. Flat-top, pointed cutaway, mahogany back and sides, bound body. Sunburst finish.
| 1950-1958 | | $2,300 | $2,600 |

CF-100E
1951-1958. CF-100 with a single-coil pickup.
| 1950-1958 | | $2,500 | $3,500 |

Challenger I
1983-1985. Single cutaway Les Paul-shaped solidbody, one humbucker pickup, bolt-on maple neck with rosewood fingerboard and dot markers. Silver finish standard.
| 1983-1985 | | $400 | $425 |

Challenger II
1983-1985. Single cutaway Les Paul-shaped solidbody, two humbucker pickups, bolt-on maple neck with rosewood fingerboard and dot markers. Various colors.
| 1983-1985 | | $400 | $450 |

Chet Atkins CE
1981-1995. CE stands for 'Classical Electric'. Single cutaway, multi-bound body, rosewood board with standard width nut, Gold hardware, various colors. In 1995, the Atkins CE and CEC were consolidated into one model, the Chet Atkins CE/CEC, with an ebony fingerboard with a standard (CE) and classical (CEC) nut.
| 1981-1995 | | $900 | $1,000 |

Chet Atkins CEC
1981-1995. Same as CE but with ebony board and 2" classical width nut, Black or Natural. In 1995, the Atkins CE and CEC were consolidated into one model, the Chet Atkins CE/CEC, with an ebony fingerboard with a standard (CE) and classical (CEC) nut.
| 1981-1995 | | $1,100 | $1,300 |

Chet Atkins Country Gentleman
1986-present. Thinline archtop, single rounded cutaway, two humbuckers, multi-bound, Gold hardware, Bigsby. Brown or Red Wine.
| 1986-1995 | | $1,700 | $2,200 |

Chet Atkins SST
1987-present. Steel string acoustic/electric solidbody, single cutaway, bridge transducer pickup, active bass and treble controls, gold hardware.
| 1986-2001 | | $1,000 | $1,200 |

Chet Atkins SST-12
1990-1994. Similar to 6-string model, mahogany/spruce body, preamp circuit controls single transducer pickup. Natural or Ebony finish.
| 1990-1994 | | $1,500 | $1,700 |

Chet Atkins Tennessean
1990-present. Single rounded cutaway archtop, two humbuckers, F-holes, bound body.
| 1990-1999 | | $1,300 | $1,500 |

Chicago 35
1994-1995. Flat-top dreadnought, round shoulders, mahogany back and sides, prewar script logo.
| 1994-1995 | Natural,
factory electronics | $950 | $1,050 |

Citation
1969-1971. 17" full-depth body, single cut archtop, 1 or 2 floating pickups, fancy inlay, natural or sunburst. Only 8 shipped for '69-'71. Reissued the first time '79-'83 and as part of the Historic Collection in '93.
| 1969-1971 | | $11,000 | $15,000 |

Citation (1st reissue)
1979-1983. Reissue of 1969-'71 model. Reintroduced in '93 as part of Gibson's Historic Collection.
| 1979-1983 | | $11,000 | $15,000 |

Citation (2nd reissue)
1993-present. Limited production via Gibson's Historic Collection, natural or sunburst.
| 1994-1999 | Natural | $11,000 | $14,000 |
| 1994-1999 | Sunburst | $11,000 | $14,000 |

Corvus I
1982-1984. Odd-shaped solidbody with offset V-type cut, bolt maple neck, rosewood 'board, 1 humbucker. Standard finish was Silver Gloss, but others available at an additional cost.
| 1982-1984 | | $300 | $350 |

Corvus II
1982-1984. Same as Corvus I, but with 2 humbuckers, 2 volume controls, 1 master tone control.
| 1982-1984 | | $400 | $450 |

Corvus III
1982-1984. Same as Corvus I, but with 3 single-coil pickups, master volume and tone control, 5-way switch.
| 1982-1984 | | $550 | $600 |

Country-Western
(See SJN)

Crest Gold
1969-1971. Double cut thinline archtop, Brazilian rosewood body, 2 mini-humbuckers, bound top and headstock, bound F-holes, gold-plated parts.
| 1969-1971 | | $2,500 | $3,000 |

Crest Silver
1969-1972. Double cutaway thinline archtop, Brazilian rosewood body, two mini-humbuckers, bound top and headstock, bound F-holes, silver-plated parts.
| 1969-1972 | | $2,000 | $2,500 |

Dove
1962-1994. Flat-top acoustic, maple back and sides, square shoulders.
1962-1964	Sunburst	$3,700	$4,500
1963-1964	Natural	$4,000	$5,000
1965	Natural	$3,700	$4,500
1965	Sunburst	$3,300	$4,200
1966	Natural	$3,200	$4,100
1966	Sunburst	$2,900	$3,800
1967	Natural	$2,500	$3,500

1986 Gibson Corvus

Gibson Dove

GUITARS

1960s Gibson EMS-1235

1956 Gibson ES-5

MODEL YEAR	FEATURES	EXC. COND. LOW	HIGH
1967	Sunburst	$2,400	$3,300
1968	Natural	$2,400	$3,100
1968	Sunburst	$2,200	$2,800
1969-1970	Natural	$2,000	$2,500
1969-1970	Sunburst	$1,900	$2,400
1971-1984	Natural	$1,600	$2,200
1971-1984	Sunburst	$1,500	$2,100
1984-1989	Sunburst, black, natural	$1,300	$1,600
1990-1999	Natural	$1,200	$1,400
1990-1999	Sunburst	$1,200	$1,400

Dove "Dove In Flight" (Custom Shop)

1996-1998		$2,500	$2,900

Dove Commemorative
1994-1996. Natural.

1994-1996		$1,500	$2,000

EAS Deluxe
1992-1994. Single cut flat-top acoustic/electric, solid flamed maple top, three-band EQ.

1992-1994	Vintage Cherry Sunburst	$825	$950

EBS(F)-1250 Double Bass
1962-1970. Double cutaway SG-type solidbody, doubleneck with bass and six-string. Originally introduced as the EBSF-1250 because of a built-in fuzztone, which was later deleted. Only 22 made.

1962-1964		$7,000	$9,000
1965-1966		$5,000	$7,000
1967-1969		$4,500	$6,000
1970		$3,500	$5,000

EDS-1275 Double 12
1958-1968, 1977-1990. Double cut doubleneck with one 12- and one six-string. Thinline hollowbody until late-'62, SG-style solidbody '62 on.

1958-1959	Black or Cherry	$15,000	$19,000
1958-1959	Sunburst	$12,000	$14,000
1958-1959	White	$16,000	$20,000
1960-1962	Black or Cherry	$14,000	$18,000
1960-1962	Sunburst	$11,000	$13,000
1960-1962	White	$15,000	$19,000
1968	Black or Cherry	$5,000	$7,000
1968	Jimmy Page exact specs	$7,000	$12,000
1968	White	$6,000	$8,000
1977-1979	Sunburst, Walnut, or White	$2,200	$3,200
1980-1991	Sunburst, Walnut, or White	$2,000	$2,400
1995-2000	Various colors	$1,900	$2,200

EDS-1275 Double 12 (Historic Collection)
1991-1994. Historic Collection reissue.

1991-1994	White	$1,900	$2,300

EDS-1275 Double 12 Centennial
1994. Guitar of the Month (May), Gold medallion on back of headstock, Gold hardware.

1994	Cherry	$1,900	$2,300

EMS-1235 Double Mandolin
1958-1968. Double cutaway, doubleneck with one regular six-string and one short six-string (the mandolin neck). Thinline hollowbody until late-1962, SG-style solidbody 1962-1968. Black, Sunburst or

MODEL YEAR	FEATURES	EXC. COND. LOW	HIGH
White. Total of 61 shipped.			
1958-1961		$10,000	$15,500
1962-1964		$5,000	$7,500
1965-1968		$3,000	$4,500

ES-5
1949-1955. Single cutaway archtop, three P-90 pickups. Renamed ES-5 Switchmaster in 1955.

1949-1955	Natural	$7,000	$8,000
1949-1955	Sunburst	$6,500	$7,500

ES-5 Switchmaster
1956-1962. Renamed from ES-5. Single cutaway (rounded until late-'60, pointed after) archtop, 3 P-90s until end of '57, humbuckers after, switchmaster control. The PAF pickups in this model are worth as much as the rest of the guitar. We have listed a non-original '58 with replaced pickups to demonstrate how value is reduced when the original PAFs are removed.

1956-1957	Natural, P-90s	$7,200	$8,200
1956-1957	Sunburst, P-90s	$6,000	$7,000
1957-1960	Natural, humbuckers	$10,200	$11,200
1957-1960	Sunburst, humbuckers	$9,000	$10,000
1957-1960	Sunburst, non-original pickups	$4,500	$5,500
1960-1962	Pointed Florentine cutaway	$9,000	$10,000

ES-5/ES-5 Switchmaster Custom Shop Historic
1995-2002.

1995-2002	ES-5, P-90s	$2,900	$3,000
1995-2002	Switchmaster, humbuckers	$2,900	$3,000

ES-100
1938-1941. Archtop, one pickup, bound body. Sunburst. Renamed ES-125 in 1941.

1938-1941		$900	$1,200

ES-120 T
1962-1970. Archtop, thinline, one F-hole, bound body, one pickup. Sunburst.

1962-1966		$850	$950
1967-1970		$550	$750

ES-125
1941-1943, 1946-1970. Archtop, non-cutaway, one pickup. Sunburst. Renamed from ES-100.

1941-1943	Blade pickup	$1,100	$1,300
1946-1950	1st non-adj., P-90s	$1,100	$1,400
1951-1964	Adj. P-90s with poles	$1,000	$1,200

ES-125 C
1966-1970. Wide body archtop, single pointed cutaway, 1 pickup, sunburst.

1966-1970		$900	$1,200

ES-125 CD
1966-1970. Wide body archtop, single cutaway, two pickups. Sunburst.

1966-1970		$1,400	$1,600

ES-125 D
1957. Limited production (not mentioned in catalog), two pickup version of thick body ES-125. Sunburst.

1957		$1,300	$1,500

MODEL YEAR FEATURES	EXC. COND. LOW	HIGH

ES-125 T
1956-1969. Archtop thinline, non-cutaway, one pickup, bound body. Sunburst.

| 1956-1964 | $1,000 | $1,600 |
| 1965-1969 | $900 | $1,500 |

ES-125 T 3/4
1957-1970. Archtop thinline, short-scale, non-cutaway, one pickup. Sunburst.

| 1957-1964 | $700 | $900 |
| 1965-1970 | $500 | $700 |

ES-125 TD
1957-1963. Archtop thinline, non-cutaway, two pickups. Sunburst.

| 1957-1963 | $1,250 | $1,500 |

ES-125 TC
1960-1970. Archtop thinline, single pointed cutaway, bound body, one P-90 pickup. Sunburst.

| 1960-1964 | $1,500 | $1,600 |
| 1965-1970 | $1,400 | $1,600 |

ES-125 TDC or ES-125 TCD
1960-1971. Archtop thinline, single pointed cutaway, two P-90 pickups. Sunburst.

1960-1964	$1,500	$2,100
1965-1966	$1,300	$2,000
1966-1971	$1,100	$2,000

ES-130
1954-1956. Archtop, non-cutaway, one pickup, bound body. Sunburst. Renamed ES-135 in 1956.

| 1954-1956 | $1,100 | $1,500 |

ES-135
1956-1958. Renamed from ES-130, non-cut archtop, 1 pickup, sunburst. Name reused on a thin body in the 1990s.

| 1956-1958 | $1,100 | $1,500 |

ES-135 (thinline)
1991-present. Single cut archtop thinline, laminated maple body, available with 2 humbuckers or 2 P-90s, chrome or gold hardware, sunburst.

| 1991-2002 | $900 | $1,200 |

ES-140 (3/4)
1950-1956. Archtop, single cutaway, one pickup, bound body, short-scale.

| 1950-1956 | Natural option | $1,800 | $2,500 |
| 1950-1956 | Sunburst | $1,300 | $2,000 |

ES-140 3/4 T
1957-1968. Archtop thinline, single cutaway, bound body, one pickup, short-scale. Sunburst.

| 1957-1968 | $1,300 | $2,000 |

ES-150
1936-1942, 1946-1956. Historically important archtop, non-cutaway, bound body, Charlie Christian bar pickup from 1936-1939, various metal covered pickups starting in 1940. Sunburst.

1936-1939	Charlie Christian pickup	$4,000	$5,000
1940-1942	Metal covered pickup	$3,000	$4,000
1946-1956	P-90 pickup	$1,500	$2,000

ES-150 DC
1969-1975. Archtop, double rounded cutaway, two humbuckers, multi-bound.

| 1969-1975 | Cherry or Walnut | $1,900 | $2,100 |
| 1969-1975 | Natural | $2,100 | $2,500 |

ES-165 Herb Ellis Model
1991-present. Single pointed cutaway hollowbody, one humbucker, gold hardware. Cherry, Ebony or Sunburst.

| 1991-1995 | $1,300 | $1,700 |

ES-175
1949-1971. Archtop, single pointed cutaway, one pickup (P-90 from 1949-early-1957, humbucker early-1957-1971), multi-bound.

1949-1951	Natural	$4,000	$4,800
1949-1951	Sunburst	$3,400	$4,400
1952-1956	Natural, P-90	$3,800	$4,600
1952-1956	Sunburst, P-90	$3,500	$3,900
1957-1959	Natural, humbucker	$5,500	$6,500
1957-1959	Sunburst, humbucker	$5,000	$5,500
1960	Sunburst	$4,800	$5,200
1961	Sunburst	$4,600	$5,000
1962	Sunburst	$4,200	$4,700
1963	Sunburst	$4,000	$4,500
1964	Sunburst	$3,700	$4,300
1965	Sunburst	$3,400	$4,100
1966	Natural	$3,200	$3,900
1966	Sunburst	$3,100	$3,700
1967-1969	Various colors	$3,100	$3,500
1970-1971	Various colors	$2,000	$2,800

ES-175 D
1951-present. Archtop, single cutaway, two pickups (P-90s from 1953-early-1957, humbuckers early-1957 on). Humbucker pickups were converted from PAF-sticks to Pat. No.-stickers in 1962. Different models were converted at different times. An ES-175 model, made during the transitional time, with PAFs, will fetch more. In some of the electric-archtop models, the transition period may have been later than 1962. Cataloged as the ES-175 Reissue since '91.

1952-1956	Natural	$5,500	$6,500
1952-1956	Sunburst	$4,500	$5,500
1957-1959	Natural, humbuckers	$7,500	$8,500
1957-1959	Sunburst, humbuckers	$7,000	$7,500
1960	Natural	$6,700	$7,700
1960	Sunburst	$6,300	$7,200
1961	Natural	$6,400	$7,400
1961	Sunburst	$6,000	$7,000
1962	Natural	$5,500	$6,500
1962	Sunburst	$5,000	$6,000
1963	Natural	$5,000	$6,000
1963	Sunburst	$4,500	$5,500
1964	Natural	$4,500	$5,500
1964	Sunburst	$4,000	$5,000
1965	Natural	$4,000	$5,000
1965	Sunburst	$3,600	$4,500
1965	Sunburst, Bigsby	$3,500	$4,000

Gibson ES-125 T

1958 Gibson ES-175

GUITARS

Gibson ES-225 TDN

1968 Gibson ES-330

MODEL YEAR	FEATURES	EXC. COND. LOW	HIGH
1966	Natural	$3,300	$4,100
1966	Sunburst	$3,200	$3,900
1967-1969	Various colors	$3,200	$3,700
1970-1972	Various colors	$2,200	$3,000
1973-1979	Various colors	$1,800	$2,400
1980-1989	Various colors	$1,600	$2,200
1990-1997	Various colors	$1,600	$2,000
1998-1999	Various colors, flamed top	$1,800	$2,200
2000-2003	Various colors	$2,000	$2,500

ES-175 CC

1978-1979. Archtop, single cutaway, one Charlie Christian pickup. Sunburst or Walnut.

1978-1979		$2,200	$2,500

ES-175 T

1976-1980. Archtop thinline, single pointed cutaway, two humbuckers. Various colors.

1976-1980		$2,200	$2,400

ES-225 T

1955-1959. Thinline, single pointed cutaway, one P-90 pickup, bound body and neck.

1955-1959	Natural	$1,700	$2,000
1955-1959	Sunburst	$1,500	$1,800

ES-225 TD

1956-1959. Thinline, single cutaway, two P-90s, bound body and neck.

1956-1959	Natural	$1,900	$2,200
1956-1959	Sunburst	$1,700	$2,000

ES-250

1939-1940. Archtop, carved top, special Christian pickup, multi-bound, high-end appointments.

1939-1940	Natural, Christian pickup	$18,000	$20,000
1939-1940	Sunburst, Christian pickup	$8,000	$10,000

ES-295

1952-1958. Single pointed cutaway archtop, 2 pickups (P-90s from 1952-late-1958, humbuckers after), gold finish, gold-plated hardware.

1952-1957	P-90 pickups	$6,000	$7,000
1957-1958	Humbuckers	$12,000	$17,000

ES-295 (reissue)

1990-1993. Reissue of ES-295, gold finish, 2 P-90 pickups, Bigsby.

1990-1993		$2,300	$2,500

ES-295 '52 Historic Collection

1993-2000. Higher end reissue of 1952 ES-295. Antique Gold finish, 2 P-90 pickups, Bigsby.

1994-1995		$2,400	$2,600

ES-300

1940-1942, 1945-1953. Archtop, non-cutaway, F-holes, had four pickup configurations during its run. Sunburst.

1940-1942	One pickup	$2,600	$3,600
1945-1948	One pickup	$2,400	$3,000
1949-1953	Two pickups	$2,400	$3,000

ES-320 TD

1971-1974. Thinline archtop, double cutaway, two single-coil pickups, bound body. Cherry, Natural, or Walnut finish.

1971-1974		$950	$1,100

ES-325 TD

1972-1978. Thinline archtop, double cutaway, two mini-humbuckers, one F-hole, bound body. Cherry or Walnut.

1972-1978		$1,000	$1,200

ES-330 T (single pickup)

1959-1963. Double rounded cutaway, thinline, 1 pickup, bound body and neck. In the '60s came with either an original semi-hard case (better than chip board) or a hardshell case. Prices quoted are for hardshell case; approximately $100 should be deducted for the semi-hard case.

1959-1961	Natural	$3,000	$4,000
1959-1961	Sunburst	$2,500	$3,000
1962-1963	Cherry or Sunburst	$2,100	$2,500

ES-330 TD (two pickups)

1959-1972. Double rounded cutaway, thinline, 2 pickups, bound body and neck. In the '60s came with either an original semi-hard case (better than chip board) or a hardshell case. Prices noted for the hardshell case; approximately $100 should be deducted for the semi-hard case.

1959-1960	Natural	$3,500	$4,500
1959-1960	Sunburst	$3,000	$3,500
1961	Cherry or Sunburst	$3,000	$3,500
1962-1964	Cherry or Sunburst	$2,700	$3,300
1965-1969	Various colors	$2,500	$3,300
1969-1972	Various colors, long neck	$2,200	$3,000

ES-335 Studio

1986-1991. No F-holes, two Dirty Fingers humbucking pickups, bound body. Cherry or Ebony.

1986-1991		$1,300	$1,500

ES-335 TD

1958-1981. The original design ES-335 has dot fingerboard inlays and a stop tailpiece. In mid-1962, block inlays replaced the dots. In late-'64, the stop tailpiece was replaced with a trapeze tailpiece. The ES-335 TD was replaced by the ES-335 DOT in '81.

1958	Natural, unbound neck	$35,000	$50,000
1958	Natural, unbound neck, Bigsby	$25,000	$35,000
1958	Sunburst, bound neck	$25,000	$30,000
1958	Sunburst, bound neck, Bigsby	$17,000	$25,000
1958	Sunburst, unbound neck	$26,000	$31,000
1958	Sunburst, unbound neck, Bigsby	$18,000	$27,000
1959	Natural, bound neck	$35,000	$50,000
1959	Natural, bound neck, Bigsby	$25,000	$35,000
1959	Sunburst	$25,000	$30,000
1959	Sunburst, factory Bigsby	$17,000	$25,000
1960	Cherry, factory Bigsby	$14,000	$16,000

MODEL YEAR	FEATURES	EXC. COND. LOW	HIGH
1960	Cherry, factory stop tail	$19,000	$22,000
1960	Natural	$30,000	$40,000
1960	Natural, factory Bigsby	$23,000	$27,000
1960	Sunburst, factory Bigsby	$14,000	$16,000
1960	Sunburst, factory stop tail	$19,000	$22,000
1961	Cherry, factory Bigsby	$9,000	$12,000
1961	Cherry, factory stop tail	$14,000	$18,000
1961	Sunburst, factory Bigsby	$9,000	$12,000
1961	Sunburst, factory stop tail	$15,000	$19,000
1962	Cherry, blocks, PAFs	$10,000	$15,000
1962	Cherry, blocks, pat. Pickups	$9,000	$11,000
1962	Cherry, dots, PAFs	$11,000	$16,000
1962	Cherry, dots, pat. Pickups	$10,000	$12,000
1962	Sunburst, blocks, PAFs	$11,000	$16,000
1962	Sunburst, blocks, pat. Pickups	$10,000	$12,000
1962	Sunburst, dots, PAFs	$12,000	$17,000
1962	Sunburst, dots, pat. Pickups	$11,000	$13,000
1963	Cherry	$7,000	$11,000
1963	Sunburst	$8,000	$12,000
1963	Sunburst, factory Bigsby	$5,500	$7,500
1964	Cherry	$7,000	$11,000
1964	Cherry, factory Bigsby	$5,500	$7,500
1964	Cherry, with Maestro	$5,500	$7,500
1964	Sunburst	$8,000	$12,000
1964	Sunburst, factory bigsby	$5,500	$7,500
1964	Sunburst, with Maestro	$5,500	$7,500
1965	Cherry, trapeze tailpiece	$4,500	$5,500
1965	Cherry, with Maestro	$4,500	$5,500
1965	Sunburst, trapeze tailpiece	$4,500	$5,500
1966	Burgundy Metallic (unfaded)	$4,500	$5,500
1966	Cherry	$3,500	$4,500
1966	Cherry, factory Bigsby	$3,500	$4,500
1966	Pelham Blue (unfaded)	$5,000	$7,000
1966	Sunburst	$3,500	$4,500
1967	Burgundy Metallic	$4,200	$4,900

MODEL YEAR	FEATURES	EXC. COND. LOW	HIGH
1967	Various colors	$3,300	$4,200
1968	Various colors	$3,200	$4,200
1969	Various colors	$2,500	$3,300
1970	Various colors	$2,400	$3,100
1971	Various colors	$2,100	$2,600
1972-1976	Various colors	$2,000	$2,500
1977-1978	Various colors, coil tap	$1,900	$2,300
1979	Various colors	$1,700	$2,100
1980-1981	Various colors	$1,200	$1,700

ES-335 TD CRR
1979. Country Rock Regular, a 335 with two stereo pickups, coil-tap. Sunburst.

1979		$1,650	$1,900

ES-335 Dot
1981-1990. Reissue of 1960 ES-335 and replaces ES-335 TD. Now called the ES-335 Reissue.

1982-1990	Black, Cherry, Sunburst, White	$1,700	$2,000
1982-1990	Natural Blond	$1,800	$2,100
1986-1990	Highly figured wood	$2,300	$2,500

ES-335 Dot CMT
1983-1985. Custom Shop ES-335 Dot with curly maple top and back, full-length center block, Gold hardware. Various colors.

1983-1985		$2,000	$2,500

ES-335 Dot Reissue
1991-present. Continuation of the ES-335 DOT and TD. A block inlay version, called the ES-335 Block, is also currently available. Black, cherry, natural blond, sunburst or white.

1991-1999	Black, Cherry, Sunburst, White	$1,600	$1,900
1991-1999	Highly figured wood	$2,000	$2,400
1991-1999	Natural Blond	$1,800	$2,000
2000-2001	Various colors	$1,600	$2,000

ES-335-12
1965-1971. 12-string version of the 335.

1965-1966	Cherry or Sunburst	$1,900	$2,300
1967-1969	Various colors	$1,600	$2,000

ES-335 '59 Historic Collection
Historical Series based upon 1959 ES-335 dot neck, figured maple top, nickel hardware, replica Orange label, cherry.

1998		$2,300	$2,600

ES-335 '63 Historic Collection
Historical Series based upon 1962 ES-335 with small block markers, maple top, nickel hardware, replica Orange label, cherry.

2000-2001		$2,000	$2,300

ES-335 Centennial
1994. Centennial edition, Gold medallion in headstock, diamond inlay in tailpiece, cherry.

1994		$4,000	$4,500

ES-335 Custom Shop
1980s-1990s. Gibson Custom Shop logo on the back of the headstock.

1984	White, gold hardware, 1984 only	$1,700	$1,900

GUITARS

Gibson ES-335

1960s Gibson ES-335-12

1960 Gibson ES-345TD

Gibson ES-355

MODEL YEAR	FEATURES	EXC. COND. LOW	HIGH
1994	Blue sparkle, dot neck	$2,200	$2,500

ES-335 Pro

1979-1981. Two humbucking pickups with exposed coils, bound fingerboard, cherry or sunburst.

MODEL YEAR	FEATURES	EXC. COND. LOW	HIGH
1979-1981		$1,300	$1,500

ES-335 Showcase Edition

1988. Guitar of the Month series, limited production, Transparent White/Beige finish, Black gothic-style hardware, EMG pickups.

MODEL YEAR	FEATURES	EXC. COND. LOW	HIGH
1988		$1,400	$1,500

ES-340 TD

1968-1973. The 335 with a laminated maple neck, master volume and mixer controls.

MODEL YEAR	FEATURES	EXC. COND. LOW	HIGH
1968-1969	Various colors	$2,200	$2,700
1970-1973	Various colors	$1,700	$2,200

ES-345 TD

1959-1983. The 335 with Vari-tone, stereo, 2 humbuckers, gold hardware, double parallelogram inlays, stop tailpiece 1959-1964 and 1982-1983, trapeze tailpiece 1965-1982.

MODEL YEAR	FEATURES	EXC. COND. LOW	HIGH
1959	Cherry, Bigsby	$10,000	$12,000
1959	Cherry, optional stud tail	$12,000	$14,000
1959	Natural, Bigsby	$20,000	$25,000
1959	Natural, optional stud tail	$30,000	$35,000
1959	Sunburst, Bigsby	$12,000	$14,000
1959	Sunburst, optional stud tail	$12,000	$14,000
1960	Cherry, optional stud tail	$11,000	$13,000
1960	Chrrry, Bigsby	$9,000	$11,000
1960	Natural, Bigsby	$15,000	$20,000
1960	Natural, optional stud tail	$25,000	$30,000
1960	Sunburst, Bigsby	$11,000	$13,000
1960	Sunburst, optional stud tail	$11,000	$13,000
1961	Cherry, Bigsby	$9,000	$11,000
1961	Cherry, optional stud tail	$11,000	$13,000
1961	Sunburst, Bigsby	$11,000	$13,000
1961	Sunburst, optional stud tail	$11,000	$13,000
1962-1964	Cherry, Bigsby, pat. No.	$7,000	$9,000
1962-1964	Sunburst, Bigsby, pat. No.	$7,000	$9,000
1965-1967	Various colors	$3,500	$5,500
1968	Various colors	$3,000	$4,500
1969	Various colors	$2,900	$3,600
1970	Various colors	$2,700	$3,400
1971	Various colors	$2,400	$3,100
1972-1976	Various colors	$2,200	$2,900
1977-1983	Various colors	$2,100	$2,800

MODEL YEAR	FEATURES	EXC. COND. LOW	HIGH

ES-347 TD/ES-347 S

1978-1993. A 335-style with Gold hardware, tune-o-matic bridge, two Spotlight double-coil pickups, coil-tap switch, bound body and neck. Name changed to ES-347S in 1987.

MODEL YEAR	FEATURES	EXC. COND. LOW	HIGH
1978-1986		$1,500	$2,000
1987-1993	ES-347 S	$1,500	$2,000

ES-350

1947-1956. Originally the ES-350 Premier, full body archtop, single cutaway, one P-90 pickup until end of 1948, two afterwards.

MODEL YEAR	FEATURES	EXC. COND. LOW	HIGH
1947-1956	Natural	$5,000	$6,000
1947-1956	Sunburst	$4,500	$5,500

ES-350 T

1955-1963. McCarty era, called the ES-350 TD in early-1960s. Thinline archtop, single cutaway (round 1955-1960 and 1977-1981, pointed 1961-1963), 2 P-90 pickups 1955-1956, humbuckers after, gold hardware.

MODEL YEAR	FEATURES	EXC. COND. LOW	HIGH
1956	Natural, two P-90s	$4,500	$5,400
1956	Sunburst, two P-90s	$4,000	$4,900
1957-1959	Natural, humbuckers	$6,000	$7,000
1957-1959	Sunburst, humbuckers	$5,500	$6,500
1960-1963	Natural	$5,000	$6,000
1960-1963	Sunburst	$4,500	$5,500

ES-350 T (2nd issue)

1977-1981. Norlin era, second issue of ES-350 T.

MODEL YEAR	FEATURES	EXC. COND. LOW	HIGH
1977-1981	Natural	$3,000	$3,800
1977-1981	Sunburst	$2,700	$3,500

ES-355 Centennial

1994. Custom Shop guitar of the month in June 1994, high-end custom appointments, gold-plated hardware. Sunburst.

MODEL YEAR	FEATURES	EXC. COND. LOW	HIGH
1994	Sunburst	$4,000	$4,500

ES-355 TD

1958-1970. A 335-style with large block inlays, multi-bound body and headstock, 2 humbuckers. The 355 model was standard with a Bigsby, Sideways or Maestro vibrato. Non-vibrato models were an option. The prices shown assume a vibrato tailpiece. A factory stop tailpiece was considered an advantage and will fetch more. Early examples have factory Bigsby vibratos, early '60s have sideways vibratos, and late '60s have Maestro vibratos. Cherry finish was the standard finish.

MODEL YEAR	FEATURES	EXC. COND. LOW	HIGH
1958-1962	Cherry, PAFs, stop tail	$19,000	$22,000
1958-1962	Cherry, PAFs, vibrato	$10,000	$14,000
1963-1964	Cherry, pat # pickups	$5,000	$7,000
1965	Burgundy metallic (unfaded)	$5,500	$6,500
1965	Cherry	$4,500	$5,500
1965	Sunburst	$4,500	$5,500
1966	Burgundy Metallic (unfaded)	$5,400	$6,400
1966	Cherry	$4,400	$5,400
1966	Sunburst	$4,400	$5,400

MODEL YEAR	FEATURES	EXC. COND. LOW	HIGH
1967	Burgundy Metallic (unfaded)	$5,000	$6,000
1967	Cherry	$4,000	$5,000
1967	Sunburst	$4,000	$5,000
1968-1969	Various colors	$3,500	$4,500

ES-355 TDSV

1959-1982. Stereo version of ES-335 with Vari-tone switch. A mono version was available but few were made. The 355 model was standard with a Bigsby, Sideways or Maestro vibrato. Non-vibrato models were an option. The prices shown assume a vibrato tailpiece. A factory stop tailpiece was considered an advantage and will fetch more. Early examples have factory Bigsby vibratos, early-'60s have Sideways vibratos and late-'60s have Maestro vibratos. Cherry finish was standard; Walnut became available in 1969.

1959-1960	Bigsby	$9,000	$13,000
1961-1962	Sideways, late PAFs	$7,000	$11,000
1963-1964	Maestro, pat # pickups	$6,000	$8,000
1965		$5,000	$6,000
1966		$4,500	$5,500
1967-1969	Maestro '67-'68, Bigsby '69	$4,000	$5,000
1970-1979	Bigsby	$2,500	$3,500

ES-369

1982. A 335-style with two exposed humbucker pickups, coil-tap. Sunburst.

1982		$1,300	$1,700

ES-775

1990-1993. Single cut hollowbody, 2 humbuckers, gold hardware. Ebony, natural or sunburst.

1990-1993		$2,500	$2,800

ES-Artist

1979-1985. A 335-style double cutaway thinline, semi-hollowbody, no F-holes, with two humbuckers, active electronics, Gold hardware. Ebony, Fireburst or Sunburst.

1979-1985		$1,400	$2,400

EST-150

1937-1940. Tenor version of ES-150. Renamed ETG-150 in 1940. Sunburst.

1937-1940		$2,500	$3,000

ETG-150

1940-1942, 1947-1971. Renamed from EST-150. Tenor version of ES-150, one pickup. Sunburst.

1947-1971		$1,200	$1,300

Everly Brothers

1962-1972. Jumbo flat-top, huge double pickguard, star inlays. Natural is optional in 1963 and becomes the standard color in 1968. Reintroduced as the J-180 Everly Brothers in 1986.

1962-1964	Black	$7,000	$8,000
1963	Natural option	$7,000	$8,000
1965-1967	Black	$5,000	$5,500
1968-1969	Natural replaces Black	$2,800	$3,200
1970-1972	Natural	$2,700	$3,000

Explorer

1958-1959, 1963. Some 1958s shipped in 1963. Korina body, 2 humbuckers. The Explorer market is a very specialized and very small market, with few genuine examples available and a limited number of high-end buyers. The Explorer and Flying V markets are similar in that respect. The slightest change to the original specifications can mean a significant drop in value. The narrow price ranges noted are for all original, untouched examples that have the original guitar case and a strong verifiable provenance.

1958-1959		$125,000	$160,000
1963		$100,000	$135,000

Explorer (Limited Edition Korina)

1976. Limited edition korina body replaces standard mahogany body. Natural.

1976		$2,500	$3,500

Explorer (Mahogany body)

1976-1982. Mahogany body, 2 humbucking pickups.

1976-1982		$1,400	$1,700

Explorer Korina

1982-1984. Korina body and neck, two humbucking pickups, gold hardware, standard eight-digit serial (versus the inked serial number on the Heritage Explorer of the same era).

1982-1984		$2,600	$2,800

Explorer Heritage

1983. Reissue of 1958 Explorer, Korina body, gold hardware, inked serial number, only 100 made.

1983	Black	$2,600	$2,800
1983	Natural	$3,000	$3,400
1983	White	$2,600	$2,800

Explorer (Alder body)

1983-1989. Alder body, 2 humbuckers, maple neck, ebony fingerboard, dot inlays, triangle knob pattern. Referred to as Explorer 83 in 1983.

1983-1989	Custom color limited runs	$900	$1,300
1983-1989	Standard finishes	$700	$800

Explorer '76/X-plorer

1990-present. Mahogany body and neck, rosewood fingerboard, dot inlays, two humbucking pickups. Name changed to X-plorer in 2002.

1990-1999	Standard finish	$750	$900
1998	Sunburst or Natural limited run	$950	$1,200

Explorer 90 Double

1989-1990. Mahogany body and neck, one single-coil and one humbucker, strings-through-body.

1989-1990		$500	$700

Explorer Centennial

1994 only. Les Paul Gold finish, 100 year banner inlay at 12th fret, diamonds in headstock and gold-plated knobs, Gibson coin in rear of headstock. Only 100 made.

1994		$3,000	$3,800

Explorer CMT/The Explorer

1981-1984. Maple body, exposed-coil pickups, TP-6 tailpiece.

1981-1984		$800	$1,100

Explorer Gothic

1998-2003. Gothic Series with black finish and hardware.

1998-2003		$650	$950

1967 Gibson Everly Brothers

1958 Gibson Explorer

1964 Gibson Firebird I

Gibson Firebird V

Explorer II (E/2)

1979-1983. Five-piece maple and walnut laminate body sculptured like V II, ebony fingerboard with dot inlays, two humbucking pickups, gold-plated hardware. Natural finish.

Year	Features	Low	High
1979-1983		$750	$1,000
1979-1983	Figured maple top option	$1,400	$1,600

Explorer III

1984-1985. Alder body, three P-90 pickups, two control knobs.

Year	Features	Low	High
1984-1985	Chrome hardware	$600	$900
1984-1985	Chrome hardware, locking trem	$550	$750
1985	Black hardware, Kahler	$600	$800

F-25 Folksinger

1963-1971. 14-1/2" flat-top, mahogany body, most have double white pickguard. Natural.

Year	Features	Low	High
1963-1964		$1,200	$1,500
1965-1969		$1,100	$1,300
1970-1971		$900	$1,100

Firebird I

1963-1969. Reverse body and one humbucking pickup 1963-mid-1965, non-reversed body and two P-90 pickups mid-1965-1969.

Year	Features	Low	High
1963	Sunburst, reverse	$4,500	$6,000
1964	Cardinal Red, reverse	$5,500	$6,500
1964	Sunburst, reverse	$3,500	$5,200
1965	Cardinal Red, reverse	$5,400	$6,400
1965	Golden Mist, non-reverse	$3,300	$4,300
1965	Sunburst, non-reverse	$2,200	$3,200
1965	Sunburst, reverse	$3,300	$4,800
1966	Sunburst, non-reverse	$2,100	$3,100
1967	Sunburst, non-reverse	$2,000	$3,000
1968	Sunburst, non-reverse	$1,900	$2,900
1969	Sunburst, non-reverse	$1,800	$2,800

Firebird I 1963 Reissue Historic Collection

1999-present. Neck-through, reverse body, Firebird logo on pickguard.

Year	Features	Low	High
1999	Sunburst	$1,500	$1,600
2002	Blue Swirl limited edition	$1,800	$2,200

Firebird I Custom Shop

1991-1992. Limited run from Custom Shop, reverse body, one pickup, gold-plated. Sunburst.

Year	Features	Low	High
1991		$1,400	$1,500

Firebird I/Firebird 76

1980-1982. Reintroduced Firebird 76 but renamed Firebird I.

Year	Features	Low	High
1980-1982		$1,400	$2,000

Firebird II/Firebird 2

1981-1982. Maple body with figured maple top, 2 full size active humbuckers, TP-6 tailpiece.

Year	Features	Low	High
1981-1982		$1,400	$1,600

Firebird III

1963-1969. Reverse body and two humbucking pickups 1963-mid-1965, non-reversed body and three P-90 pickups mid-1965-1969.

Year	Features	Low	High
1963	Cardinal Red	$6,800	$8,000
1963	Golden Mist	$6,800	$8,000
1963	Polaris White	$6,800	$8,000
1963	Sunburst	$5,000	$6,500
1964	Cardinal Red, reverse	$7,000	$8,500
1964	Polaris White, reverse	$7,000	$8,500
1964	Sunburst, reverse	$4,500	$6,000
1965	Frost Blue, reverse	$7,000	$8,500
1965	Inverness Green, non-reverse	$4,500	$6,500
1965	Sunburst, non-reverse	$2,700	$3,500
1965	Sunburst, reverse	$3,700	$5,100
1966	Sunburst, non-reverse	$2,300	$3,300
1967	Frost Blue	$3,100	$4,500
1967-1969	Pelham Blue	$3,000	$4,400
1967-1969	Sunburst	$2,200	$3,200

Firebird V

1963-1969,1994-present. Two humbucking pickups, reverse body 1963-mid-1965, non-reversed body mid-1965-1969.

Year	Features	Low	High
1963	Pelham Blue	$8,800	$10,000
1963	Sunburst	$6,300	$8,500
1964	Cardinal Red, reverse	$7,300	$9,500
1964	Sunburst, reverse	$5,500	$6,500
1965	Cardinal Red, reverse	$7,500	$9,000
1965	Sunburst, non-reverse	$3,200	$4,000
1965	Sunburst, reverse	$4,300	$5,500
1966	Sunburst, non-reverse	$2,900	$3,600
1967-1969	Sunburst	$2,800	$3,500

Firebird V Celebrity Series

1990-1993. Reverse body, Gold hardware, two humbuckers. Various colors.

Year	Features	Low	High
1990-1993		$1,100	$1,500

Firebird V Guitar Trader Reissue

1982. Guitar Trader commissioned Firebird reissue. Only 15 made..

Year	Features	Low	High
1982	Sunburst	$1,500	$2,000
1982	White	$2,000	$2,500

Firebird V Medallion

1972-1973. Reverse body, 2 humbuckers, Limited Edition medallion mounted on body.

Year	Features	Low	High
1972-1973		$3,800	$4,300

MODEL YEAR	FEATURES	EXC. COND. LOW	HIGH

Firebird V Reissue/Firebird Reissue

1990-present. Based on Firebird V specs, reverse body, several colors available with Cardinal Red optional in 1991.

1990-2002	Various colors	$1,200	$1,300
1991-2002	Cardinal Red option	$1,300	$1,450

Firebird V-12

1966-1967. Non-reverse Firebird V-style body with standard six-on-a-side headstock and split diamond headstock inlay (like ES-335-12 inlay), dot markers, special twin humbucking pickups (like mini-humbuckers).

1966-1967	Custom color	$4,700	$6,200
1966-1967	Sunburst	$3,500	$4,000

Firebird VII

1963-1969. Three humbucking pickups, reverse body 1963-mid-1965, non-reversed body mid-1965-1969. Sunburst standard.

1963		$9,500	$12,500
1964		$9,000	$10,500
1965	Reverse	$8,500	$9,500
1966	Non-reverse	$4,500	$6,500
1967		$4,300	$6,300
1968		$4,200	$6,200
1968	Custom color	$6,000	$8,500

Firebird VII (Historic/Custom Shop)

1997-present. Standard color is Vintage Sunburst.

1997	Sunburst	$2,300	$3,100
1997-1998	Frost Blue	$2,500	$3,500

Firebird VII (Reissue production model)

2003		$2,200	$3,000

Firebird VII Centennial

1994 only. Headstock medallion. Sunburst.

1994		$3,000	$3,800

Firebird 76

1976-1978. Reverse body, Gold hardware, two pickups.

1976	Bicentennial White	$2,400	$3,000
1977-1978		$1,500	$2,400

FJ-N Jumbo Folk Singer

1963-1967. Square shoulders, jumbo flat-top. Natural finish with Deep Red on back and sides.

1963-1964		$1,500	$1,700
1965-1967		$1,200	$1,500

Flamenco 2

1963-1967. Natural spruce top, 14 3/4", cypress back and sides, slotted headstock, zero fret.

1963-1967		$500	$700

Flying V

1958-1959, 1962-1963. Only 81 shipped in '58 and 17 in '59. Guitars made from leftover parts and sold in '62-'63. Natural korina body, string-through-body design.

As with any ultra high-end instrument, each instrument should be evaluated on a case-by-case basis. The Flying V market is a very specialized market, with few untouched examples available, and a limited number of high-end buyers. The Explorer and Flying V markets are similar in that respect. The price ranges

noted are for all-original, excellent condition guitars with the original Flying V case. The slightest change to the original specifications can mean a significant drop in value. The narrow price ranges noted are for all original, untouched examples that have the original guitar case and a strong provenance.

1958-1959		$85,000	$125,000

Flying V (Mahogany body)

1966-1967, 1969-1970, 1975-1980. Mahogany body, stud tailpiece.

1966-1967	Cherry or Sunburst	$10,000	$15,000
1969-1970	Cherry or Sunburst	$9,000	$13,000
1975	Various colors	$2,900	$3,200
1976	Various colors	$2,500	$2,900
1979	Silverburst	$2,900	$3,100
1979	Various colors	$2,300	$2,500
1980	Various colors	$2,200	$2,400

Flying V (Mahogany string-through-body)

1981-1982. Mahogany body, string-through-body design. Only 100 made, most in white, some red or black possible.

1981-1982	Black, Red or White	$1,600	$2,000

Flying V Heritage

1981-1982. Limited edition based on '58 specs, korina body, four colors available.

1981-1982	Natural	$2,700	$3,100
1981-1982	Various colors	$2,600	$3,800

Flying V (Korina)

1983. Name changed from Flying V Heritage.

1983	Natural	$2,600	$3,000
1983	Various colors	$2,600	$3,800

Flying V 90 Double

1989-1990. Mahogany body, stud tailpiece, one single-coil and one double-coil humbucker, Floyd Rose tremolo. Ebony, Silver or White.

1989-1990		$500	$700

Flying V Reissue/'67 Flying V/V Factor X

1990-present. Called Flying V Reissue first year, then '67 Flying V until '03, then V Factor X. Mahogany body.

1990-1999	Various colors	$800	$1,000
1993	Cardinal Red (custom)	$1,100	$1,300

Flying V '98

1998. Mahogany body, 1958 style controls, gold or chrome hardware.

1998		$750	$900

Flying V CMT/The V

1981-1985. Maple body with a curly maple top, two pickups, stud tailpiece. Natural or Sunburst.

1981-1985		$800	$1,100

Flying V Custom (Limited Edition)

2002. Appointments similar to Les Paul Custom, including Black finish, 40 made.

2002		$3,000	$3,700

Flying V Gothic/'98 Gothic

1998-2003. Satin black finish, black hardware, moon and star markers.

1998-2000		$650	$950

1964 Gibson Firebird VII

1958 Gibson Flying V

Gibson Flying V Medallion

1970s Gibson Heritage

MODEL YEAR	FEATURES	EXC. COND. LOW	HIGH

Flying V Historic Collection
1991-present. Recreation of the original 1958 Flying V, Gold hardware. Natural korina.

| 1991-1999 | | $4,000 | $6,000 |

Flying V I/V 83/Flying V (no pickguard)
1981-1988. Introduced as Flying V I, then renamed Flying V '83 in 1983. Called Flying V from 1984 on. Alder body, two exposed humbuckers, maple neck, ebony fingerboard, dot inlays, Black rings, no pickguard, Ebony or Ivory finish, designed for lower-end market.

| 1981-1988 | | $650 | $1,000 |

Flying V2
1979-1982. Five-piece maple and walnut laminate sculptured body, Ebony fingerboard with dot inlays, two V-shaped pickups (two Dirty Fingers humbuckers towards end of run), gold-plated hardware. Natural.

| 1979-1982 | | $1,400 | $1,600 |

Flying V Primavera
1994. Primavera (Light Yellow/White mahogany) body, gold-plated hardware.

| 1994 | Natural Yellow/White | $1,400 | $1,500 |
| 1994 | Various special colors | $1,200 | $1,300 |

Hendrix Hall of Fame Flying V
Late-1991-1993. Limited Edition (400 made), numbered. Black.

| 1991-1993 | | $1,700 | $1,900 |

Lonnie Mack Flying V
1993-1994. Mahogany body with Lonnie Mack-style Bigsby vibrato. Cherry.

| 1993-1994 | | $2,600 | $2,900 |

Futura
1982-1984. Deep cutout solidbody, two humbucker pickups, Gold hardware. Black, White or Purple.

| 1982-1984 | | $550 | $700 |

GB-1
1919-1923. Guitar-banjo, six-string neck, Walnut. Renamed GB-5 in 1923.

| 1919-1923 | | $1,250 | $1,700 |

Gospel
1973-1979. Flat-top, square shoulders, laminated maple back and sides, arched back. "Dove of Peace" headstock inlay, Natural.

| 1973-1979 | | $900 | $1,100 |

Gospel Reissue
1992-1997. Flat-top, cutaway with laminated mahogany back and sides and arched back. Natural or Sunburst.

| 1992-1997 | | $800 | $1,000 |

GY (Army-Navy)
1918-1921. Slightly arched top and back, low-end budget model.

| 1918 | Sheraton Brown | $750 | $1,100 |

Harley Davidson Limited Edition
1994-1995. Body 16" wide, flat-top, Harley Davidson in script and logo, 1500 sold through Harley dealers.

| 1994-1995 | Black | $2,000 | $3,000 |

Heritage
1964-1982. Flat-top dreadnought, square shoulders, rosewood back and sides (Brazilian until 1967, Indian 1968 on), bound top and back. Natural finish.

| 1964-1968 | Brazilian rosewood | $2,500 | $3,000 |
| 1968-1982 | Indian rosewood | $1,400 | $1,700 |

Heritage-12
1968-1970. Flat-top dreadnought, 12 strings, Indian rosewood back and sides, bound top and back. Natural finish.

| 1968-1970 | | $1,200 | $1,600 |

HG-00 (Hawaiian)
1932-1942, 1991-present. Hawaiian version of L-00. 14-3/4" flat-top, mahogany back and sides, bound top, natural.

| 1937-1942 | | $1,500 | $2,500 |

HG-20 (Hawaiian)
1929-1933. Hawaiian, 14-1/2" dreadnought-shaped, maple back and sides, round soundhole and 4 F-holes.

| 1929-1933 | | $2,000 | $2,500 |

HG-22 (Hawaiian)
1929-1932. Dreadnought, 14 inches, Hawaiian, round soundhole and four F-holes, White paint logo, very small number produced.

| 1929-1932 | | $2,500 | $2,700 |

HG-24 (Hawaiian)
1929-1932. 16" Hawaiian, rosewood back and sides, round soundhole plus 4 F-holes, small number produced.

| 1929-1932 | | $3,500 | $4,500 |

HG-Century (Hawaiian)
1937-1938. Hawaiian, 14-3/4" L-C Century of Progress.

| 1937-1938 | | $2,500 | $2,700 |

Howard Roberts Artist
1976-1980. Full body single cut archtop, soundhole, 1 humbucker, gold hardware, ebony fingerboard, various colors.

| 1976-1980 | | $2,100 | $2,300 |

Howard Roberts Artist Double Pickup
1979-1980. Two pickup version of HR Artist, various colors.

| 1979-1980 | | $2,300 | $2,500 |

Howard Roberts Custom
1974-1981. Full body single cut archtop, soundhole, 1 humbucker pickup, chrome hardware, rosewood fingerboard, various colors.

| 1974-1981 | | $1,900 | $2,100 |

Howard Roberts Fusion
1979-1988. Single cut semi-hollowbody, 2 humbuckers, chrome hardware, ebony fingerboard, TP-6 tailpiece, various colors. Renamed Howard Roberts Fusion IIL in 1988.

| 1979-1988 | | $1,400 | $1,600 |

Howard Roberts Fusion IIL
1988-1990. Renamed from Howard Roberts Fusion. Same specs. Renamed Howard Roberts Fusion III in 1991. Ebony, cherry or sunburst.

| 1988-1990 | | $1,400 | $1,600 |

The *Vintage Guitar Price Guide* shows low to high values for items in all-original excellent condition, and, where applicable, with original case or cover.

MODEL YEAR	FEATURES	EXC. COND. LOW	HIGH
Howard Roberts Fusion III			

1991-present. Renamed from Howard Roberts Fusion IIIL. Same specs except for fingerstyle tailpiece and gold hardware. Ebony or sunburst.

MODEL YEAR	FEATURES	EXC. COND. LOW	HIGH
1991-1999		$1,400	$1,600

Hummingbird

1960-present. Flat-top acoustic, square shoulders, mahogany back and sides, bound body and neck.

MODEL YEAR	FEATURES	EXC. COND. LOW	HIGH
1960	Cherry Sunburst, 156 shipped	$3,700	$4,300
1961-1962	Cherry Sunburst, 1000 shipped	$3,500	$4,000
1962-1963	Cherry Sunburst, maple option	$3,500	$4,000
1963-1964	Cherry Sunburst, 2700 shipped	$3,000	$3,500
1965-1966	Cherry Sunburst or Natural	$2,500	$3,100
1967-1968	Screwed pickguard	$2,200	$2,800
1969-1970	Natural or Sunburst	$1,600	$2,300
1971-1980	Double X, block markers	$1,400	$1,800
1981-1983	Non-volute neck	$1,300	$1,700
1984	Double para. Markers	$1,100	$1,300
1985-1988	Single X	$1,200	$1,400
1989-2003	25 1/2" scale	$1,200	$1,400

J-25

1983-1985. Flat-top, laminated spruce top, synthetic semi-round back, Ebony fingerboard. Natural or Sunburst.

MODEL YEAR	FEATURES	EXC. COND. LOW	HIGH
1983-1985		$350	$450

J-30

1985-1993. Dreadnought-size flat-top acoustic, mahogany back and sides, Sunburst. Renamed J-30 Montana in 1994.

MODEL YEAR	FEATURES	EXC. COND. LOW	HIGH
1985-1993		$950	$1,050

J-30 Montana

1994-1997. Renamed from J-30. Dreadnought-size flat-top acoustic, mahogany back and sides. Sunburst.

MODEL YEAR	FEATURES	EXC. COND. LOW	HIGH
1994-1997		$1,100	$1,200

J-40

1971-1982. Dreadnought flat-top, mahogany back and sides. Economy satin finish.

MODEL YEAR	FEATURES	EXC. COND. LOW	HIGH
1971-1982	Natural satin finish	$750	$850

J-45

1942-1982, 1984-1993, 1999-present. Dreadnought flat-top, mahogany back and sides, round shoulders until 1968 and 1984 on, square shoulders 1969-1982. Sunburst finish (see J-50 for Natural version) then Natural finish also available in 1990s. Renamed J-45 Western in 1994, renamed Early J-45 in 1997 then renamed J-45 in 1999. The prices noted are for all-original crack free instruments. A single professionally repaired minor crack that is nearly invisible will reduce the value only slightly. Two or more, or unsightly repaired cracks will devalue an otherwise excellent original acoustic instrument. Repaired cracks should be evaluated on a case-by-case basis.

MODEL YEAR	FEATURES	EXC. COND. LOW	HIGH
1942	Sunburst, banner logo	$4,600	$5,000
1943	Sunburst, banner logo	$4,500	$4,900
1944	Sunburst, banner logo	$4,400	$4,800
1945	Sunburst, banner logo	$4,400	$4,700
1946	Sunburst, banner logo	$4,000	$4,600
1947	Sunburst	$3,700	$4,500
1948	Sunburst	$3,500	$4,400
1949	Sunburst	$3,300	$4,300
1950-1953	Sunburst	$3,000	$4,200
1954-1955	Sunburst	$2,900	$3,800
1956-1957	Sunburst	$2,700	$3,400
1958-1959	Sunburst	$2,600	$3,100
1960-1962	Sunburst	$2,400	$2,700
1963	Sunburst	$2,300	$2,700
1964	Sunburst	$2,200	$2,700
1965	Sunburst	$1,900	$2,500
1966	Sunburst	$1,800	$2,200
1967	Sunburst	$1,600	$2,000
1968	Black, round shoulders	$1,800	$2,200
1968	Sunburst, round shoulders	$1,500	$1,900
1969	Sunburst, round shoulders	$1,400	$1,800
1969	Sunburst, square shoulders	$1,300	$1,700
1970	Sunburst, square shoulders	$1,200	$1,500
1971	Sunburst	$1,100	$1,500
1972	Sunburst	$1,000	$1,400
1973	Sunburst	$900	$1,300
1974	Sunburst	$900	$1,200
1975-1981	Sunburst	$800	$900
1984-1993	Various colors	$800	$1,000

J-45 Buddy Holly Limited Edition

1995. 250 made.

MODEL YEAR	FEATURES	EXC. COND. LOW	HIGH
1995		$1,600	$1,700

J-45 Celebrity

1985. Acoustic introduced for Gibson's 90th anniversary, spruce top, rosewood back and sides, ebony fingerboard, binding on body and fingerboard. Only 90 made.

MODEL YEAR	FEATURES	EXC. COND. LOW	HIGH
1985		$1,400	$1,700

J-45 Western

1994-1997. Previously called J-45. Name changed to Early J-45 in 1997.

MODEL YEAR	FEATURES	EXC. COND. LOW	HIGH
1994-1997		$1,100	$1,300

J-45/Early J-45

1997-1999. J-45 model name for 1997 and 1998.

MODEL YEAR	FEATURES	EXC. COND. LOW	HIGH
1997-1999		$1,100	$1,500

J-50

1942, 1945-1981, 1990-1995, 1998-present. Dreadnought flat-top, mahogany back and sides, round shoulders until 1968, square shoulders after. Natural finish (see J-45 for Sunburst version).

MODEL YEAR	FEATURES	EXC. COND. LOW	HIGH
1942		$4,600	$5,000

Gibson Hummingbird

'40s Gibson J-45

1973 Gibson J-50 Deluxe

Gibson J-185

MODEL YEAR	FEATURES	EXC. COND. LOW	HIGH
1945		$4,400	$4,700
1946		$4,000	$4,600
1947		$3,700	$4,500
1948		$3,500	$4,400
1949		$3,300	$4,300
1950-1953		$3,000	$4,200
1954-1955		$2,900	$3,800
1956-1957		$2,700	$3,400
1958-1959		$2,600	$3,100
1960-1962		$2,500	$2,800
1963		$2,400	$2,700
1964		$2,200	$2,700
1965		$1,900	$2,500
1966		$1,800	$2,200
1967		$1,600	$2,000
1968	Round shoulders	$1,500	$1,900
1969	Round shoulders	$1,400	$1,800
1969	Square shoulders	$1,300	$1,700
1970	Square shoulders	$1,200	$1,500
1971		$1,100	$1,500
1972		$1,000	$1,400
1973		$900	$1,300
1974		$900	$1,200
1975-1981		$800	$900
1990-1995		$800	$1,000
1998-2001		$1,100	$1,400

J-55 (Jumbo 55) Limited Edition
1994 only. Sixteen inch flat-top, spruce top, mahogany back and sides, 100 made. Sunburst.

| 1994 | | $1,500 | $1,700 |

J-55 (reintroduced)
1973-1982. Flat-top, laminated mahogany back and sides, arched back, square shoulders, sunburst. See Jumbo 55 listing for '39-'43 version.

| 1973-1982 | | $900 | $1,000 |

J-60
1992-1999. Solid spruce top dreadnought, square shoulders, Indian rosewood back and sides, multiple bindings, natural or sunburst.

| 1992-1999 | | $1,000 | $1,100 |

J-60 Curly Maple
1993 and 1996. Curly maple back and sides, limited edition from Montana shop. Natural.

| 1993 | | $2,000 | $2,500 |

J-100
1970-1974, 1985-1997, 2003-present. Flat-top jumbo, multi-bound top and back, black pickguard, dot inlays, mahogany back and sides. '80s version has maple back and sides, dot inlays and tortoise shell guard. Current model has maple back and sides, no pickguard, and J-200 style block fingerboard inlays.

1970-1974	Mahogany	$1,400	$1,700
1985-1989	Maple	$1,200	$1,500
1990-1997		$1,100	$1,300

J-100 Xtra
1991-1997, 1999-2003. Jumbo flat-top, mahogany back and sides, moustache bridge, dot inlays, various colors. J-100 Xtra Cutaway also available. Reintroduced in '99 with maple back and sides and single bound body.

| 1991-1997 | | $1,100 | $1,300 |

J-160E
1954-1979. Flat-top jumbo acoustic, one bridge P-90 pickup, tone and volume controls on front. Sunburst finish. Reintroduced as J-160 in 1990.

1954-1961		$3,500	$4,000
1962	Beatles' vintage June '62	$3,700	$5,000
1963		$3,600	$4,100
1964	Lennon's 2nd model	$3,700	$4,500
1965		$3,300	$3,700
1966		$3,200	$3,500
1967		$2,900	$3,100
1968		$2,600	$2,800
1969		$1,900	$2,100
1970		$1,400	$1,800
1971-1979		$1,300	$1,500

J-160E (reissue)
1991-1997. Reintroduced J-160E with solid spruce top, solid mahogany back and sides.

| 1991-1997 | | $1,500 | $1,800 |

J-180/Everly Brothers/The Everly Brothers
1986-present. Reissue of the '62-'72 Everly Brothers model. Renamed The Everly Brothers ('92-'94), then The Everly ('94-'96), then back to J-180. Black.

1986-1991		$1,100	$1,400
1992-1994	Everly Brothers	$1,100	$1,400
1994-1999	The Everly	$1,400	$1,600

J-185
1951-1959. Flat-top jumbo, figured maple back and sides, bound body and neck.

1951-1956	Natural	$7,400	$8,500
1951-1956	Sunburst	$7,000	$8,000
1957-1959	Natural	$7,200	$8,300
1957-1959	Sunburst	$6,800	$7,800

J-185 (Reissue)
1990-1995, 1999-present. Flat-top jumbo, figured maple back and sides, bound body and neck, natural or sunburst. Limited run of 100 between 1991-1992.

| 1990-1995 | | $1,700 | $2,000 |

J-185 EC
1999-present. Acoustic/electric, rounded cutaway. Sunburst.

| 1999-2002 | | $1,600 | $1,900 |

J-200/SJ-200
1947-1996. Labeled SJ-200 until ca.1954. Super Jumbo flat-top, maple back and sides. See SJ-200 for 1938-1942 rosewood back and sides model. Called J-200 Artist for a time in the mid-1970s. Renamed '50s Super Jumbo 200 in 1997 and again renamed SJ-200 Reissue in 1999. Standard finish is Sunburst.

1947-1949	Natural option	$9,500	$11,500
1947-1949	Sunburst	$8,500	$10,500
1950-1954	Natural option	$8,500	$10,500
1950-1954	Sunburst	$7,500	$9,500
1955-1959	Natural option	$8,000	$10,000
1955-1959	Sunburst	$7,000	$9,500
1960	Natural	$7,000	$9,500
1960	Sunburst	$6,500	$8,500
1961-1963	Natural option	$6,500	$8,500

MODEL YEAR	FEATURES	EXC. COND. LOW	HIGH
1961-1963	Sunburst	$5,500	$7,500
1964	Natural	$5,500	$7,000
1964	Sunburst	$4,500	$6,500
1965	Natural or Sunburst	$4,000	$5,500
1966-1967	Natural or Sunburst	$3,500	$4,000
1968	Natural or Sunburst	$3,000	$3,500
1969	Natural or Sunburst	$2,700	$3,000
1970-1972	Natural or Sunburst	$2,500	$2,800
1973	Natural or Sunburst	$2,000	$2,600
1974-1992	Natural or Sunburst	$1,800	$2,500
1992-1996	Natural or Sunburst	$1,900	$2,500

J-200 Celebrity
1985-1987. Acoustic introduced for Gibson's 90th anniversary, spruce top, rosewood back, sides and fingerboard, binding on body and fingerboard. Sunburst. Only 90 made.

1985-1987		$2,500	$3,200

J-250 R
1972-1973, 1976-1978. A J-200 with rosewood back and sides, Sunburst. Only 20 shipped from Gibson.

1972-1973		$2,000	$2,600
1976-1978		$1,800	$2,100

JG-0
1970-1972. Economy square shouldered jumbo, follows Jubilee model in 1970.

1970-1972		$650	$750

JG-12
1970. Economy square shouldered jumbo 12-string, follows Jubilee-12 model in 1970.

1970		$550	$650

Johnny Smith
1961-1989. Single cutaway archtop, one humbucking pickup, Gold hardware, multiple binding front and back.

1961-1963	Natural or Sunburst	$8,000	$9,000
1963-1964	Natural or Sunburst	$6,500	$7,500
1965-1967	Natural or Sunburst	$5,500	$6,500
1968-1969	Natural or Sunburst	$5,000	$6,000
1970-1989	Natural or Sunburst	$4,500	$5,500

Johnny Smith Double
1963-1989. Single cutaway archtop, two humbucking pickups, Gold hardware, multiple binding front and back.

1963-1964	Natural or Sunburst	$7,000	$8,000
1965-1967	Natural or Sunburst	$6,000	$7,000
1968-1969	Natural or Sunburst	$5,500	$6,500
1970-1989	Natural or Sunburst	$5,000	$6,000

Jubilee
1969-1970. Flat-top, laminated mahogany back and sides, single bound body. Natural with Black back and sides.

1969-1970		$750	$800

Jubilee Deluxe
1970-1971. Flat-top, laminated rosewood back and sides, multi-bound body. Natural finish.

1970-1971		$900	$1,000

Jubilee-12
1969-1970. Flat-top, 12 strings, laminated mahogany back and sides, multi-bound. Natural.

1969-1970		$600	$700

Jumbo
1934-1936. Gibson's first Jumbo flat-top, mahogany back and sides, round shoulders, bound top and back, Sunburst. Becomes the 16" Jumbo 35 in late-1936.

1934-1936		$14,000	$16,000

Jumbo 35/J-35
1936-1942. Jumbo flat-top, mahogany back and sides, silkscreen logo, Sunburst. Reintroduced as J-35, square-shouldered dreadnought, in 1983.

1936		$8,500	$9,500
1937		$8,000	$9,000
1938-1939		$7,500	$8,500
1940-1942		$7,000	$8,000

Jumbo 55/J-55
1939-1943. Flat-top dreadnought, round shoulders, mahogany back and sides, pearl inlaid logo, Sunburst. Reintroduced in 1973 as J-55.

1939-1943		$13,000	$15,000

Jumbo Centennial Special
1994. Reissue of 1934 Jumbo, 100 made.

1994	Natural	$2,000	$2,200

Junior Pro
1987-1989. Single cutaway, mahogany body, KB-X tremolo system one humbucker pickup, Black chrome hardware, various colors.

1987-1989		$350	$400

Kalamazoo Award Model
1978-1981. Single cutaway archtop, bound F-holes, multi-bound top and back, one mini-humbucker, gold-plated hardware, woodgrain pickguard with bird and branch abalone inlay.

1978-1981	Natural, highly figured	$15,000	$16,000
1978-1981	Sunburst, highly figured	$16,000	$17,000

L-0
1926-1933, 1937-1942. Acoustic flat-top, maple back and sides 1926-1927, mahogany after.

1926-1933	Amber Brown	$2,000	$2,500
1937-1942	Various colors	$2,000	$2,500

L-00
1932-1946. Acoustic flat-top, mahogany back and sides, bound top to 1936 and bound top and back 1937 on.

1932-1939	Black or Sunburst	$2,500	$3,000
1940-1946	Natural or Sunburst	$2,500	$3,000

L-00/Blues King
1991-1997. Mahogany back and sides, spruce top, Ebony or Sunburst.

1991-1997		$1,100	$1,400

L-1 (archtop)
1902-1925. Acoustic archtop, single-bound top, back and soundhole. Name continued on flat-top model in '26.

1902-1907	Standard 12.5" body	$1,100	$1,300
1908-1925	Standard 13.5" body	$1,200	$1,400

1961 Gibson Johnny Smith

1981 Gibson Kalamazoo Award

1930 Gibson L-2

1915 Gibson L-4

MODEL YEAR	FEATURES	EXC. COND. LOW	HIGH

L-1 (flat-top)
1926-1937. Acoustic flat-top, maple back and sides 1926-1927, mahogany after.

1926-1927	13 1/2" maple body, 12 frets	$2,200	$2,800
1928-1930	13 1/2" mahogany body, 12 frets	$2,200	$2,800
1931	14 3/4" mahogany body	$2,200	$2,800
1932-1937	14 frets	$2,200	$2,800

L-2 (archtop)
1902-1926. Round soundhole archtop, pearl inlay on peghead, 1902-1907 available in three body sizes: 12.5" to 16", 1924-1926 13.5" body width.

| 1902-1907 | Standard 12.5" body | $1,300 | $1,500 |
| 1924-1926 | Standard 13.5" body | $1,400 | $1,600 |

L-2 (flat-top)
1929-1935. Acoustic flat-top, rosewood back and sides except for mahogany in 1931, triple-bound top and back. Limited edition model in 1994.

1929-1930	Natural, 14 3/4" body, 13 frets	$2,500	$3,300
1931	Argentine Gray, 13 frets	$2,500	$3,300
1932-1933	Natural, 13 frets	$2,500	$3,300
1934-1935	Natural, 14 frets	$2,500	$3,300

L-3 (archtop)
1902-1933. Acoustic archtop, available in three sizes: 12 1/2", 13 1/2", 16".

1902-1907	Standard 12.5" body	$1,500	$1,700
1908-1926	Standard 13.5" body	$1,600	$1,800
1927-1929	Oval soundhole	$1,800	$2,100

L-4
1912-1956. Acoustic archtop, 16" wide.

1912-1927	Oval soundhole	$1,900	$2,100
1928-1934	Round soundhole	$2,000	$2,200
1935-1945	F-holes	$1,900	$2,100
1946-1956	Crown peghead inlay, triple bound	$2,000	$2,400

L-4 C/L-4 CN
1949-1971. Single cutaway acoustic archtop.

1949-1959	Natural	$2,900	$3,100
1949-1959	Sunburst	$2,700	$2,900
1960-1965	Natural	$2,800	$3,000
1960-1965	Sunburst	$2,600	$2,800
1966-1969	Sunburst	$2,400	$2,600
1969-1971	Sunburst	$2,000	$2,400

L-4 CES
1958,1969, 1986-present. Single pointed cutaway archtop, two humbuckers, Gold parts, Natural or Sunburst. Now part of Gibson's Custom Collection.

| 1986-2003 | | $2,000 | $2,400 |

L-5
1922-1958. Acoustic archtop, non-cutaway, multiple bindings, Lloyd Loar label until 1924, 17" body by 1935, Master Model label until 1927. Sunburst with Natural option later.

| 1922-1924 | Lloyd Loar label | $45,000 | $55,000 |
| 1924 | Lloyd Loar signed (Mar-Dec) | $50,000 | $60,000 |

MODEL YEAR	FEATURES	EXC. COND. LOW	HIGH
1925-1927	Master Model label	$20,000	$25,000
1928	Last dot markers	$15,000	$23,000
1929	Early 1929	$9,000	$11,000
1929-1930	Block markers	$8,500	$10,500
1931-1932	Standard trapeze	$7,500	$9,000
1933-1934	16" body	$7,000	$8,500
1935-1940	17" body	$6,000	$7,500
1939-1940	Natural option	$7,000	$9,000
1946-1949	Natural option	$7,000	$8,000
1946-1949	Sunburst	$5,000	$6,000
1950-1958	Natural	$5,000	$7,000
1950-1958	Sunburst	$4,000	$6,000

L-5 Premier/L-5 P
1939-1947. Introduced as L-5 Premier (L-5 P) and renamed L-5 C in 1948. Single rounded cutaway acoustic archtop.

| 1939-1940 | Natural option | $17,000 | $20,000 |
| 1939-1940 | Sunburst | $16,000 | $17,000 |

L-5 C
1948-1982. Renamed from L-5 Premier (L-5 P). Single rounded cutaway acoustic archtop. Sunburst.

1948		$12,500	$15,000
1949		$12,000	$14,500
1950-1959		$11,500	$12,500
1960-1962		$9,000	$10,000
1964-1965		$8,000	$9,000
1966-1967		$7,500	$8,800
1968		$6,800	$8,500
1969		$5,600	$7,400
1970-1972		$5,000	$6,700
1973-1975		$4,400	$5,600
1976-1982		$3,700	$5,200

L-5 CES
1951-present. Electric version of L-5 C, single round cutaway (pointed mid-1960-1969), archtop, two pickups (P-90s 1951-1953, Alnico Vs 1954-mid-1957, humbuckers after). Now part of Gibson's Historic Collection.

1951-1957	Natural, single coils	$15,000	$20,000
1951-1957	Sunburst, single coils	$13,000	$16,000
1958-1960	Natural, humbuckers	$20,000	$30,000
1958-1960	Sunburst, humbuckers	$15,000	$20,000
1961-1962	Natural, PAFs	$15,000	$20,000
1961-1962	Sunburst, PAFs	$12,000	$15,000
1963-1964	Natural, pat. #	$13,000	$15,000
1963-1964	Sunburst, pat. #	$10,000	$12,000
1965-1969	Natural	$7,500	$9,500
1965-1969	Sunburst	$6,500	$8,500
1970-1972	Various colors	$6,000	$7,000
1973-1992	Various colors	$5,500	$6,500

The *Vintage Guitar Price Guide* shows low to high values for items in all-original excellent condition, and, where applicable, with original case or cover.

MODEL YEAR	FEATURES	EXC. COND. LOW	HIGH

L-5 CES Custom Shop Historic Collection
1990s. Historic Collection Series. Sunburst.

1990s	100th Anniversary, Black	$6,000	$6,500
1990s	Sunburst	$5,000	$6,000

L-5 CT (George Gobel)
1959-1961. Single cutaway, thinline archtop acoustic. Some were built with pickups, Cherry. Currently available in Gibson's Historic Collection.

1959-1961		$15,000	$19,000

L-5 CT (reissue)
1998-present. Natural.

1998		$4,500	$5,500

L-5 S
1972-1985, 2004-present. Single cut solidbody, multi-bound body and neck, gold hardware, 2 pickups (low impedence '72-'74, humbuckers '75 on). Offered in natural, cherry sunburst or vintage sunburst. One humbucker version reissued in 2004 from Gibson's Custom, Art & Historic division.

1972-1974	Natural, gold hardware, low impedence	$3,200	$3,500
1972-1974	Sunburst, low impedence pickups	$2,700	$3,300
1975-1980	Natural, gold hardware, humbuckers	$3,500	$4,500
1975-1980	Sunburst, humbuckers	$3,000	$4,000

L-5 Studio
1996-2000. Normal L-5 dual pickup features, marble-style pickguard.

1996-2000	Translucent finish	$2,500	$3,000

L-5 Wes Montgomery Custom Shop
1993-present. Various colors.

1993-1999		$4,300	$4,600

L-6 S
1973-1975. Single cutaway solidbody, two humbucking pickups, stop tailpiece, Cherry or Natural. Renamed L-6 S Custom in 1975.

1973-1975		$700	$800

L-6 S Custom
1975-1980. Renamed from the L-6 S. Single cutaway solidbody, two humbucking pickups, stop tailpiece, Cherry or Natural.

1975-1980		$700	$800

L-6 S Deluxe
1975-1981. Single cutaway solidbody, two humbucking pickups, strings-through-body design, Cherry or Natural.

1975-1981		$700	$800

L-7
1932-1956. Acoustic archtop, bound body and neck, fleur-de-lis peghead inlay, 16" body 1932-1934, 17" body X-braced top late-1934.

1932-1934	16" body	$2,400	$3,200
1935-1939	17" body, X-braced	$2,500	$3,300
1940-1950	Natural or Sunburst	$2,300	$3,100
1951-1956	Natural or Sunburst	$2,200	$3,000

L-7 C
1948-1972. Single cut acoustic archtop, triple-bound top, sunburst or natural finish. Gibson revived the L-7 C name for a new acoustic archtop in 2002.

1948-1949	Natural	$4,300	$4,900
1948-1949	Sunburst	$3,600	$4,300
1950-1951	Natural	$4,100	$4,700
1950-1951	Sunburst	$3,400	$4,100
1952-1964	Natural	$3,300	$3,800
1952-1964	Sunburst	$2,900	$3,600
1965-1967	Sunburst	$2,800	$3,200
1968-1971	Sunburst	$2,700	$3,000

L-10
1929-1939. Acoustic archtop, single-bound body and fingerboard.

1929-1933	Black, 16"	$2,300	$3,000
1934-1939	Black or Sunburst, 17", X-braced	$2,800	$3,300

L-12
1930-1955. Acoustic archtop, single-bound body, pickguard, neck and headstock, gold-plated hardware. Sunburst.

1930-1934	16" body	$3,000	$3,400
1935-1938	17" body, X-braced	$3,000	$3,400
1939-1941	Parallel top braced	$3,000	$3,400
1946-1955	Post-war production	$2,800	$3,200

L-12 Premier/L-12 P
1947-1950. L-12 with rounded cutaway. Sunburst.

1947-1950		$4,400	$4,700

L-30
1935-1943. Acoustic archtop, single-bound body. Black or Sunburst.

1935-1943		$1,000	$1,400

L-37
1937-1941. 14-3/4" acoustic archtop, flat back, single-bound body and pickguard, sunburst.

1937-1941		$1,000	$1,400

L-48
1946-1971. 16" acoustic archtop, single-bound body, sunburst.

1946-1965		$900	$1,100
1966-1971		$600	$800

L-50
1932-1971. 14 3/4" wide acoustic archtop, flat or arched back, round soundhole or F-holes, pearl logo pre-war, decal logo post-war, Sunburst.

1932-1933	14 3/4" body, round hole	$1,100	$1,600
1946-1965	Decal logo, trapezoid inlay	$1,000	$1,400
1966-1971		$800	$1,200

L-75
1932-1939. 14 3/4" archtop with round soundhole and flat back, size increased to 16" with arched back in 1935, small button tuners, dot markers, lower-end style trapeze tailpiece, pearl script logo. Sunburst.

1932-1934	14 3/4" body	$1,700	$2,200
1935-1939	16" body	$2,300	$2,700

1955 Gibson L-5 CN

Gibson L-50

Gibson Le Grande

1953 Gibson Les Paul Model

MODEL YEAR	FEATURES	EXC. COND. LOW	HIGH

L-C Reissue
Pearloid headstock and fingerboard.

1994		$2,100	$2,300

L-Century (L-C)
1933-1941. Curly maple back and sides, bound body, White pearloid fingerboard and peghead (all years) and headstock (until 1938). Sunburst.

1933-1941		$3,400	$3,700

Le Grande
1993-present. Electric archtop, 17", formerly called Johnny Smith.

1993-2003		$6,000	$7,500

Les Paul

Here are the various guitars that bear the Les Paul name, beginning with the original Les Paul Model. All other variations are listed alphabetically as follows:

Les Paul Model
'52 Les Paul Goldtop
'54 Les Paul Goldtop
'56 Les Paul Goldtop
'57 Les Paul Goldtop
'57 Les Paul Jr. Historic Collection
'58 Les Paul Flametop
'59 Les Paul Flametop
'60 Corvette
'60 Les Paul Flametop
'60 Les Paul Jr. Historic Collection
Jimmy Page Signature Les Paul Custom Shop
Les Paul 25/50 Anniversary
Les Paul 25th Silver Anniversary (Guitar Center)
Les Paul 30th Anniversary
Les Paul 40th Anniversary (from 1952)
Les Paul 40th Anniversary (from 1959)
Les Paul 55
Les Paul (All Maple)
Les Paul Ace Frehley Signature
Les Paul Artisan
Les Paul Artist/L.P. Artist/Les Paul Active
Les Paul Centennial ('56 LP Standard Goldtop)
Les Paul Centennial ('59 Les Paul Special)
Les Paul Classic
Les Paul Classic Plus
Les Paul Classic Premium Plus
Les Paul Custom
Les Paul Custom '54
Les Paul Custom (Custom Shop)
Les Paul Custom 20th Anniversary
Les Paul Custom 35th Anniversary
Les Paul Custom Historic '54
Les Paul Custom Historic '57 Black Beauty/2-pickup
Les Paul Custom Historic '57 Black Beauty/3-pickup
Les Paul Custom Historic '68
Les Paul Custom Lite
Les Paul Custom Plus
Les Paul Custom SG 30th Anniversary
Les Paul DC Pro

Les Paul DC Standard
Les Paul DC Standard Plus
Les Paul DC Studio
Les Paul Deluxe
Les Paul Deluxe Hall of Fame
Les Paul Deluxe Limited Edition
Les Paul Dickey Betts Red Top
Les Paul Elegant
Les Paul Gary Moore Model
Les Paul Guitar Trader Reissue
Les Paul Heritage 80
Les Paul Heritage 80 Award
Les Paul Heritage 80 Elite
Les Paul Jimmy Page Model
Les Paul Jimmy Wallace Reissue
Les Paul Jr.
Les Paul Jr. 3/4
Les Paul Jr. Double Cutaway
Les Paul Jumbo
Les Paul KM
Les Paul Leo's Reissue
Les Paul Limited Edition
Les Paul Old Hickory
Les Paul Personal
Les Paul Pro-Deluxe
Les Paul Professional
Les Paul Recording
Les Paul Reissue Flametop
Les Paul Reissue Goldtop
Les Paul Signature
Les Paul SmartWood Standard
Les Paul SmartWood Studio
Les Paul Special
Les Paul Special (reissue)
Les Paul Special 3/4
Les Paul Special Centennial
Les Paul Special Custom Shop
Les Paul Special Double Cutaway
Les Paul Spotlight Special
Les Paul Standard (Sunburst)
Les Paul Standard (SG body)
Les Paul Standard (reintroduced)
Les Paul Standard '58
Les Paul Standard '82
Les Paul Standard Lite
Les Paul Strings and Things Standard
Les Paul Studio
Les Paul Studio Custom
Les Paul Studio Gem
Les Paul Studio Gothic
Les Paul Studio Lite
Les Paul Tie Dye Custom Shop
Les Paul TV
Les Paul TV 3/4
Les Paul Ultima
The Les Paul
The Paul
The Paul II
The Paul Firebrand Deluxe

MODEL YEAR	FEATURES	EXC. COND. LOW	HIGH

Les Paul Model

1952-1958. The Goldtop, two P-90 pickups until mid-1957, humbuckers after, trapeze tailpiece until late-1953, stud tailpiece/bridge 1953-mid-1955, Tune-o-matic bridge 1955-1958. Renamed Les Paul Standard in 1958.

1952	1st made, unbound neck	$9,000	$15,000
1952	5/8" knobs	$8,000	$10,000
1952	5/8" knobs, all Gold option, trapeze	$8,000	$10,000
1953	1/2" knobs, early-'53 trapeze	$7,500	$9,500
1953	1/2" knobs, mid-'53 wrap-around	$10,000	$13,000
1953	1/2" knobs, late-'53 wrap-around	$13,000	$15,000
1954-1955	All Gold option, wrap-around	$16,000	$21,000
1954-1955	Bigsby (factory)	$10,000	$13,000
1954-1955	Wrap-around	$15,000	$20,000
1955-1957	All Gold option, Tune-o-matic, P-90s	$22,000	$26,000
1955-1957	Tune-o-matic, all mahogany body	$19,000	$22,000
1955-1957	Tune-o-matic, P-90s	$21,000	$25,000
1957-1958	All mahogany, stud tail, humbuckers	$36,000	$49,000
1957-1958	Bigsby, humbuckers	$35,000	$40,000
1957-1958	Stud tail, humbuckers	$40,000	$55,000

'52 Les Paul Goldtop

1990s-present. By 1998 The Gibson Historic Collection offered guitars reissued "with incredible accuracy." Goldtop finish, two P-90s, '52-style trapeze tailpiece/bridge.

1997		$1,700	$2,000

'54 Les Paul Goldtop

1990s-present. Goldtop finish, two P-90s, '53-'54 stud tailpiece/bridge.

1997		$1,700	$2,000

'56 Les Paul Goldtop

1991-present. Renamed from Les Paul Reissue Goldtop. Goldtop finish, two P-90 pickups. Now part of Gibson's Historic Collection.

1991-1999		$1,800	$2,000
2000-2002		$1,900	$2,100

'57 Les Paul Goldtop

1993-present. Goldtop finish, two humbuckers. Now part of Gibson's Historic Collection.

1993-1999		$1,800	$2,000

'57 Les Paul Jr. Historic Collection

1998-present. High quality Historic reissue of '57 slab body, double cutaway Les Paul Jr.

1990s	TV Yellow	$1,000	$1,400

'58 Les Paul Flametop

Part of Gibson's Historic Collection. Sunburst.

2001		$2,900	$3,500

'59 Les Paul Flametop

1991-present. Renamed from Les Paul Reissue Flametop. Flame maple top, two humbuckers, thick 1959-style neck. Sunburst finish. Part of Gibson's Historic Collection. By 1998 Gibson guaranteed only AAA Premium grade maple tops would be used.

1991-2002		$3,000	$3,600

'60 Corvette (Custom shop)

1995-1997. Custom Shop Les Paul, Chevrolet Corvette styling from 1960, distinctive styling, offered in six colors.

1995-1997		$6,000	$7,000

'60 Les Paul Flametop

1991-1999. Renamed from Les Paul Reissue Flametop. Flame maple top, two humbuckers, thinner neck. Sunburst finish. Part of Gibson's Historic Collection.

1991-1999		$3,000	$3,600

'60 Les Paul Jr. Historic Collection

Introduced in 1992. High quality Historic reissue of 1960 slab body, double cut Les Paul Jr., cherry.

1992-1999		$1,000	$1,400

Jimmy Page Signature Les Paul Custom Shop

2004. Introduced at the January 2004 NAMM Show, 175 instrument production, the first 25 were personally inspected, played-in, and autographed by Jimmy Page. Initial retail price for first 25 was $25,000. The remaining 150 instruments had an initial retail price of $16,400, cosmetically aged by Tom Murphy to resemble Page's No. 1 Les Paul. Intricate details based on Page's No. 1 include mods to that model, color fade, instrument weight to be within a few ounces of No. 1, top flamed in the center with slab cut attribution on the edges as per No. 1's top, very exacting neck size and profile per No. 1.

2004	1st 25 made	$20,000	$25,000
2004	Factory order 26-150	$12,000	$16,400

Les Paul 25/50 Anniversary

1978-1979. Regular model with 25/50 inlay on headstock. Sunburst.

1978-1979	Moderate flame	$2,500	$3,000
1978-1979	Premium flame	$3,000	$5,000

Les Paul 25th Silver Anniversary (Guitar Center)

1978. Special order of 50 Les Paul Customs with Metallic Silver top, back, sides and neck. Commissioned by Guitar Center of California, most have 25th Anniversary etched in tailpiece.

1978		$2,200	$2,500

Les Paul 30th Anniversary

1982-1984. Features of a 1958 Les Paul Goldtop, 2 humbuckers, Thirtieth Anniversary inlay on 19th fret.

1982-1984		$2,200	$2,500

1957 Gibson Les Paul Model

Gibson Jimmy Page Signature Les Paul

1956 Gibson Les Paul Custom

*2001 Gibson Les Paul
DC Standard*

MODEL YEAR	FEATURES	EXC. COND. LOW	HIGH

Les Paul 40th Anniversary (from 1952)
1991-1992. Black finish, 2 soapbar P-100 pickups, gold hardware, stop tailpiece, 40th Anniversary inlay at 12th fret.

1991-1992		$1,800	$2,000

Les Paul 40th Anniversary (from 1959)
1999. Reissue Historic, highly figured.

1999		$3,300	$3,700

Les Paul 55
1974, 1976-1981. Single cut Special reissue, 2 pickups.

1974	Sunburst	$700	$900
1976-1981	Sunburst or Wine Red	$700	$900

Les Paul (All Maple)
1984. Limited run, all maple body, Super 400-style inlay, Gold hardware.

1984		$3,200	$3,400

Les Paul Ace Frehley Signature
1997-2001. Ace's signature inlay at 15th fret, 3 humbuckers, sunburst.

1997-2001		$2,800	$3,000

Les Paul Artisan
1976-1982. Carved maple top, 2 or 3 humbuckers, gold hardware, hearts and flowers inlays on fingerboard and headstock, ebony, sunburst or walnut.

1976-1982		$1,900	$2,400

Les Paul Artist/L.P. Artist/Les Paul Active
1979-1982. Two humbuckers (3 optional), active electronics, gold hardware, 3 mini-switches, multibound.

1979	Sunburst	$1,300	$1,500
1980-1982	Ebony or Sunburst	$1,300	$1,500

Les Paul Bird's-Eye Standard
Bird's-eye top, Gold hardware, two humbucking pickups.

1999	Transparent Amber	$1,850	$1,950

Les Paul Centennial ('56 LP Standard Goldtop)
1994. Part of the Guitar of the Month program commemorating Gibson's 100th year, limited edition of 100. Goldtop Les Paul mahogany body with 1956-style configuration, Gold hardware, Gold truss rod plate, Gold medallion, engraved Light-Gold pickguard.

1994		$5,000	$6,000

Les Paul Centennial ('59 Les Paul Special)
1994. Part of the Guitar of the Month program commemorating Gibson's 100th year, limited edition. Slab body Les Paul Special-style configuration, 100 made, Gold hardware, P-90 pickups, Gold medallion, commemorative engraving in pickguard. Cherry.

1994		$3,500	$4,000

Les Paul Classic
1990-1998, 2001. Has 1960 on pickguard (not on later models), two exposed humbucker pickups, Les Paul Model on peghead until 1993, Les Paul Classic afterwards.

1990-1996	Various colors, plain top	$1,400	$1,700
1990-1998	All Gold neck and body	$1,700	$1,900

Les Paul Classic Plus
1991-1996, 1999-2000. Les Paul Classic with fancier maple top, two exposed humbucker pickups.

1991-1996	Price depends on top figure	$1,700	$2,200

Les Paul Classic Premium Plus
1993-1996, 2000-2002. Les Paul Classic with AAA-grade flame maple top, two exposed humbucker pickups.

1992-1996	Price depends on top figure	$2,200	$2,800

Les Paul Custom
1953-1963 (renamed SG Custom late-1963), 1968-present. Les Paul body shape except for SG body 1961-1963, two pickups (three humbuckers mid-1957-1963 and 1968-1970, three pickups were optional various years after).

1953-1957	Single-coil PUs	$10,000	$14,000
1953-1957	Single-coils with factory Bigsby	$8,000	$12,000
1957-1960	Humbuckers	$15,000	$22,000
1957-1960	Humbuckers with factory Bigsby	$13,000	$18,000
1961-1963	White, SG body	$8,000	$9,000
1968-1969	Black, 1-piece body	$6,500	$8,500
1968-1969	Black, 3-piece body	$5,000	$6,500
1970-1972	2 PUs, neck volute	$2,000	$2,400
1970-1972	Volute, 3 PUs	$2,400	$2,700
1973-1974	Volute, 2 PUs	$1,800	$2,300
1973-1974	Volute, 3 PUs	$2,000	$2,500
1975-1976	Volute, 2 PUs	$1,500	$2,000
1977-1978	Volute, 2 PUs	$1,600	$1,800
1977-1978	Volute, 3 PU option	$1,900	$2,200
1979-1982	2 Pus	$1,600	$1,800
1979-1982	Silverburst, volute, 2 PUs	$2,400	$2,600
1983-1985	2 Pus	$1,500	$1,700
1983-1985	Black, 3 PU option	$1,700	$1,900
1986-1989	Various colors	$1,400	$1,700
1990-1999	Various colors	$1,400	$1,700
2000-2002	Various colors	$1,400	$1,900

Les Paul Custom '54
1972-1973. Reissue of 1954 Custom, Black finish, Alnico V and P-90 pickups.

1972-1973	Black	$3,000	$3,500

Les Paul Custom (Custom Shop)
1997-present. Handbuilt Custom Shop quality, Gold hardware.

1997-1999	Faded Cherry, Gold hardware	$1,700	$1,800

Les Paul Custom 20th Anniversary
1974. Regular two-pickup Custom, with Twentieth Anniversary inlay at 15th fret. Black or White.

1974		$2,200	$2,400

Les Paul Custom 35th Anniversary
1989. Gold hardware, three pickups, carved, solid mahogany body and neck, 35th Anniversary inlay on headstock. Black.

1989		$2,200	$2,400

MODEL YEAR	FEATURES	EXC. COND. LOW	HIGH

Les Paul Custom Historic '54
1990s Historic Collection, 1954 appointments and pickup configuration. Black.

| 1997-2000 | Gold hardware | $1,900 | $2,100 |

Les Paul Custom Historic '57 Black Beauty/2-pickup
1991-present. Black finish, Gold hardware, two humbucker pickups. Part of Gibson's Historic Collection.

| 1991-1999 | | $1,800 | $2,000 |

Les Paul Custom Historic '57 Black Beauty/3-pickup
1991-present. Black finish, Gold hardware, three humbucker pickups. Part of Gibson's Historic Collection.

| 1991-1999 | | $1,900 | $2,100 |

Les Paul Custom Historic '68
Historic Collection, Ebony block marked fretboard, Gold hardware, flamed maple top available, two pickups.

| 2000-2001 | Flamed natural | $2,100 | $2,300 |

Les Paul Custom Lite
1987-1990. Full-thickness carved maple top, ebony fingerboard, pearl block position markers, Gold hardware, PAF pickups, bound neck, headstock and body. Black.

| 1987-1990 | | $1,500 | $1,800 |

Les Paul Custom Lite (Show Case Ed.)
1988. Showcase Edition, only 200 made, Gold top.

| 1988 | | $1,700 | $2,000 |

Les Paul Custom Plus
1991-1998. Regular Custom with figured maple top. Sunburst finish or colors.

| 1991-1998 | | $1,700 | $2,300 |

Les Paul DC Pro
1997-1998. Custom Shop, body like a 1959 Les Paul Junior, carved highly figured maple top, various options.

| 1998-1998 | | $1,700 | $2,000 |

Les Paul DC Standard
1998-1999. Offset double cut, highly flamed maple top, mahogany set-neck, translucent lacquer finishes in various colors, typical Les Paul Model stencil logo on headstock and 'Standard' notation on truss rod cover. Reintroduced as Les Paul Standard DC Plus in 2001.

| 1998-1999 | | $1,000 | $1,300 |

Les Paul DC Standard Plus
2001-present. Reintroduction of LP DC Standard, flamed top, gold hardware.

| 2001-2002 | Cherry | $950 | $1,100 |

Les Paul DC Studio
1997-1999. DC Series double cutaway like late '50s models, carved maple top, two humbucker pickups. Various colors.

| 1997-1999 | | $650 | $750 |

Les Paul Deluxe
1969-1985. In 1969, the goldtop Les Paul Standard was renamed the Deluxe. Two mini-humbuckers (regular humbuckers optional in mid-'70s). Mid-'70s

Sparkle tops, made at the request of the Sam Ash chain, are worth more than standard finishes. The market slightly favors the Goldtop finish, but practically speaking condition is more important than finish, such that all finishes fetch about the same amount (with the exception of the sparkle finish). Initially, the Deluxe was offered only as a Goldtop and the first year models are more highly prized than the others. Cherry sunburst was offered in 1971, cherry in '71-'75, walnut in '71-'72, brown sunburst in '72-'79, natural in 1975, red sparkle in 1975 only, blue sparkle in '75-'77, wine red/see-through red offered '75-'85. In '99, the Deluxe was reissued for its 30th anniversary.

1969	Goldtop	$3,000	$3,800
1970	Goldtop	$2,000	$2,800
1971-1975	Various colors	$1,900	$2,300
1975	Red Sparkle, fewer made	$3,500	$4,500
1975-1977	Blue Sparkle, more made	$3,000	$3,500
1976-1979	Various colors	$1,700	$2,100
1980-1985	Various colors	$1,700	$1,900

Les Paul Deluxe Hall of Fame
1991. All Gold.

| 1991 | | $1,700 | $1,900 |

Les Paul Deluxe Limited Edition
1999-2002. Limited edition reissue with Les Paul Standard features and Deluxe mini-humbuckers, Black.

| 1999-2002 | | $1,300 | $1,500 |

Les Paul Dickey Betts Red Top
2003. Transparent Red, Gold hardware.

| 2003 | | $2,500 | $3,000 |

Les Paul Elegant (Custom Shop)
1996-present. Custom Shop highly flamed maple top, abalone Custom Shop headstock inlay.

| 1996-1999 | | $2,100 | $2,400 |

Les Paul Gary Moore Model
2000-2002. Signature Series model, Gary Moore script logo on truss rod cover, flamed maple top.

| 2000-2002 | | $1,700 | $2,000 |

Les Paul Guitar Trader Reissue
1982-1983. Special order flametop Les Paul by the Guitar Trader Company, Redbank, NJ. Approximately 47 were built. The first 15 guitars "ordered" received original PAFs, all were double black bobbins (except one Zebra and one double white), three of the guitars were made in the 1960-style. The PAF equipped models were based on order date and not build date. The serial number series started with 9 1001 and a second serial number was put in the control cavity based upon the standard Gibson serial number system, which allowed for exact build date identification.

Gibson's pickup designer in the early-1980s was Tim Shaw and the pickups used for the last 32 guitars have been nicknamed "Shaw PAFs." After Gibson's short run for Guitar Trader, 10 non-Gibson "replica" or "bootleg" Les Pauls were made. These GT "bootleg" guitars have a poorly done Gibson logo and other telltale issues.

| 1982-1983 | Actual PAFs
installed | $8,000 | $8,500 |

Gibson Les Paul Deluxe (blue sparkle)

Gibson Les Paul Guitar Trader

Gibson Les Paul Heritage 80

Gibson Les Paul Joe Perry

MODEL YEAR	FEATURES	EXC. COND. LOW	HIGH
1982-1983	Shaw PAFs	$5,000	$5,500
1983	"Bootleg" Les Paul	$1,500	$2,500

Les Paul Heritage 80
1980-1982. Copy of 1959 Les Paul Standard, curly maple top, mahogany body, rosewood fingerboard, sunburst.

1980-1982		$2,600	$3,100

Les Paul Heritage 80 Award
1982. Ebony fingerboard, one-piece mahogany neck, gold-plated hardware, sunburst.

1982		$3,200	$3,800

Les Paul Heritage 80 Elite
1980-1982. Copy of 1959 Les Paul Standard. Quilted maple top, mahogany body and neck, ebony fingerboard, chrome hardware. Sunburst.

1980-1982		$3,000	$3,300

Les Paul Jimmy Page Model
1995-1999. Jimmy Page signature on pickguard, mid-grade figured top, push-pull knobs for phasing and coil-tapping, Grover tuners, gold-plated hardware. This is not the 2004 issued Custom Shop Jimmy Page Signature Series Les Paul (see separate listing).

1995	Highly figured, 1st year	$3,700	$4,000
1995	Low to moderate figure, 1st year	$3,300	$3,700
1996-1999	Highly figured	$3,500	$3,800
1996-1999	Low to moderate figure	$3,000	$3,500

Les Paul Jimmy Wallace Reissue
1978-1997. Les Paul Standard '59 reissue with Jimmy Wallace on truss rod cover, special order by dealer Jimmy Wallace, figured maple top, Sunburst.

1978-1983	Kalamazoo-made	$4,000	$5,000
1983-1989	Nashville-made	$3,500	$4,000
1990-1997		$3,500	$4,000

Les Paul Joe Perry Model
1997-2001. Unbound slab body with push-pull knobs and Joe Perry signature below bridge, Bone-Yard logo model with typical Les paul Standard bound body, configuration and appointments.

1997-2001	Bone-Yard option with logo	$2,300	$2,600
1997-2001	Unbound standard model	$1,400	$1,700

Les Paul Jr.
1954-1963, 1986-1992. One P-90 pickup, single cutaway solidbody '54-mid-'58, double cutaway '58-early-'61, SG body '61-'63. Renamed SG Jr. in '63. Reintroduced as single cut for '86-'92. Reissued as the 1957 Les Paul Jr. Single Cutaway in '98.

1954	Sunburst, single cut	$3,300	$3,800
1955-1958	Sunburst, single cut	$3,200	$3,700
1959-1961	Cherry, double cut, normal fade	$2,800	$3,500
1959-1961	Cherry, double cut, unfaded	$3,400	$4,000
1961-1963	Cherry, SG body	$1,700	$2,400

MODEL YEAR	FEATURES	EXC. COND. LOW	HIGH

Les Paul Jr. 3/4
1956-1961. One P-90 pickup, short-scale, single cutaway solidbody 1954-mid-1958, double cutaway 1958-early-1961.

1956-1958	Sunburst, single cut	$2,100	$2,300
1958-1959	Cherry, double cut	$1,800	$2,000
1960-1961	Cherry, double cut	$1,700	$2,200

Les Paul Jr. Double Cutaway
1986-1992, 1995-1996. Copy of 1950s double cutaway Jr., Cherry or Sunburst. Reissued as the 1957 Les Paul Jr. Double Cutaway in '98.

1986-1992		$800	$950

Les Paul Jumbo
1969-1970. Single rounded cutaway, flat-top dreadnought acoustic/electric, one pickup, rosewood back and sides. Natural.

1969-1970		$2,600	$2,800

Les Paul KM (Kalamazoo Model)
1979. Regular Les Paul Standard with two exposed humbuckers, KM on headstock, sunburst, approximately 1500 were made in the Kalamazoo plant.

1979		$1,700	$2,700

Les Paul Leo's Reissue
1980-1985. Special order from Gibson's Nashville facility for Leo's Music, Oakland, CA. Identified by serial number with L at the beginning, flamed maple top. About 800 guitars were made, with about 400 being exported to Japan. Kalamazoo-made Leo's have a 2nd serial number in the control cavity. Nashville-made Leo's do not have a 2nd serial number.

1980-1983	Kalamazoo-made	$4,300	$4,700
1983-1985	Nashville-made	$3,800	$4,200

Les Paul Limited Edition (3-tone)
1997. Limited Edition stamped on the back of the headstock, Les Paul Standard configuration with 'cloud' inlay markers, two-piece three-tone Sunburst finish over non-figured maple top.

1997		$2,000	$2,200

Les Paul Old Hickory
1998 only. Limited run of 200. Tulip poplar body from The Hermitage, Custom-style trim.

1998		$2,500	$3,800

Les Paul Personal
1969-1972. Two angled, low impedence pickups, phase switch, Gold parts. Walnut finish.

1970		$1,100	$1,200

Les Paul Pro-Deluxe
1978-1982. Two P-90 pickups, chrome-plated hardware. "Pro" engraved on truss rod cover, various colors.

1978-1982		$1,300	$1,600

Les Paul Professional
1969-1971, 1977-1979. Single cutaway, two angled, low impedence pickups, carved top. Walnut finish.

1969-1971		$1,100	$1,200

Les Paul Recording
1971-1980. Two angled, low impedence pickups, high/low impedence selector switch. Various colors.

1971-1980		$1,100	$1,200

MODEL YEAR	FEATURES	EXC. COND. LOW	HIGH

Les Paul Reissue Flametop
1983-1990. Flame maple top, two humbuckers, thicker 1959-style neck. Sunburst finish. Renamed '59 Les Paul Flametop in 1991.

| 1983-1990 | Highly figured | $3,000 | $3,500 |

Les Paul Reissue Goldtop
1983-1991. Goldtop finish, two P-100 pickups. Renamed '56 Les Paul Goldtop in 1991.

| 1983-1989 | | $1,500 | $1,700 |
| 1990-1991 | | $1,600 | $1,900 |

Les Paul Signature
1973-1978. Thin semi-hollowbody, double cutaway, two low impedence pickups, F-holes. Various colors.

| 1973-1978 | | $1,800 | $2,000 |

Les Paul SmartWood Standard
1996-2002. Smartwood Series. Figured maple top, mahogany body, Smartwood on truss rod cover.

| 1996-2002 | Antique Natural | $1,000 | $1,200 |

Les Paul SmartWood Studio
2002-present. Released December 2002 as part of Les Paul Exotics guitar series. Muiracatiara (Muir) top and mahogany back. Preciosa (Prec) fingerboard, initial production will use Muir wood until replaced by another exotic wood, full-depth body style, Studio model appointments including pearl-style dot markers.

| 2002-2003 | . | $800 | $900 |

Les Paul Special
1955-1959. Slab solidbody, two pickups (P-90s in 1950s, P-100 stacked humbuckers on later version). Single cutaway until end of 1958, double in 1959. The 1989 reissue is a single cutaway. Renamed SG Special in late-1959.

| 1955-1959 | TV Yellow | $6,000 | $7,500 |
| 1959 | Cherry (mid- to late-'59) | $5,500 | $6,500 |

Les Paul Special (reissue)
1989-1998. Briefly introduced as Les Paul Junior II but name changed to Special in the first year. Single cutaway, two P-100 stacked humbucking pickups, tune-o-matic bridge, TV Yellow. In 1990 there was a run of 300 with LE serial number. Renamed Special SL in 1998.

| 1989-1998 | | $800 | $1,000 |

Les Paul Special 3/4
1959. Slab solidbody, two P-90 pickups, double cutaway, short-scale. Cherry finish. Renamed SG Special 3/4 in late-1959.

| 1959 | | $4,000 | $4,500 |

Les Paul Special Centennial
1994 only. 100 made, double cut, cherry, 100 year banner at the 12th fret, diamonds in headstock and in gold-plated knobs, gold-plated Gibson coin in back of headstock.

| 1994 | | $3,400 | $3,700 |

Les Paul Special Custom Shop
1999-present. Custom Shop decal on back of headstock. Black.

| 1999 | | $1,100 | $1,200 |

Les Paul Special Double Cutaway
1976-1979, 1993-1998. Double cut, 2 pickups (P-90s in 1970s, P-100 stacked humbuckers in later version). Various colors.

| 1976-1979 | | $1,100 | $1,500 |
| 1993-1998 | | $1,000 | $1,200 |

Les Paul Spotlight Special
1983-1984. Curly maple and walnut top, two humbuckers, Gold hardware, multi-bound top, Custom Shop Edition logo. Natural or Sunburst.

| 1983-1984 | | $2,000 | $2,200 |

Les Paul Standard (Sunburst)
1958-1960, special order 1972-1975. Les Paul Sunbursts from '58-'60 should be individually valued based on originality, color and the amount and type of figure in the maple top. Changed tuners or a Bigsby removal will drop the value. The noted price ranges are guidance valuations. Each '58-'60 Les Paul Standard should be evaluated on a case-by-case basis. As is always the case, the low and high range are for an all original, excellent condition, undamaged guitar. About 70% of the '58-'60 Les Paul Standards have relatively plain maple tops. Approximately 15% came with the Bigsby tailpiece. The majority of '58-'60 Les Paul Standards have moderate or extreme color fade.

Wider fret wire was introduced in early-'59. White bobbins were introduced in early- to mid-'59. Double ring Kluson Deluxe tuners were introduced in late-'60. It has been suggested that all '58-'60 models have two-piece centerseam tops. This implies that one-piece tops, three-piece tops and off-centerseam tops do not exist.

Sunburst language includes terms such as: arching medullary grain, swirling medullary grain, ribbon-curl, chevrons, Honey-Amber, receding red aniline, pinstripe, bookmatched, double-white bobbins, zebra bobbins, black bobbins, fiddleback maple, unburst finish, Honeyburst, lemon drop, quarter sawn, blistered figure, width of gradation, flat sawn, Teaburst, Bigsby-shadow, rift sawn, heel size, aged clear lacquer, three-dimensional figure, intense fine flame, tag-shadow, red pore filler, eastern maple fleck, medium-thick flame, shrunk tuners, wave and flame, flitch-matched, elbow discoloration, ambered top coat, natural gradation, grain orientation, script oxidation, asymmetrical figure Tangerineburst, Greenburst, and bird's-eye. As in any ultra high-end valuation, each instrument should be evaluated on a case-by-case basis. The 'burst market is heavily influenced by "buyer's preference" and "high-end bias."

The bobbins used for the pickup winding were either black or white. The market has determined that white bobbin PAFs are the most highly regarded. Generally speaking, in 1958 bobbins were black, in 1959 the bobbin component transitioned to white and some guitars have one white and one black bobbin (aka zebra). In 1960, there were zebras and double blacks returned.

For the 2005 Price Guide, a more user friendly format has been used. Rather than listing separate line items for fade and wood, the Guide lists discounts

Gibson Les Paul
Smartwood Studio

1959 Gibson
Les Paul Standard

2002 Gibson Les Paul Standard

Gibson Les Paul Studio

and premiums as follows. The price ranges shown below are for instruments with excellent color, excellent wood, with the original guitar case. The following discounts and premiums should be considered.

An instrument with a plain top should be discounted about 50%.

An instrument with an average top should be discounted about 30%.

An instrument with moderate or total fade should be discounted about 10%.

An instrument with a factory Bigsby should be discounted about 10%-15%.

Original jumbo frets are preferred over original small frets and are worth +10%.

An instrument with a non-original Les Paul case is woth $2,500 less.

MODEL YEAR	FEATURES	LOW	HIGH
1958	Highly flamed, strong color	$145,000	$210,000
1959	Highly flamed, strong color	$185,000	$250,000
1960	Highly flamed, strong color	$145,000	$210,000

Les Paul Standard (SG body)
1961-1963 (SG body those years). Renamed SG Standard in late-1963.

1961-1962	Cherry, side vibrola, PAFs	$6,500	$7,500
1962	Ebony block tailpiece	$7,500	$8,000
1963	Cherry	$6,000	$6,500

Les Paul Standard (reintroduced then renamed)
1968-1969. Comes back as a Goldtop with P-90s for 1968-1969 (renamed Les Paul Deluxe, 1969). Available as special order Deluxe 1972-1976.

1968	P-90s, small headstock	$6,500	$7,500
1968-1969	P-90s, large headstock	$5,000	$6,000

Les Paul Standard (reintroduced)
1976-present. Available as special order Deluxe 1972-1976. Reintroduced with two humbuckers 1976-present.

1972	Goldtop special order, P-90s	$2,500	$2,800
1972	Sunburst special order, P-90s	$2,500	$2,800
1973	Special order	$2,500	$2,800
1974	Sunburst special order, humbuckers	$2,600	$3,000
1974	Sunburst special order, P-90s	$2,500	$2,800
1975	Special order	$2,500	$2,900
1976	Sunburst	$1,700	$1,900
1976	Wine Red	$1,500	$1,700
1977	Sunburst	$1,600	$1,800
1978	Natural	$1,600	$1,800
1978	Sunburst	$1,600	$1,800
1979	Brown Sunburst	$1,600	$1,800
1979	Cherry Sunburst	$1,600	$1,800
1979	Goldtop	$1,700	$1,900

MODEL YEAR	FEATURES	LOW	HIGH
1979	Natural	$1,600	$1,800
1979	Wine Red	$1,600	$1,800
1980	Black	$1,600	$1,800
1980	Natural	$1,600	$1,800
1980	Sunburst	$1,600	$1,800
1980	Sunburst, mild flame	$1,700	$2,000
1980	Wine Red	$1,600	$1,800
1981	Sunburst	$1,600	$1,800
1981	Wine Red	$1,600	$1,800
1982	Black	$1,600	$1,800
1982	Brown Sunburst	$1,600	$1,800
1982	Cherry Sunburst	$1,600	$1,800
1982	Goldtop	$1,700	$1,900
1982	Wine Red	$1,600	$1,800
1983	Black	$1,500	$1,700
1983	Natural	$1,500	$1,700
1983	Sunburst	$1,500	$1,700
1984	Sunburst	$1,500	$1,700
1985	Black	$1,500	$1,700
1985	Wine Red	$1,500	$1,700
1986	Sunburst	$1,400	$1,700
1987	Various colors	$1,400	$1,700
1988	Various colors	$1,400	$1,700
1989	Various colors	$1,400	$1,700
1990-1999	Limited Edition colors	$1,600	$2,000
1990-1999	Various colors	$1,400	$1,700
2000-2002	Various colors	$1,400	$1,900

Les Paul Standard '58
1971-1975. Goldtop, called the '58, but set up like a 1954 Goldtop with two soapbar pickups and stop tailpiece.

1971-1975		$3,800	$4,900

Les Paul Standard '82
1982. Standard 82 on truss rod cover, made in Kalamazoo, "Made in USA" stamp on back of the headstock, generally quilted maple tops.

1982		$2,800	$3,800

Les Paul Standard Lite
1999-2001. A member of DC body-style, renamed from DC Standard in 1999, reintroduced as Les Paul Standard DC Plus in 2001. Various translucent finishes. Available in 2004 under this name also.

1999-2001		$900	$1,000

Les Paul Strings and Things Standard
1975-1978. Special order flamed maple top Les Paul Standard model, built for Chris Lovell, owner of Strings and Things, a Gibson dealer in Memphis. Approximately 28 were built. Authentication of a Strings and Things Les Paul is difficult due to no diffinitive attributes. Valuation should be on a case-by-case basis. Sunburst.

1975-1978	2-piece top	$4,500	$5,000
1975-1978	3-piece top	$2,500	$3,000

Les Paul Studio
1983-present. Alder body, two humbuckers.

1983-1999	Various colors	$850	$1,000
2000-2002	Transparent Red	$800	$900

MODEL YEAR	FEATURES	EXC. COND. LOW	HIGH

Les Paul Studio Custom

1984-1985. Alder body, two humbucking pickups, multi-bound top, gold-plated hardware. Various colors.

1984-1985		$900	$1,000

Les Paul Studio Gem

1996-1998. Limited edition with Les Paul Studio features, but using P-90 pickups instead of humbucker pickups, plus trapezoid markers and gold hardware.

1996-1998		$750	$850

Les Paul Studio Gothic

2000s. Gothic Black.

2000-2001		$700	$750

Les Paul Studio Lite

1987-1998. Carved maple top, mahogany back and neck, two humbucker pickups. Various colors.

1987-1998		$800	$950

Les Paul Tie Dye Custom Shop

2002. Limited series of one-off colorful finishes, Custom Shop logo.

2002		$3,300	$3,700

Les Paul TV

1954-1959. Les Paul Jr. with limed mahogany (TV Yellow) finish, single cutaway until mid-1958, double cutaway after. Renamed SG TV in late-1959.

1955-1958	Single cut	$5,000	$6,000
1958-1959	Double cut	$5,000	$6,000

Les Paul TV 3/4

1954-1957. Limed mahogany (TV Yellow) Les Paul Jr. 3/4. Short-scale, single cutaway.

1954-1957		$2,500	$3,750

Les Paul Ultima

1996-present. Custom Shop model, quilted Sunburst top, fancy inlay, abalone trim.

1990s		$5,000	$6,000

The Les Paul

1976-1980. Figured maple top, two humbuckers, Gold hardware, rosewood binding, pickguard, fingerboard, knobs, cover plates, etc. Natural or rosewood finishing, Natural only by 1979.

1976-1980	Natural or Rosewood	$11,000	$12,000

The Paul

1978-1982. Walnut body, two exposed humbuckers.

1978-1982		$675	$725

The Paul II

1996-1998. Mahogany body, two humbucking pickups, rosewood dot neck. Renamed The Paul SL in 1998.

1996-1998		$400	$500

The Paul Firebrand Deluxe

1980-1982. Single cutaway mahogany solidbody, rough Natural finish, Gibson branded in headstock, two exposed humbuckers.

1980-1982	Pelham Blue	$600	$700
1980-1982	Rough Natural	$400	$600

LG-0

1958-1974. Flat-top acoustic, mahogany, bound body, rosewood bridge 1958-1961 and 1968-1974, plastic bridge 1962-1967. Natural.

1958-1961	Rosewood bridge	$800	$1,200
1962-1964	Plastic bridge	$700	$950
1965-1967	Plastic bridge	$550	$850
1968-1969	Rosewood bridge	$500	$750
1970-1974		$400	$700

LG-1

1943-1968. Flat-top acoustic, spruce top, mahogany back and sides, bound body, rosewood bridge 1943-1961, plastic bridge after. Examples seen to 1974. Sunburst.

1943		$1,500	$2,000
1944		$1,400	$1,900
1945		$1,400	$1,700
1946		$1,300	$1,600
1947-1949		$1,100	$1,600
1950-1961		$1,000	$1,400
1962-1965		$900	$1,300
1966-1968		$800	$1,100

LG-2

1942-1962. Flat-top acoustic, spruce top, mahogany back and sides (some with maple 1943-1946), banner headstock 1942-1946, bound body, X-bracing. Sunburst finish. Replaced by B-25 in 1962.

1942		$2,300	$2,800
1943		$2,200	$2,700
1944		$2,100	$2,600
1945		$2,000	$2,500
1946		$1,900	$2,400
1947-1949		$1,800	$2,300
1950-1961		$1,600	$2,100
1962	Ajustable bridge	$1,300	$1,800

LG-2 3/4

1949-1962. Short-scale version of LG-2 flat-top, wood bridge. Sunburst.

1949-1962		$1,400	$1,800

LG-2 H

1945-1955. Flat-top, Hawaiian. Natural or Sunburst.

1945-1955		$1,400	$1,900

LG-3

1942-1964. Flat-top acoustic, spruce top, mahogany back and sides, bound body. Natural finish. Replaced by B-25 N.

1942		$2,500	$3,000
1943		$2,400	$2,900
1944		$2,300	$2,800
1945		$2,200	$2,700
1946		$2,100	$2,600
1947-1949		$2,000	$2,500
1950-1962	Wood bridge	$1,750	$2,300
1962-1964	Plastic bridge	$1,500	$2,000

LG-12 (12-string)

1967-1973. 14-1/8" wide, mahogany back and sides, bound top, natural.

1967-1969	Adjustable saddle	$700	$900
1970-1974	Set saddle	$600	$800

Mach II

1990-1991. Renamed from U-2, offset double cut, 2 single coils and 1 humbucking pickup.

1990-1991		$650	$750

Marauder

1975-1980. Single cut solidbody, pointed headstock, 2 pickups, bolt-on neck, various colors.

1975-1980		$550	$600

1950s Gibson Les Paul TV

Gibson Les Paul Ultima

The *Vintage Guitar Price Guide* shows low to high values for items in all-original excellent condition, and, where applicable, with original case or cover.

GUITARS

1970 Gibson Melody Maker

1978 Gibson RD Artist

MODEL YEAR	FEATURES	EXC. COND. LOW	HIGH

Melody Maker
1959-1971. Slab solidbody, one pickup, single cutaway until 1961, double 1961-1966, SG body 1966-1971. Reintroduced as single cutaway in 1986-1993.

1959	Sunburst	$800	$1,250
1960	Sunburst	$750	$1,100
1961	Sunburst, single cut	$700	$1,000
1962	Cherry, double cut	$650	$950
1962	Sunburst, double cut	$650	$950
1963	Cherry, double cut	$600	$900
1964	Cherry	$600	$850
1964	Sunburst	$600	$850
1965-1966	Cherry, double cut	$550	$800
1966	Blue or Red, SG body	$700	$1,050
1967-1969	Blue or Red	$650	$1,000
1968-1970	Walnut option	$650	$1,000

Melody Maker 3/4
1959-1970. Short-scale version.

1959-1965	Melody Maker body	$500	$750
1966-1970	SG body	$700	$850

Melody Maker D
1960-1970. Two pickup version of Melody Maker. Reintroduced as Melody Maker Double in 1977.

1960	Sunburst, single cut	$950	$1,200
1961	Sunburst, single cut	$900	$1,150
1962	Sunburst, double cut	$850	$1,100
1963	Cherry, double cut	$800	$1,000
1964	Cherry, double cut	$750	$900
1965-1966	Cherry, double cut	$700	$850
1966	Blue or Red, SG body	$1,000	$1,100
1967-1969	Blue, Red or White, SG body	$950	$1,150
1968-1970	Walnut option, SG body	$950	$1,150

Melody Maker Double
1977-1983. Reintroduction of Melody maker D. Double cutaway solidbody, two pickups. Cherry or Sunburst.

1977-1983		$600	$700

Melody Maker III
1965-1971. SG-style double cutaway solidbody, three pickups. Various colors.

1967-1969		$1,100	$1,350
1970-1971		$1,000	$1,300

Melody Maker 12
1967-1971. SG-style solidbody, 12 strings, two pickups. Red, White or Pelham Blue.

1967-1971		$1,050	$1,100

MK-35
1975-1978. Mark Series flat-top acoustic, mahogany back and sides, Black-bound body. Natural or Sunburst.

1975-1978		$650	$750

MK-53
1975-1978. Mark Series flat-top acoustic, maple back and sides, multi-bound body. Natural or Sunburst.

1975-1978		$750	$850

MK-72
1975-1978. Mark Series flat-top acoustic, rosewood back and sides, Black-bound body. Natural or Sunburst.

1975-1978		$850	$950

MK-81
1975-1978. Mark Series flat-top acoustic, rosewood back and sides, multi-bound body, Gold tuners, high-end appointments. Natural or Sunburst.

1975-1978		$900	$1,000

Moderne Heritage
1981-1983. Limited edition with approximately 143 made. Korina body, two humbucking pickups, Gold hardware.

1981-1983	Black or White	$2,500	$2,700
1981-1983	Natural	$2,900	$3,200

Nick Lucas
1928-1938. Flat-top acoustic, multi-bound body and neck, sunburst. Reintroduced in 1991 and '99.

1928	Mahogany, 12-fret, 13 1/3"	$5,500	$6,500
1928	Rosewood, 12-fret, 13 1/2"	$6,500	$7,500
1929-1933	Rosewood, 13-fret, 14 3/4"	$7,500	$8,500
1934-1938	Maple, 14-fret, 14 3/4"	$6,500	$7,500

Nick Lucas Reissue
1991-1992, 1999-present. Limited edition flat-top acoustic. Sunburst.

1991-1992		$1,500	$1,650

Nighthawk Custom
1993-1998. Flame maple top, Ebony fingerboard, Gold hardware, single/double/mini pickups.

1993-1998	Fireburst	$950	$1,050

Nighthawk Special
1993-1998. Single cut solidbody, figured maple top, double-coil and mini-pickup or with additional single-coil options, dot marker inlay. Cherry, ebony or sunburst.

1993-1998		$500	$600

Nighthawk Standard
1993-1998. Single cut solidbody, figured maple top, 2 or 3 pickups, double-parallelogram inlay. Amber, fireburst or sunburst.

1993-1998		$800	$900

Nouveau NV6T-M
1986-1987. A line of Gibson flat-tops with imported parts assembled and finished in the U.S. Acoustic dreadnought, bound maple body, Natural.

1986-1987		$375	$450

RD Artist
1978-1982. Double cut solidbody, two humbuckers, TP-6 tailpiece, active electronics, ebony 'board, block inlays, gold-plated parts, various colors. Called just RD (no Artist) in '81 and '82.

1978-1982		$900	$1,200

MODEL YEAR	FEATURES	EXC. COND. LOW	HIGH

RD Custom
1977-1979. Double cut solidbody, two humbuckers, stop tailpiece, active electronics, dot inlays, maple 'board, chrome parts. Natural or Walnut.

1977-1979		$900	$1,100

RD Standard
1977-1979. Double cut solidbody, two humbuckers, stop tailpiece, rosewood 'board, dot inlays, chrome parts. Natural, Sunburst or Walnut.

1977-1979		$900	$1,000

Roy Smeck Radio Grande Hawaiian
1934-1939. Dreadnought acoustic flat-top, rosewood back and sides, bound body and neck. Natural.

1934-1939		$6,500	$8,000

Roy Smeck Stage Deluxe Hawaiian
1934-1942. Dreadnought acoustic flat-top, mahogany back and sides, bound body. Natural.

1934-1942		$4,000	$6,000

S-1
1976-1980. Single cutaway solidbody, pointed headstock, three single-coil pickups, similar to the Marauder. Various colors.

1976-1980		$600	$700

SG
Following are the various, listed alphabetically, bearing the SG name:

'63 Corvette Sting Ray (Custom shop)
1996-1997. SG-style body carved to simulate split rear window on '63 Corvette, "Sting Ray" inlay, 150 instruments built. Offered in Black, White, Silver or Red.

1996-1997	Black	$3,500	$4,500

SG '61 Reissue
1993-present. Double cutaway SG body, two humbuckers, Cherry. See SG Reissue for 1986-1987, and SG '62 Reissue for 1988-1991.

1993-2002		$850	$1,200

SG '62 Reissue Showcase Edition
1988. Guitar of the month, bright Blue Opaque finish, 200 made.

1988		$1,000	$1,300

SG '62 Reissue/SG Reissue
1986-1991. Called SG Reissue 1986-1987, SG '62 Reissue 1988-1991, and SG '61 Reissue 1993-present. Cherry.

1986-1987	SG reissue	$850	$1,200
1988-1991	'62 reissue	$850	$1,200

SG 90 Double
1988-1990. SG body, updated electronics, graphite reinforced neck, two pickups. Cherry, Turquoise or White.

1988-1990		$500	$650

SG 90 Single
1988-1990. SG body, updated electronics, graphite reinforced neck, one humbucker pickup. Cherry, Turquoise or White.

1988-1990		$450	$600

SG Corvette Sting Ray L.E. (Custom Shop)
1996 only. SG-style body, Sting Ray inlay, 150 instruments built, offered in Black, Red or Silver.

1996		$2,000	$2,200

SG Custom
1963-1980. Renamed from Les Paul Custom, three humbuckers, vibrato. Made with Les Paul Custom plate from 1961-1963 (see Les Paul Custom). White finish until 1968, Walnut and others after.

1963	White, pat. #	$6,500	$9,000
1964	White	$5,500	$8,500
1965	White	$5,000	$7,500
1966	White	$4,500	$7,000
1967	White	$3,500	$4,500
1968	White	$3,000	$4,500
1969	Walnut	$2,500	$3,500
1969	White	$3,000	$4,000
1970-1973	Walnut	$2,000	$2,800
1970-1973	White option	$2,800	$3,500
1974-1976	Various colors	$2,000	$2,800
1977-1980	Various colors	$1,800	$2,600

SG Custom '67 Reissue/Les Paul SG '67 Custom
1991-1993. The SG Custom '67 Reissue has a Wine Red finish. The Les Paul SG '67 Custom (1992-1993) has a Wine Red or White finish.

1991-1993		$1,700	$1,800

SG Deluxe
1971-1972, 1981-1985, 1998-present. The 1970s models were offered in Natural, Cherry or Walnut finishes. Reintroduced in 1998 with three Firebird mini-humbucker-style pickups in Black, Ice Blue or Red finishes..

1971-1972	Cherry	$1,300	$1,600
1971-1972	Natural or Walnut	$1,100	$1,400
1981-1985	Various colors	$700	$800
1998-1999	Various colors	$800	$900

SG Exclusive
1979. SG with humbuckers, coil-tap and rotary control knob, block inlay, pearl logo (not decal), Black/Ebony finish.

1979		$900	$1,000

SG Firebrand
1980-1982. Double cut mahogany solidbody, rough natural finish, Gibson branded in headstock, 2 exposed humbuckers, Firebrand logo on "The SG (Standard)" model.

1980-1982		$600	$750

SG I
1972-1977. Double cut mahogany body, one mini-humbucker pickup (some with SG Jr. P-90). Cherry or Walnut.

1972-1977		$650	$900

SG II
1972-1976. Double cut mahogany body, two mini-humbucker pickups (some SG IIs in 1975 had regular humbuckers). Cherry or Walnut.

1972-1976		$700	$950

1976 Gibson S-1

1963 Gibson SG Custom

Gibson SG Junior

MODEL YEAR	FEATURES	LOW	HIGH

SG III

1972-1974. Replaces SG-250. Double pointed cut mahogany body, 2 mini-humbucker pickups. The SG III was the sunburst version of the II. Some shipped as late as 1979.

| 1972-1974 | | $700 | $950 |

SG Jr.

1963-1971, 1991-1994. One pickup, solidbody.

1963	Alpine White	$2,400	$2,600
1963	Cherry	$1,800	$2,100
1964	Cherry	$1,600	$1,900
1964	White	$2,300	$2,500
1965	Cherry	$1,500	$1,700
1965	White	$2,200	$2,400
1966	Cherry	$1,500	$1,600
1966	White	$2,100	$2,300
1967	Cherry	$1,400	$1,500
1967	White	$1,700	$2,000
1968	Cherry	$1,200	$1,400
1968	White	$1,500	$1,800
1969	Cherry	$1,100	$1,300
1970	Cherry	$1,000	$1,200
1971	Cherry or Walnut	$900	$1,100
1991-1994	Various colors	$700	$900

SG Les Paul Custom

1987-1992. Three pickups. Called the SG '90 Les Paul Custom towards the end of its run.

| 1987-1989 | Antique Ivory | $1,500 | $1,800 |
| 1990-1992 | White | $1,300 | $1,600 |

SG Les Paul Custom 30th Anniversary

1991. SG body, 3 humbuckers, Gold hardware, TV Yellow finish, 30th Anniversary on peghead.

| 1991 | | $1,500 | $2,000 |

SG Pete Townshend Signature (Historic/Custom Shop)

2000-2003. SG Special with 1970 specs, large guard, two cases, cherry red.

| 2000-2003 | | $2,200 | $2,400 |

SG Pro

1971-1973. Two P-90 pickups, tune-o-matic bridge, vibrato. Cherry, Mahogany or Walnut.

| 1971-1973 | Cherry | $1,200 | $1,400 |
| 1971-1973 | Mahogany or Walnut | $1,000 | $1,200 |

SG Special

1959-1978, 1986-1996, 2000-2001. Rounded double cut for 1959-1960, switched to SG body early-1961. Two P-90s 1959-1971, 2 mini-humbuckers 1972-1978, 2 regular size humbuckers on current version. Reintroduced variation to the SG line in 1986-1999, then reintroduced again in 2000.

1959	Cherry, slab, high neck pickup	$4,500	$5,000
1960	Cherry, slab, lower neck pickup	$5,000	$5,500
1961	Cherry, SG body	$3,200	$3,800
1962	Cherry	$2,900	$3,200
1962	White	$3,500	$3,800
1963	Cherry	$2,600	$2,900
1963	White	$3,400	$3,700
1964	Cherry	$2,500	$2,800

Gibson SG Pete Townshend Signature

MODEL YEAR	FEATURES	LOW	HIGH
1964	White	$3,200	$3,500
1965	Cherry	$2,100	$2,300
1965	White	$2,700	$2,900
1966	Cherry, large guard	$1,900	$2,100
1966	Cherry, small guard	$2,000	$2,200
1966	White, large guard	$2,300	$2,500
1966	White, small guard	$2,500	$2,700
1967	Cherry	$1,800	$2,000
1967	White	$2,100	$2,300
1968-1971	Cherry	$1,400	$1,700
1972-1975	Cherry or Walnut	$1,200	$1,400
1976-1978	Cherry or Walnut	$1,000	$1,200
1986-1996	Various colors	$650	$750
2000-2001	Cherry	$600	$700

SG Standard

1963-1981, 1983-present. Les Paul Standard changes to SG body, 2 humbuckers, some very early models have optional factory Bigsby.

1963	Cherry	$5,500	$7,000
1964	Cherry	$5,000	$6,500
1965	Cherry	$5,000	$6,000
1965	Pelham Blue (faded)	$5,000	$7,000
1965	Pelham Blue (unfaded)	$7,000	$10,000
1966	Cherry	$4,000	$5,000
1967	Burgundy Metallic	$4,500	$6,000
1967	Cherry	$2,500	$3,500
1967	White	$3,500	$5,000
1968	Cherry	$2,500	$3,500
1969	Cherry, engraved lyre	$2,000	$3,000
1970	Cherry, engraved lyre	$1,900	$2,500
1970	Cherry, non-lyre tailpiece	$1,500	$2,000
1971	Cherry	$1,300	$1,800
1972-1975	New specs and colors	$1,300	$1,600
1976-1981	New color line-up	$1,100	$1,400
1983-1999		$850	$1,000

SG Standard Korina

1993-1994. Korina version of SG Standard, limited run, natural.

| 1993-1994 | | $1,600 | $2,000 |

SG Tommy Iommi Signature (Historic/Custom Shop)

1999-2003. Signature humbucking pickups without poles, cross inlay markers, ebony or wine red.

| 1999 | | $1,800 | $2,200 |

SG TV

1959-1968. Les Paul TV changed to SG body. Double rounded cutaway solidbody for 1959-1960, SG body 1961-1968, one pickup, limed mahogany (TV yellow) finish.

| 1959-1961 | TV Yellow, slab body | $4,200 | $4,800 |
| 1961-1963 | White, SG body | $2,400 | $2,600 |

MODEL YEAR	FEATURES	EXC. COND. LOW	HIGH

SG-100
1971-1972. Double cut solidbody, 1 pickup, cherry or walnut.

| 1971-1972 | Melody Maker pickup | $500 | $850 |
| 1971-1972 | P-90 pickup option | $900 | $1,150 |

SG-200
1971-1972. Two pickup version of SG-100 in black, cherry or walnut finish. Replaced by SG II.

| 1971-1972 | Melody Maker pickups | $600 | $900 |

SG-250
1971-1972. Two pickup version of SG-100 in cherry sunburst. Replaced by SG III.

| 1971-1972 | Melody Maker pickups | $600 | $900 |

SG-X (All American)
1995-1999. Renamed the SG-X in 1998, previously part of the all American series, SG body with single bridge humbucker. Various colors.

| 1995-1999 | | $500 | $550 |

The SG
1979-1980. Normal SG specs, solid walnut body and neck, ebony 'board, 2 exposed-coil humbuckers, model name logo on truss rod. Firebrand logo added in 1980, refer to SG Firebrand listing.

| 1979-1980 | | $650 | $750 |

The SG (Standard)
1983-1987. Normal SG specs, exposed humbucker pickups, model name logo on truss rod, walnut neck and walnut body, Natural and other colors.

| 1983-1987 | | $650 | $750 |

SJ (Southern Jumbo)
1942-1969,1991-1996. Flat-top, Sunburst standard, Natural optional starting in 1954 (Natural finish version called Country-Western starting in 1956), round shoulders (changed to square in 1962). Catalog name changed to SJ Deluxe in 1970, refer to that listing.

1942-1944		$4,800	$5,500
1947-1948		$4,000	$5,000
1949-1950		$3,500	$4,500
1951-1955		$3,200	$4,300
1954-1956	Natural option, round shoulder	$3,500	$4,500
1954-1956	Sunburst round shoulder	$3,100	$4,000
1956-1961	Round shoulder	$2,800	$3,600
1962-1964	Square shoulder	$2,600	$2,900
1965-1966		$2,300	$2,700
1967-1968		$2,000	$2,500
1969	Below belly bridge	$1,700	$2,000

SJ Deluxe (Southern Jumbo)
1970-1978. SJ name changed to SJ Deluxe in catalog, along with a series of engineering changes.

1970-1971	Non-adj. Saddle	$1,400	$1,700
1972-1973	Unbound fingerboard	$1,100	$1,500
1974-1978	4-ply to binding	$850	$950

SJ-100 1939 Centennial
1994. Acoustic flat-top, limited edition. Sunburst

| 1994 | | $1,500 | $1,800 |

SJ-200 Ray Whitley/J-200 Custom Club
1994-1995. Based on Ray Whitley's late-1930s J-200, including engraved inlays and initials on the truss rod cover. Only 37 made. One of the limited edition models the Montana division released to celebrate Gibson's 100th anniversary.

| 1994-1995 | | $7,000 | $9,000 |

SJN (Country-Western)
1956-1969. Flat-top, Natural finish version of SJ, round shoulders 1956-1962, square shoulders after that. Called the SJN in 1960 and 1961, the SJN Country Western after that. Catalog name changed to SJN Deluxe in 1970, refer to that listing.

1956-1961	Round shoulders	$3,200	$4,000
1962-1964	Square shoulders	$2,900	$3,200
1965-1966	Square shoulders	$2,700	$3,000
1967-1968	Square shoulders	$2,500	$2,800
1969	Below belly bridge	$1,900	$2,200

SJN Deluxe (Country-Western Jumbo)
1970-1978. SJN name changed to SJN Deluxe in catalog, along with a series of engineering changes.

| 1970-1971 1972-1973 | Non-adj. Saddle/ Unbound fingerboard | $1,600 $1,300 | $1,900 $1,500 |
| 1974-1978 | 4-ply to binding | $900 | $1,000 |

Sonex-180 Custom
1980-1982. Two Super humbuckers, coil-tap, maple neck, ebony board, single cut, body of "Multi-Phonic" synthetic material. Various colors.

| 1980-1982 | | $450 | $550 |

Sonex-180 Deluxe
1980-1984. Hardwood neck, rosewood board, single cut, body of "Multi-Phonic" synthetic material, two pickups, no coil-tap. Various colors.

| 1980-1984 | | $400 | $500 |

Spirit I
1982-1988. Double rounded cut, 1 pickup, chrome hardware, various colors.

| 1982-1988 | | $350 | $450 |

Spirit II XPL
1985-1987. Double cut solidbody, Kahler trem, 2 pickups, various colors.

| 1985-1987 | | $400 | $550 |

SR-71
1987-1989. Floyd Rose tremolo, 1 humbucker, 2 single-coil pickups, various colors. Wayne Charvel designed.

| 1987-1989 | | $400 | $550 |

Style O
1902-1925. Acoustic archtop, oval soundhole, bound top, neck and headstock. Various colors.

| 1910-1925 | | $4,000 | $4,800 |

Style U Harp Guitar
1902-1939. Acoustic 6-string, with 10 or 12 sub-bass strings, maple back and sides, bound soundhole. Black.

| 1915-1919 | | $5,500 | $6,500 |

1983 Gibson The SG

1983 Gibson Sonex 180 Deluxe

*1959 Gibson
Super 400C*

Gibson Tal Farlow

MODEL YEAR	FEATURES	EXC. COND. LOW	HIGH

Super 300 (non-cutaway)
1948-1955. Acoustic archtop, non-cut, bound body, neck and headstock, sunburst.

1948-1955		$3,500	$5,000

Super 300 C (cutaway)
1954-1958. Acoustic archtop, rounded cut, bound body, neck and headstock, sunburst with Natural option.

1954-1957	Sunburst	$5,500	$7,000

Super 400
1934-1941, 1947-1955. Acoustic archtop, non-cutaway, multi-bound, F-holes. Sunburst (see Super 400 N for Natural version).

1934-1935		$11,000	$13,500
1936-1940		$9,500	$11,000
1941-1947		$8,000	$9,500
1948-1955		$8,000	$9,000

Super 400 N
1940, 1948-1955. Natural finish version of Super 400, non-cut, acoustic archtop.

1940		$9,000	$13,000
1948-1950		$8,500	$12,000
1951-1952		$7,500	$10,500

'39 Super 400 Historical Collection
1993-2000. Reissue of non-cutaway 1939 version. Part of Gibson's Historic Collection.

1993-1995	Sunburst	$5,500	$6,500
1993-1995	Wine Red Burgundy	$4,500	$5,000

Super 400 P (Premium)
1939-1941. Acoustic archtop, single rounded cutaway, 1939 model fingerboard rests on top, sunburst finish.

1939		$26,000	$28,000
1940-1941		$24,000	$26,000

Super 400 PN (Premium Natural)
1939-1940. Rounded cutaway, 1939 fingerboard rests on top, Natural finish.

1939		$40,000	$50,000
1940		$36,000	$45,000

Super 400 C
1948-1982. Introduced as Super 400 Premier, acoustic archtop, single cut, sunburst finish (Natural is called Super 400 CN).

1948-1957		$12,000	$16,000
1958-1959		$11,000	$14,000
1960-1963		$11,000	$13,000
1964-1965		$10,000	$12,000
1966-1969		$7,000	$10,000
1970-1974		$6,000	$8,000
1975-1982		$5,000	$7,000

Super 400 CN
1940-1941, 1950-1987. Natural finish version of Super 400 C.

1952-1959		$14,000	$16,000
1960-1964		$13,000	$15,000
1965-1969		$10,000	$12,000
1970-1977		$6,000	$8,000

Super 400 CES
1951-present. Electric version of Super 400 C. Archtop, single cut (round 1951-1960 and 1969-present, pointed 1960-1969), 2 pickups (P-90s 1951-1954, Alnico Vs 1954-1957, humbuckers 1957 on). Sunburst (Natural version called Super 400 CESN). Now part of Gibson's Historic Collection.

1951-1953	P-90 pickups	$14,000	$18,000
1954-1956	Alnico V pickups	$15,000	$19,000
1957-1959	Humbucker pickups	$16,000	$21,000
1960-1962		$14,000	$17,000
1963-1964		$13,000	$15,000
1965-1966		$8,500	$12,000
1967-1969		$7,500	$10,000
1970-1974		$7,000	$9,500
1975-1979		$6,500	$8,000
1980-1987		$5,500	$7,000

Super 400 CESN
1952-present. Natural version of Super 400 CES. Now part of Gibson's Historic Collection.

1952		$20,000	$25,000
1953-1956	Single-coils	$18,500	$22,000
1957-1960	Humbuckers	$30,000	$35,000
1961	Sharp cut introduced	$28,000	$30,000
1962	PAFs	$23,000	$25,000
1963-1964	Pat. #	$18,000	$20,000
1965-1966		$13,000	$15,000
1967-1969		$11,000	$13,000
1970-1982		$6,000	$10,000

Super Jumbo 100
1939-1943. Jumbo flat-top, mahogany back and sides, bound body and neck, Sunburst. Reintroduced as J-100 with different specs in 1984.

1939-1943		$16,000	$22,000

Super Jumbo/Super Jumbo 200
1938-1947. Initially called Super Jumbo in 1938 and named Super Jumbo 200 in 1939. Name then changed to J-200 (see that listing) by '47 (with maple back and sides) and SJ-200 by the '50s. Named for super large jumbo 16 7/8" flat-top body, double braced with rosewood back and sides, sunburst finish.

1938-1939		$40,000	$55,000
1940-1942		$40,000	$50,000

Super V CES
1978-1993. Archtop, L-5 with a Super 400 neck. Natural or Sunburst.

1978-1993		$5,000	$5,500

Tal Farlow
1962-1971, 1993-present. Full body, single cutaway archtop, two humbucking pickups, triple-bound top. Reintroduced 1993, now part of Gibson's Historic Collection.

1962-1964	Viceroy Brown	$7,500	$8,700
1965-1966	Viceroy Brown	$7,000	$7,900
1967-1969	Viceroy Brown	$6,000	$7,000
1970-1971	Viceroy Brown	$4,800	$5,800
1993-1999	Cherry or Viceroy Brown	$2,700	$3,000
1993-1999	Natural, figured wood	$2,900	$3,400

The *Vintage Guitar Price Guide* shows low to high values for items in all-original excellent condition, and, where applicable, with original case or cover.

GUITARS

MODEL YEAR	FEATURES	EXC. COND. LOW	HIGH

TG-0 (L-0 based)
1927-1933. Acoustic tenor based on L-0, mahogany body. Light Amber.
1927-1933 $1,200 $1,300

TG-0 (LG-0 based)
1960-1974. Acoustic tenor based on LG-0, mahogany body. Natural.
1960-1964 $650 $750
1965-1969 $550 $650
1970-1974 $450 $550

TG-00 (tenor flat-top based on L-00)
1932-1943. Tenor flat-top based on L-00.
1932-1943 $1,000 $1,200

TG-1
1927-1937. Acoustic flat-top, tenor guitar based on L-1, mahogany back and sides, bound body. Sunburst.
1927-1937 $1,400 $1,500

TG-7
1934-1940. Tenor based on the L-7. Sunburst.
1934-1940 $1,600 $1,700

TG-25/TG-25 N
1962-1970. Acoustic flat-top, tenor guitar based on B-25, mahogany back and sides. Natural or Sunburst.
1962-1964 $700 $800
1965-1969 $600 $700
1970 $500 $600

TG-50
1934-1958. Acoustic archtop, tenor guitar based on L-50, mahogany back and sides. Sunburst.
1934-1940 $1,000 $1,200
1947-1949 $800 $1,100
1950-1958 $700 $900

Trini Lopez Deluxe
1964-1970. Double pointed cutaway, thinline archtop, two humbuckers, triple-bound. Sunburst.
1964-1970 $2,500 $3,000

Trini Lopez Standard
1964-1970. Double rounded cutaway, thinline archtop, two humbuckers, tune-o-matic bridge, trapeze tailpiece, single-bound. Cherry, Sparkling Burgundy and Pelham Blue finishes.
1964-1970   Cherry $1,800 $2,500
1964-1970   Sparkling Burgundy option $2,000 $2,700

U-2
1987-1989. Double cut, 1 humbucker and 2 single-coil pickups, ebony or red. Renamed Mach II in 1990-1991.
1987-1991 $650 $750

U-2 Showcase Edition
1988. November 1988 Guitar of the Month series, 250 made.
1988 $750 $900

US-1/US-3
1986-1991. Double cut maple top with mahogany back, 3 humbucker pickups (US-1), or three P-90s (US-3), standard production and Custom Shop.
1986-1991   US-3, P-90s $500 $650

USA Map Guitar
1983, 1985. Body cutout like lower 48, 2 humbuckers, limited run promotion. 1983 version in natural mahogany or red, white and blue. 1985 version red, white and blue stars and stripes on a white background.
1983   Natural $1,900 $2,100
1983   Red, white and blue $2,100 $2,400
1985 $2,200 $2,500

Victory MV II (MV 2)
1981-1984. Asymetrical double cutaway with long horn, 3-way slider, maple body and neck, rosewood fingerboard, two pickups.
1981-1984 $600 $1,100

Victory MV X (MV 10)
1981-1984. Double cut solidbody, 3 humbucking pickups, 5-way switch. Various colors.
1981-1984 $700 $1,200

XPL Custom
1985-1986. Explorer-like shape, exposed humbuckers, locking tremolo, bound maple top. Sunburst or White.
1985-1986 $550 $650

Giffin
1977-1988, 1997-present. Professional and premium grade, production/custom, hollow-, semi-hollow-, and solidbody guitars built by luthier Roger Giffin in West San Fernando Valley, California. For '77-'88, Giffin's shop was in London. From '88 to '93, he worked for the Gibson Custom Shop in California as a Master Luthier. In '97, Giffin set up shop in Sweden for a year, moving back to California in the Spring of '98. He also built small numbers of instruments during '67-'76 and '94-'96 (when he had a repair business).

Gigliotti
2000-present. Premium grade, production/custom, electric guitars with a metal plate top and tone chambers and designed by Patrick Gigliotti in Tacoma, Washington.

Gila Eban Guitars
1979-present. Premium grade, custom, classical guitars built by luthier Gila Eban in Riverside, Connecticut.

Gilbert Guitars
1965-present. Custom classical guitars by luthiers John Gilbert and William Gilbert in Paso Robles, California. Son William has handled all production since 1991.

Girl Brand Guitars
Premium-grade, production/custom, guitars built by luthier Chris Larsen in Tucson, Arizona.

Gitane
2003-present. Classic Selmer-Maccaferri style jazz guitars made in China for Saga.

1967 Gibson Trini Lopez

Girl Brand Crossroadsgirl

Gittler

Godin LG signature

MODEL YEAR	FEATURES	EXC. COND. LOW	HIGH

Gittler

1974-ca.1985. Minimalistic electric guitar designed by Allan Gittler, consisting basically of a thin rod with frets welded to it. A total of 560 were built, with Gittler making the first 60 in the U.S. from '74 to the early '80s. The remainder were made around '85 in Israel by the Astron corporation under a licensing agreement. Three Gittler basses were also built. Gittler emigrated to Israel in the early '80s and changed his name to Avraham Bar Rashi. He died in 2002. An U.S.-made Gittler is the only musical instrument in the Museum of Modern Art in New York.

Metal-skeleton Gittler

1971-1982		$2,500	$3,500
1982-1985		$1,500	$2,000

Godin

1987-present. Intermediate and professional grade, production, solidbody electrics and nylon and steel string acoustic/electrics from luthier Robert Godin. They also build basses and mandolins. Necks and bodies are made in La Patrie, Quebec with final assembly in Berlin, New Hampshire. Godin is also involved in the Seagull, Norman, and Patrick & Simon brand of guitars.

A-6

1996-2004. Single cut acoustic/electric.

1996-2004		$425	$450

Acousticaster

1987-present. Thin line single cut acoustic/electric, maple neck, various colors.

1987-1999		$500	$550
2000-2003		$600	$650

Acousticaster Deluxe

1994-2003. Mahogany neck Acousticaster.

1994-2003		$550	$650

Artisan ST I/ST I

1992-1998. Offset double cut solidbody, birdseye maple top, 3 pickups.

1992-1998		$550	$600

G-1000

1993-1996. Double cut with long bass horn, gold hardware, single-single-humbucker configuration.

1993-1996		$400	$425

Glissentar

2000-present. Electric/acoustic nylon 11-string, solid cedar top, chambered maple body, fretless.

2000	Natural	$450	$500

Jeff Cook Signature

1994. Quilted maple top, light maple back, two twin rail and one humbucker pickups.

1994		$550	$600

LG

1995-present. Single cut carved slab mahogany body, 2 Tetrad Combo pickups ('95-'97) or 2 Duncan SP-90 pickups ('9-present), satin lacquer finish.

1997-2001		$375	$450

MODEL YEAR	FEATURES	EXC. COND. LOW	HIGH

LGXT

1997-present. Single cut silver leaf maple carved solidbody, 2 Duncan humbuckers. Various quality tops offered.

1997-2000	AA top	$900	$1,000
1997-2000	AAA top	$1,100	$1,250
1997-2000	Standard top	$800	$900

Multiac Series

1994-present. Thinline electric with solid spruce top, RMC Sensor System electronics, available in either nylon string or steel string versions, built-in EQ, program up/down buttons.

1994-1999	Duet Nylon, classical	$800	$925
1994-1999	Steel string, single cut	$800	$925
2000-2003	Steel string, single cut	$825	$950

Radiator

1999-present. Single cutaway, dual pickup, pearloid top, dot markers.

1999-2002		$300	$325

Golden Hawaiian

1920s-1930s. Private branded lap guitar most likely made by one of the many Chicago makers for a small retailer, publisher, cataloger, or teaching studio.

Guitars

1920s	Sunburst	$250	$450
1930s	Sunburst	$250	$450

Goodall

1972-present. Premium grade, custom flat-tops and nylon-strings, built by luthier James Goodall originally in California and, since 1992, in Kailua-Kona, Hawaii.

Full-Size Acoustic

1980s		$2,000	$2,500

Gordon-Smith

1979-present. Intermediate and professional grade, production/custom, semi-hollow and solidbody guitars built by luthier John Smith in Partington, England.

Gower

1955-1960s. Built in Nashville by Jay Gower, later joined by his son Randy. Gower is also associated with Billy Grammer and Grammer guitars.

G-55-2

1960s. J-50 square shoulder-style flat-top, triple abalone rosette, abalone fretboard trim, small block markers.

1960s	Natural	$1,100	$1,250

G-65 Flat-Top

1960s. J-45 square shoulder-style flat-top, lower belly bridge with pearl dots on bridge, dot markers.

1960s	Sunburst	$700	$1,050

Solidbody Electric

Mosrite influenced odd-shaped body, double pickup, bolt-on neck, Bigsby bridge, high output single-coil pickups.

1960s		$500	$750

MODEL		EXC. COND.	
YEAR	FEATURES	LOW	HIGH

Goya

1955-present. Brand initially used by Hershman Musical Instrument Company of New York City, New York, in mid-'50s for acoustic guitars made in Sweden by Levin, particularly known for its classicals. From '58 to '61 they imported Hagstrom-made electrics labeled as Goya. By '63 the company had become the Goya Musical Instrument Corporation, marketing primarily Goya acoustics. Goya was purchased by Avnet, Inc., prior to '66, when Avnet purchased Guild Guitars. In '69, Goya was purchased by Kustom which offered the instruments until '71. Probably some '70s guitars were made in Japan. The brand name purchased by C.F. Martin in the late-'70s, with Japanese-made acoustic guitars, solidbody electric guitars and basses, banjos and mandolins imported in around '78 and continuing through the '80s. The brand is currently used on Korean-made acoustic and acoustic/electric guitars, banjos and mandolins.

Classical Guitars

1960s		$300	$400

Folk Guitars

1960s	12-String	$250	$350
1960s	6-String	$250	$350

Model 80/Model 90 Sparkle Top

1959-1962. Les Paul single cutaway-style body, replaceable modular pickup assembly. Sparkle top.

1959-1962		$600	$700

Panther S-3

1960s. Double cut solidbody, 3 pickups, Panther S-3 Goya logo, volume and tone knobs with 6 upper bass bout switches, bolt-on neck.

1960s		$500	$600

Rangemaster

1967-1969. Double cut with two offset double-coil pickups and lots of buttons. Made by EKO.

1967-1969	Sunburst	$500	$600

Graf, Oskar

1970-present. Luthier Oskar Graf builds his premium grade, production/custom flat-top, classical, and flamenco guitars in Clarendon, Ontario. He also builds basses and lutes.

Grammer

1965-1970. Founded by Bill Grammer then sold to Ampeg.

G-10

1965-1970. Solid Brazilian rosewood back and sides, solid spruce top, large crown-shaped bridge, pearl dot markers, Natural.

1965-1970		$1,250	$1,700

G-20

1965-1970. Natural.

1965-1970		$1,250	$1,700

G-30

1965-1970. Natural.

1965-1970		$1,250	$1,700

MODEL		EXC. COND.	
YEAR	FEATURES	LOW	HIGH

G-58

1965-1970. Top-of-the-line Grammer, Brazilian rosewood back and sides, Adirondack spruce top.

1965-1970		$1,600	$2,100

S-30

1965-1970. Solid spruce top, solid ribbon mahogany back and sides.

1965-1970		$1,000	$1,250

Granata Guitars

1989-present. Luthier Peter Granata builds his professional grade, custom, flat-top and resonator guitars in Oak Ridge, New Jersey.

Graveel

Production/custom, solidbody guitars built by luthier Dean Graveel in Indianapolis, Indiana.

GRD

1978-1982. High-end acoustic and electric guitars produced in Charles Fox's Guitar Research & Design Center in Vermont. GRD introduced the original thin-line acoustic-electric guitar to the world at the 1978 Winter NAMM show.

Greco

1960s-present. Brand name used in Japan by Fuji Gen Gakki, maker of many Hoshino/Ibanez guitars; thus often Greco guitars are similar to Ibanez. During the '70s the company sold many high high-quality copies of American designs, though by '75 they offered many weird-shaped original designs, including the Iceman and carved people shapes. By the late-'70s they were offering neck-through-body guitars. Currently owned by Kanda Shokai and offering solidbody, hollowbody and acoustic guitars.

Electric Archtop Guitars

1960s		$250	$450

Electric Beetles Violin-Shape Copy

1960s		$250	$550

Electric Solidbody Guitars

1960s		$250	$550

Folk 12-String Hummingbird Copy

1960s		$200	$300

Green, Aaron

1990-present. Premium and presentation grade, custom, classical and flamenco guitars built by luthier Aaron Green in Waltham, Massachusetts.

Greene & Campbell

2002-present. Jeff Greene and Dean Campbell build their intermediate and professional grade, production/custom, solidbody guitars in Westwood, Massachusetts. Greene also built guitars under his own name.

Greene, Jeffrey

2000-2002. Professional grade, production/custom, electric solidbody guitars built by lutheir

60s Goya Rangemaster

1981 Oskar Graf Opus

Greenfield Philmore

1966 Gretsch Anniversary

MODEL		EXC. COND.	
YEAR	FEATURES	LOW	HIGH

Jeffrey Greene in West Kingston, Rhode Island. He now works with Dean Campbell building the Greene & Campbell line of guitars.

Greenfield Guitars

1997-present. Premium grade, production/custom, flat-top, classical, and electric archtop guitars built by luthier Michael Greenfield in Montreal, Quebec.

Gretsch

1883-present. Currently Gretsch offers intermediate, professional, and premium grade, production, acoustic, solidbody, hollowbody, double neck, resonator and Hawaiian guitars. They also offer basses and lap steels. Previous brands included Gretsch, Rex, 20th Century, Recording King (for Montgomery Ward), Dorado (Japanese imports).

Founded by Friedrich Gretsch in Brooklyn, NY, making drums, banjos, tambourines, and toy instruments which were sold to large distributors including C. Bruno and Wurlitzer. Upon early death of Friedrich, son Fred Gretsch Sr. took over business at age 15. By the turn of century the company was also making mandolins. In the '20s, they were distributing Rex and 20th Century brands, some made by Gretsch, some by others such as Kay. Charles "Duke" Kramer joins Gretsch in '35. In '40 Gretsch purchased Bacon & Day banjos. Fred Gretsch, Sr. retired in '42 and was replaced by sons Fred, Jr. and Bill. Fred departs for Navy and Bill runs company until his death in '48, when Fred resumes control. After the war the decision was made to promote the Gretsch brand rather than selling to distributors, though some jobbing continues. Kramer becomes Chicago branch manager in '48.

In '67 Baldwin of Cincinnati buys Gretsch. During '70-'72 the factory relocates from Brooklyn to Booneville, Arkansas and company headquarters moves to Cincinnati. A '72 factory fire drastically reduces production for next two years. In '78 Baldwin buys Kustom amps and sells Gretsch to Kustom's Charlie Roy, and headquarters are moved to Chanute, Kansas. Duke Kramer retires in '80. Guitar production ends '80-'81. Ca. '83 ownership reverts back to Baldwin and Kramer was asked to arrange the sale of the company. In '84 Fred Gretsch III was contacted and in '85 Gretsch guitars came back to the Gretsch family and Fred Gretsch Enterprises, Ltd (FGE). Initial Gretsch Enterprise models were imports made by Japan's Terada Company. In '95, some U.S.-made models were introduced.

As of January 1, 2003, Fred Gretsch Enterprises, Ltd granted Fender Musical Instruments Corporation the exclusive rights to develop, produce, market and distribute Gretsch guitars worldwide where FMIC is responsible for all aspects of the Gretsch stringed instrument product lines and brandnames, including development of new products. Fred Gretsch consulted during the changeover and on product development and quality control.

MODEL		EXC. COND.	
YEAR	FEATURES	LOW	HIGH

12-String Electric Archtop (6075/6076)

1967-1972. 16 inch double cutaway, 2 Super Tron pickups, 17 inch body option available. Sunburst (6075) or Natural (6076).

| 1967 | | $1,800 | $2,100 |

Anniversary 6124/6125

1958-1972. Single cut hollowbody archtop, one pickup (Filtron 1958-1960, Hi-Lo Tron 1961 on), bound body. Named for Gretsch's 75th anniversary.

1958-1959	Green 2-tone, 6124	$1,500	$1,800
1958-1959	Sunburst, 6125	$1,300	$1,700
1960-1961	Green 2-Tone, 6124	$1,500	$1,800
1960-1961	Sunburst, 6125	$1,200	$1,600
1962-1964	Green or Tan, 6124	$1,100	$1,400
1962-1964	Sunburst, 6125	$1,000	$1,300
1965-1972	Green or Tan, 6124	$1,000	$1,300
1965-1972	Sunburst, 6125	$900	$1,200

Astro-Jet (6126)

1965-1967. Solidbody electric, double cut, 2 pickups, vibrato, 4/2 tuner arrangement. Red top with Black back and sides.

| 1965-1967 | | $1,000 | $1,500 |

Atkins Axe (7685/7686)

1976-1980. Solidbody electric, single pointed cut, 2 pickups. Ebony stain (7685) or red rosewood stain (7686). Called the Super Axe with added on-board effects.

| 1976-1980 | | $1,000 | $1,250 |

Atkins Super Axe/Super Axe (7680/7681)

1976-1981. Single pointed cut solidbody with built-in phaser and sustain, 5 knobs, 3 switches. Red rosewood (7680) or ebony (7681) stains.

| 1976-1981 | Ebony or | | |
| | Red rosewood | $1,300 | $1,700 |

Bikini Doubleneck

1961-1962. Solidbody electric. Separate 6-string and bass neck-body units that slid into one of three body "butterflies" - one for the six-string only (6023), one for bass only (6024), one for double neck (six and bass - 6025). Components could be purchased separately. Prices here are for both necks and all three bodies.

| 1961-1962 | | $1,500 | $1,800 |

Black Hawk (6100/6101)

1967-1972. Hollowbody archtop, double cutaway, two pickups, G tailpiece or Bigsby vibrato, bound body and neck. Sunburst (6100) or Black (6101).

| 1967-1972 | | $1,600 | $1,800 |

Bo Diddley (6138)

2000-present. Reproduction of rectangle-shaped, semi-hollow guitar originally made for Diddley by Gretsch.

| 2000 | Firebird Red | $1,400 | $1,600 |

Brian Setzer Signature (G6120-SSL)

1994-present. Hollowbody electric, double cut, 2 Alnico PAF Filtertron pickups, based on the classic Gretsch 6120. Formerly called the Brian Setzer Nashville and currently marked as the Brian Setzer Hot Rod in various colors.

| 1994-1999 | Western Orange | $1,650 | $1,800 |

MODEL YEAR	FEATURES	EXC. COND. LOW	HIGH

Broadkaster (hollowbody)
1975-1980. Double cut archtop hollowbody, 2 pickups, natural or sunburst.

1975-1980		$900	$1,200

Broadkaster (solidbody)
1975-1979. Double cutaway, maple body, two pickups, bolt-on neck. Natural (7600) or Sunburst (7601).

1975-1979		$500	$550

BST 1000 Beast
1979-1980. Single cut solidbody, bolt-on neck, mahogany body. Available with 1 pickup in Walnut stain (8210) or Red stain (8216) or 2 pickups in walnut (7617, 8215, 8217) or red stain (8211).

1979-1980		$425	$500

BST 2000 Beast
1979. Symmetrical double cut solidbody of mahogany, 2 humbucking pickups, bolt-on neck, Walnut stain (7620 or 8220) or Red stain (8221).

1979		$475	$525

BST 5000 Beast
1979-1980. Asymmetrical double cutaway solidbody, neck-through, walnut and maple construction, two humbucking pickups, stud tailpiece. Natural walnut/maple (8250).

1979-1980		$500	$550

Burl Ives (6004)
1949-1955. Flat-top acoustic, mahogany back and sides, bound body. Natural top (6004).

1949-1955		$450	$600

Chet Atkins Country Gentleman (6122/7670)
1957-1981. Hollowbody, single cutaway to late-1962 and double after, two pickups, painted F-holes until 1972, real after. Mahogany finish (6122). Model number changes to 7670 in 1971.

1957-1960	Single cutaway	$5,000	$6,300
1961		$4,700	$6,200
1962	Single cutaway	$4,200	$4,900
1963	Double cutaway	$2,600	$3,400
1964		$2,500	$3,300
1965		$2,400	$3,200
1966		$2,300	$3,100
1967-1969		$2,300	$3,000
1970		$2,200	$2,900
1971-1981	Becomes the 7670	$1,700	$2,300

Chet Atkins Hollowbody (6120)
1954-1964. Archtop electric, single cut to '61, double after, 2 pickups, vibrato, F-holes (real to '61 and fake after), G brand on top '54-'56. Orange finish (6120). Renamed Chet Atkins Nashville in '64.

1954-1956	G brand, single cut	$6,000	$8,000
1957-1959	No G brand	$5,500	$7,000
1960	Single cutaway	$5,000	$6,300
1961	Single cutaway	$4,700	$6,000
1961-1964	Double cutaway	$2,500	$3,200

Chet Atkins Junior
1970. Archtop, single cutaway, one pickup, vibrato, open F-holes, double-bound body. Orange stain.

1970		$900	$1,150

Chet Atkins Nashville (6120)
1964-1970. Replaced Chet Atkins Hollowbody (6120). Electric archtop, double cut, 2 pickups, Amber Red (Orange). Renumbered 7660 in '71 (see below). Reissued in '90 as the Nashville.

1964		$2,500	$3,000
1965-1968		$2,400	$2,700
1969-1970		$2,300	$2,600

Chet Atkins Nashville (7660)
1971-1980. Previously numbered 6120. Electric archtop, double cutaway, two pickups, Amber Red (Orange). Reissued as Nashville in the 1990s.

1971		$2,200	$2,600
1972		$1,900	$2,300
1973-1977		$1,800	$2,200
1978-1980		$1,500	$1,900

Chet Atkins Solidbody (6121)
1955-1963. Solidbody electric, single cutaway, maple or knotty pine top, two pickups, Bigsby vibrato, G brand until 1957, multi-bound top, brown mahogany. Orange finish (6121).

1955-1957	G brand	$4,600	$5,600
1958	No G brand	$4,500	$5,500
1959	No G brand	$4,400	$5,300
1960	No G brand	$4,300	$5,200
1961-1963	No G brand	$4,000	$5,000

Chet Atkins Tennessean (6119)
1958-1970. Archtop electric, single cutaway, one pickup until 1961 and two after, vibrato. Renumbered as the 7655 in 1971 (see following).

1958		$2,600	$3,000
1959		$2,500	$2,900
1960	1 pickup	$2,400	$2,800
1961-1964	2 pickups	$2,300	$2,600
1965		$2,100	$2,400
1966-1967		$2,050	$2,250
1968-1970		$1,600	$1,900

Chet Atkins Tennessean (7655)
1971-1980. Renumbered from Tennesseean 6119 (see above). Archtop electric, single cutaway, two pickups, vibrato.

1971-1972		$1,600	$1,900
1973-1980		$1,400	$1,800

Clipper (6186)
1958-1975. Archtop electric, single cutaway, Sunburst, one pickup (6186) until 1972 and two pickups (6185) from 1972-1975. Also available in one pickup Natural (6187) from 1959-1961.

1958-1961	Natural or Sunburst	$900	$1,100
1962-1967	Sunburst	$900	$1,100
1968-1971	Sunburst, 1 pickup	$800	$900
1972-1975	Sunburst, 2 pickups	$875	$975

Committee (7628)
1977-1980. Neck-through electric solidbody, double cutaway, walnut and maple body, two pickups, four knobs. Natural.

1977-1980		$500	$650

1979 Gretsch BST 1000

1967 Gretsch Chet Atkins Nashville

1963 Gretsch Corvette

*1959 Gretsch
Double Anniversary*

MODEL YEAR	FEATURES	EXC. COND. LOW	HIGH
Constellation			

1955-1960. Renamed from Synchromatic 6030 and 6031. Archtop acoustic, single cutaway, G tailpiece, humped block inlay.

MODEL YEAR	FEATURES	LOW	HIGH
1955-1956		$1,800	$2,300
1957-1958		$1,700	$2,200
1959-1960		$1,500	$2,000
Convertible (6199)			

1955-1958. Archtop electric, single cutaway, one pickup, multi-bound body, G tailpiece. Renamed Sal Salvadore in 1958.

1955-1958		$2,200	$2,400
Corsair			

1955-1960. Renamed from Synchromatic 100. Archtop acoustic, bound body and headstock, G tailpiece. Available in Sunburst (6014), Natural (6015) or Burgundy (6016).

1955-1960		$900	$1,300
Corvette (hollowbody)			

1955-1959. Renamed from Electromatic Spanish. Archtop electric, one pickup, F-holes, bound body, 'Electromatic' on headstock. Sunburst.

1955-1959		$1,100	$1,400
Corvette (solidbody)			

1961-1972, 1976-1978. Double cut slab solidbody, 1 pickup for '61-'68, and 2 pickups available by '63-'72 and '76-'78. From late-'61 through '63 a Twist option was offered featuring a Red candy stripe pickguard.

1961-1962		$700	$900
1961-1963	Twist pickguard	$900	$1,000
1963-1965	Custom color	$900	$1,200
1963-1965	Standard finish	$650	$850
1966-1969		$600	$800
1970-1972		$500	$600
1976-1978		$350	$500
Country Club			

1954-1981. Renamed from Electro II Cutaway. Archtop electric, single cutaway, two pickups (Filter Trons after 1957), G tailpiece, multi-bound.

1954-1956	Cadillac Green or Natural	$3,000	$4,300
1954-1956	Sunburst	$2,000	$3,300
1957-1958	Cadillac Green or Natural	$3,500	$4,800
1957-1958	Sunburst	$2,500	$3,800
1959	Cadillac Green or Natural	$3,500	$4,500
1959	Sunburst	$2,400	$3,500
1960	Cadillac Green	$3,300	$4,400
1960	Sunburst	$2,400	$3,500
1961	Natural	$3,000	$4,000
1961	Sunburst	$2,300	$3,300
1962-1963	Cadillac Green or Natural	$3,000	$4,000
1962-1963	Sunburst	$2,200	$3,200
1964	Cadillac Green	$2,800	$4,000
1964	Sunburst	$2,200	$2,800
1965-1967	Sunburst or Walnut	$1,900	$2,500
1970	Black	$1,900	$2,400

MODEL YEAR	FEATURES	EXC. COND. LOW	HIGH
1971	Various colors	$1,900	$2,300
1972	Various colors	$1,900	$2,100
1973-1981	Various colors	$1,800	$2,000
Country Club 1955 (G6196-1955)(FGE)			

1995-present. U.S-made reissue of Country Club, single cutaway, twin DeArmond pickups. Natural finish.

1995-2000		$2,500	$2,900
Country Roc (7620)			

1974-1978. Single cutaway solidbody, two pickups, belt buckle tailpiece, western scene fretboard inlays, G brand, tooled leather side trim.

1974-1978		$1,400	$1,800
Deluxe Chet (7680/7681)			

1973-1974. Electric archtop with rounded cutaway, Autumn Red (7680) or Brown Walnut (7681) finishes.

1973-1974		$2,500	$2,700
Double Anniversary			

1958-1976. Archtop electric, single cut, 2 pickups, stereo optional until '63, green two-tone or sunburst.

1958-1959	Sunburst or green	$2,000	$2,500
1960-1961	Sunburst or green	$1,800	$2,300
1962-1964	Sunburst or green	$1,700	$2,200
1965-1968	Sunburst	$1,400	$1,900
1965-1969	Green 2-tone	$1,500	$2,000
1969	Sunburst	$1,300	$1,800
1974	Sunburst	$1,200	$1,700
1975-1976	Sunburst	$1,100	$1,600
Duo-Jet			

1953-1971. Solidbody electric, single cut until '61, double after, 2 pickups. Black (6128) with a few special ordered in green. Sparkle finishes were offered '63-'66. Reissued in '90.

1953-1956	Black	$4,000	$5,000
1956-1957	Cadillac Green	$6,000	$7,400
1957	Black	$3,800	$4,800
1958-1960	Black	$3,000	$4,000
1961-1962	Double cutaway	$2,500	$3,300
1963		$2,300	$3,100
1964		$2,100	$2,800
1965-1967		$2,000	$2,600
1968-1969	Super Trons	$1,800	$2,400
1970-1971	Super Trons	$1,600	$2,300
Duo-Jet Reissue			

1990-present. Reissue of the 1950s solidbody, Black.

1990-2000		$1,000	$1,300
Eldorado (6040/6041)			

1955-1970, 1991-1997. Renamed from Synchromatic 400. Archtop acoustic, single cutaway, triple-bound fretboard and peghead.

1955-1959	Natural, 6041	$2,500	$2,900
1955-1959	Sunburst, 6040	$2,200	$2,600
1960	Natural, 6041	$2,300	$2,700
1960	Sunburst, 6040	$2,000	$2,400
1964	Natural, 6041	$2,200	$2,600
1964	Sunburst, 6040	$1,900	$2,300
1966	Natural, 6041	$2,000	$2,400
1966	Sunburst, 6040	$1,800	$2,200
1969	Sunburst	$1,700	$2,100

The *Vintage Guitar Price Guide* shows low to high values for items in all-original excellent condition, and, where applicable, with original case or cover.

MODEL YEAR	FEATURES	EXC. COND. LOW	HIGH

Electro II Cutaway (6192/6193)
1951-1954. Archtop electric, single cutaway, Melita bridge by 1953, two pickups, F-holes. Renamed Country Club in 1954.

1951-1954	Natural, 6193	$3,000	$3,500
1951-1954	Sunburst, 6192	$2,800	$3,300

Electromatic Spanish (6185/6185N)
1940-1955. Hollowbody, 17" wide, one pickup. Renamed Corvette (hollowbody) in 1955.

1950-1955	Sunburst, 6185	$1,000	$1,300

Jet Fire Bird (6131)
1955-1971, 1990-present. Solidbody electric, single cutaway until 1961, double 1961-1971, two pickups. Black body with Red top. Reissued in 1990.

1955-1956		$3,900	$4,700
1957-1958		$3,600	$4,500
1959		$3,300	$4,200
1960	Single cutaway	$2,500	$3,500
1961	Double cutaway	$2,500	$3,500
1962		$2,400	$3,400
1963-1964		$2,300	$3,300
1967		$1,800	$2,150
1968-1971	Super Trons	$1,700	$2,050

Jimmie Rodgers (6003 flat-top)
1959-1962. Fourteen inch flat-top with round hold, mahogany back and sides. Renamed Folk Singing in 1963.

1959-1962		$400	$700

Jumbo Synchromatic 125F (flat-top)
1947-1955. 17" flat-top, triangular soundhole, bound top and back, metal bridge anchor plate, adjustable wood bridge. Natural top with sunburst back and sides or optional Translucent White-Blond top and sides.

1947-1955	Natural	$1,500	$2,000
1947-1955	White-Blond option	$1,500	$2,000

Model 25 (acoustic archtop)
1933-1939. 16" archtop, no binding on top or back, dot markers, sunburst.

1933-1939		$700	$900

Model 30 (acoustic archtop)
1939-1949. Sixteen-inch archtop, top binding, dot markers. Sunburst.

1939-1949		$800	$1,000

Model 35 (acoustic archtop)
1933-1949. Sixteen-inch archtop, single-bound top and back, dot markers. Sunburst.

1933-1949		$900	$1,100

Model 65 (acoustic archtop)
1933-1939. Archtop acoustic, bound body. Amber.

1933-1939		$1,000	$1,200

Model TW300T (Traveling Wilburys)
1988-1990. Promotional guitar, solidbody electric, single cutaway, one and two pickups, six variations, graphics.

1988-1990		$250	$300

Monkees
1966-1969. Hollowbody electric, double cutaway, two pickups, Monkees logo on pickguard, bound top, F-holes and neck, vibrato. Red.

1966-1969		$1,450	$1,850

New Yorker
Ca.1949-1970. Archtop acoustic, F-holes. Sunburst.

1949-1951		$650	$850
1952-1954		$600	$800
1955-1959		$550	$750
1960-1965		$500	$700
1966-1970		$450	$650

Princess (6106)
1963. Corvette-type solidbody double cut, 1 pickup, vibrato, gold parts. Colors available werewWhite/grape, blue/white, pink/white, or white/gold. Often sold with the Princess amp.

1963	White/Gold	$1,400	$1,600

Rally (6104/6105)
1967-1969. Archtop, double cutaway, two pickups, vibrato, racing strip on truss rod cover and pickguard. Green or Yellow.

1967-1969		$1,500	$1,700

Rambler (6115)
1957-1961. Small body electric archtop, single cutaway, one pickup, G tailpiece, bound body and headstock.

1957-1961		$1,100	$1,300

Rancher
1954-1980. Flat-top acoustic, triangle soundhole, western theme inlay, G brand until 1961 and 1975 and after, Golden Red (Orange). Reissued in 1990.

1954-1955	G brand	$4,000	$5,200
1956-1957		$4,000	$5,200
1958-1961	G brand	$3,500	$4,700
1962-1964	No G brand	$3,000	$4,300
1965-1966	No G brand	$3,000	$4,200
1967-1969	No G brand	$2,500	$3,500
1970-1975	G brand	$2,500	$3,300
1976-1980	G brand	$2,500	$3,300

Roc I (7635)
1974-1976. Solidbody of mahogany, single cutaway, Duo-Jet-style body, one pickup, bound body and neck.

1974-1976		$650	$850

Roc II (7621)
1974-1977. Electric solidbody, single cutaway, two pickups, Duo-Jet-style body, bound body and neck.

1974-1977		$750	$950

Roc Jet
1969-1980. Electric solidbody, single cutaway, two pickups, adjustamatic bridge. Black or Pumpkin.

1970-1972		$1,050	$1,150
1973-1976		$950	$1,050
1977-1980		$900	$1,000

Round-Up (6130)
1954-1960. Electric solidbody, single cutaway, two pickups, G brand, belt buckle tailpiece. Orange.

1954-1956		$9,000	$9,500
1957-1960		$8,000	$9,000

Round-Up Reissue
1990-1995. Based on the 1950s model. Western Orange.

1990-1995		$1,200	$1,300

1973 Gretsch Roc Jet

1954 Gretsch Roundup (6130)

The **Vintage Guitar Price Guide** shows low to high values for items in all-original excellent condition, and, where applicable, with original case or cover.

1954 Gretsch Silver Jet (6129)

1973 Gretsch Super Chet

MODEL YEAR	FEATURES	EXC. COND. LOW	HIGH

Sal Fabraio (cat's-eye) (6117)
1964-1968. Double cutaway thin electric archtop with distinctive cat's-eye F-holes, two pickups, order for resale by guitar teacher Sal Fabraio.

1964-1968	Sunburst	$1,800	$2,000

Sal Salvador (6199)
1958-1968. Renamed from Convertible. Electric archtop, single cutaway, one pickup, triple-bound neck and headstock. Sunburst (6199)

1958-1959		$2,100	$2,300
1960-1962		$2,000	$2,200
1963-1964		$1,900	$2,100
1965-1966		$1,600	$1,800
1967-1968		$1,500	$1,700

Sho Bro Hawaiian
1969-1978. Flat-top acoustic, non-cutaway, square neck, resonator, multi-bound, lucite fretboard.

1969-1978		$650	$700

Sho Bro Spanish
1969-1978. Flat-top acoustic, single cutaway or non-cutaway, round neck, multi-bound, resonator.

1969-1978		$650	$900

Silver Jet (6129)
1954-1963. Solidbody electric, single cutaway until 1961, double 1961-1963, two pickups. Duo-Jet with Silver Sparkle top. Reissued in 1990.

1954-1956	Single cutaway	$4,500	$5,500
1957-1958	Single cutaway	$4,300	$5,300
1959-1960	Single cutaway	$3,500	$4,500
1961-1963	Double cutaway	$3,000	$4,000

Silver Jet 1957 Reissue (G6129-1957)
1990-present. Reissue of single cutaway 1950s Silver Jet, Silver Sparkle.

1990-1993		$1,200	$1,300
1994-1996		$1,300	$1,400
1997-1999		$1,400	$1,500

Southern Belle (7176)
1983. Electric archtop, Country Gentleman parts from the late-1970s assembled in Mexico and marketed as Southern Belle, based upon Belle (6122).

1983	Walnut	$1,000	$1,100

Sparkle Jet
1994-present. Electric solidbody, single cutaway, two pickups, Duo-Jet with Sparkle finish.

1995-1999		$1,000	$1,200

Streamliner Double Cutaway
1968-1973. Reintroduced from single cutaway model. Electric archtop, double cutaway, two pickups, G tailpiece. Cherry or Sunburst.

1968-1969		$1,100	$1,300
1970-1973		$900	$1,200

Streamliner Single Cutaway (6189/6190/6191)
1955-1959. Electric archtop, single cut, maple top, G tailpiece, 1 pickup, multi-bound. Bamboo Yellow (6189), sunburst (6190), or natural (6191). Name reintroduced as a double cutaway in '68.

1955-1959		$1,900	$2,100

Sun Valley (6010/7515/7514)
1959-1977. Flat-top acoustic, laminated Brazilian rosewood back and sides, multi-bound top, Natural or Sunburst.

1959-1964		$650	$850
1965-1969		$550	$750
1970-1977		$500	$600

Super Chet (7690/7690-B/7691/7691-B)
1972-1980. Electric archtop, single rounded cutaway, two pickups, Gold hardware, mini control knobs along edge of pickguard, Autumn Red or Walnut.

1972-1976		$2,100	$2,900
1977-1980		$1,900	$2,400

Synchromatic 75
1939-1949. Acoustic archtop, F-holes, multi-bound, large floral peghead inlay.

1939-1949		$1,000	$1,500

Synchromatic 100
1939-1955. Renamed from No. 100F. Acoustic archtop, double-bound body, Amber, Sunburst or Natural. Renamed Corsair in 1955.

1939-1949		$1,000	$1,500
1950-1955		$900	$1,200

Synchromatic 160
1939-1943, 1947-1951. Acoustic archtop, cat's-eye soundholes, maple back and sides, triple-bound, Natural or Sunburst.

1939-1943		$1,100	$1,600
1947-1951		$900	$1,300

Synchromatic 200
1939-1949. Acoustic archtop, cat's-eye soundholes, maple back and sides, multi-bound, gold-plated hardware, Amber or Natural.

1939-1949		$1,400	$1,900

Synchromatic 300
1939-1955. Acoustic archtop, cat's-eye soundholes until 1951and F-holes after, multi-bound, Natural or Sunburst.

1939-1949		$2,400	$3,000
1950-1955		$2,200	$2,400

Synchromatic 400
1940-1955. Acoustic archtop, cat's-eye soundholes until 1951and F-holes after, multi-bound, Gold hardware, Natural or Sunburst.

1940-1949		$5,300	$6,800
1950-1955		$5,000	$6,500

Synchromatic 6038
1951-1955. Acoustic archtop, single cutaway, G tailpiece, multi-bound bound, Sunburst. Natural version is 6039. Renamed Fleetwood in 1955.

1951-1955		$1,500	$1,900

Synchromatic Limited Model G450
1997. Acoustic archtop, hand carved spruce top, floating pickup, Sunburst, only 50 were to be made.

1997		$1,100	$1,400

Synchromatic Limited Model G450 M
1997. Maple top version of the G450, Sunburst.

1997		$1,200	$1,500

MODEL YEAR	FEATURES	EXC. COND. LOW	HIGH

Synchromatic Sierra
1949-1955. Renamed from Synchromatic X75F (see below). Acoustic flat-top, maple back and sides, triangular soundhole. Sunburst.

1949-1955		$1,000	$1,500

Synchromatic X75F
1947-1949. Acoustic flat-top, maple back and sides, triangular soundhole. Sunburst. Renamed Synchromatic Sierra in 1949 (see above).

1947-1949		$1,000	$1,500

TK 300 (7624/7625)
1977-1981. Double cutaway maple solidbody, one humbucker, bolt-on neck, six-on-a-side tuners, hockey stick headstock, Autumn Red or Natural.

1977-1981		$500	$700

Town and Country (6021)
1954-1959. Renamed from Jumbo Synchromatic 125 F. Flat-top acoustic, maple back and sides, triangular soundhole, multi-bound.

1954-1959		$1,500	$2,000

Van Eps 7-String (6079/6080)
1968-1978. Electric archtop, single cutaway, two pickups, seven strings, Sunburst or Walnut.

1968-1978	Sunburst	$2,500	$3,500

Viking (6187/6188/6189)
1964-1975. Electric archtop, double cutaway, two pickups, vibrato, Cadillac Green, Natural or Sunburst.

1964-1967		$1,500	$2,000
1968-1969		$1,400	$1,900
1970-1975		$1,000	$1,650

Wayfarer Jumbo (6008)
1969-1971. Flat-top acoustic dreadnought, non-cutaway, maple back and sides, multi-bound.

1969-1971		$450	$650

White Falcon 6136 Mono (single cutaway)
1955-1961. Single cutaway archtop, two pickups, non-stereo option (stereo is 6137), White. Continued 1974-1978 as 7593.

1955		$22,000	$28,000
1956		$21,000	$27,000
1957		$20,000	$26,000
1958		$19,000	$23,000
1959-1961		$18,000	$22,000

White Falcon 6137 Stereo (single cutaway)
1958-1961. Project-O-Sonic Stereo version of single cutaway model.

1959-1961		$18,000	$22,000

White Falcon 7593 (single cutaway)
1974-1978. Single cutaway archtop, two pickups. White.

1974-1975		$3,600	$4,600
1976-1977		$3,300	$4,200

White Falcon (double cutaway)
1962-1981. Double cutaway archtop, two pickups, stereo or non-stereo. White.

1962		$8,000	$10,000
1963		$7,800	$9,800
1964		$7,000	$9,000
1965		$6,000	$8,500
1966		$5,500	$7,500
1967		$5,000	$7,000
1968		$4,800	$6,800
1969		$4,700	$5,500
1970		$4,300	$5,000
1971		$3,900	$4,700
1972		$3,900	$4,700
1974		$3,700	$4,600
1975		$3,600	$4,500
1976-1980		$3,500	$4,300
1981	Stereo doublecut 7595	$3,300	$4,100

White Falcon 1955 Custom USA (G6136-1955)(FGE)
1995-1999. Single cut, DynaSonic pickups, gold Sparkle appointments, rhinestone embedded knobs, solid spruce carved top, White.

1995-1999		$4,000	$4,700

White Falcon 1955 Single Cutaway G6136
1990-present. Single and double cut versions of the White Falcon, issued under different model numbers and variations on the name. White, Silver or Black. Model numbers include 6136 (G tailpiece) and 7593 (Gretsch Bigsby tailpiece) (both initially called the I, 1990 on), 7594 (initially called the II, 1991 on), G6136 (1994 on), G6136BK (Black Falcon 1995-1999), G6136SL (Silver Falcon single cutaway, 1955 reissue 1996-1997), G7584SL (Silver Falcon double cutaway 1996-1997).

1990-1999	White	$1,700	$2,100

White Falcon II G7594 (double cutaway)
1991-present. Import from Japan, double cutaway, standard Bigsby vibrato, White.

1991-1999		$1,800	$2,100

White Penguin (6134)
1955-1964. Electric solidbody, single cut until '62, double '62-'64, 2 pickups, fewer than 100 made, white, gold sparkle bound, gold-plated parts. Some high-end guitar dealers make the following point about the White Penguin: "Find a real one!" This quote is not considered to be a casual or idle remark. More than any other model, there seems a higher concern regarding forgery vs. authentic.

1956-1958		$75,000	$90,000
1959-1960		$65,000	$85,000
1961-1962	Single cutaway	$65,000	$75,000
1962-1964	Double cutaway	$60,000	$75,000

White Penguin (reissue)(FGE)
1996-present. White finish, single cutaway, Metalflake Orange binding, Gold hardware including the DeArmond-style Dynasonic pickups, jeweled control knobs, space control bridge, ebony fingerboard with Grover Imperial stairstep Cadillac tailpiece.

1996-1999		$2,800	$3,300

Griffin String Instruments
1976-present. Luthier Kim Griffin builds his professional and premium grade, production/custom, parlor, steel-string, and classical guitars in Greenwich, New York.

1940s Gretsch Synchromatic 400

1957 Gretsch White Falcon

GUITARS

Grimes 25th Anniversary

1959 Guild Aristocrat M-75

MODEL YEAR	FEATURES	EXC. COND. LOW	HIGH

Grimes Guitars

1974-present. Premium and presentation grade, custom, flat-tops, nylon-strings, archtops, semi-hollow electrics made by luthier Steve Grimes originally in Port Townsend, Washington, and since 1982 in Kula, Hawaii.

Groove Tools

2002-present. Korean-made, production, intermediate grade, 7-string guitars offered by Conklin Guitars of Springfield, Missouri.

Grosh, Don

1993-present. Professional and premium grade, production/custom, solid and semi-hollow body guitars built by luthier Don Grosh in Santa Clarita, California. He also builds basses. Grosh worked in production for Valley Arts from '84-'92. Guitars generally with bolt necks until '03 when set-necks were added to the line.

Retro Classic

1993-present. Classic offset double cut solidbody, 3 pickups.

2001		$1,800	$2,000

Retro Vintage T

1993-present. Classic single cut solidbody, '50s (early) black guard, higher-end boutique quality.

2001		$1,800	$2,000

Gruen Acoustic Guitars

1999-present. Luthier Paul Gruen builds his professional grade, custom steel-string guitars in Chapel Hill, North Carolina. His speciality is his E.Q. model, which features five soundholes, four of which can be plugged with wooden stoppers to give different tonal balances.

Guernsey Resophonic Guitars

1989-present. Production/custom, resonator guitars built by luthier Ivan Guernsey in Marysville, Indiana.

Guild

1952-present. Professional and premium grade, production/custom, acoustic, acoustic/electric, hollowbody and semi-hollowbody guitars. Founded in New York City by jazz guitarist Alfred Dronge, employing many ex-Epiphone workers. The company was purchased by Avnet, Inc., in '66 and the Westerly, Rhode Island factory was opened in '68. Hoboken factory closed in '71 and headquarters moved to Elizabeth, New Jersey. Company was Guild Musical Instrument Corporation in '86 but was in bankruptcy in '88. Purchased by Faas Corporation, New Berlin, Wisconsin, which became the U.S. Musical Corporation. The brand was purchased by Fender Musical Instrument Corporation in '95. The Guild Custom Shop opened in Nashville in '97. The Guild Custom Shop remains in Nashville, while all other Guild U.S. production has been moved to Corona, California.

MODEL YEAR	FEATURES	EXC. COND. LOW	HIGH

Aragon F-30

1954-1986. Acoustic flat-top, spruce top, laminated maple arched back (mahogany back and sides by 1959). Reintroduced as just F-30 in 1998.

1954-1969		$900	$1,200
1970-1986		$600	$800

Aragon F-30 NT

1959-1985. Natural finish version of F-30. Acoustic flat-top, spruce top, maple back and sides.

1960		$900	$1,200
1984		$600	$800

Aristocrat M-75

1955-1963, 1967-1968. Electric archtop, single cutaway, two pickups, Blond or Sunburst. Name changed to Bluesbird M-75 in 1968.

1955-1959		$2,300	$2,600
1960-1963		$2,100	$2,400

Artist Award

1961-1999. Renamed from Johnny Smith Award. Electric archtop, single cutaway, floating DeArmond pickup (changed to humbucker in 1980), multi-bound, Gold hardware. Sunburst or Natural.

1961-1969		$3,900	$4,400
1970-1979		$3,900	$4,400
1980-1989		$3,500	$4,000
1990-1999		$3,200	$3,700

Bluegrass D-25

1968-1999. Flat-top, mahogany top until '76, spruce after, mahogany back and sides, various colors. Called Bluegrass D-25 M in late-'70s and '80s. Listed as D-25 in '90s.

1968-1989		$600	$750
1990-1999		$550	$700

Bluegrass D-25-12

1987-1992, 1996-1999. 12-string version of D-25.

1987-1992		$650	$750

Bluegrass D-35

1966-1988. Acoustic flat-top, spruce top and mahogany back and sides, rosewood fingerboard and bridge, Natural.

1966-1969		$800	$950
1970-1979		$700	$850
1980-1988		$650	$850

Bluegrass F-47

1963-1976. 16 inch narrow-waist style, mahogany sides and back. Acoustic flat-top, spruce top, mahogany back and sides, bound rosewood fingerboard and bridge, Natural.

1966		$1,100	$1,300

Bluegrass Jubilee D-40

1963-1992. Acoustic flat-top, spruce top, mahogany back and sides, rosewood fingerboard and bridge, Natural.

1963-1969		$950	$1,000
1970-1979		$900	$1,000
1980-1992		$850	$950

MODEL		EXC. COND.	
YEAR	FEATURES	LOW	HIGH

Bluegrass Jubilee D-40 C

1975-1991. Acoustic flat-top, single Florentine cutaway, mahogany back and sides, rosewood fingerboard and bridge, Natural.

1975-1979		$900	$1,000
1980-1991		$850	$950

Bluegrass Jubilee D-44

1965-1972. Acoustic flat-top, spruce top, pearwood back and sides, ebony fingerboard, rosewood bridge.

1965-1969		$950	$1,050
1970-1972		$900	$1,000

Bluegrass Jubilee D-44M

1971-1985. Maple back and sides version.

1971-1979		$800	$1,050
1980-1985		$750	$1,000

Bluegrass Special D-50

1963-1993. Acoustic flat-top, spruce top, rosewood back and sides, ebony fretboard, multi-bound.

1963-1969		$1,500	$2,300
1970-1979		$1,500	$2,000
1980-1993		$1,200	$1,500

Bluesbird M-75 (hollowbody)

1968-1970. Reintroduced from Aristocrat M-75. Thinbody electric archtop of maple, spruce or mahogany, single cutaway, two pickups. Reintroduced as a solidbody in 1970.

1968-1970		$950	$1,250

Bluesbird M-75 (solidbody)

1970-1978. Solidbody version of hollodbody Bluesbird M-75. Mahogany body, rounded cutaway, two pickups.

1970-1978		$950	$1,250

Bluesbird M-75 (solidbody reintroduced)

1984-1988. Brian Setzer design, poplar body, single cut, 2 pickups, vibrato. Reintroduced with different specs in '97.

1984-1988		$600	$700

Brian May BHM-1

1984-1987. Electric solidbody, double cutaway, vibrato, three pickups, bound top and back, Red or Green. Brian May Pro, Special and Standard introduced in 1994.

1984-1987		$2,000	$2,200

Brian May Pro

1994-1995. Electric solidbody, double cutaway, vibrato, three pickups, bound top and back, various colors.

1994-1995		$1,500	$1,700

Burnside HA-1

Solidbody, two pickups, non-locking tremolo.

1987		$250	$300

Burnside SO-1

Solidbody, three pickups, locking-nut tremolo.

1987		$250	$300

CA-100 Capri

1956-1973. Acoustic archtop version of CE-100, sharp Florentine cutaway, solid spruce top, laminated maple back and sides, rosewood 'board and bridge, nickel-plated metal parts, natural or sunburst.

1956-1969		$1,200	$1,400
1970-1973		$1,100	$1,300

Capri CE-100

1956-1985. Electric archtop, single Florentine cutaway, one pickup (two pickups by 1983), maple body, Waverly tailpiece. Sunburst. In 1959-1982 CE-100 D listed with two pickups.

1956-1969		$1,200	$1,400
1970-1979		$1,100	$1,300
1980-1985		$1,000	$1,200

Capri CE-100 D

1956-1982. Electric archtop, single Florentine cutaway, two pickups, maple body, Waverly tailpiece (D dropped, became the Capri CE-100 in 1983).

1956-1969		$1,500	$1,700
1970-1979		$1,400	$1,600
1980-1982		$1,300	$1,500

Citron X-92

1984. Electric solidbody, detachable body section, three pickups.

1984		$250	$300

Cordoba X-50

1961-1970. Electric archtop non-cutaway, laminated maple body, rosewood fingerboard, one pickup, nickel-plated parts, Sunburst. Also came as a slimline model called the Cordoba T-50 Slim.

1961-1970		$800	$950

Custom F-412 12-String

1968-1986. Special order only from 1968-1974, then regular production. Twelve-string version of F-50, acoustic flat-top, spruce top, maple back and sides, arched back, ebony fingerboard, bound neck, Gold hardware. Natural finish.

1968-1974		$1,600	$1,800
1975-1979		$1,400	$1,600
1980-1986		$1,300	$1,500

Custom F-512 12-String

1968-1986, 1990. Acoustic flat-top, 12 strings, spruce top, rosewood back and sides, bound neck, abalone inlays.

1968-1969		$1,500	$1,700
1970-1979		$1,400	$1,600
1980-1986		$1,300	$1,500

Custom Shop 45th Anniversary

1997 only. The Guild Custom Shop opened in Nashville, TN in 1997, two years after Fender Musical Instruments purchased Guild. The Guild Custom Shop remains in Nashville, while all other Guild production has been moved to Corona, CA. The 45th Anniversary features all solid wood, a spruce top and maple back and sides, with high-end appointments.

1997	Natural,		
	Gold hardware	$2,000	$2,500

D-6 (D-6 E/D-6 HG/D-6 HE)

1992-1995. Flat-top, 15 3/4", mahogany back and sides, Natural satin non-gloss finish, options available.

1992-1995		$600	$650

1970s Guild Bluesbird

Guild Brian May BHM-1

1997 Guild D-55

Guild Duane Eddy Deluxe DE-500

MODEL YEAR	FEATURES	EXC. COND. LOW	HIGH
D-15			

1983-1988. Part of Mahogany Rush Series. Dreadnought, mahogany body and neck, rosewood fingerboard, dot inlay, peaked logo, unbound, Mahogany or Woodgrain Red satin finishes (gloss by 1987).

1983-1988		$500	$600
D-17			

1983-1986. 15 3/4" dreadnought, mahogany top, back, and sides.

1983-1986		$500	$600
D-30			

1987-1999. Acoustic flat top, spruce-top, laminated maple back and solid maple sides, rosewood fingerboard, multi-bound, various colors.

1987-1989		$800	$1,000
1990-1999		$750	$950
D-46			

1980-1985. Dreadnought-size acoustic, ash back, sides, and neck, spruce top, ebony fingerboard, ivoroid binding top and back. Originally offered in Natural or Sunburst.

1980-1985		$800	$950
D-55			

1968-1987, 1990-present (Special Order 1968-1973, regular production after). Dreadnought-size acoustic, spruce top, rosewood back and sides, scalloped bracing, gold-plated tuners. Called the TV Model in earlier years, Sunburst or Natural.

1968		$1,800	$2,700
1969	13 made	$1,700	$2,200
1973		$1,500	$1,700
1974		$1,300	$1,600
1975-1990		$1,200	$1,600
D-60			

1987-1990, 1998-2000. Renamed from D-66. Rosewood back and sides, 15 3/4", scalloped bracing, multi-bound top, slotted diamond inlay, G shield logo.

1987-1990		$1,500	$1,700
1998-1999		$1,400	$1,600
D-66			

1984-1987. Rosewood back and sides, 15 3/4", scalloped bracing. Renamed D-60 in 1987.

1984-1987	Amber	$1,500	$1,700
D-70			

1981-1985. Dreadnought acoustic, spruce top, Indian rosewood back and sides, multi-bound, ebony fingerboard with mother-of-pearl inlays.

1981-1985		$1,900	$2,100
D-212 12-String			

1981-1983. Twelve-string version of D-25, laminated mahogany back and sides. Natural, Sunburst or Black. Renamed D-25-12 in 1987, reintroduced as D-212 1996-present.

1981-1983	Sunburst	$900	$1,100
D-412 12-String			

1990-1997. Dreadnought, 12 strings, mahogany sides and arched back, satin finished, natural.

1990-1997		$900	$1,100

MODEL YEAR	FEATURES	EXC. COND. LOW	HIGH
DCE-1 True American			

1993-1999. Acoustic/electric flat-top, single rounded cutaway, laminated mahogany back and sides. Natural satin finish (high gloss optional by 1998).

1993-1999		$750	$850
Del Rio M-30			

1959-1964. Flat-top, 15", all mahogany body, satin non-gloss finish.

1959-1964		$800	$1,200
Detonator			

1987-1988. Electric solidbody, double cutaway, three pickups, bolt-on neck, Guild/Mueller tremolo system, Black hardware.

1987-1988		$200	$250
Duane Eddy Deluxe DE-500			

1962-1974, 1984-1987. Electric archtop, single rounded cutaway, two pickups (early years and 1980s version have DeArmonds), Bigsby, master volume, spruce top with maple back and sides. Available in Blond (BL) or Sunburst (SB).

1962		$4,000	$5,500
1963		$3,900	$5,400
1964-1965		$3,800	$5,300
1966-1974		$3,600	$5,100
1984-1987		$2,800	$3,500
Duane Eddy Standard DE-400			

1963-1974. Electric archtop, single rounded cutaway, two pickups, vibrato, Natural or Sunburst. Less appointments than DE-500 Deluxe.

1963		$3,000	$4,000
1964		$2,900	$3,900
1965		$2,800	$3,800
1966		$2,600	$2,800
DV-6			

1995-1999. Acoustic flat-top, spruce top, solid mahogany back and sides, rosewood board, mahogany neck, satin finish.

1995-1999		$700	$900
DV-52			

1993-2001. Acoustic flat-top, spruce top, solid rosewood back and sides, ebony board and bridge, mahogany neck, satin finish.

1993-2001		$900	$1,100
Economy M-20			

1958-1965, 1969-1973. Mahogany body, acoustic flat-top, Natural or Sunburst satin finish.

1958-1965		$700	$1,000
1970-1973		$500	$800
F-5 CE			

1992-2001. Acoustic/electric, single rounded cutaway, rosewood back and sides. Natural, Black or Sunburst finish.

1992-2001		$900	$1,100
F-45 CE			

1983-1992. Acoustic/electric, single pointed cutaway, active EQ, preamp, spruce top, mahogany back and sides, rosewood fingerboard, natural finish.

1983-1992		$900	$1,000

The *Vintage Guitar Price Guide* shows low to high values for items in all-original excellent condition, and, where applicable, with original case or cover.

MODEL YEAR	FEATURES	EXC. COND. LOW	HIGH

F-47RCE Grand Auditorium
2000s. Flat top acoustic cutaway with on-board electronics.

2000s		$1,300	$1,400

F-212 12-String
1968-1982. Acoustic flat-top jumbo, 12 strings, spruce top, mahogany back and sides.

1968-1969		$1,000	$1,200
1970-1979		$900	$1,100
1980-1982		$800	$1,000

Freshman M-65
1958-1973. Electric archtop, single cutaway, mahogany back and sides, one single-coil pickup. Sunburst or Natural top.

1958-1959		$1,000	$1,200
1960-1969		$950	$1,100
1970-1973		$900	$1,000

Freshman M-65 3/4
1958-1973. Short-scale version of M-65, electric archtop, single rounded cutaway, one pickup.

1958-1959	Natural or Sunburst	$950	$1,100
1960-1969	Cherry, Natural or Sunburst	$900	$1,000
1970-1973	Cherry or Sunburst	$850	$900

FS-46 CE
1983-1986. Flat-top acoustic/electric, pointed cutaway, Black, Natural or Sunburst.

1983-1986		$600	$700

G-5P
1988-ca.1989. Handmade in Spain, cedar top, gold-plated hardware.

1988-1989		$550	$600

G-37
1973-1986. Acoustic flat-top, spruce top, laminated maple back and sides, rosewood fingerboard and bridge. Sunburst or Natural top.

1973-1986		$700	$900

G-41
1974-1978. Acoustic flat-top, spruce top, mahogany back and sides, rosewood fingerboard and bridge, 20 frets.

1975-1978		$800	$1,000

G-75
1975-1977. Acoustic flat-top, 3/4-size version of D-50, spruce top, rosewood back and sides, mahogany neck, ebony fingerboard and bridge.

1975-1977		$650	$850

G-212 12-String
1974-1983. Acoustic flat-top 12-string version of D-40, spruce top, mahogany back and sides. Natural or Sunburst.

1974-1983		$800	$1,100

G-212 XL 12-String
1974-1983. Acoustic flat-top, 12 strings, 17" version of G-212.

1974-1983		$800	$1,100

G-312 12-String
1974-1987. Acoustic flat-top 12-string version of the D-50, spruce top, rosewood back and sides.

1974-1987		$1,000	$1,100

George Barnes AcoustiLectric
1962-1972. Electric archtop, single cutaway, solid spruce top, curly maple back and sides, multi-bound, two humbuckers, gold-plated hardware. Sunburst or Natural finish.

1962-1972		$2,900	$3,200

GF-30
1987-1991. Acoustic flat-top, maple back, sides and neck, multi-bound..

1987-1991		$750	$950

GF-50
1987-1991. Acoustic flat-top, rosewood back and sides, mahogany neck, multi-bound.

1987-1991		$800	$1,100

Granada X-50
1954-1961. Electric archtop, non-cutaway, laminated all maple body, rosewood fingerboard and bridge, nickel-plated metal parts, one pickup, Sunburst. Renamed Cordoba X-50 in 1961.

1955-1959		$850	$950
1960-1961		$800	$900

Jet Star S-50
1963-1970. Electric solidbody, double cutaway, mahogany or alder body, one pickup, vibrato optional by 1965, asymmetrical headstock until 1965. Reintroduced as S-50 in 1972-1978 with body redesigned to Gibson SG-style.

1963-1970	Red	$450	$600

JF-30
1987-2004. Jumbo 6-string acoustic, spruce top, laminated maple back, solid maple sides, multi-bound.

1987-1999		$750	$900
2000-2003		$850	$950

JF-30E
1998-2004. Fishman electronics version of the JF-30.

1998-2004		$950	$1,050

JF-30-12
1987-2004. 12-string version of the JF-30.

1987-2004		$950	$1,000

JF-50 R
1987-1988. Jumbo six-string acoustic, rosewood back and sides, multi-bound.

1987-1988		$800	$1,000

JF-55-12 (12 String)
1991-2001. Jumbo 12-string with high-end appointments.

1991-2001		$1,400	$1,600

JF-65 R
1987. Renamed from Navarre F-50 R. Jumbo flat-top acoustic, spruce top, rosewood back and sides, multi-bound, gold-plated tuners. Reintroduced as JF-55 in 1989.

1987		$1,000	$1,300

JF-65-12
1987-2001. Jumbo flat-top 12-string, spruce top, laminated maple back and solid maple sides, multi-bound, gold tuners. Natural or Sunburst.

1987-2001		$1,100	$1,300

Guild JF-30

1964 Guild Jet Star S-50

Guild Nightbird

1955 Guild Manhattan X-175

MODEL YEAR	FEATURES	EXC. COND. LOW	HIGH

Liberator Elite
1988. Limited Edition, top-of-the-line, set-neck, off-set double cut solidbody, figured maple top, mahogany body, rising-sun inlays, 3 active Bartolini pickups.

| 1988 | | $850 | $1,000 |

M-80 CS
1975-1984. Solidbody, double cutaway, two pickups, has M-80 on truss rod cover. Called just M-80 from 1980-1984.

| 1975-1984 | | $650 | $700 |

Manhattan X-170 (Mini-Manhattan X-170)
1985-2002. Called Mini-Manhattan X-170 in '85-'86. Electric archtop hollowbody, single rounded cutaway, maple body, F-holes, two humbuckers, block inlays, gold hardware, Natural or Sunburst.

| 1985-1989 | | $1,200 | $1,400 |
| 1990-1999 | | $1,250 | $1,450 |

Manhattan X-175 (Sunburst)

1954-1959		$2,000	$2,300
1960-1969		$1,900	$2,200
1970-1979		$1,600	$1,900

Manhattan X-175/X-175 B
1954-1985. Electric archtop, single rounded cutaway, laminated spruce top, laminated maple back and sides, two pickups, chrome hardware. Sunburst (X-175) or Natural (X-175B) finishes.

1954-1959		$2,100	$2,400
1960-1969		$2,000	$2,300
1970-1976		$1,800	$2,100

Mark I
1961-1973. Acoustic flat-top classical, Honduras mahogany body, rosewood fingerboard and bridge, satin finish, slotted headstock.

| 1961-1969 | | $300 | $400 |
| 1970-1973 | | $275 | $375 |

Mark II
1961-1986. Acoustic flat-top classical, spruce top, Honduras mahogany back and sides, rosewood fingerboard and bridge, satin finish, slotted headstock.

1961-1969		$350	$450
1970-1979		$350	$425
1980-1986		$300	$400

Mark III
1961-1986. Acoustic flat-top classical, spruce top, Peruvian mahogany back and sides, rosewood fingerboard and bridge, satin finish, slotted headstock, bound top and back.

1961-1969		$550	$650
1970-1979		$500	$600
1980-1986		$450	$550

Mark IV
1961-1986. Acoustic flat-top classical, rosewood or flamed pearwood back and sides, rosewood fingerboard and bridge, satin finish, slotted headstock.

1961-1969		$800	$900
1970-1979		$700	$800
1980-1986		$650	$750

Mark V
1961-1987. Rosewood or maple back and sides 1961-1978, rosewood only 1978 on.

1961-1969		$1,000	$1,200
1970-1979		$900	$1,100
1980-1987		$800	$1,000

Navarre F-50
1954-1986, 1994-1995. Acoustic flat-top, spruce top, curly maple back and sides, rosewood fingerboard and bridge, 17" rounded lower bout, laminated arched maple back. Renamed JF-65 M in 1987, and back to Navarre F-50 in 1994.

1957-1962	Pearl block markers added	$2,000	$2,600
1963-1969	Ebony fingerboard added	$1,800	$2,400
1970-1975		$1,700	$2,000
1976-1979		$1,600	$1,900
1980-1986		$1,500	$1,800
1994-1995		$1,100	$1,300

Navarre F-50 R
1965-1986. Rosewood version of F-50, flat spruce top, rosewood back and sides, fingerboard and bridge. Renamed JF-65 R in 1987.

1965-1969		$1,900	$2,500
1970-1975		$1,800	$2,100
1976-1979		$1,700	$2,000
1980-1986		$1,600	$1,900

Nightbird
1985-1987. Electric solidbody, single sharp cutaway, tone chambers, two pickups, multi-bound, Black or Gold hardware. Renamed Nightbird II in 1987.

| 1985-1987 | | $1,300 | $1,400 |

Nightbird I
1987-1988. Like Nightbird but with chrome hardware, less binding and appointments, two pickups, coil-tap, phaser switch.

| 1987-1988 | | $1,100 | $1,300 |

Nightbird II
1987-1992. Renamed from Nightbird. Electric solidbody, single sharp cutaway, tone chambers, two pickups, multi-bound, Black hardware. Renamed Nightbird X-2000 in 1992.

| 1987-1992 | | $1,300 | $1,400 |

Nightbird X-2000
1992-1996. Renamed from Nightbird II.

| 1992-1996 | | $1,300 | $1,400 |

Polara S-100
1963-1970. Electric solidbody, double cutaway, mahogany or alder body, rosewood fingerboard, two pickups, built-in stand until '70, asymmetrical headstock. In '70, Polara dropped from title (see S-100 Standard). Renamed back to Polara S-100 in '97.

| 1963-1970 | | $900 | $1,100 |

Roy Buchanan T-200
1986. Single cut solidbody, 2 pickups, pointed six-on-a-side headstock, poplar body, bolt-on neck, gold and brass hardware.

| 1986 | | $550 | $650 |

The *Vintage Guitar Price Guide* shows low to high values for items in all-original excellent condition, and, where applicable, with original case or cover.

MODEL YEAR	FEATURES	EXC. COND. LOW	HIGH

S-60
1976-1980. Electric solidbody, double cutaway, one pickup, all mahogany body, rosewood fingerboard.

1976-1980		$375	$400

S-60 D
1977-1981. S-60 with two DiMarzio pickups.

1977-1981		$400	$500

S-65 D
1980-1981. Electric solidbody, double cut, 3 DiMarzio pickups, rosewood fingerboard.

1980-1981		$400	$500

S-90
1972-1977. Double cut SG-like body, 2 humbuckers, dot inlay, chrome hardware.

1972-1977		$600	$700

S-100 Standard
1970-1978. Redesigned Polara S-100 with offset double cutaway, two pickups, SG-style body. S-100 name is reissued in 1994-1997 then renamed Polara S-100 in 1997-present.

1970-1978		$800	$1,000

S-100 Reissue
1994-1997. Renamed Polara in 1997.

1994-1997		$600	$700

S-261
Ca.1985. Double cut maple body, black Kahler tremolo, 1 humbucker and 2 single-coil pickups, rosewood fingerboard.

1985		$350	$450

S-280 Flyer
1983-1984. Double cut poplar body, 2 humbuckers or 3 single-coils, maple or rosewood neck, dot markers.

1983-1984		$375	$450

S-281 Flyer
1983-1988. Double cut poplar body S-280 with locking vibrato, optional pickups available.

1983-1988		$375	$450

S-300 D
1977-1982. Same as S-300, but with a DiMarzio PAF and Super Distortion humbucker pickups.

1977-1987	Natural	$550	$600

Savoy A-150 (Sunburst)
1958-1973. Sunburst, acoustic archtop version of X-150, available with floating pickup.

1958-1961		$1,350	$1,650

Savoy A-150 (Natural)
1958-1973. Natural finish, acoustic archtop version of X-150, available with floating pickup.

1958-1961		$1,350	$1,650

Savoy X-150
1954-1965, 1998-present. Electric archtop, single rounded cutaway, spruce top, maple back and sides, rosewood fingerboard and bridge, one single-coil pickup. Sunburst, Blond or Sparkling Gold finish. Reintroduced in 1998.

1954-1961		$1,400	$1,700

Slim Jim T-100
1958-1973. Electric archtop thinline, single cutaway, laminated all-maple body, rosewood fingerboard and bridge, Waverly tailpiece, one pickup, Natural or Sunburst.

1958-1960		$900	$1,100
1961-1969		$800	$1,000
1970-1973		$700	$800

Slim Jim T-100 D
1958-1973. Semi-hollowbody electric, single Florentine cutaway, thinline, two-pickup version of the T-100, Natural or Sunburst.

1958-1959		$1,000	$1,200
1960-1969		$900	$1,100
1970-1973		$800	$1,000

Songbird S-4
1987-1991. Designed by George Gruhn. Flat-top, mahogany back, spruce top, single pointed cutaway, pickup with preamp, multi-bound top, Black, Natural or White.

1987-1991		$600	$750

Standard F-112 12-String
1968-1982. Acoustic flat-top, 12 strings, spruce top, mahogany back, sides and neck.

1968-1969		$950	$1,150
1970-1979		$900	$1,100
1980-1982		$850	$1,050

Standard F-212XL 12-String
1966-1986. 17" body.

1966-1969		$1,000	$1,200
1970-1979		$900	$1,100
1980-1986		$800	$1,000

Starfire I
1960-1964. Electric archtop, single cutaway thinline, laminated maple or mahogany body, bound body and neck, one pickup.

1960-1961	Starfire Red	$800	$1,000
1962-1964		$700	$900

Starfire II
1960-1976, 1997-2001. Electric archtop, single cutaway thinline, laminated maple or mahogany body, bound body and rosewood neck, two pickups. Reissued 1997-present.

1960-1961	Sunburst	$1,100	$1,300
1962-1966	Sunburst	$1,000	$1,200
1967-1969	Starfire Red	$900	$1,100
1970-1975	Sunburst	$800	$1,000

Starfire III
1960-1974, 1997-present. Electric archtop, single cut thinline, laminated maple or mahogany body, bound body and rosewood neck, 2 pickups, Guild or Bigsby vibrato, Starfire Red. Reissued 1997.

1960-1961	Starfire Red	$1,200	$1,400
1962-1966		$1,100	$1,300
1967-1969		$1,000	$1,200
1970-1973		$700	$1,000
1997-1999	Reissue model	$900	$1,100

1999 Guild Polara S-100

Guild Starfire II

Guild Starfire IV

Guild Stratford X-375

MODEL YEAR	FEATURES	EXC. COND. LOW	HIGH

Starfire IV

1963-1987, 1991-present. Thinline, double cut semi-hollowbody, laminated maple or mahogany body, F-holes, 2 humbuckers, rosewood 'board, cherry or sunburst. Reissued in '91.

1963-1966		$1,500	$2,000
1967-1969		$1,400	$1,900
1970-1975		$1,300	$1,800
1976-1979		$1,300	$1,800
1980-1987		$900	$1,400
1998-1999	Reissue	$1,000	$1,200

Starfire IV Special (Custom Shop)

2002	Nashville		
	Custom Shop	$1,900	$2,000

Starfire V

1963-1973, 1999-2002. Same as Starfire IV but with block markers, Bigsby and master volume. Natural or Sunburst finish. Reissued in '99.

1963-1966		$1,700	$2,200
1967-1969		$1,600	$2,100
1970-1973		$1,500	$2,000

Starfire VI

1964-1979. Same as Starfire IV but with high appointments such as ebony fingerboard, pearl inlays, Guild/Bigsby vibrato, Natural or Sunburst.

1964-1966		$2,900	$3,400
1967-1969		$2,800	$3,300
1970-1975		$2,700	$3,200
1976-1979		$2,600	$3,000

Starfire XII

1966-1973. Electric archtop, 12 string, double cut, maple or mahogany body, set-in neck, 2 humbuckers, harp tailpiece.

1966-1967		$1,600	$1,900
1968-1969		$1,500	$1,800
1970-1973		$1,400	$1,700

Stratford A-350

1956-1973. Acoustic archtop, single rounded cutaway, solid spruce top with solid curly maple back and sides, rosewood fingerboard and bridge (changed to ebony by 1960). Sunburst.

1956-1959		$2,200	$2,500
1960-1965		$2,100	$2,400
1966-1969		$2,000	$2,300
1970-1973		$1,900	$2,200

Stratford A-350B

1956-1973. A-350 in blond/natural finish option.

1956-1959		$2,200	$2,500
1960-1965		$2,100	$2,400
1966-1969		$2,000	$2,300
1970-1973		$1,900	$2,200

Stratford X-350

1953-1965. Electric archtop, single rounded cutaway, laminated spruce top with laminated maple back and sides, rosewood fingerboard, the pickups, six push-button pickup selectors. Sunburst finish (Natural finish is X-375).

1953-1959		$2,300	$2,900
1960-1965		$2,000	$2,500

Stratford X-375/X-350 B

1953-1965. Electric archtop, single cutaway, spruce top, curly maple back and sides, rosewood fingerboard and bridge, three pickups, one volume and one tone control, six push-button pickup selectors. Natural finish (Sunburst is X-350). Renamed X-350 B in 1958.

1953-1959		$2,400	$3,000
1960-1965		$2,100	$2,600

Stuart A-500

1956-1969. Acoustic archtop single cutaway, 17" body, A-500 Sunburst, available with Guild logo, floating DeArmond pickup.

1956-1959		$2,000	$2,200

Stuart A-500B/A-550

1956-1959. A-550 in Natural finish. 1960-1969 A-500B, Natural finish, available with Guild logo, floating DeArmond pickup.

1956-1959		$2,200	$2,400

Stuart X-500

1953-1994. Electric archtop, single cutaway, laminated spruce top, laminated curly maple back & sides, 2 pickups. Blond version called the X-550 or X-500B.

1953-1959		$2,700	$3,200
1960-1964		$2,500	$2,900
1965-1969		$2,300	$2,700
1970s		$2,100	$2,700
1980s		$1,900	$2,200

Stuart X-550/X-500 B

1953-1994. 1959 model number X-550. 1960-1994 model number X-500B, natural blond finish.

1953-1959		$2,800	$3,400
1960-1964		$2,600	$3,100
1965-1969		$2,400	$2,900
1970s		$2,200	$2,700
1980s		$2,000	$2,400

Studio 301

1968-1970. Thinline, semi-hollow archtop Starfire-style but with sharp horns, single pickup, Cherry or Sunburst.

1968-1970		$1,000	$1,200

Studio 302

1968-1970. Electric archtop thinline, double sharp cutaway, laminated maple body, rosewood fingerboard and bridge, two pickups, Cherry or Sunburst.

1968-1970		$1,300	$1,500

Studio 303

1968-1970. Thinline, semi-hollow archtop with sharp horns, 302 model with added Bigsby vibrato, Cherry or Sunburst.

1968-1970		$1,300	$1,500

T-250

1986-1988. Single cut body and pickup configuration with banana-style headstock.

1986-1988		$600	$650

Thunderbird S-200

1963-1968. Electric solidbody, offset double cutaway, built-in rear guitar stand, AdjustoMatic bridge and vibrato tailpiece, two humbucker pickups until changed to single-coils in 1966.

MODEL YEAR	FEATURES	EXC. COND. LOW	HIGH
1963-1965	Humbuckers	$900	$1,200
1966-1968	Single-coils	$700	$900

Troubador F-20

1956-1987. Acoustic flat-top, spruce top with maple back and sides (mahogany 1959 and after), rosewood fingerboard and bridge, Natural or Sunburst.

1956-1959		$750	$850
1960-1969		$700	$800
1970-1979		$650	$750
1980-1987		$600	$700

TV Model D-55/D-55

1968-current. Special order 1968 to 1973. Regular production 1973-1987. Reintroduced 1990s.

1968-1969		$1,800	$2,700
1970-1979		$1,500	$1,700
1980-1987		$1,200	$1,600
1990s		$1,400	$1,600
2000s		$1,400	$1,600

Valencia F-40

1954-1983. Acoustic flat-top, rounded lower bout, spruce top, maple back and sides, rosewood fingerboard and bridge. Sunburst finish.

1954-1959		$900	$1,000
1960-1969		$850	$950
1970-1979		$800	$900
1980-1983		$750	$850

X-79 Skyhawk

1981-1986. Four-point solidbody, two pickups, coil-tap or phase switch, various colors.

1981-1986		$550	$650

X-80 Skylark/Swan

1982-1986. Explorer-style body with two deep cutaways, banana-style six-on-a-side headstock, renamed Swan in '85.

1982-1986		$850	$1,000

X-88 Flying Star "Motley Crue"

1984-1986. Explorer meets Flying V pointy four-point star body, rocketship meets spearhead headstock on bolt-on neck, one pickup, optional vibrato.

1984-1986	Pearl White	$475	$600

X-100/X-110

1953-1954. Guild was founded in 1952, so this is a very early model, 17" non-cutaway, single-col soapbar neck pickup, X-100 Sunburst finish, X-110 Natural Blond finish.

1953-1954	X-100 Sunburst	$1,300	$1,500
1953-1954	X-110 Natural	$1,400	$1,600

X-161/X-160B Savoy

1989-1993. X-160 Savoy with Bigsby, Black or Sunburst.

1989-1993		$1,100	$1,300

X-160 Savoy

1989-1993. No Bigsby, Black or Sunburst.

1989-1993		$1,100	$1,300

X-700

1994-2000. Rounded cutaway, 17", solid spruce top, laminated maple back and sides, gold hardware, Natural or Sunburst.

MODEL YEAR	FEATURES	EXC. COND. LOW	HIGH
1994-2000		$2,200	$2,300

Gurian

1965-1981. Luthier Michael Gurian started making classical guitars on a special order basis, in New York City. In 1969, he started building steel-string guitars as well. 1971 brought a move to Hinsdale, Vermont, and with it increased production.

JM
Mahogany, jumbo body with relatively wide waist (versus D-style or SJ-style), herringbone/rope trim.

1970s		$1,500	$1,700

JR3
Rosewood back and sides, U.S.A.- made

1970s		$1,800	$2,000

S-2-M
Mahogany, acoustic.

1970s		$1,000	$1,200

S-3-M
Mahogany.

1970s		$1,000	$1,200

S-3-R
Indian rosewood.

1970s		$1,300	$1,500

Guyatone

1933-present. Made in Tokyo by Matsuki Seisaku-jo, founded by Hawaiian guitarists Mitsuo Matsuki and Atsuo Kaneko (later of Teisco). Guya brand Rickenbacker lap copies in '30s. After a hiatus for the war ('40-'48), Seisakujo resumes production of laps and amps as Matsuki Denki Onkyo Kenkyujo. In '51 the Guyatone brand is first used on guitars, and in '52 they changed the company name to Tokyo Sound Company. Guyatones are among the earliest U.S. imports, branded as Marco Polo, Winston, Kingston and Kent. Other brand names included LaFayette and Bradford. Production and exports slowed after '68. Little is known about post-'60s guitars.

For early imports the following should be kept in mind: The guitar should be fully original and not have missing parts, the guitar should play and work well, the pickups should not be too weak, the guitar should have the original guitar case. The prices below are for fully original, excellent condition, fully functional guitars with cases.

Electric Hollowbody Archtops
Various models.

1950s		$300	$450
1960s		$350	$500

Electric Solidbody Guitars
Various models.

1950s		$300	$450
1960s		$350	$500

Guild X-88D Flying Star

Guild X-700 Stuart

Hagstrom HL-550

Hallmark SweptWing

MODEL YEAR	FEATURES	EXC. COND. LOW	HIGH

Hagenlocher, Henner

1996-present. Luthier Henner Hagenlocher builds his premium grade, custom, nylon-string guitars in Granada, Spain.

Hagstrom

1958-1983, 2004-present. Currently production solidbody, semi-hollowbody and acoustic guitars. Founded by Albin Hagström (b. 1905-d. 1952) of Älvdalen, Sweden, who began importing accordions in 1921 and incorporated in '25. The name of the company was changed to A.B. Hagström, Inc. in '38, and an American sales office was established in '40. Electric guitar and bass production began in '58 with plastic-covered hollowbody De Luxe and Standard models, which were single cut guitars with a patented design. The guitars were imported into the U.S. by Hershman Music of New York as Goya 90 and 80 from '58-'61. Bass versions were imported in '61. Following a year in the U.S., Albin's son Karl-Erik Hagström took over the company as exclusive distributor of Fender in Scandinavia; he changed the U.S. importer to Merson Musical Instruments of New York (later Unicord in 1965), and redesigned the line. The company closed doors in 1983. In '04 American Music & Sound started manufacturing and distributing the Hagstrom brand under license from AB Albin Hagström.

Corvette
1963-1967. Offset double cut solidbody, 3 single-coil pickups, multiple push-button switches, spring vibrato, called the Condor on U.S. imports.

1963-1967	Red	$800	$975

D'Aquisto (Jimmy D'Aquisto Model)
1969, 1976-1979. The Jimmy, designed by James D'Aquisto, electric archtop, F-holes, 2 pickups, sunburst.

1976-1979		$700	$825

H-12 Electric 12-String/Viking XII
1965-1967. Double cutaway, two pickups, 12 strings.

1965-1967		$400	$525

Impala
1963-1967. 2 pickup version of the Corvette.

1963-1967		$700	$775

Model I
1965-1971. Small double cut solidbody, 2 single-coils. Early models have plastic top.

1965-1971	Rare finish	$600	$800
1965-1971	Standard finish	$500	$525

Model II/F-200 Futura/H II
1965-1972, 1975-1976. Offset double cut slab body with beveled edge, 2 pickups. Called F-200 Futura in U.S., Model II elsewhere, '75-'76 called H II. F-200 reissued in '04.

1965-1972		$300	$475

Model III/F-300 Futura/H III
1965-1972, 1977. Offset double cut slab body with beveled edge, 3 pickups. Called F-300 Futura in U.S., Model III elsewhere, '77 called H III.

1965-1972		$300	$475
1977		$300	$475

MODEL YEAR	FEATURES	EXC. COND. LOW	HIGH

Super Swede
1979-1983, 2004-present. Glued-in neck upgrade of Swede. '04 version is maple top upgrade of Swede.

1979-1983		$800	$975

Swede
1970-1982, 2004-present. Bolt-on neck, single cut solidbody, black, cherry or natural. '04 version is set-neck.

1970-1982		$700	$825

Viking
1965-1968, 1972-1975, 2004-present. Double cut thinline, 2 f-holes. Also advertised as the V-1.

1965-1968		$500	$575
1972-1975		$500	$575

Hallmark

1965-1967, 2004-present. Imported and U.S.-made, intermediate, professional and premium grade, production/custom, guitars and basses from luthiers Bob Shade and Bill Gruggett, and located in Greenbelt, Maryland. The brand was originally founded by Joe Hall in Arvin, California, in '65. Hall had worked for Semie Moseley (Mosrite) and had also designed guitars for Standel in the mid-'60s. Bill Grugget, who also built his own line of guitars, was the company's production manager. Joe Hall estimates that less than 1000 original Hallmark guitars were built. The brand was revived by Shade in '04.

Sweptwing
1965-1967. Pointed body, sorta like a backwards Flying V.

1965		$425	$525

Hamer

1974-present. Intermediate, professional and premium grade, production/custom, electric guitars made in the U.S. and overseas. Hamer also make basses and the Slammer line of instruments. Founded in Arlington Heights, Illinois, by Paul Hamer and Jol Dantzig. Prototype guitars built in early-'70s were on Gibson lines, with first production guitar, the Standard (Explorer shape), introduced in '75. Hamer was puchased by Kaman Corporation (Ovation) in '88. The Illinois factory was closed and the operations were moved to the Ovation factory in Connecticut in '97.

Artist/Archtop Artist/Artist Custom
1995-present. Similar to Sunburst Archtop with semi-solid, F-hole design. Named Archtop Artist, then renamed Artist (with stop tailpiece)/Artist Custom in 1997.

1995-2003	Artist, Sunburst	$1,200	$1,350

Blitz
1982-1984 (1st version), 1984-1990 (2nd version). Explorer-style body, two humbuckers, three-on-a-side peghead, dot inlays, choice of tremolo or fixed bridge. Second version same except has angled six-on-a-side peghead and Floyd Rose tremolo.

1982-1984	3-on-side peghead	$450	$850
1984-1990	6-on-a-side peghead	$450	$700

MODEL YEAR FEATURES	EXC. COND. LOW	HIGH

Californian
1987-1997. Solidbody double cut, bolt neck, 1 humbucker and 1 single-coil, Floyd Rose tremolo.
| 1987-1989 | $450 | $850 |
| 1990-1997 | $450 | $700 |

Californian Custom
1987-1997. Downsized contoured body, offset double cut, neck-through-body, optional figured maple body, Duncan Trembucker and Trem-single pickups.
| 1987-1989 | $450 | $850 |
| 1990-1997 | $450 | $700 |

Californian Elite
1987-1997. Downsized contoured body, offset double cutaway, optional figured maple body, bolt-on neck, Duncan Trembucker and Trem-single pickups.
| 1987-1989 | $400 | $800 |
| 1990-1997 | $400 | $650 |

Centaura
1989-1995. Contoured body of alder or swamp ash, offset double cutaway, bolt-on neck, one humbucker and two single-coil pickups, Floyd Rose trem.
| 1989-1995 Sunburst | $450 | $650 |

Chaparral
1985-1987 (1st version), 1987-1994 (2nd version). Contoured body, offset double cut, glued maple neck, angled peghead, 1 humbucker and 2 single-coils, trem. Second version has bolt neck with a modified peghead.
| 1985-1987 Set-neck | $375 | $700 |
| 1987-1994 Bolt-on neck | $375 | $550 |

Daytona
1993-1997. Contoured body, offset double cut, bolt maple neck, dot inlay, 3 single-coils, Wilkinson VSV trem.
| 1993-1997 | $500 | $550 |

Diablo
1992-1997. Contoured alder body, offset double cut, bolt maple neck, rosewood board, dot inlays, reversed peghead '92-'94, 2 pickups, tremolo.
| 1992-1997 | $450 | $500 |

Duo-Tone
1993-present. Acoustic/electric semi-hollowbody, double cutaway, bound top, glued-in neck, rosewood fingerboard, 2 Humbuckers and EQ.
| 1993-1999 | $500 | $550 |

Eclipse
1994-1999. Asymmetrical double cut slab mahogany body, glued neck, 3-on-a-side peghead, rosewood board, dot inlays, 2 Duncan Mini-Humbuckers.
| 1994-1999 Cherry | $650 | $700 |

FB I
1986-1987. Reverse Firebird-style body, glued-in neck, reverse headstock, one pickup, rosewood board with dot inlays. Also available in non-reverse body.
| 1986-1987 | $350 | $450 |

FB II
1986-1987. Reverse Firebird-style, glued-in neck, ebony fingerboard with boomerang inlays, angled headstock, two humbuckers, Floyd Rose trem. Also available as a 12-string.
| 1986-1987 | $450 | $500 |

Korina Standard
1995-1996. Limited run, Korina Explorer-type body, glued-in neck, angled peghead, two humbuckers.
| 1995-1996 | $900 | $1,200 |

Maestro
1990. Offset double cut, 7 strings, tremolo, bolt-on maple neck, 3 Seymour Duncan rail pickups.
| 1990 | $650 | $750 |

Miller Music Guitar
1985-1986. Miller Music graphic art (White letters on Red background), double cutaway.
| 1985-1986 | $1,100 | $1,400 |

Mirage
1994-1998. Double cutaway carved figured koa wood top. Initially with three single-coil pickups, dual humbucker option in 1995.
| 1994-1998 Transparent flamed top | $1,000 | $1,150 |

Monaco Elite
2003-present. Single cut solidbody, 2 humbuckers, 3 in-line control knobs, tune-o-matic-style bridge, mother-of-pearl inlaid "victory" position markers, carved flamed maple cap over mahogany body.
| 2003 Sunburst | $1,200 | $1,350 |

Phantom A5
1982-1884 (1st version), 1985-1986 (2nd version). Contoured offset double cutaway, glued-in neck, three-on-a-side peghead, one triple-coil and one single-coil pickups. Second version same but with six-on-a-side peghead and Kahler tremolo.
| 1982-1984 | $475 | $625 |

Phantom GT
1984-1986. Contoured body, offset double cutaway, glued-in fixed neck, six-on-a-side peghead, one humbucker, single volume control.
| 1984-1986 | $375 | $525 |

Prototype
1981-1985. Contoured mahogany body, double cutaway with one splitable triple-coil pickup, fixed bridge, three-on-a-side peghead. Prototype II has extra pickup and tremolo.
| 1981-1985 | $650 | $750 |

Scarab I
1984-1986. Multiple cutaway body, six-on-a-side peghead, one humbucker, tremolo, rosewood or ebony fingerboard, dot inlays.
| 1984-1986 | $400 | $550 |

Scarab II
1984-1986. Two humbucker version of the Scarab.
| 1984-1986 | $400 | $550 |

Scepter
1986-1990. Explorer-type body, ebony fingerboard with boomerang inlays, angled six-on-a-side peghead, Floyd Rose trem.
| 1986-1990 | $350 | $500 |

Special
1980-1983 (1st version), 1984-1985 (Floyd Rose version), 1992-1997 (2nd version). Double cut solidbody, flame maple top, glued neck, 3-on-a-side peghead, two humbuckers. Rose version has mahogany body with

Hamer Duo-Tone

Hamer Monaco

GUITARS

Hamer Studio

Harmony Buck Owens

MODEL YEAR	FEATURES	EXC. COND. LOW	HIGH

ebony board. The second version is all mahogany and has tune-o-matic bridge, stop tailpiece and Duncan P-90s.

1980-1983	1st version	$500	$800
1984-1985	With Floyd Rose	$450	$750
1992-1997	2nd version	$400	$700

Special FM

1993-1997. Special with flamed maple top and dual humbuckers. Renamed the Special Custom in '97.

| 1993-1997 | | $800 | $900 |

Standard

1974-1985, 1995-1999. Explorer-shaped body, maple top, bound or unbound body, glued neck, angled headstock, either unbound neck with dot inlays or bound neck with crown inlays, 2 humbuckers. Reissued in '94 with same specs but unbound mahogany body after '97. Higher dollar Standard Custom still available.

1974-1979		$1,500	$1,950
1980-1985		$1,200	$1,500
1995-1999		$700	$1,400

Steve Stevens I

1984-1992. Introduced as Prototype SS, changed to Steve Stevens I in 1986, contoured double cut, six-on-a-side headstock, dot or crown inlays, one humbucker and two single-coil pickups.

| 1984-1992 | | $650 | $700 |

Steve Stevens II

1986-1987. One humbucker and one single-coil version.

| 1986-1987 | | $600 | $650 |

Studio

1993-present. Double cut, flamed maple top on mahogany body, dual humbucker pickups, Cherry or Natural.

| 1993-1999 | | $700 | $850 |

Sunburst

1977-1983, 1990-1992. Double cutaway bound solidbody, flamed maple top, glue-in neck, bound neck and crown inlays optional, three-on-a-side headstock, two humbuckers.

| 1977-1983 | | $900 | $1,200 |
| 1990-1992 | | $900 | $1,200 |

Sunburst Archtop

1991-present. Sunburst model with figured maple carved top, two humbuckers. Offered under various names:

Standard - unbound neck and dot inlays, tune-o-matic and stop tailpiece 1991-1993.

Custom - a Standard with bound neck and crown inlays 1991-1993.

Archtop - bound neck with crown inlays 1994-1997.

Studio Custom - bound neck with crown inlays 1997-present.

Studio - unbound body, by 1995 stud wrap-around tailpiece 1993-present.

Archtop GT - Gold top with P-90 soapbar-style pickups 1993-1997.

| 1991-1997 | | $900 | $1,200 |

MODEL YEAR	FEATURES	EXC. COND. LOW	HIGH

T-51

1993-1997. Classic single cut southern ash body, 2 single-coils.

| 1993-1997 | | $650 | $750 |

T-62

1991-1995. Classic offset double cut solidbody, tremolo, pau ferro board, Lubritrak nut, locking tuners, 3-band active EQ.

| 1991-1995 | | $650 | $750 |

TLE

1986-1992. Single cut mahogany body, maple top, glued neck, 6-on-a-side headstock, rosewood board, dot inlays, 3 pickups.

| 1986-1992 | | $650 | $750 |

TLE Custom

1986-1992. Bound, single cutaway solidbody with maple top, glued-in neck, angled headstock, ebony fingerboard with boomerang inlays, three pickups.

| 1986-1992 | | $650 | $750 |

Harmony

1892-1976, late 1970s-present. Huge, Chicago-based manufacturer of fretted instruments, mainly budget models under the Harmony name or for many other American brands and mass marketers. Harmony was at one time the largest guitar builder in the world. In its glory days, Harmony made over one-half of the guiltars built in the U.S. But by the early-'70s, the crash of '60s guitar boom and foreign manufacturers brought an end to the company. The company lasted from 1892 until 1976, with 1965 being Harmony's peak year.

The Harmony brand appeared on Asian-built intruments starting in the late '70s to the '90s with sales mainly is mass-retail stores. In 2000, the Harmony brand was distributed by MBT International. In '02, former MBT International marketing director Alison Gillette announced the launch of Harmony Classic Reissue Guitars and Basses.

Many Harmony guitars have a factory order number on the inside back of the guitar. The FON often contains the serial number. Most older Harmony acoustics and hollowbodies have a date ink-stamped inside the body. DeArmond made most of the electronic assemblies used on older Harmony electrics, and they often have a date stamped on the underside.

Archtone H1215

1950s. Lower-end archtop.

| 1950s | Sunburst | $100 | $200 |

Blond H62

1950s-1960s. Thin body, dual pickup archtop, curly maple back and sides, spruce top. Blond.

| 1950s | | $500 | $800 |
| 1960s | | $400 | $700 |

Brilliant Cutaway H1310

1962-1965. 16-1/2" body (Grand Auditorium), acoustic archtop cutaway, block markers.

| 1962-1965 | Sunburst | $450 | $550 |

MODEL YEAR	FEATURES	EXC. COND. LOW	HIGH

Broadway H954
1930s-1971. 15-3/4" body, acoustic archtop, dot markers, sunburst.

1960s	Sunburst	$250	$350

Buck Owens
Acoustic flat-top. red, white and blue.

1969		$500	$900

Cremona
1930s-1952. Full-size archtop line, Harmony and Cremona logo on headstock, natural. Cutaways became available in '53.

1940s		$100	$250

Espanada H63/H64
1950s-1960s. Thick body, single cutaway, jazz-style double pickups. Black finish with White appointments.

1950s		$500	$800
1960s		$400	$700

Grand Concert H165
1960s. Flat-top, all mahogany body.

1960s		$200	$250

H72/H72V Double Cutaway Hollowbody
1966-1971. 2 pickups, multiple bindings, cherry red, H72V has Bigsby.

1969	Burgundy	$250	$450

H75 Double Cutaway Hollowbody
1960-1970. 3 pickups, multi-bound body, 3-part F-holes, block inlays, bolt neck, Brown Sunburst.

1960-1970		$500	$700

H76 Double Cutaway Hollowbody
Late-1960s. Triple pickups, 335-style body, Bigsby vibrato tailpiece. Sunburst.

1960s		$500	$700

H77 Double Cutaway Hollowbody
1964-1970. Same as H75, but in cherry sunburst.

1964-1970		$500	$700

H78 Double Cutaway Hollowbody
Late-1960s. Triple pickups, 335-style body, Bigsby vibrato tailpiece. Cherry.

1960s		$500	$700

H79 Double Cutaway Hollowbody 12-String
1966-1970. Unique slotted headstock, 335-12-style body, cherry finish.

1966-1970		$600	$800

Hollywood H37/H39/H41
Auditorium-sized 15 3/4" non-cutaway electric archtop, H37 has a single pickup and Bronze finish, H39 has a single pickup and Brown Mahogany shaded finish, H41 has dual pickups and Brown finish.

1960		$175	$350

Master H945 (acoustic archtop)
1965-1966. 15" (Auditorium) acoustic archtop, block markers, music note painted logo on headstock.

1965-1966	Sunburst	$200	$300

Meteor H70/H71
1958-1966. Single rounded cut 2" thin body, 2 pickups, 3-part f-holes, block inlays, bolt neck, H70 sunburst, H71 natural (ended '65). Lefty offered '65-'66. Reintroduced as H661 and H671 (without Meteor name) in '72-'74.

1958-1965	H71	$300	$600
1958-1966	H70	$300	$600

MODEL YEAR	FEATURES	EXC. COND. LOW	HIGH

Montclair
Archtop acoustic.

1960		$225	$300

Monterey H1456/H1457/H1325/H950/H952
1930s-1974. Line of Auditorium and Grand Auditorium acoustic archtop models. Not all Monterey models were made during the whole period.

1955	Model H952		
	Colorama	$300	$400
1963		$225	$300

Patrician F63
Archtop.

1940s		$250	$350

Rebel H81 (single pickup)
1968-1971. Single pickup version of Rebel, brown sunburst.

1968-1971		$175	$275

Rebel H82/H82G
Listed as a new model in 1971. Thin body, hollow tone chamber, double cutaway, 2 pickups, H82 sunburst, H82G Avacado shading (renumbered as H682 and H683 in '72).

1971		$200	$300

Rocket H53/H54/H56/H59
1959-1973. Single cut, F-holes, dot inlays, 2-tone brown sunburst ('59-'62) or red sunburst ('63 on). Came with 1 pickup (Rocket I H53 '59-'71), 2 pickups (Rocket II H54 has two pickups, Rocket VII H56 has two pickups and vibrato, Rocket III H59 has three pickups. Rockets were single cutaway, Brown Sunburst in the early-1960s and double cutaway Red Sunburst in the early-1970s.

1950s	1 pickup	$200	$350
1950s	2 pickups	$200	$450
1950s	3 pickups	$500	$650
1960s	2 pickups	$200	$450
1960s	3 pickups	$500	$650
1965-1973	1 pickup	$200	$350

Roy Smeck H73
1964-1967. Modified double cut 2" thin body, bolt neck, 3-part f-holes, 2 pickups, vibrato.

1964-1967		$250	$450

Silhouette De Luxe Double H19
1964-1967. Double cut solidbody, deluxe pickups, block markers, advanced vibrato.

1965-1967	Sunburst	$325	$400

Silhouette H14/H15/H17
1964-1967. Double cut solidbody, H14 single pickup, H15 dual pickup, H17 dual with vibrato. The H17 was offered until '66.

1964-1966	H14	$150	$200
1964-1966	H15	$200	$300
1964-1966	H17	$225	$325

Singing Cowboys H1057
Western chuck-wagon scene stencil top, "Singing Cowboys" stenciled on either side of upper bouts. Brown background versus earlier Supertone version that had Black background.

1950s		$175	$300

Harmony H-82G Rebel

1930s Harmony Patrician

1959 Harmony Sovereign

Heiden Dreadnought

MODEL YEAR	FEATURES	EXC. COND. LOW	HIGH

Sovereign Jumbo Deluxe H1266
1960s-1970s. Jumbo nearly D-style, 16" wide body with out-size pickguard, Natural.

| 1960s | | $500 | $600 |
| 1970s | | $450 | $550 |

Sovereign Jumbo H1260
1960s-1970s. Jumbo shape, 16" wide body, Natural.

| 1960s | | $450 | $550 |
| 1970s | | $400 | $500 |

Sovereign Western Special Jumbo H1203
1960s-1970s. Fifteen inch wide body, 000-style.

| 1960s | | $500 | $600 |

Stratotone Deluxe Jupiter H49
1958-1968. Single cut, tone chamber construction, 2 pickups, bound spruce top, curly maple back and 6 control knobs.

| 1958-1959 | | $300 | $450 |

Stratotone Mars Electric H45/H46
1958-1968. Single cut, tone chamber construction, H45 with 1 pickup and sunburst finish, H46 with 2 pickups.

| 1958-1959 | | $200 | $350 |

Stratotone Mercury Electric H47/H48
1958-1968. Single cut, tone chamber construction, H47 with 1 pickup, block inlay and curly maple sunburst top, H48 is the same with a blond top.

| 1958-1959 | | $250 | $400 |

TG1201 Tenor
Spruce top, two-on-a-side tuners, Sovereign model tenor. Natural

| 1950s | | $200 | $300 |

Harptone
1893-ca. 1975. The Harptone Manufacturing Corporation was located in Newark, New Jersey. They made musical instrument cases and accessories and got into instrument production from 1934 to '42, making guitars, banjos, mandolins, and tiples. In '66 they got back into guitar production, making the Standel line from '67 to '69. Harptone offered flat-tops and archtops under their own brand until the mid-'70s when the name was sold to the Diamond S company, which owned Micro-Frets.

E-6N
D-style body, spruce top and mahogany back and sides, unique Harptone headstock, Natural.

| 1970 | | $850 | $950 |

Hayes Guitars
1993-present. Professional and premium grade, production/custom, steel and nylon string guitars made by luthier Louis Hayes in Paonia, Colorado.

Haynes
1865-early 1900s. The John C. Haynes Co. of Boston, also made the Bay State brand.

Parlor Guitar
1900s-1920s. Small 12 1/2" parlor guitar with typical narrow bouts, spruce top, Brazilian rosewood back and sides, multicolored wood marquetry trim, Natural.

| 1910 | | $800 | $900 |

MODEL YEAR	FEATURES	EXC. COND. LOW	HIGH

Heartfield
1989-1994. Founded as a joint venture between Fender Musical Instrument Corporation (U.S.A.) and Fender Japan (partnership between Fender and distributors Kanda Skokai and Yamano Music) to build and market more advanced designs (built by Fuji Gen-Gakki). First RR and EX guitar series and DR Bass series debut in '90. Talon and Elan guitar series and Prophecy bass series introduced in '91. The brand was dead by '94.

Elan
1989-1994. Carved-style bound double cut body, flamed top, dual humbuckers, offset PRS-style headstock.

| 1989-1994 | | $400 | $500 |

EX
1990-1994. EX models have three single-coil pickups and Floyd Rose tremolo.

| 1990-1994 | | $200 | $300 |

Talon
1989-1994. Strat-style body with wedge-triangle headstock, dot markers, hum/single/hum pickup configuration.

| 1989-1994 | Blue | $200 | $300 |

Heiden Stringed Instruments
1974-present. Luthier Michael Heiden builds his premium grade, production/custom, flat-top guitars in Chilliwack, British Columbia. He also builds mandolins.

Heit Deluxe
Ca. 1967-1970. Imported from Japan by unidentified New York distributor. Many were made by Teisco, the most famous being the Teisco V-2 Mosrite copy.

Acoustic Archtop Guitars
1967-1970. Various models.

| 1967-1970 | | $100 | $200 |

Electric Solidbody Guitars
1967-1970. Various models.

| 1967-1970 | | $90 | $150 |

Hemken, Michael
1993-present. Luthier Michael Hemken builds his premium grade, custom, archtops in St. Helena, California.

Heritage
1985-present. Professional, premium, and presentation grade, production/custom, hollow, semi-hollow, and solidbody guitars built in Kalamazoo, Michigan. They have also made banjos, mandolins, flat-tops, and basses in the past. Founded by Jim Deurloo, Marvin Lamb, J.P. Moats, Bill Paige and Mike Korpak, all former Gibson employees who did not go to Nashville when Norlin closed the original Gibson factory in 1984.

MODEL YEAR	FEATURES	EXC. COND. LOW	HIGH

Eagle
1986-present. Single rounded cut semi-hollowbody, mahogany body and neck, one jazz pickup, F-holes.

| 1986-1999 | Sunburst | $1,250 | $1,700 |
| 2000-2003 | | $1,500 | $2,000 |

Eagle Custom
Eagle with custom inlays.

| 2001 | | $1,800 | $2,400 |

Gary Moore Model
1989-1991. Single cut solidbody, two pickups, chrome hardware, sunburst.

| 1989-1991 | | $1,700 | $2,300 |

Golden Eagle
1985-present. Single cut hollowbody, back inlaid with mother-of-pearl eagle and registration number, multi-bound ebony board with mother-of-pearl cloud inlays, bound F-holes, gold-plated parts, ebony bridge inlaid with mother-of-pearl, mother-of-pearl truss rod cover engraved with owner's name, one Heritage jazz pickup, multi-bound curly maple pickguard.

| 1985-1999 | | $2,200 | $2,600 |
| 2000-2003 | | $2,500 | $3,000 |

H-140 CM
1985-present. Single pointed cutaway, solidbody with bound curly maple top, two humbucking pickups, chrome parts.

| 1985-1994 | Curly maple top | $700 | $750 |
| 1985-1994 | Goldtop | $700 | $750 |

H-147
1990-1991. Single cut solidbody, two humbuckers, mahogany body, mother-of-pearl block inlays, Black or Gold hardware.

| 1990-1991 | Black | $600 | $650 |

H-150 C/H-150 CM
1985-present. Single rounded cutaway solidbody, curly maple top, 2 pickups, chrome parts.

| 1985-1999 | Cherry Sunburst | $800 | $850 |

H-157 Ultra
Les Paul Custom-style, large block markers, figured maple top.

| 1993-1994 | | $1,200 | $1,300 |

H-204 DD
1986-1989. Single cutaway solidbody of mahogany, curly maple top, one-piece mahogany neck, 22-fret rosewood fingerboard.

| 1986-1989 | | $450 | $550 |

H-207 DD
1986-1989. Double cutaway solidbody of mahogany, curly maple top, one-piece mahogany neck, 22-fret rosewood fingerboard.

| 1986-1989 | | $450 | $550 |

H-357
1989-1994. Firebird copy, neck-through-body.

| 1989-1990 | | $1,900 | $2,100 |

H-535
1987-present. Double cutaway semi-hollowbody archtop, rosewood fingerboard, two humbucker pickups.

1987-1999		$900	$1,100
1987-1999	Flamed maple top	$1,100	$1,200
2000-2003		$1,100	$1,300

H-550
1990-present. Single cut hollow body, laminated maple top and back, multiple bound top, white bound pickguard, F-holes, 2 humbuckers.

| 1996-2000 | | $1,700 | $2,100 |

H-555 ASB
1989-2003. Like 535, but with maple neck, ebony board, pearl and abalone inlays.

| 1989-2003 | | $1,300 | $1,500 |

H-575
1987-present. Single sharp cut hollow body, solid maple top and back, cream bound top and back, wood pickguard, f-holes, 2 humbuckers.

| 1987-1999 | | $1,200 | $1,400 |

H-576
1990-present. Single rounded cut hollow body, laminated maple top and back, multiple bound top, single bound back and f-holes and wood pickguard, 2 humbuckers.

| 1990-1999 | | $1,100 | $1,300 |

HFT-445
1987-2000. Flat-top acoustic, mahogany back and sides, spruce top, maple neck, rosewood board.

| 1987-2000 | | $500 | $700 |

Johnny Smith
1989-2001. Custom hand-carved 17" hollowbody, single cutaway, F-holes, one pickup.

| 1989-1999 | Optional colors | $2,800 | $3,300 |
| 1989-1999 | Sunburst | $2,500 | $3,000 |

Millennium Eagle 2000
2000-present. Single cut semi-solidbody, multiple bound curly maple top, single bound curly maple back, f-holes, 2 humbuckers.

| 2000-2001 | | $1,100 | $1,300 |

Millennium SAE
2000-present. Single cut semi-solidbody, laminated arch top, single cream bound top and back, f-holes, 2 humbuckers.

| 2000-2001 | | $1,100 | $1,200 |

Parsons Street
1989-1992. Offset double cut, curly maple top on mahogany body, single/single/hum pickups, pearl block markers, sunburst or natural.

| 1989-1992 | | $650 | $750 |

Roy Clark
1992-present. Thinline, single cut semi-hollow archtop, gold hardware, 2 humbuckers, block markers.

| 1992-2002 | Cherry Sunburst | $1,600 | $1,900 |

SAE Custom
1992-2000. Single cut maple semi-hollow body, f-holes, 2 humbuckers and 1 bridge pickup.

| 1992-2000 | | $950 | $1,050 |

Super Eagle
1988-present. 18 inch body, single cutaway electric archtop.

| 1989-1999 | Optional colors | $2,800 | $3,000 |
| 1989-1999 | Sunburst | $2,600 | $2,700 |

Heritage H-140

Heritage Johnny Smith

The *Vintage Guitar Price Guide* shows low to high values for items in all-original excellent condition, and, where applicable, with original case or cover.

Hoffman dreadnaught

1967 Höfner Committee

MODEL YEAR	FEATURES	EXC. COND. LOW	HIGH

Sweet 16
1987-present. Single cut maple semi-hollowbody, spruce top, 2 pickups, pearl inlays.

1987-2000	Optional colors	$2,300	$2,800
1987-2000	Sunburst	$2,000	$2,600

Hill Guitar Company
1972-1980, 1990-present. Luthier Kenny Hill builds his professional and premium grade production/custom, classical and flamenco guitars in Felton, California and Michoacan, Mexico.

Hirade Classical
1968-present. Professional grade, production, classical guitars built in Japan by Takamine. The late Mass Hirade was the founder of the Takamine workshop. He learned his craft from master luthier Masare Kohno. Hirade "represents Takamine's finest craftsmanship and material." Solid tops.

H-5
Solid cedar top, laminate rosewood body.

1980s		$1,000	$1,100

H-8
1989-1996. Solid spruce top, solid rosewood body.

1989-1996		$1,300	$1,400

HD-5C
Solid cedar top, rosewood laminate body, cutaway, pickup and preamp.

1980s		$1,000	$1,100

Hoffman Guitars
1971-present. Premium grade, custom flat-tops and harp guitars built by luthier Charles Hoffman in Minneapolis, Minnesota.

Höfner
1887-present. Budget, intermediate, and professional grade, production, archtop, acoustic, and classical guitars built in Germany and the Far East. They also produce basses and bowed-instruments. Founded by Karl Hofner in Schonbach, Germany. Sons Josef and Walter joined the company in 1919 and '21 and expanded the market worldwide. The company started producing guitars in '25. They moved the company to Bavaria in '50 and are currently located in Hagenau.

Beatle Electric Model 459TZ
1966-1967. Violin-shaped 500/1 body, block-stripe position markers, transistor-powered flip-fuzz and treble boost.

1960s	Sunburst	$1,500	$1,700

Beatle Electric Model 459VTZ
1966-1967. Violin-shaped 500/1 body, same as Model 459TZ except with vibrato tailpiece.

1960s	Sunburst	$1,500	$1,700

Beatle Electric Model G459TZ Super
1966-1967. Violin-shaped 500/1 body, deluxe version of Model 459TZ, including flamed maple sides and narrow grain spruce top, gold hardware, and elaborate inlays and binding.

1960s	Natural Blond	$1,700	$1,900

Beatle Electric Model G459VTZ Super
1966-1967. Violin-shaped 500/1 body, same as G459TZ Super but with vibrato tailpiece and narrow grain spruce top, gold hardware.

1960s	Natural Blond	$1,700	$1,900

Club Model 126
1954-1970. Mid-sized single cutaway Guild Bluesbird or Les Paul-style body, dot markers, flamed maple back and sides, spruce top, listed with Hofner "Professional Electric Series."

1960s	Sunburst	$500	$700

Committee Model 4680 Thin Electric
1961-1968. Thinline archtop single cut Byrdland-style body, dual pickups, split-arrowhead markers, no vibrato, Sunburst.

1961-1968		$1,200	$1,400

Deluxe Model 176
1964-1983. Double cut, 3 pickups, polyester varnished sunburst finish, vibrola tailpiece. Similar to Model 175 polyester varnished red and gold version.

1960s		$500	$700

Galaxy Model 175
1963-1966. Double cut, 3 pickups, red and gold vinyl covering, fancy red-patch pickguard, vibrola. Similar to Model 176 polyester varnished sunburst version.

1963-1966	Red and Gold vinyl	$1,300	$1,600
1963-1966	Sunburst	$1,200	$1,500

Golden Hofner
1959-1963. Single cut archtop, blond, 2 pickups, f-holes.

1959-1963		$1,100	$1,300

Jazzica Custom
2000-present. Full body, single soft cutaway, acoustic/electric archtop, carved German spruce top.

2000-2001	Sunburst	$1,500	$1,600

Model 172 II (R) (S) (I)
1962-1963. Double cut body, polyester varnished wood (S) or scruff-proof red (R) or white (I) vinyl, 2 pickups, vibrato.

1961-1962		$400	$500

Model 173 II (S) (I)
1962-1963. Double cut body, polyester varnished wood (S) or scuffproof vinyl (I), 3 pickups, vibrato.

1962-1963	White vinyl	$375	$475
1962-1963	Gold foil vinyl	$500	$600

Model 180 Shorty Standard
1982. Small-bodied, single cut, solidbody, 1 pickup, travel guitar. The Shorty Super had a built-in amp and speaker.

1982		$250	$400

Model 457 President
1959-1972. Single cut thinline archtop, 2 pickups, non-vibrato.

1959-1965		$700	$1,000
1966-1972		$600	$900

Model 470SE2 (electric archtop)
1961-1993. Large single rounded cutaway electric archtop on Hofner's higher-end they call "superbly flamed maple (back and sides), carved top of best spruce," 2 pickups, 3 control knobs, gold hardware, pearl inlay. Natural finish only.

1969-1977		$1,100	$1,300

MODEL		EXC. COND.	
YEAR	FEATURES	LOW	HIGH

Model 471SE2 (electric archtop)
1969-1977. Large single pointed cutaway electric archtop, flamed maple back and sides, spruce top, black celluloid binding, ebony board, pearl inlays, blond finish. Sunburst version of the 470SE2.

1969-1977		$1,100	$1,300

Model 491 Flat-Top
1960s-1970s. J-45 slope shoulder body style, spruce top, mahogany back and sides, shaded Sunburst.

1970s		$300	$450

Model 496 Jumbo Flat-Top
1960s. J-185-style body with selected spruce top and highly flamed maple back and sides, gold-plated hardware, ornamented vine pattern pickguard.

1960s	Sunburst	$900	$1,100

Model 514-H Classical Concert
1960s. Concert model, lower-end of the Hofner classical line.

1960s	Natural	$200	$300

Model 4575VTZ/Verythin (Professional extra thin)
1965-1976. Extra-thinline acoustic, double cut, 3 pickups, vibrato arm, ruby-red or sunburst, includes treble boost and flip-fuzz, straight-line markers.

1960s	Ruby Red, 2 pickups	$750	$850
1960s	Rudy Red, 3 pickups	$850	$950

Verythin Standard
2000-present. Update of the 1960s Verythin line.

2000-2002		$850	$950

Model 4600/V2 (Professional extra thin)
1968-1970. Thinline acoustic, double cut, 2 pickups, vibrato arm, dot markers, sunburst.

1968-1970	Sunburst	$500	$700

Hohner
1857-present. Budget and intermediate grade, production, acoustic and electric guitars. They also have basses, ukes and mandolins. Matthias Hohner, a clockmaker in Trossingen, Germany, founded Hohner in 1857, making harmonicas. Hohner has been offering guitars and basses at least since the early '70s. HSS was founded in 1986 as a distributor of guitars and other musical products. By 2000, Hohner was also offering the Crafter brands of guitars.

Alpha Standard
Designed by Klaus Scholler. Solidbody, stereo outputs, Flytune tremolo.

1980s		$200	$300

Jacaranda Rosewood Dreadnought
Flat-top acoustic.

1970s		$200	$350

L 59/L75
Late-1970s-1980s. Classic single cut solidbody, 2 humbuckers, 59 has upgrade maple body with maple veneer top.

1970s		$200	$300

Miller Beer Guitar
Solidbody, shaped like Miller beer logo.

1980s		$300	$400

Professional
1980s. Single cut solidbody, maple neck, extra large pickguard.

1980s	Natural	$200	$300

SE-35
1989-mid-1990s. ES-335-style, 22 frets, graphite nut, two humbucker pickups.

1989-1994	Natural	$300	$400

ST Victory
1987-mid-1990s. Part of the Professional Series. Double cut solid maple body, reverse headstock, tremolo, humbucker pickup.

1987-1994	Blue	$200	$300

Holiday
Student-level, private-branded similar to Stella but may have solid tops.

Hollenbeck Guitars
1970-present. Luthier Bill Hollenbeck builds his premium grade, production/custom, hollow and semi-hollow body acoustics and electric guitars in Lincoln, Illinois.

Holman
1966-1968. Built by the Holman-Woodell guitar factory in Neodesha, Kansas. The factory was started to build guitars for Wurlitzer, but that fell through by '67.

Hondo
1969-1987, 1991-present. Budget grade, production, imported acoustic, classical and electric guitars. They also offer basses and mandolins. Originally imported by International Music Corporation (IMC) of Fort Worth, Texas, founded by Jerry Freed and Tommy Moore and named after a small town near San Antonio, Texas. Early pioneers of Korean guitarmaking, primarily targeted at beginner market. Introduced their first electrics in '72. Changed brand to Hondo II in '74. Some better Hondos made in Japan '74-'82/'83. In '85 IMC purchases major interest in Jackson/Charvel, and the Hondo line was supplanted by Charvels. '87 was the last catalog before hiatus. In '88 IMC was sold and Freed began Jerry Freed International and in '91 he revived the Hondo name. Acquired by MBT International in '95, specializing in student-level instruments.

Acoustic Flat-Top Guitars
1969-1987, 1991-present.

1970s		$150	$250

Electric Hollowbody Guitars (misc.)
1969-1987, 1991-present.

1980s		$250	$400

Electric Solidbody Guitars (misc.)
1969-1987, 1991-present.

1969-1987		$250	$400
1991-1999		$150	$250

Hohner G3T Headless

Hollenbeck Jazz Reflections

1978 Hondo II Longhorn

Thomas Humphrey La Catalina

MODEL YEAR	FEATURES	EXC. COND. LOW	HIGH

H 752 Fame
1990s. Single cut solidbody, Black single-ply pick-guard, maple neck.

| 1990s | Blond | $150 | $225 |

H 756 BTS Fame
1990s. Double cut solidbody, white pickguard, maple body, rosewood or maple fingerboard, Natural or Sunburst.

| 1990s | | $150 | $225 |

Longhorn 6/12 Doubleneck copy
1970s-1980s. Copy of Danelectro Longhorn 6/12 Doubleneck guitar, Dano coke bottle-style headstock.

| 1980s | White Sunburst | $600 | $800 |

Longhorn Copy
Ca. 1978-1980s. Copy of Danelectro Long Horn guitar, Dano Coke bottle-style headstock.

| 1970s | Brown | $350 | $450 |

M 16 "Rambo-Machine Gun"
1970s-1980s. Machine gun body-style, matching machine gun-shaped guitar case, black or red.

| 1970s | | $400 | $600 |
| 1980s | | $400 | $600 |

Hopf
1906-present. Intermediate, professional, premium, and presentation grade, production/custom, classical guitars made in Germany. They also make basses, mandolins and flutes.

The Hopf family of Germany has a tradition of instrument building going back to 1669, but the modern company was founded in 1906. Hopf started making electric guitars in the mid-1950s. Some Hopf models were made by others for the company. By the late-1970s, Hopf had discontinued making electrics, concentrating on classicals.

Explorer Standard
1960s. ES-335-style body with sharp horns, center block, dual mini-humbucker-style pickups.

| 1960s | | $400 | $500 |

Saturn Archtop
1960s. Offset cutaway, archtop-style soundholes, two pickups.

| 1960s | White | $500 | $700 |

Super Deluxe Archtop
1960s. Archtop, 16 3/4", cat's-eye soundholes, carved spruce top, flamed maple back and sides.

| 1960s | Sunburst | $600 | $800 |

Horabe
Classical and Espana models made in Japan.

Model 25 Classical
Solid top.

| 1960s | | $400 | $600 |

Model 40 Classical
Solid cedar top, rosewood back and sides.

| 1960s | | $600 | $800 |

Model 60 Classical
1980s. German spruce top, solid Indian rosewood rims.

| 1980s | | $800 | $1,200 |

Hoyer
1874-present. Intermediate grade, production, flat-top, classical, electric, and resonator guitars. They also build basses. Founded by Franz Hoyer, building classical guitars and other instruments. His son, Arnold, added archtops in the late-1940s, and solidbodies in the 1960s. In 1967, Arnold's son, Walter, took over, leaving the company in 1977. The company changed hands a few times over the following years. Walter started building guitars again in 1984 under the W.A. Hoyer brand, which is not associated with Hoyer.

Junior
Early-1960s. Solidbody with unusual sharp horn cutaway, single neck pickup, bolt-on neck, dot markers, Arnold Hoyer logo on headstock, shaded Sunburst.

| 1960s | | $450 | $500 |

Soloist Electric
Single cutaway archtop, two pickups, teardrop F-holes, Sunburst.

| 1960-1962 | | $450 | $550 |

Electric Solidbody Guitars
| 1950s | | $150 | $300 |

Humphrey, Thomas
1970-present. Premium and presentation grade, custom, nylon-string guitars built by luthier Thomas Humphrey in Gardiner, New York. In 1996 Humphrey began collaborating with Martin Guitars, resulting in the Martin C-TSH and C-1R. Often the inside back label will indicate the year of manufacture.

Classical
Brazilian or Indian rosewood back and sides, spruce top, traditionally-based designs evolved over time with Millenium becoming a benchmark design in 1985, values can increase with new designs. Valuations depend on each specific instrument and year and type of construction. Price ranges are guidance only; each instrument should be evaluated on a case-by-case basis.

| 1976-1984 | | $5,000 | $7,000 |

Millenium (classical)
1985-present. Professional performance-grade high-end classical guitar with innovative taper body design and elevated fingerboard. Tops are generally spruce (versus cedar) with rosewood back and sides.

| 1995-1996 | | $8,000 | $13,000 |

Huss and Dalton Guitar Company
1995-present. Luthiers Jeff Huss and Mark Dalton build their professional and premium grade flat-tops and banjos in Staunton, Virginia.

Ibanez
1932-present. Budget, intermediate, and professional grade, production/custom, acoustic and electric guitars. They also make basses, amps, mandolins, and effects.

MODEL		EXC. COND.	
YEAR	FEATURES	LOW	HIGH

Founded in Nagoya, Japan, by Matsujiro Hoshino as book and stationary supply, retailing musical instruments in 1909. He began importing instruments in 1921. His son Yoshitaro became president in '27 and began exporting. Manufacturing of Ibanez instruments began in '32. The company's factories were destroyed during World War II, but the business was revived in '50. Junpei Hoshino, grandson of founder, became president in '60; a new factory opened called Tama Seisakusho (Tama Industries). Brand names by '64 included Ibanez, Star, King's Stone, Jamboree and Goldentone, supplied by 85 factories serving global markets. Sold acoustic guitars to Harry Rosenblum of Elger Guitars ('59-ca.'65) in Ardmore, Pennsylvania, in early-'60s. Around '62 Hoshino purchased 50% interest in Elger Guitars, and ca. '65 changed the name to Ibanez.

Jeff Hasselberger headed the American guitar side beginning '73-'74, and the company headquarters are moved to Cornwells Heights, PA in '74. By '75 the instruments are being distributed by Chesbro Music Company in Idaho Falls, Idaho, and Harry Rosenblum sells his interest to Hoshino shortly thereafter. Ca. '81, the Elger Company becomes Hoshino U.S.A. An U.S. Custom Shop was opened in '88. Most glued-neck guitars from 1970s are fairly rare.

Dating: copy guitars begin ca. 1971. Serial numbers begin 1975 with letter (A-L for month) followed by 6 digits, the first two indicating year, last four sequential (MYYXXXX). By 1988 the month letter drops off. Dating code stops early-1990s; by 1994 letter preface either F for Fuji or C for Cort (Korean) manufacturer followed by number for year and consecutive numbers (F4XXXX=Fuji, C4XXXX=Cort, 1994).

470 S/S470
1991-present. Offset double cut mahogany solidbody, single-single-hum pickups until about '95 (470 S), hum-single-hum (S470) afterwards.

1991-1999		$375	$425

540 S/Pro 540S/Saber 540 S
1987-1994. Offset double cut mahogany solidbody, solid maple neck, rosewood board, dot inlays, single-single-hum pickups. Called the Pro 540S in '87, the Saber 540S in '88. There was also a double humbucker model (541S-HH).

1992-1997		$500	$600

540 S FM/S540FM
1992-1997. Mahogany solidbody, flame maple top, solid maple neck, rosewood board, single-single-hum pickups until '94 (540SFM), hum-single-hum (S540FM) afterwards.

1992-1997		$600	$800

540 S LTD/S540LTD
1990-1999. Offset double cut mahogany solidbody, solid maple neck, bound rosewood board, sharktooth inlays, hum-single-hum pickups. Model changed to S540LTD in '94

1990-1999		$600	$800

AE40
1994-1996. Acoustic/electric, single cut with piezo, mahogany back and sides, spruce top.

1994-1996		$300	$350

AH-10 (Allan Holdsworth)
1985-1986. Offset double cut solidbody, bolt neck, single bridge humbucker, dot markers, various colors.

1985-1986		$300	$400

Artcore Electric Hollowbody (China)
2002-2004. All Artcore semi-acoustic guitars have mahogany necks, rosewood fingerboards, 24 3/4" scale with 22 frets, dual Artcore medium output pickups, Gibson-style knobs and toggle, F-holes with binding.

2002-2004		$125	$200

Artcore United Electric Hollowbody (China/Japan)
2002-present. Body made in China and assembled in Japan, mid-level price point, dual Artcore medium output pickups, Gibson-style knobs and toggle, F-holes with binding.

2002-2004		$475	$525

Artist AM70
1980s. Small double cut body, F-holes, 2 non-adjustable pole black humbuckers.

1980s		$800	$900

Artist Doubleneck AR1200
1981-1984. Solid ash body, six/twelve strings, three-ply maple neck, Super 58 pickups, Gold hardware.

1981-1984		$1,000	$1,300

Artist Model 2612
1974-1977. Early Artist series, double cutaway solidbody, Black finish, Gold hardware, no vibrato.

1974-1977		$800	$950

Artist Model 2617
1974-1977. Early Artist series, double cutaway solidbody, Blond ash bookmatched, set-neck, German carved top. Abalonaid trim, later would evolve iinto the Professional model.

1974-1977		$950	$1,100

Artist Model 2618
Ca. 1977. Standard double cutaway Artist solidbody shape, abalone dot markers, Gold hardware.

1977		$700	$850

AS80
1994-2002. ES-335-style body and layout, dot markers, chrome hardware.

1994-2002		$375	$400

AS100
1980s. ES-335 style, dot markers, toggle switch located in the normal spot near the control knobs.

1980s	Sunburst	$1,100	$1,250

AS200
1979-2001. ES-335 style, block markers, toggle switch located on upper treble bout. Replaced by the JSM100 in 2002.

1979-1990	Sunburst	$1,100	$1,250

AX125
2001-present. Double cut solidbody, 2 humbuckers, bolt neck.

2001-2002		$100	$200

Ibanez AR-1200 Doubleneck Arist

1977 Ibanez Artist Professional

1982 Ibanez Destroyer II

Ibanez George Benson GB10

MODEL YEAR	FEATURES	EXC. COND. LOW	HIGH
Blazer			
1980-1999. Offset double cut, 2 mini-switches for coil tap and phase, various colors.			
1980-1999	Matching headstock	$200	$300
Bob Weir Model 2681			
1975-1980. Double cut solidbody of carved solid ash, maple neck, ebony board with tree-of-life inlay, gold-plated Super 70 pickups. Only three to six of these were ever produced.			
1975-1980		$1,500	$2,000
Bob Weir Standard Model 2680			
1976-1980. Double cut solidbody of carved solid ash, maple neck, ebony board, dot markers, gold-plated Super 70 pickups, production model.			
1976-1980		$900	$1,000
Concert CN-200			
1978-1979. Carved maple top, mahogany body, seven layer Black/White binding, bolt-on neck, Super 80 pickups.			
1978-1979		$300	$450
Concert CN-250			
1978-1979. Carved maple top, mahogany body, seven layer Black/White binding, bolt-on neck, rosewood board with vine inlay, Super 80 pickups.			
1978-1979		$325	$425
Concord 699			
1970s. D-style flat-top, all maple including neck and fretboard.			
1970s	Natural	$400	$500
Custom Agent 2405 (Scroll Les Paul)			
1973-1977. Built as special order, known as scroll headstock Les Paul.			
1973-1977		$1,100	$1,600
Custom Agent 2675			
1975-1980. Carved maple top, fancy inlays, six strings, maple neck and ebony fretboard with pearl inlays, scroll peghead.			
1975-1980	Sunburst	$1,000	$1,200
Deluxe			
Two pickups.			
1976-1980		$300	$400
Deluxe 12-String			
Two pickups.			
1977		$425	$500
Destroyer II			
1982-1986. Explorer-style large basswood body, some models had set-necks and some had bolt-on, two pickups. In 1984 smaller body hard rock version introduced.			
1982-1986	Black	$525	$600
Destroyer Phil Collen			
Mid-1980s. Explorer body style, three humbucking pickups.			
1985		$550	$600
EX-370 FM			
1988-1994. Double cut solidbodies with long thin horns, various models, all models may not be included.			
1988-1994		$250	$400
EX-1700			
1993-1994. Offset double cut solidbody, 3 pickups, bound body.			
1993-1994		$250	$350
EX-3700			
1993-1994. Offset double cut solidbody, 3 pickups, bound maple top.			
1993-1994		$250	$350
FA-100 NT			
Late 1970s. Hollowbody ES-175-style, single cut, 2 pickups, F-holes, block inlays.			
1978		$900	$1,100
FG-360S			
Introduced in 1973. Les Paul Standard copy with bolt-on neck, trapezoid markers, maple top.			
1970s	Sunburst	$350	$375
GAX70			
1997-present. Symmetrical double cut, 2 humbuckers, bolt-on neck, dot markers.			
1997-2000	Natural	$175	$200
GAX75			
2001-present. GAX70 with Downshifter bridge.			
2001		$175	$200
George Benson GB-10			
1977-present. Single cut, laminated spruce top, flame maple back and sides, 2 humbuckers, three-piece set-in maple neck, ebony board.			
1970s	Blond	$1,500	$2,000
1970s	Sunburst	$1,400	$1,800
1980s	Blond	$1,400	$1,800
1980s	Sunburst	$1,300	$1,700
1990s	Blond	$1,300	$1,700
1990s	Sunburst	$1,200	$1,600
George Benson GB-20			
1977-1983. Much larger than GB-10, laminated spruce top, flame maple back and sides, one pickup.			
1977-1983		$1,300	$1,700
George Benson GB-100 Deluxe			
1993-1996. GB-10 with high-end appointments including flamed maple top, pearl binding, sunburst finish pickguard, pearl vine inlay tailpiece, gold hardware, 2 mini-humbuckers.			
1993-1996		$2,400	$2,800
Iceman IC-200			
1978-1980. Set-neck, two humbuckers, four knobs, angled block inlays, 555 made.			
1978-1980	Sunburst	$500	$700
Iceman IC-300			
1995-2003. Reintroduced line, made in Korea, standard model without tremolo.			
1995-2003		$450	$500
Iceman IC-300 Artist			
1978-1979. Korina body, engraved twin Super 80 pickups, 137 made.			
1978-1979		$500	$700
Iceman IC-350			
1995-1996. Reintroduced line, made in Korea, version with tremolo.			
1995-1996		$400	$450

MODEL YEAR	FEATURES	EXC. COND. LOW	HIGH

Iceman IC-500
1994. Limited production primarily for Japanese domestic market.

1994		$800	$900

Iceman IC-2663/2663 SL/2663 TL (original Iceman)
1976. The original Iceman debuting in the 1976 catalog.

1976		$500	$700

Iceman PS-10 (Paul Stanley)
1978-1979. Limited edition Paul Stanley model, abalone trim, Stanley's name engraved at 21st fret. Reintroduced in 1977 with upgraded model names.

1978-1979	Natural korina	$1,400	$1,600
1978-1979	Sunburst or Black	$1,300	$1,500

IMG-2010 Guitar Controller MIDI
1985-1987. Similar to Roland GR-707, slim triangle-wedge body with treble horn.

1985-1987		$350	$450

JEM 10th Anniversary
1996. Limited Edition signature Steve Vai model, bolt-on neck, vine metal pickguard, vine neck inlays, vine headstock art.

1996		$1,000	$1,600

JEM 777 VBK
1987-1996. Limited production variation of JEM 777.

1987-1996	Black, Green hardware	$1,700	$1,900

JEM 777 VSK
1987-1996. Basswood body with "Monkey Grip" through-body handle, maple neck, tilted headstock, two humbuckers and one single-coil pickups. Limited editions available in Loch Ness Green, signed and numbered by co-designer Steve Vai.

1987-1989		$1,200	$1,400
1990-1996		$1,200	$1,400

JEM 90th Anniversary
1997. Limited Edition signature Seve Vai model, textured Silver finish, chrome pickguard.

1997		$1,500	$2,000

JEM DNA (limited edition)
2000. Blood Red Swirl marble finish using Steve Vai's blood in the paint.

2000		$3,500	$4,000

Joe Pass Model JP-20
1982-1990. Full body, single cutaway, one pickup, abalone and pearl split block inlay, JP inlay on headstock.

1982-1990	Sunburst	$1,500	$1,700

JPM-100 John Petrucci/JPM 100 P-3
1998-1999. Offset double cut solidbody, 2 pickups, available in multi-color art finish.

1998-1999	Custom art finish	$1,500	$2,000

Lee Ritenour LR-10
1981-1987. Flame maple body, set-in neck bound in Cream, Quick Change tailpiece, 2 pickups, Dark Red Sunburst. Body filled with foam to illuminate feedback.

1981-1987		$700	$900

MODEL YEAR	FEATURES	EXC. COND. LOW	HIGH

M340
1978-1980s. Flat-top, spruce top, flamed maple back and sides, maple board.

1978-1982		$350	$450

Maxxas
1987-1988. Solid body (Maxxas MX2) or with internal sound chambers (MX3, '88 only), 2 pickups, all-access neck joint system.

1987-1988		$700	$800

Model 600 Series
1970-1978. Copy era acoustic flat-tops with model numbers in the 600 Series, basically Gibson square shoulder dreadnought. Copies included Hummingbird (683 and 684) and Dove (693) pickguard reproductions. There were also copies of Martins with natural tops and Fender Kingmans with the six-on-a-side Kingman headstock (647). And there were 12-string copies as well. A Vintage Series of Martin copies were also offered.

1970-1978		$300	$600

Model 700 Series
1970-1978. Acoustic flat-tops, upgraded models such as the Brazilian Scent 750, with more original design content than 600 Series.

1970-1978		$300	$700

Model 1453
1971-1973. ES-175 D copy, replaced by Model 2355 in 1973.

1971-1973		$1,150	$1,300

Model 1912
1974-1976. Has ES-355 styling and appointments but without varitone. Sunburst finish.

1974-1976		$900	$1,000

Model 2020
1970-1971. Initial offering of the copy era. Offset double cut, two unusual rectangular pickups, block markers, raised nailed-on headstock logo, sunburst.

1970-1971		$500	$700

Model 2335
1974-1977. Copy of the ES-175, Sunburst.

1974-1977		$900	$1,000

Model 2341
1974-1976. Part of "Oldies Series" of faithful reproductions, Les Paul Custom copy.

1974-1976		$500	$700

Model 2345/2345S/2345W
1974-1976. SG copy, Walnut finish, with Bigsby copy or stop tailpiece (2345S), version with three pickups.

1974-1976		$400	$600

Model 2346
1974-1976. Part of "Oldies Series," SG Standard copy with Maestro vibrato copy.

1974-1976		$400	$600

Model 2348
1974-1979. Mahogany body, bolt-on neck, two pickups, like Firebrand Firebird.

1974-1979		$550	$700

Model 2350
1971-1977. Les Paul Custom copy, bolt-on neck, Black, gold hardware, a Cherry Sunburst finish (2350 Custom) was offered by '74.

1971-1977		$500	$600

Ibanez JEM 777

1970 Ibanez Model 2020

Ibanez Model 2375

Ibanez PF 1055

MODEL YEAR	FEATURES	EXC. COND. LOW	HIGH

Model 2355/2355M
1973-1977. ES-175 copy in Sunburst or M model in Natural maple.

| 1973-1977 | | $1,150 | $1,300 |

Model 2359 Destroyer
1975-1977. Explorer copy, Korina body.

| 1975-1977 | | $700 | $1,000 |

Model 2369 (Futura/Moderne)
1975-1977. Korina Moderne.

| 1975-1977 | | $900 | $1,200 |

Model 2370
1972. ES-345 Sunburst, the Cherry finish is the Model 2363R introduced in 1973.

| 1972 | | $750 | $950 |

Model 2374 Crest
1974. ES-355-style, Walnut finish.

| 1974 | | $700 | $900 |

Model 2375 Silver Series/Strato
1971-1978. Replaced earlier copy of Fender Strat, three traditional pickups.

| 1971-1978 | Sunburst | $350 | $550 |

Model 2377
1974. SG Pro copy, short production run, dot markers, Bigsby copy.

| 1974 | | $350 | $400 |

Model 2383
1974-1975. SG Custom copy, White or Walnut finish, three humbucker-style pickups, gold hardware, Bigsby copy.

| 1974-1975 | Walnut | $400 | $800 |
| 1974-1975 | White | $450 | $850 |

Model 2384
1974-1975. Fender Telecaster Thinline copy variant with dual humbuckers, ash body.

| 1974-1975 | | $400 | $500 |

Model 2387 (Rocket Roll/Rocket Roll Sr.)
1975-1977. Nearer-copy of Flying V, set-neck, dot markers, gold-covered pickups.

| 1975-1977 | | $900 | $1,100 |

Model 2390
1974-1975. ES-345 copy, Walnut finish.

| 1974-1975 | | $700 | $900 |

Model 2395
1974-1975. ES-345 copy variant with maple fingerboard and Natural finish.

| 1974-1975 | | $700 | $900 |

Model 2397
1974-1975. Variant with ES-335-style body, low impedance electronics, trapezoid markers, Goldtop.

| 1974-1975 | | $700 | $900 |

Model 2401
1974-1975. Goldtop hollowbody Les Paul Signature copy with bolt-on neck.

| 1974-1975 | | $700 | $900 |

Model 2402/2402DX
1974-1975. SG-style 6/12 doubleneck, DX model has gold hardware.

| 1974-1975 | | $600 | $900 |

Model 2404
1974-1975. SG guitar and bass doubleneck copy. Walnut in '74, white finish available in '75.

| 1974-1975 | | $600 | $1,100 |

Model 2406
1975-1976. SG doubleneck copy with two six-string necks. Cherry finish.

| 1974-1975 | | $600 | $1,100 |

Model 2407
1975-1978. Fender Stratocaster doubleneck copy.

| 1975-1978 | | $700 | $800 |

Model 2451
1975-1976. L-6 S copy with maple fingerboard, in Black or Natural finish.

| 1974-1975 | | $350 | $500 |

Model 2453
1975-1979. Copy of the Howard Roberts Custom, round soundhole, arched curly maple top, maple back and sides, maple laminate set-neck, rosewood 'board, pearl block markers, one pickup, fancy tailpiece, gold hardware. Burgundy or Sunburst.

| 1975-1979 | | $800 | $1,100 |

Model 2454
1974-1975. ES-335 TD copy, set-neck, small block markers, Byrdland-style tailpiece. Cherry finish over ash.

| 1974-1975 | | $500 | $1,000 |

Model 2455
1974-1975. L-5 CES copy.

| 1974-1975 | | $1,100 | $1,800 |

Model 2460
1971-1977. L-5 copy.

| 1971-1977 | | $800 | $1,200 |

Model 2461
1976-1979. Johnny Smith copy, laminated spruce top, curly maple back and sides, set-in neck, ebony 'board, pearl blocks, two pickups, gold hardware, Sunburst or Natural.

| 1976-1979 | | $1,700 | $1,900 |

Model 2630
1976-1979. ES-335 copy, Sunburst. Reintroduced as AS200 in 1980.

| 1976-1979 | | $500 | $1,000 |

Musician MC-400
1978-1980. Ash top with maple and mahogany back, seven-piece laminated maple/walnut neck-through-body, ebony fretboard, Gold plating.

| 1978-1980 | | $500 | $700 |

Performer PG-400AV
1978-1979. Maple top and mahogany back, set-in (high end) or bolt-on (low end) bound neck, rosewood or ebony fingerboard, Super 70 pickup.

| 1978-1979 | Set-neck | $300 | $400 |

PF-12
1990s. D-style flat-top with stylized rosette, Natural finish, rosewood board with dot markers, glued bridge.

| 1990s | | $325 | $375 |

MODEL YEAR	FEATURES	EXC. COND. LOW	HIGH

PF-100
1978-1979. Les Paul copy, mahogany back/maple top, bolt-on bound maple neck, two humbucker pickups, Black.

1978-1979		$300	$500

PF-200
1978-1979. Mahogany back and maple top, 22-fret bound maple bolt-on neck, Super 70 pickup, Sunburst.

1978-1979		$300	$450

PF-300
1978-1980. Les Paul copy, mahogany back and maple top, maple bolt-on or set-in bound neck, Super 70 pickup.

1978-1980	Bolt-on neck	$350	$550
1978-1980	Set-neck	$450	$650

PL-1770
Part of Pro Line series.

1980s	Red/Orange Metallic	$400	$500

PL-2550
Part of the Pro Line series. Pushbuttons allow user to present two separate sounds, two single-coil and one humbucker pickups.

1980s		$250	$350

PM-20 Pat Metheny
1997-1999. Double cut semi-hollow body, f-holes, 1 pickup, rosewood board.

1997-1999		$900	$1,000

PR-1660PW
Mid-1980s. Randy Rhodes-style body, dual humbucking pickups, White.

1985		$250	$275

RG220B
1994-1999. Offset double cut solidbody, 2 humbuckers.

1994-1999		$350	$400

RG270
1994-2001. Offset double cut solidbody, pointy headstock, 2 humbuckers, dot markers, various colors.

1994-2001		$250	$300

RG470
1993-2002. Double long thin pointy horn cutaway solidbody, 3 pickups, dot markers.

1993-2000		$300	$350

RG520/RG520 QS
1997-2002. Offset double cut basswood (QS is mahogany) solidbody, 2 humbucers, dot markers.

1997-2002		$450	$550

RG550/RG550 DX
1988-2001. Pointy headstock, long thin pointy horn double cutaway solidbody, hum-single-hum. Black (RG550) or Purple (RG550DX-'91-'94 only).

1988-1994	Blue or Purple DX	$500	$550

RG570
1989-2002. Double long pointy cut, 3 pickups, black hardware.

1989-2002		$325	$375

RG1200
1992. Offset double cut solidbody, 3 pickups, flame maple top.

1992		$450	$500

RGT42
2001-present. Double long thin pointy horn cutaway solidbody, 2 humbuckers, dot markers, locking tremolo.

2001		$400	$450

Roadstar/Roadstar II
1983-1989. Offset double cut, split into several different model series in late-'80s to early-'90s.

1983-1989		$275	$325

Roadster
1979-1983. Offset double cut, maple fretboard, bolt-on neck, satin finish body. Replaced by Roadstar series in '83.

1979-1983		$275	$325

Rocket Roll II RR440
1982-1986. Flying V body but with six-on-a-side headstock, pearloid block markers.

1982-1986	Sunburst	$275	$325

RT650
1993. RT Series, offset double cutaway with long slim horns, bolt-on maple neck with rosewood fretboard, dot markers, flamed top.

1993		$400	$500

RX20/GRX20
1994-present. Offset double cut maple or agatis solidbody, 2 humbuckers, trem, became the alderbodied GRX in '99.

1994-1999		$175	$225

SS40 LTD
1990s.

1990s		$600	$800

Studio ST300
1978-1980. Maple/ash body, active tone system, tri-sound switch, natural, gold hardware, 2 pickups.

1978-1980		$400	$600

Studio ST50
1979-1980. Set-neck, small offset SG-style mahogany solidbody, 2 pickups.

1979-1980		$400	$500

Talman TC420
1994-1999. Offset double cut solidbody, bolt-on neck, three-on-a-side tuners, two humbuckers, dot markers.

1994-1999	Black or Green	$350	$425

Talman TC620
1994-1997. Two stacked P-90 looking humbucker version of the Talman series solidbodies. The BP version was black with pearloid guard.

1994-1997		$275	$375

Talman TC630
1994-1998. Offset double cut solidbody, three-on-a-side tuners, three lipstick pickups, dot markers.

1994-1998	Black or Ivory	$400	$475

Universe 7-String UV7/UV77
1990-1998. Several UV seven-string guitar models with different appointments, long slim pointed horns.

1990-1998	UV7 and UV77, various colors	$1,000	$1,200
1990-1998	UV7 P, White	$900	$1,000

1984 Ibanez Roadstar

Ibanez PM-120 Pat Metheny

Imperial Tonmaster Elite

MODEL YEAR	FEATURES	EXC. COND. LOW	HIGH
Universe Steve Vai	*1997.*		
1997		$1,250	$1,350
Universe UV-777LNG	*1990s. Universe model in Lockness Green (LNG), offset double cut solidbody with long slim horns.*		
1991		$1,800	$2,000
USGR-1 Custom Shop (U.S.A.)	*1992 only. Snakeskin finish.*		
1992		$700	$800
V-300BS	*1978-1980s. Part of the Vintage Series. Acoustic dreadnought, spruce top, mahogany back and sides. Sunburst finish.*		
1978		$200	$300
Y2K Joe Satriani	*2000. Clear see-through plexi-style body.*		
2000		$1,800	$2,200

Imperial

Ca.1963-ca.1970. Imported by the Imperial Accordion Company of Chicago, Illinois. Early guitars made in Italy. By ca. 1966 switched to Japanese guitars.

Electric Solidbody Guitars

1963-1968. Italian-made until 1966, then Japanese-made, includes the Tonmaster line.			
1963-1968		$100	$250

J Burda Guitars

Flat-top guitars built by luthier Jan Burda in Berrien Springs, Michigan.

Jan Burda Flat-Top

1990s. Solid spruce top, figured walnut back and sides, flamed maple peghead, no logo, U.S.-made.			
1990s	Natural	$800	$900

J.B. Player

1980s-present. Budget and intermediate grade, production, imported acoustic, acoustic/electric, and solidbody guitars. They also offer basses, banjos and mandolins. Founded in United States. Moved production of guitars to Korea but maintained a U.S. Custom Shop. MBT International/Musicorp took over manufacture and distribution in '89.

JBA-2000

1994-1997. Solid-top acoustic, herringbone binding, abalone inlays, Gold hardware.			
1994-1997		$125	$250

PG-121

1992-1996. Offset double cut solidbody, 3 pickups, various colors.			
1992-1996	Various colors	$125	$250

J.R. Zeidler Guitars

1977-present. Luthier John Zeidler builds his premium and presentation grade, custom, flat-top, 12-string, and archtop guitars in Wallingford, Pennsylvania. He also builds mandolins.

J.R. Zeidler Auditorium

Auditorium Cutaway

Introduced in 1982. Sitka or Adirondack spruce top, Indian rosewood sides, gold hardware.			
1990s		$4,800	$5,200

Concert

1990s. Spruce top, Indian rosewood back and sides. The name does not denote the size, which approximates 00 Grand Concert.			
1992		$6,000	$6,400

J.T. Hargreaves Basses And Guitars

1995-present. Luthier Jay Hargreaves builds his premium grade, production/custom, classical and steel string guitars in Seattle, Washington. He also builds basses.

Jack Daniel's

2004-present. Acoustic and electric guitar models with custom Jack Daniel's artwork on the body and headstock, built by Peavey for the Jack Daniel Distillery. There is also an amp model.

Jackson

1980-present. Currently Jackson offers intermediate, professional, and premium grade, production, electric guitars. They also offer basses. Founded as Charvel by Wayne Charvel in Azusa, California in '76. In '78 Grover Jackson bought out Charvel and moved it to San Dimas. Jackson made custom-built bolt-on Charvels. In '82 the pointy, tilt-back Jackson headstock became standard. The Jackson logo was born in '80 and used on a guitar designed as Randy Rhoad's first flying 'V'. Jacksons were neck-through construction. The Charvel trademark was licensed to IMC in '85. IMC moved the Jackson factory to Ontario, CA in '86. Grover Jackson stayed with Jackson/Charvel until '89 (see Charvel in the Guitar section). On October 25, 2002, Fender Musical Instruments Corp (FMIC) took ownership of Jackson/Charvel Manufacturing Inc.

DR3

1996-2001. Dinky Reverse. Double cut solidbody, reverse headstock, triangle markers, dual humbuckers, locking vibrato, various colors, made in Japan. Flamed maple top available.			
1996-1999		$325	$400

DR5

1996 only. Offset double cut solidbody, 2 Kent Armstrong humbuckers, rosewood board, dot markers.			
1996		$325	$400

JSX94

1994-1995. Offset double cut solidbody, single/single/hum, rosewood board, dot markers.			
1994-1995		$250	$350

Kelly Custom

1984-early 1990s. Neck-through solidbody, Kahler tremolo, 2 humbuckers, ebony fingerboard with shark's tooth inlays, bound neck and headstock.			
1984-1993		$500	$775

MODEL YEAR	FEATURES	EXC. COND. LOW	HIGH

Kelly Pro
1994-1995. Pointy-cut solidbody, neck-thru, 2 humbuckers, bound ebony 'board, sharkfin inlays.

1994-1995		$500	$775

Kelly Standard
1993-1995. Pointy-cut solidbody, bolt neck, 2 humbuckers, dot markers.

1993-1995		$450	$725

Kelly XL
1994-1995. Pointy-cut solidbody, bolt neck, 2 humbuckers, bound rosewood 'board, sharkfin inlays.

1994-1995		$500	$775

King V Pro
1993-1995. Soft V-style neck-thru solidbody, sharkfin markers, 2 humbuckers.

1993-1995		$475	$675

King V STD
1993-1995. Bolt neck version of King V.

1993-1995		$250	$350

Phil Collen
1989-1991, 1993-1995. Offset double-cut maple neck-thru solidbody, six-on-a-side tuners, one volume, bound ebony 'board, U.S.-made. Early version has poplar body, 1 humbucker; later version with basswood body, 1 single-coil and 1 humbucker.

1993-1995		$900	$1,100

Phil Collen PC1 (U.S.-made)
1996-present. Quilt maple top, bolt-on maple neck, maple board, koa body '96-'00, mahogany body '01-present, 1 humbucker and 1 single coil '96-'97, humbucker, stacked humbucker, and single coil '98-present.

1996-2000		$1,000	$1,200

Phil Collen PC3 (Import)
1996-2001. Downscale version of Collen model, poplar body, bolt neck, humbucker\single\single.

1996-2000		$450	$500

PS2
1994-2000. Offset double cut solidbody, single/single/hum, rosewood fingerboard, dot markers.

1994-2000		$150	$175

PS3
1994-2000. Rhoads wedge-style body, two humbuckers, rosewood fingerboard, dot markers.

1994-2000		$150	$175

Randy Rhoads (Import/bolt-on neck)

1990s		$300	$350

Randy Rhoads (U.S.-made)
1983-present. V-shaped neck-thru solidbody, two humbuckers. Originally made at San Dimas plant, serial numbers RR 0001 to RR 1929. Production moved to the Ontario plant by 1987, serial numbers RR 1930 to present in sequential order.

1983-1986	Kahler trem	$1,400	$1,600
1983-1986	Rose trem or string-through	$1,900	$2,100
1987-1989	Early Ontario production	$900	$1,200
1990-1999	Ontario production	$800	$1,000

Randy Rhoads Limited Edition
1992 only. Sharkfin-style maple neck-through body, gold hardware, White with Black pinstriping, block inlays, six-on-a-side tuners, U.S.-made. Only 200 built.

1992		$1,200	$1,500

RR1T (Custom Shop)
2002 only. 50 made, Randy Rhoads body.

2002		$1,400	$1,600

Soloist
1986-1990. Double-cut, neck-thru, string-thru solidbody, two humbuckers, bound rosewood 'board, U.S.-made. Replaced by the Soloist USA in '90.

1986	San Dimas build	$1,000	$1,500
1987-1990		$900	$1,050

Soloist Custom
1993-1995. Double cut, neck-thru solidbody, one humbucker and two single-coils, bound ebony 'board, shark's tooth inlays, U.S.-made.

1993-1995		$850	$950

Soloist Student J1 (U.S.-made)
1986-1999. Double cut neck-thru solidbody, Seymour Duncan single-single-hum pickups, rosewood 'board, dot inlays, no binding.

1986-1999	Ontario-built	$700	$850

Soloist USA
1990-1995. Replaces Soloist, sharkfin markers, single-single-hum.

1990-1995		$900	$1,050

Warrior USA
1990-1992. Four point neck-thru solidbody, 1 humbucker and 1single-coil, triangle markers, active electronics, U.S.-made. The Warrior Pro was Japanese version.

1990-1992	Red	$1,000	$1,500

Warrior Pro (Import)
1990-1992. Japanese version.

1990-1992		$225	$300

Jacobacci

1930s-1994. Founded in France by Italian Vincent Jacobacci and originally building basso-guitars, banjos, and mandolins. Sons Roger and Andre joined the company and encouraged pop to add lapsteels and electric and regular acoustic guitars around 1952. The guitars are sometimes labeled as "Jaco" and, from ca. '54 to ca. '66, as "Jaco Major." In '58 the company introduced aluminum neck models, and in '59 their first solidbodies. In the '60s they also made instruments branded Royal, Texas, Ohio, Star and made instruments for Major Conn and other companies. By the mid '60s, they were producing mainly jazz style guitars.

James R. Baker Guitars

1996-present. Luthier James R. Baker builds his premium grade, custom, archtops in Shoreham, New York.

Jackson Phil Collen

1970s Jacobacci doubleneck

Jay Turser J-200 Serpent

Jerry Jones Electric Sitar

MODEL YEAR	FEATURES	EXC. COND. LOW	HIGH

James Tyler

Early 1980s-present. Luthier James Tyler builds his professional and premium grade, custom/production, solidbody guitars in Van Nuys, California, and also has a model built in Japan. He also builds basses.

Janofsky Guitars

1978-present. Production classical and flamenco guitars built by luthier Stephen Janofsky in Amherst, Massachusetts.

Jaros

1995-present. Professional and premium grade, production/custom, solidbody and acoustic/electric guitars built by father and son luthiers Harry and Jim Jaros in Rochester, Pennsylvania.

Jay Turser

1997-present. Budget and intermediate grade, production, imported acoustic, acoustic/electric, electric and resonator guitars. They also offer basses and amps. Designed and developed by Tommy Rizzi for Music Industries Corp.

JT-134

2001-present. Single cut semi-solidbody, 2 humbuckers.

2001		$175	$250

JT-134DC

2001-present. Double cut semi-solidbody, 2 humbuckers.

2001		$225	$300

JT-200 Serpent

2001-present. Single cut solidbody, bookmatched flamed maple top, multi-piece abalone and mother-of-pearl serpent inlay on fretboard.

2001		$300	$350

JT-270F

2001-present.

2001-2004		$200	$250

Jeff Traugott Guitars

1991-present. Premium and presentation grade, custom, flat-top, nylon-string, and acoustic/electric guitars built by luthier Jeff Traugott, in Santa Cruz, California.

Jeremy Locke Guitars

1985-present. Premium grade, production/custom, classical and flamenco guitars built by luthier Jeremy Locke in Coomera, South East Queensland, Australia.

Jeronimo Pena Fernandez

1967-present. Luthier Jeronimo Pena Fernandez started building classical guitars in Marmolejo, Spain, in the 1950s. In '67, he went full-time and soon became well-known for his fine work. He is now retired, but still builds a few guitars a year.

MODEL YEAR	FEATURES	EXC. COND. LOW	HIGH

Classical

Brazilian rosewood back and sides, cedar top, full-size classical guitar, higher-end luthier.

1960-1990s		$5,000	$8,000

Jerry Jones

1981-present. Intermediate grade, production, semi-hollow body electric guitars and sitars from luthier Jerry Jones, built in Nashville, Tennessee. They also build basses.

Electric Sitar

1990-present. Buzz-bar sitar bridge, individual pickup for sympathetic strings. Custom color gator finish.

1991-2000		$450	$500

Longhorn Guitarlin

1989-present. Large cutaway Guitarlin-style body.

1994-2000	Sunburst	$450	$500

Neptune Electric 12-String

1993-present. Single cut, 3 pickups.

1994-2000		$800	$900

Jersey Girl

1991-present. Premium grade, production/custom, solidbody guitars made in Japan. They also build effects.

Jim Redgate Guitars

1992-present. Luthier Jim Redgate builds his premium grade, custom, nylon-string classical guitars in Belair, Adelaide, South Australia.

John Le Voi Guitars

1970-present. Production/custom, gypsy jazz, flat-top, and archtop guitars built by luthier John Le Voi in Lincolnshire, United Kingdom. He also builds mandolin family instruments.

John Price Guitars

1984-present. Custom classical and flamenco guitars built by luthier John Price in Australia.

Johnson

Mid-1990s-present. Budget, intermediate and professional grade, production, acoustic, classical, acoustic/electric, resonator and solidbody guitars imported by Music Link, Brisbane, California. Johnson also offers basses, amps, mandolins, ukuleles and effects.

Jon Kammerer

1995-present. Luthier Jon Kammerer builds his professional grade, custom, acoustic and electric guitars in Keokuk, Iowa. He also builds the Sinister Custom Shop Bass for Sinister Guitars.

Jones

See TV Jones listing.

MODEL		EXC. COND.	
YEAR	FEATURES	LOW	HIGH

Jordan

1981-present. Professional and premium grade, custom, flat-top and archtop guitars built by luthier John Jordan in Concord, California. He also builds electric violins and cellos.

K & S

1992-1998. Hawaiian-style and classical guitars distributed by George Katechis and Marc Silber and handmade in Paracho, Mexico. A few 16" wide "Leadbelly" Model 12-strings were made in Oakland, California by luthier Stewart Port. K & S also offered mandolins, mandolas and ukes. In '98, Silber started marketing guitars under the Marc Silber Guitar Company brand and Katechis continued to offer instruments under the Casa Montalvo brand.

Kakos, Stephen

1975-present. Luthier Stephen Kakos builds his premium grade, production/custom, classical guitars in Mound, Minnesota.

Kalamazoo

1933-1942, 1965-1970. Budget brand built by Gibson. Made flat-tops, solidbodies, mandolins, lap steels, banjos and amps. Amps and solidbodies were built '65-'67.

KG-1/KG-1 A
1965-1969. Offset double cut (initial issue) or SG-shape (second issue), one pickup, Model 1 A with spring vibrato, Red, Blue or White.

1965-1969		$100	$200

KG-2/KG-2 A
1965-1970. Offset double cut (initial shape) or SG-shape, two pickups, Model 2 A with spring vibrato. Red, Blue or White.

1965-1970		$275	$325

KG-11
1933-1941. Flat-top, all mahogany, 14" with no pickguard. Sunburst.

1933-1941		$350	$550

KG-14
1936-1940. Flat-top L-0-size, mahogany back and sides, with pickguard. Sunburst.

1936-1940		$600	$750

KG-21
1936-1941. Fifteen inch archtop (bent, not curved), dot markers, bound top. Sunburst.

1936-1941		$450	$650

KG-31
1935-1940. Archtop L-50-size, 16" body, non-carved spruce top, mahogany back and sides.

1935-1940		$550	$700

KTG-14 Senior
1936-1940. Flat-top L-0-size tenor, mahogany back and sides, bound top. Sunburst.

1936-1940		$200	$350

Kamico

Brand started in 1947. Flat-top acoustic guitars. Low-end budget brand made by Kay Musical Instrument Company and sold through various distributors.

Acoustic Flat-Tops
1940s. Made by Kay.

1940s		$150	$250

Kapa

Ca. 1962-1970. Begun by Dutch immigrant and music store owner Kope Veneman in Hyattsville, Maryland whose father had made Amka guitars in Holland. Kapa is from K for Kope, A for son Albert, P for daughter Patricia, and A for wife Adeline. Crown shield logo from Amka guitars. The brand included some Hofner and Italian imports in '60. Ca. '66 Kapa started offering thinner bodies. Some German Pix pickups ca. '66. Thinlines and Japanese bodies in '69. Kapa closed shop in '70 and the parts and equipment were sold to Micro-Frets and Mosrite. Later Veneman was involved with Bradley copy guitars imported from Japan. Approximately 120,000 Kapas were made.

Challenger
1962-1970. Had a three way toggle from 1962-1966/67 and two on/off switches from 1966/67-1970.

1962-1970		$250	$400

Cobra
1962-1970. One pickup.

1962-1970		$250	$400

Continental
1966-1970. Offset double cutaway.

1966-1970		$250	$400

Continental 12-String
1966-1970.

1966-1970		$250	$400

Minstrel
1968-1970. Teardrop-shaped, three pickups.

1968-1970		$250	$400

Minstrel 12-String
1968-1970. Teardrop-shaped, 12 strings.

1968-1970		$250	$400

Wildcat
1962-1970. Mini offset double cut, three pickups, mute.

1962-1970		$250	$400

Kathy Wingert Guitars

1996-present. Luthier Kathy Wingert builds her premium grade, production/custom, flat-tops in Rancho Palos Verdes, California.

Kawai

1927-present. Kawai is a Japanese piano and guitar maker. They started offering guitars around '56 and they were imported into the U.S. carrying many different brand names, including Kimberly and Teisco. In '67 Kawai purchased Teisco. Odd-shaped guitars were offered from late-'60s through the mid-'70s. Few imports carrying the Kawai brand until

Kalamazoo KG--14

Kathy Wingert OO Cutaway

Kawai KS-700

1957 Kay Barney Kessel

MODEL YEAR	FEATURES	EXC. COND. LOW	HIGH

the late-'70s; best known for high quality basses. By '90s they were making plexiglass replicas of Teisco Spectrum 5 and Kawai moon-shaped guitar. Kawai recently quit offering guitars and basses.

Acoustic Hollowbody Archtops
1956-1990s.

1960s		$200	$250

Electric Archtop Guitars
1956-1990s.

1960s		$250	$300
1970s		$250	$300

Kay

Ca. 1931 (1890)-present. Originally founded in Chicago, Illinois as Groehsl Company (or Groehsel) in 1890, making bowl-backed mandolins. Offered Groehsl, Stromberg, Kay Kraft, Kay, Arch Kraft brand names, plus made guitars for S.S.Maxwell, Old Kraftsman (Spiegel), Recording King (Wards), Supertone (Sears), Silvertone (Sears), National, Dobro, Custom Kraft (St.Louis Music), Hollywood (Shireson Bros.), Oahu and others. In 1921 the name was changed to Stromberg-Voisinet Company. Henry Kay "Hank" Kuhrmeyer joined the company in '23 and was secretary by '25. By the mid-'20s the company was making many better Montgomery Ward guitars, banjos and mandolins, often with lots of pearloid. First production electric guitars and amps are introduced with big fanfare in '28; perhaps only 200 or so made. Last "Stromberg" instruments seen in '32.

Kuhrmeyer becomes president and the Kay Kraft brand was introduced in '31, probably named for Kuhrmeyer's middle name, though S-V had used Kay brand on German Kreuzinger violins '28-'36. By '34, if not earlier, the company is changed to the Kay Musical Instrument Company. A new factory was built at 1640 West Walnut Street in '35. The Kay Kraft brand ends in '37 and the Kay brand is introduced in late-'36 or '37. Violin Style Guitars and upright acoustic basses debut in '38. In '40 the first guitars for Sears, carrying the new Silvertone brandname, are offered.

Kamico budget line introduced in '47 and Rex flat-tops and archtops sold through Gretsch in late-'40s. Kuhrmeyer retires in '55 dies a year later. Sidney M. Katz becomes president, Bob Keyworth vice-president in '55. New gigantic factory in Elk Grove Village, Illinois opens in '64. Seeburg purchased Kay in '66 and sold it to Valco in '67. Valco/Kay went out of business in '68 and its assets were auctioned in '69. The Kay name went to Sol Weindling and Barry Hornstein of W.M.I. (Teisco Del Rey) who began putting Kay name on Teisco guitars. By '73 most Teisco guitars are called Kay. Tony Blair, president of Asian-American Mfg. Co., purchased the Kay nameplate in '80, with a market focus on first-time buyers. Currently distributed in the U.S. by A.R. Musical Enterprises. See *Guitar Stories, Volume II* by Michael Wright, for a complete history of Kay with detailed model listings.

Artist K48 (archtop)
1947-1951. Non-cutaway archtop, 17" solid spruce top with figured maple back and sides, split block inlays, sunburst or black.

1947-1951		$900	$1,300

Barney Kessel Artist
1957-1960. Single cut, 15 1/2" body, one (K6701) or two (K6700) pickups, Kelvinator headstock, sunburst or blond.

1957-1960		$1,000	$1,700

Barney Kessel Pro
1957-1960. 13" hollowbody, single cut, Kelvinator headstock, ebony fingerboard with pearl inlays, White binding, one or two pickups, Sunburst.

1957-1960		$1,000	$2,000

K20 (archtop)
1939-1942. 16" archtop, solid spruce top, maple back and sides, sunburst.

1939-1942		$250	$300

K22 (flat-top)
1950s. Similar to Gibson J-100 17", spruce top, mahogany back and sides.

1955-1959		$400	$600

K26 (flat-top)
1955-1959. J-200 copy, block markers, Natural.

1955-1959		$500	$700

K44 (archtop)
1947-1951. Non-cut archtop, solid spruce top, 17" curly maple veneered body, block markers, sunburst.

1947-1951		$400	$500

K45 (archtop)
1952-1954. Non-cut archtop, 17" body, engraved tortoiseshell-celluloid headstock, large block markers, natural.

1952-1954		$450	$550

K46 (archtop)
1947-1951. Non-cut archtop, solid spruce top, 17" curly maple-veneered body, double-eighth note headstock inlay, sunburst.

1947-1951		$500	$600

K48/K21 Jazz Special (solidbody)
Late-1960s. Slim solidbody with three reflective pickups, garden spade headstock, fancy position Circle K headstock logo.

1968	White	$400	$500

K100 Vanguard (slab solidbody)
1961-1966. Offset double cut slab body, genuine maple veneered top and back over hardwood body, sunburst.

1961-1966		$125	$175

K102 Vanguard (slab solidbody)
1961-1966. Double pickup version of the K100, sunburst.

1961-1966		$150	$200

K300 Double Cutaway Solid Electric
1962-1966. 2 single-coils, block inlays, some with curly maple top and some with plain maple top, natural.

1962-1966		$525	$575

MODEL		EXC. COND.	
YEAR	FEATURES	LOW	HIGH

K535 (thinline double cutaway)
1961-1965. Double cut, 2 pickups, vibrato, sunburst.

| 1961-1965 | Sunburst | $350 | $400 |

K592 (thinline electric)
1962-1966. Thinline semi-acoustic/electric, double Florentine cut, 2 or 3 pickups, Bigsby vibrato, pie-slice inlays.

| 1962-1966 | Cherry | $450 | $500 |

K1961 (solidbody thinline)
1960-1965. Part of the Value Leader line, thinline single cut, hollowbody, identified by the single chrome-plated checkered body length guardplate on the treble side of the strings, laminated maple body, hard rock maple neck, dot markers, 1 neck pickup.

| 1960-1965 | Sunburst | $300 | $450 |

K1962 (solidbody thinline)
1960-1965. Dual pickup version of K1961.

| 1960-1965 | Sunburst | $425 | $475 |

K1963 (solidbody thinline)
1960-1965. Triple pickup version of K1961.

| 1960-1965 | Sunburst | $425 | $600 |

K1982 Style Leader/Jimmy Reed
1960-1965. Part of the Style Leader mid-level Kay line. Sometimes dubbed Jimmy Reed of 1960s. Easily identified by the long brushed copper dual guardplates on either side of the strings. Brown or gleaming Golden Blond (Natural) finish, laminated curly maple body, 2 pickups, simple script Kay logo.

| 1960-1965 | | $425 | $500 |

K1983 Style Leader/Jimmy Reed
1960-1965. 3 pickup version of the K1982, brown or natural.

| 1960-1965 | | $425 | $600 |

K3500 Student Concert (flat-top)
1966-1968. 14 1/2", solid spruce top, laminated maple back and sides.

| 1966-1968 | | $75 | $100 |

K5113 Plains Special (flat-top)
1968. Solid spruce top, laminated mahogany back and sides.

| 1968 | | $150 | $200 |

K5160 Auditorium (flat-top)
1957-1965. 15"inch auditorium-size, laminated construction.

| 1957-1965 | | $100 | $125 |

K6100 Country (flat-top)
1950s-1960s. Jumbo flat-top, spruce x-braced top, mahogany back and sides.

| 1957-1962 | Natural | $300 | $400 |

K6116 Super Auditorium (flat-top)
1957-1965. Super Auditorium-size, laminated figured maple back and sides, solid spruce top..

| 1957-1965 | Sunburst | $125 | $175 |

K6130 Calypso (flat-top)
1960-1965. 15 1/2"flat-top with narrow waist, slotted headstock.

| 1960-1965 | Natural | $200 | $300 |

K6533 Value Leader (single arched)
1961-1965. Value Leader was the budget line of Kay, full body, 1 pickup, archtop, sunburst.

| 1961-1965 | | $200 | $300 |

K6535 Value Leader (double arched)
1961-1965. Value Leader was the budget line of Kay, full body, 2 pickups, archtop, sunburst.

| 1961-1965 | | $200 | $300 |

K7000 Artist (classical)
1960-1965. Highest-end of Kay classical series, fan bracing, spruce top, maple back and sides.

| 1960-1965 | | $350 | $450 |

K7010 Concerto (classical)
1960-1965. Entry level of Kay classical series.

| 1960-1965 | | $125 | $175 |

K7010 Maestro (classical)
1960-1965. Middle level of Kay classical series.

| 1960-1965 | | $200 | $300 |

K8127 Solo Special (flat-top)
1957-1965. Kay's professional grade flat-top, narrow waist jumbo, block markers.

| 1957-1965 | | $450 | $550 |

K8110 Master (flat-top)
1957-1960. 17"inch master-size which was largest of the series, laminated construction.

| 1957-1960 | | $125 | $175 |

Speed Demon K571
1961-1965. Thinline semi-acoustic/electric, single pointed cutaway, 1 pickup, some with Bigsby vibrato. There was also a Speed Demon solidbody.

| 1961-1965 | | $350 | $500 |

Speed Demon K572
1961-1965. 2 pickup version of the Speed Demon thinline.

| 1961-1965 | | $400 | $600 |

Speed Demon K573
1961-1965. 3 pickup version of the Speed Demon.

| 1961-1965 | | $450 | $700 |

Swingmaster K671/K672
1961-1965. Single rounded cutaway semi-hollowbody, 1 (K671) or 2 (K672) pickups.

| 1961-1965 | K671, 1 pickup | $600 | $800 |
| 1961-1965 | K672, 2 pickups | $700 | $900 |

Thin Twin K161 "Jimmy Reed"
1952-1958. Cutaway semi-hollow, 2 pickups, bird's-eye maple, often called the Jimmy Reed, sunburst.

| 1952-1958 | | $500 | $700 |

Upbeat K8995
1958-1960. Less expensive alternative to Barney Kessel Jazz Special, 2 pickups, sunburst.

| 1958-1960 | | $700 | $1,200 |

Kay Kraft

Ca. 1931-1937. First brand name of the Kay Musical Instrument Company as it began its transition from Stromberg-Voisinet Company to Kay (see Kay for more info).

Kay Kraft Recording King

| 1931-1937 | | $300 | $500 |

1950s Kay Upbeat

Kay Kraft acoustic

Knutson Songbird

1995 Kendrick Townhouse

MODEL		EXC. COND.	
YEAR	FEATURES	LOW	HIGH

Keller Custom Guitars

1994-present. Professional grade, production/custom, solidbody guitars built by luthier Randall Keller in Mandan, North Dakota.

Keller Guitars

1975-present. Premium grade, production/custom, flat-tops made by luthier Michael L. Keller in Rochester, Minnesota.

Kendrick

1989-present. Premium grade, production/custom, solidbody guitars built in Texas. Founded by Gerald Weber in Pflugerville, Texas and currently located in Kempner, Texas. Mainly known for their handmade tube amps, Kendrick also offers speakers and effects.

Kent

1961-1969. Imported from Japan by Buegeleisen and Jacobson of New York, New York. Manufacturers unknown but many early guitars were made by Guyatone and Teisco.

Acoustic Flat-Tops
1961-1969.

1961-1969		$100	$150

Acoustic/Electric Guitars
1961-1969.

1961-1969		$150	$250

Electric 12-String
1960s. Thinline 335-type electric with double pointy cutaways, 12 strings, slanted dual pickup

1965-1969	Sunburst	$250	$450

Semi-Hollow Electric
1960s. Thinline 335-type electric with offset double pointy cutaways, slanted dual pickups, various colors.

1962-1969		$250	$450

Solidbody Electrics
1962-1969. Models include Polaris I, II and III, Lido, Copa and Videocaster.

1962-1969	Century Red	$100	$200

Kevin Ryan Guitars

1989-present. Premium grade, custom, flat-tops built by luthier Kevin Ryan in Westminster, California.

Kiesel

See Carvin.

Kimberly

Late-1960s-early-1970s. Private branded import made in the same Japanese factory as Teisco.

May Queen
1960s. Same as Teisco May Queen with Kimberly script logo on headstock and May Queen Teisco on the pickguard.

1960s		$400	$600

MODEL		EXC. COND.	
YEAR	FEATURES	LOW	HIGH

Kingston

Ca. 1958-1967. Imported from Japan by Jack Westheimer and Westheimer Importing Corporation of Chicago. Early examples made by Guyatone and Teisco.

Electric Hollowbodies
1958-1967. Imported from Japan.

1958-1967		$100	$175

Kinscherff Guitars

1990-present. Luthier Jamie Kinscherff builds his premium grade, production/custom, flat-top guitars in Austin, Texas.

Klein Acoustic Guitars

1972-present. Luthiers Steve Klein and Steven Kauffman build their production/custom, premium and presentation grade flat-tops in Sonoma, California. They also build basses

Klein Electric Guitars

1988-present. Steve Klein added electrics to his line in 1988. In 1995, he sold the electric part of his business to Lorenzo German, who continues to produce professional grade, production/custom, solidbody guitars in Linden, California. He also builds basses.

Solidbody Electric (import)

1960s		$200	$400

Knutsen

1890s-1920s. Luthier Chris J. Knutsen of Tacoma and Seattle, Washington, experimented with and perfected Hawaiian and harp guitar models.

Convertible
1909-1914. Flat-top model with adjustable neck angle that allowed for a convertible Hawaiian or Spanish setup.

1909-1914		$1,800	$2,000

Harp Guitar
1900s. Normally 11 strings with fancy purfling and trim.

1900-1910		$6,000	$7,000

Knutson Luthiery

1981-present. Professional and premium grade, custom, archtop and flat-top guitars built by luthier John Knutson in Forestville, California. He also builds basses and mandolins.

Koll

1990-present. Professional and premium grade, custom/production, solidbody, chambered, and archtop guitars built by luthier Saul Koll, originally in Long Beach, California, and since '93, in Portland, Oregon. He also builds basses.

MODEL YEAR	FEATURES	EXC. COND. LOW	HIGH

Kona

1920s. Acoustic Hawaiian guitars sold by C.S. Delano, and thought to be made by Herman Weissenborn. Weissenborn appointments in line with style number, with thicker body and solid neck construction.

Style 3
Koa.

1920s		$2,700	$3,200

Style 4
Brown koa.

1920s		$3,500	$4,000

Koontz

1970-late 1980s. Luthier Sam Koontz started building custom guitars in the late '50s. Starting in '66 Koontz, who was associated with Harptone guitars, built guitars for Standel. In '70, he opened his own shop in Linden, New Jersey, building a variety of custom guitars. Koontz died in the late '80s. His guitars varied greatly and should be valued on a case-by-case basis.

Kramer

1976-1990, 1997-present. Budget and intermediate grade, production, imported acoustic, acoustic/electric, semi-hollow and solidbody guitars. They also offer basses, amps and effects.

Founded by New York music retailer Dennis Berardi, ex-Travis Bean sales rep Gary Kramer and ex-Norlin executive Peter LaPlaca. Initial financing provided by real estate developer Henry Vaccaro. Parent company named BKL Corporation (Berardi, Kramer, LaPlaca), located in Neptune City, New Jersey. The first guitars were designed by Berardi and luthier Phil Petillo and featured aluminum necks with wooden inserts on back to give them a "wooden" feel. Guitar production commenced in late-'76.

Control passed to Guitar Centers of Los Angeles for '79-'82, which recommended switch to more economical wood necks. Aluminum necks were phased out during the early-'80s, and were last produced in '85. In '89, a new investment group was brought in with James Liati as president, hoping for access to Russian market, but the company went of business in late-'90.

In '95 Henry Vaccaro and new partners revived the company and designed a number of new guitars in conjunction with Phil Petillo. However, in '97 the Kramer brandname was sold to Gibson. In '98, Henry Vaccaro released his new line of aluminum-core neck, split headstock guitars under the Vacarro brand name.

Non-U.S.A.-made models include the following lines: Aerostar, Ferrington, Focus, Hundred (post-'85 made with three digits in the 100-900), Showster, Striker, Thousand (post-'85 made with four digits in the 1000-9000), XL (except XL-5 made in '80s). Serial numbers for import models include:

Two alpha followed by four numbers: for example AA2341 with any assortment of letters and

numbers.

One alpha followed by five numbers: for example B23412.

Five numbers: for example 23412.

Model number preceeding numbers: for example XL1-03205.

The notation "Kramer, Neptune, NJ" does indicate U.S.A.-made production.

Most post-'85 Kramers were ESP Japanese-made guitars. American Series were ESP Japanese components that were assembled in the U.S.

The vintage/used market makes value distinctions between U.S.-made and import models. Headstock and logo shape can help identify U.S. versus imports as follows:

Traditional or Classic headstock with capital K as Kramer: U.S.A. '81-'84.

Banana (soft edges) headstock with all caps KRAMER: U.S.A. American Series '84-'86.

Pointy (sharp cut) headstock with all caps KRAMER: U.S.A. American Series '86-'87.

Pointy (sharp cut) headstock with downsized letters Kramer plus American decal: U.S.A. American Series '87-'94.

Pointy (sharp cut) headstock with downsized letters Kramer but without American decal, is an import.

100-ST (import)
1985-late-1980s. Offset double cut, 1 slanted bridge humbucker, maple bolt-on neck, rosewood 'board, dot markers.

1985-1987		$250	$300

250-G Aluminum Neck
1977-1979. Offset double cut, tropical woods, aluminum neck, dot markers, 2 pickups.

1977-1979		$350	$500

300-HST (import)
1988-1991. Offset double cut body, pointy-style headstock with large Kramer logo.

1988-1991		$200	$300

450-G Aluminum Neck
1977-1979. Offset double cutaway, tropical woods, aluminum neck, ebonol fingerboard, 20 Petillo frets + zero fret, two pickups, three-way switch, stop tailpiece.

1977-1979	Natural koa	$350	$500

650-G Artist Aluminum Neck
1977-1980. Aluminum neck, ebonol fingerboard, double cutaway solidbody, two humbuckers.

1977-1980		$450	$550

Aerostar ZX Series (import)
1986-1989. Offset double cut solidbodies, pointy six-on-a-side headstock. Models include the 1 humbucker ZX10, 2 humbucker ZX20, 3 single coil ZX30, and hum/single/single ZX30H.

1986-1989	ZX10	$100	$150
1986-1989	ZX20	$110	$160
1986-1989	ZX30	$110	$160
1986-1989	ZX30H	$120	$170

1964 Kent No. 540

1977 Kramer 650G

1979 Kramer DMZ-2000

1980 Kramer Gene Simmons Axe

MODEL YEAR	FEATURES	EXC. COND. LOW	HIGH

Baretta
1984-1986. Offset double cutaway, banana six-on-a-side headstock, one pickup, Floyd Rose trem, Black hardware, U.S.A.-made.

| 1984-1986 | Snakeskin finish | $625 | $775 |
| 1984-1986 | Standard opaque finish | $600 | $700 |

DMZ 1000 Custom
1978-1981. Double cutaway with larger upper horn, aluminum neck, two pickups. Changed to thin-horned double cutaway by mid-1980.

| 1978-1981 | | $400 | $500 |

DMZ 2000 Custom
1978-1981. Solidbody double cutaway with larger upper horn, bolt-on aluminum T-neck, slot headstock, two splitable pickups.

| 1978-1981 | Black | $425 | $525 |

DMZ 3000 Custom
1978-1981. Solidbody double cutaway with larger upper horn, aluminum neck, slot headstock, three single-coil pickups, stop tailpiece.

| 1978-1981 | | $450 | $550 |

DMZ 6000G Custom
1978-1981. Offset double cutaway, bird's-eye maple/burled walnut, aluminum neck, two humbuckers, active preamp, stop tailpiece.

| 1978-1981 | | $450 | $550 |

Duke Custom/Standard (headless)
1981-1982. Headless aluminum neck, 22-fret neck, one pickup, Floyd Rose trem.

| 1981-1982 | | $400 | $450 |

Duke Special (headless)
1982-1985. Headless aluminum neck, two pickups, tuners on body.

| 1982-1985 | | $400 | $450 |

E.E. Pro I
1987-1988. Designed by Elliot Easton. Offset double cut, six-on-a-side headstock, Floyd Rose trem, 2 single-coils and 1 humbucker

| 1987-1988 | | $400 | $450 |

E.E. Pro II
1987-1988. Same as E.E. Pro I, but with fixed-bridge tailpiece, three pickups, five-position switching and master volume.

| 1987-1988 | | $400 | $450 |

Ferrington
1985-1990. Acoustic-electric, offered in single and double cutaway, bolt-on electric-style neck, transducers, made in Korea.

| 1985-1990 | | $300 | $400 |

Focus 1000 (import)
1984-1988. Offset double cut, banana six-on-a-side headstock (pointy droopy headstock in '87), 1 humbucker, Rose trem. Import from Japan.

| 1984-1988 | | $275 | $350 |

Focus 2000 (import)
1984-1988. Same as Focus 1000, but with classic six-on-a-side headstock and 2 humbuckers. Banana headstock in '85, pointy droopy headstock in '87.

| 1984-1988 | | $275 | $375 |

Focus 3000 (import)
1984-1988. Same as Focus 2000, but with hum/single/single pickups. Banana headstock in '85, pointy droopy headstock in '87.

| 1984-1988 | | $275 | $400 |

Focus 4000 (import)
1984-1986. Offset double cut with 3 single coils for '84; Vanguard V shape with 2 humbuckers for '85-'86.

| 1984-1986 | | $275 | $400 |

Focus 6000 (import)
1986-1988. Same as Focus 3000, but with hum/single/single pickups and 5-way switch. Pointy droopy headstock in '87.

| 1986-1988 | | $275 | $400 |

Focus Classic (import)
1986-1989. Offset double cut, six-on-a-side headstock, 3 single-coils, Floyd Rose trem.

| 1986-1989 | | $250 | $400 |

Gene Simmons Axe
1980-1981. Axe-shaped guitar, aluminum neck, 1 humbucker, slot headstock, stop tailpiece, 25 were made.

| 1980-1981 | | $2,000 | $3,500 |

Gorky Park (import)
1986-1989. Triangular balalaika, bolt-on maple neck, pointy droopy six-on-a-side headstock, one pickup, Floyd Rose trem. Red with iron sickle graphics, tribute to Russian rock. Reissued in late-1990s.

| 1986-1989 | | $400 | $600 |

Nightswan
1987-1990. Offset double cut, six-on-a-side headstock, 2 Duncan humbuckers, Floyd Rose.

| 1987-1990 | Blue Metallic | $750 | $850 |

Pacer
1982-1984. Offset double cut, six-on-a-side headstock, 3 single coils, bolt-on maple neck and 'board.

| 1982-1984 | | $500 | $600 |

Pacer Custom
1981-1986. Offset double cut, bolt-on maple neck with maple cap, 2 humbuckers, translucent finish, gold hardware.

| 1981-1986 | | $550 | $650 |

Pacer Deluxe
1983-1986. Pacer with hum/single/single pickups.

| 1981-1986 | | $550 | $650 |

ProAxe (U.S.A.-made)
1989-1990. Offset double cut, sharp pointy headstock, dot markers, 2 or 3 pickups.

| 1989-1990 | | $450 | $600 |

Striker (import)
1984-1989. Korean imports, offset doube cut, single-single-double pickup layout, various colors. Series included Striker 100, 200, 300, 400, 600 and 700 Bass.

1984-1989	Striker 100	$200	$250
1984-1989	Striker 200	$210	$260
1984-1989	Striker 300	$220	$270
1985-1989	Striker 400	$240	$290
1986-1989	Striker 600	$250	$300

MODEL YEAR	FEATURES	EXC. COND. LOW	HIGH

Vanguard Series

1981-1986, 1999-present. U.S.A.-made or American Series (assembled in U.S.). Flying V shape, 1 humbucker, aluminum (Special '81-'83) or wood (Custom '81-'83) neck. Added for '83-'84 were the Imperial (wood neck, 2 humbuckers) and the Headless (alum neck, 1 humbucker). For '85-'86, the body was modified to a Jackson Randy Rhoads style V body, with a banana headstock and 2 humbuckers. In '99 this last design was revived as an import.

1981-1986		$400	$500

Voyager

1980s. Kramer and Voyager Series logo on headstock.

1982-1983		$400	$500

XKG-10

1980s. Aluminum neck, Flying V-style body.

1980		$325	$425

XL-5 Custom

1980-1981. Asymmetrical double cutaway, aluminum neck, 2 pickups, three-way switch, coil-tap, phase, BadAss.

1980-1981		$1,100	$1,400

Kramer-Harrison, William

1977-present. Luthier William Kramer-Harrison builds his premium grade, custom, classical and flat-top guitars in Kingston, New York.

Kubicki

1973-present. Kubicki is best known for their Factor basses, but did offer a few guitar models in the early '80s. See Bass section for more company info.

Kustom

1968-present. Founded by Bud Ross in Chanute, Kansas, and best known for the tuck-and-roll amps, Kustom also offered guitars from '68 to '69. See Amp section for more company info.

Electric Hollowbody Guitars

1968-1969. Hollowed-out two-part bodies; includes the K200A (humbucker, Bigsby), the K200B (single-coils, trapeze tailpiece), and the K200C (less fancy tuners), various colors.

1960s		$700	$800

Kyle, Doug

1990-present. Premium grade, custom, Selmer-style guitars made by luthier Doug Kyle in England.

La Baye

1967. Designed by Dan Helland in Green Bay, Wisconsin and built by the Holman-Woodell factory in Neodesha, Kansas. Introduced at NAMM and folded when no orders came in. Only 45 prototypes made. A few may have been sold later as 21st Century.

2x4 6-String

1967. Narrow plank body, controls on top, two pickups, trem. A 12-string version was also made.

1967		$800	$900

LA Guitar Factory

1997-present. Founded by Ari Lehtela and Luke Lukuer in Charlotte, North Carolina. Lehtela became the sole owner in 2000. From '97 to '03, LA offered production and custom models. Currently, Lehtela uses the LA Guitar Factory brand on his professional and premium grade, production, solidbody and tone chambered guitars and basses. He markets his premium grade, custom guitars - mainly jazz body carved tops - under Lehtela guitarCraft.

La Scala

Ca. 1920s-1930s. La Scala was another brand of the Oscar Schmidt Company of New Jersey, and was used on guitars, banjos, and mandolins.

Lace Music Products

1979-present. Intermediate and professional, production, electric guitars from Lace Music Products, a division of Actodyne General Inc. which was founded by Don Lace Sr., inventor of the Lace Sensor Pickup. In '96 Lace added amplifiers and in 2001 they added guitars. In '02, they also started offering the Rat Fink brand of guitars.

Lado

1973-present. Founded by Joe Kovacic, Lado builds professional and premium grade, production/custom, solidbody guitars in Lindsay, Ontario. Some model lines are branded "J. K. Lado." They also build basses.

Lafayette

Ca. 1963-1967. Sold through Lafayette Electronics catalogs. Early Japanese-made guitars from pre-copy era, generally shorter scale beginner guitars. Many made by Guyatone, some possibly by Teisco.

Acoustic Thinline Archtop Guitars

1963-1967. Various models.

1963-1967		$100	$200

Lakeside (Lyon & Healy)

Late-1800s-early-1900s. Mainly catalog sales of guitars and mandolins from the Chicago maker. Marketed as a less expensive alternative to the Lyon & Healy Washburn product line.

Harp Guitar - Jumbo Style G3740

Early-1900s. Spruce top, rosewood finished birch back and sides, two six-string necks with standard tuners, one neck is fretless without dot markers, rectangular bridge.

1917	Natural	$1,500	$3,000

Kustom K-200

1967 La Baye 2x4

Larrivee DM-03E

Larson Brothers Euphanon

MODEL YEAR	FEATURES	EXC. COND. LOW	HIGH

Langejans Guitars

1971-present. Premium grade, production/custom, flat-top, 12-string, and classical guitars built by luthier Delwyn Langejans in Holland, Michigan.

Larrivee

1968-present. Professional and premium grade, production/custom, acoustic, acoustic/electric, and classical guitars built in Vancouver, British Columbia. Founded by Jean Larrivee, who apprenticed under Edgar Monch in Toronto. He built classic guitars in his home from '68-'70 and built his first steel string guitar in '71. Moved company to Victoria, BC in '77 and to Vancouver in '82. In '83, he began building solidbody electric guitars until '89, when focus again returned to acoustics.

Up to 2004, Larrivee used the following model designations: 05 Mahogany Standard, 09 Rosewood Standard, 10 Deluxe, 19 Special, 50 & 60 Standard (unique inlay), 70 Deluxe, and 72 Presentation. The 2004 designations used are: 01 Parlor, 03 Standard, 05 Select Mahogany, 09 Rosewood Artist, 10 Rosewood Deluxe, 19 California Anniv. Special Edition Series, 50 Traditional Series, 60 Traditional Series, E = Electric, R = Rosewood.

C-10 Deluxe
Late-1980s-1990s. Sitka spruce top, Indian rosewood back and sides, sharp cutaway, fancy binding.

1989		$1,500	$1,700

C-72 Cutaway Presentation
Spruce top, Indian rosewood back and sides, sharp cutaway, ultra-fancy abalone and pearl hand-engraved headstock.

1990s	Mermaid headstock	$2,500	$3,000

C-72 Presentation
Spruce top, Indian rosewood back and sides, non-cut Style D, ultra-fancy abalone and pearl hand-engraved headstock.

1990s	Jester headstock	$2,000	$2,500

D-10 Deluxe
2000s. Spruce top, rosewood rims, abalone top and soundhole trim.

2000s		$1,600	$2,000

D-70 Deluxe

1990s		$1,500	$2,000

L-09 Rosewood Standard
All solid wood construction, East Indian rosewood back and sides, African ebony board and bridge, wood binding and rosette mosaic, fine grain Sitka spruce top.

1990s		$1,000	$1,500

L-72 Presentation Custom
Mid- to late-1990s. Spruce top, Indian rosewood rims, ornate vase and vine inlays.

1990a		$3,000	$3,500

Parlor Walnut
Early 2000s. Spruce top, solid walnut back and sides.

2002		$400	$500

MODEL YEAR	FEATURES	EXC. COND. LOW	HIGH

RS-4 CM Carved Top
1988-1989. Carved top solidbody, curly maple top, single-single-humbucker pickups, sunburst or translucent finishes.

1988-1989		$900	$1,200

Larson Brothers (Chicago)

1900-1944. Carl and August Larson built guitars under a variety of names, (refer to Stetson, Maurer and Prairie State listings).

Laskin

1973-present. Luthier William "Grit" Laskin builds his premium and presentation grade, custom, steel-string, classical, and flamenco guitars in Toronto, Ontario. Many of his instruments feature extensive inlay work.

Classical
All solid wood, German spruce top, Indian rosewood back and sides, portrait headstock inlay.

1980s		$3,000	$4,000

Flamenco
All solid wood, spruce top, cypress back and sides, ebony friction pegs.

1980s		$2,500	$3,000

Jumbo Brazilian
All solid wood, bear claw sitka spruce top, Brazilian rosewood back and sides, double loon headstock inlay.

1980s		$2,500	$3,000

Jumbo Cutaway
Indian rosewood back and sides, spruce top, double abalone rosette, woman and candle deluxe headstock inlay.

1992	Natural	$7,000	$8,000

Leach Guitars

1980-present. Luthier Harvey Leach builds his professional and premium grade, custom, flat-tops, archtops, and solidbody electrics in Cedar Ridge, California. He also builds basses.

Lehmann Stringed Instruments

1971-present. Luthier Bernard Lehmann builds his professional and premium grade, production/custom, flat-top, archtop, classical and Gypsy guitars in Rochester, New York. He also builds lutes, vielles and rebecs.

Lehtela guitarCraft

2003-present. Premium grade, custom, guitars - mainly jazz body carved tops - built by luthier Ari Lehtela in Charlotte, North Carolina. Markets his non-custom models under LA Guitar Factory.

Les Stansell Guitars

1980-present. Luthier Les Stansell builds his premium grade, custom, nylon-string guitars in Pistol River, Oregon.

MODEL		EXC. COND.	
YEAR	FEATURES	LOW	HIGH

Linc Luthier

Professional and premium grade, custom/production, electric and acoustic guitars built by luther Linc Luthier in Upland, California. He also builds basses and double-necks.

Lindert

1986-present. Luthier Chuck Lindert makes his intermediate and professional grade, production/custom, Art Deco-vibe electric guitars in Chelan, Washington.

Line 6

1996-present. Professional grade, production, imported solidbody and acoustic modeling guitars able to replicate the tones of a variety of instruments. Line 6 also builds effects and amps.

Lopez, Abel Garcia

1985-present. Luthier Abel Garcia Lopez builds his premium grade, custom, classical guitars in Mexico.

Loprinzi

1972-present. Professional and premium grade, production/custom, classical and steel-string guitars built in Clearwater, Florida. They also build ukes. Founded by Augustino LoPrinzi and his brother Thomas in New Jersey. The guitar operations were taken over by AMF/Maark Corp. in '73. LoPrinzi left the company and again started producing his own Augustino Guitars, moving his operations to Florida in '78. AMF ceased production in '80, and a few years later, LoPrinzi got his trademarked name back.

LM-15
Mahogany back and sides.

1970s		$700	$800

LR-15
Rosewood.

1973		$1,200	$1,300

LR-15-12

1975		$1,200	$1,300

LR-20
Classical, solid spruce top, 3-piece Indian rosewood back.

1973		$1,200	$1,300

Lord

Mid-1960s. Acoustic and solidbody electric guitars imported by Halifax.

Acoustic Guitars
Various models.

1960s		$75	$175

LTD

1995-present. Intermediate grade, production, Korean-made solidbody guitars offered by ESP. They also offer basses. See ESP for models.

MODEL		EXC. COND.	
YEAR	FEATURES	LOW	HIGH

Lucas Custom Instruments

1989-present. Premium and presentation grade, production/custom, flat-tops built by luthier Randy Lucas in Columbus, Indiana.

Lucas, A. J.

1990-present. Luthier A. J. Lucas builds his production/custom, classical and steel string guitars in Lincolnshire, England.

Lyle

Ca. 1969-1980. Imported by distributor L.D. Heater of Portland, Oregon. Generally higher quality Japanese-made copies of American designs by unknown manufacturers, but some early ones, at least, were made by Arai and Company.

Acoustics
1969-1980. Various models.

1969-1980		$100	$175

Electric Thinline Archtop Guitars
1969-1980. Various models.

1969-1980		$125	$200

Lyon & Healy

In the 1930s, Lyon & Healy was an industry giant. It operated a chain of music stores, and manufactured harps (their only remaining product), pianos, Washburn guitars and a line of brass and wind instruments. (See Washburn, American Conservatory, Lakeside, and College brands.)

Lyric

1996-present. Luthier John Southern builds his professional and premium grade, custom, semi-hollow and solidbody guitars in Tulsa, Oklahoma. He also builds basses.

M. Campellone Guitars

See listing under Campellone Guitars

Maccaferri

1923-1990. Built by luthier and classical guitarist Mario Maccaferri (b. May 20, 1900, Cento, Italy; d. 1993, New York) in Cento, Italy; Paris, France; New York, New York; and Mount Vernon, New York. Maccaferri was a student of Luigi Mozzani from 1911 to 1928. His first catalog was in '23, and included a cutaway guitar. He designed Selmer guitars in '31. Maccaferri invented the plastic clothespin during World War II and used that technology to produce plastic ukes starting in '49 and Dow Styron plastic guitars in '53. He made several experimental plastic electrics in the '60s and plastic violins in the late-'80s.

See Guitar Stories Volume II, by Michael Wright, for a complete history of Maccaferri with detailed model listings.

Line 6 Variax Acoustic

1912 Larson Bros./Dyer harp guitar

Maccaferri G-40

Mark Lacey Arch Nouveau

MODEL YEAR	FEATURES	EXC. COND. LOW	HIGH

G40 Deluxe Arched Top
1953-1958. Plastic construction.

1953-1958		$200	$275

Showtime Classical
1959-1969. Plastic construction, no decoration by 1965.

1959-1969		$175	$225

Magnatone
Ca. 1937-1971. Founded as Dickerson Brothers in Los Angeles, California and known as Magna Electronics from '47, with Art Duhamell president. Brands include Dickerson, Oahu (not all), Gourley, Natural Music Guild, Magnatone. In '59 Magna and Estey merged and in '66 the company relocated to Pennsylvania. In '71, the brand was taken over by a toy company.

Cyclops
1930s. Dobro-made resonator guitar.

1930s		$500	$650

Tornado
1965-1966. Offset double cut body, 3 DeArmond pickups, vibrato.

1965-1966		$400	$600

Typhoon
1965-1966. Double cut solidbody, three DeArmond pickups, vibrato.

1965-1966		$400	$600

Zephyr
1965-1966. Double cut with two DeArmond single-coil pickups, metallic finish, vibrato.

1965-1966		$400	$550

Mako
1985-1989. Line of solidbody guitars from Kaman (Ovation, Hamer). They also offered basses and amps.

LX2
1985-1989. Explorer copy with bolt-on neck, exposed humbuckers, dot markers.

1985-1989		$150	$250

Various Solidbody Guitars
1980s. Imports with bolt-on necks.

1985-1989		$150	$250

Manuel Contreras
1962-1994. Luthier Manuel Gonzalez Contreras worked with José Ramírez III, before opening his own shop in Madrid, Spain, in 1962.

Manuel Contreras II
1986-Present. Professional grade, production/custom, nylon string guitars made in Madrid, Spain, by luthier Pablo Contreras, son of Manuel.

Manuel Rodriguez and Sons, S.L.
1905-present. Professional, premium, and presentation grade, custom flat-top and nylon-string guitars from Madrid, Spain.

MODEL YEAR	FEATURES	EXC. COND. LOW	HIGH

Manzanita Guitars
1993-present. Custom, steel-string, Hawaiian, and resonator guitars built by luthiers Manfred Pietrzok and Moritz Sattler in Rosdorf, Germany.

Manzer Guitars
1976-present. Luthier Linda Manzer builds her premium and presentation grade, custom, steel-string, nylon-string, and archtop guitars in Toronto, Ontario.

Mapson
1995-present. Luthier James L. Mapson builds his premium and presentation grade, production/custom, archtops in Santa Ana, California.

Marc Silber Guitar Company
1998-present. Intermediate and professional grade, production, flat-top, nylon-string, and Hawaiian guitars designed by Marc Silber and made in Mexico. These were offered under the K & S Guitars and/or Silber brands for 1992-'98. Silber also has ukuleles.

Marchione Guitars
1993-present. Premium and presentation grade, custom, archtops and solidbodies built by Stephen Marchione originally in New York City, but currently in Houston, Texas.

Marco Polo
1960-ca.1964. Imported from Japan by Harry Stewart and the Marco Polo Company of Santa Ana, CA. One of the first American distributors to advertise inexpensive Japanese guitars. Manufacturers unknown, but some acoustics by Suzuki, some electrics by Guyatone.

Acoustic Hollowbody Guitars
1960-1964. Various models.

1960s		$100	$200

Mark Lacey Guitars
1974-present. Luthier Mark Lacey builds his premium and presentation archtops and flat-tops in Nashville, Tennessee.

Mark Wescott Guitars
1980-present. Premium grade, custom, flat-tops, built by luthier Mark Wescott in Marmora, New Jersey.

Marling
Ca. 1975. Budget line instruments marketed by EKO of Recanati, Italy; probably made by them, although possibly imported.

Acoustic Guitars
1975. Includes the steel-string S.110, and the dreadnoughts W.354 Western, and W.356 Western.

1975		$75	$100

MODEL YEAR	FEATURES	EXC. COND. LOW	HIGH

Electric Guitars
1975. Includes the E.400 (semi-acoustic/electric), E.490 (LP-style), E.480 (single cut-style), and the 460 (Manta-style).

| 1975 | | $75 | $150 |

Martelle
1934. Private brand attributed to Gibson and some to Kay.

De Luxe
1934. Gibson 12-fret round shoulder Jumbo construction, mahogany back and sides, Sunburst, Hawaiian or Spanish option.

| 1934 | | $8,000 | $9,000 |

Martin
1833-present. Intermediate, professional, premium, and presentation grade, production/custom, acoustic, acoustic/electric, and resonator guitars. Founded in New York City by Christian Frederick Martin, former employee of J. Staufer in Vienna, Austria. Moved to Nazareth, Pennsylvania in 1839. Early guitars were made in the European style, many made with partners John Coupa, Charles Bruno and Henry Schatz. Scalloped X-bracing was introduced in the late-1840s. The dreadnought was introduced in 1916 for the Oliver Ditson Company, Boston; and Martin introduced their own versions in 1931.

Martin model size and shape are indicated by the letter prefix (e.g., 0, 00, 000, D, etc.); materials and ornamentation are indicated by number, with the higher the number, the fancier the instrument (e.g., 18, 28, 35, etc.). Martin offered electric thinline guitars from '61-'68 and electric solidbodies from '78-'82. The Martin Shenandoah was made in Asia and assembled in U.S. Japanese Martin Sigma ('72-'73) and Korean Martin Stinger ('85 on) imported solidbodies. See Michael Wright's Guitar Stories Vol. II for more information on Martin's electric guitars.

0-15
1935, 1940-1943, 1948-1961. All mahogany, unbound rosewood fingerboard, slotted peghead and 12-fret neck until 1934, solid peghead and 14-fret neck thereafter. Natural Mahogany.

1935	2 made, maple/birch	$2,400	$2,600
1940-1943		$1,600	$1,900
1948-1949		$1,500	$1,800
1950-1959		$1,200	$1,400
1960-1961		$1,100	$1,200

0-15 T
1960-1963. Tenor with Style 15 appointments. Natural mahogany.

| 1960-1963 | | $800 | $1,000 |

0-16
1961 only. Six made.

| 1961 | | $1,700 | $1,900 |

0-16 NY
1961-1995. Mahogany back and sides, 12 frets, slotted peghead, unbound extra-wide rosewood fingerboard. Natural.

1961-1969		$1,400	$1,500
1970-1979		$1,200	$1,400
1980-1989		$1,100	$1,300
1990-1995		$1,000	$1,250

0-17
1906-1917, 1929-1948, 1966-1968. First version has mahogany back and sides, three Black soundhole rings, rosewood bound back, unbound ebony fingerboard, 12 frets, slotted peghead. Second version (1929 and on) is all mahogany, three White-Black-White soundhole rings, top bound until 1930, thin Black backstripe, 12 frets and slotted peghead until 1934, solid peghead and 14 frets thereafter. Natural Mahogany.

1906-1917	Gut	$1,500	$1,800
1929-1934	Bar frets, 12 fret-style	$1,700	$2,000
1934-1939	T-frets, 14 fret-style	$1,900	$2,200
1940-1945		$1,700	$2,100
1946-1948		$1,600	$1,900
1966	One made	$1,400	$1,700
1968	Six made	$1,200	$1,600

0-17 H
1930, 1935-1941. Hawaiian, mahogany back and sides, 12 frets clear of body. Natural.

| 1930 | 60 made | $1,600 | $1,700 |
| 1935-1941 | | $1,600 | $1,700 |

0-17 T
1932-1960. Mahogany back and sides, tenor. Natural.

| 1932-1949 | | $1,100 | $1,600 |
| 1950-1960 | Mahogany | $900 | $1,600 |

0-18
1898-1996. Rosewood back and sides until 1917, mahogany back and sides after, Adirondack spruce top until 1946. Slotted peghead and 12 frets until 1934, solid peghead and 14 frets after 1934. Braced for steel strings in 1923, improved neck in late-1934, non-scalloped braces appear late-1944. Natural.

1898-1922	Gut string bracing	$2,500	$2,800
1923-1939	Braced for steel in 1923	$2,900	$3,200
1940-1944	Scalloped braces	$2,700	$3,000
1945-1949		$2,000	$2,600
1950-1959		$1,900	$2,300
1960-1969		$1,200	$2,200
1970-1979		$1,100	$1,300
1980-1989		$1,000	$1,200
1990-1996		$900	$1,100

0-18 G (Classical)
1960s. Special order classical nylon string model. Natural.

| 1961 | | $1,200 | $2,200 |

1935 Martin O-15

1930 Martin 0-18

1923 Martin 0-21

1957 Martin 00-18

MODEL YEAR	FEATURES	EXC. COND. LOW	HIGH
0-18 K			
1918-1935. Hawaiian, all koa wood, braced for steel strings in 1923, T-frets and steel T-bar neck in late-1934. Natural.			
1918-1922		$2,400	$2,600
1923-1927	Steel string bracing	$2,600	$2,800
1928-1935		$2,700	$2,900
0-18 T			
1929-1995. Mahogany body, spruce top, tenor. Natural.			
1929-1939		$1,300	$1,900
1940-1959		$1,200	$1,800
1960-1964		$1,150	$1,350
1965-1969		$1,100	$1,300
1970-1979		$1,000	$1,200
1980-1989		$900	$1,100
1990-1995		$800	$1,000
0-21			
1898-1948. Rosewood back and sides, Adirondack spruce top until 1946, 12 frets, braced for steel strings in 1923, T-frets and steel T-bar neck in late-1934, non-scalloped braces in late-1944. Natural.			
1898-1926	Gut string bracing	$2,800	$3,000
1927-1943	Steel string bracing	$2,900	$3,500
1944-1948	Non-scalloped bracing	$2,350	$2,850
0-26			
1850-1890. Rosewood back and sides, ivory-bound top, rope-style purfling.			
1850-1890		$2,900	$3,200
0-27			
1850-1898.			
1850-1898		$3,700	$4,300
0-28			
1870s-1931, 1937 (six made), 1969 (one made). Brazilian rosewood back and sides, braced for steel strings in 1923, herringbone binding until 1937. Natural.			
1870-1927		$4,500	$5,500
1928-1931		$5,000	$6,000
0-28 K			
1917-1931, 1935. Hawaiian, all koa wood, braced for steel strings in 1923. Natural.			
1917	Spruce top option	$4,400	$5,400
1917-1924	Figured koa	$4,400	$5,400
1925-1931	Steel string bracing	$4,900	$5,900
0-28 T			
1930-1931. Tenor neck.			
1930-1931		$2,800	$3,500
0-30			
1899-1921. Brazilian rosewood back and sides, ivory-bound body, neck and headstock.			
1899-1921		$4,700	$5,700
0-42			
1870s-1942. Brazilian rosewood back and sides, 12 frets. Natural.			
1890-1926	Braced for gut strings	$11,000	$12,000
1927-1930	Steel string bracing	$12,000	$13,000

MODEL YEAR	FEATURES	EXC. COND. LOW	HIGH
0-45			
1904-1939. Brazilian rosewood back and sides, natural, special order only for '31-'39..			
1904-1928	Braced for gut strings	$18,000	$24,000
1929-1930	Steel string bracing	$25,200	$33,600
00-16 C			
1962-1977, 1980-1981. Classical, mahogany back and sides, five-ply bound top, satin finish, 12 frets, slotted peghead. Natural.			
1962-1969		$1,000	$1,200
1970-1977		$800	$1,100
1980-1981	2 made	$800	$1,100
00-17			
1908-1917, 1930-1960, 1982-1988. Mahogany back and sides, 12 frets and slotted headstock until 1934, solid headstock and 14 frets after 1934, Natural Mahogany. Reissued in 2002 with a high gloss finish.			
1908-1917	Limited production	$1,800	$2,000
1930-1939		$2,000	$2,300
1940-1944		$1,900	$2,200
1945-1949		$1,800	$2,100
1950-1960		$1,700	$1,900
2002	Reissue model	$1,000	$1,100
00-17 H			
1934-1935. Hawaiian set-up, mahogany body, no binding.			
1934-1935		$1,900	$2,200
00-18			
1898-1995. Rosewood back and sides until 1917, mahogany after, braced for steel strings in 1923, improved neck in late-1934, war-time design changes 1942-1946, non-scalloped braces in late-1944, Adirondack spruce top until 1946. Natural.			
1898-1922		$4,000	$4,500
1923-1939	Braced for steel in '23	$4,500	$5,500
1934-1939	Sunburst option	$5,000	$6,100
1942-1943	Ebony rod	$4,500	$4,800
1944	Scalloped braces early '44	$4,000	$4,500
1944-1946	Non-scalloped braces	$3,200	$3,300
1946	Steel bar neck	$3,300	$3,400
1947-1949		$3,000	$3,100
1950-1952		$2,700	$3,000
1953-1959		$2,500	$2,800
1960-1962		$2,200	$2,600
1963-1965		$2,000	$2,300
1966	Black guard late '66	$1,500	$2,000
1966	Tortoise guard early '66	$1,600	$2,100
1967		$1,400	$1,900
1968		$1,300	$1,800
1969		$1,200	$1,600
1970-1979		$1,000	$1,200
1980-1989		$900	$1,000
1990-1995		$900	$1,000

GUITARS

MODEL YEAR	FEATURES	EXC. COND. LOW	HIGH

00-18 C
1962-1995. Renamed from 00-18 G in 1962. Mahogany back and sides, classical, 12 frets, slotted headstock. Natural.

1962-1969		$1,400	$1,600
1970-1979		$1,200	$1,400

00-18 E
1959-1964. Flat top Style 18, single neck pickup and two knobs, heavier bracing. Natural.

1959-1964		$2,400	$2,600

00-18 G
1936-1962. Mahogany back and sides, classical, Natural. Renamed 00-18 C in 1962.

1936-1939		$1,600	$2,500
1940-1949		$1,500	$2,300
1950-1962		$1,300	$1,600

00-18 Gruhn Limited Edition
1995. Sitka spruce top, C-shaped neck profile, 25 made.

1995		$1,400	$1,600

00-18 H
1935-1941. Hawaiian, mahogany back amd sides, 12 frets clear of body, Natural. The Price Guide is generally for all original instruments. The H conversion is an exception, because converting from H (Hawaiian-style) to 00-18 specs is considered by some to be a favorable improvement and something that adds value.

1935-1941		$3,500	$4,000
1935-1941	Converted to Spanish	$4,000	$5,500

00-18 SH (Steve Howe)
1999-2000. Limited edition run of 250.

1999-2000		$2,400	$2,600

00-21
1898-1996. Brazilian rosewood back and sides, changed to Indian rosewood in 1970, dark outer binding, unbound ebony fingerboard until 1947, rosewood from 1947, slotted diamond inlays until 1944, dot after. Natural.

1898-1926	Braced for gut strings	$5,000	$6,000
1927-1931	Braced for steel in '27	$7,500	$8,500
1932-1939		$7,000	$8,000
1934-1939	Sunburst option	$6,800	$7,800
1940-1944	Scalloped braces	$6,500	$7,500
1944-1949	Non-scalloped braces	$4,500	$5,000
1950-1959		$4,000	$4,500
1960-1965		$3,500	$4,000
1966-1969	Brazilian rosewood, Black guard	$3,300	$3,800
1970-1979	Indian rosewood	$1,300	$1,600
1980-1989		$1,200	$1,500
1990-1996		$1,100	$1,400

00-21 H
Special order limited production.

1914	One made	$6,500	$7,000
1952	One made	$6,500	$7,000
1955	One made	$6,500	$7,000

00-21 NY
1961-1965. Brazilian rosewood back and sides, no inlay. Natural.

1961-1965		$3,000	$3,500

00-28
1898-1941, 1958 (one made), 1977 (one made), 1984 (two made). Brazilian rosewood back and sides, changed to Indian rosewood in 1977, herringbone purfling through 1941, White binding and unbound fingerboard after 1941, no inlays before 1901, diamond inlays from 1901 to 1941, dot after. Natural.

1898-1924	Gut strings	$8,000	$11,000
1925-1931	Braced for steel in '25	$9,000	$13,000
1932-1941	Special order	$9,000	$13,000
1958-1984	Special order	$1,400	$3,000

00-28 C
1966-1995. Renamed from 00-28 G. Brazilian rosewood back and sides, changed to Indian rosewood in 1970, classical, 12 frets. Natural.

1966-1969	Brazilian rosewood	$3,000	$4,000
1970-1979	Indian rosewood	$1,500	$1,800

00-28 G
1936-1962. Brazilian rosewood back and sides, classical, Natural. Only 17 made. Reintroduced as 00-28 C in 1966.

1936-1939		$5,500	$6,000
1940-1949		$5,000	$5,500
1951-1962		$4,000	$5,000

00-28 K (Hawaiian)
1919-1921, 1926-1933. Koa back and sides, Hawaiian set-up.

1919-1921	34 made	$6,500	$7,000
1926-1933	1 made per year	$7,000	$9,000

00-40 H
1928-1939. Hawaiian, Brazilian rosewood back and sides, 12 frets clear of body, Natural. H models are sometimes converted to standard Spanish setup. In higher-end models this can make the instrument more valuable to some people.

1928-1939		$9,000	$13,000
1928-1939	Converted to Spanish	$12,000	$16,000

00-40 K
Few were made (only 6). Figured koa, Natural.

1918	1 made	$19,000	$21,000
1930	5 made	$19,000	$21,000

00-42
1898-1942, 1973 (one made), 1994-1996. Brazilian rosewood back and sides, Indian rosewood in 1973, pearl top borders, 12 frets, ivory bound peghead until 1918, ivoroid binding after 1918. Natural.

1898-1926	Gut strings	$14,000	$17,000
1927-1942	Steel strings	$15,000	$21,000
1973	1 made	$2,300	$3,200
1994-1996		$2,100	$2,900

00-42 K
1919. Koa body, one made.

1919		$20,000	$22,000

Martin 00-18V

Martin 00-21GE

1927 Martin 00-45

1936 Martin 000-18

00-44 Soloist/Olcott-Bickford Artist Model
1913-1939. Custom-made in small quantities, Brazilian rosewood, ivory or faux-ivory-bound ebony fingerboard.

MODEL YEAR	FEATURES	EXC. COND. LOW	HIGH
1913-1939		$23,000	$43,000

00-45
1904-1938, 1970-1995. Brazilian rosewood back and sides, changed to Indian rosewood in 1970, 12 frets and slotted headstock until 1934 and from 1970 on 14 frets, and solid headstock from 1934-1970. Natural.

1904-1927	Gut string bracing	$25,000	$35,000
1928-1938	Steel string bracing	$35,000	$45,000

00-45 K
1919. One made.

1919	1 made	$25,000	$35,000

00-45 Stauffer Commemorative Limited Edition
1997. Stauffer six-on-a-side headstock, 45-style appointments, 00-size body, Sitka spruce top, Brazilian rosewood back and sides.

1997		$8,000	$10,000

000-1 R
1996-2002. Solid spruce top with laminated Indian rosewood sides.

1996-1999		$650	$900

000-15 Auditorium
1997-present. All solid wood mahogany body, dot markers, Natural.

1997-1999		$650	$700

000-16
1989-1995. Acoustic, mahogany back and sides, diamonds and squares inlaid. Name changed to 000-16 T Auditorium in 1996. Sunburst.

1989-1995		$1,200	$1,400

000-16 T
1996-1999. All solid wood mahogany back and sides, higher appointments than 000-15.

1996-1999		$800	$1,000

000-18
1911-present (none in 1932-1933). Rosewood back and sides until 1917, mahogany back and sides from 1917, longer scale in 1924-1934, 12 frets clear of body until 1933, changed to 14 frets in 1934. Improved neck late-1934, war-time changes 1941-1946, non-scalloped braces in late-1944, switched from Adirondack spruce to Sitka spruce top in 1946 (though some Adirondack tops in 1950s and 1960s), natural. Now called the 000-18 Auditorium.

1924-1931	25.5" scale, 12-fret clear	$7,000	$9,000
1934-1939	24.5" scale, 14-fret clear	$10,000	$12,000
1934-1939	Sunburst option	$10,000	$12,000
1940-1941		$8,000	$10,000
1942-1944	Scalloped braces	$6,000	$8,000
1943	Sunburst option	$7,500	$8,500
1944-1946	Non-scalloped braces	$4,000	$5,300
1947-1949		$3,800	$5,200

MODEL YEAR	FEATURES	EXC. COND. LOW	HIGH
1950-1952		$3,200	$4,000
1953-1959		$3,000	$3,500
1960-1962		$2,900	$3,400
1963-1965		$2,600	$2,900
1966	Black guard late '66	$2,200	$2,600
1966	Tortoise guard early '66	$2,400	$2,700
1967	Last of Maple bridgeplate	$2,000	$2,400
1968		$1,800	$2,200
1969		$1,500	$1,800
1970-1979		$1,200	$1,300
1980-1989		$1,100	$1,200
1990-1999		$1,000	$1,100
2000-2002		$1,000	$1,100

000-21
1902-1924 (22 made over that time), 1931(2), 1938-1959, 1965 (1), 1979 (12). Brazilian rosewood back and sides, changed to Indian rosewood in 1970. Natural.

1902-1937	Low production mostly gut	$12,000	$14,000
1938-1941	Pre-war specs	$14,000	$16,000
1942-1944	Ebony rod, scalloped	$13,000	$15,000
1944-1946	Non-scalloped	$8,500	$10,500
1947-1949	Herringbone, non-scalloped	$5,500	$7,500
1950-1959		$5,000	$6,000
1965	1 made	$5,500	$6,500
1979	12 made	$1,200	$1,400

000-28
1902-present. Brazilian rosewood back and sides, changed to Indian rosewood in 1970, herringbone purfling through 1941, White binding and unbound fingerboard after 1941, no inlays before 1901, slotted diamond inlays from 1901-1944, dot after, 12 frets until 1932, 14 frets 1931 on (both 12 and 14 frets were made during 1931-1932). Natural.

1902-1927	Gut strings	$22,000	$28,000
1928-1931	12 frets	$28,000	$32,000
1931-1932	14 frets	$27,000	$31,000
1931-1936	14 frets	$20,000	$27,000
1933		$26,000	$30,000
1934-1936		$24,000	$29,000
1937-1939		$22,000	$27,000
1940-1941		$21,000	$24,000
1942-1944	Scalloped braces	$19,000	$22,000
1944-1946	Herringbone, non-scalloped	$12,000	$17,000
1947-1949	Start of non-herringbone '47	$7,500	$9,000
1950-1952		$6,500	$8,000
1953-1958	Last of Kluson early '58	$6,000	$6,500
1958-1959	Grover tuners late '58	$5,500	$6,000
1960-1962		$5,000	$5,500
1963-1965		$4,500	$5,000
1966	Black guard late '66	$3,900	$4,400

MODEL YEAR	FEATURES	EXC. COND. LOW	HIGH
1966	Tortoise guard early '66	$4,000	$4,500
1967	Last of maple bridgeplate	$3,900	$4,400
1968	Rosewood bridgeplate	$3,500	$4,300
1969	Last of Brazilian rosewood	$3,400	$4,200
1970-1979	Indian rosewood	$1,400	$1,700
1980-1989	Indian rosewood	$1,400	$1,600
1990-1999	Indian rosewood	$1,300	$1,500
2000-2002		$1,250	$1,500

000-28 C
1962-1969. Brazilian rosewood back and sides, classical, slotted peghead. Natural.

1962-1969		$3,200	$4,400

000-28 EC Eric Clapton Signature
1996-present. Sitka spruce top, Indian rosewood back and sides, herringbone trim. Natural.

1996-1999		$1,900	$2,400

000-28 ECB Eric Clapton Brazilian
2003. Limited edition, 2nd edition of EC Signature Series with Brazilian rosewood.

2003		$6,500	$7,500

000-28 G
1937-1955. Special order, very limited production.

1937-1940	3 made	$9,000	$18,000
1946-1949	10 made	$7,500	$9,000
1950-1955	4 made	$6,000	$8,000

000-28 Golden Era
1996 only. Sitka spruce top, rosewood back and sides, scalloped braces, herringbone trim, 12-fret model. Natural.

1996		$2,800	$3,200

000-41
1996. Customshop style 000-41.

1996		$2,600	$2,700

000-42
1918, 1921-1922, 1925, 1930, 1934, 1938-1943. Brazilian rosewood back and sides. Natural.

1918-1934	Special order	$32,000	$36,000
1938-1943		$36,000	$41,000

000-42 EC Eric Clapton
1995. Style 45 pearl-inlaid headplate, ivoroid bindings, Eric Clapton signature, 24.9" scale, flat top, Sunburst top price is $8320 (1995 price). Only 461 made.

1995		$7,000	$8,000

000-45
1906, 1911-1914, 1917-1919, 1922-1942, 1971-1993. Brazilian rosewood back and sides, changed to Indian rosewood in 1970, 12-fret neck and slotted headstock until 1934 (but seven were made in 1970 and one in 1975), 14-fret neck and solid headstock after 1934. Natural.

1922-1927	Braced for gut strings	$45,000	$55,000
1928-1929	Braced for steel string	$55,000	$65,000
1930-1933		$65,000	$75,000
1934-1936	14 frets, C.F.M. inlaid	$75,000	$85,000
1937-1939		$73,000	$83,000
1940-1942		$70,000	$80,000

000-45 JR (Jimmie Rodgers) Golden Era
1997. Adirondack spruce top, Brazilian rosewood back and sides, scalloped high X-braces, abalone trim, Natural, 100 made.

1997		$9,000	$11,000

000-C16
1990-1995. Cutaway acoustic, mahogany back and sides, diamonds and squares inlay. Name changed to 000-C16T Auditorium in 1996.

1990-1995		$1,000	$1,200

0000-28 Custom
1998. Jumbo-size 0000 cutaway body, Indian rosewood, sitka spruce top.

1998		$2,900	$3,000

0000-28 H
1997-2000. Jumbo-size 0000 body, 28 herringbone trim.

1997-2000		$2,200	$2,400

0000-28 H-AG Arlo Guthrie 30th Anniversary
1999. Indian rosewood back and sides, 30 made, 0000 jumbo-size.

1999		$4,000	$4,200

1-17
1906-1917 (1st version), 1931-1934 (2nd version). First version has spruce top, mahogany back and sides. Second version has all mahogany with flat Natural finish.

1906-1917		$1,300	$1,600
1930-1934		$1,500	$1,800

1-18
1899-1927

1899-1927		$2,200	$2,600

1-21
1860-1926. Initially offered in size 1 in the 1860s, ornate soundhole rings.

1860-1899		$2,600	$2,800
1900-1926		$2,700	$2,900

1-26
1950-1890. Rosewood back and sides, ivory-bound top, rope-style purfling.

1850-1890		$2,700	$3,000

1-27
1880-1907.

1880-1907		$3,500	$4,100

1-28
1880-1923. Style 28 appointments including Brazilian rosewood back and sides.

1900-1923		$4,200	$5,200

1-45
1904-1919. Only six made, slotted headstock and Style 45 appointments.

1904-1919		$16,000	$20,000

Martin 000-28 EC

Martin 000-45 JR

Martin D12-28

Martin DC-1E

MODEL YEAR	FEATURES	EXC. COND. LOW	HIGH
2-15			
1939-1964. All mahogany body, dot markers.			
1939	Special order	$1,100	$1,300
2-17			
1910, 1922-1938. 1910 version has spruce top, mahogany back and sides. 1922 on, all mahogany body. No body binding after 1930.			
1910	6 made	$1,500	$1,800
1922-1930		$1,300	$1,600
2-17 H			
1927-1931. Hawaiian, all mahogany, 12 frets clear of body.			
1927-1931		$1,400	$1,700
2-24			
1857-1898.			
1857-1898		$2,600	$2,900
2-27			
1857-1907. Brazilian rosewood back and sides, pearl ring, zigzag back stripe, ivory bound ebony fingerboard and peghead.			
1857-1899		$3,300	$4,000
1900-1907		$3,300	$4,000
2-28 T			
1929-1930. Tenor neck, Brazilian rosewood back and sides, herringbone top purfling.			
1929-1930		$2,000	$2,500
2-30			
1902-1921. Similar to 2-27.			
1902-1921	7 made	$3,600	$4,200
2-34			
1870-1898. Similar to 2-30.			
1870-1898		$3,600	$4,200
2 1/2-17			
1856-1897, 1909-1914. The first Style 17s were small size 2 1/2 and 3, these early models use Brazilian rosewood.			
1890-1897		$1,500	$1,800
1909-1914		$1,300	$1,600
2 1/2-18			
1865-1923. Parlor-size body with Style 18 appointments.			
1865-1898		$2,100	$2,500
1901-1923		$2,100	$2,500
3-17			
1856-1897, 1908 (one made). The first Style 17s were small size 2 1/2 and 3. The early models use Brazilian rosewood, spruce top, bound back, unbound ebony fingerboard.			
1890-1897		$1,400	$1,700
1908	1 made	$1,400	$1,700
5-15 T			
1949-1963. All mahogany, non-gloss finish, tenor neck.			
1949-1963		$1,000	$1,500
5-17 T			
1927-1949. All mahogany, tenor neck.			
1927-1949		$1,100	$1,600

MODEL YEAR	FEATURES	EXC. COND. LOW	HIGH
5-18			
1898-1989. Rosewood back and sides (changed to mahogany from 1917 on), 12 frets, slotted headstock.			
1898-1922	Gut strings	$1,900	$2,300
1923-1939	Braced for steel in '23	$2,100	$2,500
1940-1944		$2,000	$2,400
1945-1949		$1,900	$2,300
1950-1959		$1,800	$2,000
1960-1969		$1,500	$1,800
1970-1989		$1,000	$1,500
5-21 T			
1926-1928. Tenor guitar with 21-styling.			
1926-1928		$1,900	$2,400
5-28			
2001-2002. Special edition, 1/2-size parlor guitar size 15 with Terz tuning (2 1/1 steps), Indian rosewood back and sides.			
2001-2002		$1,700	$2,100
7-28			
1980-1995, 1997-2002. Seven/eighths body size of a D-model, Style 28 appointments.			
1980-1995		$1,700	$2,100
1997-2002		$1,700	$2,100
C-1			
1931-1942. Acoustic archtop, mahogany back and sides, spruce top, round hole until 1933, F-holes appear in 1932, bound body. Sunburst.			
1931-1933	Round, 449 made	$1,900	$2,100
1932-1942	F-hole, 786 made	$1,900	$2,100
C-2			
1931-1942. Acoustic archtop, Brazilian rosewood back and sides, carved spruce top, round hole until 1933, F-holes appear in 1932, zigzag back stripe, multi-bound body, slotted-diamond inlay. Sunburst.			
1931-1933	Round, 269 made	$2,500	$3,200
1932-1942	F-hole, 439 made	$2,500	$3,200
C-2 Conversion			
1931-1942. The Vintage Guitar Price Guide lists original, excellent condition instruments. A C-2 Conversion is an exception. The C-2 archtop was not and continues to be generally less popular than a flat top with similar appointments. C series archtops and H series Hawaiians converted to Spanish setup flat tops have more appeal to some players and collectors. The C-2 Conversion requires removal of the arched top and installation of a high quality spruce top. Appointments may vary.			
1931-1942	High-end appointments	$6,000	$11,000
C-3			
1931-1933. Rosewood back and sides.			
1931-1933	Round, 53 made	$4,200	$5,300
1932-1933	F-hole, 58 made	$4,200	$5,300
D-1			
1992-present. Name first used for the prototype of the D-18, made in 1931. Name revived for current model with mahogany body, "A-frame" bracing, available as an acoustic/electric.			
1992-1999		$550	$600

MODEL YEAR	FEATURES	EXC. COND. LOW	EXC. COND. HIGH

D3-18
1991. Sitka spruce top, 3 piece mahogany back, 80 piece limited edition.

1991		$1,800	$2,400

D12-18
1973-1995. Mahogany back and sides, 12 strings, 14 frets clear of body, solid headstock.

1973-1979		$1,300	$1,400
1980-1989		$1,200	$1,300
1990-1995		$1,100	$1,300

D12-20
1964-1991. Mahogany back and sides, 12 strings, 12 frets clear of body, slotted headstock.

1964-1969		$1,500	$1,900
1970-1979		$1,400	$1,500
1980-1991		$1,300	$1,400

D12-28
1970-present. Indian rosewood back and sides, 12 strings, 14 frets clear of body, solid headstock.

1970-1979		$1,500	$1,800
1980-1989		$1,500	$1,700
1990-1999		$1,400	$1,600

D12-35
1965-1995. Brazilian rosewood back and sides, changed to Indian rosewood in 1970, 12 strings, 12 frets clear of body, slotted headstock.

1965-1969	Brazilian rosewood	$2,900	$3,400
1970-1979	Indian rosewood	$1,500	$1,800
1980-1989		$1,500	$1,700
1990-1995		$1,400	$1,600

D12-45 (special order)
1970s. Special order instrument, not a standard catalog item, with D-45 appointments, Indian rosewood.

1970-1979		$4,500	$5,500

D12XM
1999-2000. 12 string version of the DXM.

1999-2000		$350	$450

D-15
1997-present. All mahogany body.

1997-2002		$475	$550

D-16 A
1987-1990. North American ash back and sides, solid spruce top, scalloped bracing, rosewood fingerboard and bridge, solid mahogany neck.

1987-1990		$1,000	$1,200

D-16 GT
1999-present. D-16 T specs with mahogany back and sides, but with glossy top instead of satin.

1999		$650	$800

D-16 H
1991-1995. Full-size dreadnought, mahogany back and sides with satin finish, herringbone marquetry, vintage X-bracing, scalloped braces, optional acoustic pickup or active preamp system. Replaced by D-16 T in 1996.

1991-1995		$1,000	$1,200

D-16 M
1986, 1988-1990. Mahogany back and sides, non-gloss satin finish.

1988-1990		$800	$900

D-16 T
1995-2002. Solid spruce top, solid mahogany back and sides, scalloped braces, satin finish.

1995-2002		$850	$950

D-16 TR
1995-2002. Indian rosewood version of 16 T.

1995-2002		$1,200	$1,300

D-18
1932-present. Mahogany back and sides, spruce top, Black back stripe, 12-fret neck, changed to 14 frets in 1934.

1932-1933	12-fret neck	$22,000	$25,000
1934-1939	14-fret neck	$17,000	$22,000
1940-1941		$13,000	$16,000
1942-1944	Scalloped braces	$9,700	$13,000
1944-1946	Non-scalloped braces	$6,000	$8,500
1947-1949		$5,000	$6,500
1950-1952		$4,000	$5,000
1953-1959		$3,500	$4,500
1960-1962		$3,200	$4,000
1963-1965		$2,800	$3,300
1966	Black guard late '66	$2,300	$2,700
1966	Tortoise guard early '66	$2,500	$2,800
1967	Last of maple bridgeplate	$2,100	$2,500
1968	Rosewood bridgeplate	$1,900	$2,300
1969		$1,600	$1,900
1970-1979		$1,300	$1,600
1980-1989		$1,200	$1,300
1990-1999		$1,100	$1,300
2000-2002		$1,100	$1,200

D-18 E
1958-1959. D-18 factory built with DeArmond pickups which required ladder bracing (reducing acoustic volume and quality).

1958-1959		$2,900	$3,200

D-18 GE (Golden Era)
1995. Part of the Golden Era Series, copy of 1937 D-18, 272 made.

1995		$1,800	$2,300

D-18 LE
1986-1987. Limited Edition, quilted or flamed mahogany back and sides, scalloped braces, Gold tuners with ebony buttons.

1986-1987		$1,700	$1,900

D-18 MB
1990. Limited Edition Guitar of the Month, flame maple binding, Engelmann spruce top signed by shop foremen, X-brace. Total of 99 sold.

1990		$1,600	$1,800

D-18 S
1967-1993. Mahogany back and sides, 12-fret neck, slotted headstock. Majority of production before 1977, infrequent after that.

1967-1969		$1,600	$2,500
1970-1979		$1,300	$1,600
1980-1993		$1,100	$1,300

1990s Martin D-16H

Martin D-18

Martin D-18V

1966 Martin D-35

D-18 V (Vintage)
1992. Guitar of the month, low-profile neck, scalloped braces, bound. Total of 218 sold.

1992		$1,700	$1,800

D-18 VM/V
1996-present. 14 fret vintage series, mahogany body. "M" dropped from name in '99.

1996-1999		$1,400	$1,500

D-18 VMS
1996-2002. VM with 12 fret neck and slotted headstock.

1996-1999		$1,500	$1,750

D-19
1977-1988. Deluxe mahogany dreadnought, optional mahogany top, multi-bound but unbound rosewood fingerboard.

1977-1988		$1,200	$1,400

D-21
1955-1969. Brazilian rosewood back and sides, rosewood fingerboard, chrome tuners.

1955-1958	Klusons to early '58	$5,200	$6,200
1958-1959	Grover tuners late '58	$4,800	$5,700
1960-1962		$4,400	$5,300
1963-1965		$4,100	$4,900
1966-1967		$3,800	$4,500
1968-1969		$3,200	$3,800

D-25 K
1980-1989. Dreadnought-size with koa back and sides and spruce top.

1980-1989		$1,500	$1,700

D-25 K2
1980-1989. Same as D-25K, but with koa top and Black pickguard.

1980-1989		$1,600	$1,800

D-28
1931-present. Brazilian rosewood back and sides (changed to Indian rosewood in 1970), 1936 was the last year for the 12-fret model, 1944 was the last year for scalloped bracing, 1947 was the last year herringbone trim was offered, Natural. Ultra high-end D-28 Martin guitar (pre-1947) valuations are very sensitive to structural and cosmetic condition. Finish wear and body cracks for ultra high-end Martin flat tops should be evaluated on a case-by-case basis. Small variances within the 'excellent condition' category can lead to notable valuation differences.

1931-1932		$55,000	$65,000
1933		$50,000	$60,000
1934-1936	14-fret neck	$35,000	$45,000
1937-1939		$30,000	$40,000
1940-1941		$29,000	$35,000
1942-1944	Scalloped braces	$25,000	$29,000
1944-1946	Herringbone, non-scalloped	$15,000	$21,000
1947-1949	Non-herringbone starting '47	$9,500	$11,000
1950-1952		$7,500	$9,000
1953-1958	Klusons to early '58	$7,000	$7,500
1958-1959	Grover tuners late '58	$6,500	$7,000

1960-1962		$6,000	$6,500
1963-1965		$5,500	$6,000
1966	Black guard late '66	$4,900	$5,400
1966	Tortoise guard early '66	$5,000	$5,500
1967	Last of maple bridgeplate	$4,800	$5,300
1968	Rosewood bridgeplate	$4,000	$4,800
1969	Last of Brazilian rosewood	$3,900	$4,700
1970-1979	Indian rosewood	$1,700	$2,000
1980-1989		$1,700	$1,900
1990-1999		$1,400	$1,600
2000-2002		$1,400	$1,600

D-28 (1935 Special)
1993. Guitar of the Month, 1935 features, Indian rosewood back and sides, peghead with Brazilian rosewood veneer.

1993		$1,600	$2,200

D-28 50th Anniversary
1983. Stamped inside 1833-1983 150th Anniversary, Indian rosewood back and sides.

1983		$1,500	$1,800

D-28 E
1959-1964. Electric, Brazilian rosewood back and sides, two DeArmond pickups, Natural.

1959-1964		$3,400	$3,600

D-28 GE (Golden Era)
1999-2002. GE (Golden Era), Brazilian rosewood.

1999-2002		$5,400	$6,000

D-28 LSH
1991. Guitar of the Month, Indian rosewood back and sides, herringbone trim, snowflake inlay, zigzag back stripe.

1991		$1,600	$1,800

D-28 P
1988-1990. P stands for low-profile neck, Indian rosewood back and sides.

1988-1990		$1,200	$1,500

D-28 S
1954-1993. Rosewood back and sides, 12-fret neck.

1954-1965		$5,000	$6,500
1966-1969	Brazilian rosewood	$3,900	$5,400
1970-1979	Indian rosewood	$1,700	$2,000
1980-1993		$1,700	$1,900

D-28 V
1983-1985. Brazilian rosewood back and sides, Limited Edition, herringbone trim, slotted diamond inlay.

1983-1985		$4,000	$5,000

D-2832 Shenandoah
1984-1992. Dreadnought acoustic, Thinline pickup, spruce top, V-neck, laminated rosewood sides, three-piece rosewood back.

1984-1992		$500	$700

D-35
1965-present. Brazilian rosewood back and sides, changed to Indian rosewood in 1970, three-piece back, Natural with Sunburst option.

1965		$4,000	$5,000

MODEL YEAR	FEATURES	EXC. COND. LOW	HIGH
1966		$3,500	$4,000
1967		$3,400	$3,800
1968		$3,000	$3,400
1969	Brazilian rosewood	$2,900	$3,300
1970-1979	Indian rosewood	$1,700	$2,000
1970-1979	Sunburst option	$1,800	$2,100
1980-1989		$1,600	$1,800
1980-1989	Sunburst optioin	$1,700	$1,900
1990-1999		$1,300	$1,500
2000s		$1,400	$1,500

D-35 S
1966-1993. Brazilian rosewood back and sides, changed to Indian rosewood in 1970, 12-fret neck, slotted peghead.

1966-1969	Brazilian rosewood	$2,900	$4,000
1970-1979	Indian rosewood	$1,700	$2,000
1980-1989		$1,600	$1,800
1990-1993		$1,300	$1,500

D-3532 Shenandoah
1984-1993. Dreadnought acoustic, spruce top, V-neck, laminated rosewood sides, three-piece rosewood back.

1984-1993		$600	$900

D-37 K
1980-1995. Dreadnought-size, koa back and sides, spruce top.

1980-1995		$2,000	$2,200

D-37 K2
1980-1995. Same as D-37 K, but has a koa top and Black pickguard.

1980-1995		$2,000	$2,200

D-41
1969-present. Brazilian rosewood back and sides for the first ones in 1969 then Indian rosewood, bound body, scalloped braces, Natural.

1969	Brazilian rosewood	$8,000	$14,000
1970-1979	Indian rosewood	$3,000	$3,500
1980-1989		$2,600	$3,000
1990-1999		$2,200	$2,500
1990-1999	Sunburst option	$2,300	$2,700
2000-2002		$2,100	$2,300

D-41 BLE
1989. Guitar of the Month, Brazilian rosewood back and sides, inlaid abalone binding on top, soundhole, fingerboard and headstock, hexagon fingerboard inlays, abalone C.F. Martin headstock logo. Total of 58 sold.

1989		$2,800	$3,800

D-42
1996-present. Dreadnought, Indian rosewood back and sides, spruce top, pearl rosette and inlays, snowflake fingerboard inlays, Gold tuners, gloss finish.

1996-2002		$2,600	$2,800

D-42 K/D-42 K2
2000s. All koa body, figured top.

2000s		$2,100	$2,300

D-42 LE
1988 only. D-42-style, limited edition (75 sold), scalloped braces, low profile neck.

1988		$2,100	$2,500

D-42 V
1985. Vintage Series, 12 made, Brazilian rosewood, scalloped braces.

1985		$7,500	$9,000

D-45
1933-1942 (96 made), 1968-present. Brazilian rosewood back and sides, changed to Indian rosewood during 1969. The pre-World War II Martin D-45 is one of the "holy grails." The noted price ranges are guidance pricing only. A pre-war D-45, or any ultra-expensive vintage guitar, should be evaluated on a case-by-case basis. The price ranges are for all-original guitars in excellent condition. These ranges are for a crack-free guitar. Unfortunately, many older acoustics have a crack or two. Because of these cracks, ultra-expensive acoustics are generally more difficult to evaluate than ultra-expensive solidbody electrics. Technically, a repaired body crack makes a guitar non-original, but the vintage market generally considers a professionally repaired crack to be original. Crack width, length and depth can vary, therefore extra attention to detail is suggested.

1936	Only 2 made	$190,000	$240,000
1937	Only 2 made	$175,000	$220,000
1938	Only 9 made	$170,000	$210,000
1939	Only 14 made	$160,000	$175,000
1940	Only 19 made	$150,000	$170,000
1941	Only 24 made	$140,000	$160,000
1942	Only 19 made	$130,000	$150,000
1968-1969	Brazilian rosewood	$25,000	$27,000
1970-1974	Indian rosewood, 105 made	$6,200	$6,600
1975-1979		$5,800	$6,300
1980-1987		$5,500	$6,000
1988-1989	Scalloped braces, low profile	$4,400	$5,000
1990-1999		$4,200	$4,500
2000-2002		$4,200	$4,500

D-45 (1939 Reissue)
High-grade spruce top, figured Brazilian rosewood back and sides, high X and scalloped braces, abalone trim, Natural, Gold tuners.

1992		$11,000	$14,000

D-45 200th Anniversary (C.F. Martin Sr. Deluxe)
1996 only. Commemorative model for C.F. Martin Sr.'s birth in 1796, Brazilian Deluxe Edition, Natural.

1996		$13,000	$15,000

D-45 Custom
Brazilian rosewood back and sides.

1991-1992		$5,000	$10,000

D-45 Deluxe
1993 only. Guitar of the Month, Brazilian rosewood back and sides, figured spruce top, inlay in bridge and pickguard, "Tree of Life" inlay on fingerboard, pearl borders and back stripe, Gold tuners with large Gold buttons. Total of 60 sold.

1993		$15,000	$17,000

Martin D-41

1997 Martin D-45

Martin D-50 Koa

1963 Martin F-65

MODEL YEAR	FEATURES	EXC. COND. LOW	HIGH

D-45 Gene Autry
1994 only. Gene Autry inlay (two options available), Natural.

1994		$12,000	$17,000

D-45 S
1969-1993. Brazilian rosewood back and sides, 12-fret neck, S means slotted peghead, only 50 made.

1988-1993		$6,000	$8,000

D-45 Steven Stills Signature
2002. Limited edition of 91.

2002		$12,000	$14,000

D-45 V
1983-1985. Brazilian rosewood back and sides, scalloped braces, snowflake inlay, Natural. Name revived in '99.

1983-1985		$12,000	$13,000

D-45 VR
1997-Present. Scalloped braces, high X-bracing, vintage aging toner, snowflake inlay. Name changed to D-45 V in '99.

1997-2001		$5,000	$5,500

D-62
1989-1995. Dreadnought, flamed maple back and sides, spruce top, chrome-plated enclosed Schaller tuners.

1989-1995		$1,600	$2,000

D-62 LE
1986. Flamed maple back and sides, spruce top, snowflake inlays, Natural, Guitar of the Month October 1986.

1986		$1,800	$2,200

D-76
1975-1976. Limited Edition, Indian rosewood back and sides, three-piece back, herringbone back stripe, pearl stars on fingerboard, eagle on peghead. Only 200 made in 1975 and 1,976 made in 1976.

1976		$2,700	$3,000

DC-1 E/DC-1 M (cutaway)
1995-present. Cutaway design, all solid wood, mahogany back and sides, spruce top, transducer pickup.

1995-1999		$800	$900

DM
1990-present. Solid sitka spruce top, laminated mahogany back and sides, dot markers, Natural satin.

1990-1999		$500	$600

DXM
1998-present. Wood composite mahogany laminate D body, solid wood neck, decal rosette, screened headstock logo, unique DX bracing.

1998-2001		$375	$425

E-18
1979-1982. Offset double cutaway, maple and rosewood laminate solidbody, two DiMarzio pickups, phase switch, Natural.

1979-1982		$600	$800

MODEL YEAR	FEATURES	EXC. COND. LOW	HIGH

EM-18
1979-1982. Offset double cutaway, maple and rosewood laminate solidbody, two exposed-coil humbucking pickups, coil split switch.

1979-1982		$600	$800

EMP-1
1998-1999. Employee series designed by Martin employee team, cutaway solid spruce top, ovangkol wood back and sides with rosewood middle insert (D-35-style insert), on-board pickup.

1998-1999		$1,900	$2,200

F-1
1940-1942. Mahogany back and sides, carved spruce top, multi-bound, F-holes. Sunburst.

1940-1942	91 made	$1,900	$2,200

F-2
1940-1942.

1940-1942	46 made	$2,300	$3,000

F-7
1935-1942. Brazilian rosewood back and sides, F-holes, carved top, back arched by braces, multi-bound. Sunburst top finish.

1935-1942		$6,000	$7,000

F-9
1935-1941. Highest-end archtop, Brazilian rosewood, Martin inlaid vertically on headstock, seven-ply top binding, 45-style back strip. Sunburst.

1935-1941		$10,000	$14,000

F-50
1961-1965. Single cutaway thinline archtop with laminated maple body, one pickup.

1961-1965		$1,100	$1,300

F-55
1961-1965. Single cutaway thinline archtop with laminated maple body, two pickups.

1961-1965		$1,100	$1,400

F-65
1961-1965. Electric archtop, double cutaway, F-holes, two pickups, square-cornered peghead, Bigsby. Sunburst.

1961-1965		$1,400	$1,700

GT-70
1966-1968. Electric archtop, bound body, F-holes, single cutaway, two pickups, tremolo. Burgundy or Black finish.

1966-1968		$1,100	$1,400

GT-75
1966-1968. Electric archtop, bound body, F-holes, double cutaway, two pickups, tremolo. Burgundy or Black finish.

1966-1968		$1,400	$1,700

Hawaiian X
2002-present. Hawaiian scene painted on top, similar to the Cowboy guitar model, limited edition of 500.

2002		$800	$1,000

HD-28 (Standard Series)
1976-present. Indian rosewood back and sides, scalloped bracing, herringbone purfling.

1976-1979		$1,700	$2,000
1980-1989		$1,600	$1,900

MODEL YEAR	FEATURES	EXC. COND. LOW	HIGH
1990-1999		$1,500	$1,800
2000-2002		$1,500	$1,800

HD-28 BLE
1990. Guitar of the Month, Brazilian rosewood back and sides, herringbone soundhole ring, low profile neck (LE), chrome tuners.

1990		$4,000	$5,000

HD-28 GM LSH
1994. "Grand Marquis" Guitar of the Month, rosewood back and sides, large soundhole with double herringbone rings, snowflake inlay in bridge.

1994		$2,500	$3,000

HD-28 LE
1985. Guitar of the Month, rosewood back and sides, scalloped bracing, herringbone top purfling, diamonds and squares fingerboard inlay, V-neck.

1985		$2,500	$2,800

HD-28 MP
1990. Bolivian rosewood back and sides, scalloped braces, herringbone top purfling, zipper back stripe, low profile neck.

1990		$1,500	$1,800

HD-28 P
1987-1989. Rosewood back and sides, scalloped braces, herringbone, low profile neck (P), zigzag back stripe.

1987-1989		$1,500	$1,800

HD-28 VR/V
1996-present. 14 fret vintage series, rosewood body. "R" dropped from name in '99.

1996-2000		$1,700	$1,800

HD-282 R
1994 only.

1994		$1,360	$1,700

HD-2832 Shenandoah
1983-1993. Herringbone trim version of the D-2832.

1983-1993		$500	$700

HD-35
1978-present. Indian rosewood back and sides, herringbone top trim, zipper back stripe.

1978-1979		$1,700	$2,000
1980-1989		$1,600	$1,800
1990-1999		$1,600	$1,700

HOM-35
1989. Herringbone Orchestra Model Guitar of the Month, scalloped braces, three-piece Brazilian rosewood back, bookmatched sides, 14-fret neck. Only 60 built.

1989		$4,500	$5,000

J-1 Jumbo
1997-2002. Jumbo body with mahogany back and sides.

1997-2002		$850	$900

J-18/J-18M
1987-1996. J-size body with Style 18 appointments, natural. Called J-18M for '87-'89.

1987-1996		$1,200	$1,300

J-40
1990-present. Called J-40 M from 1985-1989. Jumbo, Indian rosewood back and sides, triple-bound fingerboard, hexagonal inlays.

1990-1999		$1,800	$2,200

J-40 M
1985-1989. Jumbo, Indian rosewood back and sides, triple-bound fingerboard, hexagonal inlays. Name changed to J-40 in 1990.

1985-1989		$1,800	$2,200

J-65/J-65 M/J-65 E
1985-1995. Jumbo acoustic featuring maple back and sides, gold-plated tuners, scalloped bracing, ebony fingerboard, tortoiseshell-style binding.

1985-1995		$1,800	$2,200

J12-40
1985-1996. Called J12-40 M from '85-'90. Rosewood back and sides, 12 strings, 16" jumbo size, 14-fret neck, solid peghead, gold tuners.

1996		$1,500	$1,800

J12-65
1985-1995. Called J12-65m for '84-'90. Jumbo-style 65 12-string, spruce top, figured maple back and sides, gold-plated tuning machines, scalloped bracing, ebony board, tortoiseshell-style binding. Natural.

1985-1995		$1,500	$1,800

M-21 Custom
December 1984. Guitar of the Month, low profile neck M-Series, Indian rosewood back and sides, special ornamentation.

1984		$1,800	$2,100

M-36
1978-1997. Indian rosewood back and sides, bound fingerboard, low profile neck, multi-bound, White-Black-White back stripes.

1978-1997		$1,400	$1,500

M-38
1977-1996. Indian rosewood back and sides, multi-bound, low profile neck, gold-plated tuners, stained top.

1977-1996		$1,900	$2,100

MC-28
1981-1996. Rosewood back and sides, single cutaway acoustic, oval soundhole, scalloped braces. Natural.

1981-1996		$1,500	$1,600

MC-68
1985-1995. Auditorium-size acoustic, rounded cutaway, maple back and sides, Gold tuners, scalloped bracing, ebony fingerboard, tortoiseshell-style binding. Natural or Sunburst.

1985-1995		$1,600	$1,700

MTV-1 Unplugged
1996. Body is 1/2 rosewood and 1/2 mahogany, scalloped bracing, MTV logo on headstock.

1996		$1,600	$1,700

1966 Martin GT-75

Martin J-40

GUITARS

1927 Martin 0M-28

1937 Martin R-18

MODEL YEAR	FEATURES	EXC. COND. LOW	HIGH

N-10
1968-1995. Classical, mahogany back and sides, fan bracing, wood marquetry soundhole ring, unbound rosewood fingerboard, 12-fret neck and slotted peghead from 1970.

1968-1969	Short-scale	$1,300	$1,700
1970-1979	Long-scale	$1,200	$1,500
1980-1989	Long-scale	$1,150	$1,400
1990-1995	Long-scale	$1,050	$1,300

N-20
1968-1995. Classical, Brazilian rosewood back and sides (changed to Indian rosewood in 1969), multi-bound, 12-fret neck, solid headstock (changed to slotted in 1970). Natural.

1968-1969	Brazilian rosewood, short-scale	$2,500	$3,500
1970-1979	Indian rosewood, long-scale	$1,500	$1,800
1980-1989	Long-scale	$1,400	$1,700
1990-1995	Long-scale	$1,300	$1,600

OM-18
1930-1934. Orchestra Model, mahogany back and sides, 14-fret neck, solid peghead, banjo tuners (changed to right-angle in 1931).

1930-1933	Natural	$12,000	$15,000
1934	Sunburst option	$13,000	$16,000

OM-18 V
1999-present. Vintage features.

1999-2002		$1,500	$1,800

OM-21 (Standard Series)
1992-1997. Triple 0-size, 15 1/8", spruce top, rosewood back and sides. Natural.

1992-1997		$1,200	$1,300

OM-28
1929-1933. Orchestra Model, Brazilian rosewood back and sides, 14-fret neck, solid peghead, banjo tuners (changed to right-angle in 1931). Reintroduced with Indian rosewood in 1990.

1929-1930	Small guard, banjo tuners	$32,000	$35,000
1931-1933	Large guard	$25,000	$28,000

OM-28 (reissue)
1990-1996. Indian rosewood back and sides.

1990-1996		$1,800	$2,200

OM-28 PB (Perry Bechtel)
1993. Guitar of the Month, signed by Perry Bechtel's widow Ina, spruce top, Indian rosewood back and sides, zigzag back stripe, chrome tuners, V-neck, only 50 made.

1993		$5,000	$5,300

OM-28 VR
1990-1996. Orchestra Model, reintroduced OM-28 with rosewood back and sides.

1990-1996		$1,800	$2,100

OM-42 PS (Paul Simon)
1997. Bookmatched sitka spruce top, Indian rosewood back and sides, 42 and 45-style features, low profile PS neck, 500 made.

1997		$4,000	$4,300

MODEL YEAR	FEATURES	EXC. COND. LOW	HIGH

OM-42 Reissue
1999-present. Indian rosewood back and sides, Style 45 snowflake markes, rounded neck profile.

1999-2002		$2,600	$2,750

OM-45 Deluxe/OM-45
1930-1933. OM-style, 45 level appointments with pearl inlay in pickguard and bridge. Only 14 OM-45 Deluxe instruments made. Regular OM-45 with normal 45-style appointments. Condition is critically important on this or any ultra high-end instrument, minor flaws are critical to value.

1930	OM-45 Deluxe	$90,000	$120,000
1930-1933	OM-45	$75,000	$90,000

OM-45 Deluxe Reissue
1994.

1994		$4,000	$4,200

Custom OM-45 Deluxe (custom shop)
1998-1999. Limited custom shop run of 14, Adirondack spruce and typical Style 45 appointments.

1998-1999		$14,000	$15,000

OMC-28
1990. Guitar of the Month with rounded cutaway, Gold tuners, low profile neck, pearl Martin script logo in headstock, label signed by C.F. Martin IV.

1990		$1,700	$2,100

R-17
1934-1942. All mahogany, archtop and back, three-segment F-holes (changed to one-segment in 1937), 12-fret neck. Sunburst finish.

1934-1942	940 made	$800	$1,100

R-18
1933-1942. Spruce arched top (carved top by 1937), mahogany back and sides, 14-fret neck, bound top. Sunburst.

1933-1942	1,928 made	$1,400	$1,800

SPD-16 TR
Special Edition D-body cutaway, all solid wood with spruce top, rosewood back and sides, abalone snowflake markers.

1996		$1,200	$1,300

Stauffer
1830s-ca.1850s. One of C.F. Martin's earliest models, distinguished by the scrolled, six-on-a-side headstock. Ornamentation varies from guitar to guitar.

1830s	Plain, no ivory	$3,000	$7,000
1830s	Very fancy, ivory board and bridge	$5,000	$12,000

Marvel
Ca. 1950s- ca. 1960s. Brand name used for budget instruments marketed by Peter Sorkin Company in New York, New York. Sorkin manufactured and distributed Premier guitars and amplifiers made by its Multivox subsidiary.

Marvel instruments were primarily beginner-grade. Brand disappears by mid-1960s.

Electric Solidbody Guitars
1950s-mid-1960s. Various models.

1950s		$125	$225

MODEL		EXC. COND.	
YEAR	FEATURES	LOW	HIGH

Mason

1936-1939. Henry L. Mason on headstock, wholesale distribution, similar to Gibson/Cromwell, pressed wood back and sides.

Student/Intermediate Student Guitars

1936-1939. Various flat-top and archtop student/budget models.

1936-1939		$300	$700

Maton

1946-present. Intermediate and professional grade, production/custom, acoustic, acoustic/electric, hollow body and solidbody guitars built in Box Hill, Victoria, Australia. Founded by Bill May and his brother Reg and still run by the family. Only available in USA since '82.

Mauel Guitars

1995-present. Luthier Hank Mauel builds his premium grade, custom, flat-tops in Auburn, California.

Maurer

1900-1944. Robert Maurer's Chicago-based woodworking shop was bought by Larson Brothers in 1900, but the Maurer name was retained. Low-end and high quality models were offered.

13" Acoustic Flat-Top (Standard)

Early-1900s. Rosewood back and sides, spruce top, 12 3/4", made by Larson Brothers of Chicago.

1910		$2,000	$3,000

13" Higher-End Flat-Top (Brazilian)

Early-1900s. Spruce top, 13 5/8", Brazilian rosewood back and sides, high-end pearl appointments, slotted headstock.

1910	Natural	$4,000	$5,000

14" Flat-Top (Brazilian)

1920s-1930s. Mid-sized (about 14") with Brazilian rosewood back and sides, attractive appointments.

1920s	Abalone trim	$6,500	$8,500
1930s		$6,500	$8,500

14" Flat-Top (Mahogany)

1920s-1930s. Mid-sized (about 14") with mahogany back and sides, standard appointments.

1930s		$3,000	$4,000

15" High-end Flat-Top (Brazilian)

Early-1900s. Brazilian rosewood back and sides, tree of life inlay, 15", pearl-bound.

1920s		$9,000	$11,500

McAlister Guitars

1997-present. Premium grade, custom, flat-tops built by luthier Roy McAlister in Watsonville, California.

McCollum Guitars

1994-present. Luthier Lance McCollum builds his premium grade, custom, flat-top and harp guitars in Colfax, California.

McCurdy Guitars

1983-present. Premium grade, production/custom, archtops built by luthier Ric McCurdy originally in Santa Barbara, California and, since 1991, New York, New York.

McGill Guitars

1976-present. Luthier Paul McGill builds his premium grade, production/custom, classical, resonator, and acoustic/electric guitars in Nashville, Tennessee.

MCI, Inc

1967-1990s. MusiConics International (MCI), of Waco, Texas, introduced the world to the Guitorgan, invented by Bob Murrell. Later, they also offered effects and a steel guitar. In the '90s, a MIDI version was offered. MCI was also involved with the Daion line of guitars in the late '70s and early '80s.

GuitOrgan B-35

1970s (ca. 1976-1978?). Duplicated the sounds of an organ and more. MCI bought ES-335-style guitars from others (Univox) and outfitted them with lots of switches and buttons. Each fret has six segments that correspond to an organ tone. There was also a B-300 version.

1976		$1,200	$1,700

McInturff

1996-present. Professional and premium grade, production/custom, solidbody guitars built by luthier Terry C. McInturff in Holly Springs, North Carolina. McInturff spent 17 years during guitar repair and custom work before starting his own guitar line.

Taurus Standard

Single cutaway, carved flamed maple top on chambered mahogany body, dual humbucker pickups, Gold hardware.

1996-2001	Sunburst	$1,800	$2,100

McPherson Guitars

1981-present. Premium grade, production, flat-tops built by luthier Mander McPherson in Sparta, Wisconsin.

Mean Gene

1988-1990. Heavy metal style solidbodies made by Gene Baker, who started Baker U.S.A. guitars in '97, and Eric Zoellner in Santa Maria, California. They built around 30 custom guitars.

Megas Guitars

1989-present. Luthier Ted Megas builds his premium grade, custom, archtop and solidbody guitars, originally in San Franciso, and currently in Portland, Oregon.

McCollum flat-top

McInturff Sportster

Mercurio T3

Metropolitan Glendale Deluxe

MODEL YEAR	FEATURES	EXC. COND. LOW	HIGH

Melancon

Professional and premium garde, custom/production, solid and semi-hollow body guitars built by luthier Gerard Melancon in Thibodaux, Louisiana. They also build basses.

Mello, John F.

1973-present. Premium grade, production/custom, classical and ftat-top guitars built by luthier John Mello in Kensington, California.

Melophonic

1960s. Brand built by the Valco Company of Chicago.

Resonator Guitar

Valco-made.

1965		$500	$700

Melville Guitars

1988-present. Luthier Christopher Melville builds his premium grade, custom, flat-tops in Milton, Queensland, Australia.

Menkevich Guitars

1970-present. Professional and premium grade, production/custom, classical and flamenco guitars built by luthier Michael Menkevich in Elkins Park, Pennsylvania.

Mercurio

Luthier Peter Mercuio builds his custom/production solidbody guitars, featuring his interchangeable PickupPak system to swap pickups, in Chanhassen, Minnesota.

Mermer Guitars

1983-present. Luthier Richard Mermer builds his premium grade, production/custom, steel-string, nylon-string, and Hawaiian guitars in Sebastian, Florida.

Merrill Brothers

1998-present. Premium grade, production/custom, steel-string and harp guitars built by luthiers Jim and Dave Merrill in Williamsburg, Virginia.

Mesrobian

1995-present. Luthier Carl Mesrobian builds his professional and premium grade, custom, archtop guitars in Salem, Massachusetts.

Messenger

1967-1968. Built by Musicraft, Inc., originally of 156 Montgomery Street, San Francisco, California. The distinguishing feature of the Messengers is a metal alloy neck which extended through the body to the tailblock, plus mono or stereo outputs. Sometime before March '68 the company relocated to Astoria, Oregon. Press touted "improved" magnesium neck, though it's not clear if this constituted a change from '67. Brand disappears after '68.

MODEL YEAR	FEATURES	EXC. COND. LOW	HIGH

Electric Hollowbody Archtop Guitar

1967-1968. Symmetrical vague ES-330 body shape, metal neck with rosewood fingerboards, stereo.

1967-1968	Rojo Red	$2,000	$2,500

Metropolitan

1995-present. Professional and premium grade, production/custom, retro-styled solidbodies designed by David Wintz reminiscent of the '50s National Res-o-glas and wood body guitars. They feature full-scale set-neck construction and a wood body instead of Res-o-glas. Wintz also makes Robin and Alamo brand instruments.

Glendale Custom

1997-present. Single cut, African fakimba body, set-neck, two pickups, various colors.

1997		$1,500	$1,700

Glendale Custom Acoustic

1997-present. Single cut, African fakimba body, set-neck, three pickups including piezo.

1997		$2,000	$2,300

Glendale Deluxe

1997-present. Single cut, African fakimba body, set-neck, two pickups, dot markers.

1997		$900	$1,100

Glendale Super Acoustic

1997-present. Single cut, flamed maple top, three pickups including piezo, Gold hardware.

1997		$3,000	$3,500

Tanglewood Custom

1996-present. Map-shape basswood body, German body carve front and back, 2 humbuckers, bound ebony 'board, butterfly inlays, various colors.

1996-1997		$1,500	$1,700

Tanglewood Custom Acoustic

1996-present. Tanglewood Custom with added piezo bridge pickup, various colors.

1996-1997		$2,000	$2,300

Tanglewood Deluxe

1996-present. Similar to Custom, but with unbound rosewood 'board, dot inlays, German body carve on top only.

1996		$900	$1,100

Westport Custom

1997-present. Single cut, three pickups, art deco design, African fakimba body, set-neck, various colors.

1997		$1,500	$1,700

Westport Custom Acoustic

1997-present. Single cut, three pickups, art deco design, African fakimba body, set-neck.

1997		$2,000	$2,300

Westport Deluxe

1997-present. Single cut, two humbuckers.

1997		$900	$1,000

Westport Super Acoustic

1997-present. Single cut, three pickups with piezo, art deco design, Africa fakimba body, set-neck.

1997		$3,200	$3,500

MODEL YEAR	FEATURES	EXC. COND. LOW	HIGH

Michael Dunn Guitars

1968-present. Luthier Michael Dunn builds his production/custom Maccaferri-style guitars in New Westminster, British Columbia. He also offers a harp uke and a Weissenborn- or Knutsen-style Hawaiian guitar, and has built archtops.

Michael Kelly

1999-present. Intermediate and professional grade, production, acoustic, solidbody and archtop guitars imported by Mailbox Music of Clearwater, Florida. They also offer mandolins and basses.

Michael Lewis Instruments

1992-present. Luthier Michael Lewis builds his premium and presentation grade, custom, archtop guitars in Grass Valley, California. He also builds mandolins.

Michael Silvey Custom Guitars

2003-present. Solidbody electric guitars built by Michael Silvey in North Canton, Ohio.

Microfrets

1967-1967-1975, 2004-present. Professional grade, production, electric guitars built in Myersville, Maryland. They also build basses. Founded by Ralph S. Jones, Sr. in Frederick, Microfrets offered over 20 models of guitars that sported innovative designs and features, with pickups designed by Bill Lawrence. The brand was revived, again in Frederick, by Will Meadors and Paul Rose in '04.

Baritone Signature
1971. Baritone version of Signature Guitar, sharply pointed double cut, with or without f-holes, single or double dot inlays.
1971 — $350 $600

Baritone Stage II
1971-ca. 1975. Double cut, 2 pickups.
1971-1975 — $350 $600

Calibra I
1969-1975. Double cut, 2 pickups, f-hole.
1969-1975 — $450 $500

Covington
1967-1969. Offset double cut, 2 pickups, f-hole.
1967-1969 — $600 $800

Golden Comet
1969-1971. Double cut, 2 pickups, f-hole.
1969-1971 — $400 $600

Golden Melody
1969-1971. Offset double cut, 2 pickups, f-hole, M-shaped metal design behind tailpiece.
1969-1971 — $550 $800

Huntington
1969-1975. Double cut, 2 pickups.
1969-1975 — $550 $800

Orbiter
1967-1969. Odd triple cut body, thumbwheel controls on bottom edge of pickguard.
1967-1969 — $550 $800

Plainsman
1967-1969. Offset double cut, 2 pickups, f-hole, thumbwheel controls on bottom edge of pickguard.
1967-1969 — $700 $900

Signature
1967-1969. Double cut, 2 pickups.
1967-1969 — $300 $600

Spacetone
1969-1971. Double cut, 2 pickups.
1969-1971 — $450 $700

Stage II
1969-1975. Offset double cut, 2 pickups.
1969-1975 — $350 $600

Swinger
1971-1975. Offset double cut, 2 pickups.
1971-1975 — $450 $700

Wanderer
1969. Double cutaway, two pickups.
1969 — $350 $600

Mike Lull Custom Guitars

1995-present. Professional and premium grade, production/custom, guitars built by luthier Mike Lull in Bellevue, Washington. He also builds basses.

Milburn Guitars

1990-present. Luthiers Orville and Robert Milburn build their premium grade, custom, classical guitars in Sweet Home, Oregon.

Minarik

Luthier M.E. Minarik builds his professional and premium grade, custom/production, solid and chambered body guitars in Van Nuys, California.

Mirabella

1997-present. Professional and premium grade, custom archtops, flat-tops, hollowbody, and solidbody guitars built by luthier Cristian Mirabella in Babylon, New York. He also builds mandolins and ukes.

MJ Guitar Engineering

1993-present. Professional and premium grade, production/custom, hollow-body, chambered and solidbody guitars built by luthier Mark Johnson in Rohnert Park, California. He also builds basses.

Modulus

1978-present. Founded by Geoff Gould in the San Francisco area, currently built in Novato, California. Modulus currently offers professional grade, production/custom, solidbody electric guitars. They also build electric basses.

Genesis 2/2T
1996-present. Double cutaway, long extended bass horn alder body, bolt-on carbon fiber/red cedar neck, hum-single-single pickups, locking vibrato (2T model), various colors.
1996-1999 — $1,000 $1,200

1972 Microfrets Calibra I

Mike Lull SX

Monteleone Eclipse

Moonstone M-80

MODEL YEAR	FEATURES	EXC. COND. LOW	HIGH

Moll Custom Instruments

1996-present. Luthier Bill Moll builds his professional and premium grade, archtops in Springfield, Missouri. He has also built violins, violas and cellos.

Monrad, Eric

1993-present. Premium, custom, flamenco and classical guitars built by luthier Eric Monrad in Healdsburg, California.

Montalvo

See listing under Casa Montalvo.

Monteleone

1976-present. Presentation grade, production/custom, archtop guitars built by Luthier John Monteleone in Islip, New York.

Eclipse
17" electric archtop, natural orange.

1991-1992	Natural Orange	$13,000	$18,000
2003	Natural	$18,000	$23,000

OM-42
1970s. Styled like an old Martin OM, spruce top, Brazilian rosewood back.

1975		$10,000	$14,000

Radio City
18" acoustic archtop cutaway, art deco fretboard inlays, golden blond.

1996	Golden Blond	$18,000	$23,000

Moon (Japan)

1979-present. Professional and premium grade, production/custom, guitars made in Japan. They also build basses.

Moon (Scotland)

1979-present. Intermediate, professional and premium grade, production/custom, acoustic and electric guitars built by luthier Jimmy Moon in Glasgow, Scotland. They also build mandolin family instruments.

Moonstone

1972-present. Professional, premium, and presentation grade production/custom flat-top, solid and semi-hollow electric guitars, built by luthier Steve Helgeson in Eureka, California. He also builds basses. Higher unit sales in the early-'80s. Some models have an optional graphite composite neck built by Modulus.

Eclipse Deluxe
1979-1983. Figured bird's-eye body, offset double cutaway, neck-through, Gold hardware, diamond markers. Natural finish.

Eclipse Standard
1979-1983. Figured wood body, offset double cutaway, neck-through, dot markers, standard maple neck. Natural finish.

1979-1983		$1,500	$1,900

MODEL YEAR	FEATURES	EXC. COND. LOW	HIGH

Explorer
1980-1983. Figured wood body, Explorer-style, neck-through, standard maple neck. Natural finish.

1980-1983		$1,500	$1,900

Flaming V
1980-1984. Figured wood body, Flying V-style, neck-through, standard maple neck. Natural finish.

1980-1984		$1,500	$1,900

M-80
1980-1984. Figured wood 335-style body, standard maple or optional graphite neck. Natural finish.

1980s	Optional graphite neck	$2,000	$3,000
1980s	Standard maple neck	$1,800	$2,000

Vulcan Deluxe
1979-1983. Figured maple carved-top body, offset double cutaway, diamond markers, standard maple neck. Natural finish.

1979-1983		$1,600	$2,300

Vulcan Standard
1979-1983. Mahogany carved-top body, offset double cutaway, dot markers, standard maple neck. Natural finish.

1979-1983		$1,500	$2,200

Morales

Ca.1967-1968. Made in Japan by Zen-On. Not heavily imported into the U.S., if at all.

More Harmony

1930s. Private branded by Dobro for Dailey's More Harmony Music Studio. Private branding was common in the 1930s for the Chicago makers, who branded for catalog companies, teaching studios, publishers, and music stores. More Harmony silk-screen logo on the headstock.

More Harmony Dobro
1930s. Fourteen inch wood body with upper bout F-holes and metal resonator.

1930s	Sunburst	$600	$700

Morgaine Guitars

1994-present. Luthier Jorg Tandler builds his professional and premium grade, production/custom electrics in Germany.

Morgan Monroe

1999-present. Intermediate grade, production, acoustic, acoustic/electric and resonator guitars made in Korea and distributed by SHS International of Indianapolis, Indiana. They also offer mandolins, basses, banjos, and fiddles.

Morris

1970s-present. Intermediate, professional and premium grade, production, acoustic guitars imported by Moridaira of Japan. Morris guitars were first imported into the U.S. from the early '70s to around '90. They are again being imported into the U.S. starting in 2001.

GUITARS

MODEL YEAR	FEATURES	EXC. COND. LOW	HIGH

000 Copy
1970s. Brazilian rosewood laminate body, import.

1970s		$300	$400

D-45 Copy
Brazilian laminate body.

1970s		$400	$500

Mortoro Guitars
1992-present. Luthier Gary Mortoro builds his premium grade, custom, archtop guitars in Miami, Florida.

Mosrite
The history of Mosrite has more ups and downs than just about any other guitar company. Founder Semie Moseley had several innovative designs and had his first success, at age 19, building double-neck guitars for super picker Joe Maphis and protégé Larry Collins. Next came the Ventures, who launched the brand nationally by playing Mosrites and featuring them on album covers. At its '60s peak, the company was turning out around 1,000 guitars a month. The company ceased production in '69, and Moseley went back to playing gospel concerts and built a few custom instruments during the '70s.

In the early-'80s, Mosrite again set up shop in Jonas Ridge, North Carolina, but the plant burned down in November, '83, taking about 300 guitars with it. In early-'92, Mosrite relocated to Booneville, Arkansas, producing a new line of Mosrites, of which 96% were exported to Japan, where the Ventures and Mosrite have always been popular. Semie Moseley died, at age 57, on August 7, '92 and the business carried on until finally closing its doors in '93. The Mosrite line has again been revived by Japan's Mosrite of California, which offers intermediate and premium grade, production, reissues. Throughout much of the history of Mosrite, production numbers were small and model features often changed. As a result, exact production dates are difficult to determine.

Brass Rail
1970s. Double cut solidbody, has a brass plate running the length of the fingerboard.

1970s		$800	$900

Celebrity 1
Late-1960s-1970s. Thick hollowbody, two pickups.

1970s	Sunburst	$850	$950

Celebrity 2 Standard
Late-1960s-1970s. Thin hollowbody, two pickups. In the 1970s, it came in a Standard and a Deluxe version.

1970s		$850	$950

MODEL YEAR	FEATURES	EXC. COND. LOW	HIGH

Celebrity 3
Late-1960s. Thin hollowbody, double cutaway, two pickups, F-holes.

1960s		$850	$950

Combo Mark 1
1966-1968. Bound body, one F-hole.

1966-1968		$1,400	$1,600

D-40 Resonator Guitar
1960s.

1960s		$700	$900

D-100 Californian
1960s. Double cut resonator guitar, 2 pickups.

1967		$800	$1,100

Joe Maphis Mark 1
1960s. Double cutaway solidbody, two pickups.

1960s	Natural	$1,000	$1,500

Joe Maphis Mark XVIII
1960s. Six/twelve doubleneck solidbody, double cutaway, two pickups on each neck, Moseley tremolo on six-string.

1960s		$3,000	$4,000

Mosrite 1988
1988-early-1990s. Has traditional Mosrite body styling, Mosrite pickups and bridge.

1988-1990		$500	$800

Ventures 12-String
1966-1968. Double cutaway solidbody, 12 strings.

1967		$1,500	$1,800

Ventures Mark V
1963-1968. Double cutaway solidbody.

1960s		$1,800	$2,000

Ventures Model
1963-1968. Double cutaway solidbody, triple-bound body 1963, no binding after, Vibramute for 1963-1964, Moseley tailpiece 1965-1968.

1963	Blue, bound	$5,700	$7,000
1963	Red, bound	$5,700	$7,000
1963	Sunburst, bound	$5,200	$6,500
1964	Blue, Vibramute	$4,700	$6,500
1964	Red, Vibramute	$4,700	$6,500
1964	Sunburst, Vibramute	$4,700	$6,000
1965	Blue, Moseley tailpiece	$3,700	$4,500
1965	Blue, Vibramute	$4,700	$6,500
1965	Red, Moseley tailpiece	$3,700	$4,500
1965	Red, Vibramute	$4,700	$6,500
1965	Sunburst, Moseley tailpiece	$3,700	$4,000
1965	Sunburst, Vibramute	$4,700	$6,000
1966	Moseley tailpiece	$3,200	$3,800
1967	Moseley tailpiece	$2,900	$3,500
1968	Moseley tailpiece	$2,400	$3,000

Mossman
1965-present. Professional and premium grade, production/custom, flat-top guitars built in Sulphur Springs, Texas. They have also built acoustic basses. Founded by Stuart L. Mossman in Winfield, Kansas. In '75, fire destroyed one company

Mosrite Ventures 12-String

'60s Mosrite Celebrity

1976 Mossman Southwind

Music Man Steve Morse

MODEL YEAR	FEATURES	EXC. COND. LOW	HIGH

building, including the complete supply of Brazilian rosewood. They entered into an agreement with C.G. Conn Co. to distribute guitars by '77. 1200 Mossman guitars in a Conn warehouse in Nevada were ruined by being heated during the day and frozen during the night. A disagreement about who was responsible resulted in cash flow problems for Mossman. Production fell to a few guitars per month until the company was sold in '86 to Scott Baxendale. Baxendale sold the company to John Kinsey and Bob Casey in Sulphur Springs in '89.

Flint Hills
1970-mid-1980s. Flat-top acoustic, rosewood back and sides.

1970-1979		$1,400	$1,600

Great Plains
1970-mid-1980s. Flat-top, Indian rosewood, herringbone trim.

1970-1979		$1,400	$1,600

Southwind
1976-ca. 1986, mid-1990s-2002. Flat-top, abalone trim top.

1976-1979		$1,600	$1,800

Tennessee
1975-1979. D-style, spruce top, mahogany back and sides, rope marquetry purfling, rope binding.

1975-1979		$1,200	$1,500

Tennessee 12-String
1975-1979.

1975-1979		$1,200	$1,500

Winter Wheat
1976-1979, mid-1990s-present. Flat-top, abalone trim. Natural finish.

1976-1979		$1,600	$1,800

Winter Wheat 12-String
1976-1979. Twelve-string version of Winter Wheat, Natural.

1976-1979		$1,600	$1,800

Mozzani
Built in shops of Luigi Mozzani (b. March 9, 1869, Faenza, Italy; d. 1943) who opened lutherie schools in Bologna, Cento and Rovereto in 1890s. By 1926 No. 1 and 2 Original Mozzani Model Mandolin (flat back), No. 3 Mandola (flat back), No. 4 6-String Guitar, No. 5 7-, 8-, and 9-String Guitars, No. 6 Lyre-Guitar.

Acoustic Flat-Top Guitars

1920s		$250	$400

Murph
1965-1966. Mid-level electric semi-hollow and solidbody guitars built by Pat Murphy in San Fernado, California. Murph logo on headstock.

Electric Solidbody Guitars

1965-1966		$600	$850

Electric XII

1965-1966		$650	$850

Music Man
1972-present. Professional grade, production, solidbody guitars built in San Luis Obispo, California. They also build basses. Founded by ex-Fender executives Forrest White and Tom Walker in Orange County, California. Music Man originally produced guitar and bass amps based on early Fender ideas using many former Fender employees. They contracted with Leo Fender's CLF Research to design and produce a line of solidbody guitars and basses. Leo Fender began G & L Guitars with George Fullerton in '82. In '84, Music Man was purchased by Ernie Ball and production was moved to San Luis Obispo.

Axis
1996-present. Offset double cut solidbody, figured maple top, basswood body, 2 humbucker pickups, Floyd Rose.

2000s		$950	$1,050

Edward Van Halen
1990-1995. Basswood solidbody, figured maple top, bolt-on maple neck, maple fingerboard, binding, two humbuckers. Named changed to Axis.

1991-1995		$2,000	$2,200

Sabre I
1978-1982. Offset double cut solidbody, maple neck, 2 pickups. Sabre I comes with a flat fingerboard with jumbo frets.

1978-1982		$600	$700

Sabre II
1978-1982. Sabre I with an oval 7 1/2" radius fingerboard.

1978-1982		$600	$700

Silhouette
1986-present. Offset double cutaway, contoured beveled solidbody, various pickup configurations.

1987-1995		$750	$850

Steve Morse Model
1987-present. Solidbody, 4 pickups, humbuckers in the neck and bridge positions, 2 single-coils in the middle, special pickup switching, six-bolt neck mounting, maple neck.

1987-1995		$800	$900

Stingray I
1976-1982. Offset double cutaway solidbody, flat fingerboard radius.

1976-1979		$600	$800
1980-1982		$600	$700

Stingray II
1976-1982. Offset double cutaway solidbody, rounder fingerboard radius.

1976-1979		$700	$800
1980-1982		$600	$700

Musicvox
1996-present. Intermediate grade, production, Korean-made retro-vibe guitars and basses from Matt Eichen of Cherry Hill, New Jersey.

MODEL		EXC. COND.	
YEAR	FEATURES	LOW	HIGH

Nady

Wireless sound company Nady Systems offered guitars and basses with built-in wireless systems for 1985-'87. Made by Fernandes in Japan until '86, then by Cort in Korea.

Napolitano Guitars

1993-present. Luthier Arthur Napolitano builds his professional and premium grade, custom, archtop guitars in Allentown, New Jersey.

Nashville Guitar Company

1985-present. Professional and premium grade, custom, flat-top guitars built by luthier Marty Lanham in Nashville, Tennessee. He has also built banjos.

Custom Slide

Weissenborn Hawaiian copy with hollow neck, Natural koa.

1997		$3,200	$3,500

National

Ca. 1927-present. Founded in Los Angeles as the National String Instrument Corporation by John Dopyera, George Beauchamp, Ted Kleinmeyer and Paul Barth. In '29 Dopyera left to start the Dobro Manufacturing Company with Rudy and Ed Dopyera and Vic Smith. The Dobro company competed with National until the companies re-united. Beauchamp and Barth then left National to found Ro-Pat-In with Adolph Rickenbacker and C.L. Farr (later becoming Electro String Instrument Corporation, then Rickenbacher). In '32 Dopyera returns to National and National and Dobro start their merger in late-'33, finalizing it by mid-'34. Throughout the '30s, National and Dobro maintained separate production, sales and distribution. National Dobro moved to Chicago in '36. In Chicago, archtop and flat top bodies are built primarily by Regal and Kay; after '37 all National resonator guitar bodies made by Kay. L.A. production is maintained until around '37, although some assembly of Dobros continued in L.A. (primarily for export) until '39 when the L.A. offices are finally closed. By ca. '39 the Dobro brand disappears.

In '42, the company's resonator production ceased and Victor Smith, Al Frost and Louis Dopyera buy the company and change name to Valco Manufacturing Company. Post-war production resumes in '46. Valco is purchased by treasurer Robert Engelhardt in '64. In '67, Valco bought Kay, but in '68 the new Valco/Kay company went out of business. In the Summer of '69 the assets, including brandnames, were auctioned off and the National and Supro names were purchased by Chicago-area distributor/importer Strum 'N' Drum (Noble, Norma brands). The National brand is used on copies in early- to mid-'70s, and the brandname went into hiatus by the '80s.

In '88 National Resophonic Guitars is founded in San Luis Obispo, California, by Don Young,

with production of National-style resonator guitars beginning in '89 (see following). In the '90s, the National brand also resurfaces on inexpensive Asian imports.

National Resonator guitars are categorized by materials and decoration (from plain to fancy): Duolian, Triolian, Style 0, Style 1, Style 2, Style 3, Style 4, Don #1, Style 97, Don #2, Don #3, Style 35.

National guitars all have serial numbers which provide clues to date of production. This is a complex issue. This list combines information included in George Gruhn and Walter Carter's *Gruhn's Guide to Vintage Guitars* (Miller Freeman, 1993), which was originally provided by Bob Brozman and Mike Newton, with new information provided by Mike Newton.

Pre "Chicago" numbers

A101-A450	1935-1936

"Chicago" numbers

A prefix (some may not have the prefix)	1936-mid-1997
B prefix	Mid-1937-1938
C prefix	Late-1938-1940
G prefix up to 200	Ea. 1941-ea. 1942
G suffix under 2000	Ea. 1941-ea. 1942
G suffix 2000-3000s (probably old parts)	1943-1945
G suffix 4000s (old parts)	Late 1945-mid-1947
V100-V7500	1947
V7500-V15000	1948
V15000-V25000	1949
V25000-V35000	1950
V35000-V38000	1951
X100-X7000	1951
X7000-X17000	1952
X17000-X30000	1953
X30000-X43000	1954
X43000-X57000	1955
X57000-X71000	1956
X71000-X85000	1957
X85000-X99000	1958
T100-T5000	1958
T5000-T25000	1959
T25000-T50000	1960
T50000-T75000	1961
T75000-T90000	1962
G100-G5000	1962
T90000-T99000	1963
G5000-G15000	1963
G15000-G40000	1964
1 prefix	1965-ea. 1968
2 prefix	Mid-1968

Aragon De Luxe

1939-1942. Archtop with resonator (the only archtop resonator offered), spruce top and maple back and sides.

1939-1942	Light Brown	$4,700	$6,200

1985 Nady Lightning

1955 National Debonaire

GUITARS

National Bel-Aire

1960 National Glenwood

MODEL YEAR	FEATURES	EXC. COND. LOW	HIGH

Bel-Aire
1953-1961. Single pointed cut archtop, 2 pickups until '57, 3 after, master tone knob and jack, bound body, sunburst.

1953-1961		$700	$950

Bluegrass 35
1963-1965. Acoustic, non-cutaway single-cone resonator, Res-O-Glas body in Arctic White.

1963-1965		$600	$900

Bobbie Thomas
Ca.1967-1968. Double cutaway thinline hollowbody, bat-shaped F-holes, two pickups, Bobbie Thomas on pickguard, vibrato.

1967-1968		$300	$600

Bolero
1956-1957. Les Paul-shape, control knobs mounted on pickguard, single pickup, trapeze tailpiece.

1956-1957	Sunburst	$550	$700

California
1949-1955. Electric hollowbody archtop, multi-bound, F-holes, trapeze tailpiece, one pickup. Natural.

1949-1955		$650	$950

Club Combo
1952-1955, 1959-1961. Electric hollowbody archtop, two pickups, rounded cutaway.

1952-1955		$700	$1,000
1959-1961		$950	$1,050

Don Style 1
1934-1936. Plain body with engraved borders, pearl dot inlay, 14 frets, single-cone.

1934-1936	Silver (nickel-plated)	$4,000	$6,000

Don Style 2
1934-1936. Geometric Art Deco body engraving, 14 frets, single-cone, fancy square pearl inlays and pearloid headstock overlay.

1934-1936	Silver (nickel-plated)	$5,000	$9,000

Don Style 3
1934-1936. Same as Style 2 but more elaborate floral engravings, fancy pearl diamond inlays, 14 frets, single-cone, only a very few made.

1934-1936	Silver (nickel-plated)	$6,500	$10,000

Duolian
1930-1939. Acoustic steel body, frosted paint finish until '36, mahogany-grain paint finish '37-'39, round neck, square neck available in '33, 12-fret neck until 1934 then 14-fret.

1930-1934	Round neck, 12 frets	$2,300	$2,500
1935-1939	Round neck, 14 frets	$2,000	$2,400

Estralita
1934-1942. Acoustic with single-cone resonator, mahogany top and back, F-holes, multi-bound.

1934-1942	Shaded Brown	$800	$1,100

MODEL YEAR	FEATURES	EXC. COND. LOW	HIGH

Glenwood
1954-1958. Les Paul-shaped solidbody, wood body, not fiberglass, single cutaway, multi-bound, two pickups. Renamed Glenwood Deluxe with Bigsby in 1959.

1954-1958	Natural	$1,200	$1,300

Glenwood 95
1962-1964. Glenwood 98 without third bridge-mount pickup.

1962-1964	Vermillion Red/ Flame Red	$1,900	$2,400

Glenwood 98
1964-1965. USA map-shaped solidbody of molded Res-O-Glas, 2 regular and 1 bridge pickups, vibrato. Pearl white finish.

1964-1965	Pearl White	$2,100	$2,600

Glenwood 99
1962-1965. USA map-shaped solidbody of molded Res-O-Glas, two regular and one bridge pickups, butterfly inlay. Snow white.

1964-1965	Sea Foam Green '64	$2,900	$3,500

Glenwood Deluxe
1959-1961. Renamed from Glenwood. Les Paul-shaped solidbody, wood body, not fiberglass, multi-bound, two pickups, vibrato.

1959-1961	Factory Bigsby	$1,300	$1,500

Model 1155
1948-1961. Flat top acoustic with Gibson body, mahogany back and sides, bolt-on neck.

1948-1961		$800	$1,000

Newport 82
1963-1965. Renamed from Val-Pro 82. USA map-shaped Res-O-Glas, one pickup. Red finish.

1963-1965		$1,200	$1,700

Newport 84
1963-1965. Renamed from Val-Pro 84. USA map-shaped Res-O-Glas, one regular and one bridge pickup. Sea Foam Green finish.

1963-1965		$1,500	$1,900

Newport 88
1963-1965. Renamed from Val-Pro 88. USA map-shaped Res-O-Glas, two regular and one bridge pickup. Black finish.

1963-1965		$1,600	$2,000

Reso-phonic
1956-1964. Pearloid-covered, single cut semi-solid-body acoustic, single resonator, maroon or white. Also a non-cut, square neck version was offered, which is included in these values.

1956-1964	Round neck	$700	$900
1956-1964	Square neck	$600	$800

Silvo (electric Hawaiian)
1937-1941. Nickel-plated metal body, flat-top with small upper bout, F-holes, square neck, two knobs on either side of rectangular pickup, multiple straight line art over dark background on body, Roman numeral parallelogram markers, National badge logo on headstock, Silvo name on coverplate.

1937-1941	Silver	$2,300	$3,500

MODEL YEAR	FEATURES	EXC. COND. LOW	HIGH

Studio 66
1961-1964. Electric solidbody of Res-O-Glas, single cutaway, one pickup. Renamed Varsity 66 in 1964.

1961-1962	Sand Buff, bridge pickup	$1,100	$1,400
1963-1964	Jet Black, neck pickup	$1,100	$1,400

Style O
1930-1942. Acoustic single-cone brass body (early models had a steel body), Hawaiian scene etching, 12-fret neck 1930-1934, 14-fret neck 1935 on, round (all years) or square (1933 on) neck.

1930-1934	Round neck, 12 frets	$3,000	$3,500
1933-1942	Square neck	$2,000	$2,500
1935-1942	Round neck, 14 frets	$3,500	$4,000

Style 1 Tricone
1927-1943. German silver body tricone resonator, ebony fingerboard, mahogany square (Hawaiian) or round (Spanish) neck, plain body, 12-fret neck until 1934, 14-fret after.

1927-1932	Round neck	$4,000	$6,000
1928-1932	Square neck	$2,200	$2,700

Style 1 Tricone Plectrum
1928-1935. Twenty-six inch scale versus the 23" scale of the tenor.

1928-1935		$2,400	$3,000

Style 1 Tricone Tenor
1928-1935. Tenor, four strings, 23" scale, square neck is Hawaiian, round neck is Spanish.

1928-1935		$2,200	$2,800

Style 2 Tricone
1927-1942. German silver body tricone resonator, Wild Rose engraving, square (Hawaiian) or round (Spanish) neck, 12-fret neck until 1934, 14-fret after.

1930s	Round neck	$9,000	$12,000
1930s	Square neck	$3,000	$4,000

Style 2 Tricone Plectrum
1928-1935. Twenty-six inch scale versus the 23" scale of the tenor.

1928-1935		$3,500	$4,500

Style 2 Tricone Tenor
1928-1935. Tenor.

1928-1935		$3,500	$4,500

Style 3 Tricone
1928-1941. German silver body tricone resonator, Lily-of-the-Valley engraving, square (Hawaiian) or round (Spanish) neck, 12-fret neck until 1934, 14-fret after. Reintroduced with a nickel-plated brass body in 1994.

1930s	Round neck	$14,000	$16,000
1930s	Square neck	$4,000	$6,000

Style 3 Tricone Plectrum
1928-1935. 26" scale versus the 23" scale of the tenor.

1928-1935		$4,000	$6,000

Style 3 Tricone Tenor
1928-1939.

1928-1939		$4,000	$5,500

Style 4 Tricone
1928-1940. German silver body tricone resonator, chrysanthemum etching. 12-fret neck until 1934, 14-fret after. Reissued in 1995 with same specs.

1930s	Round neck	$23,000	$25,000
1930s	Square neck	$6,500	$8,000

Style 35
1936-1942. Brass body tricone resonator, sand-blasted minstrel and trees scene, 12 frets, square (Hawaiian) or round (Spanish) neck.

1936-1942	Round neck	$7,000	$10,000
1936-1942	Square neck	$3,600	$5,000

Style 97
1936-1940. Nickel-plated brass body tricone resonator, sandblasted scene of female surfrider and palm trees, 12 frets, slotted peghead.

1930s	Round neck	$8,000	$10,000
1930s	Square neck	$4,500	$6,000

Style N
1930-1931. Nickel-plated brass body single-cone resonator, plain finish, 12 frets.

1930-1931		$3,500	$5,000

Triolian
1928-1941. Single-cone resonator, wood body replaced by metal body in 1929, 12-fret neck and slotted headstock 1928-1934, changed to 14-fret neck in 1935 and solid headstock in 1936, round or square (1933 on) neck available.

1928-1936	Various colors	$2,500	$2,700
1937	Fake rosewood grain finish	$2,000	$2,400

Trojan
1934-1942. Single-cone resonator wood body, F-holes, bound top, 14-fret neck.

1934-1942	Round neck	$1,100	$1,300

Val-Pro 82
1962-1963. USA map-shaped Res-O-Glas, one pickup, red finish. Renamed Newport 82 in 1963.

1962-1963	Vermillion Red	$1,100	$1,600

Val-Pro 84
1962-1963. USA map-shaped Res-O-Glas, one regular and one bridge pickup, Snow White finish. Renamed Newport 84 in 1963.

1962-1963		$1,400	$1,800

Val-Pro 88
1962-1963. USA map-shaped Res-O-Glas, two regular and one bridge pickup, black finish. Renamed Newport 88 in 1963.

1962-1963		$1,700	$2,100

Varsity 66
1964-1965. Renamed from Studio 66 in 1964. Molded Res-O-Glas, one pickup, two knobs.

1964-1965	Beige	$1,100	$1,400

Westwood 72
1962-1964. USA map-shaped solid hardwood body (not fiberglas), one pickup.

1962-1964	Cherry red	$700	$1,000

Westwood 75
1962-1964. USA map-shaped solid hardwood body (not fiberglas), one regular and one bridge pickup. Cherry-to-black Sunburst finish.

1962-1964	Cherry Sunburst	$800	$1,100

1930s National Style N

National Westwood 75

Novax Expression Classic

1960s Norma Solidbody

MODEL YEAR	FEATURES	EXC. COND. LOW	HIGH

Westwood 77
1962-1965. USA map-shaped solid hardwood body (not fiberglas), two regular and one bridge pickup.

| 1962-1963 | Blonde-Ivory | $900 | $1,200 |

National Reso-Phonic
1988-present. Professional and premium grade, production/custom, single cone, acoustic-electric, and tricone guitars (all with resonators), built in San Luis Obispo, California. They also build basses and ukes. McGregor Gaines and Don Young formed the National Reso-Phonic Guitar Company with the objective of building instruments based upon the original National designs.

Reso-Lectric R-2
1993-1996. Thin single-cutaway body with single-cone resonator, maple veneer top, lipstick neck pickup, pearloid or tortoiseshell celluloid pickguard.

| 1993-1996 | | $600 | $800 |

Nickerson Guitars
1983-present. Luthier Brad Nickerson builds his professional and premium grade, production/custom, archtop and flat-top guitars in Northampton, Massachusetts.

Noble
Ca. 1950-ca. 1969. Instruments made by others and distributed by Don Noble and Company of Chicago. Plastic-covered guitars made by EKO debut in '62. Aluminum-necked Wandré guitars added to the line in early-'63. By ca. '65-'66 the brandname is owned by Chicago-area importer and distributor Strum 'N' Drum and used mainly on Japanese-made solidbodies. Strum 'N' Drum bought the National brand name in '69 and imported Japanese copies of American designs under the National brand and Japanese original designs under Norma through the early '70s. The Noble brand disappears at least by the advent of the Japanese National brand, if not before.

Acoustic Archtop Guitars
1950-1969. Various models.

| 1960s | | $175 | $275 |

Norma
Ca.1965-1970. Imported from Japan by Strum 'N Drum, Inc. of Chicago (see Noble brand info). Early examples were built by Tombo, most notably sparkle plastic covered guitars and basses.

Electric Solidbodies
1965-1970. Type of finish has affect on value.

| 1965-1970 | Non-sparkle finish | $150 | $350 |
| 1965-1970 | Blue, red or gold sparkle | $400 | $500 |

Norman
1972-present. Intermediate grade, production, acoustic and acoustic/electric guitars built in LaPatrie, Quebec. Norman was the first guitar production venture luthier Robert Godin was involved

with. He has since added the Seagull, Godin, and Patrick & Simon brands of instruments.

Northworthy Guitars
1987-present. Professional and premium grade, production/custom, flat-top and electric guitars built by luthier Alan Marshall in Ashbourne, Derbyshire, England. He also builds basses and mandolins.

Norwood
1960s budget imports.

Electric Solidbodies
1960s. Offset double cut body, three soapbar-style pickups, Norwood label on headstock.

| 1960s | | $125 | $175 |

Novax Guitars
1989-present. Luthier Ralph Novak builds his fanned-fret professional and premium grade, production/custom, solidbody and acoustic guitars in San Leandro, California. He also builds basses.

Nyberg Instruments
1993-present. Professional grade, custom, flat-top and Maccaferri-style guitars built by luthier Lawrence Nyberg in Hornby Island, British Columbia. He also builds mandolas, bouzoukis and citterns.

O'Hagan
1979-1983. Designed by clarinetist and importer Jerol O'Hagan in St. Louis Park, Minnesota. Primarily neck-through construction, most with German-carved bodies. In '81 became Jemar Corporation and in '83 it was closed by the I.R.S., a victim of recession.

SN=YYM(M)NN (e.g., 80905, September '80, 5th guitar); or MYMNNN (e.g., A34006, April 1983, 6th guitar). Approximately 3000 total instruments were made with the majority being NightWatches (approx. 200 Twenty Twos, 100-150 Sharks, 100 Lasers; about 25 with bird's-eye maple bodies).

Laser
1981-1983. Solidbody, double cutaway, maple or walnut body, set-thru neck, three single-coil Schaller pickups.

| 1981-1983 | | $350 | $450 |

Shark
1979-1983. Explorer-looking solidbody.

| 1979-1983 | | $350 | $450 |

Twenty Two
1980-1983. Flying V copy, two humbuckers.

| 1980-1983 | | $350 | $450 |

Oahu
1926-1985, present. The Oahu Publishing Company and Honolulu Conservatory, based in Cleveland, Ohio was active in the sheet music and student instrument business in the '30s. An instrument, set of instructional sheet music, and lessons were

MODEL YEAR	FEATURES	EXC. COND. LOW	HIGH

offered as a complete package. Lessons were often given to large groups of students. Instruments, lessons, and sheet music could also be purchased by mail order. The Oahu Publishing Co. advertised itself as "The World's Largest Guitar Dealers." Most '30s Oahu guitars were made by Kay.

Guitar Models from the Mid-'30s include: 71K (jumbo square neck), 72K (jumbo roundneck), 68B (jumbo, vine body decoration), 68K (deluxe jumbo square neck), 69K (deluxe jumbo roundneck), 65K and 66K (mahogany, square neck), 64K and 67K (mahogany, roundneck), 65M (standard-size, checker binding, mahogany), 53K (roundneck, mahogany), 51 (black, Hawaiian scene, pearlette fingerboard), 51K (black, pond scene decoration), 52K (black, Hawaiian scene decoration), 50 and 50K (student guitar, brown). The brand has been revived on a line of tube amps.

Round Neck 14" Flat-Top
1930s. Spruce top, figured maple back and sides, thin logo.

1932		$1,000	$1,400

Style 50K Student Guitar
Student-size guitar, Brown finish.

1935		$200	$250

Style 65M
Standard-size mahogany body, checker binding, Natural Brown.

1933		$250	$350

Style 68K De Luxe Jumbo (square neck)
Hawaiian, 15 1/2" wide, Brazilian back and sides, spruce top, fancy pearl vine inlay, abalone trim on top and soundhole, rosewood pyramid bridge, fancy pearl headstock inlay, butterbean tuners, ladder-braced, Natural. High-end model made for Oahu by Kay.

1935		$3,500	$4,000

Odessa
1981-1990s. Budget guitars imported by Davitt & Hanser (BC Rich). Mainly acoustics in the '90s, but some electrics early on.

Iceman Copy
1981-mid-1980s. Iceman body, dual humbuckers, checker rope-style top binding, block markers, Sunburst.

1980s		$150	$175

Ohio
1959-ca. 1965. Line of electric solidbodies and basses made by France's Jacobacci company, which also built under its own brand. Sparkle finish, bolt-on aluminum necks, strings-thru-body design.

Old Kraftsman
Ca. 1930s-ca. 1960s. Brandname used by the Spiegel catalog company for instruments made by other American manufacturers, including Kay and even Gibson. The instruments were of mixed quality, but some better grade instruments were comparable to those offered by Wards.

MODEL YEAR	FEATURES	EXC. COND. LOW	HIGH

Archtops
1930s-1960s. Various models.

1930s	17", Stauffer-style headstock	$550	$650
1950s		$275	$375
1960s		$250	$350

Thin Twin Jimmy Reed Model

1950s		$450	$650

Olson Guitars
1977-present. Luthier James A. Olson builds his presentation grade, custom, flat-tops in Circle Pines, Minnesota.

D Custom
1977-present. D-style, Sitka spruce top, Indian rosewood back and sides, fancy pearl appointments, Natural.

1980s		$7,000	$8,000

D Cutaway
1977-present. D-style with sharp cutaway, Sitka spruce top, Indian rosewood back and sides.

1980s		$7,000	$8,000

Omega
1996-present. Luthier Kevin Gallagher builds his premium grade, custom/production acoustic guitars in East Saylorsburg, Pennsylvania.

MJ02C
1996-present. Jumbo flat-top cutaway, high-end appointments, Brazilian rosewood, flying bird markers.

1996-1999		$3,000	$3,300

Opus
1975-1976. Line of flattops made by Harmony. The original Harmony company closed soon after these were produced.

Orpheum
1897-1942, 1944-early 1970s, 2001-present. Currently intermediate grade, production, acoustic and resonator guitars. They also offer mandolins. Orpheum originally was a brandname of Rettberg and Lange, who made instruments for other companies as well. William Rettberg and William Lange bought the facilities of New York banjo maker James H. Buckbee in 1897. Lange went out on his own in '21 to start the Paramount brand. He apparently continued using the Orpheum brand as well. He went out of business in '42. In '44 the brand was acquired by New York's Maurice Lipsky Music Co. who used it primarily on beginner to medium grade instruments, which were manufactured by Regal, Kay, and United Guitar (and maybe others). In the early '60s Lipsky applied the brandname to Japanese imports. Lipsky dropped the name around '67. The brand was revived in '01 by Tacoma Guitars.

Omega MJ

1999 Olson SJ

Oscar Schmidt OE

Ovation Breadwinner

MODEL YEAR	FEATURES	EXC. COND. LOW	HIGH

Cutaway Thin Electric (Kay Thin Twin K-161)
Introduced 1952-1953 by Kay and also sold as the Orpheum Cutaway Thin Electric. Two tube/bar pickups, four knobs, block markers, curly maple top and back, mahogany sides.

1953	Natural	$450	$650

Orpheum Special (Regal-made)
1930s slot head, Dobro-style wood body, metal resonator.

1930s	Sunburst	$900	$1,100

Ultra Deluxe Professional Cutaway Model 899
1950s. 17" cutaway, two pickups, 2 knobs, maple back and sides, top material varies, dot markers, finishes as follows: E-C copper, E-G gold, E-G-B gold-black sunburst, E-B blond curly maple, E-S golden orange sunburst.

1953	All finishes	$1,300	$2,000

Oscar Schmidt
1879-ca. 1939, 1979-present. Budget and intermediate grade, production, acoustic, acoustic/electric, and electric guitars distributed by U.S. Music Corp. (Washburn, Randall, etc.). They also offer mandolins, banjos, ukes and the famous Oscar Schmidt autoharp.

The original Oscar Schmidt Company, Jersey City, NJ, offered banjo mandolins, tenor banjos, guitar banjos, ukuleles, mandolins and guitars under their own brand and others (including Sovereign and Stella). By the early 1900s, the company had factories in the U.S. and Europe producing instruments. Oscar Schmidt was also an early contributor to innovative mandolin designs and the company participated in the 1900-1930 mandolin boom. The company hit hard times during the Depression and was sold to Harmony by the end of the '30s. In '79, Washburn acquired the brandname and it is now part of U.S. Music.

Stella Model No. 501D
Decalmania top.

1921		$150	$250

Otwin
1950s-1960s. A brand name used on electric guitars made by the Musima company of East Germany. Musima also produced guitars under their own brand name.

Outbound Instruments
1990-2002. Intermediate grade, production, travel-size acoustics from the Boulder, Colorado-based company.

Ovation
1966-present. Intermediate and professional grade, production, acoustic and acoustic/electric guitars built in the U.S. They also build basses and mandolins.

Ovation's parent company, helicopter manufac-

MODEL YEAR	FEATURES	EXC. COND. LOW	HIGH

turer Kaman Corporation, was founded in 1945 by jazz guitarist and aeronautical engineer Charles Huron Kaman in Bloomfield, Connecticut. In the '60s, after losing a government contract, Kaman began looking to diversify. When offers to buy Martin and Harmony were rejected, Kaman decided to use their helicopter expertise (working with synthetic materials, spruce, high tolerances) and designed, with the help of employee and violin restorer John Ringso, the first fiberglass-backed ("Lyracord") acoustic guitars in '65. Production began in '66 and the music factory moved to New Hartford, Connecticut, in '67. Early input was provided by fingerstyle jazz guitarist Charlie Byrd, who gave Kaman the idea for the name "ovation." C. William Kaman II became president of the company in '85. Kaman Music purchased Hamer Guitars in '88, and Trace Elliot amplifiers (U.K.) in '90.

Adamas 1587
1979-1998. Carbon top, walnut, single cutaway, bowl back, binding, mini-soundholes.

1985	Black Sparkle	$1,500	$2,000

Adamas 1687
1977-1998. Acoustic/electric, carbon top, non-cutaway, bowl back, mini-soundholes.

1990	Sunburst	$1,700	$2,000

Adamas II 1881 NB-2
1993-1998. Acoustic/electric, single cutaway, shallow bowl.

1990s	Brown	$1,500	$2,000

Anniversary Electric 1657
1978. Deep bowl, acoustic/electric, abalone inlays, gold-plated parts, carved bridge, for Ovation's 10th anniversary. They also offered an acoustic Anniversary.

1978		$600	$800

Balladeer Artist 1121 (shallow bowl)
1968-1990. Acoustic, non-cutaway with shallow bowl, bound body.

1972	Natural	$350	$450

Balladeer Custom 1112 (deep bowl)
1976-1990. Acoustic, deep bowl, diamond inlays.

1976-1990	Natural	$400	$500

Balladeer Custom 12-String Electric 1655/1755
1982-1994. Twelve-string version of Balladeer Custom Electric.

1982-1994	Sunburst	$400	$500

Balladeer Custom Electric 1612/1712
1976-1990. Acoustic/electric version of Balladeer Custom, deep bowl.

1976-1990	Natural	$400	$500

Breadwinner 1251
1971-1983. Axe-like shaped single cutaway solidbody, two pickups, textured finish, Black, Blue, Tan or White.

1971-1983		$450	$650

Celebrity CC-57
1990-1996. Laminated spruce top, shallow bowl, mahogany neck.

1990-1996	Black	$250	$300

MODEL YEAR	FEATURES	LOW	HIGH

Classic 1613/1713
1971-1993. Acoustic/electric, non-cutaway, deep bowl, no inlay, slotted headstock, Gold tuners.

| 1971-1993 | Natural | $500 | $600 |

Classic 1663/1763 (deep bowl)
1982-1998. Acoustic/electric, single cutaway, deep bowl, cedar top, EQ, no inlay, slotted headstock, Gold tuners.

| 1982-1998 | . | $550 | $650 |

Classic 1863 (shallow bowl)
1989-1998. Acoustic/electric, single cutaway, shallow bowl, no inlay, cedar top, EQ, slotted headstock, Gold tuners.

| 1989-1998 | . | $550 | $650 |

Collectors Series
1982-present. Limited edition, different model featured each year and production limited to that year only. The year designation is marked at the 12th fret.

1984	Ebony stain	$800	$1,000
1985	Autumn Sunburst	$800	$1,000
1988	Gray Metallic	$800	$1,000
1991	25th Anniversary	$800	$1,000
1991	Black Sparkle	$800	$1,000
1993		$800	$1,000
1994	Natural	$800	$1,000
1996	Burgundy	$800	$1,000
1997		$800	$1,000
2002	African Cherry	$800	$1,000

Contemporary Folk Classic Electric 1616
1974-1990. Acoustic/electric, no inlay, slotted headstock. Natural or Sunburst.

| 1974-1990 | Natural | $300 | $400 |

Country Artist 6773 Classic Electric
1990s. Classic electric, soft cutaway, solid spruce top, slotted headstock, Ovation pickup system.

| 1990s | Natural | $900 | $1,000 |

Country Artist Electric 1624
Introduced in 1971. Acoustic/electric, non-cutaway, shallow bowl, slotted headstock, no inlay, chrome tuners.

| 1971-1975 | Natural | $500 | $600 |

Custom Legend 1659/1759
1980-present. Acoustic/electric, 12 strings, abalone top border, fingerboard binding, abalone floral inlay, Gold tuners. Natural or Sunburst.

| 1986 | | $700 | $800 |

Deacon 1252
1973-1980. Axe-shaped solidbody electric, active electronics, diamond fret markers.

| 1973-1980 | Sunburst | $450 | $550 |

Deacon 12-String 1253
1975. Axe-shaped solidbody, diamond inlay, two pickups. Only a few made.

| 1975 | | $450 | $550 |

Elite 1718 (deep bowl)
1982-1997. Acoustic/electric, non-cutaway, deep bowl, solid spruce top, Adamas-type soundhole, volume and tone controls, stereo output.

| 1990 | Sunburst | $650 | $750 |

Elite 1768 (deep bowl)
1990-1998. Deep bowl cutaway acoustic/electric.

| 1990s | Natural | $650 | $750 |

Elite 1868 (shallow bowl)
1983-present. Acoustic/electric, cutaway, shallow bowl.

| 1990 | Sunburst | $650 | $750 |

Elite Doubleneck
1989-1990s. Six- and twelve-string necks, could be ordered with a variety of custom options.

| 1989 | | $700 | $900 |

Glen Campbell 12-String 1118 (K-1118)
1968-1982. Acoustic, 12 strings, shallow bowl version of Legend, Gold tuners, diamond inlay.

| 1968-1982 | | $600 | $700 |

Glen Campbell Artist Balladeer 1127
1968-1990. Acoustic, shallow bowl, diamond inlay, Gold tuners.

| 1975 | Natural | $450 | $500 |

Hurricane 12-String K-1120
1968-1969. ES-335-style electric semi-hollowbody, double cutaway, 12 strings, F-holes, two pickups.

| 1968 | | $400 | $500 |

Josh White 1114
1967-1970, 1972-1983. Designed by and for folk and blues singer Josh White, has wide 12-fret to the body neck, dot markers, classical-style tuners.

| 1967-1970 | | $500 | $700 |
| 1972-1983 | | $400 | $600 |

Legend 1117
1972-1999. Deep bowl acoustic, five-ply top binding, Gold tuners, various colors (most Natural).

| 1972-1999 | | $400 | $500 |

Legend 1717
1990-1998. Acoustic/electric, five-ply top binding, various colors.

| 1990-1998 | | $700 | $750 |

Legend 12-String 1866
1989-present. Acoustic/electric, cutaway, 12 strings, shallow bowl, five-ply top binding.

| 1989-1999 | Black | $600 | $750 |

Legend 1869
1994. Acoustic/electric, cutaway, super shallow bowl.

| 1994 | Natural | $600 | $750 |

Legend Cutaway 1667
1982-1996. Acoustic/electric, cutaway, deep bowl, abalone, Gold tuners.

| 1982-1989 | | $600 | $750 |
| 1990-1996 | | $600 | $750 |

Legend Electric 1617
1972-1998. Acoustic/electric, deep bowl, abalone, Gold tuners, various colors.

| 1972-1998 | | $400 | $500 |

Pacemaker 12-String Electric 1615
1972-late-1970s.

| 1972-1977 | | $600 | $700 |

Ovation Deacon 12-string

Ovation Hurricane

Ovation Viper EA68

*Pantheon Bourgeois
Vintage Dreadnought*

MODEL YEAR	FEATURES	EXC. COND. LOW	HIGH

Patriot Bicentennial

*1976. Limited run of 1776 guitars, Legend Custom model with drum and flag decal and "1776*1976" decal on lower bout.*

| 1976 | | $700 | $900 |

Pinnacle

1990-1992. Spruce or sycamore top, broad leaf pattern rosette, mahogany neck, piezo bridge pickup.

| 1990-1992 | Sunburst | $400 | $500 |

Pinnacle Shallow Cutaway

1990-1994. Pinnacle with shallow bowl body and single cutaway.

| 1990-1994 | Sunburst | $450 | $550 |

Preacher 12-String 1285

1975-1983. Double cutaway solidbody, 12 strings, two pickups.

| 1975-1983 | | $400 | $500 |

Preacher 1281

1975-1982. Solidbody, mahogany body, double cutaway, two pickups.

| 1975-1982 | | $400 | $500 |

Preacher Deluxe 1282

1975-1982. Double cutaway solidbody, two pickups with series/parallel pickup switch and mid-range control.

| 1975-1982 | | $450 | $550 |

Thunderhead 1460

1968-1972. Double cutaway, two pickups, Gold hardware, phase switch, master volume, separate tone controls, pickup balance/blend control, vibrato.

| 1968-1972 | | $350 | $450 |

Tornado 1260

1968-1973. Same as Thunderhead without phase switch, with chrome hardware.

| 1968-1973 | | $400 | $500 |

UK II 1291

1980-1982. Single cutaway solidbody, two pickups, body made of Urelite on aluminum frame.

| 1980-1982 | | $600 | $800 |

Ultra GS

1985. Double cut solidbody electrics, 1, 2, or 3 pickups.

| 1985 | | $175 | $225 |

Viper 1271

1975-1982. Single cutaway, two single-coil pickups.

| 1975-1982 | | $350 | $450 |

Viper EA 68

1994-present. Thin acoustic/electric, single cutaway mahogany body, spruce top over sound chamber with multiple upper bout soundholes.

| 1994-1999 | Black | $600 | $700 |

Viper III 1273

1975-1982. Single cutaway, three single-coil pickups.

| 1975-1982 | | $500 | $600 |

P. W. Crump Company

1975-present. Luthier Phil Crump builds his custom flat-top guitars in Arcata, California. He also builds mandolin-family instruments.

MODEL YEAR	FEATURES	EXC. COND. LOW	HIGH

Palen

1998-present. Premium grade, production/custom, archtop guitars built by luthier Nelson Palen in Beloit, Kansas.

Pantheon Guitars

2000-present. Patrick Theimer created Pantheon which offers premium grade, production/custom, flat-tops built by seven luthiers (including Dana Bourgeois) working in an old 1840s textile mill in Lewiston, Maine.

Paramount

1930s. Private brand made by Martin for the banjo company.

Style L

1930s. Small body with resonator added, limited production to about 36 instruments.

| 1930s | | $3,000 | $3,500 |

Parker

1992-present. U.S.-made and imported intermediate, professional, and premium grade, production/custom, solidbody guitars featuring a thin skin of carbon and glass fibers bonded to a wooden guitar body. They also build basses. Located northwest of Boston, Parker was founded by Ken Parker and Larry Fishman (Fishman Transducers). Korg USA committed money to get the Fly Deluxe model into production. Production started July '93. Parker announced the opening of the Parker Custom Shop January 1, 2003 to produce custom special build instruments and non-core higher-end models that were no longer available as a standard product offering. In early '04, Parker was acquired by U.S. Music Corp.

Concert

1997 only. Solid Sitka spruce top, only piezo system pickup, no magnetic pickups. Transparent Butterscotch.

| 1997 | | $1,300 | $1,400 |

Fly Artist

1998-1999. Solid Sitka spruce top, vibrato, Deluxe-style electronics. Transparent Blond finish.

| 1998-1999 | | $1,600 | $1,800 |

Fly Classic

1996-1998, 2000-present. One-piece Honduras mahogany body, basswood neck, electronics same as Fly Deluxe.

| 1996-1998 | Transparent Cherry | $1,000 | $1,200 |
| 2000-2002 | Transparent Cherry | $1,100 | $1,300 |

Fly Deluxe

1993-present. Ultra-thin poplar body, basswood neck, two pickups a Fishman transducer in bridge, various colors. The guitar weighs only five pounds. Early models, '93-'96, were offered with or without vibrato, then the non-vibrato model was discontinued. The Deluxe normally came with a quality gig bag, but also offered with a hardshell case, which would add about $50 to the values listed.

| 1993-1999 | | $900 | $1,100 |
| 2000-2003 | | $1,100 | $1,400 |

MODEL YEAR	FEATURES	EXC. COND. LOW	HIGH

Fly Supreme
1996-1999. One-piece flame maple body, electronics same as the Fly Deluxe, includes hard molded case.

| 1990s | Highly flamed Butterscotch | $2,000 | $2,500 |

NiteFly/NiteFly NFV1/NFV3/NFV5
1996-1999. Three single-coil pickups NiteFly, Fishman piezo system, bolt-on neck, maple body for '96-'98, ash for '99, various colors. Called the NiteFly in '96, NiteFly NFV1 ('97-'98), NiteFly NFV3 ('98), NiteFly NFV5 ('99).

| 1997-1998 | | $450 | $600 |

NiteFly/NiteFly NFV2/NFV4/NFV6/SA
1996-present. Two single-coil and one humbucker pickup NiteFly, Fishman piezo system, bolt-on neck, maple body for '96-'98, ash for '99-present, various colors. Called the NiteFly in '96, NiteFly NFV2 ('97-'98), NiteFly NFV4 ('98), NiteFly NFV6 ('99), NiteFly SA (2000-present).

| 1990s | | $550 | $700 |

P-38
2000-2003. NiteFly-style ash body, bolt-on maple neck, rosewood board, vibrato, piezo bridge pickup and active Parker Alnico humbucker and two single-coils, gig bag, various colors.

| 2000-2003 | | $350 | $450 |

P-44
2002-2003. NiteFly-style mahogany body, flamed maple top, bolt-on maple neck, rosewood board, vibrato, piezo bridge pickup and two special Parker humbucker pickups, various colors.

| 2002-2003 | Sunburst | $400 | $550 |

Tulipwood Limited Edition
1998. Limited build of 35 guitars, standard Deluxe features with tulipwood body.

| 1998 | | $1,300 | $1,400 |

Paul Reed Smith
1985-present. Intermediate, professional and premium grade, production/custom, solid and semi-hollow body guitars made in the U.S. and imported. They also build basses. Paul Reed Smith built his first guitar in '75 as an independent study project in college and refined his design over the next 10 years. After building two prototypes and getting several orders from East Coast guitar dealers, Smith was able to secure the support necessary to start PRS. The initial PRS models retailed around the $2,000 price point which was an untapped market in the mid-'80s. In 2001 PRS introduced the Korean-made SE Series.

10th Anniversary
1995. Only 200 made, offset double cut, carved maple figured top, mahogany body, ebony board, mother-of-pearl inlays, abalone purfling, gold McCarty pickups, either 22-fret wide-fat or wide-thin mahogany neck, 10th Anniversary logo.

| 1995 | | $4,500 | $6,500 |

Artist/Artist I/Artist 24
1991-1994. Carved maple top, offset double cut mahogany body, 24-fret neck, bird markers, less than 500 made. A different Custom 24 Artist package was subsequently offered in the 2000s.

| 1991-1994 | | $3,500 | $4,000 |

Artist II/Artist 22
1993-1995. Curly maple top, mahogany body and neck, maple purfling on rosewood 'board, inlaid maple bound headstock, abalone birds, 22 frets, gold hardware. Short run of less than 500 instruments.

| 1993-1995 | | $3,500 | $4,000 |

Artist III
1996-1997. Continuation of the 22-fret neck with some changes in materials and specs, figured maple tops, short run of less than 500 instruments.

| 1996-1997 | Black Cherry | $3,000 | $3,500 |

Artist Limited
1994-1995. Like the Artist II with 14-Carat gold bird inlays, abalone purfling on neck, headstock and truss rod cover, Brazilian rosewood 'board. 165 made.

| 1994-1995 | | $5,000 | $5,500 |

CE 22
1994-2000. Double cut carved alder (1995) or mahogany (post 1995) body, bolt-on maple neck with rosewood 'board, dot inlays, two humbuckers, chrome hardware, translucent colors. Options include vibrato and gold hardware and custom colors.

| 1994-2000 | Standard features | $1,100 | $1,400 |
| 1994-2000 | Upgrade options | $1,200 | $1,500 |

CE 22 Maple Top
1994-present. CE 22 with figured maple top, upgrade options included gold hardware, custom colors or 10 top.

1994-1999	Standard features	$1,200	$1,500
1994-1999	Upgrade options	$1,300	$1,700
2000-2003	Upgrade options	$1,300	$1,700

CE 24 (Classic Electric, CE)
1988-2000. Double cut alder body, carved top, 24-fret bolt-on maple neck, two humbuckers, dot inlays. Upgrade options included gold hardware, custom colors or 10 top.

1988-1989	Standard features	$1,100	$1,400
1988-1989	Upgrade options	$1,200	$1,500
1990-1999	Standard features	$1,100	$1,400
1990-1999	Upgrade options	$1,200	$1,500
2000-2003	Standard features	$1,100	$1,400
2000-2003	Upgrade options	$1,200	$1,500

CE 24 Maple Top (CE Maple Top)
1989-present. CE 24 with figured maple top, 24-fret fingerboard, upgrade options may include any or all the following: Gold hardware, custom colors or 10 top.

1989	Standard features	$1,200	$1,500
1989	Upgrade options	$1,300	$1,600
1990-1999	Standard features	$1,200	$1,500
1990-1999	Upgrade options	$1,300	$1,600
2000-2003	Standard features	$1,200	$1,500
2000-2003	Upgrade options	$1,300	$1,600

Parker P-44

PRS Custom 22

PRS Custom 24

PRS McCarty Standard

MODEL YEAR	FEATURES	EXC. COND. LOW	HIGH
Custom 22 (mahogany)			

1993-present. Offset double cut solid mahogany body, 22-fret set-neck, opaque finish, chrome hardware, upgrade options include gold hardware and/or custom color.

1993-1999		$1,400	$1,800
Custom 22 (maple top)			

1993-present. Custom 22 with flamed or quilted maple top on mahogany body, 22-fret set-neck, upgrade option is gold hardware. Normally the quilt top is higher than flamed top.

1993-2003	Standard features	$1,600	$2,000
1993-2003	Upgrade options	$1,900	$2,400
Custom (Custom 24/PRS Custom)			

1985-present. Double cut solidbody, curly maple top, mahogany back and neck, pearl and abalone moon inlays, 24 frets, two humbuckers, trem. Options include quilted or 10 Top, bird inlays, and gold hardware.

1985	Standard features	$4,000	$5,500
1985	Upgrade options	$4,500	$6,000
1986	Standard features	$3,700	$5,000
1986	Upgrade options	$4,200	$5,500
1987	Standard features	$3,500	$4,500
1987	Upgrade options	$4,000	$5,000
1988	Standard features	$3,000	$3,500
1988	Upgrade options	$4,000	$4,500
1989	Standard features	$2,500	$3,000
1989	Upgrade options	$2,600	$3,100
1990	Standard features	$2,500	$3,000
1990	Upgrade options	$2,600	$3,100
1991	Upgrade options	$2,600	$3,100
1992	Upgrade options	$2,000	$2,500
1993	Upgrade options	$2,000	$2,400
1994	Upgrade options	$1,900	$2,400
1995	Standard features	$1,700	$2,200
1995	Upgrade options	$1,800	$2,300
1996-1999	Standard features	$1,500	$2,000
1996-1999	Upgrade options	$1,600	$2,100
2000-2003	Upgrade options	$1,800	$2,100
Custom 24 (mahogany)			

1985-present. Offset double cut solid mahogany body, 24-fret set-neck, opaque finish, chrome hardware, upgrade options include Gold hardware and custom colors.

1990s		$1,400	$1,800
Custom 24 (walnut)			

1992. Two made, seamless matched walnut over mahogany.

1992		$4,500	$5,500
Dragon I			

1992. 22 frets, PRS Dragon pickups, wide-fat neck, gold hardware, board inlay of a dragon made of 201 pieces of abalone, turquoise and mother-of-pearl. Limited production of 50 guitars.

1992		$20,000	$25,000
Dragon II			

1993. 22 frets, PRS Dragon pickups, wide-fat neck, gold hardware, fingerboard inlay of a dragon made of 218 pieces of gold, coral, abalone, malachite, onyx and mother-of-pearl. Limited production of 100 guitars.

1993		$17,000	$20,000

MODEL YEAR	FEATURES	EXC. COND. LOW	HIGH
Dragon III			

1994. Carved maple top, mahogany back, 22 frets, PRS Dragon pickups, wide-fat neck, gold hardware, fingerboard inlay of a dragon made of 438 pieces of gold, red and green abalone, mother-of-pearl, mammoth ivory, and stone. Limited production of 100 guitars.

1994		$17,000	$20,000
Dragon 2000			

1999-2000. Three-D dragon inlay in body versus neck inlay of previous models, limited production of 50 guitars.

1999-2000		$12,000	$18,000
Dragon 2002			

2002. Limited edition of 100 guitars, ultra-inlay work depicting dragon head on the guitar's body.

2002		$10,000	$18,000
EG II			

1991-1995. Double cut solidbody, bolt-on neck, 3 single-coils, single/single/humbucker, or hum/single/hum pickup options.

1991-1995		$1,000	$1,200
EG II Maple Top			

1991-1995. EG II with figured maple top, chrome hardware.

1991-1995		$1,500	$1,700
EG 3			

1990-1991. Double cut solidbody, bolt-on 22-fret neck, 3 single-coil pickups.

1990-1991	Flamed 10 top	$1,300	$1,500
1990-1991	Opaque finish	$900	$1,100
EG 4			

1990-1991. Similar to EG 3 with single/single/hum pickup configuration.

1990-1991		$1,100	$1,300
Golden Eagle			

1997-1998. Very limited production, eagle head and shoulders carved into lower bouts, varied high-end appointments.

1997-1998		$18,000	$25,000
Limited Edition			

1989-1991, 2000. Double cut, semi-hollow mahogany body, figured cedar top, gold hardware, less than 300 made. In 2000, single cut, short run of five Antique White and five black offered via Garrett Park Guitars.

2000	White, single cutaway	$2,200	$2,400
McCarty Model			

1994-present. Mahogany body with figured maple top, upgrade options may include a 10 top, Gold hardware, bird inlays.

1994-1999	Standard features	$1,600	$2,000
1994-1999	Upgrade options	$2,000	$2,300
2000-2003	Standard features	$1,700	$2,100
McCarty Archtop (spruce)			

1998-2000. Deep mahogany body, archtop, spruce top, 22-fret set-neck.

1998-2000	Chrome hardware	$1,800	$2,400
1998-2000	Gold hardware	$1,900	$2,500

MODEL YEAR	FEATURES	EXC. COND. LOW	HIGH

McCarty Archtop Artist
1998-2002. Highest grade figured maple top and highest appointments.

1998	Gold hardware	$4,500	$5,500

McCarty Archtop II (figured maple)
1998-2000. Deep mahogany body, archtop, figured maple top, 22-fret set-neck.

1998-2000	Flamed 10 top, chrome hardware	$2,200	$2,800
1998-2000	Flamed 10 top, gold hardware	$2,300	$3,000
1998-2000	Quilted 10 top	$2,300	$3,000

McCarty Hollowbody/Hollowbody I
1998-present. Medium deep mahogany hollowbody, spruce top, 22-fret set-neck, chrome hardware.

1998-1999	Standard features	$1,800	$2,400
1998-1999	Upgrade options	$2,000	$2,600

McCarty Hollowbody (spruce)
2000-present. Similar to Hollowbody I.

2000	Standard features	$1,700	$2,100
2000	Upgrade options	$2,000	$2,300

McCarty Hollowbody II
1998-present. Medium deep mahogany hollowbody, figured maple top, 22-fret set-neck, chrome hardware.

1998-2001		$2,500	$3,500

McCarty Soapbar (maple)
1998-present. Soapbar with figured maple top option, nickel hardware.

1998		$1,700	$1,900

McCarty Soapbar/Soapbar Standard
1998-present. Solid mahogany body, P-90-style 'soapbar' pickups, 22-fret set-neck, nickel-plated hardware, upgrade options may include gold hardware and bird inlays.

1994-1999	Standard features	$1,500	$1,700
1994-1999	Upgrade options	$1,700	$1,900

PRS Guitar
1985-1986. Set-neck, solid mahogany body, 24-fret 'board, two humbuckers, chrome hardware, renamed Standard from '87-'98 then Standard 24 from '98. PRS with opaque finish and matching headstock.

1985-1986	Sunburst	$4,500	$8,500

Rosewood Ltd.
1996. Mahogany body with figured maple top, one-piece rosewood neck with ultra-deluxe tree-of-life neck inlay, Gold hardware.

1996	Tree-of-life inlay	$9,000	$10,000

Santana
1995-1998. Solid-mahogany body, slightly wider lower bout than other models, figured maple top, 24-fret set-neck, symmetric Santana headstock versus usual PRS offset headstock design, unique body purfling at bookmatch glue joint and between pickup mounts, chrome and nickel-plated hardware, limited production special order.

1995-1998	Yellow	$5,000	$6,000

Santana II
1998-present. Three-way toggle replaces former dual mini-switches, special order only.

1998-1999	Yellow	$3,800	$4,200

Santana SE
2001-present. Solid mahogany body, set mahogany neck, 2 humbuckers, thin diagonal line position markers.

2001-2002		$375	$400

Signature/PRS Signature
1987-1991. PRS-shape solid mahogany body with figured maple top, set-neck, 24 frets. Hand-signed signature on headstock. Limited run of 1,000 guitars.

1987-1991		$5,000	$6,000

Single Cut
2000-2004. Single cut design, mahogany body, maple top, 22-fret fingerboard, upgrade options may include either or all of the followong: 10 top flamed maple, gold hardware, bird inlays.

2000-2004	Standard features	$1,600	$1,800
2000-2004	Upgrade options	$1,900	$2,100

Standard
1987-1998. Set-neck model, solid mahogany body, 24-fret fingerboard, dual humbucker pickups, chrome hardware. Originally called PRS Guitar from 1985-1986 (see that listing). Renamed Standard 24 from 1998.

1987-1989		$1,500	$2,000
1987-1989	Limited custom color	$2,000	$2,500
1990-1998		$1,200	$1,500

Standard 22
1994-present. Solid mahogany body, 22-fret set-neck.

1994-1999		$1,200	$1,400
2000-2003		$1,400	$1,600

Standard 24
1998-present. Renamed from Standard, solid mahogany body, 24-fret set-neck.

1998-1999		$1,200	$1,400

Studio Maple Top
1990-1991. Mahogany solidbody, bird fingerboard inlays, two single-coil and one humbucking pickups, tremolo, transparent finish.

1990-1991		$2,300	$2,600

Swamp Ash Special
1996-present. Solid swamp ash body, 22-fret bolt-on maple neck, three pickups, upgrade options available.

1996-2003	Figured maple neck option	$1,300	$1,600

Tremonti SE (import)
2002-present. Single cut, contoured mahogany body, 2 humbuckers, stop tailpiece.

2002-2003		$350	$375

Pawar
1999-present. Founded by Jay Pawar, Jeff Johnston and Kevin Johnston in Willoughby Hills, Ohio, Pawar builds professional and premium grade, production/custom, solidbody guitars that feature the Pawar Positive Tone System with over 20 single coil and humbucker tones.

PRS Santana SE

Pawar Stage

1990 Peavey Destiny

1999 Peavey Wolfgang Special

MODEL YEAR	FEATURES	EXC. COND. LOW	HIGH

Stage Turn of the Century
1999-present. Chambered swamp ash double cut solidbody, figured maple top, bass-side scroll horn, set-neck.

2000		$1,400	$1,500

Peavey
1965-present. Headquartered in Meridan, Mississippi, Peavey builds budget, intermediate, professional, and premium grade, production/custom, electric guitars. They also build basses, amps, PA gear, effects and drums. Hartley Peavey's first products were guitar amps. He added guitars to the mix in '78.

Axcelerator/AX
1994-1998. Offset double cutaway swamp ash or poplar body, bolt-on maple neck, dot markers, AX with locking vibrato, various colors.

1994-1998		$250	$325

Cropper Classic
1995-present. Single cut solidbody, 1 humbucker and 1 single coil, figured maple top over thin mahogany body.

1995-2002		$400	$500

Defender
1994-1995. Double cut, solid poplar body, two humbuckers and one single-coil pickup, locking Floyd Rose tremolo, metallic or pearl finish.

1994-1995		$125	$150

Destiny
1989-1992. Double cut, mahogany body, maple top, neck-through-bridge, maple neck, three integrated pickups, double locking tremolo.

1989-1992		$225	$300

Destiny Custom
1989-1992. Destiny with figured wood and higher-end appointments, various colors.

1989-1992		$350	$450

Detonator AX
1995-1998. Double cut, maple neck, rosewood board, dot markers, hum/single/hum pickups.

1995-1998	Black	$250	$300

EVH Wolfgang
1996-present. Offset double cut arched top body, bolt-on neck, offered with stop tailpiece or Floyd Rose vibrato. Also offered with quilted or flamed maple top upgrade option.

1996-1999	Flamed maple	$750	$850
1996-1999	Standard top	$450	$700

EVH Wolfgang Special
1997-present. Offset double cut lower-end Wolfgang model, various opaque finishes, flamed top optional.

1997-1999	Flamed maple top	$450	$600
1997-1999	Standard finish	$400	$500

Falcon/Falcon Active/Falcon Custom
1987-1992. Double cut, 3 pickups, passive or active electronics, Kahler locking vibrato.

1987-1992	Custom color	$275	$375
1987-1992	Standard color	$200	$300

MODEL YEAR	FEATURES	EXC. COND. LOW	HIGH

Firenza
1994-1999. Offset double cut, bolt-on neck, single-coil pickups.

1994-1999		$225	$300

Firenza AX
1994-1999. Upscale Firenza Impact with humbucking pickups.

1994-1999		$325	$400

Generation S-1/S-2
1988-1994. Single cut, maple cap on mahogany body, bolt-on maple neck, six-on-a-side tuners, active single/hum pickups, S-2 with locking vibrato system.

1988-1994		$225	$300

Horizon/Horizon II
1983-1985. Extended pointy horns, angled lower bout, maple body, rear routing for electronics, two humbucking pickups. Horizon II has added 'blade' pickup.

1983-1985		$150	$200

Hydra Doubleneck
1985-1989. Available as a custom order, 12/6-string necks each with two humbuckers, three-way pickup select.

1985-1989		$400	$500

Impact 1/Impact 2
1985-1987. Offset double cut, Impact 1 has higher-end synthetic fingerboard, Impact 2 with conventional rosewood fingerboard.

1985-1987		$200	$250

Mantis
1984-1989. Hybrid X-shaped solidbody, one humbucking pickup, trem, laminated maple neck.

1984-1989		$150	$200

Milestone 12-String
1985-1986. Double offset cut, 12 strings.

1985-1986		$200	$250

Milestone/Milestone Custom
1983-1986. Offset double cut.

1983-1986		$125	$175

Mystic
1983-1989. Double cut, 2 pickups, stop tailpiece initially, later Power Bend vibrato, maple body and neck.

1983-1989		$175	$200

Nitro I Active
1988-1990. Active electronics.

1988-1990		$250	$300

Nitro I/II/III
1986-1989. Offset double cut, banana-style headstock, one humbucker (I), two humbuckers (II), or single/single/hum pickups (III).

1986-1989	Nitro I	$150	$200
1986-1989	Nitro II	$175	$225
1986-1989	Nitro III	$200	$250

Odyssey
1990-1994. Single cut, figured carved maple top on mahogany body, humbuckers.

1990-1994		$450	$550

Odyssey 25th Anniversary
1990. Single cut body, limited production.

1990		$600	$700

MODEL YEAR FEATURES	EXC. COND. LOW	HIGH
Patriot		
1983-1987. Double cut, single bridge humbucker.		
1983-1987	$100	$150
Patriot Plus		
1983-1987. Double cut, 2 humbuckers, bi-laminated maple neck.		
1983-1987	$150	$175
Patriot Tremolo		
1986-1990. Double cut, single bridge humbucker, tremolo, replaced the standard Patriot.		
1986-1990	$100	$175
Predator/Predator AX/Predator DX		
1985-1988, 1990-2000. Double cut poplar body, two pickups until '87, three after, vibrato.		
1985-1988	$125	$200
1990-2000	$125	$225
Raptor		
1997-present. Offset double cut solidbody, 3 single-coils, 2 knobs and toggle.		
1997-2002	$120	$130
Razer		
1983-1989. Double cut with arrowhead point for lower bout, two pickups, one volume and two tone controls, stop tailpiece or vibrato.		
1983-1989	$250	$400
T-15		
1981-1983. Offset double cut, bolt-on neck, dual ferrite blade single-coil pickups.		
1981-1983 Natural	$150	$200
T-15 Amp-In-Case		
1981-1983. Amplifier built into guitar case and T-15 guitar.		
1981-1983	$200	$300
T-25		
1979-1985. Synthetic polymer body, two pickups, Cream pickguard. Sunburst finish.		
1979-1985	$150	$200
T-25 Special		
1979-1985. Same as T-25, but with super high output pickups, phenolic fingerboard, Black/White/Black pickguard. Ebony Black finish.		
1979-1985	$150	$200
T-26		
1982-1986. Same as T-25, but with 3 single-coil pickups and five-way switch.		
1982-1986	$175	$225
T-27		
1981-1983. Offset double cut, bolt-on neck, dual ferrite blade single-coil pickups.		
1981-1983	$175	$225
T-30		
1982-1985. Short-scale, 3 single-coil pickups, five-way select. By 1983 amp-in-case available.		
1982-1985	$150	$175
T-60		
1978-1988. Contoured offset double cut, ash body, six-in-line tuners, two humbuckers, through-body strings. By 1987 maple bodies. Finishes include natural, sunburst and some black.		
1978-1988	$175	$200

MODEL YEAR FEATURES	EXC. COND. LOW	HIGH
T-1000 LT		
1992-1994. Double cut, two single-coils and humbucker with coil-tap.		
1992-1994	$175	$225
Tracer Custom		
1989-1990. Tracer with two single/hum pickups and extras.		
1989-1990	$150	$200
Tracer/Tracer II		
1987-1994. Offset scooped double cut with extended pointy horns, poplar body, one pickup, Floyd Rose.		
1987-1994	$125	$175
Vandenberg Quilt Top		
1989-1992. Vandenberg Custom with quilted maple top, 2 humbuckers, glued-in neck, quilted maple top, mahogany body and neck.		
1989-1992	$700	$1,100
Vandenberg Signature		
1988-1992. Double cut, reverse headstock, bolt-on neck, locking vibrato, various colors.		
1988-1992	$400	$600
Vortex I/Vortex II		
1986. Streamlined Mantis with two pickups, three-way, Kahler locking vibrato. Vortex II has Randy Rhoads Sharkfin V.		
1986	$250	$300

Pegasus Guitars and Ukuleles

1977-present. Premium grade, custom steel-string guitars built by luthier Bob Gleason in Kurtistown, Hawaii, who also builds ukulele family instruments.

Penco

Ca. 1974-1978. Generally high quality Japanese-made copies of American acoustic, electric and bass guitars. Probably (though not certainly) imported into Philadelphia during the copy era. Includes Martin- and Gibson-style dreadnoughts with laminated woods, bolt-neck copies of the Gibson Les Paul, Fender Stratocaster, Telecaster and Rickenbacker 4001 bass, mandolins and banjos.

MODEL YEAR FEATURES	EXC. COND. LOW	HIGH
Acoustic Flat-Tops		
1974-1978. Various models.		
1974-1978	$150	$200
Electric Solidbodies		
1974-1978. Various models.		
1974-1978	$200	$250

Pensa (Pensa-Suhr)

1982-present. Premium grade, production/custom, solidbody guitars built in the U.S. They also build basses. Rudy Pensa, of Rudy's Music Shop, New York City, started building Pensa guitars in '82. In '85 he teamed up with John Suhr to build Pensa-Suhr instruments. Name changed back to Pensa in '96.

MK 1 (Mark Knopfler)

1985-present. Offset double cut solidbody, carved flamed maple bound top, 2 single-coils and 1 humbucker, gold hardware, dot markers, bolt-on neck.
1985-1992	$1,800	$2,200

1978 Peavey T-60

Peavey Razer

Phantom Deluxe

1959 Premier Custom

MODEL YEAR	FEATURES	EXC. COND. LOW	HIGH

Suhr Custom
1985-1989. Two-piece maple body, bolt-on maple neck with rosewood fingerboard. Custom order basis with a variety of woods and options available.
| 1985-1989 | Flamed maple top | $1,600 | $2,000 |

Suhr Standard
1985-1989. Double cut, single/single/hum pickup configuration, opaque solid finish normally, dot markers.
| 1985-1989 | | $1,200 | $1,400 |

Perlman Guitars
1976-present. Luthier Alan Pearlman builds his premium grade, custom, steel-string and classical guitars in San Francisco, California.

Perry Guitars
1982-present. Premium grade, production/custom, classical guitars built by luthier Daryl Perry in Winnipeg, Manitoba. He also builds lutes.

Petillo Masterpiece Guitars
1965-present. Luthiers Phillip J. and David Petillo build their intermediate, professional and premium grade, custom, steel-string, nylon-string, 12-string, resonator, archtop, and Hawaiian guitars in Ocean, New Jersey.

Petros Guitars
1992-present. Premium grade, production/custom, flattop, 12-string, and nylon-string guitars built by luthier Bruce Petros in Kaukauna, Wisconsin.

Apple Creek
1992-1999.
| 1992-1999 | | $2,400 | $3,400 |

Phantom Guitar Works
1992-present. Intermediate grade, production/custom, classic Phantom, and Teardrop shaped solid and hollowbody guitars assembled in Clatskanie, Oregon. They also offer basses and the MandoGuitar. Phantom was established by Jack Charles, former lead guitarist of the band Quarterflash. Some earlier guitars were built overseas.

Pimentel and Sons
1951-present. Luthiers Lorenzo Pimentel and sons build their professional, premium and presentation grade, flattop, jazz, cutaway electric, and classical guitars in Albuquerque, New Mexico.

Flamenco
1960s. Spruce top, cyprus back and sides.
| 1960s | | $950 | $1,250 |

W1 Classical
1970s. Cedar top, walnut back and sides.
| 1970s | | $800 | $900 |

Player
1984-1985. Player guitars featured interchangable pickup modules that mounted through the back of the guitar. They offered a double cut solidbody with various options and the pickup modules were sold separately. The company was located in Scarsdale, New York.

Pleasant
Late 1940s-ca.1966. Solidbody electric guitars, obviously others. Japanese manufacturer. Probably not imported into the U.S.

Electric Solidbodies
1940s-1966. Various models.
| 1950s | | $125 | $200 |

Prairie State
Mid-1920s. Larson Brothers brand, basically a derivative of Maurer & Company, but advertised as "a new method of guitar construction." The Prairie State equivalent models were slightly more expensive than the Maurer models (on average 5% to 10% more). Prairie State guitars were also promoted "reinforced with steel" and "the tube or support near the top withstands the strain of the strings, leaving the top or sound-board free and resilient." One or more steel tubes are noticable running from the neck block to the tail block, when looking through the round soundhole. These guitars were advertised as being suitable for playing steel (high nut and steel strings). Steel strings were the rage in the 1920s (re: Martin finally converting all guitar models to steel strings by 1928).

1932 Prairie State Catalog Models - description and prices:
Style 225 Concert	$65.00
Style 425 Auditorium	$70.00
Style 426 Style 425 Steel	$70.00
Style 427 Reinforced Neck	$75.00
Style 428 Style 427 Steel	$75.00
Style 235 Concert with trim	$80.00
Style 335 Grand Concert + trim	$83.00
Style 435 Auditorium with trim	$85.00
Style 340 Grand Concert fancy	$90.00
Style 350 Grand Concert fancy	$97.00
Style 440 Auditorium fancy trim	$93.00
Style 450 Auditorium fancy trim	$100.00

Small Higher-End Flat-Top
Mid-1920s. Spruce top, 13 5/8" scale, Brazilian rosewood back and sides, high-end pearl appointments, slotted headstock.
| 1920s | Natural | $4,000 | $5,000 |

Mid-Size Mid to High End Flat-Top
Mid-1920s. Fifteen inch spruce X-braced top, Brazilian rosewood back and sides, solid headstock, mid- to high-end appointments.
| 1920s | | $5,500 | $6,500 |

Premier
Ca.1938-ca.1975, 1990s-present. Budget and intermediate grade, production, import guitars. They also offer basses.

Brands originally offered by Premier include Premier, Multivox, Marvel, Belltone and Strad-O-Lin. Produced by Peter Sorkin Music Company in Manhattan, New York City, NY, who began in

MODEL		EXC. COND.	
YEAR	FEATURES	LOW	HIGH

Philadelphia, relocating to NYC in '35. First radio-sized amplifiers and stick-on pickups for acoustic archtops were introduced by '38. After World War II, they set up the Multivox subsidiary to manufacture amplifiers ca. '46. First flat-top with pickup appeared in '46. Most acoustic instruments made by United Guitar Corporation in Jersey City, NJ. Ca. 1957 Multivox acquires Strad-O-Lin. Ca.'64-'65 their Custom line guitars are assembled with probably Italian bodies and hardware, Japanese electronics, possibly Egmond necks from Holland. By ca. '74-'75, there were a few Japanese-made guitars, then Premier brand goes into hiatus.

The rights to the Premier brand are held by Entertainment Music Marketing Corporation in New York. The Premier brand reappears on some Asian-made solidbody guitars and basses beginning in the '90s. In-depth model details are provided by John Brinkmann.

Bantam Custom
1950s-1960s. Model below Special, single cut archtop, dot markers, early models with White potted pickups, then metal-covered pickups, and finally Japanese-made pickups (least valued).

1950s		$550	$650
1960s		$550	$650

Bantam Deluxe
1950s-1960s. Single cut archtop, fully bound, sparkle knobs, early models with white potted pickups, then metal-covered pickups, and finally Japanese-made pickups (least valued), block markers, single or double pickups (deduct $100 for single pickup instrument).

1950s	Blond	$1,000	$1,200
1950s	Sunburst	$900	$1,000
1960s	Blond	$1,000	$1,200
1960s	Sunburst	$900	$1,000

Bantam Special
1950s-1960s. Model below Deluxe, single cut archtop, dot markers, early models with White potted pickups, then metal-covered pickups, and finally Japanese-made pickups (least valued), single or double pickup models offered (deduct $100 for single pickup instrument).

1950s		$650	$750
1960s		$650	$750

Custom (solidbody scroll models)
1958-1970. Notable bass scroll cut, various models with various components used, finally import components only.

1958-1970	1 pickup	$350	$500
1958-1970	2 pickups	$450	$600
1958-1970	3 pickups	$550	$700

Deluxe Archtop (L-5-style)
1950s-1960s. Full body 17 1/4" archtop, square block markers, single cutaway, early models with White potted pickups, later into the 1960s metal pickups.

1950s	Blond	$1,100	$1,600
1950s	Sunburst	$1,100	$1,400
1960s	Blond	$1,100	$1,600
1960s	Sunburst	$1,100	$1,400

Semi-Pro 16" Archtop
1950s-early-1960s. Thinline electric 16" archtop with 2 1/4" deep body, acoustic or electric.

1950s	Acoustic non-electric	$650	$750
1950s	Electric	$750	$850
1960s	Acoustic non-electric	$650	$750
1960s	Electric	$750	$850

Semi-Pro Bantam Series (thinline)
1960s. Thinline electric archtop with 2 3/4" deep body, offered in cutaway and non-cutaway models.

1960s		$250	$350

Special Archtop (L-5-style)
1950s-1960s. Full body 17 1/4" archtop, less fancy than Deluxe, single cutaway, early models with White potted pickups, later into the 1960s metal pickups.

1950s		$800	$1,000
1960s		$800	$1,000

Studio Six Archtop
1950s-early-1960s. Sixteen inch wide archtop, single pickup, early pickups White potted, changed later to metal top.

1950s		$500	$600
1960s		$500	$600

Queen Shoals Stringed Instruments
1972-present. Luthier Larry Cadle builds his production/custom, flattop, 12-string, and nylon-string guitars in Clendenin, West Virginia.

Queguiner, Alain
1982-present. Custom flattops, 12-strings, and nylon-strings built by luthier Alain Quiguiner in Paris, France.

R.C. Allen
1951-present. Luthier R. C. "Dick" Allen builds professional and premium grade, custom hollow-body and semi-hollowbody guitars in El Monte, California. He has also built solidbody guitars.

Rahan
1999-present. Professional grade, production/custom, solidbody guitars built by luthiers Mike Curd and Rick Cantu in Houston, Texas.

Rahbek Guitars
2000-present. Professional and premium grade, production/custom, solidbody electrics built by luthier Peter Rahbek in Copenhagen, Denmark.

RainSong
1991-present. Professional grade, prodution, all-graphite acoustic guitars built in Woodinville, Washington. The guitars were developed after years of research by luthier engineer John Decker with help from luthier Lorenzo Pimentel, engineer Chris Halford, and sailboard builder George Clayton. The company was started in Maui, but has since moved to Woodinville.

Premier Deluxe E-621

Rainsong WS1000

José Ramirez R2 Classial

Rat Fink RF 2

MODEL YEAR	FEATURES	EXC. COND. LOW	HIGH

Jazz
1996-1999. Single cut jazz box, single neck pickup.

| 1996-1999 | Opaque White | $2,100 | $2,500 |

WS-1000/Windsong Cutaway
1999-present. Jumbo cutaway body, onboard electronics.

| 1999-2002 | | $1,200 | $1,300 |

WS-2000 12-String
1999-2001. 12-string version of Windsong Cutaway.

| 1999-2001 | | $1,200 | $1,400 |

Ramirez
1882-present. Founded by José Ramírez, the company is now in its fourth generation of family ownership in Madrid, Spain.

1A
1970s. Classical.

| 1970s | | $5,000 | $5,500 |

De Camera
1980s. Classical, cedar top, Brazilian rosewood back and sides.

| 1980s | | $5,000 | $5,500 |

Flamenco
European spruce top, cyprus back and sides.

| 1960-1969 | | $3,500 | $4,000 |

R4 Classical
1995-1997. All solid wood, western red cedar top, rosewood back and sides.

| 1995-1997 | | $1,100 | $1,400 |

Randy Reynolds Guitars
1996-present. Luthier Randy Reynolds builds his premium grade, production/custom classical and flamenco guitars in Colorado Springs, Colorado.

Rarebird Guitars
1978-present. Luthier Bruce Clay builds his professional and premium grade, production/custom, acoustic, electric solidbody and hollowbody guitars and mini guitars in Arvada, Colorado. He also builds basses.

Rat Fink
2002-present. Intermediate grade, production, guitars from Lace Music Products, the makers of the Lace Sensor pickup, featuring the artwork of Ed "Big Daddy" Roth. They also offer basses and amps.

Solidbody Guitars
2002-present. Various models, double cut solidbody, dual humbuckers, opaque finish, dot markers.

| 2002 | Hot Rod paint job | $100 | $125 |

Recording King
1936-1941. Brand name used by Montgomery Ward for instruments made by various American manufacturers, including Kay, Gibson and Gretsch. Generally mid-grade instruments. M Series are Gibson-made archtops.

MODEL YEAR	FEATURES	EXC. COND. LOW	HIGH

M-2
1936-1941. Gibson-made archtop with carved top and F-holes, maple back and sides.

| 1936-1941 | | $500 | $700 |

M-3
1936-1941. Gibson-made archtop, F-holes, maple back and sides, carved top.

| 1936-1941 | | $800 | $1,100 |

M-5
1936-1941. Gibson-made archtop with F-holes, maple back and sides, trapeze tailpiece, checkered top binding.

| 1936-1938 | 16" body | $1,000 | $1,400 |
| 1939-1941 | 17" body | $1,400 | $1,600 |

M-6
1938-1939. M-5 with upgraded gold hardware.

| 1938-1939 | | $1,600 | $1,800 |

Model K
1938-1939. Renamed from Carson Robison model, 14 3/4" flat-top, mahogany back and sides.

| 1938-1939 | | $800 | $1,100 |

Ray Whitley (rosewood)
1939-1940. Made by Gibson, high-quality model in the Recording King line, round shoulder flat-top with Brazilian rosewood back and sides, 5-piece maple neck, Ray Whitley stencil script logo on peghead, Recording King logo on peghead, pearl crown inlay on peghead, fancy inlaid markers.

| 1939-1940 | | $16,000 | $20,000 |

Regal
Ca. 1884-1966, 1987-present. Intermediate and professional grade, production, acoustic and wood and metal body resonator guitars. They also build basses.

Originally a mass manufacturer founded in Indianapolis, Indiana, the Regal brand was first used by Emil Wulschner & Son. In 1901 new owners changed the company name to The Regal Manufacturing Company. The company was moved to Chicago in 1908 and renamed the Regal Musical Instrument Company. Regal made brands for distributors and mass merchandisers as well as marketing its own Regal brand. Regal purchased the Lyon & Healy factory in '28. Regal was licensed to co-manufacture Dobros in '32 and became the sole manufacturer of them in '37 (see Dobro for those instruments). Most Regal instruments were beginner-grade; however, some very fancy archtops were made during the '30s. The company was purchased by Harmony in '54 and absorbed. From '59 to '66, Harmony made acoustics under the Regal name for Fender. In '87 the Regal name was revived on a line of resonator instruments by Saga.

Concert Folk H6382
1960s. Regal by Harmony, solid spruce top, mahogany back and sides, dot markers.

| 1960s | Natural | $250 | $300 |

MODEL YEAR FEATURES	EXC. COND. LOW	HIGH

Deluxe Dreadnought H6600
1960s. Regal by Harmony. Solid spruce top, mahogany back and sides, bound top and back, rosewood fingerboard, dot markers.

1960s	Natural	$250	$350

Dreadnought 12-String H1269
1960s. Regal by Harmony. Solid spruce top, 12-string version of Deluxe.

1960s	Natural	$250	$350

Model 27
1933-1942. Birch wood body, mahogany or maple, two-tone Walnut finish, single-bound top.

1933-1942		$600	$1,000

Model 45
1933-1937. Spruce top and mahogany back and sides, bound body.

1933-1937	Square neck	$900	$1,300

Model 75
1939-1940. Metal body.

1939-1940	Square neck	$1,000	$1,500

Spirit Of '76
1976. Red-White-Blue, flat-top.

1976		$200	$400

Renaissance
1978-1980. Plexiglass solidbody electric guitars and basses. Founded in Malvern, Pennsylvania, by John Marshall (designer), Phil Goldberg and Daniel Lamb. Original partners gradually leave and John Dragonetti takes over by late-1979. The line is redesigned with passive electronics on guitars, exotic shapes, but when deal with Sunn amplifiers falls through, company closes.

Fewer than 300 of first series made, plus a few prototypes and several wooden versions; six or so prototypes of second series made. SN=M(M)YYXXXX: month, year, consecutive number.

Brand name currently used on a line of guitars and basses made by Rick Turner in Santa Cruz, California.

Electric Plexiglass Solidbody Guitar
1978-1980. Models include the SPG (1978-79, DiMarzio pickups, active electronics), T-200G (1980, "Bich-style" with two passive DiMarzio pickups), and the S-200G (1980, double cutaway, two DiMarzio pickups, passive electronics).

1978-1980		$400	$600

Renaissance Guitars
1994-present. Professional grade, custom, semi-acoustic flat-top, nylon-string and solidbody guitars built by luthier Rick Turner in Santa Cruz, California. He also builds basses.

Model T
1996-present. Mahogany, single fade-away cutaway, Kay Kraft-style body, bolt-on neck, horseshoe pickup.

1996-1999		$800	$1,000

RS-6
1997-present. Acoustic/electric, solid cedar top, semi-hollow rosewood body, no soundhole, bolt-on maple neck.

1997-2000		$1,100	$1,300

Reuter Guitars
1984-present. Professional and premium grade, custom, flat-top, 12-string, resonator, and Hawaiian guitars built by luthier John Reuter, the Director of Training at the Roberto-Venn School of Luthiery, in Tempe, Arizona.

Reverend
1996-present. Intermediate grade, production, guitars built in Warren, Michigan, by luthier Joe Naylor, who also founded Naylor Amps. They also build basses and amps. Reverend offered effects for 2000-'04.

Semi-Hollow Electric
1997-present. Offset double cutaway semi-hollow-body, bolt-on maple neck, with various pickup options, various colors. Models include Avenger, Commando, Hitman, Rocco, Slingshot and Spy, variations of a similar theme. By 2004 the Workhorse Series included the Avenger TL, Commando, and Slingshot Custom, which were all factory-direct instruments.

1997-1999	Various models and options	$500	$650
2000s	Workhorse Series	$400	$475

Rex
1930s-1940s. Generally beginner-grade guitars made by Harmony and Kay and sold through Fred Gretsch distributors.

Acoustic Flat-Top Guitars
1940s. Various models.

1940s		$250	$350

Ribbecke Guitars
1972-present. Premium and presentation grade, custom thinline, flat-top, and archtop guitars built by luthier Tom Ribbecke in Healdsburg, California.

Rich and Taylor
1993-1996. Custom acoustic and electric guitars and banjos from luthiers Greg Rich and Mark Taylor (Crafters of Tennessee).

Richter Mfg.
1930s. One of many Chicago makers of the era.

Small 13" Guitar
1930s. Typical small 13" lower bout body, slotted headstock, decalmania art over Black finish, single dot markers.

1930s		$350	$450

Renaissance Model T

Reverend Rocco

Rick Turner Model One

Rickenbacker Combo 400

Rick Turner

1979-1981, 1990-present. Rick Turner has a long career as a luthier, electronics designer and innovator. He also makes the Renaissance line of guitars in his shop in Santa Cruz, California.

Rickenbacker

1931-present. Professional and premium grade, production/custom, acoustic and electric guitars built in California. They also build basses. Founded in Los Angeles as Ro-Pat-In by ex-National executives George Beauchamp, Paul Barth and National's resonator cone supplier Adolph Rickenbacher. Rickenbacher was born in Basel, Switzerland in 1886, emigrated to the U.S. and moved to Los Angeles in 1918, opening a tool and die business in 1920.

In the mid-'20s, Rickenbacher began providing resonator cones and other metal parts to George Beauchamp and Louis Dopyera of National String Instrument Corporation and became a shareholder in National. Beauchamp, Barth and Harry Watson came up with wooden "frying pan" electric Hawaiian lap steel for National in '31; National was not interested, so Beauchamp and Barth joined with Rickenbacher as Ro-Pat-In (probably for ElectRO-PATent-INstruments) to produce Electro guitars. Cast aluminum frying pans were introduced in '32. Some Spanish guitars (flat top, F-holes) with Electro pickups were produced beginning in '32.

Ro-Pat-In changes their name to Electro String Instrument Corporation in '34, and brand becomes Rickenbacher Electro, soon changed to Rickenbacker, with a "k." Beauchamp retires in '40. There was a production hiatus during World War II. In '53, Electro was purchased by Francis Cary Hall (born 1908), owner of Radio and Television Equipment Company (Radio-Tel) in Santa Ana, CA (founded in '20s as Hall's Radio Service, which began distributing Fender instruments in '46). The factory was relocated to Santa Ana in '62 and the sales/distribution company's name is changed from Radio-Tel to Rickenbacker Inc. in '65.

1950s serial numbers have from four to seven letters and numbers, with the number following the letter indicating the '50s year (e.g., NNL8NN would be from 1958). From '61 to '86 serial numbers indicate month and year of production with initial letter A-Z for the year A=1961, Z=1986) followed by letter for the month A-M (A=January) plus numbers as before followed by a number 0-9 for the year (0=1987; 9=1996).

Combo 400

1956-1958. Double cut tulip body shape, neck-through-body, one pickup, Gold anodized pickguard, 21 frets. Replaced by Model 425 in 1958.

Model Year	Features	Exc. Cond. Low	High
1956-1958	Black (216 made)	$1,000	$2,000
1956-1958	Blue Turquoise (53 made)	$1,500	$3,000
1956-1958	Cloverfield Green (53 made)	$1,500	$3,000

Model Year	Features	Exc. Cond. Low	High
1956-1958	Montezuma Brown (41 made)	$1,500	$3,000
1956-1958	OT other custom (4 made)	$1,500	$4,000

Combo 600

Modified double cut-away.

Model Year	Features	Exc. Cond. Low	High
1954-1957	Blond/White (46 made)	$1,500	$3,000
1956-1958	OT/Blue Turquoise (16 made)	$1,500	$3,500

Combo 800

1954-1959. Offset double cut, 1 horseshoe pickup until late-1957, second bar type after. Called the Model 800 in the 1960s.

Model Year	Features	Exc. Cond. Low	High
1954-1959	Blond/White (89 made)	$1,500	$3,000
1954-1959	Blue or Green (15 made)	$1,500	$3,500

Combo 850

1957-1959. Extreme double cutaway, one pickup until 1958, two after, Maple or Turquoise. Called Model 850 in the 1960s.

Model Year	Features	Exc. Cond. Low	High
1957-1959	Autumnglo (2 made)	$1,500	$3,500
1957-1959	Blue or Green (15 made)	$1,500	$3,000
1957-1959	Mapleglo (21 made)	$1,500	$2,000
1957-1959	White (1 made)	$1,500	$4,000

Combo 950

1957-1974. Double cut tulip body shape, 3/4 size, 2 pickups.

Model Year	Features	Exc. Cond. Low	High
1957-1974	Common colors	$1,200	$2,000

Electro Spanish (Model B Spanish)

1935-1943. Small guitar with a lap steel appearance played Spanish-style. Hollow bakelite body augmented with five chrome plates. Called the Model B circa 1940.

Model Year	Features	Exc. Cond. Low	High
1935-1936		$4,000	$4,800
1938-1939		$3,800	$4,600
1940-1943	Model B	$3,600	$4,400

Electro ES-17

1964-1975. The Electro line was manufactured by Electro String Instruments and distributed by Radio-Tel. The Electro logo rather than Rickenbacker appeared on the headstock. The Electro line included the short-scale ES-16 and standard-scale ES-17. The ES-17 has a glued-in neck, cutaway, one pickup.

Model Year	Features	Exc. Cond. Low	High
1964-1969	Fireglo	$800	$1,000
1970-1975		$500	$700

Model 230 Hamburg

1983-1991. Offset double cutaway, two pickups, dot inlay, rosewood fingerboard, chrome-plated hardware.

Model Year	Features	Exc. Cond. Low	High
1983		$500	$600

Model 320

1958-1992. Short-scale hollowbody, three pickups, F-holes optional in 1961 and standard in 1964 and optional again in 1979.

Model Year	Features	Exc. Cond. Low	High
1958-1968	5 made	$10,000	$20,000
1970-1989		$700	$1,100

MODEL YEAR	FEATURES	EXC. COND. LOW	HIGH

Model 325

1958-1975, 1985-1992. This was a low production model, with some years having no production. In the mid-1960s, the 325 was unofficially known as the "John Lennon Model" due to the guitar's high exposure on the "Ed Sullivan Show" and in the Saturday Evening Post.

1958-1960	29 made	$5,000	$15,000
1964-1965	Fireglo (24 Fireglo, 3 Black)	$5,000	$12,000
1966	Fireglo or Black (40 made)	$5,000	$10,000
1966	Mapleglo (6 made)	$5,000	$12,000
1968	10 made	$4,000	$8,000
1970-1979		$1,300	$1,800
1980-1992		$1,000	$1,700

Model 325 JL

1989-1993. John Lennon Limited Edition, three vintage Ric pickups, vintage vibrato, maple body; 3/4-size rosewood neck. A 12-string and a full-scale version are also available.

1989-1990		$2,000	$2,500

Model 325C58

2002. Designed as near-copy of the 1958-made model that John Lennon saw in Germany.

2002		$1,400	$1,600

Model 330

1958-present. Thinline hollowbody, two pickups, slash soundhole. Natural or Sunburst.

1958-1959	56 made	$2,000	$3,000
1960-1969	Many made in 1966	$1,600	$2,500
1984-1999		$800	$1,000
2000-2003		$850	$950

Model 330/12

1965-present. Thinline, two pickups, 12-string version of Model 300.

1964-1965		$2,000	$4,000
1966		$1,500	$3,000
1968-1969		$1,400	$2,200
1980s-90s		$1,000	$1,300

Model 331 Light Show

1970-1975. Model 330 with translucent top with lights in body that lit up when played, needed external transformer. The first offering's design, noted as Type 1, had heat problems and a fully original one is difficult to find. The 2nd offering's design, noted as Type 2, was a more stable design and is more highly valued in the market.

1970-1971	Type 1 1st edition	$6,000	$8,000
1972-1975	Type 2 2nd edition	$7,500	$10,000

Model 335 Capri

1958-1960. Thinline, two pickups, vibrato. The Capri Model name is technically reserved for the 1958 to mid-1960s vintage, these models had a two inch depth. Ca. Mid-1960 the body depth was reduced to 1 1/2". Rickenbacker dropped the Capri name in 1960.

1958-1959	Fireglo	$3,500	$4,500
1958-1959	Natural	$3,500	$4,500
1960	Fireglo	$3,200	$4,200

Model 335

1961-1978. Thinline, 2 pickups, vibrato. Called the 330VB from 1985-1997.

1966-1967	Fireglo	$1,900	$2,300

Model 340

1958-present. Thin semi-hollowbody, through-body maple neck, two single-coil pickups, sharp point horns. Very limited production 1958-1965, with first notable volume of 45 units starting in 1966.

1958	1 made	$3,000	$5,000
1962	1 made	$3,000	$5,000
1963	1 made	$3,000	$5,000
1964	2 made	$3,000	$5,000
1965	4 made	$3,000	$5,000
1966	43 made	$2,500	$4,000
2000		$675	$825

Model 345 Capri

1958-1960. Thinline 330-345 series, version with three pickups and vibrato tailpiece. The Capri Model name is technically reserved for the 1958 to mid-1960s vintage, these models had a two inch depth. Body depth was reduced to 1 1/2" circa mid-1960 and Capri name was dropped.

1958-1960	97 made	$3,500	$5,500

Model 345

1961-1974. Thinline 330-345 series, version with three pickups and vibrato tailpiece. In the mid-1960s Jetglo Black was a very unusual color, caution advised.

1961-1962	23 made	$3,000	$4,000
1964-1966		$2,000	$3,000
1974	Dual humbuckers, slant frets	$900	$1,300

Model 350 Liverpool

1983-1997. Thinline, three pickups, vibrato, no soundhole.

1983-1989		$800	$1,000

Model 350V63 (Liverpool)

1984-present. 355 JL without signature and drawing, Liverpool added to name for 1995-1996.

2002		$1,200	$1,500

Model 355 JL

1991-1992. John Lennon model, signature and drawing on pickguard.

1991-1992		$2,100	$2,600

Model 355/12 JL

1991-1998. Limited production of 1000 units.

1991-1998		$2,500	$3,000

Model 360

1958-present. Deluxe thinline, two pickups, slash soundhole.

1958-1959		$2,300	$3,000
1960-1963		$2,000	$2,800
1964	Very early NS new style	$2,000	$3,000
1965-1969	NS new style body, rounded horns	$2,000	$2,800
1970-1972		$1,800	$2,300
1973-1977		$1,400	$1,900
1978-1979		$1,300	$1,700
1980-1989		$1,000	$1,200

Rickenbacker 325

Rickenbacker 331 Light Show

1967 Rickenbacker 375

1961 Rickenbacker Model 450

MODEL YEAR	FEATURES	EXC. COND. LOW	HIGH
1990-1994		$1,000	$1,100
1995-1999		$900	$1,000

Model 360 WB
1991-1998. Two pickups, double bound body, vibrato optional.

1991-1998	Non-vibrato	$1,000	$1,300
1991-1998	Vibrato option	$1,000	$1,300

Model 360/12
1964-present. Deluxe thinline, two pickups, 12-string version of Model 360, Rick-O-Sound stereo.

1964-1965	36 + 480 made	$2,800	$3,700
1966	1164 made	$2,500	$3,500
1967-1969		$2,500	$3,000
1967-1969	Custom or rare color	$3,000	$3,500
1970-1979		$1,200	$1,700
1980-1999		$900	$1,200
2000-2001		$1,000	$1,200

Model 360/12V64
1985-2001. Deluxe thinline with 1964 features, two pickups, 12 strings, slanted plate tailpiece.

1985-2001		$1,500	$2,300

Model 365
1958-1974. Deluxe thinline, two pickups, vibrato. Called Model 360 VB from 1984-1997.

1958-1959	Late	$2,300	$3,300
1960-1963		$2,000	$3,000
1964-1969		$2,100	$2,700
1970-1974		$2,000	$2,500

Model 365 F
1960 and 1962. Thin full-body (F designation) with recorded production only in 1960.

1960	10 made	$4,000	$5,000
1962	2 made	$4,000	$5,000

Model 366/12 Convertible
1966-1974. Two pickups, 12 strings, comb-like device that converts it to a six-string. Production only noted in 1968, perhaps available on custom order basis.

1966	7 made	$2,400	$3,400
1968	125 made	$2,400	$3,400

Model 370
1958-1990, 1994-present. Deluxe thinline, three pickups. Could be considered to be a dealer special order item from 1958-1967 with limited production (1958=0, 1959=4, 1960=0, 1961=3, 1962-1967=0, then started more regularly in 1968).

1959	4 made	$4,000	$6,000
1961	3 made	$3,750	$6,000
1968-1969	Larger scale production	$2,500	$3,500
1970s		$1,200	$2,000
1980s		$1,300	$1,500
1990s		$1,300	$1,450

Model 370/12
1965-1990, 1994-present. Not regular production until 1980, deluxe thinline, three pickups, 12 strings. Could be considered to be a dealer special order item in the 1960s and 1970s with limited production.

1966	5 made	$3,500	$6,500
1985-1990		$1,000	$1,500
1994-2003		$1,000	$1,300

MODEL YEAR	FEATURES	EXC. COND. LOW	HIGH

Model 370/12 Limited Edition (Roger McGuinn)
1988. Roger McGuinn model, 1000 made, higher-quality appointments.

1988		$3,500	$4,500

Model 375
1958-1974. Deluxe thinline, three pickups, vibrato.

1958-1959	16 made	$3,500	$4,500
1960-1964	42 made	$4,000	$4,200
1965-1970	Sporadic limited production	$3,000	$4,000

Model 381
1958-1963,1969-1974. Double cutaway archtop, two pickups, slash soundhole, solid pickguard. Reintroduced in 1969 with double split-level pickguard.

1958-1963	Light sporadic production	$4,000	$5,000
1969-1974	Various colors, some rare	$2,000	$4,000

Model 381 JK
1988-1997. John Kay model, 2 humbuckers, active electronics, stereo and mono outputs.

1988-1997		$1,500	$2,500

Model 381/12V69
1987-present. Reissue of 381/12, deep double cutaway carved body from single piece of maple, sound cavity is carved inside body, cat's-eye soundhole, 21-fret rosewood fingerboard; triangle inlays, vintage-style pickups, bridge with 12 individually adjustable saddles. Finishes include Fireglo, Mapleglo and Jetglo.

1987-1999		$1,500	$2,000

Model 381V68
1987-1990. Renamed V69 in 1991.

1987-1990		$1,700	$1,900

Model 381V69
1991-1998. Reissue of vintage 381, originally called 381V68.

1991-1998		$1,700	$1,900

Model 420
1965-1983. Non-vibrato version of Model 425, single pickup.

1958-1964	Light sporadic production	$1,200	$1,600
1965-1969		$1,000	$1,400
1970-1983		$1,000	$1,200

Model 425
1958-1973. Double cutaway solidbody, one pickup. Sunburst.

1958-1959		$1,200	$1,600
1960-1965		$1,100	$1,500
1966-1969		$1,000	$1,400
1970-1973		$1,100	$1,200

Model 450
1958-1984. Replaces Combo 450. 2 pickups (3 optional '62-'77), cresting wave body shape.

1958-1959	Small consistent production	$2,000	$2,500
1960-1965	Small consistent production	$1,800	$2,000

MODEL YEAR	FEATURES	EXC. COND. LOW	HIGH
1966-1969	Small consistent production	$1,500	$1,800
1970-1979		$1,300	$1,600
1980-1984		$800	$1,200

Model 450/12

1964-1985. Double cutaway solidbody, 12-string version of Model 450, two pickups.

1964	12 made	$2,000	$2,500
1965	336 made	$1,800	$2,200
1966	1164 made	$1,500	$2,000
1967-1969		$1,500	$2,000
1970-1979		$1,300	$1,600
1980-1985		$1,000	$1,300

Model 456/12 Convertible

1968-1978. Double cutaway solidbody, two pickups, comb-like device to convert it to six-string.

1968-1969		$1,500	$2,000
1970-1978		$1,300	$1,600

Model 460

1961-1985. Double cutaway solidbody, two pickups, neck-through-body, deluxe trim.

1961-1965	Small consistent production	$1,500	$2,600
1966-1969		$1,300	$2,300
1970-1979		$1,200	$1,900
1980-1985		$1,000	$1,600

Model 480

1973-1984. Double cutaway solidbody with long thin bass horn in 4001 bass series style, two pickups, cresting wave body and headstock, bolt-on neck.

1973-1979		$950	$1,000
1980-1984		$850	$900

Model 615

1962-1977. Double cutaway solidbody, two pickups, vibrato.

1962-1965	Very small consistent production	$2,000	$3,000
1966-1969		$1,900	$2,400
1970-1977		$1,800	$2,200

Model 620

1974-present. Double cutaway solidbody, deluxe binding, two pickups, neck-through-body.

1974-1979		$1,100	$1,200
1980-1989		$1,000	$1,100
1980-1989	Custom color option	$1,400	$1,500
1990-1999		$900	$1,000

Model 620/12

1981-present. Double cutaway solidbody, two pickups, 12 strings, standard trim.

1981-1989		$1,100	$1,300
1990-1999		$900	$1,200
2000-2003		$900	$1,200

Model 625

1962-1977. Double cut solidbody, deluxe trim, two pickups, vibrato.

1962-1965		$2,500	$2,700
1966-1969		$2,400	$2,600
1970-1977		$2,100	$2,300

MODEL YEAR	FEATURES	EXC. COND. LOW	HIGH

Model 650A Atlantis

1991-2004. Cresting wave maple solidbody, neck-thru, 2 pickups, chrome hardware.

1991-2000		$700	$750

Model 650D Dakota

1993-2004. Like Atlantis but with hand-rubbed oil finished walnut body.

1993-2000		$625	$675

Model 650S Sierra

1993-2004. Like Dakota but with all-gold plated hardware, knobs and pickguard.

1993-2000		$625	$725

Model 660/12 TP

1991-1997. Tom Petty model, 12 strings, cresting wave body, two pickups, deluxe trim. Limited run of 1000.

1991-1997		$1,600	$1,800

Robert Cefalu

1998-present. Luthier Robert Cefalu builds his professional grade, production/custom, acoustic guitars in Buffalo, New York. The guitars have an "RC" on the headstock.

Robert Guitars

1981-present. Luthier Mikhail Robert builds his premium grade, production/custom, classical guitars in Summerland, British Columbia.

Robertson Guitars

1995-present. Luthier Jeff Robertson builds his premium grade, production/custom flat-top guitars in South New Berlin, New York.

Robin

1982-present. Professional and premium grade, production/custom, guitars from luthier David Wintz and built in Houston, Texas. Most guitars were Japanese-made until '87; American production began in '88. Most Japanese Robins were pretty consistent in features, but the American ones were often custom-made, so many variations in models exist. They also make Metropolitan (since '96) and Alamo (since '00) brandname guitars.

Artisan

1985-late 1980s. Double cut bound mahogany solidbody, 2 humbuckers, bound rosewood board.

1985	Sunburst, flame top	$600	$700

Avalon Classic

1994-present. Les Paul copy, figured maple top, exposed humbucking pickups, two knobs, upper bass bout toggle.

1994-2000		$1,200	$1,500

Medley Special

1992-1995. Ash body, maple neck, rosewood board, 24 frets, various pickup options.

1992-1995		$400	$500

Medley Standard

1985-present. Offset double cut ash solidbody, bolt neck, originally with hum-single-single pickups, but now also available with 2 humbuckers.

1985-1992	Swamp ash	$500	$600

Rickenbacker Model 650

Robin Avalon Classic

GUITARS

Robin Ranger Custom

Rowan Cimarron

MODEL YEAR	FEATURES	EXC. COND. LOW	HIGH

Octave
1982-1990s. Tuned an octave above standard tuning, full body size with 15 1/2" short-scale bolt maple neck. Japanese-made production model until '87, U.S.-made custom shop after.

1990s		$500	$800

Raider I
1985-1991. Double cut solidbody, 1 humbucker, maple neck, either maple or rosewood board.

1985-1991	Sunburst	$350	$450

Raider II
1985-1991. Raider I but with two humbuckers.

1985-1991	Sunburst	$400	$500

Raider III
1985-1991. Raider I but with 3 single-coils.

1985-1992	Sunburst	$450	$500

Ranger Custom
1982-1986, 1988-present. Swamp ash bound body, bolt on maple neck, rosewood or maple board, 2 single coils and 1 humbucker, made in Japan until '86, U.S.-made after.

1986	U.S.-made	$550	$700

RDN-Doubleneck Octave/Six
1982-1985. Six-string standard-scale neck with 3 pickups, six-string octave neck with 1 pickup, double cut solidbody.

1982-1985	Black	$450	$650

Soloist
1982-1986. Mahogany double cut solidbody, carved bound maple top, set neck, 2 humbuckers. Only about 125 made.

1985		$400	$550

Wrangler
1990s. Classic '50s single cutaway slab body, three Rio Grande pickups, opaque finish.

1990s		$400	$800

Rogands
Late 1960s. Produced by France's Jacobacci company and named after brothers Roger and Andre. Short-lived brand; the brothers made instruments under several other brands as well.

Rogue
2001-present. Budget and intermediate grade, production, acoustic, resonator and sitar guitars. They also offer amps, mandolins, banjos, effects, ukes and basses.

Roland
Best known for keyboards, effects, and amps, Roland offered synthesizer-based guitars and basses from 1977 to '86.

GR-707 Synth Guitar
1983-1986. Slab-wedge asymmetrical body, bass bout to headstock support arm, two humbucker pickups, multi-controls.

1983-1986	Silver	$1,100	$1,250

GS-500 Synth Guitar/Module
1977-1986. Three pickups.

1977-1980	Sunburst	$800	$1,100

Rono
1967-present. Luthier Ron Oates builds his professional and premium grade, production/custom, flat-top, jazz, Wiesenborn-style, and resonator guitars in Boulder, Colorado. He also builds basses and mandolins.

Rowan
1997-present. Professional and premium grade, production/custom, solidbody and acoustic/electric guitars built by luthier Michael Rowan in Garland, Texas.

Royal
ca. 1954-ca. 1965. Line of jazz style guitars made by France's Jacobacci company, which also built under its own brand.

Royden Guitars
1996-present. Professional grade, production/custom, flat-tops and solidbody electrics built by luthier Royden Moran in Peterborough, Ontario.

RS Guitarworks
1994-present. Professional grade, production/custom, solid and hollowbody guitars built by luthier Roy Bowen in Winchester, Kentucky.

Rubio, German Vasquez
1993-present. Luthier German Vasquez Rubio builds his professional and premium grade, production/custom classical and flamenco guitars in Los Angeles, California.

Ruck, Robert
1966-present. Premium grade, custom classical and flamenco guitars built by luthier Robert Ruck in Kalaheo, Hawaii.

Custom Classical
1966-present. Premium grade classical with solid spruce top and solid rosewood back and sides.

1990s		$7,000	$8,000

Running Dog Guitars
1994-present. Luthier Rick Davis builds his professional and premium grade, custom flat-tops in Richmond, Vermont.

Rustler
1993-ca. 1996. Solidbody electrics with hand-tooled leather bound and studded sides and a "R" branded into the top, built by luthier Charles Caponi in Mason City, Iowa.

RWK
1991-present. Luthier Bob Karger builds his intermediate grade, production/custom, solidbody electrics and travel guitars in Highland Park, Illinois.

GUITARS

MODEL YEAR	FEATURES	EXC. COND. LOW	HIGH

S. B. Brown Guitars
1994-present. Custom flat-tops made by luthier Steve Brown in Fullerton, California.

S. B. MacDonald Custom Instruments
1988-present. Professional and premium grade, custom/production, flat-top, resonator, and solid-body guitars built by luthier Scott B. MacDonald in Huntington, New York.

S.D. Curlee
1975-1982. Founded in Matteson, Illinois by music store owner Randy Curlee, after an unsuccessful attempt to recruit builder Dan Armstrong. S.D. Curlee guitars were made in Illinois, while S.D. Curlee International instruments were made by Matsumoku in Japan. The guitars featured mostly Watco oil finishes, often with exotic hardwoods, and unique neck-through-bridge construction on American and Japanese instruments. These were the first production guitars to use a single-coil pickup at the bridge with a humbucker at the neck, and a square brass nut. DiMarzio pickups. Offered in a variety of shapes, later some copies. Approximately 12,000 American-made basses and 3,000 guitars were made, most of which were sold overseas. Two hundred were made in '75-'76; first production guitar numbered 518.

Electric Solidbody Guitars
1975-1982. Models include the '75-'81Standard I, II and III, '76-'81? International C-10 and C-11, '80-'81 Yanke, Liberty, Butcher, Curbeck, Summit, Special, and the '81-'82 "Destroyer", "Flying V."
1975-1982 $400 $550

Sadowsky
1980-present. Professional and premium grade, production/custom, solidbody, archtop, and electric nylon-string guitars built by luthier Roger Sadowsky in Brooklyn, New York. He also builds basses. In 1996, luthier Yoshi Kikuchi started building Sadowsky Tokyo instruments in Japan.

T Custom Copy
2000s $2,000 $2,100

Vintage Style
Swamp ash body, Barden pickups, vintage-style gears, bridge, control plate and pickguard.
1982   Sunburst $1,000 $1,200

Saga
Saga Musical Instruments, of San Francisco, distributes a wide variety of instruments and brands, occasionally including their own line of solidbody guitars called the Saga Gladiator Series (1987-'88, '94-'95). In the 2000s, Saga also offered component kits ($90-$130) that allowed for complete assembly in "white wood."

Durango DF-360 Series
2004-present. Grand concert size, laminated spruce top, laminated mahogany back and sides.
2004 $100 $125

Gladiator Series
1994-1995. Offset double cut, pointed headstock solidbodies, solid alder bodies, maple necks. Models included the SSG-3 (red), SG-1 (blue) and SG-2 (white).
1994-1995 $125 $150

Sahlin Guitars
1975-present. Luthier Eric Sahlin builds his premium grade, custom, classical and flamenco guitars in Spokane, Washington.

Samick
1958-2001, 2002-present. Budget, intermediate and professional grade, production, imported acoustic and electric guitars. They also offer basses, mandolins, ukes and banjos. Samick also distributes Abilene and Silvertone brand instruments.

Samick started out producing pianos, adding guitars in '65 under other brandnames. In '88 Samick greatly increased their guitar production. The Samick line of 350 models was totally closed out in 2001. A totally new line of 250 models was introduced January 2002 at NAMM. All 2002 models have the new compact smaller headstock and highly styled S logo.

FV-450
1996-2001. Flying V style solidbody, 2 humbuckers.
1996-2001 $250 $325

HF-650
1994-2001. L-5 style jazz archtop, 2 humbuckers, gold hardware, maple body.
1994-2001 $500 $600

SW-218 CE (acoustic cutaway)
1996-2001. Cutaway D-style, piezo bridge pickup, unusual laser cut soundhole cover.
1996-2001   Natural $200 $300

Sand Guitars
1979-present. Luthier Kirk Sand opened the Guitar Shoppe in Laguna Beach, California in 1972 with James Matthews. By 1979, he started producing his own line of premium grade, production/custom-made flat-tops.

Santa Cruz
1976-present. Professional, premium and presentation grade, production/custom, flat-top, 12-string, and archtop guitars from luthier Richard Hoover in Santa Cruz, California. Founded by Hoover, Bruce Ross and William Davis. Hoover became sole owner in 1989. Custom ordered instruments with special upgrades may have higher values than the ranges listed here.

D 12-Fret
1994-present. 15 ½" scale, 12-fret neck, slotted headstock, round shoulders, spruce top, mahogany back and sides, notch diamond markers, herringbone trim and rosette. Special order models will vary in value and could exceed the posted range.
1990s   Natural $2,200 $2,600

1976 S.D. Curlee Standard

Sadowsky T Custom

*Santa Cruz
Tony Rice Professional*

Schecter Diamond Ultra

MODEL YEAR	FEATURES	EXC. COND. LOW	HIGH

D Koa
1980s-1990s. Style D with koa back and sides.
| 1990s | | $2,300 | $2,500 |

D PW
2001-present. Pre-war D-style.
| 2001-2002 | | $1,500 | $1,700 |

F
1976-present. 15 and 7/8 inch scale with narrow waist, Sitka spruce top, Indian rosewood back and sides.
| 1990s | Natural | $2,200 | $2,600 |

FJZ/Archtop
Early 1980s-present. Spruce top, curly maple body, ebony board, floating pickup, f-holes. Originally called the FJZ, but by mid-'90s, called the Archtop. Available in 16-, 17-, and 18-inch bodies and with many options..
| 1990s | 17 inch sunburst | $5,500 | $7,000 |

H
1976-present. Parlor size acoustic, offered in cutaway and non-cutaway versions, and options included koa, rosewood or maple, special inlays, slotted headstock, and shallow or deep bodies.
1980s		$2,200	$2,600
1990s		$2,000	$2,400
2000s		$1,800	$2,200

H Cutaway
1985-1996. Cutaway version of the H parlor guitar.
| 195-1990 | | $2,500 | $3,000 |

OM (Orchestra Model)
1987-present. Orchestra model acoustic, Sitka spruce top, Indian rosewood (Brazilian optional) back and sides, herringbone rosette, scalloped braces.
1987-1989	Brazilian rosewood	$4,200	$5,000
1987-1989	Indian rosewood	$1,500	$1,700
1990-1999	Brazilian rosewood	$4,000	$4,800
1990-1999	Indian rosewood	$1,500	$1,700

Tony Rice
1997-present. Dreadnought-size, Indian rosewood body, Sitka spruce top, solid peghead, zigzag back stripe, pickup optional.
| 1990s | | $2,000 | $2,400 |
| 2000s | | $2,000 | $2,300 |

Tony Rice Professional
1997-present. Brazilian rosewood back and sides, carved German spruce top, zigzag back stripe, solid peghead.
| 1990s | | $4,000 | $4,500 |

Vintage Jumbo/VJ
2000-present. 16 inch scale, round shouldered body, Sitka spruce, figured mahogany back and sides.
| 1990s | Natural | $2,000 | $2,500 |

Sawchyn Guitars
1972-present. Professional and premium grade, production/custom, flat-top and flamenco guitars and mandolins built by luthier Peter Sawchyn in Regina, Saskatchewan.

MODEL YEAR	FEATURES	EXC. COND. LOW	HIGH

Schaefer
1997-present. Premium grade, production/custom electric archtops handcrafted by luthier Edward A. Schaefer, who was located in Fort Worth, Texas, until '03 and is currently in Duluth, Minnesota.

Schecter
1974-present. Intermediate, professional and premium grade, production/custom, acoustic and electric guitars. They also offer basses. Guitar component manufacturer founded in California by four partners (David Schecter's name sounded the best), later offering complete instruments. The company was bought out and moved to Dallas in the early '80s. By '88 the company was back in California and in '89 was purchased by Hisatake Shibuya. Schecter Custom Shop guitars are made in Burbank, California and their Diamond Series is made in South Korea.

Avenger
1997-present. Offset double cutaway with long pointed bass horn, arched mahogany body, bolt-on neck, six-on-a-side tuners, dual humbucker pickups.
| 1997 | Custom color | $500 | $700 |
| 1997 | Sunburst | $400 | $500 |

Avenger 7
1997-present. Offset double cutaway with long pointed bass horn, arched mahogany body, bolt-on neck, six-on-a-side tuners, dual humbucker pickups, seven-string option.
| 1997-2000 | Custom color | $750 | $950 |

Diamond A1
1997-2000. Offset double cutaway with long pointed bass horn, arched mahogany body, bolt-on neck, various colors.
| 1997-2000 | | $300 | $375 |

Diamond A7
1997-2000. Seven strings, offset double cutaway with long pointed bass horn, arched mahogany body, bolt-on neck, various colors.
| 1997-2000 | | $325 | $400 |

Scheerhorn
1989-present. Professional and premium grade, custom, resonator and Hawaiian guitars built by luthier Tim Scheerhorn in Kentwood, Michigan.

Acoustic/Electric (Resophonic)
Small body resophonic, solid flamed maple body, resonator with spider bridge, mini-humbucker and transducer pickups.
| 1997 | Red Sunburst | $2,400 | $2,600 |

Schoenberg
1986-present. Premium grade, production/custom, flat-tops offered by Eric Schoenberg of Tiburon, California. From 1986-'94 guitars made to Schoenberg's specifications by Martin. From 1986-'90 constructed by Schoenberg's luthier and from 1990-1994 assembled by Martin but voiced and inlaid in the Schoenberg shop. Current mod-

MODEL YEAR	FEATURES	EXC. COND. LOW	HIGH

els made to Schoenberg specs by various smaller shops.

000-30

1990-1994. Martin-assembled, 12 frets to the body, Brazilian rosewood back and sides, six made.

1990-1994		$7,500	$8,500

OM Model

1990s-present. Specifications can vary, specific valuation on a case-by-case basis. The value noted is Style 28.

1990s	Brazilian rosewood	$7,000	$8,000

Soloist

1986-1994. Adirondack spruce top, Brazilian rosewood back and sides.

1986-1994	Brazilian rosewood	$7,000	$8,000

Schon

1986-1991. Designed by guitarist Neal Schon, early production by Charvel/Jackson building about 200 in the San Dimas factory. The final 500 were built by Larivee in Canada. Leo Knapp also built custom Schon guitars from '85-'87, and '90s custom-made Schon guitars were also available.

Standard (Canadian-made)

1987-1991. "Made in Canada" on headstock.

1987-1988	Single cutaway	$300	$400
1989-1991	Reverse double cutaway	$300	$400

Standard (U.S.A.-made)

1986 only. San Dimas/Jackson model, single cutaway, pointy headstock shape, "Made in U.S.A." on headstock.

1986		$1,100	$1,500

Schramm Guitars

1990-present. Premium grade, production/custom, classical and flamenco guitars built by luthier David Schramm in Clovis, California.

Schroder Guitars

1993-present. Luthier Timothy Schroder builds his premium grade, production/custom, archtops in Northbrook, Illinois.

Schwartz Guitars

1992-present: Premium grade, custom, flat-top guitars built by luthier Sheldon Schwartz in Concord, Ontario.

ScoGo

2001-present. Professional and premium grade, production/custom, solidbody guitars built by luthier Scott Gordon in Parkesburg, Pennsylvania.

Seagull

1980-present. Intermediate grade, production, acoustic and acoustic/electric guitars built in Canada. Seagull was founded by luthier Robert Godin, who also has the Norman, Godin, and Patrick & Simon brands of instruments.

Sebring

1980s-mid-1990s. Korean-made budget electric guitars imported by Vega Music International of Brea, California.

335 Copy

ES-335-style semi-hollowbody.

1990s		$200	$300

JS20

1980s. Large body, dual pickup, copy of L-5 CES archtop.

1980s		$300	$400

Solidbody Copy

1980s. Offset double cutaway classic, three single-coil copy.

1980s		$150	$250

Seiwa

Early 1980s. Entry-level to mid-level Japanese electric guitar and basses, logo may indicate "since 1956."

Century Crown

1980s. Classic offset double cut copy.

1980s		$150	$250

Sekova

Mid-1960s-mid-1970s. Entry level instruments imported by the U.S. Musical Merchandise Corporation of New York.

Grecian

1960s		$150	$250

Serge Guitars

1995-present. Luthier Serge Michaud builds his production/custom, classical, steel string, resophonic and archtop guitars in Breakeyville, Quebec.

Sexauer Guitars

1967-present. Premium and presentation grade, custom, steel-string, 12-string, nylon-string, and archtop guitars built by luthier Bruce Sexauer in Petaluma, California.

Shanti Guitars

1985-present. Premium and presentation grade, custom, steel-string, 12-string, nylon-string and archtop guitars built by luthier Michael Hornick in Avery, California.

Shelley D. Park Guitars

1991-present. Luthier Shelley D. Park builds her professional grade, custom, nylon- and steel-string guitars, in Vancouver, British Columbia.

Sheppard Guitars

1993-present. Luthier Gerald Sheppard builds his professional and premium grade steel-string guitars in Kingsport, Tennessee.

Schoenberg Soloist

1968 Sekova Grecian

MODEL YEAR	FEATURES	EXC. COND. LOW	HIGH

Sho-Bro resonator

Shifflett

1990-present. Luthier Charles Shifflett builds his premium grade, production/custom, flat-top, classical, flamenco, resophonic, and harp guitars in High River, Alberta. He also builds basses and banjos.

Sho-Bro

1969-1978. Spanish and Hawaiian style resonator guitars made by Sho-Bud in Nashville and distributed by Gretsch. Designed Shot Jackson and Buddy Emmons.

Grand Slam
1978. Acoustic, spruce top, mahogany neck, Jacaranda sides and back, and mother-of-pearl inlays, abalone soundhole purfling.

1978		$400	$500

Resonator
1972-1978. Flat-top style guitar with metal resonator with two small circular grilled soundholes.

1972-1978		$500	$600

Sigma

1970-present. Budget and intermediate grade, production, import acoustic guitars distributed by C.F. Martin Company.

DR-28 H
1970-1996. Dreadnaught, laminated rosewood back and sides, herringbone binding.

1980s		$350	$500

DR-35 H
1970-1996. D-35 copy, imported.

1970s		$350	$500

GCS-6
Grand concert semi-narrow waist body, laminated spruce top, mahogany back and sides.

1994	Natural	$150	$200

Signet

Ca. 1973. Acoustic flat-top guitars, imported from Japan by Ampeg/Selmer.

Acoustic Flat-Tops
1973. Various models.

1973		$75	$150

Silber

1992-1998. Solid wood, steel-string guitars designed by Marc Silber, made in Paracho, Mexico, and distributed by K & S Music. Silber continues to offer the same models under the Marc Silber Guitar Company brand.

Silvertone

1941-ca. 1970, present. Brand name of Sears instruments which replaced their Supertone brand in 1941. The Silvertone name was used on Sears phonographs, records and radios as early as the 'teens, and on occasional guitar models. When Sears divested itself of the Harmony guitar subsidiary in '40 it turned to other suppliers including Kay. In '40 Kay-made archtops and Hawaiian electric lap steels

'60s Silvertone semi-hollow-body

appeared in the catalog bearing the Silvertone brand, and after 1941-1942, all guitars, regardless of manufacturer, were called Silvertone.

Sears offered Danelectro-made solidbodies in the fall of '54. Danelectro hollowbodies appeared in '56. By '65, the Silvertones were Teisco-made guitars from W.M.I., but never sold through the catalog. First imports shown in catalog were in '69.

By '70, most guitars sold by Sears were imports and did not carry the Silvertone name. Currently, Samick offers a line of amps under the Silvertone name.

Amp-In-Case
The one pickup guitar, introduced in 1962, came with a smaller wattage amp without tremolo. The two pickup model, introduced in 1963, came with a higher-watt amp with tremolo and better quality Jensen speaker. Gray Tolex covered the guitar-amp case.

1960s	1 pickup	$250	$350
1960s	2 pickups	$350	$450

Belmont
1950s. Single cutaway solidbody, double pickup.

1958	Black	$250	$375

Espanada
Bigsby, two pickups.

1960s	Black	$200	$425

Estrelita
Semi-hollowbody archtop, two pickups, Harmony-made.

1960s	Black	$200	$425

Gene Autry Melody Ranch
1941-1955. 13 inch Harmony made acoustic, Gene Autry signature on belly, cowboy roundup stencil, same as earlier Supertone Gene Autry Roundup.

1940s		$250	$450

Meteor
Single cutaway, one pickup.

1950s	Sunburst	$200	$350

Student-level 13" Flat-Top
Harmony-made, 13" lower bout.

1960s		$50	$75

Simon & Patrick

1985-present. Intermediate and professional grade, production, acoustic and acoustic/electric guitars built in Canada. S&P was founded by luthier Robert Godin and named after his sons. He also produces the Seagull, Godin, and Norman brands of instruments.

Skylark

1981. Solidbody guitars made in Japan and distributed by JC Penney. Two set-neck models and one bolt neck model were offered. Most likely a one-time deal as brand quickly disappeared.

Electric Set-neck Solidbodies
1981. Double cut, 2 humbuckers, gold hardware, active electronics.

1981		$175	$225

MODEL YEAR	FEATURES	EXC. COND. LOW	HIGH

Electric Bolt-neck Solidbody
1981. Double cut, 2 humbuckers, chrome hardware, regular electronics.

1981		$125	$150

Slammer
1990-present. Budget and intermediate grade, production, guitars imported by Hamer. They also offer basses. Originally Slammers were upscale copies of Hamer models made in Korea. In '96, production of a more budget line was switched to Indonesia.

Slingerland
1930s-mid-1940s. The parent company was Slingerland Banjo and Drums, Chicago. The company offered other stringed instruments into the 1940s. They also marketed the May Bell brand. The guitars were made by other companies. Slingerland Drums is now owned by Gibson.

Nitehawk
1930s. Sixteen inch arch top, 'Nitehawk" logo on headstock, fancy position neck markers.

1930s		$500	$700

Songster Archtop
1930s.

1930s		$400	$550

Smart Musical Instruments
1986-present. Luthier A. Lawrence Smart builds his professional and premium grade, custom, flat-top guitars in McCall, Idaho. He also builds mandolin-family instruments.

Smith, George
1959-present. Custom classical and flamenco guitars built by luthier George Smith in Portland, Oregon.

Smith, Lawrence K.
1989-present. Luthier Lawrence Smith builds his professional and premium grade, production/custom, flat-top, nylon-string, and archtop guitars in Thirrow, New South Wales, Australia.

Somogyi, Ervin
1971-present. Luthier Ervin Somogyi builds his presentation grade, production/custom, flat-top, flamenco, and classical guitars in Oakland, California.

SonFather Guitars
1994-present. Luthier David A. Cassotta builds his production/custom, flattop, 12-string, nylon-string and electric guitars in Rocklin, California.

Southwell Guitars
1983-present. Premium grade, custom, nylon-string guitars built by luthier Gary Southwell in Nottingham, England.

Sovereign
ca.1920-ca.1938. Sovereign was originally a brandname of The Oscar Schmidt Company of Jersey City, NJ, and used on guitars, banjos and mandolins. In the late 1930s, Harmony purchased several trade names from the Schmidt Company, including Sovereign and Stella. Sovereign then ceased as a brand, but Harmony continued using it on a model line of Harmony guitars.

Specimen Products
1984-present. Luthier Ian Schneller builds his professional and premium grade, production/custom, aluminum and wood body guitars in Chicago, Illinois. He also builds basses, ukes, amps and speaker cabs.

Spector/Stuart Spector Design
1975-1990 (Spector), 1991-1998 (SSD), 1998-present (Spector SSD). Known mainly for basses, Spector offered U.S.-made guitars during 1975-'90 and '96-'99, and imports for '87-'90 and '96-'99. Since 2003, they again offer U.S.-professional grade, production, solidbody guitars. See Bass Section for more company info.

St. George
Mid to late 1960s. Early Japanese brand imported possibly by Buegeleisen & Jacobson of New York, New York.

Electric Solidbody
1960s. Early Japanese import duplicate of Zim Gar model, top mounted controls, three pickups, bolt-on neck.

1960s	Sunburst	$75	$150

St. Moritz
1960s. Imported from Japan by unidentified distributor. Manufacturers unknown, but some appear to be either Teisco or Kawai. Generally shorter scale beginner guitars, some with interesting pickup configurations.

Electric Thinline Archtop Guitars
Various models.

1960s		$100	$175

Stahl
1900-1944. Made in association with Larson Brothers. Valuation based on style number.

Style 4 Flat-Top
1930s. Mahogany body.

1930s		$2,500	$3,000

Style 5 Flat-Top
1930s. Mahogany body.

1930s		$2,500	$3,000

Style 6 Orchestra Special Flat-Top
1930s. Rosewood body.

1929-1930		$4,500	$6,500

Slingerland Songster

Spector Arc 6

1968 Standel 510

Steinberger GM-4

MODEL YEAR / FEATURES	EXC. COND. LOW	HIGH

Style 7 Special Solo Flat-Top
1930s. 13 1/2 inch scale, choice rosewood body, White spruce top, fancy appointments.

1930s	$5,000	$7,000

Style 8 Special Solo Flat-Top
1930s. Choicest rosewood body, finest White spruce top, fancy appointments.

1930s	$6,000	$8,000

Style 9 Artist Special Flat-Top
1930s. Choicest rosewood body, finest White spruce top, fancy appointments.

1930s	$7,000	$9,000

Stambaugh
1995-present. Luthier Chris Stambaugh builds his professional grade, custom/production, solid-body guitars in Stratham, New Hampshire. He also builds basses.

Standel
1952-1974, 1997-present. Amp builder Bob Crooks offered instruments under his Standel brandname three different times during the '60s. In '61 Semie Moseley, later of Mosrite fame, made two guitar models and one bass for Standel, in limited numbers. Also in '61, Standel began distributing Sierra steels and Dobro resonators, sometimes under the Standel name. In '65 and '66 Standel offered a guitar and a bass made by Joe Hall, who also made the Hallmark guitars. In '66 Standel connected with Sam Koontz, who designed and produced the most numerous Standel models (but still in relatively small numbers) in Newark, NJ. These models hit the market in '67 and were handled by Harptone, which was associated with Koontz. By '70 Standel was out of the guitar biz. See Amp section for more company info.

Custom Deluxe Solidbody 101/101X
1967-1968. Custom with better electronics, 101X has no vibrato. Sunburst, Black, Pearl White and Metallic Red.

1967-1968	$900	$1,200

Custom Deluxe Thin Body 102/102X
1967-1968. Custom with better electronics, 102X has no vibrato. Offered in Sunburst and five solid color options.

1967-1968	$1,000	$1,300

Custom Solidbody 201/201X
1967-1968. Solidbody, two pickups, vibrola, two pointed cutaways, headstock similar to that on Fender XII, 201X has no vibrato. Sunburst, black, pearl white and metallic red.

1967-1968	$700	$900

Custom Thin Body 202/202X
1967-1968. Thin body 335-style, headstock similar to that on Fender XII, 202X has no vibrato. Offered in Sunburst and five solid color options.

1967-1968	$800	$1,000

Starfield
1992-1993. Solidbody guitars from Hoshino (Ibanez) made in the U.S. and Japan. U.S. guitars are identified as American models; Japanese ones as SJ models. Hoshino also used the Starfield name on a line of Japanese guitars in the late '70s. These Starfields had nothing to do with the '90s versions and were not sold in the U.S.

Altair SJ (Japanese made)
1992-1993. Offset double cut solidbody, 3 pickups.

1992-1993	$275	$300

Stauffer
1800s. Old World violin and guitar maker, Georg Stauffer. Valid attributions include "signed or labeled by the maker" indicating the guitar was actually made by Stauffer, as opposed to "attributed to Stauffer or one of his contemporaries."

Guitar

1830	Fancy model, pearl trim	$10,000	$11,000

Stefan Sobell Musical Instruments
1982-present. Premium grade, production/custom, flattop, 12-string, and archtop guitars built by luthier Stefan Sobell in Hetham, Northumberland, England. He also builds mandolins, citterns and bouzoukis.

Steinberger
1979-present. Currently Steinberger offers budget, intermediate, and professional grade, production, electric guitars. They also offer basses. Founded by Ned Steinberger, who started designing NS Models for Stuart Spector in '76. In '79, he designed the L-2 headless bass. In '80, the Steinberger Sound Corp. was founded. Steinberger Sound was purchased by the Gibson Guitar Corp. in '87, and in '92, Steinberger relocated to Nashville.
Headless model codes for '85-'93 are:
First letter is X for bass or G for guitar.
Second letter is for body shape: M is regular offset double cut guitar body; L is rectangle body; P is mini V shaped body.
Number is pickup designation: 2 = 2 humbuckers, 3 = 3 single coils, 4 = single/single/humbucker.
Last letter is type of tremolo: S = S-Trem tremolo; T = Trans-Trem which cost more on original retail.

GL-4S
1987-1990. Rectangle L body, 2 single-coils and 1 humbucker, headless, S-Trem tremolo..

1987-1990	$650	$900

GP-3(S)(T)
1987-1988. P Series mini-V body, headless, 3 single-coils, available with S-Trem (S) or Trans-trem (T).

1987-1988	$500	$650

MODEL		EXC. COND.	
YEAR	FEATURES	LOW	HIGH

Steinegger

1976-present. Premium grade, custom steel-string flat-top guitars built by luthier Robert Steinegger in Portland, Oregon.

Ike Everly Model

1982-2001. Everly inlaid on front of headstock, body style similar to Gibson Everly Model, large star inlay, typically large double pickguard, Black finish, maple sides with flamed maple back.

1990s		$3,600	$4,000

Style D-28

Brazilian rosewood, herringbone trim.

1990s		$5,000	$6,000

Stella

Founded in 1879, Stella was a brand name of the Oscar Schmidt Company and was used on low-mid to mid-level instruments. Oscar Schmidt produced all types of stringed instruments and was very successful in the 1920s. Company salesmen reached many rural areas and Stella instruments were available in general stores, furniture stores, and dry goods stores, ending up in the hands of musicians such as Leadbelly and Charlie Patton. Harmony acquired the Stella brandname in '39 and built thousands of instruments with that name in the '50s and '60s. Harmony dissolved in '74. The Stella brand has been reintroduced by MBT International.

00 Style

Early-1900s. Oak body flat-top.

1908		$800	$1,000

Harp Guitar

Early-1900s.

1915		$1,500	$2,500

Singing Cowboy

Late-1990s. Copy of Supertone (Black background)/Silvertone/Harmony Singing Cowboy, import with laminated wood construction and ladder bracing.

2000	Stencil over Black	$50	$75

Stetson & Co.

Early-1900s. Larson Brothers brand (similar to Maurer or Prairie State).

Small Higher-End Flat-Top

Early-1900s. 13 5/8" lower bout, spruce top, Brazilian rosewood back and sides, high-end pearl appointments, slotted headstock.

1910	Natural	$3,000	$4,000

Strad-O-Lin

Ca.1920s-ca.1960s. The Strad-O-Lin company was operated by the Hominic brothers in New York, primarily making mandolins for wholesalers. Around '57 Multivox/Premier bought the company and also used the name on guitars, making both electrics and acoustics. Premier also marketed student level guitars under the U.S. Strad brand.

MODEL		EXC. COND.	
YEAR	FEATURES	LOW	HIGH

Stromberg

1906-1955, 2001-present. Intermediate and professional grade, production, archtop guitars inported by Larry Davis.

Founded in Boston by master luthier Charles Stromberg, a Swedish immigrant, building banjos and drums. Son Harry joined the company in 1907and stayed until '27. Son Elmer started in 1910 at age 15. The shop was well known for tenor banjos, but when the banjo's popularity declined, they began building archtop orchestra model guitars. The shop moved to Hanover Street in Boston in 1927 and began producing custom order archtop guitars, in particular the 16" G-series and the Deluxe. As styles changed the G-series was increased to 17 3/8" and the 19" Master 400 model was introduced in '37. Stromberg designs radically changed around 1940, most likely when Elmer took over guitar production. Both Charles and Elmer died within a few months of each other in '55.

Larry Davis of WD Music Products revived the Stromberg name and introduced a series of moderately priced jazz guitars in June, 2001. The models are crafted by a small Korean shop with component parts supplied by WD.

Deluxe

1927-1955. Non-cutaway, 16" body to 1934, 17 3/8" body after 1935, also sometimes labeled "Delux."

1927-1930		$10,000	$11,000
1931-1939		$12,000	$13,000
1940-1955		$12,000	$13,000

G-1

1927-1955. Non-cutaway, 16" body to 1935, 17 3/8" body after 1935.

1927-1935	Sunburst, 16" body	$10,000	$11,000
1936-1955	Sunburst, 17 3/8" body	$10,000	$11,000

G-3

Early 1930s. Archtop, 16 3/8", three segment F-holes, ladder bracing, gold hardware, engraved tailpiece, eight-ply pickguard, five-ply body binding, laminate maple back, fancy engraved headstock with Stromberg name, less total refinement than higher-end Stromberg models.

1932-1935		$11,000	$12,000

Master 300

1937-1955. Nineteen inch non-cutaway.

1937-1955	Natural	$30,000	$45,000
1937-1955	Sunburst	$25,000	$40,000

Master 400

1937-1955. 19" top-of-the-line non-cutaway, the most common of Stromberg's models..

1937-1955	Natural	$35,000	$55,000
1937-1955	Sunburst	$30,000	$50,000

Master 400 Cutaway

1949. Only seven cutaway Strombergs are known to exist.

1949	Natural	$70,000	$90,000

Stella/Harmony

1940 Stromberg Master 400 Cutaway

Supertone Gene Autry

1965 Supro S-555

MODEL YEAR	FEATURES	EXC. COND. LOW	HIGH

Stromberg-Voisinet

1921-ca.1932. Marketed Stromberg (not to be confused with Charles Stromberg of Boston) and Kay Kraft brand names, plus guitars of other distributors and retailers. Stromberg was the successor to the Groehsl Company (or Groehsel) founded in Chicago, Illinois in 1890; and the predecessor to the Kay Musical Instrument Company. In 1921, the name was changed to Stromberg-Voisinet Company. Henry Kay "Hank" Kuhrmeyer joined the company in '23 and was secretary by '25. By the mid-'20s, the company was making many better Montgomery Ward guitars, banjos and mandolins, often with lots of pearloid.

Joseph Zorzi, Philip Gabriel and John Abbott left Lyon & Healy for S-V in '26 or '27, developing two-point Venetian shape, which was offered in '27. The first production of electric guitars and amps was introduced with big fanfare in 1928; perhaps only 200 or so made. The last "Stromberg" acoustic instruments were seen in '32. The Kay Kraft brand was introduced by Kuhrmeyer in '31 as the company made its transition to Kay (see Kay). See Guitar Stories Volume II, by Michael Wright, for a complete history of Stromberg-Voisinet/Kay with detailed model listings.

Archtop Deluxe

1920s-1930s. Venetian cutaways, oval soundhole, decalomania art on top, trapeze tailpiece. Later offered under the Kay-Kraft brand.

1930s	Light Sunburst	$500	$600

Archtop Standard

1920s-1930s. Venetian cutaways, oval soundhole, no decalomania art, plain top, trapeze tailpiece. Later offered under the Kay-Kraft brand.

1930s	Light Sunburst	$450	$550

Stuart Custom Guitars

2004-present. Professional and premium grade, production/custom, solid and semi-hollow body guitars built by luthier Fred Stuart in Riverside, California. Stuart was a Senior Master Builder at Fender. He also builds pickups.

Superior Guitars

1987-present. Intermediate grade, production/custom Hawaiian, flamenco and classical guitars made in Mexico for George Katechis Montalvo of Berkeley Musical Instrument Exchange. They also offer mandolin-family instruments.

Supertone

1914-1941. Brand used by Sears, Roebuck and Company for instruments made by various American manufacturers, including especially its own subsidiary Harmony (which it purchased in 1916). When Sears divested itself of Harmony in 1940, instruments began making a transition to the Silvertone name. By 1941 the Supertone name was gone.

MODEL YEAR	FEATURES	EXC. COND. LOW	HIGH

Acoustic Flat-Top (high-end appointments)

1920s	Pearl trim 00-42 likeness	$1,200	$2,300
1920s	Pearl trim, Lindbergh model	$1,200	$1,900

Acoustic Flat-Tops (13" wide, non-stencil)

1930s		$150	$300

Gene Autry Roundup

1932-1939. Harmony made acoustic, Gene Autry signature on belly, cowboy roundup stencil, 13" body until '35, then 14".

1932-1939		$250	$450

Lone Ranger

1936-1941. Black with red and silver Lone Ranger and Tonto stencil, silver-painted fretboard, 13 1/2" wide. "Hi-Yo Silver" added in '37, changed to "Hi-Ho Silver" in '38.

1936-1941		$200	$300

Singing Cowboys

1938-1943. Stencil of guitar strumming cowboys around chuck wagon and campfire, branded Silvertone after '41.

1938-1943		$250	$300

Supertone 'Wedge'

1930s. Triangle-shaped 'wedge' body, laminate construction, Blue-Silver Supertone label inside sound chamber, art decals on body.

1930s		$200	$250

Supro

1935-1968. Budget brand of National Dobro Company. Some Supro models also sold under the Airline brand for Montgomery Ward. In 1942 Victor Smith, Al Frost and Louis Dopyera bought National and changed the name to Valco Manufacturing Company. Valco Manufacturing Company name changed to Valco Guitars, Inc., in '62. Company treasurer Robert Engelhardt bought Valco in '64. In '67 Valco bought Kay and in '68 Valco/Kay went out of business. In the summer of '69, Valco/Kay brand names and assets were sold at auction and the Supro and National names purchased by Chicago-area importer and distributor Strum N" Drum (Norma, Noble). The Supro name was never used on imports. In the early-'80s, ownership of the Supro name was transferred to Archer's Music, Fresno, California. Some Supros assembled from new-old-stock parts.

Belmont

1955-1964. For '55-'60, 12" wide, single cut, one neck pickup, two knobs treble side in pickguard, reverse-stairs tailpiece, No-Mar plastic Maroon-colored covering. For '60, size increased to 13 1/2" wide. For '62-'64, Res-o-glas fiberglas was used for the body, a slight cutaway on bass side, one bridge pickup, two knobs on opposite sides. Polar White.

1955-1959	Black or White No-Mar	$600	$850
1960-1962	Black or White No-Mar	$600	$850

MODEL YEAR	FEATURES	EXC. COND. LOW	HIGH
1961-1964	Polar White Res-o-glas	$900	$1,200

Bermuda

1962 only. Slab body (not beveled), double pickups, dot markers, Cherry glass-fiber finish.

1962		$800	$1,000

Collegian Spanish

1939-1942. Metal body, 12 frets. Moved to National line in 1942.

1939-1942	Maple	$1,000	$1,200

Coronado/Coronado II

1961-1967. Listed as II in 1962. 15 1/2" scale, single cut Gibson thinline-style, two pickups with four knobs and slider. Natural blond spruce top. Changed to slight cutaway on bass side in 1962 when renamed II.

1961-1962	Blond, Natural spruce top	$1,000	$1,250
1963-1967	Black fiberglass	$1,200	$1,700

Dual-Tone

1954-1966. The Dual Tone had several body style changes, all instruments had dual pickups. '54, 11 1/4" body, No Mar Arctic White plastic body ('54-'62). '55, 12" body. '58, 13" body. '60, 13 1/2" body. '62, Res-o-glas Ermine White body, light cutaway on bass side.

1954-1961	Arctic White No-Mar	$700	$1,000
1962-1964	Ermine White Res-o-glas	$900	$1,300

Folk Star

1964-1967. Molded Res-o-glas body, single-cone resonator, dot inlays.

1964-1967	Fire Engine Red	$600	$900

Kingston

1962-1963. Double cutaway slab body, bridge pickup, glass-fiber Sand finish, similar to same vintage Ozark.

1962-1963		$400	$500

Martinique

1962-1967. Single cutaway, 13 1/2" wide, two standard and one bridge pickup, six knobs on bass side, one knob and slider on treble side, block markers, cataloged as "Supro's finest electric," Val-Trol script on pickguard, Bigsby vibrato tailpiece. Ermine White Polyester Glas.

1962-1967	Blue	$1,700	$2,200
1962-1967	Ermine White	$1,700	$2,200

Ozark

1952-1954, 1958-1967. Non-cutaway, one pickup, dot inlay, White pearloid body. Name reintroduced in 1958 as a continuation of model Sixty with single cutaway, Dobro tailpiece.

1952-1954	White pearloid	$400	$500
1958-1961	Red	$400	$500
1962-1967	Jet Black or Fire Bronze	$400	$500

Ranchero

1948-1960. Full body electric archtop, neck pickup, dot markers, bound body.

1948-1960	Sunburst	$600	$700

Sahara

1960-1964. 13 1/2" body-style similar to Dual Tone, single pickup, two knobs.

1960-1964	Sand-Buff	$600	$900
1960-1964	Wedgewood Blue	$600	$900

Silverwood/Val-Trol

1960-1962. Single cut, 13 1/2" wide, two standard and one bridge pickups, six knobs on bass side, one knob and slider on treble side, block markers, cataloged as "Supro's finest electric." Natural Blond. Val-Trol script on pickguard. Renamed Martinique in 1962.

1960-1962		$1,250	$1,500

Sixty

1955-1958. Single cutaway, single pickup, becomes Ozark in 1958.

1955-1958	White No-Mar plastic	$400	$500

Special 12

1958-1960. Single cut, replaces Supro Sixty, neck pickup pickguard mounted.

1958-1960		$400	$500

Super

1958-1964. 12" wide single cut body style like mid-1950s models, single bridge pickup, short-scale. Ivory.

1958-1964		$400	$450

Super Seven

1965-1967. Offset double cut solidbody, short scale, middle pickup.

1965-1967	Calypso Blue	$350	$400

Suprosonic 30

1963-1967. Introduced as Suprosonic, renamed Suprosonic 30 in 1964. Double cutaway, single neck pickup, vibrato tailpiece, more of a student model, Holly Red.

1963-1967		$450	$550

Tremo-Lectric

1965. Fiberglas hollowbody, two pickups, unique built-in electric tremolo (not mechanical), Wedgewood Blue finish, multiple controls associated with electric tremolo.

1965		$1,000	$1,500

White Holiday/Holiday

1963-1967. Introduced as Holiday, renamed White Holiday in 1964. Fiberglas double cut, vibrato tailpiece, single bridge pickup. Dawn White.

1963-1967		$1,000	$1,500

SX

See listing for Essex.

Tacoma

1995-present. Intermediate, professional, and premium grade, production, acoustic guitars produced in Tacoma, Washington. They also build acoustic basses and mandolins.

1963 Supro Thermo-Lectric

Tacoma RM6C

Tacoma Papoose P1

1994 Takamine PSF-94

MODEL YEAR	FEATURES	EXC. COND. LOW	HIGH

C1C/C1CE Chief
1997-present. Cutaway flat-top with upper bass bout soundhole, solid cedar top, mahogany back and sides, rosewood board. Sides laminated until 2000, solid after, CE is acoustic/electric.

1997-2000		$375	$400
1997-2000	Fishman electronics	$575	$625

DM9
2000-present. D-style, solid spruce top, mahogany back and sides, satin finish.

2000	Natural	$375	$400

DR20
1997-2003. D-style, solid Sitka spruce top, solid rosewood back and sides, herringbone trim, abalone rosette.

1997-2003	Natural	$500	$600

Papoose P1
1995-present. Travel-size mini-flat-top, all solid wood, mahogany back and sides, cedar top, Natural satin finish.

1995-1999		$200	$250

Papoose P2
1995-2002. The P2 features solid rosewood back and sides.

1995-2002		$350	$450

PM15
1997-1998. Solid spruce top, solid mahogany back and sides.

1997-1998		$475	$575

Thunderchief CB10E4
2000-present. 17 3/4 flat-top, solid spruce top, solid mahogany back, laminated mahogany sides, rounded cutaway, bolt-on neck, natural satin finish, factory Fishman Prefix Plus pickup system (E4), dot markers.

2000		$700	$750

Takamine
1962-present. Intermediate and professional grade, production, steel and nylon string, acoustic and acoustic/electric guitars. They also make basses. Takamine is named after a mountain near its factory in Sakashita, Japan. Mass Hirade joined Takamine in '68 and revamped the brand's designs and improved quality. In '75, Takamine began exporting to other countries, including U.S. distribution by Kaman Music (Ovation). In '78, Takamine introduced acoustic/electric guitars. They offered solidbody electrics and some archtops for '83-'84.

Acoustic Electrics (laminate construction)
All laminate (plywood) construction, non-cutaway, standard features, pickup and preamp.

1980s		$200	$400
1990s		$200	$400

Acoustic Electrics (solid top)
Solid wood top, sides and back can vary, cutaway, standard features, preamp and pickup.

1980s		$400	$900
1990s		$400	$900

MODEL YEAR	FEATURES	EXC. COND. LOW	HIGH

Acoustic Electric Cutaways (laminate)
All laminate (plywood) construction, cutaway, standard features, pickup and preamp.

1980s		$200	$400
1990s		$200	$400

Classical Guitars (solid top)
Solid wood (often cedar) top, classical, sides and back can vary.

1980s		$400	$600
1990s		$400	$600

Collectors (limited edition)
Each year a different limited edition collector's guitar is issued.

1997 - solid top, koa body, cutaway, Natural finish, preamp and pickup.

1998-2001 - solid top, rosewood body, cutaway, Natural finish, preamp and pickup.

1990s		$900	$1,100

Taku Sakashta Guitars
1994-present. Premium and presentation grade, production/custom, archtop, flat-top, 12-sting, and nylon-string guitars, built by luthier Taku Sakashta in Sebastopol, California.

Taylor
1974-present. Intermediate, professional, premium, and presentation grade, production/custom, steel and nylon string, acoustic and acoustic/electric guitars built in El Cajon, California. Founded by Bob Taylor, Steve Schemmer and Kurt Listug in Lemon Grove, California, the company was originally named the Westland Music Company, but was soon changed to Taylor (Bob designed the guitars and it fit on the logo). Taylor and Listug bought out Schemmer in '83.

Bob Taylor was the first commercially successful guitar maker to harness CAD/CAM CNC technology for acoustic guitars. The CNC technology allowed Taylor to build a less expensive guitar model without resorting to offshore manufacturing. Taylor's CNC-based intermediate priced all wood acoustic was the Model 410. Soon other builders followed Bob Taylor's lead.

Baby
1996-present. Solid spruce top, 3/4 dreadnought, mahogany laminated back and sides until '99, sapele laminate after.

1997-2003		$150	$250

Baby Mahogany (M)
1998-present. Solid mahogany top version of Baby, mahogany laminated back and sides until '99, sapele laminate after.

1998-2003		$250	$350

Baby Rosewood
2000-2003. Laminated Indian rosewood back and sides version, solid Sitka spruce top.

2000-2003		$250	$350

MODEL YEAR	FEATURES	EXC. COND. LOW	HIGH

Big Baby

2000-present. 15/16-size dreadnought, solid Sitka spruce top, sapele-mahogany laminated back and sides, satin finish, gig bag.

| 2000-2001 | | $350 | $450 |

Model 310 Dreadnought

1998-present. D-style solid spruce top, sapele-mahogany back and sides.

| 1998-2003 | | $700 | $800 |

Model 310ce Dreadnought

1998-present. D-style Venetian cutaway, solid spruce top, sapele-mahogany back and sides, onboard electronics.

| 1998-2003 | | $800 | $900 |

Model 312ce Grand Concert

1998-present. Grand Concert Venetian cutaway, solid spruce top, sapele-mahogany back and sides, onboard electronics.

| 1998-2003 | | $700 | $850 |

Model 314 Grand Auditorium

1998-present. Mid-size Grand Auditorium-style, solid spruce top, sapele-mahogany back and sides.

| 1998-2003 | | $700 | $900 |

Model 314ce Grand Auditorium

1998-present. Grand Auditorium Venetian cutaway, solid spruce top, sapele-mahogany back and sides, onboard electronics.

| 1998-2003 | | $800 | $900 |

Model 315ce Jumbo

1998-present. Jumbo-style Venetian cutaway, solid spruce top, sapele-mahogany back and sides, onboard electronics.

| 1998-2003 | | $900 | $1,000 |

Model 355 Jumbo 12-String

1998-present. Jumbo 12-string, solid spruce top, sapele-mahogany back and sides.

| 1998-2003 | | $900 | $1,000 |

Model 355ce Jumbo 12-String

1998-present. Jumbo 12-string cutaway, solid spruce top, sapele-mahogany back and sides, onboard electrics.

| 1998-2003 | | $950 | $1,050 |

Model 410 Dreadnought

1991-present. D-style, solid spruce top, mahogany back and sides until 1998, African ovangkol back and sides after 1998.

| 1991-2003 | | $800 | $900 |

Model 410ce Dreadnought

1991-present. Cutaway, solid spruce top, mahogany back and sides until 1998, African ovangkol back and sides after 1998.

| 1991-2003 | Satin | $900 | $1,000 |

Model 412 Grand Concert

1991-1998. Solid spruce top, mahogany back and sides until 1998, African ovangkol back and sides after 1998.

| 1991-1998 | | $700 | $800 |

Model 412ce Grand Concert

1998-present. Cutaway electric version replaced the 412 in '98.

| 1998-2003 | | $800 | $900 |

Model 414 Grand Auditorium

1998-present. Solid Sitka spruce top, ovangkol back and sides, pearl dot inlays.

| 1998-2003 | Natural | $900 | $1,000 |

Model 414ce Grand Auditorium

1998-present. Cutaway version, solid Sitka spruce top, ovangkol back and sides, pearl dot inlays.

| 1998-2003 | Natural | $1,000 | $1,100 |

Model 415 Jumbo

1998-present. Solid Sitka spruce top, ovangkol back and sides, pearl dot inlays.

| 1998-2003 | | $800 | $900 |

Model 420

1990-1997. D-style, Sitka spruce top, maple back and sides.

| 1990-1997 | Natural | $800 | $900 |

Model 455 12-String

2001-present. Solid Sitka spruce top, ovangkol back and sides, dot markers.

| 2001-2003 | | $900 | $1,000 |

Model 455ce 12-String

2001-present. Cutaway electric version, solid Sitka spruce top, ovangkol back and sides, dot markers, onboard electronics.

| 2001-2003 | | $1,000 | $1,100 |

Model 510 Dreadnought

1978-present. All solid wood, spruce top, mahogany back and sides.

| 1978-1979 | | $1,000 | $1,250 |
| 1980-2003 | | $1,000 | $1,100 |

Model 510ce Dreadnought

1978-1998. Cutaway version of Model 510.

| 1978-1998 | | $1,250 | $1,350 |

Model 512 Grand Concert

1978-2000. Solid Engelmann spruce top, solid American mahogany back and sides, dot markers.

| 1978-2000 | | $1,100 | $1,300 |

Model 512ce Grand Concert

1978-present. Solid Engelmann spruce top, solid American mahogany back and sides, dot markers.

| 1978-1998 | | $1,200 | $1,400 |

Model 514c Grand Auditorium

1990-1998. Venetian cutaway, solid spruce or solid red cedar top, mahogany back and sides, no electronics.

| 1990-1998 | Natural | $1,300 | $1,500 |

Model 514ce Grand Auditorium

1998-present. Venetian cutaway, solid red cedar top, mahogany back and sides, onboard electronics.

| 1998 | | $1,400 | $1,600 |

Model 555 Jumbo 12-String

1994-present. Solid Sitka spruce top, solid mahogany back and sides, higher-end appointments.

| 1994-2003 | | $1,300 | $1,500 |

Model 555ce Jumbo 12-String

1994-present. Cutaway, solid Sitka spruce top, solid mahogany back and sides, higher-end appointments, onboard electronics.

| 1994-2003 | | $1,400 | $1,600 |

Taylor 310ce

Taylor 512ce

Taylor 712

Taylor 912ce

MODEL YEAR FEATURES	EXC. COND. LOW	HIGH
Model 610 Dreadnought		
1978-1998. Solid spruce top, solid maple back and sides, generally with Amber stained finishes.		
1978-1998	$1,200	$1,300
Model 610ce Dreadnought		
1998-present. Solid spruce top, solid maple back and sides, generally with opaque finishes, onboard electronics.		
1998-2003	$1,300	$1,500
Model 612ce Grand Concert		
1998-present. Solid spruce top, solid maple back and sides, generally with opaque finish, onboard electronics.		
1998-2003	$1,500	$1,600
Model 614 Grand Auditorium		
1978-1998. Solid spruce top, solid maple back and sides, generally with Amber stained finishes.		
1978-1998	$1,400	$1,500
Model 614ce Grand Auditorium		
1998-present. Solid spruce top, solid maple back and sides, generally with opaque finish, onboard electronics.		
1998-2003	$1,500	$1,600
Model 655 Jumbo 12-String		
1978-1991, 1996-present. Solid spruce top, solid maple back and sides, generally with Amber stained finishes.		
1978-1991	$1,500	$1,600
1996-1998	$1,500	$1,600
Model 655ce Jumbo 12-String		
1998-present. Solid spruce top, solid maple back and sides, generally with opaque finish, onboard electronics.		
1998-2003	$1,600	$1,800
Model 710		
1977-present. Dreadnought-size, rosewood back and sides, spruce top.		
1977-2003	$1,400	$1,500
Model 712 Grand Concert		
1984-present. Grand Concert small body, solid wood, non-cutaway, rosewood back and sides, spruce top, cedar soundboard.		
1984-2003	$1,400	$1,500
Model 712ce Grand Concert		
2000-present. Cutaway, Engelmann spruce top, rosewood back and sides, onboard electronics.		
2000-2003	$1,400	$1,600
Model 755 12-String		
1990-1998. D-style, 12 strings, solid spruce top, rosewood back and sides.		
1990-1998 Natural	$1,400	$1,600
Model 810 Dreadnought		
1975-present. Classic original Taylor design - early model.		
1975-2003	$1,300	$1,800
Model 810ce Dreadnought		
1998-present. Cutaway, solid Sitka spruce top, Indian rosewood back and sides, onboard electronics.		
1998-2003	$1,400	$1,900

MODEL YEAR FEATURES	EXC. COND. LOW	HIGH
Model 815c Jumbo		
1993-1998. Cutaway, no electronics, solid Sitka spruce top, Indian rosewood back and sides.		
1993-1998	$1,300	$1,500
Model 815ce Jumbo		
1998-present. Cutaway, solid Sitka spruce top, Indian rosewood back and sides, onboard electronics.		
1998-2003	$1,400	$1,600
Model 855 Jumbo 12-String		
1993-present. Jumbo (J-200-style) 12-string, solid Sitka spruce top, rosewood back and sides.		
1993-2003 Natural	$1,500	$1,700
Model 912c Grand Concert		
1993-2002. Rosewood back and sides, abalone.		
1993-2002	$2,200	$2,400
Model K10 Koa Dreadnought		
1983-present. Acoustic dreadnought, koa back and sides, spruce top, distinctive binding.		
1990s	$1,800	$2,100
Model K20 Koa Dreadnought		
1983-1992. Non-cutaway D-style, koa body, abalone rosette.		
1983-1992	$1,300	$1,500
Model K20c Koa Dreadnought		
1998-2002. Cutaway, koa body, Engelmann spruce top optional.		
1998-1999	$1,800	$2,000
Model LKSM6 12-String		
1997-present. Jumbo 12-string, spruce top, American mahogany back and sides.		
1997-2002	$1,400	$1,600
Model PS15 Jumbo		
1996-present. Solid Engelmann spruce top, Brazilian rosewood back and sides, scalloped X-bracing, high-end appointments.		
1996-2003	$4,000	$5,000
Model W10 Dreadnought		
1998-present. Claro walnut back and sides, optional tops include Sitka spruce, western red cedar, or claro walnut.		
1998-2003	$1,200	$1,400

Teisco

1946-1974, 1994-present. Founded in Tokyo, Japan by Hawaiian and Spanish guitarist Atswo Kaneko and electrical engineer Doryu Matsuda, the original company name was Aoi Onpa Kenkyujo; Teisco was the instrument name. Most imported into U.S. by Chicago's W.M.I. Corporation and Jack Westheimer beginning ca. '63-'64, some early ones for New York's Bugeleisen and Jacobson. Brandnames made by the company include Teisco, Teisco Del Rey, Kingston, World Teisco, Silvertone, Kent, Kimberly and Heit Deluxe.

In '56, the company's name was changed to Nippon Onpa Kogyo Co., Ltd., and in '64 the changed again to Teisco Co., Ltd. In January '67, the company was purchased by Kawai. After '73, the brandname was converted to Kay in U.S.; Teisco went into hiatus in Japan until being revived in the early-'90s with plexiglass reproductions of the

Spectrum 5 (not available in U.S.). Some older Teisco Del Rey stock continued to be sold in U.S. through the '70s.

EG-27
Two pickups.
1960s ... $100 ... $200

K-4L/ET-460 Super Deluxe
1966-1969. Solidbody electric.
1966-1969 ... $200 ... $400

May Queen
1968-1969. Cutaway teardrop with F-hole body, two pickups, tremolo tailpiece.
1968-1969 Black ... $400 ... $600
1968-1969 Red ... $500 ... $700

Spectrum II
1968-1969. Solidbody electric, two pickups.
1968-1969 ... $200 ... $300

Spectrum V
1966-1969. Solidbody Electric.
1966-1969 ... $300 ... $500

Tele-Star
1965-ca.1972. Imported from Japan by Tele-Star Musical Instrument Corporation of New York, NY. Primarily made by Kawai, many inspired by Burns designs, some in cool sparkle finishes.
Electric Hollowbody Archtop Guitars
1967-1970.
1967-1970 Various models ... $100 ... $200

Tennessee
1970-1993, 1996-present. Luthier Mark Taylor builds his professional and premium grade, production/custom, acoustic guitars in Old Hickory, Tennessee. He also builds mandolins, banjos and the Tut Taylor brand of resophonic guitars. Mark and his father Robert "Tut" Taylor started making the Tennessee brand of acoustic and resophonic guitars, banjos, and mandolins in 1971. In '77, Tut left the company and Mark continued on as Crafters of Tennessee. In '93, Mark and Greg Rich started building instruments as Rich and Taylor. In '96, Mark resumed production under the Tennessee brand.

Texas
1959-ca. 1965. Line of aluminum neck electric solidbodies and basses made by France's Jacobacci company, which also built under its own brand. 1, 2, or 3 pickups.

Thompson Guitars
1980-present. Luthier Ted Thompson builds his professional and premium grade, production/custom, flat-top, 12-string, and nylon-string guitars in Vernon, British Columbia.

Thorn Custom Guitars
2000-present. Professional and premium grade, custom/production, solid- and hollowbody electrics built by luthiers Bill Thorn and his sons Bill, Jr. and Ron in Glendale, California. They started Thorn Custom Inlay in the early '90s to do custom inlay work for other builders. In '00, they added their own line of guitars.

Threet Guitars
1990-present. Premium grade, production/custom, flat-tops built by luthier Judy Threet in Calgary, Alberta.

Timeless Instruments
1980-present. Luthier David Freeman builds his professional, premium and presentation grade, custom, flattop, 12-string, nylon-string, and resonator guitars in Tugaske, Saskatchewan. He also builds mandolins and dulcimers.

Timm Guitars
1997-present. Professional grade, custom, flattop, resonator and travel guitars built by luthier Jerry Timm in Auburn, Washington.

Timtone Custom Guitars
1993-present. Luthier Tim Diebert builds his premium grade, custom, solidbody, chambered-body and acoustic guitars in Grand Forks, British Columbia. He also builds basses and lap steels.

Tippin Guitar Co.
1978-present. Professional, premium and presentation grade, production/custom, flattop guitars built by luthier Bill Tippin in Marblehead, Massachusetts.

Tobias
1977-present. Known mainly for basses, Tobias did offer guitar models in the '80s. See Bass Section for more company info.

Tokai
1947-present. Japan's Tokai Company started out making a keyboard harmonica that was widely used in Japanese schools. In the late '60s, Tokai hooked up with Tommy Moore, a successful instrument merchandiser from Fort Worth, Texas, and by '70 they were producing private label and OEM guitars. The guitars were sold in the U.S. under the brandnames of various importers. By the '70s, the Tokai name was being used on the instruments. Today Tokai continues to offer electrics, acoustics, and electric basses made in Japan and Korea.
ASD 403 Custom Edition
Double cut solidbody, two single-coil/one humbucker pickups, locking tremolo.
1980s ... $350 ... $450
AST 56
Maple neck, three pickups, various colors.
1980s Various colors ... $350 ... $450

Teisco Spectrum 5

1982 Tokai AST-56

GUITARS

MODEL YEAR	FEATURES	EXC. COND. LOW	HIGH

Tony Nobles Tricone

1970s Travis Bean

Tom Anderson Guitarworks

1984-present. Professional and premium grade, production/custom, solidbody, semi-solidbody and acoustic guitars built by luthier Tom Anderson in Newbury Park, California.

Classic
1984-present. Double cut solidbody, classic 3 pickup configuration. Colors and appointments can vary.

1984-1989		$1,200	$1,600
1990-1999		$1,200	$1,600
2000-2003		$1,200	$1,600

Cobra
1993-present. Single cut solid mahogany body with figured maple top.

1993-2002		$1,500	$1,800

Drop Top
1992-present. Double cut solidbody, single/single/humbucker pickups, various specs.

1992-1999		$1,500	$1,800

Hollow Classic
1996-present. Ash double cut with tone chambers, 3 pickups.

1996-1999		$1,400	$1,700

Tony Nobles

1990-present. Professional and premium grade, custom, acoustic and electric guitars built by luthier Tony Nobles in Wimberley, Texas. Tony writes a monthly repair article for Vintage Guitar magazine.

Torres (Antonio de Torres Jurado)

19th Century luthier most often associated with the initial development of the Classical Spanish guitar.

Toyota

1972-?. Imported from Japan by Hershman of New York, NY. At least one high-end acoustic designed by T. Kurosawa was ambitiously priced at $650.

Electric Hollowbody Archtop Guitars
1970s. Various models.

1970s		$100	$200

Traphagen, Dake

1972-present. Luthier Dake Traphagen builds his premium grade, custom, nylon-string guitars in Bellingham, Washington.

Traugott Guitars

1991-present. Premium grade, production/custom, flattop and acoustic/electric guitars built by luthier Jeff Traugott in Santa Cruz, California.

Travis Bean

1974-1979, 1999. Aluminum-necked solidbody electric guitars and basses. The company was founded by motorcycle and metal-sculpture enthusiast Travis Bean and guitar repairman Marc

McElwee in Southern California; soon joined by Gary Kramer (see Kramer guitars). Kramer left Travis Bean in '75 and founded Kramer guitars with other partners. Guitar production began in mid-'76. The guitars featured carved aluminum necks with three-and-three heads with a "T" cutout in the center and wooden fingerboards. Some necks had bare aluminum backs, some were painted Black. A total of about 3,650 instruments were produced. Travis Bean guitar production was stopped in the summer of '79. The company started production again in '99 with updated versions of original designs and new models.

Serial numbers were stamped on headstock and were more-or-less consecutive. Original retail prices were $895 to $1195.

TB-1000 Artist
1974-1979. Aluminum neck with T-slotted headstock, double cut 335-size archtop body, two humbucking pickups, four controls, block markers on fingerboard.

1974-1979		$1,400	$1,600

TB-1000 Standard
1976-1979. Aluminum neck with T-slotted headstock, double cutaway body, two humbucking pickups, four controls, small pickguard, dot markers on fingerboard.

1976-1979		$1,400	$1,600

TB-3000 Wedge Guitar
1976-1979. Aluminum neck with T-slotted headstock, triangle-shaped body, two humbucking pickups, four controls, block markers on fingerboard.

1976-1979		$1,500	$1,800

Triggs

1992-present. Luthiers Jim Triggs and his son Ryan build their professional and premium grade, production/custom, archtop, flat-top, and solidbody guitars originally in Nashville, and, since '98, in Kansas City, Kansas. They also build mandolins.

Byrdland
17 inch Byrdland-style, single cut, 2 humbuckers, flamed maple top, back and sides.

1997	Natural	$2,800	$3,200

Excel
17 inch archtop cutaway, carved spruce top, flamed maple back and sides, Excel logo.

1999	Sunburst	$5,700	$6,000

New Yorker
18 inch archtop cutaway, carved spruce top, figured maple back and sides, Empire State New Yorker logo. Blond or Sunburst.

1992-2000		$6,000	$7,500

True North Guitars

1994-present. Luthier Dennis Scannell builds his premium grade, custom, flat-tops in Waterbury, Vermont.

MODEL YEAR	FEATURES	EXC. COND. LOW	HIGH

True Tone

1960s. Guitars, basses and amps retailed by Western Auto, manufactured by Chicago guitar makers like Kay. The brand was most likely gone by '68.

Double Cutaway Electric Archtop (K592)

1960s. Made by Kay and similar to their K592 double cut thinline acoustic, 2 pickups, Bigsby tailpiece, burgundy red.

1960s		$400	$450

Jazz King (K573 Speed Demon)

1960s. Kay's K573 Speed Demon, three pickups, thinline archtop electric with F-hole, eighth note art on pickguard.

1960s	Sunburst	$400	$650

Rock 'n Roll Electric (K100)

1960s. Kay's K100, slab body, single pickup, but with a bright Red multiple lacquer finish.

1960s	Red	$175	$225

Solidbody (K300 Kay)

1960s. Made by Kay and similar to their K300, double cut, dual pickups and vibrola arm.

1960s	Red	$475	$525

Speed Master (K6533 Value Leader Archtop)

1960s. Made by Kay and similar to their K6533 full-body electric archtop Value Leader line, eighth note art pickguard.

1960s	Sunburst	$150	$250

Tucker

2000-present. Founded by John N. "Jack" Tucker, John Morrall, and David Killingsworth, Tucker builds professional and premium grade, production/custom, albizzia wood solidbody guitars in Hanalei, Hawaii. They also build basses.

Tut Taylor

Line of professional and premium grade, production/custom, resophonic guitars built by luthier Mark Taylor of Crafters of Tennessee in Old Hickory, Tennessee. Brand named for his father, dobro artist Tut Taylor. Taylor also builds the Tennessee line of guitars, mandolins and banjos and was part of Rich and Taylor guitars for 1993-'96.

TV Jones

1993-present. Professional and premium grade, production/custom, hollow, chambered, and solid body guitars built by luthier Thomas Vincent Jones originally in California, now in Poulsbo, Washington. The instruments have either Jones or TV Jones inlaid on the headstock. He also builds pickups.

Unique Guitars

2003-present. Professional and premium grade, production/custom, solidbody guitars built by luthier Joey Rico in California. He also builds basses. Joey is the son of Bernie Rico, the founder of BC Rich guitars.

Univox

1964-1978. Univox started out as an amp line and added guitars around '68. Guitars were imported from Japan by the Merson Musical Supply Company, later Unicord, Westbury, NY. Many if not all supplied by Arai and Company (Aria, Aria Pro II), some made by Matsumoku. Univox Lucy ('69) first copy of lucite Ampeg Dan Armstrong. Generally mid-level copies of American designs.

Acoustic Flat-Tops

1969-1978. Various models.

1970s		$100	$250

Bi-Centennial

1976. Offset double cut, heavily carved body, brown stain, 3 humbucker-style pickups.

1976		$500	$800

Electric Hollowbodies

Various models.

1970s		$300	$500

Electric Solidbodies

Includes Flying V, Mosrite and Hofner violin-guitar copies.

1970s		$300	$500

USA Custom Guitars

1999-present. Professional and premium grade, custom/production, solidbody electric guitars built in Tacoma, Washington. USA also does work for other luthiers.

Vaccaro

1997-2002. Founded by Henry Vaccaro, Sr., one of the founders of Kramer Guitars. They offered intermediate and professional grade, production/custom, aluminum-necked guitars designed by Vaccaro, former Kramer designer Phil Petillo, and Henry Vaccaro, Jr., which were made in Asbury Park, New Jersey. They also built basses.

Valco

Valco, from Chicago, was a big player in the guitar and amplifier business. Their products were private branded for other companies like National, Supro, Airline, Oahu, and Gretsch.

Valencia

1985-present. Budget grade, production, classical guitars imported by Rondo Music of Union, New Jersey.

Valley Arts

Ca. 1977-present. Production/custom, semi-hollow and solidbody guitars built in Nashville. Valley Arts originally was a Southern California music store where partner Mike McGuire taught and did most of the repairs. Around '77, McGuire and Valley Arts started making custom instruments on a large scale. By '83, they opened a separate manufacturing facility to build the guitars. In '92 Samick acquired half of the company with McGuire staying on for a year as a consultant. Samick offered made-in-the-U.S.

Unique X-1

1970 Univox Lucy

Valley Arts Brent Mason

Veleno Original

production and custom models under the Valley Arts name. As of 2002, Valley Arts is a division of Gibson Guitar Corp., which builds the guitars in Nashville. They reintroduced the line in January, '02.

California Pro (U.S.-made)
1983-2002. Double cut body, six-on-a-side tuners, single/single/humbucker, two knobs and switch, serial number begins with CAL.

MODEL YEAR	FEATURES	EXC. COND. LOW	HIGH
1990-1999	Green Opaque	$475	$550

Optek Fretlight (U.S.-made)
Double cut body, about 126 LED lights in fretboard controlled by a scale/chord selector.

1990	Black Opaque	$475	$550

Standard Pro (U.S.-made)
1990-1993. Double cut body, six-on-a-side tuners, single/single/humbucker, two knobs and switch, serial number begins with VA.

1990-1993		$475	$550

Vantage
1977-present. Budget and intermediate grade, production, acoustic and electric guitars. They also build basses. Instruments from Japan from '77-'90 and from Korea from '90-present.

Electric Solidbodies
Student- to mid-level instruments, various models.

1970s		$200	$250

Hollowbody
1980s. Rounded cutaway, block markers, humbucking pickups, upper bass bout toggle.

1980s	Sunburst	$400	$500

Vega
1903-1980s, 1989-present. The name 'Vega' means 'star' and a star logo is often seen on the original Vega guitars. The original Boston-based company was purchased by C.F. Martin in 1970. In '80, Martin sold the Vega trademark to Korea's Galaxy Trading Company. The Deering Banjo Company, in Spring Valley, California acquired the brand name in 1989 and uses it (and the star logo) on a line of banjos.

C-series Archtops
1930-1950s. Several different C-model numbers, mid-level archtops including carved solid tops with bookmatched figured maple backs, Natural or Sunburst.

1930s		$900	$1,100
1940s		$900	$1,100
1950s	Cutaway	$1,000	$1,200

Duo-Tron Electric Archtop
1940s-1950s. Mid-level large body non-cutaway archtop, single pickup, block markers, Natural or Sunburst.

1940s		$1,200	$1,500
1950s		$1,200	$1,500

FT-90 (flat-top)
1960s. 15 inch body with narrow waist, dot markers, Vega logo.

1960s	Natural	$500	$600

Parlor Guitar
Early-1900s. Small parlor-sized instrument, Brazilian rosewood back and sides. Styles vary, fancy appointments associated with higher-end models, including binding, purfling and inlays.

MODEL YEAR	FEATURES	EXC. COND. LOW	HIGH
1900s	Mid-level	$1,700	$2,200
1914	Higher-end	$2,100	$2,700

Profundo Flat-Top
1940s-1950s. Flat top D-style body, spruce top.

1940s-50s	Mahogany back & sides	$1,400	$1,700
1940s-50s	Rosewood back & sides	$2,800	$3,200

Solidbody Electrics (import)
1970s-1980s. Solidbody copies of classic designs. Vega script logo on headstock, bolt-on necks.

1970s		$250	$350

Vega, Charles
1993-present. Luthier Charles Vega builds his premium, production/custom, nylon-string guitars in Baltimore, Maryland.

Veillette
1991-present. Luthier Joe Veillette (of Veillette-Citron fame) builds his professional grade, production/custom, acoustic, acoustic/electric, electric 6- and 12-string and baritone guitars in Woodstock, New York. He also builds basses and mandolins.

Gryphon MK IV (12-string)
2002-present. Hi-tuned 12 string, 18 1/2"-scale solidbody (like 1960s Vox Phantom 12), under-saddle piezo.

2002		$1,050	$1,250

Veillette-Citron
1975-1983. Founded by Joe Veillette and Harvey Citron who met at the NY College School of Architecture in the late '60s. Joe took a guitar building course from Michael Gurian and by the Summer of '76, he and Harvey started producing neck-thru solidbody guitars and basses. Veillette and Citron both are back building instruments.

Veleno
1967, 1970-1977, 2003-present. Premium and presentation grade, production/custom, all-aluminum electric solidbody guitars built by luthier John Veleno in St. Petersburg, Florida. First prototype in '67. Later production begins in late-'70 and lasts until '75 or '76. The guitars were chrome or gold-plated, with various anodized colors. The Traveler Guitar was the idea of B.B. King; only 10 were made. Two Ankh guitars were made for Todd Rundgren in '77. Only one bass was made. Approximately 185 instruments were made up to '77 and are sequentially numbered. In 2003, John Veleno reintroduced his brand. See *Guitar Stories Volume II*, by Michael Wright, for a complete history of Veleno guitars.

MODEL YEAR	FEATURES	EXC. COND. LOW	HIGH

Original (Aluminum Solidbody)
1973-1976. V-headstock, chrome and aluminum.

1973-1976		$7,000	$9,000

Traveler Guitar
1973-1976. Limited production of about a dozen instruments, drop-anchor-style metal body.

1973-1976		$9,500	$11,000

Ventura
1970s. Import copies distributed by C. Bruno (Kaman). Models include copies of the Howard Roberts, ES-335, SG, Flying V, Les Paul Special slab body, L-5, Barney Kessel, ES-175, and various Les Pauls. Acoustic copies include Dove, J-200, D-style, and Classical.

V-1003
1970s. Copy of Les Paul Custom.

1970s		$250	$350

V-1007
1970s. Sharp-pointed single cutaway, double pickups, block markers, ES-175 copy.

1970s		$350	$500

Versoul, LTD
1989-present. Premium grade, production/custom steel-string flat-top, acoustic/electric, nylon-string, resonator, solidbody, and baritone guitars built by luthier Kari Nieminen in Helsinki, Finland. He also builds basses and sitars.

Victor Baker Guitars
1998-present. Professional and premium grade, custom, carved archtop, flattop and solidbody electric guitars built by luthier Victor Baker in Philadelphia, Pennsylvania.

Vivi-Tone
1933-ca. 1936. Founded in Kalamazoo, Michigan, by former Gibson designer Lloyd Loar, Walter Moon and Lewis Williams, Vivi-Tone built acoustic archtop guitars as well as some of the earliest electric solidbodies. They also built amps, basses, and mandolins.

Guitar
1930s. Deep archtop-style body with F-holes on the backside and magnetic bridge pickup.

1930s	Rare model	$2,100	$3,500
1930s	Sunburst, standard model	$1,700	$2,100

Vox
1957-1972, 1982-present. Name introduced by Jennings Musical Instruments (JMI) of England. First Vox products were amplifiers brought to the market in 1958 by Tom Jennings and Dick Denny. Guitars were introduced in '61, with an Echo Unit starting the Vox line of effects in '63. Guitars and basses bearing the Vox name were offered from 1961-'69 (made in England and Italy), '82-'85 (Japan), '85-'88 (Korea), and for '98-2001 (U.S.). Vox products are currently distributed in the U.S. by Korg USA.

MODEL YEAR	FEATURES	EXC. COND. LOW	HIGH

Special thanks to Jim Rhoads of Rhoads Music in Elizabethtown, PA, for help on production years of these models.

Apollo
1967-1968. Single sharp cutaway, 1 pickup, distortion, treble and bass booster. Available in Sunburst or Cherry.

1967-1968		$500	$700

Bobcat
1963-1968. Double cut semi-hollowbody, block markers, 3 pickups, vibrato, 2 volume and 2 tone controls.

1963-1968		$650	$750

Bossman
1967-1968. Single rounded cutaway, 1 pickup, distortion, treble and bass booster. Available in Sunburst or Cherry.

1967-1968		$450	$550

Bulldog
1966. Solidbody double cutaway.

1966		$600	$850

Delta
1967-1968. Solidbody, 2 pickups, distortion, treble and bass boosters, vibrato, 1 volume and 2 tone controls. Available in White only.

1967-1968		$1,000	$1,300

Folk XII
1966-1969. D-style 12-string flat-top, large three point pickguard, block markers.

1966-1969	Natural	$450	$550

Guitar-Organ
1966. Standard Phantom with oscillators from a Continental organ installed inside. Plays either organ sounds, guitar sounds, or both. Weighs over 20 pounds.

1966		$1,300	$1,800

Mando Guitar
1966. Made in Italy, 12-string mandolin thing.

1966		$1,300	$1,600

Mark III
1998-2001. Teardrop reissue.

1998-2001		$700	$750

Mark IX
1965-1966. Solidbody teardrop-shaped, 9 strings, 3 pickups, vibrato, 1 volume and 2 tone controls.

1965	Sunburst	$800	$950

Mark VI
1965-1967. Teardrop-shaped solidbody, three pickups, vibrato, one volume and two tone controls.

1965-1967	Sunburst	$1,000	$1,200

Mark VI Reissue
1998-2001.

1998-2001		$700	$750

Mark XII
1965-1967. Teardrop-shaped solidbody, 12 strings, 3 pickups, vibrato, 1 volume and 2 tone controls.

1965-1967	Sunburst	$900	$1,000

Phantom VI
1962-1967. Five-sided body, 6 strings, 3 pickups, vibrato, 1 volume and 2 tone controls.

1962-1964	English-made	$1,900	$2,100
1965-1967	Italian-made	$1,200	$1,400

Versoul Buxom 6

Vox Mark VI

Vox Phantom XII

1965 Wandré Model Karak

MODEL YEAR	FEATURES	EXC. COND. LOW	HIGH
Phantom XII			
1964-1967. Five-sided body, 12 strings, 3 pickups, vibrato, 1 volume and 2 tone controls.			
1964	English-made	$1,900	$2,100
1965-1967	Italian-made	$1,200	$1,300
Spitfire			
1965-1967. Solidbody double cut, 3 pickups, vibrato tailpiece.			
1965-1967		$425	$500
Starstream			
1967-1968. Teardrop-shaped hollowbody, 2 pickups, distortion, treble and bass boosters, wah-wah, vibrato, 1 volume and 2 tone controls, three-way pickup selector. Available in Cherry or Sandburst.			
1967-1968		$1,000	$1,200
Starstream XII			
1967-1968. Teardrop-shaped hollowbody, 12 strings, 2 pickups, distortion, treble and bass boosters, wah-wah, vibrato, 1 volume and 2 tone controls, three-way pickup selector. Available in Cherry or Sandburst.			
1967-1968		$1,000	$1,200
Stroller			
1961-1966. Made in England, solidbody, single bridge pickup, Hurricane-style contoured body, dot markers.			
1961-1966	Red	$300	$400
Student Prince			
1965-1967. Mahogany body thinline archtop electric, 2 knobs, dot markers, made in Italy.			
1965-1967		$300	$400
Super Ace			
1963-1965. Solidbody double cutaway.			
1963-1965		$300	$400
Super Lynx			
1965-1967. Similar to Bobcat but with 2 pickups and no vibrola, double cut, 2 pickups, adjustable truss rod, 2 bass and 2 volume controls.			
1965-1967		$600	$800
Super Lynx Deluxe			
1965-1967. Super Lynx with added vibrato tailpiece.			
1965-1967		$600	$800
Super Meteor			
1965-1967. Solidbody double cutaway.			
1965-1967		$250	$300
Tempest XII			
1965-1967. Solidbody double cut, 12 strings, 3 pickups.			
1965-1967		$450	$550
Thunder Jet			
1960s-style with single pickup and vibrato arm.			
1960s		$500	$625
Tornado			
1965-1967. Thinline archtop, single pickup, dot markers.			
1965-1967	Sunburst	$300	$350
Typhoon			
1965-1967. Hollowbody single cut, 2 pickups, three-piece laminated neck.			
1965-1967		$350	$450

MODEL YEAR	FEATURES	EXC. COND. LOW	HIGH
Ultrasonic			
1967-1968. Hollowbody double cut, 2 pickups, distortion, treble and bass boosters, wah-wah, vibrato, 1 volume and 2 tone controls, three-way pickup selector. Available in Sunburst or Cherry.			
1967-1968		$650	$850
Viper			
1968. Double cut thinline archtop electric, built-in distortion.			
1968		$1,000	$1,200

Walker

1994-present. Premium and presentation grade, production/custom, flat-top and archtop guitars built by luthier Kim Walker in North Stonington, Connecticut.

Wandre (Davoli)

Ca. 1956/57-1969. Solidbody and thinline hollowbody electric guitars and basses created by German-descended Italian motorcycle and guitar enthusiast, artist, and sculptor from Milan, Italy, Wandre Pioli. Brand names include Wandre (pronounced "Vahn-dray"), Davoli, Framez, JMI, Noble, Dallas, Avalon, Avanti I and others. Until '60, they were built by Pioli himself; from '60-'63 built in Milan by Framez; '63-'65 built by Davoli; '66-'69 built in Pioli's own factory.

The guitars originally used Framez pickups, but from '63 on (or earlier) they used Davoli pickups. Mostly strange shapes characterized by neck-through-tailpiece aluminum neck with plastic back and rosewood fingerboard. Often multi-color and sparkle finishes, using unusual materials like linoleum, fiberglass and laminates, metal bindings. Often the instruments will have numerous identifying names but usually somewhere there is a Wandre "blob" logo.

Distributed early on in the U.K. by Jennings Musical Industries, Ltd. (JMI) and in the U.S. by Don Noble and Company. Model B.B. dedicated to Brigitte Bardot. Among more exotic instruments were the minimalist Krundaal Bikini guitar with a built-in amplifier and attached speaker, and the "pogo stick" Swedenbass. These guitars are relatively rare and highly collectible.

Warrior

1995-present. Professional, premium, and presentation grade, production/custom, acoustic and solidbody electric guitars built by luthier J.D. Lewis in Roseville, Georgia. Warrior also builds basses.

Washburn (Lyon & Healy)

1880s-ca.1949. Washburn was founded in Chicago as one of the lines for Lyon & Healy to promote high quality stringed instruments, circa 1880s. The rights to manufacture Washburns were sold to J.R. Stewart Co. in '28, but rights to Washburn name were sold to Tonk Brothers Of Chicago. In the Great depression (about 1930), J.R. Stewart Co. was

MODEL YEAR	FEATURES	EXC. COND. LOW	HIGH

hit hard and declared bankruptcy. Tonk Brothers bought at auction all Stewart trade names, then sold them to Regal Musical Instrument Co. Regal built Washburns by the mid-'30s. The Tonk Brothers still licensed the name. These Washburn models lasted until ca. '49. In '74 the brand resurfaced.

Model 1897
High-end appointments, plentiful pearl, 18 frets, slightly larger than parlor size.

| 1910 | Natural | $2,500 | $3,500 |

Model 1915
Brazilian rosewood back and sides.

| 1928 | | $1,800 | $2,500 |

Style 188
Rosewood back and sides with full pearl fingerboard inlaid with contrasting colored pearl. Pearl on edges and around soundhole.

| 1890s | | $4,000 | $4,500 |

Washburn

1974-present. Budget, intermediate, professional, and premium grade, production/custom, acoustic and electric guitars made in the U.S., Japan, and Korea. They also make basses, amps, banjos and mandolins. Originally a Lyon & Healy brand, the Washburn line was revived in '74, promoted by Beckman Musical Instruments. Beckman sold the rights to the Washburn name to Fretted Instruments, Inc. in '76. Guitars originally made in Japan and Korea, but production moved back to U.S. in '91. Currently Washburn is part of U.S. Music.

AF-40 Ace Frehley
1985-1988. Four-pointed solidbody, pointy headstock, one pickup, locking trem, Red lightning bolt starting on body and going half way up neck.

| 1985-1988 | | $500 | $800 |

D-42 SW Harvest
1983-1989. Flat-top, spruce top, rosewood back, sides and pickguard, maple binding, purfling. Name currently used on similar model.

| 1983-1989 | | $400 | $450 |

D-42 SW Harvest Deluxe
1983-1989. Same as Harvest, but with abalone trim and cat's-eye board inlays, Gold tuners. Name currently used on similar model.

| 1983-1989 | | $450 | $600 |

D-50S
1978-ca. 1985. Dreadnought, herringbone trim, rosewood back and sides, pearl inlays.

| 1978-1985 | | $350 | $450 |

D-55 SW
1995. Limited run of 200 made by Dana Bourgeois, Lewiston, ME, rosewood back and sides, Sitka spruce top.

| 1995 | Koa back & sides | $1,700 | $2,100 |
| 1995 | Rosewood back & sides | $1,600 | $1,900 |

DC-80E
1988-1992. Extended cutaway, dreadnought, cedar top, on-board preamp.

| 1988-1992 | | $450 | $550 |

Mirage
1983-1985. Single cut acoustic/electric classical.

| 1983-1985 | | $250 | $300 |

Monterey 12-String
Early 1980s. Thin body, 12 strings.

| 1981 | | $250 | $350 |

Spirit DL
1983-1985. Single cut acoustic/electric folk/classical.

| 1983-1985 | | $250 | $300 |

Watkins/WEM

1957-present. Watkins Electric Music (WEM) was founded by Charlie Watkins. Their first commercial product was the Watkins Dominator (wedge Gibson stereo amp shape) in '57. They made the Rapier line of guitars and basses from the beginning. Watkins offered guitars and basses up to 1982.

Wayne

1998-present. Professional and premium grade, production/custom, solidbody guitars built by luthiers Wayne and Michael (son) Charvel in Paradise, California. They also build lap steels.

Webber

1988-present. Professional grade, production/custom flat-top guitars built by luthier David Webber in North Vancouver, British Columbia.

000 12-Fret
1990s. 15 1/4" lower bout 000-style, 12-fret to the body slot-head neck, Sitka spruce top, Indian rosewood back and sides, W logo on headstock.

| 1990s | | $1,300 | $1,600 |

D
1990s. 15 ½" D-style, spruce top, rosewood back and sides, W logo on headstock.

| 1990s | Natural | $1,300 | $1,600 |

Wechter

1984-present. Intermediate, professional and premium grade, production/custom, flat-top, 12-string, and nylon string guitars from luthier Abe Wechter in Paw Paw, Michigan. The Elite line is built in Paw Paw, the others in Asia. He also offers basses. Until 1994 he built guitars on a custom basis. In '95, he set up a manufacturing facility in Paw Paw to produce his new line. Wechter was associated with Gibson Kalamazoo from the mid-'70s to '84.

Pathmaker 12
1994-present. Double cutaway, acoustic flat-top, 12 strings with onboard electronics.

| 1994-1999 | Natural gloss | $800 | $1,000 |

Pathmaker Elite
1994-present. Double cutaway, acoustic/electric flat-top, cedar top, walnut back and sides.

| 1994-1999 | Sunburst | $800 | $1,000 |

1910 Washburn Style 1897

1978 Washburn Southern Jumbo

1930s Weissenborn

Westone Corsair

MODEL YEAR	FEATURES	EXC. COND. LOW	HIGH

Pathmaker Standard
1994-present. Double cutaway, acoustic flat-top, solid Sitka spruce top, solid mahogany back and sides or optional rosewood back and sides.

| 1994-1999 | Natural gloss | $800 | $1,000 |

Weissenborn
1910s-1937, present. Hermann Weissenborn was well-established as a violin and piano builder in Los Angeles by the early 1910s. Around 1920, he added guitars, ukes and steels to his line. Most of his production was in the '20s and '30s until his death in 1937. He made tenor, plectrum, parlor, and Spanish guitars, ukuleles, and mandolins, but is best remembered for his koa Hawaiian guitars that caught the popular wave of Hawaiian music. That music captivated America after being introduced to the masses at San Francisco's Panama Pacific International Exposition which was thrown in 1915 to celebrate the opening of the Panama Canal and attended by more than 13 million people. He also made instruments for Kona and other brands. The Weissenborn brand has been revived on a line of reissue style guitars.

Style #1 Hawaiian
Koa, no binding, 3 wood circle soundhole inlays.

| 1920s | | $3,000 | $3,500 |

Style #2 Hawaiian
Koa, black celluloid body binding, white wood fingerboard binding, rope soundhole binding.

| 1920s | | $3,500 | $4,000 |

Style #3 Hawaiian
Koa, rope binding on top, fingerboard, and soundhole.

| 1920s | | $4,000 | $4,500 |

Style #4 Hawaiian
Koa, rope binding on body, fingerboard, headstock and soundhole.

| 1920s | | $4,500 | $5,000 |

Style A Spanish
Koa, no binding, 3 wood circle soundhole inlays.

| 1924 | | $2,000 | $3,000 |

Style B Spanish
Koa, black celluloid body binding, white wood fingerboard binding, rope soundhole binding.

| 1924 | | $2,500 | $3,500 |

Style C Spanish
Koa, rope binding on top, fingerboard, and soundhole.

| 1924 | | $3,000 | $4,000 |

Style D Spanish
Koa, rope binding on body, fingerboard, headstock and soundhole.

| 1924 | | $4,000 | $5,000 |

Wendler
1999-present. Intermediate and professional grade, production/custom, solidbody, electro-acoustic guitars from luthier Dave Wendler of Ozark Instrument Building in Branson, Missouri. He also builds basses. In '91, Wendler patented a pickup system that became the Taylor ES system.

Westbury-Unicord
1978-ca. 1983. Imported from Japan by Unicord of Westbury, New York. High quality original designs, generally with two humbuckers, some with varitone and glued-in necks.

Deluxe
1978-1981. Double cut solidbody, 2 exposed humbuckers.

| 1978-1981 | White | $350 | $450 |

Standard
1978-1981. Double cut solidbody, 2 exposed humbuckers, dot markers, Westbury logo on headstock.

| 1978-1981 | Sunburst | $300 | $350 |

Westone
1970s-1990, 1996-2001. Made by Matsumoku in Matsumoto, Japan and imported by St. Louis Music. Around '81, St. Louis Music purchased an interest in Matsumoku and began to make a transition from its own Electra brandname to the Westone brandname previously used by Matsumoku. In the beginning of '84, the brandname became Electra-Westone with a phoenix bird head surrounded by circular wings and flames. By the end of '84 the Electra name was dropped, leaving only Westone and a squared-off bird with W-shaped wings logo. Electra, Electra-Westone and Westone instruments from this period are virtually identical except for the brand and logo treatment. Many of these guitars were made in very limited runs and are relatively rare. From '96 to '01, England's FCN Music offered Westone branded electric and acoustic guitars. The electrics were built in England and the acoustics came from Korea.

Matsumoku-made guitars feature a serial number in which the first one or two digits represent the year of manufacture. Electra-Westone guitars should begin with either a 4 or 84.

Corsair
1989-1990, 1996-2001. Double cut solidbody endorsed by Steve Lynch, built-in DSR-5 Harmonic Enhancer, 2 humbuckers. Name revived on English-built model in 1996.

| 1989-1990 | | $175 | $250 |

Pantera II
1986-1990. Like the Trevor Rabin III, but with two humbuckers and finer features.

| 1990-1990 | | $250 | $350 |

Thunder I
Early-mid 1980s. Double cut solidbody, 2 humbuckers.

| 1980s | | $200 | $250 |

Weymann
1864-1940s. H.A. Weymann & Sons was a musical instrument distributor located in Philadelphia that marketed various stringed instruments, but mainly known for banjos. Some guitar models made by Regal and Vega, but they also built their own instruments.

Parlor Guitar
1904-ca. 1920. Small 14 5/8" body parlor-style, fancy pearl and abalone trim, fancy fretboard markers.

| 1910 | Natural | $3,000 | $4,000 |

MODEL YEAR	FEATURES	EXC. COND. LOW	HIGH

Wilkanowski

Early-1930s-mid-1940s. W. Wilkanowski primarily built violins. He did make a few dozen guitars which were heavily influenced by violin design concepts and in fact look very similar to a large violin with a guitar neck.

Violin-Shaped Acoustic
1930-1945.

1930-1945	Violin Brown	$18,000	$22,000

Wilkins

1984-present. Custom guitars built by luthier Pat Wilkins in Van Nuys, California. Wilkins also does finish work for individuals and a variety of other builders.

Wilson Brothers Guitars

2004-present. Production electric and acoustic guitars. They also build basses. Founded by Ventures guitarist Don Wilson.

Windsor

Ca. 1890s-ca. 1914. Brandname used by Montgomery Ward for flat top guitars and mandolins made by various American manufacturers, including Lyon & Healy and, possibly, Harmony. Generally beginner-grade instruments.

Acoustic Flat-Top Guitars
1890s-1914.

1900s		$200	$300

Winston

Ca. 1963-1967. Imported from Japan by Buegeleisen and Jacobson of New York. Manufacturers unknown, but some are by Guyatone. Generally shorter scale beginner guitars.

Electric Thinline Archtop Guitars
Ca.1963-1967.

1960s		$150	$250

Worland Guitars

1997-present. Professional grade, production/custom, flat-top, 12-string, and harp guitars built by luthier Jim Worland in Rockford, Illinois.

WRC Music International

1989-mid-1990s. WRC Music International by Wayne Richard Charvel, who was the original founder of Charvel Guitars.

Wright Guitar Technology

1993-present. Luthier Rossco Wright builds his unique intermediate grade, production, travel/practice steel-string and nylon-string guitars in Eugene, Oregon.

Wurlitzer

Wurlitzer marketed a line of American-made guitars in the 1920s. They also offered American- and foreign-made guitars starting in 1965. The American ones were built from '65-'66 by the Holman-Woodell guitar factory in Neodesha, Kansas. In '67, Wurlitzer switched to Italian made Welson guitars.

Model 2077 (Martin 0-K)
1920s. Made by Martin for Wurlitzer who had full-line music stores in most major cities. Size 0 with top, back and sides made from koa wood, limited production of about 28 instruments.

1920s	Natural	$5,000	$5,500

Model 2090 (Martin 0-28)
1920s. Made by Martin for Wurlitzer who had full-line music stores in most major cities. Size 0 with appointments similar to a similar period Martin 0-28. Limited production of about 11 instruments. Wurlitzer branded on the back of the headstock and on the inside back seam. Martin name also branded on inside seam.

1920s	Natural	$7,000	$8,000

Wild One "Stereo"
1960s. Two pickups, blond.

1960s		$400	$550

Xtone

2004-present. The ESP-made Xtone Paramount models are single or double cut, semi-hollow, set-neck, archtops with 2 humbuckers.

Yamaha

1946-present. Budget, intermediate, professional, and presentation grade, production/custom, acoustic, acoustic/electric, and electric guitars. They also build basses, amps, and effects. The Japanese instrument maker was founded in 1887. Began acoustic guitar production in 1946. Solidbody electric production began in '66. Production shifted from Japan to Taiwan (Yamaha's special-built plant) in '84, though some high-end guitars still made in Japan. Some Korean production began in '90s.

AE-11
1966-1974. Single cut, arched top, glued neck, 2 pickups.

1966-1974	Natural	$500	$700

AE-12
1973-1977. Single cut thinline archtop.

1973-1977		$500	$800

AE-18
1973-1977. AE-12 with upgrade inlays and gold hardware.

1973-1977		$550	$850

AE-500
1998-2000. Solidbody with rounded cutaway horn, 2 humbuckers, pearloid guard, dot markers.

1998-2000		$275	$375

APX-4
1992-1995. Acoustic/electric cutaway flat-top.

1992-1995		$400	$500

Wright Guitar Technology SoloEtte

Yamaha AEX-1500

GUITARS

Yamaha FG-433S

Yamaha SA-2000

MODEL YEAR	FEATURES	EXC. COND. LOW	HIGH
APX-10			
1987-1994. Acoustic/electric flat-top cutaway, 2 pickups, stereo two-way. Called APX-10T if ordered with rosewood back and sides.			
1987-1994		$450	$550
DW-8 VRS			
1999-2002. D-style flat-top, sunburst, solid spruce top, higher-end appointments like abalone rosette and top purfling.			
1999-2002		$475	$575
Eterna Acoustic			
1983-1994. Folk style acoustics, there were 4 models.			
1983-1994		$200	$250
FG-260			
1970s. Martin D12-20 copy.			
1970s		$250	$300
FG-340			
1990s. Bound top flat-top.			
1990s		$300	$350
FG-345			
1983-1994. Bound top flat-top.			
1983-1994		$300	$350
FG-410			
1984-1994. Flat-top acoustic; the 410E had a pickup.			
1984-1994		$300	$350
FG-412SB II 12-String			
1983-1994. 12-string flat top.			
1983-1994	Sunburst	$300	$400
FG-430A			
1984-1994. D-style flat-top.			
1984-1994		$350	$400
FG-1500			
Flat-top, Brazilian rosewood.			
1973		$400	$500
G-245S			
1981-1985. Classical, solid spruce top, rosewood back and sides.			
1981-1985		$200	$350
G-255S			
1981-1985. Classical, spruce top, Indian rosewood back and sides.			
1981-1985		$300	$450
Image Custom			
1989-1992. Electric double cut, flamed maple top, active circuitry, LED position markers.			
1989-1992		$300	$400
L-8 Acoustic			
1984-1996. Solid top D-style acoustic.			
1984-1996		$300	$350
Pacifica (standard features)			
1980s-1990s. Offset double cut with longer horns, dot markers.			
1980s		$200	$350
1990s		$200	$350
RGX Standard			
1988-1992. Electric, carved maple top, bolt-on neck, 3 pickups, bypass switch.			
1988-1992		$200	$250

MODEL YEAR	FEATURES	EXC. COND. LOW	HIGH
RGX-610M			
1987-1992. Electric, basswood body, maple board, one high-output Alnico II humbucker.			
1987-1992		$200	$300
RGZ-312			
1989-1992. Offset double cut solid body, bolt neck, 2 single-coils and 1 humbucker, dot markers.			
1989-1992		$300	$350
RGZ-820R			
1993-1994. Blues Saraceno Signature Model, bolt neck, 2 humbuckers, dot markers.			
1993-1994		$400	$500
SA-700			
1980s. ES-335-style with stud mounted tailpiece (vs. trapeze), dot markers, dual humbuckers, SA (Super Axe) Series, Super Axe script logo on headstock, SA700 logo on bell cap truss rod cover.			
1980s		$800	$950
SA-2000			
1979-1984. ES-335-style electric archtop, stud mounted tailpiece (vs. trapeze), block markers, 2 humbuckers, SA (Super Axe) Series, gold hardware. Sunburst or burgundy finish.			
1979-1984		$850	$1,000
SBG-200			
1983-1992. Solidbody, glued neck, unbound, dot inlays on rosewood 'board, gold hardware, white top.			
1983-1992		$200	$350
SBG-2000			
1983-1992. Electric, double cut beveled body, set-neck, 2 pickups.			
1983-1992		$250	$350
SBG-2100			
1984-1992. Double cut solidbody, set-neck.			
1984-1992		$200	$350
SE-250			
1986-1992. Electric, offset double cut, 2 pickups.			
1986-1992		$200	$350
SE-350 H			
1986-1992. Solidbody, offset double cut, 2 humbuckers.			
1986-1992		$200	$350
SG/SBG-3000/SG-3000 Custom/Professional			
1982-1985. Similar to SG-2000, but with solid mahogany body wings, higher output humbuckers, and abalone purfling on top.			
1982-1985		$800	$900
SG-3			
1965-1966. Early double cut solidbody with sharp horns, bolt-, 3 hum-single pickup layout, large white guard, rotor controls, tremolo.			
1965-1966		$850	$950
SG-20			
1972-1973. Bolt-on neck, slab body, single cutaway, single pickup.			
1972-1973		$300	$400

SG-30
1973-1976. Slab Katsura wood solidbody, bolt neck, 2 humbuckers, dot inlays.
1973-1976 $350 $450

SG-30A
1973-1976. Slab maple solidbody, bolt neck, 2 humbuckers, dot inlays.
1973-1976 $350 $450

SG-35
1973-1976. Slab mahogany solidbody, bolt neck, 2 humbuckers, parallelogram inlays.
1973-1976 $350 $500

SG-35A
1974-1976. Slab maple solidbody, bolt neck, 2 humbuckers, parallelogram inlays.
1973-1976 $350 $500

SG-40
1972-1973. Bolt-on neck, carved body, single cut.
1972-1973 $350 $500

SG-45
1972-1976. Glued neck, single cut, bound flat-top.
1972-1976 $450 $650

SG-50
1974-1976. Slab Katsura wood solidbody, glued neck, 2 humbuckers, dot inlays, large pickguard.
1974-1976 $450 $650

SG-60
1972 only. Bolt-on neck, carved body, single cut.
1972 $400 $500

SG-60T
1973 only. SG-60 with large cast vibrato system.
1973 $300 $500

SG-65
1972-1976. Glued neck, single cut, bound flat-top.
1972-1976   Set-neck $450 $650

SG-70
1974-1976. Slab maple solidbody, glued neck, 2 humbuckers, dot inlays, large pickguard.
1974-1976 $450 $650

SG-80
1972 only. Bolt-on neck, carved body, single cut.
1972 $400 $600

SG-80T
1973 only. SG-68 with large cast vibrato system.
1973 $400 $600

SG-85
1972-1976. Glued neck, single cutaway, bound flat-top.
1972-1976 $450 $650

SG-90
1974-1976. Carved top mahogany solidbody, glued neck, elevated pickguard, bound top, dot inlays, chrome hardware.
1974-1976 $600 $700

SG-175
1974-1976. Carved top mahogany solidbody, glued neck, elevated pickguard, abalone bound top, abalone split wing or pyramid inlays, gold hardware.
1974-1976 $700 $800

SG-500/SBG-500
1976-1978, 1981-1983. Carved unbound maple top, double pointed cutaways, glued neck, 2 exposed humbuckers, three-ply bound headstock, bound neck with clay split wing inlays, chrome hardware. Reissued as the SBG-500 (800S in Japan) in '81.
1976-1978   SG-500 $600 $700
1981-1983   SBG-500 $600 $700

SG-700
1976-1978. Carved unbound maple top, double pointed cutaways, glued neck, 2 humbuckers, 3-ply bound headstock, bound neck with clay split wing inlays, chrome hardware.
1976-1978 $700 $800

SG-700S
1999-2001. Set neck, mahogany body, 2 humbuckers with coil tap.
1999-2001 $500 $600

SG-1000/SBG-1000
1976-1983 ('84 in Japan). Carved maple top, double pointed cutaways, glued neck, 2 humbuckers, 3-ply bound headstock, unbound body, bound neck with clay split wing inlays, gold hardware. Export model name changed to SBG-1000 in '80.
1976-1979   SG-1000 $700 $800
1980-1983   SBG-1000 $700 $800

SG-1500
1976-1979. Carved maple top, double pointed cutaways, laminated neck-thru-body neck, laminated mahogany body wings, 2 humbuckers, 5-ply bound headstock and body, bound neck with dot inlays, chrome hardware. Name used on Japan-only model in the 1980s.
1976-1979 $800 $900

SG-2000/SBG-2000/SG-2000S
1976-1984 (1988 in Japan). Carved maple top, double pointed cutaways, laminated neck-thru-body neck, laminated mahogany body wings, 2 humbuckers, 5-ply bound headstock and body, bound neck with abalone split wing inlays, gold hardware. In '80, the model was changed to the SBG-2000 in the U.S., and the SG-2000S everywhere else except Japan (where it remained the SG-2000). Export model renamed SBG-2100 in 1984.
1976-1984 $850 $950

SG-3000/SBG-3000/Custom Professional
1982-1985. SG-2000 upgrade with higher output pickups and abalone purfling on top.
1982-1985 $800 $900

SHB-400
1981-1985. Solidbody electric, set-in neck, two pickups.
1981-1985 $300 $400

SSC-500
1983-1992. Solidbody electric, three pickups, set-in neck.
1983-1992 $300 $400

Yamaha SG-30

Yamaha SG-1500

1983 Zemaitis Metal-Front

Zion The Fifty

MODEL YEAR	FEATURES	EXC. COND. LOW	HIGH

Weddington Classic
1989-1992. Electric solidbody, redesigned set-in neck/body joint for increased access to the higher frets.

1989-1992		$350	$450

Yanuziello Stringed Instruments
1980-present. Production/custom resonator and Hawaiian guitars built by luthier Joseph Yanuziello, in Toronto, Ontario.

Zeiler Guitars
1992-present. Custom flat-top, 12-string, and nylon-string guitars built by luthier Jamon Zeiler in Cincinnati, Ohio.

Zemaitis
1960-1999, 2004-present. Tony Zemaitis (born Antanus Casimere Zemaitis) began selling his guitars in 1960. He emphasized simple light-weight construction and was known for hand engraved metal front guitars. Each hand-built guitar was a unique instrument. Ron Wood was an early customer and his use of a Zemaitis created a demand for the custom-built guitars. Approximately 6 to 10 instruments were built each year. Tony retired in '99, and passed away in '02 at the age of 67. In '04, Japan's Kanda Shokai, with the endorsement of Tony Zemaitis, Jr., started building the guitars again.

Acoustic Models
1965	Acoustic 12-string, 1st year	$23,000	$27,000
1980s	Acoustic 12-String D-hole	$14,000	$16,000
1980s	Acoustic 12-string heart-hole	$25,000	$30,000
1980s	Acoustic 6-string D-hole	$14,000	$16,000
1980s	Acoustic 6-string heart-hole	$20,000	$30,000

Electric Models
1980s	Disc-front	$20,000	$25,000
1980s	Metal-front	$25,000	$30,000
1980s	Pearl-front	$30,000	$40,000
1994	"Black Pearl"	$35,000	$40,000
1995	Disc-front 40th Anniversary	$30,000	$40,000

Zen-On
1946-ca.1968. Japanese manufacturer. By 1967 using the Morales brand name. Not heavily imported into the U.S., if at all (see Morales).

Acoustic Hollowbody Guitars
1946-1968. Various models.

1950s		$100	$175

Zeta
1982-present. Zeta has made solid, semi-hollow and resonator guitars, many with electronic and MIDI options, in Oakland, California over the years, but currently offer basses, amps and violins.

Zim-Gar
1960s. Imported from Japan by Gar-Zim Musical Instrument Corporation of Brooklyn, New York. Manufacturers unknown. Generally shorter scale beginner guitars.

Electric Solidbody Guitars
1960s.

1960s	Sunburst	$125	$200

Zimnicki, Gary
1980-present. Luthier Gary Zimnicki builds his professional and premium grade, custom, flat-top, 12-string, nylon-string, and archtop guitars in Allen Park, Michigan.

Zion
1980-present. Professional and premium grade, production/custom, semi-hollow and solidbody guitars built by luthier Ken Hoover, originally in Greensboro, North Carolina, currently in Raleigh.

Classic
1989-present. Double cut solidbody, six-on-a-side headstock, opaque finish, various pickup options, dot markers.

1990s	Custom quilted top	$600	$750
1995	Opaque finish	$400	$550

Graphic
1980s-1994. Double cut basswood body, custom airbrushed body design, bolt-on neck.

1990s	Green Frost Marble	$775	$925

Radicaster
1987-1990s. Double cut basswood body, graphic finish, bolt-on neck, various pickup configurations.

1990s	Marble finish	$575	$725

The Fifty
1994-present. Single cut ash solidbody, two single coils, bolt-on neck.

1990s	Custom figured top	$625	$750
1990s	Natural, plain top	$475	$625

Zolla
1979-present. Professional grade, production/custom, electric guitars built by luthier Bill Zolla in San Diego, California. Zolla also builds basses, necks and bodies.

Zon
1981-present. Currently luthier Joe Zon only offers basses, but he also built guitars from '85-'91. See Bass Section for more company info.

Basses

Photo: Steve Evans. Instrument courtesy of Steve Evans.

Acoustic Black Widow

Alamo Titan

MODEL YEAR	FEATURES	EXC. COND. LOW	HIGH

Acoustic

Ca. 1965-ca. 1987. Mainly known for solidstate amps, the Acoustic Control Corp. of Los Angeles, did offer guitars and basses from around '69 to late '74. The brand name was revived a few years ago by Samick for a line of amps.

Black Widow Bass

1969-1970, 1972-1974. Around '69 Acoustic offered the AC600 Black Widow Bass (in both a fretted and fretless version) which featured an unique black equal double cutaway body with German carve, an "Ebonite" fingerboard, two pickups, each with one row of adjustable polepieces, a zero fret, and a protective "spider design" pad on back. Also available was the AC650 short-scale. The '72-'74 version had the same body design, but had a rosewood 'board and only one pickup with two rows of adjustable pole pieces (the '72s had a different split-coil pickup with four polepieces, two front and two back). Acoustic outsourced the production of the basses, possibly to Japan, but at least part of the final production was by Semie Moseley.

1972-1974		$600	$800

Airline

1958-1968. Brandname for Montgomery Ward. Built by Kay, Harmony and Valco.

Electric Solidbody Basses

1960s	Various models	$200	$300

Pocket 3/4 Bass (Valco/National)

1962-19646. Airline brand of double cutaway 'Pocket Bass,' short-scale, two pickups, one acoustic bridge and one neck humbucker. Sunburst and other colors.

1962-1968		$600	$700

Alamo

1947-1982. Founded by Charles Eilenberg, Milton Fink, and Southern Music, San Antonio, TX. Distributed by Bruno & Sons. See *Guitar Stories Volume II*, by Michael Wright, for a complete history of Alamo with detailed model listings.

Eldorado Bass (Model 2600)

1965-1966. Solidbody, one pickup, angular offset shape, double cutaway.

1965-1966		$200	$250

Titan Bass

1963-1970. Hollowbody, one pickup, angular offset shape.

1963-1970		$200	$250

Alembic

1969-present. Professional, premium, and presentation grade, production/custom, 4-, 5-, and 6-string basses built in Santa Rosa, California. They also build guitars. Established in San Francisco as one of the first handmade bass builders. Alembic basses come with many options concerning woods (examples are maple, bubinga, walnut, vermilion, wenge, zebrawood), finishes, inlays, etc., all of which affect the values listed here. These dollar amounts should be used as a baseline guide to values for Alembic.

MODEL YEAR	FEATURES	EXC. COND. LOW	HIGH

Anniversary Bass

1989. Twentieth Anniversary limited edition, walnut and vermillion with a walnut core, five-piece body, five-piece neck-through. Only 200 built.

1989		$1,900	$2,100

Custom Shop Built Basses

1969-present. Various one-off and/or custom built instruments. Each instrument should be evaluated individually. Prices are somewhat speculative due to the one-off custom characteristics and values can vary greatly.

1978	Dragon Doubleneck	$8,000	$12,000
2000	Stanley Clarke Custom	$3,000	$5,000

Distillate 4 Bass

1980s		$900	$1,500

Distillate 5 Bass

1979-1991. Exotic woods, active electronics.

1980s		$1,000	$1,600

Elan 4 Bass

1985-1996. Available in 4-, 5-, 6- and 8-string models, three-piece through-body laminated maple neck, solid maple body, active electronics, solid brass hardware. Offered in a variety of hardwood tops and custom finishes.

1985-1996	Light Brown quilted maple	$800	$1,300

Elan 5 Bass

1985-1996. Available in 4-, 5-, 6- and 8-string models, three-piece through-body laminated maple neck, solid maple body, active electronics, solid brass hardware. Offered in a variety of hardwood tops and custom finishes.

1985-1996	Coco bolo upgrade	$1,500	$2,400

Epic 5-String Bass

Five-string version, large pointed bass horn.

1997		$1,000	$1,400

Epic Bass

1993-present. Special edition mahogany body with various tops, extra large pointed bass horn, maple/walnut veneer set-neck. Available in 4-, 5-, and 6-string versions.

1997-1998	Natural highly flamed maple	$900	$1,100

Essence 4 Bass

1991-present. Mahogany body with various tops, extra large pointed bass horn, walnut/maple laminate neck-through.

1995	Natural highly flamed maple	$1,500	$1,600

Essence 5 Bass

1991-present. Mahogany body with various tops, extra large pointed bass horn, walnut/maple laminate neck-through.

1990s	Natural highly flamed maple	$1,600	$1,900

Essence 6 Bass

1991-present. Mahogany body with various tops, extra large pointed bass horn, walnut/maple laminate neck-through.

1992		$1,400	$1,700

MODEL YEAR	FEATURES	EXC. COND. LOW	HIGH

Exploiter Bass
1980s. Explorer-style 4-string body, figured wood, neck-through design.

| 1984-1988 | Transparent, figured maple | $1,400 | $2,000 |

Persuader Bass
1983-1991.

| 1987 | | $700 | $900 |

Series I Bass
1971-present. Mahogany body with various tops, maple/purpleheart laminate neck-through, active electronics. Available in three scale lengths and with 4, 5 or 6 strings.

1970s	Medium- or long-scale	$2,200	$2,800
1970s	Short-scale	$2,000	$2,600
1980s	Medium- or long-scale	$2,200	$2,500
1980s	Short-scale	$2,000	$2,700

Series II Bass
Generally custom-made option, each instrument valued on a case-by-case basis, guidance pricing only.

| 1990s | | $4,000 | $7,000 |

Spoiler Bass
1981-1999. Solid mahogany body, maple neck-through, four strings, active electronics.

| 1980s | Various high-end wood options | $1,400 | $1,700 |
| 1990s | Various high-end wood options | $1,400 | $1,700 |

Spoiler 6-String Bass

| 1980s | Various high-end wood options | $1,500 | $1,900 |

Stanley Clarke Signature Standard Bass
1990-present. Neck-through body, active electronics, 24-fret ebony 'board, mahogany body with maple, bubinga, walnut, vermilion, or zebrawood top, 4-, 5-, and 6-string versions.

| 1990 | | $2,000 | $2,200 |

Alvarez
1965-present. Imported by St. Louis Music.

Electric Solidbody Basses (mid-level)
1990s. Import copies of Tobias and other high-end brands, many with long cutaway horns.

| 1990s | | $350 | $450 |

American Conservatory (Lyon & Healy)
Late-1800s-early-1900s. Mainly catalog sales guitars and mandolins from the Chicago maker. Mid-level Lyon & Healy offering, above their Lakeside brand, and generally under their Washburn brand.

Monster Bass G2740
Early-mid-1900s. Six-string acoustic flat-top, spruce top, birch back and sides with rosewood stain, Natural. Their catalog claimed it was "Indespensable to the up-to-date mandolin and guitar club."

| 1917 | | $3,000 | $5,000 |

MODEL YEAR	FEATURES	EXC. COND. LOW	HIGH

Ampeg
1949-present. Ampeg was founded on a vision of an amplified bass peg, which evolved into the Baby Bass. Ampeg has sold basses on and off throughout its history.

AEB-1 Bass
1966-1967. F-holes through-body, fretted, scroll headstock, pickup in body, sunburst. Reissued as the AEB-2 for 1997-1999.

| 1966-1967 | | $1,700 | $2,000 |

ASB-1 Devil Bass
1966-1967. Long-horn body, fretted, triangular F-holes through the body, Fireburst.

| 1966-1967 | | $2,000 | $3,000 |

AUB-1 Bass
1966-1967. Same as AEB-1, but fretless. Sunburst. Reissued as the AUB-2 for 1997-1999.

| 1966-1967 | | $1,700 | $2,000 |

AUSB-1 Devil Bass
1966-1967. Same as ASB-1 Devil Bass, but fretless.

| 1966-1967 | | $2,000 | $3,000 |

BB-4 Baby Bass
1962-1971. Electric upright slim-looking bass that is smaller than a cello. Available in sunburst, white, red, black, and a few turquoise. Reissued as the ABB-1 Baby Bass for 1997-1999.

| 1962-1971 | Solid color | $2,500 | $3,000 |
| 1962-1971 | Sunburst | $2,000 | $2,500 |

BB-5 Baby Bass
1964-1971. Five-string version.

| 1964-1971 | Sunburst | $2,500 | $3,000 |

Dan Armstrong Lucite Bass
1969-1971. Clear solid lucite body, did not have switchable pickups like the Lucite guitar.

| 1969-1971 | | $1,300 | $1,900 |

Dan Armstrong Lucite Bass Reissue
1998-2001. Lucite body, Dan Armstrong Ampeg block lettering on pickguard.

| 1998-2001 | | $750 | $850 |

GEB-101 Little Stud Bass
1973-1975. Import from Japan, 1960s Precision Bass-style body and controls, two-on-a-side tuners.

| 1973-1975 | | $300 | $400 |

GEB-750 Big Stud Bass
1973-1975. Import from Japan. Offset double cut solidbody, two-on-a-side tuners.

| 1973-1975 | | $300 | $400 |

Andreas
1995-present. Aluminium-necked, solidbody guitars and basses built by luthier Andreas Pichler in Dollach, Austria.

Angelica
1967-1975. Student and entry-level imports from Japan.

Electric Solidbody Basses
Japanese imports.

| 1970s | Various models | $100 | $175 |

Alembic Series I

Ampeg AEB-1

1976 Aria Mach 1

Artinger 5-string

MODEL YEAR	FEATURES	EXC. COND. LOW	HIGH

Apollo
Ca. 1967-1972. Entry-level instruments imported from Japan by St. Louis Music.
Electric Hollowbody Basses
Japanese imports.

1970s		$100	$175

Applause
1976-present. Kaman Music's entry-level Ovation-styled brand. The instruments were made in the U.S. until around 1982, when production was moved to Korea.
Acoustic/Electric AE-40 Bass
Cutaway, flat-top acoustic/electric bass. Natural.

1980s		$250	$300

Arbor
Late-1980s. Student to mid-level near copy imports by Midco International.
Electric Basses
1980s. Various models.

1980s		$200	$300

Aria/Aria Pro II
1960-present. Budget and intermediate grade, production, acoustic, solidbody, hollowbody and upright basses. They also make guitars, mandolins, and banjos. Originally branded as Aria; renamed Aria Pro II in '75.
Electric Basses
Various styles and appointments.

1980s		$250	$350

Armstrong, Rob
1971-present. Custom basses made in Coventry, England, by luthier Rob Armstrong. He also builds mandolins, flat-tops, and parlor guitars.

Artinger Custom Guitars
1997-present. Professional and premium grade, production/custom, basses built by luthier Matt Artinger in Emmaus, Pennsylvania. He also builds builds hollow, semi-hollow, and chambered solidbody guitars.

Audiovox
Ca. 1935-ca. 1950. Paul Tutmarc's Audiovox Manufacturing, of Seattle, Washington, was a pioneer in electric lap steels, basses, guitars and amps. Tutmarc is credited with inventing the electric bass guitar in 1935, which his company started selling in the late '30s.

Austin
1999-present. Budget and intermediate grade, production, basses imported by St. Louis Music. They also offer guitars, mandolins and banjos.

MODEL YEAR	FEATURES	EXC. COND. LOW	HIGH

Baldwin
1965-1970. The giant organ company got into guitars and basses in '65 when it bought Burns Guitars of England and sold those models in the U.S. under the Baldwin name.
Baby Bison Bass
1966-1970. Scroll head, 2 pickups, black, red or white finishes.

1960s		$800	$950

Bison Bass
1965-1970. Scroll headstock, 3 pickups, black or white finishes.

1960s		$1,100	$1,300

G.B. 66 Bass
1965-1970. Bass equivalent of G.B. 66 guitar, covered bridge tailpiece.

1960s		$500	$600

Shadows Bass
1965-1970. Named after Hank Marvin's backup band, solidbody, 3 slanted pickups, white finish.

1965-1970		$700	$750

Vibraslim Bass
1965-1970. Thin body, scroll head, 2 pickups, sunburst.

1960s		$550	$650

Barclay
1960s. Generally shorter-scale, student-level imports from Japan.
Electric Solidbody Basses
Various colors.

1960s		$125	$175

Bass Collection
1985-1992. Mid-level imports from Japan, distributed by Meisel Music of Springfield, New Jersey. Sam Ash Music, New York, sold the remaining inventory from '92 to '94.
SB301 Bass
1985-1992. Offset double cut, bolt-on neck, ash or alder body.

1988		$250	$350

SB302 Bass
1985-1992. Offset double cut, bolt-on fretless neck, ash or alder body.

1988		$250	$350

SB305 5-String Bass
1985-1992. Offset double cut, bolt-on neck, ash or alder body.

1988		$300	$425

SB401 Bass
1985-1992. Offset double cut, bolt-on neck, basswood body, active electronics.

1988		$400	$525

SB402 Bass
1985-1992. Offset double cut, bolt-on fretless neck, basswood body, active electronics.

1988		$400	$525

BASSES

MODEL YEAR FEATURES	EXC. COND. LOW	HIGH
SB405 5-String Bass		
1985-1992. Offset double cut, bolt-on neck, basswood body, active electronics.		
1988	$500	$625
SB501 Bass		
1985-1992. Offset double cut, bolt-on neck, alder body, active electronics.		
1988	$500	$625
SB601 Bass		
1985-1992. Offset double cut, bolt-on neck, maple/ walnut body, active electronics.		
1988	$600	$725

BC Rich

1966-present. Budget, intermediate, and premium grade, production/custom, import and U.S.-made basses. They also offer guitars.

Bich Bass		
1976-1998. Solidbody, neck-through, 2 pickups.		
1980s	$800	$1,000
Bich Supreme 8-String Bass		
Late-1970s-early-1980s.		
1978-1982	$1,700	$1,800
Eagle Bass (import)		
B.C. Rico and NJ Series imports.		
1980s	$250	$300
Eagle Bass (U.S.A. assembly)		
1977-1996. Curved double cut solidbody, natural.		
1977-1979	$1,100	$1,300
1980-1989	$1,000	$1,300
Innovator Bass		
Late-1980s-1990s. Solidbody with long bass horn, active P & J-style pickups, diamond inlay.		
1985-1990s	$275	$325
Ironbird Bass		
1984-1998. Kinda star-shaped, neck-through, solidbody, 2 pickups, active electronics, diamond inlays.		
1980s	$600	$800
Mockingbird Bass		
1976-present.		
1980s	$1,200	$1,500
Mockingbird Bass (NJ Series)		
1983-present. Import model.		
1980s	$300	$375
Nighthawk Bass		
1979-ca.1980. Bolt-neck.		
1970s	$500	$700
Seagull Bass		
1972-1998.		
1972-1979	$800	$1,200
1980-1989	$700	$1,100
1990-1998	$600	$1,000
Son Of A Rich Bass		
1977-ca.1981. Basically a bolt-neck Bich, U.S. made.		
1977-1981	$800	$950
Virgin Bass (NJ Series)		
1987-1993. Import from Japan and Korea.		
1987-1993	$300	$350

MODEL YEAR FEATURES	EXC. COND. LOW	HIGH
Warlock Bass		
1981-present.		
1980s	$800	$1,100
Warlock Bass (Platinum Series)		
1987-1998. Import version of Warlock model.		
1987-1998	$300	$375

Black Jack

1960s. Entry-level and mid-level imports from Japan.

Electric Solidbody Basses		
Various colors.		
1960s	$100	$200

Blade

1987-present. Intermediate and professional grade, production, solidbody basses from luthier Gary Levinson, who started Levinson Music Products Ltd. in Switzerland in '87. He also builds guitars.

Bradford

1960s. House brand of W.T. Grant department store, often imported.

Electric Solidbody Basses		
Various colors.		
1960s	$100	$200

Brian Moore

1992-present. Brian Moore added basses in 1997 and they offer professional grade, production, solidbody basses. They also build guitars and mandolins.

Brice

1985-present. Budget grade, production, electric and acoustic basses imported by Rondo Music of Union, New Jersey.

Bunker

1961-present. Luthier Dave Bunker builds intermediate, professional, and premium grade, production/custom, basses in Port Angeles, Washington. He also builds guitars.

Burns

Late 1950s-1970, 1992-present. Intermediate and professional grade, production, basses built in England. They also build guitars.

Nu-Sonic Bass		
1968	$400	$500

Campellone

1978-present. Archtop guitar builder Mark Campellone, of Smithfield, Rhode Island, built basses in the 1970s.

Carvin

1946-present. Intermediate and Professional grade, production/custom, acoustic and electric basses. They also build guitars and amps.

1988 BC Rich Bich Bass

1979 Carvin LB-50

BASSES

Conklin Groove Tools 4

Cort C5

MODEL YEAR	FEATURES	EXC. COND. LOW	HIGH
Solidbody Electric LB-Series Basses			
1980-1990s		$300	$500
V-220 Bass			
1980s		$300	$500

Chandler
1984-present. Premium grade, production/custom, solidbody 12-string electric basses built by luthiers Paul and Adrian Chandler in Chico, California. He also builds guitars, lapsteels and pickups.

Charles Shifflett Acoustic Guitars
1990-present. Luthier Charles Shifflett builds his premium grade, custom, acoustic basses in High River, Alberta. He also builds flat-top, classical, flamenco, resophonic, and harp guitars, and banjos.

Charvel
1978-present. U.S.-made from '78 to '85 and a combination of imports and U.S.-made post-'85.

850 XL Bass
1988-1991. 4-string, neck-through-body, active electronics.

1988-1991		$300	$400

CX-490 Bass
1991-1994. Double cut, 4-string, bolt neck.

1991-1994		$175	$225

Eliminator Bass
1990-1991. Offset double cut, active electronics, bolt neck.

1990-1991		$200	$250

Fusion V Bass
1989-1991. 5-string, offset double cut with extreme bass horn.

1989-1991	Pearl White	$500	$700

Model 1 Bass
1986-1989. Double cut, bolt neck, 1 pickup.

1986-1989		$175	$225

Model 2 Bass
1986-1989. Double cut, bolt neck, 2 pickups.

1986-1989		$250	$350

Model 3 Bass
1986-1989. Neck-through-body, 2 single-coil pickups, active circuitry, master volume, bass and treble knobs.

1986-1989		$300	$350

Model 5 Bass
1986-1989. Double cut, P/J pickups.

1986-1989		$350	$400

Star Bass
Early 1980s. Four-point solidbody, 1 pickup, brass hardware, one piece maple neck.

1980s		$400	$700

Surfcaster Bass
1991-1994. Semi-hollow, lipstick tube pickups.

1991-1994		$500	$800

Cipher
1960s. Student market import from Japan.

Electric Solidbody Basses
1960s. Japanese imports.

1960s		$100	$175

Citron
1995-present. Luthier Harvey Citron (of Veillette-Citron fame) builds his professional and premium grade, production/custom basses in Woodstock, New York. He also builds solidbody guitars.

Clevinger
1982-present. Established by Martin Clevinger, Oakland, California. Mainly specializing in electric upright basses, but has offered bass guitars as well.

Upright Solidbody Electric Bass
1982-present. Straight vertical-shaped compact body. Several options available that can increase values. Black.

1980s		$2,400	$2,600

College Line
One of many Lyon & Healy brands, made during the era of extreme design experimentation.

Monster Bass (Style 2089)
Early-1900s. 22" lower bout, flat-top guitar/bass, natural.

1915		$3,000	$5,000

Conklin
1984-present. Intermediate, professional, and premium grade, production/custom basses from luthier Bill Conklin, of Springfield, Missouri. Conklin also offers guitars. Conklin instruments are made in the U.S. and overseas.

GT-4 (Groove Tools) Bass
2001-present. Offset double cut with large bass horn, bolt neck, clear hard finish.

2001		$500	$550

GT-7 (Groove Tools) Bass
2001-present. Offset double cut with large bass horn, bolt neck, 7 strings, clear hard finish.

2001		$800	$850

M.E.U. (Mobile Electric Upright) Bass
1995-present. Cello-style hollowbody, played in an upright position, four-string or five-string option.

1995	Four strings	$1,100	$1,300

Conrad
Ca. 1968-1978. Student and mid-level copies imported by David Wexler, Chicago, Illinois.

Model 40096 Acoustical Slimline Bass
EB-2 copy, import, two pickups.

1973		$175	$300

Model 40177 Violin-Shaped Bass
Scroll headstock, import, two pickups.

1974		$125	$225

MODEL YEAR	FEATURES	EXC. COND. LOW	HIGH
Model 40224 Bumper Bass			
Ampeg Dan Armstrong lucite copy, import.			
1973		$225	$275
Professional Bass			
Copy of Fender Jazz Bass, import.			
1974		$150	$250
Professional Bison Bass			
EB-3 copy, import, two pickups.			
1974		$150	$250

Cort

1973-present. North Brook, Illinois-based Cort offers intermediate and professional grade, production, acoustic and solidbody electric basses built in Korea. They also offer guitars.

MODEL YEAR	FEATURES	EXC. COND. LOW	HIGH
Electric Solidbody Bass			
Various models.			
1973-1999		$100	$300

Crafter

2000-present. Intermediate grade, production, acoustic/electric bass from Hohner. They also offer guitars.

Crestwood

1970s. Copy models imported by La Playa Distributing Company of Detroit. Product line includes copies of the popular classical guitars, flat-tops, electric solidbodies and basses of the era.

MODEL YEAR	FEATURES	EXC. COND. LOW	HIGH
Electric Basses			
1970s. Includes near copies of the EB-2 (Crestwood model 2048), Beatle Bass (2049), Telecaster Bass (2079), Les Paul Bass (2090), SG EB-3 Bass (2092), Solidbody Bass (2093), and the Jazz Bass (2098).			
1970s		$100	$300

Crown

1960s. Violin-shaped hollowbody electrics, solidbody electric guitars and basses, possibly others. Imported from Japan.

MODEL YEAR	FEATURES	EXC. COND. LOW	HIGH
Electric Solidbody Basses			
Japanese imports.			
1960s		$100	$300

Cumpiano

1974-present. Professional and premium grade, custom steel-string and nylon-string guitars, and acoustic basses built by luthier William Cumpiano in Northampton, Massachusetts.

Custom

1980s. Line of solidbody guitars and basses introduced in the early-1980s by Charles Lawing and Chris Lovell, owners of Strings & Things in Memphis.

D'Agostino

1976-early 1990s. Import company established by Pat D'Agostino. Solidbodies imported from EKO Italy '77-'82, Japan '82-'84, and in Korea for '84 on. Overall, about 60% of guitars were Japanese, 40% Korean.

MODEL YEAR	FEATURES	EXC. COND. LOW	HIGH
Electric Solidbody Basses			
Various models.			
1970s		$250	$350

Daion

1978-1985. Higher quality copy imports from Japan. Original designs introduced in '80s.

MODEL YEAR	FEATURES	EXC. COND. LOW	HIGH
Savage Bass			
1980-1985. Maple neck, rosewood board, 22 nickel-silver frets.			
1980-1985		$300	$600

Daisy Rock

2001-present. Budget and intermediate grade, production, full-scale and 3/4 scale, solidbody, semi-hollow, and acoustic/electric basses. Founded by Tish Ciravolo as a Division of Schecter Guitars, initial offerings included daisy and heart-shaped electric guitars and basses.

Danelectro

1946-1969, 1997-present. Danelectro offered basses throughout most of its early history. In '96, the Evets Corporation, of San Clemente, California, introduced a line of Danelectro effects, amps, basses and guitars, and many reissues of earlier instruments soon followed. In early '03, Evets discontinued the guitar and amp lines, but still offers Danelectro effects.

MODEL YEAR	FEATURES	EXC. COND. LOW	HIGH
Model 1444L Bass			
Ca.1958-ca.1964. Two pickups, masonite body, single cut. Copper.			
1958-1959		$600	$750
1960-1962		$550	$700
1963-1964		$500	$650
Model 3412 Shorthorn Bass			
1958-ca.1966. Coke bottle headstock, one pickup. Copper finish.			
1958-1959		$600	$650
1960-1962		$550	$600
1963-1964		$500	$550
1965-1966		$450	$500
Model 3612 Shorthorn 6-string Bass			
1958-ca.1966. Coke bottle headstock, one pickup. Copper finish.			
1958-1959		$850	$1,000
1960-1962		$800	$950
1963-1964		$700	$850
1965-1966		$600	$750
Model 4423 Longhorn Bass			
1958-ca.1966. Coke bottle headstock, two pickups. Copper finish.			
1958-1959		$1,350	$1,400
1960-1962		$1,300	$1,350
1963-1964		$1,100	$1,150
1965-1966		$1,000	$1,050
'58 Longhorn Bass Reissue/Longhorn Pro			
1997-2003. Reissues of classic Longhorn bass.			
1997-2003		$200	$250

Cort Curbow 4-string

Danelectro 4423 Longhorn Bass

BASSES

DiPinto Belvedere

1967 EKO Rocket IV

MODEL		EXC. COND.	
YEAR	FEATURES	LOW	HIGH

UB-2 6-String Bass
Ca.1956-ca.1959. Single cutaway, two pickups.

1956-1959		$850	$1,000

Dave Maize Acoustic
1991-present. Luthier Dave Maize builds his premium grade, production/custom, acoustic basses in Cave Junction, Oregon. He also builds flat-tops.

Dean
1976-present. Intermediate and professional grade, production, solidbody, hollowbody, acoustic, and acoustic/electric, basses made overseas. They also offer guitars, banjos, mandolins, and amps.

Baby ML Bass
1982-1986. Downsized version of ML, U.S.-made.

1982-1986		$300	$400

Mach V Bass
1985-1986. U.S.-made pointed solidbody, 2 pickups, rosewood 'board.

1985-1986		$400	$600

ML Bass
1977-1986. Flying V/Explorer combo body style, fork headstock.

1977-1983	U.S.A.-made	$600	$900
1984-1986	Korean import	$200	$300

Dean Markley
The string and pickup manufacturer offered a limited line of guitars and basses for a time in the late '80s.

Vintage Bass
1987. Maple neck, maple or ash body, maple or rosewood 'board, solidbody, either split P-type or a P-J combination pickups.

1987		$250	$375

DeTemple
1995-present. Premium grade, production/custom, solidbody electric bassess built by luthier Michael DeTemple in Sherman Oaks, California. He also builds guitars.

Dillon
1975-present. Professional and premium grade, custom, acoustic basses built by luthier John Dillon in Taos, New Mexico. He also builds guitars.

Dingwall
1988-present. Luthier Sheldon Dingwall, Saskatoon, Canada, started out producing guitar bodies and necks, eventually offering complete guitars and basses. Currently Dingwall offers professional to premium grade, production/custom 4, 5, and 6-string basses featuring the Novax Fanned-Fret System.

DiPinto
1995-present. Intermediate and professional grade, production retro-vibe basses from luthier Chris DiPinto of Philadelphia, Pennsylvania. He also builds

MODEL		EXC. COND.	
YEAR	FEATURES	LOW	HIGH

guitars. Until late '99, all instruments built in the U.S., since then built in Korea and the U.S.

Domino
Ca. 1967-1968. Imported from Japan by Maurice Lipsky Music of New York, mainly copies, but some original designs.

Beatle Bass
1967-1968. Beatle Bass-style.

1967		$100	$250

Fireball Bass
1967-1968. Vox Phantom IV copy.

1967		$100	$250

Dorado
Ca. 1972-1973. Name used briefly by Baldwin/Gretsch on line of Japanese imports.

Electric Solidbody Basses
Japanese imports.

1970s		$100	$200

Dragonfly
1994-present. Professional grade, production/custom, acoustic basses built by luthier Dan Richter in Roberts Creek, British Columbia. He also builds guitars and dulcitars.

Earthwood
1972-1985. Acoustic designs by Ernie Ball with input from George Fullerton. One of the first to offer acoustic basses.

Acoustic Bass
1972-1985. Big bodied acoustic bass alternative between Kay double bass and solidbody Fender bass.

1978		$900	$1,150

EKO
1959-1985. Built by the Oliviero Pigini Company, Italy. Importers included LoDuca Brothers, Milwaukee, Wisconsin.

Cobra Bass II
1967-ca.1969. Offset double cut solidbody, 2 pickups.

1967-1969		$300	$350

Kadett Bass
1967-1978. Red or sunburst.

1967-1978		$275	$325

Model 1100/2 Bass
1961-1966. Jaguar-style plastic covered solidbody, 2 pickups, sparkle finish.

1961-1966		$450	$550

Model 995/2 Violin Bass
1966-ca.1969.

1966-1969		$400	$500

Rocket IV/Rokes Bass
1967-early-1970s. Rocket-shape design, solidbody, says "Rokes" on the headstock. The Rokes were a popular English band that endorsed EKO guitars. Marketed as the Rocket IV in the U.S. and as the Rokes in Europe. Often called the Rok. Sunburst, 1 pickup.

1967-1971		$450	$850

MODEL YEAR	FEATURES	EXC. COND. LOW	HIGH

Electra

1971-1984. Imported from Japan by St. Louis Music.

MPC Outlaw Bass

1970s. Has 2 separate modules that plug in for different effects, neck-through-body.

1970s		$200	$450

Other Electric Solidbody Basses

Japanese imports, various models.

1970s		$150	$450

Emperador

1966-1992. Student-level imports of Westheimer Musical Instruments. Early models appear to be made by either Teisco or Kawai; later models were made by Cort.

Electric Solidbody Basses

Japanese imports. Various models.

1960s		$100	$250

Engelhardt

Engelhardt specializes in student acoustic basses and cellos and is located in Elk Grove Village, Illinois.

EM-1 Maestro Bass

A popular school model upright acoustic bass, spruce top, curly maple back, rosewood trimmings, 3/4 size. Sunburst.

1970s		$400	$600

Supreme Bass

Professional quality 3/4 size upright bass, spruce top, curly maple back, ebony trimmings.

1970		$1,000	$1,600

Epiphone

1928-present. Intermediate and professional grade, production, acoustic and electric basses. Epiphone didn't add basses until 1959, after Gibson acquired the brand. The Gibson Epiphones were American-made until '69, then all imports until into the '80s, when some models were again made in the U.S.

B-5 Acoustic Bass Viol

1950s. Three-fourths size laminate construction.

1950s		$3,500	$3,700

EB-0 Bass

1998-present. SG body style, 1 pickup, bolt-on neck.

1998-2002		$200	$350

EB-3 Bass

1999-present. SG body style, 2 pickups.

1999-2002		$300	$400

EBM-4 Bass

1991-1998. Alder body, maple neck, split humbucker, white.

1991-1998		$300	$400

Embassy Deluxe Bass

1963-1969. Solidbody, double cut, 2 pickups, tune-o-matic bridge, cherry finish.

1963-1964		$1,100	$1,400
1965-1966		$900	$1,400

1967-1968		$850	$1,350
1969		$800	$1,300

Newport Bass (one pickup model)

1961-1970. Double cut solidbody, 1 pickup (2 pickups optional until 1963), two-on-a-side tuners until 1963, four-on-a-side after that. Cherry.

1961		$1,200	$1,400
1962		$1,000	$1,200
1963-1965		$800	$1,000
1966-1968		$600	$800
1969		$500	$700

Rivoli Bass (double pickup)

1970 only. Double pickup Epiphone version of Gibson EB-2D.

1970	Sunburst	$1,100	$1,400

Rivoli Bass (single pickup)

1959-1970. ES-335-style semi-hollowbody bass, two-on-a-side tuners, 1 pickup (2 in 1970). Reissued in 1994 as the Rivoli II.

1959		$2,300	$2,700
1960		$2,100	$2,500
1961		$2,000	$2,500
1963-1965		$1,200	$1,500
1966-1969	All finishes	$1,000	$1,500
1970	All finishes	$900	$1,100

Thunderbird IV Bass

1997-present. Reverse-style mahogany body, 2 pickups, sunburst.

1997-2002		$350	$550

Viola Bass

1990s-present. Beatle Bass copy, sunburst.

1990s		$450	$500

ESP

1975-present. Intermediate, professional, and premium grade, production/custom, electric basses. Japan's ESP (Electric Sound Products) made inroads in the U.S. market with mainly copy styles in the early '80s, mixing in original designs over the years. In the '90s, ESP opened a California-based Custom Shop.

B-1 Bass

1990s. Vague DC-style slab solidbody with bolt-on neck, ESP and B-1 on headstock.

1990s		$500	$550

Horizon Bass

1987-1993. Offset double cut solidbody, 4- and 5-string versions, active electronics, 34" scale.

1987-1993	Four Strings	$400	$500

Essex (SX)

1985-present. Budget grade, production, electric basses imported by Rondo Music of Union, New Jersey. They also offer guitars.

Evergreen Mountain

1971-present. Professional grade, custom, acoustic basses built by luthier Jerry Nolte in Cove, Oregon. He also builds guitars and mandolins.

1967 Epiphone Embassy

Epiphone Rivoli

1966 Fender Bass V

1963 Fender Bass VI

MODEL YEAR	FEATURES	EXC. COND. LOW	HIGH

Farnell

1989-present. Luthier Al Farnell builds his professional grade, production, solidbody basses in Ontario, California. He also offers his intermediate grade, production, "C" Series which is imported from China. He also builds guitars.

Fender

1946-present. Intermediate, professional, and premium grade, production/custom, electric and acoustic basses made in the U.S. and overseas. Leo Fender is the father of the electric bass. The introduction of his Precision Bass in late 1951 changed forever how music was performed, recorded and heard. Leo followed with other popular models of basses that continue to make up a large part of Fender's production. Please note that all the variations of the Jazz and Precision Basses are grouped under those general headings.

Bass V

1965-1970. Five strings, double cut, 1 pickup, dot inlay '65-'66, block inlay '66-'70.

Year	Features	Low	High
1965	Candy Apple Red, Lake Placid Blue	$2,500	$2,700
1965	Olympic White	$2,500	$2,600
1965	Sunburst	$2,000	$2,100
1966	Candy Apple Red	$2,400	$2,600
1966	Ice Blue Metallic	$2,600	$3,000
1966	Ocean Turquoise	$2,600	$3,000
1966	Olympic White	$2,200	$2,400
1966	Sunburst	$1,700	$2,100
1967	Lake Placid Blue	$2,200	$2,400
1967	Sunburst	$1,700	$2,000
1968-1970	Sunburst	$1,600	$2,000

Bass VI

1961-1975. Six strings, Jazzmaster-like body, 3 pickups, dot inlay until '66, block inlay '66-'75. Reintroduced as Japanese-made Collectable model '95-'98.

Year	Features	Low	High
1961	Blond	$5,000	$6,000
1961	Sunburst	$3,500	$4,500
1962	Blond, Lake Placid Blue, Olympic White	$4,500	$5,500
1962	Black, Daphne Blue, Sonic Blue	$5,000	$6,000
1963	Burgundy Mist, Sherwood Green	$6,000	$7,000
1962	Dakota Red, Fiesta Red, Inca Silver, Shoreline Gold	$5,500	$6,500
1962	Foam Green, Shell Pink, Surf Green	$6,500	$7,500
1962	Sunburst	$3,500	$4,500
1963	Black, blond, Candy Apple Red, Lake Placid Blue	$4,500	$5,500
1963	Sunburst	$3,300	$4,300
1964	Lake Placid Blue	$3,400	$4,400
1964	Sunburst	$3,200	$3,800

MODEL YEAR	FEATURES	EXC. COND. LOW	HIGH

Year	Features	Low	High
1965	Candy Apple Red, Lake Placid Blue	$3,200	$3,600
1965	Sunburst	$3,100	$3,400
1966	Sunburst, block inlay	$2,900	$3,300
1966	Sunburst, dot inlay	$2,800	$3,200
1967	Sunburst, block inlay	$2,600	$3,100
1968	Sunburst	$2,600	$3,100
1969	Sunburst	$2,500	$2,900
1970	Sunburst	$2,400	$2,700
1971	Sunburst	$2,300	$2,600
1971	Sunburst	$2,200	$2,600
1972	Olympic White	$2,800	$3,200
1973	Sunburst	$2,100	$2,500
1974-1975	Sunburst	$1,900	$2,300

Bass VI Reissue

1995-1998. Import, sunburst.

Year	Features	Low	High
1995-1998		$900	$1,000

BG-29 Bass

1995-present. Acoustic flat-top bass, single cut, two-on-a-side tuners, Fishman on-board comtrols, black.

Year	Features	Low	High
1995-2000		$350	$400

Bullet Bass (B30, B34, B40)

1982-1983. Alder body, 1 pickup, offered in short- and long-scale, red or walnut. U.S.-made, replaced by Japanese-made Squire Bullet Bass.

Year	Features	Low	High
1982-1983		$350	$500

Coronado I Bass

1966-1970. Thinline, double cut, 1 pickup, dot inlay, sunburst and cherry red were the standard colors, but custom colors could be ordered.

Year	Features	Low	High
1966-1970	Cherry red, sunburst	$800	$1,100
1966-1970	White custom color	$850	$1,150
1966-1970	Other custom colors	$1,100	$1,300

Coronado II Bass

1967-1972. Two pickups, block inlay, sunburst and cherry red standard colors, but custom colors could be ordered. Only Antigua finish offered from '70 on.

Year	Features	Low	High
1967-1969	Cherry red, sunburst	$900	$1,200
1967-1969	Custom color white	$950	$1,250
1967-1969	Other custom colors	$1,100	$1,400
1967-1969	Wildwood finish	$1,100	$1,400
1968-1972	Antigua	$900	$1,200

HM Bass IV

1989-1991. Japanese-made, 4 strings, basswood body, no pickguard, 3 Jazz Bass pickups, 5-way switch, master volume, master TBX, sunburst.

Year	Features	Low	High
1989-1991		$400	$425

HM Bass V

1989-1991. Five string version of HM, sunburst.

Year	Features	Low	High
1989-1991		$450	$475

HMT Acoustic/Electric Bass

1992. Double cut, f-hole, shark fin markers, 1 split P-bass style pickup, blend control.

Year	Features	Low	High
1992	Various colors	$675	$725

Jazz Bass

The following are the various Jazz Bass models. The main American-made models are listed first, with the others alphabetically as follows:

MODEL YEAR	FEATURES	EXC. COND. LOW	HIGH
Jazz Bass			
Standard Jazz Bass			
American Standard Jazz Bass			
American Series Jazz Bass			
American Series Jazz Bass V			
'62 Custom Shop Jazz Bass			
'62 Jazz Bass			
'64 Custom Shop Jazz Bass			
'75 Jazz Bass American Vintage Series			
50th Anniversary 5-String Jazz Bass			
American Deluxe Jazz Bass			
American Deluxe Jazz V Bass			
Custom Classic Jazz IV Bass			
Deluxe Jazz Bass (active)			
Deluxe V Jazz Bass (active)			
Foto Flame Jazz Bass			
Geddy Lee Signature Jazz Bass			
Gold Jazz Bass			
Jazz Bass Special (import)			
Jazz Plus Bass			
Jazz Plus V Bass			
Marcus Miller Signature Jazz Bass			
Noel Redding Signature Jazz Bass			
Squire Jazz Bass			
Standard Jazz Bass (later model)			
Standard Jazz Fretless Bass (later model)			
Standard Jazz V Bass (later model)			
Ventures Limited Edition Jazz Bass			

Jazz Bass

1960-1981. Two stack knobs '60-'62, 3 regular controls '62 on. Dot markers '60-'66, block markers from '66 on. Rosewood fingerboard standard, but maple available from '68 on. With the introduction of vintage reissue models in '81, Fender started calling the American-made version the Standard Jazz Bass. That became the American Standard Jazz Bass in '88 and then became the American Series Jazz Bass in 2000.

The custom colors listing are for unfaded or very slightly faded examples. Moderately faded examples will approximate values somewhat below the low end of the value range. A heavily faded example will be worth much less than the ranges shown, even if the heavily faded example is otherwise in excellent, original condition. A heavily faded example will have a tint that is unlike an unfaded example. Fade does not always mean 'lighter tint'. For example, a heavily faded Lake Placid Blue can turn dark green. A heavily faded instrument will fetch a value that is slightly higher than a standard Sunburst example.

Post 1971 Jazz Bass values are affected more by condition than color or neck option. The Jazz Bass was fitted with a three-bolt neck or bullet rod in late-1974. Prices assume a three-bolt neck starting in 1975.

Custom color Fenders can be forged and bogus finishes have been a problem. As the value of custom color Fenders has increased, so has the problem of bogus non-original finishes. The prices in the Guide are for factory original finishes in excellent condition. The prices noted do not take into account market factors such as fake instruments, which can have the

effect of lowering a guitar's market value unless the guitar's provenance can be validated.

MODEL YEAR	FEATURES	EXC. COND. LOW	HIGH
1960	Sonic Blue	$18,000	$21,000
1960	Sunburst, stack knob	$14,000	$17,000
1960	Surf Green	$19,000	$23,000
1960	White	$15,000	$18,000
1961	Dakota Red, Fiesta Red, stack knobs	$17,000	$19,000
1961	Daphne Blue, Sonic Blue, stack knobs	$15,000	$18,000
1961	Lake Placid Blue, stack knobs	$13,000	$16,000
1961	Sunburst, stack knobs	$13,000	$15,000
1962	Stack knob, blond, black, LP Blue, Oly White	$12,000	$15,000
1962	Stack knob, Burgundy Mist, Sherwood Green	$17,000	$19,000
1962	Stack knob, Dakota Red, Fiesta Red, Inca Silver, Shoreline Gold	$16,000	$18,000
1962	Stack knob, Daphne Blue, Sonic Blue	$14,000	$17,000
1962	Stack knob, Foam Green, Surf Green	$18,000	$20,000
1962	Stack knob, Shell Pink	$20,000	$22,000
1962	Stack knob, sunburst	$12,000	$14,000
1962	3 knob, blond, black, LP Blue, Oly White	$10,000	$13,000
1962	3 knob, Burgundy Mist, Sherwood Green	$14,000	$17,000
1962	3 knob, Dakota Red, Fiesta Red, Inca Silver, Shoreline Gold	$13,000	$16,000
1962	3 knob, Daphne Blue, Sonic Blue	$12,000	$15,000
1962	3 knob, Foam Green, Surf Green	$15,000	$18,000
1962	3 knob, Shell Pink	$17,000	$20,000
1962	3 knob, sunburst	$9,000	$11,000
1963	Blond, Lake Placid Blue	$9,000	$11,000
1963	Coral Pink, matching headstock	$18,000	$20,000
1963	Dakota Red, matching headstock	$12,000	$14,000
1963	Olympic White, matching headstock	$9,000	$11,000
1963	Sunburst	$8,000	$10,000

1963 Fender Jazz Bass

1961 Fender Jazz Bass

The *Vintage Guitar Price Guide* shows low to high values for items in all-original excellent condition, and, where applicable, with original case or cover.

BASSES

1961 Fender Jazz Bass

1975 Fender Jazz Bass

MODEL YEAR	FEATURES	EXC. COND. LOW	HIGH
1963	Sonic Blue	$11,000	$13,000
1964	Black, blond, Olympic White	$9,000	$11,000
1964	Burgundy Mist	$12,000	$15,000
1964	Candy Apple Red, LP Blue, matching headstock	$9,000	$11,000
1964	Dakota Red, matching headstock	$11,000	$13,000
1964	Fiesta Red	$11,000	$13,000
1964	Sherwood Green	$13,000	$15,000
1964	Sonic Blue	$10,000	$12,000
1964	Sunburst	$7,000	$9,000
1965	Black	$7,500	$9,000
1965	Burgundy Mist	$9,000	$13,000
1965	Candy Apple Red, LP Blue, matching headstock	$8,000	$9,000
1965	Dakota Red, Fiesta Red	$8,500	$9,500
1965	Firemist Gold, matching headstock	$9,000	$12,000
1965	Ice Blue Metallic	$9,000	$11,000
1965	Lake Placid Blue, matching headstock	$7,000	$8,000
1965	Olympic White	$7,500	$8,500
1965	Sonic Blue, matching headstock	$8,500	$11,000
1965	Sunburst	$6,500	$7,000
1966	Black, Candy Apple Red, block markers	$6,500	$8,500
1966	Candy Apple Red, dot markers	$7,000	$8,700
1966	Foam Green, Sonic Blue, dot markers	$8,000	$9,500
1966	Ice Blue Metallic	$7,500	$9,000
1966	Lake Placid Blue, matching headstock	$7,000	$8,600
1966	Olympic White, block markers, match headstock	$6,000	$7,000
1966	Olympic White, dot markers	$6,500	$8,500
1966	Shoreline Gold	$8,500	$9,500
1966	Sonic Blue, block markers	$7,500	$9,000
1966	Sonic Blue, dot markers	$8,000	$9,500
1966	Sunburst, block markers	$5,000	$5,500
1966	Sunburst, dot markers	$5,400	$6,000
1967	Olympic White, Candy Apple Red, block markers	$4,500	$7,000
1967	Sonic Blue, block markers	$6,000	$7,500
1967	Sunburst, block markers	$4,000	$4,500

MODEL YEAR	FEATURES	EXC. COND. LOW	HIGH
1968	Black, Candy Apple Red, Lake Placid Blue, Sonic Blue	$4,500	$6,500
1968	Cream	$3,500	$4,500
1968	Firemist Silver	$4,900	$6,700
1968	Natural, sunburst	$3,600	$4,100
1969	Candy Apple Red, Lake Placid Blue	$4,200	$6,200
1969	Cream	$3,300	$4,300
1969	Natural, sunburst	$3,400	$4,000
1969	Olympic White, matching headstock	$4,200	$6,200
1969	Sherwood Green, Sonic Blue	$4,000	$6,000
1970	Black, blond, Oly White	$3,300	$3,800
1970	Sunburst	$3,000	$3,500
1971	Black	$3,200	$3,400
1971	Candy Apple Red, Lake Placid Blue	$3,300	$3,800
1971	Sunburst	$2,700	$3,000
1972	Black, Candy Apple Red, Oly White	$2,300	$2,800
1972	Lake Placid Blue	$2,300	$2,900
1972	Natural, sunburst	$2,000	$2,600
1973	Black	$2,300	$2,500
1973	Blond, fretless	$2,000	$2,300
1973	Lake Placid Blue	$2,300	$2,800
1973	Natural, sunburst	$2,000	$2,400
1973	Olympic White	$2,200	$2,500
1973	Walnut brown	$2,100	$2,300
1974	Black, blond	$2,000	$2,300
1974	Brown, maple board	$1,900	$2,200
1974	Natural, maple neck	$2,000	$2,400
1974	Olympic White	$2,100	$2,400
1974	Sunburst	$1,700	$2,300
1974	Walnut	$1,600	$2,200
1975	Black, Oly White	$1,800	$2,100
1975	Natural	$1,700	$1,900
1975	Sunburst	$1,600	$2,000
1975	Walnut	$1,500	$1,900
1976	Black	$1,600	$1,900
1976	Natural, maple neck	$1,500	$1,800
1976	Sunburst	$1,600	$2,000
1976	Sunburst, maple neck	$1,700	$2,100
1977	Black, brown, maple neck	$1,600	$1,900
1977	Natural, maple neck	$1,500	$1,800
1977	Sunburst	$1,600	$2,100
1977	White	$1,600	$1,900
1978	Antigua	$1,800	$2,100
1978	Black, brown/walnut, white	$1,600	$1,900
1978	Natural, maple neck	$1,500	$1,800
1978	Sunburst	$1,600	$2,100
1978	Wine Red	$1,500	$1,800
1979	Natural	$1,400	$1,900
1979	Sunburst, transparent red	$1,300	$1,800
1980	Antigua	$1,700	$2,000

The *Vintage Guitar Price Guide* shows low to high values for items in all-original excellent condition, and, where applicable, with original case or cover.

MODEL YEAR	FEATURES	EXC. COND. LOW	HIGH
1980	Black	$1,400	$1,800
1980	Natural, sunburst	$1,300	$1,700
1981	Black	$1,100	$1,600
1981	Black and Gold Collector's Edition	$1,300	$1,700
1981	International colors	$1,000	$1,500
1981	Sunburst	$1,000	$1,500

Standard Jazz Bass

1981-1988. Replaced Jazz Bass ('60-'81) and replaced by the American Standard Jazz Bass in '88. Name now used on import version.

1981-1982	Various colors	$1,100	$1,400
1981-1988	Mary Kaye Blond, gold trim	$1,000	$1,300
1982-1984	Top mounted input jack	$700	$900
1985	Japan import, no U.S. mfg.	$500	$700
1986-1988	Various colors	$800	$1,100

American Standard Jazz Bass

1988-2000. Replaced Standard Jazz Bass ('81-'88) and replaced by the American Series Jazz Bass in '00. Various colors.

1988-2000		$600	$800

American Series Jazz Bass

2000-present. Replaces American Standard Jazz Bass.

2000-2004		$650	$700

American Series Jazz Bass V

2000-present. 5 string version.

2000-2004		$650	$700

'62 Custom Shop Jazz Bass

Available as N.O.S., Closet Classic, or Relic version.

2000s	Relic option	$1,800	$2,000

'62 Jazz Bass

1982-present. U.S.A.-made, reissue of 1962 Jazz Bass.

1982-1985	Standard colors	$1,000	$1,200
1986-1989	Standard colors	$950	$1,100
1990-1999	Rare colors	$1,100	$1,300
1990-2003	Standard colors	$950	$1,050

'64 Custom Shop Jazz Bass

Available as N.O.S., Closet Classic, or Relic version.

2000s	N.O.S. option	$1,600	$1,700

'75 Jazz Bass American Vintage Series

Maple neck with black block markers.

2000s		$1,225	$1,275

50th Anniversary 5-String Jazz Bass

1995-1996. Sunburst, rosewood 'board.

1995-1996		$700	$1,000

American Deluxe Jazz Bass

1998-present. Made in the U.S.A., active electronics, alder or ash body. Alder body colors are sunburst or transparent red, ash body colors are white, blond, transparent teal green or transparent purple.

1998-2000	Various colors	$800	$900

American Deluxe Jazz V Bass

1998-present. 5-string model, various colors.

1998-2000		$800	$950

Custom Classic Jazz IV Bass

2000s		$1,000	$1,050

Deluxe Jazz Bass (active)

1995-present. Made in Mexico, active electronics, various colors.

1995-2004		$500	$525

Deluxe V Jazz Bass (active)

1995-present. Made in Mexico, various colors.

1995-2000		$400	$450

Foto Flame Jazz Bass

1995. Japanese import, alder and basswood body with Foto Flame figured wood image.

1995		$600	$700

Geddy Lee Signature Jazz Bass

1998, 2004. Limited run import in'98, part of Artist Series in '04.

1998	Black	$500	$600
2004	Artist Series	$700	$750

Gold Jazz Bass

1981-1984. Gold finish and gold-plated hardware.

1981-1984		$1,000	$1,200

Jazz Bass Special (import)

1984-1991. Japanese-made, Jazz/Precision hybrid, Precision-shaped basswood body, Jazz neck (fretless available), 2 P/J pickups.

1984-1991		$400	$500

Jazz Plus Bass

1990-1994. Alder body, 2 Lace Sensors, active electronics, rotary circuit selector, master volume, balance, bass boost, bass cut, treble boost, treble cut, various colors.

1990-1994		$600	$700

Jazz Plus V Bass

1990-1994. 5-string version.

1990-1994		$650	$750

Marcus Miller Signature Jazz Bass

1998-present. Japanese import, sunburst.

1998-2004		$600	$650

Noel Redding Signature Jazz Bass

1997. Limited Edition import, artist signature on pickguard.

1997	Sunburst, rosewood	$600	$650

Squire Jazz Bass

1990s-present. Jazz bass import, without cover plates, various colors.

1990s		$175	$200
2000s		$150	$180

Standard Jazz Bass (later model)

1988-present. Imported from various countries. Not to be confused with '81-'88 American-made model with the same name.

1988-1999		$275	$375
2000-2004		$325	$375

Standard Jazz Fretless Bass (later model)

Import model.

2000-2004		$300	$350

Standard Jazz V Bass (later model)

Import model.

2000-2004		$300	$350

Fender American Series Jazz Bass

Fender '62 Jazz Bass

The **Vintage Guitar Price Guide** shows low to high values for items in all-original excellent condition, and, where applicable, with original case or cover.

1971 Fender Mustang Bass

1953 Fender Precision Bass

MODEL YEAR	FEATURES	EXC. COND. LOW	HIGH

Ventures Limited Edition Jazz Bass
1996. Made in Japan, part of Ventures guitar and bass set, dark purple.

1996		$1,000	$1,150

JP-90 Bass
1990-1994. Two P/J pickups, rosewood fretboard, poplar body, black or red.

1990-1994		$550	$600

Musicmaster Bass
1970-1983. Shorter scale, solidbody, one pickup. Various colors.

1970-1983		$425	$500

Mustang Bass
1966-1982. Shorter scale, solidbody, 1 pickup. Offered in standard and competition colors. "Competition" colors refer to racing stripes on the body.

1966-1969		$1,000	$1,300
1970-1982		$800	$1,000

Performer Bass
1985-1986. Swinger-like body style, active electronics, various colors.

1985-1986		$875	$925

Precision Bass
The following are the various Precision Bass models. The main American-made models are listed first, with the others alphabetically as follows:

Precision Bass
Standard Precision Bass
American Standard Precision Bass
American Series Precision Bass
'51 Precision Bass
'55 Custom Shop Precision Bass
'57 Precision Bass
'57 Precision Bass (import)
'62 Precision Bass
'62 Precision Bass (import)
40th Anniversary Custom Shop Precision Bass
50th Anniversary Precision Bass
American Deluxe Precision Bass
Elite I Precision Bass
Elite II Precision Bass
Foto Flame Precision Bass
Gold Elite I Precision Bass
Gold Elite II Precision Bass
Precision Bass (import - Japan)
Precision Bass Lyte
Precision Bass Special
Precision U.S. Deluxe/Plus Deluxe Bass
Precision U.S. Plus/Plus Bass
Standard Precision Bass (later model)
Walnut Elite I Precision Bass
Walnut Elite II Precision Bass
Walnut Precision Bass Special

Precision Bass
1951-1981. Slab body until '54. One-piece maple neck standard until '59, optional after '69. Rosewood fingerboard standard '59 on (slab until mid-'62, curved after). Blond finish standard until '54, sunburst standard after that (two-tone '54-'58, three-tone after '58).

Replaced by the Standard Precision Bass in '81-'85, then the American Standard Precision in '88-'00. Renamed American Series Precision Bass in '00.

The custom colors listings are for unfaded or very slightly faded examples. Moderately faded examples will approximate values somewhat below the low end of the value range. A heavily faded example will be worth much less than the ranges shown, even if the heavily faded example is otherwise in excellent, original condition. A heavily faded example will have a tint that is unlike an unfaded example. Fade does not always mean 'lighter tint'. For example, a heavily faded Lake Placid Blue can turn dark Green. A heavily faded instrument will fetch a value that is slightly higher than a standard Sunburst example.

Custom color Fenders can be forged and bogus finishes have been a problem. As the value of custom color Fenders has increased, so has the problem of bogus non-original finishes. The prices in the Guide are for factory original finishes in excellent condition. The prices noted do not take into account market factors such as fake instruments, which can have the effect of lowering a guitar's market value unless the guitar's provenance can be validated.

Unlike the Jazz and Telecaster Basses, the Precision Bass was never fitted with a three-bolt neck or bullet rod.

MODEL YEAR	FEATURES	EXC. COND. LOW	HIGH
1951	Butterscotch blond, slab body	$9,500	$10,500
1952	Butterscotch blond, slab body	$9,000	$10,000
1953	Butterscotch blond, slab body	$8,800	$9,800
1954	Butterscotch blond, slab body	$8,500	$9,500
1954	Blond, contour body	$7,000	$8,500
1955	Blond, contour body	$6,500	$8,000
1956	Blond, contour body	$6,500	$8,000
1956	Sunburst	$6,000	$7,000
1957	Blond, last full year	$6,500	$8,000
1957	Sunburst, white guard early '57	$6,000	$7,000
1957	Sunburst, anodized guard late '57	$6,000	$7,000
1958	Blond option	$6,500	$8,000
1958	Sunburst, anodized guard	$6,000	$7,000
1959-1960	Sunburst or blond	$6,000	$7,000
1961	Blond (see-thru)	$6,000	$7,000
1961	Dakota Red	$9,500	$10,500
1961	Daphne Blue	$8,500	$9,500
1961	Lake Placid Blue, Olympic White	$6,500	$7,500
1961	Sunburst, slab rosewood	$5,500	$6,500
1962	Slab board, black	$6,500	$7,500
1962	Slab, blond	$6,000	$7,000
1962	Slab, Burgundy Mist	$10,500	$12,500

MODEL YEAR	FEATURES	EXC. COND. LOW	HIGH
1962	Slab, Dakota Red, Fiesta Red, Inca Silver, Shoreline Gold	$9,500	$11,500
1962	Slab, Daphne Blue	$8,500	$10,500
1962	Slab, Foam Green	$11,500	$13,500
1962	Slab, Lake Placid Blue, Oly White	$6,500	$7,800
1962	Slab, Shell Pink	$13,500	$16,300
1962	Slab, Sherwood Green	$10,500	$12,700
1962	Slab, Sonic Blue	$8,500	$10,300
1962	Slab, Surf Green	$11,500	$14,000
1962	Slab, sunburst	$5,500	$6,700
1962	Curved board, black, blond	$5,500	$6,500
1962	Curved, Burgundy Mist	$9,000	$11,000
1962	Curved, Dakota Red, Fiesta Red, Inca Silver	$8,500	$10,500
1962	Curved, Daphne Blue	$7,500	$9,500
1962	Curved, Foam Green	$10,500	$12,500
1962	Curved, Lake Placid Blue, Oly White	$5,500	$6,600
1962	Curved, Shell Pink	$11,500	$13,800
1962	Curved, Sherwood Green	$9,000	$10,800
1962	Curved, Shoreline Gold	$8,100	$9,800
1962	Curved, Sonic Blue	$7,300	$8,700
1962	Curved, Surf Green	$9,800	$11,800
1962	Curved, sunburst	$4,700	$5,700
1963	Blond, Lake Placid Blue, Oly White	$5,400	$6,500
1963	Candy Apple Red	$6,400	$7,800
1963	Dakota Red, Fiesta Red	$8,000	$9,700
1963	Sunburst	$4,500	$5,400
1964	Blond, Oly White	$5,100	$6,200
1964	Burgundy Mist	$7,700	$9,300
1964	Candy Apple Red	$5,300	$6,400
1964	Fiesta Red	$7,500	$9,100
1964	Lake Placid Blue	$5,400	$6,500
1964	Sherwood Green, Shoreline Gold	$7,600	$9,200
1964	Sunburst	$4,500	$5,400
1965	Black	$5,500	$6,600
1965	Blond	$4,300	$5,200
1965	Burgundy Mist	$6,500	$7,900
1965	Candy Apple Red, LP Blue, Oly White	$4,500	$5,500
1965	Charcoal Frost	$5,800	$7,000
1965	Fiesta Red, Sherwood Green	$6,000	$7,300
1965	Sunburst	$3,800	$4,800
1966	Candy Apple Red	$4,000	$4,800

MODEL YEAR	FEATURES	EXC. COND. LOW	HIGH
1966	Firemist Gold, Ice Blue Metallic, Sherwood Green	$5,500	$6,600
1966	Lake Placid Blue	$4,500	$5,500
1966	Olympic White	$4,300	$5,200
1966	Sunburst	$3,500	$4,000
1967	Candy Apple Red	$3,700	$4,500
1967	Sunburst	$3,000	$4,000
1968	Black	$3,100	$3,900
1968	Candy Apple Red	$3,300	$4,500
1968	Sunburst	$3,000	$4,000
1969	Black, rosewood or maple neck	$2,600	$3,100
1969	Candy Apple Red, LP Blue, Oly White	$2,800	$3,300
1969	Firemist Gold	$4,000	$4,500
1969	Sunburst	$2,500	$3,000
1970	Olympic White	$2,500	$2,800
1970	Sonic Blue	$3,600	$3,900
1970	Sunburst, maple cap on maple	$2,900	$3,200
1970	Sunburst, rosewood	$2,300	$2,700
1971	Black	$2,100	$2,400
1971	Firemist Gold, Sonic Blue	$3,000	$3,200
1971	Lake Placid Blue	$2,300	$2,600
1971	Natural, Oly White	$1,900	$2,200
1971	Sunburst	$2,000	$2,300
1972	Black, all necks	$1,900	$2,100
1972	Blond, Oly White, all necks	$2,000	$2,200
1972	Candy Apple Red, LP Blue, all necks	$2,100	$2,300
1972	Sonic Blue, all necks	$3,000	$3,200
1972	Sunburst, all necks	$1,800	$2,200
1972	Walnut, all necks	$1,700	$2,100
1973-1974	Black, blond, natural, walnut	$1,500	$2,000
1973-1974	CA Red, LP Blue	$1,700	$2,200
1973-1974	Olympic White	$1,700	$2,000
1973-1974	Sunburst	$1,600	$2,000
1975-1976	Black, blond, Oly White, sunburst	$1,400	$1,700
1975-1976	Natural, walnut	$1,300	$1,600
1977-1979	Antigua	$1,500	$1,700
1977-1979	Black, blond	$1,100	$1,600
1977-1979	Natural, Oly White, wine	$1,100	$1,500
1977-1979	Sunburst	$1,200	$1,600
1977-1979	Walnut	$1,000	$1,400
1980-1981	Antigua, International colors	$1,200	$1,500
1980-1981	Arctic White, black	$1,000	$1,400
1980-1981	Natural, wine	$900	$1,100
1980-1981	Sunburst	$1,000	$1,200

Standard Precision Bass
1981-1985. Replaces Precision Bass, various colors. Replaced by American Standard Precision '88-'00. The Standard name is used on import Precision model for '88-present.

1981-1985		$800	$1,000

Fender '57 Precision Bass

1978 Fender Precision Bass (Antigua)

The *Vintage Guitar Price Guide* shows low to high values for items in all-original excellent condition, and, where applicable, with original case or cover.

BASSES

Fender '51 Precision Bass

Fender Standard Precision Bass

MODEL YEAR	FEATURES	EXC. COND. LOW	HIGH

American Standard Precision Bass
1988-2000. Replaces Standard Precision Bass, replaced by American Series Precision in '00.

1988-1989	Blond, gold hardware	$1,000	$1,100
1990-2000	Various colors	$700	$900

American Series Precision Bass
2000-present. Replaces American Standard Precision Bass, various colors.

2000-2002		$650	$800

'51 Precision Bass
2003-present. Import from Japan, does not include pickup or bridge covers as part of the package, blond or sunburst.

2003		$275	$225

'55 Custom Shop Precision Bass
2003-present. '55 specs including oversized pickguard, one-piece maple neck/fretboard, preproduction bridge and pickup covers, single-coil pickup. Offered in N.O.S., Closet Classic or highest-end Relic.

2003	Closet Classic option	$1,700	$1,800

'57 Precision Bass
1982-present. U.S.-made reissue, various colors.

1982-2000		$1,000	$1,200

'57 Precision Bass (import)
1984-1986. Foreign-made.

1984-1986		$450	$600

'62 Precision Bass
1982-present. U.S.A.-made reissue of 1962 Precision, alder body.

1982-1989	Mary Kaye Blond, gold hardware	$1,100	$1,300
1982-1989	Standard colors	$1,000	$1,200
1990-1999	Rare colors	$1,100	$1,300
1990-1999	Standard colors	$950	$1,050
1999	Mars Music custom color	$1,100	$1,300
2000-2003	Standard colors	$950	$1,050

'62 Precision Bass (import)
1984-1986. Foreign-made, black.

1984-1986		$450	$600

40th Anniversary Custom Shop Precision Bass
1991. 400 made, quilted amber maple top, gold hardware.

1991		$1,400	$1,700

50th Anniversary Precision Bass
2001. Commemorative certificate with date and serial number, butterscotch finish, ash body, maple neck, black guard.

2001		$825	$925

American Deluxe Precision Bass
1998-present. Made in U.S.A., active electronics, alder or ash body. Alder body colors - sunburst or transparent red. Ash body colors - white blond, transparent teal green or transparent purple.

1998-2000		$700	$875

Elite I Precision Bass
1983-1985. The Elite Series feature active electronics and noise-cancelling pickups. Ash body, 2 pickups, various colors.

1983-1985		$700	$900

MODEL YEAR	FEATURES	EXC. COND. LOW	HIGH

Elite II Precision Bass
1983-1985. Ash body, 2 pickups, various colors.

1983-1985		$750	$950

Foto Flame Precision Bass
1995. Made in Japan, simulated woodgrain finish, natural or sunburst.

1995		$500	$575

Gold Elite I Precision Bass
1983-1985. The Elite Series feature active electronics and noise-cancelling pickups. Gold-plated hardware version of the Elite Precision I, 1 pickup.

1983-1985		$700	$900

Gold Elite II Precision Bass
1983-1985. Two pickup version.

1983-1985		$750	$950

Precision Bass (import - Japan)
1984-1986. Traditional styling, various colors.

1984-1986		$300	$450

Precision Bass Lyte
1992-2001. Japanese-made, smaller, lighter basswood body, 2 pickups, sunburst.

1992-2001		$500	$575

Precision Bass Special
1980-1983, 1997-present. Active electronics, gold-plated brass hardware, 1 split-coil pickup. '90s version similar, but with chrome hardware and made in Mexico.

1997-1999	Various colors (Mexico)	$350	$450

Precision U.S. Deluxe/Plus Deluxe Bass
1991-1994. P-style bass with P-bass and Jazz bass pickups, concentric knobs, no pickguard models available, various colors.

1991-1994		$550	$650

Precision U.S. Plus/Plus Bass
1989-1992. P-style bass with P-bass and Jazz bass pickup, various model variations.

1989-1992		$850	$900

Standard Precision Bass (later model)
1988-present. Traditional style, import, currently made in Mexico. Not to be confused with '81-'1985 American-made model with the same name.

1988-1999		$300	$350

Walnut Elite I Precision Bass
1983-1985. The Elite Series feature active electronics and noise-cancelling pickups. Walnut body, 1 pickup, rosewood fingerboard, natural.

1983-1985		$650	$850

Walnut Elite II Precision Bass
1983-1985. Two pickup version.

1983-1985		$700	$900

Walnut Precision Bass Special
1980-1983. Precision Bass Special with a walnut body, natural.

1980-1983		$900	$1,200

Squire Bullet Bass
1980s. Japanese-made, Squire-branded, replaces Bullet Bass, black.

1980s		$200	$250

MODEL YEAR	FEATURES	EXC. COND. LOW	HIGH

Stu Hamm Urge Bass (U.S.A.)
1992-1999. Contoured Precision-style body with smaller wide treble cutaway, J and P pickups, various colors.

1992-1999		$750	$850

Stu Hamm Urge II Bass (U.S.A.)
1999-present. Made in the U.S.A.

1999-2004		$900	$1,000

Telecaster Bass
1968-1979. Slab solidbody, 1 pickup, fretless option '70. Blond and custom colors available (Pink Paisley or Blue Floral '68-'69).

1968	Black	$2,200	$2,600
1968	Blond	$2,000	$2,400
1968	Blue Floral, Paisley	$5,500	$6,000
1969	4-bolt, single-coil	$2,000	$2,400
1970	4-bolt, single-coil	$1,900	$2,200
1971	4-bolt, single-coil	$1,800	$2,000
1972	4-bolt, single-coil	$1,500	$1,800
1973-1974	3-bolt, humbucker	$1,400	$1,800
1975-1976	3-bolt, humbucker	$1,250	$1,600
1977-1978	3-bolt, humbucker	$1,050	$1,500

Fernandes
1969-present. Intermediate and professional grade, production, solidbody basses. Established 1969 in Tokyo. Early efforts were classical guitars, but they now offer a variety of guitars and basses.

APB-40 Bass
1990s. High-end-style copy with opaque finish, extended long bass horn, P-Bass and J-Bass dual pickups.

1990s		$350	$450

FRB-80 Bass
FRB Series basses have active electronics. The FRB-80 has slotted neck joint construction.

1988		$250	$350

P-Bass Copy
1970s. Early import P-Bass features.

1970s		$275	$325

TEB-1 Bass
1993-1996.

1993-1996		$300	$400

Fina
Production acoustic basses built at the Kwo Hsiao Music Wooden Factory in Huiyang City, Guang Dong, mainland China. They also build guitars.

Fleishman Instruments
1974-present. Premium and presentation grade, acoustic and solidbody basses made by luthier Harry Fleishman in Sebastopol, California. He also offers electric uprights, designed by him and built in China. Fleishman also designs basses for others and is the director of Luthiers School International. He also builds guitars.

MODEL YEAR	FEATURES	EXC. COND. LOW	HIGH

Framus
1946-1975, 1996-present. Professional and premium grade, production/custom, guitars and basses made in Germany. Founded by Fred Wilfer, Erlangen, Germany in '46. Relocated to Bubenreuth in '54, and to Pretzfeld in '67. Imported into the U.S. by Philadelphia Music Company in the '60s. Brand revived in '96 by Fred's son Hans Peter Wilfer, who also founded Warwick basses and is distributed in the U.S. by Dana B. Goods.

Electric Upright Bass
1950s. Full-scale neck, triangular body. Black.

1958		$1,400	$1,600

Star Bass 5/150 (Bill Wyman)
1959-1968. Early flyer says, "Bill Wyman of the Rolling Stones prefers the Star Bass." The model name was later changed to Framus "Stone" Bass. Single cut semi-hollow body, 2 pickups.

1959-1965	Sunburst, Black Rose	$700	$900
1966-1968	Sunburst	$600	$800

Strato Starbass 5/156
Ca. 1963-ca. 1972. Double cut solidbody, 2 pickups, beige, cherry or sunburst.

1963-1972		$250	$350

Upright Bass Viol
Carved top.

1946		$3,000	$5,000

Fylde
1973-present. Luthier Roger Bucknall builds his professional and premium grade, production/custom acoustic basses in Penrith, Cumbria, United Kingdom. He also builds guitars, mandolins, mandolas, bouzoukis, and citterns.

G & L
1980-present. Intermediate and professional grade, production/custom, electric basses made in the U.S. In '03, G & L introduced the Korean-made G & L Tribute Series. A Tribute logo is clearly identified on the headstock. They also build guitars.

ASAT Bass
1989-present. Single cut solidbody, active and passive modes, 2 humbuckers.

1989-1991	About 400 made	$600	$725
1992-2003		$500	$600

ASAT Commemorative Bass
1991-1992. About 150 made, 4-string ASAT commemorating Leo Fender's life.

1991-1992		$1,400	$1,600

ASAT Semi-Hollow Bass
2001-present. Semi-hollowbody style on ASAT bass.

2001-2003		$650	$800

Climax Bass
1992-1996. Single active humbucker MFD pickup.

1992-1996		$450	$550

El Toro Bass
1983-1991. Double cut solidbody, 2 active, smaller, humbucker pickups, sunburst.

1983-1991		$600	$850

1968 Fender Telecaster Bass (Paisley)

1980 G&L ASAT Bass

BASSES

G&L SB-2

Gibson EB-0

MODEL YEAR / FEATURES	EXC. COND. LOW	HIGH
Interceptor Bass		
1984-1991. Sharp pointed double cut solidbody, 2 active, smaller humbuckers, sunburst.		
1984-1991	$700	$1,000
L-1000 Bass		
1980-1994. Offset double cut solidbody, 1 pickup.		
1980-1994	$550	$750
L-1500 Bass/L-1500 Custom Bass		
1997-present.		
1997-2003	$500	$600
L-1505 Bass		
1998-present. Five-string version, single MFD humbucker.		
1998-2003	$600	$650
L-2000 Bass		
1980-present. Offset double cut solidbody, 2 pickups, active electronics. Originally, the L-2000 was available with active (L-2000E) or passive (L-2000) electronics.		
1980-1982	$700	$850
1983-1991 Leo signature	$700	$850
1992-2003	$600	$650
L-2000 Custom Bass		
1997. Ash top, wood-grain binding upgrade.		
1997	$700	$800
L-2000 Fretless Bass		
1980-1981.		
1980-1981	$800	$900
L-2000(E) Bass		
1980-1982. Offset double cut solidbody, 2 pickups, active electronics. Originally, the L-2000 was available with active (L-2000E) or passive (L-2000) electronics.		
1980-1982	$750	$850
L-2500 Bass		
1997-present. Five strings, 2 MFD humbuckers.		
1997-2003	$600	$800
L-2500 Custom Bass		
1997. Ash top, wood-grain binding upgrade.		
1997	$700	$850
L-5000 Bass		
1988-1992. Offset double cut solidbody, G & L Z-shaped split-humbucking pickup, 5 strings. Approximately 400 made.		
1988-1992	$500	$650
L-5500 Bass		
1993-1997. Alder body, 5-string.		
1993-1997	$600	$700
L-5500 Custom Bass		
1997. Ash top, wood-grain binding upgrade.		
1997	$650	$750
LB-100 Bass		
1993-2000. Follow-up to earlier Legacy Bass.		
1993-2000	$450	$550
Legacy Bass		
1992-1993. Offset double cut solidbody, 1split-coil pickup. Renamed LB-100 in '93.		
1992-1993	$450	$550

MODEL YEAR / FEATURES	EXC. COND. LOW	HIGH
Lynx Bass		
1984-1991. Offset double cut solidbody, 2 single-coils, black.		
1984-1991	$475	$600
SB-1 Bass		
1982-2000. Solidbody, maple neck, body and fingerboard, split-humbucker, 1 tone and 1 volume.		
1982-1984 Single J-Bass style pickup	$450	$600
1985-2000 Single P-Bass style pickup	$400	$550
SB-2 Bass		
1982-present. Maple neck with tilt adjustment, 1 split-coil humbucking and 1 single-coil bridge pickups.		
1982-1984 2 P-style pickups	$450	$600
1988-2003 One P & on J style PU	$500	$550

G.L. Stiles

1960-1994. Built by Gilbert Lee Stiles primarily in the Miami, Florida area. He also built guitars.

Electric Solidbody Basses

Various models.

1970s	$300	$425

Gibson

1902-present. Professional grade, production, U.S.-made electric basses. Gibson got into the electric bass market with the introduction of their Gibson Electric Bass in '53 (that model was renamed the EB-1 in '58 and reintroduced under that name in '69). Many more bass models followed. Gibson's Custom Colors can greatly increase the value of older instruments. Custom Colors offered from '63 to '69 are Cardinal Red, Ember Red, Frost Blue, Golden Mist Metallic, Heather Metallic, Inverness Green, Kerry Green, Pelham Blue Metallic, Polaris White, Silver Mist Metallic.

EB-0 Bass

1959-1979. Double cut slab body with banjo-type tuners in '59 and '60, double cut SG-type body with conventional tuners from '61 on, 1 pickup. Faded Custom Colors are of less value.

Year	Features	LOW	HIGH
1959-1960	Cherry, slab body	$2,500	$2,700
1961	Cherry, SG body	$1,700	$1,900
1962	Cherry	$1,500	$1,700
1963-1965	Cherry	$1,300	$1,500
1966-1968	Cherry	$1,100	$1,300
1968	Black	$1,200	$1,400
1968	Burgundy Metallic (unfaded)	$2,200	$2,400
1968	Burgundy Metallic (faded)	$1,500	$1,800
1968	Pelham Blue (unfaded)	$2,200	$2,400
1968-1969	Pelham Blue (faded)	$1,500	$1,800
1969-1971	Cherry	$1,000	$1,200
1972-1974	Cherry	$900	$1,100
1975-1979	Cherry	$700	$900

MODEL YEAR	FEATURES	EXC. COND. LOW	HIGH

EB-0 F Bass
1962-1965. EB-0 with added built-in fuzz. Cherry.

1962		$1,500	$1,700
1963-1965		$1,300	$1,500

EB-0 L Bass
1969-1979. 34.5 inch scale version of the EB-0.

1969	Various colors	$900	$1,100
1970-1971	Various colors	$850	$1,000
1972-1974	Various colors	$700	$900
1975-1979	Various colors	$550	$700

EB-1 Bass
1969-1972. The Gibson Electric Bass ('53-'58) is often also called the EB-1 (see Electric Bass). Violin-shaped mahogany body, 1 pickup, standard tuners.

1969-1972		$1,700	$1,900

EB-2 Bass
1958-1961, 1964-1972. ES-335-type semi-hollow-body, double cut, 1 pickup, banjo tuners '58-'60 and conventional tuners '60 on.

1958	Sunburst, banjo tuners	$2,300	$2,700
1959	Natural, banjo tuners	$2,400	$2,800
1959	Sunburst, banjo tuners	$2,200	$2,600
1960	Sunburst, banjo tuners	$2,100	$2,600
1961	Sunburst, conventional tuners	$1,700	$2,300
1964	Sunburst	$1,400	$1,700
1965	Sunburst	$1,300	$1,600
1966-1969	Various colors	$1,100	$1,600
1967-1969	Sparkling Burgundy option	$1,400	$2,000
1970-1972	Various colors	$900	$1,200

EB-2 D Bass
1966-1972. Two pickup version of EB-2, cherry, sunburst, or walnut.

1966-1969	Various colors	$1,600	$1,900
1970-1972	Sunburst	$1,200	$1,500

EB-3 Bass
1961-1979. SG-style solidbody, 2 humbuckers, solid peghead '61-'68 and '72-'79, slotted peghead '69-'71, cherry or walnut.

1961-1965		$1,800	$2,000
1966-1968		$1,700	$1,900
1969	Slotted peghead, various colors	$1,600	$1,800
1970-1971	Various colors	$1,500	$1,700
1972-1974	Various colors	$1,400	$1,600
1975-1979	Various colors	$1,200	$1,400

EB-3 L Bass
1969-1972. 34.5" scale version of EB-3, cherry, natural, or walnut.

1969	Various colors	$1,300	$1,500
1970-1971	Various colors	$1,200	$1,400
1972	Various colors	$1,100	$1,300

EB-4 L Bass
1972-1975. SG-style, 1 humbucker, 34.5" scale, Cherry or Walnut.

1972-1975		$900	$1,200

MODEL YEAR	FEATURES	EXC. COND. LOW	HIGH

EB-6 Bass
1960-1966. Introduced as semi-hollowbody 335-style six-string with 1 humbucker, changed to SG-style with 2 pickups in '62.

1960	Sunburst, 335-style	$6,200	$7,000
1961	Sunburst, 335-style	$6,300	$6,900
1962-1964	Cherry, SG-style	$5,500	$6,700
1965-1966	Cherry, SG-style	$5,000	$6,000

Electric Bass EB-1
1953-1958. Introduced as Gibson Electric Bass in '53, but was called the EB-1 by Gibson in its last year of '58. Thus, the whole line is commonly called the EB-1 by collectors. Reissued in '69 as the EB-1 (see EB-1 listing). Brown.

1953-1958		$3,500	$4,500

Explorer Bass
1984-1987. Alder body, 3-piece maple neck, ebony board, dot inlays, 2 humbuckers, various colors.

1984-1987		$700	$800

Flying V Bass
1981-1982 only. Solidbody, Flying V body.

1981-1982	Blue stain or Ebony	$1,200	$1,600
1981-1982	Silverburst	$2,200	$2,600

Gibson IV Bass
1986-1988. Mahogany body and neck, double cut, 2 pickups, black chrome hardware.

1986-1988	Various colors	$450	$600

Gibson V Bass
1986-1988. Double cut, 5 strings, 2 pickups.

1986-1988		$650	$850

Grabber Bass (G-1)
1974-1982. Double cut solidbody, 1 pickup, bolt maple neck, maple board, various colors.

1974-1982		$575	$700

Grabber III Bass (G-3)
1975-1982. Double cut solidbody, 3 pickups, bolt maple neck, maple board, nickel-plated hardware, various colors.

1975-1982		$600	$750

Les Paul Bass
1970-1971. Single cut solidbody, 2 pickups, walnut finish. Renamed Les Paul Triumph Bass '71-'79.

1970-1971		$1,300	$1,500

Les Paul Signature Bass
1973-1979. Double cut semi-hollowbody, 1 pickup, sunburst or gold (gold only by '76).

1973-1975	Sunburst	$2,400	$2,600
1973-1979	Gold	$2,300	$2,500

Les Paul Special LPB-1 Bass
1991-present. Two pickups, ebony 'board, active electronics, also available as 5-string.

1991-1999	Alpine White	$500	$600

Les Paul Triumph Bass
1971-1979. Renamed from Les Paul Bass.

1971-1979	Various colors	$1,100	$1,300
1973-1974	White optional color	$1,200	$1,500

1968 Gibson EB-3

Gibson EB-4L

Gibson L-9 Ripper

1965 Gibson Thunderbird II

Q-80 Bass
1986-1988. Victory Series body shape, 2 pickups, bolt neck, black chrome hardware. Renamed Q-90 in '88.

1986-1988		$500	$600

Q-90 Bass
1988-1992. Renamed from Q-80. Mahogany body, 2 active humbuckers, maple neck, ebony board.

1988-1992		$500	$600

RD Artist Bass
1977-1982. Double cut solid maple body, laminated neck, 2 pickups, active electronics, string-through-body, block inlays, various colors.

1977-1982		$700	$800

RD Artist Custom Bass
1977-1982. Custom option with bound top, low production.

1977-1982	Sunburst, mild figure	$850	$1,000

RD Standard Bass
1977-1979. Double cut solid maple body, laminated neck, 2 pickups, regular electronics, string-through-body, dot inlays. Various colors.

1977-1979		$700	$800

Ripper Bass
1974-1982. Introduced as L-9 S Bass in '73. Double cut solidbody, glued neck, 2 pickups, string-through-body.

1974-1982	Various colors	$550	$700
1975-1981	Various colors, fretless	$550	$750

Thunderbird II Bass
1963-1969. Reverse solidbody until '65, non-reverse solidbody '65-'69, 1 pickup, custom colors available. Reintroduced with reverse body for '83-'84.

1963	Sunburst, reverse body	$4,000	$5,000
1964	Sunburst, reverse body	$4,000	$4,500
1964	Pelham Blue Metallic, reverse body	$4,500	$5,000
1965	Inverness Green, non-reverse body	$3,500	$4,500
1965	Sunburst, reverse body	$3,300	$4,300
1966	Sunburst, non-reverse body	$2,300	$2,800
1967	Sunburst, non-reverse body	$2,100	$2,700
1968	Cardinal Red, non-reverse body	$3,100	$3,800
1968	Sunburst, non-reverse body	$2,100	$2,600
1969	Sunburst, non-reverse body	$2,100	$2,500

Thunderbird IV Bass
1963-1969. Reverse solidbody until '64, non-reverse solidbody '65-'69, 2 pickups, custom colors available. Reintroduced with reverse body for '86-present (see Thunderbird IV Bass Reissue).

1963	Sunburst, reverse body	$5,000	$6,500
1964	Frost Blue, reverse body	$6,500	$7,500
1964	Pelham Blue Metallic, reverse body	$6,500	$7,500
1964	Sunburst, reverse body	$5,000	$6,000
1965	Cardinal Red, non-reverse body	$5,000	$6,000
1965	Inverness Green, non-reverse body	$5,000	$6,500
1965	Sunburst, reverse body	$4,800	$5,800
1966	Sunburst, non-reverse body	$3,300	$3,800
1966	White, non-reverse body	$4,300	$5,300
1967	Sunburst, non-reverse body	$3,000	$3,500
1968	Sunburst, non-reverse body	$2,900	$3,400
1969	Sunburst, non-reverse	$2,700	$3,300

Thunderbird IV Bass (reissue)
1987-present. Has reverse body and 2 pickups. Sunburst.

1980s		$1,100	$1,300
1990s		$1,000	$1,200

Thunderbird 76 Bass
1976 only. Reverse solidbody, 2 pickups, rosewood fingerboard, various colors.

1976		$1,800	$2,500

Thunderbird 79 Bass
1979 only. Reverse solidbody, 2 pickups.

1979	Sunburst	$1,500	$1,800

Victory Artist Bass
1981-1985. Double cut solidbody, 2 humbuckers, active electronics, various colors.

1981-1985		$400	$500

Victory Custom Bass
1982-1984. Double cut solidbody, 2 humbuckers, passive electronics, limited production.

1982-1984		$400	$500

Victory Standard Bass
1981-1986. Double cut solidbody, 1 humbucker, active electronics, various colors.

1981-1986		$375	$450

Godin
1987-present. Intermediate and professional grade, production, solidbody electric and acoustic/electric basses from luthier Robert Godin. They also build guitars and mandolins.

Gold Tone
1993-present. Wayne and Robyn Rogers build their intermediate grade, production/custom acoustic basses in Titusville, Florida. They also offer lap steels, mandolins, banjos and banjitars.

BASSES

MODEL YEAR	FEATURES	EXC. COND. LOW	HIGH

Goya

1955-1996. Originally imports from Sweden, brand later used on Japanese and Korean imports

Electric Solidbody Basses

Various models.

1960s		$250	$350

Graf, Oskar

1970-present. Luthier Oskar Graf builds his premium grade, production/custom upright solidbody and acoustic basses in Clarendon, Ontario. He also builds guitars and lutes.

Greco

1960s-present. Currently owned by Kanda Shokai, of Japan, and offering solidbody basses. They also offer guitars. Early bass models were copies of popular brands, but the by the '70s original designs appear.

Beatle Bass Copy

1970s		$200	$300

Gretsch

1883-present. Intermediate and professional grade, production, solidbody, hollow body, and acoustic/electric basses. Gretsch came late to the electric bass game, introducing their first models in the early '60s.

Bikini Doubleneck

1961-1962. Solidbody electric, separate 6-string and bass-neck body units that slid into one of three body "butterflies"--one for the 6-string only (6023), one for bass only (6024), one for doubleneck (6 and bass-6025). Components could be purchased separately. Prices here are for bass neck and one body.

1961-1962		$800	$1,000

Broadkaster Bass (7605/7606)

1975-1979. Double cut solidbody, 1 pickup, bolt-on maple neck, natural (7605) or sunburst (7606).

1975-1979		$650	$850

Committee Bass (7629)

1977-1980. Double cut walnut and maple soldibody, neck-through, 1 pickup, natural.

1977-1980		$550	$750

Model 6070 Bass (double cutaway)

1968-1971. Country Gentleman thinline archtop double cut body, fake F-holes, 1 pickup, gold hardware.

1968-1971		$1,000	$1,200

Model 6071 Bass (single cutaway)

1968. Single cut hollowbody, fake F-holes, 1 pickup, padded back, red mahogany.

1968-1971		$900	$1,100

Model 6072 Bass (double cutaway)

1968-1971. 2 pickup version of 6070 Bass.

1968-1971		$1,300	$1,500

Model 6073 Bass (single cutaway)

1968-1971. Two pickup version of Model 6071 Bass, red mahogany.

1968		$1,000	$1,200

Grosh, Don

1993-present. Professional grade, production/custom, solidbody basses built by luthier Don Grosh in Santa Clarita, California. He also builds guitars.

P4 Custom Bass

1998-present. Offset double cut 4-string solidbody.

2003		$950	$1,050

Guild

1952-present. Guild added electric basses in the mid-'60s and offered them until '02.

Ashbory Bass

1986-1988. 18" scale, total length 30", fretless, silicone rubber strings, active electronics, low-impedance circuitry.

1986-1988		$400	$550

B-4 E Bass

1993-1999. Acoustic/electric single cut flat-top, mahogany sides with arched mahogany back, multi-bound, gold hardware until '95, chrome after.

1993-1995	Gold hardware	$850	$650
1996-1999	Chrome	$800	$900

B-30 E Bass

1987-1999. Single cut flat-top acoustic/electric, mahogany sides, arched mahogany back, multi-bound, fretless optional.

1987-1999		$1,150	$1,250

B-50 Acoustic Bass

1975-1987. Acoustic flat-top, mahogany sides with arched mahogany back, spruce top, multi-bound. Renamed B-30 in '87.

1976-1987		$1,000	$1,300

B-301 A Bass

1977-1981. Ash body B-301 Bass.

1977-1981		$550	$650

B-301 Bass

1976-1981. Double cut mahogany solidbody, 1 pickup, chrome-plated hardware.

1976-1981		$500	$650

B-302 AF Bass

1977-1981. Ash body and fretless board B-302.

1977-1981		$550	$650

B-302 Bass

1976-1981. Double cut mahogany solidbody, 2 pickups, chrome-plated hardware.

1976-1981		$550	$650

Jet Star Bass

1964-1970 (limited production '68-'70). Offset double cut solidbody, short treble horn, 1 pickup, 2-on-a-side tuners '64-'66 and 4 in-line tuners '66-'70.

1964-1966	2 on side tuners	$800	$900
1967-1970	4 in-line	$750	$850

JS I Bass

1970-1976. Single pickup version of JS II.

1970-1976		$450	$750

JS II Bass

1970-1976. Double cut solidbody, 2 pickups, mini-switch, selector switch. Renamed JS Bass 2 in '73 with carved oak leaf design available.

1970-1976		$550	$850

1978 Gretsch TK-300

Guild Ashbory

BASSES

1967 Guild Starfire Bass

Hagstrom 8-string

MODEL YEAR FEATURES	EXC. COND. LOW	HIGH

M-85 I BluesBird Bass
1972-1973. Single cut archtop, 1 humbucker, Chesterfield headstock inlay, mahogany.

| 1972-1973 | $600 | $750 |

M-85 II BluesBird Bass
1972-1976. 2 humbucker version of M-85, cherry mahogany.

| 1972-1976 | $850 | $1,050 |

MB-801 Bass
1981-1982. Double-cut solidbody, 1 pickup, dot inlays.

| 1981-1982 | $450 | $650 |

SB-601 Pilot Bass
1983-1988. Offset double cut solidbody, bolt-on neck, 1 pickup, poplar body.

| 1983-1988 | $500 | $650 |

SB-602 Pilot Bass (P-602)
1983-1993. 2 pickup SB-601 Pilot Bass. Listed as P-602 in last few years of run.

| 1983-1993 | $550 | $700 |

SB-602 Pilot V (5-String) Bass
1983-1988. 5-string version of 602.

| 1983-1988 | $550 | $700 |

Starfire Bass
1965-1975. Double cut semi-hollow thinbody, 1 pickup, mahogany neck, chrome-plated hardware, cherry or sunburst.

| 1965-1969 | $1,100 | $1,400 |
| 1970-1975 | $1,000 | $1,200 |

X-701 Bass
1982-1984. Body with 4 sharp horns with extra long bass horn, 1 pickup, various metallic finishes.

| 1982-1984 | $750 | $850 |

X-702 Bass
1982-1984. 2 pickup version of X-701.

| 1982-1984 | $850 | $950 |

Guyatone
1933-present. Large Japanese maker which also produced instruments under the Marco Polo, Winston, Kingston, Kent, LaFayette, and Bradford brand names.

Electric Solidbody Basses
Various models.

| 1960s | $250 | $400 |

Hagstrom
1921-1983. This Swedish guitar company first offered electric basses in '61.

8-String Bass
1967-1969. Double cut solidbody, 2 pickups, various colors.

| 1967-1969 | $1,000 | $1,200 |

Model I B Bass
1965-1966, 1971-1973. Double cut solidbody, 2 pickups.

| 1965-1966 | $400 | $500 |

Model II B/F-400 Bass
1965-1970. Offset double cut solidbody, 2 pickups. Called F-400 in U.S., II B elsewhere.

| 1965-1970 | $450 | $550 |

MODEL YEAR FEATURES	EXC. COND. LOW	HIGH

Swede 2000 Bass (with synth)
1977. Circuitry on this Swede bass connected to the Ampeg Patch 2000 pedal so bass would work with various synths.

| 1977 | $700 | $800 |

Swede Bass
1971-1976. Single cut solidbody, block inlays, 2 pickups cherry.

| 1971-1976 Cherry | $700 | $800 |

Hamer
1975-present. Intermediate and professional grade, production/custom, acoustic and electric basses. Founded in Arlington Heights, Illinois, by Paul Hamer and Jol Dantzig, Hamer was purchased by Kaman in '88.

12-String Short-Scale Bass
1978-1996. Four sets of 3 strings - a fundamental and 2 tuned an octave higher, maple and mahogany solidbody, 30.5" scale.

| 1970s | $1,000 | $1,450 |

Blitz Bass
1982-1990. Explorer-style solidbody, 2 pickups, bolt-on neck.

| 1982-1988 | $450 | $550 |
| 1989-1990 | $400 | $500 |

Chaparral Bass
1986-1995, 2000-present. Solidbody, 2 pickups, glued-in neck, (later basses have bolt-on neck).

| 1986-1995 | $550 | $650 |

Chaparral 5-String Bass
1987-1995. Five strings, solidbody, 2 pickups, glued-in neck. Later basses have five-on-a-side reverse peghead.

| 1980s | $600 | $700 |

Chaparral Max Bass
1986-1995. Chaparral Bass with figured maple body, glued-in neck and boomerang inlays.

| 1986-1995 | $550 | $675 |

CruiseBass
1982-1990, 1995-1999. J-style solidbody, 2 pickups, glued neck ('82-'90) or bolt neck ('95-'99). Also available as a 5-string.

| 1982-1990 | $500 | $650 |

CruiseBass 5
1982-1989. Five-string version, various colors.

| 1982-1989 | $500 | $650 |

FBIV Bass
1985-1987. Reverse Firebird shape, 1 P-Bass Slammer and one J-Bass Slammer pickup, mahogany body, rosewood board, dots.

| 1985-1987 | $500 | $700 |

Standard Bass
1975-1984. Explorer-style bound body with 2 humbuckers.

| 1970s | $750 | $850 |
| 1980s | $450 | $650 |

Harmony
1892-1976. Harmony once was one of the biggest instrument makers in the world, making guitars and basses under their own brand and for others.

MODEL YEAR	FEATURES	EXC. COND. LOW	HIGH

H-22 Bass
Introduced in 1970. Single cutaway.

1970s	Sunburst	$300	$500

Rocket Bass
1960s-1970s. First models single cut, later models double cut, similar to Rocket guitar.

1960s	Sunburst	$375	$475

Hartke
Hartke offered a line of wood and aluminum-necked basses from 2000 to 2003.

Heartfield
1989-1994. Distributed by Fender, imported from Japan.

DR-4 Bass
1989-1994. Double cut solidbody, graphite reinforced neck, 2 single-coils, 4 strings. Available in 5- and 6-string models.

1989-1994		$250	$350

Heit Deluxe
Ca. 1967-1970. Imported from Japan, many were made by Teisco.

Hofner
1887-present. Professional grade, production, basses. They also offer guitars and bowed instruments. Hofner basses, made famous in the U.S. by one Paul McCartney, are made in Germany.

JB-59 Upright Jazz Bass
Electric solidbody, 3/4-size, solid mahogany, pickup, preamp.

1980s		$1,000	$1,300

Model 185 Solid Bass
1962-ca. 1970. Classic offset double cut solidbody, 2 double-coil pickups.

1960s		$375	$450

Model 500/1 Beatle Bass
1956-present. Semi-acoustic, bound body in violin shape, glued-in neck, 2 pickups, sunburst. Currently listed as the 500/1 Cavern '61 Electric Bass Guitar.

1956-1959		$2,500	$3,500
1960-1962		$2,800	$3,800
1960-1962	Lefty	$3,500	$4,500
1963		$2,500	$3,500
1963	Lefty	$3,200	$4,200
1964		$2,400	$3,200
1964	Lefty	$2,800	$3,800
1965		$2,400	$3,000
1965	Lefty	$2,600	$3,600
1966		$2,200	$3,000
1966	Lefty	$2,400	$3,500
1967		$1,800	$2,500
1968-1969		$1,700	$2,200
1970-1973		$1,600	$2,100
1970-1973	Lefty	$1,800	$2,300
1974-1979		$1,200	$1,700

Model 500/1 1964-1984 Reissue
1984. "1964-1984" neckplate notation.

1984		$1,550	$1,650

MODEL YEAR	FEATURES	EXC. COND. LOW	HIGH

'63 Model 500/1 Beatle Bass
1994-present.

1990s	Lefty	$1,300	$1,400

Model 500/2 Bass
1965-1970. Similar to the 500/1, but with "Club" body Hofner made for England's Selmer, sunburst. Club Bass has been reissued.

1965-1970		$1,400	$1,700

Model 500/5 Bass
1959-1979. Single cut body with Beatle Bass-style pickups, sunburst.

1960s		$1,800	$2,000

Model 5000/1 Super Beatle Bass (G500/1)
1968-present. Bound ebony board, gold-plated hardware, natural finish. The version with active circuit is called G500/1 Super Beatle. Reissued in '94

1971-1972		$1,450	$1,650

President Bass
Made for England's Selmer, single cut archtop, 2 pickups, sunburst.

1961-1965		$1,500	$2,000
1968-1969		$1,100	$1,300
1970-1972		$1,000	$1,200

Hohner
1857-present. Intermediate and professional grade, production, solidbody basses. Hohner has been offering basses at least since the early '70s. They also offer guitars, banjos, mandolins and ukes.

B-Bass
1990-present. Solid maple neck-thru-body, rosewood board, 2 pickups, several options.

1990s		$300	$450

B2AFL Bass
1990-1994. Headless, 2 humbuckers, active circuitry, fretless.

1990-1994		$250	$300

HAB-1 Acoustic/Electric Bass
1990-1993. Rounded triangular soundhole, medium-size dreadnought, single cut.

1990-1993		$250	$375

Jack Bass
1989-1994. Headless, offset body, 2 pickups, active tone circuitry.

1989-1994		$300	$400

JJ Bass
Late 1980s-1991. Sunburst solid maple body, 2 pickups, active tone circuitry.

1980s		$250	$325

Hondo
1969-1987, 1991-present. Budget grade, production, imported acoustic and electric solidbody basses. They also offer guitars and mandolins.

Electric Solidbody Basses
Various models.

1970s		$125	$250
1980s		$100	$200
1990s		$75	$150

1963 Höfner 500/1

Hondo Artist 8-string

BASSES

Ibanez SR-500

Jackson C20 Concert

MODEL YEAR	FEATURES	EXC. COND. LOW	HIGH

H 1181 Longhorn Bass
Ca. 1978-1980s. Copy of Danelectro Longhorn Bass, 1 split pickup.

1970s		$450	$550

Hopf
1906-present. Hopf currently mainly offers classical guitars and mandolins. From the mid-'50s to the late-'70s, Hopf offered electric basses made in their own factory and by others.

Hoyer
1874-present. Intermediate grade, production, electric basses. They also build guitars.

Ibanez
1932-present. Intermediate and professional grade, production, solidbody basses. They also have guitars, amps, and effects.

Axstar 1000 AXB Bass
1986-1987. Headless alder solidbody, one-piece maple neck-thru-body, ebony 'board, two low impedance pickups.

1986-1987		$375	$425

Axstar 50 AXB Bass
1986-1987. Headless solidbody, one-piece maple neck, rosewood 'board, 2 humbuckers.

1986-1987		$275	$350

Axstar 60 AXB Bass
1986-1987. Headless solidbody, one-piece maple neck, ebony 'board, two low impedance pickups.

1986-1987		$275	$350

Axstar 65 AXB Bass
1986-1987. 5-string version of the 60 AXB.

1986-1987		$275	$350

BTB500 Bass
1999-2000. Offset double cutaway ash solidbody, 2 pickups, extra long bass horn, dot markers.

1999-2000		$500	$600

Destroyer X Series Bass
1983-1986. Explorer-style body, P and J-style pickups, dot markers, X Series notation on headstock, bolt-on neck, black.

1983-1986	Black	$375	$425

Model 2030 Bass
1970-1973. First copy era bass modeled after the Jazz Bass.

1972	Sunburst	$325	$375

Musician EQ Bass
1978-1979. Offset double cut solidbody, 2 pickups, EQ, ash and mahogany body, ebony 'board, dot inlays. Became the MC900.

1978-1979		$400	$550

Musician MC800 Bass
1979-1980. Offset double cut solidbody, 2 pickups, laminated neck.

1979-1980		$350	$450

Musician MC900 Bass
1979-1980. MC800 with 3-band EQ.

1979-1980		$400	$500

MODEL YEAR	FEATURES	EXC. COND. LOW	HIGH

Newport Bass
1974-1975. Copy of a Mapleglo Rickenbacker 4001 Bass.

1975	Mapleglo (Blond)	$800	$850

PL 5050 Bass
ca. 1985-ca. 1988. Part of the Pro Line Series.

1980s		$200	$350

Roadstar II Bass
1982-1987. Solidbody basses, includes several variations.

1982-1987		$250	$350

Rocket Roll Bass
1974-1976. Korina solidbody, Flying V-shape. Natural.

1970s		$850	$1,000

SB-900 Bass
1990-1993. Ultra slim solidbody.

1990-1993		$300	$375

SR-500 Bass
1993-1996. Offset double cut with typical long extended bass horn, P and J-style active pickups, bolt-on neck.

1993-1996		$350	$450

SR-505 5-String Bass
1993 only. Five strings, long extended bass horn, dot markers.

1993		$450	$550

Imperial
Ca.1963-ca.1970. Imported by the Imperial Accordion Company of Chicago, Illinois. Early guitars made in Italy, but by ca. '66 Japanese-made.

Electric Solidbody Basses
1960s. Various models.

1960s		$150	$225

Hollowbody Bass
1960s. Hollowbody with sharp double cutaways.

1960s		$250	$275

J.B. Player
1980s-present. Intermediate grade, production, imported, acoustic/electric and solidbody basses. They also offer guitars, banjos and mandolins.

J. T. Hargreaves
1995-present. Luthier Jay Hargreaves builds his premium grade, production/custom, acoustic basses, in Seattle, Washington. He also builds guitars.

Jackson
1980-present. Intermediate, professional, and premium grade, production, solidbody basses. They also offer guitars. Founded by Grover Jackson, who owned Charvel.

Concert C5P 5-String (import)
1998-2000. Bolt neck, dot inlay, chrome hardware.

1998-2000		$150	$175

MODEL YEAR	FEATURES	EXC. COND. LOW	HIGH

Concert Custom Bass (U.S.-made)
1984-1995. Neck-through Custom Shop bass.

1984-1989		$650	$700
1990-1995		$500	$600

Concert EX 4-String (import)
1992-1995. Bolt neck, dot inlay, black hardware.

1992-1995		$175	$250

Concert V 5-String (import)
1992-1995. Bound neck, shark tooth inlay.

1992-1995		$200	$300

Concert XL 4-String (import)
1992-1995. Bound neck, sharktooth inlay.

1992-1995		$200	$300

Piezo Bass
1986. 4 piezoelectric bridge pickups, neck-through, active EQ, shark tooth inlays. Student model has rosewood board, no binding. Custom Model has ebony board and neck and headstock binding.

1986		$300	$450

Jay Turser
1997-present. Intermediate grade, production, imported semi-hollow and solidbody basses. They also offer guitars and amps.

Jerry Jones
1981-present. Intermediate grade, production, semi-hollow body electric basses from luthier Jerry Jones, and built in Nashville, Tennessee. They also build guitars and sitars.

Longhorn Bass 6
1988-present. Reproduction of the Danelectro longhorn design, six strings, two lipstick-tube pickups, 30" scale, 24-fret poplar neck.

1988-1999		$500	$600

Johnson
Mid-1990s-present. Budget and intermediate grade, production, solidbody and acoustic basses imported by Music Link, Brisbane, California. They also offer guitars, amps, mandolins and effects.

Juzek
Violin maker John Juzek was originally located in Prague, Czeckoslovakia, but moved to West Germany due to World War II. Prague instruments considered by most to be more valuable. Many German instruments were mass produced with laminate construction and some equate these German basses with the Kay laminate basses of the same era. Juzek still makes instruments.

Master Art Series 3/4 Bass
Upright bass.

1964		$7,000	$8,000

Prague 3/4 Bass
Upright bass, carved top.

1920		$6,000	$7,000

Kalamazoo
1933-1942, 1965-1970. Kalamazoo was a brandname Gibson used on one of their budget lines. They also used the name on electric basses from '65 to '67.

Electric Basses

1960s	Bolt-on neck	$250	$400

Kapa
Ca. 1962-1970. Kapa was founded by Kope Veneman in Maryland.

Minstrel Bass
1968-1970. Teardrop shape, thinline.

1968-1970		$250	$350

Kawai
1927-present. Japanese instrument manufacturer Kawai started offering guitars under other brandnames around '56. There were few imports carrying the Kawai brand until the late-'70s; best known for high quality basses. Kawai recently quit offering guitars and basses.

Electric Solidbody Basses

1960s		$150	$300

F2B Bass
1987-1999. Laminated body, active, neck-through, gold-plated tuners, various options.

1980s		$400	$500

KRB 55 Bass
1986-mid 1990s. Maple neck, rosewood board, 3+1 tuners, black hardware.

1980s		$300	$400

KRB 105 Bass
1987-mid 1990s. Carbon-graphite neck, 34" scale.

1980s		$400	$500

KRB 120 Bass
1987-mid 1990s. Carbon-graphite neck, 34" scale, active circuitry.

1980s		$400	$500

Kay
Ca. 1931-present. Currently, budget grade, production, imported basses. Kay introduced upright acoustic laminate basses and 3/4 viols in '38 and electric basses in '54. See Guitar Stories Volume II, by Michael Wright, for a complete history of Kay with detailed model listings.

C1 Concert String Bass
1938-1967. Standard (3/4) size student bass, laminated construction, spruce top, figured maple back and sides, shaded light brown.

1940s		$1,500	$1,900
1950s		$1,400	$1,800
1960s		$1,300	$1,700

K-5935 Bass
1966-1968. Renumbered from 5930, plain style, double cut solidbody.

1966-1968		$300	$500

Jerry Jones Longhorn 6

'60s Kay bass

Ken Smith Black Tiger

1979 Kramer DMZ 6000B

MODEL YEAR	FEATURES	EXC. COND. LOW	HIGH

M-1 (Maestro) String Bass

1952-late-1960s. Standard (3/4) size bass, laminated construction, spruce top and curly maple back and sides. Model M-3 is the Junior (1/4) size bass. Model M-1 B has a Blond finish. Other models include the S-51 B Chubby Jackson Five-String Bass and the S-9 Swingmaster.

1960s		$1,500	$1,900

M-5 (Maestro) String Bass

1957-late-1960s. Five strings.

1960s		$1,700	$2,100

Ken Smith

See listing under "Smith."

Kent

1961-1969. Imported from Japan by Buegeleisen and Jacobson of New York, New York. Manufacturers unknown but many early instruments by Guyatone and Teisco.

Electric Solidbody Basses

1962-1969. Import models include 628 Newport, 634 Basin Street, 629, and 635.

1960s		$100	$200

Semi-Hollow Electric EB-2 Copy Bass

1960s. Offset soft cutaway EB-2 copy, single pickup, two control knobs.

1960s		$175	$275

Kingston

Ca. 1958-1967. Imported from Japan by Westheimer Importing Corp. of Chicago. Early examples by Guyatone and Teisco.

Electric Solidbody Basses

Various models.

1960s		$100	$150

Klein Acoustic Guitars

1972-present. Luthiers Steve Klein and Steven Kauffman build their production/custom, premium and presentation grade acoustic basses in Sonoma, California. They also build guitars.

Klein Electric Guitars

1988-present. Lorenzo German produces his professional grade, production/custom, basses in Linden, California. He also builds guitars.

Knutson Luthiery

1981-present. Professional grade, custom, electric upright basses built by luthier John Knutson in Forestville, California. He also builds guitars and mandolins.

Koll

1990-present. Professional and premium grade, custom/production, solidbody and chambered basses built by luthier Saul Koll, originally in Long Beach, California, and since '93, in Portland, Oregon. He also builds guitars.

MODEL YEAR	FEATURES	EXC. COND. LOW	HIGH

Kramer

1976-1990, 1997-present. Budget grade, production, imported solidbody basses. They also offer guitars. Kramer's first guitars and basses featured aluminum necks with wooden inserts on back. Around '80 they started to switch to more economical wood necks and aluminum necks were last produced in '85. Gibson acquired the brandname in '97.

250-B Special Bass

1977-1979. Offset double cut, aluminum neck, Ebonol fingerboard, zero fret, one single-coil, natural.

1977-1979		$350	$550

450-B Bass

Late-'70s-early-'80s. Aluminum neck, burled walnut body, 2 humbucking pickups, natural walnut.

1970s		$350	$550

650-B Artist Bass

1977-1980. Double cut, bird's-eye maple/burled walnut, aluminum neck, zero fret, mother-of-pearl crowns, 2 humbuckers.

1977-1980		$350	$550

BKL Bass

Eight strings, 2 DiMarzio pickups, 2 octaves.

1980		$500	$600

DMZ 4000 Bass

1978-1982. Bolt-on aluminum neck, slot headstock, double cut solidbody, active EQ and dual-coil humbucking pickup, dot inlay.

1978-1981		$500	$600
1982	Bill Wyman-type	$500	$900

DMZ 4001 Bass

1979-1980. Aluminum neck, slot headstock, double cut solidbody, 1 dual-coil humbucker pickup, dot inlay.

1979-1980		$400	$500

DMZ 5000 Bass

1979-1980. Double cut solidbody, aluminum neck, slotted headstock, 2 pickups, crown inlays.

1979-1980		$400	$550

DMZ 6000B Bass

1979-1980. Double cut, aluminum neck, slotted headstock, 2 pickups, crown inlays.

1979-1980		$400	$550

Duke Custom/Standard Bass

1981-1983. Headless, aluminum neck, 1 humbucker.

1981-1983		$400	$450

Duke Special Bass

1982-1985. Headless, aluminum neck, 2 pickups.

1982-1985		$400	$450

Duke Special Fretless Bass

1982-1985. Fretless version of Special.

1982-1985		$400	$550

Ferrington KFB-1/KFB-2 Acoustic Bass

1987-1990. Acoustic/electric, bridge-mounted active pickup, tone and volume control, various colors. KFB-1 has binding and diamond dot inlays; the KFB-2 no binding and dot inlays. Danny Ferrington continued to offer the KFB-1 after Kramer closed in '90.

1987-1990		$350	$500

MODEL		EXC. COND.	
YEAR	FEATURES	LOW	HIGH

Ferrington Signature Acoustic Bass
1990. Acoustic/electric, bridge-mounted active pickup, 4-band EQ, glued neck, various colors.

1990		$450	$600

Focus 7000 Bass
1986-1987. Offset double cut solidbody, P and double Jazz pickups, Japanese-made.

1986-1987		$250	$350

Focus K-77 Bass
1984-1986. Offset double cut solidbody, 1 pickup, Japanese-made.

1984-1986		$225	$350

Focus K-88 Bass
1984-1986. Two pickup Focus.

1984-1986		$225	$350

Forum I Bass
1988-1990. U.S.-made double cut, through-neck, arched top, active EMG or passive Seymour Duncan pickups.

1988-1990		$275	$350

Gene Simmons Axe Bass
1980-1981. Axe-shaped bass, slot headstock.

1980-1981		$2,300	$2,800

Pacer Bass
1982-1984. Offset double cut solidbody.

1982-1984		$400	$500

Ripley Five-String Bass
1984-1987. Offset double cut, 5 strings, stereo, pan pots for each string, front and back pickups for each string, active circuitry.

1984-1987		$450	$550

Stagemaster Custom Bass
1981-1985, 1987-1990. First version had an aluminum neck (wood optional). Later version was neck-through-body, bound neck, either active or passive pickups.

1987-1990		$350	$525

Striker 700 Bass
1985-1989. Offset double cut, Korean-import, 1 pickup until '87, 2 after. Striker name was again used on a bass in '99.

1985-1987	One pickup	$200	$275
1988-1989	Two pickups	$200	$300

XL 8 Bass
1980-1981. Odd shaped double cut solidbody 8-string, aluminum neck, 2 pickups, tuners mounted on both headstock and body.

1980-1981		$700	$800

XL 24 Bass
1980-1981. Odd shaped double cut solidbody 4-string, aluminum neck, 2 pickups.

1980-1981		$350	$450

ZX-70 Aerostar Series (import)
1986-1989. Offset double cut solidbody, 1 pickup.

1986-1989		$200	$300

KSD
2003-present. Intermediate grade, production, imported bass line designed by Ken Smith (see Smith listing) and distributed by Brooklyn Gear.

Kubicki
1973-present. Professional and premium grade, production/custom, solidbody basses built by luthier Phil Kubicki in Santa Barbara, California. Kubicki began building acoustic guitars when he was 15. In '64 at age 19, he went to work with Roger Rossmeisl at Fender Musical Instrument's research and development department for acoustic guitars. Nine years later he moved to Santa Barbara, California, and established Philip Kubicki Technology, which is best known for its line of Factor basses and also builds acoustic guitars, custom electric guitars, bodies and necks, and mini-guitars and does custom work, repairs and restorations.

Ex Factor 4 Bass
1985-present. Solidbody, maple body, bolt-on maple neck, 2 pickups, active electronics.

1980s		$800	$1,100

Factor 4 Bass
1985-present. Solidbody, maple body, bolt-on maple neck, fretless available, 4 strings, 2 pickups, active electronics.

1980s		$800	$1,100

Factor 5-String Bass
1985-ca.1990. Solidbody, bolt-on maple neck, fretless available, 5 strings, 2 pickups, active electronics.

1980s		$800	$1,100

Kustom
1968-present. Founded by Bud Ross in Chanute, Kansas, and best known for the tuck-and-roll amps, Kustom also offered guitars and basses from '68 to '69.

Electric Hollowbody Basses
1968-1969. Various colors.

1968-1969		$650	$850

La Baye
1967. Short-lived brand out of Green Bay, Wisconsin and built by the Holman-Woodell factory in Neodesha, Kansas.

Model 2x4 II Bass
1967. Very low production, dual pickups, long-scale, small rectangle solidbody, sometimes referred to as the Bass II.

1967		$1,100	$1,400

Model 2x4: Mini-Bass
1967. Short-scale, one pickup, small rectangle solidbody.

1967		$800	$900

LA Guitar Factory
1997-present. Luthier Ari Lehtela builds his professional grade, production, solidbody and tone chambered basses in Charlotte, North Carolina. He also builds guitars.

Lado
1973-present. Founded by Joe Kovacic, Lado builds professional and premium grade, produc-

1980 Kramer XL-8

1990 Kubicki Ex Factor 4

Lakland Jerry Scheff signature

Martin B-40

MODEL YEAR	FEATURES	EXC. COND. LOW	HIGH

tion/custom, solidbody basses in Lindsay, Ontario. Some model lines are branded "J. K. Lado." They also build guitars.

Lafayette
Ca. 1963-1967. Sold through Lafayette Electronics catalogs.

Lakland
1994-present. Professional and premium grade, production/custom, solid and hollowbody basses from luthier Dan Lakin in Chicago, Illinois. Lakland basses are built in the U.S. and overseas (Skyline series).

4 - 63 Classic Bass
1994-2002. Offset double cut alder body, large bass horn, bolt-on neck, various colors.

1990s		$1,700	$1,900

4 - 63 Deluxe Bass
1994-2002. Offset double cut figured maple top on ash body, large bass horn, bolt-on neck, various colors.

1990s		$1,900	$2,100

4 - 63 Standard Bass
1994-2002. Offset double cut swamp ash body, large bass horn, bolt-on neck, various colors.

1990s		$1,700	$1,900

4 - 94 Classic Bass
1994-present. Offset double cut alder body, large bass horn, bolt-on neck, various colors.

1990s		$1,700	$1,900

4 - 94 Deluxe Bass
1994-present. Offset double cut, figured maple top on ash body with large bass horn, bolt-on neck, various colors.

1990s		$1,900	$2,100

4 - 94 Standard Bass
1994-present. Offset double cut swamp ash body with large bass horn, bolt-on neck, various colors.

1990s		$1,600	$1,800

Larrivee
1968-present. Founded by Jean Larrivee in Toronto and currently located in Vancouver, British Columbia, Larrivee has offered several acoustic basses over the years.

RB-2 Carved Top Bass
Carved Top Series. Sunburst or translucent finishes.

1987		$900	$1,000

RB-2-5 CM Carved Top Bass
Carved Top Series. Sunburst or translucent finishes.

1987		$700	$900

RB-2-6 CM Carved Top Bass
Carved Top Series. Sunburst or translucent finishes.

1987		$700	$900

MODEL YEAR	FEATURES	EXC. COND. LOW	HIGH

Leach
1980-present. Luthier Harvey Leach builds his premium grade, custom, acoustic basses in Cedar Ridge, California. He also builds guitars.

LTD
1995-present. Intermediate grade, production, Korean-made solidbody basses offered by ESP. They also offer guitars.

Lyle
Ca. 1969-1980. Japanese instruments imported by distributor L.D. Heater in Portland, Oregon.

Electric Solidbody Basses
Various models.

1970s		$100	$200

Lyric
1996-present. Luthier John Southern builds his professional and premium grade, custom, basses in Tulsa, Oklahoma. He also builds guitars.

Mako
1985-1989. Line of solidbody basses from Kaman (Ovation, Hamer). They also offered guitars and amps.

Marco Polo
1960- ca.1964. One of the first inexpensive Japanese brands to be imported into the U.S.

Solidbody Basses
Various models.

1960s		$100	$200

Marling
Ca. 1975. Budget line instruments marketed by EKO of Recanati, Italy; probably made by them, although possibly imported.

Electric Solidbody Basses
Models include the E.495 (copy of LP), E.485 (copy of Tele), and the E.465 (Manta-style).

1970s		$100	$150

Martin
1833-present. Professional grade, production, acoustic basses made in the U.S. In 1978, Martin re-entered the electric market and introduced their solidbody EB-18 and EB-28 Basses. In the '80s they offered Stinger brand electric basses. By the late '80s, they started offering acoustic basses.

B-40 Acoustic Bass
1989-1996. Jumbo-size, spruce top and Indian rosewood back and sides, mahogany neck, ebony fingerboard, built-in pickup and volume and tone controls. The B-40B had a pickup.

1989-1996	B-40B	$1,400	$1,700
1989-1996	Without pickup	$1,200	$1,500

BASSES

MODEL		EXC. COND.	
YEAR	FEATURES	LOW	HIGH

B-65 Acoustic Bass
1989-1993. Jumbo-size, spruce top, maple back and sides, mahogany neck, ebony fingerboard with 23 frets, built-in pickup and volume and tone controls, Natural.

1989-1993		$1,200	$1,500

EB-18 Bass
1979-1982. Electric solidbody, neck-through, one pickup, Natural.

1979-1982		$450	$750

EB-28 Bass
1980-1982. Electric solidbody.

1980-1982		$550	$850

SBL-10 Bass
Stinger brand solidbody, maple neck, 1 split and 1 bar pickup.

1980s		$100	$225

Marvel
1950s-mid-1960s. Brand name used for budget instruments marketed by Peter Sorkin Company in New York, New York.

Electric Solidbody Basses
Various models.

1950s	Various models	$100	$200

Messenger
1967-1968. Built by Musicraft, Inc., Messengers featured a neck-thru metal alloy neck.

Bass
1967-1968. Metal alloy neck. Messenger mainly made guitars - they offered a bass, but it is unlikely many were built.

1967		$1,500	$2,000

Messenger Upright
Made by Knutson Luthiery, see that listing.

Michael Kelly
1999-present. Intermediate grade, production, acoustic/electric basses imported by Mailbox Music of Clearwater, Florida. They also offer mandolins and guitars.

Microfrets
1967-1975, 2004-present. Manufactured in Frederick, Maryland, Microfrets sported innovative designs and features. Brand revived in '04.

Husky Bass
1971-1974/75. Double cut, 2 pickups, two-on-a-side tuners.

1970-1975		$450	$550

Signature Bass
1969-1975. Double cut, 2 pickups, two-on-a-side tuners.

1969-1975		$450	$650

Stage II Bass
1969-1975. Double cutaway, two pickups, two-on-a-side tuners.

1969-1975		$550	$650

Mike Lull Custom Guitars
1995-present. Professional and premium grade, production/custom, basses built by luthier Mike Lull in Bellevue, Washington. He also builds guitars.

MJ Guitar Engineering
1993-present. Luthier Mark Johnson builds his professional grade, production/custom, chambered basses in Rohnert Park, California. He also builds guitars.

Modulus
1978-present. Founded by aerospace engineer Geoff Gould, Modulus currently offers professional and premium grade, production/custom, solidbody basses built in California. They also build guitars.

Bassstar SP-24 Active Bass
1981-ca. 1990. EMG Jazz Bass pickups, active bass and treble circuits.

1980s		$550	$650

Quantum-4/SP/SPi Bass
1986-present. 4-string, 35" scale, bolt-on graphite neck, 2 pickups. The original Quantum 4 (1982) was neck-thru.

1980s		$550	$650

Quantum-5/SPX/SPi Bass
1987-present. 5-string, 35" scale, bolt-on graphite neck, 2 pickups. The original Quantum 5 (1982) was neck-thru.

1980s		$550	$650

Quantum-5/TBX Bass
1982-1996. Neck-through-body version of the 5-string Quantum, 2 pickups.

1980s		$550	$650

Quantum-6/SPi Bass
1989-present. 6-string, 35" scale, bolt-on graphite neck, 2 pickups. The original Quantum 6 (1982) was neck-thru.

1989		$550	$650

Mollerup Basses
1984-present. Luthier Laurence Mollerup builds his professional grade, custom/production, electric basses and electric double basses in Vancouver, British Columbia. He has also built guitars.

Moon
1979-present. Professional grade, production/custom, basses made in Japan. They also build guitars.

J-J 130 Bass
1980s-1990s. Solidbody of walnut, alder, Canadian white ash, padauk, or other exotic wood, optional active circuitry.

1980s		$550	$650

J-J 165 Bass
1980s-1990s. Solidbody of walnut, alder, Canadian white ash, padauk, or other exotic wood, optional active circuitry.

1980s		$550	$650

Martin EB-18

Mollerup Orca 6-string

BASSES

Moonstone Exploder

1979 Music Man Sabre Bass

MODEL YEAR	FEATURES	EXC. COND. LOW	HIGH

J-J 180 Bass
1980s-1990s. Solidbody of walnut, alder, Canadian white ash, padauk, or other exotic wood, optional active circuitry.

| 1980s | | $550 | $650 |

Moonstone
1972-present. Luthier Steve Helgeson builds his premium grade, production/custom, acoustic and electric basses in Eureka, California. He also builds guitars.

Exploder Bass
1980-1983. Figured wood body, Explorer-style neck-through-body.

| 1980-1983 | | $1,300 | $1,700 |

Morales
Ca.1967-1968. Made in Japan by Zen-On and not heavily imported into the U.S.

Electric Solidbody Basses
Various models.

| 1967-1968 | | $100 | $250 |

Morgan Monroe
1999-present. Intermediate grade, production, acoustic/electric basses made in Korea and distributed by SHS International of Indianapolis, Indiana. They also offer mandolins, guitars, banjos, and fiddles.

Mosrite
Semie Moseley's Mosrite offered various bass models throughout the many versions of the Mosrite company.

Brut Bass
Late-1960s. Assymetrical body with small cutaway on upper treble bout.

| 1960s | | $950 | $1,000 |

Celebrity Bass
1965-1969. ES-335-style semi-thick double cut body with F-holes, 2 pickups.

1965-1966	Custom color	$750	$1,450
1965-1967	Sunburst	$550	$850
1968	Red	$550	$850
1969	Sunburst or red	$450	$800

Joe Maphis Bass
1966-1969. Ventures-style body, hollow without F-holes, 2 pickups.

| 1966-1969 | Natural | $950 | $1,350 |

V-II Bass
1973-1974. Ventures-style, 2 humbuckers, sunburst.

| 1973-1974 | | $650 | $950 |

Ventures Bass
Two pickups.

1965	Blue or red	$1,450	$2,000
1965	Sunburst	$1,550	$1,900
1966	Sunburst	$1,350	$1,900
1967-1968	Sunburst, red sparkle, or blue metallic	$1,250	$1,700

MODEL YEAR	FEATURES	EXC. COND. LOW	HIGH
1969	Sunburst	$1,150	$1,600
1970	Sunburst	$750	$1,000
1971-1972	Sunburst	$750	$950

MTD
1994-present. Intermediate, professional, and premium grade, production/custom, electric basses built by luthier Michael Tobias (who founded Tobias Basses in '77) in Kingston, New York.

Music Man
1972-present. Intermediate and professional grade, production, electric basses. They also build guitars.

Cutlass I Bass
1982-1987. Ash body, graphite neck, string-through-body.

| 1982-1987 | | $1,100 | $1,500 |

Cutlass II Bass
1982-1987.

| 1982-1987 | | $1,400 | $1,600 |

Sabre Bass
1978-ca.1991. Double cutaway solidbody bass, three-and-one tuning keys, two humbucking pickups, onboard preamp, Natural.

| 1978-1979 | | $800 | $1,000 |
| 1980-1991 | | $600 | $900 |

Stingray Bass
1976-present. Offset double cutaway solidbody, one pickup, three-and-one tuners, string-through until '80, various colors.

1976-1979		$1,600	$2,200
1980-1989		$1,100	$1,800
1990-1999		$900	$1,000

Stingray 5-String Bass
1987-present. Active electronics, bird's-eye maple bolt-on neck, one humbucking pickup, three-band EQ.

| 1992 | | $800 | $1,000 |

Musicvox
1996-present. Intermediate grade, production, Korean-made retro-vibe guitars and basses from Matt Eichen of Cherry Hill, New Jersey.

Nady
Wireless sound company Nady Systems offered guitars and basses with built-in wireless systems for 1985-'87. The neck-thru bass was made by Fernandes in Japan and was only available for about a year.

National
Ca. 1927-present. National offered electric basses in the '60s when Valco owned the brandname.

N-850 Bass
1967-1968. Semi-hollow double cut (similar to EB-2-style), art deco F-holes, 2 pickups, block markers, bout control knobs.

| 1967 | Sunburst | $800 | $900 |

MODEL YEAR	FEATURES	EXC. COND. LOW	HIGH

Val-Pro 85 Bass
1961-1962. Res-O-Glas body shaped like the U.S. map, 2 pickups, snow white. Renamed National 85 in '63.

1961-1962		$900	$1,200

National Reso-Phonic
1988-present. Professional grade, production/custom, acoustic and acoustic/electric resonator basses built in San Luis Obispo, California. They also build guitars and ukes.

New York Bass Works
Luthier David Segal builds his professional and premium grade, production/custom, electric basses in New York.

Noble
Ca. 1950-ca. 1969. Distributed by Don Noble and Company of Chicago. Made by other companies.

Electric Solidbody Basses
Various models.

1950s		$150	$300

Norma
Ca.1965-1970. Imported from Japan by Chicago's Strum and Drum.

Electric Solidbody Basses
Various models.

1960s		$100	$225

Northworthy
1987-present. Professional and premium grade, production/custom, acoustic and electric basses built by luthier Alan Marshall in Ashbourne, Derbyshire, England. He also builds guitars and mandolins.

Novax
1989-present. Luthier Ralph Novak builds his fanned-fret professional grade, production/custom, solidbody basses in San Leandro, California. He also builds guitars.

O'Hagan
1979-1983. Designed by Jerol O'Hagan in St. Louis Park, Minnesota.

Electric Solidbody Basses
1979-1983. Models include the Shark Bass, NightWatch Bass, NightWatch Regular Bass, and the Twenty Two Bass.

1980s		$350	$450

Old Kraftsman
1930s-1960s. Brandname used by the Spiegel Company. Instruments made by other American manufacturers.

Electric Solidbody Basses
Various models.

1950s		$150	$300

Ovation
1966-present. Intermediate and professional grade, production, acoustic/electric basses. Ovation offered electric solidbody basses early on and added acoustic basses in the '90s.

Celebrity Bass
1990-1993. Deep bowl back, cutaway, acoustic/electric.

1990-1993		$350	$450

Magnum I Bass
1974-1980. Odd-shaped mahogany solidbody, 2 pickups, mono/stereo, mute, sunburst, red or natural.

1974-1980		$600	$750

Magnum II Bass
1974-1980. Magnum I with battery-powered preamp and three-band eq.

1974-1980		$600	$750

Typhoon II Bass
1968-1971. Semi-hollowbody, 2 pickups, red or sunburst.

1968-1971		$600	$750

PANaramic
1960s. Imported from Italy by U.S. distributor.

Electric Bass
1960s. Double cut solidbody, 2 pickups, dot markers.

1960s		$350	$450

Parker
1992-present. Premium grade, production/custom, solidbody electric basses. They also build guitars.

Paul Reed Smith
1985-present. PRS added basses in '86, but by '92 had dropped the models. In 2000 PRS started again offering professional and premium grade, production, solidbody electric basses. Bird inlays can add $100 or more to the values of PRS basses listed here.

Bass-4
1986-1992. Set neck, 3 single-coil pickups, hum-cancelling coil, active circuitry, 22-fret Brazilian rosewood board.

1986-1987		$1,500	$1,800
1988-1992		$1,400	$1,700

Bass-5
1986-1992. 5-string, set-neck, rosewood 'board, 3 single-coil pickups, active electronics. Options include custom colors, bird inlays, fretless 'board.

1986-1987		$1,500	$1,800
1988-1992		$1,400	$1,700

CE Bass 4
1990-1991. Solidbody, maple bolt-on neck, alder body, rosewood 'board, 4-string.

1990-1991		$900	$1,100

CE Bass 5
1990-1991. 5-string solidbody, maple bolt-on neck, alder body, rosewood 'board.

1990-1991		$1,000	$1,300

'77 Ovation Magnum II

Parker Fly Mojo bass

PRS Curly Bass 4

Peavey Rudy Sarzo bass

MODEL YEAR	FEATURES	EXC. COND. LOW	HIGH

Curly Bass-4
1986-1992. Double-cut solidbody, curly maple top, set maple neck, Brazilian rosewood board (ebony on fretless), 3 single-coil and 1 hum-cancelling pickups, various grades of maple tops, moon inlays.

1986-1987		$1,800	$2,200
1988-1992		$1,700	$2,100

Curly Bass-5
1986-1992. 5-string version of Curly Bass-4.

1986-1987		$2,000	$2,400
1988-1992		$1,900	$2,300

Peavey
1965-present. Intermediate and professional grade, production/custom, electric basses. They also build guitars and amps. Hartley Peavey's first products were guitar amps and he added guitars and basses to the mix in '78.

Axcelerator Bass
1994-1998. J-bass styling with longer thinner horns, 2 humbuckers, stacked control knobs, bolt-on neck, dot markers.

1994-1998		$200	$400

Dyna-Bass
1987-1993. Double cut solidbody, active electronics, 3-band EQ, rosewood board.

1987-1993		$300	$400

Dyna-Bass Limited
1987-1990. Neck-through-body, ebony board, flamed maple neck/body construction, purple heart strips, mother-of-pearl inlays.

1987-1990		$375	$475

Forum Bass
1994-1995. Double cut solidbody, rosewood board, dot inlays, 2 humbuckers.

1994-1995		$250	$325

Forum Plus Bass
1994. Forum Bass with added active electronics.

1994		$275	$350

Foundation Bass
1984-2002. Double cut solidbody, 2 pickups, maple neck.

1980s		$275	$400

Foundation S Active Bass
1987-1991. Similar to Foundation S Bass with added active circuitry, provides low-impedance output, 2 pickups.

1987-1991		$275	$400

Foundation S Bass
1986-1991. Two split-coil pickups, maple body, rosewood board, black hardware, black painted headstock.

1986-1991		$200	$300

Fury Bass
1986-1999. Double cut solidbody, rosewood board, 1 split-coil humbucker.

1986-1999		$150	$250

MODEL YEAR	FEATURES	EXC. COND. LOW	HIGH

Fury Custom Bass
1986-1993. Fury Bass with black hardware and narrow neck.

1986-1993		$250	$350

Patriot Bass
1984-1988. General J-bass styling with larger thinner horns, 1 single-coil, maple neck.

1984-1988		$150	$200

Patriot Custom Bass
1986-1988. Patriot with rosewood neck, matching headstock.

1986-1988		$250	$300

RJ-4 Bass
1989-1991. Randy Jackson Signature model, neck-through-body, 2 split-coil active pickups, ebony board, mother-of-pearl position markers.

1989-1991		$400	$500

Rudy Sarzo Signature Bass
1988-1993. Double cut solidbody, active EQ, ebony fingerboard, 2 pickups.

1988-1993		$400	$600

T-20FL Bass
1980s. Fretless solidbody, 1 pickup.

1982		$250	$350

T-40 Bass
1978-ca.1988. Double cut solidbody, 2 pickups.

1978-1988		$250	$350

T-40FL Bass
1980s. Fretless T-40.

1980s		$250	$350

T-45 Bass
1982-1986. T-40 with one humbucking pickup, and a mid-frequency rolloff knob.

1980s		$250	$350

TL-Five Bass
1988-1998. 5-string, neck-through-body, gold hardware, active humbuckers, EQ, flamed maple neck and body.

1988-1998		$500	$700

TL-Six Bass
1989-1998. 6-string version of TL-5.

1989-1998		$750	$800

Pedulla
1975-present. Professional and premium grade, production/custom, electric basses made in Rockland, Massachusetts. Founded by Michael Pedulla, Pedulla offers various upscale options which affect valuation so each instrument should be evaluated on a case-by-case basis. Unless specifically noted, the following listings have standard to mid-level features. High-end options are specifically noted; if not, these options will have a relatively higher value than those shown here.

Buzz-4/Buzz-5 Bass
1984-present. Double cut neck-through solidbody, fretless, long-scale, maple neck and body wings, 2 pickups, preamp, some with other active electronics, various colors. 4-string and 5-string versions.

1984-1999		$1,200	$1,400

MODEL YEAR	FEATURES	EXC. COND. LOW	HIGH

Interceptor Bass
1980s. Double cutaway, maple/walnut laminated neck-through.

1980s		$1,000	$1,300

MVP Bass
1984-present. Fretted version of Buzz Bass.

1980s	Flame top	$1,100	$1,500
1980s	Standard top	$1,000	$1,300

MVP-5 Bass
1984-present. Five-string version of MVP Bass.

1980s		$1,000	$1,300

MVP-6 Bass
1984-present. Six-string version of MVP Bass.

1980s		$1,100	$1,400

Orsini Wurlitzer 4-String Bass
Mid-1970s. Body style similar to late-'50s Gibson double cut slab body SG Special, neck-through, 2 pickups. Sold by Boston's Wurlitzer music store chain.

1970s	Natural	$900	$1,500

Quilt Ltd. Bass
Neck-through-body with curly maple centerstrip, quilted maple body wings, 2 Bartolini pickups, available in fretted or fretless 4- and 5-string models.

1987		$1,100	$1,500

Rapture 4-String/5-String Series Bass
1995-present. Solidbody with extra long thin bass horn and extra short treble horn, various colors.

1995-1999		$800	$1,300

Series II Bass
Bolt-on neck, rosewood board, mother-of-pearl dot inlays, Bartolini pickups.

1987		$600	$900

Thunderbass 4-String/5-String Series Bass
1993-present. Solidbody with extra long thin bass horn and extra short treble horn.

1993-1999	AAA top	$2,000	$2,200
1993-1999	Standard features	$1,500	$1,800

Pensa (Pensa-Suhr)

1982-present. Premium grade, production/custom, solidbody basses built in the U.S. They also build guitars.

Phantom Guitar Works

1992-present. Intermediate grade, production/custom, solid and hollowbody basses assembled in Clatskanie, Oregon. They also build guitars and the MandoGuitar.

Phantom Bass
1995-present. Classic 5-sided Phantom body shape, 2 humbuckers.

1995-2000		$375	$425

Premier

Ca.1938-ca.1975, 1990s-present. Budget and intermediate grade, production, import basses. They also offer guitars. Originally American-made instruments, but by the '60s imported parts were being used. Current models are imports.

Bantam Bass
1950-1970. Small body, single cut short-scale archtop electric, torch headstock inlay, sunburst.

1950-1970		$400	$600

Electric Solidbody Basses
Various models.

1960s		$175	$325

Rarebird Guitars

1978-present. Luthier Bruce Clay builds his professional grade, production/custom, electric solidbody and hollowbody basses in Arvada, Colorado. He also builds guitars.

Rat Fink

2002-present. Intermediate grade, production, basses from Lace Music Products, the makers of the Lace Sensor pickup, featuring the artwork of Ed "Big Daddy" Roth. They also offer guitars and amps.

Regal

Ca. 1884-1966, 1987-present. Intermediate grade, production, acoustic wood body resonator basses from Saga. They also build guitars.

Renaissance

1978-1980. Plexiglass solidbody electric guitars and basses made in Malvern, Pennsylvania.

Plexiglas Bass
1978-1980. Plexiglas bodies and active electronics, models include the DPB bass (double cut, 1 pickup, '78-'79), SPB (single cut, 2 pickups, '78-'79), T-100B ("Bich-style," 1 pickup, '80), S-100B (double cut, 1 pickup, '80), and the S-200B (double cut, 2 pickups, '80).

1978-1980		$400	$650

Renaissance Guitars

1994-present. Professional grade, custom, acoustic and solidbody basses built by luthier Rick Turner in Santa Cruz, California. He also builds guitars.

RB-4
1997-present. "Ampli-Coustic" bass, cedar top, walnut back and sides, maple neck, rosewood 'board, piezo bridge pickup, preamp, also available as fretless.

1997		$1,100	$1,300

Reverend

1996-present. Intermediate grade, production, basses built in Warren, Michigan, by luthier Joe Naylor, who also founded Naylor Amps. They also build guitars, amps and effects.

Rumblefish
1998-present. Offset double cut, J-style neck and bridge pickups, 2 volumes, 1 master tone.

1998-2000		$500	$600

Phantom BW

Reverend Rumblefish PJ

BASSES

Rickenbacker 4001 V63

1979 Rickenbacker 4005

MODEL YEAR	FEATURES	EXC. COND. LOW	HIGH

Rick Turner

1979-1981, 1990-present. Rick Turner has a long career as a luthier, electronics designer and innovator. He also makes the Renaissance line of guitars in his shop in Santa Cruz, California.

Electric Bass
Mahogany.

1979-1981		$750	$850

Rickenbacker

1931-present. Professional grade, production/custom, electric basses. They also build guitars. Rickenbacker introduced their first electric bass in '57 and has always been a strong player in the bass market.

Model 2030 Hamburg Bass
1984-1997. Double rounded cutaway, 2 pickups, active electronics.

1984-1989		$550	$750
1990-1997		$500	$700

Model 3000 Bass
1975-1984. Double rounded cutaway, 30" scale, 1 pickup, brown sunburst.

1975-1984		$550	$850

Model 3001 Bass
1975-1984. Same as Model 3000 but with longer 33-1/2" scale, wine red.

1975-1984		$650	$800

Model 4000 Bass
1957-1985. Cresting wave body and headstock, 1 horseshoe pickup (changed to regular pickup in '64), neck-through-body.

1957-1959	Autumnglo	$4,000	$5,500
1960	Fireglo	$4,000	$5,000
1961	Fireglo, Mapleglo	$4,000	$5,000
1962-1964	Fireglo	$4,000	$5,000
1965-1966	Fireglo	$3,200	$4,000
1968	Black	$3,200	$4,000
1970-1979	Various colors	$1,100	$1,500
1980-1985	Various colors	$1,000	$1,300

Model 4000L (Light Show) Bass
1970-1975. Model 4000 with translucent top with lights in body that lit up when played, needed external transformer.

1970-1975		$3,500	$7,500

Model 4001 Bass
1961-1965, 1968-1986. Fancy version of 4000, 1 horseshoe magnet pickup (changed to regular pickup in '64) and 1 bar magnet pickup, triangle inlays, bound neck.

1961-1965	Fireglo	$4,000	$5,500
1963-1965	Mapleglo	$4,000	$5,900
1968	Mapleglo	$2,500	$3,800
1969	Mapleglo	$2,500	$3,700
1970	Mapleglo	$2,000	$3,000
1971	All colors	$2,000	$2,900
1972	All colors	$1,800	$2,000
1973	All colors	$1,800	$1,900
1974	All colors	$1,400	$1,800
1975	All colors	$1,300	$1,600
1976-1977	All colors	$1,200	$1,500
1978-1979	All colors	$1,100	$1,500
1980-1983	All colors	$1,000	$1,400
1984-1986	All colors	$900	$1,200

Model 4001 CS Bass
1991-1997. Chris Squire signature model.

1991-1997		$1,900	$2,000

Model 4001 V63 Bass
1984-2000. Vintage '63 reissue of Model 4001, horseshoe-magnet pickup.

1985-2000	Mapleglo	$1,400	$1,600

Model 4001-S Bass
1964-1985. Same as Model 4000, but with 2 pickups, export model.

1980s	Special order	$1,000	$1,500

Model 4002 Bass
1967-1985. Cresting wave body and headstock, 2 humbuckers, black 'guard, checkerboard binding.

1980-1985		$2,500	$2,700

Model 4003 Bass
1979-1998. Similar to Model 4001, split pickguard, deluxe features.

1979-1989		$1,000	$1,300
1990-1998		$900	$1,200

Model 4003 Blackstar Bass
1988-1997. Black finish version of Tuxedo Bass, black knobs, chrome and black hardware.

1988-1997		$1,000	$1,200

Model 4003 Tuxedo Bass
1980-1997. Non-deluxe feature version of Model 4003, white body with black 'guard and hardware.

1980-1997		$800	$1,000

Model 4003-S/5 Bass
1987-1997. 5 string Model 4003-S, 2 pickups.

1987-1997	Fireglo	$1,100	$1,400

Model 4003-S/8 Bass
1987-1997. 8 string 4003-S.

1987-1997		$1,200	$1,500

Model 4004C Cheyenne/Cheyenne II
1993-2000. Cresting wave, maple neck-thru body with walnut body and head wings, gold hardware, dot inlay. Maple top added in '99. Replaced by 4004Cii Cheyenne II.

1993-1998		$950	$1,000
1999	Maple top	$975	$1,000

Model 4004Cii Cheyenne II
2000-present. Continuation of maple top Cheyenne Bass.

2000s		$975	$1,000

Model 4005 Bass
1965-1984. New style double cut hollowbody, 2 pickups, R tailpiece, cresting wave headstock.

1966	Fireglo	$4,000	$5,000
1967	Mapleglo	$4,200	$5,000
1968	Black	$3,500	$5,000
1970-1979	Various colors	$2,000	$3,000

Model 4005 WB Bass
1966-1983. Old style Model 4005 with white-bound body.

1966	Mapleglo	$4,500	$5,500
1967-1969	Various colors	$4,500	$5,200

MODEL YEAR	FEATURES	EXC. COND. LOW	HIGH
Model 4005-8 Bass			
Late-1960s. 8 string Model 4005.			
1960s	Fireglo	$4,500	$5,200
1960s	Mapleglo	$4,500	$5,500
Model 4008 Bass			
1975-1983. 8 strings, cresting wave body and head-stock.			
1975-1983		$1,100	$1,300
Model 4080 Doubleneck Bass			
1975-1992. Bolt-on 6- and 4-string necks.			
1975-1979	Mapleglo	$2,500	$3,500
1980-1992		$2,000	$3,000

Rob Allen

1997-present. Professional grade, production/custom, lightweight basses made by luthier Robert Allen in Santa Barbara, California.

Robin

1982-present. Founded by David Wintz and located in Houston, Texas, Robin built basses until 2000. Most basses were Japanese-made until '87; American production began in '88. They continue to build guitars and also make Metropolitan (since 1996) and Alamo (since 2000) brand guitars.

Freedom Bass

1984-1986. Offset double cut, active treble and bass EQ controls, 1 pickup.

1984-1986		$400	$500

Freedom Bass I Passive

1986-1989. Non-active version of Freedom Bass, 1 humbucker. Passive dropped from name in '87.

1986-1989		$450	$550

Medley Bass

1984-1989. Reverse headstock, deep cutaways, 2 pickups.

1984-1989		$400	$550

Ranger Bass

1984-1997. Vintage style body with P-style and J-style pickup configuration, dot markers, medium scale from '84 to '89 and long scale from '90 to '97.

1984-1997		$750	$850

Rock Bass

2002-present. Chinese-made, intermediate and professional grade, production, bolt-neck solidbody basses from the makers of Warwick basses.

Roland

Best known for keyboards, effects, and amps, Roland offered synthesizer-based guitars and basses from 1977 to '86.

Rono

1967-present. Luthier Ron Oates builds his professional and premium grade, production/custom, acoustic and solidbody basses in Boulder, Colorado. He also builds guitars and mandolins.

S.D. Curlee

1975-1982. S.D. Curlee instruments were made in Illinois; S.D. Curlee International instruments

were made in Japan.

Electric Solidbody Basses

1975-1981.

1970s		$250	$400

Sadowsky

1980-present. Professional and premium grade, production/custom, solidbody basses built by luthier Roger Sadowsky in Brooklyn, New York. He also builds guitars. In 1996, luthier Yoshi Kikuchi started building Sadowsky Tokyo instruments in Japan; those basses are now available in the U.S.

Samick

1958-2001, 2002-present. Budget, intermediate, and professional grade, production, imported acoustic and electric basses. They also offer guitars, mandolins, ukes and banjos.

Various Models

1965-1999		$100	$250

Schecter

1976-present. Intermediate and professional grade, production/custom, electric basses made in the U.S. and overseas. They also offer guitars. Schecter basses are built in the U.S. and their Diamond Series is made in Korea.

Bass

1980s		$300	$500

Shifflett

1990-present. Luthier Charles Shifflett builds his premium grade, custom, acoustic basses in High River, Alberta. He also guitars and banjos.

Silvertone

1941- ca.1970, present. Brandname used by Sears. Instruments were U.S.-made and imported.

Bass VI

One lipstick pickup.

1960s		$500	$600

Sinister

2003-present. Intermediate and professional grade, custom/production, solidbody basses built for Sinister Guitars by luthier Jon Kammerer.

Slammer

1990-present. Budget and intermediate grade, production, basses imported by Hamer. They also offer guitars.

Smith

1978-present. Professional and premium grade, production/custom, electric basses built by luthier Ken Smith in Perkasie, Pennsylvania. Earlier models had "Ken Smith" on headstock, recent models have a large 'S' logo. He also designs the imported KSD line of basses.

1977 S.D. Curlee

1960s Silvertone bass

BASSES

Spector Spectorcore 4

Steinberger XL-2

B.T. Custom VI Bass
1985-present. 6 strings, double cut, neck-through-body.

MODEL YEAR	FEATURES	EXC. COND. LOW	HIGH
1985-1999	Natural	$1,600	$1,700

Various Basses
American-made Smiths.

1978-2000		$1,700	$3,500

Specimen Products
1984-present. Luthier Ian Schneller builds his professional and premium grade, production/custom, aluminum and wood body basses in Chicago, Illinois. He also builds guitars, ukes, amps and speaker cabs.

Spector/Stuart Spector Design
1975-1990 (Spector), 1991-1998 (SSD), 1998-present (Spector SSD). Imtermediate, professional, and premium grade, production/custom, basses made in the U.S., the Czech Republic, Korea, and China. Stuart Spector's first bass was the NS and the company quickly grew to the point where Kramer acquired it in '85. After Kramer went out of business in '90, Spector started building basses with the SSD logo (Stuart Spector Design). In '98 he recovered the Spector trademark.

Bob 4 Bass
1996-1999. Offset deep double cut swamp ash or alder body, bolt-on neck, various colors, SSD logo on headstock.

1996-1999		$800	$900

Bob 5 Bass
1996-1999. 5 string version of Bob Bass.

1996-1999		$900	$1,000

NS-1 Bass
1977-1980. Offset double cut solidbody, neck-through, 1 pickup, gold hardware.

1977-1979		$1,000	$1,300
1980		$900	$1,100

NS-2 Bass
1979-present. 2 pickup version of NS.

1979-1999		$1,000	$1,200

St. Moritz
1960s. Japanese imports, generally shorter-scale, beginner basses.

Electric Solidbody Basses
Various models.

1960s		$100	$200

Stambaugh
1995-present. Luthier Chris Stambaugh builds his professional grade, custom/production, solidbody basses in Stratham, New Hampshire. He also builds guitars.

Standel
1952-1974, 1997-present. Amp builder Bob Crooks offered instruments under his Standel brand name three different times during the '60s. See Guitar section for production details. See Amp section for more company info.

Custom Solidbody 501 Bass
1967-1968. Solidbody, 1 pickup, various colors.

MODEL YEAR	FEATURES	EXC. COND. LOW	HIGH
1967-1968		$600	$800

Custom Deluxe Solidbody 401 Bass
1967-1968. Custom with higher appointments, various colors.

1967-1968		$800	$1,100

Custom Thinbody 502 Bass
1967-1968. Thin solidbody, 2 pickups, various colors.

1967-1968		$700	$900

Custom Deluxe Thinbody 402 Bass
1967-1968. Custom with higher appointments, various colors.

1967-1968		$900	$1,200

Steinberger
1979-present. Steinberger offers budget and intermediate grade, production, electric basses. They also offer guitars.

Q-4 Bass
1990-1991. Composite neck, Double Bass system, headless with traditional-style maple body, low-impedance pickups.

1990-1991		$650	$850

Q-5 Bass
1990-1991. 5-string version of Q Bass.

1990-1991		$750	$950

XL-2 Bass
1984-1993. Rectangular composite body, 4-string, headless, 2 pickups.

1984-1989		$1,000	$1,200
1990-1993		$900	$1,100

XL-2GR Bass
1985-1990. Headless, Roland GR synthesizer controller.

1985-1990		$950	$1,150

XM-2 Bass
1986-1992. Headless, double cut maple body, 4-string, 2 low-impedance pickups, optional fretted, lined fretless or unlined fretless.

1986-1992		$850	$1,050

Stewart Basses
2000-present. Luthier Fred Stewart builds his premium grade, custom/production, solidbody basses in Charlton, Maryland. He has also built guitars since '94.

Stinger
See Martin listing.

Supro
1935-1968. Supro was a budget brand for the National Dobro Company. Supro offered only two bass models in the '60s.

MODEL YEAR	FEATURES	EXC. COND. LOW	HIGH

Pocket Bass
1960-1968. Double cut, neck pickup and bridge mounted pickup, semi-hollow, short-scale, black.

1960-1968		$600	$800

Tacoma
1995-present. Professional grade, production, acoustic basses produced in Tacoma, Washington. They also build acoustic guitars and mandolins.

Takamine
1962-present. Intermediate, professional and premium grade, production, acoustic and acoustic/electric basses. They also make guitars. They offered solidbody electrics for '83-'84.

Taylor
1974-present. Professional and premium grade, production, acoustic basses built in El Cajon, California.

AB1 Bass
1996-2003. Acoustic/electric, Sitka spruce top, Imbuia walnut back and sides, designed for 'loose' woody sound.

1996-2003		$1,300	$1,400

AB2 Bass
1996-2003. Acoustic/electric, all Imbuia walnut body.

1996-2003		$1,300	$1,400

AB3 Bass
1998-2003. Acoustic/electric, Sitka spruce top, maple back and sides.

1998-2003		$1,400	$1,500

Teisco
1946-1974, 1994-present. The Japanese Teisco line started offering basses in '60.

EB-100 Bass
1968-1969. One pickup, white pickguard.

1968-1969	Blue	$100	$200

EP-200 B Bass
1968-1969. Semi-hollowbody.

1968-1969		$150	$250

Tele-Star
1965-ca.1972. Imported from Japan by Tele-Star Musical Instrument Corporation of New York. Primarily made by Kawai, many inspired by Burns designs, some in cool sparkle finishes.

Electric Solidbody Basses
Various models.

1960s		$100	$200

Timtone Custom Guitars
1993-present. Luthier Tim Diebert builds his premium grade, custom, solidbody and chambered-body basses in Grand Forks, British Columbia. He also builds guitars and lap steels.

Tobias
1977-present. Founded by Mike Tobias in Orlando, Florida. Moved to San Francisco for '80-'81, then to Costa Mesa, eventually ending up in Hollywood. In '90, he sold the company to Gibson which moved it to Burbank. In '92, the company was moved to Nashville. Mike left the company in '92 and started a new business in '94 called MTD where he continues to make electric and acoustic basses. In '99, production of Tobias basses was moved overseas. In late '03, Gibson started again offering U.S.-made Tobias instruments; they are made in Conway, Arkansas, in the former Baldwin grand piano facility. Currently Tobias offers imported and U.S.-made, intermediate and professional grade, production, acoustic and electric basses.

Basic B-4 Bass
1984-1999. 30", 32", or 34" scale, neck-through-body in alder, koa or walnut, 5-piece laminated neck.

1984-1989		$1,500	$2,500

Classic C-4 Bass
1978-1999. 1 or 2 pickups, active or passive electronics, two-octave rosewood board. Available in short-, medium-, and long-scale models.

1978-1989		$1,800	$3,000

Classic C-5 Bass
1985-1999. 30", 32" or 34" scale, alder, koa or walnut body, bookmatched top, ebony or phenolic board, hardwood neck.

1985-1989		$1,800	$3,000

Classic C-6 Bass
ca. 1986-1999. Flamed maple and padauk neck, alder body, padauk top, ebony board, active electronics, 32" or 34" scale.

1986-1989		$2,000	$3,200

Growler GR-5 Bass
1996-1999. 5-string, offset double cut, bolt neck, various colors.

1996-1999		$800	$900

Killer Bee KB-5 Bass
1991-1999. Offset double cut, swamp ash or lacewood body, various colors.

1991-1999		$1,400	$1,700

Model T Bass
1989-1991. Line of 4- and 5-string basses, 3-piece maple neck-through-body, maple body halves, active treble and bass controls. Fretless available.

1989-1991		$1,100	$1,300

Signature S-4 Bass
1978-1999. Available in 4-, 5-, and 6-string models, chrome-plated milled brass bridge.

1978-1989		$2,000	$2,300

Standard ST-4 Bass
1992-1995. Japanese-made, 5-piece maple neck-thru, swamp ash body wings.

1992-1995		$1,000	$1,200

Toby Deluxe TD-4 Bass
1994-1996. Offset double cut, bolt neck, various colors.

1994-1996	Various colors	$600	$700

1968 Teisco EB-200

Tobias Classic 4

Univox Hi Flyer

1968 Vox Constellation

Toby Deluxe TD-5 Bass
1994-1996. 5-string, offset double cut, bolt neck, various colors.

1994-1996	Various colors	$600	$700

Tokai
1947-present. Tokai started making guitars and basses around '70 and by the end of that decade they were being imported into the U.S. Today Tokai offers electrics, acoustics, and electric basses made in Japan and Korea.

Vintage Bass Copies
1970s-1980s. Tokai offered near copies of classic U.S. basses.

1970s	$400	$550

Tonemaster
1960s. Imported from Italy by U.S. distributor with typical '60s Italian sparkle plastic finish and push-button controls, bolt-on neck.

Electric Bass
Sparkle finish.

1960s	$500	$600

Travis Bean
1974-1979, 1999. The unique Travis Bean line included a couple of bass models. Travis Bean produced some new instruments in '99.

TB-2000 Bass
Aluminum neck with T-slotted headstock. Longer horned, double cutaway body, two pickups, four controls, dot markers, various colors.

1970s	$1,400	$1,600

True Tone
1960s. Western Auto retailed this line of basses, guitars and amps which were manufactured by Chicago builders makers like Kay. The brand was most likely gone by '68.

Electric Basses

1960s	$150	$300

Unique Guitars
2003-present. Professional and premium grade, production/custom, solidbody basses built by luthier Joey Rico in California. He also builds guitars.

Univox
1964-1978. Univox started out as an amp line and added guitars and basses around '69. Guitars were imported from Japan by the Merson Musical Supply Company, later Unicord, Westbury, New York. Generally mid-level copies of American designs.

'Lectra Bass (model 1970F)
1969-ca. 1973. Violin bass, walnut.

1970s	$250	$350

Bicentennial Carved P-Bass (Aria)
1976. Carved Eagle in body, matches Univox Bicentennial Carved Strat, brown stain, maple board.

1976	$600	$800

Hi Flyer Bass
1969-1977. Mosrite Ventures Bass copy, 2 pickups, rosewood board.

1969-1977	$350	$450

Precisely Bass
1971-ca. 1975. Copy of Fender P-Bass.

1971-1975	$200	$300

Stereo Bass
1976-1977. Rickenbacker 4001 Bass copy, model U1975B.

1976-1977	$350	$450

Vaccaro
1997-2002. They offered intermediate and professional grade, production/custom, aluminum-necked basses built in Asbury Park, New Jersey. They also built guitars.

Vantage
1977-present. Intermediate grade, production, electric basses imported from Korea (from Japan until '90). They also offer guitars.

Model 895B Bass (Alembic-style 4-string)
1970s-1980s. Double cut, high quality wood, neck-through-body.

1970s	$400	$450

Veillette
1991-present. Luthier Joe Veillette (of Veillette-Citron fame) builds his professional and premium grade, production/custom, electric basses in Woodstock, New York. He also builds guitars and mandolins.

Veillette-Citron
1975-1983. Founded by Joe Veillette and Harvey Citron who met at the NY College School of Architecture in the late '60s. Joe took a guitar building course from Michael Gurian and by the Summer of '76, he and Harvey started producing neck-thru solidbody guitars and basses. Veillette and Citron both are back building instruments.

Standard Bass
1975-1983. Maple body.

1975-1983	Maple	$1,100	$1,300

Ventura
1970s. Import classic bass copies distributed by C. Bruno (Kaman).

Vintage Bass Copies

1970s	$300	$400

Versoul, LTD
1989-present. Production/custom acoustic/electric and solidbody basses built by luthier Kari Nieminen in Helsinki, Finland. He also builds guitars and sitars.

Vox
1957-1972, 1982-present. The first Vox products were amplifiers brought to market in '58 by Tom Jennings and Dick Denny. By '61 they had added

MODEL YEAR	FEATURES	EXC. COND. LOW	HIGH

instruments to the line. Guitars and basses bearing the Vox name were offered from 1961-'69 (made in England, Italy), '82-'85 (Japan), '85-'88 (Korea), and for '98-2001 (U.S.). Special thanks to Jim Rhoads of Rhoads Music in Elizabethtown, PA, for help on production years of these models.

Apollo IV Bass
1967-1969. Single cut hollowbody, bolt-on maple neck, 1 pickup, on board fuzz, booster, sunburst.
1967-1969 $650 $750

Astro IV Bass
1967-1969. 2 pickups.
1967-1969 $750 $850

Clubman Bass
1961-1966. Double cut 2 pickup solidbody.
1961-1966 $300 $400

Constellation IV Bass
1967-1968. Teardrop-shaped body, 2 pickups, 1 F-hole, 1 set of controls, treble, bass and distortion boosters.
1967-1968 $600 $800

Cougar Bass
1963-1967. Double-cut 335-style body, 2 F-holes, 2 pickups, 2 sets of controls, sunburst.
1963-1967 $600 $700

Delta IV Bass
1967-1968. 5-sided body, 2 pickups, 1 volume and 2 tone controls, distortion, treble and bass boosters.
1967-1968 $650 $850

Mark IV Bass
1963-1969. Teardrop-shaped body, 2 pickups, 1 set of controls.
1963-1969 $900 $1,000

Panther Bass
1967-1968. Double cut solidbody, 1 slanted pickup, rosewood board.
1967-1968 $400 $600

Phantom IV Bass
1963-1969. 5-sided body, 2 pickups, 1 set of controls.
1963-1964   English made $1,300 $1,800
1965-1969   Italian made $1,100 $1,300

Saturn IV Bass
1967-1968. Single cut, 2 F-holes, 1 set of controls, 1 pickup.
1967-1968 $500 $700

Sidewinder IV Bass (V272)
1967-1968. Double-cut 335-style body, 2 F-holes, 2 pickups, 1 set of controls, treble, bass, and distortion boosters.
1967-1968 $600 $800

Stinger Bass
1968. Teardrop-shaped, boat oar headstock.
1968 $600 $800

Wyman Bass
1966. Teardrop-shaped body, 2 pickups, 1 F-hole, 1 set of controls, sunburst.
1966 $700 $900

Wandre (Davoli)
Ca. 1956/57-1969. Italian-made guitars and basses.

Warrior
1995-present. Professional and premium grade, production/custom, solidbody basses built by luthier J.D. Lewis in Roseville, Georgia. He also builds guitars.

Warwick
1982-present. Professional and premium grade, production/custom, electric and acoustic basses made in Markneukirchen, Germany; founded by Hans Peter Wilfer, whose father started Framus guitars.

Jack Bruce Signature Bass
1990-1991, 2001. Based on Thumb Bass, '01 version a limited edition with 50 fretted and 50 unfretted made..
1990-1991 $1,700 $1,900

Streamer I-5 Bass
1984-present. 5-string, gold hardware, active electronics.
1990s $1,500 $1,900

Thumb Bass
1980s-present. Walnut, neck-through, double cut solidbody, 2 pickups.
1980s $1,300 $1,700

Washburn
1974-present. Intermediate and professional grade, production, acoustic and electric basses. Washburn instruments were mostly imports early on, U.S. production later, currently a combination of both. Washburn also offers guitars, mandolins, and amps.

Electric Basses
1974-present. Various electric models.
1974-1999 $300 $500

Watkins
1957-present. Watkins Electric Music (WEM) was founded by Charlie Watkins. Their first commercial product was the Watkins Dominator amp in '57. They made the Rapier line of guitars and basses from the beginning. Watkins offered guitars and basses up to '82.

Rapier Bass
Two pickups, British-made.
1960s   Red $400 $500

Wechter
1984-present. Professional grade, production/custom acoustic basses built by luthier Abe Wechter in Paw Paw, Michigan. He also offers U.S-made and import guitars.

Wendler
1999-present. Luthier Dave Wendler, of Ozark Instrument Building, builds his intermediate and professional grade, production/custom, solidbody, electro-acoustic basses in Branson, Missouri. He also builds guitars.

1960s Vox Mark IV

Warwick Streamer Stage 1

BASSES

1983 Yamaha BB-2000

Zon Tribute

Westbury-Unicord

1978-ca. 1983. Japanese imports by Unicord.

Electric Solidbody Basses

Various models.

MODEL YEAR	FEATURES	EXC. COND. LOW	HIGH
1980s		$150	$250

Westone

1970s-1990. Imported from Japan by St. Louis Music.

Electric Solidbody Basses

Various models.

1980s		$150	$250

Winston

Ca. 1963-1967. Imported by Buegeleisen & Jacobson of New York.

Electric Solidbody Basses

1960s		$100	$200

Wurlitzer

1970s. Private branded by Pedula for the Wurlitzer music store chain. Manufacturer and retailer were both based in Massachusetts. Refer to Pedulla listing.

Yamaha

1946-present. Budget, intermediate, professional and premium grade, production, electric basses. They also build guitars. Yamaha began producing solidbody instruments in '66.

Attitude Custom Bass

1990-1994. Part of the Sheehan Series.

1990s		$600	$800

Electric Basses

1966-present. Standard electric models fall within the range shown.

1966-1999		$250	$500

Zemaitis

1960-1999, 2004-present. Tony Zemaitis began selling his guitars in '60 and he retired in '99. He emphasized simple lightweight construction and his instruments are known for hand engraved metal fronts. Each hand-built custom guitar was a unique instrument. Approximately 10 custom guitars were built each year. In '04, Japan's Kanda Shokai, with the endorsement of Tony Zemaitis, Jr., started building the guitars again.

Electric Bass

1970s	Heart hole (2 made)	$26,000	$30,000
1980s	1/2 metal & spruce	$14,000	$16,000
1980s	Metal-fron 4-string	$18,000	$20,000

Zen-On

1946-ca.1968. Japanese-made. By '67 using the Morales brandname. Not heavily imported into the U.S., if at all (see Morales).

Electric Solidbody Basses

Various models.

MODEL YEAR	FEATURES	EXC. COND. LOW	HIGH
1950s		$100	$200

Zeta

1982-present. Professional and premium grade, production/custom, acoustic, electric and upright basses, with MIDI options, made in Oakland, California. They also make guitars, amps and mandolins.

Crossover 4 (Model XB-304) Bass

1990s-present. Sleek offset body design, bolt-on neck, playable as strap-on or upright.

1990s		$1,500	$1,700

Jazz Standard Uprite Bass

1990s-present. Hourglass-shaped body, bass-viol-size version of sleek electric violin, active electronics.

1990s		$2,400	$2,600

Zim-Gar

1960s. Japanese imports from Gar-Zim Musical Instrument Corporation of Brooklyn, New York.

Electric Solidbody Basses

Various models.

1960s		$100	$175

Zolla

1979-present. Professional grade, production/custom, electric basses built by luthier Bill Zolla in San Diego, California. Zolla also builds guitars, necks and bodies.

BZ-1 Bass

1988-present. Offset double cut solidbody, 2 pickups, offered in 4-, 5-, and 6-string versions.

1980s		$400	$600

Zon

1981-present. Luthier Joe Zon builds his professional and premium grade, production/custom, solidbody basses in Redwood City, California. Zon started the brand in Buffalo, New York and relocated to Redwood City in '87.

Legacy Elite VI Bass

1989-present. 6-string, 34" scale carbon-fiber neck, Bartolini pickups, ZP-2 active electronics.

1989		$1,000	$1,200

Scepter Bass

1984-1993. Offset body shape, 24 frets, 1 pickup, tremolo.

1984-1993		$900	$1,100

BASSES

Amps

AMPS

1977 Acoustic 125

1977 Acoustic 135

Aguilar DB 680 Bass Preamp

MODEL YEAR	FEATURES	EXC. COND. LOW	HIGH

Acoustic

Ca. 1965-ca. 1987, 2001-present. The Acoustic Control Corp., of Los Angeles, was mostly known for solidstate amplifiers. Heads and cabinets were sold separately with their own model numbers, but were also combined (amp sets) and marketed under a different model number (for example, the 153 amp set was the 150b head with a 2x15" cabinet). The brand was revived by Samick in '01 for a line of amps.

114 Amp
Ca. 1977-mid- 1980s. Solidstate, 50 watts, 2x10", reverb, master volume.

1978-1984		$200	$325

115 Amp
1977-1978. Solidstate, 1x12", 50 watts, reverb, master volume.

1977-1978		$225	$350

116 Bass Amp
1978-mid-1980s. Solidstate, 75 watts, 1x15", power boost switch.

1978-1984		$250	$350

120 Amp Head
1977-mid-1980ss. Solidstate head, 125 watts.

1977-1984		$200	$250

124 Amp
1977-mid-1980s. Solidstate, 4x10", five-band EQ, 100 watts, master volume.

1977-1984		$275	$350

125 Amp
1977-mid-1980s. Solidstate, 2x12", five-band EQ, 100 watts, master volume.

1977-1984		$275	$350

126 Bass Amp
1977-mid-1980s. Solidstate, 100 watts, 1x15", five-band EQ.

1977-1984		$275	$350

134 Amp
1972-1976. Solidstate, 100-125 watts, 4x10" combo.

1972-1976	125 watts	$275	$400

135 Amp
1972-1976. Solidstate, 125 watts, 2x12" combo, reverb, tremolo.

1972-1976		$275	$400

136 Amp
1972-1976. Solidstate, 125 watts, 1x15" combo.

1972-1976		$275	$400

140 Bass Head
1972-1976. Solidstate, 125 watts, two channels.

1972-1976		$200	$225

150 Amp Head
1960s-1976. Popular selling model, generally many available in the used marked. Solidstate, 110 watts until '72, 125 watts after.

1968-1976		$200	$225

150b Bass Head
1960s-1971. Bass amp version of 150 head.

1968-1971		$175	$200

153 Bass Amp Set
1960s-1971. 150b head (bass version of 150) with 2x15" 466 cabinet, 110 watts.

1968-1971		$300	$400

165 Amp
1979-mid-1980s. All tube combo, switchable to 60 or 100 watts, Brown Tolex.

1979-1984		$275	$350

220 Bass Head
1977-1980s. Solidstate, five-band EQ, either 125 or 160 watts, later models 170 or 200 watts, black Tolex.

1977-1984	170 or 200 watts	$200	$250

230 Amp Head
1977-1980s. Solidstate head, 125/160 watts, five-band EQ.

1977-1984		$200	$250

260 Amp Head
1960s-1971. Solidstate, 275 watt, stereo/mono.

1968-1971		$225	$275

270 Amp Head
1970s. 400 watts.

1970s		$250	$325

320 Bass Head
1977-1980s. Solidstate, five-band EQ, 160/300 watts, 2 switchable channels, black Tolex.

1977-1984		$275	$325

360 Bass Head
1960s-1971. One of Acoustic's most popular models, 200 watts. By '72, the 360 is listed as a "preamp only."

1968-1971		$400	$500

370 Bass Head
1972-1977. Solidstate bass head, 365 watts early on, 275 later.

1972-1977	275 or 365 watts	$275	$400

402 Cabinet
1977-1980s. 2x15" bass cab, black Tolex, black grille.

1977-1984		$200	$250

450 Amp Head
1974-1976. 170 watts, five-bank EQ, normal and bright inputs.

1974-1976		$200	$250

455 Amp Set
1974-1976. 170 watt 450 head with 4x12" cabinet. Black.

1974-1976	Black	$400	$500

470 Amp Head
1974-1977. 170 watt, dual channel.

1974-1977		$250	$350

G20-110 Amp
1981-mid-1980s. Solidstate, 20 watts, 1x10". The G series was a lower-priced combo line.

1981-1985		$100	$200

G20-120 Amp
1981-mid-1980s. Solidstate, 20 watts, 1x12".

1981-1985		$125	$225

G60-112 Amp
1981-mid-1980s. Solidstate, 60 watts, 1x12".

1981-1985		$150	$250

MODEL YEAR	FEATURES	EXC. COND. LOW	HIGH

G60-212 Amp
1981-mid-1980s. Solidstate, 60 watts, 2x12".
1981-1985 $175 $275

G60T-112 Amp
1981-1987. Tube, 60 watts, 1x12".
1981-1985 $300 $375

Tube 60 Amp
1986-1987. Combo, 60 watts, 1x12", spring reverb, bright switch, master volume control, effects loop.
1986-1987 $300 $375

ADA
1977-2002. ADA (Analog/Digital Associates) was located in Berkeley, California, and introduced its Flanger and Final Phase in '77. The company later moved to Oakland and made amplifiers, high-tech signal processors, and a reissue of its original Flanger.

B-500 B Bass Power Biamp
1989-1995. 500 watts, in bi-amp mode the two outputs drive cabinets of 4 to 16 ohms.
1989-1995 $375 $425

Aguilar
1995-present. U.S.-made tube and solidstate amp heads, cabinets, and pre-amps from New York, New York.

DB 359 Bass Amp Head
1998-present. Rack mount tube amp, 200 watts.
1998-2000 $850 $1,000

DB 680 Bass Preamp
1996-present. Rack mount tube preamp.
1996-2000 $850 $1,000

Aiken Amplification
2000-present. Tube amps, combos, and cabinets built by Randall Aiken in Buford, Georgia.

Airline
Ca. 1958-1968. Brand name for Montgomery Ward, built by Kay, Harmony, and Valco.

Large Tube Amps
1960s   Various models $250 $375
Small Tube Amps
1960s   Various models $175 $250

Alamo
1947-1982. Founded by Charles Eilenberg, Milton Fink, and Southern Music, San Antonio, Texas, and distributed by Bruno and Sons. Alamo started producing amps in '49 and the amps were all-tube until '73; solidstate preamp and tube output from '73 to ca. '80; all solidstate for ca. '80 to '82. See Guitar Stories Volume II, by Michael Wright, for a complete history of Alamo with detailed model listings.

Birch "A" Combo Amps
1949-1962. Birch wood cabinets with A-shaped grill cutout, two to five tubes. Models include the Embassy Amp 3, Jet Amp 4, Challenger Amp 2, Amp 5, and the Montclair.
1949-1962 $175 $275

MODEL YEAR	FEATURES	EXC. COND. LOW	HIGH

Bass Tube Amps
1960-1972. Leatherette covered, all tube, 20 to 35 watts, 15" speakers, combo or piggyback. Some with Lansing speaker option. Models include the Paragon Special, Paragon Bass, Piggyback Band, Piggyback Bass, Fury Bass, and Paragon Bass (piggyback).
1960-1972 $200 $300

Small Tube Amps
1960-1972. Leatherette covered, all tube, 3 to 10 watts, 6" to 10" speakers, some with tremolo. Models include the Jet, Embassy, Challenger, Capri, Fiesta, Dart, and Special.
1960-1972 $200 $300

Mid-power Tube Amps
1960-1970. Leatherette covered, all tube, 15 to 30 watts, 12" or 15" speakers, some with tremolo and reverb. Some with Lansing speaker option. Models include Montclair, Paragon, Paragon Band, Titan, and Futura.
1960-1970 $250 $350

Twin Speaker and Piggyback Tube Amps
1962-1972. Leatherette covered, all tube, up to 45 watts, 8", 10", 12" or 15" speaker configurations, some with tremolo and reverb. Some with Lansing speaker option. Models include the Electra Twin Ten, Century Twin Ten, Futuramic Twin Eight, Galaxie Twin Twelve, Galaxie Twin Twelve Piggyback, Piggyback Super Band, Alamo Pro Reverb Piggyback, Futura, Galaxie Twin Ten, Twin-Ten, and Band Piggyback.
1962-1972 $300 $400

Bass Solidstate Preamp-Tube Output Amps
1973-ca.1979. Solidstate preamp section with tube output section, 35 or 40 watts, 15" speakers, combo or piggyback. Models include the Paragon Bass, Paragon Bass Piggyback, Paragon Country Western Bass, Paragon Super Bass, and the Fury Bass.
1973-1979 $150 $250

Small Solidstate Preamp-Tube Output Amps
1973-ca.1979. Solidstate preamp section with tube output section, three to 12 watts, 5" to 12" speaker, some with reverb. Models include the Challenger, Capri, Special, Embassy, Dart, and Jet.
1973-1979 $100 $175

Mid-powered Solidstate Preamp-Tube Output Amps
1973-ca.1979. Solidstate preamp section with tube output section, 25 watts, 12" speaker, with reverb and tremolo. Models include the Montclair.
1973-1979 $150 $200

Twin & Combo Solidstate Preamp-Tube Output Amps
1973-ca.1979. Solidstate preamp section with tube output section, 20 or 70 watts, 10", 12" and 15" speaker configurations, some with reverb and tremolo. Models include the 70 watt Paragon Super Reverb piggybacks, the 45 watt Futura 2x12, and the 20 watt Twin-Ten.
1973-1979 $150 $225

Aiken Invader MKII

'60s Alamo Jet

1962 Alamo 2566 Century Twin Ten

Alesis Wildfire 60

Alessandro Redbone Special

Allen Old Flame combo

MODEL YEAR	FEATURES	EXC. COND. LOW	HIGH

Solidstate Amps
ca. 1980-1982. All solidstate.
1980-1982 — $75 — $125

Alesis
1992-present. Alesis has a wide range of products for the music industry, including digital modeling guitar amps. They also offer guitar effects.

Alessandro
1998-present. Tube amps built by George Alessandro in Huntingdon Valley, Pennsylvania. Founded in '94 as the Hound Dog Corporation, in '98 the company name was changed to Alessandro. The Redbone ('94) and the Bloodhound ('96) were the only models bearing the Hound Dog mark. Serial numbers are consecutive regardless of model (the earliest 20-30 did not have serial numbers). In '98 the company converted to exotic/high-end components and the name changed to Alessandro High-End Products. In '01, he added the Working Dog brand line of amps.

Bloodhound Amp Head
1996-1998. Stained wood amp cabinet, 55 watts with El-34 power tubes, 12AX7 preamp tubes.
1996-1998 — $1,300 — $1,600

Redbone Amp Head
1994-1998. Stained hardwood amp cabinet, 55 watts with EL-34 power tubes, octal preamp tubes.
1994-1998 — $1,400 — $1,700

Allen Amplification
1998-present. Tube combo amps, heads and cabinets built by David Allen in Walton, Kentucky. He also offers the amps in kit form and produces replacement and upgrade transformers and a tube overdrive pedal.

Class Act Combo Amp
1999-2003. 7 watt, 1x10" tube combo.
2000s — $400 — $500

Old Flame Amp Head
1998-present. Head only, black Tolex, silver grille, white control knobs, 40 watts, 6L6 power tubes.
1998-2002 — $550 — $700

Aloha
Late-1940s. Electric lap steel and amp Hawaiian outfits made for the Dallas-based Aloha.

Ampeg
1949-present. Ampeg is primarily known for their bass amps. In the eastern Uunited States, Ampeg was Fender's greatest challenger in the '60s and '70s bass amplifier market. St. Louis Music currently offers a line of Ampeg guitars and amps.

Amp Covering Dates
Wood veneer — 1946-1949
Smooth Brown — 1949-1952
Dot Tweed — 1952-1954
Tweed — 1954-1955
Rough Gray — 1957-1958

MODEL YEAR	FEATURES	EXC. COND. LOW	HIGH

Rough Tan — 1957-1958
Cream — 1957-1958
Light Blue — 1958
Navy Blue — 1958-1962
Blue check — 1962-1967
Black pebble — 1967
Smooth Black — 1967-1980
Rough Black — 1967-1985

AC12 Amp
1970. 20 watts, 1x12", accordion amp that was a market failure and dropped after one year.
1970 — $325 — $400

AP3550 Amp
1992-1993. Rackmount solidstate head, 350 watts or 200 watts, black metal.
1992-1993 350 watts — $250 — $275

B-2R Bass Head
1994-present. Two hundred watts.
1994-2002 — $400 — $500

B-3 Amp
1995-2001. Solidstate head, 150 watts, 1x15".
1995-2001 — $375 — $450

B-12 N Portaflex Amp
1961-1965. 25 watts, 2x12", two 6L6 power tubes.
1961-1965 — $850 — $1,000

B-12 XT Portaflex Amp
1965-1969. Tube, 50 watts, 2x12", reverb, vibrato, two 7027A power tubes.
1965-1969 — $750 — $900

B-15 N (NB, NC, NF) Portaflex Amp
1960-1970. Introduced as B-15 using two 6L6 power tubes, B-15 N in 1961, B-15 NB in 1962, B-15 NC with rectifier tube in 1964, B-15 NF with fixed-bias two 6L6 power tubes and 30 watts in 1967, 1x15".
1960-1965 — $900 — $1,050
1966-1970 — $800 — $950

B-15 NC Portaflex Amp (2nd version)
1967-1968. A different version than the 1964 to 1967 version. 50 watts, two 7027A power tubes, column 2x15" cabinet.
1967-1968 — $800 — $950

B-15 R Portaflex Amp (reissue)
1990s. Reissue of 1965 Portaflex 1x15". Blue check.
1990s — $775 — $850

B-15 S Portaflex Amp
1971-1977. 60 watts, two 7027A power tubes, 1x12".
1971-1977 — $800 — $950

B-18 N Portaflex Amp
1964-1969. Bass, 50 watts, 1x18".
1964-1965 — $900 — $1,000
1966-1969 — $850 — $950

B-2 Bass Amp
1994-present. Solidstate, 200 watts, 1x15" combo or 4x8" combo, Black vinyl, Black grille, large A logo.
1994-2000 1x15" — $500 — $600

B-25 Amp
1969 only. 55 watts, two 7027A power tubes, 2x15", no reverb, guitar amp.
1969 — $750 — $900

MODEL YEAR	FEATURES	EXC. COND. LOW	HIGH

B-25B Bass Amp
1969-1980. Bass amp, 55 watts, two 7027A power tubes, 2x15" bass speakers.

| 1969 | | $750 | $900 |

B-3158B Bass Amp
1990s. Solidstate, 100 watts, 1x15", Black vinyl, Black grille, large A logo.

| 1990s | | $525 | $575 |

B-50R Rocket Bass Amp (reissue)
1996-present. 50 watts, 1x12" combo, vintage-style Blue check cover.

| 1996-1999 | | $275 | $300 |

B-100R Rocket Bass Amp (reissue)
1996-present. Solidstate, 100 watts, 1x15" combo bass amp, vintage-style blue check cover.

| 1996-1999 | | $325 | $350 |

BT-15 Amp
1966-1968. Ampeg introduced solidstate amps in '66, the same year as Fender. Solidstate, 50 watts, 1x15", generally used as a bass amp. The BT-15D has two 1x15" cabinets. The BT-15C is a 2x15" column portaflex cabinet.

| 1966-1968 | | $300 | $350 |

BT-18 Amp
1966-1968. Ampeg introduced solidstate amps in '66, the same year as Fender. Solidstate, 50 watts, 1x18", generally used as a bass amp. The BT-18D has two 1x15" cabinets. The BT-18C is a 2x18" column portaflex cabinet.

| 1966-1968 | | $250 | $300 |

ET 1 Echo Twin Amp
1961-1964. Tube, 30 watts, 1x12", stereo reverb.

| 1961-1964 | | $600 | $700 |

ET 2 Super Echo Twin Amp
1962-1964. Tube, 2x12", 30 watts, stereo reverb.

| 1962-1964 | | $650 | $750 |

G-12 Gemini I Amp
1964-1971. Tube, 1x12", 22 watts, reverb.

| 1964-1971 | | $500 | $575 |

G-15 Gemini II Amp
1965-1968. Tube, 30 watts, 1x15", reverb.

| 1965-1968 | | $500 | $575 |

G-110 Amp
1978-1980. Solidstate, 20 watts, 1x10", reverb, tremolo.

| 1978-1980 | | $250 | $350 |

G-115 Amp
1979-1980. Solidstate, 175 watts, 1x15" JBL, reverb and tremolo, designed for steel guitar.

| 1979-1980 | | $300 | $400 |

G-212 Amp
1973-1980. Solidstate, 120 watts, 2x12".

| 1973-1980 | | $350 | $450 |

GS-12 Rocket 2 Amp
1965-1968. This name replaced the Reverberocket 2 (II), 15 watts, 1x12".

| 1965-1968 | | $400 | $500 |

GS-12-R Reverberocket 2 Amp
1965-1969. Tube, 1x12", 18 watts, reverb. Called the Reverberocket II in 1968 and 1969, then Rocket II in 1969.

| 1965-1969 | | $400 | $500 |

GS-15-R Gemini VI Amp
1966-1967. 30 watts, 1x15", single channel, considered to be "the accordion version" of the Gemini II.

| 1966-1967 | | $450 | $550 |

GT-10 Amp
1971-1980. Solidstate, 15 watts, 1x10", basic practice amp with reverb.

| 1971-1980 | | $250 | $350 |

GV-22 Gemini 22 Amp
1969-1972. Tube, 30 watts, 2x12".

| 1969-1972 | | $450 | $525 |

J-12 Jet Amp
1958-1972 (no 1964-66 models). 20 watts, 1x12".

| 1958-1963 | | $400 | $500 |
| 1967-1972 | Model reappears | $350 | $450 |

J-12 A Jet Amp

| 1960s | | $400 | $500 |

J-12 D Jet Amp
Jet Amp with solidstate rectifier.

| 1964-1966　. | | $400 | $500 |

J-12 T Jet Amp

| 1964-1965 | | $400 | $500 |

M-12 Mercury Amp
1957-1965. 15 watts, 2 channels, Rocket 1x12".

| 1957-1959 | | $600 | $700 |
| 1960-1965 | | $550 | $650 |

M-15 Big M Amp
1959-1965. 20 watts, 2x6L6 power, 1x15".

| 1959 | | $600 | $700 |
| 1960-1965 | | $550 | $650 |

R-12 Rocket Amp
1957-1963. 12 watts, 1x12", one channel.

| 1957-1963 | | $500 | $600 |

R-12-B Rocket Amp
1964. 12 watts, 1x12", follow-up to the R-12 Rocket.

| 1964 | | $500 | $600 |

R-12-R Reverberocket Amp
1961-1965.

| 1961-1965 | | $475 | $525 |

R-12-R Reverberocket Amp (reissue)
1996-present. 50 watts, two EL34 power tubes, 1x12" (R-212R is 2x12").

| 1996-1999 | | $350 | $375 |

R-12-R-B Reverberocket Amp
1964 variant. 7591A power tubes replace R-12-R 6V6 power tubes.

| 1964 | | $475 | $525 |

R-12-R-T Reverberocket Amp
1965 variant. 7591A or 7868 power tubes.

| 1965 | | $475 | $525 |

R-212-R Reverberocket Combo 50 Amp (reissue)
1996-present. 50 watts, 2x12", all tube reissue, vintage-style blue ckeck cover, vintage-style grille.

| 1996-1999 | | $325 | $375 |

1960s Ampeg GV-22

1959 Ampeg J-12 Jet

1965 Ampeg R-12-R-T Reverberocket

AMPS

Ampeg SVT 350

Ampeg SVT

Ampeg SVT-4 Pro

MODEL YEAR	FEATURES	EXC. COND. LOW	HIGH
SB-12 Portaflex Amp			
1965-1971. 22 watts, 1x12", designed for use with Ampeg's Baby Bass, black.			
1965-1971		$600	$700
SBT Amp			
1969-1971. 120 watts, 1x15", bass version of SST Amp.			
1969-1971		$700	$800
SE-412 Cabinet			
Four 12" speakers.			
1996-1999		$300	$350
SJ-12-R/SJ-12-RT Super Jet Amp			
1996-present. 50 watts, tube, 1x12", SJ-12-RT has tremolo added.			
1996-1999		$300	$350
SS-35 Amp			
1987-1992. Solidstate, 35 watts, 1x12", Black vinyl, Black grille, large A logo.			
1990		$150	$200
SS-70 Amp			
1987-1990. Solidstate, 70 watts, 1x12".			
1990		$300	$350
SS-70 C Amp			
1987-1992. Solidstate, 70 watts, 2x10", chorus, Black vinyl, Black grille, large A logo.			
1990		$300	$350
SVT 100T Bass Combo Amp			
1990-1992. Solidstate, ultra-compact bass combo, 100 watts, 2x8".			
1990-1992		$400	$450
SVT 200T Head Amp			
1987 only. Solidstate, 200 watts to eight ohms or 320 watts to four ohms.			
1987		$375	$475
SVT 350 Head Amp			
1995-present. Solidstate head, 350 watts, graphic EQ.			
1990s		$375	$475
SVT 400 Amp			
1987-1997. Solidstate, 400 watts per side, rack-mountable head with advanced (in 1987) technology.			
1990s		$400	$500
SVT Bass Amp Set			
1969-1985. 300 watt head with matching two 8x10" cabs.			
1969-1972	Original matching set	$2,200	$2,800
1973-1979	Original matching set	$2,100	$2,500
1980-1985	Original matching set	$2,000	$2,300
SVT Bass Cabinets			
1969-1985. Two 8x10" cabs only.			
1969-1985		$800	$1,000
SVT Bass Head Amp			
1969-1985. 300 watt head only.			
1969-1972		$1,400	$1,800
1973-1979		$1,300	$1,500
1980-1985		$1,200	$1,300

MODEL YEAR	FEATURES	EXC. COND. LOW	HIGH
SVT-II Pro Bass Head Amp			
1992-present. 300 watts, rack-mountable, all tube circuit similar to original SVT, black metal.			
1992-1999		$1,200	$1,300
SVT-III Pro Bass Head Amp			
1993-present. Tube preamp section and MOS-FET power section, 350 watts, rack-mountable, black metal.			
1993-2003		$650	$800
SVT-4 Pro Bass Head Amp			
1997-present. Hybrid rack-mountable, all tube pre-amp, MOS-FET power section yielding, 1600 watts.			
1997-1999		$800	$900
V-2 Amp Set			
1971-1980. 60 watt head with 4x12" cab, black Tolex.			
1971-1980		$700	$850
V-2 Head Amp			
1971-1980. 60 watt tube head.			
1971-1980		$300	$450
V-4 4x12" Cab			
1970s. Single 4x12" cabinet only.			
1970-1980		$350	$400
V-4 Amp Stack			
1970-1980. 100 watts, wih two 4x12" cabs.			
1970-1980	Head and cabs	$950	$1,100
1970-1980	Head only	$450	$650
V-4-B Bass Head Amp			
1972-1980. Bass version of V-4 without reverb.			
1972-1980		$450	$650
V-7-SC Amp			
1981-1985. Tube, 100 watts, 1x12", master volume, channel switching, reverb.			
1981-1985		$450	$600
VH-70 Amp			
1991-1992. 70 watts, 1x12" combo with channel switching.			
1991-1992		$300	$350
VH-140C Amp			
1992-1995. Varying Harmonics (VH) with Chorus (C), two 70-watt channel stereo, 2x12".			
1992-1995		$350	$375
VH-150 Head Amp			
1991-1992. 150 watts, channel-switchable, reverb.			
1991-1992		$325	$375
VL-502 Amp			
1991-1995. 50 watts, channel-switchable, all tube.			
1991-1995		$300	$400
VL-1001 Head Amp			
1991-1993. 100 watts, non-switchable channels, all tube.			
1991-1993		$300	$350
VL-1002 Head Amp			
1991-1995. 100 watts, channel-switchable, all tube.			
1991-1995		$350	$450
VT-120 Combo Amp			
1989-1992. Tube, 6L6 power, 120 watts, 1x12", also offered as head only.			
1989-1992		$550	$650

MODEL YEAR	FEATURES	EXC. COND. LOW	HIGH

VT-120 Head Amp
1989-1992. 120 watts, 6L6 tube head.

1989-1992		$450	$550

VT-22 Amp
1970-1980. 100 watt combo version of V-4, 2x12".

1970-1980		$700	$800

VT-40 Amp
1971-1980. 60 watt combo, 4x10".

1971-1980		$700	$800

VT-60 Combo Amp
1989-1991. Tube, 6L6 power, 60 watts, 1x12".

1989-1991		$500	$600

VT-60 Head Amp
1989-1991. Tube head only, 6L6 power, 60 watts.

1989-1991		$400	$500

Anderson Amplifiers
1993-present. Tube amps and combos built by Jack Anderson in Gig Harbor, Washington.

Aria/Aria Pro II
1960-present. The Japanese instrument builder offered a range of amps from around '79 to '89.

Ashdown Amplification
1999-present. Founded in England by Mark Gooday after he spent several years with Trace Elliot, Ashdown offers amps, combos, and cabinets.

Audiovox
Ca. 1935-ca. 1950. Paul Tutmarc's Audiovox Manufacturing, of Seattle, Washington, was a pioneer in electric lap steels, basses, guitars and amps.

Auralux
2000-present. Founded by Mitchell Omori and David Salzmann, Auralux builds effects and tube amps in Highland Park, Illinois.

Bad Cat Amplifier Company
2000-present. The company was founded in Corona, California by James and Debbie Heidrich with Mark Sampson as the chief designer and engineer. Bad Cat offers class A combo amps, heads, cabinets and effects.

Baldwin
Piano maker Baldwin started offered amplifiers from '65 to '70. The amps were solidstate with "organ-like" pastel-colored pushbutton switches.

Exterminator Amp
1965-1970. Solidstate, 100 watts, 2x15"/2x12"/2x7", four feet vertical combo cabinet, reverb and tremolo, Supersound switch and slide controls.

1965-1970		$550	$650

Model B1 Bass Amp
1965-1970. Solidstate, 45 watts, 1x15"/1x12", two channels.

1965-1970		$250	$300

Model B2 Bass Amp
1965-1970. Solidstate, 35 watts, 1x15", two channels.

1965-1970		$225	$275

Model C1 Custom (Professional) Amp
1965-1970. Solidstate, 45 watts, 2x12", reverb and tremolo, Supersound switch and slide controls.

1965-1970		$300	$350

Model C2 Custom Amp
1965-1970. Solidstate, 40 watts, 2x12", reverb and tremolo.

1960s		$250	$300

Barcus-Berry
1964-present. Pickup maker Barcus-Berry offered a line of amps from '75 to '79.

Bedrock
1984-1997. Tube amp company founded by Brad Jeter and Ron Pinto in Nashua, New Hampshire. They produced 50 amps carrying the brand name Fred before changing the company name to Bedrock in '86. Around '88, Jay Abend joined the company, eventually becoming President. In '88, Evan Cantor joined the company as an amp designer. In '90, Jeter left Bedrock and, shortly after, Pinto and Abend moved the company to Farmington, Massachusetts. The company closed in '97.

Blue Tone Amplifiers
2002-present. Founded by Alex Cooper in Worcestershire, England, Blue Tone offers comb amps employing their "virtual valve technology."

Bogner
1988-present. Tube combos, amp heads, and speaker cabinets from builder Reinhold Bogner of North Hollywood, California.

Brand X
Small solidstate combo amps from Fender Musical Instruments Corporation.

Bruno (Tony)
1995-present. Tube combos, amp heads, and speaker cabinets from builder Tony Bruno of Cairo, New York.

Underground 30 Combo Amp
1995-present. 35 watts, 1x12", no reverb.

1995-1999		$1,100	$1,200

Budda
1995-present. Amps, combos, and cabinets from San Rafael, California. They also produce effects pedals.

Burriss
Bob Burriss builds custom and production tube amps in Lexington, Kentucky. He also builds effects.

Ashdown Peacemaker 60

Bad Cat Hot Cat 15

Budda Superdrive Series II 80 Watt Head

Callaham EL34 Amp

Carr Mercury

Chicago Blues Box Roadhouse

MODEL YEAR	FEATURES	EXC. COND. LOW	HIGH

Callaham

1989-present. Tube amp heads built by Bill Callaham in Winchester, Virginia. He also builds solidbody electric guitars.

Carlsbro

1959-present. Guitar, bass, and keyboard combo amps, heads and cabinets from Carlsbro Electronics Limited of Nottingham, England. They also offer PA amps and speaker cabinets.

Carr Amplifiers

1998-present. Steve Carr started producing amps in his Chapel Hill, North Carolina amp repair business in '98. The company is now located in Pittsboro, North Carolina, and makes tube combo amps, heads, and cabinets.

Hammerhead Amp

2000-present. Class A, 2xEL34 power tubes, 25 watts with 1x12", 25 watts with 2x10" or 25 watts with 2x12".

2000-2002	1x12"	$900	$950
2000-2002	2x10"	$950	$1,050
2003	2x12"	$1,000	$1,100

Imperial Combo Amp

2002-2004. 60 watts, with 1x15", 2x12" or 4x10".

2002-2004	1x15"	$1,400	$1,600
2002-2004	2x12"	$1,400	$1,600
2002-2004	4x10"	$1,500	$1,700

Rambler Combo Amp

1999-present. Class A, 2x6L6 power tubes, 28 watts with 1x12", 2x10", 2x12" or 1x15" speakers.

1999-2003	1x12"	$1,200	$1,400
1999-2003	1x15"	$1,300	$1,500
1999-2003	2x10"	$1,300	$1,500
1999-2003	2x12"	$1,300	$1,500

Slant 6V (Dual 6V6) Amp

1998-present. 40 watt, 2 channel, combo amp, 2x12" or 1x15". Also available as a head.

1998-2002		$1,500	$1,600

Carvin

1946-present. Founded in Los Angeles Lowell C. Kiesel who sold guitars and amps under the Kiesel name until late-'49, when the Carvin brand name is introduced. They added small tube amps to their product line in '47 and today offers a variety of models. They also build guitars and basses.

212 Bel Air Amp

1999-2002. Part of the Vintage Tube series, 2x12", 50 watts, dual channels with separate controls, tube-driven spring reverb, tweed.

1999-2002		$325	$400

Amp

1950s. Tweed, 4x10".

1950s		$300	$450

Pro-Bass II Amp Head

1986-ca.1989. Available in 100- and 300-watt models, preamp, noise gate, EQ, effects loop.

1986-1989	100 watts	$225	$300

MODEL YEAR	FEATURES	EXC. COND. LOW	HIGH

R600 Bass Amp Head

1998-present. 600 watts, ohm output selectors, 9-slider EQ, black cover, red knobs.

1998-2003		$300	$400

RL6815 Bass Combo Amp

1998-present. R600 amp with 1x15" + 2x8" and horn tweeter.

1998-2003		$550	$600

SX 100 Combo Amp

1987-present. 100 watts, 1x12" solidstate combo.

1988-2000		$150	$175

SX 200 Combo Amp

1987-present. 150 watts, solidstate combo, 2x12".

1987-2003		$175	$200

VT-50 Vintage Amp

1995-2001. EL84 power, 50-watt head designed to be mated with the 410 Speaker System.

1995-2001		$225	$300

VT-112 Amp

Ca. 1977-ca.1981. Tube, 1x12", seven-band equalizer.

1970s		$225	$275

VT-212 Combo Amp

Ca. 1977-ca.1981. 100 watts (4xEL34s), 2x12".

1970s		$250	$325

X-60 Amp

1984-1991. 60 watt combo, reverb, 1x12".

1984-1991		$250	$325

XB-112 Amp

1981-ca. 1984. 30 watts, 1x12".

1981-1984		$275	$325

XV-112 Amp

1981-1995. Tube, 100 watts, 1x12" speakers.

1981-1995		$275	$325

XV-112E Amp

1981-1990. XV-112 with ElectroVoice speakers, black tolex. Was originally also available in an oak cabinet.

1981-1990	Black	$300	$350

XV-212 Amp

1981-1995. Tube, 100 watts, 2x12".

1981-1995		$325	$375

XV-212E Amp

1981-1990. XV212 with Electro-Voice speakers.

1981-1990		$350	$400

Chicago Blues Box

2001-present. Tube combo amps built by Dan Bulter of Butler Custom Sound in Elmhurst, Illinois.

Clark Amplification

Hand-wired, tweed-era replica amplifiers from builder Mike Clark, of Cayce, South Carolina.

Tyger Amp (non-reverb)

2000-present. Classic tweed Fender 5E7 Bandmaster circuit, 3x10", 35 watts.

2000	Tweed	$1,000	$1,150

Tyger Amp (reverb)

2000-present. Tyger Amp with optional three-knob reverb, and three-position power attenuator.

2000	Tweed	$1,200	$1,350

MODEL		EXC. COND.	
YEAR	FEATURES	LOW	HIGH

Comins

1992-present. Archtop luthier Bill Comins, of Willow Grove, Pennsylvania, introduced a Comins combo amp, built in collaboration with George Alessandro, in '03.

Crate

1979-present. Solidstate and tube amplifiers distributed by St. Louis Music.

Solidstate Amps

Various student to mid-level amps, up to 150 watts.

1970s		$100	$150
1980s		$100	$150

Vintage Club 50/VC 50 Amp

1994-1999. 50 watt tube head.

1994-1999		$190	$225

Vintage Club 5212/VC-5212 Amp

1994-2001. 50 watts, 2x12" tube combo, white (earlier) or black vinyl cover, black grille.

1994-2001		$200	$250

Vintage Club 5310/VC-5310

1994-1997. 50 watts, all tube, 3x10".

1994-1997		$250	$300

Cruise Audio Systems

1999-present. Founded by Mark Altekruse, Cruise offers amps, combos, and cabinets built in Cuyahoga Falls, Ohio

Da Vinci

Late-1950s-early-1960s. Another one of several private brands (for example, Unique, Twilighter, Titano, etc.) that Magnatone made for teaching studios and accordian companies.

Model 250 Amp

1958-1962. Similar to Magnatone Model 250 with about 20 watts and 1x12".

1958-1962		$475	$550

Danelectro

1946-1969, 1997-present. Founded in Red Bank, New Jersey, by Nathan I. "Nate" or "Nat" Daniel. His first amps were made for Montgomery Ward in '47, and in '48 he began supplying Silvertone Amps for Sears. His own amps were distributed by Targ and Dinner as Danelectro and S.S. Maxwell brands. In '96, the Evets Corporation, of San Clemente, California, reintroduced the Danelectro brand on effects, amps, basses and guitars. In early '03, Evets discontinued the guitar and amp lines, but still offers effects.

Cadet Amp

Tube, 6 watts, 1x6".

1955-1959		$175	$225
1960-1963		$150	$175
1964-1966		$125	$150
1967-1969		$100	$125

Centurion Model 275 Amp

Two 6V6 power tubes for approximately 15-18 watts, 1x12", Gray cover.

1959-1960		$200	$300

DM-10 Amp

Five watts, 1x6".

1960s		$125	$150

DM-25 Amp

35 watts, 1x12".

1960s		$250	$275

DS-50 Amp

1967-1969. 50 watts, 3x10" piggyback set, reverb and tremolo, suitable for bass accordion.

1967-1969		$375	$425

DS-100 Amp

1967-1969. 100 watts, piggyback, 6x10" Jensens, reverb, tremolo, suitable for bass accordion.

1967-1969		$500	$550

Model 68 Special Amp

1950s. 20 watts, 1x12", light Tweed-fabric cover, light grille, leather handle, script Danelectro plexi-plate logo.

1950s		$200	$300

Model 98 Twin 12 Amp (Series D)

1954-ca.1957. Blond tweed-style cover, brown control panel, 2x12", vibrato speed and strength, rounded front Series D.

1954-1957		$500	$700

Model 217 Twin 15 Amp

1960s. Combo amp, 100 watts, 2x15" Jensen C15P speakers, Black cover, White-Silver grille, two channels with tremolo.

1962		$400	$500

Viscount Model 142 Amp

Late-1950s. Combo amp, lower watts, 1x12", light cover, Brown grille, vibrato.

1959		$250	$300

Dean

1976-present. Acoustic, electric, and bass amps made overseas. They also offer guitars, banjos, mandolins, and basses.

Dean Markley

The string and pickup manufacturer added a line of amps in 1983. Distributed by Kaman, they now offer combo guitar and bass amps and PA systems.

K-15 Combo Amp

1980s. Solidstate, 10 watts, 1x6", recently reintroduced.

1980s		$70	$80

K-20 Amp

1980s. Solidstate, 10 to 20 watts, 1x8", master volume, overdrive switch.

1980s		$70	$80

K-50 Amp

1980s. 25 watts, 1x10", master volume, reverb.

1980s		$95	$120

K-75 Amp

1980s. 35 watts, 1x12", master volume, reverb.

1980s		$120	$145

Cruise MQ4212

Danelectro Commando

Danelectro Model 78 Maestro

Demeter TGA2-C50-112

Dr. Z Maz 18

Eden WT800 Time Traveler

MODEL YEAR	FEATURES	EXC. COND. LOW	HIGH

Demeter

1980-present. James Demeter founded the company as Innovative Audio and renamed it Demeter Amplification in '90. Located in Van Nuys, California. First products were direct boxes. By '85, amps were added. Currently they build amp heads, combos, and cabinets. They also have pro audio gear and guitar effects.

Diaz

Early 1980s-2002. Cesar Diaz restored amps for many of rock's biggest names, often working with them to develop desired tones. Along the way he produced his own line of high-end custom amps and effects. Diaz died in '02; his family resumed production of effects in '04.

Dickerson

1937-1947. Dickerson was founded by the Dickerson brothers in 1937, primarily for electric lap steels and small amps. Instruments were also private branded for Cleveland's Oahu company, and for the Gourley brand. By '47, the company changed ownership and was renamed Magna Electronics (Magnatone).

Oasis Amp

1940s-1950s. Blue pearloid cover, 1x10", low wattage. Dickerson silk-screen logo on grille with Hawaiian background.

1940s		$150	$225

Dr. Z Amps

1988-present. Mike Zaite started producing his Dr. Z line of amps in the basement of the Music Manor in Maple Heights, Ohio. The company is now located in its own larger facility in the same city. Dr. Z offers combo amps, heads and cabinets.

Duca Tone

The Duca Tone brand was distributed by Lo Duca Brothers, Milwaukee, Wisconsin, which also distributed EKO guitars in the U.S.

Tube Amp

Twelve watts, 1x12".

1950s		$400	$475

Dumble

1963-present. Made by Howard Alexander Dumble, an early custom-order amp maker from California. Initial efforts were a few Mosrite amps for Semie Moseley. First shop was in '68 in Santa Cruz.

Overdrive Special Amp and Cabinet

100 watts, 1x12", known for durability, cabinets vary.

1970s	Black	$13,000	$15,000
1980s	Black	$13,000	$15,000
1990s	Black	$13,000	$15,000

Earth Sound Research

Earth Sound was a product of ISC Audio of Huntington, New York, and offered a range of amps, cabinets and PA gear starting in the '70s.

2000 G Half-Stack Amp

1970s. 100 watts plus cab.

1970s		$500	$650

Amps

Various lower to mid-level amplifiers KT and MV Series.

1970s	Various models	$275	$350

Cabinets

Various cabinets.

1970s		$200	$250

Eden

1976-present. Founded by David Nordschow in Minnesota as a custom builder, Eden now offers a full line of amps, combos, and cabinets for the bassist, built in Mundelein, Illinois. In 2002, the brand became a division of U.S. Music Corp (Washburn, Randall). They also produce the Nemesis brand of amps.

Egnater

1980-present. Tube amps, combos, preamps and cabinets built in Michigan by Bruce Egnater.

EKO

1959-1985. In '67 EKO added amps to their product line, offering three piggyback and four combo amps, all with dark covering, dark grille, and the EKO logo. The amp line may have lasted into the early '70s.

Electar

1996-present. The Gibson owned Electar brand offers tube and solidstate amps, PA gear and wireless systems. Epiphone had a line of Electar amps in the 1930s.

Electro-Harmonix

1968-1981, 1996-present. Electro-Harmonix offered a few amps to go with its line of effects. See Effects section for more company info.

Freedom Brothers Amp

Introduced in 1977. Small AC/DC amp with two 5-1/2" speakers. E-H has reissued the similar Freedom amp.

1977		$140	$170

Mike Matthews Dirt Road Special Amp

25 watts, 1x12" Celestion, built-in Small Stone phase shifter.

1977		$325	$400

Elk

Late-1960s. Japanese-made by Elk Gakki Co., Ltd. Many were copies of American designs.

AMPS

MODEL YEAR	FEATURES	EXC. COND. LOW	HIGH

Custom EL 150L Amp
Late-1960s. Piggy-back set, all-tube with head styled after very early Marshall and cab styled after large vertical Fender cab.
| 1968 | | $375 | $425 |

Guitar Man EB 105 (Super Reverb) Amp
Late-1960s. All-tube, reverb, copy of Blackface Super Reverb.
| 1968 | | $300 | $325 |

Twin Amp 60/Twin Amp 50 EB202
Late-1960s. All-tube, reverb, copy of Blackface Dual Showman set (head plus horizontal cab) but named Twin.
| 1968 | | $375 | $425 |

Viking 100 VK 100 Amp
Late-1960s. Piggy-back set, head styled after very early Marshall and cab styled after very large vertical Fender cab.
| 1968 | | $375 | $425 |

Emery Sound
1997-present. Founded by Curt Emery in El Cerrito, California, Emery Sound specializes in custom-made low wattage tube amps.

Epiphone
1928-present. Epiphone offered amps into the mid-'70s and reintroduced them in '91 with the EP series. Currently they offer tube and solid-state amps. The price ranges listed for excellent condition, all original amps though tubes may be replaced without affecting value. Many amps have missing or broken logos. The prices listed are for amps with fully intact logos. A broken or missing logo can diminish the value of an amp. Amps with a changed handle, power cord, and especially a broken logo should be taken on a case-by-case basis.

E-30B Amp
1972-1975. Solidstate model offered similarly to Gibson G-Series (not GA-Series), 30 watts, 2x10", 4 knobs.
| 1972-1975 | | $150 | $200 |

E-60 Amp
1972-1975. Solidstate, 3 watts, 1x10", volume and tone knobs.
| 1972-1975 | | $75 | $100 |

E-70 Amp
1971-1975. Solidstate, tremolo, 1x10" speakes, 3 knobs.
| 1972-1975 | | $85 | $125 |

EA-12 RVT Futura Amp
1962-1967. Low- to mid-power, 4x8", '60s gray Tolex, light grille.
| 1962-1967 | | $650 | $750 |

EA-14 RVT Ensign Amp
1965-1969. Gray Tolex, silver-gray grille, 50 watts, 2x12", split C logo.
| 1965-1969 | Gray Tolex | $450 | $550 |

EA-15 RVT Zephyr Amp
1961-1965. 14 or 20 watts, 1x15", gray Tolex, light grille, split C logo on panel, tremolo and reverb, script Epiphone logo lower right grille.
| 1961-1965 | | $300 | $500 |

EA-16 RVT Regent Amp
1965-1969. 25 watts, 1x12", gray vinyl, gray grille, tremolo, reverb. Called the Lancer in first year.
| 1965-1969 | | $400 | $500 |

EA-26 RVT Electra Amp
1965-1969. Gray Tolex, reverb, tremolo, footswitch, 1x12".
| 1965-1969 | | $300 | $400 |

EA-32 RVT Comet Amp
1965-1967. 1x10", trem, reverb.
| 1965-1967 | | $300 | $400 |

EA-33 RVT Galaxie Amp
1963-1964. Gray Tolex, gray grille, 1x10".
| 1963-1964 | | $350 | $450 |

EA-35 Devon Amp
1961-1963. 1x10" until '62, 1x12" with trem in '63.
| 1961-1963 | | $300 | $350 |

EA-50 Pacemaker Amp
1961-1969. 1x8" until '62, 1x10" after. EA-50T with trem added in '63. Non-trem version dropped around '67.
| 1961-1969 | | $200 | $250 |

EA-300 RVT Embassy Amp
1965-1969. 90 watts, 2x12", gray vinyl, gray grille, tremolo, reverb.
| 1965-1969 | | $550 | $650 |

EA-500T Panorama
1963-1967. 65 watts, head and large cabinet, tremolo, one 15" and one 10" until '64, one 15" and 2x10" after.
| 1964-1967 | | $300 | $600 |

EA-600 RVT Maxima Amp
1966-1969. Solidstate Epiphone version of Gibson GSS-100, gray vinyl, gray grille, two 2x10" cabs and hi-fi stereo-style amp head.
| 1966-1969 | | $500 | $550 |

Fender
1946-present. Leo Fender's early manufacturing focus was on P.A. systems and he attempted to improve the inferior offerings of the day. Western Swing and Hawaiian music were popular at the time and he wanted to supply those musicians with superior products. Fender contributed many ground-breaking instruments, but Leo's primary passion was amplifiers, and of all his important contributions to musicians, none exceed those he made to the electric tube amplifier.

Fender Tweed amp circuits are highly valued because they defined the tones of Rock and Roll. Fender Blackface models remained basically the same until mid-'67. Some Silverface circuits remained the same as the Blackface circuits, while others were changed in the name of reliability. Fender amps ruled the business until things changed in the late-'60s when powerful arena amps

Emery Sound Superbaby

Epiphone Electar Zephyr

1966 Epiphone EA-14 RVT Ensign

Fender Acoustasonic SFX II

1964 Fender Bandmaster head

Late-'50s Fender Bassman

were introduced by Marshall.

Price Guide values are for all original, excellent condition amps. Small differences in an amp's condition can generate larger differences in selling prices. Non-original speakers will significantly reduce a pre-'68 amp's value. Reconed speakers will reduce the value, but a reconed speaker is preferable to a replacement speaker. Multi-speaker amps generally have matching speaker codes. Different speaker codes require explanation. Fender leather handles are often broken and replaced. A replacement handle drops the value of an amp. Tweed was not the best covering, being prone to stains and damage. Grille cloths should have no tears and a single tear can drop the value of an amp. Each tweed amp should be evaluated on a case-by-case basis, and it is not unusual for a tweed amp to have a wide range of values. Alnico speaker replacement is more significant than ceramic speaker replacement. Fender converted to ceramic about '62. Speaker replacement is of less concern in post-'70 Fender amps.

The speaker code found on the frame of an original speaker will identify the manufacturer, and the week and year that the speaker was assembled. The speaker code is typically six (sometimes seven) digits. The first three digits represent the Electronics Industries Association (E.I.A.) source code which identifies the manufacturer. For example, a speaker code 220402 indicates a Jensen speaker (220), made in '54 (4) during the second week (02) of that year. This sample speaker also has another code stamped on the frame. ST654 P15N C4964 indicates the model of the speaker, in this case it is a P15N 15" speaker. The sample speaker also had a code stamped on the speaker cone, 4965 l, which indicates the cone number. All of these codes help identify the originality of the speaker. The value ranges provided in the Guide are for amps with the original speaker and original speaker cone.

Most Fender speakers from the '50s will be Jensens (code 220). By the late-'50s other suppliers were used. Their supplier's codes are as follows: Oxford (code 465), C.T.S. (code 137), Utah (code 328). JBL speakers were first used in the late-'50s Vibrasonic, and then in the Showman series, but JBL did not normally have a E.I.A. source code. An amp's speaker code should be reconciled with other dating info when the amp's original status is being verified.

75 Combo Amp

1980-1983. Tube, 75 watts, 1x15".

1980-1983	$400	$450

85 Combo Amp

1988-1992. Solidstate, 85 watts, 1x10", Black cover, Silver grille.

1988-1992	$200	$250

Acoustasonic Jr. Amp

1998-2000. Acoustic technology, 2x40 watts, 2x8" and Piezo horn. Brown Tolex and Wheat grille.

1998	$300	$325

Acoustasonic SFX/SFX II Amp

1998-present. SFX technology, 32 stereo digital present effects, 2x80 watts, 1x10" and 1x8", and Piezo horn, brown Tolex and wheat grille.

1998-2002	$400	$425

Bandmaster Amp

1953-1974. Wide-panel 1x15" combo 1953-1954, narrow-panel 3x10" combo 1955-1960, Tolex 1960, Brownface with 1x12" piggy back speaker cabinet 1961, 2x12" 1962, Blackface 1962-1967, Silverface 1968-1974.

1953-1954	Tweed, 1x15"	$3,500	$4,500
1955-1958	Tweed, 3x10"	$4,500	$6,500
1959-1960	Tweed, 3x10"	$5,000	$7,000
1960	Brown Tolex, 3x10"	$4,500	$5,500
1961	Rough White and Oxblood, 1x12"	$1,600	$2,000
1961-1962	Rough White and Oxblood, 2x12"	$1,500	$1,900
1963-1964	Smooth White and Gold, 2x12"	$1,400	$1,700
1964-1967	Black Tolex, 2x12"	$1,100	$1,500
1967-1969	Silverface, 2x12"	$850	$950
1970-1974	Silverface, 2x12"	$550	$750

Bandmaster Cabinet

1961-1975. Two 12" speakers.

1961-1963	Blond Tolex	$700	$900
1964-1967	Blackface horizontal	$400	$550
1967-1970	Silverface vertical cabinet	$350	$400

Bandmaster Head Amp

1961-1975. Non-reverb model.

1961-1962	Rough White Tolex	$700	$900
1963-1964	Smooth White Tolex	$700	$900
1964-1967	Blackface, Black Tolex	$500	$650
1967-1969	Silverface	$350	$450
1970-1971	Silverface, Black Tolex	$300	$400

Bandmaster Reverb Amp

1968-1981. Cabinet for 2x12", 45 watts, Silverface.

1968-1972	$800	$1,000
1973-1981	$700	$900

Bandmaster Reverb Head Amp

1968-1981. Reverb, 45 watts.

1969-1972	$500	$650
1973-1981	$400	$550

Bantam Bass Amp

1970-1972. 50 watts, large unusual 1x10" Yahama speaker.

1971-1972	$350	$450

Bassman Amp

1952-1971. Tweed TV front combo, 1x15" in '52, wide-panel '53-'54, narrow-panel and 4x10" '54-'60, Tolex, brownface with 1x12" in piggyback cabinet '61, 2x12" cabinet '61-'62, Blackface '63-'67, Silverface '67-'71, 2x15" cabinet '68-'71. Renamed the Bassman 50 in '72.

1952	TV front, 1x15"	$3,500	$4,500
1953-1954	Wide panel, 1x15"	$3,500	$4,500

AMPS

MODEL YEAR	FEATURES	EXC. COND. LOW	HIGH
1955-1957	Tweed, 4x10", two inputs	$5,000	$7,000
1957-1958	Tweed, 4x10", four inputs	$5,000	$7,000
1959-1960	Tweed, 4x10", four inputs	$5,500	$7,500
1961	White and Oxblood, 1x12"	$1,800	$2,200
1961-1962	White and Oxblood 2x12"	$1,700	$2,100
1963-1964	White and Gold, 2x12"	$1,500	$1,900
1964-1967	Black Tolex, 2x12"	$1,100	$1,500
1968-1969	Silverface, 2x15"	$800	$900
1970-1971	Silverface, 2x15"	$550	$750

Bassman Cabinet

1964-early-1967. Blackface, 2x12" small horizontal cab, replaced in 1967 with larger vertical cab.

1961-1963	Blond Tolex	$700	$900
1964-1967	Blackface	$400	$550

Bassman Head Amp

1961-1962	Rough White Tolex	$900	$1,100
1963-1964	Smooth White Tolex	$900	$1,100
1964-1967	Blackface, Black Tolex	$500	$650
1967-1969	Silverface, Black Tolex	$350	$450
1970-1971	Silverface, Black Tolex	$300	$400

Bassman '59 Reissue Amp

1990-present. Tube, 45 watts, 4x10", Tweed covering.

1990		$625	$725

Bassman 10 Amp

1972-1982. 4x10" combo, silver face and 50 watts for '72-'80, black face and 70 watts after.

1972-1980	50 watts	$300	$450
1981-1982	70 watts	$350	$450

Bassman 20 Amp

1982-1985. Tubes, 20 watts, 1x15".

1982-1985		$250	$350

Bassman 50 Amp

1972-1976. 50 watts, 2x12".

1972-1976		$350	$450

Bassman 70 Amp

1977-1979. 70 watts, 2x15".

1977-1979		$350	$450

Bassman 100 Amp

1972-1979. Tube, 100 watts, 4x12".

1972-1979		$450	$550

Bassman 135 Amp

1979-1983. Tube, 135 watts, 4x10".

1979-1983		$450	$550

Bassman 300 Amp Head

2000s. All tube, 300 watts, Black cover, Black metal grille.

2000		$650	$750

Bassman 400 Combo Amp

2000-present. Solidstate, 350 watts with 2x10" plus horn, combo, black cover, black metal grille.

2000-2002	Amp and cab	$500	$600
2000-2002	Head only	$300	$425

Bassman Bassbreaker (Custom Shop)

Ca. Early-2000 (not offered by 2004 when the '59 Bassman LTD was introduced). Classic Bassman 4x10" configuration.

2000s		$750	$800

Blues De Ville Amp

1993-1996. All tube Tweed Series, 60 watts, 4x10" (optional 2x12" in '94), reverb, high-gain channel, Tweed covered (blond Tolex optional '95 only).

1993-1996	Tweed, 4x10", 60 watts	$450	$525
1994-1996	Tweed, 2x12", 60 watts	$450	$525
1995	Blond Tolex, 4x10"	$500	$550

Blues Deluxe Amp

1993-1996. All tube Tweed Series, 40 watts, 2 5881 output tubes, reverb, 1x12", tweed covering (blond Tolex optional '95 only).

1993-1996	Tweed	$350	$450
1995	Blond	$400	$500

Blues Junior Amp

1995-present. All tube, 15 watts, 1x10", spring reverb, tweed in '95, black Tolex with silver grille '96 on.

1995-2000		$250	$325

Bronco Amp

1968-1974, 1993-2001. One 8" speaker, all tube, 5 watts until '72, 6 watts for '72-'74. '90s issue is 15 watts, solidstate, tweed covering (Blond Tolex was optional for '95 only).

1968-1974		$275	$375

Bullet Amp

1994-present. Solidstate, 15 watts, 1x8", with or without reverb.

1994-2000	With reverb	$100	$125

Capricorn Amp

1970-1972. Solidstate, 105 watts, 3x12".

1970-1972		$200	$300

Champ Amp

1953-1982. Renamed from the Champion 600. Tweed until '64, black tolex after, 3 watts in '53, 4 watts '54-'64, 5 watts '65-'71, 6 watts '72-'82, 1x6" until '57, 1x8" after.

1953-1954	Wide panel, 1x6"	$500	$750
1955-1956	Narrow panel, tweed, 1x6"	$550	$800
1956-1964	Narrow panel, tweed, 1x8"	$800	$1,000
1964	Old cab, black, 1x8"	$700	$900
1964-1967	New cab, black Tolex, 1x8"	$400	$550
1968-1972	Silverface, 1x8"	$250	$350
1973-1982	Silverface, 1x8"	$200	$325

Champ II Amp

1982-1985. 18 watts, 1x10".

1982-1985		$300	$400

Champ 12 Amp

1986-1992. Tube, 12 watts, overdrive, reverb, 1x12".

1986-1992	Black	$225	$325
1986-1992	Red, white, gray or snakeskin	$300	$350

Fender Blues Junior

1960 Fender Champ

1986 Fender Champ 12

AMPS

Fender Concert II 112

1955 Fender Deluxe

Fender Cyber-Twin

MODEL YEAR	FEATURES	LOW	HIGH

Champion 110 Amp
1993-2000. Solidstate, 25 watts, 1x10", 2 channels, black Tolex, silver grille.

1993-2000		$145	$185

Champion 600 Amp
1949-1953. Replaced the Champion 800, 3 watts, 1x6", two-tone Tolex, TV front. Replaced by the Champ.

1949-1953		$500	$750

Concert Amp
1960-1965, 1992-1995. Introduced with 40 watts and 4x10", brown Tolex until '63, blackface '63-'65. In '62 white Tolex was ordered by Webbs Music (CA) instead of the standard Brown Tolex. A wide range is noted for this "rare" White Tolex, and each amp should be valued on a case-by-case basis. In '60, the very first brown Tolex had a pink tint but only on the first year amps. Reissued in '92 with 60 watts and a 1x12".

1960	Brown (pink) Tolex	$1,600	$1,900
1961-1963	Brown Tolex	$1,600	$1,900
1962	White Tolex (Webb Music)	$1,800	$3,800
1963-1965	Blackface	$1,100	$1,500

Concert 112 Amp
1982-1985. Tube, 60 watts, 1x12".

1982-1985		$575	$675

Concert 210 Amp
1982-1985. Tube, 60 watts, 2x10".

1982-1985		$600	$700

Concert 410 Amp
1982-1985. Tube, 60 watts, 4x10".

1982-1985		$650	$750

Cyber Twin Combo Amp
2000-present.

2000-2003		$725	$825

Deluxe Amp
1948-1981. Name changed from Model 26 ('46-'48). 10 watts (15 by '54 and 20 by '63), 1x12", TV front with tweed '48-'53, wide-panel '53-'55, narrow-panel '55-'60, brown Tolex with brownface '61-'63, black Tolex with blackface '63-'66.

1948-1952	Tweed, TV front	$1,500	$2,200
1953-1954	Wide panel	$1,500	$2,200
1955-1956	Narrow panel, smaller cab	$2,000	$2,700
1956-1960	Narrow panel, slightly larger cab	$2,200	$2,800
1961-1963	Brown Tolex	$1,500	$1,700
1964-1966	Black Tolex	$900	$1,400

Deluxe Reverb Amp
1963-1981. Blackface '63-'67, silverface '68-'80. Mid-80 the blackface with silver grille option was introduced and lasted through '82. Discontinued in favor of Deluxe Reverb II.

1963-1967	Blackface	$2,000	$2,300
1968-1972	Silverface	$900	$1,200
1973-1980	Silverface	$700	$1,100
1980-1981	Blackface	$700	$1,100

Deluxe Reverb '65 Reissue Amp
1993-present. Blackface reissue, 22 watts, 1x12".

1993-1999	Black Tolex	$550	$650

1993-1999	Blond (limited production)	$600	$700

Deluxe Reverb II Amp
1982-1986. Updated Deluxe Reverb with 2x6V6 power tubes, all tube preamp section, black Tolex, blackface, 20 watts, 1x12".

1982-1983		$575	$675

Deluxe 85 Amp
1988-1993. Solidstate, 65 watts, 1x12", black Tolex, silver grille, Red Knob Series.

1988-1993		$200	$300

Deluxe 112 Amp
1992-1995. Solidstate, 65 watts, 1x12", Black Tolex with Silver grille.

1992-1995		$225	$300

Deluxe 112 Plus Amp
1995-2000. 90 watts, 1x12", channel switching.

1995-2000		$225	$325

Dual Professional Amp
1994-2002. Custom Shop amp, all tube, point-to-point wiring, 100 watts, 2x12" Celestion Vintage 30s, fat switch, reverb, tremolo, white Tolex, Oxblood grille.

1994-2002		$1,400	$1,500

Dual Showman Amp
1962-1969. Called the Double Showman for the first year. White Tolex (black available from '64), 2x15", 85 watts. Reintroduced '87-'94 as solidstate, 100 watts, optional speaker cabs.

1962	Rough Blond and Oxblood	$2,000	$2,500
1963	Smooth Blond and Wheat	$1,700	$2,300
1964-1967	Black Tolex, horizontal cab	$1,500	$1,900
1968	Blackface, large vertical cab	$1,000	$1,400
1968-1969	Silverface	$900	$1,000

Dual Showman Head Amp
1962-1969. Dual Showman head with output transformer for 2x15" (versus single Showman's 1x15" output ohms), Blackface '62-'67, the late-'67 model logo stipulated "Dual Showman" while the '62-early-'67 head merely stated Showman (could be a single Showman or Dual Showman), '68-'69 Silverface.

1962-1963	Blond	$1,100	$1,400
1964-1968	"Dual Showman" Blackface	$1,000	$1,200
1968-1969	Silverface	$550	$650

Dual Showman Reverb Amp
1968-1981. Black Tolex with Silver grille, Silverface, 100 watts, 2x15".

1968-1972		$900	$1,200
1973-1981		$800	$1,100

Dual Showman Reverb Head Amp
1968-1981. Amp only.

1969-1972	Includes TFL5000 series	$600	$750
1973-1981		$500	$650

MODEL YEAR	FEATURES	EXC. COND. LOW	HIGH

Frontman 15B Amp
1997-2002. 15 watts, 1x8" combo bass amp.

1997-2002		$75	$85

Frontman 25R Amp
1997-present. 25 watts, 1x10" student combo amp, 2 channels, reverb, EQ.

1997-2000		$90	$100

H.O.T. Amp
1990-1996. Solidstate, 25 watts, 1x10", gray carpet cover (black by 1992), black grille.

1990-1996		$80	$90

Harvard Amp (tube)
1956-1961. Tweed, 10 watts, 1x10", two knobs volume and roll-off tone, some were issued with 1x8".

1956-1961		$1,000	$1,300

Harvard Amp (solidstate)
1980-1983. Reintroduced from tube model. black Tolex with blackface, 20 watts, 1x10".

1980-1983		$100	$150

Harvard Reverb Amp
1981-1982. Solidstate, 20 watts, 1x10", reverb, replaced by Harvard Reverb II in 1983.

1981-1982		$150	$200

Harvard Reverb II Amp
1983-1985. Solidstate, black Tolex with blackface, 20 watts, 1x10", reverb.

1983-1985		$150	$200

Hot Rod De Ville 212 Amp
1996-present. Updated Blues De Ville. Tube, 60 watts, black Tolex, 2x12".

1996-2000		$475	$550

Hot Rod De Ville 410 Amp
1996-present. Tube, 60 watts, black Tolex, 4x10".

1996-2000		$475	$550

Hot Rod Deluxe Amp
1996-present. Updated Blues Deluxe. Tube, 40 watts, black Tolex (tweed optional by 1998), 1x12".

1996-2000		$400	$500

J.A.M. Amp
1990-1996. Solidstate, 25 watts, 1x12", four pre-programmed sounds, Gray carpet cover (Black by 1992).

1990-1996		$95	$105

Libra Amp
1970-1972. Solidstate, 105 watts, 4x12" JBL speakers, Black Tolex.

1970-1972		$300	$400

London Reverb Head Amp
1983-1985. Solidstate head, 100 watts.

1983-1985		$175	$275

London 185 Amp
1988-1992. Solidstate, 160 watts, black Tolex.

1988-1992	Head only	$200	$250

London Reverb 112 Amp
1983-1986. Solidstate, 100 watts, black Tolex, 1x12".

1983-1986		$250	$350

London Reverb 210 Amp
1983-1986. Solidstate, 100 watts, black Tolex, 2x10".

1983-1986		$275	$375

M-80 Amp
1989 1994. Solidstate, 90 watts, 1x12".

1989-1994		$200	$275

M-80 Bass Amp
1991-1994. Solidstate, bass and keyboard amp, 160 watts, 1x15".

1991-1994		$200	$250

M-80 Chorus Amp
1990-1994. Solidstate, stereo chorus, two 65-watt channels, 2x12".

1990-1994		$200	$275

Model 26 Amp
1946-1947. Tube, 10 watts, 1x10", hardwood cabinet. Sometimes called Deluxe Model 26, renamed Deluxe in 1948.

1946-1947		$2,000	$3,000

Montreux Amp
1983-1985. Solidstate, 100 watts, 1x12", Black Tolex with Silver grille.

1983-1985		$250	$350

Musicmaster Bass Amp
1970-1983. Tube, 12 watts, 1x12", Black Tolex.

1970-1972	Silverface	$250	$350
1973-1980	Silverface	$250	$300
1981-1983	Blackface	$250	$300

PA-100 Amp
100 watts.

1970s		$300	$500

Performer 650 Amp
1993-1995. Solidstate hybrid amp with single tube, 70 watts, 1x12".

1993-1995		$250	$300

Performer 1000 Amp
1993-1995. Solidstate hybrid amp with a single tube, 100 watts, 1x12".

1993-1995		$275	$325

Princeton Amp
1948-1979. Tube, 4.5 watts (12 watts by '61), 1x8" (1x10" by '61), tweed '48-'61, brown '61-'63, black with blackface '63-'69, silverface '69-'79.

1948-1953	Tweed, TV front	$900	$1,200
1953-1954	Tweed, wide panel	$900	$1,200
1955-1961	Tweed, narrow panel	$950	$1,200
1961-1963	Brown Tolex	$800	$1,000
1963-1967	Blackface	$550	$650
1968-1972	Silverface	$400	$475
1973-1979	Silverface	$375	$450

Princeton Chorus Amp
1988-1996. Solidstate, 2x10", two channels at 25 watts each, Black Tolex. Replaced by Princeton Stereo Chorus in 1996..

1988-1996		$275	$325

Princeton Reverb Amp
1964-1981. Tube, black Tolex, Blackface until 1967, Silverface after.

1964-1967	Blackface	$900	$1,200
1968-1972	Silverface	$700	$800
1973-1979	Silverface	$600	$700
1980-1981	Blackface	$600	$700

Fender Hot Rod Deluxe

'70s Fender Musicmaster Bass

AMPS

1957 Fender Princeton Amp

The ***Vintage Guitar Price Guide*** shows low to high values for items in all-original excellent condition, and, where applicable, with original case or cover.

Fender Pro Junior

Fender Pro Reverb

1980s Fender Showman Amp

MODEL YEAR	FEATURES	EXC. COND. LOW	HIGH
Princeton Reverb II Amp			
1982-1985. Tube amp, 20 watts, 1x12", black Tolex, silver grille, distortion feature.			
1982-1985		$500	$575
Princeton 112 Amp			
1993-1995. Solidstate, 40 watts, 1x12", Black Tolex.			
1993-1995		$150	$200
Pro 185 Amp			
1989-1991. Solidstate, 160 watts, 2x12", Black Tolex.			
1989-1991		$250	$300
Pro Amp			
1947-1965. Called Professional '46-'48. 15 watts (26 by '54 and 25 by '60), 1x15", tweed TV front '48-'53, wide-panel '53-'54, narrow-panel '55-'60, brown Tolex and brownface '60-'63, black and blackface '63-'65.			
1947-1953	Tweed, TV front	$2,500	$3,500
1953-1954	Wide panel	$2,500	$3,500
1955	Narrow panel (old chassis)	$2,500	$3,500
1955-1959	Narrow panel (new chassis intro'd.)	$3,000	$4,000
1960-1962	Brown Tolex	$1,500	$1,800
1963-1965	Black Tolex	$1,400	$1,700
Pro Reverb Amp			
1965-1982. Tube, Black Tolex, 40 watts (45 watts by 1972, 70 watts by 1981), 2x12", Blackface 1965-1969 and 1981-1983, Silverface 1969-1981.			
1965-1967	Blackface	$1,500	$2,000
1968-1972	Silverface	$900	$1,000
1973-1980	Silverface	$650	$900
1981-1982	Blackface	$650	$900
Pro Reverb Amp (reissue Pro Series)			
2002-present. 50 watts, 1x12", 2 modern designed channels - clean and high gain.			
2002		$750	$850
Pro Reverb Amp (solidstate)			
1967-1969. Fender's first attempt at solidstate design, the attempt was unsuccessful and many of these models will overheat and are known to be unreliable. 50 watts, 2x12", upright vertical comb cabinet.			
1967-1969		$300	$350
Pro Junior Amp			
1994-present. All tube, 2 EL84 tubes, 15 watts, 1x10" Alnico Blue speaker, tweed until '95, black Tolex '96 on.			
1994-1999		$275	$300
Prosonic Amp			
1996-2001. Custom Shop combo, 60 watts, two channels, three-way rectifier switch, 2x10" Celestion or separate cab with 4x12", tube reverb, black, red or green.			
1996-1999		$700	$800
Prosonic Head Amp			
1996-2001. Amp head only version.			
1996-1999		$500	$650
Quad Reverb Amp			
1971-1978. Black Tolex, silverface, 4x12", tube, 100 watts.			
1971-1978		$500	$675

MODEL YEAR	FEATURES	EXC. COND. LOW	HIGH
R.A.D. Amp			
1990-1996. Solidstate, 20 watts, 1x8", gray carpet cover until 1992, black after.			
1990-1996		$50	$60
R.A.D. Bass Amp			
1992-1994. 25 watts, 1x10", renamed BXR 25.			
1992-1994		$50	$65
Satellite SFX Amp			
1998-2000. Extension amp/cab, with a variety of digital effects, to be used with another amp, 1x12", black Tolex.			
1998-2000		$225	$250
Scorpio Amp			
1970-1972. Solidstate, 56 watts, 2x12", black Tolex.			
1970-1972		$250	$300
Showman 12 Amp			
1960-1966. Piggyback cabinet with 1x12", 85 watts, blond Tolex (changed to black in '64), maroon grille '61-'63 (gold grille '63-'64, silver grille '64-'67).			
1960-1962	Rough blond and Oxblood	$2,100	$2,800
1963-1964	Smooth blond and gold	$1,800	$2,500
1964-1966	Black	$1,500	$1,900
Showman 15 Amp			
1960-1968. Piggyback cabinet with 1x15", 85 watts, blond Tolex (changed to black in '64), maroon grille '61-'63 (gold grille '63-'64, silver grille '64-'67).			
1960-1962	Rough blond and Oxblood	$2,100	$2,800
1963-1964	Smooth blond and gold	$1,800	$2,500
1964-1967	Blackface	$1,500	$1,900
1967-1968	Silverface	$750	$900
Showman 112 Amp			
1983-1987. Solidstate, 2 channels, 200 watts, reverb, 4 button footswitch, 5-band EQ, effects loop, 1x12".			
1983-1987		$300	$425
Showman 115 Amp			
1983-1987. Solidstate, 1x15", 2 channels, reverb, EQ, effects loop, 200 watts, black Tolex.			
1983-1987		$300	$450
Showman 210 Amp			
1983-1987. Solidstate, two channels, reverb, EQ, effects loop, 2x10", 200 watts, Black Tolex.			
1983-1987		$300	$450
Showman 212 Amp			
1983-1987. Solidstate, two channels, reverb, EQ, effects loop, 2x12", 200 watts, Black Tolex.			
1983-1987		$325	$475
Sidekick 10 Amp			
1983-1985. Small solidstate Japanese or Mexican import, 10 watts, 1x8".			
1983-1985		$50	$75
Sidekick Reverb 20 Amp			
1983-1985. Small solidstate Japanese or Mexican import, 20 watts, reverb, 1x10".			
1983-1985		$75	$85

MODEL YEAR	FEATURES	EXC. COND. LOW	HIGH

Sidekick Reverb 30 Amp
1983-1985. Small solidstate Japanese or Mexican import, 30 watts, 1x12", reverb.

| 1983-1985 | | $90 | $105 |

Sidekick Reverb 65 Amp
1986-1988. Small solidstate Japanese or Mexican import, 65 watts, 1x12".

| 1986-1988 | | $100 | $125 |

Squire SKX 15 Amp
1990-1992. Solidstate, 15 watts, 1x8".

| 1990-1992 | | $35 | $50 |

Squire SKX 15R Amp
1990-1992. Solidstate, 15 watts, 1x8", reverb.

| 1990-1992 | | $50 | $65 |

Stage Lead/Stage Lead II Amp
1983-1985. Solidstate, 100 watts, 1x12", reverb, channel switching, Black Tolex. Stage Lead II has 2x12".

| 1983-1985 | 1x12" | $200 | $275 |
| 1983-1985 | 2x12" | $225 | $300 |

Studio Lead Amp
1983-1986. Solidstate, 50 watts, 1x12", Black Tolex.

| 1983-1986 | | $200 | $275 |

Super Amp
1947-1963, 1992-1997. Introduced as Dual Professional in 1946, renamed Super '47. Two 10" speakers, 20 watts (30 watts by '60 with 45 watts in '62), Tweed TV front '47-'53, wide-panel '53-'54, narrow-panel '55-'60, brown Tolex '60-'64. Reintroduced '92-'97 with 4x10", 60 watts, black Tolex.

1947-1952	Tweed, V front	$3,300	$3,700
1953-1954	Tweed, wide panel	$2,500	$3,500
1955	Tweed, narrow panel, 6L6 tubes	$3,000	$4,000
1956-1957	Tweed, narrow panel, 5E4, 6V6 tubes	$2,700	$3,500
1957-1960	Tweed, narrow panel, 6L6 tubes	$3,000	$4,000
1960	Pink/Brown metal knobs	$2,000	$2,500
1960-1962	Brown, Oxblood then Tan, 6G4 tubes	$1,900	$2,400

Super Reverb Amp
1963-1982. 4x10" speakers, blackface until '67 and '80-'82, silverface '68-'80.

1963-1967	Blackface	$1,800	$2,000
1967-1972	Silverface	$1,000	$1,200
1973-1980	Silverface, no MV	$750	$1,000
1981-1982	Blackface	$750	$1,000

Super Reverb '65 Reissue Amp
2001-present. 45 watts, all tube, 4x10", blackface cosmetics.

| 2001-2003 | | $800 | $850 |

Super 60 Amp
1989-1993. Red Knob series, 1x12", 60 watts, earlier versions with red knobs, later models with black knobs.

| 1989-1993 | | $250 | $350 |

Super 112 Amp
1990-1993. Red Knob series, 1x12", 60 watts, earlier versions with red knobs, later models with black knobs, originally designed to replace the Super60 but the Super 60 remained until 1993.

| 1990-1993 | | $250 | $350 |

Super 210 Amp
1990-1993. Red Knob series, 2x10", 60 watts, earlier versions with red knobs, later models with black knobs.

| 1990-1993 | | $300 | $400 |

Super (4x10") Amp
1992-1997. 60 watts, 4x10", black Tolex, silver grille, blackface control panel.

| 1992-1997 | | $550 | $600 |

Super Champ Amp
1982-1986. Black Tolex, 18 watts, blackface, 1x10".

| 1982-1986 | | $450 | $550 |

Super Champ Deluxe Amp
1982-1986. Solid oak cabinet, 18 watts, upgrade 10" Electro-Voice speaker, see-through brown grille cloth.

| 1982-1986 | | $900 | $1,000 |

Super Six Reverb Amp
1970-1979. Large combo amp based on the Twin Reverb chassis, 100 watts, 6x10", Black Tolex.

| 1970-1979 | | $650 | $750 |

Super Twin (non-reverb) Amp
1975-1976. 180 watts (using 6x6L6 power tubes), 2x12", distinctive dark grille.

| 1975-1976 | | $400 | $500 |

Super Twin Reverb Amp
1976-1980. 180 watts (using 6x6L6 power tubes), 2x12", distinctive dark grille.

| 1976-1980 | | $500 | $600 |

Taurus Amp
1970-1972. Solidstate, 42 watts, 2x10" JBL, Black Tolex, Silver grille, JBL badge.

| 1970-1972 | | $250 | $300 |

Tonemaster Head Amp
1993-2002. Custom Shop, hand-wired high-gain head, 100 watts, two channels, effects loop.

| 1993-1999 | | $800 | $900 |

Tonemaster Set Amp
1993-2002. Custom Shop, hand-wired head with Tonemaster 2x12" or 4x12" cabinet.

| 1993-1999 | Blond and Oxblood | $1,300 | $1,400 |
| 1993-1999 | Custom color Red | $1,400 | $1,500 |

Tonemaster 212 Cabinet
1993-2002. Custom Shop extension cabinet for Tonemaster head, blond Tolex, Oxblood grille, 2x12" Celestion Vintage 30.

| 1993-1999 | | $400 | $500 |

Tonemaster 412 Cabinet
1993-2002. Custom Shop extension cabinet for Tonemaster head, blond Tolex, 4x12" Celestion Vintage 30.

| 1993-1999 | | $400 | $500 |

Fender '65 Super Reverb

1959 Fender Super Amp

1969 Fender Super Reverb

1964 Fender Twin Reverb Amp

Fender '65 Twin Reverb reissue

1963 Fender Vibroverb Amp

MODEL YEAR	FEATURES	EXC. COND. LOW	HIGH
Tremolux Amp			
1955-1966. Tube, Tweed, 1x12" 1955-1960, white Tolex with piggyback 1x10" cabinet 1961-1962, 2x10" 1962-1964, black Tolex 1964-1966.			
1955-1960	Tweed, 1x12", narrow panel	$1,800	$2,200
1961	Rough White and Oxblood, 1x10"	$1,500	$2,200
1961-1962	Rough White and Oxblood, 2x10"	$1,500	$1,700
1963-1964	Smooth White and Gold, 2x10"	$1,400	$1,600
1964-1966	Black Tolex, 2x10"	$1,300	$1,500
Twin Amp			
1952-1963, 1996-present. Tube, 2x12"; 15 watts, tweed wide-panel '52-'55; narrow-panel '55-'60; 50 watts '55-'57; 80 watts '58; brown Tolex '60; white Tolex '61-'63. Reintroduced in '96 with black Tolex, spring reverb and output control for 100 watts or 25 watts.			
1953-1954	Tweed, wide-panel	$4,500	$5,500
1955-1957	Tweed, 50 watts	$5,000	$6,000
1958-1959	Tweed, 80 watts	$6,500	$9,000
1960	Brown Tolex, 80 watts	$6,500	$8,500
1960-1962	Rough White and Oxblood	$5,500	$6,500
1963	Smooth White and Gold	$5,000	$6,000
Twin Reverb Amp			
1963-1982. Black Tolex, 85 watts (changed to 135 watts in '81), 2x12", blackface '63-'67 and '81-'82, silverface '68-'80. Reverb reintroduced as Twin in '96.			
1963-1967	Blackface	$2,000	$2,300
1968-1972	Silverface, no master vol.	$1,000	$1,200
1973-1975	Silverface, master volume	$800	$1,000
1976-1980	Silverface, push/pull	$700	$950
1981-1982	Blackface	$700	$950
Twin Reverb '65 Reissue Amp			
1992-present. Black Tolex, 2x12", 85 watts.			
1992-1999	High or low output	$700	$800
Twin Reverb Amp (solidstate)			
1966-1969. 100 watts, 2x12", black Tolex.			
1966-1969		$350	$500
Twin Reverb II Amp			
1983-1985. Black Tolex, 2x12", 105 watts, channel switching, effects loop, blackface panel, silver grille.			
1983-1985		$700	$800
Twin "The Twin"/"Evil Twin" Amp			
1987-1992. 100 watts, 2x12", red knobs, most black Tolex, but white, red and snakeskin covers offered.			
1987-1992		$650	$750
Ultimate Stereo Chorus DSP Amp			
Solidstate, 2x65 watts, 2x12", 32 built-in effect variations, Blackface cosmetics.			
1999		$325	$400
Ultra Chorus Amp			
Introduced in 1993. Solidstate, 2x65 watts, 2x12", standard control panel with chorus.			
1990s		$275	$350

MODEL YEAR	FEATURES	EXC. COND. LOW	HIGH
Vibrasonic Amp			
1959-1963. First amp to receive the new brown Tolex and JBL, 1x15", 25 watts.			
1959-1963		$1,800	$2,200
Vibrasonic Custom Amp			
1995-1997. Custom Shop designed for steel guitar and guitar, blackface, 1x15", 100 watts.			
1995-1997	Blackface	$700	$800
Vibro-Champ Amp			
1964-1982. Black Tolex, 4 watts, (5 watts 1969-1971, 6 watts 1972-1980), 1x8", blackface 1964-1968, silverface 1969-1980.			
1964-1967	Blackface	$550	$650
1968-1972	Silverface	$300	$400
1973-1981	Silverface	$275	$375
1982	Blackface	$275	$375
Vibro-King Amp			
1993-present. Custom Shop combo, blond Tolex, 60 watts, 3x10", vintage reverb, tremolo, single channel, all tube.			
1993-1999		$1,200	$1,400
Vibro-King 212 Cabinet			
1993-present. Custom Shop extension cabinet, blond Tolex, 2x12" Celestion GK80.			
1993-1999		$400	$500
Vibrolux Amp			
1956-1964. Narrow-panel, 10 watts, tweed with 1x10" '56-'61, brown Tolex and brownface with 1x12" and 30 watts '61-'62, black Tolex and blackface '63-'64.			
1956-1961	Tweed, 1x10"	$1,500	$1,700
1961-1962	Brown Tolex, 1x12", 2x6L6	$1,700	$2,000
1963-1964	Black Tolex, 1x12"	$1,700	$2,000
Vibrolux Reverb Amp			
1964-1982. Black Tolex, 2x10", Blackface and 35 watts 1964-1969, Silverface and 40 watts 1970-1979. Reissued in 1996 with Blackface and 40 watts.			
1964-1967	Blackface	$2,300	$2,600
1968-1972	Silverface	$1,100	$1,400
1973-1980	Silverface	$900	$1,200
1981-1982	Blackface	$900	$1,200
Vibrolux Reverb (reissue) Amp			
1996-present. 40 watts, 2x10", all tube, black or blond Tolex.			
1996-1999	Blond and Tan	$700	$800
1996-2003	Black and Silver	$700	$850
Vibrolux Reverb Amp (solidstate)			
1968-1969. Black Tolex, 35 watts, 2x10".			
1968-1969		$300	$350
Vibrosonic Reverb Amp			
1972-1981. Black Tolex, 100 watts, 1x15", silverface.			
1972-1981		$650	$750
Vibroverb Amp			
1963-1964. Brown Tolex with 35 watts, 2x10" and brownface '63, black Tolex with 1x15" and blackface '64-'65.			
1963	Brown Tolex, 2x10"	$5,000	$6,000
1964	Black Tolex, 1x15"	$2,500	$4,000

MODEL		EXC. COND.	
YEAR	FEATURES	LOW	HIGH

Vibroverb '63 Reissue Amp
1990-1995. 40 watts, 2x10", reverb, vibrato, brown Tolex.

1990s		$700	$750

Yale Reverb Amp
1983-1985. Solidstate, black Tolex, 50 watts, 1x12", silverface.

1983-1985		$225	$275

Flot-A-Tone
Ca. 1946-early 1960s. Flot-A-Tone was located in Milwaukee, Wisconsin, and made a variety of tube guitar and acordion amps.

Large Amp
Four speakers.

1960s		$525	$800

Small Amp
One eight inch speaker.

1962		$300	$400

Fred
1984-1986. Before settling on the name Bedrock, company founders Brad Jeter and Ron Pinto produced 50 amps carrying the brand name Fred in Nashua, New Hampshire.

Fuchs Audio Technology
2000-present. Andy Fuchs started the company, located in Bloomfield, New Jersey, in '99 to rebuild and modify tube amps. In 2000 he started production of his own brand of amps, offering combos and heads from 10 to 150 watts. They also custom build audiophile and studio tube electronics.

Fulton-Webb
Ca. 1977-present. Steve Fulton and Bill Webb build their tube amp heads, combos and cabinets in Austin, Texas.

Gallien Krueger
1969-present. Gallien-Krueger has offered a variety of bass and guitar amps, combos and cabinets and is located in San Jose, California.

2100CEL Digital Stereo Guitar Combo Amp
1989-1991. 200 watts (100 per channel), 2x8", EQ, compression, chorus and reverb.

1989-1991		$300	$400

212GS Amp
1986-ca.1989. 140 watt mono or 70 watt stereo, 2x12", black carpet.

1986-1989		$275	$325

250ML Amp
Small practice amp, 2x4-1/2", chorus and echo.

1986-1989		$275	$325

Garnet
Mid 1960s-1989. In the mid '60's, "Gar" Gillies started the Garnet Amplifier Company with his two sons, Russell and Garnet, after he started making PA systems in his Canadian radio and TV repair shop. The first PA from the new company was for Chad Allen & the Expressions (later known as The Guess Who). A wide variety of tube amps were offered and all were designed by Gar, Sr. The company also produced the all-tube effects The Herzog, H-zog, and two stand alone reverb units designed by Gar in the late '60s and early '70s. The company closed in '89, due to financial reasons caused largely by a too rapid expansion. Gar still repairs and designs custom amps.

GDS Amplification
1998-present. Tube amps, combos and speaker cabinets from builder Graydon D. Stuckey of Flint, Michigan. GDS also offers amp kits.

Genesis
Genesis was a 1980s line of student amps from Gibson.

B40 Amp
1984-late-1980s. Bass combo with 40 watts.

1984-1989		$125	$175

G10 Amp
1984-late-1980s. Combo amp with 10 watts.

1984-1989		$75	$125

G25 Amp
1984-late-1980s. Combo amp with 25 watts.

1984-1989		$100	$150

G40R Amp
1984-late-1980s.Combo amp with 40 watts, reverb.

1984-1989		$150	$200

Genz Benz
1983-present. Founded by Jeff and Cathy Genzler and located in Scottsdale, Arizona, the company offers guitar, bass, and PA amps and speaker cabinets. In late 2003, Genz Benz was acquired by Kaman (Ovation, Hamer, Takamine).

George Dennis
1991-present. Founded by George Burgerstein, original products were a line of effects pedals. In '96 they added a line of tube amps. The company is located in Prague, Czech Republic, and the products are distributed in the U.S. by Midco International.

Gerhart
2000-present. Production/custom, amps and cabinets from builder Gary Gerhart of West Hills, California. He also offers an amp in kit form.

Germino
2002-present. Tube amps, combos and cabinets built by Greg Germino in Graham, North Carolina.

Gibson
1880s (1902)-present. Gibson has offered a variety of amps since the mid-'30s to the present under the Gibson brandname and others. The price ranges

Fuchs OD Supreme

Genz Benz El Diablo 60C

Germino Lead 55

AMPS

1960s Gibson Atlas

Gibson EH-185

'55 Gibson GA-5 Les Paul Junior

MODEL YEAR	FEATURES	EXC. COND. LOW	HIGH

listed are for excellent condition, all original amps though tubes may be replaced with affecting value. The prices listed are for amps with fully intact logos. A broken or missing logo can diminish the value of the amp. Amps with a changed handle, power cord, and especially a broken logo should be taken on a case-by-case basis.

Atlas IV Amp
1963-1967. Piggyback head and cab, introduced with trapezoid shape, changed to rectangular cabs in 1965-1966 with black cover, simple circuit with four knobs, no reverb or tremolo, mid-power with 2x6L6, 1x15".

1963-1965	Brown	$450	$650
1966-1967	Black	$450	$650

Atlas IV L Amp
1967. Atlas with Lansing speakers, offered only in 1967, black cover.

1967		$450	$650

Atlas Medalist Amp
1964-1967. Combo version with 1x15".

1964-1967		$450	$650

BR-1 Amp
1945-1949. 15 watts, 1x12" field-coil speaker, brown leatherette cover, rectangular metal grille with large G.

1945-1949		$350	$450

BR-3 Amp
1946-1947. 12 watts, 1x12" Utah field-coil speaker (most BR models used Jensen speakers).

1946-1947		$300	$400

BR-4 Amp
1946-1947. 14 watts, 1x12" Utah field-coil speaker (most BR models used Jensen speakers).

1946-1947		$350	$450

BR-6 Amp
1946-1956. 10 to 12 watts, 1x10", brown leatherette, speaker opening split by cross panel with G logo, bottom mounted chassis with single on-off volume pointer knob.

1946-1947	Verticle cab	$300	$400
1948-1956	Horizontal cab	$250	$325

BR-9 Amp
1948-1953. Cream leatherette, 10 watts, 1x8". Originally sold with the BR-9 lap steel. Renamed GA-9 in 1954.

1948-1953		$225	$300

EH-100 Amp
1936-1941. Electric-Hawaiian companion amp, 1x10"

1936-1941		$400	$500

EH-125 Amp
1941-1942. One 12" speaker, rounded shoulder cab, brown cover in 1941 and dark green in 1942, leather handle.

1941	Brown	$425	$525
1942	Dark green	$425	$525

EH-150 Amp
1935-1941. Electric-Hawaiian companion amp, 1x12".

1935	13 3/4" sq. cab	$500	$600

MODEL YEAR	FEATURES	EXC. COND. LOW	HIGH
1936-1937	14 3/4" sq. cab	$500	$600
1937-1942	15 3/8" round cab	$500	$600

EH-185 Amp
1939-1942. One 12" speaker, tweed cover with black and orange vertical stripes, round speaker opening with higher oblong opening, marketed as companion amp to the EH-185 Lap Steel.

1939-1942		$550	$650

Falcon Medalist Amp (hybrid)
1967. Transitional tube 1x12" combo amp from GA-19 tube Falcon to the solidstate Falcon, Falcon logo and Gibson logo on front panel, brown control panel, dark cover and dark grille, vertical combo cabinet.

1967		$250	$300

G-10 Amp
1972-1975. Solidstate, 10 watts, 1x10", no trem or reverb.

1972-1975		$75	$125

G-20 Amp
1972-1975. Solidstate with trem, 1x10", 10 watts.

1972-1975		$100	$175

G-30 Amp
1972. Solidstate without trem or reverb, 1x12", 15 watts.

1972		$125	$200

G-35 Amp
1975. Solidstate, 30 watts, 1x12".

1975		$150	$250

G-40 Amp
1972. Solidstate with trem and reverb, 1x12", 20 watts.

1972		$200	$300

G-50 Amp
1972. Solidstate with trem and reverb, 1x12", 40 watts.

1972		$225	$325

G-60 Amp
1972. Solidstate with trem and reverb, 1x15", 60 watts.

1972		$225	$325

G-70 Amp
1972. Solidstate with trem and reverb, 2x12", 60 watts.

1972		$250	$350

G-80 Amp
1972. Solidstate with trem and reverb, 4x10", 60 watts.

1972		$250	$350

GA-5 Les Paul Jr. Amp
1954-1957. Tan fabric cover (mottled brown by '47), 7" oval speaker, 4 watts. Renamed Skylark in 1958.

1954-1957		$200	$300

GA-5 Skylark Amp
1957-1967. Gold cover (brown by '63 and black by '66), 1x8" (1x10" from '64 on), 4.5 watts (10 watts from '64 on), tremolo. Often sold with the Skylark Lap Steel.

1957-1962	Gold, 4.5 watts, 1x8"	$200	$275
1963	Brown, 4.5 watts, 1x8"	$200	$250

AMPS

MODEL YEAR	FEATURES	EXC. COND. LOW	HIGH
1964	Brown, 10 watts, 1x10"	$200	$250
1965-1967	Black, 10 watts, 1x10"	$200	$250

GA-5 T Skylark Amp
1960-1967. Tremolo, 4.5 watts, gold covering and 1x8" until '63, brown '63-'64, black and 1x10" after.

1961-1962	Gold, 4.5 watts, 1x8"	$250	$300
1963	Brown, 4.5 watts, 1x8"	$250	$300
1964	Brown, 10 watts, 1x10"	$250	$300
1965-1967	Black, 10 watts, 1x10"	$250	$300

GA-6 Amp
1956-1959. Replaced the BR-6, 8 to 12 watts, 1x12", 'Gibson 6' above the grill. Renamed GA-6 Lancer in '60.

1956-1959		$300	$400

GA-6 Lancer Amp
1960-1962. Renamed from GA-6, 1x12", tweed cover, three knobs.

1960-1962		$500	$600

GA-8 Discoverer Amp
1962-1964. Renamed from GA-8 Gibsonette. Gold fabric cover, 1x12", 10 watts.

1962-1964		$275	$400

GA-8 Gibsonette Amp
1952-1962. Tan fabric cover (gold by 1958), 1x10", 8 watts (nine watts by 1958). Name changed to GA-8 Discoverer in 1962.

1952-1957	Gibsonette logo on front	$325	$400
1958-1959	Gibson logo on front	$325	$400
1960-1962	Gibson logo upper right front	$325	$400

GA-8T Discoverer Amp
1960-1967. Gold fabric cover, 1x10", 9 watts (tan cover, 1x12" and 15 watts by 1963), tremolo.

1960-1962	9 watts, 1x10"	$300	$450
1963-1967	15 watts, 1x12"	$300	$450

GA-9 Amp
1954-1961. Renamed from BR-9. Tan fabric cover, 8 watts, 1x10". Often sold with the BR-9 Lap Steel.

1954-1961		$300	$350
1956-1957	Gibson 9 logo	$300	$350
1958-1961	Metal handle	$300	$350

GA-14 Titan Amp
1959-1961. About 15 watts using 2x6V6 power tubes, 1x10", tweed cover.

1959-1961		$450	$550

GA-15 RV (Custom Shop) Amp
2002. Custom Shop built, 15 watts, 1x12", quilted maple cabinet in natural finish, companion amp to Custom Shop L-5C or Super 400 set.

2002		$1,900	$2,100

GA-15 RV Goldtone Amp
1999-present. 15 watts, Class A, 1x12", spring reverb.

1999-2002		$300	$425

GA-15 RVT Explorer amp
1965-1967. Tube, 1x10", tremolo, reverb, black vinyl.

1965-1967		$300	$350

GA-17 RVT Scout Amp
1963-1965. Low power, 1x12", reverb and tremolo.

1963-1964	Brown	$300	$475
1965	Black	$275	$450

GA-18 Explorer Amp
1959. Tube, 14 watts, 1x10". Replaced in '60 by the GA-18T Explorer.

1959		$450	$550

GA-18T Explorer Amp
1959-1964. Tweed, 14 watts, 1x10", tremolo.

1959-1962		$550	$650
1963-1964		$300	$400

GA-19 RVT Falcon Amp
1961-1966. One of Gibson's best selling amps. Initially tweed covered, followed by smooth brown, textured brown, and black. Each amp has a different tone. One 12" Jensen with deep-sounding reverb and tremolo.

1961-1962	Tweed	$600	$700
1961-1963	Smooth brown	$400	$450
1964	Textured brown	$350	$425
1965-1966	Black	$350	$425

GA-20/GA-20 Crest Amp
1950-1962. Brown leatherette (two-tone by 1955 and tweed by 1960), tube, 12 watts early, 14 watts later, 1x12". Renamed Crest in 1960.

1952-1954	Brown, 14 watts	$550	$700
1955-1958	Two-Tone, 14 watts	$600	$725
1959-1962	Tweed/Crest, 14 watts	$650	$750

GA-20 RVT Minuteman Amp
1965-1967. Black, 14 watts, 1x12", tube, reverb, tremolo.

1965-1967		$350	$500

GA-20 T Amp
1956-1962. Tube, 16 watts, tremolo, 1x12". Renamed Ranger in 1960.

1956-1958	Two-tone	$650	$750
1959-1962	Tweed	$700	$800

GA-25 Amp
1947-1948. Brown, 1x12" and 1x8", 15 watts. Replaced by GA-30 in 1948.

1947-1948		$400	$500

GA-25 RVT Hawk Amp
1963-1967. Reverb, tremolo, 1x15".

1963	Smooth brown	$400	$500
1964	Rough brown	$300	$500
1965-1967	Black	$300	$500

GA-30 Amp
1948-1961. Brown until 1954, two-tone after, Tweed in 1960, 1x12" and 1x8", 14 watts. Renamed Invader in 1960.

1948-1954	Brown	$600	$700
1955-1958	Two-tone	$650	$750
1959	Tweed	$700	$800

GA-30 RV Invader Amp
1961-1962. Tweed, 1x12" and 1x8", 14-16 watts, reverb but no trem.

1961-1962		$900	$1,100

Gibson GA-15 RVT Explorer

1965 Gibson GA-19RVT Falcon

1962 Gibson GA-20T Ranger

'54 Gibson GA-40
Les Paul Amp

1959 Gibson GA-55
RVT Ranger

1962 Gibson GA-200
Rhythm King

MODEL YEAR	FEATURES	EXC. COND. LOW	HIGH

GA-30 RVT Invader Amp
1962-1964. Updated model with reverb and tremolo, dual speakers 1x12" and 1x8", first issue in tweed.

1962	Tweed	$800	$1,000
1963	Smooth brown	$500	$600
1964	Rough brown	$500	$600

GA-35 RVT Lancer Amp
1966-1967. Black, 1x12", tremolo, reverb.

1966-1967		$400	$500

GA-40 Les Paul Amp
1952-1960. Introduced in conjunction with the Les Paul Model guitar. 1x12" Jensen speaker, 14 watts on early models and 16 watts later, recessed leather handle using spring mounting (the handle is easily broken and an unsimilar replacement handle is more common than not). Two-tone leatherette covering, '50s checkerboard grille ('52-early-'55), Les Paul script logo on front of the amp ('52-'55), plastic grille insert with 'LP' monogram, Gold Gibson logo above grille. Cosmetics changed dramatically in early/mid-'55. Renamed GA-40 T Les Paul in '60.

1952-1955	Brown two-tone, LP grille	$900	$1,200
1955-1956	Mottled Gray two-tone	$900	$1,200
1957-1959	Two-tone	$900	$1,200
1959-1960	Tweed	$800	$1,000

GA-40 T Les Paul Amp
1960-1965. Renamed from GA-40 Les Paul, 1x12", 16 watts, tremolo. Renamed Mariner in 1965-1967.

1961	Tweed	$800	$900
1962-1963	Smooth Brown	$600	$650
1964-1965	Rough Brown	$400	$500

GA-45 RVT Saturn Amp
1965-1967. 2x10", mid power, tremolo, reverb.

1965-1967		$450	$550

GA-50 T Amp
1948-1955. Brown leatherette, 25 watts, 1x12" and 1x8", tremolo.

1948-1955		$1,000	$1,100

GA-55 RVT Ranger Amp
1965-1967. Black cover, 4x10", tremolo, reverb.

1965-1967		$550	$650

GA-55/GA-55 V Amp
1954-1958. With or without vibrato, 2x12", 20 watts.

1954-1958	GA-55 V with vibrato	$1,500	$1,700

GA-70 Country and Western Amp
1955-1958. 25 watts, 1x15", two-tone, long-horn cattle western logo on front, advertised to have extra bright sound.

1955-1958		$1,200	$1,500

GA-75 Amp
1950-1955. Mottled Brown leatherette, 1x15", 25 watts.

1950-1955		$900	$1,100

GA-75 L Recording Amp
Mid-1960s. One 15" Lansing speaker, no reverb, no tremolo, two channels, dark cover, gray grille.

1966		$500	$600

GA-75 Recording Amp
Mid-1960s. Two 10" speakers, no reverb, no tremolo, two channels, dark cover, gray grille.

1966		$500	$600

GA-77 Amp
1954-1960. Brown Tolex, 1x15" JBL, 25 watts, two 6L6 power tubes, near top-of-the-line for the mid-1950s.

1954-1958	Two-tone	$1,000	$1,200
1959-1960	Tweed	$1,000	$1,200

GA-77 RET Amp
1964-1967. Two 10" speakers, reverb, echo, tremolo.

1964-1967		$500	$600

GA-79 RV Amp
1960-1962. Stereo-reverb, 2x10", 30 watts.

1960-1961	Tweed	$1,700	$2,400
1962	Gray tolex	$1,500	$2,200

GA-79 RVT Multi-Stereo Amp
1961-1967. Introduced as GA-79 RVT, Multi-Stereo was added to name in '61. Stereo-reverb and tremolo, 2x10", tweed (black and brown also available), 30 watts.

1961-1962	Gray	$1,500	$2,200
1963-1964	Textured Brown	$1,500	$2,200
1965-1967	Black	$1,300	$1,800

GA-80 T Vari-Tone Amp
1959-1961. 25 watts, 1x15", 2 channels, described as "6-in-1 amplifier with improved tremolo," 6 Vari-Tone pushbottons which give "six distinctively separate sounds," 7 tubes, tweed cover.

1959-1961		$1,100	$1,400

GA-83 S Stereo-Vibe Amp
1959-1961. Interesting stereo amp with front baffle mounted 1x12" and 4x8" side-mounted speakers (2 on each side), 35 watts, Gibson logo on upper right corner of the grille, tweed cover, brown grill (late '50s Fender-style), three pointer knobs and 3 round knobs, 4 inputs.

1959-1961		$1,500	$2,200

GA-85 Bass Reflex Amp
1957-1958. Removable head, 25 watts, 1x12", very limited production.

1957-1958		$600	$800

GA-90 High Fidelity Amp
1953-1960. 25 watts, 6x8", 2 channels, advertised for guitar, bass, accordion, or hi-fi.

1953-1960		$1,000	$1,300

GA-95 RVT Apollo Amp
1965-1967. 90 watts, 2x12", black vinyl, black grille, tremolo, reverb.

1965-1967		$550	$650

GA-100 Bass Amp
1960-1963. Tweed, 35 watts, 1x12" cabinet, tripod was available for separate head.

1960-1963		$600	$700

GA-200 Rhythm King Amp
1957-1962. Introduced as GA-200, renamed Rhythm King in 1960, two-channel version of GA-400. Bass amp, 60 watts, 2x12".

1957-1959	Two-tone	$1,500	$1,700
1959-1962	Tweed	$1,500	$1,700

The *Vintage Guitar Price Guide* shows low to high values for items in all-original excellent condition, and, where applicable, with original case or cover.

MODEL YEAR	FEATURES	EXC. COND. LOW	HIGH

GA-400 Super 400 Amp
1957-1962. 60 watts, 2x12", 3 channels, same size as GA-200 cab, one more tube than GA-200.

1957-1959	Two-tone	$1,550	$1,750
1959-1962	Tweed	$1,550	$1,750

GSS-100 Amp
1966-1967. Solidstate, 100 watts, two 24"x12" 2x10" sealed cabs, black vinyl cover, silver grille, 8 Black knobs and 3 red knobs, slanted raised Gibson logo. Speakers prone to distortion.

1966-1967	$500	$550

GSS-50 Amp
1966-1967. Solidstate, 50 watts, 2x10" combo, reverb and tremolo, black vinyl cover, silver grille, no grille logo.

1966-1967	$400	$450

LP-1/LP-2 Amp Set
1970. Les Paul model, piggyback amp and cab set, LP-1 head and LP-2 4x12" plus 2 horns cab, large vertical speaker cabinet, rather small compact 190 watt solidstate amp head.

1970	$300	$400

Medalist 2/12 Amp
Late-1960s-1970. Vertical cab, 2x12", reverb and temolo.

1970	$350	$425

Medalist 4/10 Amp
Late-1960s-1970. Vertical cab, 4x10", reverb and tremolo.

1970	$350	$425

Mercury I Amp
1963-1965. Piggyback trapezoid-shaped head with 2x12" trapezoid cabinet, tremolo, brown.

1963-1965	$300	$500

Mercury II Amp
1963-1967. Mercury I with 1x15" and 1x10", initially trapezoid cabs then changed to rectangular.

1963-1964	Brown trapezoid cabs	$300	$500
1965-1967	Black rectangular cabs	$300	$500

Plus-50 Amp
1966-1967. 50 watts, add-or/powered extension amplifier, usable with another master amplifier. Similar to GSS-100 cabinet of the same era, 2x10" cab, black vinyl cover, silver grille, slant Gibson logo.

1966-1967	$400	$500

Super Thor Bass Amp
1972-1974. Solidstate, part of the new G-Series (not GA-Series), 65 watts, 2x15", black Tolex, black grille, upright vertical cab with front control, single channel.

1972-1974	$250	$350

Thor Bass Amp
1970-1974. Solidstate, smaller 2x10" 50 watt version of Super Thor.

1970-1974	$225	$325

Titan I Amp
1963-1965. Piggyback trapezoid-shaped head and 2x12" trapezoid-shaped cabinet, tremolo.

1963-1965	$250	$500

Titan III Amp
1963-1967. Piggyback trapezoid-shaped head and 1x15" + 2x10" trapezoid-shaped cabinet, tremolo.

1963-1964	Brown	$300	$600
1965-1967	Black	$300	$600

Titan V Amp
1963-1967. Piggyback trapezoid-shaped tube head and 2x15" trapezoid-shaped cabinet, tremolo.

1963-1964	Brown	$300	$600
1965-1967	Black	$300	$600

Titan Medalist Amp
1964-1967. Combo version of Titan Series with 1x15" and 1x10", tremolo only, no reverb, Black.

1964-1967	$300	$600

Ginelle
1996-present. Rick Emery builds his tube combo amps in West Berlin, New Jersey.

Gorilla
1980s-present. Small solidstate entry-level amps, distributed by Pignose, Las Vegas.

Compact Practice Student Amp
1980s-present. Solidstate, 10 to 30 watts, compact design.

1980s	$35	$55
1990s	$35	$55
2000s	$40	$60

Goya
1955-1996. Goya was mainly known for acoustics, but offered a few amps in the '60s. The brand was purchased by Avnet/Guild in 1966 and by Martin in the late '70s.

Amps

1960s	Various models	$100	$175

Green
1993-present. Amp model line made in England by Matamp (see that brand for listing), bright green covering, large Green logo on the front.

Gretsch
1883-present. Gretsch offered amps from the '50s to '73. Initially private branded for them by Valco (look for the Valco oval or rectangular serialized label on the back). Early-'50s amps were covered in the requisite tweed, but evolved into the Gretsch charcoal gray covering. The mid-'50s to early-'60s amps were part of the Electromatic group of amps. The mid-'50s to '62 amps often sported wrap-around and slanted grilles. In '62, the more traditional box style was introduced. In '66, the large amps went piggy-back. Baldwin-Gretsch began to phase out amps effective '65, but solidstate amps continued being offered for a period of time. The 1973 Gretsch product line only offered Sonax amps, made in Canada and Sho-Bud amps made in the U.S.A.

Gibson Thor

AMPS

Ginelle El Toro Pequeno

Gorilla GG-20

1950s Gretsch Model 6169 Electromatic Twin

1964 Gretsch 6164 Variety

Groove Tubes Soul-O Single

MODEL YEAR	FEATURES	EXC. COND. LOW	HIGH

Model 6150 Compact Amp
Early-1950s-1960s. Early amps in tweed, 1960s amps in gray covering, no tremolo, single volume knob, no treble or bass knob, 1x8".

1950s	Brown tweed	$275	$325
1960s	Gray	$275	$325

Model 6151/6151 Compact Tremolo Amp
Late 1940s-late 1960s. 1x8".

1940s	Various covers	$325	$400
1950s	Various covers	$325	$400
1960s	Various covers	$325	$400

Model 6152 Compact Tremolo Reverb Amp
Ca.1964-late-1960s. 5 watts, 11x6" elliptical speaker early on, 1x12" later.

1964-1966	Elliptical speaker	$450	$550
1967-1969	Round speaker	$450	$550

Model 6154 Super-Bass Amp
Early-1960s-mid-1960s. Gray covering, 2x12", 70 watts, tube.

1963	Gray	$400	$500

Model 6156 Playboy Amp
Early-1950s-1966. Tube amp, 17 watts, 1x10" until 1961 when converted to 1x12", tweed, then gray, then finally black covered.

1950s	Tweed	$375	$500
1960-1962	Tweed, 1x10" or 1x12"	$375	$500
1963-1966	Black or gray, 1x12"	$375	$500

Model 6157 Super Bass Amp (piggyback)
Mid-late-1960s. 35 watts, 2x15" cabinet, single channel.

1960s		$375	$475

Model 6159 Super Bass/Dual Playboy Amp (combo)
Mid-late-1960s. 35 watts, tube, 2x12" cabinet, dual channel, black covering. Replaced by 6163 Chet Atkins Piggyback Amp.

1960s	Black	$425	$500

Model 6160 Chet Atkins Country Gentleman Amp
Early-late-1960s. Combo tube amp, 35 watts, 2x12" cabinet, two channels. Replaced by 6163 Chet Atkins Piggyback amp with tremolo but no reverb.

1960s		$450	$550

Model 6161 Dual Twin Tremolo Amp
Ca.1962-late-1960s. 19 watts (later 17 watts), 2x10" with 5" tweeter, tremolo.

1960s		$450	$600

Model 6161 Electromatic Twin Amp
Ca.1953-ca.1960. Gray silverflake covering, two 11x6" speakers, 14 watts, tremolo, wraparound grille 1955 and after.

1950s		$450	$600

Model 6162 Dual Twin Tremolo & Reverb Amp
Ca.1964-late-1960s. 17 watts, 2x10", reverb, tremolo. Vertical combo amp style introduced in '68.

1964-1967	Horizontal combo style	$500	$600
1968-1969	Vertical combo style	$500	$600

Model 6163 Chet Atkins Amp (piggyback)

Mid-late-1960s. 70 watts,1x12" and 1x15", black covering, tremolo, reverb.

1960s		$450	$550

Model 6164 Variety Amp
Early-mid-1960s. 35 watts, tube, 2x12".

1960s		$450	$500

Model 6165 Variety Plus Amp
Early-mid-1960s. Tube amp, 35 watts, 2x12", reverb and tremolo, separate controls for both channels.

1960s		$550	$650

Model 6166 Fury Amp
Mid-1960s. Tube combo amp, 70 watts, 2x12", separate controls for both channels, large metal handle.

1960s		$450	$550

Model 6169 Electromatic Twin Western Finish Amp
Ca.1953-ca.1960. Western finish, 14 watts, two 11x6" speakers, tremolo, wraparound grill 1955 and after.

1950s		$1,400	$2,000

Model 6169 Fury Amp (piggyback)
Late-1960s. Tube amp, 70 watts, 2x12", separate controls for both channels.

1960s		$400	$500

Model 6170 Pro Bass Amp
1966-late-1960s. 25 or 35 watts, depending on model, 1x15", vertical cabinet style (vs. box cabinet).

1966-1969		$300	$350

Model 7154 Nashville Amp
Introduced in 1969. Solidstate combo amp, 4 feet tall, 75 watts, 2x15", reverb, tremolo, magic echo.

1970s		$450	$550

Model 7155 Tornado PA System Amp
Introduced in 1969. Solidstate piggyback head and cab, 150 watts, two column speaker cabs, reverb, trem, magic echo.

1970s	2x2x15"	$450	$550
1970s	2x4x15"	$550	$650

Model 7517 Rogue Amp
1970s. Solidstate, 40 watts, 2x12", tall vertical cabinet, front control panel.

1970s		$225	$275

Groove Tubes
1979-present. Started by Aspen Pittman in his garage in Sylmar, California, Groove Tubes is now located in San Fernando. GT manufactures and distributes a full line of tubes. In '86 they added amp production and in '91 tube microphones. Aspen is also the author of the *Tube Amp Book*.

Guild
1952-present. Guild offered amps from the '60s into the '80s. Some of the early models were built by Hagstrom.

Model Four Amp
Early-1980s. 6 watts.

1980s		$100	$175

Model Five Amp
Early-1980s. 10 watts, 6.25" speaker.

1980s		$100	$175

MODEL YEAR	FEATURES	EXC. COND. LOW	HIGH

Model Six Amp
Early 1980s. Same as Model Five but with reverb.

1980s		$100	$175

Model Seven Amp
Early-1980s. Small amp for guitar, bass and keyboard, 12 watts.

1980s		$100	$175

Thunderbird Amp

1960s		$300	$375

Thunderstar Bass Amp
1960s. 50 watts, bass head or combo.

1966-1968		$450	$650

Guytron
1995-present. Tube amp heads and speaker cabinets built by Guy Hedrick in Columbiaville, Michigan.

Hagstrom
1921-1983. The Swedish guitar maker built a variety of tube and solid state amps from ca. 1961 into the '70s. They also supplied amps to Guild.

Harmony
1892-1976, late 1970s-present. Harmony was one of the biggest producers of guitars, and offered amps as well. MBT International offered Harmony amps for 2000-'02.

Small Tube Amps

1950s		$150	$250

Model H-303A Amp
1960s. Valco-made, like Supro, black covering, silver grille, large Harmony logo upper left front, 1x8", blue bottom-mounted control panel with one chicken head control knob.

1960s		$225	$300

Model H-305A Amp
1960s. Valco-made, like Supro, black covering, Harmony silver front panel.

1960s		$250	$350

Model H-415 Amp
1960s. Valco-made, like Supro, black covering, Harmony silver front panel, 20 watts, 2x10".

1960s		$300	$400

Model H-420 Amp
1960s. Valco-made, like Supro Thunderbolt, black covering, Harmony silver front panel, 20 watts, all tube combo, 1x12".

1960s		$300	$400

Small Solidstate Amps
Dark covering, dark grille.

1970s		$75	$125

Harry Joyce
1993-2000. Hand-wired British tube amps, combos, and cabinets from builder Harry Joyce. Joyce was contracted to build Hiwatt amps in England during the '60s and '70s. He passed away on January 11, 2002.

Hartke
1984-present. Made in the United States. Founded by Larry Hartke, specializing in bass amps. Since the mid-'80s, Hartke has been distributed by Samson Technologies. Hartke also offered basses in the past.

4.5 XL Cab
1994-present. XL Series, 4x10" and 5" driver rated at 400 watts, larger ported cab.

1994-2001		$350	$450

2000 Bass Head Amp
1992-present. 200 watts, tube preamp, solidstate power section, tube/solidstate switchable.

1992-2000		$250	$350

3500 Bass Head Amp
1992-present. Solidstate, 350 watts, 10-band graphic equalizer, rack-mount.

1992-2000		$300	$400

B 30 Bass Combo Amp
1999-present. Compact practice amp, 30 watts, 1x10".

1999-2000		$125	$150

Transporter 115TP Cab
1993-present. 1x15" speaker cabinet, rated at 150 watts.

1993-2000		$225	$250

Transporter 4x10" Cab
1990s. Cab with 4x10", rated at 300 watts, Black cover, Black metal grille.

1990s		$275	$350

XL115B Cab
1994-present. XL Series, 1x15" rated at 200 watts, larger cab.

1994-2000		$250	$300

Haynes
Haynes guitar amps were built by the Amplifier Corporation of America (ACA) of Westbury, New York. ACA also made an early distortion device powered by batteries. Unicord purchased the company in around 1964, and used the factory to produce its Univox line of amps, most likely discontinuing the Haynes brand at the same time.

Jazz King II Amp
1960s. Solidstate, stereo console-style, 2x12", Haynes logo upper right side.

1960s		$175	$275

Headstrong
2003-present. Tube combo amps built by Wayne Jones in Asheville, North Carolina. They also offer a range of replacement cabinets for vintage amps.

Hilgen
1960s. Mid-level amplifiers from Hilgen Manufacturing, Hillside, New Jersey. Dark Tolex covering and swiggle-lined light color grille cloth. Examples have been found with original Jensen speakers.

Harmony H-430

Hartke B120

Headstrong Blue Lamp 210

HiWatt Bulldog SA112

Holland Lil' Jimi

Holmes Pro 112

MODEL YEAR	FEATURES	EXC. COND. LOW	HIGH
Basso Grande Bass Amp Head			
1960s. Brown metallic sparkle cover, four inputs.			
1960s		$175	$200
Model T-2512 Star Amp			
1960s. 25 watts, 1x12" combo, tremolo.			
1960s		$225	$275
Model T-2513 Galaxie Amp			
1960s. 25 watts, 1x12" piggyback cabinet, tremolo.			
1960s		$225	$275

HiWatt

MODEL YEAR	FEATURES	EXC. COND. LOW	HIGH
Bulldog SA112 Amp			
1980s, 1994-present. 50 watts, combo, 1x12".			
1980s		$700	$1,000
Bulldog SA112FL Amp			
1980s. 100 watts, combo, 1x12".			
1980s		$700	$1,000
Lead 20 (SG-20) Amp Head			
1980s. Tube amp head, 30 watts, Black cover, rectangular HiWatt plate logo.			
1980s		$500	$900
Lead 50R (combo) Amp			
1980s. Combo tube amp, 50 watts, 1x12", reverb, dark cover, dark grille, HiWatt rectangular plate logo.			
1980s		$700	$900
Model DR-103 Amp Head			
1970-late-1980s, 1995-present. Tube head, 100 watts.			
1970-1977		$1,000	$1,300
1978-1988		$900	$1,200
Model DR-504 Amp Head			
1970-late-1980s, 1995-1999. Tube head amp, 50 watts.			
1970-1977		$1,000	$1,200
1978-1987		$800	$1,100
PW-50 Tube Amp			
1989-1993. Stereo tube amp, 50 watts per channel.			
1989-1993		$500	$900
S50L Amp Head			
1989-1993. Lead guitar head, 50 watts, gain, master volume, EQ.			
1989-1993		$400	$700
SE 4122 4x12 Speaker Cabinet			
1971- mid-1980s. Salt and Pepper grille cloth, 4x12" Fane speakers, 300 watts.			
1970s		$1,000	$1,300

Hoffman

1993-present. Tube amps, combos, reverb units, and cabinets built by Doug Hoffman from 1993 to '99, in Sarasota, Florida. Hoffman no longer builds amps, concentrating on selling tube amp building supplies, and since 2001 has been located in Pisgah Forest, North Carolina.

Hohner

1857-present. Matthias Hohner, a clockmaker in Trossingen, Germany, founded Hohner in 1857, making harmonicas. Hohner has been offering guitars and amps at least since the early '70s.

MODEL YEAR	FEATURES	EXC. COND. LOW	HIGH
Panther P-12 Amp			
12 watts, master volume, gain, eq.			
1980s		$65	$100
Panther P-20 Amp			
20 watts, master volume, gain, eq.			
1980s		$75	$140
Panther P-25R Amp			
25 watts, master volume, gain, eq.			
1980s		$100	$150
Panther PBK-20 Amp			
25 watts for bass/keyboard, master volume, gain, eq.			
1980s		$100	$150
Sound Producer BA 130 Bass Amp			
Dual channels, EQ, master volume, bass, middle, and treble controls for each channel.			
1980s		$80	$150
Sound Producer SP 35 Amp			
Master volume, normal and overdrive, reverb, headphone jack.			
1980s		$70	$125
Sound Producer SP 55 Amp			
Master volume, normal and overdrive, reverb, headphone jack.			
1980s		$100	$150
Sound Producer SP 75 Amp			
Master volume, normal and overdrive, reverb, headphone jack.			
1980s		$127	$175

Holland

1992-present. Tube combo amps from builder Mike Holland, originally in Virginia Beach, Virginia, and since 2000 in Brentwood, Tennessee. In 2000, Holland took Lane Zastrow as a partner, forming L&M Amplifiers, which owns the Holland brand.

Holmes

1970-late 1980s. Founded by Harrison Holmes. Holmes amplifiers were manufactured in Mississippi and their product line included guitar and bass amps, PA systems, and mixing boards. In the early '80s, Harrsion Holmes sold the company to On-Site Music which called the firm The Holmes Corp. Products manufactured by Harrison have an all-caps HOLMES logo and the serial number plate says "The Holmes Company."

MODEL YEAR	FEATURES	EXC. COND. LOW	HIGH
Performer PB-115 Bass Amp			
Sixty watts, 1x15", Black Tolex.			
1982		$100	$175
Pro Compact 210S Amp			
Sixty watts, 2x10", two channels, active EQ, Black Tolex.			
1982		$100	$175
Pro Compact 212S Amp			
Sixty watts, 2x12", two channels, active EQ, master volume knob, Black Tolex.			
1982		$100	$150

MODEL YEAR	FEATURES	EXC. COND. LOW	HIGH

Rebel RB-112 Bass Amp
Thirty-five watts, 1x12", Black Tolex
| 1982 | | $75 | $150 |

Hondo

1969-1987, 1991-present. Hondo has offered imported amps over the years. '90s models ranged from the H20 Practice Amp to the H160SRC with 160 watts (peak) and 2x10" speakers.

Amps
1970s	Various models	$25	$100
1980s	Various models	$25	$100
1990s	Various models	$25	$100

Hound Dog

1994-1998. Founded by George Alessandro as the Hound Dog Corporation. Name was changed to Alessandro in 1998 (see that brand for more info).

Hughes & Kettner

Hughes & Kettner offers a line of guitar and bass combos, heads, cabinets and tube effects, all made in Germany.

ATS MkII 112 Combo Amp
1990-1993. MOS-FET power amp, two-stage tube channel, transistorized clean channel, compressor, EQ, reverb. Available with 1x12", 2x12", or 4x12" cabinets (GL 112, GL 212, or GL 412).
| 1990-1993 | | $300 | $350 |

ATTAX 200 Stereo Amp
1990s. Combo amp, twin speakers, black vinyl, black metal grille.
| 1990s | | $375 | $425 |

ATTAX 50 Stereo Amp
1990s. Combo, twin speakers, black vinyl, black metal grille.
| 1990s | | $300 | $350 |

Fortress Bass Preamp
1990-1994. Built-in compressor, EQ, tube preamp section.
| 1990-1994 | | $150 | $200 |

Hurricane

1998-present. Tube guitar and harmonica combo amps built by Gary Drouin in Sarasota, Florida. Drouin started the company with harp master Rock Bottom, who passed away in September, '01.

Ibanez

1932-present. Ibanez added solid-state amps to thier product line in '98. They also build guitars, basses and effects.

Idol

Late-1960s. Made in Japan. Dark tolex cover, dark grille, Hobby Series with large Idol logo on front.

Hobby 10 Amp
| 1968 | | $80 | $90 |

Hobby 20 Amp
| 1968 | | $125 | $150 |

Hobby 45 Amp
| 1968 | | $175 | $200 |

Hobby 100 Amp
| 1968 | | $200 | $250 |

Model 007 Amp
| 1968 | | $35 | $45 |

Imperial

Ca.1963-ca.1970. The Imperial Accordion Company of Chicago, Illinois offered one or two imported small amps in the '60s.

Jack Daniel's

2004-present. Tube guitar amp built by Peavey for the Jack Daniel Distillery. There are also guitar models.

Jackson

1980-present. The Jackson-Charvel Company offered amps and cabinets in the late '80s and the '90s.

4x12" Cabinet
1990s. Red cone Jackson speakers in slant cabinet with see-through metal grille.
| 1990s | | $350 | $500 |

Apogee 50 Combo Amp
1980s. Two channels, lead with boost, two speakers.
| 1980s | | $800 | $1,000 |

JG-2 Head Amp
Tube head, 50 watts, two-stage preamp, midrange boost, presence, effects loop, EL-34 tubes.
| 1988 | | $300 | $450 |

JG-3 Head Amp
Tube head, 100 watts, two-stage preamp, midrange boost, presence, effects loop, EL-34 tubes.
| 1988 | | $350 | $500 |

Jay Turser

1997-present. Smaller, inexpensive imported solidstate guitar and bass amps. They also offer basses and guitars.

JMI (Jennings Musical Industries)

2004-present. Jennings built the Vox amps of the 1960s. They are back with tube amp heads and cabinets based on some of their classic models.

Johnson

Mid-1990s-present. Line of solidstate amps imported by Music Link, Brisbane, California. Johnson also offers guitars, basses, mandolins and effects.

Johnson Amplification

1997-present. Intermediate and professional grade, production, modeling amps and effects designed by John Johnson, of Sandy, Utah. The

Hughes & Kettner ATS-60

Hurricane V-30 combo

Jay Turser Classic 25RC Lead Guitar Amp

MODEL YEAR	FEATURES	EXC. COND. LOW	HIGH

1962 Kay 703

1963 Kay Vanguard 704

Kendrick Texas Crude

company is part of Harman International. In 2002, they quit building amps, but continue the effects line.

JoMama

1994-present. Tube amps and combos under the JoMama and Kelemen brands built by Joe Kelemen in Santa Fe, New Mexico.

Juke

1989-present. Tube guitar and harmonica amps built by G. R. Croteau in Troy, New Hampshire. He also built the Warbler line of amps.

Kalamazoo

1933-1942, 1965-1970. Kalamazoo was a brand Gibson used on one of their budget lines. They used the name on amps from '65 to '67.

Bass Amp

1965-1967. Enclosed back, 2x10", flip-out control panel, not as common as numerous Model 1 and 2 student amps.

1965-1967		$250	$350

Model 1 Amp

1965-1967. No tremolo, 1x10", front control panel.

1965-1967		$75	$125

Model 2 Amp

1965-1967. Same as Model 1 with tremolo, Black.

1965-1967		$100	$150

Reverb 12 Amp

1965-1967. Black vinyl cover, 1x12", reverb, tremolo.

1965-1967		$200	$300

Kay

Ca. 1931-present. Kay offered amps throughout their history up to around '68 when the brandname changed hands. See *Guitar Stories Volume II*, by Michael Wright, for a complete history of Kay with detailed model listings.

Small Tube Amps

1940s	Wood cabinet	$175	$375
1950s	Various models	$125	$175
1960s	Models K503,		
	K504, K505	$125	$175

K506 Vibrato 12" Amp

1960s. Twelve watts, 1x12", swirl grille, metal handle.

1962		$175	$275

K507 Twin Ten Special Amp

1960s. Twenty watts, 2x10", swirl grille, metal handle.

1962		$225	$325

Kay (Imported)

1980-present. Currently distributed in the U.S. by A.R. Musical Enterprises.

MODEL YEAR	FEATURES	EXC. COND. LOW	HIGH

Kelemen

1994-present. Tube amps and combos under the JoMama and Kelemen brands built by Joe Kelemen in Santa Fe, New Mexico.

Kendrick

1989-present. Founded by Gerald Weber in Austin, Texas and currently located in Kempfner, Texas. Mainly known for their handmade tube amps, Kendrick also offers guitars, speakers, and effects. At the end of '03, Weber quit taking orders for new production amps, but still builds models for J. Hale Music of Wisconsin and for a Japanese distributor. They continue to offer amp kits and guitars. Gerald writes monthly columns for *Vintage Guitar* magazine and has authored books and videos on tube amps.

2210 Amp

1993-1995. Tweed combo 2x10".

1990s		$1,200	$1,800

2410 Amp

1998-1995. 4x10" combo.

1992-1996		$1,200	$2,000

4212 Amp

1992-1995. Ttweed combo, 2x12", 80 watts.

1990s		$1,200	$2,000

Baby Huey Combo Amp

1993-1994. Low production, 2x12" with reverb and built-in features, in a vox chassis.

1990s		$1,500	$2,200

Black Gold BG-35 Amp

1997-2003. 35 watts, 1x12" or 2x10".

1996-1999		$900	$1,300

Black Gold Stereo BG-15 Amp

1998-2003. Class A, 2x15 watt output to separate output transformer and speaker.

1997-1999		$900	$1,300

Model 4000 Special Amp Head

1990-1993. Solidstate rectifiers with four 6L6GC output tubes, switchable to 120 or 60 watts, black tolex, only 25 made.

1990-1991		$800	$1,000

Texas Crude Gusher Amp

1995-1998. 50 watt head.

1994-1999	2x12"	$900	$1,400

The Gusher Combo Amp

1996-1998. 50 watts, 1x15", 2x10", or 4x10".

1990s		$1,200	$2,000

Kent

Ca. 1962-1969. Imported budget line of guitars and amps.

Model 1475 Amp

3 tubes, brown.

1960s		$40	$50

Model 2198 Amp

3 tubes, brown.

1960s		$50	$60

Model 5999 Amp

3 tubes, brown.

1960s		$60	$70

MODEL YEAR	FEATURES	EXC. COND. LOW	HIGH

Model 6104 Piggyback Amp
12 watts, brown.

1960s		$100	$125

Kiesel
See Carvin.

Kingston
1958-1967. Economy solidstate amps imported by Westheimer Importing, Chicago, Illinois.

Cat P-1 Amp
Mid-1960s. Solidstate, 3 watts, very small speaker, Cat Series amps have dark vinyl, dark grille. The original retail selling price in the mid-1960s was $25.99.

1960s		$25	$45

Cat P-2 Amp
Mid-1960s. Solidstate, 5 watts, very small speaker.

1960s		$30	$50

Cat P-3 Amp
Mid-1960s. Solidstate, 8 amps, 1x8".

1960s		$35	$55

Cat P-8 T Amp
Mid-1960s. Solidstate, 20 watts, 1x8", tremolo.

1960s		$35	$55

Cougar BA-21 Bass Amp (piggyback)
Mid-1960s. Solidstate, 60 watts, 2x12" cab, dark vinyl, light silver grille.

1960s		$50	$150

Cougar PB-5 Bass Amp (combo)
Mid-1960s. Solidstate, 15 watts, 1x8", dark vinyl cover, dark grille.

1960s		$35	$55

Lion 2000 Amp (piggyback)
Mid-1960s. Solidstate, 90 watts, 2x12" cab, dark tuck-and-roll-type cover, dark grille.

1960s		$75	$175

Lion 3000 Amp (piggyback)
Mid-1960s. Solidstate, 250 watts, 4x12" cab, dark tuck-and-roll-type cover, dark grille.

1960s		$100	$200

Lion AP-281 R Amp (piggyback)
Mid-1960s. Solidstate, 30 watts, 2x8" cab, dark vinyl cover, light silver grille.

1960s		$50	$90

Lion AP-281 R10 Amp (piggyback)
Mid-1960s. Solidstate, 30 watts, 2x10" cab, dark vinyl cover, light silver grille.

1960s		$50	$150

Kitchen-Marshall
1965-1966. Private branded for Kitchen Music by Marshall, primarily P.A. units with block logos. Limited production.

JTM 45 MKII 45-Watt Head Amp
1965-1966. Private branded for Kitchen Music, JTM 45 Marshall with Kitchen logo plate, 45 watts.

1965-1966		$5,000	$6,000

Slant 4x12 1960 Cab
1965-1966. Slant front 4x12" 1960-style cabinet with gray bluesbreaker grille, very limited production.

1965-1966	Black on green vinyl	$4,500	$5,000

KJL
1995-present. Founded by Kenny Lannes, MSEE, a professor of Electrical Engineering at the University of New Orleans. KLJ makes tube combo amps, heads and an ABY box.

KJL Dirty 30

KMD (Kaman)
1986-ca. 1990. Distributed by Kaman (Ovation, Hamer, etc.) in the late '80s, KMD offered a variety of amps and effects.

Koch
All-tube combo amps, heads, effects and cabinets built in The Netherlands.

Krank
1996-present. Founded by Tony Dow and offering tube amp heads, combos and speaker cabinets built in Tempe, Arizona. They also build effects. The company greatly upped its distribution in '03.

Koch Classictone

Kustom
1965-present. Kustom, a division of Hanser Holdings, offers guitar and bass combo amps and P.A. equipment. Founded by Bud Ross in Chanute, Kansas, who offered tuck-and-roll amps as early as '58, but began using the Kustom brand name in '65. From '69 to '75 Ross gradually sold interest in the company (in the late '70s, Ross introduced the line of Ross effects stomp boxes). The brand changed hands a few times, and by the mid-'80s it was no longer used. In 1989 Kustom was in bankruptcy court and was purchased by Hanser Holdings Incorporated of Cincinnati, Ohio (Davitt & Hanser) and by '94, they had a new line of amps available.

Prices are for excellent condition amps with no tears in the tuck-and-roll cover and no grille tears. A tear in the tuck-and-roll will reduce the value, sometimes significantly.

Kustom amp model identification can be frustrating. Kustom used series numbers, catalog numbers (the numbers in the catalogs and price lists), and model numbers (the number often found next to the serial number on the amp's back panel). Most of the discussion that follows is by series number (100, 200, 300, etc.) and catalog number. Unfortunately, vintage amp dealers use the serial number and model number, so the best way to go is to cross-check speaker and amplifier features. Model numbers were used primarily for repair purposes and were found in the repair manuals.

In many, but not all cases, the model number is the last digit of the catalog number; for example the catalog lists a 100 series Model 1-15J-l, where the last

Krank 100 Watt combo

Kustom Commander

Kustom Hustler

Kustom K-25-C

digit 1 signifies a Model 1 amplifier chassis which is a basic amp without reverb or tremolo. A Model 1-15J-2 having 2 as the last digit signifies a Model 2 amp chassis that has reverb and tremolo. In this example, Kustom uses a different model number on the back of the amp head. For the 1-15J-2, the model number on the back panel of the amp head would be K100-2, indicating a series 100 (50 watts) amp with reverb and tremolo (amp chassis Model 2).

Model numbers relate to the amplifier's schematic and electronics, while catalog numbers describe the amp's relative power rating and speaker configuration.

Amp Chasis Model Numbers (1968-1972)
Model 1	Amp (basic)
Model 2	Amp with reverb
Model 3	Amp with Harmonic Clip and Boost
Model 4	Amp with reverb, tremolo, vibrato, Harmonic Clip and Selective Boost
Model 5	P.A. with reverb
Model 6	Amp (basic) with Selectone
Model 7	Amp with reverb, tremolo, vibrato, boost (different parts)
Model 8	Amp with reverb, tremolo, vibrato, boost (different parts)

SC (Self-Contained/Combo) Series Model Numbers
K25-2	Amp with reverb
K50-2	Amp with reverb
K100-6	Amp (basic)
K100-7	Amp with reverb (or boost too?)
K100-8	Amp with reverb
K150-6	Amp (basic) with Selectone
K150-7	Amp with reverb
K150-8	Amp with reverb

K100 Series Model Numbers
K100-1	Amp (basic)
K100-2	Amp with reverb
K100-5	PA

K200 Series Model Numbers
K200-1	Amp (basic)
K200-2	Amp with reverb
K200-3	Amp with Harmonic Clip and Selective Boost
K200-4	Amp with reverb, tremolo, vibrato, Harmonic Clip and Selective Boost .
K200-5	PA
K200-6	Amp (basic) with Selectone

K400 Series Model Numbers
K400-1	Amp (basic)
K400-2	Amp with reverb
K400-3	Amp with Harmonic Clip and Selective Boost
K400-4	Amp with reverb, tremolo, vibrato, Harmonic Clip and Selective Boost .
K400-5	PA

Naugahyde Tuck & Roll 200 (1965-1967)

The very first Kustoms had only the Kustom logo without the model series on the front control panel. The early logo stipulated Kustom by Ross, Inc. The name was then updated to Kustom Electronics, Inc. 1965-1967 amp heads have a high profile/tall "forehead" area (the area on top of

the controls but below the top of the amp). This '65-'67 model has been nicknamed "the Frankenstein model." The '65-'67 catalog numbers were often four or five digits, for example J695. The first digit represents the speaker type (J = Jensen, etc.), other examples are L995, L1195, L795RV, etc. Some 1967 catalog numbers changed to two digits followed by three digits, like 4-D 140f, or 3-15C (three CTS speakers), etc. Other 1967 amps sported five like 4-15J-1 where 4 = four speakers, 15 = 15" speakers, J = Jensen, and 1 = basic amp chassis with no effects. The fifth digit indicated amp chassis options as follows: 1 = standard, 2 =reverb, tremolo 3=harmonic clipper and boost option, 4= multi-effects and boost options combined.

Naugahyde Tuck & Roll 100/200/400 (1968-1971)

In 1968 the Kustom logo also included the model series. A K100, for example would have 100 displayed below the Kustom name. These amps are easily recognized, having the Kustom logo and model series located in the middle of the control panel. The model series generally is twice the relative output wattage, for example the 100 Series is a 50-watt amp. Keep in mind, solid-state ratings are often higher than tube-amp ratings, so use the ratings as relative measurements. The Kustom catalog numbers are numerous. The key to understanding most '68-'70 number is x-xxx-x, for example 1-15L-1. The first digit represents the number of speakers (1 = 1 speaker, 2 = two speakers), the 2nd and 3rd digit represents the speaker size (15 = 15" speaker), the forth digit represents the speaker type (A = Altec Lansing, L = J.B.L., J = Jensen, C = C.T.S. Bass), the fifth digit represents the amp chassis option, for example 1 = standard, 2 = reverb and tremolo option, etc. The power units were interchangeable in production, so amps could have similar front-ends but different power units (more power and different effect options) and visa versa. Some 1968 bass amp catalog numbers were four digits, for example 2-12C, meaning two 12" CTS speakers. Again, there were several different numbers used.

Kustom also introduced the 200 and 400 amp series. The Kustom logo included the series number. The catalog numbers were similar to the 100 series, but they had a higher power rating of 100 equivalent watts (200 series), or 200 equivalent watts (400 series).

Kustom U.S. Naugahyde (tuck & roll) covers came in seven colors, as follows: Black (the most common), Cascade (blue/green), Silver (white-silver), Gold (light gold), Red, Blue, and Charcoal (gray). The Kustom Amp market historically has distinguished between black and the color options, with the color options fetching more. The market has not noticeably distinguished power and features options. Condition and color seem to be the most important features in the Kustom amp market. Gold and Cascade may be the least often seen colors. Gold may fetch more than the other colors.

MODEL YEAR	FEATURES	EXC. COND. LOW	HIGH

Naugahyde Tuck & Roll 150/250/300/500/600 (c.1971 to c.1975)

The amp heads changed slightly with a slightly slanted control panel and the Kustom logo moved from the center of the panel to the right / upper-right portion of the front panel. The covering options continued to be the tuck & roll style offered in the same variety of colors. The sales literature indicated a 150 series had 150 watts, 250 series had 250 watts, etc.

K150   PA
K300   PA

Naugahyde Tuck & Roll SC (Self Contained) Series

Most SC combo amps were rated at 150 watts, with the 1-12SC listed at 50 watts. They were offered in seven colors of tuck and roll. Again the model numbers indicate the features as follows: 4-10 SC is a 4 x 10", 2-10 SC is a 2x10", 1-12 SC is 1 x 12"

Super Sound Tuck and Roll Combo Series

The last tuck and roll combo amps with slightly smaller tucks. Amp control panel is noticeably smaller and the Kustom logo is in the right side of the amp front control panel. Includes the following model names

Charger   150 watts, 1x15"
Challenger   50 watts 1x12"
Hustler   150 watts 4x10"
Commander   150watts 2x12"
Sidewinder   150 watts 1x15" (for steel guitar)
Sidewinder   JBL 150 watts 1x15" JBL D130f (for steel guitar)

Black Vinyl (1975-c.1978)

Most think of Kustom as being only tuck and roll but by 1975 ownership changes were complete, the colorful tuck and roll was dropped in favor of the more traditional black vinyl. Product offerings included the Kustom I, II, III, and IV Lead amps. Piggyback amps with half-stacks and full-stacks were available. Bass amps included the Kustom 1, plus the Bass I, II, III, IV, and IV SRO. The products had a slant Kustom logo spelled-out and placed in a position on the grille similar to a Fender blackface baffle.

Black Vinyl "K" logo (1978-1983)

This era is easily recognized by the prominent capital K logo.

Challenger Amp

1973-1975. One 12" speaker.

1973-1975	Black	$250	$375
1973-1975	Color	$425	$475

Hustler Amp

1973-1975. Solidstate combo amp, 4x10", Super Reverb-style, tremolo, tuck and roll.

1973-1975	Black	$300	$400
1973-1975	Color options	$500	$600

K25/K25 C-2 SC Amp

1960s. SC (self-contained) Series, small combo tuck-and-roll, 1x12", solidstate, reverb, Black control panel.

1971-1973	Black	$300	$350
1971-1973	Color options	$400	$575

MODEL YEAR	FEATURES	EXC. COND. LOW	HIGH

K100-1 Amp Head

1968-1972. 50 watt, solidstate "energizer" head, offered in black or several color options, without reverb or tremolo (suffix 1).

1968-1972	Black	$150	$200
1968-1972	Color options	$250	$325

K100-1 1-15C Bass Amp Set

1968-1972. The K100-1 is the basic amp without reverb, the 1-15C is the speaker option. 50 watt solidstate head with matching 1x15" cab, black tuck and roll standard, but several sparkle colors offered, C.T.S. bass reflex speaker.

1968-1972	Black	$275	$400
1968-1972	Color options	$525	$750

K100-1 1-15L-1/1-15A-1/1-15J-1 Amp Set

1968-1972. The K100-1 is the basic amp without reverb, 50-watt solidstate head with matching 1x15" cab, black tuck and roll standard, but several colors offered, no reverb/tremolo, speaker options JBL, Altec Lansing or Jensen.

1968-1972	Black	$275	$400
1968-1972	Color options	$525	$750

K100-1 1-D140F Bass Amp

1968-1972. 50 watt solidstate head with matching 1x15" JBL D-140F cab, black tuck and roll standard, but several sparkle colors offered, no reverb or tremolo.

1968-1972	Black	$300	$425
1968-1972	Color option	$550	$775

K100-1 2-12C Bass Amp Set

1968-1972. 50 watt solidstate head with matching 2x12" cab, black tuck and roll standard, but several sparkle colors offered, C.T.S. bass reflex speakers.

1968-1972	Black	$325	$450
1968-1972	Color option	$575	$800

K100-2 Reverb/Tremolo Amp Head

1968-1972. 50 watt solidstate "energizer" head, offered in black or several color options, includes reverb (suffix 2).

1968-1972	Black	$225	$275
1968-1972	Color option	$375	$475

K100-2 1-15L-2/1-15A-2/1-15J-2 Amp Set

1968-1972. 50 watt solidstate head and matching 1x15" cab, black tuck and roll standard, but several sparkle colors offered, includes reverb/tremolo.

1968-1972	Black	$350	$475
1968-1972	Color option	$600	$800

K100-2 2-12A-2/2-12J-2 Amp Set

1968-1972. 50 watt solidstate head with matching 2x12" cab, black tuck and roll standard, but several sparkle colors offered, includes reverb/tremolo.

1968-1972	Black	$400	$525
1968-1972	Color option	$650	$850

K100-5 PA Amp Head

1968-1972. 50 watt, 2 channels with eight control knobs per channel, reverb. Kustom 100 logo located above the four high-impedance mic inputs.

1968-1972	Black	$225	$275
1968-1972	Color option	$375	$475

Kustom K-100

Kustom K-100-1-15

Kustom K-150-7

Kustom KBA-80

Kustom KLA-20

Kustom K250-2-15

MODEL YEAR	FEATURES	EXC. COND. LOW	HIGH
K100-6 SC Amp			
1970-1972. Basic combo amp with selectone, no reverb.			
1970-1972	Black	$275	$400
K100-7 SC Amp			
1970-1972. Combo amp with reverb, tremolo, vibrato and boost.			
1970-1972	Black	$300	$425
1970-1972	Color option	$550	$750
K100-8 SC Amp			
1970-1972. Combo amp with reverb, tremolo, vibrato and boost.			
1970-1972	Black	$325	$450
1970-1972	Color option	$575	$775
K100C-6 Amp			
1968-1970. Kustom 100 logo middle of the front control panel, 1x15" combo, selectone option.			
1968-1970	Black	$275	$400
K100C-8 Amp			
1968-1970. Kustom 100 logo middle of the front control panel, 4x10" combo, reverb, tremolo, vibrato.			
1968-1970	Black	$325	$450
K200-1/K200B Bass Amp Head			
1966-1972. Head with 100 relative watts, 2 channels, 4 controls and 2 inputs per channel.			
1966-1967	Color options	$375	$425
1968-1972	Color option	$350	$400
K200-1/K200B Bass Amp Set			
1966-1972. K200 head with 2x15" cab.			
1966-1972	Black	$300	$425
1966-1972	Color option	$550	$800
K200-2 Reverb/Tremolo Amp Head			
1966-1972. Head, 100 relative watts, reverb and tremolo (suffix 2).			
1966-1972	Black	$250	$300
1966-1972	Color option	$400	$500
K200-2 Reverb/Tremolo Amp and Cab Set			
1966-1972. 100 relative watts, reverb, tremolo, with 2x15" or 3x12" cabinet, available with JBL D-140F speakers, Altec Lansing (A) speakers, C.T.S. (C), or Jensen (J). K-200 series were offered with no effects (suffix 1) or with reverb and tremolo (suffix 2), also offered with Harmonic Clipper & Boost (suffix 3), and Reverb/Trem/Clipper/Boost (suffix 4). '66 and '67 models have the "high forehead" appearance versus normal appearance by '68.			
1966-1972	Black	$375	$500
1966-1972	Blue, Charcoal, Red, Silver	$625	$850
1966-1972	Cascade, Gold	$650	$875
K250 Reverb/Tremolo Amp Head			
1971-1975. 250 watts, tuck and roll cover, Kustom 250 logo on upper right section of control panel, reverb.			
1971-1975	Black	$250	$300
1971-1975	Color option	$400	$500
K250 Amp and Cab Set			
1971-1975. 250 watts, 2x15", tuck and roll cover, Kustom 250 logo on upper right section of amp control panel, reverb.			
1971-1975	Black	$375	$500
1971-1975	Color option	$625	$875

MODEL YEAR	FEATURES	EXC. COND. LOW	HIGH
K300 PA Amp and Speaker Set			
1971-1975. Includes 302 PA, 303 PA, 304 PA, 305 PA, head and two cabs.			
1971-1975	Color option	$675	$900
K400-2 Reverb/Tremolo Amp and Cab Set			
1968-1972. 200 relative watts, reverb, tremolo, with 6x12" or 8x12" cabinet, available with JBL D-140F speakers, Altec Lansing (A), C.T.S. (C), or Jensen (J). Offered with no effects (suffix 1), or with reverb and tremolo (suffix 2), also offered with Harmonic Clipper & Boost (suffix 3) and Reverb/Trem/Clipper/Boost (suffix 4). The 400 Series amplifier head came with a separate chrome amp head stand.			
1968-1972	Black	$400	$550
1968-1972	Color options	$650	$900
KBA-20 Combo Amp			
Late-1980s-early-1990s. Compact solidstate bass amp with built-in limiter, 20 watts, 1x8".			
1989-1990		$40	$75
KBA-40 Combo Amp			
Late-1980s-early-1990s. Compact solidstate bass combo amp with built-in limiter, 40 watts, 1x12".			
1989-1990		$50	$100
KBA-80 Combo Amp			
Late-1980s-early-1990s. Solidstate bass amp with built-in limiter, 80 watts, 1x15".			
1989-1990		$75	$125
KBA-160 Combo Amp			
Late-1980s-early-1990s. Solidstate bass amp with built-in limiter, 160 watts, 1x15".			
1989-1990		$100	$150
KGA-10 VC Amp			
2000s. 10 watts, 1x6.5" speaker, switchable overdrive, super-economy student amp.			
2000s		$25	$30
KLA-15 Combo Amp			
Late-1980s-early-1990s. Compact solidstate amp with built-in footswitchable overdrive, 15 watts, 1x8".			
1989-1990		$50	$100
KLA-20 Amp			
Mid-1980s-late-1980s. One 10", MOS-FET, gain, EQ, reverb, headphone jack.			
1986		$75	$100
KLA-25 Combo Amp			
Late-1980s-early-1990s. Compact solidstate amp with built-in footswitchable overdrive and reverb, 25 watts, 1x10".			
1989-1990		$75	$100
KLA-50 Combo Amp			
Late-1980s-early-1990s. Compact solidstate amp with built-in footswitchable overdrive and reverb, 50 watts, 1x12".			
1989-1990		$100	$125
KLA-75 Amp			
Mid-1980s-late-1980s. 75 watts, dual channels with independent tone and level controls, reverb, footswitching.			
1987		$100	$150

MODEL YEAR	FEATURES	EXC. COND. LOW	HIGH

KLA-100 Combo Amp
Late-1980s-early-1990s. Solidstate amp with reverb, 100-watt dual channel, 1x12".

1989-1990		$125	$175

KLA-185 Combo Amp
Late-1980s-early-1990s. Solidstate amp with reverb, 185-watt dual channel, 1x12".

1989-1990		$150	$200

SC 1-12 SC Amp
1971-1975. 50 watts, 1x12" Jensen speaker.

1971-1975	Black	$300	$350
1971-1975	Color option	$400	$575

SC 1-15 SC Amp
1971-1975. 150 watts, 1x15" C.T.S. speaker.

1971-1975	Black	$300	$375
1971-1975	Color option	$400	$575

SC 1-15AB SC Amp
1971-1975. 150 watts, 1x15" Altec Lansing speaker.

1971-1975	Black	$300	$375
1971-1975	Color option	$400	$575

SC 2-12A SC Amp
1971-1975. 150 watts, 2x12" Altec Lansing speakers.

1971-1975	Black	$350	$425
1971-1975	Color option	$575	$700

SC 2-12J SC Amp
1971-1975. 150 watts, 2x12" Jensen speakers.

1971-1975	Black	$350	$425
1971-1975	Color option	$575	$700

SC 4-10 SC Amp
1971-1975. 150 watts, 4x10" Jensen speakers.

1971-1975	Black	$350	$425
1971-1975	Color option	$575	$700

Lab Series
1977-1980s. Five models of Lab Series amps, ranging in price from $600 to $3,700, were introduced at the '77 NAMM show by Norlin (then owner of Gibson). Two more were added later. The '80s models were Lab Series 2 amps and had a Gibson logo on the upper-left front.

B120 Amp
Ca.1984. Bass combo, 120 watts, 2 channels, 1x15".

1984		$150	$250

G120 R-10 Amp
Ca.1984. Combo, 120 watts, three-band EQ, channel switching, reverb, 4x10".

1984		$300	$400

G120 R-12 Amp
Ca.1984. Combo, 120 watts, 3-band EQ, channel switching, reverb, 2x12".

1984		$225	$325

L2 Head Amp
1977-1983. Head, 100 watts, black covering.

1977-1983	Black	$200	$300

L3 Amp
1977-ca.1983. Combo, 60 watts.

1977-1983		$275	$375

L4 Head Amp
1977-1983. Solidstate, 200 watts, black cover, dark grille, large L4 logo on front panel.

1977-1983		$225	$325

L5 Amp
1977-ca.1983. Solidstate, 100 watts, 2x12".

1977-1983		$450	$550

L7 Amp
1977-1983. Solidstate, 100 watts, 4x10".

1977-1983		$450	$550

L11 Amp
1977-1983. Head only, 200 watts.

1977-1983		$200	$300

Lace Music Products
1979-present. Lace Music Products, which was founded by pickup innovator Don Lace Sr., added amplifiers in '96. They also offer amps under the Rat Fink and Mooneyes brand names.

Lace 20-watt

Lafayette
Ca. 1963-1967. Japanese-made guitars and amps sold through the Lafayette Electronics catalogs.

Small Tube Amp
Japanese-made tube, 1x12", art deco design.

1960s	Gray Speckle	$165	$200

Laney
1968-present. Founded by Lyndon Laney and Bob Thomas in Birmingham, England. Laney offered tube amps exclusively into the '80s. A wide range of solidstate and tube amps are currently being offered.

100-Watt Amp Head
1968-1969. Similar to short head Plexi Marshall amp cab, large Laney with underlined "y" logo plate on upper left front corner, Black vinyl cover, Grayish grille.

1968-1969		$1,000	$1,300

EA-120 Amp
1990s. One hundred twenty watts, 2x10", dark vinyl cover.

1990s		$325	$400

GC-30 Amp
1990s. Compact combo amp, 30 watts, dark vinyl cover, reverb, dark see-through grille.

1990s		$225	$275

GS-212 2x12" Cab
1980s-1990s. Rated at 150 watts, 2x12", slant front cab, Black vinyl cover, metal grille.

1990s		$250	$300

GS-410 4x10" Cab
1980s-1990s. Four 10" speakers, straight-front cab, Black vinyl cover, metal grille.

1990s		$250	$300

GS-412 4x12" Cab
1980s-1990s. Straight-front or slant cab, 4x12" rated at 150 watts, Black vinyl cover.

1990s		$350	$400

Laney GG 100TI

Laney VC30-212

AMPS

Line 6 Duoverb

Little Lanilei 33 watt

Little Lanilei Rotary Wave

MODEL YEAR	FEATURES	EXC. COND. LOW	HIGH

LC-15 Amp
1990s. Compact practice amp, 15 watts.

1990s		$200	$250

MY-50 Amp
All tube head, 50 watts, master volume, four-stage cascaded preamp, active boosts for treble, middle and bass.

1980s		$250	$350

MY-100 Amp
All tube head, 100 watts, master volume, four-stage cascaded preamp, active boosts for treble, middle and bass.

1980s		$300	$400

Quarter Stack Amp
All tube, 2x12", self-contained, sealed back, foot-switchable reverb and overdrive, effects loop, active tone controls with push/pull switches.

1980s		$350	$400

Legend
1978-1984. From Legend Musical Instruments of East Syracuse, New York, these amps featured cool wood cabinets. They offered heads, combos with a 1x12" or 2x12" configuration, and cabinets with 1x12", 2x12" or 4x12".

A-30 Amp
Late-1970s-early-1980s. Natural wood cabinet, compact amp.

1980s		$400	$500

A-60 Amp
Late-1970s-early-1980s. Wood cabinet and grille, transtube design dual tube preamp with solidstate power section.

1980s		$400	$500

Rock & Roll 50 Combo Amp
1978-1983. Wood compact combo, either 1x12" or 2x12" configuration, tube preamp section and solid-state power supply.

1978-1979	2x12" option	$450	$500
1978-1983	1x12" option	$400	$450

Super Lead 50 Amp
Late-1970s-early-1980s. Rock & Roll 50-watt model with added bass boost and reverb, 1x12".

1978-1983		$425	$475

Super Lead 100 Amp
Late-1970s-early-1980s. Rock & Roll 100-watt model with added bass boost and reverb, 2x12".

1978-1983		$475	$525

Leslie
Most often seen with Hammond organs, the cool Leslie rotating speakers have been adopted by many guitarists. Many guitar effects have tried to duplicate their sound. And they are still making them.

16 Rotating Speaker Cab
1960s-1970s. One 10" or 1x12" rotating speaker (requires an amp head), black vinyl cover, silver grille, Leslie 60 logo on grille.

1960s	1 cabinet	$300	$400
1970s	1 cabinet	$300	$400

60 M Rotating Speaker Cabs
1960s-1970s. Two by one by 10" rotating speaker cabs with 45-watt amp, black vinyl cover, light silver grille, Leslie logo upper left on grille.

1960s	2 cabinets	$600	$650

103 Amp
Two-speed.

1960s		$225	$275

118 Amp
One 12" Altec speaker.

1960s		$250	$325

125 Amp
Late-1960s. All tube amp with 2-speed rotating 1x12" speaker.

1960s		$225	$275

145 Amp

1960s		$400	$500

Line 6
1996-present. Founded by Marcus Ryle and Michel Doidic and specializing in digital signal processing in both effects and amps.

Little Lanilei
1997-present. Small handmade, intermediate grade, production/custom, amps made by Songworks Systems & Products of San Juan Capistrano, California. They also build a reverb unit and a rotary effect.

Louis Electric Amplifier Co.
1993-present. Founded by Louis Rosano in Bergenfield, New Jersey. Louis produces custom-built tweeds and various combo amps from 35 to 80 watts.

Maestro
Maestro amps are associated with Gibson and were included in the Gibson catalogs. For example, in the '62-'63 Orange cover Gibson catalog, tweed Maestro amps were displayed in their own section. Tweed Maestro amps are very similar to Gibson tweed amps. Maestro amps were often associated with accordions in the early-'60s but the amps featured standard guitar inputs. Gibson also used the Maestro name on a line of effects.

The price ranges listed are for excellent condition, all original amps, though tubes may be replaced without affecting value. A broken or missing logo may diminish the value of the amp. Amps with a changed handle, power cord, and especially a broken logo, should be taken on a case-by-case basis.

Amp models in '58 include the Super Maestro and Maestro, in '60 the Stereo Maestro Accordion GA-87, Super Maestro Accordion GA-46 T, Standard Accordion GA-45 T, Viscount Accordion GA-16 T, in '62 the Reverb-Echo GA-1 RT, Reverb-Echo GA-2 RT, 30 Stereo Accordion Amp, Stereo Accordion GA-78 RV.

MODEL YEAR FEATURES	EXC. COND. LOW	HIGH

GA-1 RT Reverb-Echo Amp
1961. Tweed, 1x8".
1961 $350 $450

GA-2 RT Deluxe Reverb-Echo Amp
1961. Deluxe more powerful version of GA-1 RT, 1x12", tweed.
1961 $750 $850

GA-15 RV/Bell 15 RV Amp
1961. 15 watts, 1x12", gray Sparkle.
1961 $450 $600

GA-16 T Viscount Amp
1961. 14 watts, 1x10", gray Sparkle. Gibson also had a GA-16 Viscount amp from 1959-1960.
1961 $350 $500

GA-45 Maestro Amp
1955-1960. 16 watts, 4x8", two-tone.
1955-1960 $650 $750

GA-45 RV Standard Amp
1961. 16 watts, 4x8", reverb.
1961 $900 $1,100

GA-45 T Standard Accordion Amp
1961. 16 watts, 4x8", tremolo.
1961 $700 $800

GA-46 T Super Maestro Accordion and Bass Amp
1957-1961. Based on the Gibson GA-200 and advertised to be "designed especially for amplified accordions." 60 watts, 2x12", vibrato, two-tone cover, large Maestro Super logo on top center of grille.
1957-1960 $1,400 $1,600

GA-78 Amp
1960-1961. Wedge stereo cab, 2x10".
1960-1961 $1,500 $2,000

GA-78 RV Amp
1960-1961. 30 watts, 2x10", wedge stereo cab.
1960-1961 $1,500 $2,200

Magnatone
Ca. 1937-1971. Magnatone made a huge variety of amps sold under their own name and under brands like Dickerson, Oahu (see separate listings), and Bronson. They also private branded amps for several accordion companies or accordion teaching studios. Brand names used for them include DA VINCI, PAC - AMP, PANaramic, TITANO, TONEMASTER, TWILIGHTER, and UNIQUE (see separate listings for those brands). See Guitar section for more company info.

Model 108 Varsity Amp
1948-1954. Gray pearloid cover, small student amp or lap steel companion amp.
1948-1954 $225 $300

Model 110 Melodier Amp
1953-1954. 12 watts, 1x10", brown leatherette cover, light grille.
1953-1954 $275 $350

Model 111 Student Amp
1955-1959. 2 to 3 watts, 1x8", brown leatherette, brown grille.
1955-1959 $200 $225

Model 112/113 Troubadour Amp
1955-1959. 18 watts, 1x12", brown leatherette, brown grille, slant back rear control panel.
1955-1959 $325 $400

Model 120B Cougar Bass Amp
1967-1968. Initial Magnatone entry into the solidstate market, superseded by Brute Series in 1968. 120 watts, 2x12" solidstate bass piggyback amp, naugahyde vinyl cover with polyester rosewood side panels.
1967-1968 $225 $275

Model 120R Sting Ray Reverb Bass Amp
1967-1968. Initial Magnatone entry into the solidstate market, superseded by Brute Series in 1968. 150 watts, 4x10" solidstate combo amp, naugahyde vinyl cover with polyester rosewood side panels.
1967-1968 $225 $275

Model 130V Custom Amp
1969-1971. Solidstate 1x12" combo amp.
1969-1971 $175 $200

Model 150R Firestar Reverb Amp
1967-1968. Initial Magnatone entry into the solidstate market, superseded by Brute Series in 1968. 120 watts, 2x12" solidstate combo amp, naugahyde vinyl cover with polyester rosewood side panels.
1967-1968 $225 $250

Model 180 Triplex Amp
Mid-to-late-1950s. Mid-level power using 2x6L6 power tubes, with 1x15" and 1x8" dual speakers.
1950s $325 $400

Model 192-5-S Troubadour Amp
Early-1950s. Eighteen watts, 1x12" Jensen Concert speaker, brown alligator covering, lower back control panel, 3 chicken-head knobs, Magnatone script logo on front, Troubadour script logo on back control panel.
1950s $250 $300

Model 194 Lyric Amp
1947-mid-1950s. One 12" speaker, old-style tweed vertical cab typical of 1940s.
1940s $250 $300

Model 195 Melodier Amp
1951-1954. Vertical cab with 1x10" speaker, pearloid with flowing grille slats.
1951-1954 $200 $300

Model 196 Amp
1947-mid-1950s. 5 to 10 watts, 1x12", scroll grille design, snakeskin leatherette cover.
1940s $200 $300

Model 199 Student Amp
1950s. About 6 to 10 watts, 1x8", snakeskin leatherette cover, metal handle, slant grille design.
1950s $200 $300

Model 210 Deluxe Student Amp
1958-1960. 5 watts, 1x8", vibrato, brown leatherette with V logo lower right front on grille.
1958-1960 $225 $250

Model 213 Troubadour Amp
1957-1958. 10 watts, 1x12", vibrato, brown leatherette cover, V logo lower right of grille.
1957-1958 $450 $500

Louis Electric Gattone

1958 Maestro

Magnatone Model 3802

1958 Magnatone Model 111

'50s Magnatone Troubadour

Magnatone Custom 280

MODEL YEAR	FEATURES	EXC. COND. LOW	HIGH

Model 240 SV Magna-Chordion Amp
1967-1968. Initial Magnatone entry into the solidstate market, superseded by Brute Series in 1968. 240 watts, 2x12" solidstate stereo accordion or organ amp, naugahyde vinyl cover with polyester rosewood side panels, standard input jacks suitable for guitar, reverb and vibrato, lateral (Fender Twin-style) combo cab, rear mounted controls.

1967-1968		$225	$250

Model 250 Professional Amp
1958-1960. 20 watts, 1x12", vibrato, brown leatherette with V logo lower right front of grille.

| 1958-1960 | | $475 | $550 |

Model 260 Amp
1957-1958. 35 watts, 2x12", brown leatherette, vibrato, V logo lower right front corner of grille.

| 1957-1958 | | $800 | $1,000 |

Model 262 Jupiter/Custom Pro Amp
1961-1963. 35 watts, 2x12", vibrato, brown leatherette.

| 1961-1963 | | $575 | $650 |

Model 280/Custom 280 Amp
1957-1958. 50 watts, brown leatherette covering, brown-yellow tweed grille, 2x12" plus 2x5" speakers, double V logo.

| 1957-1958 | | $850 | $1,100 |

Model 280A Amp
1958-1960. 50 watts, brown leatherette covering, brown-yellow tweed grille, 2x12" plus 2x5" speakers, V logo lower right front.

| 1958-1960 | | $800 | $950 |

Model 410 Diana Amp
1961-1963. 5 watts, 1x12", advertised as a 'studio' low power professional amp, brown leatherette cover, vibrato.

| 1961-1963 | | $300 | $350 |

Model 413 Centaur Amp
1961-1963. 18 watts, 1x12", brown leatherette cover, vibrato.

| 1961-1963 | | $450 | $500 |

Model 415 Clio Bass Amp
1961-1963. 25 watts, 4x8", bass or accordion amp, brown leatherette cover.

| 1961-1963 | | $450 | $500 |

Model 432 Amp
Mid-1960s. Compact student model, wavey-squiggle art deco-style grille, black cover, vibrato and reverb.

| 1960s | | $275 | $350 |

Model 435 Athene Bass Amp
1961-1963. 55 watts, 4x10", piggyback head and cab, brown leatherette.

| 1961-1963 | | $600 | $750 |

Model 440 Mercury Amp
1961-1963. 18 watts, 1x12", vibrato, brown leatherette.

| 1961-1963 | | $525 | $600 |

Model 450 Juno/Twin Hi-Fi Amp
1961-1963. 25 watts, 1x12" and 1 oval 5"x7" speakers, reverb, vibrato, brown leatherette.

1961-1963		$650	$800
1961-1963	Extension cab only	$375	$425

Model 460 Victory Amp
1961-1963. 35 watts, 2x12" and two oval 5"x7" speakers, early-'60s next to the top of the line, reverb and vibrato, brown leatherette.

| 1961-1963 | | $700 | $850 |

Model 480 Venus Amp
1961-1963. 50 watts, 2x12" and two oval 5"x7" speakers, early-'60s top of the line, reverb and stereo vibrato, brown leatherette.

| 1961-1963 | | $750 | $900 |

Model M6 Amp
1964 (not seen in 1965 catalog). 25 watts, 1x12", black molded plastic 'suitcase' amp.

| 1964 | | $325 | $400 |

Model M7 Bass Amp
1964-1966. 38 watts, 1x15" bass amp, black molded plastic 'suitcase' amp.

| 1964-1966 | | $325 | $400 |

Model M8 Amp
1964-1966. 27 watts, 1x12", reverb and tremolo, black molded plastic 'suitcase' amp.

| 1964-1966 | | $450 | $550 |

Model M9 Amp
1964-1966. 38 watts, 1x15", tremolo, no reverb, black molded plastic 'suitcase' amp.

| 1964-1966 | | $500 | $600 |

Model M10 Amp
1964-1966. 38 watts, 1x15", tremolo, transistorized reverb section, black molded plastic 'suitcase' amp.

| 1964-1966 | | $600 | $700 |

Model M12 Amp
1964-1966. 80 watts, 1x15" or 2x12", mid-1960s top of the line bass amp, black molded plastic 'suitcase' amp.

| 1960s | | $500 | $600 |

Model M14 Amp
1964-1966. Stereo, 75 watts, 2x12" plus 2 tweeters, stereo vibrato, no reverb, black molded plastic 'suitcase' amp.

| 1964-1966 | | $600 | $700 |

Model M15 Amp
1964-1966. Stereo 75 watts, 2x12" plus 2 tweeters, stereo vibrato, transistorized reverb, black molded plastic 'suitcase' amp.

| 1964-1966 | | $675 | $750 |

Model M27 Bad Boy Bass Amp
1968-1971. 150 watts, 1x15" and 1x15" passive speaker, reverb, vibrato, solidstate, vertical profile bass amp, part of Brute Series.

| 1968-1971 | | $275 | $300 |

Model M30 Fang Amp
1968-1971. 150 watts, 1x15", additional 1x15" passive and 1 exponential horn, solidstate, vibrato, reverb, vertical profile amp.

| 1968-1971 | | $275 | $300 |

Model M32 Big Henry Bass Amp
1968-1971. 300 watts, 2x15" solidstate vertical profile bass amp.

| 1968-1971 | | $275 | $300 |

The *Vintage Guitar Price Guide* shows low to high values for items in all-original excellent condition, and, where applicable, with original case or cover.

MODEL YEAR	FEATURES	EXC. COND. LOW	HIGH

Model M35 The Killer Amp
1968-1971. 300 watts, 2x15" and two horns, solid-state, vibrato, vertical profile amp.

1968-1971		$275	$300

Model MP-1 (Magna Power I) Amp
1966-1967. 30 watts, 1x12", dark vinyl, light grille, Magnatone-Estey logo on upper right of grille.

1966-1967		$300	$350

Model PS150 Amp
1968-1971. Powered slave speaker cabinets, 150 watts, 2x15" linkable cabinets.

1968-1971		$150	$200

Model PS300 Amp
1968-1971. Powered slave speaker cabinets, 300 watts, 2x15" (one passive) linkable cabinets.

1968-1971		$150	$200

Small Pearloid Amp
1947-1955. Pearloid (MOTO) covered low and mid power amps generally associated with pearloid lap steel sets.

1947-1955		$225	$300

Starlet Amp
1951-1952. Student model, 1x8", pearloid covering.

1951-1952		$225	$300

Starlite Model 401 Amp
Magnatone produced the mid-'60s Starlite amplifier line for the budget minded musician. Each Starlite model prominently notes the Magnatone name. The grilles show art deco wavy circles. Magnatone 1960-'63 standard amps offer models starting with 12" speakers. Starlight models offer 10" and below. Model 401 has 15 watts, 1x8" and three tubes.

1960s		$175	$200

Starlite Model 411 Amp
Mid-1960s. 15 watts, 1x8", 5 tubes, tremolo (not advertised as vibrato), art deco wavy grille.

1960s		$200	$225

Starlite Model 441A Bass Amp
Early-mid-1960s. Lower power with less than 25 watts, 1x15", tube amp.

1960s		$325	$350

Starlite Model Custom 421 Amp
Early-mid-1960s. Tube amp, 25 watts, 1x10".

1960s		$275	$350

Starlite Model Custom 431 Amp
Early-mid-1960s. Tube amp, 30 watts, 1x10", vibrato and reverb.

1960s		$375	$400

Mako
1985-1989. Line of solidstate amps from Kaman (Ovation, Hamer). They also offered guitars and basses.

Marlboro Sound Works
1970-1980s. Economy amps imported by Musical Instruments Corp., Syosset, New York. Initially, Marlboro targeted the economy compact amp market, but quickly added larger amps and PAs.

GA-2 Amp
1970s. Solidstate, 3 watts, 1x8", dark vinyl cover, dark grille, square plate logo.

1970s		$10	$25

GA-3 Amp
1970s. Solidstate, 3 watts, 1x8", tremolo.

1970s		$15	$30

GA-20B Amp
1970s. Solidstate bass/keyboard amp, 25 watts, 1x12".

1970s		$25	$75

GA-20R Amp
1970s. Solidstate, 25 watts, 1x12", tremolo and reverb.

1970s		$25	$75

GA-40R Amp
1970s. Ssolidstate, 30 watts, 1x12", tremolo and reverb.

1970s		$50	$100

Model 520B Amp
1970s. Solidstate, 25 watts, 1x15", bass/keyboard amp, dark vinyl cover, dark grille, square plate logo.

1970s		$50	$100

Model 560A Amp
1970s. Solidstate, 45 watts, 2x10".

1970s		$50	$100

Model 760A Amp
1970s. Solidstate guitar/bass/keyboard combo amp, 60 watts, 1x15".

1970s		$50	$100

Model 1200R Head Amp
1970s. 60 watts, single channel head with reverb.

1970s		$50	$100

Model 1500B Bass Head Amp
1970s. 60 watts, single channel head.

1970s		$50	$100

Model 2000 Bass Amp Set
1970s. One 1500B 60-watt head and one LS12FH 1x12" with Piezo horn cab.

1970s		$50	$100

Marshall
1962-present. Drummer Jim Marshall started building bass speaker and PA cabinets in his garage in 1960. He opened a retail drum shop for his students and others and soon added guitars and amps. When Ken Bran joined the business as service manager in '62, the two decided to build their own amps. By '63 they had expanded the shop to house a small manufacturing space and by late that year they were offering the amps to other retailers. Marshall also made amps under the Park, CMI, Narb, Big M, and Kitchen-Marshall brand names. Marshall continues to be involved in the company.

Mark I, II, III and IVs are generally '60s and '70s and also are generally part of a larger series (for example JTM), or have a model number that is a more specific identifier. Describing an amp only as Mark II can be misleading. The most important identifier is the Model Number, which

Magnatone 401-A

Magnatone Custom 450

Marlboro 560A

AMPS

Marshall AVT-20

Marshall AVT-150

Marshall AVT-275

MODEL YEAR	FEATURES	EXC. COND. LOW	HIGH

Marshall often called the Stock Number. To help avoid confusion *VG* has added the Model number as often as possible. In addition, when appropriate, *VG* has included the wattage, number of channels, master or no-master info in the title. This should help the reader more quickly find a specific amp. Check the model's description for such things as two inputs or four inputs, because this will help with identification. Vintage Marshall amps do not always have the Model/Stock number on the front or back panel, so the additional identifiers should help. The JMP logo on the front is common and really does not help with specific identification. For example, a JMP Mark II Super Lead 100 Watt description is less helpful than the actual model/ stock number. Unfortunately, many people are not familiar with specific model/stock numbers. *VG* has tried to include as much information in the title as space will allow.

Marshall amps are sorted as follows
AVT Series - new line for Marshall
Club and Country Series (Rose-Morris)-introduced in '78
JCM 800 Series - basically the '80s
JCM 900 Series - basically the '90s
JCM 2000 Series - basically the '00s
JTM Series
Micro Stack Group
Model Number/Stock Number (no specific series, basically the '60s, '70s) - including Artist and Valvestate models (Valvestate refers to specific Model numbers in 8000 Series)
Silver Jubilee Series

AVT 20 Combo Amp
2000-present. Solidstate, 20 watts, 12AX7 preamp tube, 1x10". Advanced Valvestate Technology (AVT) models have black covering and grille, and gold panel.

2000s		$200	$250

AVT 50 Combo Amp
2000-present. Solidstate, 50 watts, 1x12".

2000s		$300	$375

AVT 100 Combo Amp
2001-present. Solidstate, 100 watts, tube preamp, 1x12".

2000s		$500	$550

AVT 150 Combo Amp
2001-present. Solidstate, 100 watts, 1x12", additional features over AVT 100.

2000s		$600	$650

AVT 150 Half-Stack Amp
2000s. Solid-state 150-watt head and 4x12" slant cabinet.

2000s		$850	$900

AVT 275 Combo Amp
2000-present. Solidstate DFX stereo, 75 watts per side, 2x12".

2000s		$700	$750

MODEL YEAR	FEATURES	EXC. COND. LOW	HIGH

AVT 412/412A Cab
2000-present. Slant half-stack 4x12" cab, 200 watt load, 25 watt Celestions.

2000s		$300	$400

AVT 412B Cab
2000-present. Straight-front half-stack 4x12" cab, 200-watt load.

2000s		$275	$375

Club and Country Model 4140 Amp
1978-1982. Tubes, 100 watts, 2x12" combo, Rose-Morris era, designed for the country music market, hence the name, brown vinyl cover, straw grille.

1978-1982		$650	$900

Club and Country Model 4145 Amp
1978-1982. Tubes, 100 watts, 4x10" combo, Rose-Morris era, designed for the country music market, hence the name, Brown vinyl, straw grille.

1978-1982		$650	$900

Club and Country Model 4150 Bass Amp
1978-1982. Tubes, 100 watts, 4x10" bass combo, Rose-Morris era, designed for the country music market, hence the name, Brown vinyl cover, straw grille.

1978-1982		$600	$800

JCM 800 Model 1959 Amp Head
1981-1991. Lead head amp, 100 watts.

1981-1991		$750	$1,000

JCM 800 Model 1987 Amp Head
1981-1991. Lead head amp, 50 watts.

1981-1991		$700	$950

JCM 800 Model 2000 Amp Head
Introduced in 1981, lead head amp, 200 watts.

1980s		$750	$1,000

JCM 800 Model 2001 Amp Head
Introduced in 1981, bass head amp, 300 watts.

1980s		$750	$1,000

JCM 800 Model 2203 Amp Head
1981-1990. Lead head amp, 100 watts, master volume. JCM 800 Lead Series noted on front panel, replaced by Model 2210. Reissued in 2003.

1981-1990		$750	$1,000

JCM 800 Model 2204 Amp Head
1981-1990. 50 watts, 1 channel, 2 inputs, master volume, front panel says JCM 800 Lead Series.

1981-1990		$750	$1,000

JCM 800 Model 2204S Amp Head
1986-1987. Shorty head, 50 watts, 4x10" cab, brown grillecloth.

1986-1987		$750	$1,000

JCM 800 Model 2205 Amp Head
1983-1990. 50 watts, split channel (1 clean and 1 distortion), switchable, both channels with reverb, front panel reads JCM 800 Lead Series.

1983-1990		$750	$1,000

JCM 800 Model 2210 Amp Head
1983-1990. 100 watts.

1983-1990		$750	$1,000

JCM 800 Model 4010 Combo Amp
1980-1990. 50 watts, 1x12", reverb, single channel master volume.

1980-1990		$700	$950

MODEL		EXC. COND.	
YEAR	FEATURES	LOW	HIGH

JCM 800 Model 4103 Combo Amp
1980-1990. Lead combo amp, 50 watts, 2x12".
| 1980-1990 | | $750 | $1,000 |

JCM 800 Model 4104 Amp
1980-1990. All tube lead combo amp, 50 watts, 2x12".
| 1980-1990 | Black | $750 | $1,000 |
| 1980-1990 | White option | $900 | $1,100 |

JCM 800 Model 4210 Combo Amp
1982-1990. 50 watts, 1x12" tube combo, split-channel, single input, master volume.
| 1982-1990 | | $700 | $950 |

JCM 800 Model 4211 Combo Amp
1983-1990. Lead combo amp, 100 watts, 2x12".
| 1983-1990 | | $750 | $1,000 |

JCM 800 Model 5005 Combo Amp
1983-1990. Solidstate combo amp, 12 watts, master volume, 1x10".
| 1983-1990 | | $250 | $350 |

JCM 800 Model 5010 Combo Amp
1983-1990. Solidstate combo amp, 30 watts, master volume, 1x12".
| 1983-1990 | | $300 | $350 |

JCM 800 Model 5150 Combo Amp
1987-1991. Combo amp, 150 watts, specially designed 12" Celestion speaker, split channel design, separate clean and distortion channels, presence and effects-mix master controls.
| 1987-1991 | | $450 | $500 |

JCM 800 Model 5213 Combo Amp
1986-1991. MOS-FET solidstate combo, 2x12", channel-switching, effects loop, direct output, remote footswitch.
| 1986-1991 | | $350 | $400 |

JCM 800 Model 5215 Combo Amp
1986-1991. MOS-FET solidstate, 1x15", Accutronics reverb, effects loop.
| 1986-1991 | | $400 | $450 |

JCM 900 2100 Mark III Amp Head
1990-1993. FX loop, 100/50-watt selectable lead head.
| 1990-1993 | | $600 | $700 |

JCM 900 2100 SL-X Amp Head
1993-1998. Updated Model 2100 with added ECC83 preamp tube for more gain, JCM 900 SL-X on panel, 100/50 watts selectable.
| 1993-1998 | | $600 | $700 |

JCM 900 2500 (SL-X) Amp Head
1990-2000. 50/25 head amp, black. SL-X added in '93.
| 1990-2000 | | $600 | $700 |

JCM 900 4100 Dual Reverb Amp Head
1990-2000. 100/50 switchable head, JCM 900 on front panel, black with black front.
| 1990-2000 | | $700 | $800 |

JCM 900 4102 Combo Amp
1990-2000. Combo amp, 100/50 watts switchable, 2x12".
| 1990-2000 | | $800 | $900 |

JCM 900 4500 Amp Head
1990-2000. All tube, two channels, 50/25 watts, EL34 powered, reverb, effects loop, compensated recording out, master volume, Black.
| 1990-2000 | | $675 | $775 |

JCM 900 4501 Dual Reverb Combo Amp
1990-2000. 50/25 switchable, 1x12".
| 1990-2000 | | $800 | $900 |

JCM 900 4502 Combo Amp
1990-2000. 50/25 switchable, 2x12".
| 1990-2000 | | $850 | $950 |

JCM 2000 TSL 100 Amp
1998-present. TSL means Triple Super Lead, three channels.
| 1998-2003 | | $900 | $950 |

JTM 45 Amp (Model 1987) Head Reissue
1989-1999. Black/Green Tolex.
| 1988-1999 | | $650 | $750 |

JTM 45 Amp Head
1962-1964. Amp head, 45 watts. The original Marshall amp. Became the Model 1987 45-watt for 1965-1966.
| 1962-1964 | | $9,000 | $12,000 |

JTM 45 MK IV Model 1961 4x10 Combo Amp
1965-1966. 45 watts, 4x10", tremolo, JTM 45 MK IV on panel, Bluesbreaker association.
| 1965-1966 | | $7,000 | $10,000 |

JTM 45 MK IV Model 1962 2x12 Combo Amp
1965-1966. 45 watts, 2x12", tremolo, JTM 45 MK IV on panel, Bluesbreaker association.
| 1965-1966 | | $9,000 | $12,000 |

JTM 45 Model 1987 Mark II Lead Amp Head
1965-1966. Replaced JTM 45 Amp (1962-1964), but was subsequently replaced by the Model 1987 50-watt Head during 1966.
| 1965-1966 | | $5,000 | $6,000 |

JTM 45 Offset Limited Edition Amp Set Reissue
Introduced in 2000. Limited run of 300 units, old style cosmetics, head and offset 2x12" cab, dark vinyl cover, Light Gray grille, rectangular logo plate on front of amp and cab, Limited Edition plate on rear of cab, serial number xxx of 300.
| 2000 | 45 watts | $3,000 | $4,000 |

JTM 50 Amp (Model 1962) Bluesbreaker Reissue
1989-present. 50 watts, 2x12", Model 1962 reissue Bluesbreaker.
| 1989-1999 | | $800 | $850 |

JTM 50 MK IV Model 1961 4x10 Amp
1965-1972. 50 watts, 4x10", Bluesbreaker association, tremolo, JTM 50 MK IV on front panel to 1968, plain front panel without model description 1968-1972.
1966-1967		$7,000	$9,000
1968		$6,000	$7,000
1969		$5,000	$6,000
1970		$3,000	$4,000
1971-1972		$3,000	$3,500

Marshall TSL 100

1962 Marshall JTM 45

Marshall JTM 45 Mk II Lead

AMPS

AMPS

Marshall Super Tremolo Mk IV

Marshal 3005

Marshall 1959 Super Lead

MODEL YEAR	FEATURES	EXC. COND. LOW	HIGH

JTM 50 MK IV Model 1962 2x12 Amp
1966-1972. 50 watts, 2x12", tremolo, Bluesbreaker association, JTM 50 MK IV on front panel to 1968, plain front panel without model description 1968-1972.

1966-1967		$8,000	$10,000
1968	Plain panel	$7,000	$9,000
1969	Plain panel	$6,000	$7,000
1970	Plain panel	$3,500	$4,500
1971-1972	Plain panel	$3,500	$4,000

JTM 50 Model 1963 PA Amp Head
1965-1966. MK II PA head, block logo.

1965-1966		$2,500	$3,000

JTM 310 Amp
1995-1997. Tube combo, reverb, 30 watts, 2x10", effects loops, 5881 output sections, footswitchable high-gain modes.

1995-1997		$550	$650

JTM 612 Combo Amp
1995-1997. Tube combo amp, 60 watts, 1x12", EQ, reverb, effects loop.

1995-1997		$550	$650

Micro Stack 3005 Amp
Solidstate head, 15 watts with two 1x10" stackable cabs (one A - slant and one B - straight). Standard model is black, but was also offered in white, green, red, or silver. A Silver Jubilee version has Jubilee 25/50 logo.

1989	Black	$300	$400
1989	Green, Red, White	$400	$450
1989	Silver Jubilee/Silver	$450	$550
1990	Black	$300	$400

Mini-Stack 3210 MOS-FET Amp Head with 2x4x10"
1984-1991. Model 3210 MOS-FET head with two 4x10" cabs, designed as affordable stack.

1984-1991		$300	$400

Model 1710 Bass Cab
1990s. One 15" Speaker.

1990s		$350	$400

Model 1930 Popular Combo Amp
1969-1973. 10 watts, 1x12", tremolo.

1969-1973		$2,500	$3,000

Model 1935A 4x12" Bass Cab
1990s. Four 12" speakers cab.

1990s		$325	$375

Model 1936 2x12" Cab
1981-present. Two 12" speakers, extension straight-front cab, Black.

1990s		$275	$325

Model 1958 18-Watt Lead Amp
1966-1968. 18 watts, 2x10" combo, Bluesbreaker cosmetics, slant logo 1966 and '67, straight logo '68.

1966-1967	Non-reverb model	$6,500	$8,500
1968	Non-reverb model	$5,500	$6,000

Model 1958 20-Watt Lead Amp
1968-1972. 20 watts, 2x10" combo, tremolo.

1968		$5,000	$6,000
1969		$4,000	$4,500
1970		$3,500	$4,000
1971-1972		$3,000	$3,500

Model 1959 Super Lead Amp
1966-1981. Two channels, 100 watts, four inputs, no master volume. Plexiglas control panels until mid-1969, aluminum after. See Model T1959 for tremolo version. Early custom color versions are rare and more valuable.

1966-1969	Black, plexi	$4,500	$5,500
1966-1969	Custom color, plexi	$6,000	$8,000
1969-1970	Black, aluminum panel	$3,000	$3,500
1969-1970	Custom color, aluminum panel	$4,000	$5,000
1971-1972	Black, hand-wired, small box	$1,500	$2,000
1971-1972	Custom color, hand-wired	$2,000	$2,700
1973-1975	Black, printed C.B., large box	$1,000	$1,300
1973-1975	Custom color, printed C.B.	$1,300	$1,700
1976-1979	Black	$1,000	$1,300
1976-1979	Custom color	$1,300	$1,700
1980-1981	Black	$900	$1,100
1980-1981	Custom color	$1,200	$1,500

Model 1959 Super Lead Matching Set (Half Stack)
1966-1981 option. 100 watt head and matching color 4x12" cabinet. Plexiglass control panels made from '65 to mid-'69, followed by aluminum panel. Matching set requires that the head and cab are the exact matching set that came out of the factory as a set. A mismatched set that is of similar color but not built as a set is not applicable for this pricing. As is the case with all vintage amps, the speakers must be the factory original (untouched) speakers.

1966-1969	Black, plexi, weave	$7,500	$9,000
1966-1969	Custom color, plexi, weave	$11,500	$14,000
1969-1970	Black, aluminum, weave	$6,000	$7,000
1969-1970	Custom color, aluminum, weave	$6,500	$8,300
1971-1972	Black, hand-wired, weave	$3,700	$4,500
1971-1972	Custom color, hand-wired, weave	$5,100	$6,000
1973-1975	Black, printed C.B., large box, checkerboard	$2,400	$2,800
1973-1975	Custom color, printed C.B., large box,	$3,800	$4,400
1976-1979	Black	$2,200	$2,600
1976-1979	Custom color	$3,500	$4,000
1980-1981	Black	$2,000	$2,300
1980-1981	Custom color	$3,200	$3,600

Model 1959 Super Lead Matching Full Stack Set
1966-1981 option. Head with 100 watts and matching color slant and straight front 4x12" cabinets.

1966-1969	Black, plexi, weave	$11,000	$12,500

MODEL YEAR	FEATURES	EXC. COND. LOW	HIGH
1966-1969	Custom color, plexi, weave	$17,000	$20,000

Model 1959 SLP Reissue Amp Head
1992-present. SLP refers to Super Lead Plexi.

1990s	Black vinyl	$900	$1,100
1990s	Purple vinyl	$1,200	$1,400
1990s	White limited edition	$1,100	$1,300
2000s	Black vinyl	$900	$1,100

Model 1959 SLP Reissue Amp Set
1992-present. 100 watt Super Lead head and matching 4x12" slant cab.

1990s	Purple vinyl	$2,200	$2,500

Model 1960 4x12 Slant Speaker Cabinet
1964-1979. The original Marshall 4x12" cab designed for compact size with four 12" speakers. This first issue in 1964/1965 was a 60-watt cab, from 1965-1970 75 watts, from 1970-1979 100 watts. After 1979, models numbers contained an alpha suffix. Suffix A implies slant-angle front, suffix B implies straight-front cabinet, often the bottom cabinet of a two cabinet stack.

1966-1970	Black, weave	$2,000	$2,500
1966-1970	Custom color, weave	$4,500	$5,000
1971-1972	Black, weave	$1,800	$2,000
1971-1972	Custom color, weave	$2,600	$2,800
1973-1975	Custom color, checkerboard	$2,000	$2,200
1976-1979	Black	$700	$800
1976-1979	Custom color	$1,700	$1,800

Model 1960A 4x12 Slant Speaker Cabinet
1979-1983 (260-watts), 1984-1986 (280-watts), 1986-1990 (300-watts).

1979-1983	260 watts	$650	$800
1984-1986	280 watts, JCM 800 era	$650	$800
1986-1990	300 watts, JCM 800 era	$650	$800

Model 1960A JCM 900 4x12 Slant Speaker Cabinet
1990-2000. JCM 900 Series updated to 300 watts, stereo-mono switching.

1990-2000		$450	$650

Model 1960AV 4x12 Slant Speaker Cabinet
1990-present. JCM 900 updated, stereo/mono switching.

1990-2000	Black vinyl, Black grille	$550	$650
1990s	Red vinyl, Tan grille	$700	$800

Model 1960AX 4x12 Slant Speaker Cabinet
1990-present. Cab for Model 1987X and 1959X reissue heads.

1990-1999		$550	$650

Model 1960B 4x12 Straight Front Cabinet
1965-1970 (75 watts), 1970-1979 (100 watts), 1979-1983 (260 watts), 1983-1986 (280 watts), 1986-1990 (300 watts).

1966-1970	Black, weave	$2,000	$2,500

MODEL YEAR	FEATURES	EXC. COND. LOW	HIGH
1966-1970	Custom color, weave	$4,500	$5,000
1971-1972	Black, weave	$1,800	$2,000
1971-1972	Custom color, weave	$2,600	$2,800
1973-1975	Black, checkerboard	$900	$1,000
1973-1975	Custom color, checkerboard	$2,000	$2,200
1976-1979	Black	$700	$800
1976-1979	Custom color	$1,700	$1,800
1980-1981	Black	$600	$800
1980-1981	Custom color	$1,400	$1,800
1982-1990	Black	$550	$700
1982-1990	Custom color	$1,400	$1,600

Model 1960B JCM 900 4x12 Straight Front Cabinet
1990-2000. JCM 900 updated cabinet, stereo/mono switching, 300 watts.

1990-2000		$450	$650

Model 1960BX 4x12 Straight Front Cabinet
1990-present. Cab for Model 1987X and 1959X reissue heads.

1990s		$400	$600

Model 1960TV 4x12 Slant Cabinet
1990-present. Extra tall for JTM 45, mono, 100 watts.

1990s		$550	$650

Model 1964 Lead/Bass 50-Watt Amp Head
1973-1976. Head with 50 watts, designed for lead or bass.

1973-1976		$1,000	$1,300

Model 1967 Pig 200-Watt Amp Head
1967-early-1968 only. Head with 200 watts. The control panel was short and stubby and nicknamed the "Pig", the 200-watt circuit was dissimilar (and unpopular) to the 50-watt and 100-watt circuits.

1967-1968		$1,700	$2,000

Model 1967 Major 200-Watt Amp Head
1968-1974. 200 watts, the original Marshall 200 'Pig' was not popular and revised into the 200 'Major'. The new Major 200 was similar to the other large amps and included two channels, four inputs, but a larger amp cab.

1968		$1,800	$2,100
1969		$1,700	$2,000
1970		$1,500	$1,900
1971-1974		$1,400	$1,800

Model 1968 100-Watt Super PA Amp Head
1968-1975. P.A. head with 100 watts, two sets of four inputs (identifies P.A. configuration), often used for guitar.

1966-1969	Plexi panel	$2,400	$2,700
1969-1972	Aluminum panel	$1,500	$1,800

Model 1973 JMP Lead & Bass 20 Amp
1973 only. Front panel: JMP, back panel: Lead & Bass 20, 20 watts, 1x12" straight front checkered grille cab, head and cab Black vinyl.

1973		$1,500	$1,700

Marshall 1959 SLP Reissue

Marshall 1960A slant cab

1972 Marshall 1967 Major

AMPS

Marshall 2060 Mercury

Marshall 3203 Artist

1985 Marshall 3210 head

Model 1987 50-Watt Amp Head
1966-1981. Head amp, 50 watts, plexiglas panel until mid-1969, aluminum panel after.

Year	Features	Low	High
1966-1969	Black, plexi	$4,000	$4,500
1967-1969	Custom color, plexi	$5,500	$7,000
1969-1970	Black, aluminum panel	$2,200	$3,000
1971-1972	Hand-wired, small box	$1,200	$1,400
1973-1979	Printed C.B., large box	$1,000	$1,200
1980-1981		$900	$1,000

Model 1987 50-Watt Matching Set
Head and matching 4x12" cab, plexiglas control panels from 1965 to mid-1969, aluminum panel after.

Year	Features	Low	High
1966-1969	Custom color, plexi	$10,000	$12,000
1969	Custom color, aluminum	$5,500	$7,000

Model 1992 Super Bass Amp Head
1966-1981. 100 watts, plexi panel until mid-1969 when replaced by aluminum front panel, 2 channels, 4 inputs.

Year	Features	Low	High
1966-1969	Black, plexi	$3,500	$4,500
1966-1969	Custom color, plexi	$4,500	$7,000
1969-1970	Black, aluminum panel	$2,300	$2,800
1971-1972	Hand-wired	$1,200	$1,500
1973-1979	Printed C.B.	$1,000	$1,300
1980-1981		$900	$1,100

Model 2040 Artist 50-Watt Combo Amp
1971-1978. 50 watts, 2x12" Artist/Artiste combo model with a 'different' (less popular?) circuit.
| 1971-1978 | | $1,700 | $1,900 |

Model 2041 Artist Head and Cab Set
1971-1978. 50 watts, 2x12" half stack Artist/Artiste cab with a 'different' (less popular?) circuit.
| 1971-1978 | | $1,700 | $1,900 |

Model 2046 Specialist 25-Watt Combo Amp
1972-1973. 25 watts, 1x15" speaker, limited production due to design flaw (amp overheats).
| 1972-1973 | | $600 | $700 |

Model 2060 Mercury Combo Amp
1972-1973. Combo amp, 5 watts, 1x12", available in red or orange covering.
| 1972-1973 | Red | $700 | $800 |

Model 2061 20-Watt Lead/Bass Amp Head
1968-1973. Lead/bass head, 20 watts, plexi until 1969, aluminum after. Reissued in '04 as the Model 2061X.
| 1968-1969 | Black, plexi | $2,500 | $3,000 |
| 1969 | Black, aluminum | $1,400 | $2,000 |

Model 2078 Combo Amp
1973-1978. Solid-state, 100 watts, 4x12" combo, gold front panel, dark cover, gray grille.
| 1973-1978 | | $900 | $1,100 |

Model 2103 100-Watt 1-Channel Master Combo Amp
1975-1981. One channel, 2 inputs, 100 watts, 2x12", first master volume design, combo version of 2203 head.
| 1975-1981 | | $1,300 | $1,600 |

Model 2104 50-Watt 1-Channel Master Combo Amp
1975-1981. One channel, 2 inputs, 50 watts, 2x12", first master volume design, combo version of 2204 head.
| 1975-1981 | | $1,200 | $1,500 |

Model 2144 Master Reverb Combo Amp
1978 only. Master volume similar to 2104 but with reverb and boost, 50 watts, 2x12".
| 1978 | | $1,400 | $1,500 |

Model 2159 100-Watt 2-Channel Combo Amp
1977-1981. 100 watts, 2 channels, 4 inputs, 2x12" combo version of Model 1959 Super Lead head.
| 1977-1981 | | $1,200 | $1,400 |

Model 2203 Lead Amp Head
1975-1981. Head amp, 100 watts, two inputs, first master volume model design, often seen with Mark II logo.
| 1975-1981 | | $850 | $1,100 |

Model 2203 Lead/1960B Cab Half Stack
1975-1981. 100 watts, one channel, two inputs, first master model design, with matching 1960B straight front 4x12" cab.
| 1975-1981 | Red custom color | $1,900 | $2,100 |

Model 2204 50-Watt Amp Head
1975-1981. Head amp, 50 watts with master volume.
| 1975-1981 | | $850 | $950 |

Model 3203 Artist Amp Head
1986-1991. Tube head version of earlier 1984 Model 3210 MOS-FET, designed as affordable alternative, 30 watts, standard short cab, 2 inputs separated by 3 control knobs, Artist 3203 on front panel, black.
| 1986-1991 | | $300 | $400 |

Model 3210 MOS-FET Amp Head
1984-1991. MOS-FET solidstate head, refer to Mini-Stack listing for 3210 with 4x10" stacked cabinets. Early-1980s front panel: Lead 100 MOS-FET.
| 1984-1991 | | $200 | $300 |

Model 3310 100-Watt Lead Amp
1988-1991. Solidstate, 100 watts, lead head with channel switching and reverb.
| 1988-1991 | | $500 | $600 |

Model 4001 Studio 15 Amp
1985-1992. 15 watts using 6V6 (only model to do this up to this time), 1x12" Celestion Vintage 30 speakers.
| 1985-1992 | | $500 | $600 |

Model 5002 Combo Amp
1984-1991. Solidstate combo amp, 20 watts, 1x10", master volume.
| 1984-1991 | | $200 | $250 |

MODEL YEAR	FEATURES	EXC. COND. LOW	HIGH

Model 5005 combo Amp
1984-1991. Solidstate, 12 watts, 1x10", practice amp with master volume, headphones and line-out.

1984-1991		$150	$200

Model 5302 Keyboard Amp
1984-1988. Solidstate, 20 watts, 1x10", marketed for keyboard application.

1984-1988		$150	$200

Model 5502 Bass Amp
1984-ca.1992. Solidstate bass comb, 20 watts, 1x10" Celestion.

1984-1992		$175	$225

Model 6100 30th Anniversary Amp Head
1992-1995. All tube, 3 channels, 100 watts, EQ, gain, contour, full and half power modes, blue vinyl covering, front panel: 6100 LM Anniversary Series. Listed as JCM 900 6100 in 1995.

1992-1995		$1,100	$1,200

Model 6100 30th Anniversary Amp Set
1992-1995. Matching head with 100/50/25 watts and 4x12" cabinet (matching colors), first year was blue Tolex.

1992	Blue Tolex	$2,200	$3,000
1993-1995	Purple Tolex	$2,000	$2,200

Model 6101 LE Combo Amp
1992-1995. 1x12", 100/50/25 switchable watts, blue/purple cover, limited edition.

1992-1995		$1,300	$1,400

Model 8008 Valvestate Rackmount Amp
1991-2001. Solidstate rackmount power amp with dual 40-watt channels.

1991-2001		$175	$275

Model 8010 Valvestate VS15 Combo Amp
1991-1997. Solidstate, 10 watts, 1x8", compact size, black vinyl, black grille.

1991-1997		$150	$200

Model 8040 Valvestate 40V Combo Amp
1991-1997. Solidstate with tube preamp, 40 watts, 1x12", compact size, black vinyl, black grille.

1991-1997		$300	$400

Model 8080 Valvestate 80V Combo Amp
1991-1997. Solidstate with tube 12AX7 preamp, 80 watts, 1x12", compact size, black vinyl, black grille.

1991-1997		$300	$400

Model 8100 100-Watt Valvestate VS100H Amp Head
1991-2001. Solidstate head, 100 watts.

1991-2001		$300	$400

Model 8200 200-Watt Valvestate Amp Head
1991-1998. Solidstate reverb head, 2 100-watt channels.

1991-1998		$350	$450

Model 8240 Valvestate Stereo Chorus Amp
1992-1996. Valvestate, 80 watts (2x40 watts stereo), 2x12" combo, reverb, chorus.

1992-1996		$400	$500

Model 8280 2x80-Watt Valvestate Combo Amp
1991-1996. Valvestate solidstate, 2x80 watts, 2x12".

1991-1996		$450	$550

Model T1959 Super Lead (Trem) Amp Head
1966-1973. Head amp, 100 watts, plexi until mid-1969, aluminum after. Tremolo version of the Model 1959 Amp.

1966-1969	Black, plexi	$4,700	$5,700
1967-1969	Custom color, plexi	$6,200	$8,200
1969-1970	Black, aluminum	$3,200	$3,700
1969-1970	Custom color, aluminum	$4,200	$5,200
1971-1973	Black, hand-wired, small box	$1,500	$2,200
1971-1973	Custom color, hand-wired	$2,000	$2,900

MS-2/MS-2R Amp
1990s. One watt, battery operated, miniature piggyback amp and cab, MS-2R in Red.

1990s		$20	$30

MS-4 Amp
1990s. MS-2 with additional mini-cab, black vinyl.

1990s		$30	$50

Silver Jubilee Model 2550 50/25 (Tall) Amp Head
1987-1989. 50/25 switchable tall box head for full Jubilee stack.

1987-1989	Black	$1,000	$1,100

Silver Jubilee Model 2553 (short) 2556A (mini)
1987-1989. Short box, 100/50 watt, 2x2x12".

1987-1989		$2,000	$2,200

Silver Jubilee Model 2553 50/25 (Short) Amp Head
1987-1989. 50/25 switchable small box head for mini-short stack.

1987-1989		$800	$900

Silver Jubilee Model 2554 1x12 Combo Amp
1987-1989. 50/25 watts, 1x12" combo using 2550 chasis.

1987-1989		$1,100	$1,300

Silver Jubilee Model 2555 Amp with Full Stack
1987-1989. Silver vinyl covering, chrome control panel, 100/50 watts with two 2551A 4x12" cabinets.

1987-1989		$2,600	$2,900

Silver Jubilee Model 2555 Amp with Half Stack
1987-1989. 100/50 watts, 1x4x12".

1987-1989		$1,800	$2,000

Silver Jubilee Model 2556 4x12 Cab
1987-1989. Cab with 4x12" speakers in 3 brand name options.

1987-1989		$800	$900

Marshall 4101

Marshall 8100 VSH100H head

Marshall Model 2553 50/25 Silver Jubilee

Marshall 2558 Silver Jubilee

Matamp Green

Matchless Chief 410

MODEL YEAR	FEATURES	EXC. COND. LOW	HIGH
Silver Jubilee Model 2556A/AV 2x12 Cab			
1987-1989. Cab with 2x12" speakers with 3 brand name options.			
1987-1989		$600	$700
Silver Jubilee Model 2558 2x12 Combo Amp			
1987-1989. 50/25 watts, 2x12" combo using 2550 chasis.			
1987-1989		$1,300	$1,500
SLX Hi-Gain Master Volume Amp			
1992-mid-1990s. 100 watts, head amp.			
1990s		$700	$800

Martin

Martin has dabbled in amps a few times, under both the Martin and Stinger brand names.

MODEL YEAR	FEATURES	EXC. COND. LOW	HIGH
Stinger FX-1 Amp			
1988-1990. Ten watts, EQ, switchable solidstate tube-synth circuit, line out and footswitch jacks.			
1988		$50	$100
Stinger FX-1R Amp			
1988-1990. Mini-stack amp, 2x10", 15 watts, dual-stage circuitry.			
1989		$100	$150
Stinger FX-6B Amp			
1989-1990. Combo bass amp, 60 watts, 1x15".			
1989		$150	$200

Matamp

1966-present. Tube amps, combos and cabinets built In Huddersfield, England, bearing names like Red, Green, White, Black, and Blue. German-born Mat Mathias started building amps in England in '58 and designed his first Matamp in '66. From '69 to '73, Mathias also made Orange amps. In '89, Mathias died at age 66 and his family later sold the factory to Jeff Lewis.

MODEL YEAR	FEATURES	EXC. COND. LOW	HIGH
Green GT-120 Stack			
1990s. 120 watt GT head with 4x12" straight front cab.			
1993-1999		$1,800	$2,000

Matchless

1989-1999, 2001-present. Founded by Mark Sampson and Rick Perrotta in California. Circuits based on Vox AC-30 with special attention to transformers. A new Matchless company was reorganized in 2001 by Phil Jamison, former head of production for the original company.

MODEL YEAR	FEATURES	EXC. COND. LOW	HIGH
1x12 Speaker Cabinet			
1990s.			
1990s		$500	$700
1x15 Bass Speaker Cabinet			
1990s.			
1990s		$500	$650
2x10 2x12 Speaker Cabinet			
1990s.			
1990s		$700	$1,000
2x10 Speaker Cabinet			
1990s.			
1990s		$550	$750

MODEL YEAR	FEATURES	EXC. COND. LOW	HIGH
2x12 Speaker Cabinet			
1990s.			
1990s		$600	$800
4x10 Bass Speaker Cabinet			
1990s.			
1990s		$550	$750
4x10 Speaker Cabinet			
1990s.			
1990s		$650	$900
4x12 Speaker Cabinet			
1990s.			
1990s		$700	$1,000
Brave 40 112 Amp			
1990s. 40 watts class A, 1x12", footswitchable between high and low inputs.			
1990s		$1,300	$1,600
Brave 40 212 Amp			
1990s. 40 watts class A, 2x12", footswitchable between high and low inputs.			
1990s		$1,500	$2,000
Chief 212 Amp			
1995-1999. 100 watts class A, 2x12", reverb.			
1995-1999		$2,800	$3,100
Chief 410 Amp			
1995-1999. 100 watts class A, 4x10", reverb.			
1995-1999		$2,800	$3,300
Chief Amp Head			
1995-1999. 100 watts class A, head.			
1995-1999		$2,400	$2,800
Chieftan Amp Head			
1995-1999. 40 watts class A head.			
1995-1999		$2,000	$2,300
Chieftan 112 Amp			
1995-1999. 40 watts class A, 1x12", reverb.			
1995-1999		$2,400	$2,800
Chieftan 210 Amp			
1995-1999. 40 watts class A, 2x10", reverb.			
1995-1999		$2,400	$3,100
Chieftan 212 Amp			
1995-1999. 40 watts class A, 2x12", reverb.			
1995-1999		$2,800	$3,300
Chieftan 410 Amp			
1995-1999. 40 watts class A, 4x10", reverb.			
1995-1999		$2,800	$3,300
Clipper 15 112 Amp			
1998-1999. 15 watts, single channel, 1x12".			
1998-1999		$900	$1,300
Clipper 15 210 Amp			
1998-1999. 15 watts, single channel, 2x10".			
1998-1999		$900	$1,300
Clubman 35 Amp Head			
1993-1999. 35 watts class A head.			
1993-1999		$1,800	$2,300
DC-30 Exotic Wood Cabinet Option			
1991-1999. 30 watts, 2x12", with or without reverb, limited production.			
1991-1999	Non-reverb	$5,500	$5,800
1991-1999	With reverb	$6,000	$6,300

AMPS

MODEL YEAR	FEATURES	EXC. COND. LOW	HIGH

DC-30 Standard Cabinet
1991-1999. 30 watts, 2x12", with or without reverb.

1991-1999	Non-reverb	$3,200	$3,400
1991-1999	With reverb	$3,400	$3,800

HC-30 Amp Head
1991-1999. The first model offered by Matchless, 30 watts class A head.

1991-1999	$2,400	$2,800

Hurricane 112 Amp
1994-1997. 15 watts class A, 1x12".

1994-1997	$1,300	$1,500

Hurricane 210 Amp
1996-1997. 15 watts class A, 2x10".

1996-1997	$1,300	$1,500

Hurricane Amp Head
1997. 15 watts class A head.

1997	$1,100	$1,300

JJ-30 112 John Jorgensen Amp
1997-1998. 30 watts, DC-30 chasis with reverb and tremolo, 1x12" Celestion 30, offered in white, blue, gray sparkle Tolex or black.

1997-1998	$3,800	$4,800

Lightning 15 112 Amp
1994-1998. 15 watts class A, 1x12".

1994-1998	Non-reverb	$1,400	$1,600
1994-1998	With reverb	$1,900	$2,100

Lightning 15 210 Amp
1996-1997. 15 watts class A, 2x10".

1996-1997	Non-reverb	$1,600	$2,100
1996-1997	With reverb	$2,100	$2,600

Lightning 15 212 Amp
1996-1997. 15 watts class A, 2x12".

1996-1997	Non-reverb	$1,600	$2,100
1996-1997	With reverb	$2,100	$2,600

Lightning 15 Amp Head
1997. 15 watts class A head.

1997	$1,100	$1,500

SC-30 Exotic Wood Cabinet Option
1991-1999. 30 watts class A, 1x12", limited production.

1991-1999	Non-reverb	$5,200	$5,500
1991-1999	With reverb	$5,700	$6,000

SC-30 Standard Cabinet
1991-1999. 30 watts class A, 1x12".

1991-1999	Non-reverb	$2,700	$3,000
1991-1999	With reverb	$3,200	$3,500

Skyliner Reverb 15 112 Amp
1998-1999. 15 watts, 1x12".

1998-1999	$1,000	$1,400

Skyliner Reverb 15 210 Amp
1998-1999. 15 watts, 2x10".

1998-1999	$1,000	$1,400

Spitfire 15 112 Amp
1994-1997. 15 watts, 1x12".

1994-1997	$1,300	$1,500

Spitfire 15 210 Amp
1996-1997. 15 watts, 2x10".

1996-1997	$1,500	$1,700

Spitfire 15 Amp Head
1997. 15 watts, head.

1997	$1,100	$1,300

MODEL YEAR	FEATURES	EXC. COND. LOW	HIGH

Starliner 40 212 Amp
1999s. 40 watts, 2x12".

1999	$1,600	$2,000

Superchief 120 Amp Head
1994-1999. 120 watts class A head.

1994-1999	$2,100	$2,600

TC-30 Exotic Wood Cabinet Option
1991-1999. 30 watts, 2x10" class A, limited production.

1991-1999	Non-reverb	$5,400	$5,800
1991-1999	With reverb	$5,900	$6,300

TC-30 Standard Cabinet
1991-1999. 30 watts, 2x10" class A, low production numbers makes value approximate with DC-30.

1991-1999	Non-reverb	$2,900	$3,300
1991-1999	With reverb	$3,400	$3,800

Thunderchief Bass Amp Head
1994-1999. 200 watts class A bass head.

1994-1999	$1,000	$1,800

Thunderman 100 Bass Combo Amp
1997-1998. 100 watts, 1x15" in portaflex-style flip-top cab.

1997-1998	$1,300	$2,000

Tornado 15 112 Amp
1994-1995. Compact, 15 watts, 1x12", two-tone covering, tremolo.

1994-1995	$1,000	$1,200

Maven Peal
1999-present. Amps, combos and cabinets built by David Zimmerman in Plainfield, Vermont (the name stands for "expert sound"). Serial number format is by amp wattage and sequential build; for example, 15-watt amp 15-001, 30-watt 30-001, and 50-watt 50-001 with the 001 indicating the first amp built. S = Silver Series, no alpha = Gold Series.

Mega Amplifiers
Budget and intermediate grade, production, solidstate and tube amps from Guitar Jones, Inc. of Pomona, California.

Merlin
Rack-mount bass head built in Germany by Musician Sound Design. They also offer the MSD guitar effects.

Mesa-Boogie
1971-present. Founded by Randall Smith in San Francisco. Circuits styled on high-gain Fender-based chassis designs, ushering in the compact high-gain amp market. The following serial number information and specs courtesy of Mesa Engineering.

.50 Caliber Amp Head
Jan. 1987-Dec. 1988. Serial number series: SS3,100-SS11,499. Mesa Engineering calls it Caliber .50. Tube head amp, 50 watts, 5-band EQ, effects loop. Called the .50 Caliber Plus in 1992 and 1993.

1987-1988	$450	$500

Matchless Spitfire 112

1997 Matchless Thunderchief

Maven Peal Zeetz 0.5>50

AMPS

AMPS

Mesa-Boogie Mk 1 reissue

Mesa-Boogie Mk II B

1980 Mesa-Boogie Mk II

MODEL		EXC. COND.	
YEAR	FEATURES	LOW	HIGH

.50 Caliber+ Combo Amp
Dec. 1988-Oct. 1993. Serial number series FP11,550-FP29,080. 50 watts, 1x12" combo amp.

1988-1993		$500	$550

20/20 Amp
June 1995-present. Serial number series: TT-01. 20 to 22 watts per channel.

1995-2001		$425	$475

395 Amp
Feb. 1991-April 1992. S2,572 to S3,237.

1991-1992		$500	$550

50/50 (Fifty/Fifty) Amp
May 1989-present. Serial number series: FF001-. 100 watts total power, 50 watts per channel, front panel reads 'Fifty/Fifty', contains four 6L6 power tubes.

1989-2003		$500	$550

500 Amp
June 1991-April 1992. S2,552-.

1991-1992		$500	$550

Bass 400 Amp
Aug. 1989-Aug. 1990. Serial number series: B001-B1200. About 500 watts using 12 5881 power tubes, replaced by 400+.

1989-1990		$800	$850

Bass 400+ Amp Head
Aug. 1990-present. Serial number series: B1200-, update change to 7-band EQ at serial number B1677, uses 12 5881 power tubes to give about 500 watts.

1990-1999		$800	$850

Blue Angel Amp
June 1994-2004. Serial number series BA01-. Lower power, 1x12" combo.

1994-1999	1x12" combo	$700	$800
1994-1999	2x10" custom color	$800	$900

Buster Bass Amp Head
Dec. 1997-Jan. 2001. Serial number series: BS-1-999, 200 watts via six 6L6 power tubes (similar to Ampeg SVT).

1997-2001		$600	$700

Buster Bass Combo Amp
1999-2001. 200 watts, 2x10", wedge cabinet, black vinyl, metal grille.

1999-2001		$700	$900

Coliseum 300 Amp
Oct. 1997-2002. Serial number series: COL-01 to COL-132, 200 watts per channel using 12 6L6 power tubes, rackmount.

1997-2002		$800	$1,000

D-180 Amp Head
July 1982-Dec. 1985. Serial number series D001-D681. All tube head amp, 200 watts, preamp, switchable.

1982-1985		$625	$675

DC-3 Amp
Sept. 1994-Jan. 1999. 35 watts, 1x12". serial number series: DC3-001 to DC3-4523.

1994-1999		$550	$625

DC-5 Amp
Oct. 1993-Jan. 1999. 50 watt head, 1x12" combo. serial numbers: DC1024-DC31,941.

1993-1999		$600	$700

MODEL		EXC. COND.	
YEAR	FEATURES	LOW	HIGH

DC-10 Amp Head
May 1996-Jan. 1999. Serial number series: DCX-001 to DCX-999. Dirty/Clean (DC) 60 or 100 watts (6L6s).

1996-1999		$650	$750

Formula Preamp
July 1998-2002. Serial number series: F-01, used 15 12AX7 tubes, 3 channels.

1998-2000		$500	$550

Heartbreaker Amp
June 1996-2001. Serial number series: HRT-01-, 60 watts to 100 watts switchable, 2x12" combo, designed to switch-out 6L6s, EL34s or the lower powered 6V6s in the power section, switchable solidstate or tube rectifier.

1996-2001		$900	$1,100

M-180 Amp
April 1982-Jan. 1986. Serial number series M001-M275.

1982-1986		$400	$700

M-2000 Amp
June 1995-2003. Serial number B2K-01.

1995-1999		$500	$700

M-Pulse 360 Amp
July 2001-present. MP3-01 rackmount, silver panel.

2001-2003		$600	$650

Mk I Combo (Model A) Amp
1971-1978. The original Boogie amp, not called the Mark I until the Mark II was issued. 60 or 100 watts, 1x12", Model A serial number series: 1-2999, very early serial numbers 1-299 had 1x15".

1971-1972	1x15"	$900	$1,100
1971-1978	1x12"	$800	$1,000

Mk I Reissue Amp
Nov. 1989-present. Serial number series: H001-. 100 watts, 1x12", reissue features include figured maple cab and wicker grille.

2000-2001		$675	$800

Mk II Combo Amp
1978-1980. Late 1978 1x12", serial number sequence: 3000-5574. Effective Aug. 1980 1x15", serial number sequence: 300-559 until Mark II B replaced.

1978-1980	1x12"	$750	$1,000
1978-1980	1x15"	$750	$1,000

Mk II B Amp Head
Head only.

1981-1983		$650	$900

Mk II B Combo Amp
1980-1983. Effective Aug. 1980 1x12" models, serial number sequence 5575-110000. May 1983 1x15" models, serial number series 560-11000. The 300 series serial number series K1-K336.

1981-1983	1x12"	$750	$1,000
1981-1983	1x15"	$750	$1,000

Mk II C+ Head Amp
1983-1985. 60 watt head.

1983-1985		$800	$1,100

MODEL YEAR	FEATURES	EXC. COND. LOW	HIGH

Mk II C/Mk II C+ Amp
May 1983-March 1985. Serial number series 11001-14999 for 60 watts, 1x15", offered with optional white Tolex cover. 300 series serial numbers after C+ are in the series K337-K422.

MODEL YEAR	FEATURES	LOW	HIGH
1983-1985		$900	$1,200
1983-1985	White Tolex	$900	$1,200

Mk III Amp Head
1985-1999. 10 watts, black vinyl.

1985-1990		$800	$1,000
1990-1999	Graphic EQ model	$800	$1,000

Mk III Combo Amp
Mar. 1985-Feb. 1999. Serial number series: 15,000-28,384. 300 series serialization K500-. Graphic equalizer only Mark III since August 1990, 100 watts, 1x12" combo. Custom cover or exotic hardwood cab will bring more than standard vinyl cover cab.

1985-1990	Black	$900	$1,200
1985-1990	Custom color	$900	$1,300
1985-1991	Custom hardward cab	$1,000	$1,400
1990-1999	Graphic EQ, hardwood cab	$1,000	$1,400
1990-1999	Graphic EQ, standard cab	$900	$1,000

Mk III 1x12 Cab
Late 1980s-early 1990s. Typically sized 1x12" extension cab with open half back, black vinyl, black grille, not strictly for Mark III, usable for any Boogie with matching output specs, rated for 90 watts.

1988-1990s	Slant cab	$550	$650
1988-1990s	Straight-front cab	$550	$650

Mk III 4x12 Cab
Late-1980s-early-1990s. Half stack 4x12" slant cab with open half back or straight-front cab, not strictly for Mark III, usable for any Boogie with matching output specs, often loaded with Celestion Vintage 30s, small weave grille (not see-through crossing strips).

1988-1990s		$550	$650

Mk IV Head and Half Stack Amp Set
1991-2000. Mark IV head and matching 4x12" slant half stack cab.

1991-2000		$1,300	$1,500

Mk IV/Mark IV B Combo Amp
May 1990-present. Changed to Model IV B Feb. '95, serial number series IV001. Clean rhythm, crunch rhythm and lead modes, 40 watts, EQ, three-spring reverb, dual effects loops, digital footswitching.

1991-1999		$1,200	$1,400
2000-2003		$1,200	$1,400

Maverick Amp Head
1994-present. 35 watts, Dual Rectifier head, white/blond vinyl cover.

1994-2000		$600	$800

Maverick Combo Amp
1997-present. Dual channels, four EL84s, 35 watts, 1x12" or 2x12" combo amp, 5AR4 tube rectifier, cream vinyl covering. Serial number identification MAV. Also available as head.

1997-2000	1x12"	$750	$900
1997-2000	2x12"	$800	$950

Maverick Half Stack Amp Set
April 1994-present. Serial number series: MAV001-. 35 watts, Dual Rectifier head and half stack cab set.

1990s		$950	$1,200

Nomad 45 Combo Amp
July 1999-present. Serial number series: NM45-01. 45 watts, 1x12, 2x12" or 4x10" combo, dark vinyl cover, dark grille.

1999-2002	1x12"	$700	$800
1999-2002	2x12"	$800	$1,000
1999-2003	4x10"	$800	$1,000

Nomad 55 Combo Amp
July 1999-2004. Serial number series: NM55-01. 55 watts, 1x12", 2x12" or 4x10" combo.

1999-2001	1x12"	$800	$900
1999-2001	2x12"	$900	$1,100

Mesa-Boogie Nomad 55

Nomad 100 Amp Head
July 1999-present. 100 watts, black cover, black grille.

1999-2001		$800	$900

Nomad 100 Combo Amp
July 1999-present. 100 watts, 1x12" or 2x12" combo, black cover, black grille.

1999-2001	1x12	$900	$1,000
1999-2001	2x12"	$1,000	$1,200

Princeton Boost Fender Conversion
1970. Fender Princeton modified by Randall Smith, Boogie badge logo instead of the Fender blackface logo on upper left corner of the grille. About 300 amps were modified and were one of the early mods that became Mesa-Boogie.

1970		$1,500	$2,500

Quad Preamp
Sept. 1987-1992. Serial number series: Q001-Q2,857. Optional Quad with FU2-A footswitch Aug. 1990-Jan. 1992, serial number series: Q2,022 to Q2,857.

1987-1992	Without footswitch	$500	$600
1990-1992	With FU2-A footswitch	$600	$700

Rect-O-Verb Combo Amp
Dec. 1998-present. Serial number series R50-. 50 watts, 1x12", black vinyl cover, black grille.

1998-2001		$1,000	$1,100

Rect-O-Verb I Amp Head
Dec. 1998-2001. Serial number series: R50-. 50 watts, head with two 6L6 power tubes, upgraded April 2001 to II Series.

1998-2001		$850	$950

Rect-O-Verb II Amp Head (upgrade)
April 2001 upgrade. R5H-750.

2001-2003		$500	$550

Rect-O-Verb/Recto 4x12" Cab
1998-2001. Slant front 4x12" cab, black cover, dark grille.

1998-2001		$500	$550

Road Ready 1x15 Cabinet
1990s. 1x15" cabinet built with anvil-style road case with metal grille and castes, heavy duty.

1990s		$400	$500

Mesa-Boogie Nomad 100

Mesa-Boogie Mk IV B reissue

*1984 Mesa-Boogie
Son of Boogie*

*Mesa-Boogie
Son of Boogie combo*

Mission Amp

MODEL YEAR	FEATURES	EXC. COND. LOW	HIGH

Road Ready 2x12 Cabinet
1990s. 2x12" cabinet built into anvil-style road case with metal grille and casters, heavy duty.

1990s		$500	$600

Rocket 440 Amp
March 1999-Aug. 2000. Serial number series: R440-R44-1159. 45 watts, 4x10".

1999-2000		$600	$650

Satellite/Satellite 60 Amp
Aug. 1990-1999. Serial number series: ST001-ST841. Uses either 6L6s for 100 watts or EL-34s for 60 watts, dark vinyl, dark grille.

1990-1999		$500	$700

Solo 50 Rectifier Amp Head (Series I)
Nov. 1998-April 2001. Serial number series: R50. 50 watts, head.

1998-2001		$800	$1,000

Solo 50 Rectifier Series II
April 2001 upgrade. Serial number series: S50-1,709. Upgrades preamp section, head with 50 watts.

2001		$700	$900

Son Of Boogie Amp
May 1982-Dec. 1985. Serial number series: S100-S2390. 60 watts, 1x12", considered the first reissue of the original Mark I.

1982-1985		$400	$475

Stereo 290 (Simul 2: Ninety) Amp
June 1992-present. Serial number series: R0001-. Dual 90-watt stereo channels, rackmount.

1992-1999		$900	$1,000

Stereo 295 Amp
March 1987-May 1991. Serial number series: S001-S2673. Dual 95-watt class A/B stereo channels, rackmount. Selectable 30 watts Class A (EL-34) power tubes) power.

1987-1991		$600	$700

Strategy 400 Amp
March 1987-May 1991. Serial number series: S001-S2627. 400 to 500 watts, power amplifier with 12 6L6 power tubes.

1987-1991		$600	$750

Studio .22 Amp
Nov. 1985-1988. Serial numbers: SS000-SS11499. Black vinyl, Black grille, 22 watts, 1x12".

1985-1988		$400	$500

Studio .22+ Amp
Dec. 1988-Aug. 1993. Serial number series: FP11,500-FP28,582. 22 watts, 1x12", black vinyl cover, black grille.

1988-1993		$400	$600

Studio Caliber DC-2 Amp
April 1994-Jan. 1999. Serial number series: DC2-01-DC2-4247 (formerly called DC-2). 20 watts, 1x12" combo, dark vinyl, dark grille.

1994-1999		$500	$575

Studio Preamp
Aug. 1988-Dec. 1993. Serial number series: SP000-SP7890. Tube preamp, EQ, reverb, effects loop.

1988-1993		$325	$400

MODEL YEAR	FEATURES	EXC. COND. LOW	HIGH

Subway Reverb Rocket Amp
Jun. 1998-Aug. 2001. Serial number series: RR1000-RR2461. 20 watts, 1x10".

1998-2001		$550	$650

Subway Rocket (no reverb) Amp
Jan. 1996-July 1998. Serial number series: SR001-SR2825. No reverb, 20 watts, 1x10".

1996-1998		$500	$550

Subway/Subway Blues Amp
Sept. 1994-Aug. 2000. Serial number series: SB001-SB2,515. 20 watts, 1x10".

1994-2000		$450	$550

Trem-O-Verb Dual Rectifier Amp Head
June 1993-Jan. 2001. 100 watt head version.

1993-2001		$950	$1,100
1993-2001	Rackmount version	$950	$1,100

Trem-O-Verb Dual Rectifier 4x12 Cab
Late-1980s-early-1990s. Half stack 4x12" slant cab with open half back, or straight-front cab, not strictly for this model, useable for any Boogie with matching output specs, often loaded with Celestion Vintage 30s, small weave grille (not see-through crossing strips).

1988-1990s	Slant cab	$500	$550
1988-1990s	Straight-front cab	$500	$550

Trem-O-Verb Dual Rectifier Combo Amp
June 1993-Jan. 2001. Serial number series R- to about R-21210. 100 watts, 2x12" Celestion Vintage 30.

1993-2000		$1,150	$1,400

Trem-O-Verb Dual Rectifier Half Stack Amp
June 1993-Jan. 2001. 100 watts, head with matching 4x12" slant cab.

2001		$1,400	$1,600

Triaxis Preamp
Oct. 1991-present. Serial number series: T0001-. Five 12AX7 tube preamp, rackmount.

1991-2000		$950	$1,050

Triple Rectifier Amp Head
Three channel amp head.

2002		$1,300	$1,700

V-Twin Rackmount Amp
May 1995-June 1998. V2R-001 to V2R-2258.

1995-1998		$450	$500

Walk About M-Pulse Bass Amp Head
Sept. 2001-present. Serial number series WK-01-. Lightweight and portable at 13 pounds, 2x12AX7 + 300 MOS-FET.

2001		$400	$500

Mission Amps
1996-present. Bruce Collins' Mission Amps, located in Arvada, Colorado, produces a line of custom-made combo amps, heads, and cabinets.

Mojave Amp Works
2002-present. Tube amp heads and speaker cabinets by Victor Mason in Apple Valley, California.

MODEL		EXC. COND.	
YEAR	FEATURES	LOW	HIGH

Montgomery Ward

Amps for this large retailer were sometimes branded as Montgomery Ward, but usually as Airline (see that listing).

Higher Power 1x12" Combo Amp
1950s. 1x12", about 2x 6L6 power tubes, includes brown covered Maestro C Series with cloverleaf grille.

1950s		$275	$325

Lower Power 1x12" Combo Amp
1950s. One 12" speaker, around 12 watts, includes Model 8439.

1950s		$175	$275

Mooneyes

Budget solid state amp line from Lace Music Products. They also offer amps under the Rat Fink and Lace brand names. Lace has a Mooneyes guitar model line.

Morley

Late 1960s-present. The effects company offered an amp in the late '70s. See Effects section for more company info.

Bigfoot Amp
1979-ca.1981. Looks like Morley's '70s effects pedals. Produced 25 watts and pedal controlled volume. Amp only, speakers were sold separately.

1979-1981		$150	$250

Mountain

Mountain builds a 9-volt amp in a wood cabinet. Originally built in California, then Nevada; currently being made in Vancouver, Canada.

Multivox

Ca.1946-ca.1984. Multivox was started as a subsidiary of Premier to manufacture amps, and later, effects.

New York 1st AVE Amp
1982. 15 watts, 1x8".

1982		$50	$75

New York 6th AVE Amp
1982. 60 watts, 1x12".

1982		$75	$100

Music Man

1972-present. Music Man made amps from '73 to '83. The number preceding the amp model indicates the speaker configuration. The last number in model name usually referred to the watts. RD indicated "Reverb Distortion." RP indicated "Reverb Phase." Many models were available in head-only versions and as combos with various speaker combinations.

110 RD Fifty Amp
1980-1983. 50 watts, 1x10", reverb, distortion.

1980-1983		$400	$525

112 RD Fifty Amp
1980-1983. 50 watts, 1x12", reverb, distortion.

1980-1983		$500	$575

112 RD One Hundred Amp
1978-1983. 100 watts, 1x12", reverb, distortion.

1978-1983		$500	$575

112 RD Sixty Five Amp
1978-1983. 65 watts, 1x12", reverb, distortion.

1978-1983		$500	$575

112 RP One Hundred Amp
1978-1983. Combo amp, 100 watts, 1x12", reverb, built-in phaser.

1978-1983		$500	$575

112 RP Sixty Five Amp
1978-1983. 65 watts, 1x12", reverb, built-in phaser.

1978-1983		$500	$575

112 Sixty Five Amp
1973-1981. Combo amp, 65 watts, 1x12", reverb, tremolo.

1973-1981		$450	$550

115 Sixty Five Amp
1973-1981. Combo amp, 65 watts, 1x15", reverb, tremolo.

1973-1981		$450	$550

210 HD130 Amp
1973-1981. 130 watts, 2x10", reverb, tremolo.

1973-1981		$525	$600

210 Sixty Five Amp
1973-1981. 65 watts, 2x10", reverb, tremolo.

1973-1981		$525	$600

212 HD130 Amp
1973-1981. 130 watts, 2x12", reverb, tremolo.

1973-1981		$550	$650

212 Sixty Five Amp
1973-1981. 65 watts, 2x12", reverb, tremolo.

1973-1981		$550	$650

410 Seventy Five Amp
1982-1983. 75 watts, 4x10", reverb, tremolo.

1982-1983		$550	$650

410 Sixty Five Amp
1973-1981. 65 watts, 4x10", reverb, tremolo.

1973-1981		$550	$650

HD-130 Amp
1973-1981. Head amp, 130 watts, reverb, tremolo.

1973-1981		$400	$500

RD Fifty Amp
1980-1983. Head amp, 50 watts, reverb, distortion.

1980-1983		$350	$450

Sixty Five Amp
1973-1981. Head amp, 65 watts, reverb, tremolo.

1973-1981		$350	$450

National

Ca. 1927-present. National/Valco amps date back to the late-'30s. National introduced a modern group of amps about the same time they introduced their new Res-O-Glas "space-age" guitar models in '62. In '64, the amp line was partially redesigned and renamed. By '68, the Res-O-Glas models were gone and National introduced many large vertical and horizontal piggyback models which lasted until National's assets were assigned during bankruptcy in '69. The National name went to Chicago importer

Mojave Coyote

Music Man 212 Sixty Five

Music Man 115 Sixty Five

AMPS

AMPS

Early-'50s National/Valco

National Glenwood 90

Nemesis NC-212

MODEL		EXC. COND.	
YEAR	FEATURES	LOW	HIGH

Strum N' Drum who then advertised "National is back and better than ever." Initially, Strum N' Drum had one amp, the National GA 950 P Tremolo/Reverb piggyback.

Chicago/Valco 51 Amp
1950s. Vertical tweed cabinet, metal preamps tubes, late-1940s-early-1950s technology, 1x12".

1950s		$275	$375

Glenwood 90 Amp (Model N6490TR)
1962-1967. 35 watts, 2x12", tremolo (not listed as vibrato) and reverb.

| 1964-1967 | | $500 | $650 |

Glenwood Vibrato Amp (Model N6499VR)
1964-1967. 70 watts, 2x12", vibrato and reverb.

| 1964-1967 | | $550 | $700 |

Model 100 Amp
Tube amp, 40 watts, 1x12".

| 1940s | | $350 | $450 |

Model GA 950-P Tremolo/Reverb Piggyback Amp
1970s. Strum N' Drum/National model, solidstate, 50 watts, 2 channel 2x12" and 1x7" in 32" tall vertical cabinet, black.

| 1970s | | $150 | $250 |

Model N6800 - N6899 Piggyback Amps
1968-1969. National introduced a new line of tube amps in 1968 and most of them were piggybacks. The N6895 was sized like a Fender piggyback Tremolux, the N6875 and N6878 bass amps were sized like a 1968 Fender large cab piggyback with a 26" tall vertical cab, the N6898 and N6899 were the large piggyback guitar amps. These amps feature the standard Jensen speakers or the upgrade JBL speakers, the largest model was the N6800 for P.A. or guitar, which sported three 70-watt channels and two column speakers using a bass 2x12" + 1x3" horn cab and a voice-guitar 4x10" + 1x3" horn cab.

| 1968-1969 | Various tube models | $175 | $375 |

Model N6816 Amp (Model 16)
1968-1969. Valco-made tube amp, 6 watts, 1x10" Jensen speaker, 17" vertical cab, tremolo, no reverb, black vinyl cover and Coppertone grille, "National" spelled out on front panel.

| 1968-1969 | | $125 | $150 |

Model N6820 Thunderball Bass Amp
1968-1969. Valco-made tube amp, about 35 watts, 1x15" Jensen speaker, 19" vertical cab, black vinyl cover and coppertone grille, "National" spelled out on front panel.

| 1968-1969 | | $150 | $175 |

Model N6822 Amp (Model 22)
1968-1969. Valco-made, 6 watts tube (4 tubes) amp, 1x12" Jensen speaker, 19" vertical cab, tremolo and reverb, black vinyl cover and coppertone grille, "National" spelled out on front panel.

| 1968-1969 | | $150 | $175 |

Studio 10 Amp
1962-1967. 5 watts, 1x3", 3 tubes, 1 channel, 1 volume control, no tone control, no reverb or tremolo.

| 1962-1963 | | $300 | $350 |
| 1964-1967 | N6410 Model | $300 | $350 |

MODEL		EXC. COND.	
YEAR	FEATURES	LOW	HIGH

Westwood 16 Amp (Model N6416T)
1964-1967. 5 watts using 1 6V6 power, 2 12AX7 preamp, 1 5Y3GT rectifier, tremolo, 2x8", dark vinyl cover, silver grille.

| 1964-1967 | | $350 | $400 |

Westwood 22 Amp (Model N6422TR)
1964-1967. 5 watts, 2x8", reverb and tremolo, 1 channel, 6 tubes.

| 1964-1967 | | $350 | $400 |

Naylor Engineering
1994-present. Joe Naylor and Kyle Kurtz founded the company in East Pointe, Michigan, in the early '90s, selling J.F. Naylor speakers. In '94 they started producing amps. In '96, Naylor sold his interest in the business to Kurtz and left to form Reverend Guitars. In '99 David King bought the company and moved it to Los Angeles, then to Dallas. Currently Naylor builds tube amps, combos, speakers, and cabinets.

Nemesis
From the makers of Eden amps, Nemesis is a line of made-in-the-U.S., FET powered bass combos and extension cabinets. The brand is a division of U.S. Music Corp.

NC-200 Combo Amp
1990s. Compact style cabinet with 200 watts, solidstate, 2x10", black cover, black grille.

| 1990s | | $350 | $450 |

NC-200P Combo Amp
1990s. Compact transporter-style cabinet with 200 watts, solidstate, 4x10", black cover, black grille.

| 1990s | | $450 | $550 |

Nobel
1950-1960s. From Don Noble and Company, of Chicago, owned by Strum N' Drum by mid-'60s.

Mid-Size Tube Amp
1950s. Low- to mid-power tube amp, Noble logo on front.

| 1950s | | $300 | $375 |

Norma
1965-1970. Economy solidstate line imported and distributed by Strum N' Drum, Wheeling (Chicago), IL. As noted in the National section, Strum N' Drum acquired the National brand name in the '70s. Low values reflect the market's low demand for an import solidstate amp.

GA-93 Amp
1969-1970. 6 watts, 1x6", dark brown vinyl cover, dark brown grille.

| 1969-1970 | | $50 | $75 |

GA-97 T Amp
1969-1970. 13 watts, 1x8", dark brown vinyl cover, dark grille, tremolo.

| 1969-1970 | | $55 | $85 |

MODEL YEAR FEATURES	EXC. COND. LOW	HIGH

GA-725 B Amp
1969-1970. 38 watts, 1x10" bass speaker, dark brown vinyl cover, sparkle grille.

| 1969-1970 | $55 | $85 |

GA-918 T Amp
1969-1970. 24 watts, 1x12", dark brown vinyl cover, dark grille, tremolo and reverb.

| 1969-1970 | $65 | $95 |

GA-930 P (piggyback) Amp
1969-1970. 40 watts, 2x12", piggyback, dark vinyl cover, dark grille.

| 1969-1970 | $75 | $125 |

GA-6240 Amp
1969-1970. 50 watts, dark vinyl cover, medium light grille.

| 1969-1970 | $75 | $125 |

GAP-2 Amp
1969-1970. 3 watts, 1x4", dark brown vinyl cover, light brown grille.

| 1969-1970 | $50 | $75 |

Oahu
The Oahu Publishing Company and Honolulu Conservatory, based in Cleveland, started with acoustic Hawaiian and Spanish guitars, selling large quantities in the 1930s. As electric models became popular, Oahu responded with guitar/amp sets. The brand has been revived on a line of U.S.-made tube amps.

Lap Steel Oahu Amp
1940s-1950s. Small compact amp originally sold with Oahu student lap steels. Amp covers ranged from yellow or white luggage linen-style to red pearloid plastic.

| 1950s | $125 | $225 |

Tonemaster 230K Amp
All tube combo, 20 watts, 1x12".

| 1960s | $200 | $225 |

Tunemaster Amp
20 watts, 1x12" Jensen speaker.

| 1949 | $200 | $225 |

Oliver
Ca.1966-late-1970s. The Oliver Sound Company, Westbury, New York, was founded by former Ampeg engineer, Jess Oliver, after he left Ampeg in '65. Tube amp designs were based upon Oliver's work at Ampeg. The Oliver Powerflex Amp is the best-known design, and featured an elevator platform that would lift the amp head out of the speaker cabinet.

Model G-150R Combo Amp
Two 6L6 power tubes, reverb, tremolo, black Tolex, black grille, silver control panel, 40 watts, 1x15".

| 1970s | $400 | $500 |

Model P-500 Combo Amp
All tube combo with 15" motorized amp chassis that rises out of tall lateral speaker cabinet as amp warms up.

| 1960s | $500 | $600 |

Orbital Power Projector Amp
Late-1960s-early-1970s. Rotating speaker cabinet with horn, Leslie-like voice.

| 1970s | $500 | $600 |

Sam Ash Oliver Amp Head
Late-1960s-early-1970s. Private branded for Sam Ash Music, about 30 watts using the extinct 2x7027A power tubes, Sam Ash script logo on front grille.

| 1960s | $175 | $300 |

Orange
1969-1981, 1995-present. Orange amps and PAs were made in England by Cliff Cooper and Matthew Mathias. The Orange-colored amps were well-built and were used by many notable guitarists. Since '95, Cliff Cooper is once again making Orange amplifiers in England, with the exception of the small Crush Practice Combo amps, which are made in Korea.

Model OR 80-Watt Amp w/4x12 Bottom.
1970s. 80 watts, 4x12" straight-front cab with Orange crest on grille, light orange grille.

| 1970s | $2,000 | $3,000 |

Model OR-80 Combo Amp
1970s. About 80 watts, 2x12" combo.

| 1970s | $1,700 | $2,200 |

Model OR-120 Graphic Head Amp and Half Stack
1970s. 120 watts, 4x12" straight front cab with Orange crest on grille, light orange grille.

| 1970s | $2,200 | $3,400 |

Model OR-120 Graphic Overdrive Amp Head
120 watts.

| 1970s | $1,200 | $1,800 |

Model OR-200 212 Twin Amp
1970s. 120 watts, 2x12" combo, orange vinyl, dark grille, Orange crest on grille, reverb and vibrato, master volume.

| 1970s | $1,800 | $2,500 |

Orpheum
Late-1950s-1960s. Student to medium level amps from New York's Maurice Lipsky Music.

Small/Mid-Size Amps
Late-1950s-1960s. Two 6V6 power tubes, U.S.-made, Jensen P12R 12" speaker, light cover with gray swirl grille.

| 1959 | $150 | $225 |

Ovation
1966-present. Kaman made few amps under the Ovation name. They offered a variety of amps under the KMD brand from '85 to around '94.

Little Dude Amp
1969-ca. 1971. 100 watt solidstate combo with 1x15" and horn, matching slave unit could also be had.

| 1970s | $200 | $275 |

Oahu Tonemaster

AMPS

'70s Oliver 6200R Uniflex

Orange Model OR-120

Overbuilt Fiscus 30 W 212 combo

AMPS

Park G10

PRS HG-212

MODEL YEAR	FEATURES	EXC. COND. LOW	HIGH

Overbuilt Amps

1999-present. Tube amps and combos built by Richard Seccombe in West Hills, California.

PAC-AMP (Magnatone)

Late-1950s-early-1960s. Private branded by Magnatone, often for accordion studios.

Model 280-A Amp

1961-1963. About 50 watts, 2x12" + 2x5", brown leatherette, light brown grille, stereo vibrato, PAC-AMP nameplate logo.

1961-1963		$700	$850

PANaramic (Magnatone)

1961-1963. Private branded equivalent of '61-'63 Magnatone brown leatherette series, large PANaramic logo combining PAN in capital letters and aramic in small alpha script. Many Magnatone private brands were associated with accordion companies or accordian teaching studios. The PANaramic amp was associated with the PANaramic accordion.

Model 260/262-style Amp

1961-1963. 35 watts, 2x12", gray vinyl and light grille, vibrato, large PANaramic logo.

1961-1963		$575	$650

Model 413-style Amp

1961-1963. 18 watts, 1x12", black leatherette cover, light silver grille, vibrato, large PANaramic logo.

1961-1963		$450	$500

Model 450-style Amp

1961-1963. 20 watts, 1x12", reverb and vibrato, reverb not generally included in an early-1960s 1x12" Magnatone amp, dark vinyl, dark cross-threaded grille, large PANaramic logo.

1961-1963		$600	$750

Paris

Master Series Amps

1960s. Compact solid-state combo, 1x12", slanted Paris logo front upper left side of grille, black tolex-style cover, silver grille (like Fender blackface), rear mounted slanted control panel.

1960s		$75	$150

Park

1965-1982, 1992-2000. Park amps were made by Marshall from '65 to '82. In the '90s, Marshall revived the name for use on small solidstate amps imported from the Far East.

G-25 R Compact Amp

1990s. Student compact 25-watt guitar amp with reverb.

1997		$100	$150

Model 75 Amp Head

Head amp, 50 watts, two KT88s, small-box plexi (later aluminum), black Tolex.

1967-1969	Plexi	$3,900	$4,400
1969-1971	Aluminum panel	$2,200	$3,000

MODEL YEAR	FEATURES	EXC. COND. LOW	HIGH

Model 1206 50-Watt Amp Head

1981-1982. 50 watts, based upon JCM 800 50-watt made at the same time period.

1981-1982		$700	$950

Model 1213 100-Watt Reverb Combo Amp

1970s. 100 watts, 2x12", reverb, dark vinyl, light grille, Park logo on front with elongated P.

1970s		$1,300	$1,600

Model 1228 50-Watt Lead Head Amp

1970s. 50 watts, based upon Marshall 50-watt made at the same time period.

1970s		$1,200	$1,500

Model 2046 25-Watt Combo Amp

1970s. 25 watts, 1x15", 1970s era blue grille cloth, black Tolex, large P Park logo upper center of grille.

1970s		$1,300	$1,400

Paul Reed Smith

1985-present. In the late '80s, PRS offered two amp models. Only 350 amp units were shipped. Includes HG-70 Head and HG-212 Combo. HG stands for Harmonic Generator, effectively a non-tube, solidstate amp.

4x12" Straight-Front Cab

1989. Straight-front 4x12" black vinyl cab with silver grille, PRS logo front lower right of grille.

1989		$400	$450

HG-70 Amp Head

1989-1990. 70 watts, reverb, effects loop, noise gate. Options include 150-watt circuitry and 4x12" straight and slant cabinets, gray-black.

1989-1990		$400	$450

HG-212 Amp

1989-1990. Combo, 70 watts, 2x12", reverb, effects loop, noise gate. Options include 150-watt circuitry and 4x12" straight and slant cabinets, gray-black.

1989-1990		$500	$600

Peavey

1965-present. Hartley Peavey's first products were guitar amps. He added guitars to the mix in '78. Headquartered in Meridan, Mississippi, Peavey continues to offer a huge variety of guitars, amps, and PAs.

5150 212 Combo Amp

1995-present. Combo version of 5150 head, 60 watts, 2x12", large 5150 logo on front panel, small Peavey logo on lower right of grille.

1995-1999		$550	$600

5150 EVH Head and Cab Amp Set

1995-present. Half stack 5150 head and 4x12" cab, large 5150 logo on front of amp.

1995-1999	Cab only	$300	$375
1995-1999	Head and cab	$800	$900
1995-1999	Head only	$400	$475

Alphabass Amp

1988-1990. Rackmount all tube, 160 watts, EQ, includes 2x15" Black Widow or 2x12" Scorpion cabinet.

1988-1990		$275	$350

MODEL YEAR	FEATURES	EXC. COND. LOW	HIGH

Artist Amp
120 watts, 1x12", bright and normal channels, EQ, reverb, master volume.

| 1970s | | $200 | $300 |

Artist 110 Amp
TransTubes, 10 watts.

| 1990s | | $100 | $130 |

Artist 250 Amp
1990s. 100 watts, 1x12", solidstate preamp, 4x6L6 power tubes, black vinyl cover, black grille.

| 1990s | | $175 | $250 |

Artist VT Amp
1990s. Combo amp, 120 watts, 1x12".

| 1990s | | $200 | $300 |

Audition 20 Amp
1980s-1990s. 20 watts, single speaker combo, black vinyl and grille.

| 1980-1990s | | $50 | $100 |

Audition 30 Amp
1980s-1990s. 30 watts, 1x12" combo amp, channel switching.

| 1980-1990s | | $75 | $125 |

Audition 110 Amp
1990s. 25 watts, 1x10" combo, 2 channels.

| 1990s | | $75 | $125 |

Audition Chorus Amp
Two 10-watt channels, 2x6", channel switching, post gain and normal gain controls.

| 1980s | | $100 | $150 |

Audition Plus Amp
1980s. Solidstate, 20 watts, 1x10" compact practice amp, standard Peavey Black Tolex, Black grille and slant logo.

| 1980s | Black Tolex | $75 | $125 |

Backstage Amp
1977-mid-1980s. Master gain control, 18 watts, 1x10", three-band EQ.

| 1977-1984 | | $50 | $80 |

Backstage 30 Amp
30 watts, 1x10".

| 1980s | | $60 | $90 |

Backstage 110 Amp
Repackaged and revoiced in 1988, 65 watts, 1x10", SuperSat preamp circuitry, new power sections.

| 1980s | | $100 | $125 |

Backstage Chorus 208 Amp
1990s. 150 watts, 2x8", reverb, channel switching.

| 1990s | | $125 | $175 |

Backstage Plus Amp
1980s. 35 watts, 1x10" combo, reverb, saturation effect.

| 1980s | | $75 | $100 |

Bandit 75 Amp
Redesigned and renamed Bandit 112 in 1988. Channel switching, 75 watts, 1x12", four-band EQ, reverb, post-effects loop, Superstat.

| 1980s | | $150 | $200 |

Bandit 112/Bandit II 112 Amp
1988-2001. 80 watts, 1x12", active EQ circuit for lead channel, active controls.

| 1980s | Bandit | $175 | $225 |

| 1990s | Bandit II | $200 | $250 |

Basic 112 Bass Amp
2000s. 75 watts, 1x12" bass combo, 2000-era red border control panel.

| 2000s | | $175 | $225 |

Basic 40 Amp
40 watts, 1x12".

| 1980s | | $100 | $125 |

Basic 60 Amp
1988-1995. Solidstate combo amp, 50-60 watts, 1x12", four-band EQ, gain controls.

| 1988-1995 | Black | $150 | $175 |

Blazer 158 Amp
1995-present. 15 watts, 1x8", clean and distortion, now called the TransTube Blazer III.

| 1995-2000 | | $60 | $85 |

Bluesman Amp
1992. Tweed, 1x12" or 1x15".

| 1992 | 1x12" or 1x15" | $300 | $400 |

Bravo 112 Amp
1988-1994. All tube reverb, 25 watts, 1x12", 3-band EQ, 2 independent input channels.

| 1988-1994 | | $200 | $275 |

Classic 20 Amp
Small tube amp with 2xEL-84 power tubes, 1x10", tweed cover.

| 1990s | | $175 | $225 |

Classic 30 Amp
1994-present. Tweed, 30 watts, 1x12", EL84 tubes.

| 1994-1999 | | $275 | $325 |

Classic 50/212 Amp
1990-present. Combo, 50 watt, 2x12", EL84 tubes, reverb, high-gain section.

| 1990-2000 | | $350 | $475 |

Classic 50/410 Amp
1990-present. Combo amp, 4x10", EL84 power, reverb, footswitchable high-gain mode.

| 1990s | | $350 | $475 |

Classic 120 Amp
1988-ca.1990. Tube, 120 watts.

| 1988-1990 | | $325 | $375 |

Classic Chorus 130 Amp
Combo amp, 2x12", channel switching, two 65-watt power amps, reverb, built-in chorus and effects loops.

| 1980s | | $225 | $275 |

DECA/750 Amp
1989-ca.1990. Digital, 2 channels, 350 watts/channel, distortion, reverb, exciter, pitch shift, multi-EQ.

| 1989-1990 | | $250 | $300 |

Decade Amp
1970s. Practice amp, 10 watts, 1x8", runs on 12 volt or AC.

| 1970s | | $35 | $65 |

Delta Blues Amp
1995-present. 30 watts, tube combo, 4xEL84 tubes, 1x15", tremolo, large-panel-style cab, blond tweed.

| 1995-2000 | | $350 | $450 |

1977 Peavey Backstage 30

Peavey Bandit

Peavey Classic 50/212

Peavey Delta Blues

Peavey Musician (head)

Peavey Special 112

MODEL YEAR FEATURES	EXC. COND. LOW	HIGH
Deuce Amp *1975-1980s. 120 watts, tube amp, 2x12" or 4x10".*		
1975-1980	$200	$275
Deuce Head Amp *1975-1980s. Tube head, 120 watts.*		
1975-1980	$150	$200
Ecoustic 112 Amp *100 watts, 1x12" acoustic and mic amp, guitar input and mic input, brown vinyl, brown grille.*		
2000s	$175	$250
Encore 65 Amp *1990s. Compact solidstate amp, 1x12", reverb, channel switching.*		
1990s	$175	$225
Envoy 110 Amp *1988-2001. Solidstate, 40 watts, 1x10", Trans-Tubes.*		
1988-2001	$125	$150
Heritage VTX Amp *1980s. 130 watts, 4 6L6s, solidstate preamp, 2x12" combo.*		
1980s	$150	$200
Jazz Classic Amp *Solidstate, 210 watts, 1x15", electronic channel switching, six-spring reverb.*		
1980s	$200	$250
KB-100 Amp *Keyboard amp, 1x15".*		
1980s	$200	$250
LTD Amp *1975-1980s. Solidstate, 200 watts, 1x12" Altec or 1x15" JBL.*		
1975-1982	$200	$250
MegaBass Amp *Rackmount preamp/power amp, 200 watts per 2 channels, solidstate, EQ, effects loop, chorus.*		
1980s	$250	$350
Minx 110 Bass Amp *1988-present. Solidstate, 35 watts RMS, 1x10" heavy duty speaker.*		
1988-1999	$100	$125
Musician Amp Head *Tube head, 200 watts.*		
1970s	$150	$200
Nashville 400 Steel Guitar Amp *210 watts, 1x15" solidstate steel guitar combo amp.*		
1990s	$300	$350
Nashville 1000 Steel Guitar Amp *1x15", solidstate steel guitar combo amp.*		
1990s	$325	$375
Pacer Amp *1977-1980s. Master volume, 45 watts, 1x12", 3-band EQ.*		
1977-1985	$125	$150
ProBass 1000 Amp *Rackmount, effects loops, preamp, EQ, crossover, headphone output.*		
1980s	$150	$200

MODEL YEAR FEATURES	EXC. COND. LOW	HIGH
Rage/Rage 158 Amp *1980s-1990s. Compact practice amp, 15 watts, 1x8".*		
1980s	$75	$95
Reno 400 Amp *Solidstate, 200 watts, 1x15" with horn, four-band EQ.*		
1980s	$225	$250
Renown 112 Amp *1989-1994. Crunch and lead SuperSat, 160 watts, 1x12", master volume, digital reverb, EQ.*		
1989-1994	$200	$250
Renown 212 Amp *1989-1994. Crunch and lead SuperSat, 160 watts, 2x12", master volume, digital reverb, EQ.*		
1989-1994	$225	$275
Renown 400 Amp *Combo, 200 watts, 2x12", channel switching, Hammond reverb, pre- and post-gain controls.*		
1980s	$250	$300
Revolution 112 Amp *2000s. 100 watts, 1x12" combo, black vinyl, black grille.*		
2000s	$225	$300
Series 400 Bass Head *Solidstate, black.*		
1970s	$125	$150
Session 500 Amp *1980s. 250 watts, 1x15", standard Black with metal panels appearance.*		
1980s	$300	$400
Special 112 Amp *160 watts, 1x12", channel-switching, effects loops, EQ. In 1988, available in wedge-shaped enclosures slanted back 30 degrees.*		
1980s	$200	$250
Special 212 Amp *1990s. 160 watts, 2x12", transtube, solidstate series.*		
1990s	$250	$300
Studio Pro 112 Amp *Repackaged and revoiced in 1988. Solidstate, 65 watts, 1x12", SuperSat preamp, new power sections*		
1980s	$150	$175
TKO-75 Bass Amp *1987-1995. Solidstate, 75 watts, 1x15", EQ, compression and pre-/post-gain controls.*		
1987-1995	$125	$225
TKO-115 Bass Amp *1980s-1990s. Seventy-five watts, 1x15", solidstate, 7-band EQ, other features.*		
1987-1995	$150	$250
TNT-150 Bass Amp *Solidstate, 150 watts, 1x15", EQ, compression, chorus. In 1988, available in wedge-shaped enclosures slanted 30 degrees.*		
1980s	$200	$300
Triumph 60 Combo Amp *Tube head, effects loop, reverb, 60 watts, 1x12", multi-stage gain.*		
1980s	$150	$200

The *Vintage Guitar Price Guide* shows low to high values for items in all-original excellent condition, and, where applicable, with original case or cover.

MODEL YEAR	FEATURES	EXC. COND. LOW	HIGH

Triumph 120 Amp
Tube, 120 watts, 1x12", 3 gain blocks in preamp, low-level post-effects loop, built-in reverb.
| 1989-1990 | | $200 | $250 |

Ultra 112 Amp
1998-2002. 60 watts, 1x12", all tube 2x6L6 power, black, black grille.
| 1998-2002 | | $300 | $350 |

Ultra 410 Amp
1998-2002. 60 watts, 4x10".
| 1998-2002 | | $325 | $375 |

Vegas 400 Amp
1980s. 210 watts, 1x15", reverb, compression feature, parametric equalizer. Some musicians prefer as a steel guitar amp.
| 1980s | | $400 | $500 |

Wiggy 212 Amp
2000s. 100 watt head in mono (2x75-watt in stereo) with matching 2x12" cab, 2 EQ systems including 5-band sliders, rounded amp head cabinet.
| 2000s | | $600 | $650 |

Penn
1994-present. Tube amps, combos, and cabinets built by Billy Penn, originally in Colts Neck, New Jersey, currently in Long Branch, New Jersey.

Pignose
1972-present. Made in the U.S. Pignose Industries was started by people associated with the band Chicago, including guitarist Terry Kath, with help from designers Wayne Kimball and Richard Erlund.

7-100 Practice Amp
1972-present. The "original Pignose," 7"x5"x3" battery-powered portable amplifier, 1x5".
| 1972-1999 | | $50 | $75 |

30/60 Amp
1978-ca.1987. Solidstate, 30 watts, 1x10", master volume.
| 1978-1987 | | $125 | $175 |

60R Studio Reverb Amp
Solidstate, 30 watts.
| 1980 | | $175 | $225 |

Polytone
1960s-present. Made in North Hollywood, California, Polytone offers compact combo amps, heads, and cabinets and a pickup system for acoustic bass.

Mega-Brut Amp
1990s. Mega-Brut logo on front lower right grille, black vinyl, black screen-style grille.
| 1990s | | $275 | $325 |

Mini-Brut III Bass Amp
1990s. 80 watts, 1x15", footswitchable reverb and distortion.
| 1990s | | $275 | $325 |

Mini-Brut IV Amp
1980s-1990s. 100 watts, 1x15", footswitchable reverb and distortion.
| 1980-1990s | | $275 | $375 |

Mini-Brut V Amp
100 watts, 2x10", footswitchable reverb and distortion.
| 1980s | | $350 | $400 |

RMS Pro Series Bass Amp
Rackmount, 240 watts, 2 power amps, 2 preamps, crossover for bi-amping.
| 1985 | | $350 | $450 |

Premier
Ca.1938-ca.1975. Produced by Peter Sorkin Music Company in Manhattan. First radio-sized amplifiers introduced by '38. After World War II, established Multivox subsidiary to manufacture amplifiers ca. '46. By mid-'50s at least, the amps featured lyre grilles. Dark brown/light tan amp covering by '60. By '64 amps covered in brown woodgrain and light tan. Multivox amps were made until around '84.

B-160 Club Bass Amp
1960s. 15 to 20 watt, 1x12" Jensen speaker, '60s two-tone brown styling, 6V6 tubes.
| 1963-1968 | | $350 | $400 |

Model 50 Combo Amp
1940s-1960s. 4 to 5 watts, 1x8" similar to Fender Champ circuit with more of a vertical cab.
| 1950s | | $325 | $375 |

Model 76 Combo Amp
1950s. Suitcase latchable cabinet that opens out into two wedges, Premier 76 logo on amp control panel, two-tone Brown, lyre grille, 1x12".
| 1950s | | $450 | $550 |

Model 88N Combo Amp
1950s-early-1960s. Rectangular suitcase cabiinet, two-tone Tan and Brown, Premier and lyre logo, 25 watts, 1x12".
| 1950s | | $450 | $550 |
| 1960s | | $450 | $550 |

Model 100R Amp
Combo amp, 1x12", reverb and tremolo.
| 1960s | | $400 | $500 |

Twin 8 Amp
1960s. 20 watts, 2x8", tremolo, reverb.
| 1964-1966 | | $500 | $600 |

Twin 12 T-12R Amp
Late-1950s. Early reverb amp with tremolo, 2x12", rectangular cabinet typical of twin 12 amps (Dano and Fender), brown cover.
| 1950s | | $500 | $700 |

Quantum
1980s. Economy amps distributed by DME, Indianapolis, Indiana.

Q Terminator Economy Amps
1980s. Economy solidstate amps ranging from 12 to 25 watts and 1x6" to 1x12".
| 1980s | | $75 | $125 |

Randall
1960s-present. Randall Instruments was originally out of California and is now a division of

Penn Signature amp

Pignose 60R and 30/60

Randall RM50

AMPS

MODEL YEAR	FEATURES	EXC. COND. LOW	HIGH

Randall RG-200 ES

Washburn. They have offered a range of combo amps, heads and cabinets over the years.

Commander II Bass Amp
Solidstate, 100 watts, 2x12", reverb, tremolo.
1980-1985 — $225 — $275

Commander-HG Amp
Two footswitch selectable channels, 2x12".
1980s — $250 — $300

DAC-15 Preamp
Fifteen watts, 1x8", EQ, preamp, master volume, Clipper distortion controls.
1980s — $75 — $100

R112C Extension Cab
1980s. Open back extension cabinet 1x12", in and out, Black Tolex, Black grille.
1980s — $180 — $200

RB-125 Bass Combo Amp
One 15" speaker.
1980s — $275 — $300

RC-280 Amp
Stereo chorus, 100 watts per channel, 2x12", bright, sustain/boost, effects loop.
1980s — $175 — $275

RG-15X Amp
1990s. Compact practice amp, 15 watts, 1x8", black Tolex, black grille.
1990s — $80 — $100

RG-100 HT Amp
Solidstate, 120 watts, FET preamp circuitry, reverb, two channels, rack-mount, effects loop.
1980s — $250 — $275

RG-300 Amp Head
1980s. RG-300 logo on front, black Tolex, black grille.
1980s — $250 — $275

RG-2000 Bass Bi-Amp
150 watts into 4 ohms/low-frequency 370 watts, EQ, compressor, effects loops.
1990s — $225 — $275

RGP-1000 Preamp
Stereo chorus preamp, presence, reverb, effects loops, channel-switching.
1980s — $150 — $200

RGT-100 Amp
Late-1980s. Tube amp, 1x12", gray Tolex combo, black metal grille.
1980s — $225 — $250

Sustainer 140 Amp
Introduced in 1978 as part of new Professional Series, single-channel version of Switchmaster 150, 1x12" combo.
1970s — $200 — $250

Switchmaster 150 Amp
Introduced in 1978. Pre-set channel switching (thus the name) from totally independent foot switchable channels, dark cover, dark grille, 120 watts, 1x12" combo.
1970s — $225 — $275

Reeves

Reverend Hellhound

Rat Fink
2002-present. Tube and solid state amp line from Lace Music Products. They also offer amps under the Mooneyes and Lace brand names.

Red Bear
1994-1997. Tube amps designed by Sergei Novikov and built in St. Petersburg, Russia. Red Bear amps were distributed in the U.S. under a joint project between Gibson and Novik, Ltd. Novik stills builds amps under other brand names.

MK 60 Lead Tube Amp
1990s. Amp with 4x12" half stack, Red Bear logo on amp and cab.
1992 — $750 — $800

Reeves Amplification
2002-present. Started by Bill Jansen, Reeves builds tube amps, combos, and cabinets based on the classic British designs of Dan Reeves.

Reverend
1996-present. Joe Naylor started building amps under the Naylor brand in '94. In '96 he left Naylor to build guitars under the Reverend brand. In 2001, Reverend started offering tube amps, combos, and cabinets built in Warren, Michigan, that Naylor co-designed with Dennis Kager. He also builds guitars, basses and effects.

Rickenbacker
1931-present. Rickenbacker made amps from the beginning of the company up to the late '80s. Rickenbacker had many different models, from the small early models that were usually sold as a guitar/amp set, to the large, very cool, Transonic.

Electro-Student Amp
Late-1940s. Typical late-'40s vertical combo cabinet, 1x12" speaker, lower power using 5 tubes, bottom mounted chassis, dark gray leatherette cover.
1948-1949 — $225 — $250

Model M-8 Amp
Gray, 1x8".
1950s — $275 — $350
1960s — $250 — $325

Professional Model 200-A Amp
1938 — $250 — $350

RB30 Amp
1986. Bass combo amp, 30 watts, tilted control panel, 1x12".
1986 — $100 — $150

RB60 Amp
1986. Bass combo amp, 60 watts, tilted control panel, 1x15".
1986 — $200 — $250

RB120 Amp
1986. Bass combo amp, 120 watts, tilted control panel, 1x15".
1986 — $200 — $275

MODEL YEAR	FEATURES	EXC. COND. LOW	HIGH

Supersonic Model B-16
4x10" speakers, gray cover.
1960s		$600	$800

TR14 Amp
1978-ca.1982. Solidstate, 1x10", reverb, distortion.
| 1978-1982 | | $100 | $125 |

TR75G Amp
1978-ca.1982. 75 watts, 2x12", 2 channels.
| 1978-1982 | | $125 | $175 |

TR75SG Amp
1978-ca.1983. One 10" and one 15" speakers.
| 1978-1982 | | $175 | $250 |

TR100G Amp
1978-ca.1982. Solidstate, 100 watts with 4x12", 2 channels.
| 1978-1982 | | $175 | $275 |

Transonic Amp
1967-1970. Trapezoid shape, 2x12", head and cabinet, Rick-O-Select.
| 1967-1970 | | $800 | $1,200 |

Rivera
1985-present. Amp designer and builder Paul Rivera modded and designed amps for other companies before starting his own line in California. He offers heads, combos, and cabinets.

Clubster 40 Amp
2000-present. 40 watts, 1x12" combo, burgundy Tolex, light grille.
| 2000-2001 | | $700 | $900 |

Fandango 212 Combo Amp
2001-present. 55 watts, 2x12" tube amp.
| 2001-2002 | | $1,150 | $1,350 |

Knuckle Head 55 Amp
1995-2002. 55 watts, head amp, replaced by reverb model.
| 1995-2002 | | $600 | $700 |

Knuckle Head 100 Amp
1995-2002. 100 watt head, head amp, replaced by reverb model.
| 1995-2002 | | $650 | $750 |

Los Lobottom Amp
1999-present. 2x12" cabinet with 300 watt powered 12" subwoofer.
| 1999-2001 | | $500 | $650 |

M-60 112 Combo Amp
1989-present. 60 watts, 1x12".
| 1989-1999 | | $600 | $750 |

M-100 212 Combo Amp
1990-present. 100 watts, 2x12" combo.
| 1990s | | $750 | $850 |

M-100 Head Amp
1989-present. 100 watts, head amp.
| 1989-1999 | | $650 | $750 |

Quiana 112 Combo Amp
2000-present. Combo, 50 watts, 1x12".
| 2000-2002 | | $1,000 | $1,150 |

R-30 112 Combo Amp
1993-present. 30 watts, 1x12", compact cab, black Tolex cover, gray-black grille.
| 1993-2000 | | $400 | $650 |

R-100 212 Combo Amp
1993-present. 100 watts, 2x12".
| 1993-2000 | | $750 | $850 |

Suprema R-55 112/115 Combo Amp
2000-present. Tube amp, 55 watts, 1x12" (still available) or 1x15" (2000-2001).
| 2000-2002 1x12" | | $1,000 | $1,150 |
| 2000-2001 1x15" | | $1,050 | $1,200 |

TBR-1 Amp
1985-1999. First Rivera production model, rackmount, 60 watts.
| 1985-1999 | | $600 | $900 |

Roccaforte Amps
1993-present. Tube amps, combos, and cabinets built by Doug Roccaforte in San Clemente, California.

Rodgers
1993-present. Custom tube amps and cabinets built by Larry Rodgers in Naples, Florida.

Rogue
2001-present. Student-level solidstate import (Korea) compact amps. They also offer guitars, mandolins, banjos, effects and basses.

CG-20R Amp
2001. Solidstate, 20 watts, 1x8".
| 2001 | | $30 | $50 |

CG-30R Amp
2001-2003. Solidstate, 30 watts, 1x10".
| 2001 | | $50 | $75 |

CG-50R Amp
2001. Solidstate, 50 watts, 1x12".
| 2001 | | $75 | $125 |

CG-110R Amp
2001. Solidstate, 100 watts, 2x12".
| 2001 | | $75 | $125 |

Roland
Japan's Roland Corporation's products include amplifiers and keyboards and, under the Boss brand, effects.

AC-100 Amp
1995-present. Acoustic amp, 50 watts, 1x12" and 2x5", chorus, reverb, EQ, effects loop.
| 1995-2000 | | $200 | $250 |

Bolt 60 Amp
Early 1980s. Solidstate/tube, 1x12".
| 1980s | | $200 | $250 |

Cube 20 Amp
1978-1982. 1x8", normal and overdrive channels, headphone jack.
| 1978-1982 | | $150 | $200 |

Cube 40 Amp
1978-1980s. 1x10", 40 watts, combo, chorus added in 1983.
| 1978-1983 | | $100 | $200 |

Cube 60 Amp
1978-1980s, 2004-present. 1x12", 60 watts, combo, chorus added in 1983
| 1978-1983 | | $225 | $275 |

Rivera Knucklehead Reverb 55

Roccaforte 80 watt

1996 Roland BC-60

The *Vintage Guitar Price Guide* shows low to high values for items in all-original excellent condition, and, where applicable, with original case or cover.

Roland Spirit 10A

Savage Gläs 30

Selmer

MODEL YEAR FEATURES	EXC. COND. LOW	HIGH
Cube 60B Bass Amp		
1978-1980s. One speaker, normal and overdrive channels, headphone jack.		
1978-1983	$200	$275
Cube 100 Amp		
1978-1982. Solidstate, 100 watts, 1x12", orange cover, large Cube-100 logo on back chassis, rear-mounted controls.		
1978-1982	$250	$350
JC-50 Jazz Chorus Amp		
1980s. 50 watts, 1x12".		
1980s	$250	$350
JC-55 Jazz Chorus Amp		
1987-1994. 50 watts, 2x8", stereo chorus, preamp, reverb.		
1987-1994	$250	$350
JC-77 Jazz Chorus Amp		
1987-1994. 80 watts, 2x10".		
1987-1994	$300	$400
JC-120 Jazz Chorus Amp		
1976-present. Two channels, 120 watts, 2x12", chorus, vibrato.		
1976-1990	$350	$450
Spirit 30 Amp		
1982-late 1980s. Compact, 30 watts, 1x12".		
1980s	$100	$200
VGA3 V-Guitar Amp		
2003. 13-pin GK digital modeling amp, 50 watts, 1x12" combo.		
2003	$275	$325
VGA5 V-Guitar Amp		
2001-present. 30-pin GK digital modeling amp, 65 watts, 1x12".		
2001-2003	$425	$450
VGA7 V-Guitar Amp		
2000-present. 130 watts, 2x12", digital modeling with analog-style controls.		
2000-2003	$550	$575

Sam Ash

1960s-1970s. Sam Ash Music was founded by a young Sam Ash (formerly Ashkynase - an Austro-Hungarian name) in 1924. Ash's first store was in Brooklyn and by '66 there were about four Ash stores. During this time Ash Music private branded their own amp line which was built by Jess Oliver of Oliver Amps and based upon Oliver's Ampeg designs.

Sam Ash Oliver Amp Head
Late-1960s-early-1970s. Private branded for Sam Ash Music, about 30 watts using the extinct 2x7027A power tubes, Sam Ash script logo on front grille.
1960s	$175	$300

Savage

Tube amps and combos built by Savage Audio in Burnsville, Minnesota.

Sceptre

1960s. Canadian-made. Sceptre script logo on upper left side of grille ('60s Fender-style and placement).

MODEL YEAR FEATURES	EXC. COND. LOW	HIGH
Signet Amp		
1960s. Low power, 1x10", class-A 1x6V6 power, Signet model name on front panel.		
1960s	$125	$175

Selmer

1960s. The Selmer UK distributor offered mid- to high-level amps.

Futurama Corvette Amp
1960s. Class A low power 1x8", volume, tone, amplitude and speed tremolo controls, large script Futurama logo on front of amp, Futurama Corvette and Selmer logo on top panel.
1960s	$400	$500

Mark 2 Treble and Bass Head Amp
1960s. About 30 watts (2xEL34s), requires power line transformer for U.S. use, large Selmer logo on grille.
1960s	$500	$700

Seymour Duncan

Pickup maker Seymour Duncan, located in Santa Barbara, California, offered a line of amps from around '84 to '95.

84-40 Amp
1989-1991. Tube combo, 40 watts, 2 switchable channels, 1x12" or 2x10", gain boost.
1989-1991 1x12"	$375	$425

Bass 300 x 2 Amp
1986-1987. Solidstate, 2 channels (300 or 600 watts), EQ, contour boost switches, effects loop.
1986-1987	$325	$400

Bass 400 Amp
1986-1987. Solidstate, 400 watts, EQ, contour boost, balanced line output, effects loop.
1986-1987	$300	$350

Convertible 100 Amp
1986-1987. Solidstate, 60 watts, effects loop, spring reverb, EQ, switchable preamp modules.
1986-1987	$375	$425

Convertible 2000 Amp
1988-1995. Solidstate, 100 watts, holds five interchangeable modules, 1x12", 2 switchable channels.
1988-1995	$650	$750

KTG-2075 Stereo Amp
1989-1993. Part of the King Tone Generator Series, 2 channels with 75 watts per channel.
1989-1993	$200	$225

Sho-Bud

Introduced and manufactured by the Baldwin/Gretsch factory in 1970. Distributed by Kustom/Gretsch in the 1980s. Models include D-15 Model 7838, S-15 Model 7836, Twin Tube Model 7834, and Twin Trans Model 7832.

D15 Sho-Bud Double Amp
Introduced in 1970. Solidstate, 100 watts, dual channels, 1x15" JBL speaker.
1970s	$300	$350

MODEL YEAR	FEATURES	EXC. COND. LOW	HIGH

S15 Sho-Bud Single Amp
Introduced in 1972. 100 watts, 1x15" JBL, solidstate single channel combo.
| 1970s | | $250 | $300 |

Sho-Bass Amp
Introduced in 1972. 100 watts, 1x15", solidstate combo, black grille, black vinyl cover.
| 1970s | | $250 | $300 |

Twin Trans Amp
Introduced in 1972. 100 watts, solidstate combo, 2x12", reverb, black vinyl cover, dark grille, Sho-Bud script logo front upper right.
| 1970s | | $450 | $500 |

Twin Tube Amp
Introduced in 1972. 100 watt tube combo, 4x6L6 power, 2x12", reverb, black vinyl cover, dark grille, Sho-Bud script logo front upper right.
| 1970s | | $700 | $800 |

Siegmund Guitars & Amplifiers
1993-present. Chris Siegmund founded the company in Seattle, moving it to Austin, Texas for '95-'97, and is currently located in Los Angeles. Siegmund offers handmade tube amps and preamp pedals.

Silvertone
1941-ca. 1970, present. Brand used by Sears. All Silvertone amps were supplied by American companies up to around '66.

Model 100 Amp
Mid-late-1960s. Solidstate, piggyback amp and 2x12" cabinet with Gold-label Jensen speakers.
| 1960s | | $300 | $400 |

Model 150 Amp
Mid-late-1960s. Solidstate, piggyback amp and 6x10" cabinet with Gold-label Jensen speakers.
| 1960s | | $450 | $500 |

Model 1331 Amp
Ca.1954-ca.1957. Danelectro-made, luggage tweed, rounded front, a whole series made this style.
| 1954-1957 | | $250 | $350 |

Model 1336 (early Twin Twelve) Amp
Ca.1954-ca.1957. Danelectro-made, luggage tweed, rounded front.
| 1954-1957 | | $550 | $700 |

Model 1340 (Student Model) Amp
Early-1950s. Tan cover, brown grille with Silvertone logo, brown sides.
| 1950s | | $150 | $175 |

Model 1346 (Twin Twelve) Amp
Ca.1958-ca.1961. Danelectro-made, brown control panel, 2x12", 4x6L6 power, vibrato, leather handle, Silvertone logo on front bottom of cabinet, tan smooth leatherette cover, 2 separate speaker baffle openings.
| 1958-1961 | | $550 | $700 |

Model 1391 Amp
1950s. Blond-tan tweed-cloth cover, brown grille, single small speaker, leather handle.
| 1950s | | $150 | $225 |

Model 1392 Amp
1950s. Student amp with tremolo, five control knobs, Brown cover and Brown grille.
| 1950s | | $125 | $175 |

Model 1432 Amp
Late-1950s. 1x12", low- to mid-power, 2x6L6, late-'50s overhanging top style cabinet.
| 1950s | | $150 | $200 |

Model 1433 Combo Amp
Late-1950s. Tube, 30 watts, 2x6L6 power, 1x15", gray cover cabinet with pronounced overhanging top, light colored grille.
| 1950s | | $500 | $550 |

Model 1451 Amp
Late-1950s. 3 or 4 watts, 3 tubes, 1x6" or 1x8" speaker, brown sparkle cover, wheat grille, by Danelectro.
| 1950s | 1x6" | $125 | $150 |

Model 1457 Amp-In-Case (case only)
1960s. The amp-in-case with the electric Silvertone guitar, this is the higher powered model with tremolo and higher quality speaker.
| 1965 | Amp only (no guitar) | $100 | $150 |

Model 1459 Amp
1960s. 4 watts, 1x6" or 1x8".
| 1960s | | $100 | $125 |

Model 1463 Bass 35 Amp
1960s. Solidstate, 2x12", piggyback.
| 1960s | | $250 | $325 |

Model 1465 Head Amp
Mid-1960s. Rectangular amp head, solidstate, 50 watts, spotted gray cover, used with Twin 12 bottom.
| 1960s | | $200 | $275 |

Model 1471 Amp
One 8" speaker.
| 1960s | | $125 | $175 |

Model 1472 Amp
1960s. 15-18 watts, 2x6V6 tubes provide mid-level power, 1x12", front controls mounted vertically on front right side, dark cover with silver grille, large stationary handle, tremolo.
| 1962-1963 | | $150 | $200 |

Model 1474 Amp
1960s. Mid-power, mid-level, dual speakers, tube combo amp, gray Tolex, gray grille.
| 1960s | | $400 | $475 |

Model 1481 Amp
1960s. Low power, student amp, 1x6", gray cover, light grille, 2 controls.
| 1960s | | $125 | $150 |

Model 1482 Amp
1960s. Lower power, 1x12" combo, gray Tolex, silver grille, control panel mounted on right side vertically, tremolo.
| 1960s | | $175 | $250 |

Model 1483 Piggyback Amp
1960s. Mid-power, 1x15" piggyback tube amp, gray Tolex and gray grille.
| 1960s | | $400 | $550 |

Siegmund Midnight Blues Breaker Custom

Silvertone Model 1482

Silvertone Model 1484

SMF 15 Watter

Soldano Lucky 13

Specimen Horn Amp

AMPS

Model 1484 Twin Twelve Amp
1960s. Medium power, 2x12" piggyback tube amp, classic Silvertone colors - gray cover with light grille.

1966		$450	$600

SMF (Sonic Machine Factory)
2002-present. Tube amps and cabinets designed by Mark Sampson (Matchless, Bad Cat, Star) and Rick Hamel (SIB effects) and built in California.

Smicz Amplification
Tube combos and extenstion cabinets built by Bob Smicz in Bristol, Connecticut.

Snider Amplification
1999-present. Jeff Snider has been building various combo tube amps in San Diego, California, since '95. In '99 he started branding them with his last name.

Soldano
1987-present. Made in Seattle by amp builder Mike Soldano, the company offers a range of all-tube combo amps, heads and cabinets.

Astroverb 16 Combo Amp
1997-present. Atomic with added reverb.

1997-2002		$600	$650

Atomic 16 Combo Amp
1996-2001. Combo, 20 watts, 1x12".

1996-2001		$450	$600

Decatone Amp
1998-2002. 2x12" 100 watt combo, rear mounted controls, still available as a head.

1998-2002	With Decatrol footswitch	$2,000	$2,200
1998-2002	No footswitch	$1,600	$1,800

HR 50/Hot Rod 50 Amp Head
1992-present. 50 watt single channel head.

1992-2002		$800	$950

HR 100/Hot Rod 100 Amp Head
1994-2001. 100 watt single channel head.

1994-2001		$950	$1,100

Lucky 13 Combo Amp
2000-present. 100 watts (50 also available), 2x12" combo.

2000-2002		$1,000	$1,200

SLO-100 Super Lead Overdrive 100-Watt Amp
1988-present. First production model, super lead overdrive, 100 watts.

1988-1999	Snakeskin cover	$1,600	$1,900

Sonax
Introduced in 1972. Budget line of solidstate amps offered by Gretsch/Baldwin, made by Yorkville Sound (Traynor) in Toronto, Canada. Introduced with dark grille and dark cover.

530-B Bass Amp
30 watts, 1x12".

1970s		$125	$175

550-B Bass Amp
50 watts, 1x15".

1970s		$150	$200

720-G Amp
Student amp, 20 watts, 2x8", reverb.

1970s		$200	$250

730-G Amp
30 watts, 2x10", reverb and trem.

1970s		$300	$350

750-G Amp
50 watts, 2x12", reverb and trem.

1970s		$350	$400

770-G Amp
75 watts, 4x10", reverb and trem.

1970s		$400	$450

Songworks Systems
See listing under Little Lanilei.

Sonny Jr.
1996-present. Harmonica amplifiers built by harmonica player Sonny Jr. in conjunction with Cotton Amps in Tolland, Connecticut.

Sound City
Made in England from the late-'60s to the late-'70s, the tube Sound City amps were Marshall-looking heads and separate cabinets. They were imported, for a time, into the U.S. by Gretsch.

120/120R Amp Head
Early-late-1970s. The 120-watt head replaced the late-1960s 100-watt model.

1970s	120 no reverb	$450	$550
1970s	With reverb	$550	$650

50 PA Plus Amp
Late-1960s-late-1970s. Similar to 50 Plus but with four channels.

1970s		$450	$550

50 Plus/50R Amp Head
Late-1960s-late-1970s. Head amp, labeled 50 Plus or 50 R.

1960s		$450	$550
1970s		$450	$550

Concord Combo Amp
80 watts, 2x12" Fane speakers, Cream, basketweave grille.

1968	Cream	$500	$600

L-80 Cabinet
1970s. 4x10" inch cabinet.

1970s		$350	$400

X-60 Cabinet
1970s. 2x12" speaker cabinet.

1970s		$350	$400

Sound Electronics
Sound Electronics Corporation introduced a line of amplifiers in '65 that were manufactured in Long Island. Six models were initially offered, all with tube preamps and solidstate power sections. Their catalog did not list power wattages but did list features and speaker configurations. The initial

MODEL		EXC. COND.	
YEAR	FEATURES	LOW	HIGH

models had dark vinyl-style covers and sparkling silver grille cloth. The amps were combos with the large models having vertical cabinets, silver script 'Sound' logo on upper left of grille (same placement as Fender blackface amps). The larger models used JBL D120F and D130F speakers. Stand alone extension speakers were also available.

Various Model Amps
Mid-1960s. Includes X-101, X-101R, X-202 Bass/Organ, X-404 Bass and Organ, X-505R amps, hi-fi chassis often using 7868 power tubes.

1965		$300	$400

Sovtek
1992-present. Sovtek amps are products of Mike Matthews of Electro-Harmonix fame and his New Sensor Corporation. The guitar and bass amps and cabinets are made in Russia.

Mig 50 Head Amp
1994-present. Tube head, 50 watts.

1990s		$275	$350

Mig 60 Head Amp
1994-2001. Tube head, 60 watts, point-to-point wiring.

1990s		$325	$375

Mig 100 Head Amp
1990s. One hundred watts, tube head.

1990s		$350	$425

Mig 100B Head Amp
1996-present. Bass tube head, 100 watts.

1990s		$325	$375

Specimen Products
1984-present. Luthier Ian Schneller added tube amps and speaker cabinets in '93. He also builds guitars, basses and ukes.

Speedster
1995-2000, 2003-present. Founded by Lynn Ellsworth, offering tube amps and combos designed by Bishop Cochran with looks inspired by dashboards of classic autos. In '03, Joe Valosay and Jevco International purchased the company and revived the brand. Amps were originally built by Soldono, but are now built by Speedster in Gig Harbor, Washington.

St. George
1960s. There were Japanese guitars bearing this brand, but these amps may have been built in California.

Mid-Size Tube Amp
1965. Low power, 1x10" Jensen, 2x5065 and 2x12AX7 tubes.

1965		$175	$275

Standel
1952-1974, 1997-present. Bob Crooks started custom building amps part time in '52, going into full time standard model production in '58 in Temple City, California. In '61 Standel started distribut-

ing guitars under their own brand and others (see Guitar section for more instrument details). By late '63 or '64, Standel had introduced solidstate amps, two years before Fender and Ampeg introduced their solidstate models. In '67 Standel moved to a new, larger facility in El Monte, California. In '73 Chicago Musical Instruments (CMI), which owned Gibson at the time, bought the company and built amps in El Monte until '74. In '97 the Standel name was revived by Danny McKinney who, with the help of original Standel founder Bob Crooks and Frank Garlock (PR man for first Standel), set about reissuing some of the early models.

A-30 B Artist 30 Bass Amp
1964-early-1970s. Artist Series, the original Standel solidstate series, 80 watts, 2x15".

1964-1969		$300	$450

A-30 G Artist 30 Guitar Amp
1964-early-1970s. 80 watts, 2x15".

1964-1970s		$350	$500

A-48 G Artist 48 Guitar Amp
1964-early-1970s. 80 watts, 4x12".

1964-1970s		$450	$650

A-60 B Artist 60 Bass Amp
1964-early-1970s. 160 watts, 4x15".

1964-1970s		$400	$600

A-60 G Artist 60 Guitar Amp
1964-early-1970s. 160 watts, 4x15".

1964-1970s		$450	$650

A-96 G Artist 96 Guitar Amp
1964-early-1970s. 160 watts, 8x12".

1964-1970s		$500	$850

Model 10L8/15L12/25L15
1953-1958. Early custom made tube amps made by Bob Crooks in his garage, padded naugahyde cabinet with varying options and colors. There are a limited number of these amps, and brand knowledge is also limited, therefore there is a wide value range. Legend has it that the early Standel amps made Leo Fender re-think and introduce even more powerful amps.

1953-1958		$2,000	$3,500

S-10 Studio 10 Amp
Late-1960s-1970s. Studio Slim Line Series, solidstate, 30 watts, 1x10", dark vinyl, dark grille.

1970s		$300	$400

S-50 Studio 50 Amp
Late-1963 or early-1964-late-1960s. 60 watts, gray Tolex, gray grille, piggyback, not listed in 1969 Standel catalog.

1964		$450	$650

Star
2004-present. Tube amps and combos and speaker cabinets built by Mark Sampson in the Los Angeles area. Sampson has also been involved with Matchless, Bad Cat, and SMF amps.

Starlite
Starlite was a budget brand made and sold by Magnatone. See Magnatone for listings.

Speedster Custom

Standel Custom

Star Gain Star

AMPS

1969 Sunn 100S

1966 Supro Thunderbolt

1964 Supro Tremo-Verb

MODEL YEAR	FEATURES	EXC. COND. LOW	HIGH

Stinger
Budget line imported by Martin.

Sunn
1965-1987. Started in Oregon by brothers Conrad and Norm Sundhold (Norm was the bass player for the Kingsman). Sunn introduced powerful amps and extra heavy duty bottoms and was soon popular with many major rock acts. Norm sold his interest to Conrad in '69. Conrad sold the company to the Hartzell Corporation of Minnesota around 1972. Fender Musical Instruments acquired the brand in '85 shortly after parting ways with CBS and used the brand until 1989. They resurrected the brand again in 1998, but quit offering the name in 2002.

200S/215B Amp & Cab Set
Late-1960s. 60 watts, 2x6550 power tubes, large verticle cab with 2x15" speakers.

1969		$650	$900

Alpha 115 Amp
1980s. MOS-FET preamp section, 1x15", clean and overdrive.

1980s		$150	$225

Alpha 212 R Amp
1980s. MOS-FET preamp section, 2x12", reverb.

1980s		$150	$225

Concert Bass Head Amp
1970s. Solidstate, 200 watts.

1970s		$150	$225

Concert 215S Bass Amp Set
1970s. Solidstate head, 200 watts, Model 215S tall vertical cabinet with 2x12" Sunn label speakers, dark vinyl cover, Silver Sparkle grille.

1970s		$400	$500

Concert Lead 610S Amp Set
1970s. Solidstate, 200 watts, 6x10" piggyback, reverb and built-in distortion.

1970s		$425	$525

Model T Head Amp
Early-1970s.

1970s		$550	$800

Model T Head Amp Reissue
1999. Reissue of 1960s Model T, see through amp grille displays tubes, dark vinyl cover.

1990s		$550	$700

Model T Head Amp and Cab
1998. Head has 100 watts, 4x12" cab, reissue model.

1990s		$850	$1,100

SB-200 Amp
1985. 200 watts, 1x15", 4-band equalizer, master volume, compressor.

1985		$250	$350

Sceptre Head Amp
1968-1970s. Head amp, 60 watts, 6550 power tubes, tremolo, reverb.

1970s		$275	$350

Solarus Amp
1967-1970s. Tube amp (EL-34s), 40 watts (upgraded to 60 watts in 1969), 2x12", reverb, tremolo.

1970s		$450	$600

Sonoro Head Amp
Early-1970s. 60 watts, 2x6550 power tubes.

1970s		$400	$500

SPL 7250 Amp
Dual channels, 250 watts per channel, forced air cooling, switch-selectable peak compressor with LEDs.

1989		$250	$350

Supertone
1914-1941. Supertone was a brand used by Sears for their musical instruments. In the '40s Sears started using the Silvertone name on those products. Amps were made by other companies.

Amp

1930s		$125	$200

Supro
1935-1968. Supro was a budget brand of the National Dobro Company, made by Valco in Chicago.

Bantam 1611S Amp
1961-1964. 4 watts, 3 tubes, 1x 8" Jensen, petite, Spanish Ivory fabric cover, gold weave saran wrap grille.

1961-1964		$225	$275

Combo 1696T Amp
1961-1964. 24 watts, 6 tubes, 1x15" Jensen, Rhino-Hide covering in black and white, light grille, tremolo.

1961-1964		$375	$425

Comet 1610B Amp
1957-1959. Grey Rhino-Hide, 1x10".

1957-1959		$250	$300

Dual-Tone 1624T Amp
1961-1964. 17 watts, 1x12", 6 tubes, "organ tone tremolo."

1961-1964		$375	$500

Dual-Tone S6424T Amp
1964-1965. 17 watts, six tubes, 1x12" Jensen, restyled in 1964, tremolo, Trinidad Blue vinyl fabric cover, light color grille.

1964-1965		$375	$500

Royal Reverb 1650TR Amp
1963-1964. 17 watts, 15 tubes, 2x10" Jensens, catalog says "authentic tremolo and magic-reverberation."

1963-1964		$500	$600

Super 1606S Amp
1961-1964. 4.5 watts, 3 tubes, 1x8", black and white fabric cover, light saran wrap grille.

1961-1964		$275	$325

Thunderbolt S6420(B) Bass Amp
1964-1967. 35 watts, 1x15" Jensen, introduced in the 1964 catalog as a "no frills - no fancy extra circuits" amp. Sometimes referred to as the "Jimmy Page amp" based on his use of this amp in his early career.

1964-1967		$650	$1,150

Thunderbolt S6920 Amp
1967-1968. Redesign circuit replaced S6420B, 35 watts, 1x12".

1967-1968		$300	$350

AMPS

MODEL		EXC. COND.	
YEAR	FEATURES	LOW	HIGH

Tremo-Verb S6422 TR Amp
1964-1965. Lower power using four 12AX7 tubes, one 5Y3GT tube, one 6V6 tube (6 tubes), 1x10", tremolo and reverb.

1964-1965	Persian Red		
	vinyl cover	$650	$850

Trojan Tremolo 1616T/S6416T Amp
1961-1966. 5 watts, 4 tubes, 1x11"x6" oval (generally Rolla) speaker, 1961-1964 black and white fabric cover and saran wrap grille, 1964-1966 new larger cab with vinyl cover and light grille.

1961-1966	Trinidad Blue		
	vinyl cover	$300	$375

Vibra-Verb S6498VR Amp
1964-1965. "Supro's finest amplifier", two 35-watt channels, 1x15" and 1x10" Jensens, vibrato and reverb

1964-1965		$550	$650

SWR Sound
1984-present. Founded by Steve W. Rabe in 1984, with an initial product focus on bass amplifiers. Fender Musical Instruments Corp. acquired SWR in June, 2003.

Baby Blue Studio Bass System
1990-2003 Combo, all tube preamp, 150 watts solidstate power amp, 2x8", one 5" cone tweeter, gain, master volume, EQ, effects-blend.

1990-2003		$450	$600

Basic Black Amp
1992-1999. Solidstate, 100 watts, 1x12", Basic Black block logo on front, black Tolex, black metal grille.

1992-1999		$350	$450

Goliath Junior Amp
1988-1991. High-end driver, 2x10", 300 watts, can function as a high-fidelity monitor or as part of a bi-amp system.

1988-1991		$400	$500

Goliath Junior III Cab
1996-present. 2x10", black Tolex, black metal grille.

1996-2000		$350	$450

Studio 220 Bass Amp
1988-1995. 220 watt solidstate head, tube preamp.

1988-1995		$275	$400

Working Man 15 Bass Amp
1995-present. Combo amp, 1x15", 160 watts.

1995-2002		$350	$450

Takt
Late-1960s. Made in Japan, tube and solidstate models.

GA Series Amps
1968. GA-9 (2 inputs and 5 controls, 3 tubes), GA-10, GA-11, GA-12, GA-14, GA-15.

1968	GA-14/GA-15	$40	$50
1968	GA-9 through GA-12	$25	$35

Teisco
1946-1974, 1994-present. Japanese brand first imported into the U.S. around '63. Teisco offered both tube and solidstate amps.

Checkmate 50 Amp
Late-1950s-early-1960s. 50 watts using two 6L6 power tubes, 2x12" open back cab, reverb and tremolo, piggyback, similar looking to Silvertone Twin 12 piggyback of the same era, gray Tolex cover, light gray grille, Teisco slant logo on cab.

1960s		$400	$450

Checkmate CM-15 Amp
Late-1960s. Tube, 15 watts.

1960s		$75	$100

Checkmate CM-20 Amp
Late-1960s. Tube, 20 watts.

1960s		$100	$125

Checkmate CM-25 Amp
Late-1960s. Tube, 25 watts.

1960s		$125	$150

Checkmate CM-60 Amp
Late-1960s. Tube, 60 watts, piggyback amp and cab with wheels.

1960s		$200	$250

Checkmate CM-66 Amp
Late-1960s. Solidstate, dual speaker combo, Check Mate 66 logo on front panel.

1960s		$50	$75

Checkmate CM-100 Amp
Late-1960s. 4x6L6 power, 100 watts, piggyback with Vox-style trolley stand.

1960s		$300	$400

King 1800 Amp
Late-1960s. Tube, 180 watts, piggyback with 2 cabinets, large Teisco logo on cabinets, King logo on lower right side of one cabinet.

1960s		$400	$500

Teisco 8 Amp
Late-1960s. 5 watts

1960s		$25	$50

Teisco 10 Amp
Late-1960s. 5 watts.

1960s		$25	$50

Teisco 88 Amp
Late-1960s. 8 watts.

1960s		$50	$75

THD
1987-present. Tube amps and cabinets made in Seattle, Washington.

Titano (Magnatone)
1961-1963. Private branded by Magnatone, often for an accordion company or accordion studio, uses standard guitar input jacks.

Model 262 R Custom Amp
1961-1963. 35 watts, 2x12" + 2x5", reverb and vibrato make this one of the top of the line models, black vinyl, light silver grille.

1961-1963		$850	$1,100

Model 415 Bass Amp
1961-1963. 25 watts, 4x8", bass or accordion amp, black cover, darkish grille.

1961-1963		$450	$500

SWR Goliath Junior III cab

Teisco Checkmate 17

THD Flexi-50

AMPS

Tone King Meteor Series

Top Hat Club Royale T-20 CR

Trainwreck Express

MODEL YEAR	FEATURES	EXC. COND. LOW	HIGH

Tone King

1993-present. Tube amps, combos, and cabinets built by Mark Bartel in Baltimore, Maryland. The company started in New York and moved to Baltimore in '94.

Tonemaster (Magnatone)

Late-1950s-early-1960s. Magnatone amps private branded for Imperial Accordion Company. Prominent block-style capital "TONEMASTER" logo on front panel, generally something nearly equal to Magnatone equivalent. This is just one of many private branded Magnatones. Covers range from brown to black leatherette and brown to light silver grilles.

Model 214 (V logo) Amp
1959-1960. 10 watts, 1x12", vibrato, brown leatherette, V logo lower right corner front, large logo.

1959-1960		$450	$500

Model 260 Amp
1961-1963. About 30 watts, 2x12", vibrato, brown leatherette and brown grille, large logo on front.

1961-1963		$575	$650

Model 380 Amp
1961-1963. 50 watts, 2x12" and two oval 5"x7" speakers, vibrato, no reverb.

1961-1963		$675	$750

Top Hat Amplification

1994-present. Mostly Class A guitar amps built by Brian Gerhard in Anaheim, California. They also make an overdrive pedal.

Ambassador 100 TH-A100 Head Amp
Jan. 1999-present. 100 watts, class AB, four 6L6 tubes, reverb, dark green vinyl cover, white chickenhead knobs.

1999-2003		$1,100	$1,300

Ambassador T-35C 212 Amp
1999-present. 35 watts, 2x12" combo, reverb, master volume, blond cover, tweed-style fabric grille.

1999-2003		$1,100	$1,300

Club Deluxe Amp
1998-present. 20 watts, 6V6 power tubes, 1x12".

2000s		$800	$900

Club Royale TC-R2 Amp
Jan. 1999-present. 20 watts, class A using EL84s, 2x12".

1999-2003		$900	$1,000

Emplexador 50 TH-E50 Head Amp
Jan. 1997-present. 50 watts, class AB vint/high-gain head.

1997-2003		$1,000	$1,200

King Royale Amp
1996-present. 35 watts, class A using 4xEL84s, 2x12".

1996-2003		$1,200	$1,400

Portly Cadet TC-PC Amp
Jan. 1999-present. 5 watts, 6V6 power, 1x8", dark gray, light gray grille.

1999-2003		$450	$500

Prince Royale TC-PR Amp
Jan. 2000-2002. 5 watts using EL84 power, 1x8", deep red, light grille.

2000-2003		$500	$550

Super Deluxe TC-SD2 Amp
Jan. 2000-present. 30 watts, class A, 7591 power tubes, 2x12".

2000-2003		$1,000	$1,200

Torres Engineering

Founded by Dan Torres, the company builds tube amps, combos, cabinets and amp kits in San Mateo, California. Dan wrote monthly columns for *Vintage Guitar* magazine for many years and authored the book *Inside Tube Amps*.

Trace Elliot

1978-present. Founded in a small music shop in Essex, England. Currently owned by Gibson.

TA35CR Acoustic Guitar Amp
1994-1995. Compact lateral-style cab with 2x5", 35 watts, with reverb and chorus, dark vinyl cover, dark grille.

1994-1995		$275	$375

TA100R Acoustic Guitar Amp
1990-present. Compact lateral-style cab with 4x5", 100 watts, with reverb, dark vinyl cover, dark grille.

1990-2000		$525	$575

Vellocette Amp
1996-1998. 15 watt, tube, Class A, 1x10", green cover, round sound speaker hole.

1990s		$325	$400

Trainwreck

1983-present. Founded by Ken Fischer. Limited production, custom-made amps that are generally grouped by model. Models include the Rocket, Liverpool and Express, plus variations on those themes. Each amp's value should be evaluated on a case-by-case basis. Ken wrote many amp articles for *Vintage Guitar*.

Custom Built Amp

1980s	High-end model	$12,000	$15,000

Traynor

1963-present. Started by Pete Traynor and Jack Long in Canada and made by Yorkville Sound.

Guitar Mate Reverb YGM3 Amp
1969-1979. 40 watts, 1x12", tube amp, black Tolex, gray grille.

1969-1979		$250	$350

Mark II Bass Master Amp
1970s.

1970s		$300	$400

Mark III (YGL-3) Amp
1971-1979. All tube, 80 watts, 2x12" combo, reverb, tremolo.

1971-1979		$250	$350

YBA3 Custom Special Bass Amp Set
1967-1972. Tube head with 130 watts and 8x10" large vertical matching cab, dark vinyl cover, light grille.

1967-1972		$500	$600

MODEL		EXC. COND.	
YEAR	FEATURES	LOW	HIGH

True Tone

1960s. Guitars and amps retailed by Western Auto, manufactured by Chicago guitar makers like Kay.

Hi-Fi 4 (K503 Hot-Line Special) Amp

1960s. 4 watts from 3 tubes, gray cabinet, gray grille, metal handle.

1960s		$100	$150

Vibrato 704 Amp

1960s. Solidstate, 10 watts, 1x8", white sides and gray back, gray grille.

1960s		$125	$175

Vibrato 706 Amp

1960s. Solidstate, 15 watts, 1x15", white sides and gray back, brown grille.

1960s		$150	$200

Tube Works

Originally out of Denver, now a division of Genz Benz Enclosures of Scottsdale, Arizona. Tube Works' first products were tube guitar effects. They have added tube/solidstate amps, cabinets, and DI boxes to the product mix.

Twilighter (Magnatone)

Late-1950s-early-1960s. Magnatone amps private branded for LoDuca Brothers. Prominent block-style capital "TWILIGHTER" logo on front panel, generally something nearly equal to Magnatone equivalent. This is just one of many private branded Magnatones. Covers range from brown to black leatherette, and brown to light silver grilles.

Model 213 Amp

1961-1963. About 20 watts, 1x12", vibrato, brown leatherette and brown grille, prominent logo on front.

1961-1963		$450	$500

Model 260R Amp

1961-1963. About 18 to 25 watts, 1x12", vibrato, brown leatherette cover, large logo.

1961-1963		$475	$550

Model 280A Amp

Late-1950s-early-1960s. About 35 watts, 2x12", vibrato, brown leatherette cover, large logo.

1961-1963		$525	$625

Two-Rock

1999-present. Tube guitar amp heads, combos and cabinets built by Joe Mloganoski and Bill Krinard (K&M Analog Designs) originally in Cotati, California, currently in Rohnert Park. They also build speakers.

Emerald Pro Head Amp

2000-2001. 50 watt switchable head.

2000-2001		$1,950	$2,100

UltraSound

A division of UJC Electronics, UltraSound builds acoustically transparent amps, designed by Greg Farres for the acoustic guitarist, in Adel, Iowa.

Unique (Magnatone)

1961-1963. Private branded, typically for an accordion company or accordion studio, uses standard guitar input jacks.

Model 260R Amp

1961-1963. Based on Magnatone 260 Series amp, 35 watts, 2x12" but with reverb, black vinyl-style cover with distinctive black diamond-check pattern running through the top and sides.

1961-1963		$650	$800

Model 460 Amp

1961-1963. 35 watts, 2x12" and oval 5"x7" speakers, reverb and vibrato make it one of the top models, black vinyl, black grille.

1961-1963		$700	$850

Univox

1964-ca.1978. From '64 to early-'68, these were American-made tube amps with Jensen speakers. By '68, they were using Japanese components in American cabinets, still with Jensen speakers. Electronics were combination of tube and transistors during this time; this type lasted until the mid-'70s. Around '71, Univox introduced a line of all solidstate amps, as well.

Bass Model U130B Amp

1976-1978. 130 watts, 1x15".

1976-1978		$150	$250

Lead Model Tube Amp

1960s. Tube amp, 2x10".

1965-1969		$350	$400

Lead Model U130L Amp

1976-1978. Solidstate.

1976-1978		$100	$175

V-Series

See Crate.

Valco

Valco, from Chicago, was a big player in the guitar and amplifier business. Their products were private branded for other companies like National, Supro, Airline, Oahu, and Gretsch.

Vega

1903-present. The original Boston-based company was purchased by C.F. Martin in 1970. In '80, the Vega trademark was sold to a Korean company.

A-49 Amp

1960s. 6 watts, 1x8", tubes, tan cover.

1960s		$150	$200

Vesta Fire

1980s. Japanese imports by Shiino Musical Instruments Corp.; later by Midco International. Mainly known for effects pedals.

J-I Preamp

1980s		$50	$100

J-II Preamp

1980s		$50	$100

Traynor PM-100

Tube Works 6150 DFX

Univox U130B

AMPS

Victoria Victorilux

1963 Vox AC-2

Vox AC-50 Super Twin

MODEL YEAR	FEATURES	EXC. COND. LOW	HIGH
PT-I Power Amp			
1980s		$100	$150
PT-II Power Amp			
1980s		$150	$200

VHT

1989-present. Founded by Steven M. Fryette, VHT builds amps, combos, and cabinets in Burbank, California.

Pittbull Fifty-Twelve Amp
1994-1999. 50 watts, all tube preamp section, 1x12", 2x12" version still available.

1994-1999		$750	$850

Victor

Late-1960s. Made in Japan.

MA-25 Amp
Late-1960s. Student model, light cover, dark grille, solidstate, 6 controls, 2 inputs, script Victor logo.

1960s		$75	$100

Victoria

1994-present. Tube amps, combos, and reverb units built by Mark Baier in Naperville, Illinois.

Double Deluxe Amp
1994-present. 35 watts, 2x12".

1994-1999		$1,300	$1,400

Model 518 Amp
1990s-present. Tweed, 1x8".

2000s		$600	$700

Model 20112 Amp
1994-1999. 20 watts, 1x12", tweed.

1994-1999		$850	$900

Model 35210 Amp
1994-1999. 35 watts, 2x10", tweed.

1994-1999		$1,300	$1,400

Model 35310-T Amp
1994-present. 35 watts, 3x10".

1994-1999		$1,400	$1,500
2000s		$1,400	$1,500

Model 45410-T Amp
1994-present. 45 watts, 4x10" combo, tweed.

1994-1999		$1,400	$1,500

Model 50212-T Amp
2002-2003. New low power offering.

2000s		$1,500	$1,600

Model 80212 Amp
1994-present. 100 watts, 2x12", tweed.

1994-1999		$1,500	$1,600

Voltmaster

Trapezoid-shaped combo amps and reverb units made in Plano, Texas, in the late '90s.

Vox

1957-1972, 1982-present. Tom Jennings and Dick Denney combined forces in '57 to produce the first Vox product, the 15-watt AC-15 amplifier. The short period between '63-'65 is considered to be the Vox heyday. Vox produced tube amps in England and also the U.S. from '64 to the early part of '66. English-made tube amps were standardized between '60 and '65. U.S.-made Vox amps in '66 were solidstate. In the mid-'60s, similar model names were sometimes used for tube and solidstate amps. In '93 Korg bought the Vox name and current products are built by Marshall.

A Vox amp stand is correctly called a "trolley" and those amps that originally came with a trolley are priced accordingly, that is the price below includes the original trolley, and an amp without the trolley will be worth less than the amount shown. Smaller amps were not originally equipped with a trolley.

AC-4 Amp
1958-1965. Made in England, early Vox tube design, 3.5 watts, 1x8", tremolo.

1958-1965		$1,400	$1,600

AC-10 Amp
1960-1965. Made in England, 12 watts, 1x10", tremolo, this tube version not made in U.S. (1964-1965).

1960-1965		$1,600	$2,400

AC-10 Twin Amp
1960-1965. Made in England, also made in U.S. 1964-1965, 12 watts (two EL84s), 2x10".

1960-1965		$1,600	$2,400

AC-15 Twin Amp
1958-1965. Tube, 2x12", 18 watts.

1958-1965	Black Tolex	$3,200	$4,000
1960-1965	Custom colors	$3,700	$4,500

AC-15 TBX
1996-2000. 15 watts, top boost, 1x12" Celestion (lower cost Eminence available).

1996-2000		$900	$950

AC-30 Twin/AC-30 Twin Top Boost Amp
1960-1965. Made in England, 30-watt head, 36 watts 2x12", Top Boost includes additional treble and bass. Custom colors available in 1960-1963.

1960-1963	Custom colors	$4,500	$5,500
1960-1965		$3,500	$4,500

AC-30 Super Twin Head Amp
1960-1965. Made in England, 30-watt head.

1960-1963	Custom color	$2,800	$3,800
1960-1965	With footswitch	$2,000	$3,000

AC-30 Collector Model
1991-1992. Limited production, high-grade solid mahogany cabinet, reverb.

1991-1992		$1,900	$2,100

AC-30 Reissue
1990-present. 2x12", black or brown leatherette.

1990-1999		$900	$1,200
1990s	Blond custom color	$1,500	$1,700

AC-50 Head Amp
1960-1965. Made in England, 50-watt head, U.S. production 1964-1965 tube version is Westminster Bass, U.S. post-1966 is solidstate.

1960-1965		$1,300	$1,800

Berkeley II V108 (tube) Amp
1964-1966. U.S.-made tube amp. Revised 1966-1969 to U.S.-made solidstate model V1081, 18 watts, 2x10" piggyback.

1964-1966		$1,200	$1,400

AMPS

MODEL		EXC. COND.	
YEAR	FEATURES	LOW	HIGH

Berkeley II V1081 (solidstate) Amp
1966-1969. U.S.-made solidstate model V1081, 35 watts, 2x10" piggyback, includes trolley stand.
1966-1969 $750 $800

Berkeley III (solidstate) Amp
1966-1969. Berkeley III logo on top panel of amp.
1966-1969 $750 $800

Buckingham Amp
1966-1969. Solidstate, 70 watts, 2x12" piggyback, includes trolley stand.
1966-1969 $850 $900

Cambridge 30 Reverb Twin 210 Amp
1999-2002. 30 watts hybrid circuit, 2x10" with reverb.
1999-2002 $300 $400

Cambridge Reverb (solidstate) V1031 Amp
1966-1969. Solidstate, 35 watts, 1x10", model V1031 replaced tube version V103.
1966-1969 $600 $700

Cambridge Reverb (tube) V103 Amp
1964-1966. U.S-made tube version, 18 watts, 1x10", a Pacemaker with reverb, superceded by solidstate Model V1031 by 1967.
1964-1966 $1,000 $1,200

Churchill PA Head Amp
Late-1960s. PA head with multiple inputs.
1960s $400 $500

Climax V-125/V-125 Lead Combo Amp
1970-1991. Solidstate, 125 watts, 2x12" combo, 5-band EQ, master volume.
1970-1991 $500 $700

Defiant Amp
1966-1969. Made in England, 50 watts, 2x12" + Midax horn cabinet.
1966-1969 $1,500 $1,600

Escort Amp
1970s. AC/DC, portable.
1970s $400 $450

Essex Bass V1042 Amp
1965-1969. U.S.-made solidstate, 35 watts, 2x12".
1965-1969 $750 $750

Foundation Bass Amp
1966-1969. Solidstate, 50 watts, 1x18", made in England only.
1966-1969 $550 $650

Kensington Bass V1241 Amp
1965-1969. U.S.-made solidstate bass amp, 22 watts, 1x15", G-tuner.
1965-1969 $500 $550

Pacemaker (tube) V102 Amp
1964-1965. U.S.-made tube amp, 18 watts, 1x10", replaced by solidstate Pacemaker model V1021.
1964-1965 $800 $900

Pacemaker (solidstate) V1021 Amp
1966-1969. U.S.-made solidstate amp, 35 watts, 1x10", replaced Pacemaker model V102.
1967-1969 $400 $450

Pathfinder (tube) V101 Amp
1964-1965. U.S.-made tube amp, 4 watts, 1x18", 1966-1969 became U.S.-made solidstate V1011.
1964-1965 $700 $800

Pathfinder (solidstate) V1011 Amp
1966-1969. U.S.-made solidstate, 25 watts peak power, 1x8".
1966-1969 $350 $400

Pathfinder 10 Amp
2002-present. Compact practice amp with 1960s cosmetics, 10 watts, 6 1/2" speaker.
2002 $70 $90

Royal Guardsman V1131/V1132 Amp
1966-1969. U.S.-made solidstate, 50 watts piggy-back, 2x12" + one horn, the model below the Super Beatle V1141/V1142.
1966-1969 $850 $950

Scorpion (solidstate) Amp
1968. Solidstate, 60 watts, 4x10" Vox Oxford speaker.
1968 $600 $700

Super Beatle V1141/V1142 Amp
1966-1967. U.S.-made 120 watt solidstate, 4x12" + two horns, with distortion pedal (V1141), or without (V1142).
1966-1967 $1,900 $2,100

Viscount V1151/V1152 Amp
1966-1969. U.S.-made solidstate, 70 watts, 2x12" combo.
1966-1969 $750 $850

Westminster V118 Bass Amp
1966-1969. Solidstate, 120 watts, 1x18".
1966-1969 $600 $700

Wabash
1950s. Private branded amps distributed by the David Wexler company.
Model 1158 Amp
Danelectro-made, 1x15", two 6L6 power tubes.
1955   Tweed $175 $275

Warbler
See listing under Juke amps.

Washburn
1974-present. Imported guitar and bass amps. Washburn also offers guitars, mandolins, and basses.

Watkins
1957-present. England's Watkins Electric Music (WEM) was founded by Charlie Watkins. Their first commercial product was the Watkins Dominator (wedge Gibson stereo amp shape) in 1957, followed by the Copicat Echo in '58.
Dominator V-Front Amp
Late-1950s-1960s. 18 watts, 2x10", wedge cabinet similar to Gibson GA-79 stereo amp, tortoise and light beige cab, light grille. Requires 220V step-up transformer.
1959-1962 $1,200 $1,400

Vox Pathfinder

Vox Super Beatle

Watkins Dominator

Working Dog Rottweiler

Yamaha T100 C

Zeta AP-12

Working Dog

2001-present. Lower cost tube amps and combos built by Alessandro High-End Products (Alessandro, Hound Dog) in Huntingdon Valley, Pennsylvania.

Rottweiler Combo amp
2002-present. 40 watt, 2x12" tube combo (also available as 4x10, 2x12, 2x12, 2x8, and 2x10), reverb.

2002	2x12"	$750	$850

Yamaha

1946-present. Japan-based Yamaha started offering amps in the '60s.

Budokan HY-10G II Amp
1987-1992. Portable, 10 watts, distortion control, EQ.

1987-1992		$50	$100

G50-112 Amp
1980s. 50 watts, 1x12".

1980s		$200	$250

G100-112 Amp
1983-1992. 100 watts, 1x12" combo, black cover, striped grille.

1983-1992		$200	$250

G100-212 Amp
1983-1992. 100, 2x12" combo, black cover, striped grille.

1983-1992		$250	$300

JX30B Amp
1983-1992. Bass amp, 30 watts.

1983-1992		$150	$200

TA-20 Amp
1968-1972. Upright wedge shape with controls facing upwards, solidstate.

1968-1972		$100	$150

TA-25 Amp
1968-1972. Upright wedge shape with controls facing upwards, 40 watts, 1x12", solidstate, Black or Red cover.

1968-1972		$100	$150

TA-30 Amp
1968-1972. Upright wedge shape, solidstate.

1968-1972		$150	$200

TA-50 Amp
1971-1972. Solidstate combo, 80 watts, 2x12", includes built-in cart with wheels, black cover.

1971-1972		$200	$250

TA-60 Amp
1968-1972. Upright wedge shape, solidstate, most expensive of wedge-shape amps.

1968-1972		$225	$275

VR4000 Amp
1988-1992. 50-watt stereo, 2 channels, EQ, stereo chorus, reverb and dual effects loops.

1988-1992		$250	$300

VR6000 Amp
1988-1992. 100-watt stereo, 2 channels which can also be combined, EQ, chorus, reverb and dual effects loops.

1988-1992		$350	$400

VX-15 Amp
1988-1992. 15 watts.

1988-1992		$100	$150

YBA-65 Bass Amp
1972-1976. Solidstate combo, 60 watts, 1x15".

1972-1976		$125	$175

YTA-25 Amp
1972-1976. Solidstate combo, 25 watts, 1x12".

1972-1976		$100	$150

YTA-45 Amp
1972-1976. Solidstate combo, 45 watts, 1x12".

1972-1976		$125	$175

YTA-95 Amp
1972-1976. Solidstate combo, 90 watts, 1x12".

1972-1976		$150	$200

YTA-100 Amp
1972-1976. Solidstate piggyback, 100 watts, 2x12".

1972-1976		$200	$250

YTA-110 Amp
1972-1976. Solidstate piggyback, 100 watts, 2x12" in extra large cab.

1972-1976		$200	$250

YTA-200 Amp
1972-1976. Solidstate piggyback, 200 watts, 4x12".

1972-1976		$225	$275

YTA-300 Amp
1972-1976. Solidstate piggyback, 200 watts, dual cabs with 2x12" and 4x12".

1972-1976		$325	$375

YTA-400 Amp
1972-1976. Solidstate piggyback, 200 watts, dual cabs 2x4x12".

1972-1976		$350	$400

Zapp

Ca. 1978-early 1980s. Zapp amps were distributed by Red Tree Music, Inc., of Mamaroneck, New York.

Z-10 Amp
1978-1980s. Small student amp, 8 watts.

1979-1982		$40	$60

Z-50 Amp
1978-1980s. Small student amp, 10 watts, reverb, tremelo.

1978-1982		$50	$75

Zeta

1982-present. Solid state amps with MIDI options, made in Oakland, California. They also make basses, violins and mandolins.

316 Ace-Tone — Ampeg

ADA Flanger

ADA TFX4 Time Effects

Alesis Guitar FX

Ace-Tone

Late-1960s-early-1970s. Effects from Ace Electronic Industry, which was a part of Sakata Shokai Limited of Osaka, Japan. Ace-Tone was the precedessor to Roland and Boss.

Fuzz Master FM-1
Distortion and overdrive.
1968 — $100 / $135

Wah Master WM-1
Filter wah.
1969 — $100 / $135

Acoustyx

1977-1982. Made by the Highland Corporation of Vermont.

Image Synthesizer IS-1
1977-1982.
1977-1982 — $40 / $60

Phase Five
1977-ca.1982. Used six 'C' cell batteries!
1977-1982 — $40 / $60

ADA

1977-2002. ADA is an acronym for Analog/ Digital Associates. The company was located in Berkeley, California, and introduced its Flanger and Final Phase in 1977. The company later moved to Oakland and made amplifiers, high-tech signal processors, and a reissue of its original Flanger.

Final Phase
1977-1979. Reissued in 1997.
1977-1979 — $300 / $400

Flanger
1977-1983. Reissued in 1996.
1977-1979 With control pedal $350 / $400
1977-1979 Without control pedal $250 / $350
1980-1983 — $150 / $250

Flanger Reissue
1996-2002.
1990s — $75 / $100

MP-1
1987-1995. Tube preamp with chorus and effects loop, MIDI.
1987-1995 With foot controller $200 / $250

MP-2
Ca.1988-1995. Tube preamp with chorus, nine-band EQ and effects loop, MIDI.
1988-1995 — $140 / $190

Pitchtraq
1987. Programmable pitch transposer including octave shifts.
1987 — $200 / $250

Stereo Tapped Delay STD-1
Introduced in 1981.
1980s — $110 / $150

TFX4 Time Effects
Introduced in 1982, includes flanger, chorus, doubler, echo.
1980s — $100 / $150

Aguila

The New York, New York amp builder also offers a line of tube and solidstate pre-amps.

Alamo

1947-1982. Founded by Charles Eilenberg, Milton Fink, and Southern Music, San Antonio, TX. Distributed by Bruno & Sons. Mainly known for guitars and amps, Alamo did offer a reverb unit. See *Guitar Stories Volume II*, by Michael Wright, for a complete history of Alamo with detailed model listings.

Reverb Unit
1965-ca. 1979. Has a Hammond reverb system, balance and intensity controls. By 1973 the unit had three controls - mixer, contour, and intensity.
1965 — $175 / $275

Alesis

1992-present. Alesis has a wide range of products for the music industry, including digital processors and amps for guitars.

Effects Processors
1992-present. Various digital processors for reverb, echo, etc.
1990s — $125 / $250

Allen Amplification

1998-present. David Allen's company, located in Richwood, Kentucky, mainly produces amps, but they also offer a tube overdrive pedal.

Altair Corp.

1977-1980s. Company was located in Ann Arbor, Michigan.

Power Attenuator PW-5
1977-1980. Goes between amp and speaker to dampen volume.
1977-1980 — $100 / $125

Amdek

Mid-1980s. Amdek offered many electronic products over the years, including drum machines and guitar effects. Many of these were sold in kit form so quality of construction can vary.

Delay Machine DMK-200
1983. Variable delay times.
1983 — $75 / $125

Octaver OCK-100
1983. Produces tone one or two octaves below the note played.
1983 — $75 / $125

Ampeg

Ampeg entered the effects market in the late-'60s. Their offerings in the early-'60s were really amplifier-outboard reverb units similar to the ones offered by Gibson (GA-1). Ampeg offered a line of imported effects in '82-'83, known as the A-series (A-1 through A-9).

MODEL		EXC. COND.	
YEAR	FEATURES	LOW	HIGH

Analog Delay A-8
1982-1983. Made in Japan.

1982-1983	$40	$60

Chorus A-6
1982-1983. Made in Japan.

1982-1983	$35	$45

Compressor A-2
1982-1983. Made in Japan.

1982-1983	$35	$45

Distortion A-1
1982-1983. Made in Japan.

1982-1983	$30	$40

Echo Jet (EJ-12) Reverb
1963-1965. Outboard, alligator clip reverb unit with 12" speaker, 12 watts, technically a reverb unit. When used as a stand-alone amp, the reverb is off. Named EJ-12A in 1965.

1963-1965	$300	$350

Echo Satellite (ES-1)
1961-1963. Outboard reverb unit with amplifier and speaker alligator clip.

1961-1963	$275	$325

Flanger A-5
1982-1983. Made in Japan.

1982-1983	$40	$50

Multi-Octaver A-7
1982-1983. Made in Japan.

1982-1983	$50	$70

Over Drive A-3
1982-1983. Made in Japan.

1982-1983	$30	$40

Parametric Equalizer A-9
1982-1983. Made in Japan.

1982-1983	$30	$40

Phaser A-4
1982-1983. Made in Japan.

1982-1983	$50	$60

Phazzer
1975-1977.

1970s	$50	$70

Scrambler Fuzz
1969-1971. Distortion pedal.

1969	$90	$150

Analog Man
1994-present. Founded by Mike Piera in '94 with full-time production by 2000. Located in Bethel, Connecticut, producing Chorus, Compressor, Fuzz, and Boost pedals by 2003.

Apollo
Ca. 1967-1972. Imported by St. Louis Music, includes Fuzz Treble Boost Box, Crier Wa-Wa, Deluxe Fuzz.

Crier Wa-Wa
Ca. 1967-1972.

1970s	$60	$80

Fuzz
Ca. 1967-1972. Includes the Fuzz Treble Boost Box and the Deluxe Fuzz.

1970s	$75	$90

Arbiter
Ivor Arbiter and Arbiter Music, London, began making the circular Fuzz Face stompbox in '66. Other products included the Fuzz Wah and Fuzz Wah Face. In '68 the company went public as Arbiter and Western, later transitioning to Dallas-Arbiter. Refer to Dallas-Arbiter for listings.

Aria
1960-present. Aria provided a line of effects in the mid-1980s.

Analog Delay AD-10
1983-1985. Dual-stage stereo.

1983-1985	$60	$65

Chorus ACH-1
1986-1987. Stereo.

1980s	$30	$35

Chorus CH-5
1985-1987.

1980s	$30	$35

Chorus CH-10
1983-1985. Dual-stage stereo.

1980s	$30	$35

Compressor CO-10
1983-1985.

1980s	$30	$35

Digital Delay ADD-100
1984-1986. Delay, flanging, chorus, doubling, hold.

1980s	$50	$65

Digital Delay DD-X10
1985-1987.

1980s	$50	$65

Distortion DT-5
1985-1987.

1980s	$40	$55

Distortion DT-10
1983-1985. Dual-stage.

1980s	$40	$60

Flanger AFL-1
1986. Stereo.

1980s	$40	$55

Flanger FL-5
1985-1987.

1980s	$40	$55

Flanger FL-10
1983-1985. Dual-stage stereo.

1980s	$40	$55

Metal Pedal MP-5
1985-1987.

1980s	$30	$45

Noise Gate NG-10
1983-1985.

1980s	$20	$35

Over Drive OD-10
1983-1985. Dual-stage.

1980s	$35	$45

Parametric Equalizer EQ-10
1983-1985.

1980s	$40	$45

Ampeg Chorus

Analog Man Black Cat Superfuzz

Aria Jet Phaser RE-202

EFFECTS

The *Vintage Guitar Price Guide* shows low to high values for items in all-original excellent condition, and, where applicable, with original case or cover.

Arion Phase Shifter RE-100

Arion Compressor SCO-1

Austone Soul-O-Stomp

MODEL YEAR	FEATURES	EXC. COND. LOW	HIGH
Phase Shifter PS-10	*1983-1984. Dual-stage.*		
1980s		$40	$55
Programmable Effects Pedal APE-1	*1984-1986. Compression, distortion, delay, chorus.*		
1980s		$50	$55
Ultra Metal AUM-1	*1986.*		
1980s		$50	$60

Arion

1984-present. Imports distributed by Matthews and Ryan of Brooklyn, NY.

MODEL YEAR	FEATURES	EXC. COND. LOW	HIGH
Compressor SCO-1	*1985-present. Stereo. The "-1" was dropped on later models.*		
1980s		$30	$35
Distortion SDI-1	*1984-2002. Stereo. The "-1" was dropped on later models.*		
1980s		$25	$30
Hot Watt II	*1984-present. Headphone amp.*		
1980s		$30	$35
Metal Master SMM-1	*1984-present. Stereo. The "-1" was dropped on later models.*		
1980s		$15	$25
Over Drive SOD-1	*1984-2002. Stereo. The "-1" was dropped on later models.*		
1980s		$25	$35
Parametric EQ SPE-1	*1985-late-1980s?. Stereo.*		
1980s		$20	$25
Stereo Chorus SCH-1	*1984-present. The "-1" was dropped on later models.*		
1980s		$30	$35
Stereo Delay SAD-1	*1984-present. Analog delay.*		
1980s		$35	$45
Stereo Delay SAD-2	*Ca.1990-present.*		
1990s		$35	$45
Stereo Flanger SFL-1	*1984-present. The "-1" was dropped on later models.*		
1980s		$30	$35
Stereo Phaser SPH-1	*1984-present. The "-1" was dropped on later models.*		
1980s		$30	$35
Tube Mania	*1987-early-1990s.*		
1980s		$30	$35

Astrotone

Late 1960s. By Universal Amp, which also made the Sam Ash Fuzzz

MODEL YEAR	FEATURES	EXC. COND. LOW	HIGH
Fuzz	*Ca.1967. By Universal Amp.*		
1960s		$150	$245

ATD

Mid-1960s-early 1980s. Made by the All-Test Devices corporation of Long Beach, NY. In the mid-'60s, Richard Minz and an associate started making effects part-time, selling them through Manny's Music in New York. They formed All-Test and started making Maestro effects and transducer pickups for CMI, which owned Gibson at the time. By '75, All-Test was marketing effects under their own brandname. All-Test is still around making products for other industries, but by the early to mid-'80s they were no longer making products for the guitar.

MODEL YEAR	FEATURES	EXC. COND. LOW	HIGH
PB-1 Power Booster	*1976-ca.1980.*		
1979		$40	$55
Volume Pedal EV-1	*1979-ca.1980.*		
1979		$25	$30
Wah-Wah/Volume Pedal WV-1	*1979-ca.1981.*		
1979		$35	$55

Audio Matrix

1980s. The company was located in Escondido, California.

MODEL YEAR	FEATURES	EXC. COND. LOW	HIGH
Mini Boogee B81	*1981. Four-stage, all-tube preamp, overdrive, distortion.*		
1980s		$90	$135

Audioworks

1980s. Company was located in Niles, Illinois.

MODEL YEAR	FEATURES	EXC. COND. LOW	HIGH
F.E.T. Distortion	*1982.*		
1980s		$25	$55

Auralux

2000-present. Founded by Mitchell Omori and David Salzmann, Auralux builds effects and tube amps in Highland Park, Illinois.

Austone Electronics

1997-present. Founded by Jon Bessent and Randy Larkin, Austone offers a range of stomp boxes, all made in Austin, Texas.

MODEL YEAR	FEATURES	EXC. COND. LOW	HIGH
Overdrive and Fuzz Pedals	*1997-present. Various overdrive and fuzz boxes.*		
1997		$100	$175

Automagic

1998-present. Wah pedals and distortion boxes made in Germany by Musician Sound Design.

Avalanche

Brianizer

Late-1980s. Leslie effect, dual rotor, adjustable speed and rates.

MODEL YEAR	FEATURES	EXC. COND. LOW	HIGH
1980s		$75	$125

EFFECTS

MODEL YEAR	FEATURES	EXC. COND. LOW	HIGH

B & M
1970s. A private brand made by Sola/Color-sound.
Fuzz Unit
1970s. Long thin orange case, volume, sustain, tone knobs, on-off stomp switch.

1970s		$200	$250

Bad Cat Amplifier Company
2000-present. Founded in Corona, California, by James and Debbie Heidrich with Mark Sampson as the chief designer and engineer. Bad Cat offers class A combo amps, heads, cabinets and effects.

Bartolini
The pickup manufacturer offered a few effects in the mid-1980s.
Tube-It
1982-ca.1988. Marshall tube amplification simulator with bass, treble, sustain controls.

1980s	Red case	$65	$85

Basic Systems' Side Effects
1980s. This company was located in Tulsa, Oklahoma.
Audio Delay
1986-ca.1987. Variable delay speeds.

1986-1987		$60	$85

Triple Fuzz
1986-ca.1987. Selectable distortion types.

1986-1987		$40	$55

BBE
1985-present. BBE, located in California, currently manufactures rack-mount effects and also owns G&L Guitars.
601 Stinger
1985-ca. 1989.

1980s		$50	$65

Bell
Vibrato

1970s		$100	$150

Bennett Music Labs
Effects built in the U.S. by Bruce Bennett.

Bigsby
Bigsby has been making volume and tone pedals since the '50s. They currently offer a volume pedal.
Foot Volume and Tone Control

1950s		$100	$150

Binson
Late 1950s-1982. Binson, of Milan, Italy, made several models of the Echorec, using tubes or transistors. They also made units for Guild, Sound City and EKO.

Echorec
Ca. 1960-1979. Four knob models with 12 echo selections, 1 head, complex multitap effects, settings for Record Level, Playback and Regeneration. Includes B1, B2, Echomaster1, T5 (has 6 knobs), T5E, and Baby. Used a magnetic disk instead of tape. Guild later offered the "Guild Echorec by Binson" which is a different stripped-down version.

1960s	Tube model	$400	$700

Bixonic
1995-present. Originally distributed by Sound-Barrier Music, Bixonic is currently distributed by Godlyke, Inc.
Expandora EXP-2000
1995-2000. Analog distortion, round silver case. The EXP-2000R reissue came out in 2004.

1995-2000		$150	$170

Blackbox Music Electronics
2000-present. Founded by Loren Stafford and located in Minneapolis, Minnesota, Blackbox offers a line of effects for guitar and bass.

Blackstone Appliances
1999-prresent. Distortion effects crafted by Jon Blackstone in New York, New York.

Bon, Mfg
Bon was located in Escondido, California.
Tube Driver 204
1979-ca.1981.

1979-1981		$75	$150

Boss
1976-present. Japan's Roland Corporation first launched effect pedals in 1974. A year or two later the subsidiary company, Boss, debuted its own line. They were marketed concurrently at first but gradually Boss became reserved for effects and drum machines while the Roland name was used on amplifiers and keyboards. Boss still offers a wide line of pedals.
Acoustic Simulator AC-2
1997-present. Four modes that emulate various acoustic tones.

1997-1999		$50	$55

Auto Wah AW-2
1991-1999.

1991-1999		$40	$45

Bass Chorus CE-2B
1987-1995.

1987-1995		$40	$55

Bass Equalizer GE-7B
1987-1995. Seven-band, name changed to GEB-7 in 1995.

1987-1995		$40	$45

Bass Flanger BF-2B
1987-1994.

1987-1994		$40	$45

Bad Cat 2-Tone

BBE 601 Stinger

Blackbox Quicksilver

EFFECTS

Boss Super Chorus CH-1

Boss Compressor Sustainer CS-3

Boss Digital Delay DD-3

MODEL YEAR	FEATURES	EXC. COND. LOW	HIGH
Bass Limiter LM-2B			
1990-1994.			
1990-1994		$35	$45
Bass Limiter/Enhancer LMB-3			
1995-present.			
1990s		$35	$45
Bass Overdrive ODB-3			
1994-present.			
1994-1999		$45	$50
Blues Driver BD-2			
1995-present.			
1995-1999		$40	$45
Chorus Ensemble CE-1			
1976-1984. Vibrato and chorus.			
1976-1984	With vibrato	$150	$250
Chorus Ensemble CE-2			
1979-1982.			
1979-1982		$50	$55
Chorus Ensemble CE-3			
1982-1992.			
1982-1992		$35	$45
Chorus Ensemble CE-5			
1991-present.			
2000s		$50	$55
Compressor Sustainer CS-1			
1978-1982.			
1978-1982		$80	$95
Compressor Sustainer CS-2			
1981-1986.			
1981-1986		$75	$85
Compressor Sustainer CS-3			
1986-present.			
1986-1999		$40	$50
Delay DM-2			
1981-1984. Analog.			
1981-1984		$165	$180
Delay DM-3			
1984-1988.			
1984-1988		$140	$150
Digital Delay DD-2			
1983-1986.			
1983-1986		$95	$145
Digital Delay DD-3			
1986-present. Up to 800 ms of delay.			
1986-1999		$95	$145
Digital Delay DD-5			
1995-present. Up to two seconds of delay.			
1995-1999		$95	$145
Digital Dimension C DC-2			
1985-1989. Two chorus effects and tremolo.			
1985-1989		$110	$145
Digital Metalizer MZ-2			
1987-1992.			
1987-1992		$75	$85
Digital Reverb RV-2			
1987-1990.			
1987-1990		$110	$145
Digital Sampler/Delay DSD-2			
1985-1986.			
1985-1986		$100	$145

MODEL YEAR	FEATURES	EXC. COND. LOW	HIGH
Digital Space-D DC-3/Digital Dimension DC-3			
1988-1993. Originally called the Digital Space-D, later changed to Digital Dimension. Chorus with EQ.			
1988-1993		$130	$155
Digital Stereo Reverb RV-70			
1990s. Rack mount, MIDI control, reverb/delay, 199 presets.			
1990s		$130	$155
Distortion DS-1			
1978-1989.			
1978-1989		$40	$55
Dr. Rhythm DR-55			
1981-present. Drum machine.			
1981-1989		$150	$195
Dual Over Drive SD-2			
1993-1998.			
1993-1998		$45	$50
Dynamic Filter FT-2			
1986-1988. Auto wah.			
1986-1988		$70	$95
Enhancer EH-2			
1990-1998.			
1990-1998		$40	$45
Flanger BF-1			
1977-1980.			
1977-1980		$50	$70
Flanger BF-2			
1980-present.			
1980-1989		$50	$70
1990-1999		$40	$55
Foot Wah FW-3			
1992-1996.			
1992-1996		$40	$45
Graphic Equalizer GE-6			
1978-1981. Six bands.			
1978-1981		$45	$60
Graphic Equalizer GE-7			
1981-present. Seven bands.			
1982-1989		$50	$75
1990-1999		$45	$70
Harmonist HR-2			
1994-1999. Pitch shifter.			
1994-1999		$70	$100
Heavy Metal HM-2			
1983-1991. Distortion.			
1983-1991		$35	$50
Hyper Fuzz FZ-2			
1993-1997.			
1993-1997		$40	$45
Hyper Metal HM-3			
1993-1998.			
1993-1998		$35	$50
Limiter LM-2			
1987-1992.			
1987-1992		$35	$45
Line Selector LS-2			
1991-present. Select between two effects loops.			
1991-1999	With adapter	$65	$75

The *Vintage Guitar Price Guide* shows low to high values for items in all-original excellent condition, and, where applicable, with original case or cover.

MODEL YEAR FEATURES	EXC. COND. LOW	HIGH
Metal Zone MT-2		
1991-present. Distortion and three-band EQ.		
1991-1999	$40	$55
Multi Effects ME-5		
1990s	$100	$125
Multi Effects ME-6		
1992-1997.		
1992-1997	$100	$125
Multi Effects ME-8		
1996-1997.		
1996-1997	$100	$125
Multi Effects ME-30		
1998-2002.		
1998-2002	$100	$125
Noise Gate NF-1		
1979-1988.		
1979-1988	$50	$55
Noise Suppressor NS-2		
1987-present.		
1987-1999	$50	$55
Octaver OC-2/Octave OC-2		
1982-present. Originally called the Octaver.		
1982-1999	$50	$55
Overdrive OD-1		
1977-1985.		
1977-1979	$95	$170
1980-1985	$85	$160
Overdrive OD-3		
1997-present.		
1997-1999	$35	$40
Parametric Equalizer PQ-4		
1991-1997.		
1991-1997	$40	$65
Phaser PH-1		
1977-1981.		
1977-1981	$65	$70
Phaser PH-1R		
1982-1985. Resonance control added to PH-1.		
1982-1985	$65	$80
Pitch Sifter/Delay PS-2		
1987-1993.		
1987-1993	$75	$95
Reverb Box RX-100		
1981-mid-1980s.		
1981-1985	$60	$75
Reverb/Delay RV-2		
1980s	$70	$105
Reverb/Delay RV-3		
1994-present.		
1994-1999	$70	$105
Rocker Distortion PD-1		
1980-mid-1980s. Variable pedal using magnetic field.		
1980-1985	$50	$65
Rocker Volume PV-1		
1981-mid-1980s.		
1980-1985	$40	$55
Rocker Wah PW-1		
1980-mid-1980s. Magnetic field variable pedal.		
1980-1985	$50	$74

MODEL YEAR FEATURES	EXC. COND. LOW	HIGH
Slow Gear SG-1		
1979-1982. Reverse simulator.		
1979-1982	$250	$300
Slow Gear SG-2		
1980s. "Violin" volume swell effect.		
1980s	$60	$85
Spectrum SP-1		
1977-1981. Single band parametric EQ.		
1977-1981	$200	$300
Super Chorus CH-1		
1989-present.		
1989-1999	$40	$45
Super Distortion & Feedbacker DF-2		
1984-1994. Also labeled as the Super Feedbacker & Distortion.		
1984-1994	$70	$75
Super Over Drive SD-1		
1981-present.		
1981-1989	$45	$60
1990-1999	$30	$45
Super Phaser PH-2		
1984-2001.		
1984-1989	$45	$50
1990-1999	$40	$45
Super Shifter PS-5		
1999-present. Pitch shifter/harmonizer.		
2000s	$100	$105
Touch Wah TW-1/T Wah TW-1		
1978-1987. Auto wah. Early models were labeled as Touch Wah.		
1978-1987	$75	$100
Tremolo TR-2		
1997-present.		
1997-1999	$60	$70
Tremolo/Pan PN-2		
1990-1995.		
1990-1995	$115	$145
Turbo Distortion DS-2		
1987-present.		
1987-1999	$40	$55
Turbo Overdrive OD-2		
1985-1994. Called OD-2R after 1994, due to added remote on/off jack.		
1985-1994	$60	$75
Vibrato VB-2		
1982-1986. True pitch-changing vibrato, warm analog tone, 'rise time' control allows for slow attach, four knobs. Aqua-Blue case.		
1982-1986	$300	$400
Volume FV-50H		
1987-present. High impedance, stereo volume pedal with inputs and outputs.		
1987-1999	$45	$50
Volume FV-50L		
1987-present. Low impedance, stereo volume pedal with inputs and outputs.		
1987-1999	$30	$35
Volume Pedal FV-100		
Late-1980s-1991. Guitar volume pedal.		
1988-1991	$35	$40

Boss ME-50

Boss Metal Zone MT-2

Boss Phase Shifter PH-3

EFFECTS

Carl Martin Hydra

Catalinbread Super Chili Picoso

Colorsound Sustain Module

Budda

1995-present. Wahs and distortion pedals from San Rafael, California. They mainly produce amp heads, combos, and cabinets.

Carl Martin

1993-present. Line of effects from Søren Jongberg and East Sound Research of Denmark.

Carrotron

Late-1970s-mid-1980s. Carrotron was out of California and offered a line of effects.

Noise Fader C900B1
1980-1982.

MODEL YEAR	FEATURES	LOW	HIGH
1980-1982		$40	$45

Preamp C821B
1981-ca.1982.

1981-1982		$55	$60

Carvin

2002-2003. Carvin introduced its line of Ground Effects in '02 and discontinued them in '03.

Castle Instruments

Castle was located in New Jersey.

Phaser III
1980-1982. Offered mode switching for various levels of phase.

1980-1982		$75	$165

Cat's Eye

2001-present. Dean Solorzano and Lisa Kroeker build their analog guitar effects in Oceanside, California.

Catalinbread

2003-present. Nicholas Harris founded Catalinbread Specialized Mechanisms of Music in Seattle, Washington, in '02 to do mods and in '03 added his own line of guitar effects.

Chandler

1984-present. Located in California, Chandler Musical Instruments offers instruments, pickups, and pickguards, as well as effects.

Digital Echo
1992-2000. Rackmount, one second delay, stereo.

1992-2000		$300	$425

Tube Driver
1986-1991. Uses a 12AX7 tube.

1980s	Large Box	$140	$200
1980s	Rackmount	$60	$110
1990s	Rackmount	$60	$110

Chapman

From Emmett Chapman, maker of the Stick.

Patch of Shades
1981-Late-1980s. Wah, with pressure sensitive pad instead of pedal.

1980s		$40	$55

Chicago Iron

1998-present. Faithful reproductions of classic effects built by Kurt Steir in Chicago.

Chunk Systems

1996-present. Guitar and bass effects pedals built by Richard Cartwright in Sydney, Australia.

Clark

1960s. Built in Clark, New Jersey.

SS-600 Fuzz
1960s. Chrome-plated, volume and tone knobs, toggle switch

MODEL YEAR	FEATURES	LOW	HIGH
1960s		$125	$145

Colorsound

1965-present. Colorsound effects were produced by England's Sola Sound, which in '65 was founded by former Vox associate Larry Macari. The first product was a fuzzbox called the Tone Bender, designed by Gary Hurst and sold at Macari's Musical Exchange stores. The first readily available fuzz in Britain, it was an instant success. In the late-'60s, wah and fuzz-wah pedals were added, and by the end of the '70s, Colorsound offered 18 different effects, an amp, and accessories. Few early Colorsound products were imported into the U.S., so today they're scarce. Except for the Wah-Wah pedal, Colorsound's production stopped by the early '80s, but in '96 most of their early line was reissued by Dick Denny of Vox fame. Denny died in 2001. The brand is now owned by Mutronics who offers a rack mount combination of four classic Colorsound effects.

Flanger

1970s		$90	$100

Fuzzphase

1970s		$140	$160

Octivider

1970s		$125	$150

Overdriver
Introduced in 1972, controls for drive, treble and bass.

1970s		$150	$175

Supa Tonebender Fuzz

1970s		$175	$200

Supa Wah-Swell
1970s. Supa Wah-Swell in slanted block letters on the end of the pedal, Silver case.

1970s		$150	$250

Supaphase

1970s		$150	$175

Supasustain

1960s		$100	$150

Tonebender Jumbo (Sola Sound)

1979		$150	$200

Tremolo

1970s		$150	$175

Tremolo Reissue
1990s. Purple case.

1990s		$100	$110

MODEL YEAR	FEATURES	EXC. COND. LOW	HIGH

Wah Fuzz Straight
1970s. Aqua-Blue case, Wah-Fuzz-Straight in capital block letters on end of wah pedal.

1970s		$150	$250

Wah Wah
1970s. Dark Gray case, Wah-Wah in capital block letters on end of wah pedal.

1975		$225	$325

Wah Wah Reissue
1990s. Red case, large Colorsound letter logo and small Wah Wah lettering on end of pedal.

1990s		$100	$110

Companion
1970s. Private branded by Shinei of Japan.

Wah pedal

1970s		$100	$150

Conn
Ca. 1968-ca.1978. Band instrument manufacturer and distributor Conn/Continental Music Company, of Elkhart, Indiana, imported guitars and effects from Japan.

Strobe ST-8 Tuner
Late-1960s. Brown case.

1968		$200	$225

Crowther Audio
1976-present. Guitar effects built by Paul Crowther, who was the original drummer of the band Split Enz, in Auckland, New Zealand. His first effect was the Hot Cake.

Crybaby
See listing under Vox for early models, and Dunlop for recent versions.

Dallas Arbiter
Dallas Arbiter, Ltd., was based in London and it appeared in the late-1960s as a division of a Dallas group of companies headed by Ivor Arbiter. They also manufactured Sound City amplifiers and made Vox amps from '72 to '78. The Fuzz Face is still available from Jim Dunlop.

Fuzz Face
Introduced in 1966. The current reissue of the Dallas Arbiter Fuzz Face is distributed by Jim Dunlop USA.

1968-1969	Red	$275	$475
1970	Red	$225	$350
1970-1976	Blue	$225	$350
1977-1980	Blue	$200	$275
1981	Grey, reissue	$100	$150
1990-2000	Red, reissue	$50	$60

Fuzz Wah Face

1970s	Black	$175	$225
1990s	Reissue copy	$50	$60

Sustain

1970s		$100	$225

Treble & Bass Face

1960s		$175	$275

Trem Face
Ca.1970-ca.1975. Reissued in 1980s. Round Red case, depth and speed control knobs, Dallas-Arbiter England logo plate.

1970-1975	Red	$225	$275

Wah Baby
1970s. Gray Speckle case, Wah Baby logo caps and small letters on end of pedal.

1970s		$200	$300

Wah Face

Dan Armstrong
In 1976, Musitronics, based in Rosemont, New Jersey, introduced six inexpensive plug-in effects designed by Dan Armstrong. Perhaps under the influence of John D. MacDonald's Travis McGee novels, each effect name incorporated a color, like Purple Peaker. Shipping box labeled Dan Armstrong by Musitronics. They disappeared a few years later but were reissued by WD Products in the '90s. Since '03, Vintage Tone Project has offered the Dan Armstrong Orange Crusher. Dan Armstrong died in '04.

Blue Clipper
1976-1981. Fuzz, Blue-Green case.

1976-1981		$75	$85

Green Ringer
1976-1981. Ring Modulator/Fuzz, Green case.

1970s		$75	$85

Orange Squeezer
1976-1981. Compressor, Orange case.

1976-1981		$80	$90

Purple Peaker
1976-1981. Frequency Booster, Light Purple case.

1976-1981		$75	$85

Red Ranger
1976-1981. Bass/Treble Booster, Light Red case.

1976-1981		$75	$85

Yellow Humper
1976-1981. Yellow case.

1976-1981		$75	$85

Danelectro
1946-1969, 1996-present. The Danelectro brand was revived in '96 with a line of effects pedals. They also offer the Wasabi line of effects.

Cool Cat Chorus
1996-present.

1990s		$20	$25

Daddy-O Overdrive
1996-present.

1990s		$22	$28

Dan Echo
1998-present.

1990s		$35	$45

Fab Tone Distortion
1996-present.

1990s		$30	$40

Reverb Unit

1965		$150	$200

Dallas Arbiter Fuzz Face

Danelectro Cool Cat

Danelectro Daddy-O

EFFECTS

The *Vintage Guitar Price Guide* shows low to high values for items in all-original excellent condition, and, where applicable, with original case or cover.

DeArmond Square Wave

Digitech PDS 2730 Hot Box

Digitech Reverberator XP-400

EFFECTS

MODEL YEAR	FEATURES	EXC. COND. LOW	HIGH

Davoli
1960s-1970. Davoli was an Italian pickup and guitar builder and is often associated with Wandre guitars.
TRD
1970s. Solidstate tremolo, reverb, distortion unit.
1970s — $175 — $225

Dean Markley
The string and pickup manufacturer offered a line of effects from the '70s to the early-'90s.
Overlord Classic Tube Overdrive
1988-1991. Uses a 12AX7A tube, AC powered.
1980s — $55 — $80
Overlord III Classic Overdrive
1990-1991. Battery powered version of Overlord pedal.
1990s — $45 — $70
Voice Box 50 (watt model)
1976-1979.
1970s — $70 — $110
Voice Box 100 (watt model)
1976-1979, 1982-ca.1985.
1970s — $70 — $110
Voice Box 200 (watt model)
1976-1979.
1970s — $70 — $110

DeArmond
In 1947, DeArmond may have introduced the first actual signal-processing effect pedal, the Tremolo Control. They made a variety of effects into the '70s, but only one caught on - their classic volume pedal. DeArmond is primarily noted for pickups.
Pedal Phaser Model 1900
1974-ca.1979.
1970s — $40 — $50
Square Wave Distortion Generator
1977-ca.1979.
1970s — $100 — $135
Thunderbolt B166
1977-ca.1979. Five octave wah.
1970s — $45 — $55
Tone/Volume Pedal 610
1978-ca.1979.
1970s — $50 — $100
Tornado Phase Shifter
1977-ca.1979.
1970s — $65 — $85
Tremolo Control Model 60B
The Model 60 Tremolo Control dates from 1947 to the early-1950s. Model 60A dates from mid- to late-1950s. Model 60B, early-1960s.
1960s — $65 — $95
Twister 1930
1980. Phase shifter.
1980 — $75 — $100
Volume Pedal Model 602
1960s.
1960s — $30 — $70

Volume Pedal 1602
1978-ca.1980s.
1970s — $35 — $50
Volume Pedal 1630
1978-1980s. Optoelectric.
1970s — $40 — $50
Weeper Wah Model 1802
1970s.
1970s — $90 — $115

DeltaLab Research
Early-1980s. DeltaLab was located in Chelmsford, Massachusetts.
Acousticomputer DL-2
1980s. Delay.
1980s — $65 — $85
Delay Control Pedal DLB-1
1980s. Controls other DeltaLab pedals, chrome, Morley-looking pedal.
1980s — $30 — $40
Time Line DL-4
1980s. Delay.
1980s — $60 — $85

Demeter
1980-present. Located in Van Nuys, California, James Demeter and company build amp heads, combos, cabinets, pro audio gear and guitar effects.

Diaz
Early 1980s-2002, 2004-present. Line of effects from the "amp doctor" Cesar Diaz. Diaz died in '02; his family resumed production in '04.

DigiTech
The DigiTech/DOD company is in Utah and the effects are made in the U.S.A. The DigiTech name started as a line under the DOD brand in the early '80s; later spinning off into its own brand. They also produce vocal products and studio processors and are now part of Harman International Industries.
Digital Delay PDS 1000
1985-ca.1989. One second delay.
1985-1989 — $75 — $100
Digital Delay PDS 2000
1985-1991. Two second delay.
1985-1991 — $90 — $125
Digital Stereo Chorus/Flanger PDS 1700
1986-1991.
1986-1991 — $90 — $120
Double Play PDS 2700
1989-1991. Delay and chorus
1989-1991 — $90 — $120
Guitar Effects Processor RP 1
1980s — $90 — $100
Guitar Effects Processor RP 3
1980s — $90 — $110
Guitar Effects Processor RP 5
1980s — $90 — $120

MODEL YEAR FEATURES	EXC. COND. LOW	HIGH
Guitar Effects Processor RP 6		
1980s	$90	$150
Guitar Effects Processor RP 10		
2000s	$125	$165
Guitar Effects Processor RP 14D		
Floor unit with expression pedal, one 12AX7 tube, 100 programs, integrated amp modeling.		
2000	$275	$325
Guitar Effects Processor RP 200		
1990s	$90	$100
Hot Box PDS 2730		
1989-1991. Delay and distortion		
1989-1991	$80	$100
Modulator Pedal XP 200		
Floor unit with 61 pre-sets, including chorus, flanger, etc.		
2000	$75	$90
Multi Play PDS 20/20		
1987-1991. Multi-function digital delay.		
1987-1991	$125	$150
Multi-Effects Processor RP 100		
2000	$80	$100
Pedalverb Digital Reverb Pedal PDS 3000		
1987-1991.		
1987-1991	$100	$120
Programmable Distortion PDS 1550		
1986-1991.		
1986-1991	$45	$65
Programmable Distortion PDS 1650		
1989-1991.		
1989-1991	$45	$65
Rock Box PDS 2715		
1989-1991. Chorus and distortion.		
1989-1991	$30	$60
Sampler PDS 2000		
1990s	$70	$90
Sampler PPS 2000		
1990s	$70	$90
Two Second Digital Delay PDS 1002		
1987-1991.		
1987-1991	$75	$100
Whammy Pedal WP I		
1990-1993. Original Whammy Pedal, red case, reissued as WP IV in '00.		
1990-1993	$300	$375
Whammy Pedal WP II		
1994-1997. Can switch between two presets, black case.		
1990s	$150	$200
Whammy Pedal Reissue		
2000-present. Reissue version of classic WP-1 with added dive bomb and MIDI features.		
2000s	$120	$165

DiMarzio

The pickup maker offered a couple of effects in the late-1980s to the mid-1990s.

MODEL YEAR FEATURES	EXC. COND. LOW	HIGH
Metal Pedal		
1987-1989.		
1987-1989	$50	$60

MODEL YEAR FEATURES	EXC. COND. LOW	HIGH
Very Metal Fuzz		
Ca.1989-1995. Distortion/overdrive pedal.		
1989-1995	$55	$65

DOD

DOD Electronics started in Salt Lake City in 1974. Today, they're a major effect manufacturer with dozens of pedals made in the U.S.A. They also market effects under the name DigiTech. They are now part of Harman International Industries.

MODEL YEAR FEATURES	EXC. COND. LOW	HIGH
6 Band Equalizer EQ601		
1977-1982.		
1977-1982	$40	$60
AB Box 270		
1978-1982.		
1978-1982	$30	$40
American Metal FX56		
1985-1991.		
1985-1991	$30	$40
Analog Delay 680		
1979-1982.		
1979-1982	$85	$100
Attacker FX54		
1992-1994. Distortion and compressor.		
1992-1994	$30	$40
Bass Compressor FX82		
1987-ca.1989.		
1987-1989	$35	$40
Bass EQ FX42B		
1987-1996.		
1987-1996	$30	$40
Bass Grunge FX92		
1995-1996.		
1995-1996	$40	$45
Bass Overd2rive FX91		
1998-present.		
1998-1999	$40	$45
Bass Stereo Chorus Flanger FX72		
1987-1997.		
1987-1997	$40	$45
Bass Stereo Chorus FX62		
1987-1996.		
1987-1996	$40	$45
Bi-FET Preamp FX10		
1982-1996.		
1982-1996	$20	$30
Buzz Box FX33		
1994-1996. Grunge distortion.		
1994-1996	$45	$55
Chorus 690		
1980-ca.1982. Dual speed chorus.		
1980-1982	$80	$100
Classic Fuzz FX52		
1990-1997.		
1990-1997	$25	$35
Classic Tube FX53		
1990-1997.		
1990-1997	$35	$45
Compressor 280		
1978-ca.1982.		
1978-1982	$35	$45

DOD A-B Box 270

DOD Bass Stereo Flanger FX72

DOD Death Metal FX86

EFFECTS

DOD Equalizer FX40B

DOD Milk Box FX84

DOD Octoplus FX35

MODEL YEAR	FEATURES	EXC. COND. LOW	HIGH
Compressor FX80			
1982-1985.			
1982-1985		$30	$40
Compressor Sustainer FX80B			
1986-1996.			
1986-1996		$30	$35
Death Metal FX86			
1994-present. Distortion.			
1994-1999		$20	$30
Delay FX90			
1984-ca.1987.			
1984-1987		$40	$60
Digital Delay DFX9			
1989-ca.1990.			
1989-1990		$30	$40
Digital Delay Sampler DFX94			
1995-1997.			
1995-1997		$40	$65
Distortion FX55			
1982-1986.			
1982-1986		$20	$30
Edge Pedal FX87			
1988-1989.			
1988-1989		$30	$35
Envelope Filter 440			
1981-ca.1982. Reissued in 1995.			
1981-1982		$60	$70
Envelope Filter FX25			
1982-1997. Replaced by FX25B.			
1982-1987		$30	$40
Envelope Filter FX25B			
1981-1987			
1982-1987		$30	$40
Equalizer FX40			
1982-1986.			
1982-1986		$35	$45
Equalizer FX40B			
1987-present. Eight bands for bass.			
1987-1999		$30	$40
Fet Preamp 210			
1981-ca.1982.			
1981-1982		$30	$40
Flanger 670			
1981-1982.			
1981-1982		$65	$85
Gate Loop FX30			
1980s		$25	$35
Graphic Equalizer EQ-610			
1980-ca.1982. Ten bands.			
1980-1982		$40	$45
Graphic Equalizer EQ-660			
1980-ca.1982. Six bands.			
1980-1982		$30	$40
Grunge FX69			
1993-present. Distortion.			
1993-1999		$35	$45
Hard Rock Distortion FX57			
1987-1994. With built-in delay.			
1987-1994		$35	$45

MODEL YEAR	FEATURES	EXC. COND. LOW	HIGH
Harmonic Enhancer FX85			
1986-ca. 1989.			
1986-1989		$35	$45
I. T. FX100			
1997. Intergrated Tube distortion, produces harmonics.			
1997		$45	$55
Juice Box FX51			
1996-1997.			
1996-1997		$30	$40
Master Switch 225			
1988-ca.1989. A/B switch and loop selector.			
1988-1989		$25	$35
Meat Box FX32			
1994-1996.			
1994-1996		$35	$40
Metal Maniac FX58			
1990-1996.			
1990-1996		$35	$40
Metal Triple Play Guitar Effects System TR3M			
1994.			
1994		$35	$40
Metal X FX70			
1993-1996.			
1993-1996		$35	$40
Milk Box FX84			
1994-present.			
1994-1999		$35	$45
Mini-Chorus 460			
1981-ca.1982.			
1981-1982		$50	$70
Mixer 240			
1978-ca.1982.			
1978-1982		$20	$30
Momentary Footswitch			
Introduced in 1987, temporally engages other boxes.			
1980s		$20	$30
Noise Gate 230			
1978-1982.			
1970s		$25	$35
Noise Gate FX30			
1982-ca.1987.			
1980s		$25	$35
Octoplus FX35			
1987-1996. Octaves.			
1980s		$35	$40
Overdrive Plus FX50B			
1986-1997.			
1980s		$30	$40
Overdrive Preamp 250			
1978-1982. Reissued in 1995.			
1978-1982		$75	$95
Overdrive Preamp 250 (reissue)			
1995-1999.			
1995-1999		$35	$45
Overdrive Preamp FX50			
1982-1985.			
1982-1985		$30	$40

MODEL YEAR FEATURES	EXC. COND. LOW	HIGH
Performer Compressor Limiter 525		
1981-1984.		
1981-1984	$50	$60
Performer Delay 585		
1982-1985.		
1982-1985	$50	$60
Performer Distortion 555		
1981-1984.		
1981-1984	$30	$40
Performer Flanger 575		
1981-1985.		
1981-1985	$30	$40
Performer Phasor 595		
1981-1984.		
1981-1984	$30	$40
Performer Stereo Chorus 565		
1981-1985.		
1981-1985 FET switching	$50	$60
Performer Wah Filter 545		
1981-1984.		
1981-1984	$35	$45
Phasor 201		
1981-ca.1982. Rreissued in 1995.		
1981-1982	$60	$100
Phasor 401		
1978-1981.		
1978-1981	$60	$100
Phasor 490		
1980-ca.1982.		
1980-1982	$60	$100
Phasor FX20		
1982-1985.		
1982-1985	$30	$40
Psychoacoustic Processor FX87		
1988-1989.		
1988-1989	$30	$40
Punkifier FX76		
1997.		
1997	$40	$50
Resistance Mixer 240		
1978-ca.1982.		
1978-1982	$25	$35
Silencer FX27		
1988-ca.1989. Noise reducer.		
1988-1989	$30	$40
Stereo Chorus FX60		
1982-1986.		
1982-1986	$30	$35
Stereo Chorus FX65		
1986-1996.		
1986-1996	$30	$35
Stereo Flanger FX70		
1982-ca.1985.		
1982-1985	$30	$40
Stereo Flanger FX75		
1986-1987.		
1986-1987	$30	$40
Stereo Flanger FX75B		
1987-1997.		
1987-1997	$30	$40

MODEL YEAR FEATURES	EXC. COND. LOW	HIGH
Stereo Phasor FX20B		
1986-1999.		
1986-1999	$40	$45
Stereo Turbo Chorus FX67		
1988-1991.		
1988-1991	$30	$40
Super American Metal FX56B		
1992-1996.		
1992-1996	$30	$40
Super Stereo Chorus FX68		
1992-1996.		
1992-1996	$30	$40
Supra Distortion FX55B		
1986-present.		
1986-1999	$25	$35
Thrash Master FX59		
1990-1996.		
1990s	$25	$35
Wah-Volume FX-17 (pedal)		
1987-2000.		
1987-2000	$35	$45

Dredge-Tone

Located in Berkeley, California, Dredge-Tone offers effects and electronic kits.

Dunlop

Jim Dunlop, USA offers the Crybaby, MXR (see MXR), Rockman, High Gain, Heil Sound (see Heil), Tremolo, Jimi Hendrix, Rotovibe and Uni-Vibe brand name effects.

MODEL YEAR FEATURES	EXC. COND. LOW	HIGH
Crybaby Bass		
1985-present. Bass wah.		
1985-1999	$50	$60
Crybaby Wah Pedal 535		
1995-present. Multi-range pedal with an external boost control.		
1995-1999	$70	$80
Crybaby Wah-Wah GCB-95		
1982-present. Dunlop began manufacturing the Crybaby in 1982.		
1982-1989	$45	$60
1990-1999	$35	$45
High Gain Volume + Boost Pedal		
1983-1996.		
1983-1996	$30	$40
High Gain Volume Pedal		
1983-present.		
1983-1999	$35	$45
Jimi Hendrix Fuzz (Round)		
1987-1993.		
1987-1993	$40	$60
Rotovibe JH-4S Standard		
1989-1998. Standard is finished in bright Red enamel with chrome top.		
1989-1998	$90	$100
Tremolo Volume Plus TVP-1		
1995-1998. Pedal.		
1995-1998	$100	$120

DOD Supra Distortion FX55-B

DOD Supra Distortion FX55-C

Dunlop Jimi Hendrix Wah

Electra Stereo Chorus 504CH

Echoplex EP-4

MODEL		EXC. COND.	
YEAR	FEATURES	LOW	HIGH

Uni-Vibe UV-1
1995-present. Rotating speaker effect.

1995-1999		$150	$200
2000-2003		$190	$210

Dynacord
1950-present. Dynacord is a German company that makes audio and pro sound amps, as well as other electronic equipment and is now owned by TELEX/EVI Audio (an U.S. company), which also owns the Electro-Voice brand name. In the '60s they offered tape echo machines. In '94 a line of multi-effects processors were introduced under the Electro-Voice/Dynacord name, but by the following year they were just listed as Electro-Voice.

EchoCord
Tape echo unit, introduced in 1959.

1960s		$225	$275

Dyno
See Dytronics.

Dytronics
Mid-1970s-early 1980s. The Japanese company Dytronics made a chorus rackmount unit for electric piano called the Dyno My Piano with flying piano keys or a lightning bolt on the front. A third version, called the Songbird, had a bird's head on the front.

Ecco Fonic
The Ecco Fonic was distributed by Fender in 1958-'59.

Echo Unit
1958-1959. Reverb unit.

1958-1959	With Brown case	$250	$300

Echoplex
The Echoplex tape echo units were first sold under the Maestro brand name. After Maestro dropped the Echoplex, it was marketed under the Market Electronics name from the late-'70s-early-'80s. In the later '80s, Market Electronics was dropped from the ads and they were marketed under the Echoplex brand name. Both the Market and Echoplex brands are listed here; for earlier models see Maestro. In '94, Gibson's Oberheim division introduced a rackmount unit called the Echoplex. In '01, it was relabeled as "Gibson."

Echoplex EP3
1984-ca. 1988. Solidstate version.

1984-1988		$225	$350

Echoplex EP4
1984-1991. Solidstate version.

1984-1991		$225	$350

Echoplex EP6T
1980-ca.1988. All-tube reissue of the EP2.

1980-1988		$325	$450

Effector 13
2002-present. Tim Shortnacy builds his guitar effects in Minneapolis, Minnesota. He was located in Austin, Texas until mid-'04.

EFX
1980s. Brand name of the Los Angeles-based EFX Center; they also offered a direct box and a powered pedal box/board.

Switch Box B287
1984. Dual effects loop selector.

1984		$20	$25

Electra
1971-1984. A guitar brand name imported by St. Louis Music, Electra offered a line of effects in the late '70s.

Chorus 504CH
ca.1975-ca.1980.

1975-1980		$40	$50

Compressor 502C
1975-1980.

1975-1980		$35	$45

Distortion 500D
ca.1976-ca.1980.

1976-1980		$60	$75

Fuzz Wah
ca.1975-ca.1980.

1975-1980		$80	$100

Pedal Drive 515AC
ca.1976-ca.1980. Overdrive.

1975-1980		$30	$40

Phaser Model 501P
ca.1976-ca.1980.

1975-1980		$40	$50

Phaser Model 875
1975-ca.1980.

1975-1980		$40	$45

Roto Phase I
1975-ca.1980. Small pocket phaser.

1975-1980		$50	$70

Roto Phase II
1975-ca.1980. Pedal phasor.

1975-1980		$60	$80

Electro-Harmonix
1968-1981, 1996-present. Founded by Mike Matthews in New York City, the company initially produced small plug-in boosters such as the LPB-1. In '70, they unveiled the awe-inspiring Big Muff Pi fuzz and dozens of innovative pedals followed. After years of disputes, the nonunion E-H factory became the target of union organizers and a '81 union campaign, combining picketing and harrying of E-H employees, brought production to a halt. Matthews' financier then cut his funding, and in early '82, E.H. filed for bankruptcy. Later that year, Matthews was able to reopen and continue through '84. In '96, he again began producing reissues of many of his classic designs as well as new designs.

E-H Big Muff Pi reissue

MODEL YEAR FEATURES	EXC. COND. LOW	HIGH
3 Phase Liner *1981.*		
1981	$40	$50
5X Junction Mixer *1977-1981.*		
1977-1981	$20	$30
10 Band Graphic Equalizer *1977-1981. Includes footswitch.*		
1977-1981	$50	$65
16-Second Digital Delay *Early-1980s. Reissued in 2004.*		
1980s With foot controller	$600	$800
Attack Equalizer *1975-1981. Active EQ, a.k.a. "Knock Out."*		
1975-1981	$100	$200
Attack/Decay *1980-1981. Tape reverse simulator.*		
1980-1981	$175	$225
Bad Stone Phase Shifter *1975-1981.*		
1970s Three knobs	$170	$250
Bass Micro-Synthesizer *1981-1984. Reissued in '99.*		
1981-1984	$250	$350
Bass Micro-Synthesizer (reissue) *1999-present.*		
1999	$150	$175
Bassballs *1978-1984. Bass envelope filter/distortion. Reissued in '98.*		
1978-1984	$175	$225
Big Muff Pi *1971-1984. Sustain, floor unit. Issued in three different looks, as described below. Reissued in 1996.*		
1970s Earlier black graphics, knobs in triangle	$250	$275
1980s Red/black graphics, logo in 1" letters	$125	$175
Big Muff Pi (reissue) *1996-present. Originally made in Russia, but currently both Russian- and U.S.-made versions are available.*		
1996-1999 Russian-made	$30	$35
Black Finger Compressor Sustainer *1977. Three knobs in triangle pattern. Reissued in 2003.*		
1977	$130	$150
Clap Track *1980-1984. Drum effect.*		
1980-1984	$30	$40
Clone Theory *1977-1981. Chorus effect.*		
1977-1981	$125	$155
Crash Pad *1980-1984. Percussion synth.*		
1980-1984	$30	$50
Crying Tone Pedal *1976-1978. Wah-wah.*		
1976-1978	$170	$200

MODEL YEAR FEATURES	EXC. COND. LOW	HIGH
Deluxe Big Muff Pi *1978-1981. Sustain, AC version of Big Muff Pi, includes a complete Soul Preacher unit.*		
1978-1981	$150	$175
Deluxe Electric Mistress Flanger *1977-1983. AC. Reissued in 1996.*		
1970s	$175	$275
1980s	$125	$175
Deluxe Memory Man *1977-1983. Echo and delay, featured four knobs 1977-1978, from 1979-1983 it has five knobs and added vibrato and chorus. Reissued in 1996.*		
1977-1978 Four knobs	$250	$300
1979-1983 Five knobs	$250	$300
Deluxe Octave Multiplexer *1977-1981.*		
1977-1981	$150	$200
Digital Delay *1981-84. With digital chorus.*		
1981-1984	$225	$275
Digital Rhythm Matrix DRM-15 *1981-1984.*		
1981-1984	$150	$250
Digital Rhythm Matrix DRM-16 *1979-1983.*		
1979-1983	$150	$250
Digital Rhythm Matrix DRM-32 *1981-1984.*		
1981-1984	$150	$250
Doctor Q Envelope Follower *1976-1983. For bass or guitar. Reissued in '01.*		
1976-1983	$150	$200
2001-2003 Reissue	$25	$30
Domino Theory *1981. Sound sensitive light tube.*		
1981	$75	$115
Echo 600 *1981.*		
1981	$150	$200
Echoflanger *1977-1982. Flange, slapback, chorus, filter.*		
1977-1982	$200	$250
Electric Mistress Flanger *1976-1984.*		
1976-1984	$150	$275
Electronic Metronome *1978-1980.*		
1978-1980	$20	$25
Frequency Analyzer *1977-1984. Ring modulator. Reissued in '01.*		
1977-1984	$225	$250
Full Double Tracking Effect *1978-1981. Doubling, slapback.*		
1978-1981	$75	$125
Fuzz Wah *Introduced around 1974.*		
1970s	$150	$200
Golden Throat *1977-1984.*		
1977-1984	$200	$400

E-H Bassballs

E-H Black Finger

E-H 16-Second Delay

E-H Hot Foot

E-H Octave Multiplexer

E-H Q-Tron

MODEL YEAR	FEATURES	EXC. COND. LOW	HIGH
Golden Throat Deluxe	*1977-1979. Deluxe has a built-in monitor amp.*		
1977-1979		$200	$400
Golden Throat II	*1978-1981.*		
1978-1981		$100	$175
Guitar Synthesizer	*1981. Sold for $1,495 in May 1981.*		
1981		$250	$300
Hog's Foot Bass Booster	*1977-1980.*		
1977-1978		$60	$90
Holy Grail	*1977-1980.*		
2000s	With adapter	$75	$85
Hot Foot	*1977-1978. Rocker pedal turns knob of other E-H effects.*		
1977-1980		$55	$65
Hot Tubes	*1978-1984. Overdrive. Reissued in 2001.*		
1978-1984		$100	$150
2000s	Reissue	$60	$70
Linear Power Booster LPB-1	*1968-1983.*		
1976-1979		$45	$55
1980-1983		$30	$45
Linear Power Booster LPB-2	*Ca.1968-1983.*		
1968-1983		$65	$75
Little Big Muff Pi	*1976-1980. Sustain, one knob floor unit.*		
1976-1980		$125	$150
Low Frequency Compressor	*1977. For bass.*		
1977		$150	$175
Memory Man	*1976-1984. Analog delay. Reissued in '01.*		
1976-1979		$225	$275
1980-1984		$125	$225
Micro Synthesizer	*1978-1984. Mini keyboard phaser. Reissued in '98.*		
1978-1979		$200	$250
1980-1984		$200	$250
Micro Synthesizer (reissue)	*1998-present.*		
1998-2002		$150	$175
Mini-Mixer	*1978-1981. Mini mic mixer. Reissued in '01.*		
1978-1981		$25	$35
MiniSynthesizer	*1981-1983. Mini keyboard with phaser.*		
1981-1983		$300	$375
MiniSynthesizer With Echo	*1981.*		
1981		$350	$475
Mole Bass Booster	*1968-1978.*		
1968-1969		$50	$75
1970-1978		$35	$50

MODEL YEAR	FEATURES	EXC. COND. LOW	HIGH
Muff Fuzz Crying Tone	*1977-1978. Fuzz, wah.*		
1977-1978		$150	$240
Octave Multiplexer Floor Unit	*1976-1980.*		
1976-1980		$150	$200
Octave Multiplexer Pedal	*1976-1977. Reissued in '01.*		
1976-1977		$150	$175
Panic Button	*1981. Siren sounds for drum.*		
1981		$20	$25
Poly Chorus	*1981. Same as Echoflanger. Reissued in '99.*		
1981		$175	$225
Poly Chorus (reissue)	*1999-present. Stereo.*		
1999-2002		$125	$150
Polyphase	*1979-1981. With envelope.*		
1979-1981		$150	$200
Pulse Modulator	*Ca.1968 -ca.1972. Triple tremolo.*		
1968-1969		$225	$300
1970-1972		$175	$225
Q-Tron	*1997-present. Envelope controlled filter.*		
1997-1999		$100	$150
Q-Tron +			
2000s		$125	$150
Queen Triggered Wah	*1976-1978. Wah/Envelope Filter.*		
1976-1978		$100	$125
Random Tone Generator RTG	*1981.*		
1981		$30	$35
Rhythm 12 (rhythm machine)	*1978.*		
1978		$100	$125
Rolling Thunder	*1980-1981. Percussion synth.*		
1980-1981		$30	$40
Screaming Bird Treble Booster	*Ca.1968-1980. In-line unit.*		
1968-1980		$50	$60
Screaming Tree Treble Booster	*1977-1981. Floor unit.*		
1977-1981		$70	$80
Sequencer Drum	*1981 Drum effect.*		
1981		$35	$45
Slapback Echo	*1977-1978. Stereo.*		
1977-1978		$125	$150
Small Clone EH4600	*1983-1984. Analog chorus with depth and rate controls, purple face plate with white logo. Reissued in '99.*		
1983-1984		$150	$200

The **Vintage Guitar Price Guide** shows low to high values for items in all-original excellent condition, and, where applicable, with original case or cover.

MODEL YEAR	FEATURES	EXC. COND. LOW	HIGH
Small Clone EH4600 (reissue)			
2000-present.			
2000s		$50	$55
Small Stone Phase Shifter			
1975-1984. Reissued in 1996.			
1975-1979		$125	$200
1980-1984		$75	$125
Soul Preacher			
1977-1983. Compressor sustainer.			
1977-1983		$100	$150
Space Drum			
1980-1981. Percussion synth.			
1980-1981		$125	$175
Switch Blade			
1977-1983. A-B Box.			
1977-1983		$40	$45
Talking Pedal			
1977-1978. Creates vowel sounds.			
1977-1978		$275	$500
The Silencer			
1976-1981. Noise elimination.			
1976-1981		$50	$75
The Wiggler			
2000-present. All-tube modulator.			
2000s		$140	$150
The Worm			
2000-present. Wah/Phaser.			
2000s		$55	$65
Tube Zipper			
2001-present. Tube (two 12AX7EHs) envelope follower.			
2001-2003		$200	$225
Vocoder			
1978-1981. Modulates voice with instrument.			
1978-1981	Rackmount	$400	$500
Volume Pedal			
1978-1981.			
1978-1981		$40	$60
Y-Triggered Filter			
1976-1977.			
1976-1977		$125	$175
Zipper Envelope Follower			
1976-1978. The Tube Zipper was introduced in 2001.			
1976-1978		$150	$250

EMMA Electronic
Line of guitar effects built in Denmark.

Epiphone
Epiphone pedals are labeled "G.A.S Guitar Audio System" and were offered in the late-1980s-early-1990s.

MODEL YEAR	FEATURES	EXC. COND. LOW	HIGH
Chorus EP-CH-70			
1988-1989.			
1988-1989		$30	$35
Compressor EP-CO-20			
1988-1991.			
1980s		$30	$40

MODEL YEAR	FEATURES	EXC. COND. LOW	HIGH
Delay EP-DE-80			
1988-1989. Twenty to 400 ms of delay.			
1988-1989		$35	$45
Distortion EP-DI-10			
1988-1991.			
1980s		$30	$40
Flanger EP-FL-60			
1988-1991.			
1980s		$30	$40
Overdrive EP-OD-30			
1988-1991.			
1980s		$30	$40

Ernie Ball
Ernie Ball owned a music store in Tarzana, California, when he noticed the demand for a better selection of strings. The demand for his Slinky strings grew to the point where, in '67, he sold the store to concentrate on strings. He went on to produce the Earthwood brand of guitars and basses from '72-'85. In '84, Ball purchased the Music Man company.

MODEL YEAR	FEATURES	EXC. COND. LOW	HIGH
Volume Pedal			
1977-present.			
1970s		$40	$75
1980s		$50	$75
1990s		$60	$75

Euthymia Electronics
Line of guitar effects built by Erik Miller in Alameda, California.

EXR
The EXR Corporation was located in Brighton, Michigan.

MODEL YEAR	FEATURES	EXC. COND. LOW	HIGH
Projector SP III			
1983-ca.1984. "Psychoacoustic enhancer pedal," volume pedal/sound boost.			
1983-1984		$60	$70

Farfisa
The organ company offered effects in the 1960s.

MODEL YEAR	FEATURES	EXC. COND. LOW	HIGH
Model VIP 345 Organ			
Mid-1960s. Portable organ with Syntheslalom used in the rock and roll venue.			
1960s		$550	$650
Repeater			
1969		$70	$80
Wah/Volume			
1969		$85	$95

Fender
Although Fender has flirted with effects since the '50s (the volume/volume-tone pedal and the EccoFonic), it concentrated mainly on guitars and amps. Fender effects ranged from the sublime to the ridiculous, from the tube Reverb to the Dimension IV. The Reverb is the only effect Fender currently produces.

E-H Small Clone EH4600

E-H Wiggler

Fender Blender

EFFECTS

MODEL YEAR	FEATURES	EXC. COND. LOW	HIGH

'63 Reverb
1994-present. Reissue of the '60s 3-knob, tube, spring reverb unit. Brown Tolex with wheat grille, a few in blond with oxblood.

| 1990s | Brown Tolex | $300 | $325 |

Blender Fuzz
1968-1977. Battery operated fuzz and sustain.

| 1968-1969 | | $225 | $275 |
| 1970-1977 | | $200 | $250 |

Contempo Organ
1967-1968. Portable organ, all solidstate, 61 keys including a 17-key bass section, catalog shows with Red cover material.

| 1967-1968 | | $450 | $550 |

Dimension IV
1968-1970. Multi-effects unit using an oil-filled drum.

| 1968 | | $175 | $200 |

Echo-Reverb
1966-1970. Solidstate, echo-reverb effect produced by rotating metal disk, Black Tolex, Silver grille.

| 1966-1970 | | $200 | $290 |

Electronic Echo Chamber
1962-1968. Solidstate tape echo, up to 400 ms of delay, rectangle box with two controls 1962-1967, slanted front 1967-1968.

| 1962-1968 | | $250 | $325 |

Fuzz-Wah
1968-1984. Has "Fuzz" and "Wah" switches on sides of pedal 1968-1973, has three switches above the pedal 1974-1984.

| 1960s | Switches on side | $150 | $200 |
| 1970s | Switches above | $125 | $175 |

Phaser
1975-1977. AC powered.

| 1975-1977 | | $100 | $150 |

Reverb Unit
1961-1966, 1975-1978. Fender used a wide variety of Tolex coverings in the early-'60s as the coverings matched those on the amps. Initially, Fender used rough blond Tolex, then rough brown Tolex, followed by smooth white or black Tolex.

1961	Blond Tolex, Oxblood grille	$1,200	$1,500
1962	Blond Tolex, Oxblood grille	$1,200	$1,500
1963	Brown Tolex	$700	$1,000
1964	Black Tolex	$725	$950
1965	Black Tolex	$700	$850
1966	Black Tolex	$700	$850
1975-1978	Tube reverb reinstated	$500	$600

Tone and Volume Fool Pedal
1954-1984.

| 1960s | | $100 | $150 |

Vibratone
1967-1972. Leslie-type speaker cabinet made specifically for the guitar, two-speed motor.

| 1960s | | $650 | $900 |

FlexiSound
FlexiSound products were made in Lancaster, Pennsylvania.
F. S. Clipper
1975-ca.1976. Distortion, plugged directly into guitar jack.

| 1975-1976 | | $45 | $55 |

The Beefer
1975. Power booster, plugged directly into guitar jack.

| 1975 | | $30 | $40 |

Flip
Line of tube effects by Guyatone and distributed in the U.S. by Godlyke Distributing.

FM Acoustics
Made in Switzerland.
E-1 Pedal
1975. Volume, distortion, filter pedal.

| 1975 | | $50 | $70 |

Foxx
Foxx pedals are readily identifiable by their felt-like "fur" covering. They slunk onto the scene in 1971 and were extinct by 1978. Made by Hollywood's Ridinger Associates, their most notable product was the Tone Machine fuzz. Foxx-made pedals also have appeared under various brand names such as G and G, Guild, Yamaha and Sears Roebuck, generally without fur.

Clean Machine
1974-1978.

| 1974-1978 | | $175 | $200 |

Down Machine
1971-1977. Bass wah.

| 1971-1977 | | $175 | $200 |

Foot Phaser
1975-1977.

| 1975-1977 | | $100 | $150 |

Fuzz and Wa and Volume
1974-1978.

| 1974-1978 | | $200 | $350 |

Guitar Synthesizer I
1975.

| 1975 | | $250 | $350 |

O.D. Machine
1972-ca.1975.

| 1972-1975 | | $100 | $150 |

Phase III
1975-1978.

| 1975-1978 | | $75 | $100 |

Tone Machine
1971-1978. Fuzz with "Octave."

| 1971-1978 | | $250 | $300 |

Wa and Volume
1971-1978.

| 1971-1978 | | $140 | $160 |

Wa Machine
1971-ca.1978.

| 1971-1978 | | $125 | $150 |

Fender Electronic Echo Chamber

Fender Fuzz Wah

Foxx Wa & Volume

The *Vintage Guitar Price Guide* shows low to high values for items in all-original excellent condition, and, where applicable, with original case or cover.

MODEL YEAR	FEATURES	EXC. COND. LOW	HIGH

Framptone
2000-present. Founded by Peter Frampton, Framptone offers hand-made guitar effects.

Frantone
1994-present. Effects and accessories hand built in New York City.

Fulltone
1991-present. Fulltone effects are based on some of the classic effects of the past. Fulltone was started in Los Angeles by Michael Fuller who says the company was born out of his love for Jimi Hendrix and fine vintage pedals.

Deja Vibe
1991-present. UniVibe-type pedal, later models have a Vintage/Modern switch. Stereo version also available.

1991-1999 Mono	$200	$225

Deja Vibe II
1997-present. Like Deja Vibe but with built-in speed control. Stereo version also available.

1997-1999 Mono	$225	$250

Octafuzz
1996-present. Copy of the Tycobrahe Octavia.

1996-1999	$85	$115

Furman Sound
1993-present. Located in Petaluma, California, Furman makes audio and video signal processors and AC power conditioning products for music and other markets.

PQ3 Parametric EQ
1998-present. Rackmount preamp and equalizer.

1998-1999	$100	$150

PQ6 Parametric Stereo
1990s	$125	$175

RV1 Reverb Rackmount
1990s	$100	$150

George Dennis
1991-present. Founded by George Burgerstein, original products were a line of effects pedals. In '96 they added a line of tube amps. The company in located in Prague, Czech Republic, and the products are distributed in the U.S. by Midco International.

Gibson
Gibson did offer a few effects bearing their own name, but most were sold under the Maestro name (see that listing).

GA-3RV Reverb Unit
1964-1967. Small, compact, spring reverb unit, black tolex, gray grille.

1964-1967	$300	$400

GA-4RE Reverb-Echo Unit
1964-1967. Small, compact, lightweight accessory reverb-echo unit that produces complete reverberation and authentic echo, utilizes Gibson's "electronic memory" system for both reverb and echo, black tolex, gray grille.

1964-1967	$400	$500

Godbout
Sold a variety of effects do-it-yourself kits in the 1970s. Difficult to value because quality depends on skills of builder.

Effects Kits
1970s	$15	$25

Goodrich Sound
Late-1970s. Goodrich was located in Grand Haven, Michigan.

Match Box 33670 Line Boost
Early-1980s. Small rectangular in and out box with control knob.

1980s	$40	$45

Volume Pedal 6122
1979-ca.1980. Uses a potentiometer.

1970s	$40	$50

Volume Pedal 6400ST
1979-ca.1980. Uses a potentiometer.

1970s	$40	$50

Volume Pedal 6402
1979-ca.1980. Uses photocell.

1970s	$40	$50

Gretsch
Gretsch has offered a limited line of effects from time to time.

Controfuzz
Mid-1970s. Distortion.

1970s	$150	$170

Deluxe Reverb Unit Model 6149
1963-1969. Similar to Gibson's GA-1 introduced around the same time.

1963-1969	$400	$450

Expandafuzz
Mid-1970s. Distortion.

1970s	$130	$150

Reverb Unit Model 6144 Preamp Reverb
1963-1967. Approximately 17 watts, preamp functionality, no speaker.

1963-1967	$200	$300

Tremofect
Mid-1970s. Tremolo effect, 3-band EQ, speed, effect, bass, total, and treble knobs.

1970s	$175	$275

Guild
Guild marketed effects made by Electro-Harmonix, Foxx, WEM and Applied, in the '60s and '70s.

Copicat
1960s-1979. Echo

1970s	$250	$350

Foxey Lady Fuzz
Distortion, sustain.

1969-1975	Two knobs, made by E-H	$175	$225
1976-1977	3 knobs in row, same as Big Muff	$100	$150

Fulltone Octafuzz

Gretsch Expandafuzz

Guild Copicat

EFFECTS

Guild Tweedy Bird MM500

Guyatone Silver Machine

Hohner Tri-Dirty Booster

MODEL YEAR	FEATURES	EXC. COND. LOW	HIGH

Fuzz Wah FW-3
1975-ca.1979. Distortion, volume, wah. Made by Foxx.

1970s		$140	$160

HH Echo Unit
1976-ca.1979.

1970s		$150	$200

VW-1
1975-ca.1979. Volume, wah. Made by Foxx.

1970s		$150	$200

Guyatone
1998-present. Imported stomp boxes and tape echo units distributed by Godlyke Distributing.

HAO
Line of guitar effects built in Japan by J.E.S. International, distributed in the U.S. by Godlyke.

Heathkit
1960s. Unassembled kits sold at retail.

TA-28 Distortion Booster
1960s. Fuzz assembly kit, heavy '60s super fuzz, case-by-case quality depending on the builder.

1960s		$95	$130

Heavy Metal Products
Mid-1970s. From Alto Loma, California, products for the heavy metal guitarist.

Raunchbox Fuzz
1975-1976.

1975-1976		$60	$70

Switchbox
1975-1976. A/B box.

1975-1976		$15	$25

Heet Sound Products
1974-present. The E Bow concept goes back to '69, but a hand-held model wasn't available until '74. Made in Los Angeles.

E Bow
1977-1979, 1985-1987, 1994-present. The Energy Bow. Hand-held electro-magnetic string driver.

1970s		$45	$55

E Bow for Pedal Steels
1979. Hand-held electro-magnetic string driver.

1979		$25	$35

Heil Sound
1960-present. Founded by Bob Heil, Marissa, Illinois. Created the "talk box" technology as popularized by Peter Frampton. In the '60s and '70s Heil was dedicated to innovative products for the music industry. In the late-'70s, innovative creations were more in the Amateur Radio market, and by the '90s the focus was on the home theater market. By the 2000s, the Heil Sound brand name was offered by Jim Dunlop USA.

Talk Box
1976-ca.1980. Reissued in 1989.

1970s		$90	$110

1980s		$80	$90
1990s		$70	$80
2000s		$70	$80

High Gain
See listing under Dunlop.

Hohner
Hohner offered effects in the late-1970s.

Dirty Booster
1977-ca.1978. Distortion.

1977-1978		$40	$50

Dirty Wah Wah'er
1977-ca.1978. Adds distortion.

1977-1978		$55	$65

Fuzz Wah
1970s. Morley-like volume pedal with volume knob and fuzz knob, switch for soft or hard fuzz, Gray box with Black foot pedal.

1970s		$55	$65

Multi-Exciter
1977-ca.1978. Volume, wah, surf, tornado, siren.

1977-1978		$50	$60

Tape Echo

1970s		$190	$225

Tri-Booster
1977-ca.1978. Distortion, sustain.

1977-1978		$50	$60

Vari-Phaser
1977-ca.1978.

1977-1978		$25	$35

Vol-Kicker Volume Pedal
1977-ca.1978.

1977-1978		$20	$30

Wah-Wah'er
1977-ca.1978. Wah, volume.

1977-1978		$40	$50

HomeBrew Electronics
2001-present. Stomp box effects handmade by Joel Weaver in Glendale, Arizona.

Ibanez
Ibanez effects were introduced ca. '74, and were manufactured by Japan's Maxon Electronics. Although results were mixed at first, a more uniform and modern product line, including the now legenday Tube Screamer, built Ibanez's reputation for quality. They still produce a wide range of effects.

60s Fuzz (Soundtank)
1989-1999. Fuzz with level, tone and distortion controls, Black plastic case, Green label.

1989-1999		$25	$30

7th Heaven SH7 (Tone-Lok)
1999-2000s. Lo, high, drive and level controls, gray-silver case, blue-green label.

2000s		$30	$35

MODEL YEAR FEATURES	EXC. COND. LOW	HIGH

Acoustic Effects PT-4
2000s. Acoustic guitar enhancement floor unit with compressor/limiter, tone shaper, stereo chorus, digital reverb, with power supply.
2000s — $85 — $95

Analog Delay 202 (Rack Mount)
1980s. Rack mount with delay, doubling, flanger, stereo chorus, dual inputs with tone and level.
1980s — $150 — $160

Analog Delay AD9
1982-1985. Three control analog delay, Hot Pink metal case.
1982-1985 — $130 — $150

Analog Delay AD-80
1980-1982.
1980-1982 — $175 — $250

Analog Delay AD99
1995-1999. Analog Delay reissue, three control knobs and on/off switch, reissue winged-hand logo.
1995-1999 — $90 — $100

Analog Delay AD-100 (Table Unit)
1980s. Stand-alone table/studio unit (not rack mount) with power cord.
1980s — $175 — $190

Auto Filter AF9
1982-ca.1985. Replaces AF201 model.
1982-1985 — $150 — $175

Auto Filter AF201
1981-1982. Two min-max sliders, three mode toggle switches, Orange metal case.
1981-1982 — $150 — $175

Auto Wah AW5 (SoundTank)
1991-1999. Plastic case SoundTank series.
1991-1999 — $35 — $45

Auto Wah AW7
1999-2000s. Silver case.
1999-2000s — $25 — $30

Bass Compressor BP10
1986-1993.
1980s — $60 — $70

Bi-Mode Chorus BC-9
1984-1985. Dual channel (Bi channel) for two independent speed and width settings.
1984-1985 — $70 — $95

Chorus CS-505
1980s. Speed and depth controls, Gray-Blue case, stereo or mono input, battery or external power option.
1980s — $65 — $85

Chorus Flanger CF7 (Tone-Lok)
1999-2000s. Speed, depth, delay, regeneration controls, mode and crazy switches, Pink CF7 label.
2000s — $35 — $40

Classic Flange FL99
1995-1999. Analog reissue, silver metal case, winged-hand artwork, 4 controls, 2 footswitch buttons.
1995-1999 — $65 — $75

Classic Phase PH99
1995-1999. Analog reissue, silver metal case, winged-hand artwork, speed, depth, feedback, effect

level controls, intense and bypass footswitches.
1995-1999 — $65 — $75

Compressor CP10
1987-1993.
1980s — $40 — $60

Compressor CP-830
1976-1979.
1970s — $70 — $80

Compressor II CP-835
1980-1982.
1980-1982 — $90 — $110

Compressor Limiter CP9
1982-1985.
1980s — $80 — $100

Delay Champ CD10
1986-1989. Red case, 3 knobs.
1986-1989 — $80 — $100

Delay Echo DE-7
1999-2000s. Digital delay and analog echo combines digital and analog tones.
1999-2000s — $45 — $55

Delay Harmonizer DM-1000
1980s. Rack mount, with chorus, 9 control knobs.
1980s — $180 — $230

Delay III DDL20 Digital Delay
1986-1989. Filtering, doubling, slap back, echo S, echo M, echo L, Seafoam Green coloring on pedal.
1986-1989 — $65 — $85

Delay PDD1 (DPC Series)
1987-1988. Programmable Digital Delay (PDD) with display screen.
1987-1988 — $80 — $100

Digital Chorus DSC10
1986-1989. Three control knobs and slider selection toggle.
1986-1989 — $50 — $60

Digital Delay DL5 (SoundTank)
1992-1999. Plastic case SoundTank series.
1992-1999 — $35 — $45

Digital Delay DL10
1986-1989. Digital Delay made in Japan, Blue case, three Green control knobs, stompbox.
1986-1989 — $85 — $100

Distortion Charger DS10
1986-1989.
1986-1989 — $55 — $65

Distortion DS7
2000s. Drive, tone, and level controls, Gray case, DS7 Green label logo.
2000s — $40 — $50

Echo Machine EM5 (SoundTank)
1989-1999.
1989-1999 — $45 — $65

Fat Cat Distortion FC10
1986-1989. Three-knob pedal with distortion, tone, and level controls, made in Japan.
1986-1989 — $45 — $65

Ibanez Autowah AW7

Ibanez Bass Compressor BP-10

Ibanez Classic Phase PH-99

EFFECTS

Ibanez Flanger FL-9

Ibanez LA Metal LM7

Ibanez Noise Buster NB10

EFFECTS

MODEL YEAR	FEATURES	EXC. COND. LOW	HIGH
Flanger FFL5 (Master Series)			
1984-1985. Speed, regeneration, width, D-time controls, battery or adapter option.			
1984-1985		$30	$40
Flanger FL5 (SoundTank)			
1991-1999. Plastic case SoundTank series.			
1991-1999		$25	$35
Flanger FL9			
1982-1984. Yellow case.			
1982-1984		$55	$70
Flanger FL-301			
1979-1982. Mini flanger, three knobs, called the FL-301 DX in late '81-'82.			
1979-1982		$75	$120
Flanger FL-305			
1976-1979. Five knobs.			
1976-1979		$75	$125
Flying Pan FP-777			
1976-1979. Auto pan/phase shifter, four control knobs, phase on/off button, pan on/off button, Silver metal case with Blue trim and Flying Pan winged-hand logo.			
1976-1979		$425	$500
Fuzz FZ7 (Tone-Lok)			
1999-2000s. Drive, tone and level controls, Gray-Silver case, blue-green FZ7 label.			
2000s		$40	$50
Graphic Bass EQ BE10			
1986-1993. Latered labeled as the BEQ10.			
1986-1989		$50	$70
Graphic EQ GE9			
1982-1985. Six EQ sliders plus one overall volume slider, Turquoise Blue case.			
1982-1985		$50	$70
Graphic EQ GE10			
1986-1993. Eight sliders.			
1986-1993		$50	$70
Graphic Equalizer GE-601 (808 Series)			
1980-1982. Seven-slider EQ in Aqua Blue metal case.			
1980-1982		$70	$80
Guitar Multi-Processor PT5			
1994-1997. Floor unit, programmable with 25 presets and 25 user presets, effects include distortion, chorus, flanger, etc.			
1994-1997	Green case	$75	$95
LA Metal LM7			
1986-1989. Silver case.			
1986-1989		$35	$55
LoFi LF7 (Tone-Lok)			
1999-2000s. Four control knobs, Light Gray case, Red LF7 label.			
2000s		$20	$30
Metal Charger MS10			
1986-1989. Distortion, level, attack, punch and edge control knobs, green case.			
1986-1989		$50	$60
Metal Screamer MSL			
1984-1985. Three control knobs.			
1984-1985		$50	$60

MODEL YEAR	FEATURES	EXC. COND. LOW	HIGH
Modern Fusion MF-5 (SoundTank)			
1990s. Level, tone and distortion control knobs, battery or optional adapter.			
1990s		$45	$50
Modulation Delay DM500			
1982-1984. Rack mount.			
1982-1984		$50	$75
Modulation Delay DM1000			
1982-1984. Rack mount with delay, reverb, modulation.			
1982-1984		$85	$110
Mostortion MT10			
Late-1980s-early-1990s. Mos-FET circuit distortion pedal, five control knobs, Green case.			
1989-1991		$40	$50
Multi-Effect UE-300 (floor unit)			
1980s. Floor unit, four footswitches for super metal, digital delay, digital stereo chorus, and master power, three delay modes.			
1980s		$150	$300
Multi-effect UE-300B (floor unit)			
1983-1984. Floor unit for bass.			
1983-1984		$100	$225
Multi-Effect UE-400 (rackmount)			
1983-1985. Rackmount with foot switch.			
1980s		$175	$275
Multi-Effect UE-405 (rackmount)			
1980s. Rackmount with analog delay, parametric EQ, compressor/limiter, stereo chorus and loop.			
1980s		$200	$300
Noise Buster NB10			
1986-1989. Single frequency knob to eliminate 60-cycle hum and other outside signals, metal case.			
1986-1989		$65	$75
Overdrive II OD-855			
1974-1979. Small stomp-box with distortion knob, tone knob, and level knob, Yellow/Green case, large Overdrive II logo.			
1974-1979		$200	$300
Overdrive OD-850			
1974-1979.			
1974-1979		$200	$300
Pan Delay DPL10			
1986-1989. Royal Blue case, three Green control knobs, small stomp box, large Pan Delay logo.			
1986-1989		$90	$100
Parametric EQ PQ9			
1982-1985.			
1980s		$90	$100
Parametric EQ PQ401			
1979-1982. Three sliders and dial-in knob, Light Aqua Blue case.			
1979-1982		$100	$150
Phase Tone PT-909			
1979-1982. Blue box, three knobs, early models with flat case (logo at bottom or later in the middle) or later wedge case.			
1979-1982		$100	$130

The *Vintage Guitar Price Guide* shows low to high values for items in all-original excellent condition, and, where applicable, with original case or cover.

MODEL YEAR FEATURES	EXC. COND. LOW	HIGH

Phase Tone PT-999
1976-1978. Script logo, one knob, round footswitch, becomes PT-909.
1976-1978 $110 $140

Phase Tone PT-1000
1974-1981. Morley-style pedal phase, Light Blue case, early model of Phase Tone.
1974-1981 $150 $200

Phase Tone II PT-707
1976-1980. Blue box, one knob, script logo for first two years.
1970s $110 $140

Phaser PH5
1991-1999. Plastic case SoundTank series.
1991-1999 $25 $40

Phaser PH7 (Tone-Lok)
1999-2000s. Tone-Lok Series phaser with Silver case, speed, depth, feedback and level controls, Purple PH7 label.
1999-2003 $35 $45

Phaser PT9
1982-1985. Three control knobs, Red case.
1982-1985 $50 $75

Powerlead PL5 (SoundTank)
1989-1999. SoundTank series, metal case '89-'91, plastic case '91-'99.
1989-1991   1st issue metal case $25 $45
1991-1999   2nd later issue plastic case $15 $20

Renometer
1976-1979. Five-band equalizer with preamp.
1976-1979 $80 $90

Rotary Chorus RC99
1995-1999. Black or Silver cases available, requires power pack and does not use a battery.
1995-1999   Black case $55 $85

Session Man SS10
1988-1990. Distortion, chorus.
1988-1990 $65 $85

Session Man II SS20
1988-1990. Four control knobs + toggle, Light Pink-Purple case.
1988-1990 $60 $70

Slam Punk SP5 (SoundTank)
1991-1999. Plastic case SoundTank series.
1990s $35 $45

Smash Box SM7 (Tone-Lok)
1999-2000s.
2000s $30 $40

Sonic Distortion SD9
1982-1984.
1982-1984 $70 $80

Standard Fuzz (No. 59)
1974-1979. Two buttons (fuzz on/off and tone change).
1974-1979 $150 $200

Stereo Box ST-800
1976-1977. One input, 2 outputs for panning, small yellow case.
1976-1977 $150 $180

Stereo Chorus CS9
1982-1984.
1980s $60 $75

Stereo Chorus CSL
1985-1986.
1985-1986 $55 $65

Super Chorus CS5 (SoundTank)
1991-1999. Plastic case SoundTank series.
1991-1999 $20 $30

Super Metal SM-9
1984-1985. Distortion.
1984-1985 $75 $100

Super Stereo Chorus SC-10
1986-1993.
1980s $40 $50

Super Tube Screamer ST9
1982-1984. Four dial-in knobs, Light Green metal case.
1982-1984 $200 $300

Super Tube STL
1985-1986.
1985-1986 $65 $75

Swell Flanger SF10
1986-1989. Speed, regeneration, width and time controls, Yellow case.
1986-1989 $45 $55

Trashmetal TM5 (SoundTank)
1989-present. Tone and distortion pedal, three editions (1st edition, 2nd edition metal case, 2nd edition plastic case).
1989-1999 $15 $20

Tremolo Pedal TL-5
1980s $30 $40

Tube King TK999
1994-1995. Has a 12AX7 tube and three-band equalizer.
1994-1995   Includes power pack $125 $200

Tube King TK999US
1996-2000. Has a 12AX7 tube and three-band equalizer, does not have the noise switch of original TK999. Made in the U.S.
1996-2000   Includes power pack $125 $200

Tube Screamer TS5
1991-1999. Plastic case SoundTank series.
1990s $30 $40

Tube Screamer TS7
1999-present. Part of the Tone-Lok series, Gray-Blue case, three control knobs.
1999 $30 $40

Tube Screamer TS9
1982-1984. Reissued in 1993.
1982-1984 $150 $200

Tube Screamer TS9 Reissue
1993-present. Reissue of the '80s TS9.
1990s $70 $90

Tube Screamer Classic TS10
1986-1993.
1986-1993 $175 $200

Tube Screamer TS-808
1980-1982, 2004-present. Reissued in 2004.
1980s $400 $600

Ibanez Phase Tone PT-909

EFFECTS

Ibanez Super Metal SM-9

Ibanez TS-808

The *Vintage Guitar Price Guide* shows low to high values for items in all-original excellent condition, and, where applicable, with original case or cover.

Ibanez Turbo Tube Screamer TS9DX

Jacques Fuse Blower

Jan-Mar The Talker

EFFECTS

MODEL YEAR	FEATURES	EXC. COND. LOW	HIGH
Turbo Tube Screamer TS-9DX			
2000s. Tube Screamer circuit with added three settings for low-end.			
2000s		$75	$85
Twin Cam Chorus TC-10			
1986-1989. Four control knobs, Light Blue case.			
1986-1989		$45	$65
Virtual Amp VA3 (floor unit)			
1990s. Digital effects processor.			
1990s		$50	$70
VL10			
1986-1997. Stereo volume pedal.			
1980s		$40	$50
Wah Fuzz Standard (Model 58)			
1974-1981. Fuzz tone change toggle, fuzz on toggle, fuzz depth control, balance control, wah volume pedal with circular friction pads on footpedal.			
1974-1981		$125	$200
Wah WH10			
1989-1999.			
1989-1999		$50	$60

Intersound
Made by Intersound, Inc. of Boulder, Colorado.

MODEL YEAR	FEATURES	EXC. COND. LOW	HIGH
Reverb-Equalizer R100F			
1977-1979. Reverb and four-band EQ, fader.			
1977-1979		$60	$70

J. Everman
2000-present. Analog guitar effects built by Justin J. Everman in Richardson, Texas.

Jacques
One-of-a-kind handmade stomp boxes and production models made in France. Production models are distributed in the U.S. by Godlyke Distributing.

Jan-Mar Industries
Jan-Mar was located in Hillsdale, New Jersey.

MODEL YEAR	FEATURES	EXC. COND. LOW	HIGH
The Talker			
1976. Thirty watts.			
1976		$55	$65
The Talker Pro			
1976. Seventy-five watts.			
1976		$65	$75

Jax
1960s-1970. Japanese imports made by Shinei.

MODEL YEAR	FEATURES	EXC. COND. LOW	HIGH
Fuzz Master			
1960s		$100	$130
Vibrachorus			
Variant of Univibe.			
1969		$700	$900
Wah-Wah			
1960s		$65	$75

Jet Sounds LTD
1977. Jet was located in Jackson, Mississippi.

MODEL YEAR	FEATURES	EXC. COND. LOW	HIGH
Hoze Talk Box			
1977. Large wood box, 30 watts.			
1977		$70	$85

JHD Audio
1974-1990. Hunt Dabney founded JHD in Costa Mesa, California, to provide effects that the user installed in their amp. Dabney is still involved in electronics and builds the BiasProbe tool for tubes.

MODEL YEAR	FEATURES	EXC. COND. LOW	HIGH
SuperCube/SuperCube II			
1974-late 1980s. Plug-in sustain mod for Fender amps with reverb, second version for amps after '78.			
1970s		$50	$60

Jimi Hendrix
See listing under Dunlop.

John Hornby Skewes & Co.
Mid-1960s-present. Large English distributor of musical products which has also made their own brands, or self-branded products from others, over the years.

Johnson
Mid-1990s-present. Budget line of effects imported by Music Link, Brisbane, California. Johnson also offers guitars, amps, mandolins and basses.

Johnson Amplification
1997-present. Modeling amps and effects designed by John Johnson, of Sandy, Utah. The company is part of Harman International. In '02, they quit building amps, but continue the effects line.

Jordan
1960s. Jordan effects were distributed by Sho-Bud of Nashville

MODEL YEAR	FEATURES	EXC. COND. LOW	HIGH
Boss Tone Fuzz			
1968-1969. Plugged into guitar's output jack.			
1968-1968		$90	$100
Compressor J-700			
1960s		$70	$90
Creator Volume Sustainer			
1960s		$150	$170
Gig Wa-Wa Volume			
1960s		$100	$140
Phaser			
Black case, Yellow knobs.			
1960s	Black case	$120	$140

Kay
1931-present. Kay was once one of the largest instrument producers in the world, offering just about everything for the guitarist. See *Guitar Stories Volume II*, by Michael Wright, for a complete history of Kay with detailed model listings.

MODEL YEAR	FEATURES	EXC. COND. LOW	HIGH
Graphic Equalizer GE-5000			
1978-ca.1979.			
1978-1979		$30	$40
Rhythmer			
1970s		$30	$40
Tremolo			
1970s. Blue plastic, Japanese-made.			
1970s		$35	$45

Keeley

2001-present. Line of guitar effects designed and built by Robert Keeley in Edmond, Oklahoma. Keeley Electronics also offers a range of custom modifications for other effects.

Kendrick

1989-present. Texas' Kendrick offers guitars, amps, and effects.

MODEL YEAR	FEATURES	EXC. COND. LOW	HIGH
ABC Amp Switcher			
1990s.			
1990s		$100	$130
Buffalo Pfuz			
1990s.			
1990s		$75	$90
Model 1000 Reverb			
1991-present. Vintage style, three knobs: dwell, tone, and mix, Brown cover, Wheat grille with art deco shape.			
1990s		$350	$400
Power Glide Attenuator			
1998-present. Allows you to cut the output before it hits the amp's speakers, rackmount, metal cab.			
1990s		$175	$200

Kent

1961-1969. This import guitar brand also offered a few effects.

Kern Engineering

Located in Kenosha, Wisconsin, Kern offers pre-amps and wah pedals.

Klon

1994-present. Originally located in Brookline, Massachusetts, and now located in Cambridge, Massachusetts, Klon was started by Bill Finnegan after working with two circuit design partners on an the Centaur Professional Overdrive.

KMD (Kaman)

1986-ca. 1990. Distributed by Kaman (Ovation, Hamer, etc.) in the late '80s.

MODEL YEAR	FEATURES	EXC. COND. LOW	HIGH
Analog Delay			
1986-ca.1990.			
1980s		$60	$90
Distortion			
1987-ca.1990.			
1980s		$35	$45
Flanger			
1987-ca.1990.			
1980s		$30	$40

MODEL YEAR	FEATURES	EXC. COND. LOW	HIGH
Overdrive			
1986-ca.1990.			
1980s		$25	$35
Phaser			
1987-ca.1990.			
1980s		$35	$45
Stereo Chorus			
1987-ca.1990.			
1980s		$20	$35

Korg

The Korg effects listed below are modular effects. The PME-40X Professional Modular Effects System holds four of them and allows the user to select several variations of effects. The modular effects cannot be used alone. This system was sold for a few years starting in 1983.

MODEL YEAR	FEATURES	EXC. COND. LOW	HIGH
KAD-301 Analog Delay			
1983-ca. 1986. Modular effect.			
1980s		$50	$60
KCH-301 Stereo Chorus			
1983-ca. 1986. Modular effect.			
1980s		$35	$45
KCO-101 Compressor			
1983-ca. 1986. Modular effect.			
1980s		$40	$50
KDI-101 Distortion			
1983-ca. 1986. Modular effect.			
1980s		$40	$50
KDL-301 Dynamic Echo			
1983-ca. 1986. Modular effect.			
1980s		$75	$90
KFL-401 Stereo Flanger			
1983-ca. 1986. Modular effect.			
1980s		$40	$45
KGE-201 Graphic EQ			
1983-ca. 1986. Modular effect.			
1980s		$20	$25
KNG-101 Noise Gate			
1983-ca. 1986. Modular effect.			
1980s		$20	$25
KOD-101 Over Drive			
1983-ca. 1986. Modular effect.			
1980s		$40	$50
KPH-401 Phaser			
1983-ca. 1986. Modular effect.			
1980s		$40	$50
OCT-1 Octaver			
1980s. Octave pedal with direct level control knob and effect level control knob, stomp switch, dark case.			
1980s		$50	$60
PEQ-1 Parametric EQ			
1980s. Dial-in equalizer with gain knob, band-width knob, and frequency knob, Black case.			
1980s		$35	$40
PME-40X Professional Modular Effects System			
1983-ca. 1986. Board that holds up to four of the above modular effects.			
1980s		$100	$125

Keeley Compressor

Kendrick Power Glide

Korg Tube Works Tube Driver

EFFECTS

Line 6 MM-4

Loco Box Graphic EQ GE-06

Maestro Echoplex EP-1

EFFECTS

MODEL YEAR	FEATURES	EXC. COND. LOW	HIGH

Krank
1996-present. Tempe, Arizona, amp builder Krank also builds effects pedals.

Laney
1968-present. Founded by Lyndon Laney and Bob Thomas in Birmingham, England, this amp builder also offered a reverb unit.
Reverberation Unit
1968-1969. Sleek reverb unit, plexi-style front panel, black vinyl cover.

| 1968-1969 | | $250 | $300 |

Line 6
1996-present. Effects from Marcus Ryle and Michel Doidic who were product line designers prior to forming their own design company. A sixth company telephone line was added to their product design business to handle their own product line, thus Line 6. All prices include Line 6 power pack if applicable. They also produce amps and guitars.
AM-4 Amp Modeler
Includes power pack, box and manual, Yellow case.

| 1996-2002 | | $175 | $200 |

DL-4 Delay Modeler
Includes power pack, box and manual, Green case.

| 1996-2002 | | $175 | $200 |

DM-4 Distortion Modeler
Includes power pack, box and manual, Red case.

| 1996-2002 | | $175 | $200 |

FM-4 Filter Modeler
Includes power pack, box and manual, Purple case.

| 2000-2002 | | $175 | $200 |

MM-4 Modulation Modeler
Includes power pack, box and manual, Aqua Blue case.

| 2000-2002 | | $175 | $200 |

POD 2.0
2000s. Amp modeler.

| 2000s | | $150 | $200 |

Little Lanilei
1997-present. Best known for their small hand-made amps, Songworks Systems & Products of San Juan Capistrano, California, also offers effects bearing the Little Lanilei name.

Lock & Rock
2003-present. Line of floor pedal guitar and microphone effects produced by Brannon Electronics, Inc. of Houston, Texas.

Loco Box
1982-1983. Loco Box was a brand of effects distributed by Aria Pro II for a short period starting in '82. It appears that Aria switched the effects to their own brand in '83.

MODEL YEAR	FEATURES	EXC. COND. LOW	HIGH

Analog Delay AD-01
1982-1983.

| 1982-1983 | | $40 | $60 |

Chorus CH-01
1982-1983.

| 1982-1983 | | $50 | $60 |

Compressor CM-01
1982-1983.

| 1982-1983 | | $30 | $40 |

Distortion DS-01
1982-1983.

| 1982-1983 | | $35 | $45 |

Flanger FL-01
1982-1983.

| 1982-1983 | | $40 | $50 |

Graphic Equalizer GE-06
1982-1983.

| 1982-1983 | | $20 | $30 |

Overdrive OD-01
1982-1983.

| 1982-1983 | | $35 | $45 |

Phaser PH-01
1982-1983.

| 1982-1983 | | $40 | $50 |

Lovetone
1995-present. Hand-made analog effects from Oxfordshire, England.

Ludwig
For some reason, drum builder Ludwig offered a guitar synth in the '70s.
Phase II Guitar Synth
1970-1971. Oversized synth, mushroom-shaped footswitches.

| 1970-1971 | Vertical silver case | $300 | $450 |

M.B. Electronics
Made in San Francisco, California.
Ultra-Metal UM-10
1985. Distortion.

| 1985 | | $30 | $40 |

Maestro
Maestro was a Gibson subsidiary; the name appeared on '50s accordian amplifiers. The first Maestro effects were the Echoplex tape echo and the FZ-1 Fuzz-Tone, introduced in the early-'60s. Maestro products were manufactured by various entities such as Market Electronics, All-Test Devices, Lowrey and Moog Electronics. In the late-'60s and early-'70s, they unleashed a plethora of pedals; some were beautiful, others had "great personality." The last Maestro effects were the Silver and Black MFZ series of the late-'70s.
Bass Brassmaster BB-1
1971-ca.1974. Added brass to your bass.

| 1971-1974 | | $250 | $450 |

The Vintage Guitar Price Guide shows low to high values for items in all-original excellent condition, and, where applicable, with original case or cover.

MODEL YEAR	FEATURES	EXC. COND. LOW	HIGH

Boomerang
CA.1969-ca.1972. Wah pedal made by All-Test Devices.

| 1969-1972 | | $125 | $175 |

Boomerang BG-2
1972-ca.1976. Wah pedal made by All-Test Devices.

| 1972-1976 | | $100 | $130 |

Echoplex (EP-1)
1962/63-mid-1960s. Original model, Smaller box, tube, separate controls for echo volume and instrument volume, made by Market Electronics. Though not labeled as such, it is often referred to as the EP-1 by collectors.

| 1960s | Earlier small
Green box | $750 | $900 |

Echoplex EP-2
Mid-1960s-ca. 1970. Larger box than original, tube, single echo/instrument volume control, made by Market Electronics. Around 1970, the EP-2 added a Sound-On-Sound feature.

| 1960s | Larger Green box | $750 | $900 |

Echoplex EP-3
Ca.1970-1977. Solidstate, made by Market Electronics, Black box.

| 1970-1977 | | $400 | $450 |

Echoplex IV (EP-4)
1977-1978. Solidstate. Last version introduced by Maestro. See brand names Market Electronics and Echoplex for later models.

| 1977-1978 | | $350 | $400 |

Echoplex Sireko ES-1
ca.1971-mid-1970s. A budget version of the Echoplex, solidstate. Made by Market.

| 1971-1975 | | $250 | $300 |

Envelope Modifier ME-1
1971-ca.1976. Tape reverse/string simulator. Made by All-Test.

| 1971-1976 | | $175 | $215 |

Filter Sample and Hold FSH-1
1975-ca.1976.

| 1975-1976 | | $400 | $450 |

Full Range Boost FRB-1
1971-ca.1975. Frequency boost with fuzz. Made by All-Test.

| 1971-1975 | | $125 | $150 |

Fuzz MFZ-1
1976-1979. Made by Moog.

| 1976-1979 | | $140 | $170 |

Fuzz Phazzer FP-1
1971-1974.

| 1971-1974 | | $150 | $200 |

Fuzz-Tone FZ-1
Mid-1960s. Brown, uses two AA batteries.

| 1960s | | $150 | $200 |

Fuzz-Tone FZ-1A
Late-1960s. Brown, uses one AA battery.

| 1960s | | $150 | $200 |

Fuzz-Tone FZ-1B
Late-1960s- early-1970s. Black, uses nine-volt battery.

| 1970s | | $150 | $175 |

Fuzztain MFZT-1
1976-1978. Fuzz, sustain. Made by Moog.

| 1976-1978 | | $175 | $225 |

Mini-Phase Shifter MPS-2
1976. Volume, speed, slow and fast controls.

| 1976 | | $100 | $125 |

Octave Box OB-1
1971-ca.1975. Made by All-Test Devices.

| 1971-1975 | | $175 | $200 |

Phase Shifter PS-1
1971-1975. With or without three-button footswitch. Made by Oberheim.

| 1971-1975 | With footswitch | $200 | $250 |

Phase Shifter PS-1A
1976.

| 1976 | | $150 | $200 |

Phase Shifter PS-1B
1970s.

| 1970s | | $100 | $125 |

Phaser MP-1
1976-1978. Made by Moog.

| 1976-1978 | | $100 | $125 |

Rhythm and Sound G-2
Ca.1969-1970s. Multi-effect unit.

| 1969-1975 | | $350 | $400 |

Ring Modulator RM-1
1971-1975.

| 1971-1975 | With control pedal | $600 | $700 |

Rover Rotating Speaker
1971-ca.1973. Rotating Leslie effect that mounted on a large tripod.

| 1971-1973 | | $700 | $900 |

Stage Phaser MPP-1
1976-1978. Had slow, fast and variable settings. Made by Moog.

| 1976-1978 | | $150 | $200 |

Super Fuzz FZ-1S
1971-ca.1975. Made by All-Test Devices.

| 1971-1975 | | $200 | $250 |

Sustainer SS-2
1971-ca.1975. Made by All-Test Devices.

| 1971-1975 | | $75 | $175 |

Theramin TH-1
1971-mid-1970s. Device with two antennae, made "horror film" sound effects. A reissue "Theremin" is available from Theremaniacs in Milwaukee, Wisconsin.

| 1971-1975 | | $850 | $1,200 |

Magnatone
1937-1970s. Magnatone built very competitive amps from '57 to '66. In the early-'60s, they offered the RVB-1 Reverb Unit. The majority of Magnatone amps pre-'66 did not have on-board reverb.

Model RVB-1 Reverb Unit
1961-1966. Reverb unit that works between the guitar and amp, typical Brown leatherette cover, square box-type cabinet. From 1964-1966, battery operated, solidstate version of RVB-1, low flat cabinet.

| 1961-1963 | | $250 | $375 |
| 1964-1966 | Battery and solidstate | $175 | $300 |

Maestro Rhythm and Sound G-2

Mestro Fuzz-Tone FZ-1A

Maestro Phase Shifter PS1-A

EFFECTS

Marshall Jackhammer JH-1

Matchless Coolbox

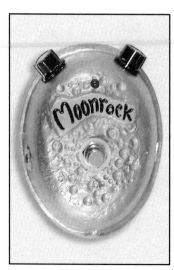

Moonrock

MODEL YEAR	FEATURES	EXC. COND. LOW	HIGH

Manny's Music

Issued by the New York-based retailer.

Fuzz

1960s		$200	$275

Market Electronics

Market, from Ohio, made the famous Echoplex line. See Maestro section for earlier models and Echoplex section for later versions.

Marshall

1962-present. The fuzz and wah boom of the '60s led many established manufacturers to introduce variations on the theme. Marshall was no exception, but its pedals never neared the popularity of their amps. They made another foray into stomp boxes in '89 with the Gov'nor distortion, and currently produce several distortion/overdrive units.

Blues Breaker (effect)

1992-1999. Replaced by Blues Breaker II in 2000.

1992-1999		$60	$75

Blues Breaker II Overdrive

2000-present. Overdrive pedal, four knobs.

2000s	Silver	$45	$70

Drive Master

1992-1999.

1992-1999		$50	$70

Guv'nor

1989-1991. Distortion. Gov'nor Plus introduced in 2000.

1989-1991		$100	$125

Power Brake

1990s		$200	$225

Shred Master

1992-1999.

1992-1999		$70	$100

Supa Fuzz

1967		$200	$280

Supa Wah

1969		$200	$300

Matchless

1989-1999, 2001-present. Matchless amplifiers offered effects in the '90s.

AB Box

1990s. Split box for C-30 series amps (DC 30, SC 30, etc.)

1990s		$200	$300

Coolbox

1990s. Tube preamp pedal.

1990s		$300	$370

Dirtbox

1990s. Tube-driven overdrive pedal.

1990s		$250	$325

Echo Box

1990s. Limited production because of malfunctioning design which included cassette tape. Black case, eight white chickhead control knobs, Echo Box script logo.

1990s	Original unreliable status	$200	$300

MODEL YEAR	FEATURES	EXC. COND. LOW	HIGH

Hotbox

1990s. Higher-end tube-driven preamp pedal.

1990s		$300	$400

Hotbox II

1990s. Higher-end tube-driven preamp pedal with more than the Hotbox I.

1990s		$350	$400

Mix Box

1990s. Four-input tube mixer pedal.

1990s		$300	$400

Reverb RV-1

1990s. Five control knobs, reverb tank in relatively large rectangular cab.

1990s	Various colors	$1,000	$1,300

Split Box

1990s. Tube AB box.

1990s	Standard AB	$250	$350

Tube Vibrato

1990s.

1990s		$300	$400

Maxon

1970s-present. Maxon was the original manufacturer of the Ibanez line of effects. Currently offering retro '70s era stomp boxes distributed in the U.S. by Godlyke.

AD-900 Analog Delay

2001-present.

2001-2003		$250	$290

OD-820 Over Drive Pro

2001-present.

2001-2003		$150	$180

Mesa-Boogie

1971-present. Mesa added pre-amps in the mid '90s.

V-Twin Preamp

Dec. 1993-present. Serial number series: V011- . One hundred watts, all tube preamp, floor unit, Silver case.

1993-1999		$200	$250

Mica

Tone Fuzz

Silver case, Black knobs.

1970s		$200	$225

Tone Surf Wah Siren

1970s. Wah pedal.

1970s		$140	$160

Wailer Fuzz

1970		$60	$70

Moog

Robert Moog, of synth fame, introduced his line of Moogerfooger analog effects in '98.

Moonrock

2002-present. Fuzz/distortion unit built by Glenn Wylie and distributed by Tonefrenzy.

MODEL YEAR FEATURES	EXC. COND. LOW	HIGH

MODEL YEAR FEATURES	EXC. COND. LOW	HIGH

Morley

Late-1960s-present. Founded by brothers Raymond and Marvin Lubow, Morley has produced a wide variety of pedals and effects over the years, changing with the trends. In 1989, the brothers sold the company to Accutronics (later changed to Sound Enhancements, Inc.) of Cary, Illinois.

ABY Switch Box
1981-ca.1985. Box.

1981-1985	$20	$25

Auto Wah PWA
1976-ca.1985.

1976-1985	$30	$40

Black Gold Stereo Volume BSV
1985-1991.

1985-1991	$30	$40

Black Gold Stereo Volume Pan BSP
1985-1989.

1985-1989	$35	$45

Black Gold Volume BVO
1985-1991.

1985-1991	$25	$35

Black Gold Wah BWA
1985-1991.

1985-1991	$40	$50

Black Gold Wah Volume BWV
1985-1989.

1985-1989	$40	$50

Chrystal Chorus

1980s	$30	$35

Deluxe Distortion DDB
1981-1991. Box, no pedal.

1980s	$45	$65

Deluxe Flanger FLB
1981-1991. Box, no pedal.

1981-1991	$60	$70

Deluxe Phaser DFB
1981-1991. Box, no pedal.

1981-1991	$45	$65

Distortion One DIB
1981-1991. Box, no pedal.

1981-1991	$40	$50

Echo Chorus Vibrato ECV
1982-ca.1985.

1982-1985	$90	$100

Echo/Volume EVO-1
1974-ca.1982.

1974-1982	$60	$70

Electro-Pik-a-Wah PKW
1979-ca.1982.

1979-1982	$60	$70

Emerald Echo

1990s	$50	$60

Jerry Donahue JD-10
Multi-effect, distortion, overdrive.

1990s	$85	$95

Power Wah PWA
1990s. Wah with boost.

1990s	$45	$55

Power Wah PWO
Ca.1969-1984.

1969-1984	$65	$75

Power Wah/Boost PWB
Introduced in 1973, doubles as a volume pedal.

1970s	$80	$90

Power Wah/Fuzz PWF
ca.1969-ca.1984.

1969-1984	$140	$150

Pro Compressor PCB
1978-1984. Stomp box without pedal, compress-sustain knob and output knob.

1980s	$50	$60

Pro Flanger PFL
1978-1984.

1978-1984	$125	$135

Pro Phaser PFA
1975-1984.

1975-1984	$70	$80

Rotating Sound Power Wah Model RWV
1974-1982.

1974-1982	$275	$325

Select-Effect Pedal SEL
Lets you control up to five other pedals.

1980s	$25	$30

Slimline Echo Volume 600
1983-1985. Twenty to 600 ms delay.

1983-1985	$50	$60

Slimline Echo Volume SLEV
1983-1985. Twenty to 300 ms delay.

1983-1985	$55	$65

Slimline Variable Taper Stereo Volume SLSV
1982-1986.

1982-1986	$90	$100

Slimline Variable Taper Volume SLVO
1982-1986.

1982-1986	$30	$50

Slimline Wah SLWA
1982-1986. Battery operated electro-optical.

1982-1986	$60	$80

Slimline Wah Volume SLWV
1982-ca.1986. Battery operated electro-optical.

1982-1986	$60	$80

Stereo Chorus Flanger CFL

1980s Footswitch	$50	$60

Stereo Volume CSV
Box, no pedal.

1980s	$35	$45

Volume Compressor VCO
1979-1984.

1979-1984	$35	$45

Volume Phaser PFV
1977-1984. With volume pedal.

1977-1984	$130	$150

Volume VOL
1975-ca.1984.

1975-1979	$35	$45
1980-1984	$30	$40

Morley ABY

Morley Jerry Donahue JD10

Morley Swivel Tone

Morley Volume/Boost VBO

Multivox Basky II

Mu-Tron III+

MODEL YEAR	FEATURES	EXC. COND. LOW	HIGH
Volume XVO			
1985-1988.			
1985-1988		$30	$40
Volume/Boost VBO			
1974-1984.			
1974-1984		$45	$60
Wah Pedal PWA			
1994		$35	$55
Wah Volume CWV			
1987-1991. Box, no pedal.			
1987-1991		$70	$80
Wah Volume XWV			
1985-ca.1989.			
1985-1989		$70	$80
Wah/Volume WVO			
1977-ca.1984.			
1977-1984		$90	$110

Mosrite

Semie Moseley's Mosrite company dipped into effects in the '60s. See the Guitar section for more company info.

Fuzzrite			
1966		$150	$175

Mu-tron

1972-ca. 1981. Made by Musitronics (founded by Aaron Newman), Rosemont, New Jersey, these rugged and unique-sounding effects were a high point of the 1970s. The Mu-Tron III appeared in '72 and more products followed, about 10 in all. Musitronics also made the U.S. models of the Dan Armstrong effects. In '78 ARP synthesizers bought Musitronics and sold Mutron products to around '81. A reissue of the Mu-Tron III was made available in '95 by NYC Music Products and distributed by Matthews and Ryan Musical Products.

Bi-Phase			
1975-ca.1981. Add $50-$75 for Opti-Pot Pedal.			
1975-1981	With 2-button footswitch	$550	$650
Flanger			
1977-ca.1981.			
1977-1981		$250	$420
III Envelope Filter			
1972-ca.1981. Envelope Filter.			
1972-1981		$250	$400
Micro V			
Ca.1975-ca.1977. Envelope Filter.			
1970s		$150	$200
Octave Divider			
1977-ca.1981.			
1977-1981		$325	$400
Phasor			
Ca.1974-ca.1976. Two knobs.			
1974-1976		$175	$225
Phasor II			
1976-ca.1981. Three knobs.			
1976-1981		$150	$200
Volume-Wah C-200			
1970s		$150	$200

MODEL YEAR	FEATURES	EXC. COND. LOW	HIGH

Multivox

New York-based Multivox offered a variety of effects in the '70s and '80s.

Big Jam 6-Band EQ			
1980-ca.1983.			
1980-1983		$20	$30
Big Jam Analog Echo/Reverb			
1980-ca.1983.			
1980-1983		$90	$100
Big Jam Bi-Phase 2			
1980-ca.1983.			
1980-1983		$35	$45
Big Jam Chorus			
1980-ca.1983.			
1980-1983		$35	$45
Big Jam Compressor			
1980-ca.1983.			
1980-1983		$30	$40
Big Jam Delay			
1982-ca.1983.			
1982-1983		$50	$60
Big Jam Distortion			
1980-ca.1983.			
1980-1983		$60	$70
Big Jam Flanger			
1980-ca.1983.			
1980-1983		$40	$50
Big Jam Jazz Flanger			
1980-ca.1983.			
1980-1983		$35	$45
Big Jam Noise Gate			
1981-ca.1983.			
1981-1983		$20	$25
Big Jam Octave Box			
1980-ca.1983.			
1980-1983		$30	$35
Big Jam Parametric EQ			
1982-ca.1983.			
1982-1983		$25	$30
Big Jam Phaser			
1980-ca.1983.			
1980-1983		$30	$40
Big Jam Space Driver			
1981-ca.1983. FET electronic switching, distortion, compression.			
1981-1983		$50	$60
Big Jam Spit-Wah			
1980-ca.1983.			
1980-1983		$30	$40
Big Jam Volume Pedal			
1982-ca.1983.			
1982-1983		$25	$30
Full Rotor MX-2			
1978-ca.1982. Leslie effect.			
1978-1982		$200	$325
Little David LD-2			
Rotary sound effector.			
1970s	With pedal	$350	$425
Multi Echo MX-201			
Tape echo unit, reverb.			
1970s		$150	$200

MODEL YEAR	FEATURES	EXC. COND. LOW	HIGH
Multi Echo MX-312			
Tape echo unit, reverb.			
1970s		$200	$250
Rhythm Ace FR6M			
Twenty-seven basic rhythms.			
1970s		$50	$70

MXR

1972-present. MXR Innovations launched its line of pedals in '72. Around '77, the Rochester, New York, company changed lettering on the effects from script to block, and added new models. MXR survived into the mid-'80s. In '87, production was picked up by Jim Dunlop. Reissues of block logo boxes can be differentiated from originals as they have an LED above the switch and the finish is slightly rough; the originals are smooth.

MODEL YEAR	FEATURES	EXC. COND. LOW	HIGH
6 Band Equalizer			
1975-1982.			
1975-1979		$60	$90
1980-1982		$50	$75
6 Band Equalizer M-109 (reissue)			
1987-present. Reissued by Jim Dunlop.			
1987-1999		$40	$45
10 Band Graphic Equalizer			
1975-1981.			
1975-1981	With AC power cord	$90	$125
Analog Delay			
1976-1981.			
1976-1981	Green case, power cord	$200	$230
Blue Box			
1972-ca.1978. Octave pedal, M-103.			
1970s	Earlier script logo	$200	$250
Blue Box (reissue)			
1995-present. Reissued by Jim Dunlop. Produces an octave above or two octaves below.			
1995-1999		$45	$50
Commande Overdrive			
1981-1983. The Commande series featured plastic housings and electronic switching.			
1981-1983		$35	$40
Commande Phaser			
1981-1983.			
1981-1983		$85	$95
Commande Preamp			
1981-1983.			
1981-1983		$35	$40
Commande Stereo Chorus			
1981-1983.			
1981-1983		$50	$60
Commande Stereo Flanger			
1982-1983.			
1982-1983		$60	$70
Commande Sustain			
1981-1983.			
1981-1983		$50	$55
Commande Time Delay			
1981-1983.			
1981-1983		$60	$70

MODEL YEAR	FEATURES	EXC. COND. LOW	HIGH
Distortion +			
1972-1982.			
1970s	Earlier script logo	$175	$200
1980s	Block logo	$70	$95
Distortion + (Series 2000)			
1983-1985.			
1983-1985		$50	$60
Distortion + M-104 (reissue)			
1987-present. Reissued by Jim Dunlop.			
1980s		$45	$55
1990s		$40	$50
Distortion II			
1981-1983.			
1981-1983	With AC power cord	$130	$140
Dyna Comp			
1972-1982. Compressor.			
1970s	Earlier script logo, battery	$150	$175
1980s	Block logo, battery	$80	$90
Dyna Comp (Series 2000)			
1980s		$55	$65
Dyna Comp M-102 (reissue)			
1987-present. Reissued by Jim Dunlop.			
1987-1999		$40	$55
Envelope Filter			
1976-1983.			
1976-1983		$120	$130
Flanger			
1976-1983. Analog. Reissued by Dunlop in 2000s.			
1976-1979	With AC power cord	$120	$130
1980-1983	With AC power cord	$90	$100
2000s	Dunlop MXR reissue	$70	$80
Flanger/Doubler			
1979	Rackmount	$130	$140
Limiter			
1980-1982. AC, four knobs.			
1980-1982	AC power cord	$90	$100
Loop Selector			
1980-1982. A/B switch for two effects loops.			
1980-1982		$40	$50
Micro Amp			
1978-1983. Variable booster.			
1978-1983		$80	$100
Micro Chorus			
1980-1983.			
1980-1983		$105	$125
Micro Flanger			
1981-1982.			
1981-1982		$80	$100
Noise Gate Line Driver			
1974-1983.			
1970s	Script logo	$55	$65
1980s	Block logo	$50	$60
Omni			
1980s. Rack unit with floor controller, compressor, 3-band EQ, distortion, delay, chorus/flanger.			
1980s		$325	$425
Phase 45			
Ca.1976-1982.			
1970s	Script logo, battery	$75	$90
1980s	Block logo, battery	$60	$70

MXR Analog Delay

MXR Distortion +

MXR Phase 90

EFFECTS

MXR Stereo Chorus

Nobels TR-X Vintage Tremolo

Olson Reverberation Amplifier RA-844

MODEL YEAR	FEATURES	EXC. COND. LOW	HIGH
Phase 90			
1972-1982.			
1970s	Earlier script logo	$225	$275
1980s	Block logo	$125	$145
Phase 90 M-101 (reissue)			
1987-present. Reissued by Jim Dunlop.			
1987-1989	Block logo	$50	$60
1990-1999	Block logo	$40	$50
Phase 100			
1974-1982.			
1970s	Earlier script logo	$160	$180
Phaser (Series 2000)			
1982-1985. Series 2000 introduced cost cutting die-cast cases.			
1982-1985		$50	$60
Pitch Transposer			
1980s		$350	$400
Power Converter			
1980s		$40	$60
Smart Gate			
2000s. Dunlop MXR noise-gate, single control, battery powered.			
2003	Battery	$65	$75
Stereo Chorus			
1978-1985.			
1978-1979	With AC power cord	$165	$185
1980-1985	With AC power cord	$150	$160
Stereo Chorus (Series 2000)			
1983-1985. 2000 Series introduced cost cutting die-cast cases.			
1983-1985		$50	$55
Stereo Flanger (Series 2000)			
1983-1985. 2000 Series introduced cost cutting die-cast cases.			
1983-1985	Black with Blue lettering	$60	$70
Super Comp			
2000s. Dunlop MXR, three knobs, battery powered.			
2003	Battery power	$45	$55

Nobels
1997-present. Offered by Musicorp. German-designed effects.

MODEL YEAR	FEATURES	EXC. COND. LOW	HIGH
ODR-1			
1997-present. Overdrive.			
1997-2002		$70	$75
TR-X Tremolo			
1997-present. Tremolo effect using modern technology.			
1997-1999		$40	$50

Nomad
Fuzz Wah
1960s. Import from Japan, similar looking to Morley pedal with depth and volume controls and fuzz switch, Silver metal case and Black foot pedal.

1960s		$80	$90

Olson
Olson Electronics was in Akron, Ohio.

MODEL YEAR	FEATURES	EXC. COND. LOW	HIGH
Reverberation Amplifier RA-844			
1967. Solidstate, battery-operated, reverb unit, depth and volume controls, made in Japan.			
1967		$75	$100

PAIA
1967-present. Founded by John Paia Simonton in Edmond, Oklahoma, specializing in synthesizer and effects kits. PAIA did make a few complete products but they are better known for the various electronic kit projects they sold. Values on kit projects are difficult as it depends on the skills of the person who built it.

MODEL YEAR	FEATURES	EXC. COND. LOW	HIGH
Roctave Divider 5760			
Kit to build analog octave divider.			
1970s		$60	$70

Park
1970s. Made for Marshall/Park by Colorsound.

Pax
1970s. Import Maestro copies.

MODEL YEAR	FEATURES	EXC. COND. LOW	HIGH
Fuzz Tone Copy			
1970s		$130	$140
Octave Box Copy			
1970s		$120	$130

Pearl
Pearl, located in Nashville and better known for drums, offered a line of guitar effects in the '80s.

MODEL YEAR	FEATURES	EXC. COND. LOW	HIGH
Analog Delay AD-08			
1983-1985. Four knobs.			
1983-1985		$70	$80
Analog Delay AD-33			
1982-1984. Six knobs.			
1982-1984		$85	$95
Chorus CH-02			
1981-1984. Four knobs.			
1981-1984		$90	$110
Chorus Ensemble CE-22			
1982-1984. Stereo chorus with toggling between chorus and vibrato, 6 knobs.			
1982-1984		$90	$115
Compressor CO-04			
1981-1984.			
1981-1984		$50	$60
Distortion DS-06			
1982-1986.			
1982-1986		$45	$55
Flanger FG-01			
1981-1986. Clock pulse generator, ultra-low frequency oscillator.			
1981-1986		$70	$80
Graphic EQ GE-09			
1983-1985.			
1983-1985		$35	$40
Octaver OC-07			
1982-1986.			
1982-1986		$70	$80

EFFECTS

MODEL YEAR	FEATURES	EXC. COND. LOW	HIGH
Overdrive OD-05			
1981-1986.			
1981-1986		$70	$80
Parametric EQ PE-10			
1983-1984.			
1983-1984		$40	$50
Phaser PH-03			
1981-1984. Four knobs.			
1981-1984		$70	$80
Phaser PH-44			
1982-1984. Six knobs.			
1982-1984		$90	$100
Stereo Chorus CH-22			
1980s	Blue case	$70	$80
Thriller TH-20			
Exciter.			
1980s	Black case, four knobs	$180	$200

Peavey

1965-present. Peavey made stomp boxes from '87 to around '90. They offered rackmount gear after that.

MODEL YEAR	FEATURES	EXC. COND. LOW	HIGH
Accelerator Overdrive AOD-2			
1980s		$30	$40
Biampable Bass Chorus BAC-2			
1980s		$30	$40
Companded Chorus CMC-1			
1980s		$30	$40
Compressor/Sustainer CSR-2			
1980s		$35	$45
Digital Delay DDL-3			
1980s		$30	$40
Digital Stereo Reverb SRP-16			
1980s		$50	$60
Dual Clock Stereo Chorus DSC-4			
1980s		$30	$40
Hotfoot Distortion HFD-2			
1980s		$25	$35

PedalworX

2001-present. Bob McBroom and George Blekas build their guitar effects in Manorville, New York and Huntsville, Alabama. They also do modifications to wahs.

Pharaoh Amplifiers

1998-present. Builder Matt Farrow builds his effects in Raleigh, North Carolina.

Premier

Ca. 1938-ca. 1975, 1990-present. Premier offered a reverb unit in the '60s.

Reverb Unit
1961-late-1960s. Two-tone Brown, tube, footswitch.

1960s	Brown two-tone	$150	$300

Prescription Electronics

1994-present. Located in Portland, Oregon, Prescription offers a variety of hand-made effects.

MODEL YEAR	FEATURES	EXC. COND. LOW	HIGH
Yardbox			
1994-present. Patterned after the original Sola Sound Tonebender.			
1994-1999		$80	$95

Pro-Sound

The effects listed here date from 1987, and were, most likely, around for a short time.

MODEL YEAR	FEATURES	EXC. COND. LOW	HIGH
Chorus CR-1			
1980s		$20	$30
Delay DL-1			
Analog.			
1980s		$35	$45
Distortion DS-1			
1980s		$20	$30
Octaver OT-1			
1980s		$30	$40
Power and Master Switch PMS-1			
1980s		$15	$25
Super Overdrive SD-1			
1980s		$20	$30

ProCo

1974-present. Located in Kalamazoo, Michigan and founded by Charlie Wicks, ProCo produces effects, cables and audio products.

Rat
1979-1987. Fuzztone, large box until 1984. The second version was one-third smaller than original box. The small box version became the Rat 2. The current Vintage Rat is a reissue of the original large box.

1979-1984	Large box	$100	$145
1984-1987	Compact box	$50	$60

Rat 2
1987-present.

1987-1999		$45	$55
2000s		$45	$55

Turbo Rat
1989-present. Fuzztone with higher output gain.

1989-2003		$45	$55

Vintage Rat
1992-present. Reissue of early-1980s Rat.

1992-1999		$40	$50

Radial Engineering

1994-present. Radial makes a variety of products in Port Coquitlam, British Columbia, including direct boxes, snakes, cables, splitters, and, since '99, the Tonebone line of guitar effects.

Rapco

The Jackson, Missouri based cable company offers a line of switch, connection and D.I. Boxes.

The Connection AB-100
1988-present. A/B box

1988-1999		$20	$25

Real McCoy Custom

1993-present. Wahs and effects by Geoffrey Teese. His first wah was advertised as "the Real

Peavey Companded Chorus CMC-1

Pedalworx SRV808

ProCo Vintage Rat

EFFECTS

The *Vintage Guitar Price Guide* shows low to high values for items in all-original excellent condition, and, where applicable, with original case or cover.

EFFECTS

Red Witch Deluxe Moon Phaser

Rocktek Bass EQ BER-01

Roger Mayer Octavia

MODEL YEAR FEATURES	EXC. COND. LOW	HIGH

McCoy, by Teese." He now offers his custom wah pedals under the Real McCoy Custom brand. He also used the Teese brand on a line of stomp boxes, starting in '96. The Teese stomp boxes are no longer being made.

Red Witch
2003-present. Analog guitar effects, designed by Ben Fulton, and made in Paekakariki, New Zealand.

Reverend
1996-present. Reverend offered its Drivetrain effects from 2000 to '04. They also build guitars, basses and amps.

RGW Electronics
2003-present. Guitar effects built by Robbie Wallace in Lubbock, Texas.

Rockman
See listings under Scholz Research and Dunlop.

Rocktek
1986-present. Imports formerly distributed by Matthews and Ryan of Brooklyn, New York; currently handled by D'Andrea USA.

6 Band EQ GER-01
1987-present.

1986-1999	$10	$15

Bass EQ BER-01
1986-present.

1986-1999	$10	$15

Chorus CHR-01
1986-present.

1986-1999	$10	$15

Compressor COR-01
1986-present.

1980s	$10	$15

Delay ADR-02
1986-present.

1986-1999	$15	$20

Distortion DIR-01
1986-present.

1986-1999	$10	$15
2000s	$10	$15

Flanger FLR-01
1986-present.

1986-1999	$10	$15

Metal Worker MWR-01
1986-present.

1986-1999	$15	$25

Overdrive ODR-01
1986-present.

1986-1999	$10	$15

Phaser PHR-01
1986-present. Black case with white letters on green background logo.

1986-1999	$10	$15

MODEL YEAR FEATURES	EXC. COND. LOW	HIGH

Super Delay ADR-01
1986-present.

1986-1999	$10	$15

Vibrator Tremolo VIB
Ca. 1990-present.

1990-1999	$10	$15

Rocktron
1980s-present. Rocktron is a division of GHS Strings and offers a line of amps, controllers, stomp boxes, and preamps.

Austin Gold Overdrive
2000s. Light overdrive enhancement without changing guitar-amp tone, Gold case.

2000	Battery power	$30	$35

Banshee Talk Box
2000s. Includes power supply.

2000s	With power supply	$100	$110

Hush
2000s. Noise reduction, Blue case.

2000s	Battery power	$30	$40

Rampage Distortion
2000s. Sustain, high-gain and distortion, White case.

2000s	Battery power	$30	$40

Surf Tremolo
2000s.

2000s		$80	$90

Tsunami Chorus
2000s. Battery or optional AC adapter.

2000	Battery power	$40	$50

Vertigo Vibe
2000s. Rotating Leslie speaker effect.

2000	Battery power	$50	$55

XDC
1980s. Rackmount stereo preamp, distortion.

1980s	$90	$120

Roger Mayer Electronics
1964-present. Roger Mayer started making guitar effects in England in 1964 for guitarists like Jimmy Page and Jeff Beck. He moved to the U.S. in 1969 to start a company making studio gear and effects. He returned to England in 1989.

Axis Fuzz
Early 1980s-present.

1980s	$275	$375
1990s	$100	$150

Classic Fuzz
1987-present. The Fuzz Face.

1987-1999	$160	$190

Metal Fuzz
1987-1994.

1987-1994	$90	$120

Mongoose Fuzz
1987-present.

1987-1999	$140	$150

Octavia
1979-present. Famous rocket-shaped box.

1979-1985	$275	$375
1986-1999	$100	$150

MODEL YEAR	FEATURES	EXC. COND. LOW	HIGH

VooDoo-1
Ca.1990-present.

1990s		$150	$175

Roland
Japan's Roland Corporation first launched effect pedals in '74; a year or two later the subsidiary company, Boss, debuted its own line. They were marketed concurrently at first, but gradually Boss became reserved for effects and drum machines while the Roland name was used on amplifiers and keyboards.

Bee Baa AF-100
1975-ca.1980. Fuzz and treble boost.

1975-1980		$250	$300

Bee Gee AF-60
1975-ca.1980. Sustain, distortion.

1975-1980		$70	$90

Double Beat AD-50
1975-ca.1980. Fuzz wah.

1975-1980		$150	$200

Expression Pedal EV-5

1970s		$40	$45

Guitar Synth Pedal GR-33 and Pickup GK-2A
2000-present. Requires optional GK-2A pickup.

2000-2003		$450	$500

Human Rhythm Composer R-8
1980s. Drum machine, key pad entry.

1980s		$200	$275

Jet Phaser AP-7
1975-ca.1978. Phase and distortion.

1975-1978		$200	$250

Phase II AP-2
1975-ca.1980. Brown case.

1975-1980		$150	$200

Phase Five AP-5
1975-ca.1978.

1975-1978		$175	$225

Space Echo RE-101
1974-ca.1980. Tape echo and reverb.

1974-1980		$350	$500

Space Echo RE-201
1974-ca.1980. Tape echo and reverb.

1974-1980		$350	$500

Space Echo RE-301
1977-ca.1980. Tape echo and reverb.

1977-1980		$350	$500

Space Echo RE-501
Tape echo and reverb.

1970s		$400	$600

Vocoder SVC-350
Late-1970s-1980s. Vocal synthesis (vocoder) for voice or guitar, rackmount version of VP-330.

1980		$550	$600

Vocoder VP-330 Plus
Late-1970s-1980s. Analog vocal synthesis (vocoder) for voice or guitar, includes 2 1/2 octaves keyboard.

1978-1982		$700	$800

Wah Beat AW-10
1975-ca.1980.

1975-1980		$75	$100

Ross
Founded by Bud Ross, who also established Kustom, in Chanute, Kansas, in the 1970s. Ross produced primarily amplifiers. In about 1978, they introduced a line of U.S.-made effects. Later production switched to the Orient.

10 Band Graphic Equalizer

1970s		$40	$80

Compressor

1970s		$275	$325

Distortion
1978-ca.1980. Brown, made in U.S.A.

1979-1980		$75	$110

Flanger
1977-ca.1980. Red, made in U.S.A.

1977-1980		$125	$150

Phase Distortion R1
Purple, made in U.S.A.

1979	Purple	$100	$125

Phaser
1978-ca.1980. Orange, made in U.S.A.

1978-1980		$100	$125

Stereo Delay
1978-ca.1980. Made in U.S.A.

1978-1980		$110	$130

Rotovibe
See listing under Dunlop.

S. Hawk

Hawk I Fuzz

1975		$90	$110

LTD

1975	Silver case, slider	$90	$100

Sam Ash
1960s-1970s. Sam Ash Music was founded by a young Sam Ash (formerly Askynase - an Austro-Hungarian name) in '24. Ash's first store was in Brooklyn, and was relocated to a better part of town in '44. By '66, there were about four Ash stores. During this time, Ash Music private branded their own amps and effects.

Fuzzz Boxx
Ca.1967. Red, made by Universal Amplifier Company.

1967	Red case	$150	$250

Volume Wah
Italian-made.

1970s		$150	$175

Scholz Research
Started by Tom Scholz of the band Boston in the early 1980s. In 1996, Jim Dunlop picked up the Rockman line (see Dunlop).

Power Soak

1980s		$60	$80

Rockman

1980s		$45	$55

Roland Jet Phaser AP-7

Ross Distortion

Scholz Acoustic Guit Pedal

EFFECTS

SIB Mr. Echo

*Snarling Dogs
Bawl Buster Bass Wah*

*Snarling Dogs
Black Dog SDP-2*

EFFECTS

MODEL		EXC. COND.	
YEAR	FEATURES	LOW	HIGH

Rockman X100
Professional studio processor.

1980s		$65	$75

Soloist
Personal guitar processor.

1980s		$40	$50

Seamoon

1973-1977, 1997-2002. Seamoon made effects until '77, when Dave Tarnowski bought up the remaining inventory and started Analog Digital Associates (ADA). He reissued the brand in '97.

Fresh Fuzz
1975-1977. Recently reissued by ADA.

1975-1977		$100	$150

Funk Machine
1974-1977. Envelope Filter. Recently reissued by ADA.

1974-1977		$150	$220

Studio Phase
1975-1977. Phase shifter.

1975-1977		$60	$80

Shinei

Japanese imports. Shinei also made effects for Univox and probably others.

Fuzz wah

1970s		$100	$120

Resly (repeat time) Machine
Black case, three speeds.

1970s		$300	$400

Sho-Bud

1956-1980. This pedal steel company offered volume pedals as well.

Volume Pedal

1965		$90	$100

SIB

Effects pedals from Rick Hamel, who helped design SMF amps.

Siegmund Guitars & Amplifiers

1993-present. Chris Siegmund's amp company also offers preamp pedals made in Los Angeles.

Snarling Dogs

1997-present. Started by Charlie Stringer of Stringer Industries, Warren, New Jersey in '97. Stringer died in May '99. The brand is now carried by D'Andrea USA.

Whine-O Wah
1997-present. Three classic wah sounds in die-cast pedal.

1997-2002		$45	$55

Sobbat

1995-present. Line of effects from Kinko Music Company of Kyoto, Japan.

Sola/Colorsound

1965-present. Sola was founded by London's Macari's Musical Exchange in '65. Sola made effects for Vox, Marshall, Park, and B & M and later under their own Colorsound brand. Refer to Colorsound for listings and more company info.

Songbird

See Dytronics.

Speedster

1995-2000, 2003-present. Speedster added an American-made overdrive pedal to their product line in '04.

Stinger

Stinger effects were distributed by the Martin Guitar Company from 1989 to 1990.

CH-70 Stereo Chorus

1989		$25	$50

CO-20 Compressor

1989		$25	$45

DD-90 Digital Delay

1989		$25	$50

DE-80 Analog Delay

1989		$30	$60

DI-10 Distortion

1989		$35	$55

FL-60 Flanger

1989		$25	$55

OD-30 Overdrive

1989		$25	$55

TS-5 Tube Stack

1989		$35	$50

Studio Electronics

1989-present. Synth and midi developer Greg St. Regis' Studio Electronics added guitar pedal effects to their line in '03.

Supro

1935-1968. Supro offered a few reverb units in the '60s.

500 R Standard Reverb Unit
1962-1963. Outboard reverb unit.

1962-1963		$200	$300

Auxiliary Reverb S6405(R)
1964-1968. Reverb unit, offered in Rhino Hide ('64-'68) or black and grey Tolex ('66-'67).

1960s		$200	$300

Sweet Sound

1994-present. Line of effects from Bob Sweet, originally made in Trenton, Michigan, currently in Coral Springs, Florida.

Systech (Systems & Technology in Music, Inc)

Systech was located in Kalamazoo, Michigan.

MODEL YEAR	FEATURES	EXC. COND. LOW	HIGH

Envelope and Repeater
1975-late-1970s.

1975-1979		$80	$100

Envelope Follower
1975-late-1970s.

1975-1979		$100	$140

Flanger
1975-late-1970s.

1975-1979		$80	$100

Harmonic Energizer
1975-late-1970s.

1975-1979		$125	$225

Overdrive Model 1300
1975-late-1970s.

1975-1979		$80	$100

Phase Shifter Model 1200
1975-late-1970s.

1975-1979		$125	$175

T-Rex
2003-present. Made in Denmark and imported by European Musical Imports.

T.C. Electronics
1976-present. Brothers Kim and John Rishøj founded TC Electronic in Risskov, Denmark, and made guitar effects pedals for several years before moving into rack-mounted gear. Currently they offer a wide range of pro audio gear.

Booster + Distortion

1980s		$300	$425

Dual Parametric Equalizer

1980s		$250	$350

Stereo Chorus/Flanger
Introduced in 1982, and reissued in '91.

1980s		$150	$200

Sustain + Equalizer

1980s		$200	$300

T.C. Jauernig Electronics
2004-present. Tim Jauernig, of Rothschild, Wisconsin, built effects for several years before launching his T.C. Jauernig brand in '04.

Tech 21
1989-present. Tech 21 offers a variety of products out of New York City.

Sansamp
1989-present. Offers a variety of tube amp tones.

1989-1999		$100	$125

XXL Pedal
1995-2000. Distortion, fuzz.

1995-2000		$50	$60

Teese
Geoffrey Teese's first wah was advertised as "the Real McCoy, by Teese." He now offers his custom wah pedals under the Real McCoy Custom brand. The Teese brand name was used on his line of stomp boxes, starting in '96. The Teese stomp boxes are no longer being made.

Thomas Organ
The Thomas Organ Company was heavily involved with Vox from '64 to '72, importing their instruments into the U.S. and designing and assembling products, including the wah-wah pedal. Both Thomas Organ and JMI, Vox's European distributor, wanted to offer the new effect. The problem was solved by labeling the Thomas Organ wah the Crybaby. The Crybaby is now offered by Dunlop. Refer to Vox listing for Crybaby Stereo Fuzz Wah, Crybaby Wah, and Wah Wah.

Tonebone
See Radial Engineering listing.

Top Gear
Rotator
Leslie effect.

1970s		$75	$125

Top Hat Amplification
1994-present. The Anaheim, California, amp builder also offers effects.

Tremolo
See listing under Dunlop.

Tube Works
Originally out of Denver, now a division of Genz Benz Enclosures of Scottsdale, Arizona, they also offer tube/solidstate amps, cabinets, and DI boxes.

Real Tube
Ca. 1987-present. Overdrive with 12AX7A tube.

1987-1999		$80	$100

Tube Driver
1989-present. With tube.

1989-1999	With tube	$90	$110

Tycobrahe
The Tycobrahe story was over almost before it began. Doing business in 1976-1977, they produced only three pedals and a direct box, one the fabled Octavia. The company, located in Hermosa Beach, California, made high-quality, original devices, but they didn't catch on. Now, they are very collectible.

Octavia
1976-1977. Octave doubler.

1976-1977		$550	$750

Parapedal
1976-1977. Wah.

1976-1977		$550	$750

Pedalflanger
1976-1977. Blue pedal-controlled flanger.

1976-1977		$550	$750

Uni-Vibe
See listings under Univox, Vox and Dunlop.

T.C. Jauernig Luxury Drive

Tycobrahe Parapedal

Univox Univibe

EFFECTS

Univox Echo-Tech EM-200

Vesta Fire Distortion DST

Vox Clyde McCoy Wah

Univox

Univox was a brand name owned by Merson (later Unicord), of Westbury, New York. It marketed guitars and amps, and added effects in the late-'60s. Most Univox effects were made by Shinei, of Japan. They vanished in about '81.

EC-80 A Echo
Early-1970s-ca.1977. Tape echo, sometimes shown as "The Brat Echo Chamber."

Model Year	Features	Low	High
1970s		$90	$130

EC-100 Echo
Tape, sound-on-sound.

1970s		$100	$150

Echo-Tech EM-200
Disc recording echo unit.

1970s		$125	$155

Micro 41 FCM41 4 channel mixer

1970s		$40	$50

Micro Fazer
1970s. Phase shifter.

1970s		$70	$95

Noise-Clamp EX110

1970s		$40	$50

Phaser PHZ1
AC powered.

1970s		$60	$85

Pro Verb
1970s. Reverb (spring) unit, Black Tolex, slider controls for two inputs, one output plus remote output.

1970s	Black Tolex	$50	$85

Square Wave SQ150
Introduced in 1976, distortion.

1970s	Orange case	$90	$100

Superfuzz

1971	Gray box, normal bypass switch	$225	$325
1973	Unicord, various colors, large Blue bypass	$225	$325

Uni-Comp
Compression limiter.

1970s		$40	$80

Uni-Drive

1970s		$100	$180

Uni-Fuzz
1960s. Fuzz tone in Blue case, two Black knobs and slider switch.

1960s	Blue case	$275	$375

Uni-Tron 5
A.k.a. Funky Filter, envelope filter.

1975		$110	$165

Uni-Vibe
Introduced around 1969, with rotating speaker simulation, with pedal.

1960s		$800	$900
1970s		$600	$800

Uni-Wah Wah/Volume

1970s		$70	$120

Vesta Fire

Ca.1981-ca.1988. Brand name of Japan's Shiino Musical Instrument Corp.

Digital Chorus/Flanger FLCH

Model Year	Features	Low	High
1980s		$35	$40

Distortion DST

1980s		$35	$45

Flanger

1980s		$35	$45

Noise Gate

1980s		$20	$30

Stereo Chorus SCH
Foot pedal.

1980s		$25	$35

Vintage Tone Project

2003-present. Line of guitar effects made by Robert Rush and company in Lafayette, Colorado. They also build reissues of Dan Armstrong's '70s effects.

VooDoo Lab

1994-present. Line of effects offered by Digital Music Corp. of California.

Analog Chorus
1994-1999.

1994-1999		$90	$130

Bosstone
1994-1999. Based on 1960s Jordan Electronics Fuzz.

1994-1999		$60	$80

Micro Vibe
1994-1999. Uni-Vibe swirl effect.

1994-1999		$95	$100

Overdrive
1994-2000. Based on '70s overdrive.

1994-2000		$40	$60

Super Fuzz
1994-1999.

1994-1999		$60	$75

Tremolo
1994-present. Vintage trem.

1994-1999		$85	$100

Vox

1957-present. Vox offered a variety of guitars, amps, organs and effects. Circa '66, they released the Tone Bender, one of the classic fuzzboxes of all time. A year or so later, they delivered their greatest contribution to the effects world, the first wah-wah pedal. The American arm of Vox (then under Thomas Organ) succumbed in '72. In the U.K., the company was on-again/off-again.

Clyde McCoy Wah-Wah Pedal
Introduced in 1967, reissued in 2001.

1967	Clyde's picture on bottom cover	$500	$650
1968	No picture on bottom plate	$400	$550

EFFECTS

MODEL YEAR	FEATURES	EXC. COND. LOW	HIGH

Crybaby Wah

Introduced in 1968. The Thomas Organ Company was heavily involved with Vox from '64 to '72, importing their instruments into the U.S. and designing and assembling products. One product developed in conjunction with Vox was the wah-wah pedal. Both Thomas Organ and JMI, Vox's European distributor, wanted to offer the new effect. The problem was solved by labeling the Thomas Organ wah the Crybaby. The original wahs were built by Jen in Italy, but Thomas later made them in their Chicago and Sepulveda, CA plants. Thomas Organ retained the marketing rights to Vox until '79, but was not very active with the brand after '72. The Crybaby brand is now offered by Dunlop.

1960s	Jen-made	$175	$225
1970	Sepulveda-made	$100	$120

Double Sound

Jen-made, Double Sound model name on bottom of pedal, double sound derived from fuzz and wah ability.

1970s		$150	$240

King Wah

Chrome top, Italian-made.

1970s		$75	$125

Stereo Fuzz Wah

1970s		$125	$150

Tone Bender V-828

1966-1970s. Fuzz box. Reissued as the V-829 in '94.

1966	Gray	$275	$325
1969	Black	$225	$285

V-807 Echo-Reverb Unit

Solidstate, disc echo.

1967		$200	$300

V-837 Echo Deluxe Tape Echo

Solidstate, multiple heads.

1967		$200	$300

V-846 Wah

1969-1970s. Chrome top, Italian-made.

1969	Transitional Clyde McCoy	$350	$475
1970s		$200	$300

V-847 Wah

1992-present. Reissue of the original V-846 Wah.

1990s		$60	$80

Volume Pedal

Late 1960s. Reissued as the V850.

1960s		$60	$85

Wasabi

2003-present. Line of guitar effect pedals from Danelectro.

Washburn

Washburn offered a line of effects from around '83 to ca. '89.

Analog Delay AX:9

1980s		$25	$35

Flanger FX:4

1980s		$25	$35

Phaser

1980s		$30	$40

Stack in a Box SX:3

Tube-like distortion.

1980s		$25	$35

Watkins/WEM

1957-present. Watkins Electric Music (WEM) was founded by Charlie Watkins. Their first commercial product was the Watkins Dominator (wedge Gibson stereo amp shape) in 1957, followed by the Copicat Echo in 1958.

Copicat Tape Echo

1958-1970s. The Copicat has been reissued by Watkins.

1960s	Tube	$600	$1,000
1968	Solidstate	$200	$400

Way Huge Electronics

1995-1998. Way Huge offered a variety of stomp boxes, made in Sherman Oaks, California.

WD Music

Since 1978, WD Music has offered a wide line of aftermarket products for guitar players. Many effects were copies of original Dan Armstrong color series (refer to Dan Armstrong listing). Large WD logo on Armstrong copies with Strat-pickguard logo on top of pedal.

Blue Clipper

1992-present. Fuzz.

1990s		$30	$40

Orange Squeezer

1992-present. Signal compressor.

1990s	Light Orange case	$40	$45

Purple Peaker

1992-present. Mini EQ.

1990s		$40	$45

Westbury

1978-ca. 1983. Brand name imported by Unicord.

Tube Overdrive

1978-1983. 12AX7.

1978-1983		$100	$150

Whirlwind

1980s. Whirlwind called Rochester, New York, home.

Commander

Boost and effects loop selector.

1980s		$60	$80

Xotic Effects

2001-present. Hand-wired effects made in Los Angeles, California, and distributed by Prosound Communications.

Vox King Wah

Wasabi AS-1

Xotic RC Booster

Yamaha UD Stomp Modulation Delay

Zoom 505 Guitar Pedal

Zoom 506II Bass

MODEL YEAR	FEATURES	EXC. COND. LOW	HIGH

Yamaha

Yamaha offers effects as part of their musical instrument line.

Analog Delay E1005
1980s. Free standing, double space rackmount-sized, short to long range delays.

1980s	Gray case	$150	$160

Yubro

Yubro, of Bellaire, Texas, offered a line of nine effects in the mid- to late-'80s.

Analog Delay AD-800
Three hundred ms.

1980s		$60	$80

Stereo Chorus CH-600

1980s		$30	$40

Zoom

Effects line from Samson Technologies Corp of Syosset, New York.

1010 Player
1996-1999. Compact multi-effects pedal board, 16 distortions, 25 effects.

1990s		$40	$80

503 Amp Simulator
1990s.

1990s		$25	$45

504 Acoustic Pedal
1997-2000. Compact multi-effects pedal, 24 effects, tuner, replaced by II version.

1990s		$25	$45

505 Guitar Pedal
1995-2000. Compact multi-effects pedal, 24 effects, tuner, replaced by II version.

1990s		$45	$60

506 Bass Pedal
1997-2000. Compact multi-effects bass pedal, 24 effects, tuner, replaced by II version.

1990s	Black box, Orange panel	$45	$60

507 Reverb

1990s		$25	$45

Steels &
Lap Steels

1960 Alamo Embassy

1947 Dickerson-made Leilani

STEELS & LAPS

MODEL YEAR	FEATURES	EXC. COND. LOW	HIGH

Airline

Ca.1958-1968. Name used by Montgomery Ward for instruments built by Kay, Harmony and Valco.

Lap Steel

1960s	Rec-O-Glas/plastic	$500	$550

Rocket 6-String Steel

Black and White, three legs, Valco-made.

1964		$300	$375

Student 6 Steel

1950	Black	$125	$175

Alamo

1947-1982. The first musical instruments built by Alamo, of San Antonio, Texas, were lap steel and amp combos with early models sold with small birch amps. See *Guitar Stories Volume II*, by Michael Wright, for a complete history of Alamo with detailed model listings.

Hawaiian Lap Steels

1947-ca. 1967. Models include the 1950s Challenger and Futuramic Dual Eight, the 1950s and early-1960s Embassy (pear-shape) and Jet (triangular), the early-1960s Futuramic Eight and Futuramic Six, and the late-1960s Embassy (triangular Jet).

1950s		$100	$200

Alkire

1939-1950s. Founded by musician and teacher Eddie Alkire, the instruments may have been built by another company.

E-Harp 10-String Steel

1939-1950s. Similar to Epiphone lap steel with Epi-style logo, offered in lap steel or console.

1940s		$650	$975
1950s		$600	$900

Alvarez

Ca. 1966-present. Imported by St. Louis Music from mid-1960s.

Model 5010 Koa D Steel-String

1960s		$250	$350

Aria

1960-present. Aria offered Japanese-made steels and lap steels in the '60s.

Audiovox

Ca. 1935-ca. 1950. Paul Tutmarc's Audiovox Manufacturing, of Seattle, Washington, was a pioneer in electric lap steels, basses, guitars and amps.

Lap Steel

1940s		$800	$900

Lap Steel and Amp Set

1940s		$1,200	$1,300

Bigsby

1947-present. All handmade by Paul Arthur Bigsby, in Downey, California. Bigsby was a pioneer in developing pedal steels and they were generally special order or custom made and not mass produced. The original instruments were made until 1965 and should be valued on a case-by-case basis. Models include the Single Neck pedal steel, Double 8 pedal steel, 8/10 Doubleneck pedal steel, Triple 8 pedal steel (all ca. 1947-'65), and the 1957-'58 Magnatone G-70 lap steel. A solidbody guitar and a pedal steel based upon the original Paul Bigsby designs were introduced January, 2002.

Triple 8-String Neck Steel

1947-1965. Bigsby steel were generally special order or custom-made and not mass produced. Instruments should be valued on a case-by-case basis.

1947-1959	Natural	$2,500	$5,000

Blue Star

1984-present. Intermediate grade, production/custom, lap steels built by luthier Bruce Herron in Fennville, Michigan. He also builds guitars, mandolins, dulcimers, and ukes.

Bronson

George Bronson was a steel guitar instructor in the Detroit area from the 1930s to the early '50s and sold instruments under his own brand. Most instruments and amps were made by Rickenbacker, Dickerson or Valco.

Melody King Model 52 Lap Steel

Brown Bakelite body with five gold cavity covers on the top, made by Rickenbacker.

1950s		$600	$750

Carvin

1946-present. Founded by Lowell C. Kiesel who produced lapsteels under the Kiesel brandname for 1947-'50. In late '49, he renamed the instrument line Carvin after sons Carson and Galvin. Until 1977, they offered lap, console, and pedal steels with up to four necks.

Double 6 Steel With Legs

1960		$500	$600

Double 8 Steel With Legs

1960	Sunburst	$600	$700

Electric Hawaiian Lap Steel

1950s		$200	$300

Single 8 With Legs

Large block position markers, one pickup, two knobs. Blond finish.

1965		$400	$500

Chandler

1984-present. Intermediate grade, production/custom, solidbody Weissenborn-shaped electric lapsteels built by luthier Paul Chandler in Chico, California. He also builds guitars, basses and pickups.

Cromwell

1935-1939. Budget model brand built by Gibson and distributed by various mail-order businesses.

MODEL YEAR	FEATURES	EXC. COND. LOW	HIGH

Lap Steel
Charlie Christian bar pickup.

1939	Sunburst	$300	$350

Danelectro
1946-1969, 1997-present. Known mainly for guitars and amps, Danelectro did offer a few lap steels in the mid-'50s.

Lap Steels

1950s		$250	$300

Dickerson
1937-1948. Founded by the Dickerson brothers in 1937, primarily for electric lap steels and small amps. Besides their own brand, Dickerson made instruments for Cleveland's Oahu Company, Varsity, Southern California Music, Bronson, Roland Ball, and Gourley. The lap steels were often sold with matching amps, both covered in pearloid Mother-of-Toilet-Seat (MOTS). By 1948, the company changed ownership and was renamed Magna Electronics (Magnatone).

Lap Steel with matching amp
1950s. Gray Pearloid with matching amp.

1950s		$400	$550

Dobro
1929-1942, ca.1954-present. Dobro offered lap steels from 1933 to '42. Gibson now owns the brand and recently offered a lap steel.

Hawaiian Lap Steel

1930s		$300	$400

Lap Steel Guitar and Amp Set
1930s-1940s. Typical pearloid covered student six-string lap steel and small matching amp (with three tubes and single control knob).

1940	White pearloid	$400	$550

Dwight
1950s. Private branded instruments by National-Supro.

Lap Steel
1950s. Pearloid, six strings.

1950s	Gray pearloid	$300	$350

Emmons
1970s-present. Owned by Lashley, Inc. of Burlington, North Carolina.

Lashley LeGrande III Steel
2001-present. Double-neck, 8 pedals, 4 knee levers, 25th Anniversary.

2001		$2,500	$3,000

S-10 Pedal Steel
Single ten-string neck pedal steel.

1970s		$900	$1,400

English Electronics
1960s. Norman English had a teaching studio in Lansing, Michigan, where he gave guitar and steel lessons. He had his own private-branded instruments made by Valco in Chicago.

Tonemaster Lap Steel
Cream Pearloid, six strings, three legs, Valco-made.

1960s		$200	$300

Epiphone
1928-present. The then Epiphone Banjo Company was established in 1928. Best known for its guitars, the company offered steels from '35 to '58 when Gibson purchased the brand.

Century Lap Steel
1939-1957. Rocket-shaped maple body, one pickup, metal fingerboard, six, seven or eight strings. Black finish.

1939-1957		$350	$400

Console Triple-Neck Steel
1950-1958. Three necks, sunburst or natural finish.

1950-1958		$600	$800

Electar Century Lap Steel

1930s	Black	$350	$400

Electar Kent Hawaiian Lap Steel
1949-1953. Guitar-shaped maple body, six strings, lower-end of Epiphone Hawaiian line. Electar script logo below bottom of fretboard.

1949-1953		$300	$350

Electar Model M Lap Steel
1936-1939. Hawaiian setup, stair-step body, art deco, six, seven or eight strings.

1936-1939	Black	$400	$500

Electar Zenith Lap Steel
Six-string neck.

1940s	Black	$300	$400

Electar Zephyr Lap Steel
1939-1957. Maple body, metal fingerboard, six, seven or eight strings.

1930s	Black, art deco	$500	$650
1940s	Black and White, 8 strings	$500	$600
1950s	Black, 7 strings	$450	$600

Skylark Steel

1962	Natural korina	$700	$900

Solo Console Steel
1939-1954. Maple with White mahogany laminated body, Black binding, Black metal fingerboard, six, seven or eight strings.

1939-1954		$400	$450

Fender
1946-present. Fender offered lap and pedal steels from '46 to '80.

400 Pedal Steel
1958-1976. One 8-string neck with 4 to 10 pedals.

1960s	Blond	$650	$950

800 Pedal Steel
1964-1976. One 10-string neck, 6 to 10 pedals.

1964-1976	Sunburst	$600	$750

1941 Epiphone Electar Zephyr

1954 Fender Stringmaster

STEELS & LAPS

1948 Fender Princeton

1961 Fender Stringmaster

MODEL YEAR	FEATURES	EXC. COND. LOW	HIGH
1000 Pedal Steel			

1957-1976. Two 8-string necks and 8 or 10 pedals.

| 1957-1976 | Natural, 8 pedals | $800 | $1,150 |
| **2000 Pedal Steel** | | | |

1964-1976. Two 10-string necks, 10 or 11 pedals. Sunburst.

| 1964-1976 | 10 pedals | $750 | $1,200 |
| **Artist Dual 10 Pedal Steel** | | | |

1976-1981. Two 10-string necks, 8 pedals, 4 knee levers. Black or Mahogany.

| 1976-1981 | | $650 | $850 |
| **Champ Lap Steel** | | | |

1955-1980. Replaced Champion Lap Steel.

1955-1959	Tan	$700	$750
1960-1969	Tan	$650	$700
1970-1980	Tan	$500	$600
Champion Lap Steel			

1949-1955. Covered in what collectors call Mother of Toilet Seat (M.O.T.S.) finish, also known as Pearloid. Replaced by Champ Lap Steel.

1949-1955	Tan	$700	$800
1949-1955	Yellow or white pearloid	$700	$800
Deluxe Steel			

1949-1950. Strings-through-pickup, Roman numeral markers. Became the Deluxe 6 or Deluxe 8 Lap Steel in 1950.

1946	Wax	$800	$1,000
1947-1950	Blond or Walnut	$800	$1,000
Deluxe 6/Stringmaster Single Steel			

1950-1981. Renamed from the Deluxe, 6 strings, 3 legs.

1950-1959	Blond or walnut	$700	$1,000
1960-1969	Blond or walnut	$700	$1,000
1970-1981	Black or white	$700	$900
Deluxe 8/Stringmaster Single Steel			

1950-1981. Renamed from the Deluxe, 8 strings, 3 legs.

1950-1959	Blond or walnut	$700	$1,000
1960-1969	Blond or walnut	$700	$1,000
1970-1981	Black or white	$700	$900
Dual 6 Professional Steel			

1950-1981. Two 6-string necks, 3 legs optional. Blond or walnut.

1952-1981	Blond	$700	$1,000
1952-1981	Walnut	$700	$900
Dual 8 Professional Steel			

1946-1957. Two 8-string necks, 3 legs optional. Blond or walnut.

1946-1957	Blond	$900	$1,200
1946-1957	Walnut	$800	$1,000
K & F Steel			

1945-1946. Made by Doc Kauffman and Leo Fender, strings-through-pickup.

1945-1946	Black	$1,400	$2,000
Organ Button Steel			
1946-1947.			
1946-1947	Wax	$800	$950

MODEL YEAR	FEATURES	EXC. COND. LOW	HIGH
Princeton Steel			

1946-1948. Strings-through-pickup, Roman numeral markers.

| 1946-1948 | Wax | $600 | $700 |
| **Stringmaster Steel (two-neck)** | | | |

1953-1981. The Stringmaster came in 3 versions, having 2, 3 or 4 8-string necks (6-string necks optional).

1953-1959	Blond (light finish)	$1,400	$1,800
1953-1959	Walnut (dark finish)	$1,000	$1,400
1960-1969	Blond (light finish)	$1,300	$1,600
1960-1969	Walnut (dark finish)	$900	$1,300
1970-1981	Blond or dark	$900	$1,200
Stringmaster Steel (three-neck)			
1953-1981.			
1953-1959	Blond (light finish)	$2,000	$2,400
1953-1959	Walnut (dark finish)	$1,500	$2,100
1960-1969	Blond (light finish)	$1,700	$2,300
1960-1969	Walnut (dark finish)	$1,200	$1,700
1970-1981	Blond (light finish)	$1,300	$1,500
1970-1981	Walnut (dark finish)	$900	$1,200
Stringmaster Steel (four-neck)			
1953-1968.			
1953-1959	Blond (light finish)	$2,100	$2,500
1953-1959	Walnut (dark finish)	$1,600	$2,200
1960-1968	Blond (light finish)	$1,600	$1,900
1960-1968	Walnut (dark finish)	$1,300	$1,600
Studio Deluxe Lap Steel			

1956-1981. One pickup, 3 legs.

| 1956-1981 | Blond | $600 | $800 |

Framus

1946-1977, 1996-present. Imported into the U.S. by Philadelphia Music Company in the 1960s. Brand revived in 1996, and distributed in the US by Dana B. Goods.

Deluxe Table Steel 0/7

| 1973 | White | $200 | $300 |

Student Hawaiian Model 0/4

| 1973 | Red | $150 | $200 |

G.L. Stiles

1960-1994. Gilbert Lee Stiles made a variety of instruments, mainly in the Miami area. **Double-neck Pedal Steel**

| 1970s | | $400 | $550 |

Gibson

1902-present. Gibson offered steels from 1935-1968.

BR-4 Lap Steel

1947. Guitar-shaped of solid mahogany, round neck, 1 pickup, varied binding.

| 1947 | Sunburst | $375 | $425 |

BR-6 Lap Steel

1947-1960. Guitar-shaped solid mahogany body, square neck (round by 1948).

| 1950s | | $375 | $450 |

STEELS & LAPS

MODEL		EXC. COND.	
YEAR	FEATURES	LOW	HIGH

BR-9 Lap Steel
1947-1959. Solidbody, one pickup, Tan.

1947-1949	Non-adj. Poles	$300	$350
1950-1959	Adj. Poles	$400	$450
1950-1959	Matching steel and amp set	$600	$700

Century 10 Lap Steel
1948-1955. Solid maple body, 10 strings, one pickup, silver fingerboard.

| 1950s | Black | $450 | $550 |

Century 6 Lap Steel
1948-1968. Solid maple body, six strings, one pickup, silver fingerboard.

| 1950s | | $450 | $550 |

Console Grand Steel
1938-1942, 1948-1967. Hollowbody, 2 necks, triple-bound body, standard 7 and 8-string combination until 1942, double 8-string necks standard for 1948 and after.

| 1938-1942 | Sunburst | $950 | $1,100 |
| 1948-1959 | Sunburst | $950 | $1,100 |

Console Steel (C-530)
1956-1966. Replaced Consolette during 1956-1957, 2 8-string necks, 4 legs optional.

| 1955-1966 | With legs | $800 | $950 |

Consolette Table Steel
1952-1957. Rectangular body of Korina, 2 8-string necks, 4 legs. Replaced by maple-body Console after 1956.

| 1950s | Natural Korina | $950 | $1,100 |

EH-100 Lap Steel
1936-1949. Hollow guitar-shaped body, bound top, 6 or 7 strings.

| 1936-1939 | | $550 | $650 |
| 1940-1941 | | $450 | $550 |

EH-125 Lap Steel
1939-1942. Hollow guitar-shaped mahogany body, single-bound tody, metal fingerboard.

| 1939-1942 | Sunburst | $600 | $700 |

EH-150 Doubleneck Electric Hawaiian Steel
1937-1939. Doubleneck EH-150 with 7- and 8-string necks.

| 1937-1939 | | $2,200 | $2,700 |

EH-150 Lap Steel
1936-1943. Hollow guitar-shaped body, 6 to 10 strings available, bound body.

1936	1st offering metal body	$2,200	$2,800
1937-1939	Sunburst	$850	$1,000
1940-1943	Sunburst	$750	$875

EH-150 Lap Steel Matching Set (guitar and amp)
1936-1942. Both electric Hawaiian steel guitar and amp named EH-150, with matching tweed guitar case.

| 1936-1939 | Guitar with Christian pickup | $1,600 | $2,000 |
| 1940-1942 | | $1,300 | $1,600 |

EH-185 Lap Steel
1939-1942. Hollow guitar-shaped curly maple body, triple-bound body, 6, 7, 8 or 10 strings.

| 1939-1942 | Sunburst, lap steel and amp | $1,600 | $1,900 |

EH-500 Skylark Lap Steel
1956-1968. Solid korina body, 8-string available by 1958.

| 1956-1968 | Natural, 6 strings | $600 | $800 |

EH-620 Steel
1955-1967. Eight strings, 6 pedals.

| 1960s | Natural | $550 | $750 |

EH-630 Electraharp Steel
1941-1967. Eight strings, 8 pedals (4 in 1949-'67). Called just EH-630 from '56-'67.

| 1941-1956 | Sunburst | $650 | $900 |

EH-820 Steel
1960-1966. Two necks, 8 pedals, Vari-Tone selector.

| 1960s | Cherry | $650 | $950 |

Royaltone Lap Steel
1950-1952, 1956-1957. Symmetrical wavy body, volume and tone knobs on treble side of pickup, Gibson silk-screen logo, brown pickup bridge cover. Updated guitar-shaped body style for 1956-'57.

| 1950-1952 | Symmetrical body | $700 | $800 |
| 1956-1957 | Guitar-shaped body | $450 | $700 |

Ultratone Lap Steel
1946-1959. Solid maple body, plastic fingerboard, 6 strings.

| 1940s | White | $600 | $800 |
| 1950s | Dark Blue or Seal Brown | $600 | $750 |

Gold Tone
1993-present. Wayne and Robyn Rogers build their intermediate grade, production/custom lap steels in Titusville, Florida. They also offer basses, mandolins, banjos and banjitars.

Gourley
See Dickerson listing.

Gretsch
1883-present. Gretsch offered a variety of steels from 1940-1963. Gretsch actually only made one model; the rest were built by Valco. Currently they offer 2 lap steel models.

Electromatic Console (6158) Twin Neck Steel
1949-1955. Two 6-string necks with 6-on-a-side tuners, Electromatic script logo on end cover plates, 3 knobs, metal control panels and knobs, pearloid covered.

| 1949-1955 | | $650 | $850 |

Electromatic Standard (6156) Lap Steel
1950-1955.

| 1950-1955 | Brown Pearloid | $350 | $450 |

Electromatic Student (6152) Lap Steel
1949-1955. Square bottom, pearloid cover.

| 1949-1955 | Brown Pearloid | $350 | $450 |

1961 Gibson EH-500 Skylark

1950s Gretsch Electromatic

STEELS & LAPS

STEELS & LAPS

Kiesel lap steel

1950s Magnatone G-70

MODEL YEAR	FEATURES	EXC. COND. LOW	HIGH

Jet Mainliner (6147) Steel
1955-1963. Single-neck version of Jet Twin.

1955-1963		$450	$550

Jet Twin Console (6148) Steel
1955-1963. Valco-made, 2 6-string necks, 6-on-a-side tuners. Jet Black.

1955-1963	Black	$650	$850

Guyatone
1933-present. Large Japanese maker. Brands also include Marco Polo, Winston, Kingston, Kent, LaFayette and Bradford. They offered lap steels under various brands from the '30s to the '60s.

Lap Steels
1960s		$200	$300

Table Steels
Three legs, two pickups.

1960s		$300	$350

Harmony
1982-1976. Founded by Wilhelm Schultz and purchased by Sears in 1916. The company evolved into the largest producer of stringed instruments in the U.S. in the '30s. They offered electric lap steels by '36.

Lap Steels
1950s	Various models	$250	$350
1960s	Painted body	$250	$300

Roy Smeck Steel
1950s-1960s. Single neck six-string steel, Roy Smeck logo, three legs, dark finish.

1950s		$400	$500

Table Steel
1960s-1970s. Single neck with black and white plexiglass fingerboard, three legs.

1960s		$300	$400
1970s		$275	$375

K & F (Kaufman & Fender)
See listing under Fender.

Kalamazoo
1933-1942, 1946-1947, 1965-1970. Budget brand produced by Gibson in Kalamazoo, Michigan. They offered lap steels in the '30s and '40s.

Lap Steels
1938-1942, 1946-1947.

1938-1942	Sunburst	$250	$400
1946-1947	Sunburst	$250	$400

Kay
Ca. 1931-present. Huge Chicago manufacturer Kay offered steels from '36 to '60 under their own brand and others. See Guitar section for more company info or Guitar Stories Volume II, by Michael Wright, for a complete history of Kay with detailed model listings.

K-24 Deluxe Steel
1950s	Honey Sunburst	$250	$400
1960s		$250	$400

Lap Steel
1940s. Kay crest logo.

1940s	Blond	$250	$400

Lap Steel with matching amp
1940s	Dark mahogany	$400	$500
1950s	Green	$400	$500

Kiesel
1946-1949. Founded by Lowell Kiesel as L.C. Kiesel Co., Los Angeles, but renamed Carvin in 1949. Kiesel logo on the headstock.

Bakelite Lap Steel
1946. Small guitar-shaped bakelite body, single pickup, two knobs, diamond markers.

1946		$350	$500

Maestro
A budget brand made by Gibson.

Lap Steel
Pearloid, one pickup, six strings.

1940s		$250	$300
1950s		$225	$275

Magnatone
Ca. 1937-1971. Magnatone offered lap steels from '37 to '58. Besides their own brand name, they also produced models under the Dickerson, Oahu, Gourley, and Natural Music Guild brands.

Lap Steel and Amp MOTS Set
Late-1940s-mid-1950s. Matching pearloid acetate covered lap steel and small amp.

1948-1955		$550	$650

Lyric Doubleneck Lap Steel
Ca.1951-1958. Model G-1745-D-W, eight strings per neck, hardwood body.

1950s		$400	$550

Maestro Tripleneck Steel
Ca.1951-1958. Model G-2495-W-W, maple and walnut, eight strings per neck, legs.

1950s		$500	$700

Pearloid (MOTS) Lap Steels
1950s. These were often sold with a matching amp; price here is for lap steel only.

1950s		$300	$400

Marvel
1950-mid 1960s. Budget brand marketed by the Peter Sorkin Company of New York.

Electric Hawaiian Lap Steel
1950s		$125	$175

May Bell
See listing under Slingerland.

McKinney
Lap Steel
1950s	White Pearloid	$250	$350

Melobar
1970-present. Designed by Walt Smith, of Smith Family Music, Melobar instruments feature a guitar

MODEL		EXC. COND.	
YEAR	FEATURES	LOW	HIGH

body with a tilted neck, allowing the guitarist to play lap steel standing up. The instrument was developed and first made in Ed and Rudy Dopyera's Dobro factory. Most were available in 6-, 8-, or 10-string versions. Ted Smith took over operations from his father. Ted retired in late 2002.

10-String Electric Steel
1970s. Double cut guitar-shaped body, portable Melobar-style. Similar model currently offered as the Skreemr.

1970s		$700	$900

6-String Electric Steel
1990s. Solidbody cutaway body shape, portable Melobar-style.

1990s		$600	$700

Skreemr Electric Steel
Early 1990s-present. The classic Melobar in a V (Skreemr SK2000) or doublecut (Skreemr) version. Available in 6-, 8- and 10-string versions.

1990s	6-string version	$500	$600

V-10 Power-Slide Guitar
1982-early 1990s. Solidbody, Flying V-style body, tilted neck, ten strings (six- or eight-string models were available). Similar model now called the Skreemr SK2000.

1981		$700	$900

X-10 Power-Slide Guitar
1981-early 1990s. Solidbody, Explorer-style body, tilted neck, ten strings (six- or eight-string models were available). Called the Power-Slide One in early literature.

1981		$700	$900

National
Ca. 1927-present. Founded in Los Angeles as the National String Instrument Corporation in 1927, the brand has gone through many ownership changes over the years. National offered lap steels from '35 to '68.

Chicagaon Lap Steel
1948-1961. Gray pearloid, metal hand rest.

1948-1961		$300	$400

Console (Dual 8) Steel
1939-1942. Two 8-string necks, parallelogram markers. Black top with white sides.

1939-1942		$900	$1,000

Dynamic Lap Steel
1942-1968. New Yorker-style body, 6 strings, 3 detachable screw-in legs added by 1956.

1942-1968	Various colors	$300	$600

Electric Hawaiian Lap Steel
1935-1937. Cast aluminum round body, 1 pickup, square neck, 6 or 7 strings.

1935-1937	6 strings	$650	$750
1935-1937	7 strings	$700	$800

Grand Console Steel
1947-1968. Two 8-string necks, "Totem Pole" fingerboard markers.

1947-1968		$500	$700

MODEL		EXC. COND.	
YEAR	FEATURES	LOW	HIGH

New Yorker Lap Steel
1939-1967. Introduced as Electric Hawaiian model in 1935. Square end body with stair-step sides, 7 or 8 strings. Black and white finish.

1939-1949		$600	$700
1950-1959		$500	$600
1960-1967		$400	$500

Princess Lap Steel
1942-1947. Strings-through-pickup, parallelogram markers, white pearloid.

1942-1947		$300	$400

Rocket One Ten Lap Steel
1955-1958. Rocket-shaped, white finish.

1955-1958		$300	$400

Trailblazer Steel
1948-1950. Square end, numbered markers, black.

1948-1950		$300	$400

Triplex Chord Changer Lap Steel
1949-1958. Maple and walnut body, 2 knobs, natural.

1950s		$300	$400

Nioma
Regal and others (maybe Dickerson?) made instruments for this brand, most likely for a guitar studio or distributor.

Lap Steel

1930s	Pearloid	$200	$300

Oahu
1926-1985. The Oahu Publishing Company and Honolulu Conservatory, based in Cleveland, published a hughly popular guitar study course. They sold instruments to go with the lessons, starting with acoustic Hawaiian and Spanish guitars, selling large quantities in the '30s. As electric models became popular, Oahu responded with guitar-amp sets. Lap steel and matching amp sets were generally the same color; for example, yellow guitar and yellow amp, or white pearloid guitar and white amp. These sets were originally sold to students who would take private or group lessons. The instruments were made by Oahu, Valco, Harmony, Dickerson, and Rickenbacker and were offered into the '50s and '60s.

Hawaiian Lap Steel

1930s	Sunburst	$350	$425
1940s	Pearloid, Supro-made	$300	$400
1950s	Pearloid or painted	$250	$400

Lap Steel/Amp Set
See also Lap Steel Oahu Amp listing in the Guide's amp section.

1930s	Pearloid, small rectangular amp	$350	$550
1930s	Sunburst, mahogany	$350	$550
1950s	White Valco Amp, 1x10"	$300	$500
1950s	Yellow Valco Amp	$300	$500

National New Yorker

1940 Oahu Tonmaster

STEELS & LAPS

Rickenbacker seven-string

Rickenbacker Model B-6

Lolana Dual 6 Lap Steel
1950-1951. Gold hardware, two six-string necks.
1950-1951 $400 $500

Premier
Ca.1938-ca.1975, 1990s-present. Premier made a variety of instruments, including lap steels, under several brand names.

Recording King
Ca. 1930-1943. Brand used by Montgomery Ward for instruments made by Gibson, Regal, Kay, and Gretsch.
Electric Hawaiian Lap Steel
1930s $350 $450
Roy Smeck Model AB104 Steel
1938-1941. Pear-shaped body, one pickup.
1940s $350 $450

Regal
Ca. 1884-1954. Regal offered their own brand and made instruments for distributors and mass-merchandisers. The company sold out to Harmony in '54.
Acoustic Lap Steel
1970 $200 $250
Electric Hawaiian Lap Steel
1940s $150 $250
Octophone Steel
1930 $300 $500
Reso-phonic Steel
1930s. Dobro-style resonator and spider assembly, round neck, adjustable nut.
1930s $800 $1,100

Rickenbacker
1931-present. Rickenbacker produced steels from '32 to '70.
Acadamy Lap Steel
1946-1947. Bakelite student model, horseshoe pickup. Replaced by Ace.
1946-1947 $250 $350
Ace Lap Steel
1948-1953. Bakelite body, one pickup.
1948-1953 $250 $350
DC-16 Steel
1950-1952. Metal, double eight-string necks.
1950-1952 $550 $700
Electro Doubleneck Steel
1940-1953. Two Bakelite eight-string necks.
1940-1953 $800 $1,300
Electro Tripleneck Steel
1940-1953 $1,000 $1,400
Model 59 Lap Steel
1937-1943. Sheet steel body, one pickup.
1937-1943 $600 $850
Model 100 Lap Steel
1956-1970. Wood body, six strings, block markers, light or Silver Gray finish.
1950s $350 $450

Model A-22 "Frying Pan" Steel
1932-1950, 1954-1958. "Frying Pan" Electro Hawaiian Guitar. Cast aluminum body, one pickup, slotted peghead.
1932-1936 $1,300 $1,500
Model B Steel
1935-1955. Bakelite body and neck, one pickup, string-through-body, decorative metal plates, six strings.
1940s   Black $750 $850
Model BD Steel
1949-1970. Bakelite body, six strings, deluxe version of Model B. Black.
1950s $600 $700
Model CW-6 Steel
1957-1961. Wood body, grille cloth on front, six strings, three legs. Renamed JB (Jerry Byrd) model in 1961.
1960   Walnut $500 $650
Model DW Steel
1955-1961. Wood body, double six- or eight-string necks, optional three legs.
1950s   Two eight-string necks $550 $700
Model G Lap Steel
Ca.1948-1957. Chrome-plated ornate version of Silver Hawaiian, Gold hardware and trim, six or eight strings.
1950s $550 $700
Model S/NS (New Style) Steel
1946-early-1950s. Sheet steel body, one pickup, also available as a doubleneck.
1946-1949   Gray Sparkle $550 $700
Model SD Steel
1949-1953. Deluxe NS, sheet steel body, six, seven or eight strings. Copper Crinkle Finish.
1949-1953 $500 $600
Silver Hawaiian Lap Steel
1937-1943. Chrome-plated sheet steel body, one horseshoe pickup, six strings.
1930s $800 $900

Roland Ball
See Dickerson listing.

Sho-Bud
1956-1980. Founded by Shot Jackson in Nashville. Distributed by Gretsch. Baldwin bought the company in '79 and closed the factory in '80.
Maverick Pedal Steel
Ca. 1970-1980. Beginner model, burl elm cover, 3 pedals.
1970s $450 $600
Pro I
1970-1980. Three pedals, natural.
1970s   Round front pre-1976 $650 $800
1970s   Square front $800 $1,200
Pro II
1973-1980. Bird's-eye maple, double 10-string necks, natural.
1970s   Round front pre-1976 $750 $950
1970s   Square front $950 $1,350

MODEL YEAR	FEATURES	EXC. COND. LOW	HIGH
Pro III			
1975-1980. Metal necks.			
1970s	Round front pre-1976	$850	$1,000
1970s	Square front	$1,000	$1,400
Super Pro			
1977-1980. Doubleneck 10 strings, 8 floor pedals, 6 knee levers, Jet Black.			
1978		$1,400	$1,600

Silvertone

1940-1970. Brand name for instruments sold by Sears.

MODEL YEAR	FEATURES	EXC. COND. LOW	HIGH
Six-String Lap Steels			
1950s		$200	$350
1960s		$150	$225

Slingerland

1916-present. Offered by Slingerland Banjos and Drums. They also sold the May Bell brand. Instruments were made by others and sold by Slingerland in the '30s and '40s.

MODEL YEAR	FEATURES	EXC. COND. LOW	HIGH
May Bell Lap Steel			
1930s. Guitar-shaped lap steel with May Bell logo. This brand also had 1930s Hawaiian and Spanish guitars.			
1930s	Black	$200	$450

Supertone

1914-1941. Brand name for Sears which was replaced by Silvertone. Instruments made by Harmony and others.

MODEL YEAR	FEATURES	EXC. COND. LOW	HIGH
Electric Hawaiian Lap Steel			
1930s		$250	$300

Supro

1935-1968. Budget brand of the National Dobro Company.

MODEL YEAR	FEATURES	EXC. COND. LOW	HIGH
Clipper Lap Steel			
1941-1943. One pickup, bound rosewood fingerboard, dot inlay. Brown pearloid.			
1941-1943		$250	$300
Comet Lap Steel			
1947-1966. One pickup, attached cord, painted-on fingerboard, pearloid.			
1947-1949	Gray pearloid	$250	$300
1950-1966	White pearloid	$250	$300
Comet Steel (with legs)			
1950s-1960s. Three-leg six-string steel version of the lap steel, two knobs, Supro logo on cover plate, single pickup.			
1960s	Black and White	$500	$750
Console 8 Steel			
1958-1960. Eight strings, three legs. Black and White.			
1958-1960		$500	$600
Jet Airliner Steel			
1962-1964. One pickup, totem pole markings, six or eight strings, pearloid, National-made.			
1962-1964	Red	$250	$300

MODEL YEAR	FEATURES	EXC. COND. LOW	HIGH
Professional Steel			
Light Brown pearloid.			
1950s		$250	$300
Special Steel			
1955-1962. Pearloid lap steel, student model, large script "Special" logo near pickup on early models. Red until 1957, White after.			
1955-1957	Red pearloid	$250	$300
1957-1962	White pearloid	$250	$300
Spectator Steel			
1952-1954. Wood body, one pickup, painted-on fingerboard. Natural.			
1952-1954		$200	$275
Student De Luxe Lap Steel			
1952-1955. One pickup, pearloid, large script "Student De Luxe" logo located near pickup. Replaced by Special in 1955.			
1952-1955	Black and white, or red, pearloid	$250	$300
Supreme Lap Steel			
1947-1960. One pickup, painted-on fingerboard. Brown pearloid until ca.1955, then Red until ca.1958, Tulip Yellow after that.			
1940s	Brown pearloid	$250	$400
1950s	Yellow pearloid	$250	$400
Twin Lap Steel			
1948-1955. Two six-string necks, pearloid covering. Renamed Console Steel in 1955.			
1950		$400	$500

Teisco

1946-1974. The Japanese guitar-maker offered many steel models from '55 to around '67. Models offered '55-'61: EG-7L, -K, -R, -NT, -Z, -A, -S, -P, -8L, -NW, and -M. During '61-'67: EG-TW, -O, -U, -L, -6N, -8N, -DB, -DB2, -DT, H-39, H-905, TRH-1, Harp-8 and H-850.

MODEL YEAR	FEATURES	EXC. COND. LOW	HIGH
Hawaiian Lap Steels			
1950s		$100	$200

Timtone Custom Guitars

1993-present. Luthier Tim Diebert builds his professional grade, custom, lap steel guitars in Grand Forks, British Columbia. He also builds guitars and basses.

True Tone

1960s. Brand name sold by Western Auto (hey, everybody was in the guitar biz back then). Probably made by Kay or Harmony.

MODEL YEAR	FEATURES	EXC. COND. LOW	HIGH
Lap Steel			
1950s. Guitar-shaped, single cutaway, single pickup.			
1950s		$100	$200

Varsity

See Dickerson listing.

1930s Supro Hawaiin Electric

Teisco

1930s Vega

MODEL YEAR	FEATURES	EXC. COND. LOW	HIGH

Vega

1903-present. The original Boston-based company was purchased by C.F. Martin in 1970. In '80, the Vega trademark was sold to a Korean company. The company was one of the first to enter the electric market by offering products in '36 and offered lap steels into the early '60s.

DG-DB Steel
Two necks, 8 strings.

1951		$500	$600

Odell Lap Steel
White pearloid.

1950s		$250	$350

Other Lap Steels

1930s		$250	$350
1940s	Art deco-style	$250	$350

Wabash

Brand name of Larry Wexler and Company of Chicago.

Lap Steel (Hawaiian Scene tailpiece)
Twelve frets. Natural.

1950		$150	$250

MODEL YEAR	FEATURES	EXC. COND. LOW	HIGH

Wayne

1998-present. Luthiers Wayne and Michael Charvel, of Paradise, California, added intermediate grade, production, lap steel guitars to their line in '04. They also build guitars.

White

1955-1960. The White brand, named after plant manager Forrest White, was established by Fender to provide steel and small amp sets to teaching studios that were not Fender-authorized dealers. A standard guitar was planned, but never produced.

6 String Steel
1955-1956. White finish, block markers, 2 knobs, 3 legs. The 6 String Steel was usually sold with the matching White Amp Model 80. Possibly only one batch of these was made by Fender in October/November '55.

1955-1956		$600	$800

Wayne lap steel

Mandolins

366   Airline – Bertoncini

MANDOLINS

1920 American Conservatory Style A

1952 Bigsby Grady Martin Doubleneck

MANDOLINS

Airline

Ca. 1958-1968. Brand name for Montgomery Ward. Instruments were built by Kay, Harmony and Valco.

Electric Mandolin (Kay K390)

Early-1960s. In 1962 the K390 was advertised as the "Kay Professional Electric Mandolin." Venetian shape with sunburst spruce top, curly maple back and sides, tube-style pickup, white 'guard, rope-style celluloid binding.

| 1962 | | $350 | $500 |

Mandolin (lower end)

1960s. Acoustic, plainer features.

| 1960s | | $200 | $375 |

Allen

1982-present. Premium grade, production resonators, steel-string flat-tops, and mandolins built by Luthier Randy Allen, Colfax, California.

Alvarez

C.1966-present. An import brand name for St. Louis Music, Alvarez currently offers intermediate grade, production, mandolins.

Model A Mandolins

Classic F-style mandolin features, round soundhole or F-holes. Models include the A700 and A910.

| 1970s | | $300 | $550 |

American Conservatory (Lyon & Healy)

Late-1800s-early-1900s. Mainly catalog sales of guitars and mandolins from the Chicago maker. Marketed as a less expensive alternative to the Lyon & Healy Washburn product line.

Mandolin Style G2603

Early-1900s. Bowl back-style, 28 rosewood ribs (generally more ribs and use of rosewood ribs versus mahogany indicates higher quality), color corded soundhole and edge inlay, inlaid tortoise shell celluloid guard plate underneath strings and below the soundhole, bent top, butterfly headstock inlay.

| 1917 | | $300 | $375 |

Mandolin Style G2604

Early-1900s. Bowl back-style, 42 rosewood ribs (generally more ribs incidated higher quality), extra fancy color corded soundhole and edge inlay around, extra fancy inlaid tortoise shell celluloid guard plate underneath strings and below the soundhole, bent top, butterfly headstock inlay.

| 1917 | | $450 | $525 |

Andersen Stringed Instruments

1978-present. Luthier Steve Andersen builds his premium grade, production/custom mandolins in Seattle, Washington. He also builds guitars.

Applause

1994-present. Applause currently offers intermediate grade, production, mandolins. Kaman

Music's entry-level Ovation-styled import brand added mandolins in 1994.

MAE148 Mandolin

1994-present. Acoustic/electric import.

| 1990s | Black | $225 | $275 |

Aria/Aria Pro II

1960-present. Intermediate grade, production, acoustic and electric mandolins from Aria/Aria Pro II, which added Japanese and Korean mandolins to their line in '76.

AM200/BS Style A Mandolin

1994-present. Beginner-grade import, pear-shaped body, Sunburst.

| 1990s | | $175 | $250 |

AM300/BS Style F Mandolin

1990s. F-style, Sunburst.

| 1990s | | $325 | $400 |

PM750 Style F Mandolin

Mid-1970s. F-style Loar copy, Sunburst.

| 1976 | | $400 | $500 |

Armstrong, Rob

1971-present. Custom mandolins made in Coventry, England, by luthier Rob Armstrong. He also builds basses, flat-tops, and parlor guitars.

Atkin Guitars

1993-present. Luthier Alister Atkin builds his production/custom mandolins in Canterbury, England. He also builds flat-top guitars.

Austin

1999-present. Budget and intermediate grade, production, mandolins imported by St. Louis Music. They also offer guitars, basses and banjos.

Bacon & Day

Established in 1921 by David Day and Paul Bacon, primarily known for fine quality tenor and plectrum banjos in the 1920s and 1930s.

Mandolin Banjo "Orchestra"

1920s. Mandolin neck and banjo body with open back, headstock with Bacon logo.

| 1920s | | $400 | $500 |

Senorita Banjo Mandolin

| 1930s | | $400 | $600 |

Silverbell #1 Banjo Mandolin

1920s. Fancy appointments, closed-back resonator.

| 1920s | | $1,100 | $1,200 |

Beltone

1920s. A brand name of Perlberg & Halpin

Bertoncini Stringed Instruments

1995-present. Luthier Dave Bertoncini mainly builds flat-top guitars in Olympia, Washington, but has also built mandolins.

| MODEL YEAR | FEATURES | EXC. COND. LOW | HIGH |

The Vintage Guitar Price Guide shows low to high values for items in all-original excellent condition, and, where applicable, with original case or cover.

The Official Vintage Guitar Magazine Price Guide 2005

MODEL YEAR	FEATURES	EXC. COND. LOW	HIGH

Bigsby
Ca. 1947-present. Paul Arthur Bigsby built six electric mandolins.

Bishline
1985-present. Luthier Robert Bishline builds custom-made mandolins in Tulsa, Oklahoma. He also builds flat-tops, resonators and banjos.

Blue Star
1984-present. Luthier Bruce Herron builds his intermediate grade, production/custom, electric solidbody mandolins in Fennville, Michigan. He also builds guitars, lap steels, dulcimers, and ukes.

Bohmann
1878-ca.1926. Established by Czechoslavakian-born Joseph Bohmann in Chicago.
Fancy Bowl Mandolin
Spruce top, marquetry trimmed, inlay, pearl.

1890		$400	$650

Brandt
Early 1900s. John Brandt started making mandolin-family instruments in Chicago around 1898.
Mandola
1900s. Spruce top, rosewood body, scroll headstock, pearl and abalone fretboard binding.

1900		$1,200	$1,425

Presentation Mandolin
Spruce top, tortoise shell-bound.

1900s		$700	$950

Breedlove
1990-present. Founded by Larry Breedlove and Steve Henderson. Professional and premium grade, production/custom, mandolins made in Tumalo, Oregon. They also produce guitars.
K-5 Mandolin
Asymmetric carved top, maple body.

1990s		$1,600	$1,700

Olympic Mandolin
Solid spruce top, teardrop-shaped, oval soundhole, highly flamed maple back, Sunburst.

1990s		$1,200	$1,350

Brian Moore
1992-present. Moore offers premium grade, production/custom, semi-hollow electric mandolins. They also build guitars and basses.

Bruno and Sons
1834-present. Established in 1834 by Charles Bruno, primarily as a distributor, Bruno and Sons marketed a variety of brandnames, including their own; currently part of Kaman. In the '60s or '70s, a Japanese-made solidbody electric mandolin was sold under the Bruno name.

Banjo Mandolin
Open back, 10" model.

1920s		$300	$375

Bowl Back Mandolin
1890s-1920s. Brazilian rosewood, spruce, rosewood ribs.

1920s		$400	$525

Calace
1825-present. Nicola Calace started The Calace "Liuteria" lute-making workshop in 1825 on the island of Procida, which is near Naples. The business is now in Naples and still in the family.
Lyre/Harp-Style Mandolin
Late-1800s-early-1900s. Lyre/harp-style, eight strings, round soundhole, slightly bent top. Condition is important for these older instruments and the price noted is for a fully functional, original or pro-restored example.

1900		$750	$1,500

Carvin
1946-present. Carvin offered solidbody electric mandolins from around 1956 to the late '60s, when they switched to a traditional pear-shaped electric/acoustic.
MB Mandolins
1956-1968. Solidbody, one pickup. Single cutaway Les Paul shape until '64, double cutaway Jazzmaster/Strat shape after. Models include the #1-MB and the #2-MB, with different pickups.

1950s		$600	$800

Collings
1986-present. Professional and premium grade, production/custom, mandolins built in Austin, Texas. Collings added mandolins to their line in '99. They also build guitars.

Conrad
Ca. 1968-1977. Imported from Japan by David Wexler and Company, Chicago, Illinois. Mid- to better-quality copy guitars, mandolins and banjos.
Mandolin

1970s		$100	$175

Crafter
2000-present. Line of intermediate grade, production, acoustic and acoustic/electric mandolins from Hohner. They also offer guitars and a bass.

Crestwood
1970s. Copy models imported by La Playa Distributing Company of Detroit.
Mandolin
Includes models 3039 (electric A-style), 3041 (bowl back-style, flower pickguard), 3043 (bowl back-style, plain pickguard), 71820 (A-style), and 71821 (F-style).

1970s		$125	$250

Breedlove Olympic

Carvin 1-MB

MANDOLINS

D'Angelico

Dean Playmate

MODEL		EXC. COND.	
YEAR	FEATURES	LOW	HIGH

Cromwell

1935-1939. Private branded instruments made by Gibson at their Parsons Street factory in Kalamazoo. Distributed by a variety of mail order companies such as Continental, Grossman, and Richter & Phillips. Gibson private branded during the depression to keep their staff busy, and to enter the low-to-mid priced market.

GM-4 Mandolin

1935-1939. Style A with F-holes, solid wood arched top, mahogany back and sides, block capital letter Cromwell headstock logo, dot markers, elevated pickguard. Sunburst.

1935-1939		$650	$800

D'Angelico

1932-1949. Handcrafted by John D'Angelico. Models include Excel, Teardrop, and Scroll. Appointments can vary from standard to higher-end so each mandolin should be evaluated on a case-by-case basis.

Mandolin

1932-1949. Various models and appointments.

1932-1949	High-end appointments	$20,000	$25,000

D'Aquisto

1965-1995. James D'Aquisto apprenticed under D'Angelico. He started his own production in 1965.

Mandolin

1970s. Various models and appointments.

1970s	Only 3 made	$23,000	$30,000

Dean

1976-present. Intermediate grade, production, acoustic and acoustic/electric mandolins made overseas. They also offer guitars, banjos, basses, and amps.

Dearstone

1993-present. Luthier Ray Dearstone builds his professional and premium grade, custom, mandolin-family instruments in Blountville, Tennessee. He also builds guitars and violins.

DeCava Guitars

1983-present. Premium grade, production/custom, mandolins built by luthier Jim DeCava in Stratford, Connecticut. He also builds guitars, ukes, and banjos.

DeLucia

Early-1900s.

Mandolins

Early-1900s. High quality material, rosewood body, fine ornamentation.

1910s		$1,000	$1,200

Dennis Hill Guitars

1991-present. Premium grade, production/custom, mandolins built by luthier Dennis Hill in Panama City, Florida. He has also built dulcimers, guitars, and violins.

Ditson

Mandolins made for the Oliver Ditson Company of Boston, an instrument dealer and music publisher. Turn of the century and early-1900s models were bowl back-style with the Ditson label. The 1920s Ditson Style A flat back mandolins were made by Martin.

Style 1 Standard Mandolin

Size three small body, plain styling.

1922		$1,150	$1,250

Style A Mandolin

1920s. Style A flat back made by Martin, mahogany sides and back, plain ornamentation.

1920s		$700	$900

Victory Bowl Back Mandolin

1890s. Brazilian rib bowl back-style with fancy inlays.

1890s		$650	$800

Dobro

1929-1942, 1954-present. Dobro offered mandolins throughout their early era and from the '60s to the mid-'90s.

Mandolin (wood body)

Resonator on wood body.

1930s		$1,100	$1,300
1940s		$1,100	$1,300
1960s		$900	$1,100

Model 65 Mandolin

Wood body, sandblasted design.

1929		$1,200	$1,400

Eastman

1992-present. Intermediate and professional grade, production, mandolins built in China. Eastman added mandolins in '04. They also build guitars, violins, and cellos.

EKO

1961-1985. The Italian-made EKOs were imported by LoDuca Brothers of Milwaukee.

Baritone Mandolin

1960s. Baritone mandolin with ornate inlays.

1960s		$300	$400

Octave Mandolin

1960s. Octave mandolin with ornate inlays.

1960s		$275	$375

Epiphone

1928-present. Intermediate grade, production, acoustic mandolins. Epiphone has offered several mandolin-family models over the years. Those from the '30s to the '60s were U.S.-made, the later models imported.

MODEL		EXC. COND.	
YEAR	FEATURES	LOW	HIGH

Adelphi Mandolin
1932-1948. A-style body, maple back and sides, F-holes, single-bound top and back.

1945-1946		$575	$725

Recording A Mandolin

1920s	Walnut	$700	$850

Strand Mandolin
1932-1958. Walnut back and sides, F-holes, multibound, Sunburst.

1944		$600	$750

Venetian Electric Mandolin
1961-1970. Gibson-made, pear-shaped body, four pole P-90 'dog-ear' mounted pickup, volume and tone knobs, dot markers. Sunburst finish.

1961-1964		$1,400	$1,900
1965-1970		$1,200	$1,500

Zephyr Mandolin
1939-1958. A-style, electric, F-holes, maple body, one pickup, slotted block inlay.

1950s		$600	$700

Esquire
1930s. Student level instruments with painted Esquire logo and painted wood grain.

Mandolins
1930s. Laminate A-style wood body, sunburst.

1930s		$200	$225

Euphonon
1934-1944. Euphonon was a brand name of the Larson Brothers of Chicago. The brand was introduced so Larson could compete in the guitar market with the new larger body 14-fret guitar models. Production also included mandolins, and most models were A-style, with teardrop body and flat backs.

Mandolin
1934-1944. Various models and appointments, each mandolin should be evaluated on a case-by-case basis.

1934-1944		$3,500	$10,000

Everett Guitars
1977-present. Luthier Kent Everett, of Atlanta, Georgia, mainly builds guitars, but has also built mandolins.

Evergreen Mountain
1971-present. Professional grade, custom, mandolins built by luthier Jerry Nolte in Cove, Oregon. He also builds guitars and basses.

Fairbanks (A.J.)
1875-ca.1920s. Primarily known for banjos, Fairbanks also offered mandolins.

Mandolin
1890-1910. Typical late-1890s bent top-style mandolin, with decorated top and rope-style binding.

1900s	Natural	$200	$350

Fender
1946-present. Intermediate grade, production, acoustic and acoustic/electric mandolins. Fender also offered an electric mandolin for 20 years.

Mandolin
1956-1976. Electric solidbody, often referred to as the Mandocaster by collectors.

1956-1957	Blond	$2,200	$2,600
1958-1959	Sunburst	$1,900	$2,300
1960-1961	Sunburst	$1,700	$2,100
1962-1963	Sunburst	$1,600	$2,000
1964-1965	Sunburst	$1,500	$1,900
1966-1970	Sunburst	$1,300	$1,600
1971-1976	Sunburst	$1,200	$1,500

Fine Resophonic
1988-present. Professional grade, production/custom, wood and metal-bodied resophonic mandolins built by luthiers Mike Lewis and Pierre Avocat in Vitry Sur Seine, France. They also build guitars and ukes.

Flatiron
1977-present. Gibson purchased Flatiron in 1987. Production was in Bozeman, Montana until the end of 1996, when Gibson closed the Flatiron mandolin workshop and moved mandolin assembly to Nashville. Currently Flatirons are available on a special order basis.

A-5 Artist Mandolin
Teardrop shape, F-holes, flamed maple body and neck, carved spruce top, bound ebony board, gold hardware, fern headstock inlay.

1980s	Sunburst	$1,300	$1,600

A-5 Mandolin
Teardrop shape, F-holes, flamed maple body and neck, carved spruce top, unbound ebony board, nickel hardware fleur-de-lis headstock inlay.

1980s	Sunburst	$1,300	$1,600

Cadet Mandolin
Flat top, oval body, spruce top, maple body, rosewood board, nickel hardware.

1990s	Black	$350	$500

F-5 Artist Mandolin
F-style body, F-holes, flamed maple body and neck, carved spruce top, x-braced, bound ebony board, gold hardware, fern headstock inlay.

1977-1987	Sunburst, pre-Gibson	$3,000	$3,500
1988-1999	Sunburst, Gibson era	$3,000	$3,500

Festival A Mandolin
Teardrop shape, carved spruce top, maple body, ebony board, F-holes.

1990s		$900	$1,250
2000s	Gibson Nashville assembly	$1,200	$1,400

Evergreen Mountain

Flatiron A-5

Flatiron Festival

Gibson A-5

MODEL YEAR	FEATURES	EXC. COND. LOW	HIGH
Festival F Mandolin			

F-style body, F-holes, maple body and neck, carved spruce top, tone bar bracing, ebony board, nickel hardware, fern headstock inlay, top binding.

1980s	Pre-Bozeman	$1,800	$2,200
1990s		$1,600	$1,800
2000s	Gibson Nashville assembly	$1,700	$2,000

Model 1 Mandolin

Oval shape, spruce top, maple body, rosewood board.

| 1980s | Natural | $350 | $525 |

Model 2-K Mandolin

Oval body, flamed koa back and sides, spruce top, ebony fingerboard.

| 1980s | Natural | $500 | $675 |

Model 2-M Mandolin

1980s. Round teardrop body, flat top and back.

| 1980s | | $350 | $500 |

Model 3 Octave Mandolin

Oval shape, bird's-eye maple (MB) or curly maple (MC) body, spruce top, ebony board, longer scale.

| 1980s | Natural bird's-eye | $650 | $900 |

Performer F Mandolin

F-style body, F-holes, maple body and neck, carved spruce top, tone bar bracing, ebony board, nickel hardware, fern headstock inlay, top, back and headstock binding.

| 1990s | | $1,500 | $1,800 |

Fletcher Brock Stringed Instruments

1992-present. Custom mandolin-family instruments made by luthier Fletcher Brock in Ketchum, Idaho. He also builds guitars.

Fylde

1973-present. Luthier Roger Bucknall builds his intermediate and professional, production/custom mandolins and mandolas in Penrith, Cumbria, United Kingdom. He also builds guitars and basses, bouzoukis, and citterns.

G.L. Stiles

1960-1994. Built by Gilbert Lee Stiles in Florida. He also built acoustics, solidbodies, basses, steels, and banjos.

Mandolin

| 1960s | | $400 | $600 |

Gibson

1880s-present. Orville Gibson created the violin-based mandolin body-style that replaced the bowl back-type. Currently Gibson offers professional, premium and presentation grade, production/custom, mandolins.

Special Designations

Snakehead headstock: 1922-1927 with production possible for a few months plus or minus.

Lloyd Loar era: Mid-1922-late 1924 with production possible for a few months plus or minus.

MODEL YEAR	FEATURES	EXC. COND. LOW	HIGH
A Mandolin			

1902-1933. Oval soundhole, snakehead headstock 1922-1927, Loar era mid-1922-late-1924.

1902-1909	Orange Top	$1,300	$1,500
1910-1918	Orange Top	$1,500	$1,700
1918-1921	Brown	$1,700	$2,000
1922-1924	Loar era	$2,800	$3,400
1925-1933		$2,500	$2,800

A Jr. Mandolin

1920-1927. The Junior was the entry level mandolin for Gibson, but like most entry level Gibsons (re: Les Paul Junior), they were an excellent product. Oval soundhole, dot markers, plain tuner buttons. Becomes A-0 in 1927.

| 1920-1927 | Sheraton Brown | $1,250 | $1,400 |

A-0 Mandolin

1927-1933. Replaces A Jr., oval soundhole, dot inlay. Brown finish.

| 1927-1933 | | $1,250 | $1,400 |

A-00 Mandolin

1933-1943. Oval soundhole, dot inlay, carved bound top.

| 1933-1943 | Sunburst | $1,500 | $1,700 |

A-1 Mandolin

1902-1918, 1922-1927, 1933-1943. Snakehead headstock 1923-1927.

1902-1918	Orange	$1,700	$1,900
1922-1924	Loar era	$3,000	$3,600
1925-1927	Black	$2,600	$3,500
1933-1943	Sunburst, F-holes	$2,600	$3,500

A-2/A-2Z Mandolin

1902-1908, 1918-1922. A-2Z 1922-1927. Renamed A-2 1927-1928. Snakehead headstock 1923-1927. Lloyd Loar era mid-1922-late-1924.

1902-1908	Orange	$1,900	$2,100
1918-1921	Brown	$2,100	$2,300
1918-1922	White (optional)	$2,400	$2,700
1922-1924	Loar Era	$3,000	$4,000
1925-1928		$2,300	$2,500

A-3 Mandolin

1902-1922. Oval soundhole, single-bound body, dot inlay.

| 1902-1905 | Various colors | $2,000 | $2,200 |
| 1906-1922 | Various colors | $2,200 | $2,400 |

A-4 Mandolin

1902-1935. Oval soundhole, single-bound body, dot inlay, snakehead 1923-1927.

1902-1917	Various colors	$2,000	$2,500
1918-1921	Dark mahogany	$2,500	$2,800
1922-1924	Loar era	$4,500	$5,000
1925-1935	Various colors	$2,800	$3,200

A-5 Mandolin

1957-1979. Oval soundhole, maple back and sides, dot inlay, scroll headstock. Sunburst.

1957-1964		$2,300	$2,900
1965-1969		$2,200	$2,800
1970-1979		$2,000	$2,600

A-5 G Mandolin

1988-1996. Less ornate version of the A-5 L, abalone fleur-de-lis headstock inlay.

| 1988-1996 | | $1,400 | $1,650 |

MODEL YEAR	FEATURES	EXC. COND. LOW	HIGH

A-5 L Mandolin
1988-present. A-5-style body, raised fingerboard, flowerpot headstock inlay, curly maple and spruce.

1988-1999	Sunburst	$2,100	$2,300

A-12 Mandolin
1970-1979. F-holes, long neck, dot inlay, fleur-de-lis inlay. Sunburst.

1970-1979		$1,500	$1,900

A-40 Mandolin
1948-1970. F-holes, bound top, dot inlay. Natural or Sunburst.

1948-1949		$1,100	$1,400
1950-1964		$1,000	$1,300
1965-1970		$900	$1,100

A-50 Mandolin
1933-1971. A-style oval bound body, F-holes. Sunburst.

1933-1941	Larger 11.25" body	$1,400	$1,600
1942-1965	Smaller 10" body	$1,200	$1,400
1966-1971		$1,000	$1,200

A-C Century Mandolin
1935-1937. Flat back, bound body, oval soundhole.

1935-1937	Sunburst	$2,800	$3,200

Army and Navy Special Style DY/Army-Navy Mandolin
1918-1922. Lower-end, flat top and back, round soundhole, no logo, round label with model name. Reintroduced as Army-Navy (AN Custom) 1988-1996.

1918-1922	Brown stain	$850	$1,000

Bill Monroe Model F Mandolin
1995. Limited run of 200.

1995	Sunburst	$8,000	$10,000

C-1 Mandolin
1932. Flat top, mahogany back and sides, oval soundhole, painted on pickguard, a 1932 version of the Army and Navy Special. This model was private branded for Kel Kroydon in the early-1930s.

1932	Natural	$900	$1,100

EM-100/EM-125 Mandolin
1938-1943. Initially called EM-100, renamed EM-125 in 1941-1943. Style A (pear-shape) archtop body, single blade pickup, two knobs on either side of bridge, dot markers, tortoise pickguard. Sunburst.

1938-1940	EM-100	$1,800	$2,100
1941-1943	EM-125	$1,600	$1,800

EM-150 Mandolin
1936-1971. Electric, A-00 body, one Charlie Christian pickup early on, one P-90 later, bound body. Sunburst.

1936-1940	Charlie Christian pickup	$1,800	$2,400
1941-1949	Rectangular pickup	$1,500	$1,900
1949-1965	P-90 pickup	$1,500	$1,800
1966-1971	P-90 pickup	$1,200	$1,500

EM-200/Florentine Mandolin
1954-1971. Electric solidbody, one pickup, gold-plated hardware, 2 control knobs, dot markers. Sunburst. Called the EM-200 in 1960 and 1961.

1954-1960	Florentine	$2,200	$2,600
1960-1961	Renamed EM-200	$2,100	$2,500

MODEL YEAR	FEATURES	EXC. COND. LOW	HIGH
1962-1971	Renamed Florentine	$2,000	$2,400

F-2 Mandolin
1902-1934. Oval soundhole, pearl inlay, star and crescent inlay on peghead.

1902-1909	3-point	$3,000	$4,000
1910-1917	2-point	$3,000	$4,000
1918-1921	2-point	$3,500	$4,500
1922-1924	Loar era	$5,000	$6,500
1925-1934		$3,500	$4,500

F-3 Mandolin
1902-1908. Three-point body, oval soundhole, scroll peghead, pearl inlayed pickguard, limited production model. Black top with Red back and sides.

1902-1908		$3,800	$4,800

F-4 Mandolin
1902-1943. Oval soundhole, rope pattern binding. Various colors.

1902-1909	3-point	$4,000	$5,000
1910-1917	2-point	$4,000	$5,000
1918-1921	2-point	$5,000	$5,500
1922-1924	Loar era	$6,500	$8,500
1925-1943		$4,500	$5,000

F-5 Mandolin
1922-1943; 1949-1980. F-holes, triple-bound body and pickguard. The 1920s Lloyd Loar era F-5s are extremely valuable. Reintroduced in 1949 with single-bound body, redesigned in 1970.

1922-1924	Loar era	$110,000	$120,000
1925-1928	Fern, Master-built	$65,000	$70,000
1928-1929	Fern, not Master-built	$55,000	$60,000
1930-1931	Fern peghead inlay	$45,000	$50,000
1932-1935	Fern peghead inlay	$35,000	$40,000
1936-1940	Fern (limited production)	$30,000	$35,000
1940-1943	Fleur-de-lis peghead inlay	$28,000	$32,000
1949	Flower pot, mahogany neck	$8,000	$15,000
1950-1953	Flower pot, maple neck	$7,500	$8,000
1954	Flower pot peghead inlay	$7,000	$7,500
1955-1956	Flower pot peghead inlay	$6,500	$7,000
1957-1959	Flower pot peghead inlay	$6,000	$6,500
1960-1965		$4,500	$5,000
1966-1969	Sunburst	$4,000	$4,500
1971-1980	Sunburst	$3,500	$4,000

F-5 Bella Voce Mandolin
1989. Custom Shop master-built model, high-end materials and construction, engraved tailpiece with "Bella Voce F-5". Sunburst.

1989		$8,500	$8,700

F-5 L Mandolin
1978-present. Reissue of Loar F-5, gold hardware, fern headstock inlay (flowerpot inlay with silver hardware also offered for '88-'91). Sunburst.

1978-1999		$4,200	$5,000

Gibson F-4

1927 Gibson F-5

MANDOLINS

1915 Gibson K-2 mandocello

Gilchrist Model 5

MANDOLINS

MODEL YEAR	FEATURES	EXC. COND. LOW	HIGH
F-5 V Mandolin			
Varnish Cremona Brown Sunburst finish.			
1995		$6,600	$6,800
F-7 Mandolin			
1934-1940. F-holes, single-bound body, neck and pickguard, fleur-de-lis peghead inlay. Sunburst.			
1934-1937		$8,000	$9,000
F-9 Mandolin			
2000s. No frills F-5 style, carved spruce top.			
2000s		$1,800	$2,000
F-10 Mandolin			
1934-1936. Slight upgrade of the 1934 F-7 with extended fingerboard and upgraded inlay. Black finish.			
1934-1936		$7,500	$8,500
F-12 Mandolin			
1934-1937, 1948-1980. F-holes, bound body and neck, scroll inlay, raised fingerboard until 1937, fingerboard flush with top 1948-on. Sunburst.			
1934-1937		$6,500	$8,000
1948-1959		$3,500	$3,700
1960-1969		$3,000	$3,500
1970-1980		$2,000	$3,000
H-1 Mandola			
1902-1936. Has same features as A-1 mandolin, but without snakehead headstock.			
1902-1908	Orange	$2,000	$2,200
1918-1921	Brown	$2,200	$2,400
1922-1924	Loar era	$3,000	$4,000
1925-1928		$2,400	$2,600
H-1 E Mandola			
Late-1930s. Limited number built, electric with built-in adjustable bar pickup. Sunburst.			
1938		$3,600	$3,800
H-2 Mandola			
1902-1922. Has same features as A-4 mandolin.			
1902-1917	Various colors	$2,200	$2,700
1918-1921	Dark Mahogany	$2,600	$2,800
H-4 Mandola			
1910-1940. Same features as F-4 mandolin.			
1910-1921		$4,000	$5,500
1922-1924	Loar era	$6,500	$8,000
1925-1940		$5,000	$5,500
H-5 Mandola			
1923-1929 (available by special order 1929-1936), 1990-1991. Same features as the high-end F-5 Mandolin. This is a very specialized market and instruments should be evaluated on a case-by-case basis.			
1923-1924	Loar ear	$35,000	$55,000
1925-1928	Fern, Master-built	$25,000	$45,000
1928-1929	Fern, not Master-built	$25,000	$40,000
1990-1991	Limited production	$5,000	$5,500
K-1 Mandocello			
1902-1943. Same features as H-1 mandola, off & on production, special order available.			
1902-1908	Orange	$2,200	$2,400
1918-1921	Brown	$2,400	$2,600
1922-1924	Loar era	$3,200	$4,200

MODEL YEAR	FEATURES	EXC. COND. LOW	HIGH
K-2 Mandocello			
1902-1922. Same features as A-4 mandolin.			
1902-1917	Black or Red mahogany	$2,800	$3,300
1918-1922		$3,000	$3,500
K-4 Mandocello			
1912-1929 (offered as special order post-1929). Same features as F-4 mandolin. Sunburst.			
1912-1921		$6,500	$5,000
1922-1924	Loar era	$8,500	$10,000
1925-1929		$6,500	$7,000
M-6 (octave guitar)			
2000s. Six-string octave-up, short neck, A-style mandolin body. Sunburst.			
2000s		$1,200	$1,400
MB-1 Mandolin Banjo			
1922-1923, 1925-1937.			
1920s		$800	$1,050
MB-2 Mandolin Banjo			
1920-1923, 1926-1937.			
1920s		$1,000	$1,200
MB-3 Mandolin Banjo			
1923-1939.			
1920s		$1,200	$1,400
MB-4 Mandolin Banjo			
1923-1932. Fleur-de-lis inlay.			
1920s		$1,300	$1,600
Style J Mando Bass			
1912-1930 (special order post-1930). A-style body, four strings, round soundhole, bound top, dot inlay.			
1912-1930		$3,300	$3,900
Style TL-1Tenor Lute Mandolin			
1924-1926. A-style, four strings, F-holes, dot inlay. Natural top with Brown back and sides.			
1924-1926		$1,500	$1,800

Gilchrist

1978-present. Premium and prestation grade, custom, mandolins made by luthier Steve Gilchrist of Warrnambool, Australia. Custom ordered but were also initially distributed through Gruhn Guitars, Nashville, TN and then exclusively by Carmel Music Company. Designs are based upon Gibson mandolins built between 1910 and 1925.

Model 5 Mandolin

1978-present. Based on the Gibson 1922-1924 Loar-era F-5 mandolin, Gilchrist slant logo, spruce top, flamed maple back, sides, and neck, ebony board, multiple binding. Sunburst.

1978-1995	Sunburst	$12,000	$14,000
1996-2003	Sunburst	$15,000	$18,000

Givens

1962-1992. Luthier R. L. (Bob) Givens handcrafted about 800 mandolins and another 700 in a production shop. Price ranges established with assistance from Greg Boyd.

A Mandolin

1962-1975. Early production A-style.

1962-1975		$2,000	$2,700

MODEL		EXC. COND.	
YEAR	FEATURES	LOW	HIGH

A-3 Mandolin
Mid-1970s-mid-1980s. Distinguished by use of decal (the only model with Givens decal).

1975-1988		$2,000	$2,500

A-4 Mandolin
1988-1993. No fingerboard binding, simple "block-like multiple-line RL Givens" inlay, nicer maple.

1988-1993		$1,700	$2,200

A-5 Mandolin
1988-1993. Bound fingerboard, pearl headstock inlay.

1988-1993		$1,500	$2,000

A-6 (Torch) Mandolin
1988-1992. Torch inlay (the only model with this), Gold hardware, snow flake markers.

1988-1992		$2,500	$3,500

A-6 Custom Mandolin
1991-1992. Elaborate customized A-6 model.

1991-1992		$3,600	$4,200

F-5 (Fern) Mandolin
1973-1985. Givens' own version with fern ornamentation.

1973-1985		$3,500	$4,500

F-5 (Loar) Mandolin
1962-1972. Givens' own version based upon the Loar model F-5.

1962-1972		$3,500	$4,500

F-5 (Torch) Mandolin
1988-1992. Givens F-5 with torch inlay (the only F model with this).

1988-1992		$6,000	$8,000

F-5 (Wheat Straw) Mandolin
1986-1988. Givens F-5-style with Wheat Straw ornamentation.

1986-1988		$5,000	$6,200

Godin
1987-present. Intermediate grade, production, acoustic/electric mandolins from luthier Robert Godin. They also build basses and guitars.

A-8 Electric Mandolin

2003		$500	$700

Gold Tone
1993-present. Wayne and Robyn Rogers build their intermediate grade, production/custom mandolins in Titusville, Florida. They also offer lap steels, basses, banjos and banjitars.

Goya
1955-present. Korean-made mandolins. They also build guitars and banjos. Originally made in Sweden, by the late '70s from Japan, then from Korea. See Guitar section for more company info.

Mandolin

1960s		$250	$350

Gretsch
1883-present. Gretsch started offering mandolins by the early 1900s. See Guitar section for more company info. Currently Gretsch does not offer mandolins.

New Yorker Mandolin
Late 1940s-late 1950s. Teardrop shape, F-holes, arched top and back, spruce top, maple back, sides, and neck, rosewood board.

1950s		$450	$550

GTR
1974-1978. GTR (for George Gruhn, Tut Taylor, Randy Wood) was the original name for Gruhn Guitars in Nashville (it was changed in 1976). GTR imported mandolins and banjos from Japan. An A-style (similar to a current Gibson A-5 L) and an F-style (similar to mid- to late-1920s F-5 with fern pattern) were offered. The instruments were made at the Moridaira factory in Matsumoto, Japan by factory foreman Sadamasa Tokaida. Quality was relatively high but quantities were limited.

F-Style Mandolin
1974-1978. F-5 Fern copy with slant GTR logo on headstock, handmade in Japan.

1970s	Sunburst	$2,000	$2,500

Harmony
1982-1976. Founded by Wilhelm Schultz in 1892, and purchased by Sears in 1916. The company evolved into one of the largest producers of stringed instruments in the U.S. in the 1930s. See Guitar section for more company info.

Baroque H425 Mandolin
F-style arched body, close grained spruce top. Sunburst.

1970		$200	$300

Lute H331 Mandolin
1960s-1970s. A-style, flat-top and back, student level.

1960s	Sunburst	$150	$200

Monterey H410 Mandolin
A-style arched body. Sunburst.

1950s		$150	$250
1960s		$150	$250
1970s		$150	$225

Heiden Stringed Instruments
1974-present. Luthier Michael Heiden builds his premium grade, production/custom mandolins in Chilliwack, British Columbia. He also builds guitars.

Heritage
1985-present. Started by former Gibson employees in Gibson's Kalamazoo plant, Heritage offered mandolins for a number of years.

H-5 Mandolin
1986-1990s. F-style scroll body, F-holes.

1989		$2,700	$3,500

Höfner
1887-present. Old World company since 1887, offering a wide variety of products, including mandolins, particularly during the guiter boom of the 1960s.

Givens A-4

Gold Tone GM-110

MANDOLINS

Hondo mandolin

Kalamazoo A-style

MODEL YEAR	FEATURES	EXC. COND. LOW	HIGH

A-Style Mandolin
1960s. Pear-shaped A-style with cat's-eye F-holes, block-style markers, engraved headstock, "Genuine Hofner Original" and "Made in Germany" on back of headstock.

| 1968-1969 | Transparent Brown | $400 | $450 |

Hohner
1857-present. Intermediate grade, production, acoustic and acoustic/electric mandolins. They also offer guitars, basses, and ukes.

Hondo
1969-1987, 1991-present. Budget grade, production, Imported mandolins. They also offer basses and guitars. Hondo also offered mandolins from around '74 to '87.

Mandolin
1974-1987. Hondo offered F-style, A-style, and bowl back mandolin models.

| 1970s | | $100 | $125 |

Hopf
1906-present. Professional grade, production/custom, mandolins made in Germany. They also make basses, guitars and flutes.

Howe-Orme
1893-early-1900s. Edward Howe patented a guitar-shaped mandolin on November 14, 1893.

Mandola
1893-early-1900s. Guitar body-style with narrow waist, not the common mandolin F or S-style body, pressed (not carved) spruce top, mahogany back and sides, flat-top guitar-type trapeze bridge, decalomania near bridge.

| 1887 | Natural | $1,300 | $1,700 |

Ibanez
1932-present. Ibanez offered mandolins from around 1977 to the early 1980s. See Guitar section for more company info.

Model 514 Mandolin
1977-early 1980s. Arched back, spruce, rosewood, dot inlays.

| 1970s | Sunburst | $300 | $400 |

Model 521 A Mandolin
1977-early 1980s. A-style, carved top, Sunburst, F-holes, gold hardware.

| 1980 | | $250 | $350 |

Model 524 Mandolin
1977-early 1980s. F-5 copy, solid wood carved top and solid wood back.

| 1970s | Sunburst | $500 | $900 |

Imperial
1890-1922. Imperial mandolins were made by the William A. Cole Company of Boston.

Bowl Back Mandolin

| 1890s | | $250 | $350 |

J.B. Player
1980s-present. Budget grade, production, imported mandolins. They also offer basses, banjos and guitars.

J.R. Zeidler Guitars
1977-present. Luthier John Zeidler builds his premium grade, custom, mandolins in Wallingford, Pennsylvania. He also builds guitars.

John Le Voi Guitars
1970-present. Production/custom, mandolin family instruments built by luthier John Le Voi in Lincolnshire, United Kingdom. He also builds guitars.

Johnson
Mid-1990s-present. Budget and intermediate grade, production, mandolins imported by Music Link, Brisbane, California. Johnson also offers guitars, amps, basses and effects.

MA Series A-Style Mandolin
Mid-1990s-present. Import, A-style copy, plain Johnson logo on headstock. Several levels offered; the range shown is for all value levels.

| 1990s | | $100 | $200 |

MF Series F-Style Mandolin
Mid-1990s-present. Import, F-style copy, plain Johnson logo on headstock. Several levels offered; the range shown is for all value levels.

| 1990s | Sunburst | $300 | $500 |

K & S
1992-1998. Mandolins and mandolas distributed by George Katechis and Marc Silber and handmade in Paracho, Mexico. They also offered guitars and ukes.

Kalamazoo
1933-1942, 1946-1947, 1965-1970. Budget brand produced by Gibson in Kalamazoo, Michigan. They offered mandolins until '42.

Kalamazoo/Oriole A-Style Mandolin
1930s. Kalamazoo and Oriole on the headstock, KM/A-style.

| 1930s | | $800 | $1,000 |

KM-11 Mandolin
1935-1941. Gibson-made, A-style, flat top and back, round soundhole, dot inlay.

| 1930s | Sunburst | $650 | $800 |

KM-21 Mandolin
1936-1940. Gibson-made, A-style, F-holes, arched bound spruce top and mahogany back.

| 1930s | Sunburst | $800 | $1,000 |

Kay
1931-present. Located in Chicago, the Kay company made an incredible amount of instruments under a variety of brand names, including the Kay name. From the beginning, Kay offered several types of electric and acoustic mandolins. In 1969,

MODEL		EXC. COND.	
YEAR	FEATURES	LOW	HIGH

the factory closed, marking the end of American-made Kays. The brand name survives today on imported instruments. See *Guitar Stories Volume II*, by Michael Wright, for a complete history of Kay with detailed model listings.

K68/K465 Concert Mandolin
1952-1968. Pear shape, close-grain spruce top, genuine mahogany back and sides. Renamed the K465 in 1966. Kay also offered a venetian-style mandolin called the K68 in 1937-1942.

1952-1968	Natural	$250	$300

K73 Mandolin
1939-1952. Solid spruce top, maple back and sides, A-style body, F-holes, Cherry Sunburst.

1950s		$250	$300

K390/K395 Professional Electric Mandolin
1960-1968. Modified Venetian-style archtop, single pickup, F-hole, spruce top, curly maple back and sides. Sunburst finish. Renamed K395 in 1966.

1960s		$400	$600

K494/K495 Electric Mandolin
1960-1968. A-style archtop, single metal-covered (no poles) pickup, volume and tone control knobs, the K494 was originally about 60% of the price of the K390 model (see above) in 1965. Renamed K495 in 1966.

1960s	Sunburst	$300	$425

Kay Kraft
1931-1937. First brand name of the newly formed Kay Company. Brand replaced by Kay in 1937.

Mandolin
1931-1937. Kay Kraft offered Venetian and teardrop-shaped mandolins.

1930s		$250	$350

Kel Kroyden (by Gibson)
1930-1933. Private branded budget level made by Gibson.

KK-20 (Style C-1) Mandolin
1930-1933. Flat-top, near oval-shaped body, oval soundhole, Natural finish, dark finish mahogany back and sides.

1930-1933		$700	$850

Kent
1961-1969. Japanese-made instruments. Kent offered teardrop, A style, and bowlback acoustic mandolins up to '68.

Acoustic Mandolin
1961-1968. Kent offered teardrop, A-style, and bowlback acoustic mandolins up to '68.

1961-1968		$100	$150

Electric Mandolin
1964-1969. Available from '64-'66 as a solidbody electric (in left- and right-hand models) and from '67-'69 an electric hollowbody venetian-style with F-holes (they called it violin-shaped).

1964-1969		$125	$200

Kentucky (Saga M.I.)
1977-present. Brand name of Saga Musical Instruments currently offering budget, intermediate, and professional grade, production, A- and F-style mandolins.

KM-1300 Mandola
Lloyd Loar H-5 copy.

1980s		$3,400	$3,600

Kingston
Ca. 1958-1967. Japanese imports. See Guitar section for more company info.

Acoustic Mandolin

1960s		$100	$150

EM1 Electric Mandolin
1964-1967. Double cut solidbody electric, 15.75" scale, one pickup.

1960s		$125	$200

Knutsen
1890s-1920s. Luthier Chris J. Knutsen of Tacoma/Seattle, Washington.

Harp Mandolin
1910s. Harp mandolin with tunable upper bass bout with four drone strings, a standard mandolin neck. The mandolin version of a harp guitar.

1910s		$4,000	$5,000

Knutson Luthiery
1981-present. Professional and premium grade, custom, acoustic and electric mandolins built by luthier John Knutson in Forestville, California. He also builds guitars and basses.

La Scala
Ca. 1920s-1930s. La Scala was another brand of the Oscar Schmidt Company of New Jersey, and was used on guitars, banjos, and mandolins.

Lakeside (Lyon & Healy)
Late-1800s-early-1900s. Mainly catalog sales of guitars and mandolins from the Chicago maker. Marketed as a less expensive alternative to the Lyon & Healy Washburn product line.

Style G2016 12-String Mandolin
Early-1900s. Twelve-string, 18 mahogany ribs with white inlay between, celluloid guard plate, advertised as "an inexpensive instrument, possessing a good tone, correct scale, and durable construction."

1917		$300	$400

Larson Brothers
1900-1944. Made by luthiers Carl and August Larson and marketed under a variety of names including Stetson, Maurer, and Prairie State.

Bowl Back Mandolin
1900s. Neopolitan-style (bowl back) with 36 Brazilian rosewood ribs, spruce top, engraved rosewood pickguard, fancy abalone trim and headstock inlay.

1900		$500	$650

1950s Kay K73

Kentucky KM-1300 mandola

MANDOLINS

1920 Lyon & Healy Style A

1925 Martin Style E

MANDOLINS

MODEL YEAR	FEATURES	EXC. COND. LOW	HIGH

Harp-Mandolin Style 35
1920s. Harp-style body with extended upper bass bout horn without drone strings.

1920		$4,000	$6,000

Lyon & Healy
1964-ca. 1945. Lyon & Healy was a large musical instrument builder and marketer, and produced under many different brandnames.

Style A Mandocello
Scroll peghead, symmetrical two-point body. Natural.

1910s		$5,000	$9,000
1920s		$5,000	$9,000

Style A Professional Mandolin
Violin scroll peghead. Natural.

1918		$3,400	$4,200

Style B Mandolin
Maple back and sides, two-point body. Natural.

1920		$1,800	$2,200

Style C Mandolin
1920s. Like Style A teardrop Gibson body style, oval soundhole, carved spruce top, carved maple back. Natural.

1920s		$1,800	$2,200

Maccaferri
1923-1990. Mario Maccaferri made a variety of instruments over his career. He produced award-winning models in Italy and France until he fled to the U.S. due to W.W. II. He applied the new plastic to a highly successful line of instruments after the war. A mandolin was about the only stringed instument they didn't offer in plastic. His Europe-era instruments are very rare.

Mandolins/Mandolas made by Maccaferri 1928-ca. 31: No. 1 Mandolone, No. 2 Mandoloncello, No. 3 Mandola Baritono, No. 4 Mandola Tenore, No. 5 Mandola Soprano, No. 6 Mandolino, No. 7 Quartino. *See Guitar Stories Volume II*, by Michael Wright, for a complete history of Maccaferri with detailed model listings.

Martin
1986-present. Martin got into the mandolin market in 1896 starting with the typical bowl back designs. By 1914, Gibson's hot selling, innovative, violin-based mandolin pushed Martin into a flat back, bent top hybrid design. By 1929, Martin offered a carved top and carved back mandolin. Most models were discontinued in 1941, partially because of World War II. Currently Martin offers only a Backpacker mandolin.

Style 0 Mandolin
1905-1925. Bowl back-style, 18 rosewood ribs, solid peghead.

1915		$900	$1,000

MODEL YEAR	FEATURES	EXC. COND. LOW	HIGH

Style 00 Mandolin
1908-1925. Bowl back-style, nine rosewood ribs (14 ribs by 1924), solid peghead.

1908-1925		$600	$900

Style 000 Mandolin
1914 only. Bowl back, solid peghead, dot inlay, nine mahogany ribs.

1914		$500	$800

Style 1 Mandolin
1898-1924. Bowl back, German silver tuners, 18 ribs.

1910s		$1,000	$1,200

Style 2-15 Mandolin
1936-1964. Carved spruce top, maple back and sides, F-hole, single-bound back, solid headstock.

1936-1964		$1,200	$1,500

Style 2-20 Mandolin
1936-1941. Carved spruce triple-bound top and bound maple back and sides, F-hole, dot inlay.

1936-1942		$2,000	$2,200

Style 2-30 Mandolin
1937-1941. Carved spruce top and maple back and sides, multi-bound, F-holes, diamond and square inlays.

1937-1941		$3,000	$3,500

Style 5 Mandolin
1898-1920. Bowl back, vine inlay, abalone top trim.

1898-1899		$2,100	$2,500
1900-1909		$2,000	$2,500
1910-1920		$2,000	$2,500

Style 6 Mandolin
1898-1921. Bowl back, top bound with ivory and abalone, vine or snowflake inlay.

1919	Snowflake inlay	$2,500	$2,800

Style A Mandolin
1914-1995. Flat back, oval soundhole, dot inlay, solid headstock.

1914-1919		$1,000	$1,250
1920s		$1,000	$1,250
1930s		$1,000	$1,250
1940s		$900	$1,100
1950s		$800	$1,000
1960s		$800	$1,000
1970s		$700	$900
1980s		$700	$900

Style AK Mandolin
1920-1937. Koa wood version of Style A, flat back.

1920-1937		$1,000	$1,300

Style B Mandolin
1914-1946, 1981-1987. Flat back with bent top, spruce top and rosewood back and sides, herringbone back stripe, multi-bound.

1910s		$1,000	$1,400
1920s		$1,000	$1,400

Style BB Mandola
1917-1921, 1932-1939. Brazilian rosewood, herringbone trim, features like Style B mandolin. This is the only Mandola offered.

1917-1921		$1,400	$1,700

MODEL YEAR	FEATURES	EXC. COND. LOW	HIGH

Style E Mandolin
1915-1937. Flat back, rosewood back and sides, bent spruce top, Style 45 snowflake fretboard inlay and other high-end appointments. Highest model cataloged.

1915-1919		$4,000	$5,000
1920-1929		$3,500	$4,500
1930-1937		$3,500	$4,500

Maurer
Maurer Mandolins from the 1930s include Style 30 Flat Model, Style 40, Octave Mandola Style 45, Mandocello Style 50, and Mandola Tenor.
Mandolin
Brazilian rosewood, bird's-eye maple, bowl back.

1930		$1,000	$1,200

Mayflower
1904-1920s. Small builder associated with several distributors.
Bowl Back Mandolin
1901-1920s. Mid-level bowl back-style with 19 rosewood ribs and mid-level appointments.

1900s		$800	$1,100

Menzenhauer & Schmidt
1894-1904. Founded by Frederick Menzenhauer and Oscar Schmidt International. Menzenhauer created the guitar-zither in the U.S. He had several patents including one issued in September 1899 for a mandolin-guitar-zither. Control of operations quickly went to Oscar Schmidt.
12-String Mandolin
1890s. Bowl back mandolin with three strings per course that were tuned in octaves. Designed during an experimental era for mandolin-related instrumetns, 13 rosewood ribs, spruce top, inlays.

1890s		$200	$250

Michael Kelly
1999-present. Intermediate and professional grade, production, imported, acoustic and acoustic/electric mandolins. They also offer guitars and basses.

Michael Lewis Instruments
1992-present. Luthier Michael Lewis builds his premium grade, custom, mandolins in Grass Valley, California. He also builds guitars.

Mid-Missouri
1995-present. Intermediate grade, production, acoustic and electric mandloins and mandolas built by luthier Michael Dulak in Columbia, Missouri.
M Series Mandolin
1995-1999. Teardrop A-style body, solid Engleman spruce top, solid maple, mahogany or rosewood back and sides. Includes M-1, M-2 and M-4.

1995-1999		$300	$475

Mirabella
1997-present. Professional and premium grade, mandolins built by luthier Cristian Mirabella in Babylon, New York. He also builds guitars and ukes.

Monteleone
1971-present. Primarily a guitar maker, luthier John Monteleone also builds presentation grade, custom, mandolins in West Islip, New York.
10-String Cittern/Mandocello
1980s. Carved spruce top, oval soundhole, sword-excalibur headstock inlay optional.

1986	"Excalibur"		
	inlay option	$8,000	$10,000
1989	Amber Brown	$7,000	$9,000

Grand Artist Mandola

1990-1995		$24,000	$27,000

Grand Artist Style F Mandolin
1990s. Style F body, spruce top, curly maple back and sides, dot markers.

1990-1995	Sunburst	$12,000	$14,500
1996-2003		$15,000	$18,000

Style B Mandolin
1980s. Long A body style with long F-holes, flamed curly maple back and sides, elongated fretboard over body.

1988	Sunburst	$10,000	$12,000

Moon
1979-present. Intermediate and professional grade, production/custom, acoustics and acoustic/electric mandolins and mandolas built by luthier Jimmy Moon in Glasgow, Scotland. They also build guitars.

Morales
Ca.1967-1968. Japanese-made, not heavily imported into the U.S.
Electric Mandolin
1967-1968.

1967		$175	$250

Morgan Monroe
1999-present. Intermediate and professional grade, production, acoustic mandolins made in Korea and distributed by SHS International of Indianapolis, Indiana. They also offer guitars, basses, banjos, and fiddles.

Mozzani
Late-1800s-early-1900s. Founder Luigi Mozzani was an Italian (Bologna) master luthier and renowned composer and musician. There are original Mozzani-built mandolins and also factory-built instruments made later at various workshops.
Mandolin
Factory-built bowl back model.

1920s		$325	$425

Michael Kelly Dragonfly

Monteleone Grand Artist

MANDOLINS

National Style 2

Nyberg Octave Mandolin

MODEL YEAR	FEATURES	EXC. COND. LOW	HIGH

Original Bowl Back Mandolin
Late-1800s-early-1900s. Handcrafted by Luigi Mozzani, about 24 ribs, soundhole ornamentation, snowflake-like markers.

1904		$1,300	$1,550

National
Ca.1927-present. The National brandname has gone through many ownership changes. National offered resonator mandolins from around 1927 to '41. Currently, National does not offer a mandolin.

Style 0 Mandolin
1931-early-1940s. Metal body with Hawaiian scenes, single-cone resonator.

1930s	Hawaiian scene	$2,000	$3,000

Style 1 Mandolin
1928-1936. Plain metal body, tri-cone resonator.

1928-1936		$2,800	$3,200

Style 2 Mandolin
1928-1936. Metal body with rose engraving, tri-cone resonator.

1928-1936		$3,500	$4,000

Style 3 Mandolin

1930s		$4,000	$5,000

Style 97 Mandolin
1936-1940. Metal body, tri-cone resonator.

1936-1940		$3,500	$4,000

Triolian Mandolin
1928-1940. Metal body with palm trees, single-cone resonator.

1928-1940		$2,000	$2,500

Northworthy
1987-present. Professional and premium grade, production/custom, mandolin-family instruments built by luthier Alan Marshall in Ashbourne, Derbyshire, England. He also builds guitars.

Nugget
1970s-present. Luthier Mike Kemnitzer builds his premium grade mandolins in Central Lake, Michigan.

Nyberg Instruments
1993-present. Professional grade, custom, mandolins and mandolas built by luthier Lawrence Nyberg in Hornby Island, British Columbia. He also builds guitars, bouzoukis and citterns.

O'Dell
1980s. Custom builder Doug O'Dell, Ohio.

Electric Solidbody Mandolin
1980s. Double cutaway with symmetrical small horns, flamed maple top, single pickup, two control knobs.

1980s		$1,800	$1,900

Old Kraftsman
1930s-1960s. Brand name used by the Siegel Company on instruments made by Kay and others

MODEL YEAR	FEATURES	EXC. COND. LOW	HIGH

(even Gibson). Quality was mixed, but some better-grade instruments were offered.

Mandolin

1950s		$275	$375

Orpheum
Founded in the very late-1890s. An old brand name often associated with banjos, 1930s branded guitars sold by Bruno and Sons. 1950s branded guitars and mandolins sold by Maurice Lipsky Music, New York, NY.

Electric Mandolin Model 730 E
1950s. Private branded for Maurice Lipsky. Cataloged as a student model designed for ensemble playing. A-style body, single neck bar pickup, two side-mounted knobs, spruce top, maple back and sides, dot markers. Sunburst.

1950s		$400	$550

Oscar Schmidt
1879-ca. 1939, 1979-present. Currently offering budget and intermediate grade, production, mandolins. They also offer guitars, banjos, and autoharps. The original Schmidt company offered innovative mandolin designs during the 1900-1930 mandolin boom.

Mandolin Harp Style B
1890s. More zither-autoharp than mandolin, flat autoharp body with soundhole.

1890s		$100	$150

Sovereign Mandolin
1920s. Bowl back, bent top, rope-style binding, mahogany ribs, dot inlay, plain headstock.

1920s	Natural	$250	$300

Ovation
1966-present. Known for innovative fiberglass-backed bowl back acoustic and acoustic/electric guitars, Ovation added mandolins in '94 and currently offers intermediate and professional grade, production, mandolins.

Celebrity Mandolin
1994-present. Single cutaway, small typically Ovation body, with typical Ovation headstock.

1990s	Red Sunburst	$400	$475

P. W. Crump Company
1975-present. Luthier Phil Crump builds his custom mandolin-family instruments in Arcata, California. He also builds guitars.

Phantom Guitar Works
1992-present. Intermediate grade, production, solidbody MandoGuitars assembled in Clatskanie, Oregon. They also build guitars and basses.

Phoenix
1990-present. Premium grade, production/custom, mandolins built by luthier Rolfe Gerhardt (formerly builder of Unicorn Mandolins in the '70s) in South Thomaston, Maine. Gerhard's Phoenix

MODEL YEAR	FEATURES	EXC. COND. LOW	HIGH

company specializes in a two-point Style A (double cutaway) body style.

Bluegrass (double-point) Mandolin

1990-present. Double-point shallow body voiced for bluegrass music, adirondack spruce top, figured maple body.

| 1990s | Sunburst | $1,700 | $2,000 |

Premier

Ca.1938-ca.1975, 1990s-present. Brand produced by Peter Sorkin Music Company in New York City. Around 1957 the company acquired Strad-O-Lin and many of their mandolins were offered under that brand name. The Premier brand name currently appears on Asian-made solidbody guitars and basses.

Ramsey

1990s. Built by luthier John Ramsey of Colorado Springs, Colorado.

Recording King

1929-1943. Montgomery Ward house brand. Suppliers include Gibson, Kay, Regal, and Gretsch.

Mandolin (Gibson-made)

1929-1940. A-style body.

| 1930s | Sunburst | $500 | $600 |

Regal

Ca.1884-1954. Large Chicago-based manufacturer which made their own brand name and others for distributors and mass merchandisers. Absorbed by the Harmony Company in 1955.

Mandolin

| 1920s | Flat-top A-style | $400 | $500 |
| 1930s | Sunburst, standard model | $400 | $500 |

Octophone Mandolin

1920s. Octave mandolin, long body with double points, round soundhole.

| 1920s | | $800 | $1,000 |

Resonator Mandolin

| 1950s | | $400 | $500 |

Rigel

1990-present. Professional and premium grade, production/custom mandolins and mandolas built by luthier Pete Langdell in Hyde Park, Vermont.

A-Plus Oval Mandolin

1990s. A-style body, oval soundhole, dot markers.

| 1990s | Sunburst | $1,000 | $1,200 |

Model G-110 Mandolin

| 1990s | Sunburst | $2,400 | $2,600 |

Roberts

1980s. Built by luthier Jay Roberts of California.

Tiny Moore Jazz 5 Mandolin

1980s. Based on Bigsby design of the early-1950s as used by Tiny Moore, five-string electric.

| 1985 | Sunburst | $1,700 | $1,850 |

Rono

1967-present. Luthier Ron Oates builds his professional grade, production/custom, electric mandolins in Boulder, Colorado. He also builds basses and guitars.

S. S. Stewart

Late-1800s-early-1900s. S. S. Stewart of Philadelphia was primarily known for banjos. Legend has it that Stewart was one of the first to demonstrate the mass productioin assembly of stringed instruments.

Mandolin Banjo

Early-1900s. Mandolin neck and a very small open back banjo body, 'star' inlay in headstock.

| 1900s | | $350 | $450 |

Samick

1958-2001, 2002-present. Budget and intermediate grade, production, imported acoustic and acoustic/electric mandolins. They also offer guitars, basses, ukes and banjos.

Sawchyn

1972-present. Intermediate and professional grade, production/custom, mandolins built by luthier Peter Sawchyn in Regina, Saskatchewan. He also builds flat-top and flamenco guitars.

Sekova

Mid-1960s-mid-1970s. Entry level, imported by the U.S. Musical Merchandise.

Electric Mandolin

1960s-1970s. Kay-Kraft-style hollowbody with F-holes, single pickup and Sekova logo on the headstock.

| 1965-1970s | | $250 | $300 |

Silvertone

1941-ca.1970. Brand name used by Sears on their musical instruments.

Mandolin

Arched top and back.

| 1940s | Sunburst | $200 | $250 |
| 1950s | Sunburst | $200 | $250 |

Smart Musical Instruments

1986-present. Premium and presentation grade, custom, mandolin family instruments built by luthier A. Lawrence Smart in McCall, Idaho. He also builds guitars.

Sovereign

1920s-1930s. Sovereign was originally a brand name of the Oscar Schmidt company.

Mandolins

1920s. Old-style bent top.

| 1920s | | $300 | $500 |

Regal Fancy Scroll

Rigel A-Plus Oval Deluxe

MANDOLINS

MODEL YEAR	FEATURES	EXC. COND. LOW	HIGH

1920s Supertone

Stahl

William C. Stahl instruments were "made" (per their literature they were not manufactured) in Milwaukee, Wisconsin, in the early-1900s. Models included Style 4 (22 ribs) to Style 12 Presentation Artist Special. The more expensive models were generally 44-rib construction.

Bowl Back Mandolin (deluxe professional model)
Rosewood, 40 ribs.

| 1910s | | $950 | $1,250 |

Bowl Back Mandolin (mid-level)
Pearl floral design on pickguard, 32 ribs.

| 1910s | | $400 | $600 |

Stathopoulo

1903-1916. Original design instruments, some patented, by Epiphone company founder A. Stathopoulo.

A-Style Mandolin
1903-1916. A-style with higher-end appointments, bent-style spruce top, figured maple back and sides.

| 1912 | | $900 | $1,300 |

Stefan Sobell Musical Instruments

1982-present. Luthier Stefan Sobell builds his premium grade, production/custom, mandolins in Hetham, Northumberland, England. He also builds guitars, citterns and bouzoukis.

Stella

Founded in 1879, Stella was a brand name of the Oscar Schmidt Company and produced all types of stringed instruments. The company was an early contributor to innovative mandolin designs and participated in the 1900-1930 mandolin boom. Pre-World War II Stella instruments were low-mid to mid-level instruments. 1950s and '60s Stella instruments were student grade, low-end instruments. In '39, Harmony purchased the Stella name.

Banjo-Mandolin
1920s. One of several innovative designs that attempted to create a new market. Eight-string mandolin neck with a banjo body. Stella logo normally impressed on the banjo rim or the side of the neck.

| 1920s | | $150 | $250 |

Bowl Back Mandolin
1920s. Typical bowl back, bent top-style mandolin with models decalomania, about 10 (wide) maple ribs, dot markers.

| 1920s | | $100 | $250 |

Pear-Shape Mandolin
1940s-1960s. Harmony-made lower-end mandolins. Pear-shaped (Style A) flat back, oval soundhole.

1940s	Natural	$200	$250
1950s		$200	$250
1960s	Sunburst	$200	$250

Sterling

Early-1900s. Distributed by wholesalers The Davitt & Hanser Music Co.

Tacoma M-1

Stiver

Professional and premium grade, custom/production, mandolins built by luthier Lou Stiver in Pennsylvania.

Strad-O-Lin

Ca.1920s-ca.1960s. The Strad-O-Lin company was operated by the Hominic brothers in New York, primarily making mandolins for wholesalers. In the late '50s, Multivox/Premier bought the company and used the name on mandolins and guitars.

Baldwin Electric Mandolin
1950s. A-Style, single pickup, tone and volume knobs, spruce top, maple back and sides, Baldwin logo on headstock.

| 1950s | Natural | $300 | $400 |

Junior A Mandolin
1950s. A-Style, Stradolin Jr. logo on headstock, dot markers.

| 1950s | Sunburst | $300 | $400 |

Superior

1987-present. Intermediate grade, production/custom mandolin-family instruments made in Mexico for George Katechis Montalvo of Berkeley Musical Instrument Exchange. They also offer guitars.

Supertone

1914-1941. Brand name used by Sears before they switched to Silvertone. Instruments made by other companies.

Mandolin
Spruce top, mahogany back and sides, some with decalomania vine pattern on top.

| 1920s | | $250 | $350 |
| 1930s | Decalomania vine pattern | $250 | $350 |

Supro

1935-1968. Budget line from the National Dobro Company.

T30 Electric Mandolin

| 1950s | | $350 | $500 |

Tacoma

1995-present. Intermediate, professional and premium grade, production, mandolins made in Tacoma, Washington. They also build guitars and basses.

M-1 Mandolin
1990s-present. Solid spruce top, mahogany back and sides, typical Tacoma body-style with upper bass bout soundhole.

| 1990s | Natural | $375 | $425 |

M-2 Mandolin
1990s-2002. Solid spruce top, solid rosewood back and sides, typical Tacoma body-style with upper bass bout soundhole.

| 2000 | Natural | $500 | $600 |

Tennessee

1970-1993, 1996-present. Luthier Mark Taylor builds his professional and premium grade, production/custom, mandolins in Old Hickory, Tennessee. He also builds guitars, mandolins, banjos and the Tut Taylor brand of resophonic guitars.

Timeless Instruments

1980-present. Luthier David Freeman builds his intermediate grade, mandolins in Tugaske, Saskatchewan. He also builds guitars and dulcimers.

Triggs

1992-present. Luthiers Jim Triggs and his son Ryan build their professional and premium grade, production/custom, mandolins in Kansas City, Kansas. They also build guitars. They were located in Nashville until '98.

Unicorn

1970s-late 1980s. Luthier Rolfe Gerhardt (currently luthier for Phoenix Mandolins) founded Unicorn in the mid-1970s. Gerhardt built 149 mandolins before selling Unicorn to Save Sjnko in 1980. Sinko closed Unicorn in the late-1980s.

F-5 Style Mandolin

MODEL YEAR	FEATURES	EXC. COND. LOW	HIGH
1976-1980	Sunburst	$700	$1,000

Vega

1903-present. The original Boston-based company was purchased by C.F. Martin in 1970. In 1980, the Vega trademark was sold to a Korean company. Vega means "star" and a star logo is often seen on the original Vega instruments.

Lansing Special Bowl Mandolin
Spruce top, abalone, vine inlay.

1890s		$500	$700

Little Wonder Mandolin Banjo
Maple neck, resonator.

1920s		$400	$600

Mando Bass Mandolin
1910s-1920s. Large upright bass-sized instrument with bass tuners, body-style similar to dual-point A-style, scroll headstock.

1920s		$2,500	$3,500

Style 202 Lute Mandolin
Early-1900s. Basic A-style with small horns, Natural spruce top, mahogany sides and cylinder back, dot markers.

1910s		$700	$900

Style A Mandolin

1910s		$500	$600

Style K Mandolin Banjo

1910s		$400	$600
1920s		$400	$600
1930s		$400	$600

Style L Banjo Mandolin
1910s. Open back banjo body and mandolin 8-string neck.

1910s		$900	$1,000

MODEL YEAR	FEATURES	EXC. COND. LOW	HIGH

Super Deluxe Mandolin

1939	Sunburst	$700	$750

Tubaphone Style X Mandolin Banjo

1923		$700	$750

Veillette

1991-present. Luthier Joe Veillette (of Veillette-Citron fame) builds his professional grade, production/custom, mandolins in Woodstock, New York. He also builds basses and guitars.

Vinaccia

Italian-made by Pasquale Vinaccia, luthier.

Bowl Back Mandolin
High-end appointments and pickguard, 30 rosewood ribs.

1904		$2,600	$2,800

Ward

Depression era private brand by Gibson's Kalamazoo factory.

Style A Mandolin
1930s. Style A body with round soundhole and flat top and back, dot markers, mahogany back and sides, silkscreened Ward logo.

1935	Sunburst	$350	$400

Washburn (Lyon & Healy)

1880s-1949. Made by Lyon and Healy.

Bowl Back Mandolin
Lyon and Healy sold a wide variety of bowl back mandolins. Brazilian ribs with fancy inlays and bindings.

1890s	Fancy inlays and bindings	$600	$1,000
1900s	Fancy inlays and bindings	$600	$1,000
1910s	Standard appointments	$400	$500

Style A Mandolin
Brazilian rosewood.

1920s		$800	$1,000

Style E Mandolin
1915-1923. Brazilian rosewood.

1915-1923		$900	$1,100

Washburn (Post 1974)

1974-present. Currently, Washburn offers imported intermediate and professional grade, production, mandolins.

M-3 SWSB Mandolin
Gibson F-5-style, import.

1980s	Sunburst	$400	$600

M-4S Mandolin
F-5-style.

1982		$400	$600

Triggs mando

Washburn Style 115 bowlback

MANDOLINS

Weber Bitteroot

Wurlitzer Mandolin Banjo

MANDOLINS

MODEL YEAR	FEATURES	EXC. COND. LOW	HIGH

Weber

1996-present. Intermediate, professional, and premium grade, production/custom, mandolins, mandolas, and mandocellos. In 1996, Gibson moved the manufacturing of Flatiron mandolins from Bozeman, Montana, to Nashville. Many former Flatiron employees, including Bruce Weber, formed Sound To Earth, Ltd., to build Weber instruments in Belgrade, Montana.

Style F Yellowstone Mandolin
1996-present. Style F mandolin built with solid spruce top and flamed maple back and sides.

1998	Sunburst	$1,800	$2,200

Weymann

1864-1940s. H.A. Weymann & Sons was a musical instrument distributor located in Philadelphia. They also built their own instruments.

Keystone State Banjo Mandolin
Maple rim and back, ebony fretboard.

1910s		$300	$500

Model 20 Mando-Lute
1920s. Lute-style body, spruce top, flamed maple sides and back, rope binding, deluxe rosette.

1920s	Natural	$550	$750

Model 40 Mandolin Banjo
1910s-1920s. Mandolin neck on a open banjo body with a larger sized 10" head.

1920s		$450	$650

Wurlitzer

The old Wurlitzer company would have been considered a mega-store by today's standards. They sold a wide variety of instruments, gave music lessons, and operated manufacturing facilities.

Mandolin
Koa.

1920		$550	$675

Mandolin Banjo
1900s. Mandolin neck on open back banjo body, plain-style.

1900s		$200	$250

Zeta

1982-present. Professional grade, production, acoustic/electric mandolins made in Oakland, California. They also make basses, amps and violins.

Ukuleles

Aloha "Islands" Uke

Dobro resonator

Flamingo

Aero Uke

1920s. Never branded, but almost certainly produced by Chicago's Stromberg-Voisenet Company, the precursor of Kay, the Aero Uke is an instrument quite unlike any other. With its spruce-capped body resembling an old-timey airplane wing and a neck and headstock that approximate a plane's fuselage, this clever 1920s offering cashed in on the Lindbergh craze (like the Harmony Johnny Marvin model with its airplane-shaped bridge), and must have been a big hit at parties.

MODEL YEAR	FEATURES	EXC. COND. LOW	HIGH
Aero Uke			
1927	Airplane body, black deco on wing	$1,500	$1,900
1927	Airplane body, gold deco on wing	$1,700	$2,000

Aloha

1935-1960s. The Aloha brand turns up on numerous vastly different ukes. In fact, the variety of features exhibited by Aloha ukuleles leads the modern observer to believe that the ukes that bear this headstock decal were made by as many as a dozen different manufacturers, each with access to the same logo. Many were undoubtedly Island-made, with all koa bodies and some with fancy rope binding; others bear unmistakable mainland traits. Some of these have a more traditional look and are stamped "Akai" inside the soundhole, while still others, strongly resembling mainland C.F. Martins in design, typically sport a decal of the Sam F. Chang curio shop on the reverse of the headstock.

MODEL YEAR	FEATURES	EXC. COND. LOW	HIGH
Akai soprano ukulele			
1930s	Koa construction	$350	$450
Soprano ukulele			
1950s	Koa body, plain	$350	$450

Applause

1976-present. Kaman Music's entry-level Ovation-styled import brand. Applause currently offers budget-grade soprano and tenor ukuleles with their trademark arched plastic bodies.

Bear Creek Guitars

1995-present. Intermediate and professional grade traditionally styled koa ukuleles built by luthier Bill Hardin in Kula, Hawaii. He also builds guitars.

Blue Star

1984-present. Production and custom ukuleles built by luthier Bruce Herron in Fennville, Michigan. He also builds guitars, mandolins, and lap steels.

Bruno

1834-present. This New York distributor certainly subcontracted all of its ukulele production to other manufacturers, and as a result you'd be hard pressed to find two identical Bruno ukes.

MODEL YEAR	FEATURES	EXC. COND. LOW	HIGH
Soprano ukulele			
1920	Koa, rope soundhole	$250	$300
1930	Koa, rope bound body	$300	$350

DeCava Guitars

1983-present. Professional grade production and custom, ukuleles built by luthier Jim DeCava in Stratford, Connecticut. He also builds guitars, banjos, and mandolins.

Del Vecchio Dimonaco

With a design patterned after the pioneering work of Dobro and National, this Brazilian company produced a full line of resonator instruments, all constructed of native Brazilian rosewood, from the 1950's onward.

MODEL YEAR	FEATURES	EXC. COND. LOW	HIGH
Resonator ukulele			
1950	Brazilian rosewood	$600	$750
1980	Brazilian rosewood	$600	$750

Ditson

1916-1930. Don't be fooled. While some of the ukes that were commissioned by this East Coast music publisher and chain store were actually manufactured by C.F. Martin, Martin was by no means the sole supplier. The Martin-made instruments often bear a Martin brand as well as a Ditson one, or, barring that, at least demonstrate an overall similarity to the rest of the ukes in the regular Martin line, both on the inside and out.

MODEL YEAR	FEATURES	EXC. COND. LOW	HIGH
Soprano ukulele			
1922	Same appointments as Martin Style O	$700	$800
1922	Same appointments as Martin Style 1 M	$800	$900
1922	Same appointments as Martin Style 2 M	$1,100	$1,200
1922	Same appointments as Martin Style 3 M	$2,200	$2,500
1922	Same appointments as Martin Style 1 K	$1,200	$1,500
1922	Same appointments as Martin Style 2 K	$1,300	$2,000
1922	Same appointments as Martin Style 3 K	$2,200	$3,000
1922	Same appointments as Martin Style 5 K	$5,000	$6,000

Dobro

1929-1942, ca. 1954-present. The ukulele version of the popular "amplifying" resonator instruments first produced in California, the Dobro uke was offered in two sizes (soprano and tenor), two styles (f-holes and screen holes), and two colors (brown and black). Models with Dobro headstock decals are often outwardly indistinguishable from others bearing either a Regal badge or no logo at all, but a peek inside often reveals the presence of a sound well in the belly of the former, making them the more desirable of the two.

UKULELES

MODEL YEAR	FEATURES	EXC. COND. LOW	HIGH
Resonator ukulele			
1930	Wood body, f holes Regal-made	$500	$1,000
1930	Wood body, screen holes	$600	$1,000

Favilla

1890-1973. The small New York City family-owned factory that produced primarily guitars also managed to offer some surprisingly high quality ukes, the best of which rival Martin and Gibson for craftsmanship and tone. As a result, Favilla ukuleles are a real value.

MODEL YEAR	FEATURES	EXC. COND. LOW	HIGH
Baritone ukulele			
1950	Plain mahogany body	$250	$350
Soprano ukulele			
1950	Plain mahogany body	$350	$450
1950	Mahogany body, triple bound	$450	$575
1950	Teardrop-shaped, birch body	$350	$425
1950	Teardrop-shaped, stained blue	$375	$425

Fin-der

1950s. The pitch of this short-lived plastic ukulele was apparently the ease of learning, since the included instructional brochure helped you to "find" your chords with the added help of rainbow of color-coded nylon strings.

MODEL YEAR	FEATURES	EXC. COND. LOW	HIGH
Diamond head			
1950	Styrene plastic, in original box,	$150	$200

Fine Resophonic

1988-present. Intermediate and professional grade, production/custom, wood and metal-bodied resophonic ukuleles built by luthiers Mike Lewis and Pierre Avocat in Vitry Sur Seine, France. They also build guitars and mandolins.

Flamingo

1950s. If swanky designs and hot-foil stamped into the surface of these '50s swirly injection molded polystyrene ukes didn't grab you, certainly the built-in functional pitch pipe across the top of the headstock would. And I ask you, who can resist a ukulele with built-in tuner?

MODEL YEAR	FEATURES	EXC. COND. LOW	HIGH
Soprano ukulele			
1955	Brown top with white fingerboard	$125	$150
1955	White top with brown fingerboard	$125	$150

Gibson

1880s (1902)-present. A relative late-comer to the uke market, Gibson didn't get a line off the ground until 1927, fully nine years after Martin had already been in production. Even then they only produced three soprano styles and one tenor version. Worse still, they never made any ukes in koa, sticking to the easier-to-obtain mahogany.

Nonetheless, Gibson ukuleles exhibit more unintentional variety than any other major maker, with enough construction, inlay, binding, and cosmetic variations to keep collectors buzzing for many a year to come. In general, the earliest examples feature a Gibson logo in script, later shortened to just Gibson. Post-war examples adopted the more square-ish logo of the rest of the Gibson line, and, at some point in the late '50s, began sporting ink-stamped serial numbers on the back of the headstock like their guitar and mandolin brethren.

MODEL YEAR	FEATURES	EXC. COND. LOW	HIGH
UKE 1			
Soprano ukulele			
1927	Plain mahogany body	$500	$700
1951	Plain body, red SG guitar-like finish	$500	$600
UKE 2			
Soprano ukulele			
1934	Triple-bound mahogany body	$600	$800
1950	Single-bound mahogany body	$600	$700
UKE 3			
Soprano ukulele.			
1933	Dark finish, diamonds and squares inlay	$900	$1,300
TU 1			
Tenor ukulele, called the TU until 1 added in 1949.			
1930	Mahogany body, sunburst finish	$750	$900
ETU 1			
Electric tenor uke			
1949	Unbound body, square black PU, 88 made	$2,000	$3,500
ETU 3			
Electric tenor uke			
1953	Triple bound body, square PU, rare	$4,000	$6,000

Graziano

1969-present. Luthier Tony Graziano has been building ukuleles almost exclusively since 1995 in his Santa Cruz shop. Like many, he sees the uke as the instrument of the new millennium, and his entirely handmade, custom orders can be had in a variety of shapes, sizes, and woods.

Gretsch

1883-present. The first (and most desirable) ukuleles by this New York manufacturer were actually stamped with the name "Gretsch American" or with interior brass nameplates. Subsequent pieces, largely inexpensive laminate-bodied catalog offerings, are distinguished by small round "Gretsch" headstock decals, and a lack of any kerfed linings inside the bodies.

Favilla

Gibson UKE 3

Gibson ETU 1 and ETU 3

UKULELES

Gretsch

1920s Harmony Roy Smeck Vita

![Johnson UK-998]

Johnson UK-998

MODEL YEAR	FEATURES	EXC. COND. LOW	HIGH
Plain soprano ukulele			
1950	Natural mahogany body, no binding	$150	$200
Round ukulele			
1940	Round body, blue to green sunburst	$150	$200
Soprano ukulele			
1940	Koa wood body, fancy fingerboard inlay	$650	$750
1940	Mahogany body, fancy fingerboard inlay	$600	$750
1940	Unbound body, engraved rose in peghead	$800	$900
1950	Darker finish, bordered in dark binding	$250	$450

Guild

1952-present. By rights this fine East Coast shop should have produced a full line of ukes to complement its impressive flat and carved-top guitar offerings. Alas, a lone baritone model was all that they could manage. And it's a darned shame, too.

B-11 Baritone ukulele

1963-1976. Mahogany body, rosewood fingerboard.

1960s		$400	$550

Harmony

1892-1976, late 1970s-present. This manufacturer surely produced more ukuleles than all other makers put together. Their extensive line ran the gamut from artist endorsed models and ukes in unusual shapes and materials, to inexpensive but flashy creations adorned with eye-catching decals and silk screening. The earliest examples have a small paper label on the back of the headstock, and a branded logo inside the body. This was replaced by a succession of logo decals applied to the front of the headstock, first gold and black, later green, white, and black. By the '60s Harmony had become so synonymous with ukulele production that they were known around their Chicago locale as simply "the ukulele factory," as in, "Ma couldn't come to the bar-b-que on-a-counta she got a job at the ukulele factory."

Baritone ukulele

Bound mahogany body.

1960		$250	$350

Concert Ukulele

Mahogany body, bound, concert-sized.

1935		$250	$300

Johnny Marvin Tenor

1930	Sunburst mahogany, "airplane" bridge	$400	$550
1930	Flamed koa, "airplane" bridge	$550	$800

MODEL YEAR	FEATURES	EXC. COND. LOW	HIGH
Roy Smeck Concert			
Concert-sized, sunburst spruce top.			
1935		$400	$500
Roy Smeck Ukulele			
Mahogany body			
1955	Wood fingerboard	$350	$450
1955	Plastic fingerboard	$150	$200
Roy Smeck Vita Uke			
Pear-shaped body, seal-shaped f-holes.			
1926		$550	$750
Tiple			
10 steel strings, multicolored binding.			
1935		$600	$850
Ukulele			
1930	Koawood body, unbound	$250	$500
1935	Plain mahogany body, unbound	$300	$400

Johnson

Mid-1990s-present. Budget ukuleles imported by Music Link of Brisbane, California. They also offer guitars, amps, mandolins and effects. Most notable of the Johnson ukes are the National metal-bodied uke copies, which come surprisingly close to the look and feel of the originals, at an unfathomably low price.

K & S

1992-1998. Ukes distributed by George Katechis and Marc Silber and handmade in Paracho, Mexico. They also offered guitars. In '98, Silber started marketing the ukes alone, under the Marc Silber Guitar Company brand.

Kamaka

Part of the "second wave" of ukulele builders on the Hawaiian islands (after Nunes, Dias, and Santos) Kamaka distinguished itself first with ukes of extremely high quality, subsequently with the most enduring non-guitar-derived designs, the Pineapple Uke, patented in 1928. Kamaka is the only maker which has been in continuous production for nearly a hundred years, offering Hawaiian-made products from native woods in virtually every size and ornamentation.

Pineapple Uke

1925	Pineapple art painted onto top or back	$1,300	$1,500
1930	Monkeypod wood, plain, unbound	$600	$950
1930	Rope bound top only, koawood body	$800	$1,000
1935	Rope bound soundhole only	$700	$900
1960	Koa body, unbound, two "K"s logo	$500	$600
1970	Koa body, extended rosewood f'board	$350	$650

UKULELES

The *Vintage Guitar Price Guide* shows low to high values for items in all-original excellent condition, and, where applicable, with original case or cover.

MODEL YEAR	FEATURES	EXC. COND. LOW	HIGH

Concert uke
Koa body, extended rosewood f'board.

1975		$250	$500

Tenor uke
Koa body, extended rosewood f'board.

1955		$300	$750

Lili'u uke
Concert-sized koa body.

1965	8 strings	$500	$700
1985	6 strings	$500	$700

Kent
1961-1969. Large, student quality ukes of laminated construction were offered by this Japanese concern throughout the 1960s.

Baritone ukulele
Mahogany body, bound top, bound back.

1960s		$150	$200

Knutsen
1890s-1920s. While Christopher Knutsen was the inventor of flat-topped harp instruments featuring an integral sound chamber on the bass side of the body, he almost certainly left the manufacturing to others. Striking in both concept and design, Knutsen products nonetheless suffer from compromised construction techniques.

Harp ukulele
Koa body, large "horn" chamber.

1915	Unbound	$1,500	$2,500
1915	Bound	$2,000	$3,500

Harp taro patch
Koa body, as above but 8 strings, unbound.

1915		$3,000	$4,000

Kumalae
Along with Kamaka, Kumalae was also of the "second wave" of Hawaiian uke makers. Jonah Kumalae's company quickly snagged the prestigious Gold Award at the Pan Pacific Exhibition in 1915, and the headstock decals and paper labels aren't about to let you forget it, either. Many assume that these all date from exactly that year, when in fact Kumalaes were offered right up through the late 1930s.

Soprano ukulele
Figured koa body

1920	Rope bound top and back	$500	$700
1919	Bound top, back, f'board	$700	$1,000
1927	As above but with "fiddle-shaped" peghead	$800	$1,400
1930	Unbound body	$500	$700
1933	Rope bound soundhole only	$500	$700

Tenor ukulele
Koa body, unbound top, unbound back.

1930		$700	$900

MODEL YEAR	FEATURES	EXC. COND. LOW	HIGH

Lanikai
Line of budget and intermediate grade, production, koa or nato wood, acoustic and acoustic/electric, ukuleles distributed by Hohner.

Larrivee
1968-present. This mainstream guitar manufacturer has an on-again off-again relationship with the ukulele, having occasionally produced some superb examples in various sizes, woods and degrees of ornamentation.

Le Domino
This line of striking ukuleles turned the popularity of domino playing into a clever visual motif, displaying not only tumbling dominos on their soundboards and around their soundholes, but fingerboard markers represented in decal domino denominations (3, 5, 7, 10, 12, etc.). The ukuleles were, in fact, produced by at least two different companies - Stewart and Regal - but you can scarcely tell them apart.

Concert ukulele
Black-finish, white bound, dominos, concert size.

1932		$1,000	$1,200

Soprano ukulele
Domino decals.

1930	Black-finish, white bound	$500	$650
1940	Natural finish, unbound body	$150	$250

Leonardo Nunes
Leonardo was the son of Manuel, the self professed "Inventor of the Ukulele." Whether actually the originator or not, Dad was certainly on the ship that brought the inventor to the islands in 1879. Leonardo, instead of joining up and making it Manuel & Son, set out on his own to produce ukes that are virtually indistinguishable from pop's. All constructed entirely of koa, some exhibit considerable figure and rope binding finery, making them as highly desirable to collectors as Manuel's.

Soprano ukulele
Figured koa body.

1919	Bound top, back, f'board	$750	$1100
1920	Rope bound top and back	$750	$1000
1927	Bound body, f'board, and head	$1,200	$1,600
1930	Unbound body	$500	$750
1933	Rope bound soundhole only	$600	$800

Tenor ukulele
Koa body, unbound top, unbound back.

1930		$800	$1,100

Taro Patch fiddle
Koa body, unbound top, unbound back.

1930		$1,600	$2,000

Kamaka Tenor

Larrivee US-01KA

Leonardo Nunes

UKULELES

1920s Lyon & Healey Leland

1950s Maccaferri Islander

Magic Fluke Uke

Loprinzi

1972-present. Intermediate and professional grade, production/custom, ukuleles built in Clearwater, Florida. They also build guitars.

Lyon & Healy

1880s-ca.1949. During different periods several different makers constructed ukes bearing this stamp – often with an additional "Washburn" tag as well. After initial production by Lyon & Healy, instrument manufacture then apparently bounced between Regal, Stewart, and Tonk Brothers all within a span of only a few short years. Adding to the confusion, ukes surface from time to time bearing no maker's mark that can be reasonably attributed to Lyon & Healy. Suffice it to say that the best of these ukes, those displaying the highest degrees of quality and ornamentation, rival Gibson and Martin for collectability and tone and beauty.

MODEL YEAR	FEATURES	EXC. COND. LOW	HIGH
"Bell-shaped" uke	*Mahogany body.*		
c.1927		$1200	$1500
Camp Uke	Round "nissa" wood body, black binding.		
1935		$150	$250
Shrine Uke	*Triangular body, green binding.*		
1930	Mahogany body	$1,000	$1,200
1933	Koa	$1,200	$1,500
Soprano ukulele	*Mahogany body.*		
1930	Unbound	$500	$700
1932	Bound top, bound back	$500	$700
Soprano ukulele	*Koa body.*		
1927	Bound top, pearl rosette	$1,750	$2,000
1934	Bound top, bound back	$750	$850
1935	Pearl bound top and back	$5,000	$7,000
Concert ukulele	*Mahogany body, bound top, bound back.*		
1930		$1,500	$1,750
Tenor ukulele	*Mahogany body, bound top, bound back.*		
1933		$1,500	$2,200

Maccaferri

1923-1990. Between the time he designed the Selmer guitar that became instantly synonymous with Django's gypsy jazz and his invention of the plastic clothespin, guitar design genius and manufacturing impresario Mario Maccaferri created a line of stringed instruments revolutionary for their complete plastic construction. The ukuleles were by far the greatest success, and most bore the tiny Maccaferri coat of arms on their tiny headstock.

MODEL YEAR	FEATURES	EXC. COND. LOW	HIGH
Baritone ukulele	*Polystyrene cutaway body.*		
1959		$100	$200
Islander ukulele	*Polytyrene plastic body, crest in peghead.*		
1953		$100	$200
Playtune ukulele	*Polystyrene body.*		
1956		$100	$200
TV Pal ukulele	*Polystyrene plastic body.*		
1955		$100	$200
TV Pal Deluxe ukulele	*Extended fingerboard.*		
1960		$100	$200

Magic Fluke Company

1999-present. Budget grade, production, ukuleles made in New Hartford, CT. With a clever design, exceptional quality, dozens of catchy finishes, and surprisingly affordable prices, it's little wonder that these little wonders have caught on. While riding – if not almost single-handedly driving – the coming third wave of uke popularity (the 1920s and '50s were the first and the second), Dale and Phyllis Webb of the Magic Fluke, along with Phyllis' brother, author and Jumpin' Jim Beloff, are downright ukulele evangelists. The Fluke is the first new uke that you're not afraid to let the kid's monkey pick up, and with their addition of the slightly smaller Flea, they're so far the only producer of a good quality instrument to learn on.

Manuel Nunes

The self-professed father of the ukulele was at least one of the first makers to produce them in any quantity. Beginning after 1879, when he and the first boat load of Portuguese settlers landed in Hawaii, until at least the 1930s, Manuel and his son Leonardo (see Leonardo Nunes section) produced some of the most beautiful and superbly crafted ukes offered by any Island maker.

MODEL YEAR	FEATURES	EXC. COND. LOW	HIGH
Soprano ukulele	*Koa body.*		
1919	Figured koa body, bound top, back, f'board	$1,000	$1,500
1920	Rope bound top and back	$800	$1,200
1927	Bound body, f'board, and head	$1,000	$1,500
1930	Unbound body	$700	$900
1933	Rope bound soundhole only	$700	$900
Tenor ukulele	*Koa body, unbound top, unbound back.*		
1930		$900	$1,200
Taro Patch fiddle	*Koa body, unbound top, unbound back.*		
1930		$1,500	$2,000

MODEL YEAR	FEATURES	EXC. COND. LOW	HIGH

Marc Silber Guitar Company

1998-present. Mexican-made ukes from designer Marc Silber of Berkley, California. He also offers guitars. His Mexican-made "Frisco Uke" takes its inspiration from the inimitable Roy Smeck Vita Uke (see Harmony), but without the whimsy of the original.

Martin

1833-present. The C.F. Martin Company knew they wanted in on the uke craze, and toyed with some prototypes as early as 1907 or so, but didn't get around to actually getting serious until 1916. The first of these were characterized by rather more primitive craftsmanship (by stringent Martin standards), bar frets, and an impressed logo in the back of the headstock. By 1920, koa became available as a pricey option, and by the early '30s, regular frets and the familiar Martin headstock decal had prevailed. Martin single-handedly created the archetype of the mainland uke and the standard by which all competitors are measured.

Martin has recently re-entered the ukulele market, albeit tentatively, with its budget Mexican-made model S-0, and Backpacker uke.

Style 0 ukulele
Unbound mahogany body

YEAR	FEATURES	LOW	HIGH
1920	Wood pegs	$400	$550
1953	Patent pegs	$400	$600

Style 1 ukulele
Mahogany body.

1940	Rosewood bound top only	$500	$800
1950	Tortoise bound top only	$500	$800
1960	Tortoise bound top only	$450	$800
1967	Tortoise bound top only	$450	$700

Style 1C Concert uke
Concert-sized mahogany body, bound top.

| 1950 | | $100 | $1,300 |

Style 1C K Concert uke
Concert-sized koa body, bound top.

| 1950 | | $1,700 | $2,000 |

Style 1T Tenor uke
Tenor-sized mahogany body, bound top only.

| 1940 | | $1,100 | $1,500 |

Style 1K ukulele
Koa body, rosewood bound top.

| 1922 | Wood pegs | $1,500 | $1,600 |
| 1939 | Patent pegs | $1,500 | $1,700 |

Style 1 Taro Patch
Mahogany body, 8 strings, rosewood bound.

| 1933 | | $1,250 | $1,700 |

Style 1K Taro Patch
Same specs as above but koa body.

| 1940 | | $1,500 | $1,900 |

MODEL YEAR	FEATURES	EXC. COND. LOW	HIGH

Style 2 ukulele
Mahogany body, ivoroid-bound top, back.

1922		$900	$1,100
1935		$800	$1,100
1961		$800	$1,000

Style 2K ukulele
Figured koa body, bound top, back.

| 1923 | | $1,700 | $2,500 |
| 1939 | Patent pegs | $1,800 | $2,500 |

Style 2 Taro Patch
Mahogany body, 8 strings, ivoroid bound.

| 1931 | | $1,500 | $1,700 |

Style 2K Taro Patch
Same specs as above, but koa body.

| 1937 | | $1,700 | $2,500 |

Style 3 ukulele
Mahogany body.

1925	Kite inlay in headstock	$1,500	$2,500
1940	B/W lines in ebony f'board	$1,500	$2,500
1950	Extended fingerboard, dots	$1,500	$2,500

Style 3K ukulele
Figured koa body.

1924	"Bow-tie" f'board inlay	$3,500	$4,000
1932	B/W lines, diamonds, squares	$3,500	$4,000
1940	B/W lines and dot inlay	$3,500	$4,500

Style 3C K ukulele
Same specs as 3K, but in concert size.

| 1930 | | $6,000 | $9,000 |

Style 3 Taro Patch
Mahogany body, 8 strings, multiple bound.

| 1941 | | $2,000 | $3,000 |

Style 3K Taro Patch
Same specs as above, but koa body.

| 1929 | | $3,000 | $4,000 |

Style 5K ukulele
Highly figured koa body, all pearl trimmed.

| 1926 | | $6,000 | $9,000 |

Style 5M ukulele
1941. Same as 5K, but mahogany body.

| 1941 | | $10,000 | $15,000 |

Style 51 Baritone ukulele
Mahogany body, bound top and back.

| 1966 | | $1,000 | $1,500 |

Style T 15 Tiple
Mahogany body, 10 metal strings, unbound.

| 1971 | | $500 | $750 |

Style T 17 Tiple
Mahogany body, unbound top, back.

| 1950 | | $750 | $1,000 |

Style T 28 Tiple
Rosewood body, bound top, back.

| 1969 | | $1,500 | $1,700 |

Marc Silber "frisco uke"

Martin 1K Taro Patch

Martin 2M Concert

UKULELES

Michael Dunn Harpuke

Pegasus Artist Series tenor 6-string

Petersen Polk-A-Lay-Lee natural uke

MODEL YEAR	FEATURES	EXC. COND. LOW	HIGH

Michael Dunn Guitars

1968-present. Luthier Michael Dunn builds a Knutsen-style harp uke in New Westminster, British Columbia. He also builds guitars.

Mirabella

1997-present. Professional grade, custom ukuleles built by luthier Cristian Mirabella in Babylon, New York. He also builds mandolins and guitars.

National

Ca. 1927-present. To capitalize on the success of their "amplifying" guitars, the Dopyera brothers introduced mental-bodied ukuleles and mandolins as well. Large, heavy, and ungainly by today's standards, these early offerings nonetheless have their charms. Their subsequent switch to a smaller body shape produced an elegant and sweet-sounding resonator uke that soon became much sought after.

Style 1 ukulele
Nickel body.

1928	Tenor, 6 in. resonator	$2,500	$4,000
1933	Soprano	$2,500	$4,000

Style 2 ukulele
Nickel body, engraved roses.

1928	Tenor	$4,000	$5,000
1931	Soprano	$4,000	$5,000

Style 3 ukulele
Nickel body, lilies of the valley.

1929	Tenor	$4,000	$6,000
1933	Soprano	$5,000	$8,000

Style O ukulele
Metal body, soprano size, sanblasted scenes.

1931		$2,000	$2,850

Triolian ukulele

1928	Sunburst Painted body, tenor size	$1,400	$1,850
1930	Sunburst painted body, soprano size	$1,600	$2,200
1934	Wood-grained metal body, soprano size	$1,200	$1,550

National Reso-Phonic

1988-present. Successors to the National name, with the designs and patented "amplifying" resonator assemblies of the original National models, they offer professional grade, production, single cone ukuleles from their shop in San Luis Obispo, California. They also build guitars and basses.

Oscar Schmidt

1879-ca. 1939, 1979-present. The same New Jersey outfit responsible for Leadbelly's 12 string guitar offered ukes as well during the same period. Many of these were odd amalgams of materials, often combining koa, mahogany, and spruce in the same instrument. Since 1979, when the name was acquired by the U.S. Music Corp. (Washburn, Randall, etc.) they have offered a line of budget grade, production, Asian-made ukes.

MODEL YEAR	FEATURES	EXC. COND. LOW	HIGH

Soprano ukulele
Spruce top, bound mahogany body.

1930		$250	$350

Pegasus

1977-present. Professional grade, custom, ukuleles and related instruments built by luthier Bob Gleason in Kurtistown, Hawaii.

Polk-a-lay-lee

1960s. These inexplicably shaped oddities were produced by Petersen Products of Chicago circa the mid-1960s, and anecdotal Midwestern lore has it that their intent was to be offered as giveaways for the Polk Brothers, a local appliance chain. This may be how they ended up, although the gargantuan original packaging makes no reference to any such promotion. The box does call out what the optional colors were.

Many have noted the striking resemblance to the similarly named wares of the Swaggerty company (see Swaggerty) of California, who also offered brightly colored plywood-bodied ukes in clown-like oversized incarnations, but who was copying whom has yet to be determined.

Ukulele
Long "boat oar" body, uke scale, brown, natural, red, or black.

1965		$250	$350

Regal

Ca. 1884-1966, 1987-present. Like the other large 1930s Chicago makers, Harmony and Lyon & Healy, the good ukes are very very good, and the cheap ukes are very very cheap. Unlike its pals, however, Regal seems to have produced more ukuleles in imaginative themes, striking color schemes, and in more degrees of fancy trim, making them the quintessential wall-hangers. And lucky for you, there's a vintage Regal uke to suit every décor.

Carson Robison Ukulele
Top sports painted signature, cowboy scene.

1935		$500	$900

Jungle Uke
Birch body, covered in leopard skin fabric.

1950		$500	$750

Resonator ukulele
Black body, f holes, see Dobro uke.

1934		$1,200	$1,500

Soprano ukulele
Birch body.

1931	Brown sunburst	$175	$250
1931	Nautical themes, various colors	$175	$250
1945	Painted body, "victory" themes	$450	$750

Soprano ukulele
Koa body, multicolored rope bound top.

1930		$250	$300

MODEL YEAR	FEATURES	EXC. COND. LOW	HIGH
Soprano ukulele			
Mahogany body.			
1930	Multiple bound top	$450	$650
1935	Inlays	$350	$650
1940	Extended fingerboard	$250	$350
Wendell Hall Red Head			
Koa body, celebrity decal on headstock.			
1935		$400	$600
Tiple			
1930	Birch body stained dark, black binding	$350	$450
1935	Spruce top, mahogany body, fancy binding	$450	$550

Rogue

2001-present. Budget grade, production, imported ukuleles. They also offer guitars, basses, mandolins, banjos, effects and amps.

S.S. Stewart

Not much is known about the ukuleles of this Philadelphia firm, except that they were most certainly sub-contracted from another maker or makers.

MODEL YEAR	FEATURES	EXC. COND. LOW	HIGH
Soprano ukulele			
Mahogany body, bound top, bound back.			
1927		$200	$350

Samick

1958-2001, 2002-present. Budget grade, production, imported ukuleles. They also offer guitars, basses, mandolins and banjos.

Sammo

Flashy internal paper labels trumpet that these ukes (mandolins and guitars, too) were products of the "Osborne Mfg. Co. Masonic Temple, Chicago-Ill" and what the heck any of that means is still open to modern speculation. Your guess is as good as mine. Still, the high quality and often opulent degree of ornamentation that the instruments exhibit, coupled with even the vaguest implication that they were made by guys wearing fezzes and/or men who ride around in tiny cars at parades is all the reason I need to buy every one I see.

MODEL YEAR	FEATURES	EXC. COND. LOW	HIGH
Soprano ukulele			
1925	Figured maple body, 5-ply top, back binding	$300	$400
1925	Unbound koa body, fancy headstock shape	$300	$400

Silvertone

1941-ca. 1970, present. Silvertone was the house brand of Sears & Roebuck after WWII, although most (if not all) of its ukes were manufactured for them by Harmony.

MODEL YEAR	FEATURES	EXC. COND. LOW	HIGH
Soprano ukulele			
Mahogany body, Harmony-made.			
1950	Unbound	$150	$250
1950	Sunburst	$150	$250
1955	Bound	$150	$250
1960	Green	$150	$250

Slingerland

Banjo ukuleles bearing this brand (see Slingerland Banjo uke section below) were certainly made by the popular drum company of the same name (banjos being little more than drums with necks, after all). Slingerland standard ukuleles, on the other hand, bear an uncanny resemblance to the work of the Oscar Schmidt company.

MODEL YEAR	FEATURES	EXC. COND. LOW	HIGH
Soprano ukulele			
Koa body, top and soundhole rope bound.			
1920		$250	$300

Specimen Products

Since 1984, Chicago builder Ian Schneller has built some of the most offbeat, endearing – and high quality – custom ukuleles available. He also builds guitars, basses, amps and speaker cabs. He'll probably build you anything you want, if you ask him nicely enough.

Sterling

The miniscule reference buried deep within the headstock decal of a "T.B. Co." can only mean that Sterling ukulele somehow fits into the mind-numbing Tonk Bros./Lyon & Healy/Regal/S.S.Stewart manufacturing puzzle. Nonetheless, the brand must have been reserved for the cream of the crop, since the Sterling ukes that surface tend to be of the drop-dead-gorgeous variety.

MODEL YEAR	FEATURES	EXC. COND. LOW	HIGH
Soprano ukulele			
Flamed Koa, multiple fancy binding all over.			
1935		$1,200	$1,500

Stetson

Popular misconception – to say nothing of wishful thinking and greed – has it that all instruments labeled with the Stetson brand were the work of the Larson Brothers of Chicago. Now, some Stetson guitars and a very few mandolins may be genuine Larson product, but the ukuleles surely were made elsewhere.

MODEL YEAR	FEATURES	EXC. COND. LOW	HIGH
Soprano ukulele			
Mahogany body, single bound top and back			
1930		$150	$300

Supertone

1914-1940s. For whatever reason, Supertone was the name attached to Sears' musical instruments before the line became Silvertone (see above). These, too, were all Harmony made.

Regal Jungle Uke

Regal Archtop Uke

Sammo

UKULELES

Supertone Cheerleader

Weissenborn

Gibson BU 3

MODEL YEAR	FEATURES	EXC. COND. LOW	HIGH
Soprano ukulele	*Mahogany body, Harmony-made.*		
1930	Unbound	$150	$300
1940	Bound	$150	$300
Soprano ukulele	*Koa body, Harmony-made.*		
1935	Rope bound	$250	$450
1943	Unbound	$150	$350

Swaggerty

Not enough is known of this WestCoast company, except that their product line of unusually shaped four stringed novelty instruments oddly mirrors those made by Petersen Products in Chicago at the same time (see Polk-a-lay-lee). The two companies even seem to have shared plastic parts, such as fingerboards and tuners. Go figure.

Surf-a-lay-lee
Green, yellow, or orange plywood body, long "horn."

1965		$200	$350

Tabu

The "Tabu" brand on either the back of a ukulele's headstock or inside its soundhole was never an indication of its original maker. Rather, it was intended to assure the purchaser that the uke was, indeed of bona fide Hawaiian origin. So rampant was the practice of mainland makers claiming Island manufacture of their wares that in the late 'teens Hawaii launched a campaign to set the record straight, and – lucky for you – a nifty little brand was the result. The Tabu mark actually was used to mark the ukes of several different makers.

Soprano ukulele
Figured koa body.

1915	Unbound	$500	$750
1915	Rope bound	$700	$850

Vega

Famous for their banjos, the Vega name was applied to a sole baritone uke, tied with the endorsement of '50s TV crooner Arthur Godfrey.

Arthur Godfrey Baritone
Mahogany body, unbound

1955	$300	$450

Washburn

See Lyon & Healy.

Weissenborn

1910s-1937. The mainland maker famous for their hollow-necked Hawaiian guitars was responsible for several uke offerings over the course of its 20-or-so-year run. Like their six-stringed big brothers, they were the closest thing to Island design and detail to come from the mainland.

Soprano ukulele
Figured koawood body.

1920	Unbound	$1,000	$1,200
1920	Rope bound	$1,000	$1,300

MODEL YEAR	FEATURES	EXC. COND. LOW	HIGH

Weymann

Renowned for fine tenor banjos, Weyman affixed their name to a full line of soprano ukes of varying degrees of decoration, quite certainly none of which were made under the same roof as the banjos. Most were C.F. Martin knock-offs.

Soprano ukulele

1925	Mahogany body, unbound	$450	$700
1930	Koa body, fancy pearl vine f'board inlay	$1,000	$1,500

Banjo Ukuleles
Bacon

This legendary Connecticut banjo maker just couldn't resist the temptation to extend their line with uke versions of their popular banjos. As with Gibson, Ludwig, Slingerland, and Weyman, the banjo ukuleles tended to mimic the already proven construction techniques and decorative motifs of their regular banjo counterparts. In materials, finish, and hardware, most banjo ukes share many more similarities with full sized banjos than differences. The banjo ukes were simply included as smaller, plainer, variations of bnajos, much as concert, tenor, and baritone options fleshed out standard ukulele lines.

Banjo ukulele
Walnut rim, fancy fingerboard inlays.

1927		$1,000	$1,200

Silver Bell banjo ukulele
Engraved pearloid fingerboard & headstock.

1927		$1,750	$2,000

Gibson

BU 1 banjo ukulele
Small 6 in. head, flat panel resonator.

1928	$300	$500

BU 2 banjo ukulele
8 in. head, dot inlay.

1930	$500	$750

BU 3 banjo ukulele
8 in. head, diamond and square inlay.

1935	$1,000	$1,200

BU 4 banjo ukulele
8 in. head, resonator and flange.

1932	$1,000	$1,500

BU 5 banjo ukulele
8 in. head, resonator and flange, gold parts.

1937	$1,500	$2,000

Le Domino
Banjo ukulele
Resonator, decorated as Le Domino uke.

1933	$350	$500

Ludwig
Banjo ukulele

1928	Flange w/ "crown" holes, nickel plated parts	$2,500	$3,500

*The **Vintage Guitar Price Guide** shows low to high values for items in all-original excellent condition, and, where applicable, with original case or cover.*

MODEL YEAR	FEATURES	EXC. COND. LOW	HIGH
1927	As above, but with all gold plated parts	$2,500	$3,500
1930	Ivoroid headstock overlay w/ art deco detail	$1,500	$2,500

Wendell Hall Professional
Walnut resonator, flange w/ oval holes.

1927		$1,100	$2,000

Regal
Banjo ukulele
Mahogany rim, resonator, fancy rope bound.

1933		$350	$500

Richter
Allegedly, this Chicago company bought the already-made guitars, ukes, and mandolins of other manufacturers, painted and decorated them to their liking and resold them. True or not, they certainly were cranked out in a bevy of swanky colors.

MODEL YEAR	FEATURES	EXC. COND. LOW	HIGH
Banjo ukulele			
1930	Chrome plated body, two f holes in back	$200	$350
1930	As above, but entire body and neck painted	$200	$350

Slingerland
May Bell banjo ukulele
Walnut resonator with multicolored rope.

1935		$300	$400

Weymann
Banjo ukulele
Maple rim, open back, ebony fingerboard.

1926		$850	$1,000

Ludwig Banjo Uke

UKULELES

Bibliography

'50s Cool: Kay Guitars, by Jay Scott, 1992, Seventh String Press, Inc.

50 Years of Fender, by Tony Bacon, 2000, Miller Freeman Books.

Acoustic Guitars and Other Fretted Instruments, A Photographic History, by George Gruhn and Walter Carter, 1993, GPI Books.

Acoustic Guitar magazine, various issues, String Letter Publishing.

Acquired of the Angels, by Paul William Schmidt, 1998, Scarecrow Press.

American Basses, by Jim Roberts, 2003, Backbeat Books.

American Guitars, An Illustrated History, by Tom Wheeler, 1992, Harper Collins.

Ampeg - The Story Behind The Sound, by Gregg Hopkins and Bill Moore, 1999, Hal Leonard Publishing.

Amps! The Other Half of Rock 'n' Roll, by Ritchie Fliegler, 1993, Hal Leonard publishing.

The Bass Book, A Complete Illustrated History of Bass Guitars, by Tony Bacon and Barry Moorhouse, 1995, Miller Freeman Books.

The Boss Book, 2001, Hal Leonard Publishing.

The Burns Book, by Paul Day, 1990, PP Publishing and The Bold Strummer.

Classic Guitars U.S.A., by Willie G. Moseley, 1992, Centerstream.

The Classical Guitar Book, by Tony Bacon, et al., 2002, Balafon Books.

The Complete History of Rickenbacker Guitars, by Richard R. Smith, 1987, Centerstream.

Cowboy Guitars, by Steve Evans andRon Middlebrook, 2002, Centerstream.

Custom Guitars, A Complete Guide to Contempory Handcrafted Guitars, 2000, String Letter Publishing.

The Custom Guitar Shop and Wayne Richard Charvel, by Frank W/m Green, 1999, Working Musician Publications.

A Desktop Reference of Hip Vintage Guitar Amps, by Gerald Weber, 1994, Kendrick Books.

Electric Guitars and Basses, A Photographic History, by George Gruhn and Walter Carter, 1994, GPI Books.

Elektro-Gitarren Made in Germany, by Norbert Schnepel and Helmuth Lemme (German, with English translation), 1987, Musik-Verlag Schnepel-Lemme oHG.

Epiphone: The Complete History, by Walter Carter, 1995, Hal Leonard publishing.

Epiphone: The House of Stathopoulo, by Jim Fisch & L.B. Fred, 1996, Amsco Publications.

The Fender Amp Book, by John Morrish, 1995, Balafon Books and GPI Books.

Fender Amps: The First Fifty Years, by John Teagle and John Sprung, 1995, Hal Leonard Publishing.

The Fender Bass, by Klaus Blasquiz, 1990, Mediapresse.

The Fender Bass, An Illustrated History, by J.W. Black and Albert Molinaro, 2001, Hal Leonard Publishing.

The Fender Book, by Tony Bacon and Paul Day, 1992, Balafon and GPI Books.

Fender: The Sound Heard 'Round the World, by Richard R. Smith, 1995, Garfish Publishing.

The Fender Stratocaster, by Andre Duchossoir, 1988, Mediapresse.

The Fender Telecaster, by Andre Duchossoir, 1991, Hal Leonard Publishing.

G&L: Leo's Legacy, by Paul Bechtoldt, 1994, Woof Associates.

Gibson Electrics, The Classic Years, by A. R. Duchossoir, 1994, Hal Leonard Publishing.

Gibson's Fabulous Flat-Top Guitars, by Eldon Whitford, David Vinopal, and Dan Erlewine, 1994, GPI Books.

Gibson Guitars: 100 Years of An American Icon, by Walter Carter, 1994, W. Quay Hays.

The Gibson Les Paul Book, A Complete History of Les Paul Guitars, by Tony Bacon and Paul Day, 1993 Balafon Books and GPI Books.

The Gibson Super 400, Art of the Fine Guitar, by Thomas A. Van Hoose, 1991, GPI Books.

Gibson Shipping Totals 1948-1979, 1992, J.T.G.

The Gretsch Book, by Tony Bacon & Paul Day, 1996, Balafon Books and GPI Books.

Gruhn's Guide to Vintage Guitars, 2nd Edition, by George Gruhn and Walter Carter, 1999, Miller Freeman Books.

The Guild Guitar Book: The Company and the Instruments 1952-1977, by Hans Moust, 1995, GuitArchives Publications.

Guitar Identification: Fender-Gibson-Gretsch-Martin, by Andre Duchossoir, 1983, Hal Leonard Publishing Corporation.

Guitar People, by Willie G. Moseley, 1997, Vintage Guitar Books.

Guitar Player magazine, various issues, Miller Freeman.

Guitar Stories, Vol. I, by Michael Wright, 1994, Vintage Guitar Books.

Guitar Stories, Vol. II, by Michael Wright, 2000, Vintage Guitar Books.

Guitar World magazine, various issues, Harris Publications.

The Guitars of the Fred Gretsch Company, by Jay Scott, 1992, Centerstream.

Guitars From Neptune, A Definitive Journey Into Danelectro-Mania, by Paul Bechtoldt, 1995, Backporch Publications.

Guitar Graphics, Vol. 1 (Japanese), 1994, Rittor Music Mooks.

The Guru's Guitar Guide, by Tony Bacon and Paul Day, 1990, Track Record and The Bold Strummer.

The History and Artistry of National Resonator Instruments, by Bob Brozman, 1993, Centerstream.

The History of Marshall, by Michael Doyle, 1993, Hal Leonard Publishing.

The History of the Ovation Guitar, by Walter Carter, 1996, Hal Leonard publishing.

The Martin Book, by Walter Carter, 1995, Balafon Books and GPI Books.

Martin Guitars, A History, by Mike Longworth, 1988, 4 Maples Press.

Martin Guitars: An Illustrated Celebration of America's Premier Guitarmaker, by Jim Washburn & Richard Johnston, 1997, Rodale Press, Inc.

Musicial Merchandise Review magazine, various issues, Symphony Publishing.

The Music Trades magazine, various issues, Music Trades Corporation.

The Official Vintage Guitar Magazine Price Guide, all editions.

The PRS Guitar Book, by Dave Burrluck, 1999, Outline Press, London.

The Rickenbacker Book, by Tony Bacon & Paul Day, 1994, Balafon Books and GFI Books.

Stellas & Stratocasters, by Willie G. Moseley, 1994, Vintage Guitar Books.

Stompbox, by Art Thompson, 1997, Miller Freeman Books.

The Tube Amp Book, 4th Edition, by Aspen Pittman, 1993, Groove Tubes.

The Ultimate Guitar Book, by Tony Bacon and Paul Day, 1991, Alfred A. Knopf.

Vintage Guitar magazine, various issues, Vintage Guitar, Inc.

VG Classics magazine, various issues, Vintage Guitar, Inc.

The Vox Story, A Complete History of the Legend, by David Peterson and Dick Denney, 1993, The Bold Strummer, Ltd.

Washburn: Over One Hundred Years of Fine Stringed Instruments, by John Teagle, 1996, Amsco Publications.

Various manufacturer catalogs, literature, and web sites.

Dealer Directory
A GEOGRAPHICAL GUIDE

AUSTRALIA
Rics Vintage Guitars
Contact: Richard Zand-Vliet
Studio 3-13 James St.
Fremantle 6160
West Australia
Phone: international +61 8
 94332625
Phone: local 08-94332625
ric@ricsvintageguitars.com
www.ricsvintageguitars.com

CANADA
Folkway Music
Contact: Mark Stutman
163 Suffolk Street West
Guelph, Ontario N1H2J7
Phone: 519-763-5524
info@folkwaymusic.com
www.folkwaymusic.com

K.S. Sound
Contact: K. Stewart Lorriman
14-4 Westwood Blvd., #386
Upper Tantallon, Nova Scotia
 B3Z-1H3
Phone: 902-826-2026
Fax: 902-826-2067
audiorep@ns.sympatico.ca

The Twelfth Fret Inc.
Contact: Grant MacNeill and
 David Wren
2132 Danforth Avenue
Toronto, Ont., Canada M4C 1J9
Phone: 416-423-2132
Fax: 416-423-0012
sales@12fret.com
www.12fret.com

ENGLAND
Ampaholics
Contact: Paul GT
P.O. Box 542
Surrey, GU1 12F, England
Phone: +44-1483-825102
Fax: +44-1483-825102
www.ampaholics.org.uk

Watford Valves & Speakers
Contact: Derek Rocco
Bricket Wood, Street Albans.
Herts. England AL2 3TS
Phone: 44-1923-893270
Fax: 44-1923-679207

sales@watfordvalves.com
www.watfordvalves.com

ITALY
Real Vintage
Contact: Nino Fazio
via Manzoni, 13
98057 Milazzo ME, Italy
Phone: +39-090-40646
realvintage@realvintage.it
www.realvintage.it

UNITED STATES
Alabama
Elite Music Sales
Contact: Brian Hinton
1737 Eastern Blvd.
Montgomery, AL 36117
Phone: 334-215-0215
Fax: 334-215-0216
sales@elitemusicsales.com
www.elitemusicsales.com

Arizona
Antique Electronic Supply
Contact: Brian Campanella
6221 South Maple Avenue
Tempe, AZ 85283
Phone: 480-820-5411
Fax: 800-706-6789
info@tubesandmore.com
www.tubesandmore.com

CE Distribution
Contact: Noreen Cravener
6221 South Maple Avenue
Tempe, AZ 85283
Phone: 480-755-4712
Fax: 480-820-4643
info@cedist.com
www.cedist.com

Willies Music
Contact: Willie
P.O. Box 1090
Dewey, AZ 86327
Phone: 928-632-0528
Fax: 928-632-9052
Cell: 928-713-3956
willieduck@yahoo.com

Arkansas
Blue Moon Music, Inc.
Contact: Les Haynie
1904 North College

Fayetteville, AR 72703
Phone: 501-521-8163
blumnmus@aol.com
bluemoonmusic.com

Blue Moon Music, Inc.
Contact: Les Haynie
1706 South East Walton Blvd.,
 Suite A
Bentonville, AR 72712
Phone: 479-271-2455
blumnmus@aol.com
bluemoonmusic.com

California
A Brown Sound
23 Joseph Ct.
San Rafael, CA 94903
Phone: 415-479-2124
Fax: 415-479-2132
abs@abrown.com
www.abrown.com

**AA-Ibanez/Gibson Guitar
Collector**
All 1970's - '80s Japanese Relics
 - Archtops/Semi-hollows/Solids
Phone: 310-672-2432
bluesfingers@earthlink.net

Aantone's Music
Contact: Antone
36601 Newark Boulevard #11
Newark, CA 94560
Phone: 510-795-9170
Fax: 510-795-9170
aantones@pacbell.net
 www.aantones.com

Bad Cat Amps
Contact: James Heidrich
PMB #406, 2621 Green River
 Road
Corona, CA 92882
Phone: 909-808-8651
Fax: 909-279-6383
badcatamps@earthlink.net
www.badcatamps.com

Bill Lawrence Pickups
Contact: Bill or Becky Lawrence
1785 Pomona Road, Unit D
Corona, CA 92880
Phone: 909-737-5853
Fax: 909-737-7834

becky@billlawrence.com
billlawrence.com

Buffalo Bros. Guitars
Contact: Bob or Tim Page
2270-C Camino Vida Roble
Carlsbad, CA 92009
Phone: 760-431-9542
Fax: 760-431-9532
BuffaloBros@aol.com
www.buffalobrosguitars.com

**California Vintage Guitar and
Amp**
5244 Van Nuys Blvd.
Sherman Oaks, CA 91401
Phone: 818-789-8884
www.californiavintageguitaran-
 damp.com

**Chandler Musical Instru-
ments**
Contact: Paul
Phone: 530-899-1503
www.chandlerguitars.com
www.pickguards.us

Deering Banjo Co.
3733 Kenora Dr.
Spring Valley, CA 91977
Phone: 619-464-8252
Fax: 619-464-0833
info@deeringbanjos.com
www.deeringbanjos.com

Demeter Amplification
Contact: James Demeter
15730 Stagg Street
Van Nuys, CA 91406
Phone: 818-994-7658
Fax: 818-994-0647
sales@demeteramps.com
www.demeteramps.com

E*Guitars
Contact: Michael Indelicato
1446 4th St.
San Rafael, CA 94901
Phone: 415-459-2525
Fax: 415-457-7962
info@eguitars.com
www.eguitars.com

Emery Sound
Contact: Curtis Emery

Phone: 510-236-1176
www.emerysound.com

Eric Schoenberg Guitars
Contact: Eric
106 Main Street
Tiburon, CA 94920
Phone: 415-789-0846
eric@om28. com
www.om28.com

Freedom Guitar, Inc.
Contact: Dewey L. Bowen
6334 El Cajon Boulevard
San Diego, CA 92115
Phone: 800-831-5569
Fax: 619-265-1414
info@freedomguitar.com
www.freedomguitar.com

Fretted Americana
23901 Calabasas Rd., Ste 2024
Calabasas, CA 91302
Phone: 818-222-4113
Fax: 818-222-6173
vgm@frettedamericana.com
www.frettedamericana.com

Guitar Center (CA)
7425 Sunset Boulevard
Hollywood, CA 90046
Phone: 323-874-2302
323-874-1060
Fax: 323-969-9783
www.vintageguitars.net

Guitar Heaven (CA)
Contact: Frank Benna
1892 Contra Costa Boulevard
Pleasant Hill, CA 94523
Phone: 925-687-5750
guitarheaven@juno.com
www.guitarheaven.com

Koz-ax's
Contact: Jeff
Phone: 909-397-0991
jeff@kozaxs.com
www.kozaxs.com

Mercury Magnetics
Contact: Paul Patronette
Chatsworth, CA
Phone: 818-998-7791
Fax: 818-998-7835
sales@mercurymagnetics.com
www.mercurymagnetics.com

Neal's Music
Contact: Neal and Cathy Shelton
16458 Bolsa Chica Road PMB133
Huntington Beach, CA 92647

Phone: 714-901-5393
Fax: 714-901-5383
nealmuzic@aol.com
www.nealsmusic.com

Players Vintage Instruments
P.O. Box 445
Inverness, CA 94937-0445
Phone: 415-669-1107
info@vintageinstruments.com
www.vintageinstruments.com
Sales by Internet/Phone/Appointment

Soest Guitar Shop
Contact: Steve Soest
760 North Main Street Suite D
Orange, CA 92668
Phone: 714-538-0272
Fax: 714-532-4763
soestguitar@earthlink.net
www.soestguitar.com

Top Hat Amplification
Contact: Brian Gerhard
920 E. Orangethorpe Ave., Ste B
Anaheim, CA 92801
Phone: 714-447-6700
Fax: 714-447-6777
tophatamps@aol.com
www.tophatamps.com

Virtual Vintage Guitars
Contact: Jason C. Allen
Phone: 949-635-9797
sales@virtualvintageguitars.com
www.virtualvintageguitars.com

Virtuoso Polish and Cleaner
The Virtuoso Group, Inc.
P.O. Box 9775
Canoga Park, CA 91309-0775
Phone: 818-992-4733
virtuosopolish@sbcglobal.net
www.virtuosopolish.com

Wild West Guitars
Contact: Bo Harrison
1546 7th Street
Riverside, CA 92507
Phone: 909-369-7888 x205
Fax: 909-369-7371
sales@wildwestguitars.com
www.wildwestguitars.com

Wings Guitar Products, Inc.
Contact: Art Wiggs
5622 Comanche Court
San Jose, CA 95123
Phone: 408-225-2162
Fax: 408-225-5147

Connecticut
Acousticmusic.org/Serious Strings
Contact: Brian Wolfe
1238 Boston Post Road
Guilford, CT 06437
Phone: 203-458-2525
brian@seriousstrings.com
www.acousticmusic.org

Analog Man Guitar Effects
Contact: Mike Piera
36 Tamarack Avenue #343
Danbury, CT 06811
Phone: 203-778-6658
AnalogMike@aol.com
www.analogman.com

Guitar Hanger
Contact: Rick Tedesco
61 Candlewood Lake Road
Brookfield, CT 06804
Phone: 203-740-8889
Fax: 203-740-2730
sales@guitarhanger.com
www.guitarhanger.com

Delaware
ACME Guitar Works
Phone: 302-836-5301
www.acmeguitarworks.com

Florida
Andy's Guitars
Contact: Andy
1208 North Monroe Street
Tallahassee, FL 32303
Phone: 850-224-9944
Fax: 850-224-5381
info@andysguitars.com
www.andysguitars.com

Crescent City Music
Contact: Allen Glenn
111 North Summit Street
Crescent City, FL 32112
Phone/Fax: 386-698-2873
Phone: 386-698-2874
Voice Mail: 1-800-714-1664
ccmusic@crescentcitymusic.biz
www.crescentcitymusic.biz

Dixie Guitar Trader
Contact: Tom Williams
5068 North Dixie Highway
Ft. Lauderdale, FL 33334
Phone: 954-772-6900
dixieguitar@aol.com

Guitar Broker
Contact: Craig Brody
Phone: 954-385-8488

Fax: 954-349-1943
vintage@guitarbroker.com
www.guitarbroker.com

Kummer's Vintage Instruments
Contact: Timm Kummer
Phone: 954-752-6063
prewar99@aol.com
www.kummersvintage.com

Legends Music, Inc.
Contact: Kent Sonenberg
4340 West Hillsborough Avenue
Tampa, FL 33614
Phone: 813-348-0688
fax: 813-348-0689
ksonenbl@tampabay.rr.com
www.legendsmusic.com

Music Magic
Contact: Robert Graupera
6850 SW 81 Terrace
Miami, FL 33143
Phone: 305-957-6656
UsedGuitar@aol.com
www.magicguitars.com

Georgia
Atlanta Vintage Guitars
Contact: Frank Moates
561 Windy Hill Road
Smyrna, GA 30080
Phone: 770-433-1891
Fax: 770-433-1858
avg@mindspring.com
www.atlantavintageguitars.com

Dreamcatcher Guitars
Contact: Eddie Mathis
26 Webb Street Suite. 1
Roswell, GA 30075
Phone: 877-241-2359
Fax: 770-587-9962
em@gtrs4u.com
www.gtrs4u.com

Hawaii
Coconut Grove Music
Contact: Fred Oshiro
418 Kuulei Road
Kailua, HI 96734
Phone: 808-262-9977
Fax: 808-263-7052
cgmusic@lava.net
www.coconutgrovemusic.com

Illinois
Butler Custom Sound/Chicago Blues Box
770 N. Church Rd., #1
Elmhurst, IL 60126

Phone: 630-832-1983
www.chicagobluesbox.com

Chicago Music Exchange
Contact: Scott Silver
3270 North Clark Street
Chicago, IL 60657
Phone: 773-477-0830
Fax: 773-477-0427
sales@chicagomusicexchange.
 com
www.chicagomusicexchange.
 com

Guitar Works Ltd
Contact: Steve or Terry
709 Main Street
Evanston, IL 60202
Phone: 847-475-0855
Fax: 847-475-0715
guitarworksltd@aol.com
www.guitarworksltd.com

Make 'n Music
Contact: Greg
250 North Artesian
Chicago, IL 60612
Phone: 312-455-1970
makenmusic@earthlink.net

Music Gallery
Contact: Frank
2558 Greenbay Road
Highland Park, IL 60035
Phone: 847-432-6350 / 847-432-
 8883
MusicGlry@aol.com
www.musicgalleryinc.com

RWK Guitars
P.O. Box 1068
Highland Park, IL 60035
Phone: 847-432-4308
Bob@RWKGuitars.com
www.RWKGuitars.com

Indiana
WeberVST
Contact: T.A. Weber
329 E Firmin Street
Kokomo, IN 46902
Phone: 765-452-1249
Fax: 765-236-0270
www.webervst.com
www.weberspeakers.com

Kansas
E.M. Shorts Guitars
Contact: Jon Ray
2525 East Douglas Avenue
Wichita, KS 67211
Phone: 800-835-3006

Fax: 316-684-6858
wbic@wichitaband.com
www.wichitaband.com

Overland Express Guitars
Contact: David Schaefer
10739 West 109th Street
Overland Park, KS 66210
Phone: 913-469-4034
Fax: 913-469-9672
dave@overlandexpress.com
www.overlandexpress.com

Kentucky
Guitar Emporium
1610 Bardstown Road
Louisville, KY 40205
Phone 502-459-4153
Fax: 502-454-3661
guitar-emporium@mindspring.
 com
www.guitar-emporium.com

Willcutt Guitars
419 Rosemont Garden
Lexington, KY 40503
Phone: 859-276-3519
info@willcuttguitars.com
www.willcuttguitars.com

Louisianna
International Vintage Guitars
Contact: Steve Staples
1011 Magazine Street
New Orleans, LA 70130
Phone: 504-524-4557
Fax: 504-524-4665
guitars@webcorral.com
www.webcorral.com

Maryland
Garrett Park Guitars, Inc.
Contact: Rick Hogue
150 East Jennifer Road 150-0
Annapolis, MD 21401
Phone: 401-573-0500
Fax: 401-573-0502
gpguitars@toad.net
www.gpguitars.com

Guitar Exchange
Contact: Bruce Sandler
740 Frederick Road
Baltimore, MD 21228
Phone: 410-747-0122
Fax: 410-747-0525

Nationwide Guitars
Contact: Bruce Rickard
P.O. Box 2334
Columbia, MD 21045

Phone: 410-997-7440
Fax: 410-997-7440
bigredjr@comcast.net

Southworth Guitars
Contact: Gil Southworth
7845 Old Georgetown Road
Bethesda, MD 20814
Phone: 301-718-1667
Fax: 301-718-0391
southworthguitar@aol.com
www.southworthguitars.com

Massachusetts
Bay State Vintage Guitars
Contact: Craig D. Jones
295 Huntington Avenue, Room
 304
Boston, MA 02115
Phone: 617-267-6077

Cold Springs Electrical Works
Contact: Norm Moren
332 Rock Rimmon Road
Belchertown, MA 01007
Phone: 413-323-8869
 norm@coldspringselectricalwo
 rks.com
 www.coldspringselectrical-
 works.com

The Guitar Shelter
Contact: Ken Kirklewski
270 Main Street, Unit 4
Buzzards Bay, MA 02532-3257
Phone: 508-743-0663
Fax: 508-743-9400
gtrshelter@aol.com
www.guitarshelter.com

Lucchesi Vintage Instruments
Contact: Frank Lucchesi
518 Pleasant Street
Holyoke, MA 01040
Phone: 413-532-8819
Fax: 413-532-9504
LoukZ2@aol.com

The Perfect Note
Contact: Bob Ogulnick
Wales, MA 01057
Phone: 413-267-3392
Fax: 413-267-3392

RC Guitars
Contact: Corey Buckingham or
 Justin Kolack
378 Highland Avenue
Somerville, MA 02144
Phone: 617-623-7100

888-964-7100
rcg@rockcityguitar.com
www.rockcityguitar.com

Michigan
Big Bends, LLC
PO Box 324
Plainwell, MI 49080-0324
1-888-788-BEND
www.guitaristonly.com

Elderly Instruments
Contact: Stan Werbin
1100 North Washington
P.O. Box 14210 -VGF
Lansing, MI 48901
Phone: 517-372-7890
Fax: 517-372-5155
elderly@elderly.com
www.elderly.com

Huber & Breese Music
33540 Groesbeck Highway
Fraser, MI 48026
Phone: 586-294-3950
Fax: 586-294-7616
handbmusic@aol.com
www.huberbreese.com

Rockin' Daddy's
Contact: Randy Volin
P.O. Box 210368
Auburn Hills, MI 48321
Fax: 248-420-8499
randy@randyvolin.com
www.rockindaddys.com

Minnesota
Schaefer Guitars
Contact: Ed Schaefer
12 E. Superior St., Ste. 5
Duluth, MN 55802
Phone: 218-722-1766
sguitars@airmail.net
www.schaeferguitars.com

Solidbodyguitar.com
Contact: Bruce Barnes
2436 Highway 10
Mounds View, MN 55112
Phone: 763-783-0080
Fax: 763-783-0090
solidbodyguitar@quest.net
www.solidbodyguitar.com

Willie's American Guitars
254 Cleveland Avenue South
St. Paul, MN 55105
Phone: 651-699-1913
Fax: 651-690-1766
willies@ix.netcom.com
www.williesguitars.com

398

Missouri
Fly By Night Music
Contact: Dave Crocker
103 South Washington
Neosho, MO 64850-1816
Phone: 417-451-5110
Show number: 800-356-3347
crocker@joplin.com
www.texasguitarshows.com

Grubville Guitars
Contact: Glen Meyers
P.O. Box 14
Grubville, MO 63041
Phone: 636-274-4738
Fax: 636-285-9833
glencogg@aol.com
grubvilleguitars.com

Hazard Ware Inc./ Killer Vintage
Contact: Dave
P.O. Box 190561
St. Louis, MO 63119
Phone: 314-647-7795\800-646-7795
Fax: 314-781-3240
www.killervintage.com

Nashville Guitar Show
P.O. Box 271
Kirksville, MO 63501
Phone: 660-665-7172
Fax: 660-665-7450
spbgma@kvmo.net

Nevada
AJ's Music In Las Vegas
Contact: Peter Trauth
2031 W. Sunset
Henderson, NV 89014
Phone: 702-436-9300
pete@ajsmusic.com
www.ajsmusic.com

Cowtown Guitars
2797 South Maryland Parkway, Suite. 14
Las Vegas, NV 89109
Phone: 888-682-3002
Fax: 702-866-2520
www.cowtownguitars.com

New Hampshire
Guitar Gallery of New England
Contact: David Stearns
5 Route 101A #4
Amhearst, NH 03031
Phone: 603-672-9224
info@guitargallery.com
guitargallery.com

Retro Music
Contact: Jeff Firestone
38 Washington Street
Keene, NH 03431
Phone/Fax: 603-357-9732
retromusic@verizon.net
www.retroguitar.com

New Jersey
Dr. Bob's Guitar & Stringed Instrument Repair
Contact: Robert "Dr. Bob" Pinaire
By Appointment Only
Princeton, NJ Area
Phone: 609-921-1407 or 888-921-2461
Fax: 609-434-1643
swtsongman@aol.com
www.DrBobsMusic.com

Fuchs Audio Technology
Contact: Annette Fuchs
73 Collins Avenue
Bloomfield, NJ 07003-4504
Phone: 973-893-0225
sales@fuchsaudiotechnology.com
fuchsaudiotechnology.com

Golden Age Fretted Instruments
Contact: John Paul Reynolds
309 South Avenue W.
Westfield, NJ 07090
Phone: 908-301-0001
Fax: 908-301-1199
info@goldenageguitars.com
www.goldenageguitars.com

Hi Test Guitars
341 Westwind Court
Norwood, NJ 07648
Phone/Fax: 201-750-2445
By appointment Mon.-Sat. 11-6 EDT

Hoboken Vintage Guitars
Contact: Jim Pasch
164 1st Street
Hoboken, NJ 07030-3544
Phone: 201-222-8977
Fax: 201-222-9127
hoboken@extend.net
www.hobokenvintage.com

Lark Street Music
479 Cedar Lane
Teaneck, NJ 07666
Phone: 201-287-1959
Larkstreet@aol.com
www.larkstreet.com

New Jersey Guitar & Bass Center
Contact: Jay Jacus
995 Amboy Avenue
Edison, NJ 08837
Phone: 732-225-4444
Fax: 732-225-4404
NJGtrBass@aol.com
www.members.aol.com/NJGtrBass

Pick of the Ricks
Contact: Chris Clayton
17 Clementon Rd at Twin Roads Plaza
Berlin, NJ 08009
Phone: 856-767-5820
Fax: 856-627-4053
sales@pickofthericks.com
www.pickofthericks.com

New York
Bernunzio Vintage Guitars
Contact: John Bernunzio
875 East Avenue
Rochester, NY 14607
Phone: 585-473-6140
Fax: 585-442-1142
info@bernunzio.com
www.bernunzio.com

David Davidson
516-333-8700
stratguy98@aol.com

Diamond Strings
Contact: Bruce Diamond
20 Shaftsbury Rd.
Rochester, NY 14610
Phone: 585-424-3369
Fax: 585-475-1818
dstrings@rochester.rr.com
diamondstrings.com

Richard Friedman
516-635-8655
guitarparts1@aol.com

Gothic City Guitars
Contact: Charles Dellavalle
P.O. Box 123
Staten Island, NY 10310
Phone: 718-273-1691
www.GothicCityGuitars.com

Imperial Guitar and Soundworks
Contact: Bill Imperial
99 Route 17K
Newburgh, NY 12550
Phone: 845-567-0111

igs55@aol.com
www.imperialguitar.com

Keyboard Instrument Rentals
Buy & Sell Vintage Effects & Pedals
1697 Broadway Suite 504
New York, NY 10019
Phone: 212-245-0820
Fax: 212-245-8858
keyboardrentals@aol.com

Laurence Wexer Ltd.
Contact: Larry
251 East 32nd Street #11F
New York, NY 10016
Phone: 212-532-2994
info@wexerguitars.com

Ludlow Guitars
Contact: Robert Gary
164 Ludlow Street
New York, NY 10002
Phone: 212-353-1775
Fax: 212-353-1749
www.ludlowguitars.com

Mandolin Brothers, Ltd.
629 Forest Avenue
Staten Island, NY 10310
Phone: 718-981-3226/8585
Fax: 718-816-4416
mandolin@mandoweb.com
www.mandoweb.com

Manny's Music
Contact: Matt DeSilva and Richard Friedman
156 West 48th Street
New York, NY 10036
Phone: 212-819-0576
Fax: 212-391-9250
guitarparts1@aol.com

Michael's Music
Contact: Michael Barnett
29 West Sunrise Highway
Freeport, NY 11520
Phone: 5163-379-4111
Fax: 516-379-3058
info@michaelsmusic.com
www.michaelsmusic.com

Mirabella Guitars & Restorations
Contact: Cris Mirabella
P.O. Box 482
Babylon, NY 11702
Phone: 631-842-3819
Fax: 631-842-3827
mirguitars@aol.com
www.mirabellaguitars.com

Rudy's Music
Contact: Rudy
169 West 48th Street
New York, NY 10036
Phone: 212-391-1699
info@rudysmusic.com
www.rudysmusic.com

Rumble Seat Music
Contact: Eliot Michael
121 West State St.
Ithica, NY 14850
Phone: 607-277-9236
Fax: 607-277-4593
rumble@rumbleseatmusic.com
www.rumbleseatmusic.com

Sam Ash Music
Contact: David Davidson
385 Old Country Rd.
Carle Place, NY 11514
Phone: 516-333-8700
Fax: 516-333-8767
stratguy98@aol.com
www.samashmusic.com

Straight Shooter Guitars
Contact: John DeSilva
Syosset, NY
Phone: 516-993-9893
straightshooter@optonline.net

Top Shelf Music
Contact: Scott Freilich
1232 Hertell Ave.
Buffalo, NY 14216
Phone: 716-876-6544
Fax: 716-876-7343
shelftop@aol.com
www.topshelfmusic.com

Toys From The Attic
Contact: Zar Fentas
203 Mamaroneck Avenue
White Plains, NY 10601
Phone: 914-421-0069
Fax: 914-328-3852
guitars@tfta.com
www.tfta.com

North Carolina
Bee-3 Vintage
Contact: Gary Burnette
25 Arbor Lane
Ashville, NC 28805
Phone: 828-298-2197
email: bee3vintage@hotmail.com
www.bee3vintage.com

Carr Amplifiers
Contact: Steve

433 West Salisbury St.
Pittsboro, NC 27312
Phone: 919-545-0747
Fax: 919-545-0739
info@carramps.com
www.carramps.com

Coleman Music
Contact: Chip Coleman
1021 South Main Street
China Grove, NC 28023
Phone: 704-857-5705
Fax: 704-857-5709
sales@colemanmusic.com
www.colemanmusic.com

Maverick Music
Contact: Phil Winfield
1100 Kirkview Lane, Suite. 201
Charlotte, NC 28213
Phone: 704-599-3700
Fax: 704-599-3712
sales@maverick-music.com
www.maverick-music.com

Ohio
Dr. Z Amplification
www.drzamps.com

DHR Music
PO Box 43209
Cincinnati, OH 45243
Phone: 513-272-8004
Fax: 513-530-0229
dhrmusic@hotmail.com
www.dhrmusic.com

Fretware Guitars
Contact: Dave Hussung
400 South Main
Franklin, OH 45005
Phone: 937-743-1151
Fax: 937-743-9987
guitar@erinet.com
www.fretware.cc

Gary's Classic Guitars
Contact: Gary Dick
Cincinnati, OH
Phone: 513-891-0555
Fax: 513-891-9444
garysclssc@aol.com
www.garysguitars.com

Mike's Music
Contact: Mike Reeder
2615 Vine Street
Cincinnati, OH 45219
Phone: 513-281-4900
Fax: 513-281-4968
www.mikesmusicohio.com

String King Products
Contact: John Mosconi
P.O. Box 9083
Akron, OH 44305
Phone: 330-798-1055

Oklahoma
Strings West
Contact: Larry Briggs
P.O. Box 999
20 E. Main Street
Sperry, OK 74073
Phone: 800-525-7273
Fax: 918-288-2888
larryb@stringswest.com
www.stringswest.com

Oregon
Exceptional Guitars
Contact: Alan R. Buchalter
info@exceptionalguitars.com
www.exceptionalguitars.com

Kalapuya Music & Trading Co.
Contact: Tim Floro
6791/2 Main Street
Lebanon, OR 97355
Phone: 541-451-3957

McKenzie River Music
455 West 11th
Eugene, OR 97401
Phone: 541-343-9482
Fax: 541-465-9060
www.McKenzieRiverMusic.com

Pennsylvania
Alessandro (HoundDog Corp.)
Contact: George Alessandro
933 Robin Lane, P.O. Box 253
Huntington Valley, PA 19006
Phone: 215-355-6424
Fax: 215-355-6424
hounddogcorp@msn.com
www.alessandro-products.com

Guitar-Villa – Retro Music
Contact: John Slog
216A Nazareth Pike
Bethlehem, PA 18020
Phone: 610-746-9200
Fax: 610-746-9135
gvilla@guitar-villa.com
www.guitar-villa.com

Guitar-Villa – Retro Music
Contact: John Slog
30 S. Westend Boulevard.
Quakertown, PA 18951
Phone: 215-536-5800
gvilla@guitar-villa.com
www.guitar-villa.com

JH Guitars
Contact: Jim Heflybower
Pennsylvania
Phone: 610-363-9204
Fax: 610-363-8689
JHGuitars@webtv.net
www. jhguitars.com

Vintage Instruments & Frederick W. Oster Fine Violins
Contact: Fred W. Oster
1529 Pine Street
Philadelphia, PA 19102
Phone: 215-545-1000
Fax: 215-735-3634
www.vintage-instruments.com

Tennessee
Chambers Guitars
Contact: Joe
3205 West End Avenue
Nashville, TN 37209
Phone: 615-279-9540
www.ChambersGuitars.com

Gruhn Guitars
Contact: George Gruhn
400 Broadway
Nashville, TN 37203
Phone: 615-256-2033
Fax: 615-255-2021
gruhn@gruhn.com
www.gruhn.com

Guitar Heaven
Contact: Mark Murphy
5211 Hickory Hollow Parkway
107
Antioch, TN 37013
Phone: 615-717-1470
gtrheaven@aol.com
www.gtrheaven.com

Kangaroo Amp Covers
Contact: Steve Purcell
P.O. Box 120593
Nashville, TN 37212
Phone: 800-431-5537/615-361-5537
info@kangarooampcovers.com
www.kangarooampcovers.com

Music Room Guitars
Contact: Brad Gibson
5103 Kingston Pike
Knoxville, TN 37919
Phone: 865-584-0041
Toll Free: 877-584-0099
mrgknox@aol.com

Nashville Guitar Show
Contact: Chuck Stearman
P.O. Box 271

Kirksville, MO 63501
Phone: 660-665-7172
Fax: 660-665-7450
spbgma@kvmo.net

PedalDoctor FX
Contact: Tim Creek
412 Newbary Ct.
Franklin, TN 37069
Phone: 615-260-5651
doc@pedaldoctor.com
www.pedaldoctor.com

Recycled Sound Repair
226 Ripley Is Rd.
Afton, TN 37616
Phone: 423-639-3977

StringDeals.com
(a division of Guitar Heaven)
Contact: Mark Murphy
5211 Hickory Hollow Parkway
#107
Antioch, TN 37013
Phone: 615-717-0600
sales@stringdeals.com
stringdeals.com

Texas
Allparts
13027 Brittmoore Park Drive
Houston, TX 77041
Phone: 713-466-6414
allpartgtr@aol.com
www.allparts.com

Eugene's Guitars Plus
Contact: Eugene Robertson
2010 South Buckner Boulevard
Dallas, TX 75217-1823
Phone: 214-391-8677
pluspawnguitars@yahoo.com
www.texasguitarshows.com

Hill Country Guitars
Contact: Kevin Drew Davis
106 Wimberley Square
Wimberley, TX 78676-5020
Phone: 512-847-8677
www.hillcountryguitars.com

Kendrick Amplifiers
Route. 2 P.O. Box 871
Kempner, TX 76539
Phone: 512-932-3130
Fax: 512-932-3135
kendrick@kendrick-amplifiers.

com
www.kendrick-amplifiers.com

Southpaw Guitars
Contact: Jimmy
5813 Bellaire Blvd.
Houston, TX 77081
Phone: 713-667-5791
Fax: 713-667-4091
southpawguitars@sbcglobal.net
www.southpawguitars.com

Rio Grande Pickups
Contact: Alan Hill
3526 E. TC Jester Blvd.
Houston, TX 77018
Phone: 713-957-0470
Fax: 713-957-3316
sales@riograndepickups.com
www.riograndepickups.com

Texas Amigos Guitar Shows
Arlington Guitar Show (The 4
Amigos)
Contact: John or Ruth Brink-
mann
Phone: 800-329-2324
Fax: 817-473-1089
www.texasguitarshows.com

Chicago/Austin Guitar Show
Contact: Dave Crocker
Phone: 800-356-3347
Fax: 817-473-1089
crocker@joplin.com
www.texasguitarshows.com

**California World Guitar
Shows**
Contact: Larry Briggs
Phone: 800-525-7273
Fax: 918-288-2888
larryb@stringswest.com
www.texasguitarshows.com

**Van Hoose Vintage Instru-
ments**
Contact: Thomas Van Hoose
2722 Raintree Drive
Carrollton, TX 75006
Phone: (days) 972-250-2919 or
(eves) 972-418-4863
Fax: 972-250-3644
tv0109@flash.net
www.vanhoosevintage.com

Waco Vintage Instruments

Contact: John Brinkman
1275 North Main Street, Ste #4
Mansfield, TX 76063
Phone: 817-473-9144
Guitar Show Phone: 888-473-
6059

Utah
**Intermountain Guitar and
Banjo**
Contact: Leonard or Kennard
712 East 100 South
Salt Lake City, UT 84102
Phone: 801-322-4682
Fax: 801-355-4023
guitarandbanjo@earthlink.com
www.guitarandbanjo.net

Virginia
Authentic Guitars
Contact: Michael Hansen
12715-Q Warwick Blvd.
Newport News, VA 23606
Phone: 757-595-4663
www.AuthenticGuitars.com

Authentic Guitars - 2nd Store
Contact: Michael Hansen
5251-42 John Tyler Highway
Williamsburg, VA 23185
Phone: 757-259-9711
www.AuthenticGuitars.com

**Callaham Vintage Guitars &
Amps**
Contact: Bill Callaham
114 Tudor Drive
Winchester, VA 22603
Phone: 540-955-0294 - Shop
callaham@callahamguitars.com
www.callahamguitars.com

Legato Guitars
Contact: Bill Fender
107 South West Street, Suite 101
Alexandria, VA 22314
By Appointment Only
bfender@legatoguitars.com
www.legatoguitars.com

Vintage Sound
Contact: Bill Holter
P.O. Box 11711
Alexandria, VA 22312
Phone: 703-914-2126
Fax: 703-914-1044
bhvsound@vintagesound.com

www.vintagesound.com
Guitars - Amps - Effects

Washington
Emerald City Guitars
Contact: Jay Boone
83 South Washington in Pioneer
Square
Seattle, WA 98104
Phone: 206-382-0231
jayboone@emeraldcityguitars.
com

Guitarville
Contact: Tommy Steinley
19258 15th Avenue North East
Seattle, WA 98155-2315
Phone: 206-363-8188
Fax: 206-363-0478
gv@guitarville.com
www.guitarville.com

Jet City Guitars LLC
Contact: Allen Kaatz
2212 Queen Anne Ave. N., Box
134
Seattle, WA 98109
Phone: 206-361-1365
ark@jetcityguitars.com
www.jetcityguitars.com

Wisconsin
Bizarre Guitars
Contact: Brian Goff
2501 Waunona Way
Madison, WI 53713
Phone: 608-235-3561
bdgoff@terracom.net
www.bizarreguitars.com

Dave's Guitar Shop
Contact: Dave Rogers
1227 South 3rd Street
La Crosse, WI 54601
Phone: 608-785-7704
Fax: 608-785-7703
davesgtr@aol.com
www.davesguitar.com

**Dave's Guitar Shop (2nd
location)**
Contact: Dave Rogers
1801 Sherman St.
Wausau, WI 54401
Phone: 715-849-4800
davesgtr@aol.com
davesguitar.com

Page numbers indicate guitar listing unless otherwise noted

A Fuller Sound 2
Abel 2
Abilene..................... 2
Abyss 2
Ace-Tone
  Effects....................316
Acoustic.................... 2
  Amps.................248-249
  Bass.....................208
Acoustyx
  Effects....................316
ADA
  Amps.....................249
  Effects....................316
Aero Uke
  Ukuleles...................384
Agile 2
Aguilar
  Amps.....................249
  Effects....................316
Aiken Amplification
  Amps.....................249
Aims........................ 2
Airline 2-3
  Amps.....................249
  Bass.....................208
  Mandolins 366
  Lap/Steels 356
Alamo 3
  Amps.................249-250
  Bass.....................208
  Effects....................316
  Lap/Steels 356
Alamo Guitars............. 3
Alan Carruth 3
Alberico, Fabrizio 3
Alembic 3
  Bass 208-209
Alesis
  Amps.....................250
  Effects....................316
Alessandro
  Amps.....................250
Alkire
  Lap/Steels 356
Allen Amplification
  Amps.....................250
  Effects....................316
Allen Guitars 3
  Mandolins 366
Aloha 3
  Amps.....................250
  Ukuleles...................384
Alray 3
Altair Corp.
  Effects....................316
Alvarez 3-4
  Bass.....................209
  Mandolins 366
  Lap/Steels 356
Alvarez Yairi............... 4
Alvarez, Juan 4
Amdek
  Effects....................316
American Acoustech .. 4
American Archtop
Guitars 4
American
Conservatory 4

Bass 209
Mandolins 366
American Showster 4
Ampeg......................4-5
  Amps.................250-253
  Bass.....................209
  Effects................ 316-317
Analog Man
  Effects....................317
Andersen Stringed
Instruments................. 5
  Mandolins 366
Anderson Amplifiers
  Amps.....................253
Andreas.................... 5
  Bass.....................209
Angelica.................... 5
  Bass.....................209
Angus 5
Antares..................... 5
Antique Acoustics...... 5
Apollo 5
  Bass 210
  Effects....................317
Applause...................5-6
  Bass 210
  Mandolins 366
  Ukuleles...................384
Arbiter
  Effects....................317
Arbor 6
  Bass 210
Arch Kraft 6
Aria/Aria Pro II 6
  Amps.....................253
  Bass 210
  Effects................ 317-318
  Mandolins 366
  Lap/Steels 356
Aria Diamond 6
Arion
  Effects....................318
Armstrong, Rob 6
  Bass 210
  Mandolins 366
Arpeggio Korina 6
Artesano 6
Artinger Custom......... 6
  Bass 210
Ashborn 6-7
Ashdown Amplification
  Amps.....................253
Astrotone
  Effects....................318
ATD
  Effects....................318
Atkin Guitars 7
  Mandolins 366
Audio Matrix
  Effects....................318
Audiovox....................7
  Amps.....................253
  Bass 210
  Lap/Steels 356
Audioworks
  Effects....................318
Auralux
  Amps..................... 253
  Effects....................318

Austin 7
  Bass 210
  Mandolins 366
Austin Hatchet 7
Austone Electronics
  Effects....................318
Automagic
  Effects....................318
Avalanche
  Effects....................318
Avanti 7
B & M
  Effects 319
Bacon
  Banjo Ukuleles.........392
Bacon & Day...............7
  Mandolins 366
Bad Cat Amplifier
Company
  Amps..................... 253
  Effects 319
Baker U.S.A. 7
Baldwin 7-8
  Amps..................... 253
  Bass 210
Baranik Guitars 8
Barclay 8
  Bass 210
Barcus-Berry.............. 8
  Amps..................... 253
Barrington 8
Bartell of California 8
Bartolini
  Effects 319
Basic Systems' Side
Effects
  Effects 319
Bass Collection
  Bass 210-211
Bay State 8
BBE
  Effects 319
BC Rich 8-10
  Bass 211
Bear Creek Guitars ... 10
  Ukuleles...................384
Beardsell Guitars 10
Bedrock
  Amps..................... 253
Bell
  Effects 319
Beltona 10
Beltone 10
  Mandolins 366
Benedetto.............10-11
Bennett Music Labs
  Effects 319
Bently 11
Bertoncini Stringed
Instruments................ 11
  Mandolins 366
Beyond The Trees 11
Bigsby 11
  Effects 319
  Mandolins 367
  Lap/Steels 356
Bil Mitchell Guitars 11
Binson
  Effects 319

Bischoff Guitars 11
Bishline Guitars.......... 11
  Mandolins 367
Bixonic
  Effects 319
Black Cat 11
  Effects
Black Jack 11
  Bass 211
Blackbox Music
Electronics
  Effects 319
Blackshear, Tom.........12
Blackstone Appliances
  Effects 319
Blade 12
  Bass 211
Blanchard Guitars......12
Blue Star.................12
  Mandolins 367
  Lap/Steels 356
  Ukuleles...................384
Blue Tone Amplifiers
  Amps.....................253
Bluebird 12
Blueridge 12
Boaz Elkayam
Guitars 12
Bogner
  Amps.....................253
Bohmann 12
  Mandolins 367
Bolin 12
Bon, Mfg
  Effects 319
Bond 12-13
Boss
  Effects 319-321
Bourgeois.................13
Bown Guitars 13
Bozo 13
Bradford.................13-14
  Bass 211
Brand X
  Amps.....................253
Brandt
  Mandolins 367
Breedlove 14
  Mandolins 367
Brian Moore 14
  Bass 211
  Mandolins 367
Brian Stone Classical
Guitars 14
Brice
  Bass 211
Bronson
  Lap/Steels 356
Brook Guitars 14
Bruné, R. E. 14
Bruno (Tony)
  Amps.....................253
Bruno and Sons...........14
  Mandolins 367
  Ukuleles...................384
Budda
  Amps.....................253
  Effects 322

Bunker....................15
  Bass 211
Burns 15
  Bass 211
Burnside 15
Burriss
  Amps..................... 253
Burton Guitars 15
Buscarino Guitars 15
Byers, Gregory 15
C. Fox 15
CA (Composite
Acoustics) 15
Calace
  Mandolins 367
Callaham 15
  Amps.....................254
Campellone............ 15-16
  Bass 211
Carbonaro 16
Carl Martin
  Effects 322
Carlos......................16
Carlsbro
  Amps.....................254
Carr Amplifiers
  Amps.....................254
Carrotron
  Effects 322
Carvin 16-17
  Amps.....................254
  Bass 211-212
  Effects 322
  Mandolins 367
  Lap/Steels 356
Casa Montalvo............ 17
Casio 17
Castle Instruments
  Effects 322
Cat's Eye
  Effects 322
Catalinbread
  Effects 322
Chandler 17
  Bass 212
  Effects 322
  Lap/Steels 356
Chapin 17
Chapman 17
  Effects 322
Charles Fox Guitars ... 17
Charles Shifflett
Acoustic Guitars.......... 17
  Bass 212
Charvel 17-19
  Bass 212
Chicago Blues Box
  Amps.....................254
Chicago Iron
  Effects 322
Chiquita 19
Chrysalis Guitars 19
Chunk Systems
  Effects 322
Cipher 19
  Bass 212
Citron 19
  Bass 212

Page numbers indicate guitar listing unless otherwise noted

Page numbers indicate guitar listing unless otherwise noted

Page numbers indicate guitar listing unless otherwise noted

Page numbers indicate guitar listing unless otherwise noted